HARRAP'S
SPANISH
and ENGLISH
pocket
DICTIONARY

McGraw·Hill

New York   Chicago   San Francisco   Lisbon   London   Madrid   Mexico City
Milan   New Delhi   San Juan   Seoul   Singapore   Sydney   Toronto

The *McGraw·Hill* Companies

Library of Congress Cataloging-in-Publication Data

Harrap's Spanish and English pocket dictionary / [editors, Teresa
Alvarez, Liam Rodger, Elena Ron Días with Talia Bugel].
        p.   cm.
    English and Spanish.
    ISBN 0-07-145669-4
    1. Spanish language—Dictionaries—English.   2. English
language—Dictionaries—Spanish.   I. Title: Spanish and
English pocket dictionary.   II. Alvarez García, Teresa.
III. Rodger, Liam.   IV. Ron Díaz, Elena.   V. Harrap (Firm)

   PC4640.H377   2005
   463'.21—dc22   2005050468

7 8 9 10 11 12 13 14 1   5DOC/DOC   0 9 8 7

ISBN: 978-0-07-145669-2
MHID: 0-07-145669-4

This book is printed on acid-free paper.

Contents

Contributors

Editors
Teresa Álvarez
Liam Rodger
Elena Ron Díaz

with
Talia Bugel

Publishing Manager
Patrick White

Prepress Manager
Sharon McTeir

Prepress
David Reid

Preface

The Harrap's Spanish and English Pocket Dictionary aims to provide all students of Spanish (in its different regional varieties) at beginner and intermediate level with a reliable, comprehensive and user-friendly dictionary in a compact form. The clear, systematic layout of information makes the dictionary an easy-to-use tool and its coverage of vocabulary should ensure that it becomes an invaluable resource.

The dictionary covers all essential words and phrases needed and packs a wealth of vocabulary into its pages. As in all Harrap dictionaries, colloquial and idiomatic language is well represented, as are words from a wide range of specialized fields, such as information technology, sports and finance.

Extra help is provided in the form of a useful supplement comprising Spanish verb conjugation tables for regular and irregular verbs, and a list of English irregular verbs, and a Spanish conversation guide, together with guides to Spanish and English pronunciation at the beginning of the book.

Abbreviations

abbreviation	*abbr, abr*	abreviatura
adjective	*adj*	adjetivo
adverb	*adv*	adverbio
agriculture	*Agr*	agricultura
somebody, someone	*algn*	alguien
Latin American Spanish	*Am*	español de América
anatomy	*Anat*	anatomía
Andean Spanish (Bolivia, Chile Colombia, Ecuador, Peru)	*Andes*	español andino (Bolivia, Chile, Colombia, Ecuador, Perú)
approximately	*aprox*	aproximadamente
architecture	*Archit*	arquitectura
Argentinian Spanish	*Arg*	español de Argentina
architecture	*Arquit*	arquitectura
article	*art*	artículo
astronomy	*Astron*	astronomía
Australian	*Austr*	australiano
motoring	*Aut*	automóviles
auxiliary	*aux*	auxiliar
aviation	*Av*	aviación
biology	*Biol*	biología
Bolivian Spanish	*Bol*	español de Bolivia
botany	*Bot*	botánica
British English	*Br*	inglés británico
Central American Spanish	*CAm*	español centroamericano
Caribbean Spanish (Cuba, Puerto Rico, Dominican Republic, Venezuela)	*Carib*	español caribeño (Cuba, Puerto Rico, República Dominicana, Venezuela)
chemistry	*Chem*	químico
Chilean Spanish	*Chile*	español de Chile
cinema	*Cin*	cine
Colombian Spanish	*Col*	español de Colombia
commerce	*Com*	comercio
comparative	*comp*	comparativo
computers	*Comput*	informática
conditional	*cond*	condicional
conjunction	*conj*	conjunción
building industry	*Constr*	construcción
sewing	*Cost*	costura
Costa Rican Spanish	*CRica*	español de Costa Rica
Spanish from the Southern Cone region (Argentina, Uruguay, Paraguay, Chile)	*CSur*	español del Cono Sur (Argentina, Uruguay, Paraguay, Chile)
Cuban Spanish	*Cuba*	español de Cuba

cookery	*Culin*	cocina
definite	*def*	definido
defective	*defect*	defectivo
demonstrative	*dem*	demostrativo
sport	*Dep*	deporte
economics	*Econ*	economía
Ecuadorian Spanish	*Ecuad*	español de Ecuador
education	*Educ*	educación
electricity	*Elec*	electricidad
especially	*esp*	especialmente
Peninsular Spanish	*Esp*	español de España
specialist term	*Espec*	término especializado
euphemism	*Euph, Euf*	eufemismo
feminine	*f*	femenino
familiar	*Fam*	familiar
pharmacy	*Farm*	farmacia
railways	*Ferroc*	ferrocarriles
figurative use	*Fig*	uso figurado
finance	*Fin*	finanzas
physics	*Fís*	física
formal use	*Fml*	uso formal
photography	*Fot*	fotografía
feminine plural	*fpl*	plural femenino
soccer	*Ftb*	fútbol
future	*fut*	futuro
geography	*Geog*	geografía
geology	*Geol*	geología
geometry	*Geom*	geometría
present participle	*ger*	gerundio
Guatemalan Spanish	*Guat*	español de Guatemala
history	*Hist*	historia
humorous	*Hum*	humorístico
imperative	*imperat*	imperativo
imperfect	*imperf*	imperfecto
impersonal	*impers*	impersonal
printing	*Impr*	imprenta
industry	*Ind*	industria
indefinite	*indef*	indefinido
indicative	*indic*	indicativo
infinitive	*infin*	infinitivo
computers	*Informát*	informática
insurance	*Ins*	seguros
interjection	*interj*	interjección
interrogative	*interr*	interrogativo
invariable	*inv*	invariable
ironic	*Irón*	irónico
law	*Jur*	derecho
linguistics	*Ling*	lingüística
literature	*Lit*	literatura

phrase	*loc*	locución
masculine	*m*	masculino
mathematics	*Math, Mat*	matemáticas
medicine	*Med*	medicina
meteorology	*Met*	meteorología
Mexican Spanish	*Méx*	español de México
masculine or feminine	*mf/m.f*	masculino o femenino
masculine or feminine plural	*mfpl/m.fpl*	plural masculino o femenino
military	*Mil*	militar
mining	*Min*	minas
masculine plural	*mpl*	plural masculino
music	*Mus, Mús*	música
noun	*n*	nombre
nautical	*Naut, Náut*	náutica
neuter	*neut*	neutro
feminine noun	*nf*	nombre femenino
plural feminine noun	*nfpl*	nombre femenino plural
masculine noun	*nm*	nombre masculino
masculine or feminine noun	*nmf/nm.f*	nombre masculino o femenino
plural masculine noun	*nmpl*	nombre masculino plural
plural noun	*npl*	nombre plural
optics	*Opt*	óptica
ornithology	*Orn*	ornitología
Panamanian Spanish	*Pan*	español de Panamá
Paraguayan Spanish	*Par*	español de Paraguay
parliament	*Parl*	parlamento
pejorative	*Pej*	peyorativo
personal	*pers*	personal
Peruvian Spanish	*Perú*	español de Perú
pejorative	*Pey*	peyorativo
photography	*Phot*	fotografía
physics	*Phys*	física
plural	*pl*	plural
politics	*Pol*	política
possessive	*poss, pos*	posesivo
past participle	*pp*	participio pasado
preposition	*prep*	preposición
present	*pres*	presente
present participle	*pres p*	gerundio
preterite	*pret*	pretérito
Puerto Rican Spanish	*PRico*	español de Puerto Rico
pronoun	*pron*	pronombre
past tense	*pt*	pretérito
chemistry	*Quím*	químico
radio	*Rad*	radio
railways	*Rail*	ferrocarriles
Dominican Spanish	*RDom*	español de la República Dominicana

relative	*rel*	relativo
religion	*Rel*	religión
Spanish from the River Plate region (Argentina, Uruguay, Paraguay)	*RP*	español de los países ribereños del Río de la Plata
Salvadoran Spanish	*Salv*	español de El Salvador
somebody, someone	*sb*	alguien
Scottish	*Scot*	escocés
insurance	*Seg*	seguros
singular	*sing*	singular
something	*sth*	algo
subjunctive	*subj*	subjunctivo
superlative	*superl*	superlativo
bullfighting	*Taurom*	tauromaquia
technical	*Tech, Téc*	técnica
telephones	*Tel*	teléfonos
tennis	*Ten*	tenis
textiles	*Tex*	textiles
theatre	*Th*	teatro
television	*TV*	televisión
typography	*Typ*	tipografía
university	*Univ*	universidad
Uruguayan Spanish	*Urug*	español de Uruguay
American English	*US*	inglés norteamericano
usually	*usu*	usualmente
verb	*v*	verbo
Venezuelan Spanish	*Ven*	español de Venezuela
intransitive verb	*vi*	verbo intransitivo
reflexive verb	*vpr*	verbo pronominal
transitive verb	*vt*	verbo transitivo
inseparable phrasal verb	*vt insep*	verbo transitivo con partícula inseparable
separable phrasal verb	*vt sep*	verbo transitivo con partícula separable
vulgar	*Vulg*	vulgar
zoology	*Zool*	zoología
cultural equivalent	≃	equivalente cultural
registered trademark	®	marca registrada

All other labels are written in full

Spanish Pronunciation Guide

The pronunciation of most Spanish words is predictable as there is a close match between spelling and pronunciation. The table below gives an explanation of that pronunciation. In the dictionary text therefore, pronunciation is only given when the word does not follow these rules, usually because it is a word of foreign origin. In these cases, the IPA (International Phonetic Alphabet) is used (see column 2 of the table below).

Letter in Spanish	IPA Symbol	Example in Spanish	Pronunciation (example in English)
Vowels			
Note that all vowel sounds in Spanish are shorter than in English			
a	a	**a**la	Similar to the sound in "f**a**ther" but more central
e	e	**e**có	Similar to the sound in "m**e**t"
i	i	**i**ris	Like the vowel sound in "m**ea**t" but much shorter
o	o	**o**so	Like the start of "**o**we" without the 'w' sound at the end
u	u	**u**va	Like the vowel sound in "s**oo**n" but much shorter
Semiconsonants			
"i" in the diphthongs: ia, ie, io, iu	j	h**i**ato, h**i**elo, av**i**ón, v**i**uda	**y**es
"u" in the diphthongs: ua, ue, ui, uo	w	s**u**ave, f**u**ego, h**u**ida	**w**in
Consonants			
b	b	**b**omba (at beginning of word or after "m")	**b**oom
	β	a**b**ajo (all other contexts)	A "**b**" pronounced without quite closing the lips completely

Letter in Spanish	IPA Symbol	Example in Spanish	Pronunciation (example in English)
c	θ (in Spain)	ceña (before "e") cinco (before "i")	thanks (in Spain)
	s (in Latin America and southern Spain)		sun (in Latin America and southern Spain)
	k	casa (all other contexts)	cat
ch	tʃ	caucho	arch
d	d	donde (at beginning of word or after "n") aldea (after "l")	day
	ð	adorno (all other contexts)	Similar to the sound in "mother" but less strong
f	f	furia	fire
g	χ	gema (before "e") girasol (before "i")	Like an "h" but pronounced at the back of the throat (similar to Scottish "loch")
	g	gato (at beginning of word) lengua (after "n")	goose
	ɣ	agua (all other contexts)	Like a "w" pronounced while trying to say "g"
j	χ	jabalí	Like an "h" but pronounced at the back of the throat (similar to Scottish "loch")
l	l	lado	lake
ll	j	lluvia	yes
	ʒ		In some regions (eg the Rio de la Plata area of South America) it is pronounced like the "s" in "pleasure"
m	m	mano	man
n	n	nulo	no
	ŋ	manco, fango (before c and g)	parking
ñ	ŋ	año	onion

Spanish Pronunciation Guide

Letter in Spanish	IPA Symbol	Example in Spanish	Pronunciation (example in English)
p	p	**p**a**p**a	**p**ool
r	r	do**r**ado (in between vowels) habla**r** (at end of syllable or word)	A rolled "**r**" sound (similar to Scottish "**r**")
	rr	**r**osa (at beginning of word) al**r**ededor (after l) en**r**edo (after n)	A much longer rolled "**r**" sound (similar to Scottish "**r**")
rr	rr	a**rr**oyo	A much longer rolled "**r**" sound (similar to Scottish "**r**")
s	s	**s**aco	**s**ound
sh	ʃ	**sh**ow	**sh**ow
t	t	**t**ela	**t**ea
v	b	in**v**ierno (after "n")	**b**oom
	β	a**v**e (all other contexts)	A "**b**" pronounced without quite closing the lips completely
x	ks	e**x**amen	e**x**tra
y	j	a**y**er	**y**es
	ʒ		In some regions (eg the Rio de la Plata area of South America) it is pronounced like the "**s**" in "plea**s**ure"
z	θ (in Spain)	**z**apato	**th**anks (in Spain)
	s (in Latin America and southern Spain)		**s**un (in Latin America and southern Spain)

Pronunciación del inglés

Para ilustrar la pronunciación inglesa, en este diccionario utilizamos los símbolos del AFI (Alfabeto Fonético Internacional). En el siguiente cuadro, para cada sonido del inglés hay ejemplos de palabras en inglés y palabras en español donde aparece un sonido similar. En los casos en los que no hay sonido similar en español, ofrecemos una explicación de cómo pronunciar.

Carácter AFI	Ejemplo en inglés	Ejemplo en español
Consonantes		
[b]	**b**a**bb**le	**b**e**b**é
[d]	**d**ig	**d**e**d**o
[dʒ]	**g**iant, **j**ig	se pronuncia como "**ll**" en el Río de la Plata pero con una "**d**" adelante, o como "**gi**" en italiano - **Gi**ovanna
[f]	**f**it, **ph**ysics	**f**aro
[g]	**g**rey, bi**g**	**g**ris
[h]	**h**appy	"**h**" aspirada
[j]	**y**ellow	se pronuncia como "**y**" o "**ll**" en España - **y**o, **ll**uvia
[k]	**c**lay, **k**ick	**c**asa
[l]	**l**ip	**l**abio
	pi**ll**	pape**l**
[m]	**m**u**mm**y	**m**a**m**á
[n]	**n**ip, pi**n**	**n**ada
[ŋ]	si**ng**	se pronuncia como "**n**" antes de "**c**" - ba**n**co
[p]	**p**i**p**	**p**a**p**á
[r]	**r**ig, **wr**ite	sonido entre "**r**" y "**rr**"
[s]	**s**ick, **sc**ience	**s**apo
[ʃ]	**sh**ip, na**ti**on	**sh**ow
[t]	**t**ip, bu**tt**	**t**ela
[tʃ]	**ch**ip, ba**tch**	cau**ch**o
[θ]	**th**ick	**z**apato (como se pronuncia en España)
[ð]	**th**is	se pronuncia como la "**d**" de "ha**d**a" pero más fuerte

Pronunciación del inglés

Carácter AFI	Ejemplo en inglés	Ejemplo en español
[v]	**v**ague, gi**v**e	se pronuncia como "**v**" de **v**ida, con los dientes apoyados sobre el labio inferior
[w]	**w**it, **wh**y	**wh**isky
[z]	**z**ip, phy**s**ics	"**s**" con sonido zumbante
[ʒ]	plea**s**ure	se pronuncia como "**y**" o "**ll**" en el Río de la Plata - **y**o, **ll**uvia
[χ]	lo**ch**	**j**ota

Vocales

En inglés, las vocales marcadas con dos puntos son mucho más alargadas

[æ]	r**a**g	se pronuncia "**e**" con posición bucal para "**a**"
[ɑ:]	l**ar**ge	"**a**" muy alargada
[ʌ]	c**u**p	"**a**" breve y cerrada
[e]	s**e**t	se pronuncia como "**e**" de **e**lefant**e** pero más corta
[ɜ:]	c**ur**tain, w**e**re	se pronuncia como una "**e**" larga con posición bucal entre "**o**" y "**e**"
[ə]	**u**tter	se pronuncia como "**e**" con posición bucal para "**o**"
[ɪ]	b**i**g, w**o**men	"**i**" breve, a medio camino entre "**e**" e "**i**"
[i:]	l**ea**k, w**ee**	"**i**" muy alargada
[ɒ]	l**o**ck	"**o**" abierta
[ɔ:]	w**a**ll, c**o**rk	"**o**" cerrada y alargada
[ʊ]	p**u**t, l**oo**k	"**u**" breve
[u:]	m**oo**n	"**u**" muy alargada

Diptongos

[aɪ]	wh**y**, h**igh**, l**ie**	**ai**re
[aʊ]	h**ow**	**au**ra
[eə]	b**ea**r	"**ea**" pronunciado muy brevemente y con sonido de "**e**" más marcado que el de "**a**"
[eɪ]	d**ay**, m**a**ke, m**ai**n	r**ei**na
[əʊ]	sh**ow**, g**o**	"**ou**" como en COU
[ɪə]	h**e**re, g**ea**r	h**ie**lo pronunciado con el sonido de "**i**" más marcado y alargado que el de "**e**"
[ɔɪ]	b**oy**, s**oi**l	v**oy**
[ʊə]	p**oo**r	c**ue**rno pronunciado con el sonido de "**u**" más marcado y alargado que el de "**e**"

English–Spanish

Aa

A, a [eɪ] *n* (**a**) *(the letter)* A, a *f*; *Br Aut* **A road** ≃ carretera *f* nacional (**b**) *Mus* **A** la *m*

a [eɪ, *unstressed* ə] *indef art* (*before vowel or silent h* **an**) (**a**) un, una; **a man/a woman** un hombre/una mujer; **he has a big nose** tiene la nariz grande (**b**) *(omitted in Spanish)* **half a litre/an hour** medio litro/media hora; **a hundred/thousand people** cien/mil personas; **let's have a drink** vamos a beber algo; **he's a teacher** es profesor; **what a pity** qué pena (**c**) *(each)* **60 pence a kilo** 60 peniques el kilo; **to eat grapes two at a time** comer las uvas de dos en dos; **three times a week** tres veces a la semana (**d**) *(a certain)* un/una tal; **a Mr Rees phoned** llamó un tal Sr. Rees

aback [əˈbæk] *adv* **to be taken a.** quedarse de una pieza (**by** por)

abandon [əˈbændən] **1** *n* desenfreno *m*; **with reckless a.** desenfrenadamente **2** *vt (child)* abandonar; *(job)* dejar; *(project)* renunciar a

abbey [ˈæbɪ] *n* abadía *f*

abbreviation [əbriːvɪˈeɪʃən] *n* abreviatura *f*

abdicate [ˈæbdɪkeɪt] *vt & vi* abdicar

abdomen [ˈæbdəmən] *n* abdomen *m*

abduction [əbˈdʌkʃən] *n* rapto *m*, secuestro *m*

ability [əˈbɪlɪtɪ] *n (capability)* capacidad *f*, aptitud *f*; *(talent)* talento *m*

ablaze [əˈbleɪz] *adj & adv* en llamas, ardiendo

able [ˈeɪbəl] *adj (capable)* capaz; **will you be a. to come on Tuesday?** ¿podrás venir el martes?

able-bodied [eɪbəlˈbɒdɪd] *adj* sano(a); **a. seaman** marinero *m* de primera

abnormal [æbˈnɔːməl] *adj* anormal

aboard [əˈbɔːd] **1** *adv* a bordo; **to go a.** *(ship)* embarcarse; *(train)* subir **2** *prep* a bordo de

abolish [əˈbɒlɪʃ] *vt* abolir

abolition [æbəˈlɪʃən] *n* abolición *f*

abominable [əˈbɒmɪnəbəl] *adj* abominable; *(dreadful)* terrible

abortion [əˈbɔːʃən] *n Med* aborto *m*; **a. law** ley *f* del aborto; **to have an a.** abortar

about [əˈbaʊt] *adv & prep* (**a**) *(concerning)* acerca de, sobre; **a programme a. Paris** un programa sobre París; **to be worried a. sth** estar preocupado(a) por algo; **to speak a. sth** hablar de algo; **what's it a.?** *(story etc)* ¿de qué trata?; *Fam* **how a. a game of tennis?** ¿qué te parece un partido de tenis?

(**b**) *(around)* por todas partes; **don't leave things lying a.** no dejes las cosas por medio; **there's nobody a.** no hay nadie; **to look a.** mirar alrededor; **to rush a.** correr de un lado para otro; **we went for a walk a. the town** dimos una vuelta por el pueblo

(**c**) *(approximately)* más o menos; **it's a. three o'clock** son más o menos las tres; **it's a. time you got up** ya es hora de que te levantes; **it's just a. finished** está casi terminado; **she's a. forty** tiene unos cuarenta años

(**d**) **it's a. to start** está a punto de empezar; **not to be a. to do sth** no estar dispuesto(a) a hacer algo

above [əˈbʌv] *adv & prep* (**a**) *(higher than)* encima de, sobre, arriba; **100 m a. sea level** 100 m sobre el nivel del mar; **it's a. the door** está encima de la puerta; **the flat a.** el piso de arriba

(**b**) *(greater than)* superior (a);

amounts a. **£10** cantidades superiores a las 10 libras; *Fig* **a policy imposed from a.** una política impuesta desde arriba
(**c**) **a. all** sobre todo; **he's not a. stealing** es capaz incluso de robar (**d**) *(in book etc)* más arriba

above-board [ə'bʌv'bɔ:d] *adj (scheme)* legítimo(a)

above-mentioned [ə'bʌvmenʃənd] *adj* susodicho(a)

abreast [ə'brest] *adv* **to walk three a.** ir de tres en fondo; *Fig* **to keep a. of things** mantenerse al día

abroad [ə'brɔ:d] *adv* **to be a.** estar en el extranjero; **to go a.** irse al extranjero

abrupt [ə'brʌpt] *adj (manner)* brusco(a); *(tone)* áspero(a); *(change)* súbito(a)

abscess ['æbses] *n* absceso *m*; *(on gum)* flemón *m*

absence ['æbsəns] *n (of person)* ausencia *f*; *(of thing)* falta *f*

absent ['æbsənt] *adj* ausente; *Fig* **an a. look** una mirada distraída

absent-minded [æbsənt'maɪndɪd] *adj* distraído(a)

absolute ['æbsəlu:t] *adj* absoluto(a); *(failure)* total; *(truth)* puro(a); **it's an a. disgrace** es una auténtica vergüenza

absolutely [æbsə'lu:tlɪ] **1** *adv (completely)* completamente; **a. wrong** totalmente equivocado(a); **a. not** en absoluto; **you're a. right** tienes toda la razón **2** *interj* ¡desde luego!

absorb [əb'zɔ:b] *vt (liquid)* absorber; *(sound, blow)* amortiguar; *Fig* **to be absorbed in sth** estar absorto(a) en algo

abstain [əb'steɪn] *vi* abstenerse (**from** de)

abstract ['æbstrækt] **1** *adj* abstracto(a) **2** *n (of thesis etc)* resumen *m*

absurd [əb'sɜ:d] *adj* absurdo(a)

abundant [ə'bʌndənt] *adj* abundante, rico(a) (**in** en)

abuse 1 *n* [ə'bju:s] (**a**) *(ill-treatment)* malos tratos; *(misuse)* abuso *m* (**b**) *(insults)* injurias *fpl* **2** *vt* [ə'bju:z] (**a**) *(ill-treat)* maltratar; *(misuse)* abusar

de (**b**) *(insult)* injuriar

abusive [əb'ju:sɪv] *adj (insulting)* insultante

academic [ækə'demɪk] **1** *adj* académico(a); *(career)* universitario(a); *(discussion)* teórico(a); **a. year** año *m* escolar **2** *n* académico(a) *m,f*

academy [ə'kædəmɪ] *n (society)* academia *f*; *Educ* instituto *m* de enseñanza media; **a. of music** conservatorio *m*

accelerate [æk'seləreɪt] **1** *vt (engine)* acelerar; *(step)* aligerar **2** *vi (car, engine)* acelerar

accelerator [æk'seləreɪtə(r)] *n* acelerador *m*

accent ['æksənt] *n* acento *m*

accept [ək'sept] *vt & vi* aceptar; *(theory)* admitir; **do you a. that …?** ¿estás de acuerdo en que …?

acceptable [ək'septəbəl] *adj (satisfactory)* aceptable; *(tolerable)* admisible

access ['ækses] *n* acceso *m*; *Comput* **a. provider** proveedor *m* de acceso (a Internet); **a. road** carretera *f* de acceso; **to have a. to sth** tener libre acceso a algo

accessible [ək'sesəbəl] *adj (place, position)* accesible; *(person)* asequible

accessory [ək'sesərɪ] *n* (**a**) *Jur* cómplice *mf* (**b**) **accessories** accesorios *mpl*; *(for outfit)* complementos *mpl*

accident ['æksɪdənt] *n* accidente *m*; *(coincidence)* casualidad *f*; **it was an a. on my part** lo hice sin querer; **car a.** accidente *m* de carretera; **by a.** por casualidad

accidental [æksɪ'dentəl] *adj* fortuito(a); *(unintended)* imprevisto(a)

acclaim [ə'kleɪm] **1** *n* aclamación *f* **2** *vt* aclamar

acclimatize [ə'klaɪmətaɪz], *US* **acclimate** ['æklɪmeɪt] *vt* aclimatar

accommodate [ə'kɒmədeɪt] *vt* (**a**) *(guests)* alojar (**b**) **to a. sb's wishes** complacer a algn

accommodation [əkɒmə'deɪʃən] *n* (*US also* **accommodations**) *(lodgings)* alojamiento *m*

accompany [əˈkʌmpənɪ] *vt* acompañar

accomplice [əˈkʌmplɪs] *n* cómplice *mf*

accomplish [əˈkʌmplɪʃ] *vt (aim)* conseguir; *(task, mission)* llevar a cabo

accomplishment [əˈkʌmplɪʃmənt] *n* (a) *(of task)* realización *f*; *(of duty)* cumplimiento *m* (b) **accomplishments** *(talents) fpl*

accord [əˈkɔːd] **1** *n (agreement)* acuerdo *m*; **of her/his own a.** espontáneamente **2** *vt (honour etc)* conceder

accordance [əˈkɔːdəns] *n* **in a. with** de acuerdo con

according [əˈkɔːdɪŋ] *prep* **a. to** según; **everything went a. to plan** todo salió conforme a los planes

accordingly [əˈkɔːdɪŋlɪ] *adv* (a) **to act a.** *(appropriately)* obrar según y conforme (b) *(therefore)* así pues

accordion [əˈkɔːdɪən] *n* acordeón *m*

account [əˈkaʊnt] *n* (a) *(report)* informe *m*; **by all accounts** al decir de todos

(b) **I was fearful on her a.** sufría por ella; **it's of no a.** no tiene importancia; **on a. of** a causa de; **on no a.** bajo ningún concepto; **to take a. of, to take into a.** tener en cuenta

(c) *Com* cuenta *f*; **to keep the accounts** llevar las cuentas; **accounts department** servicio *m* de contabilidad; **to open/close an a.** abrir/cancelar una cuenta; **current a.** cuenta corriente; **a. number** número *m* de cuenta

▶ **account for** *vt insep (explain)* explicar

accountable [əˈkaʊntəbəl] *adj* **to be a. to sb for sth** ser responsable ante algn de algo

accountant [əˈkaʊntənt] *n Esp* contable *mf, Am* contador(a) *m,f*

accounting [əˈkaʊntɪŋ] *n* contabilidad *f*

accumulate [əˈkjuːmjʊleɪt] **1** *vt* acumular; *(fortune)* amasar **2** *vi* acumularse

accuracy [ˈækjʊrəsɪ] *n (of number etc)* exactitud *f*; *(of shot, criticism)* certeza *f*

accurate [ˈækjʊrət] *adj (number)* exacto(a); *(shot, criticism)* certero(a); *(answer)* correcto(a); *(observation)* acertado(a); *(instrument)* de precisión; *(translation)* fiel

accusation [ækjʊˈzeɪʃən] *n* acusación *f*

accuse [əˈkjuːz] *vt* acusar

accused [əˈkjuːzd] *n* **the a.** el/la acusado(a)

accustom [əˈkʌstəm] *vt* acostumbrar; **to be accustomed to doing sth** estar acostumbrado(a) a hacer algo

ace [eɪs] *n* (a) *Cards & Fig* as *m* (b) *(in tennis)* ace *m*

ache [eɪk] **1** *n* dolor *m*; **aches and pains** achaques *mpl* **2** *vi* doler; **my back aches** me duele la espalda

achieve [əˈtʃiːv] *vt (attain)* conseguir, alcanzar; *(accomplish)* llevar a cabo, realizar

achievement [əˈtʃiːvmənt] *n (attainment)* logro *m*; *(completion)* realización *f*; *(feat)* hazaña *f*

acid [ˈæsɪd] **1** *adj* ácido(a); *(taste)* agrio(a); *(remark)* mordaz; **a. rain** lluvia ácida; *Fig* **a. test** prueba decisiva **2** *n* ácido *m*

acknowledge [əkˈnɒlɪdʒ] *vt* (a) *(recognize)* reconocer; *(claim, defeat)* admitir; *(present)* agradecer; *(letter)* acusar recibo de (b) *(greet)* saludar

acknowledgement [əkˈnɒlɪdʒmənt] *n* (a) *(recognition)* reconocimiento *m*; *(of letter)* acuse *m* de recibo (b) **acknowledgements** *(in preface)* menciones *fpl*

acne [ˈæknɪ] *n* acné *m*

acoustic [əˈkuːstɪk] **1** *adj* acústico(a) **2** *npl* **acoustics** acústica *f*

acquaint [əˈkweɪnt] *vt* **to a. sb with the facts** informar a algn de los detalles; **to be acquainted with the procedure** estar al corriente de como se procede; **to be acquainted with sb** conocer a algn

acquaintance [əˈkweɪntəns] *n* (a) conocimiento *m*; **to make sb's a.**

conocer a algn (**b**) *(person)* conocido(a) *m,f*

acquire [əˈkwaɪə(r)] *vt* adquirir

acquit [əˈkwɪt] *vt* (**a**) *Jur* **to a. sb of sth** absolver a algn de algo (**b**) **to a. oneself well** defenderse bien

acre [ˈeɪkə(r)] *n* acre *m* (= aprox 40,47 áreas)

acrobat [ˈækrəbæt] *n* acróbata *mf*

acrobatic [ækrəˈbætɪk] *adj* acrobático(a)

across [əˈkrɒs] **1** *adv* a través; **the river is 30 m a.** el río mide 30 m de ancho; **to go a.** atravesar; **to run a.** atravesar corriendo **2** *prep* (**a**) a través de; **they live a. the road** viven enfrente; **to go a. the street** cruzar la calle (**b**) *(at the other side of)* al otro lado de

acrylic [əˈkrɪlɪk] *adj* acrílico(a)

act [ækt] **1** *n* (**a**) *(action)* acto *m*, acción *f*; **a. of God** caso *m* de fuerza mayor (**b**) *Jur* **a.** (*Br* **of parliament** *or US* **of Congress**) ley *f* (**c**) *Th* acto *m*; *(turn in show)* número *m*
2 *vt Th (part)* interpretar; *(character)* representar; *Fig* **to a. the fool** hacer el tonto
3 *vi* (**a**) *Th* hacer teatro; *Cin* hacer cine; *Fig (pretend)* fingir (**b**) *(behave)* comportarse (**c**) *(take action)* actuar, obrar; **to a. on sb's advice** seguir el consejo de algn (**d**) *(work)* funcionar; *(drug etc)* actuar; **to a. as a deterrent** servir de disuasivo (**e**) **to a. as director** hacer de director

▸ **act out** *vt sep* exteriorizar

▸ **act up** *vi Fam (machine)* funcionar mal; *(child)* dar guerra

acting [ˈæktɪŋ] **1** *adj* interino(a) **2** *n (profession)* teatro *m*; **he's done some a.** ha hecho algo de teatro

action [ˈækʃən] *n* (**a**) *(deed)* acción *f*; *Mil* acción de combate; **to be out of a.** *(person)* estar fuera de servicio; *(machine)* estar estropeado(a); **to take a.** tomar medidas (**b**) *Jur* demanda *f* (**c**) *Br TV* **a. replay** repetición *f*

active [ˈæktɪv] *adj* activo(a); *(energetic)* vigoroso(a); *(interest)* vivo(a);

Ling **a. voice** voz activa

activity [ækˈtɪvɪtɪ] *n (of person)* actividad *f*; *(on street etc)* bullicio *m*

actor [ˈæktə(r)] *n* actor *m*

actress [ˈæktrɪs] *n* actriz *f*

actual [ˈæktʃʊəl] *adj* real, verdadero(a)

actually [ˈæktʃʊəlɪ] *adv (really)* en efecto, realmente; *(even)* incluso, hasta; *(in fact)* de hecho

acupuncture [ˈækjʊpʌŋktʃə(r)] *n* acupuntura *f*

acute [əˈkjuːt] *adj* agudo(a); *(pain)* intenso(a); *(hearing)* muy fino(a); *(shortage)* grave; *(mind)* perspicaz

ad [æd] *n Fam* anuncio *m*

adapt [əˈdæpt] **1** *vt* adaptar (**to a**); **to a. oneself to sth** adaptarse a algo **2** *vi* adaptarse

adaptable [əˈdæptəbəl] *adj (instrument)* ajustable; **he's very a.** se amolda fácilmente a las circunstancias

adapter, adaptor [əˈdæptə(r)] *n Elec* ladrón *m*

add [æd] **1** *vt (numbers)* sumar; *(one thing to another)* añadir **2** *vi (count)* sumar

▸ **add to** *vt insep* aumentar

▸ **add up 1** *vt sep* sumar **2** *vi (numbers)* sumar; *Fig* **it doesn't a. up** no tiene sentido; **it doesn't a. up to much** no es gran cosa

addict [ˈædɪkt] *n* adicto(a) *m,f*; *Fam* **television a.** teleadicto(a) *m,f*

addicted [əˈdɪktɪd] *adj* adicto(a); **to become a. to sth** enviciarse con algo

addictive [əˈdɪktɪv] *adj* que crea adicción

addition [əˈdɪʃən] *n Math* adición *f*; *(increase)* aumento *m*; **an a. to the family** un nuevo miembro de la familia; **in a. to** además de

additional [əˈdɪʃənəl] *adj* adicional

additive [ˈædɪtɪv] *n* aditivo *m*

address [əˈdres] **1** *n* (**a**) *(on letter)* dirección *f*, señas *fpl* (**b**) *(speech)* discurso *m* **2** *vt* (**a**) *(letter)* dirigir (**b**) *(speak to)* dirigirse (**to a**); **to a. the floor** tomar la palabra (**c**) *(use form of address to)* tratar de

adept [ə'dept] **1** *adj* experto(a) (**at** en) **2** *n* experto(a) *m,f*

adequate ['ædɪkwɪt] *adj (enough)* suficiente; *(satisfactory)* adecuado(a)

adhere [əd'hɪə(r)] *vi (stick)* pegarse (**to** a)

▸ **adhere to** *vt insep (policy)* adherirse a; *(contract)* cumplir con

adhesive [əd'hi:sɪv] **1** *adj* adhesivo(a); *(sticky)* pegajoso(a); **a. tape** cinta adhesiva **2** *n* adhesivo *m*

adjacent [ə'dʒeɪsənt] *adj (building)* contiguo(a); *(land)* colindante; **a. to** contiguo(a) a

adjective ['ædʒɪktɪv] *n* adjetivo *m*

adjoining [ə'dʒɔɪnɪŋ] *adj* contiguo(a); *(land)* colindante; **the a. room** la habitación de al lado

adjourn [ə'dʒɜ:n] **1** *vt (postpone)* aplazar; *(court)* levantar **2** *vi* aplazarse (**until** hasta)

adjust [ə'dʒʌst] **1** *vt (machine etc)* ajustar; *Fig (methods)* variar **2** *vi (person)* adaptarse (**to** a)

adjustable [ə'dʒʌstəbəl] *adj* ajustable

administer [əd'mɪnɪstə(r)] *vt (country)* gobernar; *(justice)* administrar

administration [ədmɪnɪ'streɪʃən] *n (management, of justice)* administración *f; (governing body)* dirección *f; US (government)* gobierno *m*, administración *f*

administrator [əd'mɪnɪstreɪtə(r)] *n* administrador(a) *m,f*

admirable [æd'mərəbəl] *adj* admirable

admiral ['ædmərəl] *n* almirante *m*

admire [əd'maɪə(r)] *vt* admirar

admission [əd'mɪʃən] *n (a) (to school etc)* ingreso *m; (price)* entrada *f (b) (of fact)* reconocimiento *m; (confession)* confesión *f*

admit [əd'mɪt] *vt (a) (person)* dejar entrar; **to be admitted to hospital** ser ingresado(a) en el hospital **(b)** *(acknowledge)* reconocer; *(crime, guilt)* confesar

admittance [əd'mɪtəns] *n (entry)* entrada *f*

admittedly [əd'mɪtɪdlɪ] *adv* la verdad es que …

adolescent [ædə'lesənt] *n* adolescente *mf*

adopt [ə'dɒpt] *vt* adoptar; *(suggestion)* aceptar

adopted [ə'dɒptɪd] *adj* **a. child** hijo(a) *m,f* adoptivo(a)

adorable [ə'dɔ:rəbəl] *adj* encantador(a)

adore [ə'dɔ:(r)] *vt* adorar

Adriatic [eɪdrɪ'ætɪk] *adj* **the A. (Sea)** el (mar) Adriático

adult ['ædʌlt] **1** *adj (person)* adulto(a), mayor; *(film, education)* para adultos **2** *n* adulto(a) *m,f*

adultery [ə'dʌltərɪ] *n* adulterio *m*

advance [əd'vɑ:ns] **1** *n (a) (movement)* avance *m; Fig (progress)* progreso *m;* **to have sth ready in a.** tener algo preparado de antemano; **to make advances (to)** *(person)* insinuarse a; **(b)** *(loan)* anticipo *m* **2** *adj (before time)* adelantado(a); *Cin, Th* **a. bookings** reservas *fpl* por adelantado **3** *vt (a) (troops)* avanzar; *(time, date)* adelantar **(b)** *(idea)* proponer; *(opinion)* dar **4** *vi (move forward)* avanzar, adelantarse; *(make progress)* hacer progresos; *(gain promotion)* ascender

advanced [əd'vɑ:nst] *adj (developed)* avanzado(a); *(student)* adelantado(a); *(course)* superior; *Br* **A. level** = examen final o diploma en una asignatura de los estudios preuniversitarios

advantage [əd'vɑ:ntɪdʒ] *n* ventaja *f; (in tennis)* **a. Velasco** ventaja para Velasco; **to take a. of sb/sth** abusar de algn/aprovechar algo

adventure [əd'ventʃə(r)] *n* aventura *f;* **a. sport** deporte *m* de aventura

adventurous [əd'ventʃərəs] *adj* aventurero(a)

adverb ['ædvɜ:b] *n* adverbio *m*

adverse ['ædvɜ:s] *adj (effect)* desfavorable; *(conditions)* adverso(a); *(winds)* contrario(a)

advert ['ædvɜːt] *n Fam* anuncio *m*

advertise ['ædvətaɪz] **1** *vt* anunciar **2** *vi* hacer publicidad; *(in newspaper)* poner un anuncio; **to a. for sth/sb** buscar algo/a algn mediante un anuncio

advertisement [əd'vɜːtɪsmənt] *n* anuncio *m*; **advertisements** publicidad *f*

advertising ['ædvətaɪzɪŋ] **1** *n* publicidad *f*, propaganda *f*; *(in newspaper)* anuncios *mpl* **2** *adj* publicitario(a); **a. agency** agencia *f* de publicidad

advice [əd'vaɪs] *n* consejos *mpl*; **a piece of a.** un consejo; **to take legal a. on a matter** consultar el caso con un abogado; **to take sb's a.** seguir los consejos de algn

advisable [əd'vaɪzəbəl] *adj* aconsejable

advise [əd'vaɪz] *vt* aconsejar; *(on business etc)* asesorar; **I a. you to do it** te aconsejo que lo hagas

adviser [əd'vaɪzə(r)] *n* consejero(a) *m,f*; *(in business etc)* asesor(a) *m,f*

advocate 1 *n* ['ædvəkɪt] *Scot Jur* abogado(a) *m,f*; *(supporter)* defensor(a) *m,f* **2** *vt* ['ædvəkeɪt] *(reform)* abogar por; *(plan)* apoyar

aerial ['eərɪəl] **1** *adj* aéreo(a) **2** *n* antena *f*

aerobics [eə'rəʊbɪks] *n sing* aerobic *m*

aeroplane ['eərəpleɪn] *n Br* avión *m*

aerosol ['eərəsɒl] *n* aerosol *m*

aesthetic [iːs'θetɪk] *adj* estético(a)

affair [ə'feə(r)] *n (matter)* asunto *m*; *(event)* acontecimiento *m*; **that's my a.** eso es asunto mío; **business affairs** negocios *mpl*; **foreign affairs** asuntos exteriores; **love a.** aventura amorosa

affect [ə'fekt] *vt (person, health)* afectar; *(prices, future)* influir en; *(touch emotionally)* conmover

affected [ə'fektɪd] *adj (a) (unnatural)* afectado(a) **(b)** *(influenced)* influido(a) **(c)** *(touched emotionally)* conmovido(a) **(d)** *(pretended)* fingido(a)

affection [ə'fekʃən] *n* afecto *m*, cariño *m*

affectionate [ə'fekʃənɪt] *adj* cariñoso(a)

affinity [ə'fɪnɪtɪ] *n* afinidad *f*; *(liking)* simpatía *f*

affirm [ə'fɜːm] *vt* afirmar, sostener

affirmative [ə'fɜːmətɪv] **1** *adj* afirmativo(a) **2** *n* **he answered in the a.** contestó que sí

afflict [ə'flɪkt] *vt* afligir

affluent ['æflʊənt] *adj (society)* opulento(a); *(person)* rico(a)

afford [ə'fɔːd] *vt* **(a)** *(be able to buy)* permitirse el lujo de; **I can't a. a new car** no puedo pagar un coche nuevo **(b)** *(be able to do)* permitirse; **you can't a. to miss the opportunity** no puedes perderte la ocasión

affordable [ə'fɔːdəbəl] *adj (price, purchase)* asequible

Afghanistan [æf'gænɪstɑːn] *n* Afganistán

afield [ə'fiːld] *adv* **far a.** muy lejos

afloat [ə'fləʊt] *adv* **to keep a.** mantenerse a flote

afraid [ə'freɪd] *adj* **(a) to be a.** tener miedo **(of sb** a algn; **of sth** de algo); **I'm a. of it** me da miedo **(b) I'm a. not** me temo que no; **I'm a. so** me temo que sí; **I'm a. you're wrong** me temo que estás equivocado(a)

afresh [ə'freʃ] *adv* de nuevo

Africa ['æfrɪkə] *n* Africa

African ['æfrɪkən] *adj & n* africano(a) *(m,f)*

after ['ɑːftə(r)] **1** *adv* después; **soon a.** poco después; **the day a.** el día siguiente

2 *prep* **(a)** *(later)* después de; *US* **it's ten a. five** son las cinco y diez; **soon a. arriving** al poco rato de llegar; **the day a. tomorrow** pasado mañana **(b)** *(behind)* detrás de, tras; **a. you!** ¡pase usted!; **they went in one a. the other** entraron uno tras otro; **the police are a. them** la policía anda tras ellos **(c)** *(about)* por; **they asked a. you** preguntaron por ti; **what's he a.?** ¿qué pretende?

3 *conj* después (de) que; **a. it happened** después de que ocurriera

after-effect [ˈɑːtərɪfekt] *n* efecto secundario

afterlife [ˈɑːtəlaɪf] *n* vida *f* después de la muerte

aftermath [ˈɑːtəmæθ] *n* secuelas *fpl*

afternoon [ɑːftəˈnuːn] *n* tarde *f*; **good a.!** ¡buenas tardes!; **in the a.** por la tarde

after-sales service [ɑːftəseɪlzˈsɜːvɪs] *n Com* servicio *m* posventa

aftershave (lotion) [ˈɑːftəʃeɪv (ˈləʊʃən)] *n* loción *f* para después del afeitado *or Méx* rasurado

afterthought [ˈɑːftəθɔːt] *n* ocurrencia *f* tardía

afterward(s) [ˈɑːftəwəd(z)] *adv* después, más tarde

again [əˈgen] *adv* (**a**) otra vez, de nuevo; **I tried a. and a.** lo intenté una y otra vez; **to do sth a.** volver a hacer algo; **never a.!** ¡nunca más!; **now and a.** de vez en cuando; **once a.** otra vez (**b**) *(besides)* además; **then a.** por otra parte

against [əˈgenst] *prep* (**a**) *(touching)* contra (**b**) *(opposing)* contra, en contra (de); **a. the grain** a contrapelo; **it's a. the law** es ilegal (**c**) **as a.** en contraste con, comparado con

age [eɪdʒ] **1** *n* (**a**) edad *f*; **she's eighteen years of a.** tiene dieciocho años; **to be under a.** ser menor de edad; **to come of a.** llegar a la mayoría de edad; **a. limit** límite *m* de edad; **old a.** vejez *f* (**b**) *(period)* época *f*; **the Iron A.** la Edad de Hierro (**c**) *Fam (long time)* eternidad *f*; **it's ages since I last saw her** hace siglos que no la veo **2** *vt & vi* envejecer

aged¹ [eɪdʒd] *adj* de *or* a la edad de

aged² [ˈeɪdʒɪd] *npl* **the a.** los ancianos

agency [ˈeɪdʒənsɪ] *n* (**a**) *Com* agencia *f* (**b**) **by the a. of** por medio de

agenda [əˈdʒendə] *n* orden *m* del día

agent [ˈeɪdʒənt] *n* agente *mf*; *(representative)* representante *mf*

aggravate [ˈægrəveɪt] *vt (worsen)* agravar; *(annoy)* fastidiar, molestar, *RP* hinchar

aggressive [əˈgresɪv] *adj (violent)* agresivo(a), violento(a); *(dynamic)* dinámico(a)

aghast [əˈgɑːst] *adj* espantado(a)

agile [*Br* ˈædʒaɪl, *US* ˈædʒəl] *adj* ágil

agitate [ˈædʒɪteɪt] **1** *vt (shake)* agitar; *Fig (worry)* perturbar **2** *vi Pol* **to a. against sth** hacer campaña en contra de algo

agitated [ˈædʒɪteɪtɪd] *adj* inquieto(a), agitado(a); **to be a.** estar inquieto(a) *or* agitado(a)

agnostic [ægˈnɒstɪk] *n* agnóstico(a) *m,f*

ago [əˈgəʊ] *adv* **a long time a.** hace mucho tiempo; **as long a. as 1910** ya en 1910; **a week a.** hace una semana; **how long a.?** ¿hace cuánto tiempo?

agonizing [ˈægənaɪzɪŋ] *adj (pain)* atroz; *(decision)* desesperante

agony [ˈægənɪ] *n* dolor *m* muy fuerte; *(anguish)* angustia *f*; **he was in a. with his back** tenía un dolor insoportable de espalda

agree [əˈgriː] **1** *vi* (**a**) *(be in agreement)* estar de acuerdo; *(reach agreement)* ponerse de acuerdo; *(consent)* consentir; **to a. to do sth** consentir en hacer algo; **to a. with sb** estar de acuerdo con algn (**b**) *(harmonize) (things)* concordar; *(people)* congeniar; **onions don't a. with me** la cebolla no me sienta bien **2** *vt* acordar

agreeable [əˈgriːəbəl] *adj (pleasant)* agradable; *(person)* simpático(a); *(in agreement)* de acuerdo

agreement [əˈgriːmənt] *n (arrangement)* acuerdo *m*; *Com* contrato *m*; **to reach an a.** llegar a un acuerdo

agricultural [ægrɪˈkʌltʃərəl] *adj* agrícola; *(college)* de agricultura

agriculture [ˈægrɪkʌltʃə(r)] *n* agricultura *f*

aground [əˈgraʊnd] *adv* **to run a.** encallar, varar

ahead [əˈhed] *adv (forwards)* adelante; *(in front)* delante, *Am* adelante; *(early)* antes; **go a.!** ¡adelante!; **to be a.** llevar la ventaja; **to go a.** ir adelante; *Fig* **to go a. with sth** llevar algo adelante; *(start)* comenzar algo;

to get a. triunfar; **to look a.** pensar en el futuro

aid [eɪd] **1** *n* ayuda *f*; *(rescue)* auxilio *m*; **in a. of** a beneficio de; **to come to the a. of sb** acudir en ayuda de algn; **a. worker** cooperante *mf* **2** *vt* ayudar; **to a. and abet sb** ser cómplice de algn

aide [eɪd] *n* ayudante *mf*

AIDS [eɪdz] *n* (*abbr* **Acquired Immune Deficiency Syndrome**) sida *m*

ailing ['eɪlɪŋ] *adj* achacoso(a)

ailment ['eɪlmənt] *n* enfermedad *f* (leve), achaque *m*

aim [eɪm] **1** *n* *(with weapon)* puntería *f*; *(target)* propósito *m* **2** *vt* *(gun)* apuntar (**at** a *or* hacia); *(attack, action)* dirigir (**at** a *or* hacia)

▸ **aim at** *vt insep* *(target)* tirar para; **to a. at doing sth** tener pensado hacer algo

▸ **aim to** *vt insep* **to a. to do sth** tener la intención de hacer algo

aimless ['eɪmlɪs] *adj* sin objeto, sin propósito

air [eə(r)] **1** *n* (**a**) aire *m*; **to travel by a.** viajar en avión; **to throw sth up in the a.** lanzar algo al aire; *Fig* **it's still in the a.** todavía queda por resolver; *Aut* **a. bag** airbag *m*; **a. base** base aérea; **a. bed** colchón *m* hinchable; **a. conditioning** aire acondicionado; **A. Force** Fuerzas Aéreas; **a. freshener** ambientador *m*; **a. gun** pistola *f* de aire comprimido; **a. hostess** azafata *f* de vuelo, *Am* aeromoza *f*; **a. letter** carta aérea; **a. pocket** bache *m*; **a. pressure** presión atmosférica; **a. raid** ataque aéreo; **a. traffic control** control *m* de tráfico aéreo; **a. traffic controller** controlador(a) *m,f* aéreo(a)

(**b**) *Rad, TV* **to be on the a.** *(programme)* estar emitiendo; *(person)* estar transmitiendo

(**c**) *(appearance)* aspecto *m*

2 *vt* *(bed, clothes)* airear; *(room)* ventilar; *Fig (grievance)* airear; *(knowledge)* hacer alarde de

air-conditioned ['eəkɒndɪʃənd] *adj* climatizado(a)

aircraft ['eəkrɑːft] *n* (*pl* **aircraft**) avión *m*; **a. carrier** portaaviones *m inv*

airfield ['eəfiːld] *n* campo *m* de aviación

airline ['eəlaɪn] *n* línea aérea

airmail ['eəmeɪl] *n* correo aéreo; **by a.** por avión

airplane ['eəpleɪn] *n US* avión *m*

airport ['eəpɔːt] *n* aeropuerto *m*; **a. tax** tasas *fpl* de aeropuerto

airtight ['eətaɪt] *adj* hermético(a)

airy ['eərɪ] *adj* (**airier, airiest**) *(well-ventilated)* bien ventilado(a); *(vague, carefree)* ligero(a)

aisle [aɪl] *n* *(in church)* nave *f*; *(in theatre)* pasillo *m*

ajar [ə'dʒɑː(r)] *adj & adv* entreabierto(a)

alarm [ə'lɑːm] **1** *n* (**a**) alarma *f*; **a. clock** despertador *m* (**b**) *(fear)* inquietud *f*; **to cause a.** provocar temor **2** *vt* alarmar

alas [ə'læs] *interj* ¡ay!, ¡ay de mí!

Albania [æl'beɪnɪə] *n* Albania

Albanian [æl'beɪnɪən] **1** *n* (**a**) *(person)* albanés(esa) *m,f* (**b**) *(language)* albanés *m* **2** *adj* albanés(esa)

album ['ælbəm] *n* álbum *m*

alcohol ['ælkəhɒl] *n* alcohol *m*

alcoholic [ælkə'hɒlɪk] *adj & n* alcohólico(a) *(m,f)*

alcove ['ælkəʊv] *n* hueco *m*

ale [eɪl] *n* cerveza *f*; **brown/pale a.** cerveza negra/rubia

alert [ə'lɜːt] **1** *adj* alerta; *(lively)* despabilado(a)

2 *n* alerta *m*; **to be on the a.** estar alerta

3 *vt* **to a. sb to sth** avisar a algn de algo

A-level ['eɪlevəl] *n Br Educ* (*abbr* **Advanced level**) = examen final o diploma en una asignatura de los estudios preuniversitarios

algebra ['ældʒɪbrə] *n* álgebra *f*

Algeria [æl'dʒɪərɪə] *n* Argelia

Algerian [æl'dʒɪərɪən] *adj & n* argelino(a) *(m,f)*

alias ['eɪlɪəs] **1** *n* alias *m* **2** *adv* alias

alibi ['ælɪbaɪ] *n* coartada *f*

alien ['eɪlɪən] **1** *adj (foreign)* extranjero(a); *(from space)* extraterrestre; **a. to** ajeno(a) a **2** *n (foreigner)* extranjero(a) *m,f; (from space)* extraterrestre *mf*

alienate ['eɪlɪəneɪt] *vt* (**a**) **to a. sb** ofender a algn; **to a. oneself from sb** alejarse de algn (**b**) *Jur* enajenar

alight¹ [ə'laɪt] *adj (on fire)* ardiendo(a)

alight² [ə'laɪt] *vi (get off)* apearse (**from** de)

align [ə'laɪn] *vt* alinear

alike [ə'laɪk] **1** *adj (similar)* parecidos(as); *(the same)* iguales **2** *adv (in the same way)* de la misma manera, igualmente; **dressed a.** vestidos(as) iguales

alimony ['ælɪmənɪ] *n Jur* pensión alimenticia

alive [ə'laɪv] *adj* vivo(a); *Fig (teeming)* lleno(a) (**with** de); **to be a.** estar vivo(a)

all [ɔːl] **1** *adj* todo(a), todos(as); **a. year** (durante) todo el año; **a. kinds of things** todo tipo de cosas; **at a. hours** a todas horas; **at a. times** siempre; **she works a. the time** siempre está trabajando; **a. six of us were there** los seis estábamos allí **2** *pron* todo(a), todos(as); **after a.** al fin y al cabo; **a. of his work** toda su obra; **a. of us** todos(as) nosotros(as); **a. who saw it** todos los que lo vieron; **a. you can do is wait** lo único que puedes hacer es esperar; **I don't like it at a.** no me gusta en absoluto; **is that a.?** ¿eso es todo?; **most of** *or* **above a.** sobre todo; **once and for a.** de una vez por todas; **thanks − not at a.** gracias − de nada; **a. in a.** en conjunto; **that's a.** ya está; **the score was one a.** empataron a uno **3** *adv* **a. by myself** completamente solo(a); **a. at once** *(suddenly)* de repente; *(altogether)* de una vez; **a. the better** tanto mejor; **he knew a. along** lo sabía desde el principio; **it's a. but impossible** es casi imposible; **I'm not a. that tired** no estoy tan cansado(a) como eso

all-around ['ɔːləraʊnd] *adj US* = **all-round**

allegation [ælɪ'geɪʃən] *n* alegato *m*

allege [ə'ledʒ] *vt* sostener, pretender (**that** que); **it is alleged that she accepted a bribe** supuestamente aceptó un soborno

allegiance [ə'liːdʒəns] *n* lealtad *f*

allergic [ə'lɜːdʒɪk] *adj* alérgico(a) (**to** a)

allergy ['ælədʒɪ] *n* alergia *f*

alleviate [ə'liːvɪeɪt] *vt (pain)* aliviar

alley ['ælɪ] *n* callejón *m*

alliance [ə'laɪəns] *n* alianza *f*

allied ['ælaɪd] *adj* aliado(a)

alligator ['ælɪgeɪtə(r)] *n* caimán *m*

all-night ['ɔːlnaɪt] *adj (café etc)* abierto(a) toda la noche; *(vigil)* que dura toda la noche

allocate ['æləkeɪt] *vt* destinar (**to** para)

allot [ə'lɒt] *vt* asignar

allotment [ə'lɒtmənt] *n* (**a**) *(of time, money)* asignación *f* (**b**) *Br (plot of land)* huerto *m* de ocio, parcela *f (arrendada por el ayuntamiento para cultivo)*

all-out ['ɔːlaʊt] **1** *adj (effort)* supremo(a); *(attack)* concentrado(a) **2** *adv* **to go a. to do sth** emplearse a fondo para hacer algo

allow [ə'laʊ] *vt* (**a**) *(permit)* permitir; *(a request)* acceder a; **to a. sb to do sth** permitir que algn haga algo (**b**) *(allot) (time)* dejar; *(money)* destinar

▶ **allow for** *vt insep* tener en cuenta

allowance [ə'laʊəns] *n (money given)* asignación *f; US (pocket money)* paga *f;* **to make allowances for sb/sth** disculpar a algn/tener algo en cuenta; **tax a.** desgravación *f* fiscal; **travel a.** dietas *fpl* de viaje

alloy ['ælɔɪ] *n* aleación *f*

all-purpose ['ɔːlpɜːpəs] *adj (cleaner, adhesive)* multiuso

all right [ɔːl'raɪt] **1** *adj (okay)* bien; **thank you very much − that's a.** muchas gracias − de nada **2** *adv* (**a**) *(well)* bien (**b**) *(definitely)* sin duda (**c**) *(okay)* de acuerdo, vale

all-round ['ɔːlraʊnd] *adj (athlete etc)* completo(a)

allusion [ə'luːʒən] n alusión f

ally ['ælaɪ] **1** n aliado(a) m,f **2** vt **to a. oneself to/with sb** aliarse a/con algn

almighty [ɔːl'maɪtɪ] **1** adj (all-powerful) todopoderoso(a) **2** n **the A.** El Todopoderoso

almond ['ɑːmənd] n almendra f

almost ['ɔːlməʊst] adv casi

alone [ə'ləʊn] **1** adj solo(a); **can I speak to you a.?** ¿puedo hablar contigo a solas?; **let a.** ni mucho menos; **leave it a.!** ¡no lo toques!; **leave me a.** déjame en paz; **to be a.** estar solo(a) **2** adv solamente, sólo

along [ə'lɒŋ] **1** adv **come a.!** ¡anda, ven!; **he'll be a. in ten minutes** llegará dentro de diez minutos; **a. with** junto con **2** prep (the length of) a lo largo de; **to walk a. the street** andar por la calle; **it's just a. the street** está un poco más abajo

alongside [ə'lɒŋsaɪd] **1** adv Naut de costado **2** prep al lado de

aloof [ə'luːf] **1** adj (person) distante **2** adv **to keep oneself a. (from)** mantenerse a distancia (de)

aloud [ə'laʊd] adv en voz alta

alphabet ['ælfəbet] n alfabeto m

alphabetical [ælfə'betɪkəl] adj alfabético(a)

Alps [ælps] npl **the A.** los Alpes

already [ɔːl'redɪ] adv ya

alright [ɔːl'raɪt] adj & adv = all right

also ['ɔːlsəʊ] adv también, además

altar ['ɔːltə(r)] n altar m

alter ['ɔːltə(r)] **1** vt (plan) cambiar, retocar; (project) modificar; (clothing) arreglar; (timetable) revisar **2** vi cambiar, cambiarse

alteration [ɔːltə'reɪʃən] n (to plan) cambio m; (to project) modificación f; (to clothing) arreglo m; (to timetable) revisión f; **alterations** (to building) reformas fpl

alternate 1 adj [ɔːl'tɜːnɪt] alterno(a); **on a. days** cada dos días **2** vt ['ɔːltəneɪt] alternar

alternative [ɔːl'tɜːnətɪv] **1** adj alternativo(a) **2** n alternativa f; **I have no a. but to accept** no tengo más remedio que aceptar

alternatively [ɔːl'tɜːnətɪvlɪ] adv o bien; **a., you could walk** o bien podrías ir andando

although [ɔːl'ðəʊ] conj aunque

altitude ['æltɪtjuːd] n altitud f

altogether [ɔːltə'geðə(r)] adv (in total) en conjunto, en total; (completely) completamente, del todo

aluminium [æljʊ'mɪnɪəm], US **aluminum** [ə'luːmɪnəm] n aluminio m

always ['ɔːlweɪz] adv siempre

am [æm] 1st person sing pres of be

a.m. [eɪ'em] (abbr ante meridiem) a.m., de la mañana

amalgamate [ə'mælgəmeɪt] **1** vt (metals) amalgamar **2** vi (metals) amalgamarse; (companies) fusionarse

amateur ['æmətə(r)] **1** n amateur mf, aficionado(a) m,f **2** adj aficionado(a); Pej (work etc) chapucero(a)

amaze [ə'meɪz] vt asombrar, pasmar; **to be amazed at sth** quedarse pasmado(a) de algo

amazing [ə'meɪzɪŋ] adj asombroso(a), increíble

ambassador [æm'bæsədə(r)] n embajador(a) m,f

amber ['æmbə(r)] **1** n ámbar m **2** adj ambarino(a); Br **a. light** semáforo m en ámbar

ambiguous [æm'bɪgjʊəs] adj ambiguo(a)

ambition [æm'bɪʃən] n ambición f

ambitious [æm'bɪʃəs] adj ambicioso(a)

ambivalent [æm'bɪvələnt] adj ambivalente

ambulance ['æmbjʊləns] n ambulancia f; **a. man** ambulanciero m

ambush ['æmbʊʃ] **1** n emboscada f **2** vt tender una emboscada a; Fig atacar por sorpresa

amend [ə'mend] vt (law) enmendar; (error) subsanar

amends [ə'mendz] npl **to make a. to sb for sth** compensar a algn por algo

amenities [ə'miːnɪtɪz] *npl* comodidades *fpl*

America [ə'merɪkə] *n (continent)* América *f*; *(USA)* (los) Estados Unidos; **South A.** América del Sur, Sudamérica *f*

American [ə'merɪkən] *adj & n* americano(a) *(m,f)*; *(of USA)* norteamericano(a) *(m,f)*, estadounidense *(mf)*

amiable ['eɪmɪəbəl] *adj* amable, afable

amicable ['æmɪkəbəl] *adj* amistoso(a)

amid(st) ['æmɪd(st)] *prep* entre, en medio de

amiss [ə'mɪs] *adj & adv* mal; **there's sth a.** algo anda mal; **to take sth a.** tomar algo a mal

ammunition [æmjʊ'nɪʃən] *n* municiones *fpl*

among(st) [ə'mʌŋ(st)] *prep* entre

amoral [eɪ'mɒrəl] *adj* amoral

amount [ə'maʊnt] *n* cantidad *f*; *(of money)* suma *f*; *(of bill)* importe *m*

▸ **amount to** *vt insep* ascender a; *Fig* equivaler a

amp [æmp], **ampère** ['æmpeə(r)] *n* amperio *m*

ample ['æmpəl] *adj (enough)* bastante; *(more than enough)* abundante; *(large)* amplio(a)

amplifier ['æmplɪfaɪə(r)] *n* amplificador *m*

amplify ['æmplɪfaɪ] *vt (essay, remarks)* ampliar; *(current, volume)* amplificar

amputate ['æmpjʊteɪt] *vt* amputar

Amtrak ['æmtræk] *n* = compañía ferroviaria estadounidense

amuse [ə'mjuːz] *vt* divertir, entretener

amusement [ə'mjuːzmənt] *n (enjoyment)* diversión *f*; *(laughter)* risa *f*; *(pastime)* pasatiempo *m*; **a. arcade** salón *m* de juegos; **a. park** parque *m* de atracciones

an [æn, *unstressed* ən] *see* **a**

anaemic [ə'niːmɪk] *adj* anémico(a); *Fig (weak)* débil

anaesthetic [ænɪs'θetɪk] *n* anestesia *f*

analogy [ə'nælədʒɪ] *n* analogía *f*

analyse ['ænəlaɪz] *vt* analizar

analysis [ə'nælɪsɪs] *n (pl* **analyses** [ə'nælɪsiːz]) análisis *m inv*

analyst ['ænəlɪst] *n* analista *mf*; *(psychoanalyst)* psicoanalista *mf*

analyze ['ænəlaɪz] *vt US =* **analyse**

anarchist ['ænəkɪst] *n* anarquista *mf*

anarchy ['ænəkɪ] *n* anarquía *f*

anatomy [ə'nætəmɪ] *n* anatomía *f*

ancestor ['ænsestə(r)] *n* antepasado *m*

anchor ['æŋkə(r)] **1** *n Naut* ancla *f*; *Fig* áncora *f* **2** *vt Naut* anclar; *Fig (fix securely)* sujetar **3** *vi* anclar

anchovy [*Br* 'æntʃəvɪ, *Am* æn'tʃəʊvɪ] *n* anchoa *f*

ancient ['eɪnʃənt] *adj* antiguo(a)

and [ænd, *unstressed* ənd, ən] *conj* y; *(before i-, hi-)* e; **a hundred a. one** ciento uno; **a. so on** etcétera; **Bill a. Pat** Bill y Pat; **Chinese a. Indian** chino e indio; **come a. see us** ven a vernos; **four a. a half** cuatro y medio; **she cried a. cried** no paró de llorar; **try a. help me** trata de ayudarme; **wait a. see** espera a ver; **worse a. worse** cada vez peor

anemic [ə'niːmɪk] *n US =* **anaemic**

anesthetic [ænɪs'θetɪk] *n US =* **anaesthetic**

angel ['eɪndʒəl] *n* ángel *m*

anger ['æŋgə(r)] **1** *n* ira *f*, *esp Esp* enfado *m*, *esp Am* enojo *m* **2** *vt esp Esp* enfadar, *esp Am* enojar

angle ['æŋgəl] *n* ángulo *m*; *Fig* punto *m* de vista

angler ['æŋglə(r)] *n* pescador(a) *m,f* de caña

Anglican ['æŋglɪkən] *adj & n* anglicano(a) *(m,f)*

Anglo-Saxon [æŋgləʊ'sæksən] *adj & n* anglosajón(ona) *(m,f)*

angry ['æŋgrɪ] *adj (angrier, angriest)* *(person) esp Esp* enfadado(a), *esp Am* enojado(a); *(voice, letter)* airado(a); **to get a.** estar *esp Esp* enfadado(a) *or esp Am* enojado(a)

anguish ['æŋgwɪʃ] n angustia f

animal ['ænɪməl] **1** adj animal **2** n animal m; Fig bestia f

animated ['ænɪmeɪtɪd] adj (lively) animado(a)

animation [ænɪ'meɪʃən] n animación f

aniseed ['ænɪsi:d] n anís m

ankle ['æŋkəl] n tobillo m; **a. boots** botines mpl; **a. socks** calcetines mpl cortos, CSur zoquetes mpl, Col medias fpl tobilleras

annex [ə'neks] vt (territory) anexionar

anniversary [ænɪ'vɜːsərɪ] n aniversario m; **wedding a.** aniversario de bodas

announce [ə'naʊns] vt anunciar; (news) comunicar; (fact) hacer saber

announcement [ə'naʊnsmənt] n anuncio m; (news) comunicación f; (statement) declaración f

announcer [ə'naʊnsə(r)] n TV, Rad locutor(a) m,f

annoy [ə'nɔɪ] vt fastidiar, molestar, esp Am enojar; **to get annoyed** molestarse, esp Esp enfadarse, esp Am enojarse

annoying [ə'nɔɪɪŋ] adj molesto(a), fastidioso(a)

annual ['ænjʊəl] **1** adj anual **2** n (book) anuario m; (plant) anual m

annually ['ænjʊəlɪ] adv anualmente

annul [ə'nʌl] vt anular

anomaly [ə'nɒməlɪ] n anomalía f

anonymous [ə'nɒnɪməs] adj anónimo(a)

anorak ['ænəræk] n anorak m

anorexia [ænə'reksɪə] n anorexia f

another [ə'nʌðə(r)] **1** adj otro(a); **a. one** otro(a); **without a. word** sin más **2** pron otro(a); **have a.** toma otro(a); **to love one a.** quererse el uno al otro

answer ['ɑːnsə(r)] **1** n (to letter etc) contestación f; (to question) respuesta f; (to problem) solución f; **in a. to your letter** contestando a su carta; **there's no a.** (on telephone) no contestan; (at door) no abren **2** vt contestar a; (problem) resolver;

3 vi contestar, responder

▶ **answer back** vi replicar; **don't a. back!** ¡no seas respondón!

▶ **answer for** vt insep responder de; **he's got a lot to a. for** es responsable de muchas cosas

▶ **answer to** vt insep (name) responder a; (description) corresponder a

answering machine ['ɑːnsərɪŋməʃiːn] n contestador m automático

ant [ænt] n hormiga f; **a. hill** hormiguero m

antagonize [æn'tægənaɪz] vt enemistar, malquistar

Antarctic [æn'tɑːktɪk] **1** adj antártico(a); **A. Ocean** océano Antártico **2** n **the A.** la Antártida

antenna [æn'tenə] n (a) (pl antennae [æn'teniː]) (of animal, insect) antena f (b) (pl antennas) TV, Rad antena f

anthem ['ænθəm] n motete m; **national a.** himno m nacional

anthology [æn'θɒlədʒɪ] n antología f

antibiotic [æntɪbaɪ'ɒtɪk] n antibiótico m

anticipate [æn'tɪsɪpeɪt] vt (a) (expect) esperar (b) (predict) prever; (get ahead of) anticiparse a, adelantarse a

anticipation [æntɪsɪ'peɪʃən] n (expectation) esperanza f; (expectancy) ilusión f

anticlimax [æntɪ'klaɪmæks] n (disappointment) decepción f

anticlockwise [æntɪ'klɒkwaɪz] adv Br en sentido opuesto al de las agujas del reloj

antics ['æntɪks] npl payasadas fpl; (naughtiness) travesuras fpl

antidote ['æntɪdəʊt] n antídoto m

antifreeze ['æntɪfriːz] n anticongelante m

antihistamine [æntɪ'hɪstəmɪn] n antihistamínico m

antiperspirant [æntɪ'pɜːspɪrənt] n antitranspirante m

antiquated ['æntɪkweɪtɪd] adj anticuado(a)

antique [æn'ti:k] **1** *adj* antiguo(a) **2** *n* antigüedad *f*; **a. dealer** anticuario(a) *m,f*; **a. shop** tienda *f* de antigüedades

antisemitic [æntɪsɪ'mɪtɪk] *adj* (*person*) antisemita; (*beliefs, remarks*) antisemítico(a)

antiseptic [æntɪ'septɪk] *adj & n* antiséptico(a) *(m)*

antisocial [æntɪ'səʊʃəl] *adj* (*delinquent*) antisocial; (*unsociable*) insociable

anxiety [æŋ'zaɪɪtɪ] *n* (*concern*) inquietud *f*; (*worry*) preocupación *f*; (*fear*) angustia *f*; (*eagerness*) ansia *f*

anxious [æŋkʃəs] *adj* (*concerned*) inquieto(a); (*worried*) preocupado(a); (*fearful*) angustiado(a); (*eager*) ansioso(a); **to be a. about sth** estar preocupado(a) por algo

any ['enɪ] **1** *adj* (**a**) (*in questions, conditionals*) algún(una); **are there a. seats left?** ¿quedan plazas?; **have you a. apples?** ¿tienes manzanas?; **have you a. money?** ¿tienes (algo de) dinero? (**b**) (*in negative clauses*) ningún(una); **I don't have a. time** no tengo tiempo (**c**) (*no matter which*) cualquier(a); **a. doctor will say the same** cualquier médico te dirá lo mismo; **at a. moment** en cualquier momento (**d**) (*every*) todo(a); **in a. case** de todas formas **2** *pron* (**a**) (*in questions*) alguno(a); **do they have a.?** ¿tienen alguno?; **I need some paper, have you a.?** necesito papel, ¿tienes? (**b**) (*in negative clauses*) ninguno(a); **I don't want a.** no quiero ninguno(a) (**c**) (*no matter which*) cualquiera; **you can have a. (one)** coge el/la que quieras **3** *adv* **is there a. more?** ¿hay más?; **I used to like it, but not a. more** or **longer** antes me gustaba pero ya no; **is he a. better?** ¿está mejor?

anybody ['enɪbɒdɪ] *pron* (*in questions, conditionals*) alguien, alguno(a); (*in negative clauses*) nadie, ninguno(a); (*no matter who*) cualquiera; **a. but me** cualquiera menos yo; **bring a. you like** trae a quien quieras; **do you see a. over there?** ¿ves a alguien allí?; **I**

can't find a. no encuentro a nadie

anyhow ['enɪhaʊ] *adv* (**a**) (*in spite of that*) en todo caso, de todas formas; (*changing the subject*) bueno, pues (**b**) (*carelessly*) desordenadamente, de cualquier modo or forma

anyone ['enɪwʌn] *pron* = **anybody**

anyplace ['enɪpleɪs] *adv US* = **anywhere**

anything ['enɪθɪŋ] **1** *pron* (*in questions, conditionals*) algo, alguna cosa; (*in negative clauses*) nada; (*no matter what*) cualquier cosa; **a. but that** cualquier cosa menos eso; **a. else?** ¿algo más?; **can I do a. for you?** ¿puedo ayudarte en algo?; **hardly a.** casi nada; **if a., I'd buy the big one** de comprar uno compraría el grande; **to run/work like a.** correr/trabajar a más no poder **2** *adv* **is this a. like what you wanted?** ¿viene a ser éste lo que querías?

anyway ['enɪweɪ] *adv* = **anyhow** (**a**)

anywhere ['enɪweə(r)] *adv* (**a**) (*in questions, conditionals*) (*situation*) en alguna parte; (*movement*) a alguna parte; **could it be a. else?** ¿podría estar en otro sitio?
(**b**) (*in negative clauses*) (*situation*) en ninguna parte; (*movement*) a ninguna parte; (*no matter where*) dondequiera, en cualquier parte; **go a. you like** ve a donde quieras; **we aren't a. near finished** no hemos terminado ni mucho menos

apart [ə'pɑːt] *adv* (**a**) aparte; **to fall a.** deshacerse; **to take sth a.** desmontar algo (**b**) (*distant*) alejado(a); (*separate*) separado(a); **to be poles a.** ser polos opuestos; **you can't tell the twins a.** no se puede distinguir los mellizos el uno del otro (**c**) **a. from** aparte de

apartment [ə'pɑːtmənt] *n US* apartamento *m*, *Esp* piso, *Arg* departamento; **a. block** edificio *m* or bloque *m* de apartamentos or *Esp* pisos or *Arg* departamentos

apathy ['æpəθɪ] *n* apatía *f*

ape [eɪp] **1** *n* mono *m* **2** *vt* imitar, copiar

aperture ['æpətʃə(r)] *n (hole, crack)* resquicio *m*, rendija *f*; *Phot* abertura *f*

apiece [ə'piːs] *adv* cada uno(a)

apologetic [əpɒlə'dʒetɪk] *adj (remorseful)* de disculpa; **he was very a.** pidió mil perdones

apologize [ə'pɒlədʒaɪz] *vi (say sorry)* disculparse; **they apologized to us for the delay** se disculparon con nosotros por el retraso

apology [ə'pɒlədʒɪ] *n* disculpa *f*, excusa *f*; *Fam* **what an a. for a meal!** ¡vaya birria de comida!

apostle [ə'pɒsəl] *n* apóstol *m*

apostrophe [ə'pɒstrəfɪ] *n* apóstrofo *m*

appal, *US* **appall** [ə'pɔːl] *vt* horrorizar

appalling [ə'pɔːlɪŋ] *adj (horrifying)* horroroso(a); *Fam (very bad)* pésimo(a), fatal

apparatus [æpə'reɪtəs] *n* aparato *m*; *(equipment)* equipo *m*

apparel [ə'pærəl] *n US* indumentaria *f*, ropa *f*

apparent [ə'pærənt] *adj (obvious)* evidente; *(seeming)* aparente; **to become a.** ponerse de manifiesto

apparently [ə'pærəntlɪ] *adv (seemingly)* por lo visto

appeal [ə'piːl] **1** *n* (a) *(request)* solicitud *f*; *(plea)* súplica *f* (b) *(attraction)* atractivo *m*; *(interest)* interés *m* (c) *Jur* apelación *f* **2** *vi* (a) *(plead)* rogar, suplicar (**to** a); **to a. for help** solicitar ayuda (b) *(attract)* atraer; *(interest)* interesar; **it doesn't a. to me** no me dice nada (c) *Jur* apelar

appealing [ə'piːlɪŋ] *adj (moving)* conmovedor(a); *(attractive)* atractivo(a); *(tempting)* atrayente

appear [ə'pɪə(r)] *vi* (a) *(become visible)* aparecer; *(publicly)* presentarse; *(on stage)* actuar; **to a. before a court** comparecer ante un tribunal; **to a. on television** salir en la televisión (b) *(seem)* parecer; **he appears relaxed** parece relajado; **so it appears** según parece

appearance [ə'pɪərəns] *n* (a) *(becoming visible)* aparición *f*; *(publicly)* presentación *f*; *(on stage)* actuación *f*; *(before court)* comparecencia *f*; *(of book etc)* publicación *f*; **to put in an a.** hacer acto de presencia (b) *(look)* apariencia *f*, aspecto *m*; **to all appearances** al parecer

appendicitis [əpendɪ'saɪtɪs] *n* apendicitis *f*

appendix [ə'pendɪks] *n (pl* **appendices***)* apéndice *m*

appetite ['æpɪtaɪt] *n* apetito *m*; *Fig* deseo *m*

appetizing ['æpɪtaɪzɪŋ] *adj* apetitoso(a)

applaud [ə'plɔːd] *vt & vi* aplaudir

applause [ə'plɔːz] *n* aplausos *mpl*

apple ['æpəl] *n* manzana *f*; **a. tree** manzano *m*

appliance [ə'plaɪəns] *n* dispositivo *m*

applicable [ə'plɪkəbəl] *adj* aplicable

applicant ['æplɪkənt] *n (for post)* candidato(a) *m,f*; *(to court, for tickets)* solicitante *mf*

application [æplɪ'keɪʃən] *n* (a) *(of cream)* aplicación *f* (b) *(for post etc)* solicitud *f*; **a. form** solicitud; **job a.** solicitud de empleo, *(c) (effort)* aplicación *f*; **she lacks a.** no se aplica

applied [ə'plaɪd] *adj* aplicado(a)

apply [ə'plaɪ] **1** *vt* aplicar; *(brake)* echar; *(law)* recurrir a; *(force)* usar; **to a. oneself to** dedicarse a **2** *vi* (a) *(refer)* aplicarse (**to** a) (b) *(for job)* presentar una solicitud; *(for information, to court)* presentar una petición

▸ **apply for** *vt insep (post, information)* solicitar; *(tickets)* pedir

appoint [ə'pɔɪnt] *vt (person)* nombrar; *(time, place etc)* fijar, señalar

appointment [ə'pɔɪntmənt] *n* (a) *(to post)* nombramiento *m*; *(post)* cargo *m* (b) *(meeting)* cita *f*; **to make an a. with** citarse con; *(at doctor's)* pedir hora a

appraisal [ə'preɪzəl] *n* evaluación *f*

appreciate [ə'priːʃɪeɪt] **1** *vt* (a) *(be thankful for)* agradecer (b) *(understand)* entender (c) *(value)* apreciar, valorar **2** *vi (increase in value)* apreciarse

appreciation [əpriːʃɪˈeɪʃən] *n* (**a**) *(of help, advice)* agradecimiento *m*; *(of difficulty)* comprensión *f*; *(of wine etc)* aprecio *m*; *(appraisal)* evaluación *f* (**b**) *(increase in value)* apreciación *f*

appreciative [əˈpriːʃɪətɪv] *adj* *(thankful)* agradecido(a); *(responsive)* apreciativo(a)

apprehend [æprɪˈhend] *vt* *(arrest)* detener

apprehensive [æprɪˈhensɪv] *adj* *(fearful)* aprensivo(a)

apprentice [əˈprentɪs] *n* aprendiz(a) *m,f*

apprenticeship [əˈprentɪsʃɪp] *n* aprendizaje *m*

approach [əˈprəʊtʃ] **1** *n* (**a**) *(coming near)* acercamiento *m*; *(to town)* acceso *m*; **a. road** vía *f* de acceso (**b**) *(to problem)* enfoque *m*
2 *vt* *(come near to)* acercarse a; *(be similar to)* aproximarse a; *Fig (problem)* abordar; *(person)* dirigirse a; **to a. sb about sth** dirigirse a algn a propósito de algo
3 *vi* acercarse

approachable [əˈprəʊtʃəbəl] *adj* *(person)* accesible

appropriate[1] [əˈprəʊprɪət] *adj* *(suitable)* apropiado(a), adecuado(a); *(convenient)* oportuno(a)

appropriate[2] [əˈprəʊprɪeɪt] *vt (allocate)* asignar; *(steal)* apropiarse de

approval [əˈpruːvəl] *n* aprobación *f*, visto bueno; *Com* **to get sth on a.** adquirir algo sin compromiso de compra

approve [əˈpruːv] *vt* aprobar
▸ **approve of** *vt insep* aprobar

approving [əˈpruːvɪŋ] *adj (look etc)* aprobatorio(a)

approximate **1** *adj* [əˈprɒksɪmɪt] aproximado(a) **2** *vt* [əˈprɒksɪmeɪt] aproximarse a

apricot [ˈeɪprɪkɒt] *n* *(fruit)* *Esp* albaricoque *m*, *Andes, RP* damasco *m*, *Méx* chabacano *m*; **a. tree** *Esp* albaricoquero *m*, *Andes, RP* damasco *m*, *Méx* chabacano *m*

April [ˈeɪprəl] *n* abril *m*; **A. Fools' Day**

día *m* uno de abril, ≃ día de los Inocentes (28 de diciembre)

apron [ˈeɪprən] *n* delantal *m*; *(for workman)* mandil *m*

apt [æpt] *adj* (**a**) *(suitable)* apropiado(a); *(remark)* acertado(a), oportuno(a); *(name)* justo(a); *(description)* exacto(a) (**b**) **to be a. to do sth** ser propenso(a) a hacer algo

aptitude [ˈæptɪtjuːd] *n* capacidad *f*; **a. test** prueba *f* de aptitud

aptly [ˈæptlɪ] *adv* acertadamente

aquarium [əˈkweərɪəm] *n* acuario *m*

Aquarius [əˈkweərɪəs] *n* Acuario *m*

aquatic [əˈkwætɪk] *adj* acuático(a)

Arab [ˈærəb] *adj & n* árabe *(mf)*

Arabian [əˈreɪbɪən] *adj* árabe

Arabic [ˈærəbɪk] **1** *adj* árabe, arábigo(a); **A. numerals** numeración arábiga **2** *n (language)* árabe *m*

arbitrary [ˈɑːbɪtrərɪ] *adj* arbitrario(a)

arbitration [ɑːbɪˈtreɪʃən] *n* arbitraje *m*

arc [ɑːk] *n* arco *m*; **a. lamp** arco voltaico

arcade [ɑːˈkeɪd] *n* arcada *f*; *(passageway)* pasaje *m*; **shopping a.** galerías *fpl* (comerciales)

arch [ɑːtʃ] **1** *n* (**a**) *Archit* arco *m*; *(vault)* bóveda *f* (**b**) *Anat* empeine *m* **2** *vt* *(back)* arquear

archaeologist [ɑːkɪˈɒlədʒɪst] *n* arqueólogo(a) *m,f*

archaeology [ɑːkɪˈɒlədʒɪ] *n* arqueología *f*

archaic [ɑːˈkeɪɪk] *adj* arcaico(a)

archbishop [ɑːtʃˈbɪʃəp] *n* arzobispo *m*

archeologist [ɑːkɪˈɒlədʒɪst] *n US* = archaeologist

archeology [ɑːkɪˈɒlədʒɪ] *n US* = archaeology

archer [ˈɑːtʃə(r)] *n* arquero(a) *m,f*

archetypal [ˈɑːkɪtaɪpəl] *adj* arquetípico(a)

architect [ˈɑːkɪtekt] *n* arquitecto(a) *m,f*

architecture [ˈɑːkɪtektʃə(r)] *n* arquitectura *f*

archives [ˈɑːkaɪvz] *npl* archivos *mpl*

archway ['ɑ:tʃweɪ] *n (arch)* arco *m*; *(vault)* bóveda *f*; *(in church)* atrio *m*; *(passage)* pasaje *m*

arctic ['ɑ:ktɪk] **1** *adj* ártico(a); **A. Circle** círculo *m* polar Ártico **2** *n* **the A.** el Ártico

ardent ['ɑ:dənt] *adj (supporter etc)* apasionado(a); *(desire)* ardiente

ardour, *US* **ardor** ['ɑ:də(r)] *n* pasión *f*, ardor *m*

arduous ['ɑ:djʊəs] *adj* arduo(a), penoso(a)

are [ɑ:(r)] *2nd person sing pres, 1st, 2nd, 3rd person pl pres of* **be**

area ['eərɪə] *n (surface)* área *f*, superficie *f*; *(space)* extensión *f*; *(region)* región *f*; *(of town)* zona *f*; *Fig (field)* campo *m*; *US Tel* **a. code** prefijo *m* local

arena [ə'ri:nə] *n (stadium)* estadio *m*; *(bullring)* plaza *f*; *(circus)* pista *f*; *Fig (stage)* campo *m* de batalla

Argentina [ɑ:dʒən'ti:nə] *n* Argentina

arguable ['ɑ:gjʊəbəl] *adj* discutible

argue ['ɑ:gju:] **1** *vt (reason)* discutir; *(point of view)* mantener **2** *vi (quarrel)* discutir; *(reason)* argumentar, razonar; **to a. for** abogar por; **to a. against sth** ponerse en contra de algo

argument ['ɑ:gjʊmənt] *n (reason)* argumento *m* (**for** a favor de; **against** en contra de); *(quarrel)* discusión *f*, disputa *f*; **for the sake of a.** por decir algo

argumentative [ɑ:gjʊ'mentətɪv] *adj* **she's very a.** le gusta discutir por todo

Aries ['eəri:z] *n* Aries *m*

arise [ə'raɪz] *vi (pt* **arose**; *pp* **arisen** [ə'rɪzən]*) (get up)* levantarse; *(happen)* surgir; **should the occasion a.** si se presenta la ocasión

aristocracy [ærɪ'stɒkrəsɪ] *n* aristocracia *f*

aristocrat [*Br* 'ærɪstəkræt, *US* ə'rɪstəkræt] *n* aristócrata *mf*

arithmetic [ə'rɪθmətɪk] *n* aritmética *f*

ark [ɑ:k] *n* arca *f*; **Noah's A.** el arca de Noé

arm [ɑ:m] **1** *n* (**a**) brazo *m*; *(of garment)* manga *f*; **to walk. in a.** ir cogidos(as) del brazo (**b**) *Mil* **arms** armas *fpl*; **arms race** carrera armamentística; **coat of arms** escudo *m* **2** *vt* armar; **to a. oneself against sth** armarse contra algo

armaments ['ɑ:məmənts] *npl* armamentos *mpl*

armband ['ɑ:mbænd] *n (at funeral, for swimming)* brazalete *m*

armchair ['ɑ:mtʃeə(r)] *n* sillón *m*

armistice ['ɑ:mɪstɪs] *n* armisticio *m*

armour, *US* **armor** ['ɑ:mə(r)] *n (on vehicle)* blindaje *m*; **(suit of) a.** armadura *f*

armoured car, *US* **armored car** [ɑ:məd'kɑ:(r)] *n* coche *m* blindado

armpit ['ɑ:mpɪt] *n* axila *f*, sobaco *m*

army ['ɑ:mɪ] *n* ejército *m*

aroma [ə'rəʊmə] *n* aroma *m*

aromatic [ærəʊ'mætɪk] *adj* aromático(a)

arose [ə'rəʊz] *pt of* **arise**

around [ə'raʊnd] **1** *adv* alrededor; **all a.** por todos los lados; **are the children a.?** ¿están los niños por aquí?; **he looked a.** miró (a su) alrededor **2** *prep* (**a**) alrededor de; **a. the corner** a la vuelta de la esquina; **a. here** por aquí (**b**) *(approximately)* aproximadamente

arouse [ə'raʊz] *vt* despertar; *(sexually)* excitar

arrange [ə'reɪndʒ] **1** *vt* (**a**) *(order)* ordenar; *(hair, flowers)* arreglar; *Mus* adaptar (**b**) *(plan)* organizar; *(agree on)* quedar en; **to a. a time** fijar una hora; **arranged marriage** boda arreglada **2** *vi* **I shall a. for him to be there** lo arreglaré para que pueda asistir

arrangement [ə'reɪndʒmənt] *n* (**a**) *(display)* colocación *f*; *Mus* adaptación *f* (**b**) *(agreement)* acuerdo *m* (**c**) **arrangements** *(plans)* planes *mpl*; *(preparations)* preparativos *mpl*

arrears [ə'rɪəz] *npl* atrasos *mpl*; **to be in a. with the rent** estar atrasado(a) en el pago del alquiler *o Méx* de la renta; **to be paid in a.** cobrar con retraso

arrest [ə'rest] **1** n detención f; **to be under a.** estar detenido(a) **2** vt (criminal) detener; Fig (progress) frenar

arrival [ə'raɪvəl] n llegada f; **a new a.** un(a) recién llegado(a)

arrive [ə'raɪv] vi llegar (**at/in** a)

arrogance ['ærəgəns] n arrogancia f

arrogant ['ærəgənt] adj arrogante

arrow ['ærəʊ] n flecha f

arse [ɑːs] n Br Vulg (buttocks) culo m

arson ['ɑːsən] n incendio m provocado

art [ɑːt] n (**a**) arte m; (drawing) dibujo m; **the arts** las bellas artes; **arts and crafts** artes fpl y oficios mpl; **a. gallery** galería f de arte (**b**) **arts** (branch of knowledge) letras fpl

artery ['ɑːtərɪ] n arteria f

arthritis [ɑː'θraɪtɪs] n artritis f

artichoke ['ɑːtɪtʃəʊk] n alcachofa f, Am alcaucil m

article ['ɑːtɪkəl] n artículo m; **a. of clothing** prenda f de vestir; Jur **articles** contrato m de aprendizaje

articulate¹ [ɑː'tɪkjʊlɪt] adj (speech) claro(a); (person) que se expresa bien

articulate² [ɑː'tɪkjʊleɪt] vt & vi articular; (words) pronunciar; Br **articulated lorry** camión articulado

artificial [ɑːtɪ'fɪʃəl] adj artificial; (limb) postizo(a); **a. intelligence** inteligencia f artificial

artillery [ɑː'tɪlərɪ] n artillería f

artist ['ɑːtɪst] n artista mf; (painter) pintor(a) m,f

artistic [ɑː'tɪstɪk] adj artístico(a)

arty ['ɑːtɪ] adj Fam (person) = que se interesa por las artes

as [æz, unstressed əz] **1** adv & conj (**a**) (comparison) **as ... as ...** tan ... como ...; **as far as** hasta; Fig **as far as I'm concerned** por lo que a mí respecta; **as many as** tantos(as) como; **as much as** tanto(a) como; **as tall as me** tan alto(a) como yo; **as little as £5** tan sólo 5 libras; **as soon as they arrive** en cuanto lleguen; **I'll stay as long as I can** quedaré todo el tiempo que pueda; **just as big** igual de grande; **three times as fast** tres veces más

rápido; **the same as** igual que

(**b**) (manner) como; **as a rule** por regla general; **as you know** como ya sabéis; **as you like** como quieras; **do as I say** haz lo que yo te digo; **he's working as a doctor** está trabajando de médico; **I thought as much** ya me lo suponía; **it serves as a table** sirve de mesa; **leave it as it is** déjalo tal como está; **he was dressed as a pirate** iba vestido de pirata

(**c**) (while, when) mientras (que); **as a child** de niño(a); **as I was eating** mientras comía; **as we were leaving, we saw Pat** al salir vimos a Pat

(**d**) (though) aunque; **be that as it may** por mucho que así sea; **young as he is** aunque es joven

(**e**) (because) como, ya que

(**f**) (and so) igual que; **as do I** igual que yo; **as well** también

(**g**) (purpose) para; **so as to do sth** para hacer algo

(**h**) **as for my brother** en cuanto a mi hermano

(**i**) **as from, as of** a partir de

(**j**) **to act as if** actuar como si (+ subj); **it looks as if the concert is off** parece ser que no habrá concierto

(**k**) **it's late enough as it is** ya es muy tarde; **as it were** por así decirlo

(**l**) **as long as** (only if) siempre que, con tal de que

(**m**) **as regards** en cuanto a, por lo que se refiere a; **as usual** como siempre; **as yet** aún, todavía

2 rel pron **such as** tal(es) como

asap [eɪeseɪ'piː] adv (abbr **as soon as possible**) cuanto antes, lo antes posible

ascend [ə'send] vi subir, ascender

ascent [ə'sent] n subida f

ascertain [æsə'teɪn] vt averiguar, enterarse de

ash¹ [æʃ] n Bot fresno m

ash² [æʃ] n ceniza f; **a. bin,** US **a. can** cubo m de la basura; Rel **A. Wednesday** miércoles m inv de ceniza

ashamed [ə'ʃeɪmd] adj avergonzado(a), Am salvo RP apenado(a); **you ought to be a. of yourself!** ¡debería darte vergüenza or Am salvo RP pena!

ashore [ə'ʃɔː(r)] *adv (position)* en tierra; **to go a.** desembarcar; **to swim a.** nadar hacia tierra

ashtray ['æʃtreɪ] *n* cenicero *m*

Asia ['eɪʒə] *n* Asia; **A. Minor** Asia Menor

Asian ['eɪʒən] **1** *n* asiático(a) *m,f*; *Br (person from Indian subcontinent)* = persona de la India, Paquistán o Bangladesh **2** *adj* asiático(a); *Br (from Indian subcontinent)* = de la India, Paquistán o Bangladesh

aside [ə'saɪd] **1** *adv* al lado, aparte; **to cast a.** echar a un lado; **to stand a.** apartarse
2 *prep* **a. from** *(apart from)* aparte de; *(as well as)* además de
3 *n Th* aparte *m*

ask [ɑːsk] **1** *vt* **(a)** preguntar; **to a. sb a question** hacer una pregunta a algn **(b)** *(request)* pedir, solicitar; **she asked me to post it** me pidió que lo echara al buzón **(c)** *(invite)* invitar **2** *vi (inquire)* preguntar; *(request)* pedir

▸ **ask after** *vt insep* **to a. after sb** preguntar por algn

▸ **ask for** *vt insep (help)* pedir, solicitar; *(person)* preguntar por

▸ **ask out** *vt sep* **to a. sb out** invitar a algn a salir

asleep [ə'sliːp] *adj (person)* dormido(a); *(limb)* adormecido(a); **to fall a.** quedarse dormido(a)

asparagus [ə'spærəgəs] *n inv* espárragos *mpl*

aspect ['æspekt] *n* **(a)** *(of question)* aspecto *m* **(b)** *(of building)* orientación *f*

asphyxiate [æs'fɪksɪeɪt] **1** *vt* asfixiar **2** *vi* asfixiarse

aspire [ə'spaɪə(r)] *vi* **to a. to** aspirar a

aspirin ['æsprɪn] *n* aspirina *f*

ass¹ [æs] *n* asno(a) *m,f*, burro(a) *m,f*

ass² [æs] *n US Vulg* culo *m*

assailant [ə'seɪlənt] *n* agresor(a) *m,f*, atacante *mf*

assassin [ə'sæsɪn] *n* asesino(a) *m,f*

assassinate [ə'sæsɪneɪt] *vt* asesinar

assassination [əsæsɪ'neɪʃən] *n* asesinato *m*

assault [ə'sɔːlt] **1** *n Mil* ataque *m* (**on** a); *Jur* agresión *f* **2** *vt Mil* asaltar, atacar; *Jur* agredir; *(sexually)* violar

assemble [ə'sembəl] **1** *vt (people)* reunir, juntar; *(furniture)* montar **2** *vi (people)* reunirse, juntarse

assembly [ə'semblɪ] *n* reunión *f*, asamblea *f*; *Tech* montaje *m*; *Educ* = reunión de todos los profesores y los alumnos al principio de la jornada escolar; *Ind* **a. line** cadena *f* de montaje

assent [ə'sent] **1** *n (agreement)* asentimiento *m*; *(consent)* consentimiento *m*; *(approval)* aprobación *f* **2** *vi* asentir, consentir (**to** en)

assert [ə'sɜːt] *vt* afirmar; **to a. oneself** imponerse; **to a. one's rights** hacer valer sus derechos

assertion [ə'sɜːʃən] *n* afirmación *f*

assertive [ə'sɜːtɪv] *adj* enérgico(a)

assess [ə'ses] *vt (estimate value)* valorar; *(damages, price)* calcular; *(tax)* gravar; *Fig (effect)* evaluar

assessment [ə'sesmənt] *n (of value)* valoración *f*; *(of damages etc)* cálculo *m*; *(of taxes)* gravamen *m*; *Fig* juicio *m*

asset ['æset] *n* **(a)** ventaja *f*; **to be an a.** *(person)* ser de gran valor **(b)** *Fin* **assets** bienes *mpl*; **fixed assets** bienes raíces

assign [ə'saɪn] *vt (task)* asignar; *(property etc)* ceder; **to a. sb to a job** designar a algn para un trabajo

assignment [ə'saɪnmənt] *n (allocation)* asignación *f*; *(task)* tarea *f*; *(mission)* misión *f*; *(appointment)* cita *f*

assimilate [ə'sɪmɪleɪt] *vt* asimilar

assist [ə'sɪst] *vt & vi* ayudar

assistance [ə'sɪstəns] *n* ayuda *f*, auxilio *m*

assistant [ə'sɪstənt] *n* ayudante *mf*; **a. manager** subdirector(a) *m,f*; **shop a.** dependiente(a) *m,f*; *Br* **(language) a.** *(in school)* auxiliar *mf* de conversación; *(in university)* lector(a) *m,f* de lengua extranjera

associate¹ [ə'səʊʃɪeɪt] **1** *vt (ideas)* relacionar; *(companies)* asociar; **to be associated with sth** estar relacionado(a) con algo **2** *vi* **to a. with** tratar con

associate² [ə'səʊʃɪɪt] **1** adj asociado(a) **2** n (colleague) colega mf; (partner) socio(a) m,f; (accomplice) cómplice mf

association [əsəʊsɪ'eɪʃən] n asociación f; (company) sociedad f

assorted [ə'sɔːtɪd] adj surtido(a), variado(a)

assortment [ə'sɔːtmənt] n surtido m, variedad f

assume [ə'sjuːm] **1** vt (power) asumir; (attitude, name) adoptar; **an assumed name** un nombre falso **2** vi (suppose) suponer

assumption [ə'sʌmpʃən] n (a) (of power) toma f; **a. of office** toma de posesión (b) (supposition) suposición f

assurance [ə'ʃʊərəns] n (a) (guarantee) garantía f (b) (confidence) confianza f (c) Br (insurance) seguro m

assure [ə'ʃʊə(r)] vt asegurar

asterisk ['æstərɪsk] n asterisco m

asthma ['æsmə] n asma f

astonish [ə'stɒnɪʃ] vt asombrar, pasmar; **I was astonished** me quedé pasmado(a)

astonishing [ə'stɒnɪʃɪŋ] adj asombroso(a), pasmoso(a)

astonishment [ə'stɒnɪʃmənt] n asombro m; **to my a.** para gran sorpresa mía

astound [ə'staʊnd] vt asombrar, pasmar

astounding [ə'staʊndɪŋ] adj pasmoso(a), asombroso(a)

astray [ə'streɪ] adv **to go a.** extraviarse; Fig equivocarse; **to lead sb a.** llevar a algn por mal camino

astride [ə'straɪd] prep a horcajadas sobre

astrology [ə'strɒlədʒɪ] n astrología f

astronaut ['æstrənɔːt] n astronauta mf

astronomer [ə'strɒnəmə(r)] n astrónomo(a) m,f

astronomy [ə'strɒnəmɪ] n astronomía f

astute [ə'stjuːt] adj astuto(a)

asylum [ə'saɪləm] n (a) (protection) asilo m; **to seek political a.** pedir asilo político (b) **mental a.** manicomio m

at [æt, unstressed ət] prep (a) (position) a, en; **at school/work** en el colegio/ trabajo; **at the window** a la ventana; **at the top** en lo alto

(b) (direction) a; **to be angry at sb** estar esp Esp enfadado(a) or esp Am enojado(a) con algn; **to laugh at sb** reírse de algn; **to look at sth/sb** mirar algo/a algn; **to shout at sb** gritarle a algn

(c) (time) a; **at Easter/Christmas** en Semana Santa/Navidad; **at six o'clock** a las seis; **at night** Esp por la noche, Am en la noche; **at first** al principio; **at last** por fin; **at once** enseguida; **at that time** entonces; **at the moment** ahora

(d) (manner) a, en; **at best/worst** en el mejor/peor de los casos; **at hand** a mano; **at least** por lo menos; **not at all** en absoluto; (don't mention it) de nada

(e) (rate) a; **they retail at 100 euros each** se venden a 100 euros la unidad; **two at a time** de dos en dos

ate [et, eɪt] pt of **eat**

atheist ['eɪθɪɪst] n ateo(a) m,f

Athens ['æθɪnz] n Atenas

athlete ['æθliːt] n atleta mf

athletic [æθ'letɪk] **1** adj atlético(a); (sporty) deportista **2** npl **athletics** Br (track and field) atletismo m; US deportes mpl

Atlantic [ət'læntɪk] adj **the A. (Ocean)** el (océano) Atlántico

atlas ['ætləs] n atlas m

atmosphere ['ætməsfɪə(r)] n atmósfera f; Fig (ambience) ambiente m

atmospheric [ætməs'ferɪk] adj atmosférico(a)

atom ['ætəm] n átomo m; **a. bomb** bomba atómica

atomic [ə'tɒmɪk] adj atómico(a)

atrocious [ə'trəʊʃəs] adj atroz

atrocity [ə'trɒsɪtɪ] n atrocidad f

attach [ə'tætʃ] vt (stick) pegar; (fasten) sujetar; (document) adjuntar; **to a. importance to sth** dar importancia a algo; *Fig* **to be attached to** *(be fond of)* tener cariño a

attachment [ə'tætʃmənt] *n* (**a**) *Tech* accesorio *m*; *(action)* acoplamiento *m* (**b**) *(fondness)* apego *m* (**to** por) (**c**) *Comput (to e-mail)* archivo adjunto, anexo *m*

attack [ə'tæk] **1** *n* (**a**) *(assault)* ataque *m*, asalto *m*; **an a. on sb's life** un atentado contra la vida de algn (**b**) *Med* ataque *m* **2** *vt (assault)* atacar, asaltar; *Fig (problem)* abordar; *(job)* emprender; *Fig (criticize)* atacar

attacker [ə'tækə(r)] *n* asaltante *mf*, agresor(a) *m,f*

attain [ə'teɪn] *vt (aim)* lograr; *(rank, age)* llegar a

attempt [ə'tempt] **1** *n* intento *m*, tentativa *f*; **at the second a.** a la segunda; **an a. on sb's life** un atentado contra la vida de algn **2** *vt* intentar; **to a. to do sth** tratar de *or* intentar hacer algo; *Jur* **attempted murder/rape** intento *m* de asesinato/violación

attend [ə'tend] **1** *vt (be present at)* asistir a; *(care for, wait on)* atender **2** *vi (be present)* asistir; *(pay attention)* prestar atención

▸**attend to** *vt insep (business)* ocuparse de; *(in shop)* atender a

attendance [ə'tendəns] *n* asistencia *f*

attendant [ə'tendənt] *n (in cinema etc)* acomodador(a) *m,f*; *(in museum)* guía *mf*; *(in car park)* vigilante(a) *m,f*

attention [ə'tenʃən] *n* (**a**) atención *f*; **for the a. of Miss Jones** a la atención de la Srta. Jones; **pay a.!** ¡atiende!; **to pay a. to sb/sth** prestar atención a algn/algo (**b**) *Mil* **a.!** ¡firmes!; **to stand to a.** estar firmes

attentive [ə'tentɪv] *adj (listener)* atento(a); *(helpful)* solícito(a)

attic ['ætɪk] *n* ático *m*

attitude ['ætɪtjuːd] *n* actitud *f*; *(position of body)* postura *f*; **an a. of mind** un estado de ánimo

attorney [ə'tɜːnɪ] *n* (**a**) *US (lawyer)* abogado(a) *m,f*; **A. General** ≃ Ministro(a) *m,f* de Justicia; **district a.**

fiscal *mf* (**b**) *Jur* **power of a.** poderes *mpl*

attract [ə'trækt] *vt* atraer; **to a. attention** llamar la atención; **to a. a waiter's attention** llamar a un camarero

attraction [ə'trækʃən] *n* (**a**) *(power)* atracción *f* (**b**) *(attractive thing)* atractivo *m*; *(charm)* encanto *m*; *(incentive)* aliciente *m*; **the main a.** el número fuerte

attractive [ə'træktɪv] *adj* atractivo(a); *(good-looking)* guapo(a); *(idea, proposition)* atrayente

attribute¹ ['ætrɪbjuːt] *n (quality)* atributo *m*

attribute² [ə'trɪbjuːt] *vt* atribuir

aubergine ['əʊbəʒiːn] *n Br* berenjena *f*

auburn ['ɔːbən] *adj* castaño rojizo *inv*

auction ['ɔːkʃən] **1** *n* subasta *f* **2** *vt* subastar

auctioneer [ɔːkʃə'nɪə(r)] *n* subastador(a) *m,f*

audacity [ɔː'dæsɪtɪ] *n* audacia *f*

audible ['ɔːdɪbəl] *adj* audible

audience ['ɔːdɪəns] *n* (**a**) *(spectators)* público *m*; *(at concert, conference)* auditorio *m*; *(television)* telespectadores *mpl* (**b**) *(meeting)* audiencia *f*

audio-visual [ɔːdɪəʊ'vɪzjʊəl] *adj* audiovisual; **a. aids** apoyo *m* audiovisual

audit ['ɔːdɪt] **1** *n* revisión *f* de cuentas **2** *vt* revisar, intervenir

audition [ɔː'dɪʃən] **1** *n* prueba *f* **2** *vt* **to a. sb for a part** probar a algn para un papel

auditorium [ɔːdɪ'tɔːrɪəm] *n* auditorio *m*

August ['ɔːgəst] *n* agosto *m*

aunt [ɑːnt] *n (also Fam* **auntie, aunty** ['ɑːntɪ]*)* tía *f*

au pair [əʊ'peə(r)] *n* **au pair (girl)** au pair *f*

aura ['ɔːrə] *n* aura *f*; *Rel* aureola *f*

austere [ɒ'stɪə(r)] *adj* austero(a)

austerity [ɒ'sterɪtɪ] *n* austeridad *f*

Australia [ɒ'streɪlɪə] *n* Australia

Australian [ɒ'streɪlɪən] *adj & n* australiano(a) *(m,f)*

Austria ['ɒstrɪə] *n* Austria

Austrian ['ɒstrɪən] *adj & n* austríaco(a) *(m,f)*

authentic [ɔ:'θentɪk] *adj* auténtico(a)

author ['ɔ:θə(r)] *n* autor(a) *m,f*

authoritarian [ɔ:θɒrɪ'teərɪən] *adj* autoritario(a)

authority [ɔ:'θɒrɪtɪ] *n* autoridad *f*; **local a.** ayuntamiento *m*

authorization [ɔ:θəraɪ'zeɪʃən] *n* autorización *f*

authorize ['ɔ:θəraɪz] *vt* autorizar; *(payment etc)* aprobar; **to a. sb to do sth** autorizar a algn a hacer algo

autistic [ɔ:'tɪstɪk] *adj* autista

auto ['ɔ:təʊ] *n US* automóvil *m, Esp* coche *m, Am* carro *m, RP* auto *m*

autobiography [ɔ:təʊbaɪ'ɒgrəfɪ] *n* autobiografía *f*

autograph ['ɔ:təgrɑ:f] **1** *n* autógrafo *m* **2** *vt (sign)* firmar; *(book, photo)* dedicar

automatic [ɔ:tə'mætɪk] **1** *adj* automático(a) **2** *n (car) Esp* coche *m or Am* carro *m or RP* auto *m* (con cambio) automático; *(gun)* pistola automática

automobile ['ɔ:təməbi:l] *n US* automóvil *m, Esp* coche *m, Am* carro *m, RP* auto *m*

autonomous [ɔ:'tɒnəməs] *adj* autónomo(a)

autonomy [ɔ:'tɒnəmɪ] *n* autonomía *f*

autopsy ['ɔ:tɒpsɪ] *n* autopsia *f*

autumn ['ɔ:təm] *n* otoño *m*

auxiliary [ɔ:g'zɪljərɪ] *adj* auxiliar

availability [əveɪlə'bɪlɪtɪ] *n* disponibilidad *f*

available [ə'veɪləbəl] *adj (thing)* disponible; *(person)* libre

avalanche ['ævəlɑ:nʃ] *n* avalancha *f*

Ave *(abbr* **Avenue)** Av., Avda.

avenge [ə'vendʒ] *vt* vengar

avenue ['ævɪnju:] *n* avenida *f*, *Fig* vía *f*

average ['ævərɪdʒ] **1** *n* promedio *m*, media *f*; **on a.** por término medio **2** *adj* medio(a); *(condition)* regular **3** *vt* sacar la media de; **he averages**

eight hours' work a day trabaja una media de ocho horas al día

▸ **average out at** *vt insep* salir a una media de

aversion [ə'vɜ:ʃən] *n (feeling)* aversión *f*; *(thing)* bestia negra

avert [ə'vɜ:t] *vt (eyes, thoughts)* apartar **(from** de); *(accident)* impedir; *(danger)* evitar

aviation [eɪvɪ'eɪʃən] *n* aviación *f*

avid ['ævɪd] *adj (reader)* voraz

avocado [ævə'kɑ:dəʊ] *n* **a. (pear)** aguacate *m, Andes, CSur* palta *f*

avoid [ə'vɔɪd] *vt* evitar; *(question)* eludir

avoidable [ə'vɔɪdəbəl] *adj* evitable

await [ə'weɪt] *vt* esperar, *Esp* aguardar

awake [ə'weɪk] **1** *adj* despierto(a); **to be a.** estar despierto(a) **2** *vt & vi (pt* awoke, awaked; *pp* awoken, awaked) despertar

awaken [ə'weɪkən] *vt & vi (pt* awakened) *pp* awoken) = **awake 2**

award [ə'wɔ:d] **1** *n (prize)* premio *m*; *(medal)* condecoración *f*; *Jur* indemnización *f*; *(grant)* beca *f* **2** *vt (prize)* conceder, otorgar; *(medal)* dar; *(damages)* adjudicar

aware [ə'weə(r)] *adj (informed)* enterado(a); **not that I'm a. of** que yo sepa no; **to be a. of sth** ser consciente de algo; **to become a. of sth** darse cuenta de algo

awareness [ə'weənɪs] *n* conciencia *f* **(of** de)

away [ə'weɪ] *adv* **far a.** lejos; **go a.!** ¡lárgate!; **it's 3 miles a.** está a 3 millas (de distancia); **keep a. from the fire!** ¡no te acerques al fuego!; **right a.** en seguida; **to be a.** *(absent)* estar ausente; *(out)* estar fuera; **to die a.** desvanecerse; **to give sth a.** regalar algo; *(secret)* revelar algo; **to go a.** irse; *Sport* **to play a.** jugar fuera; **to turn a.** volver la cara; **to work a.** trabajar

awe [ɔ:] *n (fear)* temor *m*; *(amazement)* asombro *m*; **he was in a. of his father** le intimidaba su padre

awesome ['ɔ:səm] *adj* impresionante

awful [ˈɔːfʊl] *adj Fam* espantoso(a); **an a. lot of people** un montón de gente, *Am salvo RP* harta gente

awfully [ˈɔːfʊlɪ] *adv Fam* terriblemente

awkward [ˈɔːkwəd] *adj (clumsy)* torpe; *(object)* incómodo(a); *(moment)* inoportuno(a); *(situation)* embarazoso(a); *(problem)* difícil

awning [ˈɔːnɪŋ] *n (on ship)* toldo *m*; *(on shop)* marquesina *f*

awoke [əˈwəʊk] *pt of* **awake**

awoken [əˈwəʊkən] *pp of* **awake, awaken**

axe, *US* **ax** [æks] **1** *n* hacha *f* **2** *vt Fig (jobs)* eliminar; *(costs)* reducir; *(plan)* cancelar; *(person)* despedir

axis [ˈæksɪs] *n (pl* **axes** [ˈæksiːz]*)* eje *m*

axle [ˈæksəl] *n* eje *m*; *Tech* árbol *m*

Bb

B, b [bi:] *n* (**a**) *(the letter)* B, b *f*; *Br Aut* B road carretera secundaria (**b**) *Mus* B si *m*; **B flat** si bemol

BA [bi:'eɪ] *n* (*abbr* **Bachelor of Arts**) *(person)* licenciado(a) *m,f* en Filosofía y Letras

babble ['bæbəl] *vi (baby)* balbucear; *(brook)* murmurar

baboon [bə'bu:n] *n* zambo *m*

baby ['beɪbɪ] *n* (**a**) bebé *m, Andes* guagua *mf*, *RP* nene(a) *m,f*; *Br* **B. Buggy®** sillita *f* de paseo *or* de niño; *US* **b. buggy** *or* **carriage** cochecito *m* de niño; **b. face** cara *f* de niño (**b**) *(animal)* cría *f* (**c**) *Fam (darling)* querido(a) *m,f*

baby-sit ['beɪbɪsɪt] *vi* cuidar a niños, hacer de *Esp* canguro *or Am* babysitter

baby-sitter ['beɪbɪsɪtə(r)] *n* canguro *mf*, *Am* babysitter *mf*

bachelor ['bætʃələ(r)] *n* (**a**) soltero *m* (**b**) *Univ* licenciado(a) *m,f*; **B. of Arts/Science** licenciado(a) *m,f* en Filosofía y Letras/Ciencias

back [bæk] **1** *n* (**a**) *(of person)* espalda *f*; *(of animal)* lomo *m*; **b. to front** al revés (**b**) *(of book)* lomo *m*; *(of chair)* respaldo *m*; *(of coin)* reverso *m*; *(of hand)* dorso *m*; *(of house, car)* parte *f* de atrás (**c**) *(of stage, cupboard)* fondo *m* (**d**) *Ftb* defensa *mf* (**e**) *US* **in b. (of)** *(behind)* en la parte de atrás (de), detrás (de); *(to the rear of)* al fondo (de)
2 *adj* (**a**) *(rear)* trasero(a), de atrás; **b. door** puerta *f* de atrás; **b. seat** asiento *m* de detrás (**b**) **b. rent** alquiler *or Am* renta pendiente de pago; **b. pay** atrasos *mpl*
3 *adv* (**a**) *(to the rear)* atrás; *(towards the rear)* hacia atrás; **b. and forth** de acá para allá (**b**) **some years b.** hace unos años
4 *vt* (**a**) *(support)* apoyar, respaldar (**b**) *Fin* financiar (**c**) *(bet on)* apostar por (**d**) *(car etc)* dar marcha atrás a
5 *vi* (**a**) *(move backwards)* retroceder (**b**) *(car etc)* dar marcha atrás

▶ **back away** *vi* retirarse

▶ **back down** *vi* echarse atrás

▶ **back off** *vi* desistir

▶ **back out** *vi (withdraw)* retractarse, volverse atrás

▶ **back up 1** *vt sep* (**a**) *(support)* apoyar (**b**) *Comput (file)* hacer una copia de seguridad de **2** *vi Aut* ir marcha atrás

backache ['bækeɪk] *n* dolor *m* de espalda

backbone ['bækbəʊn] *n Anat* columna *f*

backer ['bækə(r)] *n* (**a**) *Fin* promotor(a) *m,f* (**b**) *Pol* partidario(a) *m,f* (**c**) *(person who bets)* apostante *mf*

backfire [bæk'faɪə(r)] *vi* (**a**) *Aut* petardear (**b**) *Fig* **our plan backfired** nos salió el tiro por la culata

background ['bækgraʊnd] *n* (**a**) fondo *m*; **to stay in the b.** quedarse en segundo plano; **b. music** música *f* de fondo (**b**) *(origin)* origen *m*; *(past)* pasado *m*; *(education)* formación *f* (**c**) *(circumstances)* antecedentes *mpl* (**d**) *(atmosphere)* ambiente *m*

backlash ['bæklæʃ] *n* reacción violenta y repentina

backlog ['bæklɒg] *n* **to have a b. of work** tener un montón de trabajo atrasado

backpack ['bækpæk] *n* mochila *f*

backside [bæk'saɪd] *n Fam* trasero *m*, culo *m*

backstage [bæk'steɪdʒ] *adv* entre bastidores

backup ['bækʌp] *n* (**a**) *(support)* apoyo *m*, respaldo *m*; *Comput* **b. (file)** fichero *m* de apoyo (**b**) *US (of traffic)* caravana *f*

backward ['bækwəd] **1** *adj* (**a**) *(movement)* hacia atrás (**b**) *(country)* subdesarrollado(a); *(child)* retrasado(a) **2** *adv esp US* hacia atrás

backwards ['bækwəds] *adv* hacia atrás; **to walk b.** andar de espaldas

backyard [bæk'jɑːd] *n* patio trasero; *US* jardín trasero

bacon ['beɪkən] *n* panceta *f, Méx* tocino *m, Esp* bacon *m, Esp* beicon *m*

bacteria [bæk'tɪərɪə] *npl* bacterias *fpl*

bad [bæd] **1** *adj* (**worse, worst**) (**a**) *(poor)* malo(a); **to go from b. to worse** ir de mal en peor (**b**) *(decayed)* podrido(a); **to go b.** echarse a perder (**c**) **that's too b.!** ¡qué pena! (**d**) *(wicked)* malo(a); **to use b. language** ser mal hablado(a) (**e**) *(accident)* grave; *(headache)* fuerte (**f**) *(ill)* enfermo(a) (**g**) **b. debt** deuda *f* incobrable **2** *n* lo malo

bade [beɪd] *pt of* **bid**

badge [bædʒ] *n* insignia *f; (metal disc)* chapa *f*

badger ['bædʒə(r)] **1** *n* tejón *m* **2** *vt* acosar

badly ['bædlɪ] *adv* (**a**) mal; **he did b. in the exam** le salió mal el examen; **to be b. off** andar mal de dinero (**b**) *(seriously)* gravemente (**c**) *(very much)* mucho; **to miss sb b.** echar mucho de menos a algn; **we need it b.** nos hace mucha falta

bad-mannered [bæd'mænəd] *adj* maleducado(a)

badminton ['bædmɪntən] *n* bádminton *m*

bad-tempered [bæd'tempəd] *adj* **to be b.** *(temperament)* tener mal genio; *(temporarily)* estar de mal humor

baffle ['bæfəl] **1** *vt* desconcertar **2** *n Tech* pantalla acústica

bag [bæg] *n* (**a**) *(large)* bolsa *f; (handbag)* bolso *m, Andes, RP* cartera *f, Méx* bolsa; *Fam* **bags of** montones de; **travel b.** bolsa de viaje (**b**) *(hunting)* caza *f; Fam* **it's in the b.** es cosa hecha (**c**) *Br very Fam Pej* **old b.**

(woman) bruja *f* (**d**) **bags** *(under eyes)* ojeras *fpl*

baggage ['bægɪdʒ] *n* (**a**) equipaje *m* (**b**) *Mil* bagaje *m*

baggy ['bægɪ] *adj* (**baggier, baggiest**) holgado(a); **b. trousers** pantalones anchos

bagpipes ['bægpaɪps] *npl* gaita *f*

bail¹ [beɪl] *n Jur* fianza *f;* **on b.** bajo fianza; **to stand** *or US* **post b. for** salir fiador por algn

▸**bail out** *vt sep Fig (person)* sacar de un apuro

bail² [beɪl] *vi Naut* **to b. (out)** achicar

bait [beɪt] **1** *n* cebo *m;* **to rise to the b.** tragar el anzuelo, picar **2** *vt* (**a**) *(for fishing)* cebar (**b**) *(torment)* hostigar

bake [beɪk] **1** *vt* (**a**) cocer al horno (**b**) *(harden)* endurecer **2** *vi Fam* hacer mucho calor

baked [beɪkt] *adj* al horno; **b. potato** patata *for Am* papa *f* al horno

baker ['beɪkə(r)] *n* panadero(a) *m,f*

bakery ['beɪkərɪ] *n* panadería *f*

baking ['beɪkɪŋ] *n* cocción *f;* **b. dish** fuente *f* para horno; **b. powder** levadura *f* en polvo; **b. tin** molde *m*

balance ['bæləns] **1** *n* (**a**) *(scales)* balanza *f; Fig* **to hang in the b.** estar en juego (**b**) *(equilibrium)* equilibrio *m; Pol* **b. of power** equilibrio de fuerzas (**c**) *Fin* saldo *m;* **b. of payments** balanza *f* de pagos; **b. sheet** balance *m;* **credit b.** saldo acreedor (**d**) *(remainder)* resto *m*
2 *vt* (**a**) poner en equilibrio (**on** en) (**b**) *(budget)* equilibrar; **to b. the books** hacer el balance (**c**) *(weigh up)* sopesar **3** *vi* guardar el equilibrio

▸**balance out** *vi (figures)* corresponderse

balcony ['bælkənɪ] *n* balcón *m; Th* anfiteatro *m*

bald [bɔːld] *adj* (**a**) *(person)* calvo(a) (**b**) *(tyre)* desgastado(a) (**c**) *(style)* escueto(a)

Balkans ['bɔːlkəns] *npl* **the B.** los Balcanes

ball¹ [bɔːl] *n* (**a**) *(in cricket, tennis etc)* pelota *f; Ftb* balón *m; (in billiards, golf* *etc)* bola *f; Fam* **to be on the b.** ser un espabilado; *Tech* **b. bearing** rodamiento *m* de bolas; **b. game** *(in general)* juego *m* de pelota; *US (baseball match)* partido m de béisbol *m; Fig* **it's a whole new b. game** es otra historia (**b**) *(of paper)* bola *f; (of wool)* ovillo *m*

ball² [bɔːl] *n (dance)* baile *m*

ballad ['bæləd] *n* balada *f*

ballerina [bælə'riːnə] *n* bailarina *f*

ballet ['bæleɪ] *n* ballet *m;* **b. dancer** bailarín(ina) *m,f*

balloon [bə'luːn] **1** *n* (**a**) globo *m* (**b**) *(in cartoon)* bocadillo *m* **2** *vi* hincharse; *Fig* aumentar rápidamente

ballot ['bælət] **1** *n* votación *f;* **b. box** urna *f;* **b. paper** papeleta *f* (de voto), *Chile, Méx* voto *m, Col* tarjetón *m, RP* boleta *f* **2** *vt* someter a votación

ballpark ['bɔːlpɑːk] *n* campo *m* de béisbol

ballpoint ['bɔːlpɔɪnt] *n* **b. (pen)** bolígrafo *m, Carib, Méx* pluma *f, Col, Ecuad* estereográfico *m, CSur* lapicera *f*

ballroom ['bɔːlruːm] *n* salón *m* de baile

Baltic ['bɔːltɪk] *adj* báltico(a); **the B. (Sea)** el (mar) Báltico

bamboo [bæm'buː] *n* bambú *m*

ban [bæn] **1** *n* prohibición *f* **2** *vt* (**a**) *(prohibit)* prohibir (**b**) *(exclude)* excluir

banal [bə'nɑːl] *adj* banal, trivial

banana [bə'nɑːnə] *n* plátano *m, CAm, Col* banano *m, Ven* cambur *m, RP* banana *f; Fam* **to be bananas** *(mad)* estar como una cabra *or Méx* destrompado *or RP* de la nuca

band [bænd] **1** *n* (**a**) *(strip)* tira *f; (ribbon)* cinta *f* (**b**) *(stripe)* raya *f* (**c**) *(group)* grupo *m; (of youths)* pandilla *f; (of thieves)* banda *f* (**d**) *Mus* banda *f* **2** *vi* **to b. together** unirse, juntarse

bandage ['bændɪdʒ] **1** *n* venda *f* **2** *vt* vendar

Band-aid® ['bændeɪd] *n US Esp* tirita® *f, Am* curita *f*

B & B [biːən'biː] *n Br (abbr* **bed and breakfast)** *(hotel)* = hostal familiar en el que el desayuno está incluido en el precio de la habitación

bandit ['bændɪt] *n* bandido *m*

bandwagon ['bændwægən] *n Fig* **to jump on the b.** subirse al tren

▶**bandy about** *vt sep (ideas)* propagar, difundir

bang [bæŋ] **1** *n* (**a**) *(blow)* golpe *m* (**b**) *(noise)* ruido *m; (explosion)* estallido *m; (of gun)* estampido *m*

2 *npl US* **bangs** flequillo *m, Am* cerquillo *m (corto)*

3 *vt* golpear; **to b. sth shut** cerrar algo de golpe

4 *vi* golpear; **to b. shut** cerrarse de golpe

5 *interj (blow)* ¡zas!; **b., b.!** *(of gun)* ¡pum, pum!

6 *adv Fam* justo

banger ['bæŋə(r)] *n* (**a**) *(firework)* petardo *m* (**b**) *Fam (sausage)* salchicha *f* (**c**) *Fam* **old b.** *(car)* tartana *f*

bangle ['bæŋgəl] *n* brazalete *m*

banish ['bænɪʃ] *vt* desterrar

banister ['bænɪstə(r)] *n* pasamanos *m inv*

banjo ['bændʒəʊ] *n (pl* **banjos)** banjo *m*

bank¹ [bæŋk] **1** *n* (**a**) *Com, Fin* banco *m;* **b. account** cuenta bancaria; **b. card** tarjeta bancaria; **b. clerk** empleado(a) *m,f* de banca; **b. draft** letra bancaria; *Br* **b. holiday** fiesta *f* nacional; **b. statement** extracto *m* de cuenta (**b**) *(in gambling)* banca *f* (**c**) *(store)* banco *m*

2 *vt Com, Fin* depositar, ingresar

3 *vi Com, Fin* **to b. with** tener una cuenta en

▶**bank on** *vt insep* contar con

bank² [bæŋk] **1** *n* (**a**) *(mound)* loma *f; (embankment)* terraplén *m* (**b**) *(of river)* ribera *f; (edge)* orilla *f*

2 *vt Av* ladear

3 *vi Av* ladearse

banker ['bæŋkə(r)] *n* banquero(a) *m,f*

banking ['bæŋkɪŋ] *n* banca *f*

bankrupt ['bæŋkrʌpt] **1** *adj* en quiebra; **to go b.** quebrar **2** *vt* llevar a la bancarrota

banner ['bænə(r)] *n (in demonstration)*

pancarta *f; (flag)* bandera *f*

banquet ['bæŋkwɪt] *n* banquete *m*

banter ['bæntə(r)] **1** *n* bromas *fpl* **2** *vi* bromear

baptism ['bæptɪzəm] *n* bautismo *m*

Baptist ['bæptɪst] *n* baptista *mf*, bautista *mf*

baptize [bæp'taɪz, US 'bæptaɪz] *vt* bautizar

bar [bɑː(r)] **1** *n* (**a**) *(of gold)* barra *f; (of chocolate)* tableta *f; (of soap)* pastilla *f; Com* **b. code** código *m* de barras (**b**) *(of cage)* barrote *m; Fam* **to be behind bars** estar en la cárcel (**c**) *Jur* **the B.** *Br (barristers)* = conjunto de los abogados que ejercen en tribunales superiores; *US (lawyers in general)* la abogacía (**d**) *(pub)* bar *m; (counter)* barra *f* (**e**) *Mus* compás *m*

2 *vt* (**a**) *(door)* atrancar; *(road)* cortar (**b**) *(exclude)* excluir (**from** de) (**c**) *(prohibit)* prohibir

3 *prep* salvo; **b. none** sin excepción

barbaric [bɑː'bærɪk] *adj* bárbaro(a)

barbecue ['bɑːbɪkjuː] **1** *n* barbacoa *f, Andes, RP* asado *m* **2** *vt* asar en la barbacoa

barbed [bɑːbd] *adj* (**a**) **b. wire** alambre *m* de púas (**b**) *Fig (remark)* mordaz

barber ['bɑːbə(r)] *n* barbero(a) *m,f*; **b.'s (shop)** barbería *f*

bare [beə(r)] **1** *adj* (**a**) desnudo(a); *(head)* descubierto(a); *(foot)* descalzo(a); *(room)* sin muebles; **to lay b.** poner al descubierto; **with his b. hands** sólo con las manos (**b**) *(basic)* mero(a); **the b. minimum** lo mínimo **2** *vt* desnudar; *(uncover)* descubrir

barefoot ['beəfʊt] *adj & adv* descalzo(a)

barely ['beəlɪ] *adv* apenas

bargain ['bɑːgɪn] **1** *n* (**a**) *(agreement)* pacto *m; (deal)* negocio *m*; **into the b.** por añadidura, además; **to drive a hard b.** imponer condiciones duras; **to strike a b.** cerrar un trato (**b**) *(cheap purchase)* ganga *f*; **b. price** precio *m* de oferta **2** *vi* (**a**) negociar (**b**) *(haggle)* regatear

▸ **bargain for** *vt insep* esperar, contar con

barge [bɑːdʒ] **1** *n* gabarra *f* **2** *vt Fam* **to b. into** *(room)* irrumpir en; *(person)* tropezar con

▸ **barge in** *vi Fam* (**a**) *(go in)* entrar sin permiso (**b**) *(interfere)* entrometerse

bark¹ [bɑːk] **1** *n* ladrido *m* **2** *vi (dog)* ladrar

bark² [bɑːk] *n Bot* corteza *f*

barley ['bɑːlɪ] *n* cebada *f*; **b. sugar** azúcar *m* cande

barmaid ['bɑːmeɪd] *n esp Br* camarera *f, Am* mesera *f, RP* moza *f*

barman ['bɑːmən] *n* camarero *m, Am* mesero *m, RP* mozo *m*

barn [bɑːn] *n* granero *m*; **b. dance** baile *m* popular

barnyard ['bɑːnjɑːd] *n* corral *m*

barometer [bə'rɒmɪtə(r)] *n* barómetro *m*

baron ['bærən] *n* barón *m*

baroness ['bærənɪs] *n* baronesa *f*

barracks ['bærəks] *n Mil* cuartel *m*

barrage ['bærɑːdʒ] *n* (**a**) *(dam)* presa *f* (**b**) *Mil* barrera *f* de fuego (**c**) *Fig (of questions)* lluvia *f*

barrel ['bærəl] *n* (**a**) *(of wine)* tonel *m; (of beer, oil)* barril *m* (**b**) *(of firearm)* cañón *m*

barren ['bærən] *adj* estéril; *(land)* yermo(a)

barricade [bærɪ'keɪd] **1** *n* barricada *f* **2** *vt* levantar barricadas; **to b. oneself in** parapetarse

barrier ['bærɪə(r)] *n* barrera *f*

barring ['bɑːrɪŋ] *prep* salvo, excepto; **b. a miracle** a menos que ocurra un milagro

barrister ['bærɪstə(r)] *n Br* abogado(a) *m,f (que ejerce en tribunales superiores)*

barrow ['bærəʊ] *n* carretilla *f*

bartender ['bɑːtendə(r)] *n US* camarero *m, Am* mesero *m, RP* mozo *m*

barter ['bɑːtə(r)] *vt* trocar (**for** por)

base [beɪs] **1** *n* base *f; (foot)* pie *m; (of column)* basa *f; Sport (of team)* concentración *f*; **air/naval b.** base *f* aérea/naval

2 *vt* (**a**) basar, fundar (**on** en) (**b**) *(troops)* estacionar

3 *adj* (**a**) *(despicable)* bajo(a), despreciable (**b**) *(metals)* común

baseball ['beɪsbɔːl] *n* béisbol *m*

basement ['beɪsmənt] *n* sótano *m*

bash [bæʃ] **1** *n (heavy blow)* golpetazo *m*; *(dent)* bollo *m*; *Fam (attempt)* intento *m* **2** *vt* golpear

bashful ['bæʃfʊl] *adj* tímido(a)

basic ['beɪsɪk] **1** *adj* básico(a); **b. pay** sueldo *m* base **2** *npl* **basics** lo fundamental

basically ['beɪsɪklɪ] *adv* fundamentalmente

basil [*Br* 'bæzəl, *US* 'beɪzəl] *n* albahaca *f*

basin ['beɪsən] *n* (**a**) *(for cooking)* recipiente *m*, bol *m*; *(for washing hands)* lavabo *m*, *Am* lavamanos *m inv*; *(plastic, for washing up)* palangana *f*, *Esp* barreño *m* (**b**) *(of river)* cuenca *f*

basis ['beɪsɪs] *n (pl* **bases**) base *f*; **on the b. of** en base a

basket ['bɑːskɪt] *n* cesta *f*; *(in basketball)* canasta *f*

basketball ['bɑːskɪtbɔːl] *n* baloncesto *m*

Basque [bæsk, bɑːsk] **1** *adj* vasco(a); **B. Country** País Vasco, Euskadi; **B. flag** ikurriña *f*; **B. nationalist** abertzale *mf* **2** *n* (**a**) *(person)* vasco(a) *m,f* (**b**) *(language)* vasco *m*, euskera *m*

bass¹ [bæs] *n inv (seawater)* lubina *f*; *(freshwater)* perca *f*

bass² [beɪs] **1** *n* (**a**) *(singer)* bajo *m* (**b**) *(notes)* graves *mpl*; **b. drum** bombo *m*; **b. guitar** bajo *m* **2** *adj* bajo(a)

bassoon [bə'suːn] *n* fagot *m*

bat¹ [bæt] **1** *n (in cricket, baseball)* bate *m*; *(in table tennis)* pala *f*; *Br Fam* **to do sth off one's own b.** hacer algo por cuenta propia **2** *vi (in cricket, baseball)* batear

bat² [bæt] *n Zool* murciélago *m*

bat³ [bæt] *vt Fam* **without batting an eyelid** sin pestañear

batch [bætʃ] *n (of bread)* hornada *f*; *(of goods)* lote *m*; *Comput* **b. processing** procesamiento *m* por lotes

bath [bɑːθ] **1** *n* (**a**) baño *m*; **to have a b.** bañarse; **b. towel** toalla *f* de baño (**b**) *(tub)* bañera *f*, *Am* tina *f* (**c**) *Br* **(swimming) baths** piscina *f*, *Méx* alberca *f*, *RP* pileta *f* **2** *vt* bañar

bathe [beɪð] **1** *vi* bañarse **2** *vt* (**a**) *(wound)* lavar (**b**) **he was bathed in sweat** *(covered)* estaba empapado de sudor

bathing ['beɪðɪŋ] *n* baño *m*; **b. cap** gorro *m* de baño; **b. costume** traje *m* de baño, *Col* vestido *m* de baño, *RP* malla *f*; **b. trunks** bañador *m* de hombre

bathrobe ['bɑːθrəʊb] *n* albornoz *m*

bathroom ['bɑːθruːm] *n* cuarto *m* de baño

bathtub ['bɑːθtʌb] *n* bañera *f*, *Am* tina *f*

baton ['bætən, 'bætɒn] *n* (**a**) *Mus* batuta *f* (**b**) *Br (of policeman)* porra *f* (**c**) *Sport* testigo *m*

battalion [bə'tæljən] *n* batallón *m*

batter¹ ['bætə(r)] *vt* aporrear, apalear

batter² ['bætə(r)] *n (in cricket, baseball)* bateador(a) *m,f*

batter³ ['bætə(r)] *Culin* **1** *n* pasta *f* (para rebozar); **fish in b.** pescado rebozado **2** *vt* rebozar

battered ['bætəd] *adj (car)* abollado(a); *(person)* maltratado(a)

battery ['bætərɪ] *n* (**a**) *(for torch, radio)* pila *f*; *Aut* batería *f* (**b**) *Jur* **assault and b.** lesiones *fpl*

battle ['bætəl] **1** *n* batalla *f*; *Fig* lucha *f*; **to do b.** librar batalla; *Fig* **b. cry** lema *m* **2** *vi* luchar

battlefield ['bætəlfiːld] *n* campo *m* de batalla

battleship ['bætəlʃɪp] *n* acorazado *m*

baulk [bɔːk] **1** *vt (frustrate, defeat)* frustrar, hacer fracasar **2** *vi* **to b. at sth** mostrarse reticente *or* echarse atrás ante algo

bawl [bɔːl] *vi* gritar, chillar

bay¹ [beɪ] *n Geog* bahía *f*; *(large)* golfo *m*; **B. of Biscay** golfo de Vizcaya; **B. of Bengal** golfo de Bengala

bay² [beɪ] n (**a**) *(recess)* hueco m; **b. window** ventana saprana (**b**) *(in factory)* nave f; **cargo b.** bodega f de carga

bay³ [beɪ] n laurel m

bay⁴ [beɪ] **1** vi *(dog)* aullar **2** n ladrido m; *Fig* **at b.** acorralado(a); *Fig* **to keep sb at b.** mantener a algn a raya

bayonet ['beɪənɪt] n bayoneta f

bazaar [bə'zɑː(r)] n (**a**) *(market)* bazar m (**b**) **(church) b.** *(charity sale)* rastrillo benéfico

BC [biː'siː] *(abbr* **before Christ)** a. de C.

be [biː, *unstressed* bɪ]

En el inglés hablado, y en el escrito en estilo coloquial, el verbo **be** se contrae de forma que **I am** se transforma en **I'm, he/she/it is** se transforman en **he's/she's/it's** y **you/we/they are** se transforman en **you're/we're/ they're**. Las formas negativas **is not, are not, was not** y **were not** se transforman en **isn't, aren't, wasn't** y **weren't**

1 vi *(pres 1st person sing* **am**; *3rd person sing* **is**; *2nd person sing & all persons pl* **are**; *pt 1st & 3rd persons sing* **was**; *2nd person sing & all persons pl* **were**; *pp* **been**) (**a**) ser; **he is very tall** es muy alto; **Madrid is the capital** Madrid es la capital

(**b**) *(nationality, occupation)* ser; **he's Italian** es italiano

(**c**) *(origin, ownership)* ser; **the car is Domingo's** el coche es de Domingo

(**d**) *(price)* costar; *(total)* ser; **a return ticket is £24** un billete de ida y vuelta cuesta £24; **how much is it?** ¿cuánto es?

(**e**) *(temporary state)* estar; **how are you? – I'm very well** ¿cómo estás? – estoy muy bien; **this soup is cold** esta sopa está fría; **to be cold/afraid/ hungry** *(person)* tener frío/miedo/ hambre

(**f**) *(location)* estar; **Birmingham is 200 miles from London** Birmingham está a 200 millas de Londres

(**g**) *(age)* tener; **she is thirty (years old)** tiene treinta años

2 v aux (**a**) *(with pres participle)* estar; **he is writing a letter** está escribiendo una carta; **she was singing** estaba cantando; **they are leaving next week** se van la semana que viene; **we have been waiting for a long time** hace mucho que estamos esperando

(**b**) *(passive)* ser; **he was murdered** fue asesinado; **she is allowed to smoke** se le permite fumar

(**c**) *(obligation)* **I am to see him this afternoon** debo verle esta tarde; **you are not to smoke here** no se puede fumar aquí

3 v impers (**a**) *(with* **"there")** haber; **there is, there are** hay; **there was, there were** había; **there will be** habrá; **there would be** habría; **there have been a lot of complaints** ha habido muchas quejas; **there were ten of us** éramos diez

(**b**) *(with* **"it")** **it's late** es tarde; **it is said that** se dice que; **who is it? – it's me** ¿quién es? – soy yo; **what is it?** ¿qué pasa?

(**c**) *(weather)* **it's foggy** hay niebla; **it's cold/hot** hace frío/calor

(**d**) *(time)* ser; **it's one o'clock** es la una; **it's four o'clock** son las cuatro

(**e**) *(date)* **it's the 11th/Tuesday today** hoy es el 11/martes

(**f**) *(in tag questions)* **it's lovely, isn't it?** es bonito, ¿no?; **you're happy, aren't you?** estás contento, ¿verdad? **he's not very clever, is he?** no es muy listo, ¿verdad?

(**g**) *(unreal conditions)* **if I was** or **were you …** yo en tu lugar …; **if you were a millionaire …** si fueras millonario …

(**h**) *(as past participle of* **"go")** **I've been to Paris** he estado en París

beach [biːtʃ] **1** n playa f **2** vt varar

beacon ['biːkən] n (**a**) Av, Naut baliza f (**b**) *(lighthouse)* faro m

bead [biːd] n (**a**) *(of necklace etc)* cuenta f; **glass b.** abalorio m (**b**) *(of liquid)* gota f

beak [biːk] n (**a**) *(of bird)* pico m (**b**) *Fam (nose)* nariz ganchuda

beaker ['biːkə(r)] n *(tumbler)* taza alta, jarra f

beam [bi:m] **1** n (**a**) (in building) viga f (**b**) (of light) rayo m; Phys haz m **2** vi (**a**) (sun) brillar (**b**) (smile) sonreír **3** vt (broadcast) difundir, emitir

bean [bi:n] n (vegetable) Esp alubia f, Esp judía f, Am salvo RP frijol m, Andes, RP poroto m; (of coffee) grano m; **to be full of beans** estar lleno(a) de vitalidad

bear[1] [beə(r)] (pt **bore**; pp **borne**) **1** vt (**a**) (carry) llevar; **to b. in mind** tener presente (**b**) (support) sostener (**c**) (endure) soportar, aguantar; **I can't b. him** no lo soporto (**d**) (pt **born** passive only, not followed by **by**) (give birth to) dar a luz; **he was born in Wakefield** nació en Wakefield **2** vi (turn) girar, torcer; **to b. left** girar a la izquierda

▸ **bear up** vi (endure) resistir

bear[2] [beə(r)] n (animal) oso m; **b. cub** osezno m

bearable ['beərəbəl] adj soportable

beard [bɪəd] n barba f

bearing ['beərɪŋ] n (**a**) (posture) porte m (**b**) (relevance) relación f; **to have a b. on** estar relacionado(a) con (**c**) Tech cojinete m (**d**) Naut **bearings** posición f, orientación f; **to get one's bearings** orientarse

beast [bi:st] n (**a**) bestia f; **b. of burden** bestia de carga (**b**) Fig bestia f, bruto m (**c**) **beasts** (cattle) reses fpl

beat [bi:t] (pt **beat**; pp **beaten** ['bi:tən]) **1** vt (**a**) (hit) pegar, golpear; (drum) tocar; Fam **b. it!** ¡largo!, ¡esfúmate!, RP ¡bórrate! (**b**) Culin batir (**c**) (defeat) batir, vencer; **we b. them 5-2** les ganamos 5 a 2; Fam **it beats me** (puzzle) no lo entiendo (**d**) Mus (time) marcar **2** vi (**a**) (heart) latir (**b**) (strike) dar golpes; Fam **to b. about the bush** andarse por las ramas **3** n (**a**) (of heart) latido m (**b**) Mus ritmo m, compás m (**c**) Br (of policeman) ronda f

▸ **beat down** vi (sun) apretar

▸ **beat off** vt sep rechazar

▸ **beat up** vt sep Fam dar una paliza a

beater ['bi:tə(r)] n (**a**) (in hunting) ojeador(a) m,f (**b**) (in cookery) batidora f, batidor m

beating ['bi:tɪŋ] n (**a**) (thrashing) paliza f (**b**) (defeat) derrota f (**c**) (of drum) toque m (**d**) (of heart) latido m

beautician [bju:'tɪʃən] n esteticista mf

beautiful ['bju:tɪfʊl] adj (woman) bonita, esp Esp guapa; (child, animal) bonito(a), precioso(a); (music, dress, landscape) hermoso(a), precioso(a); (smell, taste) delicioso(a)

beauty ['bju:tɪ] n belleza f, hermosura f; **b. contest** concurso m de belleza; **b. parlour** salón m de belleza; **b. queen** miss f; **b. salon** salón m de belleza; **b. spot** (on face) lunar m; (place) lugar pintoresco

beaver ['bi:və(r)] **1** n castor m **2** vi **to b. away at sth** meterse de lleno en algo

became [bɪ'keɪm] pt of **become**

because [bɪ'kɒz] **1** conj porque **2** prep **b. of** a causa de, debido a

beckon ['bekən] vt & vi llamar (con la mano); **to b. to sb** llamar a algn con señas

become [bɪ'kʌm] (pt **became**; pp **become**) **1** vi (a teacher, doctor) hacerse; (boring, jealous, suspicious) volverse; (old, difficult, stronger) hacerse; (happy, sad, thin) ponerse; **to b. interested** interesarse; **what will b. of him?** ¿qué va a ser de él? **2** vt Fml (of clothes, colour) sentar bien a

becoming [bɪ'kʌmɪŋ] adj (**a**) (dress) favorecedor(a) (**b**) (behaviour) conveniente, apropiado(a)

bed [bed] n (**a**) cama f; **to get out of b.** levantarse de la cama; **to go to b.** acostarse; **to make the b.** hacer la cama; Br **b. and breakfast** (service) cama y desayuno m; (sign) pensión; **b. linen** ropa f de cama (**b**) (of river) lecho m; (of sea) fondo m (**c**) Geol estrato m (**d**) (flower) **b.** arriate m

bedclothes ['bedkləʊðz] npl, **bedding** ['bedɪŋ] n ropa f de cama

bedraggled [bɪ'drægəld] adj (wet) mojado(a); (dirty) ensuciado(a)

bedridden ['bedrɪdən] *adj* postrado(a) en cama

bedroom ['bedruːm] *n (in house)* dormitorio *m*, habitación *f*, cuarto *m*, *CAm, Col, Méx* recámara *f*; *(in hotel)* habitación *f*, *Am* cuarto *m*, *CAm, Col, Méx* recámara *f*

bedside ['bedsaɪd] *n* **at sb's b.** al lado de la cama de algn; **b. table** mesilla *f* or mesita *f* (de noche), *Andes* velador *m*, *Méx* buró *m*, *RP* mesa *f* de luz

bedsit ['bedsɪt] *n Fam*, **bedsitter** [bed'sɪtə(r)] *n Br* estudio *m*

bedspread ['bedspred] *n* colcha *f*

bedtime ['bedtaɪm] *n* hora *f* de acostarse

bee [biː] *n* abeja *f*

beech [biːtʃ] *n* haya *f*

beef [biːf] *n* carne *f* de vaca, *Am* carne de res; **roast b.** rosbif *m*

▸ **beef up** *vt sep Fam* reforzar

beefburger ['biːfbɜːgə(r)] *n* hamburguesa *f*

beehive ['biːhaɪv] *n* colmena *f*

been [biːn, bɪn] *pp of* **be**

beer [bɪə(r)] *n* cerveza *f*; **a glass of b.** una caña

beet [biːt] *n US* remolacha *f*, *Méx* betabel *f*

beetle ['biːtəl] *n* escarabajo *m*

beetroot ['biːtruːt] *n Br* remolacha *f*, *Méx* betabel *f*

before [bɪ'fɔː(r)] **1** *conj* (**a**) *(earlier than)* antes de que *(+ subj)*, antes de *(+ infin)*; **b. she goes** antes de que se vaya; **b. leaving** antes de salir (**b**) *(rather than)* antes que *(+ infin)*
2 *prep* (**a**) *(place)* delante de; *(in the presence of)* ante (**b**) *(order, time)* antes de; **b. Christ** antes de Cristo; **b. long** dentro de poco; **b. 1950** antes de 1950; **I saw it b. you** lo vi antes que tú
3 *adv* (**a**) *(time)* antes; **I have met him b.** ya lo conozco; **not long b.** poco antes; **the night b.** la noche anterior (**b**) *(place)* delante, por delante

befriend [bɪ'frend] *vt* trabar amistad con

beg [beg] **1** *vt* (**a**) *(money etc)* pedir (**b**) *(beseech)* rogar, suplicar; **I b. your pardon!** ¡perdone usted!; **I b. your pardon?** ¿cómo ha dicho usted? **2** *vi* (**a**) *(solicit)* mendigar; *(dog)* pedir; **to b. for money** pedir limosna (**b**) **to b. for help/mercy** *(beseech)* implorar ayuda/compasión

began [bɪ'gæn] *pt of* **begin**

beggar ['begə(r)] *n* (**a**) mendigo(a) *m,f* (**b**) *Br Fam* **poor b.!** ¡pobre diablo!

begin [bɪ'gɪn] *vt & vi (pt* **began**; *pp* **begun**) empezar, comenzar; **to b. again** volver a empezar; **to b. at the beginning** empezar por el principio; **to b. doing** *or* **to do sth** empezar a hacer algo; **to b. with …** *(initially)* para empezar …

beginner [bɪ'gɪnə(r)] *n* principiante *mf*

beginning [bɪ'gɪnɪŋ] *n* (**a**) principio *m*, comienzo *m*; **at the b. of May** a principios de mayo; **from the b.** desde el principio; **in the b.** al principio (**b**) *(origin)* origen *m*

begrudge [bɪ'grʌdʒ] *vt* dar de mala gana; *(envy)* envidiar

begun [bɪ'gʌn] *pp of* **begin**

behalf [bɪ'hɑːf] *n* **on b. of**, *US* **in b. of** en nombre de, de parte de; **don't worry on my b.** no te preocupes por mí

behave [bɪ'heɪv] *vi* (**a**) *(person)* portarse, comportarse; **b. yourself!** ¡pórtate bien!; **to b. well/badly** portarse bien/mal (**b**) *(machine)* funcionar

behaviour, *US* **behavior** [bɪ'heɪvjə(r)] *n* (**a**) *(of person)* comportamiento *m*, conducta *f* (**b**) *(of machine)* funcionamiento *m*

behind [bɪ'haɪnd] **1** *prep* (**a**) detrás de; **b. sb's back** a espaldas de algn; **b. the scenes** entre bastidores; **to be b. sb** apoyar a algn; **what motive was there b. the crime?** ¿cuál fue el móvil del crimen? (**b**) **b. the times** *(less advanced than)* anticuado(a)
2 *adv* (**a**) *(in the rear)* detrás, atrás; **I've left my umbrella b.** se me ha olvidado el paraguas (**b**) **to be b. with one's**

payments *(late)* estar atrasado(a) en los pagos
3 *n Fam* trasero *m*

beige [beɪʒ] *adj & n* beige *m inv, Esp* beis *m inv*

Beijing [beɪ'ʒɪŋ] *n* Pekín

being ['biːɪŋ] *n* (**a**) ser *m* (**b**) *(existence)* existencia *f*; **to come into b.** nacer

belated [bɪ'leɪtɪd] *adj* tardío(a)

belch [beltʃ] **1** *vi (person)* eructar
2 *vt (smoke, flames)* vomitar, arrojar
3 *n* eructo *m*

Belgian ['beldʒən] *adj & n* belga *(mf)*

Belgium ['beldʒəm] *n* Bélgica

belief [bɪ'liːf] *n* (**a**) creencia *f*; **beyond b.** increíble (**b**) *(opinion)* opinión *f* (**c**) *(faith)* fe *f* (**d**) *(confidence)* confianza *f* (**in** en)

believable [bɪ'liːvəbəl] *adj* verosímil

believe [bɪ'liːv] **1** *vi* (**a**) *(have faith)* creer (**b**) **to b. in** *(be in favour of)* ser partidario(a) de (**c**) *(think)* creer; **I b. so** creo que sí **2** *vt* creer

believer [bɪ'liːvə(r)] *n* (**a**) *Rel* creyente *mf* (**b**) partidario(a) *m,f* (**in** de)

belittle [bɪ'lɪtəl] *vt (person)* menospreciar; *(problem)* minimizar

bell [bel] *n (of church)* campana *f*; *(small)* campanilla *f*; *(of school, door, bicycle etc)* timbre *m*; *(on cat)* cascabel *m*; *(on cow)* cencerro *m*; *Fig* **that rings a b.** eso me suena; **b. jar** campana de vidrio *or Esp* cristal; **b. tower** campanario *m*

bellboy ['belbɔɪ], **bellhop** ['belhɒp] *n US* botones *m inv*

bellow ['beləʊ] *vi (bull)* bramar; *(person)* rugir

belly ['belɪ] *n* (**a**) *(of person)* vientre *m*, barriga *f, Chile* guata *f*; **b. flop** panzazo *m* (**b**) *(of animal)* panza *f*

belong [bɪ'lɒŋ] *vi* (**a**) pertenecer (**to** a) (**b**) *(be a member)* ser socio(a) (**to** de); *Pol* **to b. to a party** ser miembro de un partido (**c**) *(have a proper place)* corresponder; **this chair belongs here** esta silla va aquí

belongings [bɪ'lɒŋɪŋz] *npl* efectos *mpl* personales

beloved [bɪ'lʌvɪd, bɪ'lʌvd] **1** *adj* amado(a), querido(a) **2** *n* amado(a) *m,f*

below [bɪ'ləʊ] **1** *prep* debajo de, bajo; *Am* abajo de; **b. average** por debajo de la media; **10 degrees b. zero** 10 grados bajo cero **2** *adv* abajo; **above and b.** arriba y abajo; **see b.** véase más abajo

belt [belt] **1** *n* (**a**) cinturón *m*; **blow below the b.** golpe bajo (**b**) *Tech* correa *f*, cinta *f* (**c**) *(area)* zona *f* **2** *vt Fam* pegar una paliza a
▶ **belt along** *vi Fam* ir a todo gas
▶ **belt out** *vt sep Fam (song)* cantar a voz en grito
▶ **belt up** *vi Br Fam* callarse

bemused [bɪ'mjuːzd] *adj* perplejo(a)

bench [bentʃ] *n* (**a**) *(seat)* banco *m* (**b**) *(in parliament)* escaño *m* (**c**) *Br* **the B.** *(judges)* la magistratura (**d**) *Sport* banquillo *m*

bend [bend] *(pt & pp* **bent**) **1** *vt* doblar; *(back)* encorvar; *(head)* inclinar; *Fam* **to b. the rules** hacer una excepción **2** *vi* (**a**) doblarse; *(road)* torcerse (**b**) **to b. (over)** inclinarse; *Fam* **he bends over backwards to please her** hace lo imposible por complacerla
3 *n (in river, road)* curva *f*; *(in pipe)* recodo *m*; *Br Fam* **to be round the b.** estar *Esp* majara *or Am* zafado(a)
▶ **bend down** *vi* inclinarse

beneath [bɪ'niːθ] **1** *prep (below)* bajo, debajo de; *Fig* **it's b. him** es indigno de él **2** *adv* debajo

benefactor ['benɪfæktə(r)] *n* bienhechor(a) *m,f*

beneficial [benɪ'fɪʃəl] *adj* (**a**) *(doing good)* benéfico(a) (**b**) *(advantageous)* beneficioso(a)

benefit ['benɪfɪt] **1** *vt* beneficiar
2 *vi* sacar provecho (**from** *or* **by** de)
3 *n* (**a**) *(advantage)* beneficio *m*, provecho *m*; **for the b. of** en beneficio de; **I did it for your b.** lo hice por tu bien (**b**) *(allowance)* subsidio *m*; **unemployment b.** subsidio de desempleo (**c**) *(event)* función benéfica

benevolent [bɪ'nevələnt] *adj* benévolo(a)

benign [bɪ'naɪn] *adj* benigno(a)

bent [bent] **1** *adj* (**a**) *(curved)* curvado(a) (**b**) **to be b. on doing sth** *(determined)* estar empeñado(a) en hacer algo (**c**) *Br Fam (dishonest)* deshonesto(a)
  2 *pt & pp of* **bend**
  3 *n (inclination)* inclinación *f* (**towards** hacia)

bequeath [bɪˈkwiːð] *vt Jur* legar

bereaved [bɪˈriːvd] *npl* **the b.** los familiares del/de un difunto

bereavement [bɪˈriːvmənt] *n (mourning)* duelo *m*

beret [ˈbereɪ] *n* boina *f*

Berlin [bɜːˈlɪn] *n* Berlín

berry [ˈberɪ] *n* baya *f*

berserk [bəˈsɜːk, bəˈzɜːk] *adj* **to go b.** volverse loco(a)

berth [bɜːθ] *Naut* **1** *n* (**a**) *(mooring)* amarradero *m*; *Fig* **to give sb a wide b.** evitar a algn (**b**) *(bed)* litera *f* **2** *vi* atracar

beset [bɪˈset] *vt (pt & pp* **beset***)* acosar; **it is b. with dangers** está plagado de peligros

beside [bɪˈsaɪd] *prep* (**a**) *(next to)* al lado de, junto a (**b**) *(compared with)* comparado con (**c**) **he was b. himself with joy** estaba loco de alegría; **that's b. the point** eso no viene al caso; **to be b. oneself** estar fuera de sí

besides [bɪˈsaɪdz] **1** *prep* (**a**) *(in addition to)* además de (**b**) *(except)* excepto, menos; **no one b. me** nadie más que yo **2** *adv* además

besiege [bɪˈsiːdʒ] *vt (city)* sitiar; *Fig* asediar

best [best] **1** *adj (superl of* **good***)* mejor; **b. man** ≃ padrino *m* de boda; **her b. friend** su mejor amiga; **the b. thing would be to phone them** lo mejor sería llamarles; **we had to wait the b. part of a year** tuvimos que esperar casi un año; **with b. wishes from Mary** *(in letter)* con mis mejores deseos, Mary
  2 *adv (superl of* **well***)* mejor; **as b. I can** lo mejor que pueda; **I like this one b.** éste es el que más me gusta; **the world's b. dressed man** el hombre mejor vestido del mundo
  3 *n* **the b.** el/la/lo mejor; **all the b.!** *(at the end of letter)* ¡un saludo!, *RP* cariños; **at b.** a lo más; **to be at one's b.** estar en plena forma; **to do one's b.** hacer todo lo posible; **to make the b. of sth** sacar el mejor partido de algo; **to the b. of my knowledge** que yo sepa

best-seller [bestˈselə(r)] *n* best-seller *m*

bet [bet] *(pt* **bet** *or* **betted***)* **1** *n* apuesta *f*
  2 *vt* apostar
  3 *vi* apostar (**on** por); *Fam* **you b.!** ¡y tanto!

betray [bɪˈtreɪ] *vt* (**a**) traicionar (**b**) *(be unfaithful to)* engañar (**c**) *(reveal)* revelar

betrayal [bɪˈtreɪəl] *n* traición *f*

better [ˈbetə(r)] **1** *adj* (**a**) *(comp of* **good***)* mejor; **the weather is b. than last week** hace mejor que la semana pasada; **to be no b. than ...** no ser más que ...; **to get b.** mejorar (**b**) *(healthier)* mejor (de salud) (**c**) **b. off** *(better)* mejor; *(richer)* más rico(a); **you'd be b. off going home** lo mejor es que te vayas a casa (**d**) **the b. part of the day** la mayor parte del día
  2 *adv (comp of* **well***)* (**a**) **all the b., so much the b.** tanto mejor; **b. and b.** cada vez mejor; **b. late than never** más vale tarde que nunca (**b**) **we had b. leave** más vale que nos vayamos (**c**) **to think b. of** *(plan)* cambiar de
  3 *n* mejor; **a change for the b.** una mejora; **to get the b. of sb** vencer a algn
  4 *vt* (**a**) *(improve)* mejorar (**b**) *(surpass)* superar

betting [ˈbetɪŋ] *n* apuestas *fpl*; **b. shop** quiosco *m* de apuestas

between [bɪˈtwiːn] **1** *prep* entre; **b. you and me** entre nosotros; **closed b. one and two** cerrado de una a dos **2** *adv* **in b.** *(position)* en medio; *(time)* entretanto, mientras (tanto)

beverage [ˈbevərɪdʒ] *n* bebida *f*

beware [bɪˈweə(r)] *vi* tener cuidado (**of** con); **b.!** ¡cuidado!; **b. of the dog**

(sign) cuidado con el perro

bewildered [bɪˈwɪldəd] *adj* desconcertado(a)

beyond [bɪˈjɒnd] **1** *prep* más allá de; **b. belief** increíble; **b. doubt** sin lugar a dudas; **it is b. me why ...** no comprendo por qué ...; **it's b. a joke** eso ya no tiene gracia; **she is b. caring** ya no le importa; **this task is b. me** no puedo con esta tarea **2** *adv* más allá, más lejos

bias [ˈbaɪəs] *n (tendency)* tendencia *f* (**towards** hacia); *(prejudice)* prejuicio *m*

bias(s)ed [ˈbaɪəst] *adj* parcial; **to be b. against sth/sb** tener prejuicio en contra de algo/algn

bib [bɪb] *n (for baby)* babero *m*; *(of apron)* peto *m*

Bible [ˈbaɪbəl] *n* Biblia *f*; *Fam Pej* **B. thumper** *or Br* **basher** evangelista *mf*

biblical [ˈbɪblɪkəl] *adj* bíblico(a)

bibliography [bɪblɪˈɒɡrəfɪ] *n* bibliografía *f*

biceps [ˈbaɪseps] *n* biceps *m*

bicker [ˈbɪkə(r)] *vi* reñir

bicycle [ˈbaɪsɪkəl] *n* bicicleta *f*; **b. pump** bomba *f* (de aire); **to go by b.** ir en bicicleta

bid [bɪd] **1** *vt* (a) *(pt* bid *or* bade; *pp* bid *or* bidden [ˈbɪdən]) *Literary (say)* decir; *(command)* mandar, ordenar; **to b. sb farewell** despedirse de algn (b) *(pt & pp* bid) *(at auction)* pujar **2** *vi* (*pt & pp* bid) *(at auction)* pujar (**for** por) **3** *n* (a) *(offer)* oferta *f* (b) *(at auction)* puja *f* (c) *(attempt)* intento *m*, tentativa *f*

bidder [ˈbɪdə(r)] *n* **the highest b.** el mejor postor

bide [baɪd] *vt* (*pt* bided *or* bode; *pp* bided) esperar; **to b. one's time** esperar el momento oportuno

big [bɪɡ] **1** *adj* grande (gran *before singular noun*); **a b. clock** un reloj grande; **a b. surprise** una gran sorpresa; **my b. brother** mi hermano mayor; *Fam Ironic* **b. deal!** ¿y qué?; **b. business** los grandes negocios; **b. dipper** montaña rusa; *US Astron* **B. Dipper** Osa *f* Mayor; *Fam* **b. gun, b. shot** pez gordo; **b. toe** dedo gordo del pie; *Fam* **b. top** carpa *f* **2** *adv* (a) *(on a grand scale)* a lo grande (b) *(well)* de manera excepcional

bighead [ˈbɪɡhed] *n Fam* creído(a) *m,f*, engreído(a) *m,f*

bigot [ˈbɪɡət] *n* intolerante *mf*

bigoted [ˈbɪɡətɪd] *adj* intolerante

bigwig [ˈbɪɡwɪɡ] *n Fam* pez gordo

bike [baɪk] *n Fam (abbr* **bicycle** *or* **motorbike**) *(bicycle)* bici *f*; *(motorcycle)* moto *f*; *Br* **on your b.!** *(go away)* ¡largo!, ¡piérdete!; *(don't talk nonsense)* ¡no digas *Esp* chorradas *or Am* pendejadas *or RP* pavadas!

bikini [bɪˈkiːnɪ] *n* bikini *m*

bilingual [baɪˈlɪŋɡwəl] *adj* bilingüe

bill¹ [bɪl] **1** *n* (a) *(for gas etc)* factura *f*, recibo *m* (b) *esp Br (in restaurant)* cuenta *f* (c) *Pol* proyecto *m* de ley; **B. of Rights** = las diez primeras enmiendas a la constitución estadounidense, relacionadas con la garantía de las libertades individuales (d) *US (banknote)* billete *m* de banco (e) *(poster)* cartel *m* (f) *Fin* **b. of exchange** letra *f* de cambio **2** *vt* (a) *(send bill to)* facturar (b) *Th* programar

bill² [bɪl] *n (of bird)* pico *m*

billboard [ˈbɪlbɔːd] *n (hoarding)* cartelera *f*

billiards [ˈbɪljədz] *n sing* billar *m*

billion [ˈbɪljən] *n US* mil millones *mpl*; *Br Old-fashioned* billón *m*

billow [ˈbɪləʊ] **1** *n (of water)* ola *f*; *(of smoke)* nube *f* **2** *vi (sea)* ondear; *(sail)* hincharse

bin [bɪn] *n (for storage)* cajón *m*; *Br* **bread b.** panera *f*; *Br* **(rubbish) b.** cubo *m or Am* bote *m* de la basura

binary [ˈbaɪnərɪ] *adj* **b. number** número binario

bind [baɪnd] (*pt & pp* bound) *vt* (a) *(tie up)* atar (b) *Med (bandage)* vendar (c) *(book)* encuadernar (d) *(require)* obligar (e) *(join etc)* unir

▶**bind over** *vt sep Jur* obligar legalmente

binder ['baɪndə(r)] n (file) carpeta f

binding ['baɪndɪŋ] adj (promise) comprometedor(a); (contract) vinculante

binge [bɪndʒ] n Fam borrachera f; **to go on a b.** irse de juerga

bingo ['bɪŋgəʊ] n bingo m

binoculars [bɪ'nɒkjʊləz] npl prismáticos mpl, gemelos mpl

biochemistry [baɪəʊ'kemɪstrɪ] n bioquímica f

biodegradable [baɪəʊdɪ'greɪdəbəl] adj biodegradable

biography [baɪ'ɒgrəfɪ] n biografía f

biological [baɪə'lɒdʒɪkəl] adj biológico(a); **b. warfare** guerra biológica

biology [baɪ'ɒlədʒɪ] n biología f

bird [bɜːd] n (a) pájaro m, ave f; Fig **to kill two birds with one stone** matar dos pájaros de un tiro; **they're birds of a feather** son tal para cual; **b. of prey** ave de rapiña (b) Br Fam (woman) nena f, Arg piba f

Biro® ['baɪrəʊ] n (pl Biros) Br bolígrafo m, Carib pluma f, Col, Ecuad esferográfico m, CSur lapicera f, Méx pluma f (atómica)

birth [bɜːθ] n (a) nacimiento m; (childbirth) parto m; **by b.** de nacimiento; **to give b. to a child** dar a luz a un niño; **b. certificate** partida f de nacimiento; **b. control** (family planning) control m de la natalidad; (contraception) métodos anticonceptivos; **b. rate** índice m de natalidad (b) **of noble b.** (parentage) de noble linaje

birthday ['bɜːθdeɪ] n cumpleaños m inv

birthmark ['bɜːθmɑːk] n antojo m

birthplace ['bɜːθpleɪs] n lugar m de nacimiento

biscuit ['bɪskɪt] n (a) Br (sweet, salted) galleta f; Fam **that really takes the b.!** ¡eso ya es el colmo! (b) US (muffin) tortita f, bollo m

bishop ['bɪʃəp] n (a) Rel obispo m (b) (in chess) alfil m

bit¹ [bɪt] n (a) (small piece) trozo m, pedazo m; **to smash sth to bits** hacer añicos algo (b) (small quantity) poco m;

a b. of advice un consejo; **bits and pieces** trastos mpl; Fig **b. by b.** poco a poco (c) **a b.** (slightly) un poco; **a b. longer** un ratito más; **a b. worried** un poco preocupado (d) (coin) moneda f

bit² [bɪt] n (of tool) broca f

bit³ [bɪt] n Comput bit m

bit⁴ [bɪt] pt of **bite**

bitch [bɪtʃ] **1** n (a) Zool (female) hembra f; (dog) perra f (b) Fam (spiteful woman) bruja f **2** vi Fam (complain) quejarse, Esp dar la tabarra

bite [baɪt] (pt bit; pp bitten) **1** n (a) (act) mordisco m (b) (wound) mordedura f; (insect) b. picadura f (c) (mouthful) bocado m (d) Fam (snack) bocado m **2** vt morder; (insect) picar; **to b. one's nails** morderse las uñas; Fam **to b. sb's head off** echarle una bronca a algn **3** vi morder; (insect) picar

biting ['baɪtɪŋ] adj (wind) cortante; Fig (criticism) mordaz

bitten ['bɪtən] pp of **bite**

bitter ['bɪtə(r)] **1** adj (a) amargo(a) (b) (weather) glacial; (wind) cortante (c) (person) amargado(a) (d) (struggle) enconado(a); (hatred) implacable **2** n Br (beer) = cerveza sin burbujas y de tono castaño

bitterly ['bɪtəlɪ] adv **she was b. disappointed** sufrió una terrible decepción

bizarre [bɪ'zɑː(r)] adj (odd) extraño(a); (eccentric) estrafalario(a)

blab [blæb] vi Fam parlotear; Esp largar, Méx platicar; (let out a secret) chivarse

black [blæk] **1** adj (a) (colour) negro(a); **a b. and white television** un televisor en blanco y negro; Fig **b. and blue** amoratado(a); **to put sth down in b. and white** poner algo por escrito; Av **b. box** caja negra; **b. coffee** café solo; **the B. Country** = la región de los Midlands; **b. eye** ojo morado; **b. hole** agujero negro; **b. humour** humor negro; **b. magic** magia negra; **b. market** mercado negro; esp Br **b. pudding** morcilla f; **the B. Sea** el Mar

Negro; *Fig* **b. sheep** oveja negra
(**b**) *(gloomy)* negro(a); *Fig* **a b. day** un
día aciago; *Aut* **b. spot** punto negro
2 *n* (**a**) *(colour)* negro *m* (**b**) *(person)*
negro(a) *m,f*
3 *vt* (**a**) *(make black)* ennegrecer (**b**)
(polish) lustrar (**c**) *Br (boycott)* boicotear

▶ **black out 1** *vt sep* (**a**) *(extinguish
lights in)* apagar las luces de (**b**)
(censor) censurar **2** *vi (faint)* desmayarse

blackberry ['blækbərɪ] *n* zarzamora *f*

blackbird ['blækbɜːd] *n* mirlo *m*

blackboard ['blækbɔːd] *n* pizarra *f*,
encerado *m*, *Am* pizarrón *m*

blackcurrant [blæk'kʌrənt] *n* grosella
negra *f*

blacken ['blækən] *vt* (**a**) *(make black)*
ennegrecer (**b**) *Fig (defame)* manchar

blacklist ['blæklɪst] *n* lista negra

blackmail ['blækmeɪl] **1** *n* chantaje *m*
2 *vt* chantajear

blackout ['blækaʊt] *n* (**a**) *(of lights)*
apagón *m* (**b**) *Rad, TV* censura *f* (**c**)
(fainting) pérdida *f* de conocimiento

blacksmith ['blæksmɪθ] *n* herrero *m*

bladder ['blædə(r)] *n* vejiga *f*; **gall b.**
vesícula *f* biliar

blade [bleɪd] *n* (**a**) *(of grass)* brizna *f*
(**b**) *(of knife etc)* hoja *f* (**c**) *(of propeller,
oar)* pala *f*

blame [bleɪm] **1** *n* culpa *f*; **to take the
b. for sth** asumir la responsabilidad de
algo **2** *vt* echar la culpa a; **he is to b.** él
tiene la culpa

blameless ['bleɪmlɪs] *adj (person)*
inocente; *(conduct)* intachable

blanch [blɑːntʃ] **1** *vt Culin* escaldar
2 *vi (go pale)* palidecer, ponerse
pálido(a)

bland [blænd] *adj (food)* soso(a)

blank [blæŋk] **1** *adj* (**a**) *(without
writing)* en blanco; *Fin* **b. cheque**
cheque *m* en blanco (**b**) *(empty)*
vacío(a); **a b. look** una mirada
inexpresiva (**c**) **a b. refusal** *(absolute)*
una negativa rotunda **2** *n* (**a**) *(space)*
espacio *m* en blanco; **to draw a b.** no
tener éxito (**b**) *Mil* cartucho *m* de

fogueo (**c**) *US (form)* impreso *m*

blanket ['blæŋkɪt] **1** *n* manta *f*, *Am*
cobija *f*, *Am* frazada *f*; *Fig* capa *f* **2** *adj*
general

blare [bleə(r)] *vi* resonar

▶ **blare out** *vt sep* pregonar

blasé [*Br* 'blɑːzeɪ, *US* blɑː'zeɪ] *adj* de
vuelta (de todo)

blasphemous ['blæsfəməs] *adj* blas-
femo(a)

blast [blɑːst] **1** *n* (**a**) *(of wind)* ráfaga *f*
(**b**) *(of horn etc)* toque *m*; **at full b.** a
toda marcha (**c**) *(explosion)* explosión *f*
(**d**) *(shock wave)* onda *f* de choque **2** *vt*
(**a**) *(blow up)* volar; *Br Fam* **b. (it)!**
¡maldito sea! *Fig (destroy)* arruinar
(**c**) *Fig (criticize)* criticar

blasted ['blɑːstɪd] *adj* maldito(a)

blast-off ['blɑːstɒf] *n* despegue *m*

blatant ['bleɪtənt] *adj (very obvious)*
evidente; *(shameless)* descarado(a); **a
b. lie** una mentira patente

blaze¹ [bleɪz] **1** *n* (**a**) *(burst of flame)*
llamarada *f* (**b**) *(fierce fire)* incendio *m*
(**c**) *(of sun)* resplandor *m* (**d**) *Fig (of
anger)* arranque *m* **2** *vi* (**a**) *(fire)* arder
(**b**) *(sun etc)* brillar

blaze² [bleɪz] *vt* **to b. a trail** abrir un
camino

blazer ['bleɪzə(r)] *n* chaqueta *f* sport

blazing ['bleɪzɪŋ] *adj (building)* en
llamas; *Fig* **a b. row** una discusión
violenta

bleach [bliːtʃ] **1** *n (household)* lejía *f*,
Arg lavandina *f*, *CAm, Chile, Méx, Ven*
cloro *m*, *Col* decol *m*, *Urug* jane *f* **2** *vt*
(**a**) *(whiten)* blanquear; *(fade)* descolo-
rir (**b**) *(hair)* decolorar

bleak [bliːk] *adj* (**a**) *(countryside)*
desolado(a) (**b**) *(weather)* desapacible
(**c**) *(future)* poco prometedor(a)

bleat [bliːt] **1** *n* balido *m* **2** *vi (animal)*
balar

bleed [bliːd] *(pt & pp* **bled** [bled]) **1** *vi*
sangrar **2** *vt Med* sangrar; *Fam* **to b.
sb dry** sacarle a algn hasta el último
céntimo

bleep [bliːp] **1** *n* bip *m*, pitido *m* **2** *vi*
pitar

bleeper ['bliːpə(r)] n Br buscapersonas m inv, Esp busca m, Méx localizador m, RP radiomensaje m

blemish ['blemɪʃ] n (flaw) defecto m; (on fruit) maca f; Fig mancha f; Fig **without b.** sin tacha

blend [blend] **1** n mezcla f
2 vt (mix) mezclar; (colours) armonizar
3 vi (mix) mezclarse; (colours) armonizar

blender ['blendə(r)] n Esp batidora f, Am licuadora f

bless [bles] (pt & pp **blessed** or **blest**) vt (a) bendecir; **b. you!** (when someone sneezes) ¡salud!, Esp ¡jesús! (b) **blessed with good eyesight** dotado(a) de buena vista

blessed ['blesɪd] adj (a) (holy) sagrado(a), santo(a) (b) Fam (for emphasis) dichoso(a)

blessing ['blesɪŋ] n bendición f; (advantage) ventaja f; **a mixed b.** una ventaja relativa

blew [bluː] pt of **blow**²

blind [blaɪnd] **1** adj ciego(a); **a b. man** un ciego; **a b. woman** una ciega; Fig **b. faith** fe ciega; Fig **to turn a b. eye** hacer la vista gorda; **b. alley** callejón m sin salida; **b. spot** ángulo muerto; Fam **b. date** cita f a ciegas
2 adv a ciegas; Fam **to get b. drunk** agarrar una curda
3 n (a) Br (on window) persiana f (b) pl **the b.** los ciegos
4 vt (a) cegar, dejar ciego (b) (dazzle) deslumbrar

blindfold ['blaɪndfəʊld] **1** n venda f **2** vt vendar los ojos a

blindly ['blaɪndlɪ] adv a ciegas, ciegamente

blink [blɪŋk] vi (eyes) pestañear; (lights) parpadear

blissful ['blɪsfʊl] adj (happy) feliz; (marvellous) maravilloso(a)

blister ['blɪstə(r)] **1** n (on skin) ampolla f; (on paint) burbuja f **2** vi ampollarse

blizzard ['blɪzəd] n ventisca f

bloated ['bləʊtɪd] adj hinchado(a)

blob [blɒb] n (drop) gota f; (spot) mancha f

block [blɒk] **1** n (a) bloque m; (of wood) taco m; **in b. capitals** en mayúsculas (b) Br **a b. of flats** un bloque de pisos (c) (group of buildings) manzana f, Am cuadra f (d) (obstruction) bloqueo m **2** vt (obstruct) obstruir; **to b. the way** cerrar el paso

▸ **block up** vt sep bloquear, obstruir; **to get blocked up** (pipe) obstruirse

blockage ['blɒkɪdʒ] n bloqueo m, obstrucción f; (traffic jam) atasco m

blockbuster ['blɒkbʌstə(r)] n Fam exitazo m; Cin, TV gran éxito m de taquilla; (book) éxito de ventas

bloke [bləʊk] n Br Fam tipo m, Esp tío m

blond [blɒnd] **1** n (man) rubio m, Méx güero m, CAm chele m, Carib catire m, Col mono m **2** adj rubio(a), Méx güero(a), CAm chele(a), Carib catire(a), Col mono(a)

blonde [blɒnd] adj & n rubio(a) (m,f), Méx güero(a) (m,f), CAm chele(a) (m,f), Carib catire(a) (m,f), Col mono(a) (m,f)

blood [blʌd] n (a) sangre f; **b. bank** banco m de sangre; **b. cell** glóbulo m; **b. donor** donante mf de sangre; **b. group** grupo sanguíneo; **b. pressure** tensión f arterial; US **b. sausage** morcilla f; **b. test** análisis m de sangre; **b. transfusion** transfusión f de sangre; **b. vessel** vaso sanguíneo; **blue b.** sangre azul; **high/low b. pressure** hipertensión f/hipotensión f (b) (race) sangre f, raza f

bloodshed ['blʌdʃed] n derramamiento m de sangre

bloodshot ['blʌdʃɒt] adj inyectado(a) de sangre

bloodstream ['blʌdstriːm] n corriente sanguínea

bloodthirsty ['blʌdθɜːstɪ] adj sanguinario(a)

bloody ['blʌdɪ] **1** adj (a) (bleeding) sanguinolento(a), sangriento(a); (blood-stained) ensangrentado(a); (battle, revolution) sangriento(a); Fig **to give sb a b. nose** poner a algn en su sitio (b) Br, Austr very Fam (for emphasis) maldito(a), *Esp* puñetero(a), *Méx* pinche; **a b. liar** un mentiroso de mierda; **b. hell!** ¡me cago en la mar!, ¡mierda!, *Méx* ¡en la madre!

2 *adv Br, Austr very Fam* **it's b. hot!** hace un calor del carajo *or Esp* de la leche *or RP* de mierda; **he can b. well do it himself!** ¡que lo haga él, carajo *or Esp* joder!

bloody-minded [blʌdɪ'maɪndɪd] *adj Br Fam* terco(a)

bloom [bluːm] **1** *n* (**a**) *(flower)* flor *f*; **in full b.** en flor (**b**) *(on fruit)* vello *m* **2** *vi (blossom)* florecer

blooming ['bluːmɪŋ] *adj* (**a**) *(blossoming)* floreciente (**b**) *Br Fam (for emphasis)* condenado(a)

blossom ['blɒsəm] **1** *n (flower)* flor *f* **2** *vi* florecer; *Fig* **to b. out** alcanzar la plenitud

blot [blɒt] **1** *n (of ink)* borrón *m*; *Fig* mancha *f*
2 *vt* (**a**) *(with ink)* emborronar (**b**) *(dry)* secar
3 *vi (ink)* correrse

▸ **blot out** *vt sep (memories)* borrar; *(view)* ocultar

blotch [blɒtʃ] *n (on skin)* mancha *f*, enrojecimiento *m*

blotchy ['blɒtʃɪ] *adj* (**blotchier, blotchiest**) *(skin etc)* enrojecido(a); *(paint etc)* cubierto(a) de manchas

blotting-paper ['blɒtɪŋpeɪpə(r)] *n* papel *m* secante

blouse [blaʊz] *n* blusa *f*

blow¹ [bləʊ] *n* golpe *m*; **to come to blows** llegar a las manos; **it came as a terrible b.** fue un duro golpe

blow² [bləʊ] *(pt* **blew** *; pp* **blown**) **1** *vi* (**a**) *(wind)* soplar (**b**) *(fuse)* fundirse (**c**) *(tyre)* reventar **2** *vt* (**a**) *(kiss)* mandar (**b**) *(trumpet etc)* tocar (**c**) *(one's nose)* sonarse (**d**) *(fuse)* fundir (**e**) *Br Fam (money)* fundir, *RP* fumar

▸ **blow away** *vt sep & vi* = **blow off**

▸ **blow down** *vt sep* derribar

▸ **blow off 1** *vt sep (by wind)* llevarse **2** *vi (hat)* salir volando

▸ **blow out 1** *vt sep* apagar **2** *vi* apagarse

▸ **blow over** *vi (storm)* calmarse; *(scandal)* olvidarse

▸ **blow up 1** *vt sep* (**a**) *(building)* volar (**b**) *(inflate)* inflar (**c**) *Phot* ampliar **2** *vi (explode)* explotar

blown [bləʊn] *pp of* **blow²**

blowout ['bləʊaʊt] *n Aut* reventón *m*; *Fam (meal)* comilona *f*

blowtorch ['bləʊtɔːtʃ] *n US* soplete *m*

blue [bluː] **1** *adj* (**a**) *(colour)* azul; *Fig* **once in a b. moon** de uvas a peras, *RP* cada muerte de obispo; *Fam* **to scream b. murder** gritar como un loco; **b. jeans** vaqueros *mpl*, tejanos *mpl* (**b**) *(sad)* triste; **to feel b.** sentirse deprimido(a) (**c**) *(obscene)* verde; **b. joke** chiste *m* verde
2 *n* (**a**) *(colour)* azul *m*; *Fam* **the boys in b.** los maderos (**b**) **out of the b.** *(suddenly)* de repente; *(unexpectedly)* como llovido del cielo

blueberry ['bluːbərɪ] *n* arándano *m*

blueprint ['bluːprɪnt] *n* anteproyecto *m*

bluff [blʌf] **1** *n (trick)* farol *m*; **to call sb's b.** hacer que algn ponga sus cartas encima de la mesa **2** *adj (abrupt)* brusco(a); *(forthright)* francote(a) **3** *vi* tirarse un farol; **to b. one's way through sth** hacer colar algo

blunder ['blʌndə(r)] **1** *n* metedura *f* o *Am* metida *f* de pata; *Fam* patinazo *m* **2** *vi* meter la pata, pegar un patinazo

blunt [blʌnt] **1** *adj* (**a**) *(knife)* desafilado(a); *(pencil)* despuntado(a); **b. instrument** instrumento *m* contundente (**b**) *(frank)* directo(a), francote(a); *(statement)* tajante **2** *vt (pencil)* despuntar; *(knife)* desafilar

blur [blɜː(r)] **1** *n* imagen *f* borrosa **2** *vt (shape)* desdibujar; *(memory)* enturbiar

blurred [blɜːd] *adj* borroso(a)

blurt [blɜːt] *vt* **to b. out** dejar escapar

blush [blʌʃ] **1** *n* rubor *m* **2** *vi* ruborizarse

blustery ['blʌstərɪ] *adj* borrascoso(a)

boar [bɔː(r)] *n* verraco *m*; **wild b.** jabalí *m*

board [bɔːd] **1** *n* (**a**) *(plank)* tabla *f* (**b**) *(work surface)* mesa *f*; *(blackboard)* pizarra *f*, *Am* pizarrón *m*; *(for games)* tablero *m* (**c**) *(meals)* pensión *f*; **full b.** pensión completa; **b. and lodging** or *US* **room** casa *f* y comida (**d**) *(committee)* junta *f*, consejo *m*; **b. of directors** consejo de administración; **b. room** sala *f* del consejo (**e**) *Naut* **on b.** a bordo (**f**) *Fig* **above b.** en regla; **across-the-b.** general

2 *vt (ship, plane etc)* embarcarse en, subir a

3 *vi* (**a**) *(lodge)* alojarse (**b**) *(at school)* estar interno(a)

▸ **board up** *vt sep* tapar

boarder ['bɔːdə(r)] *n* (**a**) *(in boarding house)* huésped *mf* (**b**) *(at school)* interno(a) *m,f*

boarding ['bɔːdɪŋ] *n* (**a**) *(embarkation)* embarque *m*; **b. card, b. pass** tarjeta *f* de embarque (**b**) *(lodging)* alojamiento *m*, pensión *f*; **b. house** pensión; **b. school** internado *m*

boast [bəʊst] **1** *n* jactancia *f*, alarde *m*

2 *vi* jactarse, alardear (**about** de)

3 *vt* presumir de, alardear de; **the town boasts an Olympic swimming pool** la ciudad disfruta de una piscina olímpica

boastful ['bəʊstfʊl] *adj* jactancioso(a), presuntuoso(a)

boat [bəʊt] *n* barco *m*; *(small)* barca *f*, bote *m*; *(launch)* lancha *f*; *(large)* buque *m*; *Fig* **we're all in the same b.** todos estamos en el mismo barco; **fishing b.** barco de pesca

bode¹ [bəʊd] *pt of* **bide**

bode² [bəʊd] *vt & vi* presagiar; **to b. well/ill** ser de buen/mal agüero

bodily ['bɒdɪlɪ] **1** *adj* físico(a); **b. harm** daños *mpl* corporales **2** *adv* **to carry sb b.** llevar a algn en brazos

body ['bɒdɪ] *n* (**a**) cuerpo *m*; **b. odour** olor *m* corporal (**b**) *(corpse)* cadáver *m* (**c**) *(main part)* parte *f* principal (**d**) *Aut* carrocería *f* (**e**) *(organization)* organismo *m*; *(profession)* cuerpo *m* (**f**) *(group of people)* conjunto *m*, grupo *m*

bodyguard ['bɒdɪgɑːd] *n* guardaespaldas *mf inv*

bodywork ['bɒdɪwɜːk] *n Aut* carrocería *f*

bog [bɒg] *n* (**a**) ciénaga *f* (**b**) *Br Fam (lavatory)* baño *m*, *Esp* tigre *m*

▸ **bog down** *vt sep* **to get bogged down** atascarse

bogus ['bəʊgəs] *adj* falso(a); **b. company** compañía *f* fantasma

boil¹ [bɔɪl] **1** *n* **to come to the b.** empezar a hervir

2 *vt (water)* hervir; *(food)* cocer; *(egg)* cocer, pasar por agua

3 *vi* hervir; *Fig* **to b. with rage** estar furioso(a)

▸ **boil down** *vi* reducirse (**to** a)

▸ **boil over** *vi (milk)* salirse

boil² [bɔɪl] *n Med* furúnculo *m*

boiled [bɔɪld] *adj* **b. egg** huevo cocido *or* pasado por agua

boiler ['bɔɪlə(r)] *n* caldera *f*; *Br* **b. suit** mono *m* (de trabajo), *Am* overol *m*, *CSur, Cuba* mameluco *m*

boiling ['bɔɪlɪŋ] *adj* **b. water** agua hirviendo; **it's b. hot** *(food)* quema; *(weather)* hace un calor agobiante; **b. point** punto *m* de ebullición

boisterous ['bɔɪstərəs] *adj* (**a**) *(person, party)* bullicioso(a) (**b**) *(weather)* borrascoso(a)

bold [bəʊld] *adj* (**a**) *(brave)* valiente (**b**) *(daring)* audaz (**c**) *Typ* **b. type** negrita *f*

bolster ['bəʊlstə(r)] **1** *n (pillow)* cabezal *m*, travesaño *m* **2** *vt (strengthen)* reforzar; *(support)* apoyar

bolt [bəʊlt] **1** *n* (**a**) *(on door)* cerrojo *m*; *(small)* pestillo *m* (**b**) *Tech* perno *m*, tornillo *m* (**c**) *(of lightning)* rayo *m*

2 *vt* (**a**) *(lock)* cerrar con cerrojo (**b**) *Tech* sujetar con pernos (**c**) *Fam (food)* engullir

3 *vi (person)* largarse; *(horse)* desbocarse

4 *adv* **b. upright** derecho

bomb [bɒm] **1** *n* bomba *f*; *Br Fam* **to cost a b.** costar un ojo de la cara; **car b.** coche-bomba *m*; **letter b.** cartabomba *f*; **b. disposal squad** brigada *f* de artificieros; **b. scare** amenaza *f* de bomba

2 *vt (city etc)* bombardear; *(by terrorists)* volar

3 *vi Br Fam* **to b. (along)** *(car)* ir a toda pastilla

bombard [bɒm'bɑ:d] *vt* bombardear

bombshell ['bɒmʃel] *n* (a) *Mil* obús *m* (b) *Fig (surprise)* bomba *f* (c) *Fam* **a blonde b.** una rubia explosiva

bona fide [bəʊnə'faɪdɪ] *adj* (a) *(genuine)* auténtico(a) (b) *(in good faith)* bienintencionado(a)

bond [bɒnd] **1** *n* (a) *(link)* lazo *m*, vínculo *m* (b) *Fin* bono *m* (c) *(binding agreement)* acuerdo *m*
2 *vt (stick)* pegar
3 *vi (form attachment)* unirse (**with** a)

bone [bəʊn] **1** *n* (a) *(in)* hueso *m*; *(in fish)* espina *f*; *Fig* **b. of contention** manzana *f* de la discordia; *Fig* **he made no bones about it** no trató de disimularlo; **b. china** porcelana fina (b) **bones** *(remains)* restos *mpl*; **the bare bones** lo esencial **2** *vt (meat)* deshuesar; *(fish)* quitar las espinas a
▸ **bone up on** *vt insep Fam* empollar

bonfire ['bɒnfaɪə(r)] *n* hoguera *f*, fogata *f*; *Br* **B. Night** = fiesta del 5 de noviembre en que de noche se hacen hogueras y hay fuegos artificiales

bonkers ['bɒŋkəz] *adj Br Fam* **to be b.** estar chiflado(a) *or Esp* majareta

bonnet ['bɒnɪt] *n* (a) *(child's)* gorra *f* (b) *Br (of car)* capó *m*, *CAm*, *Méx* cofre *m*

bonus ['bəʊnəs] *n* (a) *(on wages)* prima *f* (b) *Fin (on shares)* dividendo *m* extraordinario (c) *Br Ins* beneficio *m*

boo [bu:] **1** *interj* ¡bu!
2 *n* abucheo *m*
3 *vt* abuchear

boob [bu:b] *n Br Fam* (a) *(silly mistake)* metedura *f or Am* metida de pata (b) **boobs** *(breasts)* tetas *fpl*

booby-trap ['bu:bɪtræp] **1** *n (explosive device)* bomba *f* trampa *or* camuflada **2** *vt* colocar una bomba trampa

book [bʊk] **1** *n* (a) libro *m*; *Fig* **by the b.** según las reglas; **b. end** sujetalibros *m inv* (b) *(of stamps)* carpeta *f*; *(of matches)* cajetilla *f* (c) *Com* **books** cuentas *fpl* **2** *vt* (a) *(reserve)* reservar;

(return flight) cerrar (b) *(engage)* contratar (c) *(of police)* poner una multa a

▸ **book into** *vt insep (hotel)* reservar una habitación en

▸ **book out** *vi (of hotel)* marcharse

▸ **book up** *vt sep* **booked up** *(sign)* completo

bookcase ['bʊkkeɪs] *n* librería *f*, estantería *f*

booking ['bʊkɪŋ] *n esp Br (reservation)* reserva *f*; **b. office** taquilla *f*, *Am* boletería *f*

bookkeeping ['bʊkki:pɪŋ] *n Fin* contabilidad *f*

booklet ['bʊklɪt] *n* folleto *m*

bookmaker ['bʊkmeɪkə(r)] *n* corredor(a) *m,f* de apuestas

bookmark ['bʊkmɑ:k] *n* marcador *m*

bookseller ['bʊkselə(r)] *n* librero(a) *m,f*

bookshelf ['bʊkʃelf] *n* estante *m*; **bookshelves** estantería *f*

bookshop ['bʊkʃɒp] *n* librería *f*

bookstore ['bʊkstɔ:(r)] *n US* librería *f*

bookworm ['bʊkwɜ:m] *n Fam* ratón *m* de biblioteca

boom¹ [bu:m] **1** *n* (a) *(noise)* estampido *m*, trueno *m* (b) *(sudden prosperity)* boom *m*, auge *m* **2** *vi* (a) *(thunder)* retumbar; *(cannon)* tronar (b) *(prosper)* estar en auge

boom² [bu:m] *n (of microphone)* jirafa *f*

boor ['bʊə(r)] *n* grosero(a) *m,f*, cafre *mf*

boost [bu:st] **1** *n* estímulo *m*, empujón *m* **2** *vt* (a) *(increase)* aumentar (b) **to b. sb's confidence** subirle la moral a algn (c) *(tourism, exports)* fomentar (d) *(voltage)* elevar

boot¹ [bu:t] **1** *n* (a) bota *f*; *(short)* botín *m*; *Fig* **he's too big for his boots** es muy creído; *Br Fam* **to put the b. in** pisotear; *Fam* **she got the b.** la echaron (del trabajo); **b. polish** betún *m* (b) *Br (of car)* maletero *m*, *CAm*, *Méx* cajuela *f*, *CSur* baúl *m*
2 *vt Fam* (a) *Ftb (ball)* chutar (b) **to b. (out)** echar a patadas (c) *Comput* arrancar

3 *vi Comput* **to b. (up)** arrancar

boot² [bu:t] *n* **to b.** además

booth [bu:ð, bu:θ] *n* (**a**) *(in language lab etc)* cabina *f*; **telephone b.** cabina telefónica (**b**) *(at fair)* puesto *m*

booze [bu:z] *Fam* **1** *n* bebida *f*, *Esp* priva *f*, *RP* chupi *m* **2** *vi* empinar el codo, *Esp* privar, *RP* chupar

border ['bɔ:də(r)] *n* (**a**) borde *m*, margen *m* (**b**) *(frontier)* frontera *f* (**c**) *(flowerbed)* arriate *m*

▶ **border on** *vt insep* (**a**) *Geog* lindar con (**b**) *Fig* rayar en

bore¹ [bɔ:(r)] **1** *vt Tech* taladrar, perforar **2** *n* (**a**) *Tech (hole)* taladro *m* (**b**) *(of gun)* calibre *m*

bore² [bɔ:(r)] **1** *vt* aburrir **2** *n (person)* pesado(a) *m,f*, pelma *mf*; *(thing)* lata *f*, rollo *m*; **what a b.!** ¡qué rollo!

bore³ [bɔ:(r)] *pt of* **bear¹**

boredom ['bɔ:dəm] *n* aburrimiento *m*

boring ['bɔ:rɪŋ] *adj (uninteresting)* aburrido(a); *(tedious)* pesado(a), latoso(a)

born [bɔ:n] **1** *pp of* **bear**; **to be b.** nacer; **I wasn't b. yesterday** no nací ayer **2** *adj (having natural ability)* nato(a); **a b. poet** un poeta nato

borne [bɔ:n] *pp of* **bear¹**

borough ['bʌrə] *n* (**a**) *(town)* ciudad *f*; *US (municipality)* municipio *m* (**b**) *Br (constituency)* = división administrativa y electoral que comprende un municipio o un distrito urbano

borrow ['bɒrəʊ] **1** *vt* (**a**) tomar prestado; **can I b. your pen?** ¿me prestas *or* dejas tu bolígrafo? (**b**) *(ideas etc)* apropiarse **2** *vi* tomar prestado

bosom ['bʊzəm] *n* (**a**) *(breast)* pecho *m*; *(breasts)* pechos *mpl*; **b. friend** amigo(a) *m,f* del alma (**b**) *Fig* seno *m*

boss [bɒs] **1** *n* (**a**) *(head)* jefe(a) *m,f*; *(factory owner etc)* patrón(ona) *m,f* (**b**) *esp US Pol* jefe *m*; *Pej* cacique *m* **2** *vt* **to b. sb about** *or* **around** mandar sobre algn

bossy ['bɒsɪ] *adj* (**bossier, bossiest**) *Fam* mandón(ona)

botany ['bɒtənɪ] *n* botánica *f*

botch [bɒtʃ] **1** *vt* chapucear; **a botched job** una chapuza **2** *n* chapuza *f*

both [bəʊθ] **1** *adj* ambos(as), los dos/ las dos; **b. men are teachers** ambos son profesores; **hold it with b. hands** sujétalo con las dos manos

2 *pron* **b. (of them)** ambos(as), los dos/las dos; **b. of you** vosotros dos

3 *conj* a la vez; **b. England and Spain are in Europe** tanto Inglaterra como España están en Europa

bother ['bɒðə(r)] **1** *vt* (**a**) *(disturb)* molestar; *(be a nuisance to)* dar la lata a (**b**) *(worry)* preocupar; *Fam* **I can't be bothered** no tengo ganas

2 *vi* molestarse; **don't b. about me** no te preocupes por mí; **he didn't b. shaving** no se molestó en afeitarse **3** *n* (**a**) *(disturbance)* molestia *f*; *(nuisance)* lata *f* (**b**) *(trouble)* problemas *mpl* **4** *interj Br* ¡maldito sea!

bottle ['bɒtəl] **1** *n* botella *f*; *(of perfume, ink)* frasco *m*; **baby's b.** biberón *m*; **b. opener** abrebotellas *m inv* **2** *vt (wine)* embotellar; *(fruit)* enfrascar

▶ **bottle out** *vi Br Fam* encogerse

▶ **bottle up** *vt sep* reprimir

bottleneck ['bɒtəlnek] *n Aut* embotellamiento *m*, atasco *m*

bottom ['bɒtəm] **1** *adj* (**a**) *(lowest)* más bajo(a); *(drawer, shelf)* de abajo; *Aut* **b. gear** primera *f* (**b**) *(last)* último(a); **b. line** *Fin* saldo *m* final; *Fig* resultado *m* final

2 *n* (**a**) parte *f* inferior; *(of sea, garden, street, box)* fondo *m*; *(of bottle)* culo *m*; *(of page, hill)* pie *m*; *Educ* **to be (at) the b. of the class** ser el último/la última de la clase; **to touch b.** tocar fondo; *Fam* **bottoms up!** ¡salud! (**b**) **to get to the b. of a matter** llegar al meollo de una cuestión; **who is at the b. of all this?** ¿quién está detrás de todo esto? (**c**) *(buttocks)* trasero *m*

▶ **bottom out** *vi Fin* tocar fondo

bottomless ['bɒtəmlɪs] *adj (pit)* sin fondo; *(mystery)* insondable

bought [bɔ:t] *pt & pp of* **buy**

boulder ['bəʊldə(r)] *n* canto rodado

bounce [baʊns] **1** vi (**a**) (ball) rebotar (**b**) (jump) saltar (**c**) Fam (cheque) ser rechazado (por el banco)
2 vt (ball) botar
3 n (**a**) (of ball) bote m (**b**) (jump) salto m (**c**) (energy) vitalidad f

▸ **bounce back** vi (recover health) recuperarse, recobrarse

bouncer ['baʊnsə(r)] n Fam gorila m

bound¹ [baʊnd] adj (**a**) (tied up) atado(a) (**b**) (obliged) obligado(a) (**c**) **b. (up)** (linked) vinculado(a) (**with** a) (**d**) **it's b. to happen** sucederá con toda seguridad; **it was b. to fail** estaba destinado al fracaso

bound² [baʊnd] **1** vi saltar **2** n salto m

bound³ [baʊnd] pt & pp of **bind**

bound⁴ [baʊnd] adj **b. for** con destino a, rumbo a; **to be b. for** dirigirse a

boundary ['baʊndərɪ] n límite m

bounds [baʊndz] npl **beyond the b. of reality** más allá de la realidad; **her ambition knows no b.** su ambición no conoce límites; **the river is out of b.** está prohibido bajar al río

bouquet n (**a**) [buːˈkeɪ, bəʊˈkeɪ] (of flowers) ramillete m (**b**) [buːˈkeɪ] (of wine) aroma m, buqué m

bout [baʊt] n (**a**) (of work) turno m; (of illness) ataque m (**b**) (in boxing) combate m

boutique [buːˈtiːk] n boutique f, tienda f

bow¹ [baʊ] **1** vi (**a**) hacer una reverencia (**b**) (give in) ceder **2** n (with head, body) reverencia f

▸ **bow out** vi retirarse (**of** de)

bow² [bəʊ] n (**a**) Sport, Mus arco m; Fig **to have more than one string to one's b.** ser una persona de recursos (**b**) (knot) lazo m; **b. tie** Esp pajarita f, CAm, Carib, Col corbatín m, Méx corbata f de moño

bow³ [baʊ] n esp Naut proa f

bowel ['baʊəl] n (**a**) intestino m (**b**) **bowels** entrañas fpl

bowl¹ [bəʊl] n (**a**) (dish) cuenco m; (for soup) tazón m; (for washing hands) palangana f; (for washing clothes,

dishes) barreño m; (of toilet) taza f (**b**) Geol cuenca f

bowl² [bəʊl] **1** n bola f
2 vt (in cricket) lanzar
3 vi (**a**) (play bowls) jugar a los bolos (**b**) (in cricket) lanzar la pelota

▸ **bowl over** vt sep (**a**) (knock down) derribar (**b**) Fig (astonish) desconcertar

bowling ['bəʊlɪŋ] n (game) bolos mpl; **b. alley** bolera f; **b. ball** bola f (de jugar a los bolos)

box¹ [bɒks] **1** n (**a**) caja f; (large) cajón m; (of matches) cajetilla f; Th **b. office** taquilla f (**b**) Th palco m (**c**) Br Fam (television) **the b.** la tele **2** vt (pack) embalar

box² [bɒks] Sport **1** vi boxear **2** vt (hit) pegar; **to b. sb's ears** dar un cachete a algn

boxer ['bɒksə(r)] n (**a**) boxeador m (**b**) (dog) bóxer m

boxing ['bɒksɪŋ] n boxeo m, CAm, Méx box m; **b. ring** cuadrilátero m

boy [bɔɪ] n (**a**) (child) niño m, chico m; (youth) joven m; **b. band** = grupo musical juvenil compuesto por adolescentes varones; Fam **oh b.!** ¡vaya! (**b**) (son) hijo m

boycott ['bɔɪkɒt] **1** n boicot m **2** vt boicotear

boyfriend ['bɔɪfrend] n novio m; (live-in) compañero m

bra [brɑː] n sostén m, Esp sujetador m, Carib, Col, Méx brasier m, RP corpiño m

brace [breɪs] **1** n (**a**) (clamp) abrazadera f; (of drill) berbiquí m; (for teeth) aparato m (**b**) Br **braces** (for trousers) tirantes mpl **2** vt (**a**) (reinforce) reforzar (**b**) **to b. oneself (for)** prepararse or Chile, Méx, Ven alistarse (para)

▸ **brace up** vi cobrar ánimo

bracelet ['breɪslɪt] n pulsera f

bracing ['breɪsɪŋ] adj (wind) fresco(a); (stimulating) tonificante

bracket ['brækɪt] **1** n (**a**) Typ (round) paréntesis m; (square) corchete m; (curly) llave f; **in brackets** entre paréntesis (**b**) (support) soporte m; (for *lamp)* brazo *m*; *(shelf)* repisa *f* **(c)** *(for tax)* sector *m* **2** *vt* **(a)** *Ling (phrase etc)* poner entre paréntesis **(b)** *(group together)* agrupar, juntar

brag [bræg] *vi* jactarse (**about** de)

braid [breɪd] **1** *vt* trenzar **2** *n* **(a)** *Sewing* galón *m* **(b)** *esp US (plait)* trenza *f*

brain [breɪn] *n* **(a)** cerebro *m*; **she's got cars on the b.** está obsesionada por los coches; *Med* **b. death** muerte *f* cerebral; *Fig* **b. drain** fuga *f* de cerebros; **b. wave** idea *f* genial **(b)** *Fam* **brains** inteligencia *f*; **to have brains** ser inteligente; *Br* **brains** or *US* **b. trust** grupo *m* de expertos **(c)** *Culin* **brains** sesos *mpl*

brainchild ['breɪntʃaɪld] *n* invento *m*, idea *f* genial

brainstorm ['breɪnstɔːm] *n* **(a)** *(outburst)* arranque *m* **(b)** *(brainwave)* genialidad *f*, lluvia *f* de ideas

brainwash ['breɪnwɒʃ] *vt* lavar el cerebro a

brainy ['breɪnɪ] *adj* (**brainier, brainiest**) *Fam* listo(a)

brake [breɪk] **1** *n Aut (also pl)* freno *m*; **b. drum** tambor *m* del freno; **b. fluid** líquido *m* de frenos; **b. light** luz *f* de freno **2** *vi* frenar, echar el freno

bran [bræn] *n* salvado *m*

branch [brɑːntʃ] **1** *n (of tree)* rama *f*; *(of road)* bifurcación *f*; *(of science etc)* ramo *m*; *Com* **b. (office)** sucursal *f* **2** *vi (road)* bifurcarse

▸ **branch off** *vi* desviarse

▸ **branch out** *vi* diversificarse

brand [brænd] **1** *n* **(a)** *Com* marca *f*; **b. name** marca de fábrica **(b)** *(type)* clase *f* **(c)** *(on cattle)* hierro *m* **2** *vt* **(a)** *(animal)* marcar con hierro candente **(b)** *(label)* tildar

brandish ['brændɪʃ] *vt* blandir

brand-new ['brænd'njuː] *adj* flamante

brandy ['brændɪ] *n* brandy *m*, coñac *m*, *RP* cognac *m*

brash [bræʃ] *adj* **(a)** *(impudent)* descarado(a) **(b)** *(reckless)* temerario(a) **(c)** *(loud, showy)* chillón(ona)

brass [brɑːs] *n* **(a)** *(metal)* latón *m* **(b)** *Br Fam (money)* *Esp* pasta *f*, *Esp, RP* guita *f*, *Am* plata *f*, *Méx* lana *f* **(c)** *Mus* instrumentos *mpl* de metal; **b. band** banda *f* de metal

brat [bræt] *n Fam* mocoso(a) *m,f*

brave [breɪv] **1** *adj* valiente, valeroso(a) **2** *n US* **(Indian) b.** guerrero *m* indio **3** *vt* **(a)** *(face)* hacer frente a **(b)** *(defy)* desafiar

bravery ['breɪvərɪ] *n* valentía *f*, valor *m*

brawl [brɔːl] **1** *n* reyerta *f* **2** *vi* pelearse

Brazil [brə'zɪl] *n* (el) Brasil

Brazilian [brə'zɪlɪən] *adj & n* brasileño(a) *(m,f)*

breach [briːtʃ] **1** *n* **(a)** *(in wall)* brecha *f* **(b)** *(violation)* incumplimiento *m*; **b. of confidence** abuso *m* de confianza; **b. of contract** incumplimiento de contrato; **b. of the law** violación *f* de la ley; **b. of the peace** alteración *f* del orden público **(c)** *(in relations)* ruptura *f* **2** *vt* violar

bread [bred] *n* **(a)** pan *m*; **b. and butter** pan con mantequilla, *Am* pan con manteca; *Fig* **our daily b.** el pan nuestro de cada día **(b)** *Fam (money)* *Esp* pasta *f*, *Esp, RP* guita *f*, *Am* plata *f*, *Méx* lana *f*

breadboard ['bredbɔːd] *n* tabla *f* (para cortar el pan)

breadcrumb ['bredkrʌm] *n* miga *f* de pan; **breadcrumbs** pan rallado

breadline ['bredlaɪn] *n Fam* miseria *f*; **to be on the b.** vivir en la miseria

breadth [bredθ] *n* **(a)** *(width)* anchura *f*; **it is 2 m in b.** tiene 2 m de ancho **(b)** *(extent)* amplitud *f*

breadwinner ['bredwɪnə(r)] *n* cabeza *mf* de familia

break [breɪk] *(pt* **broke**; *pp* **broken**) **1** *vt* **(a)** romper; **to b. a leg** romperse la pierna; **to b. a record** batir un récord; *Fig* **to b. sb's heart** partirle el corazón a algn **(b)** *(fail to keep)* faltar a; **to b. a contract** romper un contrato; **to b. the law** violar la ley **(c)** *(destroy)* destrozar; *Fin* arruinar **(d)** *(interrupt)* interrumpir

(e) *(fall)* amortiguar (f) **she broke the news to him** le comunicó la noticia **2** *vi* (a) romperse; *(clouds)* dispersarse; *(waves)* romper (b) *(storm)* estallar (c) *(voice)* cambiar (d) *(health)* resentirse (e) **when day breaks** al rayar el alba (f) *(story)* divulgarse **3** *n* (a) *(fracture)* rotura *f*; *(crack)* grieta *f*; *(opening)* abertura *f* (b) *(in relationship)* ruptura *f* (c) *(pause)* pausa *f*, descanso *m*; *(at school)* recreo *m*; **to take a b.** descansar un rato; *(holiday)* tomar unos días libres; (d) *Fam (chance)* oportunidad *f*

▸**break away** *vi* (a) *(become separate)* desprenderse (**from** de) (b) *(escape)* escaparse

▸**break down 1** *vt sep* (a) *(door)* derribar (b) *(resistance)* acabar con (c) *(costs)* desglosar **2** *vi* (a) *Aut* tener una avería (b) *(resistance)* ceder (c) *(health)* debilitarse (d) *(weep)* ponerse a llorar

▸**break in 1** *vt sep* acostumbrar; **to b. in a pair of shoes** cogerle la forma a los zapatos **2** *vi (burglar)* entrar por la fuerza

▸**break into** *vt insep* (a) *(burgle) (house)* allanar; *(safe)* forzar (b) **to b. into song** empezar a cantar

▸**break off 1** *vt sep* partir **2** *vi* (a) *(become detached)* desprenderse (b) *(talks)* interrumpirse (c) *(stop)* pararse

▸**break out** *vi* (a) *(prisoners)* escaparse (b) *(war etc)* estallar; **she broke out in a rash** le salió un sarpullido

▸**break through 1** *vt insep* (a) *(crowd)* abrirse paso por; *(cordon)* romper (b) *(clouds)* atravesar **2** *vi* (a) *(crowd)* abrirse paso (b) *(sun)* salir

▸**break up 1** *vt sep (object)* romper; *(car)* desguazar; *(crowd)* disolver **2** *vi* (a) *(object)* romperse (b) *(crowd)* disolverse; *(meeting)* levantarse (c) *(relationship)* fracasar; *(couple)* separarse (d) *Educ* terminar

▸**break with** *vt insep (past)* romper con

breakage ['breɪkɪdʒ] *n (breaking)* rotura *f*

breakdown ['breɪkdaʊn] *n* (a) *Aut*

avería *f*; *Br* **b. truck** grúa *f* (b) **(nervous) b.** crisis nerviosa (c) *(in communications)* *Esp* fallo *m*, *Am* falla *f* (d) *(analysis)* análisis *m*; *Fin* desglose *m*

breakfast ['brekfəst] **1** *n* desayuno *m*; **to have b.** desayunar **2** *vi* desayunar

break-in ['breɪkɪn] *n* robo *m (con allanamiento de morada)*

breakthrough ['breɪkθruː] *n* paso *m* adelante, avance *m*

breast [brest] *n (chest)* pecho *m*; *(of woman)* pecho, seno *m*; *(of chicken etc)* pechuga *f*; *Fig* **to make a clean b. of it** dar la cara

breast-feed ['brestfiːd] *vt* dar el pecho a, amamantar a

breaststroke ['breststrəʊk] *n* braza *f*

breath [breθ] *n* (a) aliento *m*; *(breathing)* respiración *f*; **in the same b.** al mismo tiempo; **out of b.** sin aliento; **to catch one's b.** recobrar el aliento; **to draw b.** respirar; **under one's b.** en voz baja; *Fig* **to take sb's b. away** dejar pasmado a algn; *Aut* **b. test** alcoholemia *f* (b) **to go out for a b. of fresh air** salir a tomar el aire

Breathalyser® *Br*, **Breathalyzer**® *US* ['breθəlaɪzə(r)] *n* alcoholímetro *m*

breathe [briːð] **1** *vt* respirar; **to b. a sigh of relief** dar un suspiro de alivio **2** *vi* respirar; **to b. in** aspirar; **to b. out** espirar; **to b. heavily** resoplar

breathing ['briːðɪŋ] *n* respiración *f*; **b. space** pausa *f*, respiro *m*

breathless ['breθlɪs] *adj* sin aliento, jadeante

breathtaking ['breθteɪkɪŋ] *adj* impresionante

breed [briːd] *(pt & pp* **bred** [bred]*)* **1** *n (of animal)* raza *f*; *Fig (class)* clase *f* **2** *vt (animals)* criar; *Fig (ideas)* engendrar **3** *vi (animals)* reproducirse

breeding ['briːdɪŋ] *n* (a) *(of animals)* cría *f*; *Fig* **b. ground** caldo *m* de cultivo (b) *(of person)* educación *f*

breeze [briːz] **1** *n* brisa *f*; *Br Constr* **b. block** bloque *m* de cemento **2** *vi* **to b.**

in/out entrar/salir despreocupadamente

breezy ['bri:zı] *adj* (**breezier, breeziest**) (**a**) *(weather)* ventoso(a) (**b**) *(person)* despreocupado(a)

brew [bru:] **1** *vt (beer)* elaborar; *(hot drink)* preparar

2 *vi (tea)* reposar; *Fig* **a storm is brewing** se prepara una tormenta; *Fam* **something's brewing** algo se está cociendo

3 *n* (**a**) *(of tea)* infusión *f*; *Fam (of beer)* birra *f* (**b**) *(magic potion)* brebaje *m*

brewery ['bru:ərı] *n* cervecería *f*

bribe [braıb] **1** *vt* sobornar **2** *n* soborno *m*, *Andes, CSur* coima *f*, *CAm, Méx* mordida *f*

bribery ['braıbərı] *n* soborno *m*

brick [brık] *n* ladrillo *m*; *Br Fam Old-fashioned* **he's a b.** es un gran tipo

bricklayer ['brıkleıə(r)] *n* albañil *m*

bride [braıd] *n* novia *f*; **the b. and groom** los novios

bridegroom ['braıdgru:m] *n* novio *m*

bridesmaid ['braıdzmeıd] *n* dama *f* de honor

bridge¹ [brıdʒ] **1** *n* puente *m*; *(of nose)* caballete *m*; *(of ship)* puente de mando **2** *vt* (**a**) *(river)* tender un puente sobre (**b**) *(gap)* llenar; *Br Fin* **bridging loan** crédito *m* a corto plazo

bridge² [brıdʒ] *n Cards* bridge *m*

brief [bri:f] **1** *adj* (**a**) *(short)* breve (**b**) *(concise)* conciso(a)

2 *n* (**a**) *(report)* informe *m*; **in b.** en resumen (**b**) *Jur* expediente *m* (**c**) *Mil* instrucciones *fpl* (**d**) **briefs** *(for men)* calzoncillos *mpl*, *Chile* fundillos *mpl*, *Méx* calzones *mpl*; *(for women) Esp* bragas *fpl*, *Chile, Col, Méx* calzones *mpl*, *RP* bombacha *f*

3 *vt* (**a**) *(inform)* informar (**b**) *(instruct)* dar instrucciones a

briefcase ['bri:fkeıs] *n* cartera *f*, portafolios *m inv*

briefing ['bri:fıŋ] *n (meeting)* reunión informativa

briefly ['bri:flı] *adv* brevemente; **as b. as possible** con la mayor brevedad (posible)

brigade [brı'geıd] *n* brigada *f*

bright [braıt] *adj* (**a**) *(light, sun, eyes)* brillante; *(colour)* vivo(a); *(day)* claro(a) (**b**) *(cheerful)* alegre (**c**) *(clever)* listo(a), espabilado(a) (**d**) *(promising)* prometedor(a)

brighten ['braıtən] *vi (prospects)* mejorarse; *(face)* iluminarse

▸ **brighten up 1** *vt sep (room etc)* alegrar **2** *vi (weather)* despejarse; *(person)* animarse

brightly ['braıtlı] *adv* brillantemente

brilliant ['brıljənt] **1** *adj* brillante; *Br (excellent)* genial, *Am* salvo *RP* chévere, *Andes, CSur* macanudo(a), *Méx* padre, *RP* bárbaro(a) **2** *n* brillante *m*

brim [brım] **1** *n* borde *m*; *(of hat)* ala *f*; **full to the b.** lleno hasta el borde **2** *vi* rebosar (**with** de)

▸ **brim over** *vi* rebosar

bring [brıŋ] (*pt & pp* **brought**) *vt* (**a**) *(carry, take)* traer; *(lead)* llevar (**b**) *(cause)* provocar; **he brought it upon himself** se lo buscó (**c**) *(persuade)* convencer; **how did they b. themselves to do it?** ¿cómo llegaron a hacerlo?

▸ **bring about** *vt sep* provocar

▸ **bring along** *vt sep* traer

▸ **bring back** *vt sep* (**a**) *(return)* devolver (**b**) *(reintroduce)* volver a introducir (**c**) *(make one remember)* traerle a la memoria

▸ **bring down** *vt sep* (**a**) *(from upstairs)* bajar (**b**) *(government)* derribar; *Th* **to b. the house down** echar el teatro abajo con los aplausos (**c**) *(reduce)* rebajar

▸ **bring forward** *vt sep* (**a**) *(meeting etc)* adelantar (**b**) *(present)* presentar (**c**) *Fin* **brought forward** suma y sigue

▸ **bring in** *vt sep* (**a**) *(yield)* dar (**b**) *(show in)* hacer entrar (**c**) *(law etc)* introducir; *(fashion)* lanzar

▸ **bring off** *vt sep* lograr, conseguir

▸ **bring on** *vt sep* provocar

▸ **bring out** *vt sep* (**a**) *(publish)* publicar (**b**) *(reveal)* recalcar; **he brings out the worst in me** despierta lo peor que hay en mí

▸**bring round** *vt sep* (**a**) *(revive)* hacer volver en si (**b**) *(persuade)* convencer

▸**bring to** *vt sep* reanimar

▸**bring up** *vt sep* (**a**) *(educate)* criar, educar (**b**) *(subject)* plantear (**c**) *(vomit)* devolver

brink [brɪŋk] *n (edge)* borde *m*; *Fig* **on the b. of ruin** al borde de la ruina; **on the b. of tears** a punto de llorar

brisk [brɪsk] *adj* enérgico(a); *(pace)* rápido(a); *(trade)* activo(a); *(weather)* fresco(a)

bristle ['brɪsəl] **1** *n* cerda *f* **2** *vi* (**a**) erizarse (**b**) *(show anger)* enfurecer (**at con**)

▸**bristle with** *vt insep (be full of)* estar lleno(a) de

Britain ['brɪtən] *n* (**Great**) **B.** Gran Bretaña

British ['brɪtɪʃ] **1** *adj* británico(a); **the B. Isles** las Islas Británicas **2** *npl* **the B.** los británicos

Brittany ['brɪtənɪ] *n* Bretaña

brittle ['brɪtəl] *adj* quebradizo(a), frágil

broad [brɔːd] *adj* (**a**) *(wide)* ancho(a); *(large)* extenso(a) (**b**) **a b. hint** *(clear)* una indirecta clara (**c**) *(daylight)* pleno(a) (**d**) *(not detailed)* general (**e**) *(accent)* marcado(a), cerrado(a)

broadcast ['brɔːdkɑːst] *Rad, TV* **1** *n* emisión *f* **2** *vt (pt & pp* **broadcast**) emitir, transmitir

broaden ['brɔːdən] *vt* ensanchar

broadly ['brɔːdlɪ] *adv* en términos generales

broad-minded [brɔːd'maɪndɪd] *adj* liberal, tolerante

broccoli ['brɒkəlɪ] *n* brécol *m*

brochure ['brəʊʃə(r), 'brəʊʃjʊə(r)] *n* folleto *m*

broil [brɔɪl] *vt US* asar a la parrilla

broke [brəʊk] **1** *adj Fam* **to be b.** estar sin un centavo *or Méx* sin un peso *or Esp* sin blanca **2** *pt of* **break**

broken ['brəʊkən] **1** *adj* roto(a) **2** *pp of* **break**

broker ['brəʊkə(r)] *n* corredor *m*,

agente *mf* de Bolsa

bronchitis [brɒŋ'kaɪtɪs] *n* bronquitis *f*

bronze [brɒnz] **1** *n* bronce *m* **2** *adj (material)* de bronce; *(colour)* bronceado(a)

brooch [brəʊtʃ] *n* broche *m*

brood [bruːd] **1** *n (birds)* cría *f*; *Hum (children)* prole *m* **2** *vi (hen)* empollar; *Fig (ponder)* rumiar; *Fig* **to b. over a problem** darle vueltas a un problema

broody ['bruːdɪ] *adj* (**a**) *(pensive)* pensativo(a) (**b**) *(moody)* melancólico(a) (**c**) *Br Fam (woman)* con ganas de tener hijos

broom [bruːm] *n* (**a**) escoba *f* (**b**) *Bot* retama *f*

broth [brɒθ] *n* caldo *m*

brothel ['brɒθəl] *n* burdel *m*

brother ['brʌðə(r)] *n* hermano *m*; **brothers and sisters** hermanos

brother-in-law ['brʌðərɪnlɔː] *n* cuñado *m*

brought [brɔːt] *pt & pp of* **bring**

brow [braʊ] *n* (**a**) *(forehead)* frente *f* (**b**) *(eyebrow)* ceja *f* (**c**) *(of hill)* cima *f*

brown [braʊn] **1** *adj* (**a**) marrón, *Am* café; *(hair, eyes)* castaño(a); **b. bread** pan *m* integral; **b. paper** papel *m* de estraza; **b. sugar** azúcar moreno (**b**) *(tanned)* moreno(a)
2 *n* marrón *m*, *Am* color *m* café
3 *vt Culin* dorar; *(tan)* broncear

browse [braʊz] **1** *vi (in shop)* mirar; *(through book)* hojear
2 *vt Comput* **to b. the Web** navegar por la Web
3 *n* **to have a b. (in)** dar un vistazo (a)

bruise [bruːz] **1** *n* morado *m*, cardenal *m*
2 *vt (body)* contusionar; *(fruit)* estropear
3 *vi (body)* magullarse; *(fruit)* estropearse

brunch [brʌntʃ] *n Fam* desayunocomida *m*, *RP* brunch *m*

brunette [bruː'net] *adj & n* morena (*f*)

brush[1] [brʌʃ] **1** *n* (**a**) *(for hair, teeth)* cepillo *m*; *Art* pincel *m*; *(for housepainting)* brocha *f* (**b**) *(with the law)* roce *m*

2 vt (**a**) cepillar; **to b. one's hair** cepillarse el pelo; **to b. one's teeth** cepillarse los dientes (**b**) (touch lightly) rozar

3 vi **to b. against** rozar al pasar

▸ **brush aside** vt sep dejar de lado

▸ **brush off** vt sep Fam no hacer caso a, Esp pasar de

▸ **brush up** vt sep repasar

brush² [brʌʃ] n (undergrowth) broza f, maleza f

brush-off ['brʌʃɒf] n Fam **to give sb the b.** no hacer ni caso a algn

brusque [bruːsk, brʊsk] adj brusco(a); (words) áspero(a)

Brussels ['brʌsəlz] n Bruselas

brutal ['bruːtəl] adj brutal, cruel

brute [bruːt] **1** adj bruto(a); **b. force** fuerza bruta **2** n (animal) bruto m; (person) bestia f

BSc [biːesˈsiː] n (abbr **Bachelor of Science**) (person) licenciado(a) m,f en Ciencias

BSE [biːesˈiː] n (abbr **bovine spongiform encephalopathy**) encefalopatía f espongiforme bovina (enfermedad de las vacas locas)

bubble ['bʌbəl] **1** n burbuja f; **b. bath** espuma f de baño; **b. gum** chicle m; **soap b.** pompa f de jabón **2** vi burbujear; Culin borbotear

bubbly ['bʌblɪ] **1** adj (**bubblier, bubbliest**) efervescente **2** n Fam champán m, cava m

buck¹ [bʌk] **1** n Zool macho m; (male deer) ciervo m; (male goat) macho cabrío; Fam **to pass the b. to sb** echarle el muerto a algn **2** vi (horse) corcovear

▸ **buck up 1** vt sep Fam **b. your ideas up!** ¡espábilate! **2** vi (cheer up) animarse

buck² [bʌk] n US, Austr Fam dólar m

bucket ['bʌkɪt] **1** n balde m, Esp cubo m; Br Fam **it's raining buckets** llueve a cántaros or RP a baldes **2** vi Fam **it's bucketing (down)** llueve a cántaros or RP a baldes

buckle ['bʌkəl] **1** n hebilla f **2** vt abrochar con hebilla

3 vi (**a**) (wall, metal) combarse (**b**) (knees) doblarse

bud [bʌd] **1** n (shoot) brote m; (flower) capullo m **2** vi brotar; Fig florecer

Buddhist ['bʊdɪst] n & adj budista (mf)

budding ['bʌdɪŋ] adj en ciernes

buddy ['bʌdɪ] n US Fam Esp colega mf, Am compadre, Am hermano(a), Méx cuate

budge [bʌdʒ] vi (**a**) (move) moverse (**b**) (yield) ceder

budgerigar ['bʌdʒərɪgɑː(r)] n periquito m

budget ['bʌdʒɪt] **1** n presupuesto m; Br Pol **the B.** ≃ los Presupuestos Generales del Estado **2** vi hacer un presupuesto (**for** para)

buff¹ [bʌf] **1** adj & n (colour) color (m) de ante **2** vt dar brillo a

buff² [bʌf] n Fam (enthusiast) aficionado(a) m,f

buffalo ['bʌfələʊ] n (pl **buffaloes** or **buffalo**) búfalo m

buffer ['bʌfə(r)] **1** n (**a**) (device) amortiguador m; Rail tope m; **b. zone** zona f de seguridad (**b**) Comput memoria intermedia **2** vt amortiguar

buffet¹ ['bʊfeɪ] n (**a**) (snack bar) bar m; (at railway station) cantina f; Rail **b. car** coche m restaurante (**b**) (self-service meal) bufet m libre (**c**) (item of furniture) aparador m

buffet² ['bʌfɪt] vt golpear

bug [bʌg] **1** n (**a**) (insect) bicho m (**b**) Fam (microbe) microbio m; **the flu b.** el virus de la gripe (**c**) (hidden microphone) micrófono oculto (**d**) Comput error m **2** vt Fam (**a**) **to b. a room** ocultar micrófonos en una habitación (**b**) (annoy) fastidiar, molestar

bugger ['bʌgə(r)] **1** n Br very Fam (unpleasant person) cabrón(ona) m,f; **you silly b.** ¡qué tonto(a) eres!; **the poor b.!** ¡pobre desgraciado!; **b. all** nada de nada; **2** vt (**a**) (sodomize) sodomizar (**b**) Br very Fam **b. (it)!** ¡carajo!, Esp ¡joder!, RP ¡la puta (digo)!

buggy ['bʌgɪ] n (**a**) Br (baby's pushchair) sillita f de niño (**b**) US *(pram)* cochecito *m* (de niño)

build [bɪld] **1** *vt* (*pt & pp* **built**) construir **2** *n (physique)* tipo *m*, físico *m*

▸**build up** *vt sep (accumulate)* acumular; **to b. up a reputation** labrarse una buena reputación

builder ['bɪldə(r)] *n* constructor(a) *m,f; (contractor)* contratista *mf*

building ['bɪldɪŋ] *n* edificio *m*, construcción *f*; **b. site** obra *f*; *Br* **b. society** sociedad hipotecaria

build-up ['bɪldʌp] *n* (**a**) *(accumulation)* aumento *m*; *(of gas)* acumulación *f* (**b**) *(publicity)* propaganda *f*

built [bɪlt] *pp of* **build**

built-in ['bɪlt'ɪn] *adj* (**a**) *(cupboard)* empotrado(a) (**b**) *(incorporated)* incorporado(a)

built-up [bɪlt'ʌp] *adj* urbanizado(a)

bulb [bʌlb] *n* (**a**) *Bot* bulbo *m* (**b**) *(light bulb)* *Esp* bombilla *f*, *Andes, Méx* foco *m*, *CAm, Carib* bombillo *m*, *RP* lamparita *f*

bulge [bʌldʒ] **1** *n* protuberancia *f*; *(in pocket)* bulto *m* **2** *vi (swell)* hincharse; *(be full)* estar repleto(a)

bulimia [buː'lɪmɪə] *n Med* bulimia *f*

bulk [bʌlk] *n* (**a**) *(mass)* masa *f*, volumen *m*; *Com* **in b.** a granel; **to buy sth in b.** comprar algo al por mayor (**b**) *(greater part)* mayor parte *f*

bulky ['bʌlkɪ] *adj* (**bulkier, bulkiest**) (**a**) *(large)* voluminoso(a) (**b**) **this crate is rather b.** esta caja es un armatoste

bull [bʊl] *n* (**a**) toro *m*; *Fig* **to take the b. by the horns** agarrar *or Esp* coger el toro por los cuernos (**b**) *Fin* **b. market** mercado *m* al alza

bulldozer ['bʊldəʊzə(r)] *n* bulldozer *m*

bullet ['bʊlɪt] *n* bala *f*; **b. wound** balazo *m*

bulletin ['bʊlɪtɪn] *n* boletín *m*; *Rad, TV* **news b.** boletín de noticias; *US* **b. board** tablón *m* de anuncios

bullet-proof ['bʊlɪtpruːf] *adj* a prueba de balas; **b. vest** chaleco *m* antibalas

bullfight ['bʊlfaɪt] *n* corrida *f* de toros

bullion ['bʊljən] *n (gold, silver)* lingote *m*

bull's-eye ['bʊlzaɪ] *n (of target)* blanco *m*

bully ['bʊlɪ] **1** *n* matón *m*; *(at school)* *Esp* abusón(ona) *m,f*, *Am* abusador(a) *m,f*

2 *vt (terrorize)* intimidar; *(bulldoze)* tiranizar

3 *interj Ironic* **b. for you!** ¡bravo!

bum¹ [bʌm] *n Br Fam (bottom)* culo *m*, *Am* cola *f*

bum² [bʌm] *Fam* **1** *n* (**a**) *US (tramp)* vagabundo *m* (**b**) *(idler)* holgazán(ana) *m,f* **2** *vi* gorronear

▸**bum around** *vi Fam* vaguear

bump [bʌmp] **1** *n* (**a**) *(swelling)* chichón *m*; *(lump)* abolladura *f*; *(on road)* bache *m* (**b**) *(blow)* choque *m*, golpe *m* (**c**) *(jolt)* sacudida *f*

2 *vt* golpear; **to b. one's head** darse un golpe en la cabeza

3 *vi* chocar (**into** contra)

▸**bump into** *vt insep (meet)* tropezar con

▸**bump off** *vt sep Fam* liquidar

bumper ['bʌmpə(r)] **1** *adj* abundante; *Br* **b. issue** número *m* especial **2** *n Br (of car)* parachoques *m inv*, *Méx* defensas *fpl*, *RP* paragolpes *mpl*

bumpy ['bʌmpɪ] *adj* (**bumpier, bumpiest**) con muchos baches

bun [bʌn] *n* (**a**) *(bread)* panecillo *m*; *(sweet)* bollo *m*; *Fig Euph* **she's got a b. in the oven** está preñada (**b**) *(of hair)* moño *m*

bunch [bʌntʃ] **1** *n (of keys)* manojo *m*; *(of flowers)* ramo *m*; *(of grapes)* racimo *m*; *(of people)* grupo *m*; *(gang)* pandilla *f* **2** *vi* **to b. together** juntarse, agruparse

bundle ['bʌndəl] **1** *n (of clothes)* bulto *m*, fardo *m*; *(of papers)* fajo *m*; *(of wood)* haz *m* **2** *vt* (**a**) *(make a bundle of)* liar, atar (**b**) *(push)* empujar

bungalow ['bʌŋgələʊ] *n* chalé *m*, bungalow *m*

bungle ['bʌŋgəl] *vt* chapucear

bunk [bʌŋk] *n (bed)* litera *f*

bunker ['bʌŋkə(r)] *n* (**a**) *(for coal)*

carbonera f (**b**) *Mil* búnker *m* (**c**) *Br (on golf course)* búnker *m*

bunny ['bʌnɪ] *n Fam (baby talk)* **b. (rabbit)** conejito *m*

buoy [bɔɪ] *n* boya *f*

▸ **buoy up** *vt sep* (**a**) *(keep afloat)* mantener a flote (**b**) *(person, spirits)* alentar, animar

buoyant ['bɔɪənt] *adj* (**a**) *(object)* flotante (**b**) *Fin* con tendencia alcista (**c**) *(optimistic)* optimista

burden ['bɜːdən] **1** *n* carga *f*; *Fig* to be a b. to sb ser una carga para algn **2** *vt* cargar (**with** con)

bureau ['bjʊərəʊ] *n* (*pl* **bureaux**) (**a**) *(office)* agencia *f*, oficina *f* (**b**) *Br (desk)* escritorio *m* (**c**) *US (chest of drawers)* cómoda *f*

bureaucracy [bjʊə'rɒkrəsɪ] *n* burocracia *f*

bureaucrat ['bjʊərəkræt] *n* burócrata *mf*

burger ['bɜːgə(r)] *n Fam (hamburger)* hamburguesa *f*

burglar ['bɜːglə(r)] *n* ladrón(ona) *m,f*; **b. alarm** alarma *f* antirrobo

burgle ['bɜːgəl] *vt* robar, desvalijar

burial ['berɪəl] *n* entierro *m*

burn [bɜːn] (*pt & pp* **burnt** *or* **burned**) **1** *n* quemadura *f*
2 *vt* quemar
3 *vi* (**a**) *(fire)* arder; *(building, food)* quemarse (**b**) *(lamp)* estar encendido(a) (**c**) *(sore)* escocer

▸ **burn down 1** *vt sep* incendiar **2** *vi* incendiarse

▸ **burn out** *vi (person)* quemarse

▸ **burn up** *vt sep (energy, calories)* quemar

burner ['bɜːnə(r)] *n* quemador *m*

burning ['bɜːnɪŋ] *adj* (**a**) *(on fire)* incendiado(a); *(hot)* abrasador(a) (**b**) *(passionate)* ardiente (**c**) **a b. question** una cuestión candente

burp [bɜːp] **1** *n* eructo *m* **2** *vi* eructar

burrow ['bʌrəʊ] **1** *n* madriguera *f*; *(for rabbits)* conejera *f* **2** *vi* (**a**) hacer una madriguera (**b**) *(search)* hurgar

burst [bɜːst] (*pt & pp* **burst**) **1** *n* (**a**)

(explosion) estallido *m*; *(of tyre)* reventón *m* (**b**) *(of applause)* arranque *m*; *(rage)* arrebato *m*; **b. of gunfire** ráfaga *f* de tiros; **b. of laughter** carcajadas *fpl*
2 *vt (balloon)* reventar; *Fig* **the river b. its banks** el río se salió de madre
3 *vi* (**a**) reventarse; *(shell)* estallar (**b**) *(enter suddenly)* irrumpir (**into** en)

▸ **burst into** *vt insep* **to b. into laughter/tears** echarse a reír/a llorar

▸ **burst open** *vi* abrirse violentamente

▸ **burst out** *vi* **to b. out laughing** echarse a reír

bury ['berɪ] *vt* (**a**) enterrar; **to be buried in thought** estar absorto en pensamientos (**b**) *(hide)* ocultar

bus [bʌs] *n* (*pl* **buses**, *US* **busses**) autobús *m*, *Andes* buseta *f*, *Bol*, *RP* colectivo *m*, *CAm*, *Méx* camión *m*, *CAm*, *Carib* guagua *f*, *Urug* ómnibus *m*, *Ven* microbusete *m*; **b. conductor** cobrador(a) *m,f* de autobús; **b. driver** conductor(a) *m,f* de autobús; **b. stop** parada *f* de autobús

bush [bʊʃ] *n* (**a**) *(shrub)* arbusto *m* (**b**) *Austr* **the b.** el monte; *Fam* **b. telegraph** *Esp* radio *f* macuto, *Cuba*, *CRica*, *Pan* radio *f* bemba

bushy ['bʊʃɪ] *adj* espeso(a), tupido(a)

business ['bɪznɪs] *n* (**a**) *(commerce)* negocios *mpl*; **how's b.?** ¿cómo andan los negocios?; **to be away on b.** estar en viaje de negocios; **b. deal** negocio *m*; **b. hours** horas *fpl* de oficina; **b. trip** viaje *m* de negocios
(**b**) *(firm)* empresa *f*
(**c**) *(matter)* asunto *m*; **I mean b.** estoy hablando en serio; **it's no b. of mine** no es asunto mío; **to make it one's b. to ...** encargarse de ...; **to get down to b.** ir al grano; **to go about one's b.** ocuparse de sus asuntos

businessman ['bɪznɪsmən] *n* hombre *m* de negocios

businesswoman ['bɪznɪswʊmən] *n* mujer *f* de negocios

bust¹ [bʌst] *n* (**a**) *(of woman)* pecho *m* (**b**) *Art* busto *m*

bust² [bʌst] *Fam* **1** *vt* (**a**) *(break)*

estropear; *Esp* escacharrar (**b**) *(person)* trincar; *(place)* hacer una redada en **2** *adj* (**a**) *(broken)* **to be b.** estar estropeado(a) *or Esp* escacharra-do(a) (**b**) **to go b.** *(bankrupt)* quebrar

bustle ['bʌsəl] **1** *n (activity, noise)* bullicio *m* **2** *vi* **to b. about** ir y venir

busy ['bɪzɪ] **1** *adj* (**a**) ocupado(a), atareado(a); *(life)* ajetreado(a); *(street)* concurrido(a) (**b**) *esp US Tel* ocupado(a); **b. signal** señal *f* de comunicando **2** *vt* **to b. oneself doing sth** ocuparse haciendo algo

busybody ['bɪzɪbɒdɪ] *n* entrometido(a) *m,f*

but [bʌt] **1** *conj* (**a**) pero; **b. yet** a pesar de todo (**b**) *(after negative)* sino; **not two b. three** no dos sino tres

2 *adv* **b. for her we would have drowned** si no hubiera sido por ella, nos habríamos ahogado

3 *prep* salvo, menos; **everyone b. her** todos menos ella

butcher ['bʊtʃə(r)] **1** *n* carnicero(a) *m,f*; **b.'s (shop)** carnicería *f* **2** *vt (animals)* matar; *(people)* masacrar

butler ['bʌtlə(r)] *n* mayordomo *m*

butt[1] [bʌt] *n* (**a**) *(of rifle)* culata *f*; *(of cigarette)* colilla *f* (**b**) *US Fam (bottom)* culo *m*

butt[2] [bʌt] **1** *n (with head)* cabezazo *m* **2** *vt (hit with head)* dar un cabezazo a

▸ **butt in** *vi* entrar en la conversación

butter ['bʌtə(r)] **1** *n* mantequilla *f, RP* manteca *f*; **b. dish** mantequera *f* **2** *vt* untar con mantequilla *or RP* manteca

butterfly ['bʌtəflaɪ] *n* mariposa *f*

buttock ['bʌtək] *n* nalga *f*; **buttocks** nalgas *fpl*

button ['bʌtən] **1** *n* (**a**) *(on clothes, machine)* botón *m* (**b**) *US (badge)* chapa *f* **2** *vt* **to b. (up)** abrochar(se), abotonar(se)

buttonhole ['bʌtənhəʊl] *n* ojal *m*

buy [baɪ] **1** *n* compra *f*; **a good b.** una ganga **2** *vt (pt & pp* **bought**) (**a**) comprar; **she bought that car from a neighbour** compró ese coche a un vecino (**b**) *Fam (believe)* tragar

▸ **buy off** *vt sep* sobornar

▸ **buy out** *vt sep* adquirir la parte de

▸ **buy up** *vt sep* comprar en grandes cantidades

buyer ['baɪə(r)] *n* comprador(a) *m,f*

buzz [bʌz] **1** *n* (**a**) *(of bee)* zumbido *m*; *(of conversation)* rumor *m* (**b**) *Fam (telephone call)* telefonazo *m* **2** *vi* zumbar

buzzer ['bʌzə(r)] *n* timbre *m*

by [baɪ] **1** *prep* (**a**) *(indicating agent)* por; **composed by Bach** compuesto(a) por Bach; **a film by Almodóvar** una película de Almodóvar

(**b**) *(via)* por; **he left by the back door** salió por la puerta trasera

(**c**) *(manner)* por; **by car/train** en coche/tren; **by credit card** con tarjeta de crédito; **by day/night** de día/noche; **by chance** por casualidad; **by oneself** solo(a); **made by hand** hecho(a) a mano

(**d**) *(amount)* por; **little by little** poco a poco; **they are sold by the dozen** se venden por docenas; **to be paid by the hour** cobrar por horas; **by far** con mucho

(**e**) *(beside)* al lado de, junto a; **side by side** juntos

(**f**) **to walk by a building** *(pass)* pasar por delante de un edificio

(**g**) *(time)* para; **by now** ya; **by then** para entonces; **we have to be there by nine** tenemos que estar allí para las nueve

(**h**) *Math* por

(**i**) *(according to)* según; **is that O.K. by you?** ¿te viene bien?

(**j**) *(phrases)* **bit by bit** poco a poco; **day by day** día a día; **what do you mean by that?** ¿qué quieres decir con eso?; **by the way** a propósito

2 *adv* (**a**) **to go by** *(past)* pasar; **she just walked by** pasó de largo (**b**) **by and by** con el tiempo; **by and large** en conjunto

by-law ['baɪlɔː] *n* ley *f* municipal

bypass ['baɪpɑːs] **1** *n* (**a**) *(road)* carretera *f* de circunvalación (**b**) *Med* **b. surgery** cirugía *f* de by-pass **2** *vt* evitar

bystander ['baɪstændə(r)] *n* testigo *mf*

byte [baɪt] *n Comput* byte *m*, octeto *m*

Cc

C, c [siː] *n* (**a**) *(the letter)* C, c (**b**) *Mus* do *m* (**c**) *Educ (grade)* aprobado *m*; **to get a C** *(in exam, essay)* sacar un aprobado

C (**a**) *(abbr* **celsius** *or* **centigrade**) C, centígrado (**b**) *(abbr* **century**) s., siglo; **C16** s. XVI

cab [kæb] *n* taxi *m*; **c. driver** taxista *mf*

cabaret ['kæbəreɪ] *n* cabaret *m*

cabbage ['kæbɪdʒ] *n* col *f*, berza *f*; **red c.** (col) lombarda *f*

cabin ['kæbɪn] *n* (**a**) *(hut)* choza *f*; **log c.** cabaña *f* (**b**) *Naut* camarote *m* (**c**) *(of lorry, plane)* cabina *f*

cabinet ['kæbɪnɪt] *n* (**a**) *(item of furniture)* armario *m*; *(glass-fronted)* vitrina *f*; **c. maker** ebanista *mf* (**b**) *Pol* gabinete *m*, consejo *m* de ministros

cable ['keɪbəl] **1** *n* cable *m*; **c. car** teleférico *m*; **c. company** cableoperador(a) *m,f*; **c. TV** televisión *f* por cable **2** *vt & vi* cablegrafiar, telegrafiar

cactus ['kæktəs] *n* *(pl* **cacti** ['kæktaɪ]) cactus *m*

caddie ['kædɪ] *n* *(in golf)* cadi *m*

cadet [kə'det] *n* *Mil* cadete *m*

cadge [kædʒ] *vt & vi Fam* gorrear, *Esp, Méx* gorronear, *RP* garronear (**from** *or* **off** a)

café ['kæfeɪ], **cafeteria** [kæfɪ'tɪərɪə] *n* cafetería *f*

caffeine ['kæfiːn] *n* cafeína *f*

cage [keɪdʒ] **1** *n* jaula *f* **2** *vt* enjaular

cake [keɪk] *n* pastel *m*, tarta *f*

calamity [kə'læmɪtɪ] *n* calamidad *f*

calculate ['kælkjʊleɪt] *vt* calcular

calculated ['kælkjʊleɪtɪd] *adj* intencionado(a)

calculation [kælkjʊ'leɪʃən] *n* cálculo *m*

calculator ['kælkjʊleɪtə(r)] *n* calculadora *f*

calendar ['kælɪndə(r)] *n* calendario *m*; **c. year** año *m* natural, *Am* año *m* calendario

calf¹ [kɑːf] *n* *(pl* **calves**) *(of cattle)* becerro(a) *m,f*, ternero(a) *m,f*; *(of other animals)* cría *f*

calf² [kɑːf] *n* *(pl* **calves**) *Anat* pantorrilla *f*

calibre, US caliber ['kælɪbə(r)] *n* calibre *m*

call [kɔːl] **1** *vt* (**a**) *(on phone)* llamar, telefonear, *Am* hablar; **to c. sb names** poner verde a algn; **what's he called?** ¿cómo se llama? (**b**) *(meeting etc)* convocar; **to c. sth to mind** traer algo a la memoria

2 *vi* (**a**) *(on phone)* llamar, *Am* hablar; *Tel* **who's calling?** ¿de parte de quién? (**b**) **to c. at sb's (house)** pasar por casa de algn; **to c. for sth/sb** pasar a recoger algo/a algn (**c**) *(trains)* parar (**d**) **to c. for** *(require)* exigir; **that wasn't called for** eso no estaba justificado

3 *n* (**a**) *(shout) (of person)* llamada *f*, grito *m*, *Am* llamado *m* (**b**) *(visit)* visita *f*; **to pay a c. on sb** visitar a algn (**c**) *Tel* **(phone) c.** llamada *f*, *Am* llamado *m*; **c. box** *Br* cabina telefónica; *US* teléfono *m* de emergencia; **c. centre** centro *m* de atención telefónica

▸ **call away** *vt sep* **to be called away on business** tener que ausentarse por motivos de trabajo

▸ **call back** *vi (phone again)* volver a llamar *or Am* hablar; *(visit again)* volver

▸ **call in 1** *vt sep (doctor)* llamar **2** *vi* (**a**) **I'll c. in tomorrow** *(visit)* mañana me paso (**b**) *Naut* hacer escala (**at** en)

▸ **call off** *vt sep* suspender

▸ **call on** *vt insep* (**a**) visitar (**b**) **to c. on sb for support** recurrir a algn en busca de apoyo

▸ **call out 1** *vt sep* (**a**) *(shout)* gritar (**b**) *(doctor)* hacer venir; *(workers)* convocar a la huelga **2** *vi* gritar

▸ **call up** *vt sep* (**a**) *Tel* llamar, *Am* hablar (**b**) *Mil* llamar a filas, reclutar

caller [ˈkɔːlə(r)] *n* visita *mf*; *Tel* persona *f* que llama

callous [ˈkæləs] *adj* insensible, duro(a)

calm [kɑːm] **1** *adj* (**a**) *(weather, sea)* en calma (**b**) *(relaxed)* tranquilo(a); **keep c.!** ¡tranquilo(a)!
2 *n* (**a**) *(of weather, sea)* calma *f* (**b**) *(tranquillity)* tranquilidad *f*
3 *vt* calmar, tranquilizar
4 *vi* **to c. (down)** calmarse, tranquilizarse

calorie, calory [ˈkælərɪ] *n* caloría *f*

calves [kɑːvz] *pl of* **calf¹, calf²**

camcorder [ˈkæmkɔːdə(r)] *n* videocámara *f* (portátil)

came [keɪm] *pt of* **come**

camel [ˈkæməl] *n* camello(a) *m,f*

camera [ˈkæmərə] *n* (**a**) cámara *f or* máquina *f* fotográfica; *Cin, TV* cámara (**b**) *Jur* **in c.** a puerta cerrada

camouflage [ˈkæməflɑːʒ] **1** *n* camuflaje *m* **2** *vt* camuflar

camp¹ [kæmp] **1** *n* campamento *m*; **c. bed** cama *f* plegable; **c. site** camping *m* **2** *vi* **to go camping** ir de camping

camp² [kæmp] *adj Fam* afeminado(a); *(affected)* amanerado(a)

campaign [kæmˈpeɪn] **1** *n* campaña *f* **2** *vi* **to c. for/against** hacer campaña a favor de/en contra de

campaigner [kæmˈpeɪnə(r)] *n* defensor(a) *m,f* (**for** de)

camper [ˈkæmpə(r)] *n* (**a**) *(person)* campista *mf* (**b**) *US (vehicle)* caravana *f*

camping [ˈkæmpɪŋ] *n* **c. ground, c. site** camping *m*

campus [ˈkæmpəs] *n* campus *m*, ciudad universitaria

can¹ [kæn, *unstressed* kən] *(pt* **could**) *v aux*

El verbo **can** carece de infinitivo, de gerundio y de participio. En infinitivo o en participio, se empleará la forma correspondiente de **be able to**, por ejemplo: **he wanted to be able to speak English**; **she has always been able to swim**. En el inglés hablado, y en el escrito en estilo coloquial, la forma negativa **cannot** se transforma en **can't** y la forma negativa **could not** se transforma en **couldn't**

(**a**) *(be able to)* poder; **he could have come** podría haber venido; **I'll phone you as soon as I c.** te llamaré en cuanto pueda; **she can't do it** no puede hacerlo; **I can't understand why** no entiendo por qué

(**b**) *(know how to)* saber; **c. you ski?** ¿sabes esquiar?; **I can't speak English** no sé hablar inglés

(**c**) *(be permitted to)* poder; **he can't go out tonight** no le dejan salir esta noche (**d**) *(be possible)* poder; **she could have forgotten** puede (ser) que lo haya olvidado; **they can't be very poor** no deben ser muy pobres; **what c. it be?** ¿qué será?

can² [kæn] **1** *n* (**a**) *(of oil)* bidón *m* (**b**) *(container)* lata *f*, *Am* tarro *m*; **c. opener** abrelatas *m inv* **2** *vt (fish, fruit)* enlatar

Canada [ˈkænədə] *n* Canadá

Canadian [kəˈneɪdɪən] *adj & n* canadiense *(mf)*

canal [kəˈnæl] *n* canal *m*

canary [kəˈneərɪ] *n* canario *m*

cancel [ˈkænsəl] *vt (train, contract)* cancelar; *Com* anular; *(permission)* retirar; *(decree)* revocar

cancellation [kænsɪˈleɪʃən] *n* cancelación *f*; *Com* anulación *f*

cancer [ˈkænsə(r)] *n* (**a**) *Med* cáncer *m*; **breast c.** cáncer de mama; **c. research** cancerología *f* (**b**) **C.** *(in astrology)* Cáncer *m*

candid [ˈkændɪd] *adj* franco(a), sincero(a)

candidate [ˈkændɪdeɪt, ˈkændɪdɪt] *n* candidato(a) *m,f*; *(in exam)* opositor(a) *m,f*

candle ['kændəl] *n* vela *f*; *(in church)* cirio *m*

candlestick ['kændəlstɪk] *n* candelero *m*, palmatoria *f*; *(in church)* cirial *m*

candy ['kændɪ] *n US* caramelo *m*; **c. store** confitería *f*

candyfloss ['kændɪflɒs] *n Br* algodón *m* dulce

cane [keɪn] **1** *n* (**a**) *Bot* caña *f*; **c. sugar** azúcar *m* de caña (**b**) *(wicker)* mimbre *m* (**c**) *(walking stick)* bastón *m*; *(for punishment)* palmeta *f* **2** *vt* castigar con la palmeta

canine ['keɪnaɪn] *adj Zool* canino(a); **c. tooth** colmillo *m*

canister ['kænɪstə(r)] *n* bote *m*

cannabis ['kænəbɪs] *n* hachís *m*, cannabis *m*

canned [kænd] *adj* enlatado(a); **c. foods** conservas *fpl*

cannon ['kænən] **1** *n* (**a**) *(pl* **cannons** *or* **cannon**) cañón *m*; *Fig* **c. fodder** carne *f* de cañón (**b**) *Br (in billiards, snooker)* carambola *f* **2** *vi* chocar (**into** contra)

cannot ['kænɒt, kæ'nɒt] = **can not**

canoe [kə'nu:] *n* canoa *f*; *Sport* piragua *f*

canoeing [kə'nu:ɪŋ] *n* piragüismo *m*; **to go c.** ir a hacer piragüismo

canopy ['kænəpɪ] *n* (**a**) *(on throne)* dosel *m* (**b**) *(awning)* toldo *m*

can't [kɑ:nt] = **can not**

canteen [kæn'ti:n] *n* (**a**) *(restaurant)* cantina *f* (**b**) *Br (set of cutlery)* juego *m* de cubiertos (**c**) *(flask)* cantimplora *f*

canvas ['kænvəs] *n* (**a**) *Tex* lona *f* (**b**) *(painting)* lienzo *m*

canvass ['kænvəs] *vi* (**a**) *Pol* hacer propaganda electoral (**b**) *Com* hacer promoción, buscar clientes

canyon ['kænjən] *n* cañón *m*; **the Grand C.** el Gran Cañón

cap [kæp] **1** *n* (**a**) gorro *m*; *(soldier's)* gorra *f* (**b**) *Br Sport* **to win a c. for England** ser seleccionado(a) para el equipo de Inglaterra (**c**) *(of pen)* capuchón *m*; *(of bottle)* tapón *m* **2** *vt* (**a**) *(outdo)* superar; *Fig* **to c. it all**

para colmo (**b**) *(spending)* limitar

capability [keɪpə'bɪlɪtɪ] *n* habilidad *f*

capable ['keɪpəbəl] *adj* (**a**) *(skilful)* hábil (**b**) *(able)* capaz (**of** de)

capacity [kə'pæsɪtɪ] *n* (**a**) capacidad *f* (**b**) *(position)* puesto *m*; **in her c. as manageress** en calidad de gerente

cape¹ [keɪp] *n (garment)* capa *f*

cape² [keɪp] *n Geog* cabo *m*, promontorio *m*; **C. Horn** Cabo de Hornos; **C. Town** Ciudad del Cabo; **C. Verde** Cabo Verde

capital ['kæpɪtəl] **1** *n* (**a**) *(town)* capital *f* (**b**) *(letter)* mayúscula *f* (**c**) *Fin* capital *m* **2** *adj* (**a**) *(city)* capital (**b**) **c. punishment** pena *f* capital (**c**) **c. letter** mayúscula *f*

capitalism ['kæpɪtəlɪzəm] *n* capitalismo *m*

capitalist ['kæpɪtəlɪst] *adj & n* capitalista *(mf)*

capitalize ['kæpɪtəlaɪz] *vi Fin* capitalizar; *Fig* **to c. on sth** sacar provecho *or* beneficio de algo

Capricorn ['kæprɪkɔ:n] *n* Capricornio *m*

capsize [kæp'saɪz] **1** *vt* hacer zozobrar **2** *vi* zozobrar

capsule ['kæpsju:l] *n* cápsula *f*

captain ['kæptɪn] **1** *n* capitán *m* **2** *vt* capitanear

caption ['kæpʃən] *n (under picture)* pie *m* de foto; *Cin* subtítulo *m*

captivating ['kæptɪveɪtɪŋ] *adj* seductor(a)

captive ['kæptɪv] **1** *n* cautivo(a) *m,f* **2** *adj* cautivo(a)

captivity [kæp'tɪvɪtɪ] *n* cautiverio *m*

capture ['kæptʃə(r)] **1** *vt* (**a**) capturar, apresar; *Mil (town)* tomar (**b**) *(market)* acaparar (**c**) *Fig (mood)* captar **2** *n (of fugitive)* captura *f*; *(of town)* toma *f*

car [kɑ:(r)] *n* (**a**) coche *m*, *Am* carro *m*, *CSur* auto *m*; *Br* **c. park** parking *m*, *Esp* aparcamiento *m*; **c. wash** túnel *m* de lavado (**b**) *US Rail* coche *m*

caramel ['kærəmel] *n* azúcar *m* quemado; *(sweet)* caramelo *m*

carat ['kærət] *n* quilate *m*

caravan ['kærəvæn] *n* (**a**) *Br (vehicle)* caravana *f* (**b**) *(in desert)* caravana *f*

carbohydrate [kɑːbəʊ'haɪdreɪt] *n* hidrato *m* de carbono, carbohidrato *m*

carbon ['kɑːbən] *n* carbono *m*; **c. copy** copia *f* al papel carbón; *Fig* copia exacta; **c. dioxide** dióxido *m* de carbono; **c. paper** papel *m* carbón

card [kɑːd] *n* (**a**) tarjeta *f*; *(of cardboard)* cartulina *f*; **birthday/ Christmas c.** tarjeta de cumpleaños/ de Navidad (**b**) *(in file)* ficha *f*; *(for identification)* carné *m*, *CSur, Méx* credencial *m*; **c. index** fichero *m* (**c**) **pack of cards** baraja *f*, cartas *fpl*; **(playing) c.** naipe *m*, carta; *Fig Br* **on** or *US* **in the cards** previsto

cardboard ['kɑːdbɔːd] *n* cartón *m*; **c. box** caja *f* de cartón; **c. cutout** recortable *m*

cardigan ['kɑːdɪgən] *n* rebeca *f*

cardinal ['kɑːdɪnəl] **1** *n Rel* cardenal *m* **2** *adj* cardinal; **c. numbers** números *mpl* cardinales

care [keə(r)] **1** *vi (be concerned)* preocuparse (**about** por); **I don't c.** no me importa; *Fam* **for all I c.** me trae sin cuidado; *Fam* **he couldn't c. less** le importa un bledo **2** *n* (**a**) *(attention, protection)* cuidado *m*, atención *f*; **c. of …** *(on letter)* al cuidado de …; **medical c.** asistencia *f* médica; **to take c. of** cuidar; *(business)* ocuparse de (**b**) *(carefulness)* cuidado *m*; **take c.** *(be careful)* ten cuidado; *(as farewell)* ¡cuídate! (**c**) *(worry)* preocupación *f*

▶ **care for** *vt insep* (**a**) *(look after)* cuidar (**b**) *(like)* gustar, interesar; **would you c. for a coffee?** ¿te apetece or *Carib, Col, Méx* provoca un café?

career [kə'rɪə(r)] **1** *n* carrera *f* **2** *vi* correr a toda velocidad

carefree ['keəfriː] *adj* despreocupado(a)

careful ['keəfʊl] *adj* cuidadoso(a); *(cautious)* prudente; **be c.!** ¡ojo!; **to be c.** tener cuidado

carefully ['keəfʊlɪ] *adv (painstakingly)* cuidadosamente; *(cautiously)* con cuidado

careless ['keəlɪs] *adj* descuidado(a); *(about clothes)* desaliñado(a); *(driving)* negligente; **a c. mistake** un descuido

carer ['keərə(r)] *n* = persona que cuida de un familiar enfermo o anciano, sin que necesariamente reciba compensación económica por ello

caress [kə'res] **1** *n* caricia *f* **2** *vt* acariciar

caretaker ['keəteɪkə(r)] *n Br (of building)* conserje *m*, portero(a) *m,f*; *(of school)* conserje *m*

cargo ['kɑːgəʊ] *n (pl* **cargoes** or *US* **cargos)** carga *f*, cargamento *m*; *Naut* **c. boat** buque *m* de carga, carguero *m*

Caribbean [kærɪ'bɪən, *US* kə'rɪbɪən] *adj* caribe, caribeño(a); **the C. (Sea)** el (mar) Caribe

caricature ['kærɪkətjʊə(r)] *n* caricatura *f*

caring ['keərɪŋ] *adj* solidario(a)

carnation [kɑː'neɪʃən] *n* clavel *m*

carnival ['kɑːnɪvəl] *n* carnaval *m*

carol ['kærəl] *n* villancico *m*

carp¹ [kɑːp] *n (fish)* carpa *f*

carp² [kɑːp] *vi* refunfuñar

carpenter ['kɑːpɪntə(r)] *n* carpintero(a) *m,f*

carpentry ['kɑːpɪntrɪ] *n* carpintería *f*

carpet ['kɑːpɪt] **1** *n* alfombra *f* **2** *vt* *(floor) Esp* enmoquetar, *Am* alfombrar

carriage ['kærɪdʒ] *n* (**a**) *(horse-drawn)* carruaje *m* (**b**) *Br (of train)* vagón *m*, coche *m* (**c**) *(of gun)* cureña *f* (**d**) *(of typewriter)* carro *m* (**e**) *(of goods)* porte *m*, transporte *m*

carrier ['kærɪə(r)] *n* (**a**) *(company)* transportista *mf*; *Br* **c. bag** bolsa *f* de plástico; **c. pigeon** paloma mensajera (**b**) *Med* portador(a) *m,f*

carrot ['kærət] *n* zanahoria *f*

carry ['kærɪ] **1** *vt* (**a**) llevar; *(goods)* transportar (**b**) *(stock)* tener; *(responsibility, penalty)* conllevar, implicar (**c**) *(disease)* ser portador(a) de **2** *vi* *(sound)* oírse

▸ **carry away** *vt sep* llevarse; **to get carried away** entusiasmarse

▸ **carry forward** *vt sep Fin* **carried forward** suma y sigue

▸ **carry off** *vt sep (prize)* llevarse; *Fam* **to c. it off** salir airoso(a)

▸ **carry on 1** *vt sep* continuar; *(conversation)* mantener **2** *vi* **(a)** continuar, seguir adelante; **c. on!** ¡adelante! **(b)** *Fam (make a fuss)* hacer una escena; **don't c. on about it!** ¡no te enrolles! **(c)** *Fam* **to c. on with sb** tener un lío *or Méx* una movida *or RP* un asunto con algn

▸ **carry out** *vt sep (plan)* llevar a cabo, realizar; *(test)* verificar

cart [kɑːt] **1** *n (horse-drawn)* carro *m*; *(handcart)* carretilla *f*; *US (in supermarket)* carrito *m* **2** *vt* carretear

carton ['kɑːtən] *n (of cream etc)* caja *f*

cartoon [kɑː'tuːn] *n (strip)* tira cómica, historieta *f*; *Art* cartón *m*; *(animated)* dibujos *mpl* animados

cartridge ['kɑːtrɪdʒ] *n* **(a)** cartucho *m* **(b)** *(for pen)* recambio *m*; **c. paper** papel guarro

carve [kɑːv] *vt* **(a)** *(wood)* tallar; *(stone, metal)* cincelar, esculpir **(b)** *(meat)* trinchar

carving ['kɑːvɪŋ] *n* **(a)** *Art* talla *f* **(b)** **c. knife** *(for meat)* cuchillo *m* de trinchar

cascade [kæ'skeɪd] *n* cascada *f*

case[1] [keɪs] *n* **(a)** caso *m*; **a c. in point** un buen ejemplo; **in any c.** en cualquier caso, de todas formas; **in c. of doubt** en caso de duda; **just in c.** por si acaso **(b)** *Med* caso *m*; **c. history** historial clínico **(c)** *Jur* causa *f*

case[2] [keɪs] *n* **(a)** *(suitcase)* maleta *f*, *RP* valija *f*; *(small)* estuche *m*; *(soft)* funda *f* **(b)** **a c. of wine** una caja de botellas de vino **(c)** *Typ* **lower c.** minúscula *f*; **upper c.** mayúscula *f*

cash [kæʃ] **1** *n* dinero efectivo; **to pay c.** pagar al contado *or* en efectivo; *Br* **c. desk** caja *f*; **c. on delivery** entrega *f* contra reembolso; **c. dispenser** cajero automático; **c. register** caja registradora **2** *vt (cheque)* cobrar

▸ **cash in 1** *vi Fam Fig* **to c. in on sth** sacar provecho de algo **2** *vt sep* hacer efectivo(a)

cashew ['kæʃuː] *n* **c. (nut)** anacardo *m*

cashier [kæ'ʃɪə(r)] *n* cajero(a) *m,f*

casino [kə'siːnəʊ] *n* casino *m*

casket ['kɑːskɪt] *n (box)* cofre *m*; *US (coffin)* ataúd *m*

casserole ['kæsərəʊl] *n* **(a)** *(container)* cacerola *f* **(b)** *Culin* guisado *m*

cassette [kə'set] *n* cinta *f*, casete *f*; **c. recorder** casete *m*

cast [kɑːst] *(pt & pp* **cast)** **1** *vt* **(a)** *(net, fishing line)* echar, arrojar; *(light)* proyectar; *(glance)* lanzar; *(vote)* emitir **(b)** *Fig* **to c. doubts on sth** poner algo en duda; **to c. suspicion on sb** levantar sospechas sobre algn **(c)** *(metal)* moldear; **c. iron** hierro fundido **(d)** *Th (play)* hacer el reparto de **2** *n* **(a)** *(mould)* molde *m*; *(product)* pieza *f* **(b)** *Med* **(plaster) c.** escayola *f*, *esp Am* yeso *m* **(c)** *Th* reparto *m*

▸ **cast off** *vi Naut* soltar (las) amarras

caster sugar ['kɑːstə(r)'ʃʊgə(r)] *n Br* azúcar *m or f* extrafino(a)

cast-iron ['kɑːstaɪən] *adj* de hierro fundido

castle ['kɑːsəl] **1** *n* **(a)** castillo *m* **(b)** *(in chess)* torre *f* **2** *vi (in chess)* enrocar

castrate [kæ'streɪt] *vt* castrar

casual ['kæʒjʊəl] *adj* **(a)** *(meeting etc)* fortuito(a) **(b)** *(worker)* eventual **(c)** *(clothes)* (de) sport **(d)** *(visit)* de paso **(e)** *(person, attitude)* despreocupado(a), informal

casualty ['kæʒjʊəltɪ] *n* **(a)** *Mil* baja *f*; **casualties** pérdidas *fpl* **(b)** *(injured)* herido(a) *m,f*

cat [kæt] *n* gato(a) *m,f*; *Fig* **to let the c. out of the bag** revelar el secreto, *Esp* descubrir el pastel

catalogue, *US* **catalog** ['kætəlɒg] **1** *n* catálogo *m* **2** *vt* catalogar

catalyst ['kætəlɪst] *n* catalizador *m*

catapult ['kætəpʌlt] *n Br* tirachinas *m inv*

catastrophe [kə'tæstrəfɪ] *n* catástrofe *f*

catch [kætʃ] (*pt & pp* **caught**) **1** *vt* (**a**) *(thrown object, falling object)* atrapar, *Esp* coger, *Am* agarrar; *(fish)* pescar; *(prey, mouse, thief)* atrapar, capturar; **c. (it)!** *(when throwing something)* ¡agárralo!, *Esp* ¡cógelo!; *(train, bus)* coger, *Am* agarrar; **to c. a cold** coger un resfriado; **to c. fire** *(log)* prenderse; *(building)* incendiarse; **to c. hold of** agarrar; **to c. sb's eye** captar la atención de algn; **to c. sight of** entrever

(**b**) *(surprise)* pillar, sorprender

(**c**) *(hear)* entender

(**d**) **to c. one's breath** *(hold)* sostener la respiración; *(recover)* recuperar el aliento

2 *vi (sleeve etc)* engancharse (**on** en); *(fire)* encenderse

3 *n* (**a**) *(of ball)* parada *f*; *(of fish)* presa *f* (**b**) *(on door)* pestillo *m* (**c**) *(disadvantage)* trampa *f*

▸**catch on** *vi Fam* (**a**) *(become popular)* ganar popularidad (**b**) *(understand)* caer en la cuenta

▸**catch out** *vt sep Fam* **to c. sb out** *(discover, trick)* *Esp* pillar *or* *Am* agarrar a algn

▸**catch up** *vi* (**a**) **to c. up with sb** *(reach)* alcanzar a algn (**b**) *(with news)* ponerse al corriente (**on** de); **to c. up on sleep** recuperar el sueño perdido; **to c. up with work** ponerse al día de trabajo

catching [ˈkætʃɪŋ] *adj (disease)* contagioso(a)

catchy [ˈkætʃɪ] *adj* (**catchier**, **catchiest**) *Fam (tune)* pegadizo(a)

categoric(al) [kætɪˈɡɒrɪk(əl)] *adj* categórico(a)

category [ˈkætɪɡərɪ] *n* categoría *f*

cater [ˈkeɪtə(r)] *vi* (**a**) **to c. for** *(wedding etc)* proveer comida para (**b**) **to c. for** *(taste)* atender a

caterer [ˈkeɪtərə(r)] *n* proveedor(a) *m,f*

catering [ˈkeɪtərɪŋ] *n* abastecimiento *m* (de comidas por encargo)

caterpillar [ˈkætəpɪlə(r)] *n* (**a**) oruga *f* (**b**) **c. (tractor)** tractor *m* de oruga

cathedral [kəˈθiːdrəl] *n* catedral *f*

Catholic [ˈkæθəlɪk] *adj & n* católico(a) *(m,f)*

cattle [ˈkætəl] *npl* ganado *m* (vacuno)

caught [kɔːt] *pt & pp of* **catch**

cauliflower [ˈkɒlɪflaʊə(r)] *n* coliflor *f*

cause [kɔːz] **1** *n* (**a**) *(origin)* causa *f* (**b**) *(reason)* motivo *m* (**c**) **for a good c.** por una buena causa **2** *vt* causar; **to c. sb to do sth** hacer que algn haga algo

caution [ˈkɔːʃən] **1** *n* (**a**) *(care)* cautela *f*, prudencia *f* (**b**) *(warning)* aviso *m*, advertencia *f* (**c**) *Br Jur* reprensión *f* **2** *vt* advertir, amonestar

cautious [ˈkɔːʃəs] *adj* cauteloso(a), prudente

cavalry [ˈkævəlrɪ] *n* caballería *f*

cave [keɪv] *n* cueva *f*

▸**cave in** *vi (roof etc)* derrumbarse, hundirse

cavern [ˈkævən] *n* caverna *f*

cavity [ˈkævɪtɪ] *n* (**a**) *(hole)* cavidad *f* (**b**) *(in tooth)* caries *f inv*

CD [siːˈdiː] *n (abbr* **compact disc**) CD *m*; **CD player** (lector *m or* reproductor *m* de) CD *m*

CD-ROM [siːdiːˈrɒm] *n Comput (abbr* **compact disc read-only memory**) CD-ROM *m*

cease [siːs] **1** *vt* cesar; **to c. doing** *or* **to do sth** dejar de hacer algo **2** *vi* terminar

cease-fire [siːsˈfaɪə(r)] *n* alto *m* el fuego

cedar [ˈsiːdə(r)] *n* cedro *m*

ceiling [ˈsiːlɪŋ] *n* techo *m*

celebrate [ˈselɪbreɪt] **1** *vt (occasion)* celebrar **2** *vi* divertirse

celebration [selɪˈbreɪʃən] *n* (**a**) celebración *f* (**b**) **celebrations** festividades *fpl*

celebrity [sɪˈlebrɪtɪ] *n* celebridad *f*

celery [ˈselərɪ] *n* apio *m*

cell [sel] *n* (**a**) *(in prison)* celda *f* (**b**) *Biol, Pol* célula *f* (**c**) *Elec* pila *f*

cellar [ˈselə(r)] *n* sótano *m*; *(for wine)* bodega *f*

cello [ˈtʃeləʊ] *n* violoncelo *m*

Cellophane® [ˈseləfeɪn] *n Br* celofán *m*

cellphone ['selfəʊn] *n* teléfono *m* móvil *or Am* celular

cement [sɪ'ment] **1** *n* cemento *m*; **c. mixer** hormigonera *f* **2** *vt Constr* unir con cemento; *Fig (friendship)* cimentar

cemetery ['semɪtrɪ] *n* cementerio *m*

censor ['sensə(r)] **1** *n* censor(a) *m,f* **2** *vt* censurar

censorship ['sensəʃɪp] *n* censura *f*

census ['sensəs] *n* censo *m*

cent [sent] *n* (**a**) centavo *m*, céntimo *m* (**b**) **per c.** por ciento

centenary [sen'ti:nərɪ] *n* centenario *m*

center ['sentər] *n & vt US* = **centre**

centigrade ['sentɪɡreɪd] *adj* centígrado(a)

centimetre, *US* **centimeter** ['sentɪmi:tə(r)] *n* centímetro *m*

central ['sentrəl] *adj* central; **c. heating** calefacción *f* central; **C. America** Centroamérica; **C. American** centroamericano(a) *m,f*; *Br* **c. reservation** *(on motorway)* mediana *f*, *Col, Méx* camellón *m*

centralize ['sentrəlaɪz] *vt* centralizar

centre ['sentə(r)] **1** *n* centro *m*; **town c.** centro de la ciudad; *Ftb* **c. forward** delantero centro; *Ftb* **c. half** medio centro; *Pol* **c. party** partido *m* centrista; **sports c.** centro deportivo **2** *vt (attention etc)* centrar (**on** en)

century ['sentʃərɪ] *n* siglo *m*; **the nineteenth c.** el siglo diecinueve

ceramic [sɪ'ræmɪk] **1** *n* cerámica *f* **2** *adj* de cerámica

cereal ['sɪərɪəl] *n* cereal *m*

ceremony ['serɪmənɪ] *n* ceremonia *f*

certain ['sɜːtən] *adj* (**a**) *(sure)* seguro(a); **to be c.** estar seguro(a); **to make c. of sth** asegurarse de algo; **for c.** a ciencia cierta (**b**) **to a c. extent** hasta cierto punto (**c**) *(not known)* cierto(a); **a c. Miss Ward** una tal señorita Ward (**d**) *(true)* cierto(a)

certainly ['sɜːtənlɪ] *adv* desde luego; **c. not** de ninguna manera

certainty ['sɜːtəntɪ] *n* certeza *f*; *(assurance)* seguridad *f*

certificate [sə'tɪfɪkɪt] *n* certificado *m*; *Educ* diploma *m*

certify ['sɜːtɪfaɪ] *vt* certificar

chain [tʃeɪn] **1** *n* cadena *f*; *Fig (of events)* serie *f*; **c. of mountains** cordillera *f*; **c. reaction** reacción *f* en cadena; **c. saw** sierra mecánica **2** *vt* **to c. (up)** encadenar

chain-smoke ['tʃeɪnsməʊk] *vi* fumar un pitillo tras otro

chair [tʃeə(r)] **1** *n* (**a**) silla *f*; *(with arms)* sillón *m*; **c. lift** telesilla *m* (**b**) *(position)* presidencia *f*; *Univ* cátedra *f* **2** *vt* presidir

chairman ['tʃeəmən] *n* presidente *m*

chairperson ['tʃeəpɜːsən] *n* presidente(a) *m,f*

chalet ['ʃæleɪ] *n* chalet *m*, chalé *m*

chalk [tʃɔːk] *n (for writing)* tiza *f*, *Méx* gis *m*

▸ **chalk up** *vt sep Fam (victory etc)* apuntarse

challenge ['tʃælɪndʒ] **1** *vt* (**a**) retar, desafiar; **to c. sb to do sth** retar a algn a que haga algo (**b**) *(authority etc)* poner a prueba; *(statement)* poner en duda (**c**) *Mil* dar el alto a **2** *n* (**a**) reto *m*, desafío *m* (**b**) *Mil* quién vive *m*

challenger ['tʃælɪndʒə(r)] *n* aspirante *mf*

chamber ['tʃeɪmbə(r)] *n* (**a**) *(hall)* cámara *f*; **C. of Commerce** Cámara de Comercio (**b**) *Mus* **c. music** música *f* de cámara (**c**) *Br Jur* **chambers** gabinete *m*

chambermaid ['tʃeɪmbəmeɪd] *n* camarera *f*

champagne [ʃæm'peɪn] *n (French)* champán *m*; *(from Catalonia)* cava *m*

champion ['tʃæmpɪən] *n* campeón(ona) *m,f*; *Fig* **c. of human rights** defensor(a) *m,f* de los derechos humanos

championship ['tʃæmpɪənʃɪp] *n* campeonato *m*

chance [tʃɑːns] **1** *n* (**a**) *(fortune)* casualidad *f*, azar *m*; **by c.** por casualidad; **to take a c.** arriesgarse; **c. meeting** encuentro *m* casual (**b**) *(likelihood)* posibilidad *f*; **(the)**

chances are that ... lo más posible es que ... (**c**) *(opportunity)* oportunidad *f*; *Am* chance *f* **2** *vt* arriesgar

chancellor ['tʃɑːnsələ(r)] *n* (**a**) *(head of state, in embassy)* canciller *m* (**b**) *Univ Br* rector(a) *m,f* honorario(a); *US* rector(a) *m,f* (**c**) *Br* **C. of the Exchequer** ≃ ministro(a) *m,f* de Hacienda

chandelier [ʃændɪ'lɪə(r)] *n* araña *f* (de luces)

change [tʃeɪndʒ] **1** *vt* cambiar; **to c. gear** cambiar de marcha; **to c. one's mind/the subject** cambiar de opinión/de tema; **to c. trains** hacer transbordo; **to get changed** cambiarse de ropa; *Fig* **to c. hands** cambiar de dueño(a)
2 *vi* cambiar, cambiarse; **to c. for the better/worse** mejorar/empeorar; **to c. into** convertirse en
3 *n* (**a**) cambio *m*; **for a c.** para variar; **c. of heart** cambio de parecer; **c. of scene** cambio de aires (**b**) *(money)* cambio *m*, *Andes, CAm, Méx* sencillo *m*, *RP* vuelto *m*; **small c.** suelto *m*
▸ **change over** *vi* cambiarse

changeable ['tʃeɪndʒəbəl] *adj (weather)* variable; *(person)* inconstante

changeover ['tʃeɪndʒəʊvə(r)] *n* conversión *f*

changing ['tʃeɪndʒɪŋ] **1** *n* (**a**) **c. room** vestuario *m* (**b**) *Mil* relevo *m* (de la guardia) **2** *adj* cambiante

channel ['tʃænəl] **1** *n* (**a**) *Geog* canal *m*; *(of river)* cauce *m*; **the C. Islands** las Islas Anglonormandas; **the English C.** el Canal de la Mancha (**b**) *(administrative)* vía *f* (**c**) *TV, Rad* canal *m*, cadena *f* **2** *vt Fig (ideas etc)* canalizar, encauzar

chant [tʃɑːnt] **1** *n Rel* cántico *m*; *(of demonstrators)* slogan *m* **2** *vt & vi Rel* cantar; *(demonstrators)* corear

chaos ['keɪɒs] *n* caos *m*

chaotic [keɪ'ɒtɪk] *adj* caótico(a)

chap [tʃæp] *n Fam (man)* tipo *m*, *Esp* tío *m*; **a good c.** un buen tipo

chapel ['tʃæpəl] *n* capilla *f*

chaplain ['tʃæplɪn] *n* capellán *m*

chapter ['tʃæptə(r)] *n* (**a**) capítulo *m* (**b**) *Rel* cabildo *m*

character ['kærɪktə(r)] *n* (**a**) carácter *m* (**b**) *Fam (person)* tipo *m* (**c**) *Th* personaje *m*

characteristic [kærɪktə'rɪstɪk] **1** *n* característica *f* **2** *adj* característico(a)

charcoal ['tʃɑːkəʊl] *n* carbón *m* vegetal; *Art* **c. drawing** carboncillo *m*; **c. grey** gris marengo *or* oscuro

charge [tʃɑːdʒ] **1** *vt* (**a**) cobrar; **c. it to my account** cárguelo en mi cuenta (**b**) **to c. sb with a crime** acusar a algn de un crimen (**c**) *Mil* cargar contra (**d**) *Elec* cargar
2 *vi Elec, Mil* cargar; **to c. about** andar a lo loco
3 *n* (**a**) *(cost)* precio *m*; **free of c.** gratis (**b**) **to be in c. of** estar a cargo de; **to take c. of** hacerse cargo de (**c**) *Jur* cargo *m*, acusación *f* (**d**) *(explosive)* carga *f* explosiva (**e**) *Mil* carga *f* (**f**) *Elec* carga *f*

charity ['tʃærɪtɪ] *n* caridad *f*; *(organization)* institución *f* benéfica

charm [tʃɑːm] **1** *n* (**a**) *(quality)* encanto *m* (**b**) *(spell)* hechizo *m*; **lucky c.** amuleto *m* **2** *vt* encantar

charming ['tʃɑːmɪŋ] *adj* encantador(a)

chart [tʃɑːt] **1** *n* (**a**) *(giving information)* tabla *f*; *(graph)* gráfico *m* (**b**) *(map)* carta *f* de navegación (**c**) *Mus* **the charts** la lista de éxitos **2** *vt Av, Naut (on map)* trazar

charter ['tʃɑːtə(r)] **1** *n* (**a**) *(of institution)* estatutos *mpl*; *(of rights)* carta *f* (**b**) **c. flight** vuelo *m* chárter **2** *vt (plane, boat)* fletar

chartered accountant [tʃɑːtəd-ə'kaʊntənt] *n Br* censor(a) *m,f* jurado(a) de cuentas, *Am* contador(a) *m,f* público(a)

chase [tʃeɪs] **1** *vt* perseguir; *(hunt)* cazar **2** *n* persecución *f*; *(hunt)* caza *f*

chasm ['kæzəm] *n Geog* sima *f*; *Fig* abismo *m*

chassis ['ʃæsɪ] *n* chasis *m inv*

chaste [tʃeɪst] *adj* casto(a)

chat [tʃæt] **1** n (**a**) *(informal conversation)* charla f, CAm, Méx plática f; Br **c. show** coloquio m (**b**) Comput charla f; **c. room** sala f de conversación **2** vi (**a**) *(talk informally)* charlar, CAm, Méx platicar (**b**) Comput charlar (**to** or **with** con)

▸ **chat up** vt sep Br Fam **to chat sb up** intentar ligar con algn, RP intentar levantar a algn

chatter ['tʃætə(r)] **1** vi *(person)* parlotear; *(bird)* piar; *(teeth)* castañetear **2** n *(of person)* parloteo m; *(of birds)* gorjeo m; *(of teeth)* castañeteo m

chatty ['tʃætɪ] adj (**chattier, chattiest**) hablador(a)

chauffeur ['ʃəʊfə(r), ʃəʊ'fɜ:(r)] n Esp chófer m, Am chofer m

chauvinist ['ʃəʊvɪnɪst] adj & n chovinista *(mf)*; **male c.** machista m

cheap [tʃi:p] **1** adj barato(a); *(fare)* económico(a); *(joke)* de mal gusto; *(contemptible)* bajo(a); Fam **dirt c.** tirado(a)
  2 n Br Fam **on the c.** en plan barato
  3 adv barato

cheaply ['tʃi:plɪ] adv barato, en plan económico

cheat [tʃi:t] **1** vt engañar; **to c. sb out of sth** estafar algo a algn
  2 vi (**a**) *(at games)* hacer trampa; *(in exam etc)* copiar(se) (**b**) Fam *(husband, wife)* poner cuernos (**on** a)
  3 n *(trickster)* tramposo(a) m,f

check [tʃek] **1** vt (**a**) *(facts)* repasar; comprobar, Guat, Méx cheçar; *(tickets)* controlar; *(tyres, oil)* revisar (**b**) *(impulse)* refrenar; *(growth)* retardar (**c**) *(stop)* detener
  2 vi comprobar, Guat, Méx checar
  3 n (**a**) *(of documents etc)* revisión f; *(of facts)* comprobación f (**b**) *(in chess)* jaque m (**c**) *(pattern)* cuadro m (**d**) **to keep in c.** *(feelings)* contener; *(enemy)* mantener a raya (**e**) US = **cheque**

▸ **check in** vi *(at airport)* facturar; *(at hotel)* registrarse (**at** en)

▸ **check out 1** vi *(of hotel)* dejar el hotel **2** vt sep *(facts)* verificar

▸ **check up** vi **to c. up on sb** hacer averiguaciones sobre algn; **to c. up on sth** comprobar algo

checked [tʃekt] adj a cuadros

checkers ['tʃekərz] n sing US *(game)* damas fpl

check-in ['tʃekɪn] n **c. desk** *(at airport)* mostrador m de facturación

checking account ['tʃekɪŋ ə'kaʊnt] n cuenta f corriente

checkout ['tʃekaʊt] n *(counter)* caja f

checkpoint ['tʃekpɔɪnt] n control m

checkroom ['tʃekru:m] n US *(for coats, hats)* guardarropa m; *(for luggage)* consigna f

checkup ['tʃekʌp] n Med chequeo m, examen médico

cheek [tʃi:k] n (**a**) *(of face)* mejilla f (**b**) Fam *(nerve)* cara f; **he's got a c.!** ¡qué caradura!, Esp ¡vaya morro!

cheeky ['tʃi:kɪ] adj (**cheekier, cheekiest**) Fam fresco(a), descarado(a)

cheer [tʃɪə(r)] **1** vi aplaudir, aclamar **2** vt (**a**) *(applaud)* vitorear, aclamar (**b**) *(make hopeful)* animar
  3 n viva m; **cheers** aplausos mpl; Br Fam **cheers!** *(thank you)* ¡gracias!; *(before drinking)* ¡salud!

▸ **cheer up 1** vi animarse **2** vt sep **to c. sb up** alegrar or animar a algn

cheerful ['tʃɪəfʊl] adj alegre

cheese [tʃi:z] n queso m

cheesecake ['tʃi:zkeɪk] n tarta f de queso

chef [ʃef] n chef m

chemical ['kemɪkəl] **1** n sustancia química, producto químico **2** adj químico(a)

chemist ['kemɪst] n (**a**) químico(a) m,f (**b**) Br **c.'s (shop)** farmacia f; (**dispensing**) **c.** farmacéutico(a) m,f

chemistry ['kemɪstrɪ] n química f

cheque [tʃek] n cheque m; **to pay by c.** pagar con (un) cheque; **c. book** talonario m (de cheques); Br **c. card** = tarjeta que avala los cheques

cherry ['tʃerɪ] n cereza f

chess [tʃes] n ajedrez m

chessboard ['tʃesbɔ:d] n tablero m de ajedrez

chest [tʃest] *n* (**a**) *Anat* pecho *m* (**b**) *(for linen)* arca *f*; *(for valuables)* cofre *m*; **c. of drawers** cómoda *f*

chestnut ['tʃesnʌt] *n (tree, colour)* castaño *m*; *(nut)* castaña *f*

chew [tʃuː] *vt* masticar, mascar

chewy ['tʃuːɪ] *adj (meat, bread)* correoso(a); *(confectionery)* gomoso(a), correoso(a)

chick [tʃɪk] *n* (**a**) *(young chicken)* pollito *m* (**b**) *Fam (woman)* nena *f*, *Arg* piba *f*, *Méx* chava *f*

chicken ['tʃɪkɪn] **1** *n* (**a**) *(young chicken)* pollo *m* (**b**) *Fam (coward)* gallina *mf*, *Esp* miedica *mf* **2** *vi Fam* **to c. out** acobardarse, *Méx* ciscarse, *RP* achicarse

chickenpox ['tʃɪkɪnpɒks] *n* varicela *f*

chickpea ['tʃɪkpiː] *n* garbanzo *m*

chief [tʃiːf] **1** *n* jefe *m* **2** *adj* principal

chiefly ['tʃiːflɪ] *adv (above all)* sobre todo; *(mainly)* principalmente

chilblain ['tʃɪlbleɪn] *n* sabañón *m*

child [tʃaɪld] *n (pl* **children***)* niño(a) *m,f*; *(son)* hijo *m*; *(daughter)* hija *f*; **c. minder** = persona que cuida niños en su propia casa

childhood ['tʃaɪldhʊd] *n* infancia *f*, niñez *f*

childish ['tʃaɪldɪʃ] *adj* pueril, aniñado(a)

childlike ['tʃaɪldlaɪk] *adj* infantil

children ['tʃɪldrən] *pl of* **child**

chill [tʃɪl] **1** *n* (**a**) *Med* resfriado *m* (**b**) *(coldness)* fresco *m* **2** *adj* frío(a) **3** *vt (meat)* refrigerar; *(wine)* enfriar

chilli ['tʃɪlɪ] *n* **c. (pepper)** chile *m*, *Esp* guindilla *f*, *Andes, RP* ají *m*

chilly ['tʃɪlɪ] *adj* (**chillier, chilliest**) frío(a)

chime [tʃaɪm] **1** *n (peal)* campanada *f* **2** *vt* **to c. five o'clock** *(clock)* dar las cinco **3** *vi* sonar

▸ **chime in** *vi Fam* meter baza *or Méx, RP* la cuchara

chimney ['tʃɪmnɪ] *n* chimenea *f*; **c. sweep** deshollinador *m*

chimpanzee [tʃɪmpæn'ziː] *n* chimpancé *m*

chin [tʃɪn] *n* barbilla *f*, mentón *m*; **double c.** papada *f*

china ['tʃaɪnə] *n* loza *f*, porcelana *f*

Chinese [tʃaɪ'niːz] **1** *adj* chino(a) **2** *n* (**a**) *(person)* chino(a) *m,f* (**b**) *(language)* chino *m*

chink¹ [tʃɪŋk] *n (opening)* resquicio *m*; *(crack)* grieta *f*

chink² [tʃɪŋk] **1** *vi* tintinear **2** *n* tintineo *m*

chip [tʃɪp] **1** *n* (**a**) *(of wood)* astilla *f*; *(of stone)* lasca *f*; *(in cup)* mella *f* (**b**) *Br Culin* **chips** *Esp* patatas *or Am* papas fritas; *US* **(potato) chips** *(crisps) Esp* patatas *or Am* papas fritas *(de bolsa)* (**c**) *Comput* chip *m* (**d**) *(in gambling)* ficha *f* **2** *vt (wood)* astillar; *(stone)* resquebrajar; *(china, glass)* mellar **3** *vi (wood)* astillarse; *(china, glass)* mellarse; *(paint)* desconcharse

▸ **chip in** *vi Fam* (**a**) meterse (**b**) *(with money)* poner algo (de dinero)

chiropodist [kɪ'rɒpədɪst] *n* podólogo(a) *m,f*, *Am* podiatra *mf*

chirp [tʃɜːp] *vi (birds)* gorjear

chisel ['tʃɪzəl] *n* cincel *m*

chives [tʃaɪvz] *npl* cebolleta *f*

chlorine ['klɔːriːn] *n* cloro *m*

chocolate ['tʃɒkəlɪt] **1** *n* chocolate *m*; **chocolates** bombones *mpl* **2** *adj* de chocolate

choice [tʃɔɪs] **1** *n* elección *f*; **a wide c.** un gran surtido; **by c.** por gusto **2** *adj* selecto(a)

choir ['kwaɪə(r)] *n* coro *m*, coral *f*

choke [tʃəʊk] **1** *vt* (**a**) *(person)* ahogar (**b**) *(obstruct)* obstruir **2** *vi* ahogarse; **to c. on food** atragantarse con la comida **3** *n Aut* estárter *m*

▸ **choke back** *vt sep (emotions)* tragarse

cholesterol [kə'lestərɒl] *n* colesterol *m*

choose [tʃuːz] *(pt* **chose***; pp* **chosen***)* **1** *vt* escoger, elegir; *(decide on)* optar por **2** *vi* escoger, elegir

choos(e)y ['tʃuːzɪ] *adj* (**choosier,
choosiest**) *Fam* exigente

chop [tʃɒp] **1** *vt* (**a**) *(wood)* cortar;
(tree) talar (**b**) *Culin* cortar a pedacitos
2 *n* (**a**) *(blow)* tajo *m*; *(with axe)* hachazo *m* (**b**) *Culin* chuleta *f*

choppy ['tʃɒpɪ] *adj* (**choppier,
choppiest**) *(sea)* picado(a)

chopsticks ['tʃɒpstɪks] *npl* palillos
mpl

choral ['kɔːrəl] *adj* coral

chord [kɔːd] *n Mus* acorde *m*; *Fig* **it
strikes a c.** (me) suena

chore [tʃɔː(r)] *n* quehacer *m*, tarea *f*

chorus ['kɔːrəs] *n Mus, Th* coro *m*; *(in a
song)* estribillo *m*; **c. girl** corista *f*

chose [tʃəʊz] *pt of* **choose**

chosen ['tʃəʊzən] *pp of* **choose**

Christ [kraɪst] *n* Cristo *m*, Jesucristo *m*

christen ['krɪsən] *vt* bautizar

christening ['krɪsənɪŋ] *n* bautizo *m*

Christian ['krɪstʃən] **1** *adj* cristia-
no(a); **c. name** nombre *m* de pila **2** *n*
cristiano(a) *m,f*

Christianity [krɪstɪ'ænɪtɪ] *n* cristianismo *m*

Christmas ['krɪsməs] *n* Navidad *f*;
merry C.! ¡feliz Navidad!; **C. carol**
villancico *m*; **C. Day** día *m* de Navidad;
C. Eve Nochebuena *f*

chrome [krəʊm] *n* cromo *m*

chronic ['krɒnɪk] *adj* crónico(a)

chronological [krɒnə'lɒdʒɪkəl] *adj*
cronológico(a)

chubby ['tʃʌbɪ] *adj* (**chubbier,
chubbiest**) rellenito(a)

chuck [tʃʌk] *vt Fam* tirar, *Am* botar; **to
c. one's job in** *or* **up** dejar el trabajo; **to
c. sb out** echar a algn; **to c. sth away**
or **out** tirar *or Am* botar algo

chuckle ['tʃʌkəl] **1** *vi* reír entre dientes
2 *n* sonrisita *f*

chum [tʃʌm] *n* compinche *mf*, com-
pañero(a) *m,f*

chunk [tʃʌŋk] *n Fam* cacho *m*, pedazo
m

church [tʃɜːtʃ] *n* iglesia *f*; **to go to c.** ir
a misa; **C. of England** Iglesia Angli-
cana

churchyard ['tʃɜːtʃjɑːd] *n* cementerio
m, campo santo

churn [tʃɜːn] **1** *n* *(for butter)*
mantequera *f*; *Br (for milk)* lechera *f*
  2 *vt (butter)* hacer
  3 *vi* revolverse, agitarse
▸ **churn out** *vt sep Fam* producir en
serie

chute [ʃuːt] *n* *(channel)* conducto *m*;
(slide) tobogán *m*

CID [siːaɪ'diː] *n Br (abbr* **Criminal
Investigation Department**) = policía
judicial británica

cider ['saɪdə(r)] *n* sidra *f*

cigar [sɪ'gɑː(r)] *n* puro *m*

cigarette [sɪgə'ret] *n* cigarrillo *m*; **c.
case** pitillera *f*; **c. end** colilla *f*, *Am*
pucho *m*; **c. holder** boquilla *f*; **c.
lighter** encendedor *m*, *Esp* mechero *m*

cinder ['sɪndə(r)] *n* **cinders** cenizas
fpl; **burnt to a c.** completamente
carbonizado(a)

cinema ['sɪnɪmə] *n* (**a**) *Br (building)*
cine *m* (**b**) *(art)* cine *m*

cinnamon ['sɪnəmən] *n* canela *f*

circle ['sɜːkəl] **1** *n* (**a**) *(circle)* círculo *m*; *(of
people)* corro *m*; **in business circles**
en el mundo de los negocios (**b**) *Th*
anfiteatro *m*
  2 *vt (surround)* rodear; *(move round)*
dar la vuelta a
  3 *vi* dar vueltas

circuit ['sɜːkɪt] *n* (**a**) *(journey)*
recorrido *m* (**b**) *Elec* circuito *m* (**c**) *Br
(motor-racing track)* circuito *m*

circular ['sɜːkjʊlə(r)] *adj & n* circular
(f)

circulate ['sɜːkjʊleɪt] **1** *vt (news)*
hacer circular **2** *vi* circular

circulation [sɜːkjʊ'leɪʃən] *n* (**a**) *(of
blood)* circulación *f* (**b**) *(of newspaper)*
tirada *f*

circumcise ['sɜːkəmsaɪz] *vt* circunci-
dar

circumference [sə'kʌmfərəns] *n*
circunferencia *f*

circumstance ['sɜːkəmstəns] *n (usu
pl)* circunstancia *f*; **under no circumstances** en ningún caso; **economic
circumstances** situación económica

circus ['sɜːkəs] *n* circo *m*

citizen ['sɪtɪzən] *n* ciudadano(a) *m,f*

citrus ['sɪtrəs] *adj* **c. fruits** agrios *mpl*

city ['sɪtɪ] *n* (**a**) ciudad *f*; *US* **c. council** ayuntamiento *m*; *US* **c. hall** ayuntamiento (**b**) *Br Fin* **the C.** la City (de Londres), = el barrio financiero y bursátil de Londres

civics ['sɪvɪks] *n* (*subject*) educación *f* cívica

civil ['sɪvəl] *adj* (**a**) civil; **c. defence** defensa *f* civil; **c. rights** derechos *mpl* civiles; **c. servant** funcionario(a) *m,f*; *Pol* **c. service** administración pública (**b**) *(polite)* cortés, educado(a)

civilian [sɪ'vɪljən] *adj & n* civil *(mf)*; **c. clothing** traje *m* de paisano

civilization [sɪvɪlaɪ'zeɪʃən] *n* civilización *f*

civilized ['sɪvɪlaɪzd] *adj* civilizado(a)

claim [kleɪm] **1** *vt* (**a**) *(benefits, rights)* reclamar; *Jur (compensation)* exigir (**b**) *(assert)* afirmar **2** *n* (**a**) *(demand)* reclamación *f*; *Jur* demanda *f*; **to put in a c.** reclamar una indemnización (**b**) *(right)* derecho *m* (**c**) *(assertion)* pretensión *f*

clam [klæm] *n* almeja *f*

▸ **clam up** *vi Fam* callarse

clamber ['klæmbə(r)] *vi* trepar (**over** por)

clamour, *US* **clamor** ['klæmə(r)] **1** *n* clamor *m* **2** *vi* clamar; **to c. for** pedir a gritos

clamp [klæmp] **1** *n* *(for carpentry)* tornillo *m* de banco; *Tech* abrazadera *f*; **wheel c.** cepo *m* **2** *vt* sujetar con abrazaderas

▸ **clamp down on** *vt insep* aumentar los esfuerzos contra

clan [klæn] *n* clan *m*

clang [klæŋ] **1** *vi* sonar **2** *n* sonido metálico

clap [klæp] **1** *vi* aplaudir **2** *n* (**a**) palmada *f* (**b**) **a c. of thunder** un trueno

clapping ['klæpɪŋ] *n* aplausos *mpl*

claret ['klærət] *n Br (wine)* clarete *m*; *(colour)* burdeos *m*

clarification [klærɪfɪ'keɪʃən] *n* aclaración *f*

clarify ['klærɪfaɪ] *vt* aclarar

clarinet [klærɪ'net] *n* clarinete *m*

clarity ['klærɪtɪ] *n* claridad *f*

clash [klæʃ] **1** *vi* (**a**) *(cymbals)* sonar; *(swords)* chocar; *Fig (disagree)* estar en desacuerdo (**b**) *(colours)* desentonar (**c**) *(dates)* coincidir **2** *n* (**a**) *(sound)* sonido *m* (**b**) *(fight)* choque *m*; *Fig (conflict)* conflicto *m*

clasp [klɑːsp] **1** *n* (**a**) *(on belt)* cierre *m*; *(on necklace)* broche *m* (**b**) *(grasp)* apretón *m*; **c. knife** navaja *f* **2** *vt* *(object)* agarrar; **to c. hands** juntar las manos

class [klɑːs] **1** *n* clase *f*; **c. struggle** lucha *f* de clases; *US Educ* **c. of '84** promoción *f* de 1984; *Rail* **first/second c. ticket** billete *m* de primera/segunda (clase) **2** *vt* clasificar

classic ['klæsɪk] **1** *adj* clásico(a) **2** *n* (**a**) *(author)* autor clásico; *(work)* obra clásica (**b**) **the classics** *(literature)* las obras clásicas; **classics** *(languages)* clásicas *fpl*

classical ['klæsɪkəl] *adj* clásico(a)

classification [klæsɪfɪ'keɪʃən] *n* clasificación *f*

classified ['klæsɪfaɪd] *adj (information)* secreto(a); **c. advertisements** anuncios *mpl* por palabras

classify ['klæsɪfaɪ] *vt* clasificar

classmate ['klɑːsmeɪt] *n* compañero(a) *m,f* de clase

classroom ['klɑːsruːm] *n* aula *f*, clase *f*

classy ['klɑːsɪ] *adj Fam* con clase, elegante

clatter ['klætə(r)] **1** *vi* hacer ruido; *(things falling)* hacer estrépito **2** *n* ruido *m*, estrépito *m*

clause [klɔːz] *n* (**a**) *Jur* cláusula *f* (**b**) *Ling* oración *f*

claustrophobic [klɔːstrə'fəʊbɪk] *adj* claustrofóbico(a)

claw [klɔː] **1** *n (of bird, lion)* garra *f*; *(of cat)* uña *f*; *(of crab)* pinza *f* **2** *vt* agarrar, arañar; *(tear)* desgarrar

▸ **claw at** *vt insep* agarrar, arañar

clay [kleɪ] n arcilla f; **c. pigeon shooting** tiro m al plato

clean [kli:n] **1** adj (a) limpio(a) (b) (unmarked, pure) sin defecto; **to have a c. record** no tener antecedentes (penales) (c) (not obscene) decente

2 adv (a) **to play c.** jugar limpio; Fam **to come c.** confesarlo todo (b) Fam por completo; **it went c. through the middle** pasó justo por el medio

3 vt (room) limpiar; **to c. one's teeth** lavarse los dientes

▸ **clean out** vt sep (room) limpiar a fondo

▸ **clean up** vt sep & vi limpiar

cleaner ['kli:nə(r)] n limpiador(a) m,f

cleaning ['kli:nɪŋ] n limpieza f

cleanse [klenz] vt limpiar

clean-shaven ['kli:n'ʃeɪvən] adj (man, face) (bien) afeitado(a)

clear [klɪə(r)] **1** adj (a) claro(a); (road, day) despejado(a); **c. conscience** conciencia tranquila (b) (obvious) claro(a); **to make sth c.** aclarar algo (c) (majority) absoluto(a); (profit) neto(a) (d) (free) libre

2 adv (a) Fig **loud and c.** claramente (b) **stand c.!** ¡apártese!; **to stay c. of** evitar

3 vt (a) (room) vaciar; Com liquidar; **to c. one's throat** aclararse la garganta; **to c. the table** quitar la mesa (b) (authorize) autorizar (c) (hurdle) salvar (d) **to c. sb of a charge** exculpar a algn de un delito **4** vi (sky) despejarse

▸ **clear away** vt sep quitar

▸ **clear off** vi Br Fam largarse; **c. off!** ¡largo!

▸ **clear out** vt sep (room) limpiar a fondo; (cupboard) vaciar

▸ **clear up 1** vt sep (a) (tidy) recoger; (arrange) ordenar (b) (mystery) resolver; (misunderstanding) aclarar **2** vi (weather) despejarse; (problem) desaparecer

clearance ['klɪərəns] n (a) (of area) despeje m; Com **c. sale** liquidación f (de existencias) (b) (space) espacio m libre (c) (authorization) autorización f

clear-cut [klɪə'kʌt] adj claro(a)

clearing ['klɪərɪŋ] n (a) (in wood) claro m (b) (of rubbish) limpieza f (c) (of cheque) compensación f

clearly ['klɪəlɪ] adv (a) claramente (b) (at start of sentence) evidentemente

clef [klef] n clave f; **bass/treble c.** clave de fa/de sol

clench [klentʃ] vt (teeth, fist) apretar

clergy ['klɜːdʒɪ] n clero m

clergyman ['klɜːdʒɪmən] n clérigo m

clerical ['klerɪkəl] adj (a) Rel clerical (b) (staff, work) de oficina

clerk [klɑːk, US klɜːrk] n (a) (office worker) oficinista m,f; (civil servant) funcionario(a) m,f (b) US Com dependiente(a) m,f, vendedor(a) m,f

clever ['klevə(r)] adj (a) (person) inteligente, listo(a); **to be c. at sth** tener aptitud para algo; Br Fam Pej **c. clogs** or **dick** sabelotodo m,f, Esp listillo(a) m,f (b) (argument) ingenioso(a)

cliché ['kli:ʃeɪ] n cliché m

click [klɪk] **1** n (sound) clic m

2 vt (tongue) chasquear

3 vi **it didn't c.** (I didn't realize) no me di cuenta

client ['klaɪənt] n cliente m,f

clientele [kli:ɒn'tel] n clientela f

cliff [klɪf] n acantilado m

climate ['klaɪmɪt] n clima m

climax ['klaɪmæks] n (a) (peak) clímax m, punto m culminante (b) (sexual) orgasmo m

climb [klaɪm] **1** vt (ladder) subir a; (mountain) escalar; (tree) trepar a

2 vi (plants) trepar; Av subir; Fig (socially) ascender

3 n subida f, ascensión f

▸ **climb down** vi bajar; Fig volverse atrás

climber ['klaɪmə(r)] n alpinista m,f, Am andinista m,f

climbing ['klaɪmɪŋ] n Sport montañismo m, alpinismo m, Am andinismo m

clinch [klɪntʃ] **1** vt resolver; (deal) cerrar **2** n Fam abrazo apasionado

cling [klɪŋ] [pt & pp **clung**] vi (hang on)

agarrarse; *(clothes)* ajustarse; *(smell)* pegarse; **to c. together** unirse

clinic [ˈklɪnɪk] *n (in state hospital)* ambulatorio *m; (specialized)* clínica *f*

clinical [ˈklɪnɪkəl] *adj* **(a)** *Med* clínico(a) **(b)** *(detached)* frío(a)

clink [klɪŋk] **1** *vi* tintinear **2** *n* tintineo *m*

clip¹ [klɪp] **1** *vt (cut)* cortar; *(ticket)* picar **2** *n* **(a)** *(of film)* extracto *m* **(b)** *(with scissors)* tijeretada *f*

clip² [klɪp] **1** *n (for hair)* pasador *m; (for paper)* clip *m*, sujetapapeles *m inv; (brooch)* clip **2** *vt* sujetar

clippers [ˈklɪpəz] *npl (for hair)* maquinilla *f* para rapar; *(for nails)* cortauñas *m inv; (for hedge)* tijeras *fpl* de podar

clipping [ˈklɪpɪŋ] *n* recorte *m*

clique [kliːk] *n Pej* camarilla *f*

cloak [kləʊk] **1** *n (garment)* capa *f* **2** *vt* encubrir

cloakroom [ˈkləʊkruːm] *n* guardarropa *m; Br Euph (toilets)* servicios *mpl*

clock [klɒk] **1** *n* reloj *m* **2** *vt (race)* cronometrar

▸ **clock in, clock on** *vi* fichar (a la entrada), *Am* marcar tarjeta (a la entrada)

▸ **clock off, clock out** *vi* fichar (a la salida), *Am* marcar tarjeta (a la salida)

▸ **clock up** *vt sep (mileage)* hacer

clockwise [ˈklɒkwaɪz] *adj & adv* en el sentido de las agujas del reloj

clockwork [ˈklɒkwɜːk] *n* mecanismo *m;* **c. toy** juguete *m* de cuerda

clog [klɒg] **1** *vt* obstruir; *(pipe)* atascar; **to get clogged up** atascarse **2** *n (footwear)* zueco *m*

cloister [ˈklɔɪstə(r)] *n* claustro *m*

close¹ [kləʊs] **1** *adj* **(a)** *(in space, time)* cercano(a); *(contact)* directo(a); **c. to** cerca de; **c. together** juntos(as) **(b)** *(relationship)* estrecho(a); *(friend)* íntimo(a) **(c)** *(inspection)* detallado(a); *(watch)* atento(a) **(d)** *(contest)* reñido(a); **a c. resemblance** un gran parecido **(e)** *(air)* cargado(a); *(weather)* bochornoso(a)
2 *adv* cerca; **they live c. by** *or* **c. at**

hand viven cerca; **to stand c. together** estar apretados(as)

close² [kləʊz] **1** *vt* **(a)** cerrar; **closing time** hora *f* de cierre **(b)** *(end)* concluir, terminar; *(meeting)* levantar
2 *vi* **(a)** *(shut)* cerrar, cerrarse **(b)** *(end)* concluirse, terminarse
3 *n* fin *m*, final *m*

▸ **close down** *vi (business)* cerrar para siempre; *Br Rad, TV* finalizar la emisión

▸ **close in** *vi* **to c. in on sb** rodear a algn

closed [kləʊzd] *adj* cerrado(a); *Ind* **c. shop** = empresa que emplea solamente a miembros de un sindicato

closet [ˈklɒzɪt] *n US* armario *m*

close-up [ˈkləʊsʌp] *n* primer plano *m*

closure [ˈkləʊʒə(r)] *n* cierre *m*

clot [klɒt] **1** *n* **(a)** *(of blood)* coágulo *m; Med* **c. on the brain** embolia *f* cerebral **(b)** *Br Fam* lelo(a) *m,f, Esp* memo(a) *m,f* **2** *vi* coagularse

cloth [klɒθ] *n* tela *f*, paño *m; (rag)* trapo *m; (tablecloth)* mantel *m*

clothes [kləʊðz] *npl* ropa *f*, vestidos *mpl;* **c. brush** cepillo *m* de la ropa; **c. hanger** percha *f;* **c. horse** tendedero *m* plegable; **c. line** tendedero *m;* **c. Br peg** *or* **US pin** pinza *f*

clothing [ˈkləʊðɪŋ] *n* ropa *f*

cloud [klaʊd] **1** *n* nube *f*
2 *vt* nublar; *Fig* **to c. the issue** complicar el asunto
3 *vi* **to c. over** nublarse

cloudy [ˈklaʊdɪ] *adj* **(cloudier, cloudiest)** **(a)** *(sky)* nublado(a) **(b)** *(liquid)* turbio(a)

clove¹ [kləʊv] *n (spice)* clavo *m*

clove² [kləʊv] *n (of garlic)* diente *m*

clover [ˈkləʊvə(r)] *n* trébol *m*

clown [klaʊn] **1** *n* payaso *m* **2** *vi* **to c. (about** *or* **around)** hacer el payaso

club [klʌb] **1** *n* **(a)** *(society)* club *m;* **sports c.** club deportivo **(b)** *(nightclub)* discoteca *f*, sala *f* (de fiestas) **(c)** *(heavy stick)* garrote *m*, porra *f; (in golf)* palo *m* **(b)** *Cards* trébol *m*
2 *vt* aporrear
3 *vi* **to c. together** pagar entre varios

clue [kluː] *n (sign)* indicio *m*; *(to mystery)* pista *f*; *(in crossword)* clave *f*; *Fam* **I haven't a c.** no tengo ni idea

clump [klʌmp] *n (of trees)* grupo *m*; *(of plants)* mata *f*

clumsy ['klʌmzɪ] *adj* (**clumsier, clumsiest**) desmañado(a), torpe; *(awkward)* tosco(a)

clung [klʌŋ] *pt & pp of* **cling**

cluster ['klʌstə(r)] **1** *n* grupo *m*; *(of grapes)* racimo *m* **2** *vi* agruparse

clutch [klʌtʃ] **1** *vt* agarrar
2 *vi* **Fig to c. at straws** aferrarse a cualquier cosa
3 *n* (**a**) *Aut* embrague *m* (**b**) *Fig* **to fall into sb's clutches** caer en las garras de algn

clutter ['klʌtə(r)] *vt* **to c. (up)** llenar, atestar

cm (*abbr* **centimetre(s)**) cm

Co (**a**) *Com* (*abbr* **Company**) Cía. (**b**) *abbr* **County** condado *m*

c/o [siː'əʊ] (*abbr* **care of**) en el domicilio de

coach [kəʊtʃ] **1** *n* (**a**) *esp Br (bus)* autobús *m*, *Esp* autocar *m*; *(carriage)* carruaje *m*; **c. tour** excursión *f* en autocar (**b**) *Rail* coche *m*, vagón *m* (**c**) *Sport* entrenador(a) *m,f* **2** *vt* *Sport* entrenar; *Educ* dar clases particulares a

coal [kəʊl] *n* carbón *m*, hulla *f*; **c. bunker** carbonera *f*; **c. merchant** carbonero *m*; **c. mine** mina *f* de carbón

coalition [kəʊə'lɪʃən] *n* coalición *f*

coarse [kɔːs] *adj (material)* basto(a); *(skin)* áspero(a); *(language)* grosero(a), ordinario(a)

coast [kəʊst] *n* costa *f*, litoral *m*

coat [kəʊt] **1** *n* (**a**) *(overcoat)* abrigo *m*; *(jacket)* chaqueta *f*, *Méx* chamarra *f*, *RP* campera *f*; **c. hanger** percha *f* (**b**) *(of animal)* pelo *m* (**c**) *(of paint)* mano *f*, capa *f* **2** *vt* cubrir (**with** de); *(with liquid)* bañar (**with** en)

coating ['kəʊtɪŋ] *n* capa *f*, baño *m*

coax [kəʊks] *vt* engatusar

cob [kɒb] *n* mazorca *f*

cobbled ['kɒbəld] *adj (path, street)* adoquinado(a)

cobweb ['kɒbweb] *n* telaraña *f*

cocaine [kə'keɪn] *n* cocaína *f*

cock [kɒk] **1** *n* (**a**) *Orn* gallo *m*; *(male bird)* macho *m* (**b**) *(on gun)* percutor *m* (**c**) *Vulg (penis)* *Esp* polla *f*, *Am* verga *f*, *Chile* pico *m*, *Méx* pito *m*, *RP* pija *f* **2** *vt* *(gun)* amartillar; *(ears)* erguir

▸ **cock up** *vt sep* *Br very Fam* **to c. sth up** cagar *or Esp* joder *or Méx* madrear algo

cockerel ['kɒkərəl] *n* gallo *m* joven

cockney ['kɒknɪ] **1** *adj* = del East End londinense **2** *n* = persona del East End londinense

cockpit ['kɒkpɪt] *n* cabina *f* del piloto

cockroach ['kɒkrəʊtʃ] *n* cucaracha *f*

cocktail ['kɒkteɪl] *n* cóctel *m*; **c. lounge** bar *m*; **c. party** cóctel; **prawn c.** cóctel de gambas; **Molotov c.** cóctel Molotov

cocky ['kɒkɪ] *adj* (**cockier, cockiest**) *Fam* gallito(a), engreído(a), *Esp* chulo(a)

cocoa ['kəʊkəʊ] *n* cacao *m*

coconut ['kəʊkənʌt] *n* coco *m*

cod [kɒd] *n* bacalao *m*; **c. liver oil** aceite *m* de hígado de bacalao

code [kəʊd] **1** *n* código *m*; *(symbol)* clave *f*; *Tel* prefijo *m* **2** *vt* *(message)* cifrar, poner en clave

coerce [kəʊ'ɜːs] *vt* coaccionar

coexist [kəʊɪg'zɪst] *vi* coexistir

coffee ['kɒfɪ] *n* café *m*; **c. bar/shop** cafetería *f*; **c. break** descanso *m*; **c. table** mesita *f* de café

coffin ['kɒfɪn] *n* ataúd *m*

cog [kɒg] *n* diente *m*

cognac ['kɒnjæk] *n* coñac *m*

coherent [kəʊ'hɪərənt] *adj* coherente

coil [kɔɪl] **1** *vt* **to c. (up)** enrollar
2 *vi* enroscarse
3 *n* (**a**) *(loop)* vuelta *f*; *(of rope)* rollo *m*; *(of hair)* rizo *m* (**b**) *Br (contraceptive)* espiral *f* (**c**) *Elec* carrete *m*, bobina *f*

coin [kɔɪn] **1** *n* moneda *f* **2** *vt* (**a**) *(money)* acuñar (**b**) *Fig* **to c. a phrase** por así decirlo

coincide [kəʊɪn'saɪd] *vi* coincidir (**with** con)

coincidence [kəʊ'ɪnsɪdəns] n coincidencia f

coke [kəʊk] n (coal) coque m

colander ['kɒləndə(r)] n colador m

cold [kəʊld] **1** adj frío(a); **I'm c.** tengo frío; **it's c.** (weather) hace frío; (thing) está frío(a); Fig **to get c. feet (about doing sth)** entrarle miedo a algn (de hacer algo); **c. cream** crema f hidratante; Fig **it leaves me c.** ni me va ni me viene, Esp me deja frío(a); **c. sore** herpes m inv labial, Esp calentura f, Méx fuego m; **c. war** guerra fría

2 n (**a**) frío m (**b**) (illness) resfriado m; catarro m, Esp, Méx resfriado m, Andes, RP resfrío m; **to have a c.** estar acatarrado(a), tener un Esp, Méx resfriado or Andes, RP resfrío

coldness ['kəʊldnɪs] n (of weather, manner) frialdad f

coleslaw ['kəʊlslɔː] n ensalada f de col

collaborate [kə'læbəreɪt] vi colaborar (**with** con)

collaboration [kəlæbə'reɪʃən] n also Pej colaboración f

collapse [kə'læps] **1** vi (break down) derrumbarse; (cave in) hundirse; Fig (prices) caer en picado; Med sufrir un colapso

2 vt (table) plegar

3 n (breaking down) derrumbamiento m; (caving in) hundimiento m; Med colapso m

collar ['kɒlə(r)] **1** n (of garment) cuello m; (for dog) collar m **2** vt Fam pescar, agarrar

colleague ['kɒliːg] n colega mf

collect [kə'lekt] **1** vt (**a**) (gather) recoger (**b**) (stamps etc) coleccionar (**c**) (taxes) recaudar

2 vi (**a**) (people) reunirse (**b**) (for charity) hacer una colecta (**for** para)

3 adv US **to call sb c.** llamar or Am hablar a algn a cobro revertido

collection [kə'lekʃən] n (**a**) (of mail) recogida f; (of money) colecta f (**b**) (of stamps) colección f

collector [kə'lektə(r)] n (of stamps) coleccionista mf

college ['kɒlɪdʒ] n colegio m; Br (of university) colegio universitario; US (university) universidad f

collide [kə'laɪd] vi chocar, colisionar

collision [kə'lɪʒən] n choque m

colloquial [kə'ləʊkwɪəl] adj coloquial

colon[1] ['kəʊlən] n Typ dos puntos mpl

colon[2] ['kəʊlən] n Anat colon m

colonel ['kɜːnəl] n coronel m

colonial [kə'ləʊnɪəl] adj colonial

colony ['kɒlənɪ] n colonia f

color ['kʌlər] US = **colour**

colossal [kə'lɒsəl] adj colosal

colour ['kʌlə(r)] **1** n (**a**) color m; **what c. is it?** ¿de qué color es?; **c. film/ television** película f/televisión f en color; **c. scheme** combinación f de colores (**b**) (race) color m; **c. bar** discriminación f racial (**c**) **colours** Br Sport colores mpl; Mil (flag) bandera f

2 vt colorear

3 vt **to c. (up)** ruborizarse

colour-blind ['kʌləblaɪnd] adj daltónico(a)

coloured ['kʌləd] adj (pencils) de colores

colourful ['kʌləfʊl] adj (**a**) con muchos colores (**b**) Fig lleno(a) de color; (person) pintoresco(a)

colouring ['kʌlərɪŋ] n (colour) colorido m

column ['kɒləm] n columna f

coma ['kəʊmə] n coma m; **to go into a c.** entrar en coma

comb [kəʊm] **1** n peine m **2** vt peinar; **to c. one's hair** peinarse

combat ['kɒmbæt] **1** n combate m

2 vt (enemy, disease) combatir

3 vi combatir (**against** contra)

combination [kɒmbɪ'neɪʃən] n combinación f

combine 1 vt [kəm'baɪn] combinar

2 vi [kəm'baɪn] combinarse; (companies) asociarse

3 n ['kɒmbaɪn] (**a**) Com asociación f (**b**) **c. harvester** cosechadora f

combustion [kəm'bʌstʃən] n combustión f

come [kʌm] (pt **came**; pp **come**) vi (**a**) venir; (arrive) llegar; **coming!** ¡voy!; **to**

c. and go ir y venir; *Fig* **in years to c.** en el futuro (**b**) *(happen)* suceder; **c. what may** pase lo que pase (**c**) **I came to believe that ...** llegué a creer que ...

▸ **come about** *vi* ocurrir, suceder

▸ **come across 1** *vt insep (thing)* encontrar por casualidad; **to c. across sb** tropezar con algn **2** *vi Fig* **to c. across well** causar buena impresión

▸ **come along** *vi* (**a**) *(arrive)* venir; **c. along!** ¡vamos!, *Esp* ¡venga! (**b**) *(make progress)* progresar

▸ **come away** *vi (leave)* salir; *(part)* desprenderse (**from** de)

▸ **come back** *vi (return)* volver, *Col, Méx* regresar

▸ **come before** *vt insep* (**a**) preceder (**b**) *(court)* comparecer ante

▸ **come by** *vt insep* adquirir

▸ **come down** *vi* bajar; *(rain)* caer; *(building)* ser derribado(a); **to c. down with the flu** coger la gripe

▸ **come forward** *vi (advance)* avanzar; *(volunteer)* ofrecerse

▸ **come in** *vi* (**a**) *(enter)* entrar; **c. in!** ¡pase! (**b**) *(arrive) (train)* llegar; *(tide)* subir; *Fam Fig* **where do I c. in?** y yo ¿qué pinto? (**c**) **to c. in handy** venir bien (**d**) **to c. in for** ser objeto de

▸ **come into** *vt insep* (**a**) *(enter)* entrar en (**b**) *(inherit)* heredar

▸ **come off 1** *vt insep (fall from)* caerse de; *Fam* **c. off it!** ¡venga ya! **2** *vi* (**a**) *(fall)* caerse; *(stain)* quitarse; *(button)* caerse (**b**) *Fam (take place)* pasar; *(succeed)* salir bien; **to c. off badly** salir mal

▸ **come on** *vi* (**a**) **c. on!** *(hurry)* ¡vamos!, *Esp* ¡venga! (**b**) *(make progress)* progresar (**c**) *(rain, illness)* comenzar

▸ **come out** *vi* (**a**) salir (**of** de); *(book)* aparecer; *(product)* estrenarse; *(facts)* revelarse (**b**) *(stain)* quitarse; *(colour)* desteñir (**c**) **to c. out against/in favour of sth** declararse en contra/a favor de algo; *Br Ind* **to c. out (on strike)** declararse en huelga (**d**) *(turn out)* salir

▸ **come over 1** *vi* venir **2** *vt insep* (**a**) *(hill)* aparecer en lo alto de (**b**) *Fam* **what's c. over you?** ¿qué te pasa?

▸ **come round 1** *vt insep (corner)* dar la vuelta a **2** *vi* (**a**) *(visit)* venir (**b**) *(regain consciousness)* volver en sí (**c**) **to c. round to sb's way of thinking** dejarse convencer por algn

▸ **come through 1** *vt insep* (**a**) *(cross)* cruzar (**b**) *(illness)* recuperarse de; *(accident)* sobrevivir **2** *vi (message)* llegar

▸ **come to 1** *vi (regain consciousness)* volver en sí **2** *vt insep* (**a**) *Fig* **to c. to one's senses** recobrar la razón (**b**) *(amount to)* costar (**c**) *(arrive at)* llegar a; **to c. to an end** terminar; *Fam* **c. to that** a propósito

▸ **come under** *vt insep Fig* **to c. under fire from sb** ser criticado(a) por algn

▸ **come up** *vi* (**a**) *(rise)* subir; *(approach)* acercarse (**to** a) (**b**) *(difficulty, question)* surgir; **to c. up with a solution** encontrar una solución; **to c. up against problems** encontrarse con problemas (**c**) *(sun)* salir (**d**) **to c. up to** igualar; **to c. up to sb's expectations** satisfacer a algn (**e**) *Fam* **three chips, coming up!** ¡van tres de patatas fritas!

▸ **come upon** *vt insep* = **come across**

comeback ['kʌmbæk] *n Fam* (**a**) *(of person)* reaparición *f*; **to make a c.** reaparecer (**b**) *(answer)* réplica *f*

comedian [kə'miːdɪən] *n* cómico *m*

comedy ['kɒmɪdɪ] *n* comedia *f*

comet ['kɒmɪt] *n* cometa *m*

comfort ['kʌmfət] **1** *n* (**a**) comodidad *f*; *US* **c. station** servicios *mpl*, *Esp* aseos *mpl*, *Am* baños *mpl* (**b**) *(consolation)* consuelo *m*; **to take c. in** *or* **from sth** consolarse con algo **2** *vt* consolar

comfortable ['kʌmfətəbəl] *adj (chair, person, margin)* cómodo(a); *(temperature)* agradable

comfortably ['kʌmfətəblɪ] *adv (win)* con facilidad; **to be c. off** vivir cómodamente

comic ['kɒmɪk] **1** *adj* cómico(a); **c. strip** tira cómica, historieta *f* **2** *n* **(a)** *(person)* cómico(a) *m,f* **(b) c. (book)** *(for children)* Esp tebeo *m*, Am revista *f* de historietas; *(for adults)* cómic *m*

coming ['kʌmɪŋ] **1** *adj (year)* próximo(a); *(generation)* futuro(a) **2** *n* venida *f*, llegada *f*; **comings and goings** idas *fpl* y venidas; *Fig* **c. and going** ajetreo *m*

comma ['kɒmə] *n* coma *f*

command [kə'mɑːnd] **1** *vt* **(a)** mandar **(b)** *(respect)* infundir; *(sympathy)* merecer; *(money etc)* disponer de **2** *n* **(a)** *(order)* orden *f*; *(authority)* mando *m*; **to be at sb's c.** estar a las órdenes de algn **(b)** *(of language)* dominio *m* **(c)** *(disposal)* disposición *f* **(d)** *Comput* comando *m*, instrucción *f*

commander [kə'mɑːndə(r)] *n* comandante *m*

commandment [kə'mɑːndmənt] *n* mandamiento *m*

commemorate [kə'meməreɪt] *vt* conmemorar

commemoration [kəmemə'reɪʃən] *n* conmemoración *f*; **in c. of** en conmemoración de

commence [kə'mens] *vt & vi Fml* comenzar

commendable [kə'mendəbəl] *adj* encomiable

comment ['kɒment] **1** *n* comentario *m*; **no c.** sin comentario **2** *vi* hacer comentarios

commentary ['kɒməntərɪ] *n* comentario *m*

commentator ['kɒmənteɪtə(r)] *n* comentarista *mf*

commerce ['kɒmɜːs] *n* comercio *m*

commercial [kə'mɜːʃəl] **1** *adj* comercial; *TV* **c. break** corte publicitario **2** *n TV* anuncio *m*

commercialize [kə'mɜːʃəlaɪz] *vt* explotar

commiserate [kə'mɪzəreɪt] *vi* compadecerse **(with** de)

commission [kə'mɪʃən] **1** *n* **(a)** *Mil* despacho *m* (de oficial); **out of c.** fuera de servicio **(b)** *(of inquiry)* comisión *f*; *(job)* encargo *m* **(c)** *(payment)* comisión *f* **2** *vt* **(a)** *Mil* nombrar **(b)** *(order)* encargar **(c)** *Naut* poner en servicio

commissioner [kə'mɪʃənə(r)] *n* *(official)* comisario *m*; **c. of police** comisario de policía

commit [kə'mɪt] *vt* **(a)** *(crime)* cometer; **to c. suicide** suicidarse **(b) to c. oneself (to do sth)** comprometerse (a hacer algo) **(c) to c. sth to sb's care** confiar algo a algn

commitment [kə'mɪtmənt] *n* compromiso *m*

committee [kə'mɪtɪ] *n* comisión *f*, comité *m*

commodity [kə'mɒdɪtɪ] *n* producto *m* básico

common ['kɒmən] **1** *adj* **(a)** común; **that's c. knowledge** eso lo sabe todo el mundo; **c. law** derecho consuetudinario; **C. Market** Mercado *m* Común; **c. room** *(for students)* sala *f* de estudiantes; *(for teachers)* sala *f* de profesores **(b)** *(ordinary)* corriente **(c)** *(vulgar)* ordinario(a), maleducado(a) **2** *n (land)* terreno *m* comunal

commonly ['kɒmənlɪ] *adv* comúnmente

commonplace ['kɒmənpleɪs] *adj* corriente

Commonwealth ['kɒmənwelθ] *n Br* **the C.** la Commonwealth; **C. of Independent States** Comunidad *f* de Estados Independientes

commotion [kə'məʊʃən] *n* alboroto *m*

communal ['kɒmjʊnəl] *adj* comunal

commune¹ [kə'mjuːn] *vi (converse)* conversar íntimamente; *(with nature)* estar en comunión **(with** con)

commune² ['kɒmjuːn] *n* comuna *f*

communicate [kə'mjuːnɪkeɪt] **1** *vi* comunicarse **(with** con) **2** *vt* comunicar

communication [kəmjuːnɪ'keɪʃən] *n* **(a)** comunicación *f* **(b)** *Br Rail* **c. cord** timbre *m* de alarma

communism ['kɒmjʊnɪzəm] *n* comunismo *m*

communist ['kɒmjʊnɪst] *adj & n* comunista *(mf)*

community [kə'mju:nɪtɪ] *n* comunidad *f*; *(people)* colectividad *f*; **c. centre** centro *m* social

commute [kə'mju:t] **1** *vi* = viajar diariamente al lugar de trabajo **2** *vt Jur* conmutar

commuter [kə'mju:tə(r)] *n* = persona que viaja diariamente al lugar de trabajo

compact¹ 1 *adj* [kəm'pækt] compacto(a); *(style)* conciso(a) **2** *n* ['kɒmpækt] *(for powder)* polvera *f*

compact² ['kɒmpækt] *n Pol* pacto *m*

compact disc ['kɒmpækt'dɪsk] *n* disco compacto

companion [kəm'pænjən] *n* compañero(a) *m,f*

company ['kʌmpənɪ] *n* (**a**) compañía *f*; **to keep sb c.** hacer compañía a algn (**b**) *Com* empresa *f*, compañía *f*

comparable ['kɒmpərəbəl] *adj* comparable (**to** *or* **with** con)

comparative [kəm'pærətɪv] **1** *adj* comparativo(a); *(relative)* relativo(a) **2** *n Ling* comparativo *m*

comparatively [kəm'pærətɪvlɪ] *adv* relativamente

compare [kəm'peə(r)] **1** *vt* comparar (**to** *or* **with** con); **(as) compared with** en comparación con **2** *vi* compararse

comparison [kəm'pærɪsən] *n* comparación *f*; **by c.** en comparación; **there's no c.** no se puede comparar

compartment [kəm'pɑ:tmənt] *n* *(section)* compartimiento *m*; *Rail* departamento *m*

compass ['kʌmpəs] *n* (**a**) brújula *f* (**b**) **(pair of) compasses** compás *m* (**c**) *Fig (range)* límites *mpl*

compassion [kəm'pæʃən] *n* compasión *f*

compatible [kəm'pætəbəl] *adj* compatible

compatriot [kəm'pætrɪət] *n* compatriota *mf*

compel [kəm'pel] *vt* (**a**) *(oblige)* obligar; **to c. sb to do sth** obligar a

algn a hacer algo (**b**) *(admiration)* despertar

compensate ['kɒmpənseɪt] **1** *vt* compensar; **to c. sb for sth** indemnizar a algn de algo **2** *vi* compensar

compensation [kɒmpən'seɪʃən] *n* compensación *f*; *(for loss)* indemnización *f*

compere ['kɒmpeə(r)] *n Br* animador(a) *m,f*

compete [kəm'pi:t] *vi* competir

competent ['kɒmpɪtənt] *adj* competente

competition [kɒmpɪ'tɪʃən] *n* (**a**) *(contest)* concurso *m* (**b**) *Com* competencia *f*

competitive [kəm'petɪtɪv] *adj* competitivo(a)

competitor [kəm'petɪtə(r)] *n* competidor(a) *m,f*

compile [kəm'paɪl] *vt* compilar, recopilar

complacent [kəm'pleɪsənt] *adj* autocomplaciente

complain [kəm'pleɪn] *vi* quejarse (**of/ about** de)

complaint [kəm'pleɪnt] *n* (**a**) queja *f*; *Com* reclamación *f* (**b**) *Jur* demanda *f* (**c**) *Med* enfermedad *f*

complement 1 *n* ['kɒmplɪmənt] (**a**) complemento *m* (**b**) *Naut* dotación *f* **2** *vt* ['kɒmplɪment] complementar

complete [kəm'pli:t] **1** *adj* (**a**) *(entire)* completo(a) (**b**) *(absolute)* total **2** *vt* completar; **to c. a form** rellenar un formulario

completely [kəm'pli:tlɪ] *adv* completamente, por completo

complex ['kɒmpleks] **1** *adj* complejo(a) **2** *n* complejo *m*; **inferiority c.** complejo de inferioridad

complexion [kəm'plekʃən] *n* tez *f*; *Fig* aspecto *m*

complicate ['kɒmplɪkeɪt] *vt* complicar

complication [kɒmplɪ'keɪʃən] *n* complicación *f*

compliment 1 *n* ['kɒmplɪmənt] (**a**) cumplido *m*; **to pay sb a c.** hacerle un cumplido a algn (**b**) **compliments** saludos *mpl* **2** *vt* ['kɒmplɪment] felicitar; **to c. sb on sth** felicitar a algn por algo

complimentary [kɒmplɪ'mentərɪ] *adj* (**a**) *(praising)* elogioso(a) (**b**) *(free)* gratis

comply [kəm'plaɪ] *vi* obedecer; **to c. with** *(order)* cumplir con; *(request)* acceder a

component [kəm'pəʊnənt] **1** *n* componente *m* **2** *adj* componente; **c. part** parte *f*

compose [kəm'pəʊz] *vt & vi* (**a**) componer; **to be composed of** componerse de (**b**) **to c. oneself** calmarse

composed [kəm'pəʊzd] *adj (calm)* sereno(a)

composer [kəm'pəʊzə(r)] *n* compositor(a) *m,f*

composition [kɒmpə'zɪʃən] *n* composición *f; (essay)* redacción *f*

compost ['kɒmpɒst] *n* abono *m*

composure [kəm'pəʊʒə(r)] *n* calma *f*, serenidad *f*

compound¹ 1 *n* ['kɒmpaʊnd] compuesto *m*
  2 *adj* ['kɒmpaʊnd] compuesto(a); *(fracture)* complicado(a)
  3 *vt* [kəm'paʊnd] *(problem)* agravar

compound² ['kɒmpaʊnd] *n (enclosure)* recinto *m*

comprehend [kɒmprɪ'hend] *vt* comprender

comprehensive [kɒmprɪ'hensɪv] *adj* (**a**) *(knowledge)* amplio(a); *(study)* detallado(a) (**b**) *Ins* a todo riesgo (**c**) *Br* **c. school** ≃ instituto *m* de segunda enseñanza

compress 1 *vt* [kəm'pres] comprimir
  2 *n* ['kɒmpres] compresa *f*

comprise [kəm'praɪz] *vt* comprender; *(consist of)* constar de

compromise ['kɒmprəmaɪz] **1** *n* solución *f* negociada; **to reach a c.** llegar a un acuerdo
  2 *vi (two people)* llegar a un acuerdo; *(individual)* transigir
  3 *vt (person)* comprometer

compulsion [kəm'pʌlʃən] *n* obligación *f*

compulsive [kəm'pʌlsɪv] *adj* compulsivo(a)

compulsory [kəm'pʌlsərɪ] *adj* obligatorio(a)

computer [kəm'pjuːtə(r)] *n Esp* ordenador *m*, *Am* computadora *f*; **personal c.** ordenador personal, *Am* computadora personal; **c. programmer** programador(a) *m,f*; **c. science** informática *f*

computerize [kəm'pjuːtəraɪz] *vt* informatizar, *Am* computarizar, *Am* computadorizar

computing [kəm'pjuːtɪŋ] *n* informática *f*, *Am* computación *f*

con [kɒn] *Fam* **1** *vt* timar, *RP* cagar **2** *n* timo *m*, *Andes, RP* truchada *f*; **c. man** timador *m*, *Andes, RP* cagador *m*

conceal [kən'siːl] *vt* ocultar; *(emotions)* disimular

concede [kən'siːd] *vt* conceder

conceited [kən'siːtɪd] *adj* presuntuoso(a)

conceivable [kən'siːvəbəl] *adj* concebible

conceive [kən'siːv] *vt & vi* concebir

concentrate ['kɒnsəntreɪt] **1** *vt* concentrar **2** *vi* **to c. on sth** concentrarse en algo

concentration [kɒnsən'treɪʃən] *n* concentración *f*; **c. camp** campo *m* de concentración

concept ['kɒnsept] *n* concepto *m*

concern [kən'sɜːn] **1** *vt* (**a**) concernir, afectar; **as far as I'm concerned** por lo que a mí se refiere (**b**) *(worry)* preocupar **2** *n* (**a**) **it's no c. of mine** no es asunto mío (**b**) *(worry)* preocupación *f* (**c**) *Com* negocio *m*

concerned [kən'sɜːnd] *adj* (**a**) *(affected)* afectado(a) (**b**) *(worried)* preocupado(a) (**about** por)

concerning [kən'sɜːnɪŋ] *prep* con respecto a, en cuanto a

concert ['kɒnsət, 'kɒnsɜːt] *n Mus* concierto *m*; **c. hall** sala *f* de conciertos

concerto [kən'tʃɜːtəʊ] *n* concierto *m*

concession [kən'seʃən] n (**a**) concesión f; **tax c.** privilegio m fiscal (**b**) Com reducción f

conciliatory [kən'sɪlɪətərɪ] adj conciliador(a)

concise [kən'saɪs] adj conciso(a)

conclude [kən'klu:d] vt & vi concluir

conclusion [kən'klu:ʒən] n conclusión f; **to reach a c.** llegar a una conclusión

conclusive [kən'klu:sɪv] adj concluyente

concoction [kən'kɒkʃən] n (mixture) mezcolanza f; Pej (brew) brebaje m

concourse ['kɒŋkɔ:s] n explanada f

concrete ['kɒŋkri:t] 1 n hormigón m, Am concreto m; **c. mixer** hormigonera f 2 adj (**a**) (definite) concreto(a) (**b**) (made of concrete) de hormigón

concur [kən'kɜ:(r)] vi (**a**) **to c. with** (agree) estar de acuerdo con (**b**) (coincide) coincidir

concussion [kən'kʌʃən] n conmoción f cerebral

condemn [kən'dem] vt condenar

condensation [kɒnden'seɪʃən] n condensación f

condense [kən'dens] 1 vt condensar 2 vi condensarse

condescending [kɒndɪ'sendɪŋ] adj condescendiente

condition [kən'dɪʃən] 1 n condición f; **to be in good c.** estar en buen estado; **on c. that ...** a condición de que ...; **on one c.** con una condición; **heart c.** enfermedad cardíaca; **conditions** (circumstances) circunstancias fpl 2 vt condicionar

conditional [kən'dɪʃənəl] adj condicional

conditioner [kən'dɪʃənə(r)] n acondicionador m

condolences [kən'dəʊlənsɪz] npl pésame m; **please accept my c.** le acompaño en el sentimiento

condom ['kɒndəm] n preservativo m

condominium [kɒndə'mɪnɪəm] n US (building) = bloque de apartamentos poseídos por diferentes propietarios;

(apartment) apartamento m, Esp piso m, Arg departamento m (en propiedad)

condone [kən'dəʊn] vt perdonar, consentir

conducive [kən'dju:sɪv] adj conducente

conduct 1 n ['kɒndʌkt] (behaviour) conducta f, comportamiento m **2** vt [kən'dʌkt] (lead) guiar; (business, orchestra) dirigir; **conducted tour** visita acompañada; **to c. oneself** comportarse

conductor [kən'dʌktə(r)] n (**a**) Br (on bus) cobrador(a) m,f, RP guarda mf (**b**) US Rail revisor(a) m,f (**c**) Mus director(a) m,f (**d**) Phys conductor m

cone [kəʊn] n (**a**) cono m; **ice-cream c.** cucurucho m (**b**) Bot piña f

confectionery [kən'fekʃənərɪ] n dulces mpl

confederation [kənfedə'reɪʃən] n confederación f

confer [kən'fɜ:(r)] **1** vt **to c. a title on sb** conferir un título a algn **2** vi consultar

conference ['kɒnfərəns] n conferencia f

confess [kən'fes] **1** vi confesar; Rel confesarse **2** vt confesar

confession [kən'feʃən] n confesión f

confetti [kən'fetɪ] n confeti m

confide [kən'faɪd] vi **to c. in sb** confiar en algn

confidence ['kɒnfɪdəns] n (**a**) confianza f; **vote of c./no c.** voto m de confianza/de censura; **c. trick** camelo m (**b**) (secret) confidencia f; **in c.** en confianza

confident ['kɒnfɪdənt] adj seguro(a)

confidential [kɒnfɪ'denʃəl] adj (secret) confidencial; (entrusted) de confianza

confidently ['kɒnfɪdəntlɪ] adv con seguridad

confine [kən'faɪn] vt encerrar; Fig limitar

confirm [kən'fɜ:m] vt confirmar

confirmation [kɒnfə'meɪʃən] n confirmación f

confirmed [kən'fɜ:md] *adj* empedernido(a)

confiscate ['kɒnfɪskeɪt] *vt* confiscar

conflict 1 *n* ['kɒnflɪkt] conflicto *m* **2** *vi* [kən'flɪkt] chocar (**with** con)

conflicting [kən'flɪktɪŋ] *adj* contradictorio(a)

conform [kən'fɔ:m] *vi* conformarse; **to c. to** *or* **with** *(customs)* amoldarse a; *(rules)* someterse a

confront [kən'frʌnt] *vt* hacer frente a

confrontation [kɒnfrʌn'teɪʃən] *n* confrontación *f*

confuse [kən'fju:z] *vt* *(person)* despistar; *(thing)* confundir (**with** con); **to get confused** confundirse

confused [kən'fju:zd] *adj* *(person)* confundido(a); *(mind, ideas)* confuso(a)

confusing [kən'fju:zɪŋ] *adj* confuso(a)

confusion [kən'fju:ʒən] *n* confusión *f*

congested [kən'dʒestɪd] *adj* **(a)** *(street)* repleto(a) de gente; *(city)* superpoblado(a) **(b)** *Med* congestionado(a)

congestion [kən'dʒestʃən] *n* congestión *f*

congratulate [kən'grætjʊleɪt] *vt* felicitar

congratulations [kəngrætjʊ'leɪʃənz] *npl* felicitaciones *fpl*; **c.!** ¡enhorabuena!

congregate ['kɒŋgrɪgeɪt] *vi* congregarse

congregation [kɒŋgrɪ'geɪʃən] *n* *(group)* congregación *f*; *Rel* fieles *mpl*

congress ['kɒŋgres] *n* **(a)** *(conference)* congreso *m* **(b)** *US Pol* **C.** el Congreso *(de los Estados Unidos)*

conifer ['kɒnɪfə(r)] *n* conífera *f*

conjunction [kən'dʒʌŋkʃən] *n* conjunción *f*; *Fig* **in c. with** conjuntamente con

connect [kə'nekt] **1** *vt* **(a)** *(join)* juntar, unir; *(wires)* empalmar; *Fig* **to be connected by marriage** estar emparentado(a) por matrimonio **(b)** *(install)* instalar; *Elec* conectar **(c)** *Tel* *(person)* pasar, *Esp* poner **(d)** *Fig* *(associate)* asociar **2** *vi* unirse; *(rooms)* comunicarse; *(train, flight)* enlazar *or* empalmar (**with** con)

connected [kə'nektɪd] *adj* unido(a); *(events)* relacionado(a); *Fig* **to be well c.** *(person) (socially)* estar bien relacionado(a)

connection [kə'nekʃən] *n* **(a)** *(joint)* juntura *f*, unión *f*; *Elec* conexión *f*; *Tel* instalación *f* **(b)** *Rail* correspondencia *f* **(c)** *Fig (of ideas)* relación *f*; **in c. with** *(regarding)* con respecto a **(d)** *(person)* contacto *m*

connoisseur [kɒnɪ'sɜ:(r)] *n* conocedor(a) *m,f*

connotation [kɒnə'teɪʃən] *n* connotación *f*

conquer ['kɒŋkə(r)] *vt* *(enemy, bad habit)* vencer; *(country)* conquistar

conquest ['kɒŋkwest] *n* conquista *f*

conscience ['kɒnʃəns] *n* conciencia *f*; **to have a clear c.** tener la conciencia tranquila; **to have a guilty c.** sentirse culpable

conscientious [kɒnʃɪ'enʃəs] *adj* concienzudo(a); **c. objector** objetor(a) *m,f* de conciencia

conscious ['kɒnʃəs] *adj* *(aware)* consciente; *(choice etc)* deliberado(a)

consciousness ['kɒnʃəsnɪs] *n Med* conocimiento *m*; *(awareness)* conciencia *f*

conscript ['kɒnskrɪpt] *n* recluta *m*

conscription [kən'skrɪpʃən] *n* servicio *m* militar obligatorio

consecutive [kən'sekjʊtɪv] *adj* consecutivo(a)

consensus [kən'sensəs] *n* consenso *m*

consent [kən'sent] **1** *n* consentimiento *m*; **by common c.** de común acuerdo **2** *vi* consentir (**to** en)

consequence ['kɒnsɪkwəns] *n* consecuencia *f*

consequently ['kɒnsɪkwəntlɪ] *adv* por consiguiente

conservation [kɒnsə'veɪʃən] *n* conservación *f*

conservative [kən'sɜːvətɪv] **1** adj cauteloso(a) **2** adj & n Br Pol **C.** conservador(a) (m,f)

conservatory [kən'sɜːvətrɪ] n (**a**) (greenhouse) invernadero m (**b**) Mus conservatorio m

conserve 1 vt [kən'sɜːv] conservar **2** ['kɒnsɜːv] conserva f

consider [kən'sɪdə(r)] vt (**a**) (ponder on, regard) considerar; **to c. doing sth** pensar hacer algo (**b**) (keep in mind) tener en cuenta

considerable [kən'sɪdərəbəl] adj considerable

considerably [kən'sɪdərəblɪ] adv bastante

considerate [kən'sɪdərɪt] adj considerado(a)

consideration [kənsɪdə'reɪʃən] n consideración f; **without due c.** sin reflexión

considering [kən'sɪdərɪŋ] prep teniendo en cuenta

consignment [kən'saɪnmənt] n envío m

consist [kən'sɪst] vi **to c. of** consistir en

consistency [kən'sɪstənsɪ] n (**a**) (of actions) consecuencia f (**b**) (of mixture) consistencia f

consistent [kən'sɪstənt] adj consecuente; **c. with** de acuerdo con

consolation [kɒnsə'leɪʃən] n consuelo m; **c. prize** premio m de consolación

console¹ [kən'səʊl] vt consolar

console² ['kɒnsəʊl] n consola f

consolidate [kən'sɒlɪdeɪt] **1** vt consolidar **2** vi consolidarse

consonant ['kɒnsənənt] n consonante f

conspicuous [kən'spɪkjʊəs] adj (striking) llamativo(a); (easily seen) visible; (mistake) evidente

conspiracy [kən'spɪrəsɪ] n conjura f

conspire [kən'spaɪə(r)] vi conspirar

constable ['kʌnstəbəl] n Br policía mf; **chief c.** jefe m de policía

constant ['kɒnstənt] **1** adj constante;

(continuous) incesante; (loyal) fiel, leal **2** n constante f

constellation [kɒnstɪ'leɪʃən] n constelación f

constipated ['kɒnstɪpeɪtɪd] adj **to be c.** estar estreñido(a)

constituency [kən'stɪtjʊənsɪ] n circunscripción f electoral

constituent [kən'stɪtjʊənt] **1** adj (component) constituyente **2** n (**a**) (part) componente m (**b**) Pol votante mf

constitute ['kɒnstɪtjuːt] vt constituir

constitution [kɒnstɪ'tjuːʃən] n constitución f

constraint [kən'streɪnt] n coacción f; **to feel c. in sb's presence** sentirse cohibido(a) ante algn

construct [kən'strʌkt] vt construir

construction [kən'strʌkʃən] n construcción f

constructive [kən'strʌktɪv] adj constructivo(a)

consul ['kɒnsəl] n cónsul mf

consulate ['kɒnsjʊlɪt] n consulado m

consult [kən'sʌlt] vt & vi consultar (**about** sobre)

consultant [kən'sʌltənt] n Med especialista mf; Com, Ind asesor(a) m,f

consultation [kɒnsəl'teɪʃən] n consulta f

consume [kən'sjuːm] vt consumir

consumer [kən'sjuːmə(r)] n consumidor(a) m,f; **c. goods** bienes mpl de consumo

consumption [kən'sʌmpʃən] n (**a**) (of food) consumo m; **fit for c.** apto(a) para el consumo (**b**) Med tisis f

contact ['kɒntækt] **1** n contacto m; **c. lens** lente f de contacto, Esp lentilla f, Méx pupilente f **2** vt ponerse en contacto con

contagious [kən'teɪdʒəs] adj contagioso(a)

contain [kən'teɪn] vt contener; **to c. oneself** contenerse

container [kən'teɪnə(r)] n (**a**) (box, package) recipiente m; (bottle) envase m (**b**) Naut contenedor m

contaminate [kən'tæmɪneɪt] *vt* contaminar

contemplate ['kɒntempleɪt] *vt* (**a**) *(consider)* considerar, pensar en (**b**) *(look at)* contemplar

contemporary [kən'temprərɪ] *adj & n* contemporáneo(a) *(m,f)*

contempt [kən'tempt] *n* desprecio *m*; **to hold in c.** despreciar; **c. of court** desacato *m* a los tribunales

contend [kən'tend] **1** *vi* competir; *Fig* **there are many problems to c. with** se han planteado muchos problemas **2** *vt* afirmar

content¹ ['kɒntent] *n* contenido *m*; **table of contents** índice *m* de materias

content² [kən'tent] **1** *adj* contento(a) **2** *vt* contentar **3** *n* contento *m*; **to one's heart's c.** todo lo que uno quiera

contented [kən'tentɪd] *adj* contento(a), satisfecho(a)

contest 1 *n* ['kɒntest] concurso *m*; *Sport* prueba *f* **2** *vt* [kən'test] (**a**) *(matter)* rebatir; *(verdict)* impugnar; *Fig (will)* disputar (**b**) *Pol (seat)* luchar por

contestant [kən'testənt] *n* concursante *mf*

context ['kɒntekst] *n* contexto *m*

continent ['kɒntɪnənt] *n* continente *m*; *Br* **(on) the C.** (en) Europa

continental [kɒntɪ'nentəl] *adj* (**a**) continental; **c. shelf** plataforma *f* continental (**b**) *Br* de la Europa continental; **c. quilt** edredón *m* de pluma

contingency [kən'tɪndʒənsɪ] *n* contingencia *f*; **c. plans** planes *mpl* para casos de emergencia

contingent [kən'tɪndʒənt] *adj & n* contingente *(m)*

continual [kən'tɪnjʊəl] *adj* continuo(a), constante

continue [kən'tɪnjuː] *vt & vi* continuar, seguir; **to c. to do sth** seguir *or* continuar haciendo algo

continuous [kən'tɪnjʊəs] *adj* continuo(a)

contour ['kɒntʊə(r)] *n* contorno *m*; **c. line** línea *f* de nivel

contraception [kɒntrə'sepʃən] *n* anticoncepción *f*

contraceptive [kɒntrə'septɪv] *adj & n* anticonceptivo *(m)*

contract 1 *vi* [kən'trækt] *Phys* contraerse **2** *vt* [kən'trækt] (**a**) contraer (**b**) **to c. to do sth** *(make agreement)* comprometerse por contrato a hacer algo **3** *n* ['kɒntrækt] contrato *m*; **to enter into a c.** hacer un contrato

contractor [kən'træktə(r)] *n* contratista *mf*

contradict [kɒntrə'dɪkt] *vt* contradecir

contradictory [kɒntrə'dɪktərɪ] *adj* contradictorio(a)

contraption [kən'træpʃən] *n Fam* cacharro *m*

contrary ['kɒntrərɪ] **1** *adj* (**a**) *(opposite)* contrario(a) (**b**) [kən'treərɪ] *(awkward)* terco(a) **2** *n* **on the c.** todo lo contrario; **unless I tell you to the c.** a menos que te diga lo contrario **3** *adv* **c. to** en contra de

contrast 1 *vi* [kən'trɑːst] contrastar **2** *n* ['kɒntrɑːst] contraste *m*

contribute [kən'trɪbjuːt] **1** *vt (money)* contribuir con; *(ideas, information)* aportar **2** *vi* (**a**) contribuir; *(in discussion)* participar (**b**) *Press* colaborar (**to** en)

contribution [kɒntrɪ'bjuːʃən] *n* (**a**) *(of money)* contribución *f*; *(of ideas etc)* aportación *f* (**b**) *Press* colaboración *f*

contributor [kən'trɪbjʊtə(r)] *n (to newspaper)* colaborador(a) *m,f*

contrive [kən'traɪv] *vt* inventar, idear; **to c. to do sth** buscar la forma de hacer algo

contrived [kən'traɪvd] *adj* artificial, forzado(a)

control [kən'trəʊl] **1** *vt* controlar; *(person, animal)* dominar; *(vehicle)* manejar; **to c. one's temper** controlarse **2** *n* (**a**) *(power)* control *m*, dominio *m*;

out of c. fuera de control; **to be in c.** estar al mando; **to be under c.** *(situation)* estar bajo control; **to go out of c.** descontrolarse; **to lose c.** perder los estribos (**b**) *Aut, Av (device)* mando *m*; *Rad, TV* botón *m* de control; **c. panel** tablero *m* de instrumentos; **c. room** sala *f* de control; *Av* **c. tower** torre *f* de control

controversial [kɒntrə'vɜːʃəl] *adj* controvertido(a), polémico(a)

controversy ['kɒntrəvɜːsɪ, kən'trɒvəsɪ] *n* polémica *f*

convalescence [kɒnvə'lesəns] *n* convalecencia *f*

convenience [kən'viːnɪəns] *n* conveniencia *f*, comodidad *f*; **all modern conveniences** todas las comodidades; **at your c.** cuando le convenga; **c. food** comida precocinada; *Br* **public conveniences** *(toilets)* servicio *m* público, *Esp* aseos *mpl*, *Am* baños *mpl* públicos

convenient [kən'viːnɪənt] *adj (time, arrangement)* conveniente, oportuno(a); *(place)* bien situado(a)

convention [kən'venʃən] *n* convención *f*

conventional [kən'venʃənəl] *adj* clásico(a); *(behaviour)* convencional

converge [kən'vɜːdʒ] *vi* convergir

conversation [kɒnvə'seɪʃən] *n* conversación *f*, *CAm, Méx* plática *f*

conversion [kən'vɜːʃən] *n* *Math, Rel* conversión *f* (**to** a; **into** en)

convert **1** *vt* [kən'vɜːt] convertir **2** *n* ['kɒnvɜːt] converso(a) *m,f*

convertible [kən'vɜːtəbəl] **1** *adj* convertible **2** *n (car)* descapotable *m*, *Am* convertible *m*

convey [kən'veɪ] *vt* (**a**) *(carry)* transportar (**b**) *(sound)* transmitir; *(idea)* comunicar

conveyor [kən'veɪə(r)] *n* **c. belt** cinta transportadora

convict **1** *vt* [kən'vɪkt] declarar culpable a, condenar **2** *n* ['kɒnvɪkt] presidiario(a) *m,f*

conviction [kən'vɪkʃən] *n* (**a**) *(belief)* creencia *f*, convicción *f* (**b**) *Jur* condena *f*

convince [kən'vɪns] *vt* convencer

convincing [kən'vɪnsɪŋ] *adj* convincente

convoy ['kɒnvɔɪ] *n* convoy *m*

cook [kʊk] **1** *vt* cocinar, guisar; *(dinner)* preparar; *Fam* **to c. the books** falsificar las cuentas **2** *vi (person)* cocinar, guisar; *(food)* cocerse **3** *n* cocinero(a) *m,f*

cookbook ['kʊkbʊk] *n US* libro *m* de cocina

cooker ['kʊkə(r)] *n* cocina *f*, *Col, Méx, Ven* estufa *f*

cookery ['kʊkərɪ] *n* cocina *f*; **c. book** libro *m* de cocina

cookie ['kʊkɪ] *n US* galleta *f*

cooking ['kʊkɪŋ] *n* cocina *f*

cool [kuːl] **1** *adj* (**a**) fresco(a); **it's c.** *(weather)* hace fresquito (**b**) *Fig (calm)* tranquilo(a); *(reserved)* frío(a) **2** *n* (**a**) *(coolness)* fresco *m* (**b**) *Fam* **to lose one's c.** perder la calma **3** *vt (air)* refrescar; *(drink)* enfriar **4** *adv Fam* **to play it c.** aparentar calma

▸**cool down, cool off** *vi Fig* calmarse; *(feelings)* enfriarse

coop [kuːp] **1** *n* gallinero *m* **2** *vt* **to c. (up)** encerrar

co-op ['kəʊɒp] *n* cooperativa *f*

co-operate [kəʊ'ɒpəreɪt] *vi* cooperar

co-operation [kəʊɒpə'reɪʃən] *n* co-operación *f*

co-ordinate **1** *vt* [kəʊ'ɔːdɪneɪt] coordinar **2** *n* [kəʊ'ɔːdɪnɪt] (**a**) *Math* coordenada *f* (**b**) **co-ordinates** *(clothes)* conjunto *m*

co-ordination [kəʊɔːdɪ'neɪʃən] *n* coordinación *f*

cop [kɒp] *Fam* **1** *n (policeman)* poli *m* **2** *vt Br* **you'll c. it** te vas a ganar una buena

▸**cop out** *vi Fam* zafarse, *Esp* escaquearse, *RP* zafar

cope [kəʊp] *vi* arreglárselas; **to c. with** *(person, work)* poder con; *(problem)* hacer frente a

copier ['kɒpɪə(r)] *n (photocopying*

machine) fotocopiadora *f*

copper¹ [ˈkɒpə(r)] **1** *n (metal)* cobre *m* **2** *adj (colour)* cobrizo(a)

copper² [ˈkɒpə(r)] *n Fam* poli *mf*

copy [ˈkɒpɪ] **1** *n* (a) copia *f* (b) *(of book)* ejemplar *m* **2** *vt & vi* copiar

coral [ˈkɒrəl] *n* coral *m*; **c. reef** arrecife *m* de coral

cord [kɔːd] *n* (a) *(string)* cuerda *f*; *Elec* cordón *m* (b) *Tex (corduroy)* pana *f*; **cords** pantalones *mpl* de pana

cordial [ˈkɔːdɪəl] **1** *adj* cordial **2** *n* licor *m*

cordon [ˈkɔːdən] **1** *n* cordón *m* **2** *vt* **to c. off a street** acordonar una calle

corduroy [ˈkɔːdərɔɪ] *n* pana *f*

core [kɔː(r)] **1** *n (of fruit)* corazón *m*; *Elec* núcleo *m*; *Fig* **the hard c.** los incondicionales **2** *vt* quitarle el corazón a

cork [kɔːk] *n* corcho *m*; **c. oak** alcornoque *m*

corkscrew [ˈkɔːkskruː] *n* sacacorchos *m inv*

corn¹ [kɔːn] *n* (a) *Br (wheat)* trigo *m*; (b) *(maize)* maíz *m*, *Andes*, *RP* choclo *m*; **c. bread** pan *m* de maíz *or Andes*, *RP* choclo; **c. on the cob** mazorca *f* de maíz *or Andes*, *RP* choclo, *Méx* elote *m*

corn² [kɔːn] *n Med* callo *m*

corner [ˈkɔːnə(r)] **1** *n* (a) *(of street)* esquina *f*; *(bend in road)* curva *f*; **round the c.** a la vuelta de la esquina; *Ftb* **c. kick** córner *m*; **c.** *Br* **shop** *or US* **store** tienda pequeña de barrio (b) *(of room)* rincón *m* **2** *vt* (a) *(enemy)* arrinconar (b) *Com* acaparar **3** *vi Aut* tomar una curva

cornet [*Br* ˈkɔːnɪt, *US* kɔːˈnet] *n* (a) *Mus* corneta *f* (b) *Br (for ice cream)* cucurucho *m*

cornflakes [ˈkɔːnfleɪks] *npl* copos *mpl* de maíz, cornflakes *mpl*

cornstarch [ˈkɔːnstɑːtʃ] *n US* harina *f* de maíz *or Andes*, *RP* choclo, maicena® *f*

corny [ˈkɔːnɪ] *adj* (**cornier, corniest**) *Fam* gastado(a)

coronary [ˈkɒrənərɪ] *adj* coronario(a); **c. thrombosis** trombosis coronaria

coronation [kɒrəˈneɪʃən] *n* coronación *f*

corporal¹ [ˈkɔːpərəl] *adj* corporal; **c. punishment** castigo *m* corporal

corporal² [ˈkɔːpərəl] *n Mil* cabo *m*

corporate [ˈkɔːpərɪt] *adj* corporativo(a)

corporation [kɔːpəˈreɪʃən] *n* (a) *(business)* sociedad anónima (b) *(of city)* ayuntamiento *m*

corps [kɔː(r)] *n (pl* **corps** [kɔːz]) cuerpo *m*

corpse [kɔːps] *n* cadáver *m*

correct [kəˈrekt] **1** *vt* (a) *(mistake)* corregir (b) *(child)* reprender **2** *adj* correcto(a), exacto(a); *(behaviour)* formal

correction [kəˈrekʃən] *n* corrección *f*

correspond [kɒrɪˈspɒnd] *vi* (a) corresponder; **to c. to** equivaler a (b) *(by letter)* escribirse

correspondence [kɒrɪˈspɒndəns] *n* correspondencia *f*; **c. course** curso *m* por correspondencia

corresponding [kɒrɪˈspɒndɪŋ] *adj* correspondiente

corridor [ˈkɒrɪdɔː(r)] *n* pasillo *m*

corrosion [kəˈrəʊʒən] *n* corrosión *f*

corrugated [ˈkɒrʊgeɪtɪd] *adj* **c. iron** hierro ondulado

corrupt [kəˈrʌpt] **1** *adj (person)* corrompido(a), corrupto(a); *(actions)* deshonesto(a) **2** *vt & vi* corromper

corruption [kəˈrʌpʃən] *n* corrupción *f*

Corsica [ˈkɔːsɪkə] *n* Córcega

cosmetic [kɒzˈmetɪk] **1** *n* cosmético *m* **2** *adj* cosmético(a); **c. surgery** cirugía plástica

cosmopolitan [kɒzməˈpɒlɪtən] *adj* cosmopolita

cost [kɒst] **1** *n (price)* costo *m*, *Esp* coste *m*; **c. of living** costo *or Esp* coste de la vida; **to count the c.** considerar las desventajas; **at all costs** a toda costa **2** *vt & vi. (pt & pp* **cost**) costar, valer;

how much does it c.? ¿cuánto cuesta?; **whatever it costs** cueste lo que cueste

3 *vt (pt & pp* **costed)** *Com, Ind* calcular el costo *or Esp* coste de

costly ['kɒstlɪ] *adj* (**costlier, costliest**) costoso(a)

costume ['kɒstjuːm] *n* traje *m*; (**swimming**) **c.** traje *m* de baño, *Esp* bañador *m*, *RP* malla *f*; **c. jewellery** bisutería *f*

cosy ['kəʊzɪ] *adj* (**cosier, cosiest**) *(atmosphere)* acogedor(a); *(bed)* calentito(a); **it's c. in here** aquí se está bien

cot [kɒt] *n* (**a**) *Br (for child)* cuna *f* (**b**) *US (folding bed)* catre *m*, cama *f* plegable

cottage ['kɒtɪdʒ] *n* casa *f* de campo; **c. cheese** queso fresco; **c. industry** industria casera; *Br* **c. pie** = pastel de carne picada y puré de *Esp* patata *or Am* papa

cotton ['kɒtən] *n* algodón *m*, *Am* cotón *m*; **a c. shirt** una camisa de algodón; **c. bud** bastoncillo *m* (de algodón); *US* **c. candy** algodón dulce; *Br* **c. wool** algodón (hidrófilo)

▸ **cotton on** *vi Fam* enterarse, *Esp* coscarse, *RP* captar

couch [kaʊtʃ] *n* sofá *m*; *(in surgery)* camilla *f*

couchette [kuː'ʃet] *n Rail* litera *f*

cough [kɒf] **1** *vi* toser **2** *n* tos *f*; **c. drop** pastilla *f* para la tos; **c. mixture** jarabe *m* para la tos

▸ **cough up** *vt sep Fam (money)* poner, *Esp* apoquinar, *RP* garpar

could [kʊd] *v aux see* **can**[1]

council ['kaʊnsəl] *n (body)* consejo *m*; *Br* **c. house** vivienda *f* de protección oficial; **town c.** consejo municipal, ayuntamiento *m*

councillor, *US* **councilor** ['kaʊnsələ(r)] *n* concejal *mf*

counselling ['kaʊnsəlɪŋ] *n* apoyo *m* psicológico, orientación *f* psicológica

count[1] [kaʊnt] **1** *vt* (**a**) contar (**b**) *Fig* **to c. oneself lucky** considerarse afortunado(a)

2 *vi* contar; **that doesn't c.** eso no

vale; **to c. to ten** contar hasta diez

3 *n* (**a**) cuenta *f*; *(total)* recuento *m* (**b**) *Jur* cargo *m*

▸ **count on** *vt insep* contar con

count[2] [kaʊnt] *n (nobleman)* conde *m*

countdown ['kaʊntdaʊn] *n* cuenta *f* atrás

counter[1] ['kaʊntə(r)] *n* (**a**) *(in shop)* mostrador *m*; *(in bank)* ventanilla *f* (**b**) *(in board games)* ficha *f*

counter[2] ['kaʊntə(r)] *n* contador *m*

counter[3] ['kaʊntə(r)] **1** *adv* **c. to** en contra de

2 *vt (attack)* contestar a; *(trend)* contrarrestar

3 *vi* contestar

counterattack ['kaʊntərətæk] *n* contraataque *m*

counter-clockwise ['kaʊntə'klɒkwaɪz] *adv US* en sentido opuesto al de las agujas del reloj

counterfeit ['kaʊntəfɪt] **1** *adj* falsificado(a); **c. coin** moneda falsa

2 *n* falsificación *f*

3 *vt* falsificar

counterpart ['kaʊntəpaːt] *n* homólogo(a) *m,f*

countless ['kaʊntlɪs] *adj* innumerable, incontable

country ['kʌntrɪ] *n* (**a**) *(state)* país *m*; **native c.** patria *f* (**b**) *(rural area)* campo *m*; **c. dancing** baile *m* popular

countryman ['kʌntrɪmən] *n* (**a**) *(rural)* hombre *m* del campo (**b**) *(compatriot)* compatriota *m*

countryside ['kʌntrɪsaɪd] *n (area)* campo *m*; *(scenery)* paisaje *m*

county ['kaʊntɪ] *n* condado *m*

coup [kuː] *n (pl* **coups** [kuːz]) golpe *m*; **c. d'état** golpe de estado

couple ['kʌpəl] **1** *n* (**a**) *(of people)* pareja *f*; **a married c.** un matrimonio (**b**) *(of things)* par *m*; *Fam* **a c. of times** un par de veces **2** *vt (wagons)* enganchar

coupon ['kuːpɒn] *n* (**a**) cupón *m* (**b**) *Br Ftb* quiniela *f*

courage ['kʌrɪdʒ] *n* coraje *m*, valentía *f*

courageous [kə'reɪdʒəs] adj valeroso(a), valiente

courgette [kʊə'ʒet] n Br calabacín m, CSur zapallito m, Méx calabacita f

courier ['kʊrɪə(r)] n (a) (messenger) mensajero(a) m,f (b) (guide) guía mf turístico(a)

course [kɔːs] n (a) (of river) curso m; Naut, Av rumbo m
(b) Fig desarrollo m; **in the c. of construction** en vías de construcción; **in the c. of time** con el tiempo
(c) (series) ciclo m; **a c. of treatment** un tratamiento
(d) Educ curso m; Univ asignatura f
(e) (for golf) Esp campo m, Am cancha f; (for horse-racing) hipódromo m
(f) Culin plato m
(g) **of c.** claro, por supuesto; **of c. not!** ¡claro que no!

court [kɔːt] 1 n (a) Jur tribunal m; **c. martial** consejo m de guerra; **c. order** orden f judicial (b) (royal) corte f (c) Sport pista f, cancha f
2 vt (woman) hacer la corte a; Fig **to c. danger** buscar el peligro; Fig **to c. disaster** exponerse al desastre
3 vi (couple) tener relaciones

courteous ['kɜːtɪəs] adj cortés

courtesy ['kɜːtɪsɪ] n (a) cortesía f, educación f (b) **by c. of** por cortesía de

courthouse ['kɔːthaʊs] n US palacio m de justicia

courtroom ['kɔːtruːm] n sala f de justicia

courtyard ['kɔːtjɑːd] n patio m

cousin ['kʌzən] n primo(a) m,f; **first c.** primo(a) hermano(a)

cover ['kʌvə(r)] 1 vt (a) cubrir (**with** de); (furniture) revestir (**with** de); (with lid) tapar (b) (hide) disimular (c) (protect) abrigar (d) (distance) recorrer (e) Press investigar (f) (deal with) abarcar (g) (include) incluir
2 vi **to c. for sb** sustituir a algn
3 n (a) cubierta f; (lid) tapa f; (on bed) manta f, Am frazada f, cobija f; (of chair etc) funda f (b) (of book) tapa f; (of magazine) portada f (c) (in restaurant) cubierto m (d) (protection) abrigo m;

to take c. abrigarse; **under c.** al abrigo; (indoors) bajo techo

▸ **cover up** 1 vt sep (a) cubrir (b) (crime) encubrir 2 vi (a) (person) abrigarse (b) **to c. up for sb** encubrir a algn

coverage ['kʌvərɪdʒ] n cobertura f

coveralls ['kʌvərɔːlz] npl US mono m (de trabajo), Am overol m

covering ['kʌvərɪŋ] 1 n cubierta f, envoltura f 2 adj (letter) explicatorio(a)

cover-up ['kʌvərʌp] n encubrimiento m

cow¹ [kaʊ] n vaca f; Pej (woman) arpía f, bruja f

cow² [kaʊ] vt intimidar

coward ['kaʊəd] n cobarde mf

cowboy ['kaʊbɔɪ] n vaquero m

cower ['kaʊə(r)] vi (with fear) encogerse

cozy ['kəʊzɪ] adj US = cosy

CPA [siːpiː'eɪ] n US (abbr **certified public accountant**) Esp censor(a) m,f jurado(a) de cuentas, Am contador(a) m,f público(a)

crab [kræb] n (a) cangrejo m, Am jaiba f (b) **c. apple** manzana f silvestre

crack [kræk] 1 vt (a) (cup) partir; (bone) fracturar; (nut) cascar; (safe) forzar (b) (whip) hacer restallar (c) Fig (problem) dar con la solución de; (joke) contar
2 vi (a) (glass) partirse; (wall) agrietarse (b) (whip) restallar (c) Fam **to get cracking on sth** ponerse a hacer algo
3 n (a) (in cup) raja f; (in wall, ground) grieta f (b) (of whip) restallido m; (of gun) detonación f (c) Fam (drug) crack m
4 adj Fam de primera

▸ **crack down on** vt insep atajar con mano dura

▸ **crack up** vi Fam Fig (go mad) desquiciarse; (with laughter) partirse de risa, Méx atacarse de risa

cracker ['krækə(r)] n (a) (biscuit) galleta salada (b) (firework) petardo m

crackle ['krækəl] vi crujir; (fire) crepitar

cradle ['kreɪdəl] n (baby's) cuna f

craft [krɑːft] n (a) (occupation) oficio m; (art) arte m; (skill) destreza f (b) (cunning) maña f (c) Naut embarcación f

craftsman ['krɑːftsmən] n artesano m

craftsmanship ['krɑːftsmənʃɪp] n arte f

crafty ['krɑːftɪ] adj (craftier, craftiest) astuto(a)

cram [kræm] 1 vt atiborrar; **crammed with** atestado(a) de 2 vi Fam Educ matarse estudiando, Esp empollar, RP tragar

cramp¹ [kræmp] n Med calambre m; **cramps** retortijones mpl

cramp² [kræmp] vt (development etc) poner trabas a

cramped [kræmpt] adj atestado(a); (writing) apretado(a)

crane [kreɪn] 1 n (a) Zool grulla f común (b) (device) grúa f 2 vt estirar

crank [kræŋk] n (a) Tech manivela f (b) Fam (eccentric) tío raro

crash [kræʃ] 1 vt **to c. one's car** tener un accidente con el coche or Am carro or CSur auto
2 vi (a) (car, plane) estrellarse; (collide) chocar; **to c. into** estrellarse contra (b) Com quebrar
3 n (a) (noise) estrépito m (b) (collision) choque m; car/plane c. accidente m de coche/avión; Fig **c. course** curso intensivo; **c. helmet** casco m protector (c) Com quiebra f

crate [kreɪt] n caja f, cajón m (para embalaje)

crater ['kreɪtə(r)] n cráter m

craving ['kreɪvɪŋ] n ansia f; (in pregnancy) antojo m

crawl [krɔːl] 1 vi (baby) gatear; (vehicle) avanzar lentamente; Fig **to c. to sb** arrastrarse a los pies de algn 2 n (swimming) crol m

crayon ['kreɪɒn] n cera f

craze [kreɪz] n manía f; (fashion) moda f; **it's the latest c.** es el último grito

crazy ['kreɪzɪ] adj (crazier, craziest) Fam loco(a), chalado(a)

creak [kriːk] vi (floor) crujir; (hinge) chirriar

cream [kriːm] 1 n (a) (of milk) Esp nata f, Am crema f (de leche); **c.-coloured** color crema; Fig **the c.** la flor y nata; **c. cheese** queso m blanco para untar (b) (cosmetic) crema f 2 vt (a) (milk) desnatar (b) Culin batir; **creamed potatoes** puré m de patatas or Am papas

creamy ['kriːmɪ] adj (creamier, creamiest) cremoso(a)

crease [kriːs] 1 n (wrinkle) arruga f; (fold) pliegue m; (on trousers) raya f
2 vt (clothes) arrugar
3 vi arrugarse

create [kriːˈeɪt] vt crear

creation [kriːˈeɪʃən] n creación f

creative [kriːˈeɪtɪv] adj (person) creativo(a)

creator [kriːˈeɪtə(r)] n creador(a) m,f

creature ['kriːtʃə(r)] n (animal) criatura f

crèche [kreɪʃ, kreʃ] n Br guardería f (infantil)

credentials [krɪˈdenʃəlz] npl credenciales fpl

credibility [kredɪˈbɪlɪtɪ] n credibilidad f

credible ['kredɪbəl] adj creíble

credit ['kredɪt] 1 n (a) Com crédito m; **on c.** a crédito; **c. card** tarjeta f de crédito (b) **to give c. to sb for sth** reconocer algo a algn (c) (benefit) honor m; **to be a c. to** hacer honor a (d) Cin, TV **credits** créditos mpl 2 vt (a) Com abonar (b) (believe) creer (c) Fig atribuir; **he is credited with having** se le atribuye haber

creek [kriːk] n (a) Br cala f (b) US, Austr riachuelo m

creep [kriːp] 1 vi (pt & pp crept) andar silenciosamente; (insect) arrastrarse; (plant) trepar; **to c. up on sb** sorprender a algn 2 n Fam (unpleasant person) asqueroso(a) m,f, Br (obsequious person) pelota mf, Am arrastrado(a) m,f, Méx lambiscón(ona) m,f, RP chupamedias mf inv

creepy ['kriːpɪ] adj (creepier, creepiest) Fam espeluznante

cremation [krɪ'meɪʃən] n incineración f, cremación f

crematorium [kremə'tɔːrɪəm] n crematorio m

crept [krept] pt & pp of **creep**

crescent ['kresənt] **1** n (shape) medialuna f; Br (street) calle f en medialuna **2** adj creciente

crest [krest] n (a) (of cock, wave) cresta f; (on helmet) penacho m; (of hill) cima f (b) (heraldic) blasón m

Crete [kriːt] n Creta

crevice ['krevɪs] n grieta f, hendedura f

crew [kruː] n Av, Naut tripulación f; **c. cut** corte m al rape; **c.-neck sweater** jersey m con cuello redondo

crib [krɪb] **1** n (a) (manger) pesebre m (b) (for baby) cuna f (c) Fam (in exam) Esp, Ven chuleta f, Arg machete m, Col, Méx acordeón m **2** vt Fam (a) (copy) copiar (b) (steal) quitar

cricket¹ ['krɪkɪt] n (insect) grillo m

cricket² ['krɪkɪt] n Sport cricket m

crime [kraɪm] n delincuencia f; (offence) delito m

criminal ['krɪmɪnəl] adj & n criminal (mf); **c. law** derecho m penal; **c. record** antecedentes mpl penales

crimson ['krɪmzən] adj & n carmesí (m)

cringe [krɪndʒ] vi abatirse, encogerse

crinkle ['krɪŋkəl] vt fruncir, arrugar

cripple ['krɪpəl] **1** n lisiado(a) m,f, mutilado(a) m,f **2** vt mutilar, dejar cojo(a); Fig paralizar

crisis ['kraɪsɪs] n (pl **crises** ['kraɪsiːz]) crisis f inv

crisp [krɪsp] **1** adj crujiente; (lettuce) fresco(a); (banknote) nuevo(a); (weather) frío(a) y seco(a); Fig (style) directo(a) **2** n Br **crisps** patatas or Am papas fritas (de bolsa)

criterion [kraɪ'tɪərɪən] n (pl **criteria** [kraɪ'tɪərɪə]) criterio m

critic ['krɪtɪk] n Art, Th crítico(a) m,f

critical ['krɪtɪkəl] adj crítico(a)

critically ['krɪtɪkəlɪ] adv críticamente; **c. ill** gravemente enfermo(a)

criticism ['krɪtɪsɪzəm] n crítica f

criticize ['krɪtɪsaɪz] vt criticar

croak [krəʊk] vi (frog) croar; (raven) graznar; (person) hablar con voz ronca

crockery ['krɒkərɪ] n loza f

crocodile ['krɒkədaɪl] n cocodrilo m

crocus ['krəʊkəs] n azafrán m

crook [krʊk] **1** n (a) (of shepherd) cayado m (b) Fam caco m **2** vt (arm) doblar

crooked ['krʊkɪd] adj (a) (stick, picture) torcido(a); (path) tortuoso(a) (b) Fam (dishonest) deshonesto(a)

crop [krɒp] **1** n (a) cultivo m; (harvest) cosecha f; (of hair) mata f (b) (whip) fusta f **2** vt (hair) rapar; (grass) cortar

▸ **crop up** vi Fam surgir, presentarse

cross [krɒs] **1** n (a) cruz f (b) (breeds) cruce m, Am cruza f
2 vt (a) cruzar (b) Rel **to c. oneself** hacer la señal de la cruz; Fam **c. my heart!** ¡te lo juro!
3 vi cruzar; (roads) cruzarse; **to c. over** cruzar
4 adj (annoyed) esp Esp enfadado(a), esp Am enojado(a)

▸ **cross off, cross out** vt sep tachar, rayar

cross-country 1 adj ['krɒskʌntrɪ] **c. race** cros m **2** adv [krɒs'kʌntrɪ] campo través

crossing ['krɒsɪŋ] n cruce m; **pedestrian c.** paso m de peatones; **sea c.** travesía f

crossroads ['krɒsrəʊdz] n cruce m; Fig encrucijada f

cross-section ['krɒs'sekʃən] n sección f transversal

crossword ['krɒswɜːd] n **c. (puzzle)** crucigrama m

crotch [krɒtʃ] n entrepierna f

crouch [kraʊtʃ] vi **to c. (down)** agacharse

crow¹ [krəʊ] n cuervo m; Fig **as the c. flies** en línea recta; **c.'s-feet** patas fpl de gallo

crow² [krəʊ] **1** vi (a) (cock) cantar; Fig **to c. over sth** jactarse de algo (b) (baby) balbucir **2** n (of cock) canto m

crowbar ['krəʊbɑː(r)] n palanca f

crowd [kraʊd] **1** n muchedumbre f; Fam (gang) pandilla f, Méx bola f, RP barra f; **the c.** el populacho
2 vt (streets) llenar
3 vi apiñarse; **to c. in/out** entrar/salir en tropel

crowded ['kraʊdɪd] adj atestado(a), lleno(a)

crown [kraʊn] **1** n (**a**) (of king) corona f; **the c. jewels** las joyas de la corona (**b**) (of head) coronilla f **2** vt coronar

crucial ['kruːʃəl] adj decisivo(a)

crucifix ['kruːsɪfɪks] n crucifijo m

crucify ['kruːsɪfaɪ] vt crucificar

crude [kruːd] adj (**a**) (manners, style) tosco(a), grosero(a); (tool) primitivo(a) (**b**) **c. oil** crudo m

cruel [kruːəl] adj cruel (**to** con)

cruelty ['kruːəltɪ] n crueldad f (**to** hacia)

cruise [kruːz] **1** vi (**a**) Naut hacer un crucero (**b**) Aut viajar a velocidad constante; Av viajar a velocidad de crucero **2** n (**a**) Naut crucero m (**b**) **c. missile** misil teledirigido

crumb [krʌm] n miga f, migaja f

crumble ['krʌmbəl] **1** vt desmigar **2** vi (wall) desmoronarse; Fig (hopes) desvanecerse

crumpet ['krʌmpɪt] n = torta pequeña que se come con mantequilla

crumple ['krʌmpəl] vt arrugar

crunch [krʌntʃ] **1** vt (food) ronchar; (with feet) hacer crujir **2** n Fam **when it comes to the c.** a la hora de la verdad

crusade [kruːˈseɪd] n cruzada f

crush [krʌʃ] **1** vt aplastar; (wrinkle) arrugar; (grind) moler; (squeeze) exprimir **2** n (**a**) (of people) gentío m (**b**) **orange c.** naranjada f

crust [krʌst] n corteza f

crutch [krʌtʃ] n Med muleta f; Fig apoyo m

cry [kraɪ] (pt & pp **cried**) **1** vi (**a**) gritar (**b**) (weep) llorar
2 vt gritar; Fig **to c. wolf** dar una falsa alarma
3 n (**a**) grito m (**b**) (weep) llanto m

▶ **cry off** vi Fam rajarse

▶ **cry out** vi gritar; **to c. out for sth** pedir algo a gritos

crypt [krɪpt] n cripta f

crystal ['krɪstəl] n cristal m

cub [kʌb] n (**a**) (animal) cachorro m (**b**) (junior scout) niño m explorador

Cuba ['kjuːbə] n Cuba

cube [kjuːb] **1** n cubo m; (of sugar) terrón m; **c. root** raíz cúbica **2** vt Math elevar al cubo

cubic ['kjuːbɪk] adj cúbico(a)

cubicle ['kjuːbɪkəl] n cubículo m; (at swimming pool) caseta f

cuckoo ['kʊkuː] **1** n cuco m; **c. clock** reloj m de cuco, RP reloj m cucú **2** adj Fam (mad) **to be c.** estar pirado(a), Méx estar zafado(a)

cucumber ['kjuːkʌmbə(r)] n pepino m

cuddle ['kʌdəl] **1** vt abrazar **2** vi abrazarse

cue¹ [kjuː] n Th pie m

cue² [kjuː] n (in billiards) taco m; **c. ball** bola blanca

cuff¹ [kʌf] n (of sleeve) puño m; US (of trousers) dobladillo m; Fig **to do sth off the c.** improvisar algo

cuff² [kʌf] **1** vt (hit) dar un sopapo or Am una cachetada a **2** n (blow) cachete m, cate m

cul-de-sac ['kʌldəsæk] n callejón m sin salida

culinary ['kʌlɪnərɪ] adj culinario(a)

culminate ['kʌlmɪneɪt] vi **to c. in** terminar en

culprit ['kʌlprɪt] n culpable mf

cult [kʌlt] n culto m; **c. figure** ídolo m

cultivate ['kʌltɪveɪt] vt cultivar

cultivated ['kʌltɪveɪtɪd] adj (person) culto(a)

cultural ['kʌltʃərəl] adj cultural

culture ['kʌltʃə(r)] n cultura f

cultured ['kʌltʃəd] adj = **cultivated**

cumbersome ['kʌmbəsəm] adj (awkward) incómodo(a); (bulky) voluminoso(a)

cunning ['kʌnɪŋ] **1** adj astuto(a) **2** n astucia f

cup [kʌp] **1** n taza f; Sport copa f; **C. Final** final f de copa; **c. tie** partido m

de copa **2** vt *(hands)* ahuecar
cupboard [ˈkʌbəd] n armario m; *(on wall)* alacena f
cupcake [ˈkʌpkeɪk] n *(cake)* ≃ magdalena f
curable [ˈkjʊərəbəl] adj curable
curate [ˈkjʊərɪt] n coadjutor m
curb [kɜːb] **1** n (**a**) *(limit)* freno m (**b**) US *(kerb)* bordillo m (de la acera), Chile solera f, Col, Perú sardinel m, CSur cordón m (de la vereda), Méx borde m (de la banqueta) **2** vt *(horse)* refrenar; *Fig (public spending)* contener
cure [kjʊə(r)] **1** vt curar **2** n *(remedy)* cura f, remedio m
curiosity [kjʊərɪˈɒsɪtɪ] n curiosidad f
curious [ˈkjʊərɪəs] adj (**a**) *(inquisitive)* curioso(a) (**b**) *(odd)* extraño(a)
curl [kɜːl] **1** vt *(hair)* rizar; *(lip)* fruncir **2** vi rizarse **3** n *(of hair)* rizo m, Andes, RP rulo m; *(of smoke)* espiral f
▸ **curl up** vi enroscarse
curler [ˈkɜːlə(r)] n *(for hair)* rulo m, Chile tubo m, RP rulero m, Ven rollo m
curly [ˈkɜːlɪ] adj (**curlier, curliest**) rizado(a), Chile, Col crespo(a), Méx quebrado(a), RP enrulado(a)
currant [ˈkʌrənt] n pasa f (de Corinto)
currency [ˈkʌrənsɪ] n (**a**) moneda f; **foreign c.** divisa f (**b**) **to gain c.** cobrar fuerza
current [ˈkʌrənt] **1** adj (**a**) *(opinion)* general; *(word)* en uso; *(year)* en curso; Br **c. account** cuenta f corriente; **c. affairs** actualidad f (política); Fin **c. assets** activo m disponible (**b**) **the c. issue** *(of magazine, newspaper)* el último número **2** n corriente f
currently [ˈkʌrəntlɪ] adv actualmente
curriculum [kəˈrɪkjʊləm] n *(pl* **curricula** [kəˈrɪkjʊlə]*)* plan m de estudios; *esp Br* **c. vitae** curriculum m (vitae)
curry¹ [ˈkʌrɪ] n curry m; **chicken c.** pollo m al curry
curry² [ˈkʌrɪ] vt **to c. favour with** congraciarse con

curse [kɜːs] **1** n maldición f; *(oath)* palabrota f; *Fig* azote m **2** vt maldecir **3** vi blasfemar
cursor [ˈkɜːsə(r)] n cursor m
cursory [ˈkɜːsərɪ] adj rápido(a)
curt [kɜːt] adj brusco(a), seco(a)
curtail [kɜːˈteɪl] vt *(expenses)* reducir; *(text)* acortar
curtain [ˈkɜːtən] n cortina f; *Th* telón m; *Fig* velo m
curts(e)y [ˈkɜːtsɪ] **1** n reverencia f **2** vi hacer una reverencia (**to** a)
curve [kɜːv] **1** n curva f **2** vt encorvar **3** vi torcerse, describir una curva
cushion [ˈkʊʃən] **1** n cojín m; *(large)* almohadón m; *(of billiard table)* banda f **2** vt *Fig* amortiguar; *(person)* proteger
custard [ˈkʌstəd] n natillas fpl; **c. powder** polvos mpl para hacer natillas
custody [ˈkʌstədɪ] n custodia f; **to take into c.** detener
custom [ˈkʌstəm] n (**a**) *(habit)* costumbre f (**b**) Com clientela f
customary [ˈkʌstəmərɪ] adj habitual
customer [ˈkʌstəmə(r)] n cliente mf
customs [ˈkʌstəmz] n sing or pl aduana f; **c. duty** derechos mpl de aduana; **c. officer** agente mf de aduana
cut [kʌt] *(pt & pp* **cut***)* **1** n (**a**) corte m; *(in skin)* cortadura f; *(wound)* herida f; *(with knife)* cuchillada f (**b**) *(of meat)* clase f de carne (**c**) *(reduction)* reducción f **2** vt (**a**) cortar; *(stone)* tallar; *(record)* grabar; **to c. one's finger** cortarse el dedo; *Fig* **to c. a long story short** en resumidas cuentas; *Fig* **to c. corners** recortar presupuestos (**b**) *(reduce)* reducir (**c**) *(divide up)* dividir (**into** en) **3** vi *(of knife, scissors)* cortar
▸ **cut back** vt sep *(expenses)* reducir; *(production)* disminuir
▸ **cut down 1** vt sep *(tree)* talar **2** vt insep **to c. down on** reducir
▸ **cut in** vi *(driver)* adelantar bruscamente
▸ **cut off** vt sep *(water etc)* cortar;

(place) aislar; *(heir)* excluir; *Tel* **I've been c. off** me han cortado (la comunicación)

▸ **cut out 1** *vt sep* (**a**) *(from newspaper)* recortar; *(person)* **to be c. out for sth** estar hecho(a) para algo (**b**) *(delete)* suprimir **2** *vi (engine)* calarse

▸ **cut up** *vt sep* cortar en pedazos

cutback ['kʌtbæk] *n* reducción *f* (**in** de)

cute [kjuːt] *adj* mono(a), lindo(a); *US Fam Pej* listillo(a)

cutlery ['kʌtlərɪ] *n* cubiertos *mpl*

cutting ['kʌtɪŋ] **1** *n (from newspaper)* recorte *m*; *Rail* tajo *m* **2** *adj* cortante; *(remark)* mordaz

CV, cv [siː'viː] *n (abbr* **curriculum vitae)** CV *m*

cybercafe ['saɪbəkæfeɪ] *n Comput* cibercafé *m*

cyberspace ['saɪbəspeɪs] *n Comput* ciberespacio *m*

cycle ['saɪkəl] **1** *n* (**a**) ciclo *m* (**b**) *(bicycle)* bicicleta *f*; *(motorcycle)* moto *f* **2** *vi* ir en bicicleta

cycling ['saɪklɪŋ] *n* ciclismo *m*

cyclist ['saɪklɪst] *n* ciclista *mf*

cylinder ['sɪlɪndə(r)] *n* (**a**) cilindro *m* (**b**) *(for gas)* bombona *f*

cymbal ['sɪmbəl] *n* címbalo *m*, platillo *m*

cynical ['sɪnɪkəl] *adj* (**a**) *(sceptical)* descreído(a), suspicaz (**b**) *(unscrupulous)* desaprensivo(a), sin escrúpulos

Cyprus ['saɪprəs] *n* Chipre

cyst [sɪst] *n* quiste *m*

Czech [tʃek] **1** *adj* checo(a); **the C. Republic** la República Checa **2** *n* (**a**) *(person)* checo(a) *m,f* (**b**) *(language)* checo *m*

Dd

D, d [di:] *n* (**a**) *(the letter)* D, d *f* (**b**) *Mus* D re *m*

dab [dæb] **1** *n (small quantity)* toque *m* **2** *vt* (**a**) *(apply)* aplicar (**b**) *(touch lightly)* tocar ligeramente

dabble ['dæbəl] *vi* **to d. in politics** meterse en política

dad [dæd], **daddy** ['dædɪ] *n Fam* papá *m*

daffodil ['dæfədɪl] *n* narciso *m*

daft [dɑːft] *adj Br Fam (persona, idea)* tonto(a), *Am* sonso(a), *Am* zonzo(a)

dagger ['dægə(r)] *n* puñal *m*, daga *f*

daily ['deɪlɪ] **1** *adj* diario(a), cotidiano(a) **2** *adv* diariamente; **three times d.** tres veces al día **3** *n* (**a**) *(newspaper)* diario *m* (**b**) *Br Fam (cleaning lady)* asistenta *f*

dairy ['deərɪ] *n (on farm)* vaquería *f*; *(shop)* lechería *f*; **d. farming** industria lechera; **d. produce** productos lácteos

daisy ['deɪzɪ] *n* margarita *f*

dam [dæm] **1** *n (barrier)* dique *m*; *(lake)* presa *f* **2** *vt (water)* represar

▸ **dam up** *vt sep Fig (emotion)* contener

damage ['dæmɪdʒ] **1** *n* (**a**) daño *m*; *(to health, reputation)* perjuicio *m*; *(to relationship)* deterioro *m* (**b**) *Jur* **damages** daños *mpl* y perjuicios *mpl* **2** *vt (harm)* dañar, hacer daño a; *(spoil)* estropear; *(undermine)* perjudicar

damaging ['dæmɪdʒɪŋ] *adj* perjudicial

damn [dæm] **1** *vt* condenar; **well, I'll be damned!** ¡vaya por Dios! **2** *interj Fam* **d. (it)!** ¡maldito(a) sea! **3** *n Fam* **I don't give a d.** me importa un bledo **4** *adj Fam* maldito(a) **5** *adv Fam* muy, sumamente

damned [dæmd] *adj & adv* = **damn**

damp [dæmp] **1** *adj* húmedo(a); *(wet)* mojado(a) **2** *n* humedad *f* **3** *vt* (**a**) *(for ironing)* humedecer (**b**) **to d. (down)** *(fire)* sofocar; *Fig (violence)* frenar

dampen ['dæmpən] *vt* humedecer; *Fig* frenar

dance [dɑːns] **1** *n* baile *m*; *(classical, tribal)* danza *f*; **d. band** orquesta *f* de baile; **d. floor** pista *f* de baile; **d. hall** salón *m* de baile **2** *vi & vt* bailar

dancing ['dɑːnsɪŋ] *n* baile *m*

dandelion ['dændɪlaɪən] *n* diente *m* de león

dandruff ['dændrəf] *n* caspa *f*

Dane [deɪn] *n* danés(esa) *m,f*

danger ['deɪndʒə(r)] *n* (**a**) *(risk)* riesgo *m*; *(of war etc)* amenaza *f* (**b**) *(peril)* peligro *m*; **d. (sign)** peligro; **out of d.** fuera de peligro

dangerous ['deɪndʒərəs] *adj* peligroso(a); *(risky)* arriesgado(a); *(harmful)* nocivo(a); *(illness)* grave

dangle ['dæŋgəl] **1** *vi (hang)* colgar; *(swing)* balancearse **2** *vt (legs)* colgar; *(bait)* dejar colgado(a); *(swing)* balancear en el aire

Danish ['deɪnɪʃ] **1** *adj* danés(esa); **D. pastry** pastel *m* de hojaldre **2** *n (language)* danés *m*

dare [deə(r)] **1** *vi* atreverse, osar; **he doesn't d. be late** no se atreve a llegar tarde; **how d. you!** ¿cómo te atreves?; *esp Br* **I d. say** quizás; *Ironic* ya (lo creo) **2** *vt (challenge)* desafiar **3** *n* desafío *m*

daring ['deərɪŋ] **1** *adj* (**a**) *(bold)*

audaz, osado(a) (**b**) *(clothes)* atrevido(a) **2** *n* atrevimiento *m*, osadía *f*

dark [dɑːk] **1** *adj* (**a**) *(room, colour)* oscuro(a); *(hair, complexion)* moreno(a); *(eyes, future)* negro(a) (**b**) *Fig (gloomy)* triste (**c**) *Fig (sinister)* siniestro(a)

2 *n* (**a**) *(darkness)* oscuridad *f*, tinieblas *fpl*; **after d.** después del anochecer (**b**) *Fig* **to be in the d. (about sth)** *Esp* estar in albis (sobre algo), *Am* no tener ni idea (sobre algo)

darken ['dɑːkən] **1** *vt (sky)* oscurecer; *(colour)* hacer más oscuro(a) **2** *vi* oscurecerse; *(sky)* nublarse; *Fig (face)* ensombrecerse

darkness ['dɑːknɪs] *n* oscuridad *f*, tinieblas *fpl*

darling ['dɑːlɪŋ] *adj & n* querido(a) *(m,f)*

darn [dɑːn] **1** *vt* zurcir **2** *n* zurcido *m*

dart [dɑːt] **1** *n* (**a**) *(missile)* dardo *m* (**b**) **darts** *sing* dardos *mpl* **2** *vi (fly about)* revolotear; **to d. in/out** entrar/salir corriendo

dash [dæʃ] **1** *n* (**a**) *(rush)* carrera *f* (**b**) *esp US (race)* sprint *m* (**c**) *(small amount)* poquito *m*; *(of salt)* pizca *f*; *(of liquid)* gota *f* (**d**) *Typ* guión largo; *(hyphen)* guión

2 *vt (throw)* arrojar

3 *vi (rush)* correr; **to d. around** correr de un lado a otro; **to d. out** salir corriendo

▸**dash off** *vi* salir corriendo

dashboard ['dæʃbɔːd] *n* tablero *m* de mandos, *Esp* salpicadero *m*

data ['deɪtə, 'dɑːtə] *npl* datos *mpl*; **d. bank** *or* **base** banco *m* de datos; **d. processing** *(act)* proceso *m* de datos; *(science)* informática *f*; **d. protection act** ley *f* de informática

date¹ [deɪt] **1** *n* (**a**) *(date)* fecha *f*; **what's the d. today?** ¿a qué (fecha) estamos hoy?, ¿qué fecha es hoy?, *Am* ¿a cómo estamos?; **out of d.** *(ideas)* anticuado(a); *(expression)* desusado(a); *(invalid)* caducado(a); **to d.** hasta la fecha; *Fig* **to be up to d.** estar al día; **d. of birth** fecha de nacimiento

(**b**) *(social event)* compromiso *m*; *Fam (with girl, boy)* cita *f* (**c**) *US Fam (person dated)* ligue *m*

2 *vt (ruins)* datar

3 *vi (ideas)* quedar anticuado(a)

▸**date back to, date from** *vt insep* remontar a, datar de

date² [deɪt] *n (fruit)* dátil *m*; **d. palm** datilera *f*

dated ['deɪtɪd] *adj (idea)* anticuado(a); *(fashion)* pasado(a) de moda; *(expression)* desusado(a)

daughter ['dɔːtə(r)] *n* hija *f*

daughter-in-law ['dɔːtərɪnlɔː] *n* nuera *f*, hija política

dawdle ['dɔːdəl] *vi Fam (walk slowly)* andar despacio; *(waste time)* perder el tiempo

dawn [dɔːn] **1** *n* alba *f*, amanecer *m* **2** *vi* (**a**) *(day)* amanecer (**b**) *Fig (age, hope)* comenzar (**c**) *Fig* **suddenly it dawned on him that ...** de repente cayó en la cuenta de que ...

day [deɪ] *n* (**a**) día *m*; **one of these days** un día de éstos; **(on) the next** *or* **following d.** el *or* al día siguiente; **the d. after tomorrow** pasado mañana; **the d. before yesterday** anteayer; **the other d.** el otro día (**b**) *(daylight)* día *m*; **by d.** de día (**c**) *(era)* **in those days** en aquellos tiempos; **these days** hoy (en) día

daybreak ['deɪbreɪk] *n* amanecer *m*

daydream ['deɪdriːm] **1** *n* ensueño *m*; *(vain hope)* fantasía *f* **2** *vi* soñar despierto(a); *(hope vainly)* hacerse ilusiones

daylight ['deɪlaɪt] *n* luz *f* del día; **in broad d.** en pleno día; **to scare the (living) daylights out of sb** pegarle a algn un susto de muerte

daytime ['deɪtaɪm] *n* día *m*; **in the d.** de día

daze [deɪz] *n* aturdimiento *m*; **in a d.** aturdido(a)

dazzle ['dæzəl] *vt* deslumbrar

dead [ded] **1** *adj* (**a**) *(dead)* muerto(a); **to be d.** estar muerto(a); **d. man** muerto *m* (**b**) *(machine)* averiado(a); *(phone)* cortado(a) (**c**) *(numb)* entumecido(a);

(limb) adormecido(a); **my leg's gone d.** se me ha dormido la pierna (**d**) *(silence, secrecy)* total; **d. end** callejón *m* sin salida

2 *adv (very)* muy; *Fam* **you're d. right** tienes toda la razón; **to stop d.** pararse en seco

3 *n* **the d.** *pl* los muertos

deadline ['dedlaɪn] *n (date)* fecha *f* tope; *(time)* hora *f* tope; **we have to meet the d.** tenemos que hacerlo dentro del plazo

deadlock ['dedlɒk] *n* punto muerto

deadly ['dedlɪ] **1** *adj* (**deadlier, deadliest**) mortal; *(weapon)* mortífero(a); *(aim)* certero(a) **2** *adv (extremely)* terriblemente, sumamente

deaf [def] **1** *adj* sordo(a); *Fig* **to turn a d. ear** hacerse el sordo; **d. mute** sordomudo(a) *m,f*

2 *npl* **the d.** los sordos; **the d. and dumb** los sordomudos

deafen ['defən] *vt* ensordecer

deal [diːl] **1** *n* (**a**) *Com, Pol* trato *m*, pacto *m*; **business d.** negocio *m*, transacción *f*; **to do a d. with sb** *(transaction)* cerrar un trato con algn; *(agreement)* pactar algo con algn; *Fam* **it's a d.!** ¡trato hecho! (**b**) *(amount)* cantidad *f*; **a good d. of criticism** muchas críticas; **a good d. slower** mucho más despacio (**c**) *Cards* reparto *m* **2** *vt (pt & pp* **dealt**) (**a**) *Cards* dar (**to** a) (**b**) **to d. sb a blow** asestarle un golpe a algn

▸ **deal in** *vt insep (goods)* comerciar en, tratar en; *(drugs)* traficar con

▸ **deal out** *vt sep* repartir

▸ **deal with** *vt insep (firm, person)* tratar con; *(subject, problem)* abordar, ocuparse de; *(in book etc)* tratar de

dealer ['diːlə(r)] *n* (**a**) *Com (in goods)* comerciante *mf*; *(in drugs)* traficante *mf* (**b**) *Cards* repartidor(a) *m,f*

dealings ['diːlɪŋz] *npl* (**a**) *(relations)* trato *m* (**b**) *Com* negocios *mpl*

dealt [delt] *pt & pp of* **deal**

dear [dɪə(r)] **1** *adj* (**a**) *(loved)* querido(a); **D. Andrew** *(in letter)* Querido Andrew; *Fml* **D. Madam** Estimada señora; *Fml* **D. Sir(s)** Muy señor(es) mío(s) (**b**) *(expensive)* caro(a) **2** *n* querido(a) *m,f*; **my d.** mi vida

3 *interj* **oh d.!, d. me!** *(surprise)* ¡caramba!; *(disappointment)* ¡qué pena!

dearly [dɪəlɪ] *adv* muchísimo; *Fig* **he paid d. for his mistake** su error le costó caro

death [deθ] *n* muerte *f*; *Fml* fallecimiento *m*; *Fam* **to be bored to d.** aburrirse como una ostra; *Fam* **to be scared to d.** estar muerto(a) de miedo; *Fam Fig* **to be sick to d. of** estar hasta la coronilla de; **d. certificate** certificado *m* de defunción; **d. penalty, d. sentence** pena *f* de muerte

debatable [dɪ'beɪtəbəl] *adj* discutible

debate [dɪ'beɪt] **1** *n* debate *m*; **a heated d.** una discusión acalorada

2 *vt* (**a**) *(discuss)* discutir (**b**) *(wonder about)* dar vueltas a

3 *vi* discutir

debit ['debɪt] **1** *n* débito *m*; **d. balance** saldo negativo **2** *vt* **d. Mr Jones with £20** cargar la suma de 20 libras en la cuenta del Sr. Jones

debris ['debriː, 'deɪbriː] *n sing* escombros *mpl*

debt [det] *n* deuda *f*; **to be deeply in d.** estar cargado(a) de deudas; *Fig* **to be in sb's d.** estar en deuda con algn

debtor ['detə(r)] *n* deudor(a) *m,f*

debut ['debjuː, 'deɪbjuː] *n* debut *m*; **to make one's d.** debutar

decade [de'keɪd, 'dekeɪd] *n* decenio *m*, década *f*

decadent ['dekədənt] *adj* decadente

decaffeinated [diː'kæfɪneɪtɪd] *adj* descafeinado(a)

decay [dɪ'keɪ] **1** *n (of food, body)* descomposición *f*; *(of teeth)* caries *f inv*; *(of buildings)* desmoronamiento *m*; *Fig* decadencia *f* **2** *vi* descomponerse; *(teeth)* cariarse; *(building)* deteriorarse; *Fig* corromperse

deceased [dɪ'siːst] *adj Fml* difunto(a), fallecido(a)

deceit [dɪ'siːt] *n* (**a**) *(dishonesty)* falta *f*

de honradez, falsedad f (**b**) (trick) engaño m, mentira f

deceitful [dɪˈsiːtʊl] adj falso(a)

deceive [dɪˈsiːv] vt (mislead) engañar; (lie to) mentir

December [dɪˈsembə(r)] n diciembre m

decency [ˈdiːsənsɪ] n decencia f; (modesty) pudor m; (morality) moralidad f

decent [ˈdiːsənt] adj decente; (person) honrado(a); Fam (kind) simpático(a)

deception [dɪˈsepʃən] n engaño m

deceptive [dɪˈseptɪv] adj engañoso(a)

decide [dɪˈsaɪd] **1** vt (**a**) decidir; **to d. to do sth** decidir hacer algo (**b**) (matter, question) resolver, determinar **2** vi (reach decision) decidirse; **to d. against sth** decidirse en contra de algo

▶ **decide on** vt insep (choose) optar por

decimal [ˈdesɪməl] **1** adj decimal; **d. point** coma f (de fracción decimal) **2** n decimal m

decipher [dɪˈsaɪfə(r)] vt descifrar

decision [dɪˈsɪʒən] n (**a**) decisión f; Jur fallo m; **to come to a d.** llegar a una decisión; **to make a d.** tomar una decisión (**b**) (resolution) resolución f

decisive [dɪˈsaɪsɪv] adj (**a**) (resolute) decidido(a), resuelto(a) (**b**) (conclusive) decisivo(a)

deck [dek] **1** n (**a**) (of ship) cubierta f; **d. chair** tumbona f (**b**) (of bus) piso m; **top d.** piso de arriba (**c**) esp US (of cards) baraja f (**d**) (of record player) plato m **2** vt **to d. out** adornar

declaration [dekləˈreɪʃən] n declaración f

declare [dɪˈkleə(r)] vt declarar; (winner, innocence) proclamar; (decision) manifestar

decline [dɪˈklaɪn] **1** n (**a**) (decrease) disminución f (**b**) (deterioration) deterioro m; (of health) empeoramiento m; **to fall into d.** empezar a decaer **2** vi (**a**) (decrease) disminuir; (amount) bajar; (business) decaer (**b**) (deteriorate) deteriorarse; (health) empeorar (**c**) (refuse) negarse

3 vt (**a**) (refuse) rechazar (**b**) Ling declinar

décor [ˈdeɪkɔː(r)] n decoración f; Th decorado m

decorate [ˈdekəreɪt] vt (**a**) (adorn) decorar, adornar (**with** con) (**b**) (paint) pintar; (wallpaper) empapelar (**c**) (honour) condecorar

decoration [dekəˈreɪʃən] n (**a**) (decor) decoración f; **Christmas decorations** adornos navideños (**b**) (medal) condecoración f

decorative [ˈdekərətɪv] adj decorativo(a)

decrease 1 n [ˈdiːkriːs] disminución f; (in speed, size, price) reducción f **2** vi [dɪˈkriːs] disminuir; (strength) menguar; (price, temperature) bajar; (speed, size) reducir **3** vt [dɪˈkriːs] disminuir, reducir; (price, temperature) bajar

decree [dɪˈkriː] **1** n (**a**) Pol, Rel decreto m (**b**) esp US Jur sentencia f; **d. absolute** sentencia definitiva de divorcio; **d. nisi** sentencia provisional de divorcio **2** vt Pol, Rel decretar, pronunciar

decrepit [dɪˈkrepɪt] adj decrépito(a)

dedicate [ˈdedɪkeɪt] vt consagrar, dedicar

dedicated [ˈdedɪkeɪtɪd] adj ardiente; **d. to** entregado(a) a

dedication [dedɪˈkeɪʃən] n (act) dedicación f; (commitment) entrega f; (in book) dedicatoria f

deduce [dɪˈdjuːs] vt deducir (**from** de)

deduct [dɪˈdʌkt] vt descontar (**from** de)

deduction [dɪˈdʌkʃən] n (**a**) (conclusion) conclusión f (**b**) (subtraction) descuento m

deed [diːd] n (**a**) (act) acto m; (feat) hazaña f (**b**) Jur escritura f; **title deeds** título m de propiedad

deep [diːp] **1** adj (**a**) profundo(a); (breath, sigh) hondo(a); **it's 10 m d.** tiene 10 m de profundidad (**b**) (voice) grave (**c**) (colour) oscuro(a) (**d**) (serious) grave **2** adv **to be d. in thought** estar absorto(a); **to look d.**

into sb's eyes penetrar a algn con la mirada

deepen ['di:pən] **1** *vt (well)* profundizar, ahondar; *Fig (knowledge)* aumentar **2** *vi (river etc)* hacerse más hondo *or* profundo; *Fig (knowledge)* aumentar; *(colour, emotion)* intensificarse; *(sound, voice)* hacerse más grave

deep-freeze [di:p'fri:z] **1** *n* congelador *m* **2** *vt* congelar

deeply ['di:plɪ] *adv* profundamente; *(breathe)* hondo; **to be d. in debt** estar cargado(a) de deudas

deer [dɪə(r)] *n inv* ciervo *m*

deface [dɪ'feɪs] *vt (book, poster)* garabatear

default [dɪ'fɔ:lt] **1** *vi* (**a**) *(not act)* faltar a sus compromisos (**b**) *Jur* estar en rebeldía (**c**) *(not pay)* suspender pagos **2** *n* (**a**) *(failure to act)* omisión *f* (**b**) *(failure to pay)* incumplimiento *m* de pago (**c**) *Jur* rebeldía *f*; **in d. of** a falta de; **to win by d.** ganar por incomparecencia del adversario

defeat [dɪ'fi:t] **1** *vt* (**a**) derrotar, vencer; *(motion)* rechazar (**b**) *Fig* frustrar **2** *n* (**a**) *(of army, team)* derrota *f*; *(of motion)* rechazo *m* (**b**) *Fig* fracaso *m*

defect **1** *n* ['di:fekt] defecto *m*; *(flaw)* desperfecto *m* **2** *vi* [dɪ'fekt] desertar (**from** de); *(from country)* huir

defective [dɪ'fektɪv] *adj (faulty)* defectuoso(a); *(flawed)* con desperfectos; *(lacking)* incompleto(a)

defence [dɪ'fens] *n* (**a**) *also Pol* defensa *f*; **to come to sb's d.** salir en defensa de algn (**b**) *usu sing Jur* defensa *f* (**c**) *Sport* [*US* 'di:fens] **the d.** la defensa

defend [dɪ'fend] *vt* defender

defendant [dɪ'fendənt] *n Jur* acusado(a) *m,f*

defender [dɪ'fendə(r)] *n* defensor(a) *m,f*; *Sport* defensa *mf*

defense [dɪ'fens, 'di:fens] *n US* = **defence**

defensive [dɪ'fensɪv] **1** *adj* defensivo(a) **2** *n* **to be on the d.** estar a la defensiva

defer[1] [dɪ'fɜ:(r)] *vt* aplazar, retrasar

defer[2] [dɪ'fɜ:(r)] *vi* **to d. to** deferir a

defiance [dɪ'faɪəns] *n* (**a**) *(challenge)* desafío *m*; **in d. of** a despecho de (**b**) *(resistance)* resistencia *f*

defiant [dɪ'faɪənt] *adj (challenging)* desafiante; *(bold)* insolente

deficiency [dɪ'fɪʃənsɪ] *n* (**a**) *(lack)* falta *f*, carencia *f* (**b**) *(shortcoming)* defecto *m*

deficient [dɪ'fɪʃənt] *adj* deficiente; **to be d. in sth** carecer de algo

deficit ['defɪsɪt] *n* déficit *m*

define [dɪ'faɪn] *vt* definir; *(duties, powers)* delimitar

definite ['defɪnɪt] *adj* (**a**) *(clear)* claro(a); *(progress)* notable (**b**) *(date, place)* determinado(a); **is it d.?** ¿es seguro?

definitely ['defɪnɪtlɪ] **1** *adv* sin duda; **he was d. drunk** no cabe duda de que estaba borracho **2** *interj* ¡desde luego!

definition [defɪ'nɪʃən] *n* definición *f*; **by d.** por definición

deflect [dɪ'flekt] *vt* desviar

deformed [dɪ'fɔ:md] *adj* deforme

defraud [dɪ'frɔ:d] *vt* estafar

defrost [di:'frɒst] *vt* (**a**) *(freezer, food)* descongelar (**b**) *US (windscreen)* desempañar

defy [dɪ'faɪ] *vt* (**a**) *(person)* desafiar; *(law, order)* contravenir (**b**) *(challenge)* retar, desafiar

degenerate **1** *vi* [dɪ'dʒenəreɪt] degenerar (**into** en) **2** *adj & n* [dɪ'dʒenərɪt] degenerado(a) *(m,f)*

degrading [dɪ'greɪdɪŋ] *adj* degradante

degree [dɪ'gri:] *n* (**a**) grado *m*; **to some d.** hasta cierto punto (**b**) *(stage)* etapa *f*; **by degrees** poco a poco (**c**) *(qualification)* título *m*; *(doctorate)* doctorado *m*; **to have a d. in science** ser licenciado(a) en ciencias

dehydrated [di:haɪ'dreɪtɪd] *adj (person)* deshidratado(a); *(vegetables)* seco(a)

dejected [dɪ'dʒektɪd] *adj* desalentado(a), abatido(a)

delay [dɪˈleɪ] **1** vt (**a**) *(flight, train)* retrasar; *(person)* entretener; **delayed action** acción retardada (**b**) *(postpone)* aplazar
2 vi **don't d.** no lo deje para más tarde
3 n retraso m, *Am* demora f

delegate 1 n [ˈdelɪgɪt] delegado(a) m,f **2** vt [ˈdelɪgeɪt] delegar (**to** en); **to d. sb to do sth** encargar a algn que haga algo

delegation [delɪˈgeɪʃən] n delegación f

delete [dɪˈliːt] vt tachar, suprimir

deliberate 1 adj [dɪˈlɪbərɪt] *(intentional)* deliberado(a), intencionado(a); *(studied)* premeditado(a); *(careful)* prudente; *(unhurried)* pausado(a)
2 vt [dɪˈlɪbəreɪt] deliberar
3 vi deliberar (**on** or **about** sobre)

deliberately [dɪˈlɪbərɪtlɪ] adv *(intentionally)* a propósito; *(unhurriedly)* pausadamente

delicacy [ˈdelɪkəsɪ] n (**a**) delicadeza f (**b**) *(food)* manjar m (exquisito)

delicate [ˈdelɪkɪt] adj delicado(a); *(handiwork)* fino(a); *(instrument)* sensible; *(flavour)* sutil

delicatessen [delɪkəˈtesən] n *(shop)* = tienda de ultramarinos *or Am* enlatados de calidad

delicious [dɪˈlɪʃəs] adj delicioso(a)

delight [dɪˈlaɪt] **1** n (**a**) *(pleasure)* placer m; **he took d. in it** le encantó (**b**) *(source of pleasure)* encanto m, delicia f **2** vt encantar

delighted [dɪˈlaɪtɪd] adj encantado(a); *(smile)* de alegría; **I'm d. to see you** me alegro mucho de verte

delightful [dɪˈlaɪtfʊl] adj encantador(a); *(view, person)* muy agradable; *(meal, weather)* delicioso(a)

delinquent [dɪˈlɪŋkwənt] adj & n delincuente *(mf)*

delirious [dɪˈlɪrɪəs] adj delirante

deliver [dɪˈlɪvə(r)] vt (**a**) *(goods)* repartir, entregar; *(message)* dar; *(order)* despachar (**b**) *(blow)* asestar; *(speech, verdict)* pronunciar (**c**) *Med* ayudar en el nacimiento de (**d**) *Fml (rescue)* liberar

delivery [dɪˈlɪvərɪ] n (**a**) *(of goods)* reparto m, entrega f (**b**) *(of speech)* declamación f (**c**) *(of baby)* parto m

delude [dɪˈluːd] vt engañar; **don't d. yourself** no te hagas ilusiones

delusion [dɪˈluːʒən] n (**a**) *(state, act)* engaño m (**b**) *(false belief)* ilusión f (vana); **delusions of grandeur** delirios mpl de grandeza

de luxe [dəˈlʌks, dəˈlʊks] adj de lujo inv

demand [dɪˈmɑːnd] **1** n (**a**) solicitud f; *(for pay rise, rights)* reclamación f; *(need)* necesidad f; **on d.** a petición (**b**) *(claim)* exigencia f; **to be in d.** ser solicitado(a) (**c**) *Econ* demanda f **2** vt (**a**) exigir; *(rights)* reclamar; **to d. that …** insistir en que … (+ subj) (**b**) *(need)* requerir

demanding [dɪˈmɑːndɪŋ] adj (**a**) *(person)* exigente (**b**) *(job)* agotador(a)

demeaning [dɪˈmiːnɪŋ] adj *Fml* humillante

demo [ˈdeməʊ] n *Fam* manifestación f; **d. tape** maqueta f

democracy [dɪˈmɒkrəsɪ] n democracia f

democratic [deməˈkrætɪk] adj democrático(a); *US Pol* **D. party** partido m demócrata

demolish [dɪˈmɒlɪʃ] vt *(building)* derribar, demoler; *Fig (theory, proposal)* echar por tierra

demon [ˈdiːmən] n demonio m

demonstrate [ˈdemənstreɪt] **1** vt demostrar **2** vi *Pol* manifestarse

demonstration [demənˈstreɪʃən] n (**a**) *(proof)* demostración f, prueba f (**b**) *(explanation)* explicación f (**c**) *Pol* manifestación f

demonstrator [ˈdemənstreɪtə(r)] n manifestante mf

demoralize [dɪˈmɒrəlaɪz] vt desmoralizar

den [den] n (**a**) *(of animal)* guarida f (**b**) *Fam (study)* estudio m

denial [dɪˈnaɪəl] n (**a**) *(of charge)* desmentido m (**b**) *(of rights)* denegación f; *(of request)* negativa f

denim [ˈdenɪm] n tela f vaquera;

denims *(jeans)* vaqueros *mpl, Andes, Ven* bluyíns *nmpl, Méx* pantalones *mpl* de mezclilla; **d. skirt/shirt** falda *f*/camisa *f* vaquera

Denmark ['denmɑːk] *n* Dinamarca

denomination [dɪnɒmɪ'neɪʃən] *n* (**a**) *Rel* confesión *f* (**b**) *Fin (of coins)* valor *m*

denounce [dɪ'naʊns] *vt* denunciar; *(criticize)* censurar

dense [dens] *adj* (**a**) denso(a); *(crowd)* numeroso(a) (**b**) *Fam (stupid)* torpe

dent [dent] **1** *n* abolladura *f* **2** *vt (car)* abollar

dental ['dentəl] *adj* dental; **d. floss** hilo *m* dental; **d. surgeon** odontólogo(a) *m,f;* **d. surgery** *(place)* clínica *f* dental; *(treatment)* cirugía *f* dental

dentist ['dentɪst] *n* dentista *mf*

denture ['dentʃə(r)] *n (usu pl)* dentadura postiza

deny [dɪ'naɪ] *vt* (**a**) *(repudiate)* negar; *(rumour, report)* desmentir; *(charge)* rechazar (**b**) *(refuse)* negar

deodorant [diː'əʊdərənt] *n* desodorante *m*

depart [dɪ'pɑːt] *vi* marcharse, irse; *Fig (from subject)* desviarse (**from** de)

department [dɪ'pɑːtmənt] *n* sección *f; (in university)* departamento *m; (in government)* ministerio *m;* **d. store** grandes almacenes *mpl; US* **D. of the Interior** Ministerio *m* del Interior

departure [dɪ'pɑːtʃə(r)] *n* partida *f; Av, Rail* salida *f; Av* **d. lounge** sala *f* de embarque

depend [dɪ'pend] **1** *vi (rely)* fiarse (**on** or **upon** de) **2** *v impers (be determined by)* depender (**on** or **upon** de); **it depends on the weather** según el tiempo que haga; **that depends** según

dependant [dɪ'pendənt] *n* dependiente *mf*

dependent [dɪ'pendənt] **1** *adj* dependiente; **to be d. on sth** depender de algo **2** *n US* = **dependant**

depict [dɪ'pɪkt] *vt Art* representar; *Fig* describir

deplorable [dɪ'plɔːrəbəl] *adj* lamentable

deploy [dɪ'plɔɪ] *vt Mil* desplegar; *Fig* utilizar

deport [dɪ'pɔːt] *vt* expulsar (**from** de; **to** a)

deposit [dɪ'pɒzɪt] **1** *n* (**a**) sedimento *m; Min* yacimiento *m; (in wine)* poso *m* (**b**) *(in bank)* depósito *m; Br* **d. account** cuenta *f* de ahorros (**c**) *(returnable)* señal *f,* fianza *f; (first payment)* entrega *f* inicial, *Esp* entrada *f* **2** *vt* depositar; *(in bank account) Esp* ingresar, *Am* depositar

depot [*Br* 'depəʊ, *US* 'diːpəʊ] *n* almacén *m; Mil* depósito *m; Br (for keeping and repairing buses)* cochera *f; US (bus station)* estación *f* de autobuses, *CAm, Méx* central *f* camionera

depress [dɪ'pres] *vt* (**a**) *(person)* deprimir (**b**) *Econ (profits)* reducir; *(trade)* dificultar (**c**) *Fml (switch, lever etc)* presionar; *(clutch, piano pedal)* pisar

depressed [dɪ'prest] *adj* (**a**) *(person)* deprimido(a); **to get d.** deprimirse (**b**) *(market)* en crisis (**c**) *(surface)* hundido(a)

depression [dɪ'preʃən] *n* depresión *f*

deprive [dɪ'praɪv] *vt* privar (**of** de)

deprived [dɪ'praɪvd] *adj* necesitado(a)

depth [depθ] *n* (**a**) profundidad *f* (**b**) *Fig (of emotion)* intensidad *f; (of thought)* complejidad *f;* **to be in the depths of despair** estar completamente desesperado(a); **in d.** a fondo

deputy ['depjʊtɪ] *n* (**a**) *(substitute)* suplente *mf;* **d. chairman** vicepresidente *m;* **d. head** subdirector(a) *m,f* (**b**) *Pol* diputado(a) *m,f*

derail [dɪ'reɪl] *vt* hacer descarrilar

derelict ['derɪlɪkt] *adj* abandonado(a), en ruinas

derive [dɪ'raɪv] **1** *vt* sacar **2** *vi (word)* derivarse (**from** de); *(skill)* provenir (**from** de)

descend [dɪ'send] **1** *vi* descender; **to d. from** *(be related to)* descender de **2** *vt (stairs)* bajar

descendant [dɪ'sendənt] *n* descendiente *mf*

descent [dɪ'sent] n (**a**) descenso m (**b**) *(slope)* declive m (**c**) *(ancestry)* ascendencia f

describe [dɪ'skraɪb] vt (**a**) describir (**b**) *(circle)* trazar

description [dɪ'skrɪpʃən] n (**a**) descripción f; **to defy d.** superar la descripción (**b**) *(type)* clase f

desert[1] ['dezət] n desierto m

desert[2] [dɪ'zɜ:t] **1** vt *(place, family)* abandonar **2** vi Mil desertar (**from** de)

deserted [dɪ'zɜ:tɪd] adj desierto(a)

deserve [dɪ'zɜ:v] vt merecer, merecerse, Am ameritar

deserving [dɪ'zɜ:vɪŋ] adj *(person)* de valía; *(cause)* meritorio(a)

design [dɪ'zaɪn] **1** n (**a**) *(of car, furniture, clothes)* diseño m (**b**) *(drawing, blueprint)* plano m (**c**) *(layout)* disposición f (**d**) *(pattern)* dibujo m (**e**) Fig *(scheme)* intención f; **by d.** a propósito; Fam **to have designs on** tener puestas las miras en **2** vt diseñar

designate 1 vt ['dezɪgneɪt] (**a**) *(appoint)* designar, nombrar (**b**) Fml *(boundary)* señalar **2** adj ['dezɪgnɪt] designado(a)

designer [dɪ'zaɪnə(r)] n Art diseñador(a) m,f; **d. jeans** pantalones mpl de marca

desirable [dɪ'zaɪərəbəl] adj deseable; *(asset, offer)* atractivo(a)

desire [dɪ'zaɪə(r)] **1** n deseo m; **I feel no d. to go** no me Esp apetece or Carib, Col, Méx provoca nada ir, no tengo nada de ganas de ir **2** vt desear

desk [desk] n *(in school)* pupitre m; *(in office)* escritorio m; US **d. clerk** recepcionista mf; **d. job** trabajo m de oficina; **news d.** redacción f; **reception d.** recepción f

desktop ['desktɒp] n Comput escritorio m; **d. computer** Esp ordenador m or Am computadora de sobremesa; **d. publishing** autoedición f

desolate ['desəlɪt] adj (**a**) *(uninhabited)* desierto(a); *(barren)* yermo(a) (**b**) *(person)* desconsolado(a)

despair [dɪ'speə(r)] **1** n desesperación

f; **to drive sb to d.** desesperar a algn **2** vi desesperár(se) (**of** de)

despatch [dɪ'spætʃ] n & vt = **dispatch**

desperate ['despərɪt] adj (**a**) desesperado(a); *(struggle)* encarnizado(a) (**b**) *(need)* apremiante

desperately ['despərɪtlɪ] adv *(recklessly)* desesperadamente; *(struggle)* encarnizadamente; *(ill)* gravemente; *(in love)* locamente; *(difficult)* sumamente

despicable [dɪ'spɪkəbəl] adj despreciable; *(behaviour)* indigno(a)

despise [dɪ'spaɪz] vt despreciar, menospreciar

despite [dɪ'spaɪt] prep Fml a pesar de

dessert [dɪ'zɜ:t] n postre m; **d. wine** vino m dulce

dessertspoon [dɪ'zɜ:tspu:n] n (**a**) cuchara f de postre (**b**) **dessertspoon-(ful)** *(measure)* cucharada f de postre

destination [destɪ'neɪʃən] n destino m

destined ['destɪnd] adj (**a**) **d. to fail** condenado(a) al fracaso (**b**) *(bound)* con destino (**for** a)

destiny ['destɪnɪ] n destino m

destitute ['destɪtju:t] adj indigente

destroy [dɪ'strɔɪ] vt destruir; *(vehicle, old furniture)* destrozar

destruction [dɪ'strʌkʃən] n destrucción f; Fig ruina f

destructive [dɪ'strʌktɪv] adj *(gale etc)* destructor(a); *(tendency, criticism)* destructivo(a)

detach [dɪ'tætʃ] vt *(remove)* separar

detachable [dɪ'tætʃəbəl] adj separable (**from** de)

detached [dɪ'tætʃt] adj (**a**) *(separated)* separado(a); esp Br **d. house** casa f independiente (**b**) *(impartial)* objetivo(a)

detail [Br 'di:teɪl, US dɪ'teɪl] **1** n (**a**) detalle m, pormenor m; **without going into detail(s)** sin entrar en detalles; **details** *(information)* información f (**b**) Mil destacamento m **2** vt (**a**) *(list)* detallar, enumerar (**b**) Mil *(appoint)* destacar

detailed ['di:teɪld] *adj* detallado(a), minucioso(a)

detain [dɪ'teɪn] *vt* (**a**) *Jur* detener (**b**) *(delay)* retener

detect [dɪ'tekt] *vt* (**a**) *(error, movement)* advertir; *(difference)* notar; *(smell, sound)* percibir (**b**) *(discover)* descubrir; *(enemy ship)* detectar; *(position)* localizar

detective [dɪ'tektɪv] *n* detective *mf*; **d. story** novela policíaca

detector [dɪ'tektə(r)] *n* aparato *m* detector

detention [dɪ'tenʃən] *n (of suspect etc)* detención *f*, arresto *m*; *Educ* **to get d.** quedarse castigado(a)

deter [dɪ'tɜ:(r)] *vt (dissuade)* disuadir (**from** de); *(stop)* impedir

detergent [dɪ'tɜ:dʒənt] *n* detergente *m*

deteriorate [dɪ'tɪərɪəreɪt] *vi* deteriorarse

determine [dɪ'tɜ:mɪn] *vt* determinar

determined [dɪ'tɜ:mɪnd] *adj (person)* decidido(a); *(effort)* enérgico(a)

deterrent [dɪ'terənt] **1** *adj* disuasivo(a) **2** *n* fuerza disuasoria

detest [dɪ'test] *vt* detestar, odiar

detonate ['detəneɪt] *vt & vi* detonar

detour ['di:tʊə(r)] *n* desvío *m*

detract [dɪ'trækt] *vi* quitar mérito (**from** a)

devaluation [di:væljʊ:'eɪʃən] *n* devaluación *f*

devastate ['devəsteɪt] *vt (city, area)* asolar; *Fig (person)* desolar

devastating ['devəsteɪtɪŋ] *adj (fire)* devastador(a); *(wind, flood)* arrollador(a)

develop [dɪ'veləp] **1** *vt* (**a**) desarrollar; *(trade)* fomentar; *(skill)* perfeccionar; *(plan)* elaborar; *(habit)* contraer; *(interest)* mostrar (**b**) *(natural resources)* aprovechar; *Constr (site)* urbanizar (**c**) *Phot* revelar **2** *vi* (**a**) *(body, industry)* desarrollarse; *(system)* perfeccionarse; *(interest)* crecer (**b**) *(appear)* crearse; *(evolve)* evolucionar

developer [dɪ'veləpə(r)] *n* (**property**) **d.** inmobiliaria *f*

development [dɪ'veləpmənt] *n* (**a**) desarrollo *m*; *(of trade)* fomento *m*; *(of skill)* perfección *f*; *(of character)* formación *f* (**b**) *(advance)* avance *m* (**c**) **there are no new developments** no hay ninguna novedad (**d**) *(exploitation)* explotación *f* (**e**) *Constr* urbanización *f*

deviate ['di:vɪeɪt] *vi* desviarse (**from** de)

device [dɪ'vaɪs] *n* (**a**) aparato *m*; *(mechanism)* mecanismo *m* (**b**) *(trick, scheme)* ardid *m*

devil ['devəl] *n* diablo *m*, demonio *m*; **d.'s advocate** abogado(a) *m,f* del diablo; *Fam* **where the d. did you put it?** ¿dónde demonios lo pusiste?; **you lucky d.!** ¡vaya suerte que tienes!

devious ['di:vɪəs] *adj* (**a**) *(winding)* tortuoso(a) (**b**) *esp Pej (person)* taimado(a)

devise [dɪ'vaɪz] *vt* idear, concebir

devoid [dɪ'vɔɪd] *adj* desprovisto(a) (**of** de)

devote [dɪ'vəʊt] *vt* dedicar; **she devoted her life to helping the poor** consagró su vida a la ayuda de los pobres

devoted [dɪ'vəʊtɪd] *adj* fiel, leal (**to** a)

devotion [dɪ'vəʊʃən] *n* devoción *f*; *(to cause)* dedicación *f*

devour [dɪ'vaʊə(r)] *vt* devorar

devout [dɪ'vaʊt] *adj* devoto(a)

dew [dju:] *n* rocío *m*

diabetes [daɪə'bi:ti:z, daɪə'bi:tɪs] *n* diabetes *f*

diabetic [daɪə'betɪk] *adj & n* diabético(a) *(m,f)*

diagnose ['daɪəgnəʊz] *vt* diagnosticar

diagnosis [daɪəg'nəʊsɪs] *n* (*pl* **diagnoses** [daɪəg'nəʊsi:z]) diagnóstico *m*

diagonal [daɪ'ægənəl] *adj & n* diagonal *(f)*

diagonally [daɪ'ægənəlɪ] *adv* en diagonal, diagonalmente

diagram ['daɪəgræm] *n* diagrama *m*; *(of process, system)* esquema *m*; *(of workings)* gráfico *m*

dial ['daɪəl, daɪl] **1** n *(of clock)* esfera f; *(of radio)* cuadrante m; *(of telephone)* disco m; *(of machine)* botón m selector **2** vt & vi *Tel* marcar, *Andes, CSur* discar; *Br* **dialling** or *US* **d. code** prefijo m; *Br* **dialling** or *US* **d. tone** señal f de marcar or *Andes, CSur* discar

dialect ['daɪəlekt] n dialecto m

dialogue, *US* **dialog** ['daɪəlɒg] n diálogo m

diameter [daɪ'æmɪtə(r)] n diámetro m

diamond ['daɪəmənd] n (**a**) diamante m (**b**) *(shape)* rombo m

diaper ['daɪəpə(r)] n *US* pañal m

diarrhoea, *US* **diarrhea** [daɪə'rɪə] n diarrea f

diary ['daɪərɪ] n (**a**) diario m; **to keep a d.** llevar un diario (**b**) *Br (for appointments)* agenda f

dice [daɪs] **1** n *(pl* **dice)** dado m **2** vt *Culin* cortar en cuadritos

dictate 1 vt [dɪk'teɪt] *(letter, order)* dictar
 2 vi [dɪk'teɪt] **to d. to sb** dar órdenes a algn
 3 n ['dɪkteɪt] *Fig* **the dictates of conscience** los dictados de la conciencia

dictation [dɪk'teɪʃən] n dictado m

dictator [dɪk'teɪtə(r)] n dictador(a) m,f

dictionary ['dɪkʃənərɪ] n diccionario m

did [dɪd] pt of **do**

die [daɪ] vi morir, morirse; *Fam Fig* **to be dying for sth/to do sth** morirse por algo/de ganas de hacer algo

▸ **die away** vi desvanecerse

▸ **die down** vi *(fire)* extinguirse; *(wind)* amainar; *(noise, excitement)* disminuir

▸ **die off** vi morir uno por uno

▸ **die out** vi extinguirse

diesel ['diːzəl] n (**a**) *(oil)* gasoil m; **d. engine** motor m diesel (**b**) *Fam (vehicle)* vehículo m diesel

diet ['daɪət] **1** n *(normal food)* dieta f; *(selected food)* régimen m; **to be on a d.** estar a régimen **2** vi estar a régimen

differ ['dɪfə(r)] vi *(be unlike)* ser distinto(a); *(disagree)* discrepar

difference ['dɪfərəns] n (**a**) *(dissimilarity)* diferencia f; **it makes no d. (to me)** (me) da igual; **what d. does it make?** ¿qué más da? (**b**) *(disagreement)* desacuerdo m

different ['dɪfərənt] adj diferente, distinto(a); **you look d.** pareces otro(a)

differentiate [dɪfə'renʃɪeɪt] **1** vt distinguir, diferenciar (**from** de) **2** vi distinguir (**between** entre)

differently ['dɪfərəntlɪ] adv de otra manera

difficult ['dɪfɪkəlt] adj difícil

difficulty ['dɪfɪkəltɪ] n dificultad f; *(problem)* problema m; **to be in difficulties** estar en un apuro

dig [dɪg] *(pt & pp* **dug) 1** n (**a**) *(poke)* codazo m (**b**) *Fam (gibe)* pulla f
 2 vt (**a**) *(earth)* cavar; *(tunnel)* excavar (**b**) *Fam Fig* **to d. one's heels in** mantenerse en sus trece
 3 vi *(person)* cavar; *(animal)* escarbar

▸ **dig in** vi *Mil* atrincherarse

▸ **dig out** vt sep *Fig (old suit)* sacar; *(information)* descubrir

▸ **dig up** vt sep *(weeds)* arrancar; *(buried object)* desenterrar; *(road)* levantar; *Fig* sacar a relucir

digest 1 n ['daɪdʒest] *(summary)* resumen m **2** vt [dɪ'dʒest] *(food)* digerir; *Fig (facts)* asimilar

digestion [dɪ'dʒestʃən] n digestión f

digit ['dɪdʒɪt] n (**a**) *Math* dígito m (**b**) *Fml Anat* dedo m

digital ['dɪdʒɪtəl] adj digital; **d. television** televisión f digital

dignified ['dɪgnɪfaɪd] adj *(manner)* solemne, serio(a); *(appearance)* majestuoso(a)

dignity ['dɪgnɪtɪ] n dignidad f

dilapidated [dɪ'læpɪdeɪtɪd] adj en mal estado

dilemma [dɪ'lemə, daɪ'lemə] n dilema m

diligent ['dɪlɪdʒənt] adj *(worker)* diligente; *(inquiries, search)* esmerado(a)

dilute [daɪ'luːt] **1** vt diluir; *(wine, milk)* aguar; *Fig (effect, influence)* atenuar **2** vi diluirse

dim [dɪm] **1** adj (**dimmer, dimmest**) (**a**) *(light)* débil, tenue; *(room)* oscuro(a); *(outline)* borroso(a); *(eyesight)* defectuoso(a); *Fig (memory)* vago(a); *Fig (future)* sombrío(a) (**b**) *Fam (stupid)* tonto, corto de alcances, *Am* sonso(a)
 2 vt *(light)* bajar
 3 vi *(light)* bajarse; *(sight)* nublarse; *Fig (joy)* extinguirse

dime [daɪm] n *US* moneda f de diez centavos

dimension [daɪ'menʃən] n dimensión f

diminish [dɪ'mɪnɪʃ] vt & vi disminuir

dimple ['dɪmpəl] n hoyuelo m

din [dɪn] n *(of crowd)* alboroto m; *(of machinery)* estruendo m

dine [daɪn] vi *Fml* cenar; **to d. out** cenar fuera

diner ['daɪnə(r)] n (**a**) *(person)* comensal mf (**b**) *US (restaurant)* restaurante barato

dinghy ['dɪŋɪ] n bote m; (**rubber**) **d.** bote neumático

dingy ['dɪndʒɪ] adj (**dingier, dingiest**) (**a**) *(dark)* oscuro(a) (**b**) *(dirty)* sucio(a) (**c**) *(colour)* desteñido(a)

dining car ['daɪnɪŋkɑː(r)] n vagón m restaurante

dining room ['daɪnɪŋruːm] n comedor m

dinner ['dɪnə(r)] n *(at midday)* comida f; *(in evening)* cena f; **d. jacket** smoking m; **d. service** vajilla f; **d. table** mesa f de comedor

dinosaur ['daɪnəsɔː(r)] n dinosaurio m

dip [dɪp] **1** n (**a**) *Fam (bathe)* chapuzón m (**b**) *(of road)* pendiente f; *(in ground)* depresión f (**c**) *Culin* salsa f
 2 vt (**a**) bañar; *(spoon, hand)* meter (**b**) *Br Aut* **to d. one's headlights** poner las luces de cruce
 3 vi *(road)* bajar
 ▶ **dip into** vt insep (**a**) *(savings)* echar mano de (**b**) *(book)* hojear

diploma [dɪ'pləʊmə] n diploma m

diplomat ['dɪpləmæt] n diplomático(a) m,f

diplomatic [dɪplə'mætɪk] adj diplomático(a)

dire ['daɪə(r)] adj *(urgent)* extremo(a); *(serious)* grave

direct [dɪ'rekt, daɪ'rekt] **1** adj (**a**) directo(a); **d. current** corriente continua (**b**) **the d. opposite** todo lo contrario
 2 adv directamente
 3 vt (**a**) dirigir; **can you d. me to a bank?** ¿me puede indicar dónde hay un banco? (**b**) *Fml (order)* mandar

direction [dɪ'rekʃən, daɪ'rekʃən] n (**a**) dirección f; **sense of d.** sentido m de la orientación (**b**) **directions** *(to place)* señas fpl; **directions for use** modo m de empleo (**c**) *Th* puesta f en escena

directly [dɪ'rektlɪ, daɪ'rektlɪ] **1** adv (**a**) *(above etc)* exactamente, justo (**b**) *(speak)* francamente (**c**) *(descend)* directamente (**a**) *(come)* en seguida
 2 conj *Fam* en cuanto

director [dɪ'rektə(r), daɪ'rektə(r)] n director(a) m,f

directory [dɪ'rektərɪ, daɪ'rektərɪ] n *Tel* guía telefónica, *Am* directorio m de teléfonos; **d. enquiries** (servicio m de) información f

dirt [dɜːt] n suciedad f

dirty ['dɜːtɪ] **1** adj (**dirtier, dirtiest**) (**a**) sucio(a) (**b**) **to give sb a d. look** fulminar a algn con la mirada (**c**) *(joke)* verde; *(mind)* pervertido(a); **d. word** palabrota f; **d. old man** viejo m verde
 2 vt ensuciar

disability [dɪsə'bɪlɪtɪ] n incapacidad f, discapacidad f; **d. pension** pensión f por invalidez

disabled [dɪs'eɪbəld] **1** adj minusválido(a) **2** npl **the d.** los minusválidos

disadvantage [dɪsəd'vɑːntɪdʒ] n desventaja f; *(obstacle)* inconveniente m

disagree [dɪsə'griː] vi (**a**) *(differ)* no estar de acuerdo (**with** con); **to d. on** or **over sth** reñir por algo (**b**) *(not* *match)* discrepar (**with** de *or* con) (**c**) garlic disagrees with me el ajo no me sienta bien

disagreeable [dɪsə'griːəbəl] *adj* desagradable

disagreement [dɪsə'griːmənt] *n* (**a**) desacuerdo *m*; *(argument)* riña *f* (**b**) *(non-correspondence)* discrepancia *f*

disappear [dɪsə'pɪə(r)] *vi* desaparecer

disappearance [dɪsə'pɪərəns] *n* desaparición *f*

disappoint [dɪsə'pɔɪnt] *vt (person)* decepcionar, defraudar; *(hope, ambition)* frustrar

disappointing [dɪsə'pɔɪntɪŋ] *adj* decepcionante

disappointment [dɪsə'pɔɪntmənt] *n* decepción *f*

disapproval [dɪsə'pruːvəl] *n* desaprobación *f*

disapprove [dɪsə'pruːv] *vi* **to d. of** desaprobar

disaster [dɪ'zɑːstə(r)] *n* desastre *m*

disastrous [dɪ'zɑːstrəs] *adj* desastroso(a)

disbelief [dɪsbɪ'liːf] *n* incredulidad *f*

disc [dɪsk] *n* disco *m*; *Comput* disquete *m*; **d. jockey** disc-jockey *mf*, pinchadiscos *mf inv*

discard [dɪs'kɑːd] *vt (old things)* deshacerse de; *(plan)* descartar

discern [dɪ'sɜːn] *vt (shape, difference)* percibir; *(truth)* darse cuenta de

discerning [dɪ'sɜːnɪŋ] *adj (person)* perspicaz; *(taste)* refinado(a)

discharge *Fml* **1** *vt* [dɪs'tʃɑːdʒ] *(prisoner)* soltar; *(patient)* dar de alta a; *(soldier)* licenciar; *(employee)* despedir; *(gun)* descargar **2** *n* ['dɪstʃɑːdʒ] (**a**) *(of current, load, gun)* descarga *f*; *(of gases)* escape *m* (**b**) *(of prisoner)* liberación *f*; *(of patient)* alta *f*; *(of soldier)* licencia *f*

disciple [dɪ'saɪpəl] *n* discípulo(a) *m,f*

discipline ['dɪsɪplɪn] **1** *n* disciplina *f* **2** *vt (child)* castigar; *(worker)* sancionar; *(official)* expedientar

disclose [dɪs'kləʊz] *vt* revelar

disco ['dɪskəʊ] *n Fam (abbr disco-theque)* disco *f*

discomfort [dɪs'kʌmfət] *n* (**a**) *(lack of comfort)* incomodidad *f* (**b**) *(pain)* malestar *m* (**c**) *(unease)* inquietud *f*

disconcerting [dɪskən'sɜːtɪŋ] *adj* desconcertante

disconnect [dɪskə'nekt] *vt* desconectar (**from** de); *(gas, electricity)* cortar

discontented [dɪskən'tentɪd] *adj* descontento(a)

discotheque ['dɪskətek] *n* discoteca *f*

discount 1 *n* ['dɪskaʊnt] descuento *m* **2** *vt* [dɪs'kaʊnt] (**a**) *(price)* rebajar (**b**) *(view, suggestion)* descartar

discourage [dɪs'kʌrɪdʒ] *vt (dishearten)* desanimar; *(advances)* rechazar

discover [dɪ'skʌvə(r)] *vt* descubrir; *(missing person, object)* encontrar

discovery [dɪ'skʌvərɪ] *n* descubrimiento *m*

discredit [dɪs'kredɪt] **1** *n* descrédito *m* **2** *vt (person, régime)* desacreditar; *(theory)* poner en duda

discreet [dɪ'skriːt] *adj* discreto(a); *(distance, silence)* prudente; *(hat, house)* modesto(a)

discretion [dɪ'skreʃən] *n* discreción *f*; *(prudence)* prudencia *f*; **at the d. of ...** a juicio de ...

discriminate [dɪ'skrɪmɪneɪt] *vi* discriminar (**between** entre); **to d. against sth/sb** discriminar algo/a algn

discrimination [dɪskrɪmɪ'neɪʃən] *n* (**a**) *(bias)* discriminación *f* (**b**) *(distinction)* diferenciación *f*

discus ['dɪskəs] *n* disco *m (para lanzamientos)*

discuss [dɪ'skʌs] *vt* discutir; *(in writing)* tratar de

discussion [dɪ'skʌʃən] *n* discusión *f*

disdain [dɪs'deɪn] *Fml* **1** *n* desdén *m* **2** *vt* desdeñar

disease [dɪ'ziːz] *n* enfermedad *f*; *Fig* mal *m*

disembark [dɪsɪm'bɑːk] *vt & vi* desembarcar

disfigure [dɪsˈfɪgə(r)] vt desfigurar

disgrace [dɪsˈgreɪs] **1** n (a) *(disfavour)* desgracia f; **to be in d.** estar desacreditado(a); **to fall into d.** caer en desgracia (b) *(shame)* vergüenza f, escándalo m **2** vt deshonrar, desacreditar

disgraceful [dɪsˈgreɪsfʊl] adj vergonzoso(a)

disgruntled [dɪsˈgrʌntəld] adj contrariado(a), disgustado(a)

disguise [dɪsˈgaɪz] **1** n disfraz m; **in d.** disfrazado(a) **2** vt (a) *(person)* disfrazar (**as** de) (b) *(feelings)* disimular

disgust [dɪsˈgʌst] **1** n (a) *(loathing)* repugnancia f, asco m (b) *(strong disapproval)* indignación f **2** vt (a) *(revolt)* repugnar, dar asco a (b) *(offend)* indignar

disgusting [dɪsˈgʌstɪŋ] adj asqueroso(a), repugnante; *(behaviour, state of affairs)* intolerable

dish [dɪʃ] n *(for serving)* fuente f; *(course)* plato m; **to wash** or **do the dishes** fregar los platos

▸ **dish out** vt sep Fam *(food)* servir; *(books, advice)* repartir; **to d. it out (to sb)** *(criticize)* criticar (a algn)

▸ **dish up** vt sep *(meal)* servir

dishcloth [ˈdɪʃklɒθ] n *(for washing)* bayeta f; *(for drying)* paño m (de cocina), CAm secador m, Méx trapón m, RP repasador m

dishevelled, US **disheveled** [dɪˈʃevəld] adj *(hair)* despeinado(a); *(appearance)* desaliñado(a)

dishonest [dɪsˈɒnɪst] adj *(person)* poco honrado(a); *(means)* fraudulento(a)

dishonesty [dɪsˈɒnɪstɪ] n *(of person)* falta f de honradez

dishonourable, US **dishonorable** [dɪsˈɒnərəbəl] adj deshonroso(a)

dishtowel [ˈdɪʃtaʊəl] n paño m (de cocina), CAm secador m, Méx trapón m, RP repasador m

dishwasher [ˈdɪʃwɒʃə(r)] n lavaplatos m inv; *(person)* lavaplatos mf inv

disillusion [dɪsɪˈluːʒən] vt desilusionar

disinfect [dɪsɪnˈfekt] vt desinfectar

disinfectant [dɪsɪnˈfektənt] n desinfectante m

disintegrate [dɪsˈɪntɪgreɪt] vi desintegrarse

disinterested [dɪsˈɪntrɪstɪd] adj desinteresado(a)

disjointed [dɪsˈdʒɔɪntɪd] adj inconexo(a)

disk [dɪsk] n US disco m; Comput disquete m; **on d.** en disco; **d. drive** disquetera f, disketera f

diskette [dɪsˈket] n Comput disquete m

dislike [dɪsˈlaɪk] **1** n antipatía f, aversión f (**of** a or hacia) **2** vt tener antipatía or aversión a or hacia

dislocate [ˈdɪsləkeɪt] vt *(joint)* dislocar

dislodge [dɪsˈlɒdʒ] vt sacar

disloyal [dɪsˈlɔɪəl] adj desleal

dismal [ˈdɪzməl] adj (a) *(prospect)* sombrío(a); *(place, weather)* deprimente; *(person)* triste (b) *(failure)* horroroso(a)

dismantle [dɪsˈmæntəl] vt desmontar

dismay [dɪsˈmeɪ] **1** n consternación f **2** vt consternar

dismiss [dɪsˈmɪs] vt (a) *(idea)* descartar (b) *(employee)* despedir; *(official)* destituir (c) **to d. sb** *(from room, presence)* dar permiso a algn para retirarse (d) Jur *(case)* sobreseer

dismissal [dɪsˈmɪsəl] n (a) *(of employee)* despido m; *(of official)* destitución f (b) Jur *(of case)* sobreseimiento m

dismount [dɪsˈmaʊnt] vi Fml apearse (**from** de)

disobedient [dɪsəˈbiːdɪənt] adj desobediente

disobey [dɪsəˈbeɪ] vt & vi desobedecer; *(law)* violar

disorder [dɪsˈɔːdə(r)] n (a) *(untidiness)* desorden m (b) *(riot)* disturbio m (c) *(of organ, mind)* trastorno m; *(of speech)* defecto m

disorderly [dɪsˈɔːdəlɪ] adj (a) *(untidy)* desordenado(a) (b) *(meeting)* alborotado(a); *(conduct)* escandaloso(a)

disorganized [dɪs'ɔːɡənaɪzd] *adj* desorganizado(a)

disorient [dɪs'ɔːrɪənt], **disorientate** [dɪs'ɔːrɪenteɪt] *vt* desorientar

disown [dɪs'əʊn] *vt* desconocer

dispatch [dɪ'spætʃ] 1 *n* (a) *(official message)* despacho *m*; *(journalist's report)* reportaje *m*; *(military message)* parte *m* (b) *(of mail)* envío *m*; *(of goods)* consignación *f* 2 *vt* (a) *(mail)* enviar; *(goods)* expedir (b) *Fam (food)* zamparse; *(job)* despachar

dispel [dɪ'spel] *vt* disipar

dispensary [dɪ'spensərɪ] *n* dispensario *m*

dispense [dɪ'spens] *vt* *(supplies)* repartir; *(justice)* administrar

▸ **dispense with** *vt insep (do without)* prescindir de

dispenser [dɪ'spensə(r)] *n* máquina expendedora; **cash d.** cajero automático; **soap d.** dosificador *m* de jabón

disperse [dɪ'spɜːs] 1 *vt* dispersar 2 *vi* dispersarse; *(fog)* disiparse

display [dɪ'spleɪ] 1 *n (exhibition)* exposición *f*; *Comput* visualización *f*; *(of feelings, skills)* demostración *f*; *(of force)* despliegue *m*; **d. window** escaparate *m*, *Am* vidriera *f*, *Chile, Col, Méx* vitrina *f*; **military d.** desfile *m* militar 2 *vt* (a) mostrar; *(goods)* exponer; *Comput* visualizar (b) *(feelings)* manifestar

disposable [dɪ'spəʊzəbəl] *adj* (a) *(throwaway)* desechable (b) *(available)* disponible

disposal [dɪ'spəʊzəl] *n (of rubbish)* eliminación *f*; **at my d.** *(available)* a mi disposición

dispose [dɪ'spəʊz] 1 *vi* **to d. of** *(remove)* eliminar; *(rubbish)* tirar; *(unwanted object)* deshacerse de; *(matter)* resolver; *(sell)* vender; *(property)* traspasar 2 *vt* *Fml (arrange)* disponer

disposition [dɪspə'zɪʃən] *n* (a) *(temperament)* genio *m* (b) *Fml (arrangement)* disposición *f*

dispossess [dɪspə'zes] *vt* desposeer (**of** de)

disproportionate [dɪsprə'pɔːʃənɪt] *adj* desproporcionado(a) (**to** a)

disprove [dɪs'pruːv] *vt* refutar

dispute 1 *n* ['dɪspjuːt] *(disagreement)* discusión *f*; *(quarrel)* disputa *f*; **industrial d.** conflicto *m* laboral 2 *vt* [dɪ'spjuːt] *(claim)* refutar; *(territory)* disputar; *(matter)* discutir 3 *vi* discutir (**about** *or* **over** de *or* sobre)

disqualify [dɪs'kwɒlɪfaɪ] *vt* (a) *Sport* descalificar (b) *(make ineligible)* incapacitar

disregard [dɪsrɪ'ɡɑːd] 1 *n* indiferencia *f*; *(for safety)* despreocupación *f* 2 *vt* descuidar; *(ignore)* ignorar

disrespectful [dɪsrɪ'spektfʊl] *adj* irrespetuoso(a)

disrupt [dɪs'rʌpt] *vt (meeting, traffic)* interrumpir; *(schedule etc)* desbaratar

disruption [dɪs'rʌpʃən] *n (of meeting, traffic)* interrupción *f*; *(of schedule etc)* desbaratamiento *m*

disruptive [dɪs'rʌptɪv] *adj* **to be d.** ocasionar trastornos

dissatisfaction [dɪssætɪs'fækʃən] *n* descontento *m*, insatisfacción *f*

dissatisfied [dɪs'sætɪsfaɪd] *adj* descontento(a)

dissent [dɪ'sent] 1 *n* disentimiento *m* 2 *vi* disentir

dissertation [dɪsə'teɪʃən] *n Univ Br (for higher degree)* tesina *f*; *US (doctoral)* tesis *f*

dissident ['dɪsɪdənt] *adj & n* disidente (*mf*)

dissimilar [dɪ'sɪmɪlə(r)] *adj* distinto(a)

dissociate [dɪ'səʊʃɪeɪt] *vt* **to d. oneself** distanciarse

dissolute ['dɪsəluːt] *adj* disoluto(a)

dissolve [dɪ'zɒlv] 1 *vt* disolver 2 *vi* disolverse

dissuade [dɪ'sweɪd] *vt* disuadir (**from** de)

distance ['dɪstəns] 1 *n* distancia *f*; **in the d.** a lo lejos; *Fam* **to stay the d.**

completar la prueba **2** *vt* **to d. oneself (from)** distanciarse (de)

distant [ˈdɪstənt] *adj* (**a**) *(place, time)* lejano(a); *(look)* distraído(a) (**b**) *(aloof)* distante, frío(a)

distasteful [dɪsˈteɪstfʊl] *adj* desagradable

distil, *US* **distill** [dɪsˈtɪl] *vt* destilar

distinct [dɪˈstɪŋkt] *adj* (**a**) *(different)* diferente; **as d. from** a diferencia de (**b**) *(smell, change)* marcado(a); *(idea, intention)* claro(a)

distinction [dɪˈstɪŋkʃən] *n* (**a**) *(difference)* diferencia *f* (**b**) *(excellence)* distinción *f* (**c**) *Educ* sobresaliente *m*

distinctive [dɪˈstɪŋktɪv] *adj* distintivo(a)

distinctly [dɪˈstɪŋktlɪ] *adv* (**a**) *(clearly) (speak, hear)* claramente, con claridad (**b**) *(decidedly) (better, easier)* claramente; *(stupid, ill-mannered)* verdaderamente

distinguish [dɪˈstɪŋgwɪʃ] *vt* distinguir

distinguished [dɪˈstɪŋgwɪʃt] *adj* distinguido(a)

distort [dɪˈstɔːt] *vt (misrepresent)* deformar; *(words)* tergiversar

distract [dɪˈstrækt] *vt* distraer

distracted [dɪˈstræktɪd] *adj* distraído(a)

distraction [dɪˈstrækʃən] *n (interruption)* distracción *f*; *(confusion)* confusión *f*; **to drive sb to d.** sacar a algn de quicio

distraught [dɪˈstrɔːt] *adj (anguished)* afligido(a)

distress [dɪˈstres] **1** *n (mental)* angustia *f*; *(physical)* dolor *m*; **d. signal** señal *f* de socorro **2** *vt (upset)* apenar

distressing [dɪˈstresɪŋ] *adj* penoso(a)

distribute [dɪˈstrɪbjuːt] *vt* distribuir, repartir

distribution [dɪstrɪˈbjuːʃən] *n* distribución *f*

distributor [dɪˈstrɪbjʊtə(r)] *n* (**a**) *Com* distribuidor(a) *m,f* (**b**) *Aut* distribuidor *m*, *Esp* delco® *m*

district [ˈdɪstrɪkt] *n (of country)* región *f*; *(of town)* barrio *m*; *US* **d. attorney** fiscal *m*; **d. council** corporación *f* local; *Br* **d. nurse** practicante *mf*

distrust [dɪsˈtrʌst] **1** *n* recelo *m* **2** *vt* desconfiar de

disturb [dɪsˈtɜːb] *vt* (**a**) *(inconvenience)* molestar (**b**) *(silence)* romper; *(sleep)* interrumpir (**c**) *(worry)* perturbar (**d**) *(papers)* desordenar

disturbance [dɪsˈtɜːbəns] *n* (**a**) *(of routine)* alteración *f* (**b**) *(commotion)* disturbio *m*, alboroto *m*

disturbing [dɪsˈtɜːbɪŋ] *adj* inquietante

disuse [dɪsˈjuːs] *n* desuso *m*

ditch [dɪtʃ] **1** *n* zanja *f*; *(at roadside)* cuneta *f*; *(for irrigation)* acequia *f* **2** *vt Fam (plan, friend)* abandonar

ditto [ˈdɪtəʊ] *adv* ídem, lo mismo

dive [daɪv] **1** *n* (**a**) *(into water)* salto *m* de cabeza; *(of submarine)* inmersión *f*; *(of plane) Esp* picado *m*, *Am* picada *f*; *Sport* salto *m* (**b**) *Fam (bar)* antro *m* **2** *vi* (**a**) *(from poolside, diving board)* tirarse de cabeza; *(submarine)* sumergirse; *(plane)* lanzarse en *Esp* picado *or Am* picada; *Sport* saltar (**b**) *(move quickly)* **he dived for the phone** se precipitó hacia el teléfono

diver [ˈdaɪvə(r)] *n (person)* buceador(a) *m,f*; *(professional)* buzo *m*; *Sport* saltador(a) *m,f*

diverge [daɪˈvɜːdʒ] *vi* divergir

diverse [daɪˈvɜːs] *adj (varied)* diverso(a), variado(a); *(different)* distinto(a), diferente

diversify [daɪˈvɜːsɪfaɪ] **1** *vt* diversificar **2** *vi (company)* diversificarse

diversion [daɪˈvɜːʃən] *n* (**a**) *(distraction)* distracción *f* (**b**) *Br (detour)* desvío *m*

diversity [daɪˈvɜːsɪtɪ] *n* diversidad *f*

divert [daɪˈvɜːt] *vt* desviar

divide [dɪˈvaɪd] **1** *vt* dividir **2** *vi (road, stream)* bifurcarse **3** *n* división *f*, diferencia *f*

divine [dɪˈvaɪn] *adj* divino(a)

diving board [ˈdaɪvɪŋbɔːd] *n* trampolín *m*

division [dɪ'vɪʒən] n (**a**) división f (**b**) (sharing) reparto m (**c**) (of organization) sección f

divorce [dɪ'vɔːs] **1** n divorcio m **2** vt she divorced him, she got divorced from him se divorció de él **3** vi divorciarse

divorcé [dɪ'vɔːseɪ] n divorciado m

divorcée [dɪvɔː'siː] n divorciada f

divulge [daɪ'vʌldʒ] vt Fml divulgar, revelar

DIY [diːaɪ'waɪ] n Br (abbr **do-it-yourself**) bricolaje m

dizzy ['dɪzɪ] adj (**dizzier, dizziest**) (**a**) (person) (unwell) mareado(a) (**b**) (height, pace) vertiginoso(a)

DJ ['diːdʒeɪ] n Fam (abbr **disc jockey**) pinchadiscos mf inv, disc-jockey mf

do [duː, unstressed dʊ, də]

> En el inglés hablado, y en el escrito en estilo coloquial, las formas negativas **do not**, **does not** y **did not** se transforman en **don't**, **doesn't** y **didn't**

(3rd person sing pres **does**; pt **did**; pp **done**) **1** v aux (**a**) (in negatives and questions) (not translated in Spanish) **do you want some coffee?** ¿quieres café?; **do you drive?** ¿tienes carnet de conducir?; **don't you want to come?** ¿no quieres venir?; **he doesn't smoke** no fuma
(**b**) (emphatic) (not translated in Spanish) **Do come with us!** ¡ánimo, vente con nosotros!; **I Do like your bag** me encanta tu bolso
(**c**) (substituting main verb in sentence) (not translated in Spanish) **neither/so do I** yo tampoco/también; **I'll go if you do** si vas tú, voy yo; **I think it's dear, but he doesn't** a mí me parece caro pero a él no; **who went? – I did** ¿quién asistió? – yo
(**d**) (in question tags) **he refused, didn't he?** dijo que no, ¿verdad?; **I don't like it, do you?** a mí no me gusta, ¿y a ti?
2 vt hacer; (task) realizar; (duty) cumplir con; **to do one's best** hacer todo lo posible; **to do sth again** volver a hacer algo; **to do sth for sb**

hacer algo por algn; **to do the cooking/cleaning** cocinar/limpiar; **what can I do for you?** ¿en qué puedo servirle?; **what do you do (for a living)?** ¿a qué te dedicas?; Fam **he's done it!** ¡lo ha conseguido!

> **do**, unido a muchos nombres, expresa actividades, como **to do the gardening**, **to do the ironing**, etc. En este diccionario, estas estructuras se encuentran bajo los nombres respectivos

3 vi (**a**) (act) hacer; **do as I tell you** haz lo que te digo; **you did right** hiciste bien
(**b**) (with adverb) **he did badly in the exams** los exámenes le salieron mal; **how are you doing?** ¿qué tal?; **how do you do?** (greeting) ¿cómo está usted?; (answer) mucho gusto; **to do well** (person) tener éxito; (business) ir bien
(**c**) **£5 will do** (suffice) con 5 libras será suficiente; Fam **that will do!** ¡basta ya!
(**d**) **this cushion will do as a pillow** (be suitable) este cojín servirá de almohada; **this won't do** esto no puede ser
4 n Br Fam (party) fiesta f; (event) ceremonia f

▸ **do away with** vt insep (**a**) (abolish) abolir; (discard) deshacerse de (**b**) (kill) asesinar

▸ **do down** vt sep Br (criticize) desacreditar, menospreciar

▸ **do for** vt insep Fam (destroy, ruin) arruinar; Fig **I'm done for if I don't finish this** estoy perdido(a) si no acabo esto

▸ **do in** vt sep Fam (**a**) (kill) cargarse (**b**) esp Br **I'm done in** (exhausted) estoy hecho(a) polvo

▸ **do over** vt sep Fam (**a**) US (repeat) repetir (**b**) Br (thrash) dar una paliza a

▸ **do up** vt sep (**a**) (wrap) envolver (**b**) (belt etc) abrochar; (laces) atar (**c**) (dress up) arreglar (**d**) Fam (redecorate) renovar

▸ **do with** vt insep (**a**) **I could do with a rest** (need) un descanso no me vendría nada mal (**b**) **to have** or **be to**

do with *(concern)* tener que ver con

▶**do without** *vt insep* pasar sin, prescindir de

docile ['dəʊsaɪl] *adj* dócil; *(animal)* manso(a)

dock¹ [dɒk] **1** *n Naut* **the docks** el muelle **2** *vi* **(a)** *(ship)* atracar **(b)** *(spacecraft)* acoplarse

dock² [dɒk] *vt (reduce)* descontar

dock³ [dɒk] *n Jur* banquillo *m* (de los acusados)

doctor ['dɒktə(r)] **1** *n* **(a)** *Med* médico(a) *m,f* **(b)** *Univ* doctor(a) *m,f*; **D. of Law** doctor en derecho **2** *vt Pej (figures)* falsificar; *(text)* arreglar; *(drink etc)* adulterar

doctorate ['dɒktərɪt] *n* doctorado *m*

document ['dɒkjʊmənt] **1** *n* documento *m*; **documents** documentación *f* **2** *vt* documentar

documentary [dɒkjʊ'mentərɪ] *adj & n* documental *(m)*

dodge [dɒdʒ] **1** *vt* **(a)** *(blow)* esquivar; *(pursuer)* despistar; *Fig* eludir **(b)** *Fam* **to d. one's taxes** engañar a Hacienda **2** *vi (move aside)* echarse a un lado **3** *n* **(a)** *(movement)* regate *m* **(b)** *Fam (trick)* truco *m*

dodgy ['dɒdʒɪ] *adj* **(dodgier, dodgiest)** *Br Fam (risky)* peligroso(a), *Esp* chungo; *(untrustworthy)* dudoso; **a d. business deal** un chanchullo; **the engine sounds a bit d.** el motor no suena nada bien

does [dʌz] *3rd person sing pres of* **do**

doesn't ['dʌzənt] = **does not**

dog [dɒg] **1** *n* perro(a) *m,f* **2** *vt* acosar; **to d. sb's footsteps** seguir los pasos de algn

dogged ['dɒgɪd] *adj* obstinado(a), tenaz

doing ['duːɪŋ] *n* **(a)** *(action)* obra *f*; **it was none of my d.** yo no tuve nada que ver; *Fig* **it took some d.** costó trabajo hacerlo **(b)** **doings** *(activities)* actividades *fpl*

do-it-yourself [duːɪtjə'self] *n* bricolaje *m*

dole [dəʊl] *Fam* **1** *n Br Fam* subsidio *m* de desempleo, *Esp* paro *m*; **to be on the d.** cobrar el subsidio de desempleo *or Esp* el paro; **to go on the d.** apuntarse para cobrar el desempleo, *Esp* apuntarse al paro **2** *vt* **to d. (out)** repartir

doll [dɒl] **1** *n* **(a)** *(toy)* muñeca *f* **(b)** *US Fam (girl)* muñeca *f* **2** *vt Fam* **to d. oneself up** ponerse guapa

dollar ['dɒlə(r)] *n* dólar *m*

dolphin ['dɒlfɪn] *n* delfín *m*

domain [də'meɪn] *n* **(a)** *(sphere)* campo *m*, esfera *f*; **that's not my d.** no es de mi competencia **(b)** *(territory)* dominio *m* **(c)** *Comput* dominio *m*; **d. name** nombre *m* de dominio

dome [dəʊm] *n (roof)* cúpula *f*; *(ceiling)* bóveda *f*

domestic [də'mestɪk] *adj* **(a)** *(appliance, pet)* doméstico(a); *Br* **d. science** economía doméstica **(b)** *(home-loving)* casero(a) **(c)** *(flight, news)* nacional; *(trade, policy)* interior

dominant ['dɒmɪnənt] *adj* dominante

dominate ['dɒmɪneɪt] *vt & vi* dominar

domineering [dɒmɪ'nɪərɪŋ] *adj* dominante

domino ['dɒmɪnəʊ] *n (pl* **dominoes**) *(piece)* ficha *f* de dominó; **dominoes** *(game)* dominó *m*

donate [dəʊ'neɪt] *vt* donar

donation [dəʊ'neɪʃən] *n* donativo *m*

done [dʌn] **1** *adj* **(a)** *(finished)* terminado(a); **it's over and d. with** se acabó **(b)** *Fam (tired)* rendido(a) **(c)** *(meat)* hecho(a); *(vegetables)* cocido(a) **2** *pp of* **do**

donkey ['dɒŋkɪ] *n* burro(a) *m,f*

donor ['dəʊnə(r)] *n* donante *mf*

don't [dəʊnt] = **do not**

doom [duːm] **1** *n (fate)* destino *m* *(funesto)*; *(ruin)* perdición *f*; *(death)* muerte *f* **2** *vt (destine)* destinar; **doomed to failure** condenado(a) al fracaso

door [dɔː(r)] *n* puerta *f*; **front / back d.** puerta principal/trasera; *Fig* **behind closed doors** a puerta cerrada; **d. handle** manilla *f* (de la puerta); **d. knocker** picaporte *m*; **next d. (to)** (en) la casa de al lado (de)

doorbell ['dɔːbel] n timbre m (de la puerta)

doorknob ['dɔːnɒb] n pomo m

doorman ['dɔːmən] n portero m

doormat ['dɔːmæt] n felpudo m, esterilla f

doorstep ['dɔːstep] n peldaño m; Fig **on one's d.** a la vuelta de la esquina

door-to-door ['dɔːtə'dɔː(r)] adj a domicilio

doorway ['dɔːweɪ] n portal m, entrada f

dope [dəʊp] 1 n (a) Fam (drug) chocolate m (b) Fam (person) tonto(a) mf, Am zonzo(a) m,f 2 vt (food, drink) adulterar con drogas; Sport dopar

dormitory ['dɔːmɪtərɪ] n (a) (in school) dormitorio m (b) US (in university) colegio m mayor

dosage ['dəʊsɪdʒ] n Fml (amount) dosis f inv

dose [dəʊs] 1 n dosis f inv 2 vt (patient) medicar

dossier ['dɒsɪeɪ] n expediente m

dot [dɒt] 1 n punto m; **on the d.** en punto; Comput **d. matrix printer** impresora f matricial or de agujas 2 vt (a) Fam **to dot one's i's and cross one's t's** poner los puntos sobre las íes (b) (scatter) esparcir, salpicar

dote [dəʊt] vi **to d. on sb** chochear con algn

double ['dʌbəl] 1 adj doble; **it's d. the price** cuesta dos veces más; **d. bass** contrabajo m; **d. bed** cama f de matrimonio; Br **d. cream** Esp nata f para montar, Am crema líquida enriquecida, RP crema f doble
2 adv doble; **folded d.** doblado(a) por la mitad; **to earn d.** ganar el doble
3 n vivo retrato m; Cin, Th doble m
4 vt doblar; Fig (efforts) redoblar
5 vi (a) (increase) doblarse (b) **to d. as** (serve) hacer las veces de
► **double back** vi **to d. back on one's tracks** volver sobre sus pasos
► **double up** 1 vt sep (bend) doblar 2 vi (a) (bend) doblarse (b) (share room) compartir la habitación (with con)

double-cross [dʌbəl'krɒs] Fam 1 vt engañar, traicionar 2 n engaño m, traición f

double-glazing ['dʌbəl'gleɪzɪŋ] n doble acristalamiento m

doubt [daʊt] 1 n duda f; **beyond (all) d.** sin duda alguna; **no d.** sin duda; **there's no d. about it** no cabe la menor duda; **to be in d. about sth** dudar algo; **to be open to d.** (fact) ser dudoso(a); (outcome) ser incierto(a) 2 vt (a) (distrust) desconfiar de (b) (not be sure of) dudar; **I d. if** or **whether he'll come** dudo que venga

doubtful ['daʊtfʊl] adj (a) (future) dudoso(a), (look) dubitativo(a); **I'm a bit d. about it** no me convence del todo; **it's d. whether ...** no se sabe seguro si ... (b) (questionable) sospechoso(a)

doubtless ['daʊtlɪs] adv sin duda, seguramente

dough [dəʊ] n (a) (for bread) masa f (b) Fam (money) Esp pasta f, Esp, RP guita f, Am plata f, Méx lana f

doughnut ['dəʊnʌt] n rosquilla f, dónut® m

dove [dʌv] n paloma f

dowdy ['daʊdɪ] adj (dowdier, dowdiest) poco elegante

down [daʊn] 1 prep (a) (to or at a lower level) **d. the river** río abajo; **to go d. the road** bajar la calle (b) (along) por 2 adv (a) (to lower level) (hacia) abajo; (to floor) al suelo; (to ground) a tierra; **sales are d. by 5 per cent** las ventas han bajado un 5 por ciento; **to fall d.** caerse (b) (at lower level) abajo; **d. there** allí abajo; Fam Fig **to feel d.** estar deprimido(a); Br Fam **d. under** en Australia y Nueva Zelanda
3 adj (payment) al contado; (on property) de entrada
4 vt Fam (drink) tomarse de un trago; (food) zamparse

down-and-out ['daʊnən'aʊt] 1 adj en las últimas 2 n vagabundo(a) m,f

downcast ['daʊnkɑːst] adj abatido(a)

downfall ['daʊnfɔːl] n (of regime) caída f; (of person) perdición f

downhearted [daʊnˈhɑːtɪd] *adj* desalentado(a)

downhill [daʊnˈhɪl] **1** *adj (skiing)* de descenso; *Fam* **after his first exam, the rest were all d.** después del primer examen, los demás le fueron sobre ruedas **2** *adv* **to go d.** ir cuesta abajo; *Fig (standards)* deteriorarse

download [ˈdaʊnˈləʊd] *vt Comput* bajar, descargar

downpour [ˈdaʊnpɔː(r)] *n* chaparrón *m*

downright [ˈdaʊnraɪt] *Fam* **1** *adj (blunt) (categorical)* categórico(a); **it's a d. lie** es una mentira y gorda **2** *adv (totally)* completamente

downstairs 1 *adv* [daʊnˈsteəz] abajo; *(to ground floor)* a la planta baja; **to go d.** bajar la escalera **2** *adj* [ˈdaʊnsteəz] *(on ground floor)* de la planta baja

down-to-earth [daʊntʊˈɜːθ] *adj* realista

downtown [daʊnˈtaʊn] *adv US* en el centro (de la ciudad)

downward [ˈdaʊnwəd] **1** *adj (slope)* descendente; *(look)* hacia abajo; *Fin (tendency)* a la baja **2** *adv* = **downwards**

downwards [ˈdaʊnwədz] *adv* hacia abajo

doze [dəʊz] **1** *vi* dormitar **2** *n* cabezada *f*; **to have a d.** echar una cabezada

▸ **doze off** *vi* quedarse dormido(a)

dozen [ˈdʌzən] *n* docena *f*; **half a d./a d. eggs** media docena/una docena de huevos; *Fam* **dozens of** un montón de

Dr *(abbr* **Doctor)** Dr., Dra.

drab [dræb] *adj* **(drabber, drabbest)** (a) *(ugly)* feo(a); *(dreary)* monótono(a), gris **(b)** *(colour)* pardo(a)

draft [drɑːft] **1** *n* **(a)** borrador *m* **(b)** *US* servicio militar obligatorio **(c)** *US* = **draught 2** *vt* **(a)** hacer un borrador de **(b)** *US Mil* reclutar

drag [dræg] **1** *vt (pull)* arrastrar; **2** *vi (trail)* arrastrarse **3** *n Fam (nuisance)* lata *f*

▸ **drag off** *vt sep* llevarse arrastrando

▸ **drag on** *vi (war, strike)* hacerse interminable

▸ **drag out** *vt sep (speech etc)* alargar

dragon [ˈdrægən] *n* dragón *m*

drain [dreɪn] **1** *n* **(a)** *(for water)* desagüe *m*; *(for sewage)* alcantarilla *f* **(b)** *(grating)* sumidero *m* **(c)** *Fig* **the boys are a d. on her strength** los niños la dejan agotada
2 *vt* **(a)** *(marsh etc)* avenar; *(reservoir)* desecar **(b)** *(crockery)* escurrir **(c)** *(empty) (glass)* apurar; *Fig (capital etc)* agotar
3 *vi* **(a)** *(crockery)* escurrirse **(b)** **to d. (away)** *(liquid)* irse

drainpipe [ˈdreɪnpaɪp] *n* tubo *m* de desagüe

drama [ˈdrɑːmə] *n* **(a)** *(play)* obra *f* de teatro; *Fig* drama *m* **(b)** *(subject)* teatro *m*

dramatic [drəˈmætɪk] *adj* **(a)** *(change)* impresionante; *(moment)* emocionante **(b)** *Th* dramático(a), teatral

drank [dræŋk] *pt of* **drink**

drape [dreɪp] **1** *vt* **to d. sth over sth** colgar algo sobre algo; **draped with** cubierto(a) de **2** *n* **(a)** *(of fabric)* caída *f* **(b)** *US* cortina *f*

drastic [ˈdræstɪk] *adj* **(a)** *(measures)* drástico(a), severo(a) **(b)** *(change)* radical

draught [drɑːft] *n* **(a)** *(of cold air)* corriente *f* (de aire) **(b)** *(of liquid)* trago *m*; **d. (beer)** cerveza *f* de barril **(c)** *Br* **draughts** *(game)* damas *fpl*

draw [drɔː] *(pt* **drew**; *pp* **drawn)** **1** *vt* **(a)** *(picture)* dibujar; *(line)* trazar **(b)** *(pull)* tirar de; *(train, carriage)* arrastrar; *(curtains) (open)* descorrer; *(close)* correr; *(blinds)* bajar **(c)** *(extract)* sacar; *(salary)* cobrar; *(cheque)* librar **(d)** *(attract)* atraer; *(attention)* llamar **(e)** *Fig (strength)* sacar **(f)** *(comparison)* hacer; *(conclusion)* sacar
2 *vi* **(a)** *(sketch)* dibujar **(b)** *(move)* **the train drew into/out of the station** el tren entró en/salió de la estación; **to d. apart (from)** separarse (de) **(c)** *Sport* **they drew two all** empataron a dos
3 *n* **(a)** *(raffle)* sorteo *m* **(b)** *Sport* empate *m* **(c)** *(attraction)* atracción *f*

▸ **draw in** *vi (days)* acortarse

▶ **draw on** vt insep (savings) recurrir a; (experience) aprovecharse de

▶ **draw out** vt sep (a) (make long) alargar (b) (encourage to speak) desatar la lengua a (c) (from pocket, drawer etc) sacar

▶ **draw up** vt sep (contract) preparar; (plan) esbozar

drawback ['drɔːbæk] n desventaja f, inconveniente m

drawer ['drɔːə(r)] n cajón m

drawing ['drɔːɪŋ] n dibujo m; Br **d. pin** Esp chincheta f, Am chinche m; Fml **d. room** sala f de estar

drawl [drɔːl] 1 vi hablar arrastrando las palabras 2 n voz cansina; US **a Southern d.** un acento sureño

drawn [drɔːn] 1 adj (tired) ojeroso(a) 2 pp of **draw**

dread [dred] 1 vt temer a, tener pavor a 2 n temor m

dreadful ['dredful] adj (a) (shocking) espantoso(a) (b) Fam (awful) fatal; **how d.!** ¡qué horror!

dreadfully ['dredfulɪ] adv Fam terriblemente

dream [driːm] (pt & pp **dreamed** or **dreamt**) 1 n (a) sueño m (b) (daydream) ensueño m (c) Fam (marvel) maravilla f
2 vt soñar
3 vi soñar (**of** or **about** con)

dreary ['drɪərɪ] adj (**drearier, dreariest**) (a) (gloomy) triste (b) Fam (boring) aburrido(a), pesado(a)

drench [drentʃ] vt empapar

dress [dres] 1 n (a) (frock) vestido m (b) (clothing) ropa f; **d. rehearsal** ensayo m general; **d. shirt** camisa f de etiqueta
2 vt (a) (person) vestir; **he was dressed in a grey suit** llevaba (puesto) un traje gris (b) (salad) aderezar, Esp aliñar (c) (wound) vendar
3 vi vestirse

▶ **dress up** 1 vi (a) (in disguise) disfrazarse (**as** de) (b) (in best clothes) vestirse elegante 2 vt sep Fig disfrazar

dressing ['dresɪŋ] n (a) (bandage) vendaje m (b) (salad) **d.** aliño m (c)

d. gown bata f; **d. room** Th camerino m; Sport vestuario m; **d. table** tocador m

drew [druː] pt of **draw**

dribble ['drɪbəl] 1 vi (a) (baby) babear (b) (liquid) gotear
2 vt Sport (ball) driblar
3 n (saliva) saliva f; (of water, blood) gotas fpl

dried [draɪd] adj (fruit) seco(a); (milk) en polvo

drier ['draɪə(r)] n = **dryer**

drift [drɪft] 1 vi (a) (boat) ir a la deriva; Fig (person) ir sin rumbo, vagar; **they drifted away** se marcharon poco a poco (b) (snow) amontonarse 2 n (a) (flow) flujo m (b) (of snow) ventisquero m; (of sand) montón m (c) Fig (meaning) idea f

drill [drɪl] 1 n (a) (hand tool) taladro m; Min barrena f; **dentist's d.** fresa f; **pneumatic d.** martillo neumático (b) esp Mil instrucción f
2 vt (a) (wood etc) taladrar (b) (soldiers, children) instruir
3 vi (by hand) taladrar; (for oil, coal) perforar, sondar

drink [drɪŋk] (pt **drank**; pp **drunk**) 1 vt beber
2 vi beber; **to have sth to d.** tomarse algo; **to d. to sth/sb** brindar por algo/algn
3 n bebida f; (alcoholic) copa f

drinking ['drɪŋkɪŋ] n **d. water** agua f potable

drip [drɪp] 1 n (a) goteo m (b) Med gota a gota m inv (c) Fam (person) necio(a) m,f 2 vi gotear; **he was dripping with sweat** el sudor le caía a gotas

drive [draɪv] (pt **drove**; pp **driven**) 1 vt (a) (vehicle) conducir, Am manejar; (person) llevar (b) (power) impulsar (c) (compel) forzar, obligar; **to d. sb mad** volver loco(a) a algn; **to d. off** rechazar
2 vi Aut conducir, Am manejar
3 n (a) (trip) paseo m en coche or Am carro or CSur auto; **to go for a d.** dar una vuelta en coche or Am carro or CSur auto (b) (to house) camino m de

entrada (**c**) *(campaign)* campaña *f* (**d**) *(energy)* energía *f*, vigor *m* (**e**) *Comput* unidad *f* de disco

drivel ['drɪvəl] *n Fam Esp* chorradas *fpl*, *CAm*, *Méx* babosadas *fpl*, *Chile* leseras *fpl*, *CSur*, *Perú*, *Ven* macanas *fpl*

driven ['drɪvən] *pp of* **drive**

driver ['draɪvə(r)] *n (of car, bus)* conductor(a) *m,f*; *(of train)* maquinista *mf*, *Am* chofer *mf*; *(of lorry)* camionero(a) *m,f*; *(of racing car)* piloto *mf*; *US* **d.'s license** *Esp* carné *m* or permiso *m* de conducir, *Bol*, *Ecuad*, *Perú* brevet *m*, *Carib* licencia *f* de conducir, *Méx* licencia *f* de manejar or para conducir, *RP* permiso *m* de conductor

driveway ['draɪvweɪ] *n (to house)* camino *m* de entrada

driving ['draɪvɪŋ] **1** *n* conducción *f*, *Am* manejo *m*; *Br* **d. licence** *Esp* carné *m* or permiso *m* de conducir, *Bol*, *Ecuad*, *Perú* brevet *m*, *Carib* licencia *f* de conducir, *Méx* licencia *f* de manejar or para conducir, *RP* permiso *m* de conductor; **d. school** autoescuela *f*; **d. test** examen *m* de conducir **2** *adj* **d. force** fuerza *f* motriz

drizzle ['drɪzəl] **1** *n* llovizna *f*, *Andes*, *RP* garúa *f* **2** *vi* lloviznar, chispear, *Andes*, *RP* garuar

droop [dru:p] *vi (flower)* marchitarse; *(eyelids)* caerse

drop [drɒp] **1** *n* (**a**) *(of liquid)* gota *f*; **eye drops** colirio *m* (**b**) *(descent)* desnivel *m* (**c**) *(in price)* bajada *f*; *(in temperature)* descenso *m* **2** *vt* (**a**) *(let fall)* dejar caer; *(lower)* bajar; *(reduce)* disminuir; **to d. a hint** soltar una indirecta (**b**) *(abandon)* *(subject, charge etc)* abandonar, dejar; *Sport* **he was dropped from the team** le echaron del equipo **3** *vi (object)* caerse; *(person)* tirarse; *(voice, price, temperature)* bajar; *(wind)* amainar; *(speed)* disminuir

▸ **drop by**, **drop in** *vi Fam (visit)* pasarse (**at** por)

▸ **drop off 1** *vi Fam (fall asleep)* quedarse dormido(a) **2** *vt sep (deliver)* dejar

▸ **drop out** *vi (from college)* dejar los estudios; *(from society)* marginarse; *(from competition)* retirarse

▸ **drop round** *vi Fam* = **drop by**

drought [draʊt] *n* sequía *f*

drove [drəʊv] **1** *n (of cattle)* manada *f* **2** *pt of* **drive**

drown [draʊn] **1** *vt* (**a**) ahogar (**b**) *(place)* inundar **2** *vi* ahogarse; **he (was) drowned** murió ahogado

drowsy ['draʊzɪ] *adj* (**drowsier, drowsiest**) soñoliento(a); **to feel d.** tener sueño

drug [drʌg] **1** *n* (**a**) *(medicine)* medicamento *m* (**b**) *(narcotic)* droga *f*, estupefaciente *m*; **to be on drugs** drogarse; **d. addict** drogadicto(a) *m,f*; **d. addiction** drogadicción *f*; **d. squad** brigada *f* antidroga **2** *vt (person)* drogar; *(food, drink)* adulterar con drogas

druggist ['drʌgɪst] *n US* farmacéutico(a) *m,f*

drugstore ['drʌgstɔ:r] *n US* = establecimiento donde se compran medicamentos, periódicos, etc

drum [drʌm] **1** *n* (**a**) tambor *m*; **to play the drums** tocar la batería (**b**) *(container)* bidón *m*
　2 *vi Fig (with fingers)* tabalear
　3 *vt Fig* **to d. sth into sb** enseñar algo a algn a machamartillo

▸ **drum up** *vt sep Fam* solicitar

drummer ['drʌmə(r)] *n (in band)* tambor *mf*; *(in pop group)* batería *mf*, *Am* baterista *mf*

drumstick ['drʌmstɪk] *n* (**a**) *Mus* baqueta *f* (**b**) *(chicken leg)* muslo *m*

drunk [drʌŋk] **1** *adj* borracho(a); **to get d.** emborracharse
　2 *n* borracho(a) *m,f*
　3 *pp of* **drink**

drunkard ['drʌŋkəd] *n* borracho(a) *m,f*

drunken ['drʌŋkən] *adj (person)* borracho(a); **d. brawl** trifulca *f* de borrachos

dry [draɪ] *(pt & pp* **dried**) **1** *adj* (**drier, driest** or **dryer, dryest**) (**a**) seco(a); *US* **d. goods store** mercería *f*, tienda *f* de

confección (**b**) *(wry)* socarrón(ona)
2 *vt* secar
3 *vi* **to d. (off)** secarse

dry-clean [draɪ'kliːn] *vt* limpiar *or* lavar en seco

dryer ['draɪə(r)] *n* secadora *f*

dual ['djʊəl] *adj* doble; *Br* **d. carriageway** *(road)* (tramo *m* de) autovía *f*

dub[1] [dʌb] *vt (subtitle)* doblar (**into** a)

dub[2] [dʌb] *vt* (**a**) *(give nickname to)* apodar (**b**) *(knight)* armar

dubious ['djuːbɪəs] *adj* (**a**) *(morals etc)* dudoso(a); *(compliment)* equívoco(a) (**b**) *(doubting)* indeciso(a)

duchess ['dʌtʃɪs] *n* duquesa *f*

duck[1] [dʌk] *n* pato(a) *m,f*; *Culin* pato *m*

duck[2] [dʌk] **1** *vt* (**a**) *(submerge)* dar una ahogadilla a (**b**) *(evade)* esquivar **2** *vi* (**a**) *(evade blow)* esquivar (**b**) *Fam* **to d. (out)** rajarse

duckling ['dʌklɪŋ] *n* patito *m*

due [djuː] *adj* (**a**) *(expected)* esperado(a); **the train is d. (to arrive) at ten** el tren debe llegar a las diez (**b**) *Fml (proper)* debido(a); **in d. course** a su debido tiempo (**c**) *(owing)* pagadero(a); **how much are you d.?** *(owed)* ¿cuánto te deben? (**d**) **to be d. to** *(caused by)* deberse a; **d. to** *(because of)* debido de

duel ['djuːəl] *n* duelo *m*

duet [djuː'et] *n* dúo *m*

duffel ['dʌfəl] *n* **d. bag** petate *m*; **d. coat** trenca *f*

dug [dʌg] *pt & pp of* **dig**

duke [djuːk] *n* duque *m*

dull [dʌl] **1** *adj* (**a**) *(boring)* pesado(a); *(place)* sin interés (**b**) *(light)* apagado(a); *(weather)* gris (**c**) *(sound, ache)* sordo(a) (**d**) *(not intelligent)* tonto(a), torpe, *Am* sonso(a) **2** *vt (pain)* aliviar

duly ['djuːlɪ] *adv Fml (properly)* debidamente; *(as expected)* como era de esperar; *(in due course)* a su debido tiempo

dumb [dʌm] **1** *adj* (**a**) *Med* mudo(a) (**b**) *Fam (stupid)* tonto(a) **2** *npl* **the d.** los mudos

dumbfounded [dʌm'faʊndɪd], **dumbstruck** ['dʌmstrʌk] *adj* pasmado(a)

dummy ['dʌmɪ] *n* (**a**) *(sham)* imitación *f* (**b**) *(in shop window)* maniquí *m*; *(of ventriloquist)* muñeco *m* (**c**) *Br (for baby)* chupete *m*

dump [dʌmp] **1** *n* (**a**) *(tip)* vertedero *m*; *(for old cars)* cementerio *m* (de coches) (**b**) *Fam Pej (place)* estercolero *m*; *(town)* poblacho *m*; *(dwelling)* tugurio *m* (**c**) *Mil* depósito *m* **2** *vt* (**a**) *(rubbish)* verter; *(truck contents)* descargar (**b**) *(person)* dejar; *Com* inundar el mercado con (**c**) *Comput (transfer)* copiar de memoria interna

dumpling ['dʌmplɪŋ] *n Culin* = bola de masa hervida

dune [djuːn] *n* (**sand**) **d.** duna *f*

dung [dʌŋ] *n* estiércol *m*

dungarees [dʌŋgə'riːz] *npl* mono *m*

dupe [djuːp] **1** *vt* engañar **2** *n* ingenuo(a) *m,f*

duplex ['djuːpleks] *n US (house)* casa adosada; **d. apartment** dúplex *m inv*

duplicate 1 *vt* ['djuːplɪkeɪt] (**a**) *(copy)* duplicar; *(film, tape)* reproducir (**b**) *(repeat)* repetir **2** *n* ['djuːplɪkɪt] duplicado *m*; **in d.** por duplicado

durable ['djʊərəbəl] *adj* duradero(a)

duration [djʊ'reɪʃən] *n Fml* duración *f*

during ['djʊərɪŋ] *prep* durante

dusk [dʌsk] *n Fml* crepúsculo *m*; **at d.** al anochecer

dust [dʌst] **1** *n* polvo *m*; **d. cloud** polvareda *f*; **d. jacket** sobrecubierta *f* **2** *vt* (**a**) *(furniture)* quitar el polvo a (**b**) *(cake)* espolvorear

dustbin ['dʌstbɪn] *n Br* cubo *m* or *Am* bote *m* de la basura

duster ['dʌstə(r)] *n Br (cloth)* trapo *m* or bayeta *f* (del polvo); **feather d.** plumero *m*

dustman ['dʌstmən] *n Br* basurero *m*

dustpan ['dʌstpæn] *n* recogedor *m*

dusty ['dʌstɪ] *adj* (**dustier, dustiest**) polvoriento(a)

Dutch [dʌtʃ] **1** *adj* holandés(esa); *Fig* **D. cap** diafragma *m*

2 *n* (**a**) *pl* **the D.** los holandeses (**b**) *(language)* holandés *m*; **it's double D. to me** me suena a chino

3 *adv Fam* **to go D.** pagar cada uno lo suyo, *Esp* pagar a escote

duty ['dju:tɪ] *n* (**a**) deber *m*; **to do one's d.** cumplir con su deber (**b**) *(task)* función *f* (**c**) **to be on d.** estar de servicio; *Med, Mil* estar de guardia (**d**) *(tax)* impuesto *m*

duty-free [dju:tɪ'fri:] *adj* libre de impuestos

duvet ['du:veɪ] *n Br* edredón *m*

DVD [di:vi:'di:] *n Comput (abbr* **Digital Versatile Disk, Digital Video Disk)** DVD *m*

dwarf [dwɔ:f] **1** *n* (*pl* **dwarves** [dwɔ:vz]) *(person)* enano(a) *m,f* **2** *vt* hacer parecer pequeño(a) a

dwell [dwel] (*pt & pp* **dwelt** [dwelt]) *vi Fml* morar

▸**dwell on** *vt insep* hablar extensamente de; **let's not d. on it** olvidémoslo

dwindle ['dwɪndəl] *vi* menguar, disminuir

dye [daɪ] (*pres participle* **dyeing**; *pt & pp* **dyed**) **1** *n* tinte *m* **2** *vt* teñir; **to d. one's hair black** teñirse el pelo de negro

dying ['daɪɪŋ] *adj (person)* moribundo(a), agonizante; *Fig (custom)* en vías de desaparición

dynamic [daɪ'næmɪk] *adj* dinámico(a)

dynamite ['daɪnəmaɪt] *n* dinamita *f*

dynamo ['daɪnəməʊ] *n* dínamo *f*

dyslexia [dɪs'leksɪə] *n* dislexia *f*

Ee

E, e [iː] n (**a**) (the letter) E, e f (**b**) Mus E mi m

E [iː] n (**a**) (abbr **east**) E (**b**) Fam (abbr **ecstasy**) (drug) éxtasis m inv

each [iːtʃ] 1 adj cada; **e. day/month** todos los días/meses; **e. person** cada cual; **e. time I see him** cada vez que lo veo 2 pron (**a**) cada uno(a); **£2 e.** 2 libras cada uno; **we bought one e.** nos compramos uno cada uno (**b**) **e. other** el uno al otro; **they hate e. other** se odian

eager [ˈiːgə(r)] adj (anxious) impaciente; (desirous) deseoso(a); **e. to begin** impaciente por empezar; **to be e. for success** codiciar el éxito

eagerly [ˈiːgəlɪ] adv (anxiously) con impaciencia; (keenly) con ilusión

eagle [ˈiːgəl] n águila f

ear [ɪə(r)] n (**a**) oreja f; (sense of hearing) oído m (**b**) (of corn etc) espiga f

earache [ˈɪəreɪk] n dolor m de oídos

early [ˈɜːlɪ] (**earlier, earliest**) 1 adj (**a**) (before the usual time) temprano(a); **to have an e. night** acostarse pronto; **you're e.!** ¡qué pronto has venido! (**b**) (at first stage, period) **at an e. age** siendo joven; **in e. July** a principios de julio; **e. work** obra de juventud; **in her e. forties** a los cuarenta y pocos 2 adv (**a**) (before the expected time) temprano, Esp pronto; **earlier on** antes; **five minutes e.** con cinco minutos de adelanto (**b**) (near the beginning) **as e. as 1914** ya en 1914; **as e. as possible** tan pronto como sea posible; **to book e.** reservar con tiempo; **e. on** temprano

earmark [ˈɪəmɑːk] vt destinar (**for** para or a)

earn [ɜːn] vt (**a**) (money) ganar; **to e. one's living** ganarse la vida (**b**) (reputation) ganarse (**c**) **to e. interest** cobrar interés or intereses

earnest [ˈɜːnɪst] 1 adj serio(a), formal 2 n **in e.** de veras, en serio

earnings [ˈɜːnɪŋz] npl ingresos mpl

earphones [ˈɪəfəʊnz] npl auriculares mpl

earring [ˈɪərɪŋ] n pendiente m, Am arete m

earshot [ˈɪəʃɒt] n **out of e.** fuera del alcance del oído; **within e.** al alcance del oído

earth [ɜːθ] 1 n (**a**) tierra f; Fig **to be down to e.** ser práctico; Fam **where/why on e. ...?** ¿pero dónde/por qué demonios ...? (**b**) Br Elec toma f de tierra 2 vt Br Elec conectar a tierra

earthquake [ˈɜːθkweɪk] n terremoto m

ease [iːz] 1 n (**a**) (freedom from discomfort) tranquilidad f; **at e.** relajado(a) (**b**) (lack of difficulty) facilidad f 2 vt (pain) aliviar

▸ **ease off, ease up** vi (**a**) (decrease) disminuir (**b**) (slow down) ir más despacio

easily [ˈiːzɪlɪ] adv fácilmente; **e. the best** con mucho el mejor

east [iːst] 1 n este m; **the Middle E.** el Oriente Medio 2 adj del este, oriental; **E. Germany** Alemania Oriental 3 adv al or hacia el este

Easter [ˈiːstə(r)] n Semana Santa, Pascua f; **E. egg** huevo m de Pascua; **E. Sunday** Domingo m de Resurrección

easterly [ˈiːstəlɪ] adj (from the east) del este; (to the east) hacia al este

eastern [ˈiːstən] adj oriental, del este

eastward(s) ['i:stwəd(z)] *adv* hacia el este

easy ['i:zɪ] **(easier, easiest) 1** *adj* (**a**) *(simple)* fácil, sencillo(a) (**b**) *(unworried, comfortable)* cómodo(a), tranquilo(a); *Fam* **I'm e.!** ¡me da lo mismo!; **e. chair** butacón *m* **2** *adv* **go e. on the wine** no te pases con el vino; *Fam* **to take things e.** tomarse las cosas con calma; *Fam* **take it e.!** ¡tranquilo!

easy-going [i:zɪ'gəʊɪŋ] *adj (calm)* tranquilo(a); *(lax)* despreocupado(a); *(undemanding)* poco exigente

eat [i:t] *vt (pt* **ate**; *pp* **eaten** ['i:tən]) comer
▶ **eat away** *vt sep* desgastar; *(metal)* corroer
▶ **eat into** *vt insep* (**a**) *(wood)* roer (**b**) *Fig (savings)* consumir
▶ **eat out** *vi* comer fuera
▶ **eat up** *vt sep* (**a**) *(meal)* terminar (**b**) *Fig (petrol)* consumir; *(miles)* recorrer rápidamente

eavesdrop ['i:vzdrɒp] *vi* escuchar disimuladamente

ebb [eb] **1** *n* reflujo *m*; **e. and flow** flujo y reflujo; *Fig* **to be at a low e.** estar decaído **2** *vi* (**a**) *(tide)* bajar; **to e. and flow** subir y bajar (**b**) *Fig* **to e. away** decaer

eccentric [ɪk'sentrɪk] *adj & n* excéntrico(a) *(m,f)*

echo ['ekəʊ] **1** *n* (*pl* **echoes**) eco *m* **2** *vt (repeat)* repetir **3** *vi* resonar, hacer eco

eclipse [ɪ'klɪps] **1** *n* eclipse *m* **2** *vt* eclipsar

ecological [i:kə'lɒdʒɪkəl] *adj* ecológico(a)

economic [i:kə'nɒmɪk] *adj* económico(a); *(profitable)* rentable

economical [i:kə'nɒmɪkəl] *adj* económico(a)

economics [i:kə'nɒmɪks] *n sing (science)* economía *f*; *Educ* (ciencias *fpl*) económicas *fpl*

economize [ɪ'kɒnəmaɪz] *vi* economizar

economy [ɪ'kɒnəmɪ] *n* (**a**) *Pol* **the e.** la economía (**b**) *(saving)* ahorro *m*;

e. class clase *f* turista

ecstasy ['ekstəsɪ] *n* éxtasis *m*

edge [edʒ] **1** *n* borde *m*; *(of knife)* filo *m*; *(of coin)* canto *m*; *(of water)* orilla *f*; **on the e. of town** en las afueras de la ciudad
2 *vt Sewing* ribetear
3 *vi* **to e. forward** avanzar poco a poco

edgy ['edʒɪ] *adj* (**edgier, edgiest**) nervioso(a)

edible ['edɪbəl] *adj* comestible

Edinburgh ['edɪnbrə] *n* Edimburgo

edit ['edɪt] *vt* (**a**) *(prepare for printing)* preparar para la imprenta (**b**) *(rewrite)* corregir (**c**) *Press* ser redactor(a) de (**d**) *Cin, Rad, TV* montar; *(cut)* cortar

edition [ɪ'dɪʃən] *n* edición *f*

editor ['edɪtə(r)] *n* (*of book)* editor(a) *m,f*; *Press* redactor(a) *m,f*; *Cin, Rad, TV* montador(a) *m,f*

educate ['edjʊkeɪt] *vt* educar

educated ['edjʊkeɪtɪd] *adj* culto(a)

education [edjʊ'keɪʃən] *n* (**a**) *(schooling)* enseñanza *f*; **Ministry of E.** Ministerio *m* de Educación (**b**) *(training)* formación *f* (**c**) *(studies)* estudios *mpl* (**d**) *(culture)* cultura *f*

educational [edjʊ'keɪʃənəl] *adj* educativo(a), educacional

eel [i:l] *n* anguila *f*

eerie ['ɪərɪ] *adj* (**eerier, eeriest**) siniestro(a)

effect [ɪ'fekt] **1** *n* (**a**) efecto *m*; **in e.** efectivamente; **to come into e.** entrar en vigor; **to have an e. on** afectar a; **to take e.** *(drug)* surtir efecto; *(law)* entrar en vigor (**b**) *(impression)* impresión *f* **2** *vt Fml* provocar

effective [ɪ'fektɪv] *adj* (**a**) *(successful)* eficaz (**b**) *(real)* efectivo(a) (**c**) *(impressive)* impresionante

effectively [ɪ'fektɪvlɪ] *adv* (**a**) *(successfully)* eficazmente (**b**) *(in fact)* en efecto

efficient [ɪ'fɪʃənt] *adj* eficaz, eficiente; *(machine)* de buen rendimiento

effort ['efət] *n* (**a**) esfuerzo *m*; **to make an e.** hacer un esfuerzo, esforzarse **(b)** *(attempt)* intento *m*

e.g. [iːˈdʒiː] *(abbr* **exempli gratia)** p. ej.

egg [eg] **1** *n* huevo *m*, *CAm*, *Méx* blanquillo *m*; **e. cup** huevera *f*; **e. timer** reloj *m* de arena; **e. white** clara *f* de huevo **2** *vt* **to e. sb on (to do sth)** empujar a algn (a hacer algo)

eggplant [ˈegplɑːnt] *n US* berenjena *f*

ego [ˈiːgəʊ, ˈegəʊ] *n* **(a)** ego *m*; *Fam* **e. trip** autobombo *m* **(b)** *Fam* amor propio

egoist [ˈiːgəʊɪst] *n* egoísta *mf*

Egypt [ˈiːdʒɪpt] *n* Egipto

Egyptian [ɪˈdʒɪpʃən] *adj & n* egipcio(a) *(m,f)*

eight [eɪt] *adj & n* ocho *(m inv)*

eighteen [eɪˈtiːn] *adj & n* dieciocho *(m inv)*

eighteenth [eɪˈtiːnθ] **1** *adj & n* decimoctavo *(m,f)* **2** *n (fraction)* decimoctavo *m*

eighth [eɪtθ] **1** *adj & n* octavo(a) *(m,f)* **2** *n (fraction)* octavo *m*

eighty [ˈeɪtɪ] *adj & n* ochenta *(m inv)*

either [ˈaɪðə(r), ˈiːðə(r)] **1** *pron* **(a)** *(affirmative)* cualquiera; **e. of them** cualquiera de los dos; **e. of us** cualquiera de nosotros dos **(b)** *(negative)* ninguno/ninguna, ni el uno ni el otro/ni la una ni la otra; **I don't want e. of them** no quiero ninguno de los dos **2** *adj (both)* cada, los dos/las dos; **on e. side** en ambos lados; **in e. case** en cualquier de los dos casos **3** *conj* o; **e. ... or ...** o ... o ...; **e. Friday or Saturday** o (bien) el viernes o el sábado **4** *adv (after negative)* tampoco; **I don't want to do it e.** yo tampoco quiero hacerlo

eject [ɪˈdʒekt] **1** *vt* expulsar **2** *vi Av* eyectarse

elaborate 1 *vt* [ɪˈlæbəreɪt] **(a)** *(devise)* elaborar **(b)** *(explain)* explicar detalladamente **2** *vi* [ɪˈlæbəreɪt] explicarse; **to e. on sth** explicar algo con más detalles **3** *adj* [ɪˈlæbərɪt] **(a)** *(complicated)* complicado(a) **(b)** *(detailed)* detallado(a); *(style)* esmerado(a)

elastic [ɪˈlæstɪk] **1** *adj* elástico(a); *Fig* flexible; **e. band** goma elástica **2** *n* elástico *m*

elbow [ˈelbəʊ] **1** *n* **(a)** codo *m*; *Fig* **e. room** espacio *m* **(b)** *(bend)* recodo *m* **2** *vt* **to e. sb** dar un codazo a algn

elder¹ [ˈeldə(r)] **1** *adj* mayor **2** *n* **the elders** los ancianos

elder² [ˈeldə(r)] *n Bot* saúco *m*

elderly [ˈeldəlɪ] **1** *adj* anciano(a) **2** *npl* **the e.** los ancianos

eldest [ˈeldɪst] **1** *adj* mayor **2** *n* **the e.** el/la mayor

elect [ɪˈlekt] **1** *vt* **(a)** *Pol* elegir **(b)** *(choose)* **to e. to do sth** decidir hacer algo **2** *adj* **the president e.** el presidente electo

election [ɪˈlekʃən] **1** *n* elección *f*; **general e.** elecciones *fpl* generales **2** *adj* electoral

electorate [ɪˈlektərɪt] *n* electorado *m*

electric [ɪˈlektrɪk] *adj* **(a)** eléctrico(a); **e. blanket** manta eléctrica, *Am* frazada eléctrica; **e. chair** silla eléctrica; **e. shock** electrochoque *m* **(b)** *Fig* electrizante

electrical [ɪˈlektrɪkəl] *adj* eléctrico(a)

electrician [ɪlekˈtrɪʃən] *n* electricista *mf*

electricity [ɪlekˈtrɪsɪtɪ] *n* electricidad *f*; **e. bill** recibo *m* de la luz

electronic [ɪlekˈtrɒnɪk] *adj* electrónico(a); **e. banking** banca electrónica, telebanca *f*

electronics [ɪlekˈtrɒnɪks] **1** *n sing (science)* electrónica *f* **2** *npl (of machine)* componentes *mpl* electrónicos

elegant [ˈelɪgənt] *adj* elegante

element [ˈelɪmənt] *n* **(a)** elemento *m* **(b)** *(part)* parte *f* **(c)** *(electrical)* resistencia *f* **(d)** *Fam Fig* **to be in one's e.** estar en su salsa

elementary [elɪˈmentərɪ] *adj (basic)* elemental; *(not developed)* rudimentario(a); *(easy)* fácil; *US* **e. school** escuela primaria

elephant [ˈelɪfənt] *n* elefante *m*

elevate [ˈelɪveɪt] *vt* elevar; *(in rank)* ascender

elevator ['elɪveɪtər] n US ascensor m

eleven [ɪ'levən] adj & n once (m inv)

eleventh [ɪ'levənθ] **1** adj & n undécimo(a) (m,f) **2** n (fraction) undécimo m

elicit [ɪ'lɪsɪt] vt obtener

eligible ['elɪdʒəbəl] adj apto(a); **he isn't e. to vote** no tiene derecho al voto

eliminate [ɪ'lɪmɪneɪt] vt eliminar

elite [ɪ'liːt] n elite f

eloquent ['elɒkwənt] adj elocuente

else [els] adv (**a**) anyone e. alguien más; **anything e.?** ¿algo más?; **everything e.** todo lo demás; **no one e.** nadie más; **someone e.** otro(a); **something e.** otra cosa, algo más; **somewhere e.** en otra parte; **what e.?** ¿qué más?; **where e.?** ¿en qué otro sitio? (**b**) **or e.** (otherwise) si no

elsewhere [els'weə(r)] adv en otra parte

elude [ɪ'luːd] vt (**a**) (escape) eludir; **his name eludes me** no consigo acordarme de su nombre (**b**) (avoid) esquivar

e-mail ['iːmeɪl] Comput **1** n (system) correo m (electrónico); (message) (mensaje m por) correo (electrónico); **e. address** dirección f de correo (electrónico) **2** vt (person) enviar un correo (electrónico) a; (file) enviar por correo (electrónico)

embankment [ɪm'bæŋkmənt] n (**a**) (made of earth) terraplén m (**b**) (of river) dique m

embargo [em'bɑːgəʊ] n (pl embargoes) embargo m

embark [em'bɑːk] **1** vt (merchandise) embarcar **2** vi embarcar, embarcarse; Fig **to e. upon** emprender; (sth difficult) embarcarse en

embarrass [ɪm'bærəs] vt avergonzar, Am salvo RP apenar

embarrassing [ɪm'bærəsɪŋ] adj embarazoso(a), Am salvo RP penoso(a)

embassy ['embəsɪ] n embajada f

ember ['embə(r)] n ascua f, rescoldo m

emblem ['embləm] n emblema m

embrace [ɪm'breɪs] **1** vt (**a**) abrazar

(**b**) (accept) adoptar (**c**) (include) abarcar **2** vi abrazarse **3** n abrazo m

embroider [ɪm'brɔɪdə(r)] vt (**a**) Sewing bordar (**b**) Fig (story, truth) adornar, embellecer

embroidery [ɪm'brɔɪdərɪ] n bordado m

embryo ['embrɪəʊ] n embrión m

emerald ['emərəld] n esmeralda f

emerge [ɪ'mɜːdʒ] vi salir; (problem) surgir; **it emerged that ...** resultó que ...

emergency [ɪ'mɜːdʒənsɪ] n emergencia f; Med urgencia f; **in an e.** en caso de emergencia; **e. exit** salida f de emergencia; **e. landing** aterrizaje forzoso; **e. measures** medidas fpl de urgencia; US **e. room** sala f de urgencias; Aut **e. stop** frenazo m en seco; Pol **state of e.** estado m de excepción

emigrant ['emɪgrənt] n emigrante mf

emigrate ['emɪgreɪt] vi emigrar

eminent ['emɪnənt] adj eminente

emit [ɪ'mɪt] vt (signals) emitir; (smells) despedir; (sound) producir

emotion [ɪ'məʊʃən] n emoción f

emotional [ɪ'məʊʃənəl] adj (**a**) emocional (**b**) (moving) conmovedor(a)

emotive [ɪ'məʊtɪv] adj emotivo(a)

empathy ['empəθɪ] n identificación f

emperor ['empərə(r)] n emperador m

emphasis ['emfəsɪs] n (pl emphases ['emfəsiːz]) énfasis m; **to place e. on sth** hacer hincapié en algo

emphasize ['emfəsaɪz] vt subrayar, hacer hincapié en; (insist) insistir; (highlight) hacer resaltar

emphatic [em'fætɪk] adj (forceful) enfático(a); (convinced) categórico(a)

empire ['empaɪə(r)] n imperio m

employ [ɪm'plɔɪ] vt emplear; (time) ocupar

employee [em'plɔɪiː, emplɔɪ'iː] n empleado(a) m,f

employer [ɪm'plɔɪə(r)] n patrón(ona) m,f

employment [ɪmˈplɔɪmənt] n empleo m; **e. agency** agencia f de colocaciones; **full e.** pleno empleo

emptiness [ˈemptɪnɪs] n vacío m

empty [ˈemptɪ] **1** adj (**emptier, emptiest**) vacío(a); **an e. house** una casa deshabitada; **e. promises** promesas fpl vanas
2 vt vaciar
3 vi (**a**) vaciarse (**b**) (river) desembocar (**into** en)
4 npl **empties** envases vacíos

empty-handed [emptɪˈhændɪd] adj con las manos vacías

emulate [ˈemjʊleɪt] vt emular

enable [ɪnˈeɪbəl] vt permitir

enamel [ɪˈnæməl] n esmalte m

enchanting [ɪnˈtʃɑːntɪŋ] adj encantador(a)

encircle [ɪnˈsɜːkəl] vt rodear

enclose [ɪnˈkləʊz] vt (**a**) (surround) rodear (**b**) (fence in) cercar (**c**) (in envelope) adjuntar; **please find enclosed** le enviamos adjunto

enclosure [ɪnˈkləʊʒə(r)] n (**a**) (fenced area) cercado m (**b**) (in envelope) documento adjunto (**c**) (of racecourse) recinto m

encore [ˈɒŋkɔː(r)] **1** interj ¡otra!, ¡bis! **2** n repetición f, bis m

encounter [ɪnˈkaʊntə(r)] **1** n (meeting) encuentro m **2** vt encontrar, encontrarse con; (problems) tropezar con

encourage [ɪnˈkʌrɪdʒ] vt (**a**) (person) animar (**b**) (tourism, trade) fomentar

encouragement [ɪnˈkʌrɪdʒmənt] n estímulo m

encyclop(a)edia [ensaɪkləʊˈpiːdɪə] n enciclopedia f

end [end] **1** n (**a**) (of stick) punta f; (of street) final m; (of table) extremo m; Fig **to make ends meet** llegar a final de mes (**b**) (conclusion) fin m, final m; **in the e.** al final; **for hours on e.** hora tras hora; **to bring an e. to sth** poner fin a algo; **to put an e. to** acabar con (**c**) (aim) objetivo m, fin m
2 vt acabar, terminar
3 vi acabarse, terminarse

▸ **end up** vi terminar; **it ended up in the dustbin** fue a parar al cubo de la basura; **to e. up doing sth** terminar por hacer algo

endanger [ɪnˈdeɪndʒə(r)] vt poner en peligro

endearing [ɪnˈdɪərɪŋ] adj simpático(a)

endeavour, US **endeavor** [ɪnˈdevə(r)] **1** n esfuerzo m **2** vt intentar, procurar

ending [ˈendɪŋ] n final m

endless [ˈendlɪs] adj interminable

endorse [ɪnˈdɔːs] vt (**a**) (document, cheque) endosar (**b**) (approve) (opinion, action) apoyar, respaldar

endorsement [ɪnˈdɔːsmənt] n (**a**) (on document, cheque) endoso m (**b**) Br (on driving licence) infracción f anotada (**c**) (approval) aprobación f

endow [ɪnˈdaʊ] vt dotar; **to be endowed with** estar dotado(a) de

endurance [ɪnˈdjʊərəns] n resistencia f

endure [ɪnˈdjʊə(r)] **1** vt (bear) aguantar, soportar **2** vi perdurar

enemy [ˈenəmɪ] adj & n enemigo(a) (m,f)

energetic [enəˈdʒetɪk] adj enérgico(a)

energy [ˈenədʒɪ] n energía f

enforce [ɪnˈfɔːs] vt (law) hacer cumplir

engage [ɪnˈgeɪdʒ] vt (**a**) (hire) contratar (**b**) (attention) llamar (**c**) (in conversation) entablar

engaged [ɪnˈgeɪdʒd] adj (**a**) (betrothed) prometido(a); **to get e.** prometerse (**b**) (busy) ocupado(a); Br Tel **it's e.** está comunicando

engagement [ɪnˈgeɪdʒmənt] n (**a**) (betrothal) petición f de mano; (period) noviazgo m; **e. ring** anillo m de compromiso (**b**) (appointment) cita f (**c**) Mil combate m

engine [ˈendʒɪn] n motor m; Rail locomotora f; **e. room** sala f de máquinas; **e. driver** maquinista mf

engineer [endʒɪˈnɪə(r)] **1** n (**a**)

ingeniero(a) *m,f;* **civil e.** ingeniero de caminos **(b)** *US Rail* maquinista *mf* **2** *vt Fig (contrive)* maquinar

engineering [endʒɪˈnɪərɪŋ] *n* ingeniería *f;* **electrical e.** electrotecnia *f;* **civil e.** ingeniería civil

England [ˈɪŋɡlənd] *n* Inglaterra

English [ˈɪŋɡlɪʃ] **1** *adj* inglés(esa) **2** *n* **(a)** *(language)* inglés *m* **(b)** *pl* **the E.** los ingleses

Englishman [ˈɪŋɡlɪʃmən] *n* inglés *m*

English-speaking [ˈɪŋɡlɪʃspiːkɪŋ] *adj* de habla inglesa

Englishwoman [ˈɪŋɡlɪʃwʊmən] *n* inglesa *f*

engraving [ɪnˈɡreɪvɪŋ] *n* grabado *m*

engrossed [ɪnˈɡrəʊst] *adj* absorto(a) **(in** en)

engulf [ɪnˈɡʌlf] *vt* tragarse

enhance [ɪnˈhɑːns] *vt (beauty)* realzar; *(power, chances)* aumentar

enigma [ɪˈnɪɡmə] *n* enigma *m*

enjoy [ɪnˈdʒɔɪ] *vt* **(a)** disfrutar de; **to e. oneself** pasarlo bien **(b)** *(benefit from)* gozar de

enjoyable [ɪnˈdʒɔɪəbəl] *adj* agradable; *(amusing)* divertido(a)

enjoyment [ɪnˈdʒɔɪmənt] *n* placer *m,* gusto *m*

enlarge [ɪnˈlɑːdʒ] **1** *vt* extender, ampliar; *Phot* ampliar **2** *vi* **to e. upon a subject** extenderse sobre un tema

enlargement [ɪnˈlɑːdʒmənt] *n Phot* ampliación *f*

enlighten [ɪnˈlaɪtən] *vt* iluminar

enlist [ɪnˈlɪst] **1** *vt Mil* reclutar; **to e. sb's help** conseguir ayuda de algn **2** *vi Mil* alistarse

enormous [ɪˈnɔːməs] *adj* enorme

enormously [ɪˈnɔːməslɪ] *adv* enormemente; **I enjoyed myself e.** lo pasé genial

enough [ɪˈnʌf] **1** *adj* bastante, suficiente; **e. books** bastantes libros; **e. money** bastante dinero; **have we got e. petrol?** ¿tenemos suficiente gasolina? **2** *adv* bastante; **oddly e. ...** lo curioso es que ...; **sure e.** en efecto

3 *pron* lo bastante, lo suficiente; **e. to live on** lo suficiente para vivir; **it isn't e.** no basta; **more than e.** más que suficiente; *Fam* **I've had e.!** ¡estoy harto!

enquire [ɪnˈkwaɪə(r)] *vi* preguntar

enquiry [ɪnˈkwaɪərɪ] *n* **(a)** *(question)* pregunta *f;* **to make an e.** preguntar; **enquiries** información *f* **(b)** *(investigation)* investigación *f*

enrage [ɪnˈreɪdʒ] *vt* enfurecer

enrich [ɪnˈrɪtʃ] *vt* enriquecer

enrol, *US* **enroll** [ɪnˈrəʊl] **1** *vt* matricular, inscribir **2** *vi* matricularse, inscribirse

enrolment, *US* **enrollment** [ɪnˈrəʊlmənt] *n* matrícula *f*

ensue [ɪnˈsjuː] *vi* **(a)** *(follow)* seguir **(b)** *(result)* resultar **(from** de)

ensure [ɪnˈʃʊə(r)] *vt* asegurar

entail [ɪnˈteɪl] *vt (involve)* suponer

entangle [ɪnˈtæŋɡəl] *vt* enredar

enter [ˈentə(r)] **1** *vt* **(a)** *(go into)* entrar en; *Fig (join)* ingresar en **(b)** *(write down)* apuntar, anotar **(c)** *Comput* dar entrada a **2** *vi* entrar

▸ **enter into** *vt insep* **(a)** *(agreement)* firmar; *(negotiations)* iniciar; *(bargain)* cerrar **(b)** *(relations)* establecer; *(conversation)* entablar

enterprise [ˈentəpraɪz] *n* empresa *f;* **free e.** libre empresa; **private e.** iniciativa privada; *(as a whole)* el sector privado; **public e.** el sector público

enterprising [ˈentəpraɪzɪŋ] *adj* emprendedor(a)

entertain [entəˈteɪn] **1** *vt* **(a)** *(amuse)* divertir **(b)** *(consider)* considerar; **to e. an idea** abrigar una idea **2** *vi* tener invitados

entertainer [entəˈteɪnə(r)] *n* artista *mf*

entertainment [entəˈteɪnmənt] *n* **(a)** diversión *f* **(b)** *Th* espectáculo *m*

enthusiasm [ɪnˈθjuːzɪæzəm] *n* entusiasmo *m*

enthusiast [ɪnˈθjuːzɪæst] *n* entusiasta *mf*

enthusiastic [ɪnθjuːzɪˈæstɪk] *adj* entusiasta; *(praise)* caluroso(a); **to be e. about sth** entusiasmarse por algo

entice [ɪnˈtaɪs] *vt* seducir, atraer

entire [ɪnˈtaɪə(r)] *adj* entero(a), todo(a)

entirely [ɪnˈtaɪəlɪ] *adv* (**a**) *(completely)* totalmente (**b**) *(solely)* exclusivamente

entitle [ɪnˈtaɪtəl] *vt* (**a**) dar derecho a; **to be entitled to** tener derecho a (**b**) *(book etc)* titular

entrance¹ [ˈentrəns] *n* (**a**) entrada *f*; **e. fee** *(to museum etc)* entrada; *(to organization)* cuota *f* (**b**) *(admission)* ingreso *m*; **e. examination** examen *m* de ingreso

entrance² [ɪnˈtrɑːns] *vt* encantar

entrant [ˈentrənt] *n* *(in competition)* participante *mf*; *(applicant)* aspirante *mf*

entrée [ˈɒntreɪ] *n* Br *(first course)* entrada *f*; primer plato *m*; US *(main course)* plato principal

entrepreneur [ɒntrəprəˈnɜː(r)] *n* empresario(a) *m,f*

entrust [ɪnˈtrʌst] *vt* encargar (**with** de); **to e. sth to sb** dejar algo al cuidado de algn

entry [ˈentrɪ] *n* (**a**) *(entrance)* entrada *f*; **no e.** *(sign)* dirección prohibida (**b**) *(in competition)* participante *mf*

envelope [ˈenvələʊp] *n* sobre *m*

envious [ˈenvɪəs] *adj* envidioso(a); **to feel e.** tener envidia

environment [ɪnˈvaɪərənmənt] *n* medio *m* ambiente

environmental [ɪnvaɪərənˈmentəl] *adj* medioambiental

envisage [ɪnˈvɪzɪdʒ] *vt* *(imagine)* imaginarse; *(foresee)* prever

envoy [ˈenvɔɪ] *n* enviado(a) *m,f*

envy [ˈenvɪ] **1** *n* envidia *f* **2** *vt* envidiar, tener envidia de

ephemeral [ɪˈfemərəl] *adj* efímero(a)

epic [ˈepɪk] **1** *n* epopeya *f* **2** *adj* épico(a)

epidemic [epɪˈdemɪk] *n* epidemia *f*; Fig *(of crime etc)* ola *f*

epilepsy [ˈepɪlepsɪ] *n* epilepsia *f*

episode [ˈepɪsəʊd] *n* episodio *m*

epitaph [ˈepɪtɑːf] *n* epitafio *m*

epoch [ˈiːpɒk] *n* época *f*

equal [ˈiːkwəl] **1** *adj* igual; **to be e. to the occasion** estar a la altura de las circunstancias; **e. pay** igualdad *f* de salarios

2 *n* igual *mf*; **to treat sb as an e.** tratar a algn de igual a igual

3 *vt* *(pt & pp equalled, US equaled)* (**a**) *Math* equivaler (**b**) *(match)* igualar

equality [iːˈkwɒlɪtɪ] *n* igualdad *f*

equalize [ˈiːkwəlaɪz] **1** *vi* Ftb empatar **2** *vt* igualar

equally [ˈiːkwəlɪ] *adv* igualmente; **e. pretty** igual de bonito; **to share sth e.** dividir algo en partes iguales

equation [ɪˈkweɪʒən, ɪˈkweɪʃən] *n* Math ecuación *f*

equator [ɪˈkweɪtə(r)] *n* ecuador *m*

equilibrium [iːkwɪˈlɪbrɪəm] *n* equilibrio *m*

equip [ɪˈkwɪp] *vt* *(with tools, machines)* equipar; *(with food)* proveer

equipment [ɪˈkwɪpmənt] *n* *(materials)* equipo *m*; **office e.** material *m* de oficina

equivalent [ɪˈkwɪvələnt] *adj & n* equivalente *(m)*; **to be e. to** equivaler a, ser equivalente a

era [ˈɪərə] *n* era *f*

eradicate [ɪˈrædɪkeɪt] *vt* erradicar

erase [ɪˈreɪz] *vt* borrar

eraser [Br ɪˈreɪzə(r), US ɪˈreɪsər] *n* goma *f* de borrar

erect [ɪˈrekt] **1** *adj* (**a**) *(upright)* erguido(a) (**b**) *(penis)* erecto(a) **2** *vt* *(monument)* levantar, erigir

erode [ɪˈrəʊd] *vt* (**a**) *(rock, soil)* erosionar (**b**) *(metal)* corroer, desgastar; Fig *(power, confidence)* hacer perder

erosion [ɪˈrəʊʒən] *n* Geol erosión *f*

erotic [ɪˈrɒtɪk] *adj* erótico(a)

errand [ˈerənd] *n* recado *m*; **e. boy** recadero *m*

erratic [ɪˈrætɪk] *adj* *(performance, behaviour)* irregular; *(weather)* muy variable; *(person)* caprichoso(a)

error ['erǝ(r)] *n* error *m*, equivocación *f*

erupt [ɪ'rʌpt] *vi* (a) *(volcano)* entrar en erupción; *(violence)* estallar (b) **his skin erupted in a rash** le salió una erupción

eruption [ɪ'rʌpʃǝn] *n* erupción *f*

escalate ['eskǝleɪt] *vi (war)* intensificarse; *(prices)* aumentar; *(change)* convertirse (**into** en)

escalator ['eskǝleɪtǝ(r)] *n* escalera mecánica

escapade ['eskǝpeɪd] *n* aventura *f*

escape [ɪ'skeɪp] **1** *n* huida *f*, fuga *f*; *(of gas)* escape *m*; **e. route** vía *f* de escape **2** *vi* escaparse **3** *vt* (a) *(avoid)* evitar, huir de; **to e. punishment** librarse del castigo (b) *Fig* **his name escapes me** no recuerdo su nombre

escort 1 *n* ['eskɔːt] (a) *(companion)* acompañante *mf* (b) *Mil* escolta *f* **2** *vt* [ɪ'skɔːt] (a) *(accompany)* acompañar (b) *(protect)* escoltar

Eskimo ['eskɪmǝʊ] *adj & n* esquimal *(mf)*

especially [ɪ'speʃǝlɪ] *adv* especialmente, sobre todo

espresso [e'spresǝʊ] *n* café *m* exprés

essay ['eseɪ] *n Educ* redacción *f*

essence ['esǝns] *n* esencia *f*; **in e.** esencialmente

essential [ɪ'senʃǝl] **1** *adj* esencial, imprescindible **2** *n* necesidad básica; **the essentials** lo fundamental

establish [ɪ'stæblɪʃ] *vt* (a) *(found)* establecer; *(business)* montar (b) *Jur* **to e. a fact** probar un hecho; **to e. the truth** demostrar la verdad

established [ɪ'stæblɪʃt] *adj (person)* establecido(a); *(fact)* conocido(a)

establishment [ɪ'stæblɪʃmǝnt] *n* establecimiento *m*; **the E.** el sistema

estate [ɪ'steɪt] *n* (a) *(land)* finca *f*; *Br* **e. agent** agente *mf* inmobiliario(a); *Br* **e. (car)** ranchera *f*, *Esp* coche *m* modelo familiar (b) *Br* **(housing) e.** urbanización *f* (c) *Jur (of deceased person)* herencia *f*

esteem [ɪ'stiːm] **1** *n* **to hold sb in great e.** apreciar mucho a algn **2** *vt* estimar

esthetic [es'θetɪk] *adj US* = **aesthetic**

estimate 1 *n* ['estɪmɪt] *(calculation)* cálculo *m*; *(likely cost of work)* presupuesto *m*; **rough e.** cálculo aproximado **2** *vt* ['estɪmeɪt] calcular; *Fig* pensar, creer

estuary ['estjʊǝrɪ] *n* estuario *m*

etc [et'setrǝ] *adv (abbr* **et cetera)** etc., etcétera

etching ['etʃɪŋ] *n* aguafuerte *m*

eternal [ɪ'tɜːnǝl] *adj* eterno(a), incesante; **e. triangle** triángulo amoroso

eternity [ɪ'tɜːnɪtɪ] *n* eternidad *f*

ethical ['eθɪkǝl] *adj* ético(a)

ethics ['eθɪks] *n* ética *f*

ethnic ['eθnɪk] *adj* étnico(a)

etiquette ['etɪket] *n* protocolo *m*, etiqueta *f*

EU [iː'juː] *n (abbr* **European Union)** UE *f*

euphemism ['juːfɪmɪzǝm] *n* eufemismo *m*

euro ['jʊǝrǝʊ] *n (pl* **euros)** *(European currency)* euro *m*

Europe ['jʊǝrǝp] *n* Europa

European [jʊǝrǝ'piːǝn] *adj & n* europeo(a) *(m,f)*; **E. Union** Unión Europea

evacuate [ɪ'vækjʊeɪt] *vt* evacuar

evade [ɪ'veɪd] *vt* evadir

evaluate [ɪ'væljʊeɪt] *vt* evaluar

evangelical [iːvæn'dʒelɪkǝl] *adj* evangélico(a)

evaporate [ɪ'væpǝreɪt] **1** *vt* evaporar; **evaporated milk** leche condensada sin endulzar **2** *vi* evaporarse; *Fig* desvanecerse

evasive [ɪ'veɪsɪv] *adj* evasivo(a)

eve [iːv] *n* víspera *f*; **on the e. of** en vísperas de

even ['iːvǝn] **1** *adj* (a) *(smooth)* liso(a); *(level)* llano(a) (b) *(regular)* uniforme (c) *(equally balanced)* igual; **to get e. with sb** desquitarse con algn (d) *(number)* par (e) *(at the same level)* a nivel (f) *(quantity)* exacto(a)

2 *adv* (**a**) incluso, hasta, aun; **e. now** incluso ahora; **e. so** aun así; **e. the children knew** hasta los niños lo sabían (**b**) *(negative)* ni siquiera; **she can't e. write her name** ni siquiera sabe escribir su nombre (**c**) *(before comparative)* aun, todavía; **e. worse** aun peor (**d**) *(if)* incluso si; **e. though** aunque
3 *vt* igualar

evening ['i:vnɪŋ] *n* (**a**) *(early)* tarde *f*; *(late)* noche *f*; **in the e.** por la tarde; **tomorrow e.** mañana por la tarde; **e. class** clase nocturna; **e. dress** *(for man)* traje *m* de etiqueta; *(for woman)* traje de noche; **e. paper** periódico vespertino (**b**) *(greeting)* **good e.!** *(early)* ¡buenas tardes!; *(late)* ¡buenas noches!

evenly ['i:vənlɪ] *adv* *(uniformly)* uniformemente; *(fairly)* equitativamente

event [ɪ'vent] *n* (**a**) *(happening)* suceso *m*, acontecimiento *m* (**b**) *(case)* caso *m*; **in the e. of fire** en caso de incendio (**c**) *Sport* prueba *f*

eventful [ɪ'ventful] *adj* **an e. day** *(busy)* un día agitado; *(memorable)* un día memorable

eventual [ɪ'ventʃʊəl] *adj* *(ultimate)* final; *(resulting)* consiguiente

eventuality [ɪventʃʊ'ælɪtɪ] *n* eventualidad *f*

eventually [ɪ'ventʃʊəlɪ] *adv* finalmente

ever ['evə(r)] *adv* (**a**) nunca, jamás; **stronger than e.** más fuerte que nunca (**b**) *(interrogative)* alguna vez; **have you e. been there?** ¿has estado allí alguna vez? (**c**) *(always)* siempre; **for e.** para siempre (**d**) *(emphasis)* **how e. did you manage it?** ¿cómo diablos lo conseguiste?; **thank you e. so much** muchísimas gracias

evergreen ['evəgri:n] **1** *adj* de hoja perenne **2** *n* árbol *m*/planta *f* de hoja perenne

everlasting [evə'lɑ:stɪŋ] *adj* eterno(a)

every ['evrɪ] *adj* (**a**) *(each)* cada; **e.**

now and then de vez en cuando; **e. day** todos los días; **e. other day** cada dos días; **e. one of you** todos(as) vosotros(as); **e. citizen** todo ciudadano (**b**) **you had e. right to be angry** tenías toda la razón para estar *esp Esp* enfadado *or esp Am* enojado

everybody ['evrɪbɒdɪ] *pron* todo el mundo, todos(as)

everyday ['evrɪdeɪ] *adj* diario(a), de todos los días; **an e. occurrence** un suceso cotidiano

everyone ['evrɪwʌn] *pron* todo el mundo, todos(as)

everyplace ['evrɪpleɪs] *adv US =* **everywhere**

everything ['evrɪθɪŋ] *pron* todo; **he eats e.** come de todo; **she means e. to me** ella lo es todo para mí

everywhere ['evrɪweə(r)] *adv* en todas partes, por todas partes

evict [ɪ'vɪkt] *vt* desahuciar

evidence ['evɪdəns] *n* (**a**) *(proof)* evidencia *f* (**b**) *Jur* testimonio *m*; **to give e.** prestar declaración (**c**) *(sign)* indicio *m*, señal *f*; **to be in e.** dejarse notar

evident ['evɪdənt] *adj* evidente, manifiesto(a)

evidently ['evɪdəntlɪ] *adv* evidentemente, al parecer

evil ['i:vəl] **1** *adj* *(wicked)* malo(a), malvado(a); *(harmful)* nocivo(a); *(unfortunate)* aciago(a) **2** *n* mal *m*

evocative [ɪ'vɒkətɪv] *adj* evocador(a)

evoke [ɪ'vəʊk] *vt* evocar

evolution [i:və'lu:ʃən] *n* evolución *f*; *Biol* desarrollo *m*

evolve [ɪ'vɒlv] **1** *vi* *(species)* evolucionar; *(ideas)* desarrollarse **2** *vt* desarrollar

ewe [ju:] *n* oveja *f*

ex [eks] *n* **her ex** su ex marido; **his ex** su ex mujer

ex- [eks] *prefix* ex, antiguo(a); **ex-minister** ex ministro *m*

exact [ɪg'zækt] **1** *adj* *(accurate)* exacto(a); *(definition)* preciso(a); **this e. spot** este mismo lugar **2** *vt* exigir

exactly [ɪg'zæktlɪ] *adv* exactamente; precisamente; **e.!** ¡exacto!

exaggerate [ɪg'zædʒəreɪt] *vi & vt* exagerar

exam [ɪg'zæm] *n Fam* examen *m*

examination [ɪgzæmɪ'neɪʃən] *n* (**a**) *Educ* examen *m*; **to sit an e.** hacer un examen (**b**) *Med* reconocimiento *m* (**c**) *Jur* interrogatorio *m*

examine [ɪg'zæmɪn] *vt Educ* examinar; *(customs)* registrar; *Med* hacer un reconocimiento médico a; *Jur* interrogar

example [ɪg'zɑːmpəl] *n* ejemplo *m*; *(specimen)* ejemplar *m*; **for e.** por ejemplo

exasperate [ɪg'zɑːspəreɪt] *vt* exasperar

excavate ['ekskəveɪt] *vt* excavar

exceed [ek'siːd] *vt* exceder, sobrepasar

exceedingly [ek'siːdɪŋlɪ] *adv* extremadamente, sumamente

excel [ɪk'sel] **1** *vi* sobresalir **2** *vt* superar

excellent ['eksələnt] *adj* excelente

except [ɪk'sept] **1** *prep* excepto, salvo; **e. for the little ones** excepto los pequeños; **e. that ...** salvo que ... **2** *vt* exceptuar

exception [ɪk'sepʃən] *n* (**a**) excepción *f*; **with the e. of** a excepción de; **without e.** sin excepción (**b**) *(objection)* objeción *f*; **to take e. to sth** ofenderse por algo

exceptional [ɪk'sepʃənəl] *adj* excepcional

excerpt ['eksɜːpt] *n* extracto *m*

excess 1 *n* [ɪk'ses] exceso *m* **2** *adj* ['ekses] excedente; **e. baggage** exceso *m* de equipaje; **e. fare** suplemento *m*

excessive [ɪk'sesɪv] *adj* excesivo(a)

exchange [ɪks'tʃeɪndʒ] **1** *n* (**a**) cambio *m*; **e. of ideas** intercambio *m* de ideas; **in e. for** a cambio de (**b**) *Fin* **e. rate** tipo *m* de cambio (**c**) *(telephone)* **e.** central telefónica **2** *vt* (**a**) intercambiar; **to e. blows** golpearse (**b**) *(prisoners)* canjear

exchequer [ɪks'tʃekə(r)] *n Br* **the E.** Hacienda *f*; **Chancellor of the E.** Ministro *m* de Hacienda

excitable [ɪk'saɪtəbəl] *adj* excitable

excite [ɪk'saɪt] *vt (person)* entusiasmar, emocionar; *(stimulate)* excitar

excited [ɪk'saɪtɪd] *adj* entusiasmado(a), emocionado(a)

excitement [ɪk'saɪtmənt] *n (stimulation)* excitación *f*; *(emotion)* emoción *f*; *(commotion)* agitación *f*

exciting [ɪk'saɪtɪŋ] *adj* apasionante, emocionante

exclaim [ɪk'skleɪm] **1** *vi* exclamar **2** *vt* gritar

exclamation [eksklə'meɪʃən] *n* exclamación *f*; **e.** *Br* **mark** *or US* **point** signo *m* de admiración

exclude [ɪk'skluːd] *vt* excluir; *(from club)* no admitir

exclusive [ɪk'skluːsɪv] **1** *adj* exclusivo(a); *(neighbourhood)* selecto(a); *(club)* cerrado(a) **2** *n Press* exclusiva *f*

excruciating [ɪk'skruːʃɪeɪtɪŋ] *adj* insoportable

excursion [ɪk'skɜːʃən] *n* excursión *f*

excuse 1 *vt* [ɪk'skjuːz] (**a**) perdonar, disculpar; **e. me!** *(to attract attention)* ¡perdón!, ¡oiga (por favor)!; *(when trying to get past)* con permiso; **may I be excused for a moment?** ¿puedo salir un momento? (**b**) *(exempt)* dispensar (**c**) *(justify)* justificar **2** *n* [ɪk'skjuːs] excusa *f*; **to make an e.** dar excusas

execute ['eksɪkjuːt] *vt* (**a**) *(order)* cumplir; *(task)* realizar (**b**) *Jur* cumplir (**c**) *(person)* ejecutar

execution [eksɪ'kjuːʃən] *n* (**a**) *(of order)* cumplimiento *m*; *(of task)* realización *f* (**b**) *Jur* cumplimiento *m* (**c**) *(of person)* ejecución *f*

executive [ɪg'zekjʊtɪv] **1** *adj* ejecutivo(a) **2** *n* ejecutivo(a) *m,f*

exemplify [ɪg'zemplɪfaɪ] *vt* ejemplificar

exempt [ɪg'zempt] **1** *vt* eximir (**from** de) **2** *adj* exento(a); **e. from tax** libre de impuesto

exemption [ɪg'zempʃən] *n* exención *f*

exercise ['eksəsaɪz] **1** *n* ejercicio *m*; **e. book** cuaderno *m* **2** *vt* (**a**) *(rights, duties)* ejercer (**b**) *(dog)* sacar de paseo **3** *vi* hacer ejercicio

exert [ɪg'zɜːt] *vt (influence)* ejercer; **to e. oneself** esforzarse

exertion [ɪg'zɜːʃən] *n* esfuerzo *m*

exhale [eks'heɪl] **1** *vt (breathe)* exhalar **2** *vi* espirar

exhaust [ɪg'zɔːst] **1** *vt* agotar **2** *n (gas)* gases *mpl* de combustión; **e. pipe** tubo *m* de escape

exhausted [ɪg'zɔːstɪd] *adj* agotado(a)

exhausting [ɪg'zɔːstɪŋ] *adj* agotador(a)

exhaustive [ɪg'zɔːstɪv] *adj* exhaustivo(a)

exhibit [ɪg'zɪbɪt] **1** *n Art* objeto expuesto; *Jur* prueba *f* instrumental **2** *vt Art* exponer; *(surprise etc)* mostrar

exhibition [eksɪ'bɪʃən] *n* exposición *f*

exhilarating [ɪg'zɪləreɪtɪŋ] *adj* estimulante

exile ['eksaɪl] **1** *n* (**a**) *(banishment)* exilio *m* (**b**) *(person)* exiliado(a) *m,f* **2** *vt* exiliar

exist [ɪg'zɪst] *vi* existir; *(have little money)* malvivir

existence [ɪg'zɪstəns] *n* existencia *f*

existing [ɪg'zɪstɪŋ] *adj* existente, actual

exit ['eksɪt] **1** *n* (**a**) salida *f* (**b**) *Th* mutis *m* **2** *vi Th* hacer mutis

exorbitant [ɪg'zɔːbɪtənt] *adj* exorbitante, desorbitado(a)

exotic [ɪg'zɒtɪk] *adj* exótico(a)

expand [ɪk'spænd] **1** *vt (enlarge)* ampliar; *(gas, metal)* dilatar **2** *vi (grow)* ampliarse; *(metal)* dilatarse; *(become more friendly)* abrirse

▶ **expand on** *vt insep* ampliar

expanse [ɪk'spæns] *n* extensión *f*

expatriate 1 *adj & n* [eks'pætrɪɪt] expatriado(a) *(m,f)* **2** *vt* [eks'pætrɪeɪt] expatriar

expect [ɪk'spekt] **1** *vt* (**a**) *(anticipate)* esperar; **I half-expected that to**
happen suponía que iba a ocurrir (**b**) *(demand)* contar con (**c**) *(suppose)* suponer **2** *vi Fam* **to be expecting** estar embarazada

expectation [ekspek'teɪʃən] *n* esperanza *f*; **contrary to e.** contrariamente a lo que se esperaba

expedient [ɪk'spiːdɪənt] **1** *adj* conveniente, oportuno(a) **2** *n* expediente *m*, recurso *m*

expedition [ekspɪ'dɪʃən] *n* expedición *f*

expel [ɪk'spel] *vt* expulsar

expend [ɪk'spend] *vt* gastar

expendable [ɪk'spendəbəl] *adj* prescindible

expenditure [ɪk'spendɪtʃə(r)] *n* desembolso *m*

expense [ɪk'spens] *n* gasto *m*; **all expenses paid** con todos los gastos pagados; **to spare no e.** no escatimar gastos; *Fig* **at the e. of** a costa de; **e. account** cuenta *f* de gastos de representación

expensive [ɪk'spensɪv] *adj* caro(a), costoso(a)

experience [ɪk'spɪərɪəns] **1** *n* experiencia *f* **2** *vt (sensation)* experimentar; *(difficulty, loss)* sufrir

experienced [ɪk'spɪərɪənst] *adj* experimentado(a)

experiment [ɪk'sperɪmənt] **1** *n* experimento *m* **2** *vi* experimentar, hacer experimentos (**on** *or* **with** con)

expert ['ekspɜːt] **1** *adj* experto(a) **2** *n* experto(a) *m,f*, especialista *mf*

expertise [ekspɜː'tiːz] *n* pericia *f*

expire [ɪk'spaɪə(r)] *vi* (**a**) *(die)* expirar; *(mandate)* terminar (**b**) *Com, Ins* vencer; *(ticket)* caducar

expiry [ɪk'spaɪərɪ] *n* vencimiento *m*; **e. date** fecha *f* de caducidad

explain [ɪk'spleɪn] **1** *vt* explicar; *(clarify)* aclarar; **to e. oneself** justificarse **2** *vi* explicarse

explanation [eksplə'neɪʃən] *n* explicación *f*; *(clarification)* aclaración *f*

explanatory [ɪk'splænətərɪ] *adj* explicativo(a), aclaratorio(a)

explicit [ɪk'splɪsɪt] *adj* explícito(a)

explode [ɪk'spləʊd] **1** *vt* (a) *(bomb)* hacer explotar (b) *Fig (theory)* echar por tierra **2** *vi* *(bomb)* estallar, explotar; *Fig* **to e. with** *or* **in anger** montar en cólera

exploit 1 *n* ['eksplɔɪt] proeza *f*, hazaña *f* **2** *vt* [ek'splɔɪt] explotar

exploitation [eksplɔɪ'teɪʃən] *n* explotación *f*

explore [ɪk'splɔ:(r)] *vt* explorar

explosion [ɪk'spləʊʒən] *n* explosión *f*

explosive [ɪk'spləʊsɪv] **1** *adj* explosivo(a); **e. issue** asunto delicado **2** *n* explosivo *m*

export 1 *vt* [ɪk'spɔ:t] exportar **2** *n* ['ekspɔ:t] (a) *(trade)* exportación *f* (b) *(commodity)* artículo *m* de exportación

exporter [ek'spɔ:tə(r)] *n* exportador(a) *m,f*

expose [ɪk'spəʊz] *vt (uncover)* exponer; *(secret)* revelar; *(plot)* descubrir; **to e. oneself** exhibirse desnudo

exposure [ɪk'spəʊʒə(r)] *n* (a) *(to light, cold, heat)* exposición *f*; **to die of e.** morir de frío (b) *Phot* fotografía *f*; **e. meter** fotómetro *m* (c) *(of criminal)* descubrimiento *m*

express [ɪk'spres] **1** *adj* (a) *(explicit)* expreso(a) (b) *Br (letter)* urgente; **e. train** expreso *m* **2** *n Rail* expreso *m* **3** *vt* expresar **4** *adv* **send it e.** mándalo urgente

expression [ɪk'spreʃən] *n* expresión *f*

expressive [ɪks'presɪv] *adj* expresivo(a)

expressway [ɪk'spresweɪ] *n US* autopista *f*

expulsion [ɪk'spʌlʃən] *n* expulsión *f*

exquisite [ɪk'skwɪzɪt] *adj* exquisito(a)

extend [ɪk'stend] **1** *vt* (a) *(enlarge)* ampliar; *(lengthen)* alargar; *(increase)* aumentar; *Fig* **the prohibition was extended to cover cigarettes** extendieron la prohibición a los cigarrillos (b) *(give)* rendir, dar; **to e. a welcome to sb** recibir a algn (c) *(prolong)* prolongar **2** *vi* (a) *(stretch)* extenderse (b) *(last)* prolongarse

extension [ɪk'stenʃən] *n* (a) extensión *f*; *(of time)* prórroga *f* (b) *Constr* anexo *m*

extensive [ɪk'stensɪv] *adj* extenso(a)

extent [ɪk'stent] *n* (a) *(area)* extensión *f* (b) **to some e.** hasta cierto punto; **to a large e.** en gran parte; **to a lesser e.** en menor grado; **to such an e.** hasta tal punto

exterior [ɪk'stɪərɪə(r)] **1** *adj* exterior, externo(a) **2** *n* exterior *m*

exterminate [ɪk'stɜ:mɪneɪt] *vt* exterminar

external [ɪk'stɜ:nəl] *adj* externo(a), exterior

extinct [ɪk'stɪŋkt] *adj* extinguido(a)

extinguish [ɪk'stɪŋgwɪʃ] *vt* extinguir, apagar

extinguisher [ɪk'stɪŋgwɪʃə(r)] *n* extintor *m*

extortionate [ɪk'stɔ:ʃənɪt] *adj* desorbitado(a)

extra ['ekstrə] **1** *adj* extra; *(spare)* de sobra; **e. time** *(in soccer match)* prórroga *f* **2** *adv* extra; **e. fine** extra fino **3** *n (additional charge)* suplemento *m*; *Cin* extra *mf*; *(newspaper)* edición *f* especial

extract 1 *n* ['ekstrækt] extracto *m* **2** *vt* [ɪk'strækt] *(tooth, information)* extraer; *(confession)* arrancar

extracurricular [ekstrəkə'rɪkjʊlə(r)] *adj* extracurricular

extraordinary [ɪk'strɔ:dənərɪ] *adj* *(meeting)* extraordinario(a); *(behaviour etc)* extraño(a)

extravagance [ɪk'strævəgəns] *n* *(with money)* derroche *m*; *(of behaviour)* extravagancia *f*

extravagant [ɪk'strævəgənt] *adj* *(wasteful)* derrochador(a); *(excessive)* exagerado(a); *(luxurious)* lujoso(a)

extreme [ɪk'stri:m] **1** *adj* extremo(a); **an e. case** un caso excepcional; **to hold e. views** tener opiniones radicales **2** *n* extremo *m*; **in the e.** en sumo grado

extremist [ɪk'stri:mɪst] *n* extremista *mf*

extrovert [ˈekstrəvɜːt] *adj & n* extrovertido(a) *(m,f)*

exuberant [ɪgˈzjuːbərənt] *adj* exuberante

eye [aɪ] **1** *n* ojo *m*; *Fig* **not to take one's eyes off sb/sth** no quitar la vista de encima a algn/algo; *Fig* **to catch sb's e.** llamar la atención a algn; *Fig* **to have an e. for** tener buen ojo para; *Fig* **to turn a blind e. (to)** hacer la vista gorda (a); *Fig* **with an e. to** con miras a; **to keep an e. on sb/sth** vigilar a algn/algo; **black e.** ojo morado; *US* **e. doctor** óptico(a) *m,f*
2 *vt* observar

eyebrow [ˈaɪbraʊ] *n* ceja *f*

eyelash [ˈaɪlæʃ] *n* pestaña *f*

eyelid [ˈaɪlɪd] *n* párpado *m*

eyeliner [ˈaɪlaɪnə(r)] *n* lápiz *m* de ojos

eyeshadow [ˈaɪʃædəʊ] *n* sombra *f* de ojos

eyesight [ˈaɪsaɪt] *n* vista *f*

eyesore [ˈaɪsɔː(r)] *n* monstruosidad *f*

eyewitness [ˈaɪwɪtnɪs] *n* testigo *mf* ocular

Ff

F, f [ef] *n* (**a**) *(the letter)* F, f *f* (**b**) *Mus* F fa *m*

F [ef] *(abbr Fahrenheit)* F

fable ['feɪbəl] *n* fábula *f*

fabric ['fæbrɪk] *n* (**a**) *Tex* tejido *m* (**b**) *Constr* estructura *f*

fabulous ['fæbjʊləs] *adj* fabuloso(a)

face [feɪs] **1** *n* (**a**) cara *f*, rostro *m*; **f. to f.** cara a cara; **f. cloth** paño *m* (**b**) *(expression)* cara *f*, expresión *f*; **to pull faces** hacer muecas (**c**) *(surface)* superficie *f*; *(of card, coin)* cara *f*; *(of watch)* esfera *f*; **f. down/up** boca abajo/arriba (**d**) *(appearance)* aspecto *m*; **to lose f.** desprestigiarse; **to save f.** salvar las apariencias

2 *vt* (**a**) *(look on to)* dar a; *(be opposite)* estar enfrente de (**b**) **to f. the wall/window** *(person)* estar de cara a la pared/ventana (**c**) *(problem)* hacer frente a; **to f. up to** hacer cara a

3 *vi* (**a**) *(show, film)* dar a; **to f. towards** mirar hacia; **f. this way** vuélvase de este lado

faceless ['feɪslɪs] *adj* anónimo(a)

facelift ['feɪslɪft] *n Med* lifting *m*; *Fig* renovación *f*

facetious [fə'siːʃəs] *adj* bromista

facial ['feɪʃəl] *adj* facial

facilitate [fə'sɪlɪteɪt] *vt* facilitar

facility [fə'sɪlɪtɪ] *n* (**a**) *(ease)* facilidad *f* (**b**) *(means)* facilidades *fpl*; **credit facilities** facilidades de crédito (**c**) **facilities** *(rooms, equipment)* instalaciones *fpl*; **cooking facilities** derecho *m* a cocina

fact [fækt] *n* hecho *m*; **as a matter of f.** de hecho; **the f. that he confessed** el hecho de que confesara; **in f.** en realidad

faction ['fækʃən] *n (group)* facción *f*

factor ['fæktə(r)] *n* factor *m*

factory ['fæktərɪ] *n* fábrica *f*

factual ['fæktʃʊəl] *adj* **a f. error** un error de hecho

faculty ['fækəltɪ] *n* (**a**) facultad *f* (**b**) *US Univ* profesorado *m*, cuerpo *m* docente

fad [fæd] *n Fam (craze)* moda pasajera; *(whim)* capricho *m*

fade [feɪd] *vi (colour)* desteñirse; *(flower)* marchitarse; *(light)* apagarse

▸ **fade away** *vi* desvanecerse

▸ **fade in, fade out** *vt sep Cin, TV* fundir

fag [fæg] *n* (**a**) *Br Fam (cigarette)* pitillo *m* (**b**) *US very Fam (homosexual)* marica *m*

fail [feɪl] **1** *n* (**a**) *(in exam) Esp* suspenso *m*, *Am* reprobado *m* (**b**) **without f.** sin falta

2 *vt* (**a**) **don't f. me** no me falles (**b**) *(exam)* suspender (**c**) *(be unable)* no lograr (**d**) *(neglect)* dejar de

3 *vi* (**a**) *(show, film)* fracasar; *(in exam) Esp* suspender, *Am* reprobar; *(brakes)* fallar (**b**) *(business)* quebrar (**c**) *(health)* deteriorarse

failing ['feɪlɪŋ] **1** *n* (**a**) *(shortcoming)* defecto *m* (**b**) *(weakness)* punto *m* débil **2** *prep* a falta de

failure ['feɪljə(r)] *n* (**a**) fracaso *m* (**b**) *Com* quiebra *f* (**c**) *Educ* suspenso *m* (**d**) *(person)* fracasado(a) *m,f*

faint [feɪnt] **1** *adj* (**a**) *(sound)* débil; *(colour)* pálido(a); *(outline)* borroso(a); *(recollection)* vago(a) (**b**) *(giddy)* mareado(a)

2 *n* desmayo *m*

3 *vi* desmayarse

fair¹ [feə(r)] **1** *adj* (**a**) *(impartial)* imparcial; *(just)* justo(a); **it's not f.** no hay derecho; *Fam* **f. enough!** de acuerdo, *Esp* vale (**b**) *(hair)* rubio(a), *Méx* güero(a); *(skin)* claro(a) (**c**) *(weather)* bueno(a) (**d**) *(beautiful)* bello(a) (**e**) **a f. number** un buen número; **he has a f. chance** tiene bastantes probabilidades **2** *adv* **to play f.** jugar limpio

fair² [feə(r)] *n* (**a**) *Br (funfair)* feria *f* (**b**) **trade f.** feria de muestras

fairground ['feəgraʊnd] *n* real *m* de la feria

fairly ['feəlɪ] *adv* (**a**) *(justly)* justamente (**b**) *(moderately)* bastante

fairy ['feərɪ] *n* (**a**) hada *f*; **f. godmother** hada madrina; **f. tale** cuento *m* de hadas (**b**) *Fam Pej* marica *m*

faith [feɪθ] *n* (**a**) *Rel* fe *f* (**b**) *(trust)* confianza *f*; **in good f.** de buena fe

faithful ['feɪθfʊl] **1** *adj* fiel **2** *npl* **the f.** los fieles

faithfully ['feɪθfʊlɪ] *adv* fielmente; **yours f.** *(in letter)* le saluda atentamente

fake [feɪk] **1** *adj* falso(a)
2 *n* (**a**) *(object)* falsificación *f* (**b**) *(person)* impostor(a) *m,f*
3 *vt* (**a**) *(forge)* falsificar (**b**) *(feign)* fingir
4 *vi (pretend)* fingir

fall [fɔːl] **1** *n* (**a**) caída *f*; **f. of snow** nevada *f* (**b**) *(decrease)* baja *f* (**c**) *US (autumn)* otoño *m* (**d**) *(usu pl)* cascada *f*; **Niagara Falls** las cataratas del Niágara
2 *vi (pt* **fell***; pp* **fallen)** (**a**) caer, caerse; **they f. into two categories** se dividen en dos categorías; *Fig* **night was falling** anochecía; *Fig* **to f. short (of)** no alcanzar (**b**) *(in battle)* caer (**c**) *(temperature, prices)* bajar (**d**) **to f. asleep** dormirse; **to f. ill** caer enfermo(a), enfermar, *RP, Ven* enfermarse ; **to f. in love** enamorarse

▶ **fall back** *vi* replegarse

▶ **fall back on** *vt insep* echar mano a, recurrir a

▶ **fall behind** *vi (in race)* quedarse atrás; **to f. behind with one's work** retrasarse en el trabajo

▶ **fall down** *vi* (**a**) *(picture etc)* caerse (**b**) *(building)* derrumbarse

▶ **fall for** *vt insep* (**a**) *(person)* enamorarse de (**b**) *(trick)* dejarse engañar por

▶ **fall in** *vi* (**a**) *(roof)* desplomarse (**b**) *Mil* formar filas

▶ **fall off 1** *vi* (**a**) *(drop off)* caerse (**b**) *(part)* desprenderse (**c**) *(diminish)* disminuir **2** *vt insep* **to f. off sth** caerse de algo

▶ **fall out** *vi* (**a**) *(hair)* caerse (**b**) *Mil* romper filas (**c**) *(quarrel)* pelearse

▶ **fall over** *vi* caerse

▶ **fall through** *vi (plan)* fracasar

fallacy ['fæləsɪ] *n* falacia *f*

fallen ['fɔːlən] *pp of* **fall**

fallible ['fælɪbəl] *adj* falible

false [fɔːls] *adj* falso(a); **f. teeth** dentadura postiza; **f. alarm** falsa alarma

falsify ['fɔːlsɪfaɪ] *vt (records, accounts)* falsificar; *(story)* falsear

falter ['fɔːltə(r)] *vi* vacilar; *(voice)* fallar

fame [feɪm] *n* fama *f*

familiar [fə'mɪlɪə(r)] *adj* (**a**) *(common)* familiar, conocido(a); **his face is f.** su cara me suena (**b**) *(aware, knowledgeable)* enterado(a), al corriente (**with** de) (**c**) **to be on f. terms with sb** *(know well)* tener confianza con algn

familiarize [fə'mɪljəraɪz] *vt* (**a**) *(become acquainted)* familiarizar (**with** con); **to f. oneself with sth** familiarizarse con algo (**b**) *(make widely known)* popularizar

family ['fæmɪlɪ] *n* familia *f*; **f. allowance** subsidio *m* familiar; **f. doctor** médico *m* de cabecera; **f. man** hombre hogareño; **f. planning** planificación *f* familiar; **f. tree** árbol genealógico

famine ['fæmɪn] *n* hambre *f*, escasez *f* de alimentos

famished ['fæmɪʃt] *adj Fam* muerto(a) de hambre

famous ['feɪməs] *adj* célebre, famoso(a) (**for** por)

fan [fæn] **1** *n* (**a**) abanico *m*; *Elec*

ventilador *m* (**b**) *(person)* aficionado(a) *m,f; (of pop star etc)* fan *mf;* **f. club** club *m* de fans; **football f.** hincha *mf* **2** *vt* (**a**) abanicar (**b**) *(fire, passions)* avivar

▸ **fan out** *vi (troops)* desplegarse en abanico

fanatic [fə'nætɪk] *adj & n* fanático(a) *(m,f)*

fanciful ['fænsɪfʊl] *adj* (**a**) *(person)* caprichoso(a) (**b**) *(idea)* fantástico(a)

fancy ['fænsɪ] **1** *adj* (**fancier**, **fanciest**) de fantasía; **f. dress** disfraz *m* **2** *n* (**a**) *(imagination)* fantasía *f* (**b**) *(whim)* capricho *m*, antojo *m*; **to take a f. to sb** cogerle cariño a algn; **to take a f. to sth** encapricharse con algo **3** *vt* (**a**) *(imagine)* imaginarse; *Fam* **f. seeing you here!** ¡qué casualidad verte por aquí! (**b**) *(like, want)* apetecer; **do you f. a drink?** ¿te apetece una copa?; *Br Fam* **I f. her** ella me gusta

fanfare ['fænfeə(r)] *n* fanfarria *f*

fantastic [fæn'tæstɪk] *adj* fantástico(a)

fantasy ['fæntəsɪ] *n* fantasía *f*

far [fɑː(r)] (**farther** *or* **further**, **farthest** *or* **furthest**) **1** *adj* (**a**) *(distant)* lejano(a); **the F. East** el Lejano Oriente (**b**) **at the f. end** en el otro extremo (**c**) **the f. left** la extrema izquierda **2** *adv* (**a**) *(distant)* lejos; **f. off** a lo lejos; **farther back/north** más atrás/al norte; **how f. is it to Cardiff?** ¿cuánto hay de aquí a Cardiff?; **as f. as I know** que yo sepa; **as f. as possible** en lo posible; *Fig* **f. from complaining, he seemed pleased** lejos de quejarse, parecía contento; *Fam* **to go too f.** pasarse de la raya (**b**) *(in time)* **as f. back as the fifties** ya en los años cincuenta; **so f.** hasta ahora (**c**) *(much)* mucho; **by f.** con diferencia *or* mucho, *RP* por lejos; **f. cleverer** mucho más listo(a); **f. too much** demasiado

faraway ['fɑːrəweɪ] *adj* lejano(a), remoto(a)

farce [fɑːs] *n* farsa *f*

farcical ['fɑːsɪkəl] *adj* absurdo(a)

fare [feə(r)] **1** *n* (**a**) *(ticket price)* tarifa *f*, precio *m* del billete; *(for boat)* pasaje *m*; **half f.** media tarifa (**b**) *(passenger)* pasajero(a) *m,f* (**c**) *(food)* comida *f* **2** *vi* **how did you f.?** ¿qué tal te fue?

farewell [feə'wel] **1** *interj Literary* ¡adiós! **2** *n* despedida *f*

far-fetched [fɑː'fetʃt] *adj* rebuscado(a)

farm [fɑːm] **1** *n (small)* granja *f; (large)* hacienda *f*, *CSur* estancia *f* **2** *vt* cultivar, labrar

▸ **farm out** *vt sep* encargar fuera

farmer ['fɑːmə(r)] *n* granjero(a) *m,f*, *Am* hacendado(a) *m,f*

farmhouse ['fɑːmhaʊs] *n* granja *f*, *Am* hacienda *f*

farming ['fɑːmɪŋ] **1** *n* (**a**) *(agriculture)* agricultura *f* (**b**) *(of land)* cultivo *m*, labranza *f* **2** *adj* agrícola

farmyard ['fɑːmjɑːd] *n* corral *m*

far-reaching [fɑː'riːtʃɪŋ] *adj* de gran alcance

far-sighted [fɑː'saɪtɪd] *adj* (**a**) *(person)* con visión de futuro (**b**) *(plan)* con miras al futuro

fart [fɑːt] *Fam* **1** *n* pedo *m* **2** *vi* tirarse un pedo

farther ['fɑːðə(r)] *adj & adv comp of* far

farthest ['fɑːðɪst] *adj & adv superl of* far

fascinate ['fæsɪneɪt] *vt* fascinar

fascinating ['fæsɪneɪtɪŋ] *adj* fascinante

fascist ['fæʃɪst] *adj & n* fascista *(mf)*

fashion ['fæʃən] **1** *n* (**a**) *(manner)* manera *f*, modo *m*; **after a f.** más o menos (**b**) *(latest style)* moda *f*; **to go/be out of f.** pasar/no estar de moda; **f. designer** diseñador(a) *m,f* de modas; **f. parade** desfile *m* de modelos **2** *vt (metal)* labrar; *(clay)* formar

fashionable ['fæʃənəbəl] *adj* (**a**) de moda (**b**) *(area, hotel)* elegante

fast¹ [fɑːst] **1** *adj* (**a**) *(quick)* rápido(a) (**b**) **hard and f. rules** reglas estrictas (**c**) *(clock)* adelantado(a) **2** *adv* (**a**) rápidamente, deprisa; **how f.?** ¿a qué velocidad? (**b**) *(securely)* firmemente; **f. asleep** profundamente dormido(a)

fast² [fɑːst] **1** *n* ayuno *m* **2** *vi* ayunar

fasten ['fɑːsən] **1** *vt* (**a**) *(attach)* sujetar; *(fix)* fijar (**b**) *(belt)* abrochar; *(bag)* asegurar; *(shoelaces)* atar **2** *vi* *(dress)* abrocharse

fastener ['fɑːsənə(r)] *n* cierre *m*

fat [fæt] **1** *adj* (**fatter, fattest**) (**a**) gordo(a) (**b**) *(book, file)* grueso(a) (**c**) *(meat)* que tiene mucha grasa **2** *n* grasa *f*; **cooking f.** manteca *f* de cerdo

fatal ['feɪtəl] *adj* (**a**) *(accident, illness)* mortal (**b**) *(ill-fated)* fatal, funesto(a) (**c**) *(fateful)* fatídico(a)

fatality [fə'tælɪtɪ] *n* víctima *f* mortal

fatally ['feɪtəlɪ] *adv* **f. wounded** mortalmente herido(a)

fate [feɪt] *n* destino *m*, suerte *f*

fateful ['feɪtfʊl] *adj* fatídico(a), aciago(a)

father ['fɑːðə(r)] *n* (**a**) padre *m*; **my f. and mother** mis padres; **F. Christmas** Papá *m* Noel (**b**) *Rel* padre *m*

fatherhood ['fɑːðəhʊd] *n* paternidad *f*

father-in-law ['fɑːðərɪnlɔː] *n* suegro *m*

fatigue [fə'tiːg] *n* (**a**) *(tiredness)* fatiga *f* (**b**) *Mil* faena *f*; **f. dress** traje *m* de faena

fatten ['fætən] *vt* engordar

fattening ['fætənɪŋ] *adj* que engorda

fatty ['fætɪ] **1** *adj (food)* graso(a); *Anat (tissue)* adiposo(a) **2** *n* *Fam (person)* gordinflón(ona) *m,f*

faucet ['fɔːsɪt] *n US Esp* grifo *m*, *Chile, Col, Méx* llave *f*, *RP* canilla *f*

fault [fɔːlt] **1** *n* (**a**) *(defect)* defecto *m*; *(in merchandise)* desperfecto *m* (**b**) *(blame)* culpa *f*; **to be at f.** tener la culpa (**c**) *(mistake)* error *m* (**d**) *Geol* falla *f* **2** *vt* criticar

faultless ['fɔːltlɪs] *adj* intachable

faulty ['fɔːltɪ] *adj* defectuoso(a)

favour, US favor ['feɪvə(r)] **1** *n* (**a**) favor *m*; **in f. of** a favor de; **to be in f. with sb** gozar del favor de algn; **to ask**

sb a f. pedirle un favor a algn (**b**) **1-0 in our f.** *(advantage)* 1-0 a favor nuestro **2** *vt* (**a**) *(person)* favorecer a (**b**) *(approve)* estar a favor de

favourable, US favorable ['feɪvərəbəl] *adj* favorable

favourite, US favorite ['feɪvərɪt] *adj & n* favorito(a) *(m,f)*

favouritism, US favoritism ['feɪvərɪtɪzəm] *n* favoritismo *m*

fawn¹ [fɔːn] **1** *adj* (de) color café claro **2** *n* (**a**) *Zool* cervato *m* (**b**) color *m* café claro

fawn² [fɔːn] *vi* adular (**on** a)

fax [fæks] **1** *n (machine, message)* fax *m*; **f. modem** modem *m* fax **2** *vt* mandar por fax

fear [fɪə(r)] **1** *n* miedo *m*, temor *m*; **for f. of** por temor a; *Fam* **no f.!** ¡ni pensarlo! **2** *vt* temer; **I f. it's too late** me temo que ya es tarde **3** *vi* temer (**for** por)

fearful ['fɪəfʊl] *adj* (**a**) *(person)* temeroso(a) (**b**) *(frightening)* espantoso(a)

fearless ['fɪəlɪs] *adj* intrépido(a)

feasible ['fiːzəbəl] *adj (practicable)* factible; *(possible)* viable

feast [fiːst] *n* (**a**) banquete *m*; *Fam* comilona *f* (**b**) *Rel* **f. day** fiesta *f* de guardar

feat [fiːt] *n* hazaña *f*

feather ['feðə(r)] **1** *n* pluma *f*; **f. duster** plumero *m* **2** *vt* *Fam* **to f. one's nest** hacer su agosto

feature ['fiːtʃə(r)] **1** *n* (**a**) *(of face)* rasgo *m*, facción *f* (**b**) *(characteristic)* característica *f* (**c**) **f. film** largometraje *m* (**d**) *Press* crónica *f* especial **2** *vt* (**a**) poner de relieve (**b**) *Cin* tener como protagonista a **3** *vi* figurar

February ['febrʊərɪ] *n* febrero *m*

fed [fed] **1** *adj* *Fam* **f. up (with)** harto(a) (de) **2** *pt & pp of* **feed**

federal ['fedərəl] *adj* federal

federation [fedə'reɪʃən] *n* federación *f*

fee [fi:] *n (of lawyer, doctor)* honorarios *mpl; Ftb* **transfer f.** prima *f* de traslado; *Univ* **tuition fees** derechos *mpl* de matrícula

feeble ['fi:bəl] *adj* débil

feed [fi:d] *(pt & pp fed)* **1** *vt* (**a**) *(give food to)* dar de comer a; *Fig (fire)* alimentar; **to f. a baby** *(breast-feed)* amamantar a un bebé; *(with bottle)* dar el biberón a un bebé (**b**) *Elec* alimentar (**c**) *(insert)* introducir
  2 *vi (cows, sheep)* pacer; **to f. on sth** *(person)* comer algo
  3 *n* (**a**) *(food)* comida *f*; **cattle f.** pienso *m* (**b**) *Tech* alimentación *f*

▸ **feed up** *vt sep* cebar

feedback ['fi:dbæk] *n* (**a**) *Tech* feedback *m* (**b**) *Fig* reacción *f*

feel [fi:l] *(pt & pp* **felt**) **1** *vi* (**a**) *(emotion, sensation)* sentir; **how do you f.?** ¿qué tal te encuentras?; **I f. bad about it** me da pena; **to f. happy/uncomfortable** sentirse feliz/incómodo; **to f. cold/sleepy** tener frío/sueño
  (**b**) *(seem)* **your hand feels cold** tienes la mano fría; **it feels like summer** parece verano
  (**c**) *(opinion)* opinar; **I f. sure that ...** estoy seguro(a) de que ...
  (**d**) **I f. like an ice cream** me tomaría *or Esp* me apetece un helado, *Carib, Col, Méx* me provoca un sorbete; **to f. like doing sth** tener ganas de hacer algo
  2 *vt* (**a**) *(touch)* tocar (**b**) **she feels a failure** se siente inútil (**c**) *(notice, be aware of)* notar
  3 *n* (**a**) *(touch, sensation)* tacto *m; Fig* **to get the f. for sth** *Esp* cogerle el truco a algo, *Am* agarrar la onda a algo (**b**) *(atmosphere)* ambiente *m*

▸ **feel for** *vt insep* (**a**) *(search for)* buscar (**b**) *(have sympathy for)* compadecer

feeling ['fi:lɪŋ] **1** *n* (**a**) *(emotion)* sentimiento *m*; **ill f.** rencor *m* (**b**) *(compassion)* compasión *f* (**c**) **I had the f. that ...** *(impression)* tuve la impresión de que ... (**d**) *(sensitivity)* sensibilidad *f* (**e**) *(opinion)* opinión *f*;

to express one's feelings expresar sus opiniones **2** *adj* sensible, compasivo(a)

feet [fi:t] *pl of* **foot**

feign [feɪn] *vt* fingir

feline ['fi:laɪn] **1** *n* felino *m*, félido *m* **2** *adj* felino(a)

fell[1] [fel] *pt of* **fall**

fell[2] [fel] *vt (trees)* talar; *Fig (enemy)* derribar

fellow ['feləʊ] *n* (**a**) *(companion)* compañero(a) *m,f;* **f. citizen** conciudadano(a) *m,f;* **f. countryman/countrywoman** compatriota *mf;* **f. men** prójimos *mpl;* **f. passenger/student** compañero(a) *m,f* de viaje/estudios (**b**) *Fam (chap)* tipo *m*, tío *m* (**c**) *(of society)* socio(a) *m,f*

fellowship ['feləʊʃɪp] *n* (**a**) *(comradeship)* camaradería *f* (**b**) *Univ* beca *f* de investigación

felony ['felənɪ] *n US Law* crimen *m*, delito *m* grave

felt[1] [felt] *pt & pp of* **feel**

felt[2] [felt] *n Tex* fieltro *m*

felt-tip(ped) ['felttɪp(t)] *adj* **f. pen** rotulador *m*

female ['fi:meɪl] **1** *adj* (**a**) *Zool* hembra (**b**) *(woman)* mujer *f; (girl)* chica *f*

feminine ['femɪnɪn] *adj* femenino(a)

feminist ['femɪnɪst] *adj & n* feminista *(mf)*

fence [fens] **1** *n* cerca *f*, valla *f; Fig* **to sit on the f.** ver los toros desde la barrera **2** *vi Sport* practicar la esgrima

▸ **fence in** *vt sep* meter en un cercado

fencing ['fensɪŋ] *n Sport* esgrima *f*

fend [fend] *vi* **to f. for oneself** valerse por sí mismo

▸ **fend off** *vt sep (blow)* parar; *(question)* rehuir; *(attack)* rechazar

fender ['fendə(r)] *n* (**a**) *(fireplace)* pantalla *f* (**b**) *US Aut Esp, Bol, RP* guardabarros *mpl, Andes, CAm, Carib* guardafango *m, Méx* salpicadera *f* (**c**) *Naut* defensa *f*

ferment *vt & vi* [fə'ment] fermentar

ferocious [fə'rəʊʃəs] *adj* feroz

ferret ['ferɪt] **1** *n* hurón *m* **2** *vi* huronear, husmear

▸ **ferret out** *vt sep* descubrir

ferry ['ferɪ] **1** *n* (**a**) *(small)* barca *f* de pasaje (**b**) *(large, for cars)* transbordador *m*, ferry *m* **2** *vt* transportar

fertile ['fɜ:taɪl] *adj* fértil

fertilizer ['fɜ:tɪlaɪzə(r)] *n* abono *m*

fervent ['fɜ:vənt] *adj* ferviente

festival ['festɪvəl] *n (event)* festival *m*; *(celebration)* fiesta *f*

festive ['festɪv] *adj* festivo(a); **the f. season** las fiestas de Navidad

festivity [fe'stɪvɪtɪ] *n* **the festivities** las fiestas

fetch [fetʃ] *vt* (**a**) *(go for)* ir a buscar (**b**) *(bring)* traer (**c**) **how much did it f.?** *(sell for)* ¿por cuánto se vendió?

fete [feɪt] **1** *n* fiesta *f* **2** *vt* festejar

fetus ['fi:təs] *n US* = **foetus**

feud [fju:d] **1** *n* enemistad duradera **2** *vi* pelear

fever ['fi:və(r)] *n* fiebre *f*

feverish ['fi:vərɪʃ] *adj* febril

few [fju:] **1** *adj* (**a**) *(not many)* pocos(as); **as f. as** solamente (**b**) *(some)* algunos(as), unos(as) cuantos(as); **a f. books** unos *or* algunos libros; **she has fewer books than I thought** tiene menos libros de lo que pensaba; **for the past f. years** durante estos últimos años; **in the next f. days** dentro de unos días; **quite a f.** bastantes **2** *pron* (**a**) *(not many)* pocos(as); **there are too f.** no hay suficientes (**b**) **a f.** *(some)* algunos(as), unos(as) cuantos(as); **who has the fewest?** ¿quién tiene menos?

fiancé [fɪ'ɒnseɪ] *n* prometido *m*

fiancée [fɪ'ɒnseɪ] *n* prometida *f*

fiasco [fɪ'æskəʊ] *n (pl Br* **fiascos**, *US* **fiascoes**) fiasco *m*

fib [fɪb] *Fam* **1** *n* trola *f* **2** *vi* contar trolas

fibre, *US* **fiber** ['faɪbə(r)] *n* fibra *f*

fickle ['fɪkəl] *adj* inconstante, voluble

fiction ['fɪkʃən] *n* ficción *f*

fictional ['fɪkʃənəl] *adj* (**a**) *Lit* novelesco(a) (**b**) *(imaginative)* ficticio(a)

fictitious [fɪk'tɪʃəs] *adj* ficticio(a)

fiddle ['fɪdəl] **1** *n* (**a**) *(violin)* violín *m* *(en música folk)* (**b**) *esp Br Fam (swindle)* timo *m* **2** *vt Br Fam* amañar **3** *vi* jugutear (**with** con)

▸ **fiddle about** *vi* perder tiempo

fiddly ['fɪdlɪ] *adj Fam* laborioso(a)

fidget ['fɪdʒɪt] *vi* (**a**) moverse; **stop fidgeting!** ¡estáte quieto! (**b**) jugar (**with** con)

field [fi:ld] **1** *n* (**a**) campo *m*; **f. glasses** gemelos *mpl*; **f. marshal** mariscal *m* de campo (**b**) *Geol, Min* yacimiento *m* (**c**) **f. trip** viaje *m* de estudios; **f. work** trabajo *m* de campo **2** *vt Sport* (**a**) *(ball)* parar y devolver (**b**) *(team)* presentar

fierce [fɪəs] *adj (animal)* feroz; *(argument)* acalorado(a); *(heat, competition)* intenso(a); *(wind)* violento(a)

fiery ['faɪərɪ] *adj (temper)* fogoso(a); *(speech)* acalorado(a); *(colour)* encendido(a)

fifteen [fɪf'ti:n] *adj & n* quince *(inv)*

fifteenth [fɪf'ti:nθ] **1** *adj & n* decimoquinto(a) *(m,f)* **2** *n (fraction)* quinzavo *m*

fifth [fɪfθ] **1** *adj & n* quinto(a) *(m,f)* **2** *n (fraction)* quinto *m*

fifty ['fɪftɪ] *adj & n* cincuenta *(m inv)*

fig¹ [fɪg] *n (fruit)* higo *m*

fig² [fɪg] *(abbr* **figure**) fig

fight [faɪt] *(pt & pp* **fought**) **1** *vt* (**a**) pelear(se) con, luchar con; *(of boxer)* enfrentarse a, luchar con; *(of bullfighter)* lidiar; *Fig (corruption)* combatir (**b**) *(battle)* librar; *(war)* hacer (**c**) *(decision)* recurrir contra **2** *vi* (**a**) pelear(se), luchar (**b**) *(quarrel)* reñir; **to f. over sth** disputarse la posesión de algo (**c**) *Fig (struggle)* luchar (**for/against** por/contra) **3** *n* (**a**) pelea *f*, lucha *f*; *(in boxing)* combate *m* (**b**) *(quarrel)* riña *f* (**c**) *Fig (struggle)* lucha *f*

▸ **fight back 1** *vt sep (tears)* contener
2 *vi* contraatacar

▸ **fight off** *vt sep* **(a)** *(attack)* rechazar
(b) *(illness)* cortar

▸ **fight out** *vt sep* discutir

fighter ['faɪtə(r)] *n* **(a)** *(person)*
combatiente *mf*; *(in boxing)* púgil *m*
(b) *Fig* luchador(a) *m,f*; **f. (plane)**
(avión *m* de) caza *m*; **f. bomber**
cazabombardero *m*

figment ['fɪgmənt] *n* **it's a f. of your**
imagination es un producto de tu
imaginación

figurative ['fɪgərətɪv] *adj* figura-
do(a)

figure ['fɪgə(r), *US* 'fɪgjər] **1** *n* **(a)**
(form, outline) forma *f*, silueta *f* **(b)**
(shape, statue, character) figura *f*; **she**
has a good f. tiene buen tipo **(c)** *(in*
book) dibujo *m* **(d) f. of speech** figura
retórica *f* **(e)** *Math* cifra *f*
2 *vt US Fam* pensar, figurarse
3 *vi* **(a)** *(appear) (in list, book)* figurar
(b) *Fam (make sense)* **that figures!**
(es) normal or lógico

▸ **figure out** *vt sep Fam* comprender;
I can't f. it out no me lo explico

file [faɪl] **1** *n* **(a)** *(tool)* lima *f* **(b)**
(folder) carpeta *f* **(c)** *(archive, of*
computer) archivo *m*; **on f.** archi-
vado(a) **(d)** *(line)* fila *f*; **in single f.** en
fila india
2 *vt* **(a)** *(smooth)* limar **(b)** *(put away)*
archivar
3 *vi* **to f. past** desfilar

filing ['faɪlɪŋ] *n* clasificación *f*; **f.**
cabinet archivador *m*; *(for cards)*
fichero *m*

fill [fɪl] **1** *vt* **(a)** *(space, time)* llenar
(with de) **(b)** *(post, requirements)*
cubrir **(c)** *Culin* rellenar
2 *vi* llenarse **(with** de)
3 *n* **to eat one's f.** comer hasta
hartarse

▸ **fill in 1** *vt sep* **(a)** *(space, form)*
rellenar **(b)** *Fam (inform)* poner al
corriente **(on** de) **(c)** *(time)* pasar **2** *vi*
to f. in for sb sustituir a algn

▸ **fill out 1** *vt sep US (form)* llenar **2** *vi*
Fam engordar

▸ **fill up 1** *vt sep* llenar hasta arriba;
Fam Aut **f. her up!** ¡llénelo! **2** *vi*
llenarse

fillet ['fɪlɪt] *n* filete *m*; **f. steak** filete

filling ['fɪlɪŋ] **1** *adj* que llena mucho **2**
n **(a)** *(stuffing)* relleno *m* **(b)** *(in tooth)*
empaste *m* **(c)** *Br* **f. station** gasolinera
f, estación *f* de servicio, *Andes, Ven*
bomba *f*, *Méx* gasolinería *f*, *Perú* grifo *m*

film [fɪlm] **1** *n* **(a)** *esp Br (at cinema)*
película *f*; **f. star** estrella *f* de cine **(b)**
(layer) capa *f* **(c)** *(photographic)* **a**
(roll of) f. *(for camera)* un rollo, un
carrete
2 *vt Cin* filmar
3 *vi Cin* rodar

filter ['fɪltə(r)] **1** *n* filtro *m*; *Aut* **f. lane**
carril *m* de acceso **2** *vt* filtrar

▸ **filter through** *vi Fig* filtrarse **(to** a)

filth [fɪlθ] *n* *(dirt)* porquería *f*; *Fig*
porquerías *fpl*

filthy ['fɪlθɪ] *adj* **(filthier, filthiest)**
(a) *(dirty)* asqueroso(a) **(b)** *(obscene)*
obsceno(a)

fin [fɪn] *n Zool, Av* aleta *f*

final ['faɪnəl] **1** *adj* **(a)** *(last)* último(a),
final **(b)** *(definitive)* definitivo(a) **2** *n*
(a) *Sport* final *f* **(b)** *Univ* **finals** *Br*
exámenes *mpl* de fin de carrera; *US*
exámenes *mpl* finales

finalist ['faɪnəlɪst] *n* finalista *mf*

finalize ['faɪnəlaɪz] *vt* ultimar; *(date)*
fijar

finally ['faɪnəlɪ] *adv* *(lastly)* por
último; *(at last)* por fin

finance ['faɪnæns, fɪ'næns] **1** *n* **(a)**
finanzas *fpl* **(b) finances** fondos *mpl*
2 *vt* financiar

financial [faɪ'nænʃəl, fɪ'nænʃəl] *adj*
financiero(a); **f. crisis** crisis económica; *Br* **f. year** *(for budget)* ejercicio *m*
(económico); *(for tax)* año *m* fiscal

financier [faɪ'nænsɪə(r), fɪ'nænsɪə(r)]
n financiero(a) *m,f*

find [faɪnd] **1** *vt* (*pt & pp* **found**)
(a) *(locate)* encontrar **(b)** *(think)*
encontrar **(c)** *(discover)* descubrir **(d)**
Jur **to f. sb guilty/not guilty**
declarar culpable/inocente a algn **(e)** **I**
can't f. the courage to tell him no

tengo valor para decírselo; **I found it impossible to get away** me resultó imposible irme **2** *n* hallazgo *m*

▶ **find out 1** *vt sep* (a) *(inquire)* averiguar (b) *(discover)* descubrir **2** *vi* (a) **to f. out about sth** informarse sobre algo (b) *(discover)* enterarse

findings ['faɪndɪŋz] *npl* conclusiones *fpl*

fine¹ [faɪn] **1** *n* multa *f* **2** *vt* multar

fine² [faɪn] **1** *adj* (a) *(delicate etc)* fino(a) (b) *(subtle)* sutil (c) *(excellent)* excelente (d) *(weather)* bueno(a) (e) *(all right)* bien

2 *adv Fam* muy bien

3 *interj* ¡vale!

finger ['fɪŋgə(r)] **1** *n* dedo *m* (de la mano) **2** *vt* tocar; *Pej* manosear

fingernail ['fɪŋgəneɪl] *n* uña *f*

fingertip ['fɪŋgətɪp] *n* punta *f or* yema *f* del dedo

finish ['fɪnɪʃ] **1** *n* (a) *(end)* fin *m*; *(of race)* llegada *f* (b) *(surface)* acabado *m*

2 *vt* (a) *(complete)* acabar, terminar; **to f. doing sth** terminar de hacer algo (b) *(use up)* agotar

3 *vi* acabar, terminar; **to f. second** quedar el segundo

▶ **finish off** *vt sep* (a) *(complete)* terminar completamente (b) *Fam (kill)* rematar

▶ **finish up 1** *vt sep* acabar, agotar **2** *vi* **to f. up in jail** ir a parar a la cárcel

finished ['fɪnɪʃt] *adj* (a) *(product)* acabado(a) (b) *Fam (exhausted)* rendido(a)

finishing ['fɪnɪʃɪŋ] *adj* **to put the f. touch(es) to sth** darle los últimos toques a algo; **f. line** (línea *f* de) meta *f*; **f. school** = escuela privada de modales para señoritas

finite ['faɪnaɪt] *adj* finito(a); *(verb)* conjugable

Finland ['fɪnlənd] *n* Finlandia

Finn [fɪn] *n* finlandés(esa) *m,f*

Finnish ['fɪnɪʃ] **1** *adj* finlandés(esa) **2** *n (language)* finlandés *m*

fir [fɜ:(r)] *n* abeto *m*

fire ['faɪə(r)] **1** *n* (a) fuego *m* (b) *(accident etc)* incendio *m*; **to be on**

f. estar en llamas; **to catch f.** incendiarse; **f. alarm** alarma *f* de incendios; *Br* **f. brigade,** *US* **f. department** (cuerpo *m* de) bomberos *mpl*; **f. engine** coche *m* de bomberos; **f. escape** escalera *f* de incendios; **f. station** parque *m* de bomberos (c) *(heater)* estufa *f* (d) *Mil* fuego *m*; **to open f.** abrir fuego

2 *vt* (a) *(gun)* disparar (**at** a); *(rocket)* lanzar; *Fig* **to f. questions at sb** bombardear a algn a preguntas (b) *Fam (dismiss)* despedir

3 *vi (shoot)* disparar (**at** sobre)

firearm ['faɪərɑ:m] *n* arma *f* de fuego

fireman ['faɪəmən] *n* bombero *m*

fireplace ['faɪəpleɪs] *n* chimenea *f*; *(hearth)* hogar *m*

firewood ['faɪəwʊd] *n* leña *f*

fireworks ['faɪəwɜ:ks] *npl* fuegos *mpl* artificiales

firm [fɜ:m] **1** *adj* firme; **to be f. with sb** *(strict)* tratar a algn con firmeza **2** *n Com* empresa *f*, firma *f*

firmly ['fɜ:mlɪ] *adv* firmemente

first [fɜ:st] **1** *adj* primero(a); *(before masculine singular noun)* primer; **Charles the F.** Carlos Primero; **for the f. time** por primera vez; **in the f. place** en primer lugar; **f. aid** primeros auxilios; **f. floor** *Br* primer piso, *US* planta baja; **f. name** nombre *m* de pila **2** *adv (before anything else)* primero; **f. of all** en primer lugar

3 *n* (a) **the f.** el primero/la primera; **the f. of April** el primero *or Esp* el uno de abril (b) **at f.** al principio; **from the (very) f.** desde el principio (c) *Aut* primera *f*

first-class ['fɜ:st'klɑ:s] **1** *adj* de primera clase **2** *adv* **to travel f.** viajar en primera

firstly ['fɜ:stlɪ] *adv* en primer lugar

first-rate ['fɜ:streɪt] *adj* de primera

fish [fɪʃ] **1** *n* (*pl* **fish**) (a) pez *m*; **f. shop** pescadería *f* (b) *Culin* pescado *m*; *Br* **f. and chips** = pescado frito con patatas *or Am* papas fritas; **f.** *Br* **finger** *or US* **stick** palito *m* de pescado **2** *vi* pescar; *Fig* **to f. in one's pocket for sth**

buscar algo en el bolsillo

fisherman ['fɪʃəmən] n pescador m

fishing ['fɪʃɪŋ] n pesca f; **to go f.** ir de pesca; **f. net** red f de pesca; **f. rod** caña f de pescar; **f. tackle** aparejo m de pesca

fishmonger ['fɪʃmʌŋgə(r)] n Br pescadero(a) m,f; **fishmonger's (shop)** pescadería f

fishy ['fɪʃɪ] adj (fishier, fishiest) de pescado; Fam (suspicious) sospechoso(a)

fist [fɪst] n puño m

fit¹ [fɪt] **1** vt (a) ir bien a; **that suit doesn't f. you** ese traje no te entalla; **the key doesn't f. the lock** la llave no es de esta cerradura; Fig **she doesn't f. the description** no responde a la descripción (b) (install) colocar; **a car fitted with a radio** un coche provisto de radio

2 vi (a) (be of right size) caber (b) (facts etc) cuadrar

3 adj (a) (suitable) apto(a), adecuado(a) (**for** para); **are you f. to drive?** ¿estás en condiciones de conducir? (b) (healthy) en (plena) forma; **to keep f.** mantenerse en forma

4 n ajuste m; **to be a good f.** encajar bien

▸ **fit in 1** vi (a) he didn't f. in with his **colleagues** no encajó con sus compañeros de trabajo (b) (tally) cuadrar (**with** con) **2** vt sep (find time for) encontrar un hueco para

fit² [fɪt] n (a) Med ataque m (b) Fig arrebato m; **f. of anger** arranque m de cólera; Fig **by fits and starts** a trompicones

fitness ['fɪtnɪs] n (a) (aptitude) aptitud f, capacidad f (b) (health) (buen) estado físico

fitted ['fɪtɪd] adj empotrado(a); **f. carpet** moqueta f; **f. cupboard** armario empotrado

fitting ['fɪtɪŋ] **1** adj apropiado(a) **2** n (a) (of dress) prueba f; **f. room** probador m (b) (usu pl) accesorio m; **light fittings** apliques eléctricos

five [faɪv] adj & n cinco (m inv)

fix [fɪks] **1** n (a) Fam **to be in a f.** estar en un apuro (b) Fam (drugs) chute m **2** vt (a) (fasten) fijar, asegurar (b) (date, price) fijar; (limit) señalar (c) (repair) arreglar (d) US (food, drink) preparar

▸ **fix up** vt sep (arrange) arreglar; **to f. sb up with sth** proveer a algn de algo

fixed [fɪkst] adj (a) fijo(a) (b) Fam (match etc) amañado(a)

fixture ['fɪkstʃə(r)] n (a) Br (in football) encuentro m (b) **fixtures** (in building) accesorios mpl

fizz [fɪz] **1** n burbujeo m **2** vi burbujear

▸ **fizzle out** ['fɪzəl] vi Fam (plan) quedarse en nada or Esp en agua de borrajas

fizzy ['fɪzɪ] adj (fizzier, fizziest) (water) con gas

flabbergasted ['flæbəgɑːstɪd] adj pasmado(a)

flabby ['flæbɪ] adj (flabbier, flabbiest) fofo(a)

flag [flæg] **1** n bandera f; Naut pabellón m

2 vt Fig **to f. down a car** hacer señales a un coche para que pare

3 vi (interest) decaer; (conversation) languidecer

flagstone ['flægstəʊn] n losa f

flair [fleə(r)] n facilidad f

flake [fleɪk] **1** n (of snow) copo m; (of skin, soap) escama f; (of paint) desconchón m **2** vi (skin) descamarse; (paint) desconcharse

flamboyant [flæm'bɔɪənt] adj extravagante

flame [fleɪm] n (a) (of fire) llama f; **to go up in flames** incendiarse (b) Comput llamarada f, = mensaje ofensivo

flamingo [flə'mɪŋgəʊ] n flamenco m

flammable ['flæməbəl] adj inflamable

flan [flæn] n tarta f; **fruit f.** tarta de fruta

flank [flæŋk] **1** n (a) (of animal) ijada f (b) Mil flanco m **2** vt flanquear

flannel ['flænəl] n (a) Tex franela f (b) Br (face cloth) toallita f

flap [flæp] **1** vt *(wings, arms)* batir **2** vi *(wings)* aletear; *(flag)* ondear **3** n **(a)** *(of envelope, pocket)* solapa f; *(of tent)* faldón m **(b)** *(of wing)* aletazo m **(c)** Fam **to get into a f.** ponerse nervioso(a)

flare [fleə(r)] **1** n **(a)** *(flame)* llamarada f **(b)** Mil, Naut bengala f **2** vi **to f. (up)** *(fire)* llamear; Fig *(person)* encolerizarse; *(trouble)* estallar

flared [fleəd] adj *(trousers etc)* acampanado(a)

flash [flæʃ] **1** n **(a)** *(of light)* destello m; *(of lightning)* relámpago m; Fig **in a f.** en un santiamén **(b)** **news f.** noticia f de última hora **(c)** Phot flash m **2** adj Br Fam *(showy)* llamativo(a), ostentoso(a) **3** vt **(a)** *(torch)* dirigir **(b)** Rad, TV transmitir **4** vi **(a)** *(light)* destellar **(b)** **a car flashed past** un coche pasó como un rayo

flashback ['flæʃbæk] n flashback m

flashlight ['flæʃlaɪt] n US linterna f

flashy ['flæʃɪ] adj *(flashier, flashiest)* Fam chillón(ona)

flask [flɑːsk, flæsk] n frasco m; **(Thermos®) f.** termo m

flat [flæt] **1** adj *(flatter, flattest)* **(a)** *(surface)* llano(a) **(b)** *(beer)* sin gas **(c)** *(battery)* descargado(a); *(tyre)* desinflado(a) **(d)** *(rate)* fijo(a) **(e)** *(dull)* soso(a) **(f)** Mus **B f.** si m bemol **2** adv **(a)** **to fall f. on one's face** caerse de bruces **(b)** **in ten seconds f.** en diez segundos justos **(c)** Fam **to go f. out** ir a todo gas **3** n **(a)** Br *(apartment)* apartamento m, Esp piso m, Arg departamento m **(b)** US Aut pinchazo m

flatly ['flætlɪ] adv rotundamente

flatten ['flætən] vt **(a)** *(make level)* allanar **(b)** *(crush)* aplastar

flatter ['flætə(r)] vt **(a)** adular, halagar **(b)** *(clothes, portrait)* favorecer **(c)** **to f. oneself** hacerse ilusiones

flattering ['flætərɪŋ] adj **(a)** *(words)* halagador(a) **(b)** *(dress, portrait)* favorecedor(a)

flattery ['flætərɪ] n adulación f, halago m

flaunt [flɔːnt] vt hacer alarde de

flavour, US **flavor** ['fleɪvə(r)] **1** n sabor m **2** vt Culin sazonar **(with** con)

flavouring, US **flavoring** ['fleɪvər-ɪŋ] n condimento m; **artificial f.** aroma m artificial

flaw [flɔː] n *(failing)* defecto m; *(fault)* desperfecto m

flawed [flɔːd] adj defectuoso(a)

flawless ['flɔːlɪs] adj perfecto(a)

flea [fliː] n pulga f; **f. market** rastro m

fled [fled] pt & pp of **flee**

flee [fliː] **1** vt *(pt & pp* **fled)** huir de **2** vi huir **(from** de)

fleece [fliːs] **1** n **(a)** *(sheep's coat)* lana f **(b)** *(sheared)* vellón m **2** vt Fam *(cheat)* sangrar

fleet [fliːt] n flota f

fleeting ['fliːtɪŋ] adj fugaz

Flemish ['flemɪʃ] **1** adj flamenco(a) **2** n *(language)* flamenco m

flesh [fleʃ] n **(a)** carne f; Fig **in the f.** en persona; Fig **to be of f. and blood** ser de carne y hueso; **f. wound** herida f superficial **(b)** *(of fruit)* pulpa f

flew [fluː] pt of **fly**

flex [fleks] **1** n Br Elec cable m **2** vt *(muscles)* flexionar

flexible ['fleksɪbəl] adj flexible

flick [flɪk] **1** n movimiento rápido; *(of finger)* capirotazo m **2** vt *(with finger)* dar un capirotazo a

► **flick through** vt insep *(book)* hojear

flicker ['flɪkə(r)] **1** n **(a)** parpadeo m; *(of light)* titileo m **(b)** Fig **a f. of hope** un destello de esperanza **2** vi *(eyes)* parpadear; *(flame)* vacilar

flier ['flaɪə(r)] n aviador(a) m,f

flight [flaɪt] n **(a)** vuelo m; **f. path** trayectoria f de vuelo **(b)** *(of ball)* trayectoria f **(c)** *(escape)* huida f, fuga f; **to take f.** darse a la fuga **(d)** *(of stairs)* tramo m

flimsy ['flɪmzɪ] adj *(flimsier, flimsiest)* *(cloth)* ligero(a); *(paper)* fino(a); *(structure)* poco sólido(a);

(excuse) poco convincente

flinch [flɪntʃ] *vi (wince)* estremecerse

fling [flɪŋ] **1** *vt (pt & pp* **flung)** arrojar **2** *n Fam* **to have a f.** echar una cana al aire

flint [flɪnt] *n* (a) *(stone)* pedernal *m* (b) *(in lighter)* piedra *f* de mechero

flip [flɪp] **1** *n (flick)* capirotazo *m*; **f. chart** flip chart *m*, pizarra *f* de conferencia *(con bloc)* **2** *vt (toss)* tirar (al aire); **to f. a coin** echar a cara o cruz

flip-flop [ˈflɪpflɒp] *n* (a) *Comput* báscula *f* biestable (b) *Br (footwear)* chancla *f*

flippant [ˈflɪpənt] *adj* frívolo(a)

flipper [ˈflɪpə(r)] *n* aleta *f*

flirt [flɜːt] **1** *n* coqueto(a) *m,f* **2** *vi* flirtear, coquetear; **to f. with death** jugar con la muerte

float [fləʊt] **1** *n* (a) *(on fishing line, as swimming aid)* flotador *m* (b) *(in procession)* carroza *f* **2** *vt* (a) poner a flote (b) *(shares)* emitir; *(currency, business)* hacer flotar **3** *vi* flotar

flock [flɒk] **1** *n Zool* rebaño *m*; *Orn* bandada *f*; *Rel* grey *f*; *(crowd)* multitud *f* **2** *vi* acudir en masa

flood [flʌd] **1** *n* inundación *f*; *(of river)* riada *f*; *Fig* torrente *m* **2** *vt* inundar **3** *vi (river)* desbordarse; *Fig* **to f. in** entrar a raudales

floodlight [ˈflʌdlaɪt] *n* foco *m*

floor [flɔː(r)] **1** *n* (a) *(of room)* suelo *m*; **dance f.** pista *f* de baile (b) *(of ocean, forest)* fondo *m* (c) *(storey)* piso *m*; **first f.** *Br* primer piso, *US* planta baja; *Br* **ground f.** planta baja **2** *vt Fig* dejar perplejo(a)

floorboard [ˈflɔːbɔːd] *n* tabla *f* (del suelo)

flop [flɒp] **1** *n Fam* fracaso *m* **2** *vi* (a) **to f. down on the bed** tumbarse en la cama (b) *Fam* fracasar

floppy [ˈflɒpɪ] *adj* **(floppier, floppiest)** flojo(a); *Comput* **f. disk** disco *m* flexible

florist [ˈflɒrɪst] *n* florista *mf*; **f.'s shop** floristería *f*

flour [ˈflaʊə(r)] *n* harina *f*

flourish [ˈflʌrɪʃ] **1** *n* (a) *(gesture)* ademán *m* (teatral) (b) *(under signature)* rúbrica *f* **2** *vt (brandish)* agitar **3** *vi (thrive)* florecer; *(plant)* crecer

flow [fləʊ] **1** *n* flujo *m*; *(of river)* corriente *f*; *(of traffic)* circulación *f*; *(of capital)* movimiento *m*; *(of people, goods)* afluencia *f*; **f. chart** diagrama *m* de flujo; *Comput* organigrama *m* **2** *vi (blood, river)* fluir; *(sea)* subir; *(traffic)* circular

flower [ˈflaʊə(r)] **1** *n* flor *f*; **f. bed** arriate *m* **2** *vi* florecer

flowery [ˈflaʊərɪ] *adj Fig* florido(a)

flowing [ˈfləʊɪŋ] *adj (hair)* suelto(a); *(dress)* de mucho vuelo; *(style)* fluido(a); *(shape, movement)* natural

flown [fləʊn] *pp of* **fly**

flu [fluː] *n (abbr* **influenza)** gripe *f*

fluctuate [ˈflʌktjʊeɪt] *vi* fluctuar

fluent [ˈfluːənt] *adj* (a) **he speaks f. German** habla el alemán con soltura (b) *(eloquent)* fluido(a)

fluff [flʌf] **1** *n (down)* pelusa *f* **2** *vt Fam* **to f. sth** hacer algo mal

fluffy [ˈflʌfɪ] *adj* **(fluffier, fluffiest)** *(pillow)* mullido(a); *(toy)* de peluche; *(cake)* esponjoso(a)

fluid [ˈfluːɪd] **1** *adj (movement)* natural; *(style, prose)* fluido(a); *(situation)* incierto(a) **2** *n* fluido *m*, líquido *m*

fluke [fluːk] *n Fam* chiripa *f*; **by a f.** por chiripa

flung [flʌŋ] *pt & pp of* **fling**

flunk [flʌŋk] *vt & vi US Fam Esp* catear, *Am* reprobar, *Méx* tronar

fluorescent [flʊəˈresənt] *adj* fluorescente

fluoride [ˈflʊəraɪd] *n* fluoruro *m*

flurry [ˈflʌrɪ] *n* (a) *(of wind)* ráfaga *f*; *(of snow)* nevasca *f* (b) *Fig (bustle)* agitación *f*

flush [flʌʃ] **1** *adj* **f. with** *(level)* a ras de **2** *n (blush)* rubor *m* **3** *vt* **to f. the lavatory** tirar de la cadena

4 *vi (blush)* ruborizarse

fluster ['flʌstə(r)] *vt* **to get flustered** ponerse nervioso(a)

flute [fluːt] *n* flauta *f*

flutter ['flʌtə(r)] **1** *vi (leaves, birds)* revolotear; *(flag)* ondear **2** *n Br Fam (bet)* apuesta *f*

fly¹ [flaɪ] *(pt* **flew**; *pp* **flown) 1** *vt* **(a)** *Av* pilotar **(b)** *(merchandise, troops)* transportar **(c)** *(distance)* recorrer **(d)** *(kite)* hacer volar

2 *vi* **(a)** *(bird, plane)* volar **(b)** *(go by plane)* ir en avión **(c)** *(flag)* ondear **(d)* **to f. into a rage** montar en cólera **(e)** *Fam* **to go flying** *(fall)* caerse

3 *npl* **flies** bragueta *f*

fly² [flaɪ] *n (insect)* mosca *f*; **f. spray** spray *m* matamoscas

flying ['flaɪɪŋ] **1** *adj* volador(a); *(rapid)* rápido(a); **a f. visit** una visita relámpago; *Fig* **to come out of an affair with f. colours** salir airoso(a) de un asunto; *Fig* **to get off to a f. start** empezar con buen pie; **f. saucer** platillo *m* volante **2** *n* **(a)** *(action)* vuelo *m* **(b)** *(aviation)* aviación *f*

flyover ['flaɪəʊvə(r)] *n Br* paso elevado

foal [fəʊl] *n* potro(a) *m,f*

foam [fəʊm] **1** *n* espuma *f*; **f. bath** espuma de baño; **f. rubber** goma espuma **2** *vi* hacer espuma

focus ['fəʊkəs] **1** *vt* centrarse **(on** en)

2 *vi* enfocar; **to f. on sth** *Phot* enfocar algo; *Fig* centrarse en algo

3 *n (pl* **focuses)** foco *m*; **to be in f./ out of f.** estar enfocado(a)/desenfocado(a)

foetus ['fiːtəs] *n* feto *m*

fog [fɒg] *n* niebla *f*; *(at sea)* bruma *f*

foggy ['fɒgɪ] *adj* **(foggier, foggiest)** **it is f.** hay niebla; *Fam* **I haven't the foggiest (idea)** no tengo la más mínima idea

foglamp ['fɒglæmp], *US* **foglight** ['fɒglaɪt] *n* faro *m* antiniebla

foil [fɔɪl] **1** *n* **(a)** **aluminium f.** papel *m* de aluminio **(b)** *(in fencing)* florete *m* **2** *vt (plot)* desbaratar

fold [fəʊld] **1** *n (crease)* pliegue *m*

2 *vt* plegar, doblar; **to f. one's arms** cruzar los brazos

3 *vi* **to f. (up)** *(chair etc)* plegarse; *Com* quebrar

folder ['fəʊldə(r)] *n* carpeta *f*

folding ['fəʊldɪŋ] *adj (chair etc)* plegable

foliage ['fəʊlɪɪdʒ] *n* follaje *m*

folk [fəʊk] **1** *npl Fam* **(a)** *(people)* gente *f* **(b)** **my/your folks** mi/tu familia; *US (parents)* mis/tus padres **2** *adj* popular; **f. music** música *f* folk; **f. song** canción *f* popular

follow ['fɒləʊ] **1** *vt* seguir; *(pursue)* perseguir; *(understand)* comprender; *(way of life)* llevar **2** *vi* **(a)** *(come after)* seguir; **as follows** como sigue **(b)** *(result)* resultar; **that doesn't f.** eso no es lógico **(c)** *(understand)* entender

▸ **follow through, follow up** *vt sep (idea)* llevar a cabo; *(clue)* investigar

follower ['fɒləʊə(r)] *n* seguidor(a) *m,f*

following ['fɒləʊɪŋ] **1** *adj* siguiente **2** *n* seguidores *mpl*

folly ['fɒlɪ] *n* locura *f*, desatino *m*

fond [fɒnd] *adj (loving)* cariñoso(a); **to be f. of sb** tenerle mucho cariño a algn; **to be f. of doing sth** ser aficionado(a) a hacer algo

fondle ['fɒndəl] *vt* acariciar

fondly ['fɒndlɪ] *adv* **(a)** *(lovingly)* cariñosamente **(b)** *(naively)* **to f. imagine that...** creer ingenuamente que...

font [fɒnt] *n Rel* pila *f*.

food [fuːd] *n* comida *f*; **f. chain** cadena trófica; **f. poisoning** intoxicación alimenticia

foodstuffs ['fuːdstʌfs] *npl* productos alimenticios

fool [fuːl] **1** *n* **(a)** tonto(a) *m,f*, imbécil *mf*; **to make a f. of sb** poner a algn en ridículo **(b)** *Culin* ≃ mousse *f* de fruta

2 *vt (deceive)* engañar

3 *vi (joke)* bromear; **to f. about** *or* **around** hacer el tonto

foolish ['fuːlɪʃ] *adj* estúpido(a)

foolproof ['fuːlpruːf] *adj* infalible

foot [fʊt] **1** *n (pl* **feet)** pie *m*; *Zool* pata

f; **on f.** a pie, *Esp* andando **2** *vt (bill)* pagar

football ['fʊtbɔːl] *n* (**a**) *(soccer)* fútbol *m*; **bar f.** futbolín *m*; **f. ground** campo *m* de fútbol; **f. match** partido *m* de fútbol; *Br* **f. pools** quinielas *fpl* (**b**) *(ball)* balón *m*

footballer ['fʊtbɔːlə(r)] *n* futbolista *mf*

footbridge ['fʊtbrɪdʒ] *n* puente *m* para peatones

foothold ['fʊthəʊld] *n Fig* **to gain a f.** afianzarse en una posición

footnote ['fʊtnəʊt] *n* nota *f* a pie de página

footpath ['fʊtpɑːθ] *n (track)* sendero *m*

footstep ['fʊtstep] *n* paso *m*

footwear ['fʊtweə(r)] *n* calzado *m*

for [fɔː(r), *unstressed* fə(r)] **1** *prep* (**a**) *(intended)* para; **curtains f. the bedroom** cortinas para el dormitorio

(**b**) *(representing)* por; **a cheque f. £10** un cheque de 10 libras; **what's the Spanish f. "rivet"?** ¿cómo se dice "rivet" en español?

(**c**) *(purpose)* para; **what's this f.?** ¿para qué sirve esto?

(**d**) *(because of)* por; **famous f. its cuisine** famoso(a) por su cocina

(**e**) *(on behalf of)* por; **will you do it f. me?** ¿lo harás por mí?

(**f**) *(during)* por, durante; **I shall stay f. two weeks** me quedaré dos semanas; **I've been here f. three months** hace tres meses que estoy aquí

(**g**) *(distance)* **I walked f. 10 km** caminé 10 km

(**h**) *(at a point in time)* para; **I can do it f. next Monday** puedo hacerlo para el lunes que viene; **f. the last time** por última vez

(**i**) *(destination)* para

(**j**) *(in exchange)* por; **I got the car f. £500** conseguí el coche por 500 libras; **how much did you sell it f.?** ¿por cuánto lo vendiste?

(**k**) *(in favour of)* a favor de; **are you f. or against?** ¿estás a favor o en contra?; **to vote f. sb** votar a algn

(**l**) *(to obtain)* para; **to run f. the bus**

correr para coger el autobús; **to send sb f. water** mandar a algn a por agua

(**m**) *(with respect to)* en cuanto a; **as f. him** en cuanto a él; **f. all I know** que yo sepa

(**n**) *(despite)* a pesar de; **he's tall f. his age** está muy alto para su edad

(**o**) *(towards)* hacia, por; **his love f. you** su amor por ti

(**p**) *(as)* por; **what do you use f. fuel?** ¿qué utilizan como combustible?

(**q**) *(+ object + infin)* **it's time f. you to go** es hora de que os marchéis; **it's easy f. him to say that** le es fácil decir eso

2 *conj (since, as)* ya que, puesto que

forbid [fə'bɪd] *vt* (*pt* **forbade** [fə'bæd]; *pp* **forbidden** [fə'bɪdən]) prohibir; **to f. sb to do sth** prohibirle a algn hacer algo

force [fɔːs] **1** *n* (**a**) fuerza *f*; **by f.** por la fuerza; **to come into f.** entrar en vigor (**b**) *Mil* cuerpo *m*; **the (armed) forces** las fuerzas armadas; **the police f.** la policía **2** *vt* forzar; **to f. sb to do sth** forzar a algn a hacer algo

forceful ['fɔːsfʊl] *adj* (**a**) *(person)* enérgico(a) (**b**) *(argument)* convincente

ford [fɔːd] **1** *n* vado *m* **2** *vt* vadear

forearm ['fɔːrɑːm] *n* antebrazo *m*

forecast ['fɔːkɑːst] **1** *n* pronóstico *m* **2** *vt* (*pt & pp* **forecast** *or* **forecasted**) pronosticar

forefinger ['fɔːfɪŋgə(r)] *n* (dedo *m*) índice *m*

forefront ['fɔːfrʌnt] *n* **in the f.** a la vanguardia

forego [fɔː'gəʊ] (*pt* **forewent**; *pp* **foregone** [fɔː'gɒn]) *vt Fml* renunciar a

foreground ['fɔːgraʊnd] *n* primer plano

forehead ['fɒrɪd, 'fɔːhed] *n* frente *f*

foreign ['fɒrɪn] *adj* extranjero(a); *(trade, policy)* exterior; **f. exchange** divisas *fpl*; *Br* **the F. Office** el Ministerio de Asuntos Exteriores; **f. body** cuerpo extraño

foreigner ['fɒrɪnə(r)] *n* extranjero(a) *m,f*

foreman ['fɔːmən] *n* (**a**) *Ind* capataz *m*

(**b**) *Jur* presidente *m* del jurado

foremost ['fɔːməʊst] *adj* principal; **first and f.** ante todo

forerunner ['fɔːrʌnə(r)] *n* precursor(a) *m,f*

foresee [fɔː'siː] *vt* (*pt* **foresaw** [fɔː'sɔː]; *pp* **foreseen** [fɔː'siːn]) prever

foresight ['fɔːsaɪt] *n* previsión *f*

forest ['fɒrɪst] *n* bosque *m*

forestall [fɔː'stɔːl] *vt* (*plan*) anticiparse a; (*danger*) prevenir

foretell [fɔː'tel] (*pt & pp* **foretold** [fɔː'təʊld]) *vt* presagiar

forever [fə'revə(r)] *adv* (**a**) (*eternally*) siempre (**b**) (*for good*) para siempre (**c**) *Fam* (*ages*) siglos *mpl*

forewent [fɔː'went] *pp of* forego

foreword ['fɔːwɜːd] *n* prefacio *m*

forfeit ['fɔːfɪt] **1** *n* (*penalty*) pena *f*; (*in games*) prenda *f* **2** *vt* perder

forgave [fə'geɪv] *pt of* forgive

forge [fɔːdʒ] **1** *n* (**a**) (*furnace*) fragua *f* (**b**) (*blacksmith's*) herrería *f*
2 *vt* (**a**) (*counterfeit*) falsificar (**b**) (*metal*) forjar
3 *vi* **to f. ahead** hacer grandes progresos

forged [fɔːdʒd] *adj* (*banknote, letter*) falso(a), falsificado(a)

forgery ['fɔːdʒərɪ] *n* falsificación *f*

forget [fə'get] (*pt* **forgot**; *pp* **forgotten**) **1** *vt* olvidar, olvidarse de; **I've forgotten my key** he olvidado la llave **2** *vi* olvidarse

forgetful [fə'getfʊl] *adj* olvidadizo(a)

forgive [fə'gɪv] *vt* (*pt* **forgave**; *pp* **forgiven** [fə'gɪvən]) perdonar; **to f. sb for sth** perdonarle algo a algn

forgiveness [fə'gɪvnɪs] *n* perdón *m*

forgo [fɔː'gəʊ] *vt Fml* = forego

forgot [fə'gɒt] *pt of* forget

forgotten [fə'gɒtən] *pp of* forget

fork [fɔːk] **1** *n* (**a**) *Agr* horca *f* (**b**) (*cutlery*) tenedor *m* (**c**) (*in road*) bifurcación *f* **2** *vi* (*roads*) bifurcarse

▸ **fork out** *vt sep Fam* (*money*) aflojar, *Esp* apoquinar, *RP* garpar

forlorn [fə'lɔːn] *adj* (*forsaken*) abandonado(a); (*desolate*) triste; (*without*

hope) desesperado(a)

form [fɔːm] **1** *n* (**a**) (*shape*) forma *f* (**b**) (*type*) clase *f* (**c**) (*document*) formulario *m* (**d**) **on (top) f.** en (plena) forma; **off f.** en baja forma (**e**) *Br Educ* clase *f*; **the first f.** el primer curso
2 *vt* formar; **to f. an impression** formarse una impresión
3 *vi* formarse

formal ['fɔːməl] *adj* (**a**) (*official*) oficial; **a f. application** una solicitud en forma (**b**) (*party, dress*) de etiqueta (**c**) (*ordered*) formal (**d**) (*person*) formalista

formality [fɔː'mælɪtɪ] *n* formalidad *f*

formally ['fɔːməlɪ] *adv* oficialmente

format ['fɔːmæt] **1** *n* formato *m* **2** *vt Comput* formatear

formation [fɔː'meɪʃən] *n* formación *f*

former ['fɔːmə(r)] *adj* (**a**) (*time*) anterior (**b**) (*one-time*) antiguo(a); (*person*) ex; **the f. champion** el excampeón (**c**) (*first*) aquél/aquélla; **Peter and Lisa came, the f. wearing a hat** vinieron Peter y Lisa, aquél llevaba sombrero

formerly ['fɔːməlɪ] *adv* antiguamente

formidable ['fɔːmɪdəbəl] *adj* (*prodigious*) formidable; (*daunting*) terrible

formula ['fɔːmjʊlə] *n* fórmula *f*

formulate ['fɔːmjʊleɪt] *vt* formular

fort [fɔːt] *n* fortaleza *f*

forth [fɔːθ] *adv Fml* **and so f.** y así sucesivamente; **to go back and f.** ir de acá para allá

forthcoming [fɔːθ'kʌmɪŋ] *adj* (**a**) (*event*) próximo(a) (**b**) **no money was f.** no hubo oferta de dinero (**c**) (*communicative*) comunicativo(a)

fortieth ['fɔːtɪəθ] *n & adj* cuadragésimo(a) (*m,f*)

fortification [fɔːtɪfɪ'keɪʃən] *n* fortificación *f*

fortify ['fɔːtɪfaɪ] *vt* fortificar

fortnight ['fɔːtnaɪt] *n Br* quincena *f*

fortress ['fɔːtrɪs] *n* fortaleza *f*

fortunate ['fɔːtʃənɪt] *adj* afortunado(a); **it was f. that he came** fue una suerte que viniera

fortunately [ˈfɔːtʃənɪtlɪ] adv afortunadamente

fortune [ˈfɔːtʃən] n (a) (luck, fate) suerte f; **to tell sb's f.** echar la buenaventura a algn (b) (money) fortuna f

fortune-teller [ˈfɔːtʃəntelə(r)] n adivino(a) m,f

forty [ˈfɔːtɪ] adj & n cuarenta (m inv)

forum [ˈfɔːrəm] n foro m

forward [ˈfɔːwəd] **1** adv (a) (also **forwards**) (direction and movement) hacia adelante (b) Fig **to come f.** ofrecerse (c) **from this day f.** de ahora en adelante
2 adj (a) (movement) hacia adelante; (position) delantero(a) (b) (person) fresco(a)
3 n Sport delantero(a) m,f
4 vt (a) (send on) remitir (b) Fml (send goods) expedir (c) Fml (further) fomentar

fossil [ˈfɒsəl] n fósil m; **f. fuel** combustible m fósil

foster [ˈfɒstə(r)] **1** vt (a) (child) criar (b) Fml (hopes) abrigar; (relations) fomentar **2** adj **f. child** hijo(a) adoptivo(a); **f. father** padre adoptivo; **f. mother** madre adoptiva; **f. parents** padres adoptivos

fought [fɔːt] pt & pp of **fight**

foul [faʊl] **1** adj (a) (smell) fétido(a); (taste) asqueroso(a) (b) (deed) atroz; (weather) de perros (c) (language) grosero(a) (d) Sport **f. play** juego sucio **2** n Sport falta f
3 vt (a) (dirty) ensuciar; (air) contaminar (b) Sport cometer una falta contra

found[1] [faʊnd] pt & pp of **find**

found[2] [faʊnd] vt (establish) fundar

foundation [faʊnˈdeɪʃən] n (a) (establishment) fundación f (b) (basis) fundamento m (c) Constr **foundations** cimientos mpl

founder[1] [ˈfaʊndə(r)] n fundador(a) m,f

founder[2] [ˈfaʊndə(r)] vi (a) Fml (sink) hundirse (b) Fig (plan, hopes) fracasar

fountain [ˈfaʊntɪn] n (structure) fuente f; (jet) surtidor m; **f. pen** pluma estilográfica, CSur lapicera f fuente, Perú lapicero m

four [fɔː(r)] adj & n cuatro (m inv); **on all fours** a gatas

fourteen [fɔːˈtiːn] adj & n catorce (m inv)

fourteenth [fɔːˈtiːnθ] **1** adj & n decimocuarto(a) (m,f) **2** n (fraction) catorceavo m

fourth [fɔːθ] **1** adj & n cuarto(a) (m,f) **2** n (a) (fraction) cuarto m (b) Aut cuarta f (velocidad)

fowl [faʊl] n (pl **fowl**) ave f de corral

fox [fɒks] **1** n zorro(a) m,f **2** vt (a) (perplex) dejar perplejo(a) (b) (deceive) engañar

foyer [ˈfɔɪeɪ, ˈfɔɪə(r)] n vestíbulo m

fraction [ˈfrækʃən] n fracción f

fracture [ˈfræktʃə(r)] **1** n fractura f **2** vt fracturar

fragile [ˈfrædʒaɪl] adj frágil

fragment [ˈfrægmənt] n fragmento m

fragrance [ˈfreɪgrəns] n fragancia f, perfume m

frail [freɪl] adj frágil, delicado(a)

frame [freɪm] **1** n (a) (of window, door, picture) marco m; (of machine) armazón m; (of bicycle) cuadro m; (of spectacles) montura f; Fig **f. of mind** estado m de ánimo (b) Cin, TV fotograma m **2** vt (a) (picture) enmarcar (b) (question) formular (c) Fam (innocent person) incriminar

framework [ˈfreɪmwɜːk] n Fig **within the f. of ...** dentro del marco de ...

franc [fræŋk] n franco m

France [frɑːns] n Francia f

franchise [ˈfræntʃaɪz] n (a) Pol derecho m al voto (b) Com concesión f, licencia f

frank [fræŋk] **1** adj franco(a) **2** vt (mail) franquear

frankly [ˈfræŋklɪ] adv francamente

frantic [ˈfræntɪk] adj (anxious) desesperado(a); (hectic) frenético(a)

fraternize ['frætənaɪz] *vi* confraternizar (**with** con)

fraud [frɔːd] *n* (**a**) fraude *m* (**b**) *(person)* impostor(a) *m,f*

fraught [frɔːt] *adj* (**a**) *(full)* cargado(a) (**with** de) (**b**) *(tense)* nervioso(a)

fray¹ [freɪ] *vi* (**a**) *(cloth)* deshilacharse (**b**) *(nerves)* crisparse; **his temper frequently frayed** se irritaba a menudo

fray² [freɪ] *n* combate *m*

freak [friːk] **1** *n* (**a**) *(monster)* monstruo *m* (**b**) *Fam (eccentric)* estrafalario(a) *m,f* (**c**) *Fam (fan)* fanático(a) *m,f* **2** *adj* (**a**) *(unexpected)* inesperado(a) (**b**) *(unusual)* insólito(a)

freckle ['frekəl] *n* peca *f*

free [friː] **1** *adj* (**a**) libre; **to set sb f.** poner en libertad a algn; **f. kick** tiro *m* libre; **f. speech** libertad *f* de expresión; **f. will** libre albedrío *m* (**b**) **f. (of charge)** *(gratis)* gratuito(a); **f. gift** obsequio *m* **2** *adv* (**a**) **(for) f.** gratis (**b**) *(loose)* suelto(a) **3** *vt* (**a**) *(liberate)* poner en libertad (**b**) *(let loose, work loose)* soltar (**c**) *(untie)* desatar (**d**) *(exempt)* eximir (**from** de)

freedom ['friːdəm] *n* (**a**) *(liberty)* libertad *f*; **f. of the press** libertad de prensa (**b**) *(exemption)* exención *f*

freelance ['friːlɑːns] *adj* independiente

freely ['friːlɪ] *adv* (**a**) libremente (**b**) *(openly)* abiertamente

free-range ['friːreɪndʒ] *adj Br* de granja

freeway ['friːweɪ] *n US* autopista *f*

freeze [friːz] *(pt* **froze**; *pp* **frozen) 1** *vt* congelar **2** *n Met* helada *f*; **price f.** congelación *f* de precios; *TV, Cin* **f. frame** imagen congelada **3** *vi (liquid)* helarse; *(food)* congelarse

freezer ['friːzə(r)] *n* congelador *m*

freezing ['friːzɪŋ] *adj* (**a**) glacial (**b**) **f. point** punto *m* de congelación; **above/below f. point** sobre/bajo cero

freight [freɪt] *n* (**a**) *(transport)* transporte *m* (**b**) *(goods, price)* flete *m*; *US* **f. car** vagón *m*; *US* **f. elevator** montacargas *m inv*; **f. train** tren *m* de mercancías

French [frentʃ] **1** *adj* francés(esa); **F. bean** judía *f* verde, *Bol, RP* chaucha *f, CAm* ejote *m, Col, Cuba* habichuela *f, Chile* poroto *m* verde, *Ven* vainita *f*; **F. dressing** vinagreta *f*; *US* **F. fries** patatas *fpl* or *Am* papas *fpl* fritas; **F. window** puerta *f* vidriera **2** *n* (**a**) *(language)* francés *m* (**b**) *pl* **the F.** los franceses

Frenchman ['frentʃmən] *n* francés *m*

Frenchwoman ['frentʃwʊmən] *n* francesa *f*

frenzy ['frenzɪ] *n* frenesí *m*

frequency ['friːkwənsɪ] *n* frecuencia *f*

frequent 1 *adj* ['friːkwənt] frecuente **2** *vt* [frɪ'kwent] frecuentar

frequently ['friːkwəntlɪ] *adv* frecuentemente, a menudo

fresh [freʃ] *adj* (**a**) fresco(a); **f. water** agua *f* dulce; **f. bread** pan *m* del día (**b**) *(new)* nuevo(a) (**c**) *(air)* puro(a); **in the f. air** al aire libre (**d**) *US Fam (cheeky)* fresco(a)

freshly ['freʃlɪ] *adv* recién, recientemente

fret [fret] *vi* preocuparse (**about** por)

friction ['frɪkʃən] *n* fricción *f*

Friday ['fraɪdɪ] *n* viernes *m*

fridge [frɪdʒ] *n esp Br* nevera *f*, frigorífico *m, Andes* frigider *m, RP* heladera *f*

fried [fraɪd] *adj* frito(a)

friend [frend] *n* amigo(a) *m,f*; **a f. of mine** un(a) amigo(a) mío(a); **to make friends with sb** hacerse amigo(a) de algn; **to make friends again** hacer las paces

friendly ['frendlɪ] *adj* (**friendlier, friendliest)** *(person)* simpático(a); *(atmosphere)* acogedor(a); **f. advice** consejo *m* de amigo; **f. nation** nación amiga

friendship ['frendʃɪp] *n* amistad *f*

fright [fraɪt] *n* (**a**) *(fear)* miedo *m*; **to take f.** asustarse (**b**) *(shock)* susto *m*; **to get a f.** pegarse un susto

frighten ['fraɪtən] *vt* asustar

▶ **frighten away, frighten off** *vt sep* ahuyentar

frightened ['fraɪtənd] *adj* asustado(a); **to be f. of sb** tenerle miedo a algn

frightening ['fraɪtənɪŋ] *adj* espantoso(a)

frightful ['fraɪtfʊl] *adj* espantoso(a), horroroso(a)

frill [frɪl] *n (on dress)* volante *m*; *Fig* **frills** *(decorations)* adornos *mpl*

fringe [frɪndʒ] *n* (**a**) *Br (of hair)* flequillo *m*, *Am* cerquillo *m* (**b**) *(edge)* borde *m*; *Fig* **on the f. of society** al margen de la sociedad; **f. theatre** teatro *m* experimental; **f. benefits** extras *mpl*

frisk [frɪsk] *vt Fam (search)* registrar

frisky ['frɪskɪ] *adj* (**friskier, friskiest**) (**a**) *(children, animals)* juguetón(ona) (**b**) *(adult)* vivo(a)

fritter ['frɪtə(r)] *n* buñuelo *m*

▶ **fritter away** *vt sep* malgastar

frivolous ['frɪvələs] *adj* frívolo(a)

frizzy ['frɪzɪ] *adj* (**frizzier, frizziest**) crespo(a)

frog [frɒg] *n* rana *f*

frolic ['frɒlɪk] *vi* retozar, juguetear

from [frɒm, *unstressed* frəm] *prep* (**a**) *(time)* desde, a partir de; **f. now on** a partir de ahora; **f. Monday to Friday** de lunes a viernes; **f. the 8th to the 17th** desde el 8 hasta el 17 (**b**) *(price, number)* desde, de; **a number f. one to ten** un número del uno a diez (**c**) *(origin)* de; **a letter f. her father** una carta de su padre; **f. English into Spanish** del inglés al español; **he's f. Malaga** es de Málaga; **the train f. Bilbao** el tren procedente de Bilbao (**d**) *(distance)* de; **the town is 4 miles f. the coast** el pueblo está a 4 millas de la costa (**e**) *(out of)* de; **bread is made f. flour** el pan se hace con harina (**f**) *(remove, subtract)* a; **he took the book f. the child** le quitó el libro al niño; **take three f. five** restar tres a cinco (**g**) *(according to)* según, por; **f. what the author said** según lo que dijo el autor (**h**) *(position)* desde, de; **f. here** desde aquí (**i**) **can you tell margarine f. butter?** ¿puedes distinguir entre la margarina y la mantequilla?

front [frʌnt] **1** *n* (**a**) parte delantera; **in f. (of)** delante (de) (**b**) *(of building)* fachada *f* (**c**) *Mil, Pol, Met* frente *m* (**d**) *(seaside)* paseo marítimo (**e**) *Fig* **she put on a brave f.** hizo de tripas corazón **2** *adj* delantero(a), de delante; **f. door** puerta *f* principal; **f. seat** asiento *m* de delante

frontier ['frʌntɪə(r)] *n* frontera *f*

frost [frɒst] **1** *n* (**a**) *(covering)* escarcha *f* (**b**) *(freezing)* helada *f* **2** *vt US Culin* recubrir con azúcar glas

▶ **frost over** *vi* escarchar

frostbite ['frɒstbaɪt] *n* congelación *f*

frosty ['frɒstɪ] *adj* (**frostier, frostiest**) (**a**) **it will be a f. night tonight** esta noche habrá helada (**b**) *Fig* glacial

froth [frɒθ] **1** *n* espuma *f*; *(from mouth)* espumarajos *mpl* **2** *vi* espumar

frothy ['frɒθɪ] *adj* (**frothier, frothiest**) espumoso(a)

frown [fraʊn] *vi* fruncir el ceño

▶ **frown upon** *vt insep* desaprobar

froze [frəʊz] *pt of* **freeze**

frozen ['frəʊzən] **1** *adj (liquid, feet etc)* helado(a); *(food)* congelado(a) **2** *pp of* **freeze**

fruit [fruːt] *n* (**a**) *Bot* fruto *m* (**b**) *(apple, orange etc)* fruta *f*; **f. cake** pastel *m* con fruto seco; **f. machine** (máquina *f*) tragaperras *f inv*; **f. salad** macedonia *f* de frutas (**c**) **fruits** *(rewards)* frutos *mpl*

fruitful ['fruːtfʊl] *adj Fig* provechoso(a)

fruitless ['fruːtlɪs] *adj* infructuoso(a)

frustrate [frʌ'streɪt] *vt* frustrar

frustrating [frʌs'treɪtɪŋ] *adj* frustrante

frustration [frʌ'streɪʃən] *n* frustración *f*

fry¹ [fraɪ] (pt & pp **fried**) **1** vt freír **2** vi Fig asarse

fry² [fraɪ] npl **small f.** gente f de poca monta

frying pan ['fraɪɪŋpæn], US **frypan** ['fraɪpæn] n sartén f

ft (abbr **foot**) pie m; (abbr **feet**) pies mpl

fudge [fʌdʒ] **1** n Culin = dulce hecho con azúcar, leche y mantequilla **2** vt (figures) amañar

fuel ['fjʊəl] **1** n combustible m; (for engines) carburante m; **f. tank** depósito m de combustible **2** vt Fig (ambition) estimular; (difficult situation) empeorar

fugitive ['fjuːdʒɪtɪv] n Fml fugitivo(a) m,f

fulfil, US **fulfill** [fʊl'fɪl] vt (**a**) (task, ambition) realizar; (promise) cumplir; (role) desempeñar (**b**) (wishes) satisfacer

fulfilment, US **fulfillment** [fʊl'fɪlmənt] n (**a**) (of ambition) realización f (**b**) (of duty, promise) cumplimiento m

full [fʊl] **1** adj (**a**) lleno(a); **f. of** lleno(a) de; **I'm f. (up)** no puedo más (**b**) (complete) completo(a); **at f. speed** a toda velocidad; **f. employment** pleno empleo; **f. moon** luna llena; **f. stop** punto m
2 n **in f.** en su totalidad; **name in f.** nombre y apellidos completos
3 adv **f. well** perfectamente

full-scale ['fʊlskeɪl] adj (**a**) (model) de tamaño natural (**b**) **f. search** registro m a fondo; **f. war** guerra generalizada or total

full-time ['fʊl'taɪm] **1** adj de jornada completa **2** adv **to work f.** trabajar a tiempo completo

fully ['fʊlɪ] adv completamente

fumble ['fʌmbəl] vi hurgar; **to f. for sth** buscar algo a tientas; **to f. with sth** manejar algo con torpeza

fume [fjuːm] **1** n (usu pl) humo m **2** vi despedir humo

fun [fʌn] **1** n (amusement) diversión f; **in** or **for f.** en broma; **to have f.** divertirse, pasarlo bien; **to make f. of**

sb reírse de algn **2** adj divertido(a)

function ['fʌŋkʃən] **1** n (**a**) función f (**b**) (ceremony) acto m; (party) recepción f **2** vi funcionar

functional ['fʌŋkʃənəl] adj funcional

fund [fʌnd] **1** n (**a**) Com fondo m (**b**) **funds** fondos mpl **2** vt (finance) financiar

fundamental [fʌndə'mentəl] **1** adj fundamental **2** npl **fundamentals** los fundamentos

funeral ['fjuːnərəl] n funeral m; US **f. home** funeraria f; **f. march** marcha f fúnebre; Br **f. parlour** funeraria f; **f. service** misa f de cuerpo presente

funfair ['fʌnfeə(r)] n Br parque m de atracciones

fungus ['fʌŋgəs] n (pl **fungi** ['fʌŋgaɪ]) (**a**) Bot hongo m (**b**) Med fungo m

funnel ['fʌnəl] **1** n (**a**) (for liquids) embudo m (**b**) Naut chimenea f **2** vt (pt & pp **funnelled**, US **funneled**) Fig (funds, energy) encauzar

funny ['fʌnɪ] adj (**funnier**, **funniest**) (**a**) (peculiar) raro(a), extraño(a); **that's f.!** ¡qué raro! (**b**) (amusing) divertido(a), gracioso(a); **I found it very f.** me hizo mucha gracia (**c**) Fam (ill) mal

fur [fɜː(r)] **1** n (**a**) (of living animal) pelo m (**b**) (of dead animal) piel f (**c**) (in kettle, on tongue) sarro m **2** adj de piel; **f. coat** abrigo m de pieles

furious ['fjʊərɪəs] adj (**a**) (angry) furioso(a) (**b**) (vigorous) violento(a)

furnace ['fɜːnɪs] n horno m

furnish ['fɜːnɪʃ] vt (**a**) (house) amueblar (**b**) Fml (food) suministrar; (details) facilitar

furnishings ['fɜːnɪʃɪŋz] npl (**a**) muebles mpl (**b**) (fittings) accesorios mpl

furniture ['fɜːnɪtʃə(r)] n muebles mpl; **a piece of f.** un mueble

furrow ['fʌrəʊ] n Agr surco m; (on forehead) arruga f

furry ['fɜːrɪ] adj (**furrier**, **furriest**) (**a**) (hairy) peludo(a) (**b**) (tongue, kettle) sarroso(a)

further ['fɜːðə(r)] (comp of **far**) **1** adj (**a**) (new) nuevo(a); **until f. notice**

hasta nuevo aviso (**b**) *(additional)* otro(a), adicional (**c**) *(later)* posterior; *Br* **f. education** estudios *mpl* superiores

2 *adv* (**a**) *(more)* más; **f. back** más atrás; **f. along** más adelante (**b**) *Fml (besides)* además

3 *vt* fomentar

furthermore [fɜ:ðə'mɔ:(r)] *adv Fml* además

furthest ['fɜ:ðɪst] **1** *adj (superl of* **far***)* más lejano(a) **2** *adv* más lejos

furtive ['fɜ:tɪv] *adj* furtivo(a)

fury ['fjʊərɪ] *n* furia *f,* furor *m*

fuse [fju:z] **1** *n* (**a**) *Elec* fusible *m;* **f. box** caja *f* de fusibles (**b**) *(of bomb)* mecha *f*

2 *vi* (**a**) *Br Elec* **the lights fused** se fundieron los plomos (**b**) *Fig (merge)* fusionarse (**c**) *(melt)* fundirse

3 *vt* (**a**) *Br Elec* **a surge of power fused the lights** se fundieron los plomos y se fue la luz por una subida

de corriente (**b**) *Fig (merge)* fusionar (**c**) *(melt)* fundir

fusion ['fju:ʒən] *n* fusión *f*

fuss [fʌs] **1** *n (commotion)* jaleo *m;* **to kick up a f.** armar un escándalo; **stop making a f.** *(complaining)* deja ya de quejarte; **to make a f. of** *(pay attention to)* mimar a **2** *vi* preocuparse (**about**) por)

fussy ['fʌsɪ] *adj* (**fussier, fussiest**) exigente; *(nitpicking)* quisquilloso(a)

futile ['fju:taɪl] *adj* inútil, vano(a)

futon ['fu:tɒn] *n* futón *m*

future ['fju:tʃə(r)] **1** *n* futuro *m,* porvenir *m;* **in the near f.** en un futuro próximo; **in f.** de aquí en adelante **2** *adj* futuro(a)

fuze [fju:z] *n, vi & vt US* = **fuse**

fuzzy ['fʌzɪ] *adj* (**fuzzier, fuzziest**) (**a**) *(hair)* muy rizado(a) (**b**) *(blurred)* borroso(a)

Gg

G, g [dʒiː] *n* (**a**) *(the letter)* G, g *f* (**b**) *Mus* **G** sol *m*

G [dʒiː] *adj US Cin* ≃ (apta) para todos los públicos

gabble ['gæbəl] **1** *n* chapurreo *m* **2** *vi* hablar atropelladamente

gadget ['gædʒɪt] *n* artilugio *m*, aparato *m*

gaffe [gæf] *n* metedura *f* de pata, desliz *m*; **to make a g.** meter la pata, patinar

gag [gæg] **1** *n* (**a**) mordaza *f* (**b**) *Fam (joke)* chiste *m* **2** *vt* amordazar

gage [geɪdʒ] *n & vt US* = **gauge**

gaily ['geɪlɪ] *adv* alegremente

gain [geɪn] **1** *n* ganancia *f*, beneficio *m*; *(increase)* aumento *m* **2** *vt* ganar; *Fig* **to g. ground** ganar terreno; **to g. speed** ganar velocidad, acelerar; **to g. weight** aumentar de peso

gala ['gɑːlə, 'geɪlə] *n* gala *f*, fiesta *f*

galaxy ['gæləksɪ] *n* galaxia *f*

gale [geɪl] *n* vendaval *m*

gallant ['gælənt] *adj (brave)* valiente; *(also* [gə'lænt]) *(chivalrous)* galante

gallery ['gælərɪ] *n* (**a**) galería *f* (**b**) *Th* gallinero *m* (**c**) *(court)* tribuna *f*

gallon ['gælən] *n* galón *m* (*Br = 4,55 l; US = 3,79 l*)

gallop ['gæləp] **1** *n* galope *m* **2** *vi* galopar

gamble ['gæmbəl] **1** *n (risk)* riesgo *m*; *(risky undertaking)* empresa arriesgada; *(bet)* apuesta *f* **2** *vi (bet)* jugar; *(take a risk)* arriesgarse

gambler ['gæmblə(r)] *n* jugador(a) *m,f*

gambling ['gæmblɪŋ] *n* juego *m*

game [geɪm] **1** *n* (**a**) juego *m*; **g. of chance** juego de azar (**b**) *(match)* partido *m*; *(of bridge)* partida *f* (**c**) **games** *(sporting event)* juegos *mpl*; *Br (school subject)* deportes *mpl* (**d**) *(hunting)* caza *f*; *Fig* presa *f* **2** *adj* **g.**

for anything dispuesto(a) a todo

gang [gæŋ] *n (of criminals)* banda *f*; *(of youths)* pandilla *f*; *(of workers)* cuadrilla *f*

▸ **gang up** *vi Fam* confabularse (**on** contra)

gangster ['gæŋstə(r)] *n* gángster *m*

gangway ['gæŋweɪ] *n Naut* pasarela *f*; *Th* pasillo *m*

gaol [dʒeɪl] *n & vt Br* = **jail**

gap [gæp] *n* (**a**) abertura *f*, hueco *m*; *(blank space)* blanco *m* (**b**) *(in time)* intervalo *m*; *(emptiness)* vacío *m* (**c**) *(gulf)* diferencia *f* (**d**) *(deficiency)* laguna *f*

gape [geɪp] *vi (person)* quedarse boquiabierto(a), mirar boquiabierto(a); *(thing)* estar abierto(a)

garage ['gærɑːʒ, 'gærɪdʒ, *US* gə'rɑːʒ] *n* garaje *m*; *(for repairs)* taller mecánico; *(filling station)* gasolinera *f*, estación *f* de servicio, *Andes, Ven* bomba *f*, *Méx* gasolinería *f*, *Perú* grifo *m*

garbage ['gɑːbɪdʒ] *n US* basura *f*, *Méx* cochera *f*; *Fig* tonterías *fpl*

garbanzo [gɑː'bɑːnzəʊ] (*pl* **garbanzos**) *n US* **g. (bean)** garbanzo *m*

garbled ['gɑːbəld] *adj* embrollado(a); **g. account** relato confuso

garden ['gɑːdən] *n* jardín *m*; **g. centre** centro *m* de jardinería; **g. party** recepción *f* al aire libre

gardener ['gɑːdənə(r)] *n* jardinero(a) *m,f*

gardening ['gɑːdənɪŋ] *n* jardinería *f*; **his mother does the g.** su madre es la que cuida el jardín

gargle ['gɑːgəl] *vi* hacer gárgaras

garish ['geərɪʃ] *adj* chillón(ona)

garland ['gɑːlənd] *n* guirnalda *f*

garlic ['gɑːlɪk] *n* ajo *m*

garment ['gɑːmənt] *n* prenda *f*

garnish ['gɑːnɪʃ] *vt* guarnecer

garter ['gɑːtə(r)] *n* liga *f*

gas [gæs] **1** *n* (**a**) gas *m*; **g. cooker** cocina *f* de gas; **g. fire** estufa *f* de gas; **g. mask** careta *f* antigás; **g. ring** hornillo *m* de gas (**b**) *US* gasolina *f*, *RP* nafta *f*; **g. pump** surtidor *m* de gasolina; **g. station** gasolinera *f*, estación *f* de servicio, *Andes, Ven* bomba *f*, *Méx* gasolinería *f*, *Perú* grifo *m*; **g. tank** depósito *m* de la gasolina **2** *vt (asphyxiate)* asfixiar con gas **3** *vi Fam (talk)* charlotear

gash [gæʃ] **1** *n* herida profunda **2** *vt* hacer un corte en; **he gashed his forehead** se hizo una herida en la frente

gasoline ['gæsəliːn] *n US* gasolina *f*, *RP* nafta *f*

gasp [gɑːsp] **1** *n (cry)* grito sordo; *(breath)* bocanada *f*; *Fig* **to be at one's last g.** estar en las últimas **2** *vi (in surprise)* quedar boquiabierto(a); *(breathe)* jadear

gassy ['gæsɪ] *adj* (**gassier, gassiest**) gaseoso(a)

gastric ['gæstrɪk] *adj* gástrico(a)

gate [geɪt] *n* (**a**) puerta *f* (**b**) *(at football ground)* entrada *f*; **g. (money)** taquilla *f* (**c**) *(attendance)* entrada *f*

gateau ['gætəʊ] *n* (*pl* **gateaux** ['gætəʊz]) pastel *m* con nata

gatecrash ['geɪtkræʃ] **1** *vt* colarse en **2** *vi* colarse

gateway ['geɪtweɪ] *n* puerta *f*; *Fig* pasaporte *m*

gather ['gæðə(r)] **1** *vt* (**a**) *(collect)* juntar; *(pick)* coger; *(pick up)* recoger (**b**) *(bring together)* reunir (**c**) *(harvest)* cosechar (**d**) **to g. speed** ir ganando velocidad; **to g. strength** cobrar fuerzas (**e**) *(understand)* suponer; **I g. that ...** tengo entendido que ... **2** *vi* (**a**) *(come together)* reunirse (**b**) *(form)* formarse

▸ **gather round** *vi* agruparse

gathering ['gæðərɪŋ] **1** *adj* creciente **2** *n* reunión *f*

gauge [geɪdʒ] **1** *n* (**a**) medida *f* estándar; *(of gun, wire)* calibre *m* (**b**) *(calibrator)* indicador *m* (**c**) *Fig (indication)* indicación *f* **2** *vt* (**a**) *(measure)* medir, calibrar (**b**) *Fig (judge)* juzgar

gaunt [gɔːnt] *adj (lean)* demacrado(a); *(desolate)* lúgubre

gauze [gɔːz] *n* gasa *f*

gave [geɪv] *pt of* **give**

gay [geɪ] *adj* (**a**) *(homosexual)* gay (**b**) *(happy)* alegre

gaze [geɪz] **1** *n* mirada fija **2** *vi* mirar fijamente

GB [dʒiː'biː] *(abbr* **Great Britain)** GB

GCSE [dʒiːsiːes'iː] *n Br (abbr* **General Certificate of Secondary Education)** = certificado de enseñanza secundaria

gear [gɪə(r)] **1** *n* (**a**) *(equipment)* equipo *m* (**b**) *Fam (belongings)* bártulos *mpl* (**c**) *Fam (clothing)* ropa *f* (**d**) *Tech* engranaje *m* (**e**) *Aut* velocidad *f*, marcha *f*; **first g.** primera *f* (velocidad *f*); **g. lever** *or US* **shift** palanca *f* de cambio **2** *vt* ajustar, adaptar

gearbox ['gɪəbɒks] *n* caja *f* de cambios

geese [giːs] *pl of* **goose**

gel [dʒel] **1** *n* gel *m*; *(for hair)* gomina *f* **2** *vi Fig (ideas etc)* cuajar **3** *vt (hair)* engominar

gelatin ['dʒelətɪn] *n* gelatina *f*

gem [dʒem] *n* piedra preciosa; *Fig (person)* joya *f*

Gemini ['dʒemɪnaɪ] *n* Géminis *m inv*

gender ['dʒendə(r)] *n* género *m*

gene [dʒiːn] *n* gene *m*, gen *m*

general ['dʒenərəl] **1** *adj* general; **g. knowledge** conocimientos *mpl* generales; **in g.** en general; **the g. public** el público; **g. practitioner** médico *m* de cabecera **2** *n Mil* general *m*; *US* **g. of the army** mariscal *m* de campo

generalization [dʒenərəlaɪ'zeɪʃən] *n* generalización *f*

generalize ['dʒenərəlaɪz] *vt & vi* generalizar

generally ['dʒenərəlɪ] *adv* generalmente, en general

generate ['dʒenəreɪt] *vt* generar

generation [dʒenə'reɪʃən] n generación f; **g. gap** abismo m or conflicto m generacional

generator ['dʒenəreɪtə(r)] n generador m

generosity [dʒenə'rɒsɪtɪ] n generosidad f

genetic [dʒɪ'netɪk] adj genético(a); **g. engineering** ingeniería genética

genetics [dʒɪ'netɪks] n sing genética f

genitals ['dʒenɪtəlz] npl órganos mpl genitales

genius ['dʒiːnjəs, 'dʒiːnɪəs] n (a) (person) genio m (b) (gift) don m

gent [dʒent] n Br Fam (abbr **gentleman**) señor m, caballero m; **the gents** los servicios (de caballeros)

gentle ['dʒentəl] adj dulce, tierno(a); (breeze) suave

gentleman ['dʒentəlmən] n caballero m; **g.'s agreement** pacto m de caballeros

gently ['dʒentlɪ] adv con cuidado

genuine ['dʒenjʊɪn] adj auténtico(a), genuino(a); (sincere) sincero(a)

genuinely ['dʒenjʊɪnlɪ] adv auténticamente

geographic(al) [dʒɪə'græfɪk(əl)] adj geográfico(a)

geography [dʒɪ'ɒgrəfɪ, 'dʒɒgrəfɪ] n geografía f

geologic(al) [dʒɪə'lɒdʒɪk(əl)] adj geológico(a)

geology [dʒɪ'ɒlədʒɪ] n geología f

geometric(al) [dʒɪə'metrɪk(əl)] adj geométrico(a)

geometry [dʒɪ'ɒmɪtrɪ] n geometría f

geriatric [dʒerɪ'ætrɪk] adj geriátrico(a)

germ [dʒɜːm] n (a) Biol & Fig germen m (b) Med microbio m

German ['dʒɜːmən] 1 adj alemán(ana); **G. measles** rubeola f 2 n (a) alemán(ana) m,f (b) (language) alemán m

Germany ['dʒɜːmənɪ] n Alemania

germinate ['dʒɜːmɪneɪt] vi germinar

gesticulate [dʒe'stɪkjʊleɪt] vi gesticular

gesture ['dʒestʃə(r)] 1 n gesto m, ademán m; **it's an empty g.** es pura formalidad 2 vi gesticular, hacer gestos

get [get] (pt & pp **got**, US pp **gotten**) 1 vt (a) (obtain) obtener, conseguir; (receive) recibir; (earn) ganar (b) (fetch) (something) traer; (somebody) ir a por; **can I g. you something to eat?** ¿quieres comer algo?; **g. the police!** ¡llama a la policía! (c) (bus, train) coger; Am agarrar (d) (have done) **g. him to call me** dile que me llame; **to g. sb to agree to sth** conseguir que algn acepte algo; **to g. one's hair cut** cortarse el pelo (e) **have got, have got to** see **have** (f) Fam (understand) entender

2 vi (a) (become) ponerse; **to g. dressed** vestirse; **to g. drunk** emborracharse; **to g. married** casarse; **to g. paid** cobrar (b) **to g. to** (arrive, come to) llegar a; **to g. to know sb** llegar a conocer a algn

▸ **get about** vi (person) salir; (news) difundirse

▸ **get across** vt sep (idea etc) hacer comprender

▸ **get ahead** vi progresar

▸ **get along** vi (a) (leave) marcharse (b) (manage) arreglárselas (c) (two people) llevarse bien

▸ **get around** vi (person) salir; (travel) viajar; (news) difundirse

▸ **get at** vt insep (a) (reach) alcanzar (b) (insinuate) insinuar; **what are you getting at?** ¿a dónde quieres llegar?

▸ **get away** vi escaparse

▸ **get away with** vt insep salir impune de

▸ **get back 1** vi (a) (return) regresar, volver (b) **g. back!** (move backwards) ¡atrás! 2 vt sep (recover) recuperar; Fam **to g. one's own back on sb** vengarse de algn

▸ **get by** vi (manage) arreglárselas; **she can g. by in French** sabe defenderse en francés

▸ **get down 1** vt sep (depress) deprimir 2 vi (descend) bajar

▸ **get down to** vt insep ponerse a; **to**

g. down to the facts ir al grano

▸ **get in 1** vi (**a**) (arrive) llegar (**b**) Pol ser elegido(a) **2** vt sep (**a**) (buy) comprar (**b**) (collect) recoger

▸ **get into** vt insep Fig **to g. into bad habits** adquirir malas costumbres; **to g. into trouble** meterse en un lío

▸ **get off 1** vt insep (bus etc) bajarse de **2** vt sep (remove) quitarse **3** vi (**a**) bajarse; Fam **g. off!** ¡fuera! (**b**) **to g. off to a good start** (begin) empezar bien (**c**) (escape) escaparse

▸ **get on 1** vt insep (board) subir a **2** vi (**a**) (board) subirse (**b**) (make progress) hacer progresos; **how are you getting on?** ¿cómo te van las cosas? (**c**) **to g. on (well) (with sb)** llevarse bien (con algn) (**d**) (continue) seguir; **to g. on with one's work** seguir trabajando

▸ **get on to** vt insep (**a**) (find a person) localizar; (find out) descubrir (**b**) (continue) pasar a

▸ **get out 1** vt sep (object) sacar **2** vi (**a**) (room etc) salir (**of** de); (train) bajar (**of** de) (**b**) (escape) escaparse (**of** de); **to g. out of an obligation** librarse de un compromiso (**c**) (news) difundirse; (secret) hacerse público

▸ **get over 1** vt insep (**a**) (illness) recuperarse de (**b**) (difficulty) vencer **2** vt sep (convey) hacer comprender

▸ **get round** vt insep (**a**) (problem) salvar; (difficulty) vencer (**b**) (rule) soslayar

▸ **get round to** vt insep **if I g. round to it** si tengo tiempo

▸ **get through 1** vi (**a**) (message) llegar (**b**) Educ aprobar (**c**) Tel **to g. through to sb** conseguir comunicar con algn **2** vt insep (**a**) **to g. through a lot of work** trabajar mucho (**b**) (consume) consumir

▸ **get together 1** vi (people) juntarse, reunirse **2** vt sep (people) juntar, reunir

▸ **get up 1** vi (rise) levantarse, Am pararse **2** vt sep (wake) despertar

▸ **get up to** vt insep hacer; **to g. up to mischief** hacer de las suyas

getaway ['getəweɪ] n fuga f; **to**

make one's g. fugarse

get-together ['gettəgeðə(r)] n reunión f

ghastly ['gɑːstlɪ] adj (**ghastlier, ghastliest**) horrible, espantoso(a)

gherkin ['gɜːkɪn] n pepinillo m

ghetto ['getəʊ] n gueto m

ghost [gəʊst] n fantasma m; **g. story** cuento m de fantasmas; **g. town** pueblo m fantasma

giant ['dʒaɪənt] adj & n gigante (m)

gibe [dʒaɪb] **1** n mofa f **2** vi mofarse (**at** de)

giddy ['gɪdɪ] adj (**giddier, giddiest**) mareado(a); **it makes me g.** me da vértigo; **to feel g.** sentirse mareado(a)

gift [gɪft] n (**a**) regalo m; Com obsequio m; **g. token** vale m (**b**) (talent) don m; **to have a g. for music** estar muy dotado(a) para la música

gifted ['gɪftɪd] adj dotado(a)

gig [gɪg] n Fam Mus actuación f

gigantic [dʒaɪ'gæntɪk] adj gigantesco(a)

giggle ['gɪgəl] **1** n (**a**) risita f (**b**) (lark) broma f, diversión f **2** vi reírse tontamente

gilt [gɪlt] **1** adj dorado(a) **2** n (colour) dorado m

gimmick ['gɪmɪk] n truco m; (in advertising) reclamo m

gin [dʒɪn] n ginebra f; **g. and tonic** gin tonic m

ginger ['dʒɪndʒə(r)] **1** n jengibre m; **g. ale** ginger ale m **2** adj (**a**) de jengibre (**b**) (hair) pelirrojo(a)

gipsy ['dʒɪpsɪ] adj & n gitano(a) (m,f)

giraffe [dʒɪ'rɑːf] n jirafa f

girl [gɜːl] n (**a**) chica f, joven f; (child) niña f; Br **g. guide**, US **g. scout** exploradora f (**b**) (daughter) hija f (**c**) (sweetheart) novia f

girlfriend ['gɜːlfrend] n (**a**) (lover) novia f (**b**) (female friend) amiga f

girlish ['gɜːlɪʃ] adj (**a**) de niña (**b**) (effeminate) afeminado(a)

giro ['dʒaɪrəʊ] n Br Fam (unemployment cheque) cheque m del desempleo or Esp paro

gist [dʒɪst] *n* esencia *f*; **did you get the g. of what he was saying?** ¿cogiste la idea de lo que decía?

give [gɪv] (*pt* **gave**; *pp* **given**) **1** *n* (*elasticity*) elasticidad *f*

2 *vt* (a) dar; **to g. sth to sb** dar algo a algn; **to g. a start** pegar un salto; **to g. sb a present** regalar algo a algn; **to g. sb sth to eat** dar de comer a algn (b) (*pay*) pagar (c) (*speech*) pronunciar (d) (*grant*) otorgar; **to g. sb one's attention** prestar atención a algn (e) (*yield*) ceder; **to g. way** *Aut* ceder el paso; *Fig* ceder; (*legs*) flaquear

3 *vi* (*yield*) ceder; (*fabric*) dar de sí

▸ **give away** *vt sep* (a) repartir; (*present*) regalar (b) (*disclose*) revelar; **to g. the game away** descubrir el pastel (c) (*betray*) traicionar

▸ **give back** *vt sep* devolver

▸ **give in 1** *vi* (a) (*admit defeat*) darse por vencido(a); (*surrender*) rendirse (b) **to g. in to** ceder ante **2** *vt sep* (*hand in*) entregar

▸ **give off** *vt sep* (*smell etc*) despedir

▸ **give out** *vt sep* distribuir, repartir

▸ **give over** *vt sep* (*hand over*) entregar; (*devote*) dedicar

▸ **give up 1** *vt sep* (a) (*idea*) abandonar; **to g. up smoking** dejar de fumar (b) (*hand over*) entregar; **to g. oneself up** entregarse **2** *vi* (*admit defeat*) darse por vencido(a), rendirse

▸ **give up on** *vt insep* darse por vencido con

given ['gɪvən] **1** *adj* (a) (*particular*) dado(a); **at a g. time** en un momento dado (b) **g. to** dado(a) a

2 *conj* (a) (*considering*) dado(a) (b) (*if*) si

3 *pp of* **give**

glad [glæd] *adj* (**gladder, gladdest**) contento(a); (*happy*) alegre; **he'll be only too g. to help you** tendrá mucho gusto en ayudarle; **to be g.** alegrarse

glamorous ['glæmərəs] *adj* atractivo(a), encantador(a)

glance [glɑːns] **1** *n* mirada *f*, vistazo *m*; **at a g.** de un vistazo; **at first g. a** primera vista **2** *vi* echar un vistazo (**at a**)

▸ **glance off** *vt insep* (*of ball etc*) rebotar de

gland [glænd] *n* glándula *f*

glare [gleə(r)] **1** *n* (*light*) luz *f* deslumbrante; (*dazzle*) deslumbramiento *m*; (*look*) mirada *f* feroz **2** *vi* (*dazzle*) deslumbrar; (*look*) lanzar una mirada furiosa (**at a**)

glaring ['gleərɪŋ] *adj* (*light*) deslumbrante; (*colour*) chillón(ona); (*obvious*) evidente

glass [glɑːs] *n* (a) (*material*) vidrio *m*; **pane of g.** cristal *m* (b) (*drinking vessel*) vaso *m*; **wine g.** copa *f* (para vino) (c) **glasses** gafas *fpl*, *Am* lentes *mpl*, anteojos *mpl*; **to wear glasses** llevar gafas *or Am* lentes *or* anteojos

glaze [gleɪz] **1** *n* (*varnish*) barniz *m*; (*for pottery*) vidriado *m* **2** *vt* (a) (*windows*) acristalar; (b) (*varnish*) barnizar; (*ceramics*) vidriar (c) *Culin* glasear

gleam [gliːm] **1** *n* (a) destello *m* (b) *Fig* (*glimmer*) rayo *m* **2** *vi* brillar, relucir

glean [gliːn] *vt Fig* recoger, cosechar

glee [gliː] *n* gozo *m*

glen [glen] *n* cañada *f*

glide [glaɪd] *vi* (a) (*slip, slide*) deslizarse (b) *Av* planear

glider ['glaɪdə(r)] *n* planeador *m*

gliding ['glaɪdɪŋ] *n* vuelo *m* sin motor

glimmer ['glɪmə(r)] *n* (a) (*light*) luz *f* tenue (b) *Fig* (*trace*) destello *m*

glimpse [glɪmps] **1** *n* atisbo *m* **2** *vt* atisbar

glint [glɪnt] **1** *n* destello *m*, centelleo *m*; **he had a g. in his eye** le brillaban los ojos **2** *vi* destellar, centellear

glisten ['glɪsən] *vi* relucir, brillar

glitter ['glɪtə(r)] **1** *n* brillo *m* **2** *vi* relucir

gloat [gləʊt] *vi* jactarse; **to g. over another's misfortune** recrearse con la desgracia de otro

global ['gləʊbəl] *adj* (a) (*of the world*) mundial (b) (*overall*) global

globalization [gləʊbəlaɪ'zeɪʃən] *n*

mundialización f, globalización f

globe [gləʊb] n globo m, esfera f

gloom [gluːm] n (obscurity) penumbra f; (melancholy) melancolía f; (despair) desolación f

gloomy ['gluːmɪ] adj (**gloomier, gloomiest**) (dark) oscuro(a); (weather) gris; (dismal) deprimente; (despairing) pesimista; (sad) triste

glorious ['glɔːrɪəs] adj (momentous) glorioso(a); (splendid) magnífico(a), espléndido(a)

glory ['glɔːrɪ] n gloria f; Fig (splendour) esplendor m; Fig (triumph) triunfo m

gloss [glɒs] **1** n (**a**) (explanation) glosa f (**b**) (sheen) brillo m; **g. (paint)** pintura f brillante **2** vi glosar
► **gloss over** vt insep Fig encubrir

glossary ['glɒsərɪ] n glosario m

glossy ['glɒsɪ] adj (**glossier, glossiest**) lustroso(a); **g. magazine** revista f de lujo

glove [glʌv] n guante m; Aut **g. compartment** guantera f

glow [gləʊ] **1** n brillo m; (of fire) incandescencia f; (of sun) arrebol m; (heat) calor m; (light) luz f; (in cheeks) rubor m **2** vi brillar; (fire) arder

glowing ['gləʊɪŋ] adj (**a**) (fire) incandescente; (colour) vivo(a); (light) brillante (**b**) (cheeks) encendido(a) (**c**) Fig (report) entusiasta

glue [gluː] **1** n pegamento m, cola f **2** vt pegar (**to** a)

glum [glʌm] adj (**glummer, glummest**) alicaído(a)

glutton ['glʌtən] n glotón(ona) m,f

GM [dʒiː'em] adj (abbr **genetically modified**) transgénico(a), modificado(a) genéticamente; **GM food** (alimentos) transgénicos

GMT [dʒiːem'tiː] n (abbr **Greenwich Mean Time**) hora f del meridiano de Greenwich

gnat [næt] n mosquito m

gnaw [nɔː] vt & vi (chew) roer

go [gəʊ] (3rd person sing pres **goes**; pt **went**; pp **gone**) **1** vi (**a**) ir; **to go for a**

walk (ir a) dar un paseo
(**b**) (depart) irse, marcharse
(**c**) (function) funcionar
(**d**) (be sold) venderse
(**e**) (become) quedarse, volverse; **to go blind** quedarse ciego(a); **to go mad** volverse loco(a)
(**f**) (progress) ir, marchar; **everything went well** todo salió bien; **how's it going?** ¿qué tal (te van las cosas)?
(**g**) **to be going to** (in the future) ir a; (on the point of) estar a punto de
(**h**) (fit) caber
(**i**) (be available) quedar; **I'll take whatever's going** me conformo con lo que hay
(**j**) (be acceptable) valer; **anything goes** todo vale
(**k**) (time) pasar; **there are only two weeks to go** sólo quedan dos semanas
(**l**) (say) decir; **as the saying goes** según el dicho
(**m**) **to let sth go** soltar algo
2 vt (**a**) (travel) hacer, recorrer (**b**) **go it alone** apañárselas solo
3 n (**a**) (energy) energía f, dinamismo m (**b**) (try) intento m; **to have a go at sth** probar suerte con algo; **to have a go at sb** criticar a algn (**c**) (turn) turno m; **it's your go** te toca a ti (**d**) **to make a go of sth** tener éxito en algo
► **go about 1** vt insep (**a**) (task) emprender; **how do you go about it?** ¿cómo hay que hacerlo? (**b**) **to go about one's business** ocuparse de sus asuntos **2** vi (rumour) correr
► **go after** vt insep (pursue) ir tras
► **go against** vt insep (oppose) ir en contra de; (verdict) ser desfavorable a
► **go ahead** vi (**a**) (proceed) proceder (**b**) **we'll go on ahead** iremos delante
► **go along 1** vt insep (street) pasar por **2** vi (progress) progresar
► **go along with** vt insep (**a**) (agree with) estar de acuerdo con (**b**) (accompany) acompañar
► **go around** vi (**a**) (rumour) correr (**b**) **there's enough to go around** hay para todos
► **go away** vi marcharse

▸ **go back** *vi* (**a**) *(return)* volver, regresar (**b**) *Fig* **to go back to** *(date from)* datar de

▸ **go back on** *vt insep* **to go back on one's word** faltar a su palabra

▸ **go back to** *vt insep* volver a

▸ **go by** *vi* pasar; **as time goes by** con el tiempo

▸ **go down** *vi* (**a**) *(descend)* bajar; *(sun)* ponerse; *(ship)* hundirse (**b**) *(diminish)* disminuir; *(temperature)* bajar (**c**) *(be received)* ser acogido(a)

▸ **go for** *vt insep* (**a**) *(attack)* lanzarse sobre (**b**) *(fetch)* ir por

▸ **go in** *vi* entrar

▸ **go in for** *vt insep (exam)* presentarse a; *(hobby)* dedicarse a

▸ **go into** *vt insep* (**a**) *(enter)* entrar en; **to go into journalism** dedicarse al periodismo (**b**) *(study)* examinar; *(matter)* investigar

▸ **go off 1** *vi* (**a**) *(leave)* irse, marcharse (**b**) *(bomb)* explotar; *(gun)* dispararse; *(alarm)* sonar (**c**) *(food)* pasarse **2** *vt insep Fam* **to go off sth** perder el gusto *or* el interés por algo

▸ **go on** *vi* (**a**) *(continue)* seguir, continuar; **to go on talking** seguir hablando; *Fam* **to go on and on about sth** no parar de hablar sobre algo; *(complain)* quejarse constantemente de algo (**b**) *(time)* transcurrir, pasar (**c**) *(light)* encenderse, *Am* prenderse

▸ **go out** *vi* (**a**) *(leave)* salir; **to go out for a meal** comer *or* cenar fuera (**b**) *(boy and girl)* salir juntos (**c**) *(fire, light)* apagarse (**d**) *(tide)* bajar

▸ **go over** *vt insep (revise)* repasar

▸ **go over to** *vt insep* (**a**) acercarse a; **to go over to the enemy** pasarse al enemigo (**b**) *(switch to)* pasar a

▸ **go round** *vi* (**a**) *(revolve)* dar vueltas (**b**) **to go round to sb's house** pasar por casa de algn

▸ **go through 1** *vi (bill)* ser aprobado(a) **2** *vt insep* (**a**) *(examine)* examinar; *(search)* registrar (**b**) *(rehearse)* ensayar (**c**) *(spend)* gastar (**d**) *(list etc)* explicar (**e**) *(endure)* sufrir

▸ **go through with** *vt insep* llevar a cabo

▸ **go under** *vi* (**a**) *(ship)* hundirse (**b**) *(business)* fracasar

▸ **go up** *vi* (**a**) *(price etc)* subir (**b**) **to go up to sb** acercarse a algn (**c**) *(in a lift)* subir

▸ **go with** *vt insep* (**a**) *(accompany)* ir con (**b**) *(colours)* hacer juego con

▸ **go without** *vt insep* pasarse sin, prescindir de

go-ahead ['gəʊəhed] *n Fam* **to give sb the g.** dar luz verde a algn

goal [gəʊl] *n* (**a**) *Sport* gol *m*; **g. post** poste *m* (**b**) *(aim, objective)* meta *f*, objetivo *m*

goalkeeper ['gəʊlkiːpə(r)] *n* portero(a) *m,f*

goat [gəʊt] *n (female)* cabra *f*; *(male)* macho cabrío

gobble ['gɒbəl] *vt* engullir

goblet ['gɒblɪt] *n* copa *f*

god [gɒd] *n* dios *m*; **G.** Dios; **(my) G.!** ¡Dios mío!

goddam(n) ['gɒdæm] *US Fam* **1** *adj* maldito(a), dichoso(a), *Méx* pinche **2** *adv* **that was g. stupid!** ¡eso fue una auténtica estupidez!

goddaughter ['gɒdɔːtə(r)] *n* ahijada *f*

goddess ['gɒdɪs] *n* diosa *f*

godfather ['gɒdfɑːðə(r)] *n* padrino *m*

godmother ['gɒdmʌðə(r)] *n* madrina *f*

godsend ['gɒdsend] *n* regalo inesperado

godson ['gɒdsʌn] *n* ahijado *m*

goes [gəʊz] *3rd person sing pres of* **go**

goggles ['gɒgəlz] *npl* gafas *fpl* protectoras, *CSur* antiparras *fpl*

going ['gəʊɪŋ] **1** *adj* (**a**) *(price)* corriente; **the g. rate** el precio medio (**b**) **a g. concern** un negocio que marcha bien (**c**) **to get** *or* **be g.** marcharse (**d**) **to keep g.** resistir **2** *n* **to get out while the g. is good** retirarse antes que sea demasiado tarde

goings-on [gəʊɪŋz'ɒn] *npl Fam* tejemanejes *mpl*

gold [gəʊld] **1** *n* oro *m*; **g. leaf** pan *m* de oro; **g. medal** medalla *f* de oro; **g. mine** mina *f* de oro **2** *adj* de oro; *(colour)* oro, dorado(a)

golden ['gəʊldən] *adj* de oro; *(colour)* dorado(a); *Fig* **a g. opportunity** una excelente oportunidad; *Orn* **g. eagle** águila *f* real; *Fig* **g. handshake** indemnización *f* por despido; **g. wedding** bodas *fpl* de oro

goldfish ['gəʊldfɪʃ] *n* pez *m* de colores

gold-plated [gəʊld'pleɪtɪd] *adj* chapado(a) en oro

goldsmith ['gəʊldsmɪθ] *n* orfebre *m*

golf [gɒlf] *n* golf *m*; **g. ball** pelota *f* de golf; **g. club** *(stick)* palo *m* de golf; *(place)* club *m* de golf; **g. course** campo *m* de golf

golfer ['gɒlfə(r)] *n* golfista *mf*

gone [gɒn] **1** *adj* desaparecido(a) **2** *pp of* **go**

gong [gɒŋ] *n* gong *m*

good [gʊd] **1** *adj* (**better, best**) (**a**) *(before noun)* buen(a); *(after noun)* bueno(a); **a g. book** un buen libro; **g. afternoon/evening** buenas tardes; **g. morning** buenos días; **g. night** buenas noches; **it looks g.** tiene buena pinta; **to feel g.** sentirse bien; **to smell g.** oler bien; **to have a g. time** pasarlo bien
  (**b**) *(kind)* amable
  (**c**) *(morally correct)* correcto(a); **be g.!** ¡pórtate bien!
  (**d**) **he's g. at languages** tiene facilidad para los idiomas
  (**e**) *(attractive)* bonito(a); **g. looks** atractivo *m*, belleza *f*
  (**f**) *(propitious)* propicio(a)
  (**g**) *(character)* agradable; **he's in a g. mood** está de buen humor
2 *n* (**a**) bien *m*; **g. and evil** el bien y el mal; **to do g.** hacer el bien (**b**) *(advantage)* bien *m*, provecho *m*; **for your own g.** para tu propio bien; **it's no g.** waiting no sirve de nada esperar; **it will do you g.** te hará bien (**c**) *Com* **goods** artículos *mpl*, géneros

mpl; **goods train** tren *m* de mercancías **3** *adv* **she's gone for g.** se ha ido para siempre
4 *interj* ¡muy bien!

goodbye [gʊd'baɪ] **1** *interj* ¡adiós! **2** *n* adiós *m*, despedida *f*; **to say g. to sb** despedirse de algn

good-for-nothing ['gʊdfənʌθɪŋ] *adj & n* inútil *(mf)*

good-looking [gʊd'lʊkɪŋ] *adj* guapo(a)

goodness ['gʊdnɪs] *n* bondad *f*; **my g.!** ¡Dios mío!; **thank g.!** ¡gracias a Dios!; **for g. sake!** ¡por Dios!

goodwill [gʊd'wɪl] *n* (**a**) buena voluntad *f* (**b**) *Com (reputation)* buen nombre *m*

goose [guːs] *n (pl* **geese**) ganso *m*, oca *f*

gooseberry ['gʊzbərɪ, 'guːsbərɪ] *n* uva espina, grosella espinosa; *Br Fam* **to play g.** *Esp* hacer de carabina *or* de sujetavelas, *Méx* hacer mal tercio, *RP* estar de paleta

gooseflesh ['guːsfleʃ] *n*, **goose-pimples** ['guːspɪmpəlz] *npl* carne *f* de gallina

gorge [gɔːdʒ] **1** *n* desfiladero *m* **2** *vt & vi* **to g. (oneself) (on)** atiborrarse (de)

gorgeous ['gɔːdʒəs] *adj* magnífico(a), estupendo(a); *(person)* atractivo(a), guapo(a)

gorilla [gə'rɪlə] *n* gorila *m*

gory ['gɔːrɪ] *adj* (**gorier, goriest**) sangriento(a)

gosh [gɒʃ] *interj Fam* ¡cielos!, ¡caray!

go-slow [gəʊ'sləʊ] *n Br* huelga *f* de celo

gospel ['gɒspəl] *n* **the G.** el Evangelio; *Fam* **it's the g. truth** es la pura verdad

gossip ['gɒsɪp] **1** *n* (**a**) *(rumour)* cotilleo *m*; **g. column** ecos *mpl* de sociedad (**b**) *(person)* chismoso(a) *m,f*, cotilla *mf* **2** *vi (natter)* cotillear, chismorrear

got [gɒt] *pt & pp of* **get**

gotten ['gɒtən] *US pp of* **get**

gourmet ['gʊəmeɪ] *n* gourmet *mf*

govern ['gʌvən] *vt* (**a**) gobernar (**b**) *(determine)* determinar

government ['gʌvənmənt] n gobierno m

governor ['gʌvənə(r)] n (ruler) gobernador(a) m,f; (of prison) director(a) m,f; (of school) administrador(a) m,f

gown [gaʊn] n (dress) vestido largo; Jur, Univ toga f

GP [dʒi:'pi:] n Br (abbr **general practitioner**) médico(a) m,f de familia or de cabecera

grab [græb] **1** n agarrón m; Fam **to be up for grabs** estar disponible **2** vt (a) agarrar; **to g. hold of sb** agarrarse a algn (b) Fig **g. a bottle of wine** píllate una botella de vino (c) Fig **how does that g. you?** ¿qué te parece?

grace [greɪs] **1** n (a) gracia f (b) **to say g.** bendecir la mesa (c) **five days' g.** (reprieve) un plazo de cinco días (d) (elegance) elegancia f **2** vt (a) (adorn) adornar (b) (honour) honrar

graceful ['greɪsfʊl] adj elegante; (movement) garboso(a)

gracious ['greɪʃəs] **1** adj (a) (elegant) elegante (b) (courteous) cortés (c) (kind) amable **2** interj **good g. (me)!, goodness g.!** ¡santo cielo!

grade [greɪd] **1** n (a) (quality) grado m; (rank) categoría f; Mil rango m (b) US Educ (mark) nota f (c) US Educ (class) clase f; **g. school** escuela primaria (d) (level) nivel m (e) US **g. crossing** paso m a nivel **2** vt clasificar

gradient ['greɪdɪənt] n (graph) declive m; (hill) cuesta f, pendiente f

gradual ['grædjʊəl] adj gradual, progresivo(a)

gradually ['grædjʊəlɪ] adv poco a poco

graduate 1 n ['grædjʊɪt] Univ licenciado(a) m,f; US (from high school) ≃ bachiller mf **2** vi ['grædjʊeɪt] (a) Univ licenciarse (in en) (b) US (from high school) ≃ sacar el bachillerato

graduation [grædjʊ'eɪʃən] n graduación f; Univ **g. ceremony** ceremonia f de entrega de los títulos

graffiti [grə'fi:ti:] npl grafiti mpl

grain [greɪn] n (a) (cereals) cereales mpl (b) (particle) grano m; Fig **there's not a g. of truth in it** no tiene ni pizca de verdad (c) (in wood) fibra f; (in stone) veta f; (in leather) flor f; Fig **to go against the g.** ir a contrapelo

gram [græm] n gramo m

grammar ['græmə(r)] n gramática f; **g. (book)** libro m de gramática; Br **g. school** instituto m de enseñanza secundaria (al que sólo se accede después de superar un examen de ingreso)

grammatical [grə'mætɪkəl] adj gramatical

gramme [græm] n gramo m

grand [grænd] **1** adj (a) grande; (before singular noun) gran; **g. piano** piano m de cola (b) (splendid) grandioso(a), magnífico(a); (impressive) impresionante (c) **g. total** total m (d) Fam (wonderful) genial, Am salvo RP chévere, Méx padre, RP bárbaro(a) **2** n Fam mil libras fpl; US mil dólares mpl

grandchild ['græntʃaɪld] n nieto(a) m,f

granddad ['grændæd] n Fam abuelo m

granddaughter ['grændɔ:tə(r)] n nieta f

grandfather ['grænfɑ:ðə(r)] n abuelo m; **g. clock** reloj m de caja

grandma ['grænmɑ:] n Fam abuelita f

grandmother ['grænmʌðə(r)] n abuela f

grandpa ['grænpɑ:] n Fam abuelito m

grandparents ['grænpeərənts] npl abuelos mpl

grandson ['grænsʌn] n nieto m

grandstand ['grænstænd] n tribuna f

granite ['grænɪt] n granito m

granny ['grænɪ] n Fam abuelita f

grant [grɑ:nt] **1** vt (a) (allow) conceder, otorgar (b) (admit) admitir; **to take sb for granted** no apreciar a algn en lo que vale; **to take sth for granted** dar algo por sentado **2** n Educ beca f; (subsidy) subvención f

grape [greɪp] n uva f; **g. juice** mosto m

grapefruit ['greɪpfruːt] *n* pomelo *m*, *Am* toronja *f*

graph [grɑːf, græf] *n* gráfica *f*

graphic ['græfɪk] *adj* gráfico(a); **g. arts** artes gráficas; **g. designer** grafista *mf*

graphics ['græfɪks] *n* (**a**) *(study)* grafismo *m* (**b**) *pl Comput* gráficas *fpl*

grapple ['græpəl] **1** *vi (struggle)* luchar cuerpo a cuerpo (**with** con); *Fig* **to g. with a problem** intentar resolver un problema **2** *n (hook)* garfio *m*

grasp [grɑːsp] **1** *vt* (**a**) agarrar (**b**) *(understand)* comprender **2** *n* (**a**) *(grip)* agarrón *m* (**b**) *(understanding)* comprensión *f*; **within sb's g.** al alcance de algn

grass [grɑːs] *n* hierba *f*; *(lawn)* césped *m*; *Fig* **g. roots** base *f*

grasshopper ['grɑːshɒpə(r)] *n* saltamontes *m inv*

grassy ['grɑːsɪ] *adj* (**grassier**, **grassiest**) cubierto(a) de hierba

grate¹ [greɪt] **1** *vt Culin* rallar **2** *vi* chirriar

grate² [greɪt] *n* (**a**) *(in fireplace)* rejilla *f* (**b**) *(fireplace)* chimenea *f* (**c**) *Constr* rejilla *f*, reja *f*

grateful ['greɪtfʊl] *adj* agradecido(a); **to be g. for** agradecer

grater ['greɪtə(r)] *n Culin* rallador *m*

gratify ['grætɪfaɪ] *vt* (**a**) *(please)* complacer (**b**) *(yield to)* sucumbir a

gratifying ['grætɪfaɪɪŋ] *adj* grato(a)

grating¹ ['greɪtɪŋ] *n* rejilla *f*, reja *f*

grating² ['greɪtɪŋ] *adj* chirriante; *(tone)* áspero(a)

gratitude ['grætɪtjuːd] *n* agradecimiento *m*

gratuitous [grə'tjuːɪtəs] *adj* gratuito(a)

grave¹ [greɪv] *n* sepultura *f*, tumba *f*

grave² [greɪv] *adj (look etc)* serio(a); *(situation)* grave

gravel ['grævəl] *n* grava *f*, gravilla *f*

gravestone ['greɪvstəʊn] *n* lápida *f* sepulcral

graveyard ['greɪvjɑːd] *n* cementerio *m*

gravity ['grævɪtɪ] *n* gravedad *f*

gravy ['greɪvɪ] *n* salsa *f*, jugo *m* (de la carne)

gray [greɪ] *adj & n US* = **grey**

graze¹ [greɪz] *vi* pacer, pastar

graze² [greɪz] **1** *vt (scratch)* rasguñar; *(brush against)* rozar **2** *n* rasguño *m*

grease [griːs, griːz] **1** *n* grasa *f* **2** *vt* engrasar

greasy ['griːsɪ, 'griːzɪ] *adj* (**greasier**, **greasiest**) (**a**) *(oily)* grasiento(a); *(hair, food)* graso(a) (**b**) *(slippery)* resbaladizo(a) (**c**) *Fam (ingratiating)* pelotillero(a)

great [greɪt] **1** *adj* (**a**) grande; *(before singular noun)* gran; *(pain, heat)* fuerte; **a g. many** muchos(as); **G. Britain** Gran Bretaña; *Br* **G. Bear** Osa *f* Mayor (**b**) *Fam (excellent)* genial, *Am salvo RP* chévere, *Méx* padre, *RP* bárbaro(a); **to have a g. time** pasarlo muy bien **2** *adv Fam* muy bien, estupendamente

great-grandfather [greɪt'grænfɑːðə(r)] *n* bisabuelo *m*

great-grandmother [greɪt'grænmʌðə(r)] *n* bisabuela *f*

greatly ['greɪtlɪ] *adv* muy, mucho

Greece [griːs] *n* Grecia

greed [griːd], **greediness** ['griːdɪnɪs] *n (for food)* gula *f*; *(for money)* codicia *f*, avaricia *f*

greedy ['griːdɪ] *adj* (**greedier**, **greediest**) *(for food)* glotón(ona); *(for money)* codicioso(a) (**for** de)

Greek [griːk] **1** *adj* griego(a) **2** *n* (**a**) *(person)* griego(a) *m,f* (**b**) *(language)* griego *m*

green [griːn] **1** *n* (**a**) *(colour)* verde *m* (**b**) *(in golf)* campo *m*; **village g.** plaza *f* (del pueblo) (**c**) **greens** verdura *f*, verduras *fpl* **2** *adj* (**a**) verde; **g. bean** judía *f* verde, *Bol, RP* chaucha *f*, *CAm* ejote *m*, *Col, Cuba* habichuela *f*, *Chile* poroto *m* verde, *Ven* vainita *f*; **g. belt** zona *f* verde; *US* **g. card** *(work permit)* permiso *m* de trabajo; **g. pepper** pimiento *m* verde; **she was g. with envy** se la comía la envidia (**b**) *(inexperienced)* verde, novato(a); *(gullible)* crédulo(a) (**c**) *Pol* **G. Party** Partido *m* Verde

greenery ['gri:nərɪ] *n* follaje *m*

greengrocer ['gri:ŋgrəʊsə(r)] *n Br* verdulero(a) *m,f*

greenhouse ['gri:nhaʊs] *n* invernadero *m*; **g. effect** efecto invernadero

greet [gri:t] *vt (wave at)* saludar; *(receive)* recibir; *(welcome)* dar la bienvenida a

greeting ['gri:tɪŋ] *n* (**a**) saludo *m*; **greetings card** tarjeta *f* de felicitación (**b**) *(reception)* recibimiento *m*; *(welcome)* bienvenida *f*

grenade [grɪ'neɪd] *n* granada *f*

grew [gru:] *pt of* **grow**

grey [greɪ] **1** *adj (colour)* gris; *(hair)* cano(a); *(sky)* nublado(a); **g. matter** materia *f* gris **2** *n* (**a**) *(colour)* gris *m* (**b**) *(horse)* caballo tordo

grey-haired ['greɪheəd] *adj* canoso(a)

greyhound ['greɪhaʊnd] *n* galgo *m*

grid [grɪd] *n* (**a**) *(on map)* cuadrícula *f* (**b**) *(of electricity etc)* red *f* nacional (**c**) *(for cooking)* parrilla *f*

griddle ['grɪdəl] *n (for cooking)* plancha *f*

grief [gri:f] *n* dolor *m*, pena *f*; *Fam* **to come to g.** *(car, driver)* sufrir un accidente; *(plans)* irse al traste

grievance ['gri:vəns] *n (wrong)* agravio *m*; *(resentment)* queja *f*

grieve [gri:v] **1** *vt* apenar, dar pena a **2** *vi* apenarse, afligirse; **to g. for sb** llorar la muerte de algn

grill [grɪl] **1** *vt* (**a**) *Culin* asar (a la parrilla) (**b**) *Fam (interrogate)* interrogar duramente **2** *n Br (on cooker)* grill *m*; *(for open fire)* parrilla *f*; *(dish)* parrillada *f*

grill(e) [grɪl] *n (grating)* reja *f*

grim [grɪm] *adj* (**grimmer, grimmest**) (**a**) *(sinister)* macabro(a); *(landscape)* lúgubre (**b**) *(person)* ceñudo(a) (**d**) *Fam (unpleasant)* desagradable

grimace [grɪ'meɪs] **1** *n* mueca *f* **2** *vi* hacer una mueca

grime [graɪm] *n* mugre *f*, porquería *f*

grimy ['graɪmɪ] *adj* (**grimier, grimiest**) mugriento(a)

grin [grɪn] **1** *vi* sonreír abiertamente **2** *n* sonrisa abierta

grind [graɪnd] *(pt & pp* **ground**) **1** *vt (mill)* moler; *(crush)* triturar; *(sharpen)* afilar; *US (meat)* picar

2 *vi* (**a**) rechinar; *Fig* **to g. to a halt** *(vehicle)* pararse lentamente; *(production etc)* pararse poco a poco (**b**) *US Fam* empollar

3 *n* (**a**) *Fam* **the daily g.** la rutina cotidiana (**b**) *US Fam (studious pupil)* empollón(ona) *m,f*

grinder ['graɪndə(r)] *n (for coffee, pepper)* molinillo *m*; *(crusher)* trituradora *f*; *(for sharpening)* afilador *m*

grip [grɪp] **1** *n* (**a**) *(hold)* agarrón *m*; *(handshake)* apretón *m*; **to get to grips with a problem** superar un problema (**b**) *(handle)* *(of oar, handlebars, racket)* empuñadura *f* (**c**) *US (bag)* bolsa *f* de viaje **2** *vt* (**a**) agarrar, asir; *(hand)* apretar (**b**) *Fig (of film, story)* captar la atención de; **to be gripped by fear** ser presa del miedo

gripping ['grɪpɪŋ] *adj (film, story)* apasionante

grisly ['grɪzlɪ] *adj* (**grislier, grisliest**) espeluznante

gristle ['grɪsəl] *n* cartílago *m*, ternilla *f*

grit [grɪt] **1** *n* (**a**) *(gravel)* grava *f* (**b**) *Fam (courage)* valor *m* **2** *vt Fig* **to g. one's teeth** apretar los dientes

groan [grəʊn] **1** *n* (**a**) *(of pain)* gemido *m* (**b**) *Fam (of disapproval)* gruñido *m* **2** *vi* (**a**) *(in pain)* gemir (**b**) *Fam (complain)* quejarse (**about** de)

grocer ['grəʊsə(r)] *n* tendero(a) *m,f*; *Br* **g.'s (shop)** tienda *f* de comestibles *or* de ultramarinos, *Andes, CSur* bodega *f*, *CAm, Méx* (tienda *f* de) abarrotes *mpl*

groceries ['grəʊsərɪz] *npl* comestibles *mpl*

grocery ['grəʊsərɪ] *n esp US* **g. (store)** tienda *f* de comestibles *or* de ultramarinos, *Andes, CSur* bodega *f*, *CAm, Méx* (tienda *f* de) abarrotes *mpl*

groin [grɔɪn] *n* ingle *f*

groom [gru:m] **1** n (**a**) mozo m de cuadra (**b**) *(bridegroom)* novio m **2** vt *(horse)* almohazar; *(clothes, appearance)* cuidar

groove [gru:v] n *(furrow etc)* ranura f; *(of record)* surco m

grope [grəʊp] vi (**a**) *(search about)* andar a tientas; **to g. for sth** buscar algo a tientas (**b**) *Fam (fondle)* meter mano

gross [grəʊs] **1** adj (**a**) grosero(a); *(joke)* verde (**b**) *(fat)* obeso(a) (**c**) *(flagrant)* flagrante; *(ignorance)* craso(a) (**d**) *Com, Econ* bruto(a); **g. national product** producto nacional bruto **2** vt *Com* recaudar (en bruto)

grossly ['grəʊslɪ] adv enormemente

grotesque [grəʊ'tesk] adj grotesco(a)

ground¹ [graʊnd] **1** n (**a**) suelo m, tierra f; **at g. level** al nivel del suelo; *Br* **g. floor** planta baja (**b**) *(terrain)* terreno m (**c**) *US Elec* toma f de tierra (**d**) **grounds** *(gardens)* jardines mpl (**e**) **grounds** *(reason)* motivo m (**f**) **grounds** *(sediment)* poso m **2** vt (**a**) *Av* obligar a quedarse en tierra; *Naut* varar (**b**) *US Elec* conectar con tierra

ground² [graʊnd] **1** adj *(coffee)* molido(a); *US (meat) Esp, RP* picado(a); *Am* molido(a) **2** pt & pp of **grind**

grounding ['graʊndɪŋ] n base f; **to have a good g. in** tener buenos conocimientos de

groundwork ['graʊndwɜ:k] n trabajo preparatorio

group [gru:p] **1** n grupo m, conjunto m **2** vt agrupar, juntar (**into** en) **3** vi **to g. (together)** agruparse, juntarse

grovel ['grɒvəl] *(pt & pp* **grovelled,** *US* **groveled)** vi humillarse (**to** ante); *(crawl)* arrastrarse (**to** ante)

grow [grəʊ] *(pt* **grew;** *pp* **grown) 1** vt *(cultivate)* cultivar; **to g. a beard** dejarse (crecer) la barba **2** vi (**a**) crecer; *(increase)* aumentar (**b**) *(become)* hacerse, volverse; **to g. accustomed to** acostumbrarse a; **to g. dark** oscurecer; **to g. old** envejecer

grower ['grəʊə(r)] n cultivador(a) m,f

growl [graʊl] **1** vi gruñir **2** n gruñido m

grown [grəʊn] **1** adj crecido(a), adulto(a) **2** pp of **grow**

grown-up ['grəʊnʌp] adj & n adulto(a) *(m,f)*; **the grown-ups** los mayores

growth [grəʊθ] n (**a**) crecimiento m; *(increase)* aumento m; *(development)* desarrollo m (**b**) *Med* bulto m

grub [grʌb] n (**a**) *(larva)* gusano m (**b**) *Fam (food)* papeo m

grubby ['grʌbɪ] adj (**grubbier, grubbiest**) sucio(a)

grudge [grʌdʒ] **1** n rencor m; **to bear sb a g.** guardar rencor a algn **2** vt *(give unwillingly)* dar a regañadientes; **he grudges me my success** me envidia el éxito

grudgingly ['grʌdʒɪŋlɪ] adv a regañadientes

gruelling, *US* **grueling** ['gru:əlɪŋ] adj penoso(a)

gruesome ['gru:səm] adj espantoso(a), horrible

gruff [grʌf] adj *(manner)* brusco(a); *(voice)* áspero(a)

grumble ['grʌmbəl] **1** vi refunfuñar **2** n queja f

grumpy ['grʌmpɪ] adj (**grumpier, grumpiest**) gruñón(ona)

grunt [grʌnt] **1** vi gruñir **2** n gruñido m

guarantee [gærən'ti:] **1** n garantía f; *(certificate)* certificado m de garantía **2** vt garantizar; *(assure)* asegurar

guard [ɡɑ:d] **1** vt (**a**) *(protect)* defender, proteger; *(keep watch over)* vigilar (**b**) *(control)* guardar **2** vi protegerse (**against** de or contra) **3** n (**a**) **to be on one's g.** estar en guardia; **to catch sb off his g.** coger desprevenido a algn (**b**) *(sentry)* guardia mf; **g. dog** perro m guardián (**c**) *Br Rail* jefe m de tren; **g.'s van** furgón m de cola (**d**) *(on machine)* dispositivo m de seguridad; **fire g.** pantalla f

guardian ['ɡɑ:dɪən] n (**a**) guardián(ana) m,f; **g. angel** ángel m de la guarda (**b**) *Jur (of minor)* tutor(a) m,f

guer(r)illa [gə'rɪlə] n guerrillero(a)

m,f; **g. warfare** guerra *f* de guerrillas

guess [ges] **1** *vt & vi* (**a**) adivinar; **I guessed as much** me lo imaginaba; **to g. right/wrong** acertar/no acertar (**b**) *US Fam* pensar, suponer; **I g. so** supongo que sí **2** *n* conjetura *f*; *(estimate)* cálculo *m*; **at a rough g.** a ojo de buen cubero; **to have** *or* **make a g.** intentar adivinar

guesswork ['geswɜːk] *n* conjetura *f*

guest [gest] *n (at home)* invitado(a) *m,f*; *(in hotel)* cliente *mf*, huésped(a) *mf*; **g. artist** artista *mf* invitado(a); **g. room** cuarto *m* de los invitados

guesthouse ['gesthaʊs] *n* casa *f* de huéspedes

guidance ['gaɪdəns] *n* orientación *f*, consejos *mpl*; **for your g.** a título de información

guide [gaɪd] **1** *vt* guiar, dirigir **2** *n* (**a**) *(person)* guía *mf*; *Br* **girl g.** exploradora *f*; **g. dog** perro lazarillo (**b**) *(guidebook)* guía *f*

guided ['gaɪdɪd] *adj* dirigido(a); **g. tour** visita con guía; **g. missile** misil teledirigido

guideline ['gaɪdlaɪn] *n* pauta *f*

guild [gɪld] *n* gremio *m*

guilt [gɪlt] *n* (**a**) culpa *f* (**b**) *Jur* culpabilidad *f*

guilty ['gɪltɪ] *adj* (**guiltier, guiltiest**) culpable (**of** de); **to have a g. conscience** remorderle a uno la conciencia

guinea¹ ['gɪnɪ] *n* **g. pig** conejillo *m* de Indias, cobayo *m*; *Fig* **to act as a g. pig** servir de conejillo de Indias

guinea² ['gɪnɪ] *n Br (coin)* guinea *f* (= 21 chelines)

guise [gaɪz] *n* **under the g. of** so pretexto de

guitar [gɪ'tɑː(r)] *n* guitarra *f*

guitarist [gɪ'tɑːrɪst] *n* guitarrista *mf*

gulf [gʌlf] *n* (**a**) golfo *m*; **G. of Mexico** Golfo de Méjico; **G. Stream** corriente *f* del Golfo de Méjico; **the G. War** la guerra del Golfo (**b**) *Fig* abismo *m*

gull [gʌl] *n* gaviota *f*

gullible ['gʌləbəl] *adj* crédulo(a)

gulp [gʌlp] **1** *n* trago *m*
2 *vt* tragar; **to g. sth down** *(drink)* tomarse algo de un trago; *(food)* engullir algo
3 *vi* (**a**) *(swallow air)* tragar aire (**b**) *Fig (with fear)* tragar saliva

gum¹ [gʌm] **1** *n* goma *f* **2** *vt* pegar con goma

gum² [gʌm] *n Anat* encía *f*

gun [gʌn] *n* arma *f* de fuego; *(handgun)* pistola *f*, revólver *m*; *(rifle)* fusil *m*, escopeta *f*; *(cannon)* cañón *m*; *Fam* **the big guns** los peces gordos

▸ **gun down** *vt sep* matar a tiros

gunfire ['gʌnfaɪə(r)] *n* tiros *mpl*

gunpowder ['gʌnpaʊdə(r)] *n* pólvora *f*

gunshot ['gʌnʃɒt] *n* disparo *m*, tiro *m*

gurgle ['gɜːgəl] *vi (baby)* gorjear; *(liquid)* gorgotear; *(stream)* murmurar

gush [gʌʃ] **1** *vi* (**a**) brotar (**b**) *Fig* **to g. over sb** enjabonar a algn **2** *n (of water)* chorro *m*; *(of words)* torrente *m*

gust [gʌst] *n (of wind)* ráfaga *f*, racha *f*

gusto ['gʌstəʊ] *n* entusiasmo *m*

gut [gʌt] **1** *n* (**a**) *Anat* intestino *m* (**b**) **guts** *(entrails)* tripas *fpl*; *Fam* **to have guts** tener agallas
2 *vt* (**a**) *(fish)* destripar (**b**) *(destroy)* destruir por dentro
3 *adj Fam* **g. reaction** reacción *f* visceral

gutter ['gʌtə(r)] *n (in street)* arroyo *m*; *(on roof)* canalón *m*; *Fig* **g. press** prensa amarilla

guy¹ [gaɪ] *n Fam* tipo *m*, tío *m*

guy² [gaɪ] *n (rope)* viento *m*, cuerda *f*

guzzle ['gʌzəl] *vt & vi Fam (food etc)* zamparse; *(car)* tragar mucho

gym [dʒɪm] *Fam* (**a**) *(gymnasium)* gimnasio *m* (**b**) *(gymnastics)* gimnasia *f*; **g. shoes** zapatillas *fpl* de deporte

gymnasium [dʒɪm'neɪzɪəm] *n* gimnasio *m*

gymnastics [dʒɪm'næstɪks] *n sing* gimnasia *f*

gynaecologist, *US* **gynecologist** [gaɪnɪ'kɒlədʒɪst] *n* ginecólogo(a) *m,f*

gypsy ['dʒɪpsɪ] *adj & n* gitano(a) *(m,f)*

gyrate [dʒaɪ'reɪt] *vi* girar

Hh

H, h [eɪtʃ] *n (the letter)* H, h *f*

habit ['hæbɪt] *n* (**a**) costumbre *f* (**b**) *(garment)* hábito *m*

habitat ['hæbɪtæt] *n* hábitat *m*

habitual [həˈbɪtjʊəl] *adj* habitual; *(drinker, liar)* empedernido(a)

hack¹ [hæk] **1** *n (cut)* corte *m*; *(with axe)* hachazo *m* **2** *vt (with knife, axe)* cortar; *(kick)* dar un puntapié a

hack² [hæk] *n Fam (writer)* escritorzuelo(a) *m,f; (journalist)* gacetillero(a) *m,f*

hacker ['hækə(r)] *n Comput* pirata *mf* informático(a), hacker *mf*

had [hæd] *pt & pp of* **have**

haemorrhage ['hemərɪdʒ] *n* hemorragia *f*

haemorrhoids ['hemərɔɪdz] *npl* hemorroides *fpl*

hag [hæg] *n Pej* bruja *f*, arpía *f*

haggard ['hægəd] *adj* ojeroso(a)

haggle ['hægəl] *vi* regatear

hail¹ [heɪl] **1** *n* granizo *m*; *Fig* **a h. of bullets/insults** una lluvia de balas/ insultos **2** *vi* granizar

hail² [heɪl] **1** *vt* (**a**) *(taxi etc)* parar (**b**) *(acclaim)* aclamar **2** *vi* **to h. from** *(originate)* ser nativo(a) de

hair [heə(r)] *n (strand)* pelo *m*, cabello *m*; *(mass)* pelo, cabellos *mpl; (on arm, leg)* vello *m*; **to have long h.** tener el pelo largo

hairbrush ['heəbrʌʃ] *n* cepillo *m* (para el pelo)

haircut ['heəkʌt] *n* corte *m* de pelo; **to have a h.** cortarse el pelo

hairdo ['heəduː] *n Fam* peinado *m*

hairdresser ['heədresə(r)] *n* peluquero(a) *m,f*; **h.'s (shop)** peluquería *f*

hairdryer, hairdrier ['heədraɪə(r)] *n* secador *m* (de pelo)

hairgrip ['heəgrɪp] *n Br* horquilla *f*

hairpin ['heəpɪn] *n* horquilla *f*; **h. bend** curva muy cerrada

hairspray ['heəspreɪ] *n* laca *f* (para el pelo)

hairstyle ['heəstaɪl] *n* peinado *m*, corte *m* de pelo

hairy ['heərɪ] *adj* (**hairier, hairiest**) (**a**) *(with hair)* peludo(a) (**b**) *Fig (frightening)* enervante, espantoso(a)

half [hɑːf] **1** *n (pl* **halves**) mitad *f; Sport (period)* tiempo *m*; **he's four and a h.** tiene cuatro años y medio; **to cut in h.** cortar por la mitad

2 *adj* medio(a); **h. a dozen/an hour** media docena/hora; **h. board** media pensión; **h. fare** media tarifa; **h. term** medio trimestre

3 *adv* medio, a medias; **h. asleep** medio dormido(a)

half-caste ['hɑːfkɑːst] *adj & n* mestizo(a) *(m,f)*

half-hearted [hɑːfˈhɑːtɪd] *adj* poco entusiasta

half-hour [hɑːfˈaʊə(r)] *n* media hora

half-time [hɑːfˈtaɪm] *n* descanso *m*

half-way ['hɑːfweɪ] **1** *adj* intermedio(a) **2 halfway** [hɑːfˈweɪ] *adv* a medio camino, a mitad de camino

hall [hɔːl] *n* (**a**) *(lobby)* vestíbulo *m* (**b**) *(building)* sala *f; Br Univ* **h. of residence** residencia *f* de estudiantes, *Esp* colegio *m* mayor

hallo [həˈləʊ] *interj* ¡hola!

Hallowe(')en [hæləʊˈiːn] *n* víspera *f* de Todos los Santos

hallucination [həluːsɪˈneɪʃən] *n* alucinación *f*

hallway ['hɔːlweɪ] *n* vestíbulo *m*

halo ['heɪləʊ] *n* (**a**) *Rel* aureola *f* (**b**) *Astron* halo *m*

halt [hɔ:lt] **1** n *(stop)* alto m, parada f; **to call a h. to sth** poner fin a algo
2 vt parar
3 vi pararse

halve [hɑ:v] vt **(a)** partir por la mitad; *(reduce by half)* reducir a la mitad **(b)** *(share)* compartir

ham [hæm] n jamón m; **boiled h.** jamón de York; **Parma** or **cured h.** jamón serrano

hamburger ['hæmbɜːgə(r)] n hamburguesa f

hammer ['hæmə(r)] **1** n **(a)** martillo m; **(b)** *(of gun)* percusor m
2 vt **(a)** martillar; *(nail)* clavar; *Fig* **to h. home** insistir sobre **(b)** *Fam (defeat)* dar una paliza a
3 vi martillar, dar golpes

hammock ['hæmək] n hamaca f; *Naut* coy m

hamper¹ ['hæmpə(r)] n cesta f

hamper² ['hæmpə(r)] vt estorbar, dificultar

hamster ['hæmstə(r)] n hámster m

hand [hænd] **1** n **(a)** mano f; **by h.** a mano; **(close) at h.** a mano; **hands up!** ¡manos arriba!; **on the one/other h.** por una/otra parte; *Fig* **to get out of h.** descontrolarse; *Fig* **to wash one's hands of sth** lavarse las manos de algo; *Fig* **to give sb a h.** echarle una mano a algn; **h. grenade** granada f de mano **(b)** *(worker)* trabajador(a) m,f; *Naut* tripulante m **(c)** *(of clock)* aguja f **(d)** *(handwriting)* letra f
2 vt *(give)* dar, entregar
▸ **hand back** vt sep devolver
▸ **hand down** vt sep dejar en herencia
▸ **hand in** vt sep *(homework)* entregar; *(resignation)* presentar
▸ **hand out** vt sep repartir
▸ **hand over** vt sep entregar
▸ **hand round** vt sep repartir

handbag ['hændbæg] n Br *(woman's)* Esp bolso m, Col, CSur cartera f, Méx bolsa f

handbook ['hændbʊk] n manual m

handbrake ['hændbreɪk] n freno m de mano

handful ['hændfʊl] n puñado m

handicap ['hændɪkæp] **1** n **(a)** *Med* minusvalía f **(b)** *Sport* hándicap m, desventaja f **2** vt impedir

handicapped ['hændɪkæpt] adj **(a)** *(physically)* minusválido(a); *(mentally)* retrasado(a) **(b)** *Sport* en desventaja **(c)** *Fig* desfavorecido(a)

handicraft ['hændɪkrɑːft] n artesanía f.

handkerchief ['hæŋkətʃiːf] n pañuelo m

handle ['hændəl] **1** n *(of knife)* mango m; *(of cup)* asa f; *(of door)* pomo m; *(of drawer)* tirador m **2** vt **(a)** manejar; **h. with care** *(sign)* frágil **(b)** *(problem)* encargarse de; *(people)* tratar; *Fam (put up with)* soportar

handmade [hænd'meɪd] adj hecho(a) a mano

hand-out ['hændaʊt] n **(a)** *(leaflet)* folleto m; *Press* nota f de prensa **(b)** *(charity)* limosna f

handshake ['hændʃeɪk] n apretón m de manos

handsome ['hænsəm] adj **(a)** *(person)* guapo(a) **(b)** *(substantial)* considerable

handwriting ['hændraɪtɪŋ] n letra f

handwritten ['hændrɪtən] adj manuscrito(a), escrito(a) a mano

handy ['hændɪ] adj (**handier, handiest**) **(a)** *(useful)* útil, práctico(a); *(nearby)* a mano **(b)** *(dextrous)* diestro(a)

handyman ['hændɪmæn] n *(person good at odd jobs)* persona f habilidosa, Esp manitas mf inv

hang [hæŋ] *(pt & pp hung)* **1** vt **(a)** colgar **(b)** *(head)* bajar **(c)** *(pt & pp hanged)* ahorcar; **to h. oneself** ahorcarse **2** vi **(a)** colgar *(from de)*; *(in air)* flotar **(b)** *(pt & pp hanged)* *(criminal)* ser ahorcado(a)
▸ **hang about** vi *Fam* **(a)** perder el tiempo **(b)** *(wait)* esperar
▸ **hang around** vi *Fam* **(a)** esperar **(b)** frecuentar; **where does he h. around?** ¿a qué lugares suele ir?
▸ **hang on** vi **(a)** agarrarse **(b)** *(wait)* esperar

▶ **hang out 1** *vt sep (washing)* tender **2** *vi Fam (frequent)* frecuentar

▶ **hang together** *vi (ideas)* ser coherente

▶ **hang up** *vt sep (picture, telephone)* colgar

hanger ['hæŋə(r)] *n* percha *f*

hang-glider ['hæŋglaɪdə(r)] *n* ala delta

hang-gliding ['hæŋglaɪdɪŋ] *n* vuelo *m* libre

hangover ['hæŋəʊvə(r)] *n* resaca *f*

hang-up ['hæŋʌp] *n Fam (complex)* complejo *m*

hankie, hanky ['hæŋkɪ] *n Fam* pañuelo *m*

haphazard [hæp'hæzəd] *adj* caótico(a), desordenado(a)

happen ['hæpən] *vi* suceder, ocurrir; **it so happens that** lo que pasa es que; **if you h. to see my friend** si por casualidad ves a mi amigo

happily ['hæpɪlɪ] *adv (with pleasure)* felizmente; *(fortunately)* afortunadamente

happiness ['hæpɪnɪs] *n* felicidad *f*

happy ['hæpɪ] *adj* (**happier, happiest**) *(cheerful)* feliz, contento(a); *(fortunate)* afortunado(a); **h. birthday!** ¡feliz cumpleaños!

harass ['hærəs] *vt* acosar

harassment ['hærəsmənt, hə'ræsmənt] *n* hostigamiento *m*, acoso *m*

harbour, *US* **harbor** ['hɑːbə(r)] **1** *n* puerto *m* **2** *vt* (**a**) *(criminal)* encubrir (**b**) *(doubts)* abrigar

hard [hɑːd] **1** *adj* (**a**) duro(a); *(solid)* sólido(a); *Comput* **h. disk** disco duro; *Br Aut* **h. shoulder** *Esp* arcén *m*, *Andes* berma *f*, *Méx* acotamiento *m*, *RP* banquina *f*

(**b**) *(difficult)* difícil; **h. of hearing** duro(a) de oído; *Fam Fig* **to be h. up** estar sin blanca

(**c**) *(harsh)* severo(a); *(strict)* estricto(a); **h. drugs** droga dura; *Pol* **h. left** extrema izquierda; **h. sell** promoción *f* de venta agresiva

(**d**) **a h. worker** un trabajador concienzudo

(**e**) **h. luck!** ¡mala suerte!

(**f**) **h. evidence** pruebas definitivas; **h. currency** divisa *f* fuerte

2 *adv* (**a**) *(hit)* fuerte (**b**) *(work)* mucho

hardback ['hɑːdbæk] *n* edición *f* de tapas duras

hardball ['hɑːdbɔːl] *n US (baseball)* béisbol *m*

hard-boiled ['hɑːdbɔɪld] *adj* duro(a)

harden ['hɑːdən] **1** *vt* endurecer **2** *vi* endurecerse

hardly ['hɑːdlɪ] *adv* apenas; **h. anyone/ever** casi nadie/nunca; **he had h. begun when …** apenas había comenzado cuando …; **I can h. believe it** apenas lo puedo creer

hardware ['hɑːdweə(r)] *n* (**a**) *(goods)* ferretería *f*; *US* **h. store** *(ironmonger's)* ferretería (**b**) *Comput* hardware *m*

hardwearing [hɑːd'weərɪŋ] *adj* duradero(a)

hardworking ['hɑːdwɜːkɪŋ] *adj* muy trabajador(a)

hardy ['hɑːdɪ] *adj* (**hardier, hardiest**) *(person)* robusto(a), fuerte; *(plant)* resistente

hare [heə(r)] **1** *n* liebre *f* **2** *vi* correr muy de prisa

harm [hɑːm] **1** *n* daño *m*, perjuicio *m*; **to be out of h.'s way** estar a salvo **2** *vt* hacer daño a, perjudicar

harmful ['hɑːmfʊl] *adj* perjudicial (**to para**)

harmless ['hɑːmlɪs] *adj* inofensivo(a)

harmonica [hɑː'mɒnɪkə] *n* armónica *f*

harmonious [hɑː'məʊnɪəs] *adj* armonioso(a)

harmonize ['hɑːmənaɪz] *vt & vi* armonizar

harmony ['hɑːmənɪ] *n* armonía *f*

harness ['hɑːnɪs] **1** *n (for horse)* arreos *mpl* **2** *vt* (**a**) *(horse)* enjaezar (**b**) *Fig (resources etc)* aprovechar

harp [hɑːp] *n* arpa *f*

▶ **harp on** *vi Fam* hablar sin parar

harrowing ['hærəʊɪŋ] *adj* angustioso(a)

harsh [hɑːʃ] *adj* severo(a); *(voice)*

áspero(a); *(sound)* discordante

harvest ['hɑːvɪst] **1** *n* cosecha *f*; *(of grapes)* vendimia *f* **2** *vt* cosechar, recoger

has [hæz] *3rd person sing pres of* **have**

has-been ['hæzbiːn] *n Fam Pej* vieja gloria *f*

hassle ['hæsəl] *Fam* **1** *n* (**a**) *(nuisance)* rollo *m* (**b**) *(problem)* lío *m* (**c**) *(wrangle)* bronca *f* **2** *vt* fastidiar

haste [heɪst] *n Fml* prisa *f*; **to make h.** darse prisa

hasten ['heɪsən] *vi* apresurarse

hastily ['heɪstɪlɪ] *adv (quickly)* de prisa

hasty ['heɪstɪ] *adj* (**hastier, hastiest**) apresurado(a); *(rash)* precipitado(a)

hat [hæt] *n* sombrero *m*

hatch[1] [hætʃ] *n* escotilla *f*; **serving h.** ventanilla *f*

hatch[2] [hætʃ] **1** *vt* (**a**) *(eggs)* empollar (**b**) *Fig (plan)* tramar **2** *vi* **to h. (out)** salirse del huevo

hatchback ['hætʃbæk] *n* coche *m* de 3/5 puertas

hate [heɪt] **1** *n* odio *m* **2** *vt* odiar

hateful ['heɪtfʊl] *adj* odioso(a)

hatred ['heɪtrɪd] *n* odio *m*

haughty ['hɔːtɪ] *adj* (**haughtier, haughtiest**) altanero(a), arrogante

haul [hɔːl] **1** *n* (**a**) *(journey)* trayecto *m* (**b**) *(of fish)* redada *f* (**c**) *(loot)* botín *m* **2** *vt* (**a**) *tirar; (drag)* arrastrar (**b**) *(transport)* acarrear

▶ **haul up** *vt sep Fam (to court)* llevar

haunt [hɔːnt] **1** *n* guarida *f* **2** *vt* (**a**) *(of ghost)* aparecerse en (**b**) *Fig* atormentar (**c**) *(frequent)* frecuentar

haunted ['hɔːntɪd] *adj* encantado(a), embrujado(a)

have [hæv]

En el inglés hablado, y en el escrito en estilo coloquial, el verbo auxiliar **have** se contrae de forma que **I have** se transforma en **I've**, **he/she/it has** se transforman en **he's/she's/it's** y **you/we/they have** se transforman en **you've/we've/they've**. Las formas de pasado **I/you/he** *etc* **had** se

transforman en **I'd**, **you'd**, **he'd** *etc*. Las formas negativas **has not**, **have not** y **had not** se transforman en **hasn't**, **haven't** y **hadn't**.

(*3rd person sing pres* **has**; *pt & pp* **had**) **1** *vt* (**a**) *(possess)* tener; **h. you got a car?** ¿tienes coche?

(**b**) *(get, experience, suffer)* tener; **to h. a holiday** tomarse unas vacaciones

(**c**) *(partake of) (drink)* tomar; **to h. breakfast/lunch/dinner** desayunar/comer/cenar; **to h. a bath/shave** bañarse/afeitarse

(**d**) **to h. (got) to** *(obligation)* tener que, deber

(**e**) *(make happen)* hacer que; **I'll h. someone come round** haré que venga alguien

(**f**) *(receive)* recibir; **to h. people round** invitar a gente

(**g**) *(party, meeting)* hacer, celebrar

(**h**) **to h. a baby** tener un niño

(**i**) **we won't h. it** *(allow)* no lo consentiremos

(**j**) *(hold)* tener; *Fig* **to h. sth against sb** tener algo en contra de algn

(**k**) *Fam (deceive)* engañar

(**l**) **you'd better stay** más vale que te quedes

2 *v aux* (**a**) *(compound)* haber; **I had been waiting for half an hour** hacía media hora que esperaba; **he hasn't eaten yet** no ha comido aún; **she had broken the window** había roto el cristal; **we h. lived here for ten years** hace diez años que vivimos aquí; **so I h.!** *(emphatic)* ¡ay, sí!, es verdad; **yes I h.!** ¡que sí!

(**b**) *(tag questions)* **you haven't seen my book, h. you?** no has visto mi libro, ¿verdad?; **he's been to France, hasn't he?** ha estado en Francia, ¿verdad? *or* ¿no?

(**c**) **to h. just done** acabar de hacer

▶ **have on** *vt sep* (**a**) *(wear)* vestir (**b**) *Fam* **to h. sb on** tomarle el pelo *or Esp, Carib, Méx* vacilar a algn

▶ **have out** *vt sep Fam* **to h. it out with sb** ajustar cuentas con algn

▶ **have over** *vt sep (invite)* recibir

haven ['heɪvən] *n* puerto *m*; *Fig* refugio *m*

havoc ['hævək] *n* **to play h. with** hacer estragos en

hawk [hɔːk] *n Orn, Pol* halcón *m*

hay [heɪ] *n* heno *m*; **h. fever** fiebre *f* del heno

haystack ['heɪstæk] *n* almiar *m*

haywire ['heɪwaɪə(r)] *adj Fam* en desorden; **to go h.** *(machine etc)* estropearse; *(person)* volverse loco(a)

hazard ['hæzəd] **1** *n* peligro *m*, riesgo *m*; *(in golf)* obstáculo *m* **2** *vt Fml* arriesgar; **to h. a guess** intentar adivinar

hazardous ['hæzədəs] *adj* arriesgado(a), peligroso(a)

haze [heɪz] *n (mist)* neblina *f*; *Fig (blur)* confusión *f*

hazelnut ['heɪzəlnʌt] *n* avellana *f*

hazy ['heɪzɪ] *adj* (**hazier, haziest**) nebuloso(a)

he [hiː] *pers pron* él *(usually omitted in Spanish, except for contrast)*; HE **did it** ha sido él; **he who** el que

head [hed] **1** *n* (**a**) cabeza *f*; *(mind)* mente *f*; **£3 a h.** *(each)* 3 libras por cabeza; *Fig* **to lose one's h.** perder la cabeza; **success went to his h.** se le subió el éxito a la cabeza (**b**) *(of nail)* cabeza *f*; *(of beer)* espuma *f* (**c**) *(boss)* cabeza *m*; *(of company)* director(a) *m,f*; *Br* **h. (teacher)** director(a) *m,f* (**d**) *(of coin)* cara *f*; **heads or tails** cara o cruz **2** *adj* principal; **h. office** oficina *f* central **3** *vt* (**a**) *(list etc)* encabezar (**b**) *Ftb* cabecear

▸**head for** *vt insep* dirigirse hacia

▸**head off 1** *vi* irse **2** *vt sep (avert)* evitar

headache ['hedeɪk] *n* dolor *m* de cabeza; *Fig* quebradero *m* de cabeza

headband ['hedbænd] *n* cinta *f* para la cabeza

header ['hedə(r)] *n Ftb* cabezazo *m*

heading ['hedɪŋ] *n* título *m*; *(of letter)* membrete *m*

headlamp ['hedlæmp] *n* faro *m*

headlight ['hedlaɪt] *n* faro *m*

headline ['hedlaɪn] *n* titular *m*; **the headlines** *(on radio, TV)* los titulares

headlong ['hedlɒŋ] *adj & adv* de cabeza; **to rush h. into sth** lanzarse a hacer algo sin pensar

headmaster [hed'mɑːstə(r)] *n* director *m*

headmistress [hed'mɪstrɪs] *n* directora *f*

headphones ['hedfəʊnz] *npl* auriculares *mpl*

headquarters ['hedkwɔːtəz] *npl* (**a**) oficina *f* central, sede *f* (**b**) *Mil* cuartel *m* general

headstrong ['hedstrɒŋ] *adj* testarudo(a)

heady ['hedɪ] *adj* (**headier, headiest**) embriagador(a)

heal [hiːl] **1** *vi* cicatrizar **2** *vt (wound)* curar

health [helθ] *n* salud *f*; *Fig* prosperidad *f*; **to be in good/bad h.** estar bien/mal de salud; **your good h.!** ¡salud!; **h. foods** alimentos *mpl* naturales; **h. food shop** tienda *f* de alimentos naturales; *Br* **the H. Service** el sistema de sanidad pública británico

healthy ['helθɪ] *adj* (**healthier, healthiest**) sano(a); *(good for health)* saludable; *(thriving)* próspero(a)

heap [hiːp] **1** *n* montón *m* **2** *vt* amontonar; *Fig* **to h. praise on sb** colmar a algn de alabanzas; **a heaped spoonful** una cucharada colmada

hear [hɪə(r)] *(pt & pp* **heard** [hɜːd]) **1** *vt* (**a**) oír (**b**) *(listen to)* escuchar (**c**) *(find out)* enterarse (**d**) *Jur* ver; *(evidence)* oír **2** *vi* **to h. from sb** tener noticias de algn

hearing ['hɪərɪŋ] *n* (**a**) oído *m*; **h. aid** audífono *m* (**b**) *Jur* audiencia *f*

hearse [hɜːs] *n* coche *m* fúnebre

heart [hɑːt] *n* (**a**) corazón *m*; **h. attack** infarto *m* de miocardio; *Med* **h. failure** paro *m* cardíaco; **a broken h.** un corazón roto; **at h.** en el fondo; **to take sth to h.** tomarse algo a pecho; **to have a good h.** *(be kind)* tener buen corazón (**b**) *(courage)* valor *m*; **to**

lose h. desanimarse (**c**) *(core)* meollo *m*; *(of lettuce)* cogollo *m*

heartache ['hɑːteɪk] *n* dolor *m*, tristeza *f*

heartbeat ['hɑːtbiːt] *n* latido *m* del corazón

heart-breaking ['hɑːtbreɪkɪŋ] *adj* desgarrador(a)

heart-broken ['hɑːtbrəʊkən] *adj* hundido(a); **he's h.** tiene el corazón destrozado

heartening ['hɑːtənɪŋ] *adj* alentador(a)

hearth [hɑːθ] *n* (**a**) *(fireplace)* chimenea *f* (**b**) *Fml (home)* hogar *m*

hearty ['hɑːtɪ] *adj* (**heartier, heartiest**) *(person)* francote; *(meal)* abundante; *(welcome)* cordial; **to have a h. appetite** ser de buen comer

heat [hiːt] **1** *n* (**a**) calor *m* (**b**) *Sport* eliminatoria *f* (**c**) *Zool* **on h.** en celo **2** *vt* calentar

▸ **heat up** *vi* (**a**) *(warm up)* calentarse (**b**) *(increase excitement)* acalorarse

heated ['hiːtɪd] *adj Fig (argument)* acalorado(a)

heater ['hiːtə(r)] *n* calentador *m*

heath [hiːθ] *n (land)* brezal *m*

heather ['heðə(r)] *n* brezo *m*

heating ['hiːtɪŋ] *n* calefacción *f*

heave [hiːv] **1** *n (pull)* tirón *m*; *(push)* empujón *m*
2 *vt* (**a**) *(lift)* levantar; *(haul)* tirar; *(push)* empujar (**b**) *(throw)* arrojar
3 *vi* subir y bajar

heaven ['hevən] **1** *n* (**a**) cielo *m*; **for h.'s sake!** ¡por Dios!; **h. on earth** un paraíso en la tierra (**b**) **heavens** cielo *m* **2** *interj* **good heavens!** ¡por Dios!

heavily ['hevɪlɪ] *adv* **it rained h.** llovió mucho; **to sleep h.** dormir profundamente

heavy ['hevɪ] **1** *adj* (**heavier, heaviest**) pesado(a); *(rain, meal)* fuerte; *(traffic)* denso(a); *(loss)* grande; **h. going** duro(a); **is it h.?** ¿pesa mucho?; **a h. drinker/smoker** un(a) bebedor(a)/fumador(a) empedernido(a); *Mus* **h. metal** heavy metal *m*
2 *n Fam* gorila *m*

heavyweight ['hevɪweɪt] *n* peso pesado

Hebrew ['hiːbruː] **1** *adj* hebreo(a) **2** *n (language)* hebreo *m*

heckle ['hekəl] *vt* interrumpir

hectic ['hektɪk] *adj* agitado(a)

hedge [hedʒ] **1** *n* seto *m* **2** *vt* cercar con un seto; *Fig* **to h. one's bets** cubrirse

hedgehog ['hedʒhɒg] *n* erizo *m*

hedgerow ['hedʒrəʊ] *n* seto vivo

heed [hiːd] *n* **to take h. of** hacer caso de

heel [hiːl] *n (of foot)* talón *m*; *(of shoe)* tacón *m*; *(of palm)* pulpejo *m*; *Fig* **to be on sb's heels** pisarle los talones a algn; **high heels** zapatos *mpl* de tacón alto

hefty ['heftɪ] *adj* (**heftier, heftiest**) (**a**) *(person)* fornido(a); *(package)* pesado(a) (**b**) *(large)* grande

height [haɪt] *n* (**a**) altura *f*; *(of person)* estatura *f*; *Av* **to gain/lose h.** subir/bajar; **what h. are you?** ¿cuánto mides?; *Fig* **the h. of ignorance** el colmo de la ignorancia (**b**) *Geog* cumbre *f*

heighten ['haɪtən] *vt (intensify)* realzar; *(increase)* aumentar

heir [eə(r)] *n* heredero *m*

heiress ['eərɪs] *n* heredera *f*

heirloom ['eəluːm] *n* reliquia *f* de familia

held [held] *pt & pp of* **hold**

helicopter ['helɪkɒptə(r)] *n* helicóptero *m*

hell [hel] *n* infierno *m*; *Fam* **what the h. are you doing?** ¿qué diablos estás haciendo?; *Fam Pej* **go to h.!** ¡vete a hacer puñetas!; *Fam* **a h. of a party** una fiesta estupenda; *Fam* **she's had a h. of a day** ha tenido un día fatal

hello [hə'ləʊ, he'ləʊ] *interj* ¡hola!; *(when answering phone)* ¿sí?, ¿diga?, *Am* ¿aló?, *Méx* ¿bueno?; *(showing surprise)* ¡hala!

helm [helm] *n* timón *m*; **to be at the h.** llevar el timón

helmet ['helmɪt] *n* casco *m*

help [help] **1** n (**a**) ayuda f; **h.!** ¡socorro! (**b**) (**daily**) **h.** asistenta f **2** vt (**a**) ayudar; **can I h. you?** (in shop) ¿qué desea? (**b**) (alleviate) aliviar (**c**) **h. yourself!** (to food etc) ¡sírvete! (**d**) (avoid) evitar; **I can't h. it** no lo puedo remediar

▸ **help out** vt sep **to h. sb out** echarle una mano a algn

helper ['helpǝ(r)] n ayudante(a) m,f

helpful ['helpful] adj (person) amable; (thing) útil

helping ['helpɪŋ] n ración f; **who wants a second h.?** ¿quién quiere repetir?

helpless ['helplɪs] adj (defenceless) desamparado(a); (powerless) incapaz

helpline ['helplaɪn] n teléfono m de asistencia or ayuda

hem [hem] Sewing **1** n dobladillo m **2** vt hacer un dobladillo a

▸ **hem in** vt sep cercar, rodear

hemisphere ['hemɪsfɪǝ(r)] n hemisferio m

hemorrhage ['hemǝrɪdʒ] n US = haemorrhage

hemorrhoids ['hemǝrɔɪdz] nmpl US = haemorrhoids

hen [hen] n gallina f; Fam **h. party** reunión f de mujeres

hence [hens] adv Fml (**a**) **six months h.** (from now) de aquí a seis meses (**b**) (consequently) por lo tanto

her [hɜː(r), unstressed hǝ(r)] **1** pos adj (one thing) su; (more than one) sus; (to distinguish) de ella; **are they h. books or his?** ¿los libros son de ella o de él?; **she has cut h. finger** se ha cortado el dedo **2** pers pron (**a**) (direct object) la; **I saw h. recently** la vi hace poco (**b**) (indirect object) le; (with other third person pronouns) se; **he gave h. money** le dio dinero; **they handed it to h.** se lo entregaron (**c**) (after prep) ella; **for h.** para ella (**d**) (as subject) Fam ella; **look, it's h.!** ¡mira, es ella!

herb [hɜːb, US ɜːrb] n hierba f; **h. tea** infusión f

herbal ['hɜːbǝl] adj herbario(a); **h.**

remedies curas fpl de hierbas

herd [hɜːd] n (of cattle) manada f; (of goats) rebaño m; Fig (large group) multitud f

here [hɪǝ(r)] **1** adv aquí; **come h.** ven aquí; **h.!** ¡presente!; **h. goes!** ¡vamos a ver!; **here's to success!** ¡brindemos por el éxito!; **h. you are!** ¡toma! **2** interj **look h., you can't do that!** ¡oiga, que no se permite hacer eso!

hereafter [hɪǝr'ɑːftǝ(r)] Fml **1** adv de ahora en adelante **2** n **the h.** la otra vida, el más allá

hereditary [hɪ'redɪtǝrɪ] adj hereditario(a)

heritage ['herɪtɪdʒ] n patrimonio m; Jur herencia f

hero ['hɪǝrǝʊ] n (pl heroes) héroe m; (in novel) protagonista m; **h. worship** idolatría f

heroic [hɪ'rǝʊɪk] adj heroico(a)

heroin ['herǝʊɪn] n heroína f

heroine ['herǝʊɪn] n heroína f; (in novel) protagonista f

herring ['herɪŋ] n arenque m

hers [hɜːz] pos pron (**a**) (attribute) (one thing) suyo(a); (more than one) suyos(as); (to distinguish) de ella; **they are h., not his** son de ella, no de él (**b**) (noun reference) (one thing) el suyo/la suya; (more than one) los suyos/las suyas; **my car is blue and h. is red** mi coche es azul y el suyo es rojo

herself [hɜː'self] pers pron (**a**) (reflexive) se; **she dressed h.** se vistió (**b**) (alone) ella sola; **she was by h.** estaba sola (**c**) (emphatic) ella misma

hesitant ['hezɪtǝnt] adj vacilante

hesitate ['hezɪteɪt] vi vacilar

hesitation [hezɪ'teɪʃǝn] n indecisión f

heterosexual [hetǝrǝʊ'seksjʊǝl] adj & n heterosexual (mf)

hexagon ['heksǝgǝn] n hexágono m

hey [heɪ] interj ¡oye!, ¡oiga!

hi [haɪ] interj Fam ¡hola!

hibernate ['haɪbǝneɪt] vi hibernar

hiccup, hiccough ['hɪkʌp] n hipo m; Fam (minor problem) problemilla m; **to have hiccups** tener hipo

hide¹ [haɪd] (*pt* **hid** [hɪd]; *pp* **hidden** ['hɪdən]) **1** *vt* *(conceal)* esconder; *(obscure)* ocultar
2 *vi* esconderse, ocultarse
3 *n* puesto *m*

hide² [haɪd] *n* *(of animal)* piel *f*

hide-and-seek [haɪdən'siːk] *n* escondite *m*

hideous ['hɪdɪəs] *adj* *(horrific)* horroroso(a); *(extremely ugly)* espantoso(a)

hide-out ['haɪdaʊt] *n* escondrijo *m*, guarida *f*

hiding¹ ['haɪdɪŋ] *n* **to go into h.** esconderse

hiding² ['haɪdɪŋ] *n Fam* paliza *f*

hierarchy ['haɪərɑːkɪ] *n* jerarquía *f*

hi-fi ['haɪfaɪ] *n* hifi *m*; **h. equipment** equipo *m* de alta fidelidad

high [haɪ] **1** *adj* **(a)** alto(a); **how h. is that wall?** ¿qué altura tiene esa pared?; **it's 3 feet h.** tiene 3 pies de alto; **h. chair** trona *f*; **h. jump** salto *m* de altura; **h. wind** viento *m* fuerte;
(b) *(elevated)* elevado(a); **h. prices** precios elevados
(c) *(important)* importante; **to have a h. opinion of sb** tener muy buena opinión de algn; **h. school** instituto *m* de enseñanza media; *Br* **the H. Street** la Calle Mayor
(d) *Fam (drugged)* colocado(a)
2 *adv* alto; **to fly h.** volar a gran altura
3 *n* *(high point)* punto máximo

highbrow ['haɪbraʊ] *adj* & *n* intelectual *(mf)*

high-class ['haɪklɑːs] *adj* de alta categoría

higher ['haɪə(r)] *adj* superior; **h. education** enseñanza *f* superior

highlands ['haɪləndz] *npl* tierras altas

highlight ['haɪlaɪt] **1** *n* **(a)** *(in hair)* reflejo *m* **(b)** *(of event)* atracción *f* principal **2** *vt* **(a)** hacer resaltar **(b)** *(text)* marcar con un rotulador fosforescente

highly ['haɪlɪ] *adv* *(very)* sumamente; **to speak h. of sb** hablar muy bien de algn

Highness ['haɪnɪs] *n* alteza *mf*; **Your H.** Su Alteza

high-powered ['haɪpaʊəd] *adj* *(person)* dinámico(a)

high-rise ['haɪraɪz] *adj* **h. building** rascacielos *m inv*

high-speed ['haɪspiːd] *adj* **h. lens** objetivo ultrarrápido; **h. train** tren *m* de alta velocidad

high-tech ['haɪtek] *adj* de alta tecnología

highway ['haɪweɪ] *n US* carretera *f*, autopista *f*; *Br* **H. Code** código *m* de la circulación

hijack ['haɪdʒæk] **1** *vt* secuestrar **2** *n* secuestro *m*

hijacker ['haɪdʒækə(r)] *n* secuestrador(a) *m,f*; *(of planes)* pirata *mf* del aire

hike [haɪk] **1** *n* **(a)** *(walk)* excursión *f* **(b)** **price h.** aumento *m* de precio **2** *vi* ir de excursión

hiker ['haɪkə(r)] *n* excursionista *mf*

hilarious [hɪ'leərɪəs] *adj* graciosísimo(a)

hill [hɪl] *n* colina *f*; *(slope)* cuesta *f*

hillside ['hɪlsaɪd] *n* ladera *f*

hilly ['hɪlɪ] *adj* **(hillier, hilliest)** accidentado(a)

him [hɪm] *pers pron* **(a)** *(direct object)* lo, le; **hit h.!** ¡pégale!; **she loves h.** lo quiere **(b)** *(indirect object)* le; *(with other third person pronouns)* se; **give h. the money** dale el dinero; **give it to h.** dáselo **(c)** *(after prep)* él; **it's not like h. to say that** no es propio de él decir eso **(d)** *Fam (as subject)* él; **it's h.** es él

himself [hɪm'self] *pers pron* **(a)** *(reflexive)* se; **he hurt h.** se hizo daño **(b)** *(alone)* él solo; **by h.** solo **(c)** *(emphatic)* él mismo

hind¹ [haɪnd] *adj* trasero(a); **h. legs** patas traseras

hind² [haɪnd] *n Zool* cierva *f*

hinder ['hɪndə(r)] *vt* dificultar, estorbar; **to h. sb from doing sth** impedir a algn hacer algo

hindrance ['hɪndrəns] *n* estorbo *m*

hindsight ['haɪndsaɪt] *n* **with h.** en retrospectiva

Hindu [hɪn'duː, 'hɪnduː] *adj & n* hindú *(mf)*

hinge [hɪndʒ] **1** *n* bisagra *f*; *Fig* eje *m* **2** *vt* engoznar

▶ **hinge on** *vt insep* depender de

hint [hɪnt] **1** *n* (**a**) indirecta *f*; **to take the h.** coger la indirecta (**b**) *(clue)* pista *f* (**c**) *(trace)* pizca *f* (**d**) *(advice)* consejo *m* **2** *vi* (**a**) lanzar indirectas (**b**) *(imply)* insinuar algo

hip¹ [hɪp] *n* cadera *f*; **h. flask** petaca *f*

hip² [hɪp] *adj Fam* en la onda

hippie ['hɪpɪ] *adj & n Fam* hippy *(mf)*

hippopotamus [hɪpə'pɒtəməs] *n* hipopótamo *m*

hire ['haɪə(r)] **1** *n Br* alquiler *m*; **bicycles for h.** se alquilan bicicletas; **taxi for h.** taxi *m* libre; **h. purchase** compra *f* a plazos **2** *vt* (**a**) *Br (rent)* alquilar, *Méx* rentar (**b**) *(employ)* contratar

▶ **hire out** *vt sep (car)* alquilar, *Méx* rentar; *(people)* contratar

his [hɪz] **1** *pos adj (one thing)* su; *(more than one)* sus; *(to distinguish)* de él; **he washed h. face** se lavó la cara; **is it h. dog or hers?** ¿el perro es de él o de ella?

2 *pos pron* (**a**) *(attribute) (one thing)* suyo(a); *(more than one)* suyos(as); *(to distinguish)* de él; **they are h., not hers** son de él, no de ella (**b**) *(noun reference) (one thing)* el suyo/la suya; *(more than one)* los suyos/las suyas; **my car is blue and h. is red** mi coche es azul y el suyo es rojo

Hispanic [hɪ'spænɪk] **1** *adj* hispánico(a) **2** *n US* hispano(a) *m,f*, latino(a) *m,f*

hiss [hɪs] **1** *n* siseo *m*; *Th* silbido *m* **2** *vt & vi* silbar

historian [hɪ'stɔːrɪən] *n* historiador(a) *m,f*

historic [hɪ'stɒrɪk] *adj* histórico(a)

historical [hɪ'stɒrɪkəl] *adj* histórico(a); **h. novel** novela histórica

history ['hɪstərɪ] *n* historia *f*

hit [hɪt] **1** *n* (**a**) *(blow)* golpe *m*; **direct**

h. impacto directo; *Fam* **h. list** lista negra; *Fam* **h. man** asesino *m* a sueldo (**b**) *(success)* éxito *m*; **h. parade** lista *f* de éxitos (**c**) *Comput (visit to web site)* acceso *m*, visita *f*

2 *vt (pt & pp hit)* (**a**) *(strike)* golpear, pegar; **he was h. in the leg** le dieron en la pierna; **the car h. the kerb** el coche chocó contra el bordillo (**b**) *(affect)* afectar (**c**) **to h. the headlines** ser noticia

▶ **hit back** *vi (reply to criticism)* replicar

▶ **hit on** *vt insep* dar con; **we h. on the idea of …** se nos ocurrió la idea de …

▶ **hit out** *vi* **to h. out at sb** atacar a algn

▶ **hit upon** *vt insep* = **hit on**

hitch [hɪtʃ] **1** *n* dificultad *f* **2** *vt (fasten)* atar **3** *vi Fam (hitch-hike)* hacer autostop

▶ **hitch up** *vt sep* remangarse

hitch-hike ['hɪtʃhaɪk] *vi* hacer autostop *or* dedo

hitch-hiker ['hɪtʃhaɪkə(r)] *n* autostopista *mf*

HIV [eɪtʃaɪ'viː] *n (abbr human immunodeficiency virus)* VIH *m*; **HIV positive/negative** seropositivo(a)/seronegativo(a)

hive [haɪv] *n* colmena *f*; *Fig* lugar muy activo

hoard [hɔːd] **1** *n (provisions)* reservas *fpl*; *(money etc)* tesoro *m* **2** *vt (objects)* acumular; *(money)* atesorar

hoarding ['hɔːdɪŋ] *n (temporary fence)* valla *f*; *Br (billboard)* valla publicitaria

hoarse [hɔːs] *adj* ronco(a); **to be h.** tener la voz ronca

hoax [həʊks] *n (joke)* broma pesada; *(trick)* engaño *m*

hobby ['hɒbɪ] *n* pasatiempo *m*, afición *f*

hockey ['hɒkɪ] *n Br (on grass)* hockey *m* (sobre hierba *or Am* césped); *US (on ice)* hockey (sobre hielo)

hog [hɒg] **1** *n* cerdo *m*, puerco *m*; *Fam* **to go the whole h.** liarse la manta a la cabeza **2** *vt Fam* acaparar

hoist [hɔɪst] **1** *n (crane)* grúa *f; (lift)* montacargas *m inv* **2** *vt* levantar, subir

hold [həʊld] (*pt & pp* **held**) **1** *vt* (**a**) *(keep in hand)* aguantar, tener (en la mano); *(grip)* agarrar; *(support) (weight)* soportar; *(opinion)* sostener; **to h. sb** abrazar a algn; **to h. sb's hand** cogerle la mano a algn
(**b**) *(contain)* dar cabida a; **the jug holds a litre** en la jarra cabe un litro
(**c**) *(meeting)* celebrar; *(conversation)* mantener
(**d**) **to h. office** ocupar un puesto
(**e**) **he was held for two hours at the police station** estuvo detenido durante dos horas en la comisaría; **to h. one's breath** contener la respiración; **to h. sb hostage** retener a algn como rehén
(**f**) *Tel* **to h. the line** no colgar
2 *vi (rope)* aguantar
3 *n* (**a**) **to get h. of** *(grip)* coger, agarrar; *Fig* localizar (**b**) *Naut* bodega *f* (**c**) *(in wrestling)* llave *f*

► **hold back 1** *vt sep (crowd)* contener; *(feelings)* reprimir; *(truth)* ocultar; **I don't want to h. you back** *(delay)* no quiero entretenerte **2** *vi (hesitate)* vacilar

► **hold down** *vt sep* (**a**) *(control)* dominar (**b**) *Fam (job)* desempeñar

► **hold off** *vt sep* mantener a distancia

► **hold on** *vi* (**a**) *(keep a firm grasp)* agarrarse bien (**b**) *(wait)* esperar; *Tel* **h. on!** ¡no cuelgue!

► **hold out 1** *vt sep (hand)* tender **2** *vi (last) (things)* durar; *(person)* resistir

► **hold up** *vt sep* (**a**) *(rob) (train)* asaltar; *(bank)* atracar (**b**) *(delay)* retrasar (**c**) *(raise)* levantar (**d**) *(support)* apuntalar

holdall ['həʊldɔ:l] *n esp Br* bolsa *f (de viaje o de deporte)*

holder ['həʊldə(r)] *n* (**a**) *(receptacle)* recipiente *m* (**b**) *(owner)* poseedor(a) *m,f; (of passport)* titular *mf;* **record h.** plusmarquista *mf*

hold-up ['həʊldʌp] *n* (**a**) *(robbery)* atraco *m* (**b**) *(delay)* retraso *m; (in traffic)* atasco *m*

hole [həʊl] *n* (**a**) agujero *m; (large)* hoyo *m; (in the road)* bache *m* (**b**) *(in golf)* hoyo *m* (**c**) *Fam (of place)* antro *m*

holiday ['hɒlɪdeɪ] **1** *n (one day) Esp* (día *m* de) fiesta, *Am* feriado *m; Br (several days)* vacaciones *fpl;* **to be/ go on h.** estar/irse de vacaciones; **h. resort** lugar turístico **2** *vi Br* pasar las vacaciones; *(in summer)* veranear

holidaymaker ['hɒlɪdeɪmeɪkə(r)] *n esp Br* turista *mf; (in summer)* veraneante *mf*

Holland ['hɒlənd] *n* Holanda

hollow ['hɒləʊ] **1** *adj* (**a**) hueco(a) (**b**) *(cheeks, eyes)* hundido(a) (**c**) *Fig (insincere)* falso(a); *(empty)* vacío(a)
2 *n* hueco *m; Geog* hondonada *f*
3 *vt* **to h. (out)** hacer un hueco en

holly ['hɒlɪ] *n* acebo *m*

holy ['həʊlɪ] *adj* sagrado(a), santo(a); *(blessed)* bendito(a); **H. Ghost** Espíritu Santo; **H. Land** Tierra Santa; **H. See** Santa Sede

homage ['hɒmɪdʒ] *n* homenaje *m;* **to pay h. to sb** rendir homenaje a algn

home [həʊm] **1** *n* (**a**) casa *f,* hogar *m;* **at h.** en casa; *Fig* **make yourself at h.!** ¡estás en tu casa!; *Fig* **to feel at h.** estar a gusto; **h. banking** telebanco *m; Comput* **h. page** *(initial page)* portada *f,* página *f* inicial *or* de inicio; *(personal page)* página personal; **h. shopping** telecompra *f*
(**b**) *(institution)* residencia *f;* **old people's h.** residencia de ancianos
(**c**) *Sport* **to play at h.** jugar en casa
2 *adj* (**a**) *(domestic)* del hogar; *Br* **h. help** asistenta *f* (**b**) *Pol* interior; *Br* **H. Office** Ministerio *m* del Interior; *Br* **H. Secretary** Ministro(a) *m,f* del Interior (**c**) *(native)* natal
3 *adv* en casa; **to go h.** irse a casa; **to leave h.** irse de casa

homeland ['həʊmlænd] *n* patria *f; (birthplace)* tierra *f* natal

homeless ['həʊmlɪs] **1** *adj* sin techo **2** *npl* **the h.** los sin techo

homely ['həʊmlɪ] *adj* (**homelier, homeliest**) (**a**) *Br (person)* casero(a);

(atmosphere) familiar (**b**) *US (ugly)* feúcho(a)

home-made ['həʊmmeɪd] *adj* casero(a)

homesick ['həʊmsɪk] *adj* **to be h.** tener morriña

homeward(s) ['həʊmwəd(z)] *adv* hacia casa

homework ['həʊmwɜːk] *n* deberes *mpl*

homicide ['hɒmɪsaɪd] *n* homicidio *m*

homosexual [həʊməʊ'seksjʊəl] *adj & n* homosexual *(mf)*

honest ['ɒnɪst] *adj* honrado(a); *(sincere)* sincero(a), franco(a); *(fair)* justo(a); **the h. truth** la pura verdad

honestly ['ɒnɪstlɪ] *adv* honradamente; *(question)* ¿de verdad?; *(exclamation)* ¡hay que ver!; **h., it doesn't matter** de verdad, no tiene importancia

honesty ['ɒnɪstɪ] *n* honradez *f*

honey ['hʌnɪ] *n* miel *f*; *esp US Fam (endearment)* cariño *m*

honeymoon ['hʌnɪmuːn] *n* luna *f* de miel

honk [hɒŋk] *vi Aut* tocar la bocina

honor ['ɒnə(r)] *n US* = **honour**

honorable ['ɒnərəbəl] *adj US* = **honourable**

honorary ['ɒnərərɪ] *adj (member)* honorario(a); *(duties)* honorífico(a)

honour ['ɒnə(r)] **1** *n* (**a**) honor *m* (**b**) *US Jur* **Her H./His H./Your H.** Su Señoría *f* (**c**) *Mil* **honours** honores *mpl* (**d**) **Honours degree** licenciatura *f* superior **2** *vt* (**a**) *(respect)* honrar (**b**) *(obligation)* cumplir con

honourable ['ɒnərəbəl] *adj (person)* honrado(a); *(action)* honroso(a)

hood [hʊd] *n* (**a**) *(of garment)* capucha *f* (**b**) *Br (of car, pram)* capota *f*; *US (car bonnet)* capó *m* (**c**) *US Fam (gangster)* matón(ona) *m,f*

hoof [huːf] *n* (*pl* **hoofs** *or* **hooves**) *(of horse)* casco *m*; *(of cow, sheep)* pezuña *f*

hook [hʊk] **1** *n* (**a**) gancho *m*; *(in fishing)* anzuelo *m*; *Sewing* **hooks and eyes** corchetes *mpl*; **to take the**

phone off the h. descolgar el teléfono (**b**) *(in boxing)* gancho *m* **2** *vt* enganchar

▶ **hook up** *vt sep & vi Rad, TV, Comput* conectar (**with** con)

hooked [hʊkt] *adj* (**a**) *(nose)* aguileño(a) (**b**) *Fam (addicted)* enganchado(a) (**on** a); **to get h.** engancharse

hooligan ['huːlɪɡən] *n Fam* gamberro(a) *m,f*

hoot [huːt] **1** *n* (**a**) ululato *m*; *Fam* **hoots of laughter** carcajadas *fpl*; *Fam* **I don't care a h.** me importa un pepino (**b**) *(of car horn)* bocinazo *m* **2** *vi* (**a**) *(owl)* ulular (**b**) *(car)* dar un bocinazo; *(train)* silbar; *(siren)* pitar

hooter ['huːtə(r)] *n Br (of car)* bocina *f*; *(of ship, factory)* sirena *f*

Hoover® ['huːvə(r)] *Br* **1** *n* aspiradora *f* **2** *vt* **to h.** pasar la aspiradora por

hooves [huːvz] *pl of* **hoof**

hop[1] [hɒp] **1** *vi* saltar; **to h. on one leg** andar a la pata coja **2** *n (small jump)* brinco *m*

hop[2] [hɒp] *n Bot* lúpulo *m*

hope [həʊp] **1** *n* esperanza *f*; *(false)* ilusión *f*; **to have little h. of doing sth** tener pocas posibilidades de hacer algo **2** *vt & vi* esperar; **I h. so/not** espero que sí/no; **we h. you're well** esperamos que estés bien

hopeful ['həʊpfʊl] *adj (confident)* optimista; *(promising)* prometedor(a)

hopefully ['həʊpfʊlɪ] *adv* (**a**) *(confidently)* con optimismo (**b**) **h. the weather will be fine** *(it is hoped)* esperemos que haga buen tiempo

hopeless ['həʊplɪs] *adj* desesperado(a); *Fam* **to be h. at sports** ser negado(a) para los deportes

horde [hɔːd] *n* multitud *f*

horizon [hə'raɪzən] *n* horizonte *m*

horizontal [hɒrɪ'zɒntəl] *adj* horizontal

hormone ['hɔːməʊn] *n* hormona *f*

horn [hɔːn] *n* (**a**) cuerno *m* (**b**) *Fam Mus* trompeta *f*; **French h.** trompa *f*; **hunting h.** cuerno *m* de caza (**c**) *Aut* bocina *f*

horoscope ['hɒrəskəʊp] *n* horóscopo *m*

horrendous [hɒ'rendəs] *adj* horrendo(a)

horrible ['hɒrəbəl] *adj* horrible

horrid ['hɒrɪd] *adj* horrible

horrific [hə'rɪfɪk] *adj* horrendo(a)

horrify ['hɒrɪfaɪ] *vt* horrorizar

horror ['hɒrə(r)] *n* horror *m*; *Fam* **a little h.** un diablillo; **h. film** película *f* de miedo *or* de terror

horse [hɔːs] *n* (**a**) caballo *m*; **h. race** carrera *f* de caballos (**b**) **h. chestnut** *(tree)* castaño *m* de Indias

horseback ['hɔːsbæk] *n* **on h.** a caballo; *US* **h. riding** equitación *f*

horsepower ['hɔːspaʊə(r)] *n* caballo *m* (de vapor)

horticulture ['hɔːtɪkʌltʃə(r)] *n* horticultura *f*

hose [həʊz] *n* *(pipe)* manguera *f*

hosepipe ['həʊzpaɪp] *n* manguera *f*

hospitable ['hɒspɪtəbəl, hɒ'spɪtəbəl] *adj* hospitalario(a); **h. atmosphere** ambiente acogedor

hospital ['hɒspɪtəl] *n* hospital *m*

hospitality [hɒspɪ'tælɪtɪ] *n* hospitalidad *f*

host¹ [həʊst] **1** *n* (**a**) *(at home)* anfitrión *m* (**b**) *Th, TV* presentador *m* (**c**) *Biol* huésped *m* **2** *vt* *Th, TV* presentar

host² [həʊst] *n* *(large number)* montón *m*

hostage ['hɒstɪdʒ] *n* rehén *m*

hostel ['hɒstəl] *n* hostal *m*

hostess ['həʊstɪs] *n* (**a**) *(at home etc)* anfitriona *f* (**b**) *Th, TV* presentadora *f* (**c**) *(air)* **h.** azafata *f*

hostile ['hɒstaɪl, *US* 'hɒstəl] *adj* hostil

hostility [hɒ'stɪlɪtɪ] *n* hostilidad *f*

hot [hɒt] *adj* (**hotter, hottest**) (**a**) caliente; *Fig* **h. line** teléfono rojo (**b**) *(weather)* caluroso(a); **it's very h.** hace mucho calor; **to feel h.** tener calor (**c**) *(spicy)* picante; **h. dog** perrito *m* caliente, *Col, Méx* perro *m* caliente, *RP* pancho *m* (**d**) *(temper)* fuerte (**e**) *Fam (good)* bueno(a); **it's**

not so h. no es nada del otro mundo (**f**) *(popular)* popular

▸ **hot up** *vi* *Fam (situation, contest) Esp* calentarse, *Am* ponerse bravo(a)

hotcake ['hɒtkeɪk] *n* *US* crepe *f*, panqueque *m*, *Esp* tortita *f*

hotel [həʊ'tel] *n* hotel *m*

hot-headed [hɒt'hedɪd] *adj* impetuoso(a)

hotplate ['hɒtpleɪt] *n* *(cooker)* placa *f* de cocina; *(to keep food warm)* calientaplatos *m inv*

hound [haʊnd] **1** *n* perro *m* de caza **2** *vt* acosar

hour ['aʊə(r)] *n* hora *f*; **60 miles an h.** 60 millas por hora; **by the h.** por horas; **h. hand** manecilla *f*

hourly ['aʊəlɪ] **1** *adj* cada hora **2** *adv* por horas

house 1 *n* [haʊs] (**a**) casa *f*; **at my h.** en mi casa; *Fig* **on the h.** cortesía de la casa; **h. plant** planta *f* de interior (**b**) *Pol* **H. of Commons** Cámara *f* de los Comunes; **H. of Lords** Cámara de los Lores; *US* **H. of Representatives** Cámara de Representantes; **Houses of Parliament** Parlamento *m* (**c**) *(company)* empresa *f*; **publishing h.** editorial *f* (**d**) *Th* sala *f* **2** *vt* [haʊz] alojar; *(store)* guardar

housebound ['haʊsbaʊnd] *adj* **to be h.** estar confinado(a) en casa

household ['haʊshəʊld] *n* hogar *m*; **h. products** productos domésticos

housekeeper ['haʊskiːpə(r)] *n* ama *f* de llaves

housekeeping ['haʊskiːpɪŋ] *n* administración doméstica; **h. money** dinero *m* para los gastos domésticos

house-train ['haʊstreɪn] *vt* *(pet)* educar

house-warming ['haʊswɔːmɪŋ] *n* **h. (party)** fiesta *f* de inauguración

housewife ['haʊswaɪf] *n* ama *f* de casa

housework ['haʊswɜːk] *n* trabajo doméstico

housing ['haʊzɪŋ] *n* vivienda *f*; *Br* **h. estate** *(public housing)* ≃ viviendas *fpl* de protección oficial; *(private* *housing)* urbanización *f*, *Am* condominio *m*

hovel ['hʌvəl, 'hɒvəl] *n* casucha *f*

hover ['hɒvə(r)] *vi (bird)* cernerse; *(aircraft)* permanecer inmóvil (en el aire)

hovercraft ['hɒvəkrɑːft] *n* aerodeslizador *m*

how [haʊ] *adv* (a) *(direct question)* ¿cómo?; **h. are you?** ¿cómo estás?; *Fam* **h. come?** ¿por qué?
(b) *(indirect question)* cómo
(c) *(very)* qué; **h. funny!** ¡qué divertido!
(d) *(suggestion)* **h. about going to the cinema?** ¿te apetece ir al cine?
(e) *(quantity)* cuánto; **h. old is she?** ¿cuántos años tiene?; **h. tall are you?** ¿cuánto mides?
(f) **h. many?** ¿cuántos(as)?; **h. much?** ¿cuánto(a)?

however [haʊ'evə(r)] *adv* (a) *(nevertheless)* no obstante, sin embargo (b) *(with adjective)* **h. difficult it may be** por difícil que sea; **h. much** por mucho que *(+ subj)*

howl [haʊl] **1** *n* aullido *m* **2** *vi* aullar

HP, hp [eɪtʃ'piː] *n* (a) *Br (abbr* **hire purchase)** compra *f* a plazos (b) *(abbr* **horsepower)** cv *mpl*

HQ [eɪtʃ'kjuː] *n (abbr* **headquarters)** sede *f*, central *f*

hub [hʌb] *n Aut* cubo *m*; *Fig* eje *m*

hubcap ['hʌbkæp] *n Aut* tapacubos *m inv*

huddle ['hʌdəl] **1** *n* grupo *m* **2** *vi* **to h. (up** or **together)** acurrucarse

huff [hʌf] *n* **to be in a h.** estar de mala uva

hug [hʌg] **1** *vt* abrazar **2** *n* abrazo *m*

huge [hjuːdʒ] *adj* enorme

hull [hʌl] *n Naut* casco *m*

hullo [hʌ'ləʊ] *interj Br* ¡hola!

hum [hʌm] **1** *vt (tune)* tararear
2 *vi (bees, engine)* zumbar; *(sing)* tararear
3 *n (of bees)* zumbido *m*

human ['hjuːmən] **1** *adj* humano(a); **h. race** raza humana; **h. being** ser humano **2** *n* ser humano

humane [hjuː'meɪn] *adj* humano(a)

humanity [hjuː'mænɪtɪ] *n* (a) humanidad *f* (b) *Univ* **the humanities** las humanidades

humble ['hʌmbəl] **1** *adj* humilde **2** *vt* humillar

humid ['hjuːmɪd] *adj* húmedo(a)

humidity [hjuː'mɪdɪtɪ] *n* humedad *f*

humiliate [hjuː'mɪlɪeɪt] *vt* humillar

humiliation [hjuːmɪlɪ'eɪʃən] *n* humillación *f*

humility [hjuː'mɪlɪtɪ] *n* humildad *f*

humor ['hjuːmə(r)] *n US =* **humour**

humorous ['hjuːmərəs] *adj (writer)* humorístico(a); *(person, story)* gracioso(a), divertido(a)

humour ['hjuːmə(r)] **1** *n* humor *m* **2** *vt* seguir la corriente a

hump [hʌmp] **1** *n* (a) *(on back)* joroba *f* (b) *(small hill)* montículo *m* **2** *vt esp Br Fam (carry)* acarrear

hunch [hʌntʃ] *n Fam* corazonada *f*

hundred ['hʌndrəd] **1** *n* cien *m*, ciento *m*; *(rough number)* centenar *m*; **a h. and twenty-five** ciento veinticinco; **five h.** quinientos **2** *adj* cien; **a h. people** cien personas; **a h. percent** cien por cien; **two h. chairs** doscientas sillas

hundredth ['hʌndrədθ] *adj & n* centésimo(a) *(m,f)*

hundredweight ['hʌndrədweɪt] *n Br =* 50,8 kg; *US =* 45,36 kg

hung [hʌŋ] **1** *adj Fam* (a) **h. over** con resaca (b) **h. up** acomplejado(a) **2** *pt & pp of* **hang**

Hungarian [hʌŋ'geərɪən] *adj & n* húngaro(a) *(m,f)*

Hungary ['hʌŋgərɪ] *n* Hungría

hunger ['hʌŋgə(r)] **1** *n* hambre *f*; **h. strike** huelga *f* de hambre **2** *vi Fig* tener hambre **(for** de)

hungry ['hʌŋgrɪ] *adj* **(hungrier, hungriest)** hambriento(a); **to be h.** tener hambre; **to go h.** pasar hambre

hunk [hʌŋk] *n* (a) *(piece)* buen pedazo *m* (b) *Fam (man)* machote *m*

hunt [hʌnt] **1** *vt* cazar
2 *vi (for game)* cazar; *(search)* buscar

3 *n* caza *f*; *(search)* búsqueda *f*
▶ **hunt down** *vt sep* perseguir
hunter ['hʌntə(r)] *n* cazador(a) *m,f*
hunting ['hʌntɪŋ] *n* caza *f*; *(expedition)* cacería *f*
hurdle ['hɜːdəl] *n* *Sport* valla *f*; *Fig* obstáculo *m*
hurl [hɜːl] *vt* arrojar, lanzar
hurrah [hʊˈrɑː], **hurray** [hʊˈreɪ] *interj* ¡hurra!; **h. for John!** ¡viva John!
hurricane ['hʌrɪkən, *US* 'hʌrɪkeɪn] *n* huracán *m*
hurried ['hʌrɪd] *adj* apresurado(a); *(action etc)* hecho(a) de prisa
hurry ['hʌrɪ] **1** *vi* darse prisa, apresurarse, *Am* apurarse
 2 *vt* meter prisa a
 3 *n* **to be in a h.** tener prisa *or Am* apuro
hurt [hɜːt] *(pt & pp* **hurt**) **1** *vt* hacer daño a; *(wound)* herir; *(feelings)* ofender
 2 *vi* doler; **my arm hurts** me duele el brazo
 3 *adj (physically)* herido(a); *(mentally)* dolido(a)
hurtful ['hɜːtfʊl] *adj* hiriente
hurtle ['hɜːtəl] *vi* lanzarse; **to h. down** desplomarse
husband ['hʌzbənd] *n* marido *m*, esposo *m*
hush [hʌʃ] **1** *vt* callar; **to h. sth up** echar tierra a un asunto
 2 *n* silencio *m*
 3 *interj* ¡silencio!
husky¹ ['hʌskɪ] *adj* (**huskier, huskiest**) ronco(a)
husky² ['hʌskɪ] *n (dog)* perro *m* esquimal

hustle ['hʌsəl] **1** *vt* (**a**) *(jostle)* empujar (**b**) *Fam* meter prisa a **2** *n* bullicio *m*; **h. and bustle** ajetreo *m*
hut [hʌt] *n* cabaña *f*; *(shed)* cobertizo *m*; *Mil* barraca *f*
hybrid ['haɪbrɪd] *adj & n* híbrido(a) *(m,f)*
hydrogen ['haɪdrədʒən] *n* hidrógeno *m*
hygiene ['haɪdʒiːn] *n* higiene *f*
hygienic [haɪˈdʒiːnɪk] *adj* higiénico(a)
hymn [hɪm] *n* himno *m*; **h. book** cantoral *m*
hype [haɪp] *n Fam* campaña publicitaria, movida *f*
hyper- ['haɪpə(r)] *prefix* hiper-; **hyperactive** hiperactivo(a)
hypermarket ['haɪpəmɑːkɪt] *n Br* hipermercado *m*
hyphen ['haɪfən] *n* guión *m*
hypnotize ['hɪpnətaɪz] *vt* hipnotizar
hypochondriac [haɪpəˈkɒndrɪæk] *adj & n* hipocondríaco(a) *(m,f)*
hypocrisy [hɪˈpɒkrəsɪ] *n* hipocresía *f*
hypocrite ['hɪpəkrɪt] *n* hipócrita *mf*
hypocritical [hɪpəˈkrɪtɪkəl] *adj* hipócrita
hypothesis [haɪˈpɒθɪsɪs] *n (pl* **hypotheses** [haɪˈpɒθɪsiːz]) hipótesis *f*
hypothetic(al) [haɪpəˈθetɪk(əl)] *adj* hipotético(a)
hysterical [hɪˈsterɪkəl] *adj* histérico(a)
hysterics [hɪˈsterɪks] *npl* (**a**) ataque *m* de histeria (**b**) *Fam (of laughter)* ataque *m* de risa

Ii

I, i [aɪ] *n (the letter)* I, i *f*

I [aɪ] *pers pron* yo *(usually omitted in Spanish, except for contrast)*; **I know her** (yo) la conozco

ice [aɪs] **1** *n* hielo *m*; **i. axe** pico *m* (de alpinista); **i. cream** helado *m, Am* sorbete; **i. cube** cubito *m* de hielo; **i. hockey** hockey *m* sobre hielo; *Br* **i. lolly** polo *m*; **i. rink** pista *f* de patinaje; **i. skate** patín *m* de cuchilla **2** *vt (cake)* alcorzar

▸**ice over, ice up** *vi (pond etc)* helarse; *(windscreen, plane wings)* cubrirse de hielo

iceberg ['aɪsbɜːg] *n* iceberg *m*

icebox ['aɪsbɒks] *n* (**a**) *Br (compartment of fridge)* congelador *m* (**b**) *US (fridge)* nevera *f, Méx* refrigerador *m, RP* heladera *f*

Iceland ['aɪslənd] *n* Islandia

ice-skating ['aɪsskeɪtɪŋ] *n* patinaje *m* sobre hielo

icicle ['aɪsɪkəl] *n* carámbano *m*

icing ['aɪsɪŋ] *n* alcorza *f; Br* **i. sugar** azúcar *m Esp, Méx* glas *or Chile* flor *or RP* impalpable

icon ['aɪkɒn] *n* icono *m*

icy ['aɪsɪ] *adj* (**icier, iciest**) *(road etc)* helado(a); *Fig (smile)* glacial

ID [aɪ'diː] *n US* documentación *f;* **ID card** DNI *m*

I'd [aɪd] = **I would; I had**

idea [aɪ'dɪə] *n* (**a**) idea *f* (**b**) *(aim)* intención *f* (**c**) *(impression)* impresión *f*

ideal [aɪ'dɪəl] *adj & n* ideal (*m*)

idealistic [aɪdɪə'lɪstɪk] *adj* idealista

ideally [aɪ'dɪəlɪ] *adv* (**a**) *(perfectly)* perfectamente (**b**) *(in the best conditions)* de ser posible

identical [aɪ'dentɪkəl] *adj* idéntico(a)

identification [aɪdentɪfɪ'keɪʃən] *n*

(**a**) identificación *f* (**b**) *(papers)* documentación *f*

identify [aɪ'dentɪfaɪ] **1** *vt (body)* identificar; *(cause)* descubrir **2** *vi* identificarse (**with** con)

identity [aɪ'dentɪtɪ] *n* identidad *f;* **i. card** carné *m* de identidad; **proof of i.** prueba *f* de identidad

ideology [aɪdɪ'ɒlədʒɪ] *n* ideología *f*

idiom ['ɪdɪəm] *n* modismo *m; Fig (style)* lenguaje *m*

idiot ['ɪdɪət] *n* idiota *mf*, tonto(a) *m,f*

idiotic [ɪdɪ'ɒtɪk] *adj (behaviour)* idiota, tonto(a); *(joke, plan)* estúpido(a)

idle ['aɪdəl] **1** *adj* holgazán(ana); *(not working) (person)* desempleado(a); *(machinery)* parado(a); *(gossip)* frívolo(a); *(threat)* vano(a) **2** *vi (engine)* funcionar en vacío

▸**idle away** *vt sep (time)* desperdiciar

idol ['aɪdəl] *n* ídolo *m*

idolize ['aɪdəlaɪz] *vt* idolatrar

i.e. (*abbr* **id est**) i.e.

if [ɪf] **1** *conj* (**a**) si; **if not** si no; **if so** ser así; **if I were you** yo en tu lugar; **if only she were here!** ¡ojalá estuviera aquí! (**b**) *(whenever)* si; **if you need help, ask** siempre que necesites ayuda, pídela **2** *n* **ifs and buts** pegas *fpl*

ignition [ɪg'nɪʃən] *n* ignición *f; Aut* encendido *m;* **i. key** llave *f* de contacto

ignorance ['ɪgnərəns] *n* ignorancia *f*

ignorant ['ɪgnərənt] *adj* ignorante (**of** de); **to be i. of the facts** ignorar *or* desconocer los hechos

ignore [ɪg'nɔː(r)] *vt (warning, remark)* no hacer caso de; *(behaviour, fact)* pasar por alto

ill [ɪl] **1** *adj* (**a**) enfermo(a); **to feel i.** encontrarse mal (**b**) *(bad)* malo(a); **i.**

feeling resentimiento *m*; **i. will** mala voluntad
  2 *n* mal *m*
  3 *adv* difícilmente

I'll [aɪl] = **I shall; I will**

illegal [ɪ'li:gəl] *adj* ilegal

illegible [ɪ'ledʒɪbəl] *adj* ilegible

illegitimate [ɪlɪ'dʒɪtɪmɪt] *adj* ilegítimo(a)

illicit [ɪ'lɪsɪt] *adj* ilícito(a)

illiterate [ɪ'lɪtərɪt] *adj (person)* analfabeto(a); *Fam (uneducated)* inculto(a)

illness ['ɪlnɪs] *n* enfermedad *f*

illogical [ɪ'lɒdʒɪkəl] *adj* ilógico(a)

illuminate [ɪ'lu:mɪneɪt] *vt* (**a**) *(light up)* iluminar, alumbrar; *Fig (clarify)* aclarar (**b**) *(manuscript)* iluminar

illusion [i'lu:ʒən] *n* ilusión *f*; **to be under the i. that ...** engañarse pensando que ...

illustrate ['ɪləstreɪt] *vt* ilustrar

illustration [ɪlə'streɪʃən] *n* ilustración *f; (example)* ejemplo *m*

image ['ɪmɪdʒ] *n* imagen *f*

imaginary [ɪ'mædʒɪnərɪ] *adj* imaginario(a)

imagination [ɪmædʒɪ'neɪʃən] *n* imaginación *f; (inventiveness)* inventiva *f*

imaginative [ɪ'mædʒɪnətɪv] *adj* imaginativo(a)

imagine [ɪ'mædʒɪn] *vt (visualize)* imaginar; *(think)* suponer, imaginarse; **just i.!** ¡imagínate!

imitate ['ɪmɪteɪt] *vt* imitar

imitation [ɪmɪ'teɪʃən] **1** *n* imitación *f*, copia *f; Pej* remedo *m* **2** *adj* de imitación

immaculate [ɪ'mækjʊlɪt] *adj (clean)* inmaculado(a); *(tidy)* perfectamente ordenado(a); *(clothes)* impecable; *(work)* perfecto(a); **the I. Conception** la Inmaculada Concepción

immature [ɪmə'tjʊə(r)] *adj* inmaduro(a)

immediate [ɪ'mi:dɪət] *adj* (**a**) inmediato(a); *(urgent)* urgente (**b**) *(close)* cercano(a); *(danger)* inminente (**c**)

(cause) primero(a)

immediately [ɪ'mi:dɪətlɪ] **1** *adv* (**a**) inmediatamente (**b**) *(directly)* directamente **2** *conj* en cuanto

immense [ɪ'mens] *adj* inmenso(a), enorme

immensely [ɪ'menslɪ] *adv (rich)* enormemente; *(interesting, difficult)* sumamente

immerse [ɪ'mɜ:s] *vt* sumergir (**in** en); *Fig* **to be immersed in sth** estar absorto(a) en algo

immigrant ['ɪmɪgrənt] *adj & n* inmigrante *(mf)*

immigrate ['ɪmɪgreɪt] *vi* inmigrar

immigration [ɪmɪ'greɪʃən] *n* inmigración *f*

imminent ['ɪmɪnənt] *adj* inminente

immobile [ɪ'məʊbaɪl] *adj* inmóvil

immoral [ɪ'mɒrəl] *adj* inmoral

immortal [ɪ'mɔ:təl] *adj* inmortal

immune [ɪ'mju:n] *adj* inmune; *(exempt)* exento(a)

immunize ['ɪmjʊnaɪz] *vt* inmunizar (**against** contra)

impact ['ɪmpækt] *n* impacto *m; (crash)* choque *m*

impair [ɪm'peə(r)] *vt* perjudicar; *(sight etc)* dañar

impartial [ɪm'pɑ:ʃəl] *adj* imparcial

impassive [ɪm'pæsɪv] *adj* impasible

impatient [ɪm'peɪʃənt] *adj* impaciente; *(fretful)* irritable; **to get i.** perder la paciencia

impending [ɪm'pendɪŋ] *adj Fml* inminente

imperative [ɪm'perətɪv] **1** *adj Fml* imperativo(a); *(tone)* imperioso(a); *(urgent)* urgente **2** *n Ling* imperativo *m*

imperfect [ɪm'pɜ:fɪkt] **1** *adj* imperfecto(a); *(goods)* defectuoso(a) **2** *n Ling* imperfecto *m*

imperial [ɪm'pɪərɪəl] *adj* (**a**) imperial (**b**) *(measure)* **i. gallon** galón británico *(aprox 4,546 l)*

impersonal [ɪm'pɜ:sənəl] *adj* impersonal

impersonate [ɪm'pɜ:səneɪt] *vt* hacerse pasar por; *(famous people)* imitar

impertinent [ɪm'pɜːtɪnənt] *adj* impertinente

impetus ['ɪmpɪtəs] *n* ímpetu *m*; *Fig* impulso *m*

implant *Med* **1** *vt* [ɪm'plɑːnt] implantar **2** *n* ['ɪmplɑːnt] implantación *f*

implement 1 *n* ['ɪmplɪmənt] *(tool)* herramienta *f*; *(instrument)* instrumento *m*; **farm implements** aperos *mpl* de labranza **2** *vt* ['ɪmplɪment] *(decision, plan)* llevar a cabo; *(law, policy)* aplicar

implicate ['ɪmplɪkeɪt] *vt* implicar (**in** en)

implication [ɪmplɪ'keɪʃən] *n* implicación *f*; *(consequence)* consecuencia *f*

implicit [ɪm'plɪsɪt] *adj (implied)* implícito(a); *(trust)* absoluto(a); *(faith)* incondicional

implore [ɪm'plɔː(r)] *vt* implorar, suplicar

imply [ɪm'plaɪ] *vt* (**a**) *(involve)* implicar (**b**) *(hint)* dar a entender; *(mean)* significar

impolite [ɪmpə'laɪt] *adj* maleducado(a)

import 1 *n* ['ɪmpɔːt] (**a**) *Com (usu pl)* importación *f*; **i. duty** derechos *mpl* de importación (**b**) *Fml (meaning)* sentido *m* **2** *vt* [ɪm'pɔːt] *Com* importar

importance [ɪm'pɔːtəns] *n* importancia *f*; *(standing)* envergadura *f*; **of little i.** de poca monta

important [ɪm'pɔːtənt] *adj* importante; **it's not i.** no importa

importer [ɪm'pɔːtə(r)] *n Com* importador(a) *m,f*

impose [ɪm'pəʊz] **1** *vt* imponer (**on or upon** a) **2** *vi* **to i. on** or **upon** *(take advantage of)* abusar de

imposing [ɪm'pəʊzɪŋ] *adj* imponente, impresionante

imposition [ɪmpə'zɪʃən] *n (of tax etc)* imposición *f*; *(unfair demand)* abuso *m*; **would it be an i. if ...?** ¿le molestaría si ...?

impossibility [ɪmpɒsə'bɪlɪtɪ] *n* imposibilidad *f*

impossible [ɪm'pɒsəbəl] **1** *adj* imposible; *(person)* insoportable **2** *n*

to do the i. hacer lo imposible

impostor [ɪm'pɒstə(r)] *n* impostor(a) *m,f*

impotent ['ɪmpətənt] *adj* impotente

impractical [ɪm'præktɪkəl] *adj (person)* poco práctico(a); *(project, solution etc)* poco viable

imprecise [ɪmprɪ'saɪs] *adj* impreciso(a)

impress [ɪm'pres] *vt* (**a**) impresionar; **to i. sb favourably/unfavourably** dar a algn buena/mala impresión (**b**) *(mark)* imprimir (**on** en); *(pattern)* estampar (**on** en); *Fig* **to i. sth on sb** convencer a algn de la importancia de algo

impression [ɪm'preʃən] *n* (**a**) impresión *f*; **to be under the i. that ...** tener la impresión de que ...; **to give the i. of ...** dar la impresión de ... (**b**) *(imprint)* marca *f*; *(in snow)* huella *f* (**c**) *(imitation)* imitación *f*

impressive [ɪm'presɪv] *adj* impresionante

imprint 1 *vt* [ɪm'prɪnt] *(mark)* dejar huella (**on** en) **2** *n* ['ɪmprɪnt] (**a**) *(mark)* marca *f*; *(left by foot etc)* huella *f* (**b**) *(publisher's name)* pie *m* de imprenta

imprison [ɪm'prɪzən] *vt* encarcelar

imprisonment [ɪm'prɪzənmənt] *n* encarcelamiento *m*

improbable [ɪm'prɒbəbəl] *adj (event)* improbable; *(story)* inverosímil

improper [ɪm'prɒpə(r)] *adj* (**a**) impropio(a); *(method)* inadecuado(a) (**b**) *(indecent)* indecente; *(behaviour)* deshonesto(a) (**c**) *(wrong)* incorrecto(a)

improve [ɪm'pruːv] **1** *vt* mejorar; *(knowledge)* perfeccionar; *(mind)* cultivar; *(increase)* aumentar **2** *vi* mejorarse; *(increase)* aumentar

▶ **improve on** *vt insep* superar; *(offer, bid)* sobrepujar

improvement [ɪm'pruːvmənt] *n* mejora *f*; *(in skill)* perfeccionamiento *m*; *(increase)* aumento *m*

improvise ['ɪmprəvaɪz] *vt & vi* improvisar

impudent [ˈɪmpjʊdənt] *adj* insolente

impulse [ˈɪmpʌls] *n* impulso *m*; **to act on (an) i.** dejarse llevar por un impulso

impulsive [ɪmˈpʌlsɪv] *adj* irreflexivo(a)

impurity [ɪmˈpjʊərɪtɪ] *n* (**a**) *(of act)* deshonestidad *f* (**b**) *(usu pl) (in air, substance)* impureza *f*

in [ɪn] **1** *prep* (**a**) *(place)* en; *(within)* dentro de; **in bed** en la cama; **in Brazil** en Brasil; **in prison** en la cárcel
(**b**) *(motion)* en; **she arrived in Paris** llegó a París
(**c**) *(time) (during)* en, durante; **I haven't seen her in years** hace años que no la veo; **in May/1945** en mayo/1945; **in spring** en primavera; **in the daytime** durante el día; **in the morning** por la mañana; **at ten in the morning** a las diez de la mañana
(**d**) *(time) (within)* dentro de; **I arrived in time** llegué a tiempo
(**e**) *(time) (after)* al cabo de
(**f**) *(manner)* en; **in a loud/quiet voice** en voz alta/baja; **in fashion** de moda; **in French** en francés; **in writing** por escrito; **write in pencil** escribe con lápiz
(**g**) *(wearing)* en; **dressed in blue** vestido(a) de azul; **in uniform** de uniforme
(**h**) *(weather etc)* a, en; **in the rain** bajo la lluvia; **in the sun** al sol; **in darkness** en la oscuridad; **in daylight** a la luz del día
(**i**) *(state, emotion)* en; **in danger/public/silence** en peligro/público/silencio; **in love** enamorado(a); **in tears** llorando
(**j**) *(ratio, numbers)* de; **in threes** de tres en tres; **one in six** uno de cada seis; **2 m in length** 2 m de largo
(**k**) *(after superlative)* de; **the smallest car in the world** el coche más pequeño del mundo
(**l**) *(phrases)* **in all** en total; **in itself/himself/herself** en sí; **in that ...** dado que ...

2 *adv* **in here/there** aquí/allí dentro; **let's go in** vamos adentro; **to be in** *(at home)* estar (en casa); *(at work)* estar; *(tide)* estar alta; *Fam (in fashion)* estar de moda; **the bus is in** el autobús ha llegado; *Fam* **to be in on sth** estar enterado(a) de algo

3 *adj Fam* (**a**) *(fashionable) (place)* de moda; *(clothes)* del último grito (**b**) **an in joke** una broma privada

4 *n Fam* **ins and outs** detalles *mpl*

inability [ɪnəˈbɪlɪtɪ] *n* incapacidad *f*

inaccessible [ɪnækˈsesəbəl] *adj* inaccesible

inaccurate [ɪnˈækjʊrɪt] *adj* inexacto(a); *(statement)* erróneo(a); *(figures, total)* incorrecto(a)

inadequate [ɪnˈædɪkwɪt] *adj* (**a**) *(lacking)* insuficiente (**b**) *(not capable)* incapaz; *(unsuitable)* inadecuado(a) (**c**) *(defective)* defectuoso(a)

inanimate [ɪnˈænɪmɪt] *adj* inanimado(a)

inappropriate [ɪnəˈprəʊprɪɪt] *adj* inoportuno(a); *(behaviour)* poco apropiado(a)

inauguration [ɪnɔːgjʊˈreɪʃən] *n (of building)* inauguración *f*; *(of president)* investidura *f*

Inc, inc *US Com (abbr* **Incorporated)** ≃ S.A.

incalculable [ɪnˈkælkjʊləbəl] *adj* incalculable

incapable [ɪnˈkeɪpəbəl] *adj* incapaz

incense¹ [ˈɪnsens] *n* incienso *m*

incense² [ɪnˈsens] *vt* enfurecer, sacar de quicio

incentive [ɪnˈsentɪv] *n* incentivo *m*

incest [ˈɪnsest] *n* incesto *m*

inch [ɪntʃ] *n* pulgada *f*; *Fig* **i. by i.** poco a poco; *Fig* **she wouldn't give an i.** no quería ceder ni un ápice

▸ **inch forward** *vt sep & vi* avanzar poco a poco

incident [ˈɪnsɪdənt] *n* incidente *m*

incidental [ɪnsɪˈdentəl] *adj (accessory)* incidental, accesorio(a); *(risk)* inherente (**to** a); **i. music** música *f* de fondo

incidentally [ɪnsɪˈdentəlɪ] *adv* a propósito

incinerator [ɪn'sɪnəreɪtə(r)] *n* incinerador *m*

incision [ɪn'sɪʒən] *n* incisión *f*

incisive [ɪn'saɪsɪv] *adj (comment)* incisivo(a); *(reply)* tajante; *(mind)* penetrante

incite [ɪn'saɪt] *vt* incitar; **to i. sb to do sth** incitar a algn a hacer algo

inclination [ɪnklɪ'neɪʃən] *n* inclinación *f*; **my i. is to stay** yo prefiero quedarme

incline [ɪn'klaɪn] **1** *vt* (**a**) **I'm inclined to believe him** me inclino a creerlo; **she's inclined to be aggressive** tiende a ser agresiva (**b**) *(head etc)* inclinar
 2 *vi (slope)* inclinarse
 3 *n* ['ɪnklaɪn] *(slope)* pendiente *f*

include [ɪn'kluːd] *vt* incluir (**in** en); *(in price)* comprender (**in** en); *(in list)* figurar (**in** en)

including [ɪn'kluːdɪŋ] *prep* incluso, inclusive

inclusive [ɪn'kluːsɪv] *adj* inclusivo(a); **pages 6 to 10 i.** de la página 6 a la 10, ambas inclusive; **the rent is i. of bills** el alquiler incluye las facturas

incoherent [ɪnkəʊ'hɪərənt] *adj* incoherente

income ['ɪnkʌm] *n* ingresos *mpl*; *(from investment)* réditos *mpl*; **i. tax** impuesto *m* sobre la renta; **i. tax return** declaración *f* de la renta

incomparable [ɪn'kɒmpərəbəl] *adj* incomparable, sin par

incompatible [ɪnkəm'pætəbəl] *adj* incompatible (**with** con)

incompetent [ɪn'kɒmpɪtənt] *adj* incompetente

incomplete [ɪnkəm'pliːt] *adj* incompleto(a)

incomprehensible [ɪnkɒmprɪ'hensəbəl] *adj* incomprensible

inconceivable [ɪnkən'siːvəbəl] *adj* inconcebible

inconclusive [ɪnkən'kluːsɪv] *adj* *(vote)* no decisivo(a); *(proof)* no concluyente

inconsiderate [ɪnkən'sɪdərɪt] *adj* desconsiderado(a); **how i. of you!** ¡qué falta de consideración por tu parte!

inconsistent [ɪnkən'sɪstənt] *adj* inconsecuente; *(contradictory)* contradictorio(a); **your evidence is i. with the facts** su testimonio no concuerda con los hechos

inconspicuous [ɪnkən'spɪkjʊəs] *adj* que pasa desapercibido(a); *(discreet)* discreto(a)

inconvenience [ɪnkən'viːnɪəns] **1** *n* inconveniente *f*; *(annoyance)* molestia *f* **2** *vt (annoy)* molestar; *(cause difficulty to)* incomodar

inconvenient [ɪnkən'viːnɪənt] *adj* molesto(a); *(time)* inoportuno(a); *(design)* poco práctico(a)

incorporate [ɪn'kɔːpəreɪt] *vt* incorporar (**in** or **into** a); *(include)* incluir; *(contain)* contener

incorrect [ɪnkə'rekt] *adj* incorrecto(a)

increase 1 *n* ['ɪnkriːs] aumento *m*; *(in number)* incremento *m*; *(in price etc)* subida *f*
 2 *vt* [ɪn'kriːs] aumentar; *(price etc)* subir
 3 *vi* [ɪn'kriːs] aumentar

increasing [ɪn'kriːsɪŋ] *adj* creciente

increasingly [ɪn'kriːsɪŋlɪ] *adv* cada vez más

incredible [ɪn'kredəbəl] *adj* increíble

incredulous [ɪn'kredjʊləs] *adj* incrédulo(a)

increment ['ɪnkrɪmənt] *n* incremento *m*

incriminate [ɪn'krɪmɪneɪt] *vt* incriminar

incriminating [ɪn'krɪmɪneɪtɪŋ] *adj* incriminatorio(a)

incubator ['ɪnkjʊbeɪtə(r)] *n* incubadora *f*

incur [ɪn'kɜː(r)] *vt (blame)* incurrir en; *(risk)* correr; *(debt)* contraer; *(loss)* sufrir

incurable [ɪn'kjʊərəbəl] *adj* incurable

indebted [ɪn'detɪd] *adj* endeudado(a); *Fig (grateful)* agradecido(a); *Fig* **to be i. to sb** estar en deuda con algn

indecent [ɪn'diːsənt] *adj* indecente; **i.**

assault atentado *m* contra el pudor; **i. exposure** exhibicionismo *m*

indecisive [ɪndɪ'saɪsɪv] *adj (person)* indeciso(a); *(evidence)* poco concluyente; *(victory)* no decisivo(a)

indeed [ɪn'diːd] *adv* (**a**) *Fml (in fact)* efectivamente, en realidad (**b**) **I'm very sorry i.** lo siento de veras; **it's very hard i.** es verdaderamente difícil; **thank you very much i.** muchísimas gracias

indefinite [ɪn'defɪnɪt] *adj* indefinido(a)

indefinitely [ɪn'defɪnɪtlɪ] *adv* indefinidamente

independence [ɪndɪ'pendəns] *n* independencia *f*; *US* **I. Day** día *m* de la Independencia *(4 julio)*

independent [ɪndɪ'pendənt] *adj* independiente; *Br* **i. school** colegio *m* privado; **to become i.** independizarse

indescribable [ɪndɪs'kraɪbəbəl] *adj (pain, beauty)* indescriptible

indestructible [ɪndɪs'trʌktəbəl] *adj* indestructible

index ['ɪndeks] **1** *n (pl* **indexes** *or* **indices**) (**a**) *(in book)* índice *m*; *(in library)* catálogo *m*; **i. card** ficha *f* (**b**) *Math* exponente *m*; *Econ* índice *m* (**c**) **i. finger** dedo *m* índice **2** *vt* catalogar

India ['ɪndɪə] *n* (la) India

Indian ['ɪndɪən] *adj & n (of America)* indio(a) *(m,f)*; *Am* indígena *(mf)*; *(of India)* hindú *(mf)*; **I. Ocean** Océano Índico; **I. Summer** veranillo *m* de San Martín

indicate ['ɪndɪkeɪt] **1** *vt* indicar **2** *vi Aut* poner el intermitente

indication [ɪndɪ'keɪʃən] *n* indicio *m*

indicator ['ɪndɪkeɪtə(r)] *n* indicador *m*; *Br Aut* intermitente *m*

indifferent [ɪn'dɪfərənt] *adj* (**a**) *(uninterested)* indiferente (**b**) *(mediocre)* regular

indigestion [ɪndɪ'dʒestʃən] *n* indigestión *f*; **to suffer from i.** tener un empacho

indignant [ɪn'dɪgnənt] *adj* indignado(a); *(look)* de indignación; **to get i. about sth** indignarse por algo

indirect [ɪndɪ'rekt, ɪndaɪ'rekt] *adj* indirecto(a)

indiscreet [ɪndɪ'skriːt] *adj* indiscreto(a)

indiscriminate [ɪndɪs'krɪmɪnɪt] *adj* indiscriminado(a)

indispensable [ɪndɪ'spensəbəl] *adj* indispensable, imprescindible

indisputable [ɪndɪ'spjuːtəbəl] *adj* indiscutible, incontestable

indistinct [ɪndɪ'stɪŋkt] *adj* indistinto(a); *(memory)* confuso(a), vago(a); *(shape etc)* borroso(a)

indistinguishable [ɪndɪ'stɪŋgwɪʃ-əbəl] *adj* indistinguible

individual [ɪndɪ'vɪdjʊəl] **1** *adj* (**a**) *(separate)* individual; *(for one)* particular; *(personal)* personal (**b**) *(characteristic)* particular; *(original)* original **2** *n (person)* individuo *m*; **private i.** particular *m*

indoctrinate [ɪn'dɒktrɪneɪt] *vt* adoctrinar

Indonesia [ɪndəʊ'niːzɪə] *n* Indonesia

indoor ['ɪndɔː(r)] *adj (plant)* de interior; **i. football** fútbol *m* sala; **i. pool** piscina cubierta

indoors [ɪn'dɔːz] *adv (inside)* dentro (de casa); *(at home)* en casa; **let's go i.** vamos adentro

induce [ɪn'djuːs] *vt* (**a**) *(persuade)* inducir, persuadir (**b**) *(cause)* producir; *Med (labour)* provocar

indulge [ɪn'dʌldʒ] **1** *vt* (**a**) *(child)* consentir; *(person)* complacer; **to i. oneself** darse gusto (**b**) *(whim)* ceder a, satisfacer **2** *vi* darse el gusto (**in** de)

indulgent [ɪn'dʌldʒənt] *adj* indulgente

industrial [ɪn'dʌstrɪəl] *adj* industrial; **to take i. action** declararse en huelga; *Br* **i. estate,** *US* **i. park** polígono *m* industrial

industrialist [ɪn'dʌstrɪəlɪst] *n* industrial *mf*

industrialize [ɪn'dʌstrɪəlaɪz] *vt* industrializar; **to become industrialized** industrializarse

industrious [ɪn'dʌstrɪəs] *adj* trabajador(a)

industry ['ɪndəstrɪ] n (**a**) industria f (**b**) *(diligence)* aplicación f

inedible [ɪn'edəbəl] *adj* incomible

ineffective [ɪnɪ'fektɪv] *adj* ineficaz

ineffectual [ɪnɪ'fektʃʊəl] *adj (aim, protest)* ineficaz; *(person)* incompetente

inefficient [ɪnɪ'fɪʃənt] *adj* ineficaz; *(person)* inepto(a)

inept [ɪn'ept] *adj (person)* inepto(a); *(remark)* estúpido(a)

inequality [ɪnɪ'kwɒlɪtɪ] n desigualdad f

inert [ɪn'ɜːt] *adj* inerte

inescapable [ɪnɪ'skeɪpəbəl] *adj* ineludible

inevitable [ɪn'evɪtəbəl] *adj* inevitable

inexcusable [ɪnɪk'skjuːzəbəl] *adj* inexcusable, imperdonable

inexpensive [ɪnɪk'spensɪv] *adj* económico(a)

inexperienced [ɪnɪk'spɪərɪənst] *adj* inexperto(a)

inexplicable [ɪnɪk'splɪkəbəl] *adj* inexplicable

infallible [ɪn'fæləbəl] *adj* infalible

infamous ['ɪnfəməs] *adj* infame

infant ['ɪnfənt] n niño(a) m,f; Br **i. school** parvulario m

infantry ['ɪnfəntrɪ] n infantería f

infatuated [ɪn'fætjʊeɪtɪd] *adj* encaprichado(a)

infect [ɪn'fekt] *vt (cut)* infectar; *(water)* contaminar; *(person)* contagiar

infection [ɪn'fekʃən] n *(of cut)* infección f; *(of water)* contaminación f; *(with illness)* contagio m

infectious [ɪn'fekʃəs] *adj (disease)* infeccioso(a); *Fig* contagioso(a)

infer [ɪn'fɜː(r)] *vt* inferir (**from** de)

inferior [ɪn'fɪərɪə(r)] **1** *adj* inferior (**to** a) **2** n *Pej* inferior mf

inferiority [ɪnfɪərɪ'ɒrɪtɪ] n inferioridad f

infest [ɪn'fest] *vt* infestar, plagar (**with** de)

infidelity [ɪnfɪ'delɪtɪ] n infidelidad f

infiltrate ['ɪnfɪltreɪt] *vt* infiltrarse (**into** en)

infinite ['ɪnfɪnɪt] *adj* infinito(a)

infinitive [ɪn'fɪnɪtɪv] n infinitivo m

infinity [ɪn'fɪnɪtɪ] n infinidad f; *Math* infinito m

infirmary [ɪn'fɜːmərɪ] n hospital m

inflamed [ɪn'fleɪmd] *adj* inflamado(a); **to become i.** inflamarse

inflammable [ɪn'flæməbəl] *adj (material)* inflamable; *Fig (situation)* explosivo(a)

inflammation [ɪnflə'meɪʃən] n inflamación f

inflatable [ɪn'fleɪtəbəl] *adj* inflable

inflate [ɪn'fleɪt] **1** *vt* inflar **2** *vi* inflarse

inflation [ɪn'fleɪʃən] n inflación f

inflexible [ɪn'fleksəbəl] *adj* inflexible

inflict [ɪn'flɪkt] *vt (blow)* asestar (**on** a); *(damage)* causar (**on** a); *(defeat)* infligir (**on** a)

influence ['ɪnflʊəns] **1** n influencia f; *Fam* **to be under the i.** llevar una copa de más **2** *vt* influir en

influential [ɪnflʊ'enʃəl] *adj* influyente

influenza [ɪnflʊ'enzə] n gripe f

influx ['ɪnflʌks] n afluencia f

info ['ɪnfəʊ] n *Fam* información f

inform [ɪn'fɔːm] **1** *vt* informar (**of** or **about** de or sobre); *(police)* avisar (**of** or **about** de) **2** *vi* **to i. against** or **on** denunciar

informal [ɪn'fɔːməl] *adj* (**a**) *(occasion, behaviour)* informal; *(language, treatment)* familiar (**b**) *(unofficial)* no oficial

informality [ɪnfɔː'mælɪtɪ] n *(of occasion, behaviour)* sencillez f; *(of treatment)* familiaridad f

information [ɪnfə'meɪʃən] n información f; *(details)* detalles mpl; *(facts)* datos mpl; *(knowledge)* conocimientos mpl; *(news)* noticias fpl; **a piece of i.** un dato; **i. bureau** centro m de información; **i. (super)highway** autopista f de la información; **i. technology** informática f

informative [ɪn'fɔːmətɪv] *adj* informativo(a)

infrequent [ɪn'friːkwənt] *adj* infrecuente

infringe [ɪn'frɪndʒ] **1** *vt (law, rule)* infringir; *(copyright)* no respetar **2** *vi* **to i. on** *or* **upon** *(rights)* violar; *(privacy)* invadir

infuriating [ɪn'fjʊərɪeɪtɪŋ] *adj* exasperante

ingenious [ɪn'dʒiːnɪəs] *adj* ingenioso(a)

ingrained [ɪn'greɪnd] *adj Fig* arraigado(a)

ingredient [ɪn'griːdɪənt] *n* ingrediente *m*

inhabit [ɪn'hæbɪt] *vt* vivir en, ocupar

inhabitant [ɪn'hæbɪtənt] *n* habitante *mf*

inhale [ɪn'heɪl] **1** *vt (gas)* inhalar; *(air)* aspirar **2** *vi* aspirar; *(smoker)* tragar el humo

inherent [ɪn'hɪərənt] *adj* inherente

inherit [ɪn'herɪt] *vt* heredar (**from** de)

inheritance [ɪn'herɪtəns] *n* herencia *f*

inhibit [ɪn'hɪbɪt] *vt (freedom)* limitar; *(person)* cohibir; **to i. sb from doing sth** impedir a algn hacer algo

inhibition [ɪnhɪ'bɪʃən] *n* cohibición *f*

inhospitable [ɪnhɒ'spɪtəbəl] *adj* inhospitalario(a); *(climate, place)* inhóspito(a)

inhuman [ɪn'hjuːmən] *adj* inhumano(a)

inhumane [ɪnhjuː'meɪn] *adj* inhumano(a)

initial [ɪ'nɪʃəl] **1** *adj* inicial, primero(a)

2 *n* (**a**) inicial *f* (**b**) **initials** *(of name)* iniciales *fpl*; *(of abbreviation)* siglas *fpl*

3 *vt (pt & pp* **initialled,** *US* **initialed)** firmar con las iniciales

initially [ɪ'nɪʃəlɪ] *adv* al principio

initiate [ɪ'nɪʃɪeɪt] *vt* (**a**) iniciar; *(reform)* promover; *(lawsuit)* entablar (**b**) *(into society)* admitir (**into** en); *(into knowledge)* iniciar (**into** en)

initiative [ɪ'nɪʃətɪv] *n* iniciativa *f*

inject [ɪn'dʒekt] *vt* (**a**) *(drug etc)*

inyectar (**b**) *Fig (capital)* invertir; *(life, hope)* infundir

injection [ɪn'dʒekʃən] *n* (**a**) inyección *f* (**b**) *Fig (of capital)* inversión *f*

injure ['ɪndʒə(r)] *vt* herir; **to i. oneself** hacerse daño; *Fig (health, reputation)* perjudicar

injured ['ɪndʒəd] **1** *adj* herido(a); *Fig (look, tone)* ofendido(a) **2** *npl* **the i.** los heridos

injury ['ɪndʒərɪ] *n (hurt)* herida *f; Fig (harm)* daño *m; Sport* **i. time** (tiempo *m* de) descuento *m*

injustice [ɪn'dʒʌstɪs] *n* injusticia *f*

ink [ɪŋk] *n* tinta *f;* **invisible i.** tinta simpática

inland 1 *adj* ['ɪnlənd] (del) interior; *Br* **I. Revenue** ≃ Hacienda *f* **2** *adv* [ɪn'lænd] *(travel)* tierra adentro

in-laws ['ɪnlɔːz] *npl Fam* familia *f* política

inlet ['ɪnlet] *n* (**a**) *(in coastline)* ensenada *f,* cala *f* (**b**) *(in pipe, machine)* entrada *f,* admisión *f*

inmate ['ɪnmeɪt] *n (of prison)* preso(a) *m,f; (of hospital)* enfermo(a) *m,f; (of asylum, camp)* internado(a) *m,f*

inn [ɪn] *n (with lodging)* posada *f,* mesón *m*

innate [ɪ'neɪt] *adj* innato(a)

inner ['ɪnə(r)] *adj* (**a**) *(region)* interior; *(structure)* interno(a); **i. city** zona urbana desfavorecida; **i. tube** cámara *f* de aire (**b**) *Fig (thoughts)* íntimo(a); *(peace etc)* interior

innermost ['ɪnəməʊst] *adj (room)* más interior; *Fig (thoughts)* más íntimo(a)

innocent ['ɪnəsənt] *adj & n* inocente *(mf)*

innovation [ɪnə'veɪʃən] *n* novedad *f*

innumerable [ɪ'njuːmərəbəl] *adj* innumerable

inoculate [ɪ'nɒkjʊleɪt] *vt* inocular

inoculation [ɪnɒkjʊ'leɪʃən] *n* inoculación *f*

inpatient ['ɪnpeɪʃənt] *n* interno(a) *m,f*

input ['ɪnpʊt] *n (of resources)* inversión

f; *(of power)* entrada *f*; *Comput (of data)* input *m*, entrada

inquest ['ɪnkwest] *n* investigación *f* judicial

inquire [ɪn'kwaɪə(r)] **1** *vt* preguntar; *(find out)* averiguar **2** *vi* preguntar (**about** por); *(find out)* informarse (**about** de)

▶ **inquire after** *vt insep* preguntar por

▶ **inquire into** *vt insep* investigar, indagar

inquiry [ɪn'kwaɪərɪ] *n* (**a**) pregunta *f*; **inquiries** *(sign)* información (**b**) *(investigation)* investigación *f*

inquisitive [ɪn'kwɪzɪtɪv] *adj (curious)* curioso(a); *(questioning)* preguntón(ona)

insane [ɪn'seɪn] *adj* loco(a); *(act)* insensato(a); *Fig* **to drive sb i.** volver loco(a) a algn

inscription [ɪn'skrɪpʃən] *n (on stone, coin)* inscripción *f*; *(in book, on photo)* dedicatoria *f*

insect ['ɪnsekt] *n* insecto *m*; **i. bite** picadura *f*

insecure [ɪnsɪ'kjʊə(r)] *adj* inseguro(a)

insensitive [ɪn'sensɪtɪv] *adj* insensible

inseparable [ɪn'sepərəbəl] *adj* inseparable

insert 1 *n* ['ɪnsɜːt] encarte *m* **2** *vt* [ɪn'sɜːt] introducir

inside [ɪn'saɪd] **1** *n* (**a**) interior *m*; **on the i.** por dentro; **to turn sth i. out** volver algo al revés (**b**) *Fam* **insides** tripas *fpl*
2 ['ɪnsaɪd] *adj* interior; *Aut* **i. lane** carril *m* interior
3 *adv (be)* dentro, adentro; *(run etc)* (hacia) adentro; **to come i.** entrar
4 *prep* (**a**) *(place)* dentro de (**b**) *Fam* **i. (of)** *(time)* en menos de

insider [ɪn'saɪdə(r)] *n* **i. dealing** = uso indebido de información privilegiada y confidencial para operaciones comerciales

insight ['ɪnsaɪt] *n* perspicacia *f*

insignificant [ɪnsɪg'nɪfɪkənt] *adj* insignificante

insincere [ɪnsɪn'sɪə(r)] *adj* poco sincero(a)

insinuate [ɪn'sɪnjʊeɪt] *vt* insinuar

insipid [ɪn'sɪpɪd] *adj* soso(a), insulso(a)

insist [ɪn'sɪst] **1** *vi* insistir (**on** en); *(argue)* obstinarse (**on** en) **2** *vt* **to i. that ...** insistir en que ...

insistence [ɪn'sɪstəns] *n* insistencia *f*

insistent [ɪn'sɪstənt] *adj* insistente

in so far as [ɪnsəʊ'fɑːrəz] *adv* en tanto que

insolent ['ɪnsələnt] *adj* insolente

insoluble [ɪn'sɒljʊbəl] *adj* insoluble

insolvent [ɪn'sɒlvənt] *adj Fin* insolvente

insomnia [ɪn'sɒmnɪə] *n* insomnio *m*

inspect [ɪn'spekt] *vt* inspeccionar, examinar; *(troops)* pasar revista a

inspector [ɪn'spektə(r)] *n* inspector(a) *m,f*; *Br (on bus, train)* revisor(a) *m,f*

inspiration [ɪnspɪ'reɪʃən] *n* inspiración *f*; **to get i. from sb/sth** inspirarse en algn/algo

inspire [ɪn'spaɪə(r)] *vt* (**a**) inspirar; **to i. respect in sb** infundir respeto a algn (**b**) **to i. sb to do sth** animar a algn a hacer algo

instability [ɪnstə'bɪlɪtɪ] *n* inestabilidad *f*

install, US instal [ɪn'stɔːl] *vt* instalar

instalment, US installment [ɪn'stɔːlmənt] *n* (**a**) *(of payment)* plazo *m*; **to pay by instalments** pagar a plazos; *US* **i. plan** venta *f*/compra *f* a plazos (**b**) *(of novel, programme)* entrega *f*; *(of journal)* fascículo *m*

instance ['ɪnstəns] *n* caso *m*, ejemplo *m*; **for i.** por ejemplo; **in the first i.** en primer lugar

instant ['ɪnstənt] **1** *n (moment)* instante *m*, momento *m*; **in an i.** en un instante **2** *adj* inmediato(a); *(coffee, meal)* instantáneo(a)

instantaneous [ɪnstən'teɪnɪəs] *adj* instantáneo(a)

instantly ['ɪnstəntlɪ] *adv* inmediatamente

instead [ɪnˈsted] **1** *adv* en cambio **2** *prep* **i. of** en vez de, en lugar de

instigate [ˈɪnstɪgeɪt] *vt (strike, violence)* instigar; *(inquiry, changes)* iniciar

instinct [ˈɪnstɪŋkt] *n* instinto *m*

instinctive [ɪnˈstɪŋktɪv] *adj* instintivo(a)

institute [ˈɪnstɪtjuːt] **1** *n* instituto *m*; *(centre)* centro *m*; *(professional body)* colegio *m* **2** *vt Fml* **(a)** *(system)* establecer **(b)** *(start)* iniciar; *(proceedings)* entablar

institution [ɪnstɪˈtjuːʃən] *n* **(a)** institución *f* **(b)** *(home)* asilo *m*; *(asylum)* manicomio *m*

instruct [ɪnˈstrʌkt] *vt* instruir; *(order)* mandar; **I am instructed to say that ...** me han encargado decir que ...

instruction [ɪnˈstrʌkʃən] *n* **(a)** instrucción *f* **(b) instructions** instrucciones *fpl*; **instructions for use** modo de empleo

instructor [ɪnˈstrʌktə(r)] *n* instructor(a) *m,f*; *(of driving)* profesor(a) *m,f*

instrument [ˈɪnstrəmənt] *n* instrumento *m*; **i. panel** tablero *m* de mandos

instrumental [ɪnstrəˈmentəl] *adj* **(a)** *Mus* instrumental **(b) to be i. in sth** contribuir decisivamente a algo

insufficient [ɪnsəˈfɪʃənt] *adj* insuficiente

insulate [ˈɪnsjʊleɪt] *vt* aislar (**against** *or* **from** de)

insulation [ɪnsjʊˈleɪʃən] *n* aislamiento *m*

insulin [ˈɪnsjʊlɪn] *n* insulina *f*

insult 1 *n* [ˈɪnsʌlt] *(words)* insulto *m*; *(action)* afrenta *f*, ofensa *f* **2** *vt* [ɪnˈsʌlt] insultar, ofender

insurance [ɪnˈʃʊərəns] *n* seguro *m*; **fire i.** seguro contra incendios; **i. broker** agente *mf* de seguros; **i. company** compañía *f* de seguros; **i. policy** póliza *f* (de seguros); **private health i.** seguro médico privado

insure [ɪnˈʃʊə(r)] *vt* asegurar (**against** contra)

intact [ɪnˈtækt] *adj* intacto(a)

intake [ˈɪnteɪk] *n* **(a)** *(of air, water)* entrada *f*; *(of electricity etc)* toma *f* **(b)** *(of food, calories)* consumo *m* **(c)** *(of students, recruits)* número *m* de admitidos

integral [ˈɪntɪgrəl] **1** *adj* **(a)** *(intrinsic)* integrante **(b)** *(whole)* íntegro(a) **(c)** *Math* integral **2** *n Math* integral *f*

integrate [ˈɪntɪgreɪt] **1** *vt* integrar **2** *vi* integrarse

integrity [ɪnˈtegrɪtɪ] *n* integridad *f*, honradez *f*

intellect [ˈɪntɪlekt] *n* intelecto *m*

intellectual [ɪntɪˈlektʃʊəl] *adj & n* intelectual *(mf)*

intelligence [ɪnˈtelɪdʒəns] *n* **(a)** inteligencia *f* **(b)** *(information)* información *f*

intelligent [ɪnˈtelɪdʒənt] *adj* inteligente

intelligible [ɪnˈtelɪdʒəbəl] *adj* inteligible

intend [ɪnˈtend] *vt* **(a)** *(mean)* tener la intención de **(b) to i. sth for sb** destinar algo a algn

intended [ɪnˈtendɪd] *adj (planned)* previsto(a)

intense [ɪnˈtens] *adj* intenso(a); *(person)* muy serio(a)

intensify [ɪnˈtensɪfaɪ] *vt (search)* intensificar; *(effort)* redoblar; *(production, pollution)* aumentar

intensity [ɪnˈtensɪtɪ] *n* intensidad *f*

intensive [ɪnˈtensɪv] *adj* intensivo(a); *Med* **i. care unit** unidad *f* de vigilancia intensiva

intent [ɪnˈtent] **1** *adj (absorbed)* absorto(a); *(gaze etc)* atento(a); **to be i. on doing sth** estar resuelto(a) a hacer algo **2** *n Fml* intención *f*, propósito *m*; **to all intents and purposes** a todos los efectos

intention [ɪnˈtenʃən] *n* intención *f*

intentional [ɪnˈtenʃənəl] *adj* deliberado(a)

interact [ɪntərˈækt] *vi (people)* interrelacionarse

interactive [ɪntərˈæktɪv] *adj* interactivo(a)

intercept [ɪntə'sept] *vt* interceptar

interchange 1 *n* ['ɪntətʃeɪndʒ] (a) *(exchange)* intercambio *m* (b) *(on motorway)* cruce *m* **2** *vt* [ɪntə'tʃeɪndʒ] intercambiar (**with** con)

interchangeable [ɪntə'tʃeɪndʒəbəl] *adj* intercambiable

intercom ['ɪntəkɒm] *n* portero automático

intercourse ['ɪntəkɔːs] *n* (a) *(dealings)* trato *m* (b) *(sexual)* relaciones *fpl* sexuales

interest ['ɪntrɪst] **1** *n* (a) interés *m* (b) *(advantage)* provecho *m*; **in the i. of** en pro de (c) *Com (share)* participación *f* (d) *Fin* interés *m*; **i. rate** tipo *m* de interés **2** *vt* interesar; **he's interested in politics** le interesa la política

interesting ['ɪntrɪstɪŋ] *adj* interesante

interfere [ɪntə'fɪə(r)] *vi* (a) *(meddle)* entrometerse (**in** en); **to i. with** *(hinder)* dificultar; *(spoil)* estropear; *(prevent)* impedir (b) *Rad, TV* interferir (**with** con)

interference [ɪntə'fɪərəns] *n (meddling)* intromisión *f*; *(hindrance)* estorbo *m*; *Rad, TV* interferencia *f*

interim ['ɪntərɪm] **1** *n Fml* **in the i.** en el ínterin **2** *adj* interino(a), provisional

interior [ɪn'tɪərɪə(r)] **1** *adj* interior **2** *n* interior *m*; **i. design** diseño *m* de interiores

interlude ['ɪntəluːd] *n (break)* intervalo *m*; *Cin, Th* intermedio *m*; *Mus* interludio *m*

intermediary [ɪntə'miːdɪərɪ] *n* intermediario(a) *m,f*

intermediate [ɪntə'miːdɪɪt] *adj* intermedio(a)

intermission [ɪntə'mɪʃən] *n Cin, Th* intermedio *m*

intern 1 *vt* [ɪn'tɜːn] recluir **2** *n* ['ɪntɜːn] *US Med* médico(a) *m,f* interno(a) residente

internal [ɪn'tɜːnəl] *adj* interior; *(dispute, injury)* interno(a); *US* **I. Revenue Service** ≃ Hacienda *f*

international [ɪntə'næʃənəl] **1** *adj* internacional **2** *n Sport (player)* internacional *mf*; *(match)* partido *m* internacional

Internet ['ɪntənet] *n Comput* **the I.** Internet; **it's on the I.** está en Internet; **I. access provider** proveedor *m* de acceso a Internet; **I. service provider** proveedor *m* de (acceso a) Internet

interpret [ɪn'tɜːprɪt] **1** *vt* interpretar **2** *vi* actuar de intérprete

interpretation [ɪntɜːprɪ'teɪʃən] *n* interpretación *f*

interpreter [ɪn'tɜːprɪtə(r)] *n* intérprete *mf*

interrogate [ɪn'terəgeɪt] *vt* interrogar

interrogation [ɪnterə'geɪʃən] *n* interrogatorio *m*

interrupt [ɪntə'rʌpt] *vt & vi* interrumpir

interruption [ɪntə'rʌpʃən] *n* interrupción *f*

intersect [ɪntə'sekt] **1** *vt* cruzar **2** *vi* cruzarse

intersection [ɪntə'sekʃən] *n* (a) *(crossroads)* cruce *m* (b) *(of two lines)* intersección *f*

interstate ['ɪntəsteɪt] *n US* autopista *f* interestatal

interval ['ɪntəvəl] *n* (a) *(of time, space)* intervalo *m*; **at intervals** *(time, space)* a intervalos; *(time)* de vez en cuando (b) *Br Cin, Th* intermedio *m*

intervene [ɪntə'viːn] *vi* (a) *(person)* intervenir (**in** en) (b) *(event)* sobrevenir (c) *(time)* transcurrir

intervention [ɪntə'venʃən] *n* intervención *f*

interview ['ɪntəvjuː] **1** *n* entrevista *f*; **to give an i.** conceder una entrevista **2** *vt* entrevistar

interviewer ['ɪntəvjuːə(r)] *n* entrevistador(a) *m,f*

intestine [ɪn'testɪn] *n (usu pl)* intestino *m*; **large/small i.** intestino grueso/delgado

intimate¹ ['ɪntɪmɪt] *adj* íntimo(a); *(knowledge)* profundo(a)

intimate² ['ɪntɪmeɪt] *vt Fml* dar a entender

intimidate [ɪnˈtɪmɪdeɪt] *vt* intimidar

into [ˈɪntu:, *unstressed* ˈɪntə] *prep* (**a**) *(motion)* en, a, con; **he fell i. the water** se cayó al agua; **to go i. a house** entrar en una casa (**b**) *(state)* en, a; **to change pounds i. euros** cambiar libras en *or* por euros; **to translate sth i. French** traducir algo al francés (**c**) **to divide sth i. three** dividir algo en tres (**d**) *Fam* **to be i. sth** ser aficionado(a) a algo

intolerable [ɪnˈtɒlərəbəl] *adj* intolerable

intolerance [ɪnˈtɒlərəns] *n* intolerancia *f*

intolerant [ɪnˈtɒlərənt] *adj* intolerante

intonation [ɪntəˈneɪʃən] *n* entonación *f*

intoxicated [ɪnˈtɒksɪkeɪtɪd] *adj* borracho(a)

intransitive [ɪnˈtrænsɪtɪv] *adj* intransitivo(a)

intrigue 1 *n* [ɪnˈtri:g, ˈɪntri:g] intriga *f*
2 *vt* [ɪnˈtri:g] intrigar
3 *vi* [ɪnˈtri:g] intrigar, conspirar

introduce [ɪntrəˈdju:s] *vt* (**a**) *(person, programme)* presentar (**to** a) (**b**) *(bring in)* introducir (**into** *or* **to** en); *Com* lanzar (**into** *or* **to** a); *(topic)* proponer

introduction [ɪntrəˈdʌkʃən] *n* (**a**) *(of person, programme)* presentación *f*; *(in book)* introducción *f* (**b**) *(bringing in)* introducción *f*; *Com (of product)* lanzamiento *m*

introductory [ɪntrəˈdʌktərɪ] *adj* introductorio(a); *(remarks)* preliminar; *Com* de lanzamiento

introvert [ˈɪntrəvɜ:t] *n* introvertido(a) *m,f*

intrude [ɪnˈtru:d] *vi* entrometerse (**into** *or* **on** en); *(disturb)* molestar

intruder [ɪnˈtru:də(r)] *n* intruso(a) *m,f*

intrusion [ɪnˈtru:ʒən] *n* incursión *f*

intuition [ɪntjʊˈɪʃən] *n* intuición *f*

inundate [ˈɪnʌndeɪt] *vt* inundar (**with** de)

invade [ɪnˈveɪd] *vt* invadir

invader [ɪnˈveɪdə(r)] *n* invasor(a) *m,f*

invalid¹ [ˈɪnvəlɪd] *n (disabled person)* minusválido(a) *m,f*; *(sick person)* enfermo(a) *m,f*

invalid² [ɪnˈvælɪd] *adj* inválido(a), nulo(a)

invalidate [ɪnˈvælɪdeɪt] *vt* invalidar

invaluable [ɪnˈvæljʊəbəl] *adj* inestimable

invariably [ɪnˈveərɪəblɪ] *adv* invariablemente

invasion [ɪnˈveɪʒən] *n* invasión *f*

invent [ɪnˈvent] *vt* inventar

invention [ɪnˈvenʃən] *n* invento *m*; *(creativity)* inventiva *f*; *(lie)* mentira *f*

inventor [ɪnˈventə(r)] *n* inventor(a) *m,f*

inventory [ˈɪnvəntərɪ] *n* inventario *m*

invest [ɪnˈvest] **1** *vt* invertir (**in** en); **to i. sb with sth** conferir algo a algn **2** *vi* invertir (**in** en)

investigate [ɪnˈvestɪgeɪt] *vt (crime, subject)* investigar; *(cause, possibility)* estudiar

investigation [ɪnvestɪˈgeɪʃən] *n (of crime)* investigación *f*; *(of cause)* examen *m*

investigator [ɪnˈvestɪgeɪtə(r)] *n* investigador(a) *m,f*; **private i.** detective privado

investment [ɪnˈvestmənt] *n* inversión *f*

investor [ɪnˈvestə(r)] *n* inversor(a) *m,f*

invigorating [ɪnˈvɪgəreɪtɪŋ] *adj* vigorizante

invincible [ɪnˈvɪnsəbəl] *adj* invencible

invisible [ɪnˈvɪzəbəl] *adj* invisible

invitation [ɪnvɪˈteɪʃən] *n* invitación *f*

invite [ɪnˈvaɪt] *vt* (**a**) invitar (**to** a) (**b**) *(comments etc)* solicitar; *(criticism)* provocar; **to i. trouble** buscarse problemas

invoice [ˈɪnvɔɪs] **1** *n* factura *f* **2** *vt* facturar

invoke [ɪnˈvəʊk] *vt Fml* invocar

involuntary [ɪnˈvɒləntərɪ] *adj* involuntario(a)

involve [ɪnˈvɒlv] *vt* (**a**) *(concern)* implicar (**in** en); **the issues involved**

las cuestiones en juego; **to be involved in an accident** sufrir un accidente (**b**) *(entail)* suponer, implicar; *(trouble, risk)* acarrear

involved [ɪn'vɒlvd] *adj (complicated)* complicado(a); *Fam (romantically attached)* enredado(a), liado(a)

involvement [ɪn'vɒlvmənt] *n (participation)* participación *f*; *(in crime)* implicación *f*

invulnerable [ɪn'vʌlnərəbəl] *adj* invulnerable

inward ['ɪnwəd] **1** *adj* interior **2** *adv* = **inwards**

inwards ['ɪnwədz] *adv* hacia dentro

iodine ['aɪədiːn] *n* yodo *m*

IOU [aɪəʊ'juː] *n (abbr* **I owe you)** pagaré *m*

IQ [aɪ'kjuː] *n (abbr* **intelligence quotient)** CI *m*

IRA [aɪɑː'reɪ] *n* (**a**) *(abbr* **Irish Republican Army)** IRA *m* (**b**) *US (abbr* **individual retirement account)** cuenta *f* de retiro *or* jubilación individual

Iran [ɪ'rɑːn] *n* Irán

Iraq [ɪ'rɑːk] *n* Irak

irate [aɪ'reɪt] *adj* airado(a), furioso(a)

Ireland ['aɪələnd] *n* Irlanda; **Republic of I.** República de Irlanda

iris ['aɪərɪs] *n* (**a**) *Anat* iris *m inv* (**b**) *Bot* lirio *m*

Irish ['aɪrɪʃ] **1** *adj* irlandés(esa); **I. coffee** café *m* irlandés; **I. Sea** Mar *m* de Irlanda **2** *n* (**a**) *(language)* irlandés *m* (**b**) *pl* **the I.** los irlandeses

Irishman ['aɪrɪʃmən] *n* irlandés *m*

Irishwoman ['aɪrɪʃwʊmən] *n* irlandesa *f*

iron ['aɪən] **1** *n* (**a**) hierro *m*; **the i. and steel industry** la industria siderúrgica (**b**) *(for clothes)* plancha *f* **2** *vt (clothes)* planchar

▸ **iron out** *vt sep* (**a**) *(crease)* planchar (**b**) *Fam Fig (problem)* resolver

ironic(al) [aɪ'rɒnɪk(əl)] *adj* irónico(a)

ironing ['aɪənɪŋ] *n* (**a**) **to do the i.** planchar; **i. board** mesa *f* de la plancha (**b**) *(clothes to be ironed)* ropa *f* para

planchar; *(clothes ironed)* ropa planchada

ironmonger ['aɪənmʌŋɡə(r)] *n Br* ferretero(a) *m,f*; **i.'s (shop)** ferretería *f*

irony ['aɪrənɪ] *n* ironía *f*

irrational [ɪ'ræʃənəl] *adj* irracional

irregular [ɪ'reɡjʊlə(r)] *adj* (**a**) irregular; *(abnormal)* anormal (**b**) *(uneven)* desigual

irrelevant [ɪ'reləvənt] *adj* no pertinente

irresistible [ɪrɪ'zɪstəbəl] *adj* irresistible

irrespective [ɪrɪ'spektɪv] *adj* **i. of** sin tener en cuenta

irresponsible [ɪrɪ'spɒnsəbəl] *adj* irresponsable

irreverent [ɪ'revərənt] *adj* irreverente

irrigate ['ɪrɪɡeɪt] *vt* regar

irritable ['ɪrɪtəbəl] *adj* irritable

irritate ['ɪrɪteɪt] *vt (annoy)* fastidiar; *Med* irritar

irritating ['ɪrɪteɪtɪŋ] *adj* irritante

is [ɪz] *3rd person sing pres of* **be**

Islam ['ɪzlɑːm] *n* Islam *m*

Islamic [ɪz'læmɪk] *adj* islámico(a)

island ['aɪlənd] *n* isla *f*; **(traffic) i.** isleta *f*

isle [aɪl] *n* isla *f*

isn't ['ɪzənt] = **is not**

isolate ['aɪsəleɪt] *vt* aislar (**from** de)

isolated ['aɪsəleɪtɪd] *adj* aislado(a)

isolation [aɪsə'leɪʃən] *n* aislamiento *m*

ISP [aɪes'piː] *n Comput (abbr* **Internet Service Provider)** PSI *m*

Israel ['ɪzreɪəl] *n* Israel

Israeli [ɪz'reɪlɪ] *adj & n* israelí *(mf)*

issue ['ɪʃuː] **1** *n* (**a**) *(matter)* cuestión *f*; **to take i. with sb (over sth)** manifestar su desacuerdo con algn (en algo) (**b**) *(of magazine)* ejemplar *m* (**c**) *Fml (outcome)* resultado *m* (**d**) *Jur (offspring)* descendencia *f* **2** *vt* (**a**) *(book)* publicar; *(banknotes etc)* emitir; *(passport)* expedir (**b**) *(supplies)* repartir (**c**) *(order, instructions)* dar; *(warrant)* dictar

it [ɪt] *pers pron* (**a**) *(subject)* él/ella/ello

(usually omitted in Spanish, except for contrast); it's here está aquí

(**b**) *(direct object)* lo/la; **I don't believe it** no me lo creo; **I liked the house and bought it** me gustó la casa y la compré

(**c**) *(indirect object)* le; **give it a kick** dale una patada

(**d**) *(after prep)* él/ella/ello; **I saw the beach and ran towards it** vi la playa y fui corriendo hacia ella; **we'll talk about it later** ya hablaremos de ello

(**e**) *(abstract)* ello; **let's get down to it!** ¡vamos a ello!

(**f**) *(impersonal)* **it's late** es tarde; **it's me** soy yo; **it's raining** está lloviendo; **it's 2 miles to town** hay 2 millas de aquí al pueblo; **who is it?** ¿quién es?

Italian [ɪˈtæljən] **1** *adj* italiano(a) **2** *n* (**a**) *(person)* italiano(a) *m,f* (**b**) *(language)* italiano *m*

italic [ɪˈtælɪk] *n* cursiva *f*

Italy [ˈɪtəlɪ] *n* Italia

itch [ɪtʃ] **1** *n* picor *m*; *Fig* **an i. to travel** unas ganas locas de viajar **2** *vi* (**a**) *(skin)* picar (**b**) *Fig* anhelar; *Fam* **to be itching to do sth** tener muchas ganas de hacer algo

item [ˈaɪtəm] *n* (**a**) *(in list)* artículo *m*; *(in collection)* pieza *f*; **i. of clothing** prenda *f* de vestir (**b**) *(on agenda)* asunto *m*; *(in show)* número *m*; **news i.** noticia *f*

itemize [ˈaɪtəmaɪz] *vt* detallar

itinerary [aɪˈtɪnərərɪ] *n* itinerario *m*

its [ɪts] *pos adj (one thing)* su; *(more than one)* sus

itself [ɪtˈself] *pers pron* (**a**) *(reflexive)* se; **the cat scratched i.** el gato se arañó (**b**) *(emphatic)* él mismo/ella misma/ello mismo; *(after prep)* sí (mismo(a)); **in i.** en sí

ivory [ˈaɪvərɪ] *n* marfil *m*

ivy [ˈaɪvɪ] *n* hiedra *f*

Jj

J, j [dʒeɪ] *n (the letter)* J, j *f*

jab [dʒæb] **1** *n* pinchazo *m*; *(poke)* golpe seco **2** *vt* pinchar; *(with fist)* dar un puñetazo a

jack [dʒæk] *n* (**a**) *Aut* gato *m* (**b**) *Cards* sota *f* (**c**) *(bowls)* boliche *m*

▸**jack in** *vt sep Br Fam (job)* dejar

▸**jack up** *vt sep Fam (price, salaries)* subir

jacket ['dʒækɪt] *n* (**a**) *(coat) (formal)* chaqueta *f*, americana *f*, *Am* saco *m*; *(casual)* cazadora *f*; *(bomber jacket)* cazadora *f* (**b**) *(of book)* sobrecubierta *f*; *US (of record)* funda *f* (**c**) **j. potatoes** patatas *fpl* or *Am* papas *fpl* al horno

jackpot ['dʒækpɒt] *n* (premio *m*) gordo *m*

jagged ['dʒægɪd] *adj* dentado(a)

jail [dʒeɪl] **1** *n* cárcel *f*, prisión *f* **2** *vt* encarcelar

jam¹ [dʒæm] *n Culin* mermelada *f*

jam² [dʒæm] **1** *n (blockage)* atasco *m*; *Fam (fix)* apuro *m*
2 *vt* (**a**) *(cram)* meter a la fuerza (**b**) *(block)* atascar; *Rad* interferir
3 *vi (door)* atrancarse; *(brakes)* agarrotarse

jam-packed [dʒæm'pækt] *adj Fam (with people)* atestado(a); *(with things)* atiborrado(a)

jangle ['dʒæŋgəl] *vi* tintinear

janitor ['dʒænɪtə(r)] *n US, Scot (caretaker)* conserje *m*, bedel *m*

January ['dʒænjʊərɪ] *n* enero *m*

Japan [dʒə'pæn] *n* (el) Japón

Japanese [dʒæpə'niːz] **1** *adj* japonés(esa) **2** *n (person)* japonés(esa) *m*,*f*; *(language)* japonés *m*

jar¹ [dʒɑː(r)] *n (container)* tarro *m*; *Br Fam* **to have a j.** tomar una copa

jar² [dʒɑː(r)] *vi (sounds)* chirriar; *(appearance)* chocar; *(colours)* desentonar; *Fig* **to j. on one's nerves** ponerle a uno los nervios de punta

jargon ['dʒɑːgən] *n* jerga *f*, argot *m*

jaunt [dʒɔːnt] *n (walk)* paseo *m*; *(trip)* excursión *f*

javelin ['dʒævəlɪn] *n* jabalina *f*

jaw [dʒɔː] **1** *n* mandíbula *f* **2** *vi Fam* estar de palique

jaywalking ['dʒeɪwɔːkɪŋ] *n* imprudencia *f* peatonal

jazz [dʒæz] *n* jazz *m*

▸**jazz up** *vt sep* alegrar; *(premises)* arreglar

jealous ['dʒeləs] *adj* celoso(a); *(envious)* envidioso(a); **to be j. of ...** tener celos de ...

jealousy ['dʒeləsɪ] *n* celos *mpl*; *(envy)* envidia *f*

jeans [dʒiːnz] *npl* vaqueros *mpl*, tejanos *mpl*

Jeep® [dʒiːp] *n* jeep *m*, todo terreno *m inv*

jeer [dʒɪə(r)] **1** *n (boo)* abucheo *m*; *(mocking)* mofa *f* **2** *vi (boo)* abuchear; *(mock)* burlarse

jeering ['dʒɪərɪŋ] *adj* burlón(ona)

Jell-O®, jello ['dʒeləʊ] *n US* gelatina *f*

jelly ['dʒelɪ] *n Br (dessert)* gelatina *f*; *esp US (jam)* mermelada *f*, confitura *f*

jellyfish ['dʒelɪfɪʃ] *n* medusa *f*

jeopardize ['dʒepədaɪz] *vt* poner en peligro; *(agreement etc)* comprometer

jeopardy ['dʒepədɪ] *n* riesgo *m*, peligro *m*

jerk [dʒɜːk] **1** *n* (**a**) *(jolt)* sacudida *f*; *(pull)* tirón *m* (**b**) *Pej (idiot)* imbécil *mf*
2 *vt (shake)* sacudir; *(pull)* dar un tirón a
3 *vi (move suddenly)* dar una sacudida

jersey ['dʒɜːzɪ] *n* jersey *m*, suéter *m*,

pulóver *m*, *Andes* chompa *f*, *Urug* buzo *m*

jest [dʒest] **1** *n* broma *f* **2** *vi* bromear

Jesus ['dʒiːzəs] *n* Jesús *m*; **J. Christ** Jesucristo *m*

jet¹ [dʒet] **1** *n* (**a**) *(stream of water)* chorro *m* (**b**) *(spout)* surtidor *m* (**c**) *Av* reactor *m*; **j. engine** reactor; **j. lag** = cansancio debido al desfase horario; **j. ski** moto náutica *or* acuática **2** *vi Fam* volar

jet² [dʒet] *n* **j. black** negro(a) como el azabache

jetty ['dʒetɪ] *n* muelle *m*, malecón *m*

Jew [dʒuː] *n* judío(a) *m,f*

jeweller, *US* **jeweler** ['dʒuːələ(r)] *n* joyero(a) *m,f*; **j.'s (shop)** joyería *f*

jewellery, *US* **jewelry** ['dʒuːəlrɪ] *n* joyas *fpl*, alhajas *fpl*

Jewish ['dʒuːɪʃ] *adj* judío(a)

jibe [dʒaɪb] *n & vi* = **gibe**

jiffy ['dʒɪfɪ] *n Fam* momento *m*; **in a j.** en un santiamén; **just a j.!** ¡un momento!

jigsaw ['dʒɪgsɔː] *n (puzzle)* rompecabezas *m inv*

jingle ['dʒɪŋgəl] **1** *n Rad, TV* = canción que acompaña un anuncio **2** *vi* tintinear

jinx [dʒɪŋks] **1** *n (person)* gafe *mf* **2** *vt* gafar

jitters ['dʒɪtəz] *npl Fam* **to get the j.** tener canguelo

job [dʒɒb] *n* (**a**) trabajo *m*; *(task)* tarea *f* (**b**) *(occupation)* (puesto *m* de) trabajo *m*, empleo *m*; *(trade)* oficio *m*; *US* **j. office** oficina *f* de empleo; **j. sharing** trabajo compartido a tiempo parcial (**c**) *Fam* **we had a j. to ...** nos costó (trabajo) ... (**d**) *Br Fam* **it's a good j. that ...** menos mal que ...

jobless ['dʒɒblɪs] *adj* parado(a)

jockey ['dʒɒkɪ] **1** *n* jinete *m*, jockey *m* **2** *vi* **to j. for position** luchar para conseguir una posición aventajada

jog [dʒɒg] **1** *n* trote *m* **2** *vt* empujar; *Fig (memory)* refrescar **3** *vi Sport* hacer footing

jogging ['dʒɒgɪŋ] *n* footing *m*

john [dʒɒn] *n US Fam* **the j.** *(lavatory)* el váter

join [dʒɔɪn] **1** *vt* (**a**) juntar; **to j. forces with sb** unir fuerzas con algn (**b**) *(road)* empalmar con; *(river)* desembocar en (**c**) *(meet)* reunirse con (**d**) *(group)* unirse a; *(institution)* entrar; *(army)* alistarse a (**e**) *(party)* afiliarse a; *(club)* hacerse socio(a) de **2** *vi* (**a**) unirse (**b**) *(roads)* empalmar; *(rivers)* confluir (**c**) *(become member of political party)* afiliarse; *(become member of club)* hacerse socio(a) **3** *n* juntura *f*

▸ **join in 1** *vi* participar, tomar parte; *(debate)* intervenir **2** *vt insep* participar en, tomar parte en

▸ **join up 1** *vt sep* juntar **2** *vi (of roads)* unirse; *Mil* alistarse

joiner ['dʒɔɪnə(r)] *n Br* carpintero(a) *m,f*

joint [dʒɔɪnt] **1** *n* (**a**) juntura *f*, unión *f*; *Tech, Anat* articulación *f* (**b**) *Culin* = corte de carne para asar; *(once roasted)* asado *m* (**c**) *Fam (nightclub etc)* garito *m* (**d**) *Fam (drug)* porro *m* **2** *adj* colectivo(a); **j. (bank) account** cuenta conjunta; **j. venture** empresa conjunta

jointly ['dʒɔɪntlɪ] *adv* conjuntamente, en común

joke [dʒəʊk] **1** *n* (**a**) chiste *m*; *(prank)* broma *f*; **to play a j. on sb** gastarle una broma a algn; **to tell a j.** contar un chiste (**b**) *Fam (person)* hazmerreír *m*, payaso(a) *m,f*; **to be a j.** *(thing)* ser de chiste **2** *vi* estar de broma; **you must be joking!** ¡no hablarás en serio!

joker ['dʒəʊkə(r)] *n* (**a**) bromista *mf* (**b**) *Cards* comodín *m*

jolly ['dʒɒlɪ] **1** *adj* (**jollier, jolliest**) alegre **2** *adv Br Fam (very)* bien; **she played j. well** jugó muy bien

jolt [dʒəʊlt] **1** *n* (**a**) sacudida *f*; *(pull)* tirón *m* (**b**) *Fig (fright)* susto *m* **2** *vi* moverse a sacudidas **3** *vt* sacudir

jostle ['dʒɒsəl] *vi* dar empujones **2** *vt* dar empujones a

▸ **jot down** [dʒɒt] *vt sep* apuntar

jotter ['dʒɒtə(r)] n Br bloc m

journal ['dʒɜːnəl] n (**a**) revista f (**b**) *(diary)* diario m (**c**) *(newspaper)* periódico m

journalism ['dʒɜːnəlɪzəm] n periodismo m

journalist ['dʒɜːnəlɪst] n periodista mf

journey ['dʒɜːnɪ] **1** n viaje m; *(distance)* trayecto m **2** vi Fml viajar

joy [dʒɔɪ] n alegría f; *(pleasure)* placer m

joyful ['dʒɔɪfʊl] adj alegre, contento(a)

joyride ['dʒɔɪraɪd] n Fam paseo m en un coche robado

joystick ['dʒɔɪstɪk] n Av palanca f de mando; *(of video game)* joystick m

jubilant ['dʒuːbɪlənt] adj jubiloso(a)

jubilee ['dʒuːbɪliː] n festejos mpl; **golden j.** quincuagésimo aniversario

judge [dʒʌdʒ] **1** n juez mf, jueza f; *(in competition)* jurado m

2 vt (**a**) Jur juzgar (**b**) *(estimate)* considerar (**c**) *(competition)* actuar de juez de (**d**) *(assess)* juzgar

3 vi juzgar; **judging from what you say** a juzgar por lo que dices

judg(e)ment ['dʒʌdʒmənt] n (**a**) Jur sentencia f, fallo m (**b**) *(opinion)* juicio m (**c**) *(ability)* buen juicio m

judicial [dʒuːˈdɪʃəl] adj judicial

judo ['dʒuːdəʊ] n judo m

jug [dʒʌg] n Br jarra f; **milk j.** jarra de leche

juggle ['dʒʌgəl] vi *(perform)* hacer juegos malabares (**with** con); Fig *(responsibilities)* ajustar

juggler ['dʒʌglə(r)] n malabarista mf

juice [dʒuːs] n *(of fruit)* zumo m, Am jugo m; *(of meat)* jugo

juicy ['dʒuːsɪ] adj (**juicier, juiciest**) (**a**) jugoso(a) (**b**) Fam Fig picante

jukebox ['dʒuːkbɒks] n rocola f

July [dʒuːˈlaɪ, dʒəˈlaɪ] n julio m

jumble ['dʒʌmbəl] **1** n revoltijo m; Br **j. sale** rastrillo m benéfico **2** vt revolver

jumbo ['dʒʌmbəʊ] n **j. (jet)** jumbo m

jump [dʒʌmp] **1** n salto m; *(sudden increase)* subida repentina; Br Aut **j. leads** cables mpl de emergencia; **j. suit** mono m

2 vi (**a**) saltar, dar un salto; Fig **to j. to conclusions** sacar conclusiones precipitadas (**b**) Fig *(start)* sobresaltarse (**c**) *(increase)* aumentar de golpe

3 vt saltar; Br **to j. the queue** colarse; US **to j. rope** saltar a la comba

▶**jump at** vt insep aceptar sin pensarlo

jumper ['dʒʌmpə(r)] n (**a**) Br *(sweater)* suéter m, Esp jersey m, RP pulóver m (**b**) US *(dress)* Esp pichi m, CSur, Méx jumper m (**c**) US Aut **j. cables** cables mpl de emergencia

jumpy ['dʒʌmpɪ] adj (**jumpier, jumpiest**) Fam nervioso(a)

junction ['dʒʌŋkʃən] n *(of roads)* cruce m; Rail, Elec empalme m

June [dʒuːn] n junio m

jungle ['dʒʌŋgəl] n jungla f, selva f; Fig laberinto m; **the concrete j.** la jungla de asfalto

junior ['dʒuːnjə(r)] **1** adj (**a**) *(son of)* hijo; **David Hughes J.** David Hughes hijo (**b**) US **j. high (school)** *(between 11 and 15)* escuela secundaria; Br **j. school** *(between 7 and 11)* escuela primaria; **j. team** equipo m juvenil (**c**) *(lower in rank)* subalterno(a) **2** n (**a**) *(person of lower rank)* subalterno(a) m,f (**b**) *(younger person)* menor mf

junk [dʒʌŋk] n (**a**) Fam trastos mpl; **j. food** comida basura; **j. mail** propaganda f (por correo); **j. shop** tienda f de segunda mano (**b**) *(boat)* junco m

junkie ['dʒʌŋkɪ] n Fam yonqui mf

jury ['dʒʊərɪ] n jurado m

just [dʒʌst] **1** adj *(fair)* justo(a); Fml *(well-founded)* justificado(a)

2 adv (**a**) **he had j. arrived** acababa de llegar (**b**) *(at this very moment)* ahora mismo, en este momento; **he was j. leaving when ...** estaba a punto de salir cuando ...; **I'm j. coming!** ¡ya voy!; (**c**) *(only)* solamente; **j. in case** por si acaso; **j. a minute!** ¡un momento!

(**d**) *(barely)* por poco; **j. about** casi; **j. enough** justo lo suficiente

(**e**) *(emphatic)* **it's j. fantastic!** ¡es sencillamente fantástico!

(**f**) *(exactly)* exactamente, justo; **j. as I thought** me lo figuraba; **j. as fast as** tan rápido como

justice ['dʒʌstɪs] *n* (**a**) justicia *f*; **you didn't do yourself j.** no diste lo mejor de ti (**b**) *US (judge)* juez *mf*; *Br* **J. of the Peace** juez de paz

justifiable ['dʒʌstɪfaɪəbəl] *adj* justificable

justification [dʒʌstɪfɪ'keɪʃən] *n* justificación *f*

justify ['dʒʌstɪfaɪ] *vt* justificar

jut [dʒʌt] *vi* sobresalir; **to j. out over** proyectarse sobre

juvenile ['dʒuːvənaɪl] **1** *adj* (**a**) juvenil; **j. court** tribunal *m* de menores; **j. delinquent** delincuente *mf* juvenil (**b**) *(immature)* infantil **2** *n* menor *mf*, joven *mf*

juxtapose [dʒʌkstə'pəʊz] *vt* yuxtaponer

Kk

K, k [keɪ] *n (the letter)* K, k *f*

K (*abbr* Kilo(s)) K

kangaroo [kæŋgəˈruː] *n* canguro *m*

karate [kəˈrɑːtɪ] *n* kárate *m*

kebab [kəˈbæb] *n Culin* pincho moruno, brocheta *f*

keel [kiːl] *n* quilla *f*; *Fig* **to be on an even k.** estar en calma

▸**keel over** *vi Fam* desmayarse

keen [kiːn] *adj* (a) *(eager)* entusiasta (b) *(intense)* profundo(a) (c) *(mind, senses)* agudo(a); *(look)* penetrante; *(blade)* afilado(a); *(competition)* fuerte

keep [kiːp] (*pt & pp* **kept**) 1 *n* (a) **to earn one's k.** ganarse el pan (b) *Fam* **for keeps** para siempre

2 *vt* (a) guardar; **to k. one's room tidy** mantener su cuarto limpio (b) *(not give back)* quedarse con (c) *(detain)* detener; **to k. sb waiting** hacer esperar a algn (d) *(animals)* criar (e) *(the law)* observar; *(promise)* cumplir (f) *(secret)* guardar (g) *(diary, accounts)* llevar (h) *(prevent)* **to k. sb from doing sth** impedir a algn hacer algo (i) *(own, manage)* tener; *(shop, hotel)* llevar

3 *vi* (a) *(remain)* seguir; **k. still!** ¡estáte quieto(a)!; **to k. fit** mantenerse en forma; **to k. going** seguir adelante (b) *(do frequently)* no dejar de; **she keeps forgetting her keys** siempre se olvida las llaves (c) *(food)* conservarse

▸**keep at** *vt insep* perseverar en

▸**keep away 1** *vt sep* mantener a distancia **2** *vi* mantenerse a distancia

▸**keep back** *vt sep (information)* ocultar, callar; *(money etc)* retener

▸**keep down** *vt sep* **to k. prices down** mantener los precios bajos

▸**keep off** *vt insep* **k. off the grass** *(sign)* prohibido pisar la hierba

▸**keep on 1** *vt sep* (a) *(clothes etc)* no quitarse; **to k. an eye on sth/sb** vigilar algo/a algn (b) *(continue to employ)* no despedir a **2** *vi (continue to do)* seguir

▸**keep out 1** *vt sep* no dejar pasar **2** *vi* no entrar; **k. out!** *(sign)* ¡prohibida la entrada!

▸**keep to** *vt insep (subject)* limitarse a; **to k. to one's room** quedarse en el cuatro; **k. to the point!** ¡cíñete a la cuestión!; **to k. to the left** circular por la izquierda

▸**keep up** *vt sep* (a) mantener; **to k. up appearances** guardar las apariencias (b) **k. it up!** ¡sigue así! (c) *(prevent from sleeping)* mantener despierto(a)

▸**keep up with** *vt insep* **to k. up with the times** estar al día

keeper [ˈkiːpə(r)] *n (in zoo)* guarda *mf*; *(in record office)* archivero(a) *m,f*; *(in museum)* conservador(a) *m,f*

keeping [ˈkiːpɪŋ] *n* (a) *(care)* cuidado *m* (b) **in k. with** en armonía con; **out of k. with** en desacuerdo con

kennel [ˈkenəl] *n* caseta *f* para perros; **kennels** hotel *m* de perros

kept [kept] *pt & pp of* **keep**

kerb [kɜːb] *n Br* bordillo *m* (de la acera), *Chile* solera *f*, *Col, Perú* sardinel *m*, *CSur* cordón *m* (de la vereda), *Méx* borde *m* (de la banqueta)

kernel [ˈkɜːnəl] *n (of fruit, nut)* pepita *f*; *(of wheat)* grano *m*; *Fig* meollo *m*

kerosene, kerosine [ˈkerəsiːn] *n US* queroseno *m*

ketchup [ˈketʃəp] *n* ketchup *m*, salsa *f* de tomate

kettle [ˈketəl] *n* hervidor *m*; **that's a different k. of fish** eso es harina de otro costal

key [kiː] **1** *n* (**a**) *(for lock)* llave *f*; **k. ring** llavero *m* (**b**) *(of piano, typewriter)* tecla *f* (**c**) *Mus* tono *m*
2 *adj* clave
3 *vt Comput* teclear

▸ **key in** *vt sep Comput* introducir

keyboard ['kiːbɔːd] *n* teclado *m*

keyhole ['kiːhəʊl] *n* ojo *m* de la cerradura

khaki ['kɑːkɪ] *adj & n* caqui *(m)*

kick [kɪk] **1** *n* (*from person*) patada *f*, puntapié *m*; (*from horse etc*) coz *f*
2 *vi* (*animal*) cocear; (*person*) dar patadas
3 *vt* dar un puntapié a

▸ **kick off** *vi Fam* empezar; *Ftb* sacar

▸ **kick out** *vt sep* echar a patadas

▸ **kick up** *vt insep Fam* **to k. up a fuss** armar *or Esp* montar un alboroto

kick-off ['kɪkɒf] *n Ftb* saque *m* inicial

kid¹ [kɪd] *n* (**a**) *Zool* cabrito *m*; *Fig* **to handle sb with k. gloves** tratar a algn con guante blanco (**b**) *Fam* niño(a) *m,f*, *CAm* chavalo(a) *m,f*, *Méx* chavo(a) *mf*; **the kids** los críos

kid² [kɪd] **1** *vi Fam* tomar el pelo; **no kidding!** ¡va en serio! **2** *vt* tomar el pelo a; **to k. oneself** *(fool)* hacerse ilusiones

kidnap ['kɪdnæp] *vt* secuestrar

kidnapper ['kɪdnæpə(r)] *n* secuestrador(a) *m,f*

kidnapping ['kɪdnæpɪŋ] *n* secuestro *m*

kidney ['kɪdnɪ] *n* riñón *m*

kill [kɪl] *vt* matar; *Fig* **to k. time** pasar el rato; *Fam* **my feet are killing me!** ¡cómo me duelen los pies!

▸ **kill off** *vt sep* exterminar

killer ['kɪlə(r)] *n* asesino(a) *m,f*; **k. whale** orca *f*

killing ['kɪlɪŋ] *n* asesinato *m*; *Fig* **to make a k.** forrarse de dinero

killjoy ['kɪldʒɔɪ] *n* aguafiestas *mf inv*

kilo ['kiːləʊ] *n* kilo *m*

kilobyte ['kɪləbaɪt] *n Comput* kilobyte *m*

kilogram(me) ['kɪləʊgræm] *n* kilogramo *m*

kilometre, *US* **kilometer** [kɪ'lɒmɪtə(r)] *n* kilómetro *m*

kilt [kɪlt] *n* falda escocesa, kilt *m*

kin [kɪn] *n* familiares *mpl*, parientes *mpl*

kind¹ [kaɪnd] **1** *n* tipo *m*, clase *f*; **they are two of a k.** son tal para cual; **in k.** (*payment*) en especie; (*treatment*) con la misma moneda **2** *adv Fam* **k. of** en cierta manera

kind² [kaɪnd] *adj* amable, simpático(a); *Fml* **would you be so k. as to …?** ¿me haría usted el favor de …?

kindergarten ['kɪndəgɑːtən] *n* jardín *m* de infancia

kindly ['kaɪndlɪ] **1** *adj* (**kindlier, kindliest**) amable, bondadoso(a) **2** *adv Fml* (*please*) por favor; **k. remit a cheque** sírvase enviar cheque; **to look k. on** aprobar

kindness ['kaɪndnɪs] *n* bondad *f*, amabilidad *f*

king [kɪŋ] *n* rey *m*; (*draughts*) dama *f*

kingdom ['kɪŋdəm] *n* reino *m*

kiosk ['kiːɒsk] *n* quiosco *m*

kip [kɪp] *Br Fam* **1** *n* **to have a k.** echar un sueño **2** *vi* (*pt & pp* **kipped**) dormir

kipper ['kɪpə(r)] *n* arenque *m* ahumado

kiss [kɪs] **1** *n* beso *m*
2 *vt* besar
3 *vi* besarse

kit [kɪt] *n* (**a**) *(gear)* equipo *m*; *Mil* avíos *mpl* (**b**) *(clothing)* ropa *f* (**c**) *(toy model)* maqueta *f*

▸ **kit out** *vt sep* equipar

kitchen ['kɪtʃɪn] *n* cocina *f*; **k. sink** fregadero *m*

kite [kaɪt] *n* (**a**) *(toy)* cometa *f* (**b**) *Orn* milano *m*

kitten ['kɪtən] *n* gatito(a) *m,f*

kitty ['kɪtɪ] *n (money)* fondo *m* común; *Cards* bote *m*

kiwi ['kiːwiː] *n Bot, Orn* kiwi *m*

klutz [klʌts] *n US Fam (stupid person)* bobo(a) *m,f*, *Esp* chorra *mf*; *(clumsy person)* torpe, *Esp* patoso(a) *m,f*

km (*pl* **km** *or* **kms**) (*abbr* **kilometre(s)**) km

knack [næk] *n* to get the k. of doing sth cogerle el truquillo a algo

knackered ['nækəd] *adj Br Fam* to be k. *(tired)* estar reventado(a) *or* hecho(a) polvo; *(broken, damaged)* estar hecho(a) polvo

knapsack ['næpsæk] *n* mochila *f*

knead [ni:d] *vt* dar masaje a; *(bread etc)* amasar

knee [ni:] **1** *n* rodilla *f* **2** *vt* dar un rodillazo a

kneecap ['ni:kæp] **1** *n* rótula *f* **2** *vt* romper la rótula a

kneel [ni:l] *(pt & pp* **knelt***) vi* to k. **(down)** arrodillarse

knelt [nelt] *pt & pp of* **kneel**

knew [nju:] *pt of* **know**

knickers ['nɪkəz] *npl Br* bragas *fpl*, *Chile, Col, Méx* calzones *mpl*, *RP* bombacha *f*

knick-knack ['nɪknæk] *n Fam* chuchería *f*, baratija *f*

knife [naɪf] **1** *n (pl* **knives***)* cuchillo *m* **2** *vt* apuñalar, dar una puñalada a

knight [naɪt] **1** *n Hist* caballero *m; (in chess)* caballo *m* **2** *vt* armar caballero

knit [nɪt] *(pt & pp* **knitted** *or* **knit***)* **1** *vt* **(a)** tejer **(b)** to k. **(together)** *(join)* juntar; *Fig* to k. one's brow fruncir el ceño **2** *vi* **(a)** tejer, hacer punto **(b)** *(bone)* soldarse

knitting ['nɪtɪŋ] *n* punto *m;* k. **machine** máquina *f* de tejer; k. **needle** aguja *f* de tejer

knives [naɪvz] *pl of* **knife**

knob [nɒb] *n* **(a)** *(of stick)* puño *m; (of drawer)* tirador *m; (button)* botón *m* **(b)** *(small portion)* trozo *m*

knock [nɒk] **1** *n* golpe *m; Fig* revés *m* **2** *vt* **(a)** golpear **(b)** *Fam (criticize)* criticar
3 *vi* chocar **(against** *or* **into** contra); *(at door)* llamar **(at** a)

▸**knock down** *vt sep* **(a)** *(demolish)* derribar **(b)** *Aut* atropellar **(c)** *(price)* rebajar

▸**knock off 1** *vt sep* **(a)** tirar **(b)** *Fam* *(steal) Esp* mangar, *Am* volar **(c)** *Fam (kill)* asesinar a, *Esp* cepillarse a **2** *vi Fam* **they k. off at five** se piran a las cinco

▸**knock out** *vt sep* **(a)** *(make unconscious)* dejar sin conocimiento; *(in boxing)* poner fuera de combate, derrotar por K.O. **(b)** *(surprise)* dejar pasmado(a)

▸**knock over** *vt sep (cup)* volcar; *(with car)* atropellar

knocker ['nɒkə(r)] *n (on door)* aldaba *f*

knockout ['nɒkaʊt] *n* **(a)** *(in boxing)* K.O. *m*, knock-out *m* **(b)** *Fam* maravilla *f*

knot [nɒt] **1** *n* nudo *m; (group of people)* curro *m* **2** *vt* anudar

know [nəʊ] *(pt* **knew***; pp* **known***) vt & vi* **(a)** saber; **as far as I k.** que yo sepa; **she knows how to ski** sabe esquiar; **to get to k. sth** enterarse de algo; **to let sb k.** avisar al algn **(b)** *(be acquainted with)* conocer; **we got to k. each other at the party** nos conocimos en la fiesta

know-how ['nəʊhaʊ] *n Fam* conocimiento práctico

knowingly ['nəʊɪŋlɪ] *adv (shrewdly)* a sabiendas; *(deliberately)* deliberadamente

know-it-all ['nəʊɪtɔ:l] *n Fam* sabihondo(a) *m,f*, sabelotodo *mf*

knowledge ['nɒlɪdʒ] *n* **(a)** conocimiento *m;* **without my k.** sin saberlo yo **(b)** *(learning)* conocimientos *mpl*

knowledgeable ['nɒlɪdʒəbəl] *adj* erudito(a); k. **about** muy entendido(a) en

known [nəʊn] **1** *adj* conocido(a) **2** *pp of* **know**

knuckle ['nʌkəl] *n Anat* nudillo *m; Culin* hueso *m*

▸**knuckle down** *vi Fam* ponerse a trabajar en serio

Koran [kɔːˈrɑːn] *n* Corán *m*

Korea [kəˈriːə] *n* Corea

Ll

L, l [el] *n (the letter)* L, l *f*

lab [læb] *n Fam (abbr* **laboratory)** laboratorio *m*

label ['leɪbəl] **1** *n* etiqueta *f*; **record l.** ≃ casa discográfica **2** *vt (pt & pp* **labelled,** *US* **labeled)** poner etiqueta a

labor ['leɪbə(r)] *n US =* **labour**

laboratory [lə'bɒrətərɪ, *US* 'læbrətɔːrɪ] *n* laboratorio *m*

laborer ['leɪbərə(r)] *n US =* **labourer**

laborious [lə'bɔːrɪəs] *adj* penoso(a)

labour ['leɪbə(r)] **1** *n* **(a)** *(work)* trabajo *m* **(b)** *(workforce)* mano *f* de obra **(c)** **labours** esfuerzos *mpl* **(d) the L. Party** el Partido Laborista **(e)** *(childbirth)* **to be in l.** estar de parto
2 *adj* laboral
3 *vt (stress, linger on)* machacar; *(a point)* insistir en
4 *vi (work)* trabajar (duro)

labourer ['leɪbərə(r)] *n* peón *m*; **farm l.** peón *m* agrícola

labyrinth ['læbərɪnθ] *n* laberinto *m*

lace [leɪs] **1** *n* **(a)** *(fabric)* encaje *m* **(b) laces** cordones *mpl* **2** *vt* **(a)** *(shoes)* atar (los cordones de) **(b)** *(add spirits to)* echar licor a

▸ **lace up** *vt sep* atar con cordones

lack [læk] **1** *n* falta *f*, escasez *f*; **for l. of** por falta de
2 *vt* carecer de
3 *vi* carecer **(in** de)

lad [læd] *n Fam* chaval *m*, muchacho *m*; **(stable) l.** mozo *m* de cuadra

ladder ['lædə(r)] **1** *n* **(a)** escalera *f* (de mano); *Fig* escala *f* **(b)** *(in stocking)* carrera *f* **2** *vt* **I've laddered my stocking** me he hecho una carrera en las medias

laden ['leɪdən] *adj* cargado(a) **(with** de)

lady ['leɪdɪ] *n* señora *f*; *Pol* **First L.** primera dama; **Ladies** *(sign on WC)* Señoras; **ladies and gentlemen!** ¡señoras y señores!; **L. Brown** Lady Brown

ladybird ['leɪdɪbɜːd], *US* **ladybug** ['leɪdɪbʌg] *n* mariquita *f*

lag [læg] **1** *n* **time l.** demora *f*
2 *vi* **to l. (behind)** quedarse atrás, retrasarse
3 *vt Tech* revestir

lager ['lɑːgə(r)] *n* cerveza rubia

lagoon [lə'guːn] *n* laguna *f*

laid [leɪd] *pt & pp of* **lay**

lain [leɪn] *pp of* **lie²**

lair [leə(r)] *n* guarida *f*

lake [leɪk] *n* lago *m*

lamb [læm] *n* cordero *m*; *(meat)* carne *f* de cordero; **l. chop** chuleta *f* de cordero; **l.'s wool** lana *f* de cordero

lame [leɪm] *adj* **(a)** cojo(a) **(b)** *Fig (excuse)* poco convincente; *(argument)* flojo(a)

lament [lə'ment] **1** *n Mus* elegía *f*
2 *vt (death)* llorar, lamentar
3 *vi* llorar **(for** a), lamentarse **(over** de)

laminated ['læmɪneɪtɪd] *adj (metal)* laminado(a); *(glass)* inastillable; *(paper)* plastificado(a)

lamp-post ['læmppəʊst] *n* farola *f*

lampshade ['læmpʃeɪd] *n* pantalla *f*

lance [lɑːns] **1** *n* lanza *f*; *Br Mil* **l. corporal** cabo interino; *Med* lanceta *f*
2 *vt Med* abrir con lanceta

land [lænd] **1** *n* **(a)** tierra *f*; *(soil)* suelo *m*; **by l.** por tierra **(b)** *(country)* país *m* **(c)** *(property)* tierras *fpl*; *(estate)* finca *f*; **piece of l.** terreno *m*
2 *vt* **(a)** *(plane)* hacer aterrizar **(b)** *(disembark)* desembarcar **(c)** *Fam (obtain)* conseguir; *(contract)* ganar

(d) *Fam* **she got landed with the responsibility** tuvo que cargar con la responsabilidad (e) *Fam (blow)* asestar **3** *vi* (a) *(plane)* aterrizar (b) *(disembark)* desembarcar

▸ **land up** *vi Fam* ir a parar

landing ['lændɪŋ] *n* (a) *(of staircase)* rellano *m* (b) *(of plane)* aterrizaje *m*; **l. strip** pista *f* de aterrizaje (c) *(of passengers)* desembarco *m*; **l. stage** desembarcadero *m*

landlady ['lændleɪdɪ] *n (of flat)* dueña *f*, propietaria *f*; *(of boarding house)* patrona *f*; *(of pub)* dueña

landlord ['lændlɔːd] *n (of flat)* dueño *m*, propietario *m*; *(of pub)* patrón *m*, dueño

landmark ['lændmɑːk] *n* (a) señal *f*, marca *f*, *(well-known place)* lugar muy conocido (b) *Fig* hito *m*

landowner ['lændəʊnə(r)] *n* terrateniente *mf*

landscape ['lændskeɪp] **1** *n* paisaje *m* **2** *vt* ajardinar

landslide ['lændslaɪd] *n* desprendimiento *m* de tierras; **l. victory** victoria arrolladora

lane [leɪn] *n (in country)* camino *m*; *(in town)* callejón *m*; *(of motorway)* carril *m*; *Sport* calle *f*; *Naut* ruta *f*

language ['læŋgwɪdʒ] *n* (a) lenguaje *m*; **bad l.** palabrotas *fpl* (b) *(of a country)* idioma *m*, lengua *f*; **l. laboratory** laboratorio *m* de idiomas; **l. school** academia *f* de idiomas

languish ['læŋgwɪʃ] *vi* languidecer; *(project, plan etc)* quedar abandonado(a); *(in prison)* pudrirse

lanky ['læŋkɪ] *adj* (**lankier, lankiest**) larguirucho(a)

lantern ['læntən] *n* farol *m*

lap¹ [læp] *n Anat* regazo *m*

lap² [læp] **1** *n (circuit)* vuelta *f*; *Fig* etapa *f* **2** *vt (overtake)* doblar

lap³ [læp] (*pt & pp* **lapped**) **1** *vt (of cat)* **to l. (up)** beber a lengüetadas **2** *vi (waves)* lamer, besar

lapel [lə'pel] *n* solapa *f*

lapse [læps] **1** *n* (a) *(of time)* lapso *m* (b) *(error)* error *m*, desliz *m*; *(of memory)* fallo *m* **2** *vi* (a) *(time)* pasar, transcurrir (b) *(expire)* caducar (c) *(err)* cometer un error; *(fall back)* caer (**into** en)

laptop ['læptɒp] *n Comput* **l. (computer)** *Esp* ordenador *m* or *Am* computadora *f* portátil

larceny ['lɑːsənɪ] *n Law* (delito *m* de) robo *m* or latrocinio *m*

lard [lɑːd] *n* manteca *f* de cerdo

larder ['lɑːdə(r)] *n* despensa *f*

large [lɑːdʒ] **1** *adj* grande; *(amount)* importante; *(extensive)* amplio(a); **by and l.** por lo general **2** *n* **to be at l.** andar suelto(a); **the public at l.** el público en general

largely ['lɑːdʒlɪ] *adv (mainly)* en gran parte; *(chiefly)* principalmente

large-scale ['lɑːdʒskeɪl] *adj (project, problem etc)* de gran envergadura; *(map)* a gran escala

lark¹ [lɑːk] *n Orn* alondra *f*

lark² [lɑːk] *n Fam (joke)* broma *f*; **what a l.!** ¡qué risa!

▸ **lark about, lark around** *vi Fam* hacer el tonto

laryngitis [lærɪn'dʒaɪtɪs] *n* laringitis *f*

laser ['leɪzə(r)] *n* láser *m*; **l. printer** impresora *f* láser

lash [læʃ] **1** *n* (a) *(eyelash)* pestaña *f* (b) *(blow with whip)* latigazo *m* **2** *vt* (a) *(beat)* azotar (b) *(rain)* azotar (c) *(tie)* atar

▸ **lash out** *vi* (a) *(with fists)* repartir golpes a diestro y siniestro; *(verbally)* criticar (**at** a) (b) *Fam (spend money)* tirar or *Am salvo RP* botar la casa por la ventana

lass [læs] *n Fam* chavala *f*, muchacha *f*

last [lɑːst] **1** *adj* (a) *(final)* último(a), final; *Fam* **the l. straw** el colmo (b) *(most recent)* último(a) (c) *(past)* pasado(a); *(previous)* anterior; **l. but one** penúltimo(a); **l. month** el mes pasado; **l. night** anoche **2** *adv* (a) **when I l. saw her** la última vez que la vi (b) *(at the end)* en último lugar; *(in race etc)* último; **at (long) l.** por fin; **l. but not least** el último en orden pero no en importancia

3 *n* **the l.** el último/la última
4 *vi* (**a**) *(time)* durar; *(hold out)* aguantar (**b**) *(be enough for)* llegar, alcanzar

lasting ['lɑːstɪŋ] *adj* duradero(a)

lastly ['lɑːstlɪ] *adv* por último, finalmente

latch [lætʃ] *n* picaporte *m*, pestillo *m*

late [leɪt] **1** *adj* (**a**) *(not on time)* tardío(a); *(hour)* avanzado(a); **to be five minutes l.** llegar con cinco minutos de retraso (**b**) *(far on in time)* tarde; **in l. autumn** a finales del otoño; **in the l. afternoon** a última hora de la tarde; **she's in her l. twenties** ronda los treinta (**c**) *(dead)* difunto(a)
2 *adv* (**a**) *(not on time)* tarde; **to arrive l.** llegar tarde (**b**) *(far on in time)* tarde; **l. at night** a altas horas de la noche; **l. in life** a una edad avanzada (**c**) **as l. as 1950** todavía en 1950; **of l.** últimamente

latecomer ['leɪtkʌmə(r)] *n* tardón(ona) *m,f*

lately ['leɪtlɪ] *adv* últimamente, recientemente

lather ['lɑːðə(r)] **1** *n* *(of soap)* espuma *f*; *(horse's sweat)* sudor *m* **2** *vt* *(with soap)* enjabonar

Latin ['lætɪn] **1** *adj & n* latino(a) *(m,f)*; **L. America** América Latina, Latinoamérica; **L. American** latinoamericano(a) *(m,f)* **2** *n* *(language)* latín *m*

latitude ['lætɪtjuːd] *n* latitud *f*

latter ['lætə(r)] **1** *adj* (**a**) *(last)* último(a) (**b**) *(second of two)* segundo(a) **2** *pron* éste(a); **the former ... the l.** aquél ... éste/aquélla ... ésta

lattice ['lætɪs] *n* enrejado *m*, rejilla *f*

laudable ['lɔːdəbəl] *adj* loable

laugh [lɑːf] **1** *n* risa *f*; *(guffaw)* carcajada *f*; **for a l.** para divertirse **2** *vi* reír, reírse
▸ **laugh at** *vt insep* **to l. at sb/sth** reírse de algn/algo
▸ **laugh about** *vt insep* **to l. about sb/sth** reírse de algn/algo
▸ **laugh off** *vt sep* tomar a risa

laughable ['lɑːfəbəl] *adj (situation,* *suggestion)* ridículo(a); *(amount, offer)* irrisorio(a)

laughter ['lɑːftə(r)] *n* risa *f*

launch [lɔːntʃ] **1** *n* (**a**) *(vessel)* lancha *f* (**b**) *(of product)* lanzamiento *f* **2** *vt* (**a**) *(attack, rocket, new product)* lanzar; *(ship)* botar (**b**) *(company)* fundar; *(scheme)* iniciar

laund(e)rette [lɔːndə'ret], *US* **Laundromat**® ['lɔːndrəmæt] *n* lavandería *f*

laundry ['lɔːndrɪ] *n* (**a**) *(place)* lavandería *f* (**b**) *(dirty clothes)* ropa sucia; **to do the l.** lavar la ropa

lava ['lɑːvə] *n* lava *f*

lavatory ['lævətərɪ] *n* (**a**) excusado *m*, retrete *m* (**b**) *(room)* baño *m*; **public l.** servicios *mpl*, aseos *mpl*

lavender ['lævəndə(r)] *n* lavanda *f*

lavish ['lævɪʃ] **1** *adj* (**a**) *(generous)* pródigo(a) (**b**) *(abundant)* abundante (**c**) *(luxurious)* lujoso(a) **2** *vt* **to l. praise on sb** colmar de alabanzas a algn; **to l. attention on sb** prodigarse en atenciones con algn

law [lɔː] *n* (**a**) ley *f*; **by l.** según la ley; **l. and order** el orden público; **to lay down the l.** dictar la ley (**b**) *(as subject)* derecho *m*; **l. court** tribunal *m* de justicia (**c**) *Fam* **the l.** los maderos

lawful ['lɔːfʊl] *adj* legal; *(permitted by law)* lícito(a); *(legitimate)* legítimo(a)

lawn [lɔːn] *n* césped *m*; **l. tennis** tenis *m* sobre hierba

lawsuit ['lɔːsjuːt] *n* pleito *m*

lawyer ['lɔːjə(r)] *n* abogado(a) *m,f*; **l.'s office** bufete *m* de abogados

lax [læks] *adj (not strict)* relajado(a); *(not demanding)* poco exigente; *(careless)* descuidado(a)

laxative ['læksətɪv] *adj & n* laxante *(m)*

lay¹ [leɪ] *adj* (**a**) *Rel* laico(a) (**b**) *(non-specialist)* lego(a)

lay² [leɪ] *(pt & pp* **laid**) **1** *vt* (**a**) *(place)* poner, colocar; *(cable, trap)* tender; *(foundations)* echar (**b**) *(fire)* preparar; *(table)* poner (**c**) *(eggs)* poner **2** *pt of* **lie²**
▸ **lay down** *vt sep* (**a**) *(put down)*

poner; *(let go)* dejar; **to l. down one's arms** rendir las armas **(b)** *(establish)* fijar, imponer; *(principles)* sentar

▸ **lay into** *vt insep Fam (physically)* dar una paliza a; *(verbally)* arremeter contra

▸ **lay off 1** *vt sep (dismiss)* despedir **2** *vt insep Fam* dejar en paz

▸ **lay on** *vt sep (provide)* proveer de; *(food)* preparar

▸ **lay out** *vt sep* **(a)** *(open out)* extender **(b)** *(arrange)* disponer **(c)** *(ideas)* exponer **(d)** *(plan)* trazar **(e)** *Fam (spend)* gastar

layabout ['leɪəbaʊt] *n Fam* vago(a) *m,f*

lay-by ['leɪbaɪ] *n Br* área *f* de descanso

layer ['leɪə(r)] *n* capa *f*

layman ['leɪmən] *n* lego(a) *m,f*

layout ['leɪaʊt] *n (arrangement)* disposición *f*; *(presentation)* presentación *f*; *Typ* composición *f*; *(plan)* diseño *m*, trazado *m*

lazy ['leɪzɪ] *adj* **(lazier, laziest)** perezoso(a), holgazán(ana); **at a l. pace** a paso lento

lb *(abbr* **pound)** libra *f*

lead¹ [led] *n* **(a)** *(metal)* plomo *m* **(b)** *(in pencil)* mina *f*

lead² [liːd] *(pt & pp* **led)** **1** *n* **(a)** *(front position)* delantera *f*; *(advantage)* ventaja *f*; **to take the l.** *(in race)* tomar la delantera **(b)** *(clue)* pista *f* **(c)** *Th* primer papel *m* **(d)** *(leash)* correa *f* **(e)** *Elec* cable *m* **2** *vt* **(a)** *(conduct)* llevar, conducir **(b)** *(be the leader of)* dirigir, encabezar **(c)** *(influence)* llevar a; **this leads me to believe that** esto me lleva a creer que **(d)** *(life)* llevar **3** *vi* **(a)** *(road)* llevar, conducir **(to a) (b)** *(go first)* ir delante; *(in race)* llevar la delantera **(c) to l. to** llevar a

▸ **lead away** *vt sep* llevar

▸ **lead on 1** *vi (go ahead)* ir adelante **2** *vt sep (deceive)* engañar, timar

▸ **lead up to** *vt insep* llevar a

leader ['liːdə(r)] *n* **(a)** jefe(a) *m,f*, líder *mf*; *(in race)* líder **(b)** *Press* editorial *m*, artículo *m* de fondo

leadership ['liːdəʃɪp] *n* **(a)** *(command)* dirección *f*, mando *m*; *Pol* liderazgo *m* **(b)** *(leaders)* dirigentes *mpl*, cúpula *f*

leading ['liːdɪŋ] *adj* **(a)** *(main)* principal **(b)** *(outstanding)* destacado(a)

leaf [liːf] *n (pl* **leaves)** hoja *f*; **to turn over a new l.** hacer borrón y cuenta nueva

▸ **leaf through** *vt insep* hojear

leaflet ['liːflɪt] *n* folleto *m*

league [liːg] *n* **(a)** *(alliance)* alianza *f*; *(association)* sociedad *f*; *Fam* **to be in l. with sb** estar conchabado(a) con algn **(b)** *Sport* liga *f*

leak [liːk] **1** *n* **(a)** *(hole)* agujero *m*; *(in roof)* gotera *f* **(b)** *(of gas, liquid)* fuga *f*, escape *m*; *(of information)* filtración *f* **2** *vi* **(a)** *(container)* tener un agujero; *(pipe)* tener un escape; *(roof)* gotear; *(boat)* hacer agua **(b)** *(gas, liquid)* escaparse; *(information)* filtrarse; *(news)* trascender **3** *vt (information)* filtrar **(to a)**

leaky ['liːkɪ] *adj* **(leakier, leakiest)** *(container)* agujereado(a); *(roof)* que tiene goteras; *(ship)* que hace agua

lean¹ [liːn] *adj (meat)* magro(a); *(person)* flaco(a); *(harvest)* escaso(a)

lean² [liːn] *(pt & pp* **leaned** *or* **leant** [lent])** **1** *vi* **(a)** inclinarse **(b) to l. on/ against** apoyarse en/contra; *Fig* **to l. on sb** *(pressurize)* presionar a algn; *(depend)* depender de algn **2** *vt* apoyar **(on** en**)**

▸ **lean back** *vi* reclinarse

▸ **lean forward** *vi* inclinarse hacia delante

▸ **lean over** *vi* inclinarse

leaning ['liːnɪŋ] **1** *adj* inclinado(a) **2** *n Fig (tendency)* inclinación *f*, tendencia *f*

leap [liːp] **1** *n (jump)* salto *m*; *Fig* paso *m*; **l. year** año bisiesto **2** *vi (pt & pp* **leaped** *or* **leapt** [lept])** saltar; *Fig* **her heart leapt** su corazón dio un vuelco

▸ **leap at** *vt insep Fig (chance)* no dejar escapar

learn [lɜːn] *(pt & pp* **learned** *or* **learnt** [lɜːnt])** **1** *vt* **(a)** aprender; **to l. (how) to**

ski aprender a esquiar (**b**) **to l. that** enterarse de que **2** *vi* (**a**) aprender (**b**) **to l. about** *or* **of** *(find out)* enterarse de

learned ['lɜːnɪd] *adj* erudito(a)

learner ['lɜːnə(r)] *n (beginner)* principiante *mf*; **l. driver** aprendiz(a) *m,f* de conductor

learning ['lɜːnɪŋ] *n (knowledge)* conocimientos *mpl*; *(erudition)* saber *m*

lease [liːs] **1** *n* contrato *m* de arrendamiento; *Fig* **to give sb a new l.** *Br* **of** *or US* **on life** dar nueva vida a algn **2** *vt* arrendar

leash [liːʃ] *n* correa *f*

least [liːst] *(superl of little)* **1** *adj* menor, mínimo(a); **he has the l. time** él es quien menos tiempo tiene

2 *adv* menos; **l. of all him** él menos que nadie

3 *n* **the l.** lo menos; **at l.** por lo menos, al menos; **to say the l.** por no decir más

leather ['leðə(r)] **1** *n* piel *f*, cuero *m* **2** *adj* de piel

leave¹ [liːv] *(pt & pp* **left**) **1** *vt* (**a**) dejar; *(go away from)* abandonar; *(go out of)* salir de (**b**) **l. him alone!** ¡déjale en paz!; *Fam* **l. it to me** yo me encargo (**c**) *(bequeath)* legar (**d**) *(forget)* dejarse, olvidarse (**e**) **I have two biscuits left** me quedan dos galletas (**f**) **to be left over** sobrar

2 *vi (go away)* irse, marcharse; *(go out)* salir; **the train leaves in five minutes** el tren sale dentro de cinco minutos

▸ **leave behind** *vt sep* (**a**) dejar atrás (**b**) *(forget)* olvidarse

▸ **leave on** *vt sep* (**a**) *(clothes)* dejar puesto(a) (**b**) *(lights, radio)* dejar encendido(a) *or Am* prendido(a)

▸ **leave out** *vt sep (omit)* omitir; *Fig* **to feel left out** sentirse excluido(a)

leave² [liːv] *n* (**a**) *(permission)* permiso *m* (**b**) *(time off)* vacaciones *fpl*; *Mil* **on l.** de permiso; **l. of absence** excedencia *f* (**c**) **to take one's l. of sb** despedirse de algn

leaves [liːvz] *pl of* **leaf**

Lebanon ['lebənən] *n* (**the**) **L.** (el) Líbano

lecherous ['letʃərəs] *adj* lascivo(a)

lecture ['lektʃə(r)] **1** *n* (**a**) conferencia *f*; *Univ* clase *f*; **to give a l. (on)** dar una conferencia (sobre); **l. hall, l. room, l. theatre** sala *f* de conferencias; *Univ* aula *f* (**b**) *(rebuke)* sermón *m*

2 *vi* dar una conferencia; *Univ* dar clases

3 *vt (reproach)* sermonear

lecturer ['lektʃərə(r)] *n* conferenciante *mf*; *Br Univ* profesor(a) *m,f* de universidad

led [led] *pt & pp of* **lead²**

ledge [ledʒ] *n* (**a**) *(shelf)* repisa *f*; *(of window)* alféizar *m* (**b**) *(on mountain)* saliente *m*

ledger ['ledʒə(r)] *n* libro *m* mayor

leek [liːk] *n* puerro *m*

leer [lɪə(r)] *vi* mirar con lascivia

leeway ['liːweɪ] *n* libertad *f*; **this gives me a certain amount of l.** esto me da cierto margen de libertad

left¹ [left] **1** *adj* izquierdo(a); *Pol* **l. wing** izquierda *f*

2 *adv* a la izquierda

3 *n* (**a**) izquierda *f*; **on the l.** a mano izquierda (**b**) *Pol* **to be on the l.** ser de izquierdas

left² [left] *pt & pp of* **leave¹**

left-hand ['lefthænd] *adj* **l. drive** con el volante a la izquierda; **on the l. side** a mano izquierda

left-handed [left'hændɪd] *adj* zurdo(a)

left-luggage [left'lʌgɪdʒ] *n Br* **l. office** consigna *f*

leftovers ['leftəʊvəz] *npl* sobras *fpl*

left-wing ['leftwɪŋ] *adj* de izquierdas, izquierdista

leg [leg] *n* (**a**) *(of person)* pierna *f*; *(of animal, table)* pata *f*; *Culin (of lamb)* pierna; *(of trousers)* pernera *f* (**b**) *(stage)* etapa *f*

legacy ['legəsɪ] *n* herencia *f*, legado *m*

legal ['liːgəl] *adj* (**a**) legal; *(permitted by law)* lícito(a); **l. tender** moneda *f* de curso legal (**b**) *(relating to the law)* jurídico(a); **l. aid** asesoramiento jurídico gratuito; **l. dispute** contencioso *m*; *US* **l. holiday** fiesta *f* nacional

legalize ['li:gəlaɪz] *vt* legalizar

legally ['li:gəlɪ] *adv* legalmente

legend ['ledʒənd] *n* leyenda *f*

legendary ['ledʒəndərɪ] *adj* legendario(a)

leggings ['legɪŋz] *npl* polainas *fpl*

legible ['ledʒəbəl] *adj* legible

legislation [ledʒɪs'leɪʃən] *n* legislación *f*

legislative ['ledʒɪslətɪv] *adj* legislativo(a)

legitimate [lɪ'dʒɪtɪmɪt] *adj* legítimo(a)

leisure ['leʒə(r), *US* 'li:ʒər] *n* ocio *m*, tiempo *m* libre; **at l.** con calma; **do it at your l.** hazlo cuando tengas tiempo; **l. activities** pasatiempos *mpl*; **l. centre** centro recreativo

leisurely ['leʒəlɪ, *US* 'li:ʒərlɪ] *adj (unhurried)* tranquilo(a); *(slow)* lento(a)

lemon ['lemən] *n* limón *m*; **l. curd** crema *f* de limón; **l. juice** zumo *m* de limón; **l. tea** té *m* con limón

lemonade [lemə'neɪd] *n (still)* limonada *f*; *Br (fizzy) Esp, Arg* gaseosa *f*, *Am* gaseosa *f* de lima *or* limón

lend [lend] *vt (pt & pp* lent*)* prestar; **to l. oneself/itself to sth** prestarse a *or* para algo

lender ['lendə(r)] *n Fin* prestamista *mf*

length [leŋkθ, leŋθ] *n* **(a)** longitud *f*, largo *m*; **it is 5 m in l.** tiene 5 m de largo; *Fig* **to go to any lengths to achieve sth** hacer lo que sea para conseguir algo **(b)** *(duration)* duración *f* **(c)** *(of string)* trozo *m*; *(of cloth)* retal *m* **(d)** **at l.** *(finally)* finalmente; *(in depth)* a fondo

lengthen ['leŋkθən, 'leŋθən] **1** *vt* alargar; *(lifetime)* prolongar **2** *vi* alargarse; *(lifetime)* prolongarse

lengthy ['leŋkθɪ, 'leŋθɪ] *adj* (**length-ier, lengthiest**) largo(a); *(film, illness)* de larga duración; *(meeting, discussion)* prolongado(a)

lenient ['li:nɪənt] *adj* indulgente

lens [lenz] *n (of eye)* cristalino *m*; *(of spectacles)* lente *f*; *Phot* objetivo *m*

lent [lent] *pt & pp of* lend

lentil ['lentɪl] *n* lenteja *f*

Leo ['li:əʊ] *n* Leo *m*

leopard ['lepəd] *n* leopardo *m*

leotard ['li:ətɑːd] *n* leotardo *m*

lesbian ['lezbɪən] *adj & n* lesbiana *(f)*

less [les] **1** *adj (comp of* little*)* menos **2** *pron* menos; **the l. said about it, the better** cuanto menos se hable de eso mejor **3** *adv* menos; **l. and l.** cada vez menos **4** *prep* menos

lessen ['lesən] *vt & vi* disminuir

lesser ['lesə(r)] *adj* menor; **to a l. extent** en menor grado

lesson ['lesən] *n* **(a)** clase *f*; *(in book)* lección *f*; **Spanish lessons** clases de español **(b)** *Rel* lectura *f*

let [let] *(pt & pp* let*)* **1** *vt* **(a)** dejar, permitir; **to l. go of sth** soltar algo; **to l. sb know** avisar a algn; *Fig* **to l. oneself go** dejarse ir **(b)** *(rent out)* alquilar, *Méx* rentar; **to l.** *(sign)* se alquila **(c)** **l. alone** ni mucho menos **2** *v aux* **l. him wait** que espere; **l. me go!** ¡suéltame!; **l.'s go!** ¡vamos!, ¡vámonos!; **l.'s see** a ver

▶ **let down** *vt sep* **(a)** *(lower)* bajar; *(lengthen)* alargar **(b)** *(deflate)* desinflar **(c)** *(fail)* fallar, defraudar

▶ **let in** *vt sep* **(a)** *(admit)* dejar entrar **(b)** **to l. oneself in for** meterse en

▶ **let off** *vt sep* **(a)** *(bomb)* hacer explotar; *(fireworks)* hacer estallar **(b)** *(liquid, air)* soltar **(c)** *Fam* **to l. sb off** *(pardon)* perdonar

▶ **let on** *vi Fam* **don't l. on** *(reveal information)* no se lo digas

▶ **let out** *vt sep* **(a)** *(release)* soltar; *(news)* divulgar; *(secret)* revelar **(b)** *(air, water)* dejar salir **(c)** *(cry)* soltar **(d)** *Sewing* ensanchar

▶ **let up** *vi* cesar, parar

letdown ['letdaʊn] *n* decepción *f*

lethal ['li:θəl] *adj* letal

lethargic [lɪ'θɑːdʒɪk] *adj* aletargado(a)

letter ['letə(r)] *n* **(a)** *(of alphabet)* letra *f*; *Fig* **to the l.** al pie de la letra **(b)** *(written message)* carta *f*; *Br* **l. box**

buzón *m*; *Com* **l. of credit** carta de crédito

lettuce ['letɪs] *n* lechuga *f*

level ['levəl] **1** *adj* (**a**) *(flat)* llano(a); *(even)* nivelado(a); *(equal)* igual, parejo(a); **a l. spoonful of** una cucharada rasa de; **to be l. with** estar a nivel de; *Br* **l. crossing** paso *m* a nivel (**b**) *(steady)* estable; *(tone)* uniforme
2 *vt* (*pt & pp* **levelled**, *US* **leveled**) (**a**) nivelar, allanar (**b**) *(building)* arrasar (**c**) *(stare, criticism)* dirigir
3 *n* nivel *m*; **to be on a l. with** estar al mismo nivel que

▸ **level off, level out** *vi* estabilizarse

▸ **level with** *vt insep Fam* ser franco(a) con

lever ['liːvə(r), *US* 'levər] **1** *n* palanca *f*
2 *vt* apalancar; **to l. sth out** sacar algo con palanca

lewd [luːd] *adj* (*person*) lascivo(a); (*story*) obsceno(a)

liability [laɪə'bɪlɪtɪ] *n* (**a**) *Jur* responsabilidad *f* (**b**) *(handicap)* estorbo *m* (**c**) *Fin* **liabilities** pasivo *m*

liable ['laɪəbəl] *adj* (**a**) *Jur* responsable; *(susceptible)* sujeto(a); **to be l. for** ser responsable de (**b**) **to be l. to do sth** ser propenso(a) a hacer algo; **it's l. to happen** es muy probable que (así) suceda

liaise [lɪ'eɪz] *vi* comunicarse (**with** con)

liaison [lɪ'eɪzɒn] *n* (**a**) enlace *m*; **l. officer** oficial *mf* de enlace (**b**) *(love affair)* amorío *m*

liar ['laɪə(r)] *n* mentiroso(a) *m,f*, embustero(a) *m,f*

libel ['laɪbəl] **1** *n* libelo *m* **2** *vt* (*pt & pp* **libelled**, *US* **libeled**) difamar, calumniar

liberal ['lɪbərəl] **1** *adj* (**a**) liberal; **L. Party** Partido *m* Liberal (**b**) *(abundant)* abundante **2** *n* *Pol* **L.** liberal *mf*

liberate ['lɪbəreɪt] *vt* liberar; *(prisoner etc)* poner en libertad; **liberated woman** mujer liberada

liberation [lɪbə'reɪʃən] *n* liberación *f*

liberty ['lɪbətɪ] *n* libertad *f*; **to be at l. to say sth** ser libre de decir algo; **to**

take liberties tomarse libertades

Libra ['liːbrə] *n* Libra *m*

librarian [laɪ'breərɪən] *n* bibliotecario(a) *m,f*

library ['laɪbrərɪ] *n* biblioteca *f*

Libya ['lɪbɪə] *n* Libia

lice [laɪs] *pl of* **louse**

licence ['laɪsəns] *n* (**a**) *(permit)* licencia *f*, permiso *m*; *Aut* **l. number** matrícula *f*; *US* **l. plate** (placa *f* de la) matrícula (**b**) *(freedom)* libertad *f*; *(excessive freedom)* libertinaje *m*

license ['laɪsəns] **1** *vt* dar licencia a, autorizar **2** *n US* = **licence**

lick [lɪk] **1** *vt* lamer; **to l. one's lips** relamerse **2** *n* lamedura *f*; *Fam* **a l. of paint** una mano de pintura

licorice ['lɪkərɪs] *n US* = **liquorice**

lid [lɪd] *n* (**a**) *(cover)* tapa *f* (**b**) *(of eye)* párpado *m*

lie¹ [laɪ] **1** *vi* mentir **2** *n* mentira *f*

lie² [laɪ] **1** *vi* (*pt* **lay**; *pp* **lain**) (**a**) *(act)* echarse, acostarse; *(state)* estar echado(a), estar acostado(a); *(be buried)* yacer (**b**) *(be situated)* encontrarse, hallarse; **the valley lay before us** el valle se extendía ante nosotros (**c**) *(remain)* quedarse **2** *n* *(position)* situación *f*; *(direction)* orientación *f*

▸ **lie about, lie around** *vi* (*person*) estar tumbado(a); *(things)* estar tirado(a)

▸ **lie down** *vi* acostarse, echarse

lie-in ['laɪɪn] *n* *Fam* **to have a l.** levantarse tarde

lieu [ljuː, luː] *n* **in l. of** en lugar de

lieutenant [*Br* lef'tenənt, *US* luː'tenənt] *n* (**a**) *Mil* teniente *m* (**b**) *(deputy, assistant)* lugarteniente *m*

life [laɪf] *n* (*pl* **lives**) (**a**) vida *f*; **to come to l.** cobrar vida; **to take one's own l.** suicidarse; *Fam* **how's l.?** ¿qué tal?; **l. belt** cinturón *m* salvavidas; **l. imprisonment** cadena perpetua; **l. insurance** seguro *m* de vida; **l. jacket** chaleco *m* salvavidas; **l. style** estilo *m* de vida; **l. story** biografía *f* (**b**) *(liveliness)* vitalidad *f*

lifeboat ['laɪfbəʊt] *n* *(on ship)* bote *m*

salvavidas; *(on shore)* lancha *f* de socorro

lifeguard ['laɪfgɑːd] *n* socorrista *mf*

lifelike ['laɪflaɪk] *adj* natural; *(portrait)* fiel

lifelong ['laɪflɒŋ] *adj* de toda la vida

life-size(d) ['laɪfsaɪz(d)] *adj* (de) tamaño natural

lifetime ['laɪftaɪm] *n* vida *f*; **in his l.** durante su vida; **it's the chance of a l.** es una ocasión única

lift [lɪft] **1** *vt* (**a**) levantar; *(head etc)* alzar; *(pick up)* coger (**b**) *(troops)* transportar (**c**) *Fam (steal)* birlar
2 *vi (clouds, mist)* disiparse
3 *n* (**a**) *Br (elevator)* ascensor *m* (**b**) **to give sb a l.** llevar a algn en coche (**c**) *Fig (boost)* estímulo *m*
▸ **lift up** *vt sep* levantar, alzar

lift-off ['lɪftɒf] *n* despegue *m*

ligament ['lɪgəmənt] *n* ligamento *m*

light¹ [laɪt] **1** *n* (**a**) luz *f*; *Fig* **in the l. of** en vista de; *Fig* **to bring sth to l.** sacar algo a la luz; *Fig* **to come to l.** salir a la luz; **l. bulb** bombilla *f*; **l. switch** interruptor *m* de la luz; **l. year** año *m* luz (**b**) *(lamp)* luz *f*, lámpara *f*; *(traffic light)* semáforo *m*; *(headlight)* faro *m* (**c**) *(flame)* lumbre *f*; **to set l. to sth** prender fuego a algo; *Fam* **have you got a l.?** ¿tiene fuego?
2 *vt (pt & pp* **lighted** *or* **lit**) (**a**) *(illuminate)* iluminar, alumbrar (**b**) *(ignite)* encender
3 *adj* claro(a); *(hair)* rubio(a)
▸ **light up 1** *vt sep* iluminar, alumbrar
2 *vi* (**a**) iluminarse (**b**) *Fam* encender un cigarrillo

light² [laɪt] **1** *adj* ligero(a); *(rain)* fino(a); *(breeze)* suave; *Fig (sentence etc)* leve; *Fig* **to make l. of sth** dar poca importancia a algo **2** *adv* **to travel l.** ir ligero(a) de equipaje

lighten¹ ['laɪtən] **1** *vt* (**a**) *(colour)* aclarar (**b**) *(illuminate)* iluminar **2** *vi* aclararse

lighten² ['laɪtən] *vt* (**a**) *(weight)* aligerar (**b**) *Fig (mitigate)* aliviar; *(heart)* alegrar

lighter ['laɪtə(r)] *n* (**cigarette**) **l.**

encendedor *m*, mechero *m*

light-hearted ['laɪthɑːtɪd] *adj* alegre

lighthouse ['laɪthaʊs] *n* faro *m*

lighting ['laɪtɪŋ] *n* (**a**) *(act)* iluminación *f* (**b**) *(system)* alumbrado *m*

lightly ['laɪtlɪ] *adv* (**a**) ligeramente (**b**) **to get off l.** salir casi indemne

lightning ['laɪtnɪŋ] *n* *(flash)* relámpago *m*; *(stroke)* rayo *m*; **l. conductor** *or* **rod** pararrayos *m inv*; **l. strike** huelga *f* relámpago

like¹ [laɪk] **1** *adj* (**a**) parecido(a), semejante (**b**) *(equal)* igual
2 *adv* **(as) l. as not** a lo mejor
3 *prep* (**a**) *(similar to)* como, parecido(a) a; *(the same as)* igual que; **it's not l. her to do that** no es propio de ella hacer eso; **I've never seen anything l. it** nunca he visto cosa igual; **l. that** así; **people l. that** ese tipo de gente; **what's he l.?** ¿cómo es? (**b**) **to feel l.** *(want)* tener ganas de; **I feel l. a change** me apetece un cambio
4 *n* **brushes, combs and the l.** cepillos, peines y cosas por el estilo

like² [laɪk] **1** *vt* (**a**) **do you l. chocolate?** ¿te gusta el chocolate?; **he likes dancing** le gusta bailar; **she likes children** le gustan los niños (**b**) *(want)* querer; **whether you l. it or not** quieras o no (quieras); **would you l. a drink?** ¿te apetece tomar algo?
2 *vi* querer, gustar; **as you l.** como quieras
3 *n* gusto *m*

likeable ['laɪkəbəl] *adj* simpático(a)

likelihood ['laɪklɪhʊd] *n* probabilidad *f*

likely ['laɪklɪ] **1** *adj* (**likelier, likeliest**) probable; **he's l. to cause trouble** es probable que cause problemas; **where are you l. to be this afternoon?** ¿dónde piensas estar esta tarde? **2** *adv* probablemente; **not l.!** ¡ni hablar!

liken ['laɪkən] *vt* comparar (**to** *a or* **con**)

likeness ['laɪknɪs] *n* (**a**) semejanza *f*, parecido *m* (**b**) *(portrait)* retrato *m*

likewise ['laɪkwaɪz] *adv* (**a**) *(also)* también, asimismo (**b**) *(the same)* lo mismo, igual

liking ['laɪkɪŋ] *n (for thing)* afición *f; (for person)* simpatía *f; (for friend)* cariño *m*; **to take a l. to sth** cogerle el gusto a algo; **to take a l. to sb** coger cariño a algn

lily ['lɪlɪ] *n* lirio *m*, azucena *f*; **l. of the valley** lirio de los valles

limb [lɪm] *n* miembro *m*; *Fig* **to be out on a l.** *(in danger)* estar en peligro; *Br (isolated)* estar aislado(a)

▸ **limber up** ['lɪmbə(r)] *vi Sport* entrar en calor; *Fig* prepararse (**for** para)

lime¹ [laɪm] *n Chem* cal *f*

lime² [laɪm] *n (fruit)* lima *f; (tree)* limero *m*

limelight ['laɪmlaɪt] *n Fig* **to be in the l.** estar en el candelero

limit ['lɪmɪt] **1** *n* límite *m; (maximum)* máximo *m; (minimum)* mínimo *m* **2** *vt (restrict)* limitar

limitation [lɪmɪ'teɪʃən] *n* limitación *f*

limited ['lɪmɪtɪd] *adj* limitado(a); **l. edition** edición limitada; *Br* **l. (liability) company** sociedad anónima

limousine ['lɪməziːn, lɪmə'ziːn] *n* limusina *f*

limp¹ [lɪmp] **1** *vi* cojear **2** *n* cojera *f*

limp² [lɪmp] *adj* **(a)** *(floppy)* flojo(a) **(b)** *(weak)* débil

line¹ [laɪn] *n* **(a)** línea *f; (straight)* raya *f* **(b)** *(of writing)* renglón *m; (of poetry)* verso *m; Th* **to learn one's lines** aprenderse el papel
 (c) *(row)* fila *f; (of trees)* hilera *f; US (queue)* cola *f; Fig* **to be in l. (with)** coincidir (con); *US* **to stand in l.** *(queue)* hacer cola; *Fig* **sth along these lines** algo por el estilo; **l. dancing** baile *m* en línea, = baile al ritmo de música country en el que los participantes se colocan en hileras y dan los mismos pasos
 (d) *(rope)* cuerda *f; (wire)* cable *m*
 (e) *Tel* línea *f*; **hold the l.!** ¡no cuelgue!
 (f) *Br Rail* vía *f*
 (g) *(range of goods)* surtido *m*; **a new l.** una nueva línea

▸ **line up 1** *vt sep (arrange in rows)* poner en fila **2** *vi (people)* ponerse en fila; *(troops)* formar; *(in queue)* hacer cola

line² [laɪn] *vt (pipe etc)* revestir; *Sewing* forrar; *Fam* **to l. one's pockets** forrarse

linen ['lɪnɪn] *n* **(a)** *(cloth)* lino *m* **(b)** *(clothes)* ropa *f; (sheets etc)* ropa blanca

liner ['laɪnə(r)] *n* transatlántico *m*

line-up ['laɪnʌp] *n Sport* alineación *f*

linger ['lɪŋgə(r)] *vi* tardar; *(dawdle)* rezagarse; *(smell, doubt)* persistir; *Fig (memory)* perdurar

linguist ['lɪŋgwɪst] *n* lingüista *mf*; **he's a good l.** se le dan bien los idiomas

linguistic [lɪŋ'gwɪstɪk] *adj* lingüístico(a)

linguistics [lɪŋ'gwɪstɪks] *n sing* lingüística *f*

lining ['laɪnɪŋ] *n* forro *m*

link [lɪŋk] **1** *n* **(a)** *(of chain)* eslabón *m* **(b)** *(connection)* conexión *f; Fig* vínculo *m*; **rail l.** enlace ferroviario **(c)** **links** campo *m* de golf **2** *vt* unir

▸ **link up** *vi* unirse; *(meet)* encontrarse; *(spaceships)* acoplarse

lino ['laɪnəʊ] *n Fam* linóleo *m*

lint [lɪnt] *n (for wounds)* hilas *fpl*

lion ['laɪən] *n* león *m*

lip [lɪp] *n* **(a)** labio *m* **(b)** *(of jug)* pico *m*

lip-read ['lɪpriːd] *vt & vi* leer en los labios

lipstick ['lɪpstɪk] *n* lápiz *m* de labios

liqueur [lɪ'kjʊə(r)] *n* licor *m*

liquid ['lɪkwɪd] *adj & n* líquido(a) *(m)*

liquidate ['lɪkwɪdeɪt] *vt* liquidar

liquidize ['lɪkwɪdaɪz] *vt* licuar

liquor ['lɪkər] *n US* alcohol *m*, bebidas alcohólicas; **l. store** tienda *f* de bebidas alcohólicas

liquorice ['lɪkərɪs] *n* regaliz *m*

lisp [lɪsp] **1** *n* ceceo *m* **2** *vi* cecear

list¹ [lɪst] **1** *n* lista *f; (catalogue)* catálogo *m* **2** *vt (make a list of)* hacer una lista de; *(put on a list)* poner en una lista; **it is not listed** no figura en la lista

list² [lɪst] *Naut* **1** *n* escora *f* **2** *vi* escorar

listen ['lɪsən] *vi* escuchar; *(pay attention)* prestar atención

▸**listen out for** *vt insep* estar atento(a) a

listener ['lɪsənə(r)] *n* oyente *mf*

listless ['lɪstlɪs] *adj* apático(a)

lit [lɪt] *pt & pp of* **light**

liter ['li:tə(r)] *n US* = **litre**

literal ['lɪtərəl] *adj* literal

literally ['lɪtərəlɪ] *adv* literalmente

literary ['lɪtərərɪ] *adj* literario(a)

literate ['lɪtərɪt] *adj* alfabetizado(a)

literature ['lɪtərətʃə(r)] *n* (**a**) literatura *f* (**b**) *Fam (documentation)* folleto informativo

litigation [lɪtɪ'geɪʃən] *n* litigio *m*

litre ['li:tə(r)] *n* litro *m*

litter ['lɪtə(r)] **1** *n* (**a**) *(rubbish)* basura *f; (papers)* papeles *mpl;* **l. bin** papelera *f* (**b**) *(offspring)* camada *f* **2** *vt* ensuciar

little ['lɪtəl] **1** *adj* (**a**) pequeño(a); **a l. dog** un perrito; **a l. house** una casita; **l. finger** dedo *m* meñique (**b**) *(not much)* poco(a); **a l. cheese** un poco de queso
 2 *pron* poco *m;* **save me a l.** guárdame un poco
 3 *adv* poco; **l. by l.** poco a poco; **as l. as possible** lo menos posible

live¹ [lɪv] **1** *vi* vivir; **long l. the King!** ¡viva el Rey! **2** *vt* vivir; **to l. an interesting life** vivir una vida interesante

▸**live down** *vt sep* conseguir que se olvide

▸**live off** *vt insep* vivir de

▸**live on 1** *vt insep (food, money)* vivir de **2** *vi (memory)* persistir

▸**live through** *vt insep* vivir durante

▸**live up to** *vt insep (promises)* cumplir con; **it didn't l. up to expectations** no fue lo que se esperaba

live² [laɪv] *adj* (**a**) *(living)* vivo(a) (**b**) *TV, Rad* en directo, en vivo (**c**) *(ammunition)* real; *(bomb)* sin explotar; *Elec* con corriente; *Fam* **he's a real l. wire!** ¡éste no para nunca!

livelihood ['laɪvlɪhʊd] *n* sustento *m*

lively ['laɪvlɪ] *adj* (**livelier, liveliest**) *(person)* vivo(a); *(place)* animado(a);

Fig (interest) entusiástico(a)

liver ['lɪvə(r)] *n* hígado *m*

lives [laɪvz] *pl of* **life**

livestock ['laɪvstɒk] *n* ganado *m*

livid ['lɪvɪd] *adj* lívido(a); *Fam (angry)* furioso(a)

living ['lɪvɪŋ] **1** *adj* vivo(a) **2** *n* vida *f;* **l. conditions** condiciones *fpl* de vida; **l. expenses** dietas *fpl;* **to earn** *or* **make one's l.** ganarse la vida; **l. room** sala *f* de estar; **l. standards** nivel *m* de vida; **l. wage** sueldo mínimo

lizard ['lɪzəd] *n (large)* lagarto *m; (small)* lagartija *f*

load [ləʊd] **1** *n (cargo)* carga *f; (weight)* peso *m; Elec, Tech* carga; *Fam* **loads (of)** montones de; *Fam* **that's a l. of rubbish!** ¡no son más que tonterías!
 2 *vt* cargar

▸**load up** *vi & vt sep* cargar

loaded ['ləʊdɪd] *adj* (**a**) cargado(a) (**with** de); *Fig* **a l. question** una pregunta intencionada (**b**) *Fam* **to be l.** *(rich)* estar forrado(a)

loaf¹ [ləʊf] *n (pl* **loaves**) pan *m; (French stick)* barra *f* de pan; *(sliced)* pan de molde

loaf² [ləʊf] *vi* **to l. (about** *or* **around)** holgazanear

loan [ləʊn] **1** *n* préstamo *m; Fin* empréstito *m;* **on l.** prestado(a); *(footballer)* cedido(a) **2** *vt* prestar

loathe [ləʊð] *vt* aborrecer, odiar

loaves [ləʊvz] *pl of* **loaf**

lobby ['lɒbɪ] **1** *n* (**a**) *(hall)* vestíbulo *m* (**b**) *(pressure group)* grupo *m* de presión, lobby *m*
 2 *vt* presionar
 3 *vi* ejercer presiones

lobster ['lɒbstə(r)] *n* langosta *f*

local ['ləʊkəl] **1** *adj* local; *(person)* del pueblo; *Med* **l. anaesthetic** anestesia *f* local; *Tel* **l. call** llamada urbana; **l. government** gobierno *m* municipal **2** *n Fam* (**a**) **the locals** los vecinos (**b**) *Br (pub)* bar *m* del barrio

locality [ləʊ'kælɪtɪ] *n* localidad *f*

locally ['ləʊkəlɪ] *adv* en *or* de la localidad

locate [ləʊ'keɪt] *vt (situate)* situar, ubicar; *(find)* localizar

location [ləʊ'keɪʃən] *n* (**a**) lugar *m*, situación *f* (**b**) *Cin* **l. shots** exteriores *mpl*; **they're on l. in Australia** están rodando en Australia

lock¹ [lɒk] **1** *n* (**a**) *(on door etc)* cerradura *f*; *(bolt)* cerrojo *m*; *(padlock)* candado *m* (**b**) *(on canal)* esclusa *f*
2 *vt* cerrar con llave/cerrojo/candado
3 *vi (door etc)* cerrarse; *(wheels)* trabarse
► **lock up** *vt sep (house)* cerrar; *(jail)* meter en la cárcel

lock² [lɒk] *n Literary (of hair)* mechón *m*

locker ['lɒkə(r)] *n (cupboard)* armario ropero; *US* **l. room** vestuarios *mpl*

locket ['lɒkɪt] *n* medallón *m*

locksmith ['lɒksmɪθ] *n* cerrajero *m*

locomotive [ləʊkə'məʊtɪv] *n* locomotora *f*

locust ['ləʊkəst] *n* langosta *f*

lodge [lɒdʒ] **1** *n (gamekeeper's)* casa *f* del guarda; *(porter's)* portería *f*; *(hunter's)* refugio *m*
2 *vt* (**a**) *(accommodate)* alojar (**b**) *(complaint)* presentar
3 *vi* (**a**) *(live)* alojarse (**b**) *(get stuck)* meterse (**in** en)

lodger ['lɒdʒə(r)] *n* huésped(a) *m,f*

lodging ['lɒdʒɪŋ] *n* alojamiento *m*; **l. house** casa *f* de huéspedes

loft [lɒft] *n* desván *m*

log [lɒg] **1** *n* (**a**) *(tree)* tronco *m*; *(for fuel)* leño *m*; **l. cabin** cabaña *f* de troncos (**b**) *Naut* diario *m* de a bordo **2** *vt (record)* registrar
► **log in, log on** *vi Comput* entrar (en sistema)
► **log out, log off** *vi Comput* salir (del sistema)

logic ['lɒdʒɪk] *n* lógica *f*

logical ['lɒdʒɪkəl] *adj* lógico(a)

logistics [lə'dʒɪstɪks] *npl* logística *f*

loiter ['lɔɪtə(r)] *vi (hang about)* holgazanear; *(lag behind)* rezagarse; *(prowl)* merodear

loll [lɒl] *vi (tongue, head)* colgar

► **loll about, loll around** *vi* repantigarse

lollipop ['lɒlɪpɒp] *n* piruleta *f*; *Br Fam* **l. lady/man** = persona encargada de ayudar a cruzar la calle a los colegiales

lolly ['lɒlɪ] *n Fam* (**a**) *(sweet)* piruleta *f*; **ice(d) l.** polo *m* (**b**) *Br Fam (money) Esp* pasta *f*, *Am* plata *f*

London ['lʌndən] *n* Londres

lone [ləʊn] *adj (solitary)* solitario(a); *(single)* solo(a)

loneliness ['ləʊnlɪnɪs] *n* soledad *f*

lonely ['ləʊnlɪ] *adj* (**lonelier, loneliest**) solo(a), solitario(a)

long¹ [lɒŋ] **1** *adj* (**a**) *(size)* largo(a); **how l. is the table?** ¿cuánto tiene de largo la mesa?; **it's 3 m l.** tiene 3 m de largo; **l. jump** salto *m* de longitud (**b**) *(time)* mucho(a); **at l. last** por fin; **how l. is the film?** ¿cuánto tiempo dura la película?
2 *adv* mucho, mucho tiempo; **all day l.** todo el día; **as l. as the exhibition lasts** mientras dure la exposición; **as l. as** *or* **so l. as you don't mind** con tal de que no te importe; **before l.** dentro de poco; **how l. have you been here?** ¿cuánto tiempo llevas aquí?

long² [lɒŋ] *vi* añorar; **to l. for** anhelar

long-distance ['lɒŋdɪstəns] *adj* de larga distancia; **l. call** conferencia interurbana; **l. runner** corredor(a) *m,f* de fondo

longing ['lɒŋɪŋ] *n (desire)* anhelo *m*; *(nostalgia)* nostalgia *f*

longitude ['lɒndʒɪtjuːd] *n* longitud *f*

long-range ['lɒŋreɪndʒ] *adj (missile etc)* de largo alcance; *(weather forecast)* de largo plazo

long-sighted [lɒŋ'saɪtɪd] *adj* (**a**) *Med* présbita (**b**) *Fig* previsor(a)

long-standing ['lɒŋstændɪŋ] *adj* antiguo(a), de mucho tiempo

long-term ['lɒŋtɜːm] *adj* a largo plazo

loo [luː] *n Br Fam* baño *m*, váter *m*

look [lʊk] **1** *n* (**a**) *(glance)* mirada *f*; **to take a l. at** *(peep)* echar un vistazo a; *(examine)* examinar (**b**) *(appearance)* aspecto *m*, apariencia *f*; **I don't like the l. of it** me da mala espina (**c**) *(fashion)* moda *f* (**d**) (**good**) **looks** belleza *f*

2 *vi* (**a**) mirar, *Am* ver (**b**) *(seem)* parecer; **it looks delicious** tiene un aspecto buenísimo; **she looks like her father** *(resembles)* se parece a su padre

3 *vt* mirar

▸**look after** *vt insep* cuidar a, ocuparse de

▸**look at** *vt insep* mirar; *Fig* **whichever way you l. at it** desde cualquier punto de vista

▸**look away** *vi* apartar la mirada

▸**look back** *vi* (**a**) mirar hacia atrás; *Fig* **since then he has never looked back** desde entonces ha ido prosperando (**b**) *(remember)* recordar

▸**look down** *vi Fig* **to l. down on sth/sb** despreciar algo/a algn

▸**look for** *vt insep* buscar

▸**look forward to** *vt insep* esperar con ansia; **I l. forward to hearing from you** *(in letter)* espero noticias suyas

▸**look into** *vt insep* examinar, investigar

▸**look on** **1** *vt insep (consider)* considerar **2** *vi* quedarse mirando

▸**look onto** *vt insep* dar a

▸**look out** *vi* (**a**) **the bedroom looks out onto the garden** el dormitorio da al jardín (**b**) **l. out!** *(take care)* ¡cuidado!, ¡ojo!

▸**look over** *vt sep (examine)* revisar; *(place)* inspeccionar

▸**look round** **1** *vi* mirar alrededor; *(turn head)* volver la cabeza **2** *vt insep (house, shop)* ver

▸**look through** *vt insep* (**a**) *(window)* mirar por (**b**) *(leaf through)* hojear; *(examine)* revisar; *(check)* registrar

▸**look to** *vt insep* (**a**) *(take care of)* velar por (**b**) *(turn to)* recurrir a

▸**look up** **1** *vi* (**a**) *(glance upwards)* alzar la vista (**b**) *Fam (improve)* mejorar **2** *vt sep* (**a**) *(look for)* buscar (**b**) *(visit)* ir a visitar

▸**look upon** *vt insep* considerar

▸**look up to** *vt insep (person)* respetar

lookout ['lʊkaʊt] *n (person)* centinela *mf*; *(place)* mirador *m*; **to be on the l. for** estar al acecho de; *Fam* **that's his l.!** ¡eso es asunto suyo!

loom¹ [luːm] *n* telar *m*

loom² [luːm] *vi* alzarse; *Fig (threaten)* amenazar

loony ['luːnɪ] *adj* (**loonier, looniest**) *Fam* loco(a)

loop [luːp] **1** *n* (**a**) lazo *m* (**b**) *Comput* bucle *m* **2** *vt* (**a**) encordar (**b**) *Av* **to l. the loop** rizar el rizo

loophole ['luːphəʊl] *n Fig* escapatoria *f*

loose [luːs] *adj* (**a**) *(not secure)* flojo(a); *(papers, hair, clothes)* suelto(a); *(tongue)* desatado(a); *(baggy)* holgado(a); **to set sb l.** soltar a algn (**b**) *(not packaged)* a granel; **l. change** suelto *m* (**c**) *(not exact)* vago(a); *(translation)* libre (**d**) *(lax)* relajado(a); **a l. woman** una mujer fácil

loosen ['luːsən] **1** *vt* aflojar; *(belt)* desabrochar; *Fig (restrictions)* flexibilizar **2** *vi (slacken)* aflojarse

loot [luːt] **1** *n* botín *m* **2** *vt* saquear

looting ['luːtɪŋ] *n* saqueo *m*, pillaje *m*

lop [lɒp] *vt* podar

▸**lop off** *vt sep* cortar

lopsided [lɒp'saɪdɪd] *adj* ladeado(a)

lord [lɔːd] *n* (**a**) señor *m*; *(British peer)* lord *m*; *Br* **the (House of) Lords** la cámara de los lores; **the L. Mayor** el señor alcalde (**b**) *Rel* **the L.** El Señor; **good L.!** ¡Dios mío!; **the L.'s Prayer** el Padrenuestro (**c**) *(judge)* señoría *mf*

lorry ['lɒrɪ] *n Br* camión *m*; **l. driver** camionero(a) *m,f*; **l. load** carga *f*

lose [luːz] *(pt & pp* **lost**) **1** *vt* perder; **to l. time** *(clock)* atrasarse **2** *vi* perder; **to l. to sb** perder contra algn; **to l. out** salir perdiendo

loser ['luːzə(r)] *n* perdedor(a) *m,f*

loss [lɒs] *n* pérdida *f*; **to make a l.** perder; *Fig* **to be at a l. for words** quedarse de una pieza; **to be at a l. what to do** no saber qué hacer

lost [lɒst] **1** *adj* (**a**) perdido(a); **to get l.** perderse; *Fam* **get l.!** ¡vete a la porra!; **l. property office,** *US* **l. and found**

department oficina f de objetos perdidos (**b**) *(disoriented)* desorientado(a); *(distracted)* distraído(a); **l. in thought** ensimismado(a) **2** *pt & pp of* **lose**

lot [lɒt] n (**a**) *(fate)* suerte f (**b**) *US (plot of land)* parcela f (**c**) *(in an auction)* lote m (**d**) *(everything)* todo m; **he ate the l.** se lo comió todo (**e**) **a l. of** *(much)* mucho(a); *(many)* muchos(as); **he feels a l. better** se encuentra mucho mejor; *Fam* **lots of** montones de, cantidad de

lotion ['ləʊʃən] n loción f

lottery ['lɒtərɪ] n lotería f; **l. ticket** ≃ décimo m de lotería

loud [laʊd] **1** *adj* (**a**) *(voice)* alto(a); *(noise)* fuerte; *(laugh)* estrepitoso(a); *(applause)* clamoroso(a); *(protests, party)* ruidoso(a) (**b**) *(flashy)* chillón(ona) (**c**) *(vulgar)* hortera **2** *adv* **to read/think out l.** leer/pensar en voz alta

loudspeaker [laʊd'spiːkə(r)] n altavoz m

lounge [laʊndʒ] **1** n *Br* salón m, sala f de estar **2** *vi* hacer el vago

louse [laʊs] n *(pl* **lice***)* piojo m

lousy ['laʊzɪ] *adj* (**lousier, lousiest**) *Fam* fatal; **a l. trick** una cochinada

lout [laʊt] n gamberro m

love [lʌv] **1** n (**a**) *amor m* (**for** por); *(passion)* pasión f (**for** por); **to be in l. with sb** estar enamorado(a) de algn; **to fall in l.** enamorarse; **to make l.** hacer el amor; **(with) l. (from) Mary** *(in letter)* un abrazo, Mary; **l. affair** amorío m; **l. life** vida f sentimental (**b**) *(person)* amor m, cariño m; **my l.** mi amor (**c**) *(in tennis)* **forty l.** cuarenta a cero

2 *vt (person)* querer a, amar a; **he loves cooking/football** le encanta cocinar/el fútbol

lovely ['lʌvlɪ] *adj* (**lovelier, loveliest**) *(charming)* encantador(a); *(beautiful)* precioso(a), *Am* lindo(a); *(delicious)* riquísimo(a)

lover ['lʌvə(r)] n (**a**) *(sexual partner)* amante mf (**b**) *(enthusiast)* aficionado(a) m,f, amigo(a) m,f

loving ['lʌvɪŋ] *adj* cariñoso(a)

low¹ [ləʊ] **1** *adj* (**a**) bajo(a); *(neckline)* escotado(a) (**b**) *(in quantity)* bajo(a) (**c**) *(poor)* pobre (**d**) *(battery)* gastado(a); **l. frequency** baja frecuencia (**e**) **to feel l.** sentirse deprimido(a) (**f**) *(reprehensible)* malo(a)

2 *adv* bajo

3 n (**a**) *Met* área f de baja presión (**b**) *(low point)* punto más bajo; **to reach an all-time l.** tocar fondo

low² [ləʊ] *vi (cow)* mugir

lowdown ['ləʊdaʊn] n *Fam* pormenores *mpl*

lower ['ləʊə(r)] **1** *adj (comp of* **low¹***)* inferior; *Typ* **l. case** minúscula f; **l. class** clase baja

2 *adv comp of* **low¹**

3 *vt* bajar; *(flag)* arriar; *(reduce)* reducir; *(price)* rebajar

lowly ['ləʊlɪ] *adj* (**lowlier, lowliest**) humilde

loyal ['lɔɪəl] *adj* leal, fiel

loyalty ['lɔɪəltɪ] n lealtad f, fidelidad f

lozenge ['lɒzɪndʒ] n pastilla f

LP [el'piː] n *(abbr* **long-playing record***)* LP m

L-plate ['elpleɪt] n *Br* placa f de la "L"

Ltd *Br Com (abbr* **limited***)* S.L.

lubricate ['luːbrɪkeɪt] *vt* lubricar; *(engine)* engrasar

lucid ['luːsɪd] *adj* lúcido(a)

luck [lʌk] n suerte f; **bad l.!** ¡mala suerte!; **good l.!** ¡(buena) suerte!; **to be in l.** estar de suerte; **to be out of l.** no tener suerte; *Fig* **to push one's l.** tentar la suerte; *Fig* **to try one's l.** probar fortuna

luckily ['lʌkɪlɪ] *adv* por suerte, afortunadamente

lucky ['lʌkɪ] *adj* (**luckier, luckiest**) *(person)* afortunado(a); *(day)* de suerte; *(move)* oportuno(a); *(charm)* de la suerte; **to be lucky** tener suerte; **a l. break** una oportunidad

lucrative ['luːkrətɪv] *adj* lucrativo(a)

ludicrous ['luːdɪkrəs] *adj* absurdo(a), ridículo(a)

luggage ['lʌgɪdʒ] n equipaje m; **l.**

rack *Aut* baca *f*; *Rail* portaequipajes *m inv*

lukewarm ['lu:kwɔ:m] *adj (water etc)* tibio(a); *Fig (reception etc)* poco entusiasta

lull [lʌl] **1** *n (in storm)* calma chicha; *(in fighting)* tregua *f* **2** *vt (cause to sleep)* adormecer; **to l. sb into a false sense of security** infundir una falsa seguridad a algn

lullaby ['lʌləbaɪ] *n* canción *f* de cuna, nana *f*

lumber ['lʌmbə(r)] **1** *n* (**a**) *Br (junk)* trastos viejos (**b**) *US (wood)* maderos *mpl* **2** *vt Fam* cargar (**with** de)

lumberyard ['lʌmbəjɑːd] *n* *US* almacén *m* maderero, maderería *f*, *RP* barraca *f* maderera

luminous ['lu:mɪnəs] *adj* luminoso(a)

lump [lʌmp] **1** *n (of coal etc)* trozo *m*; *(of sugar, earth)* terrón *m*; *(in sauce)* grumo *m*; *(swelling)* bulto *m*; *Fam Fig (in throat)* nudo *m*; **l. sum** cantidad *f* global **2** *vt Fam (endure)* aguantar

▶ **lump together** *vt sep* apelotonar

lumpy ['lʌmpɪ] *adj* (**lumpier, lumpiest**) *(bed)* lleno(a) de bultos; *(sauce)* grumoso(a)

lunar ['lu:nə(r)] *adj* lunar

lunatic ['lu:nətɪk] *adj & n* loco(a) *(m,f)*; **l. asylum** manicomio *m*

lunch [lʌntʃ] **1** *n* comida *f*, almuerzo *m*; **l. hour** hora *f* de comer **2** *vi* comer, almorzar

luncheon ['lʌntʃən] *n Old-fashioned Fml* almuerzo *m*; **l. voucher** vale *m* de comida; (**pork**) **l. meat** carne *f* de

cerdo troceada, chopped *m*

lung [lʌŋ] *n* pulmón *m*

lunge [lʌndʒ] **1** *n* arremetida *f* **2** *vi* **to l. (forward)** arremeter; **to l. (out) at sb** arremeter contra algn

lurch [lɜ:tʃ] **1** *n* (**a**) *(of vehicle)* sacudida *f*; *(of person)* tambaleo *m* (**b**) *Fam* **to leave sb in the l.** dejar a algn en la cuneta **2** *vi (vehicle)* dar sacudidas; *(person)* tambalearse

lure [lʊə(r)] **1** *n (decoy)* señuelo *m*; *(bait)* cebo *m*; *Fig (charm)* aliciente *m* **2** *vt* atraer con engaños

lurid ['lʊərɪd] *adj* (**a**) *(gruesome)* espeluznante; *(sensational)* sensacionalista (**b**) *(gaudy)* chillón(ona)

lurk [lɜ:k] *vi (lie in wait)* estar al acecho; *(hide)* esconderse

luscious ['lʌʃəs] *adj (food)* delicioso(a)

lush [lʌʃ] *adj (vegetation)* exuberante

lust [lʌst] **1** *n (sexual desire)* lujuria *f*; *(craving)* ansia *f*; *(greed)* codicia *f* **2** *vi* **to l. after sth/sb** codiciar algo/ desear a algn

Luxembourg ['lʌksəmbɜ:g] *n* Luxemburgo

luxurious [lʌg'zjʊərɪəs] *adj* lujoso(a)

luxury ['lʌkʃərɪ] *n* lujo *m*; **l. flat** piso *m* de lujo

lying ['laɪɪŋ] **1** *adj* mentiroso(a) **2** *n* mentiras *fpl*

lynch [lɪntʃ] *vt* linchar

lyric ['lɪrɪk] **1** *adj* lírico(a) **2** *n* (**a**) *(poem)* poema lírico (**b**) **lyrics** *(words of song)* letra *f*

Mm

M, m [em] *n (the letter)* M, m *f*

m (**a**) *(abbr* **metre(s))** m (**b**) *(abbr* **million(s))** m

macabre [mə'kɑːbrə] *adj* macabro(a)

machine [mə'ʃiːn] **1** *n* máquina *f*; **m. gun** ametralladora *f* **2** *vt* trabajar a máquina

machinery [mə'ʃiːnəri] *n (machines)* maquinaria *f*; *(workings of machine)* mecanismo *m*

mackerel ['mækrəl] *n (pl* **mackerel)** caballa *f*

mackintosh ['mækɪntɒʃ] *n* impermeable *m*

mad [mæd] *adj* (**madder, maddest**) (**a**) loco(a); *(animal)* furioso(a); *(dog)* rabioso(a); **to go m.** volverse loco(a); *Fam* **m. cow disease** el mal de las vacas locas (**b**) *(idea, plan)* disparatado(a) (**c**) *Fam* **to be m. about sth/sb** estar loco(a) por algo/algn (**d**) *esp US Fam* **to be m. at sb** estar muy *esp Esp* enfadado(a) *or esp Am* enojado(a) con algn

madam ['mædəm] *n* señora *f*; **Dear M.** *(in letter)* Muy señora mía, Estimada señora

made [meɪd] *pt & pp of* **make**

madly ['mædlɪ] *adv Fam (extremely)* terriblemente; **to be m. in love with sb** estar locamente enamorado(a) de algn

madman ['mædmən] *n* loco *m*

madness ['mædnɪs] *n* locura *f*

magazine [mægə'ziːn] *n* (**a**) *(periodical)* revista *f* (**b**) *(in rifle)* recámara *f* (**c**) *Mil (storehouse)* alma-cén *m*; *(for explosives)* polvorín *m*

magic ['mædʒɪk] **1** *n* magia *f* **2** *adj* (**a**) mágico(a); **m. wand** varita mágica (**b**) *Fam (excellent)* genial, *Esp* guay, *Am* salvo *RP* chévere, *Méx* padrísimo(a), *RP* bárbaro(a)

magician [mə'dʒɪʃən] *n* (**a**) *(wizard)* mago(a) *m,f* (**b**) *(conjurer)* prestidigitador(a) *m,f*

magistrate ['mædʒɪstreɪt] *n Br* juez *mf* de primera instancia; **magistrates' court** juzgado *m* de primera instancia

magnet ['mægnɪt] *n* imán *m*

magnetic [mæg'netɪk] *adj* magnético(a); *Fig (personality)* carismático(a); **m. tape** cinta magnetofónica

magnificent [mæg'nɪfɪsənt] *adj* magnífico(a)

magnify ['mægnɪfaɪ] *vt* (**a**) *(enlarge)* aumentar (**b**) *Fig (exaggerate)* exagerar

mahogany [mə'hɒɡənɪ] **1** *n* caoba *f* **2** *adj* de caoba

maid [meɪd] *n* (**a**) criada *f*, *Andes, RP* mucama *f* (**b**) *Pej* **old m.** solterona *f*

maiden ['meɪdən] *adj* (**a**) *(unmarried)* soltera; **m. name** apellido *m* de soltera (**b**) *(voyage, flight)* inaugural

mail [meɪl] **1** *n* correo *m*; **by m.** por correo; **m. order** venta *f* por correo **2** *vt (post)* echar al buzón; *(send)* enviar por correo

mailbox ['meɪlbɒks] *n US* buzón *m*

maim [meɪm] *vt* lisiar

main [meɪn] **1** *adj (problem, door etc)* principal; *(square, mast, sail)* mayor; *(office)* central; *Culin* **m. course** plato *m* principal; **m. road** carretera *f* principal; *US* **M. Street** la Calle Mayor **2** *n* (**a**) *(pipe, wire)* conducto *m* principal; **the mains** *(water or gas system)* la cañería maestra; *Elec* la red eléctrica (**b**) **in the m.** por regla general

mainland ['meɪnlənd] *n* continente *m*

mainly ['meɪnlɪ] *adv* principalmente,

sobre todo; *(for the most part)* en su mayoría

maintain [meɪn'teɪn] *vt* mantener; *(conversation)* sostener; *(silence, appearances)* guardar; *(road, machine)* conservar en buen estado

maintenance ['meɪntənəns] *n* (**a**) *(of car, equipment, roads)* mantenimiento *m* (**b**) *(divorce allowance)* pensión *f*

maize [meɪz] *n* maíz *m*, *Andes, RP* choclo *m*

majesty ['mædʒɪstɪ] *n* majestad *f*

major ['meɪdʒə(r)] **1** *adj* (**a**) principal, mayor; *(contribution, operation)* importante (**b**) *Mus* mayor **2** *n* (**a**) *Mil* comandante *m* (**b**) *US Univ* especialidad *f* **3** *vi US Univ* **to m. in** especializarse en

Majorca [mə'jɔːkə] *n* Mallorca

majority [mə'dʒɒrɪtɪ] *n* mayoría *f*; **to be in the m.** ser (la) mayoría

make [meɪk] (*pt & pp* **made**) **1** *vt* (**a**) *(produce, prepare, perform)* hacer; *(manufacture)* hacer, fabricar; *(clothes, curtains)* confeccionar; *(meal)* preparar; *(payment)* efectuar; *(speech)* pronunciar; *(decision)* tomar; *(mistake)* cometer; **to be made of** ser de; **to m. a noise** hacer ruido

(**b**) *(render)* poner, volver; *(convert)* convertir (**into** en); *(appoint)* nombrar; **he made it clear that ...** dejó claro que ...

(**c**) *(force, compel)* obligar; *(cause)* causar; **to m. do with sth** arreglárselas con algo

(**d**) *(earn)* ganar; **to m. a living** ganarse la vida

(**e**) **7 and 5 m. 12** 7 y 5 son 12

(**f**) *(calculate, reckon)* calcular; **I don't know what to m. of it** no sé qué pensar de eso; **what time do you m. it?** ¿qué hora tienes?

(**g**) *(achieve)* alcanzar, conseguir

2 *vi* (**a**) hacer; **to m. sure of sth** asegurarse de algo (**b**) **she made as if to leave** hizo como si quisiera marcharse

3 *n (brand)* marca *f*

▸ **make for** *vt insep (move towards)* dirigirse hacia

▸ **make out 1** *vt sep* (**a**) *(list, receipt)* hacer; *(cheque)* extender (**b**) *(perceive)* distinguir; *(writing)* descifrar (**c**) *(understand)* entender (**d**) *(claim)* pretender **2** *vi* **how did you m. out?** ¿qué tal te fue?

▸ **make up 1** *vt sep* (**a**) *(parcel, list)* hacer; *(prescription)* preparar; *(assemble)* montar (**b**) *(story)* inventar (**c**) *(apply cosmetics to)* maquillar; *(one's face)* maquillarse (**d**) *(loss)* compensar; *(lost time)* recuperar (**e**) *(constitute)* componer (**f**) **to m. it up (with sb)** hacer las paces (con algn) **2** *vi* maquillarse

▸ **make up to** *vt sep* **to m. it up to sb for sth** compensar a algn por algo

makeshift ['meɪkʃɪft] *adj (improvised)* improvisado(a); *(temporary)* provisional

make-up ['meɪkʌp] *n* (**a**) *(cosmetics)* maquillaje *m*; **m. remover** desmaquillador *m* (**b**) *(composition)* composición *f*; *(character)* carácter *m*

malaria [mə'leərɪə] *n* malaria *f*

male [meɪl] **1** *adj (animal, plant)* macho; *(person)* varón; *(sex)* masculino; *Pej* **m. chauvinism** machismo *m* **2** *n (person)* varón *m*; *(animal, plant)* macho *m*

malfunction [mæl'fʌŋkʃən] **1** *n Esp* fallo *m*, *Am* falla *f* **2** *vi* funcionar mal

malice ['mælɪs] *n* malicia *f*; *Jur* **with m. aforethought** con premeditación

malicious [mə'lɪʃəs] *adj* malévolo(a)

malignant [mə'lɪgnənt] *adj* (**a**) *(person)* malvado(a) (**b**) *Med* maligno(a)

mall [mɔːl] *n US* centro *m* comercial

malnutrition [mælnjuː'trɪʃən] *n* desnutrición *f*

malt [mɔːlt] *n* malta *f*

mammal ['mæməl] *n* mamífero *m*

man [mæn] **1** *n (pl* **men**) (**a**) hombre *m*; **old m.** viejo *m*; **young m.** joven *m*; *Fig* **the m. in the street** el hombre de la calle (**b**) *(humanity)* el hombre (**c**) *(husband)* marido *m*; *(partner)* pareja *f* **2** *vt (boat, plane)* tripular; *(post)* servir; **manned flight** vuelo tripulado

manage ['mænɪdʒ] **1** vt (a) (company, household) llevar; (money, affairs, person) manejar (b) (succeed) conseguir; **to m. to do sth** lograr hacer algo **2** vi (cope physically) poder; (esp financially) arreglárselas; **we're managing** vamos tirando

management ['mænɪdʒmənt] n dirección f

manager ['mænɪdʒə(r)] n (a) (of company, bank) director(a) m.f. (head of department) jefe(a) m.f (b) (of pop group etc) mánager m (c) Sport entrenador m

manageress [mænɪdʒə'res] n (of shop, restaurant) encargada f; (of company) directora f

mandate ['mændeɪt] n mandato m

mane [meɪn] n (of horse) crin f; (of lion) melena f

maneuver [mə'nu:vər] n, vt & vi US = manoeuvre

mangle¹ ['mæŋgəl] n (for wringing) rodillo m

mangle² ['mæŋgəl] vt (crush) aplastar; (destroy by cutting) despedazar

mango ['mæŋgəʊ] n (pl **mangoes**) mango m

mania ['meɪnɪə] n manía f

maniac ['meɪnɪæk] n maníaco(a) m.f. **to drive like a m.** Esp conducir or Am manejar como un loco

manicure ['mænɪkjʊə(r)] **1** n manicura f **2** vt **to m. one's nails** hacerse la manicura

manifesto [mænɪ'festəʊ] n programa m electoral

manipulate [mə'nɪpjʊleɪt] vt (a) manipular (b) Fig (accounts etc) falsificar

mankind [mæn'kaɪnd] n la humanidad, el género humano

man-made ['mænmeɪd] adj (lake) artificial; (fibres, fabric) sintético(a)

manner ['mænə(r)] n (a) (way, method) manera f, modo m; **in this m.** de esta manera (b) (way of behaving) forma f de ser (c) Fml (type, class) clase f (d) (etiquette) (**good**) **manners**

buenos modales; **bad manners** falta f de educación

mannerism ['mænərɪzəm] n (gesture) gesto m; (affectation) amaneramiento m

manoeuvre [mə'nu:və(r)] **1** n maniobra f

2 vt maniobrar; (person) manejar

3 vi maniobrar

manpower ['mænpaʊə(r)] n mano f de obra

mansion ['mænʃən] n casa f grande; (in country) casa solariega

manslaughter ['mænslɔ:tə(r)] n homicidio involuntario

mantelpiece ['mæntəlpi:s] n (shelf) repisa f de chimenea; (fireplace) chimenea f

manual ['mænjʊəl] adj & n manual (m)

manufacture [mænjʊ'fæktʃə(r)] **1** vt fabricar **2** n fabricación f

manufacturer [mænjʊ'fæktʃərə(r)] n fabricante mf

manure [mə'njʊə(r)] n abono m, estiércol m

manuscript ['mænjʊskrɪpt] n manuscrito m

many ['menɪ] (**more, most**) **1** adj mucho(a)/muchos(as); **a great m.** muchísimos(as); **as m. ... as ...** tantos(as) ... como ...; **how m. days?** ¿cuántos días?; **too m.** demasiados(as) **2** pron muchos(as)

map [mæp] **1** n (of country) mapa m; (of town, bus route) plano m **2** vt trazar un mapa de

▶ **map out** vt sep (route) trazar en un mapa; Fig (future etc) planear

maple ['meɪpəl] n arce m

marathon ['mærəθən] n maratón m

marble ['mɑ:bəl] **1** n (a) (stone) mármol m (b) (glass ball) canica f **2** adj de mármol

March [mɑ:tʃ] n marzo m

march [mɑ:tʃ] **1** n (a) Mil marcha f (b) (demonstration) manifestación f

2 vi (a) marchar (b) (demonstrate) manifestarse

3 vt Mil hacer marchar

mare [meə(r)] *n* yegua *f*

margarine [mɑːdʒəˈriːn] *n* margarina *f*

margin [ˈmɑːdʒɪn] *n* margen *m*; *Fig* **to win by a narrow m.** ganar por escaso margen

marijuana, marihuana [mærɪˈhwɑːnə] *n* marihuana *f*, marijuana *f*

marinate [ˈmærɪneɪt] *vt* adobar

marine [məˈriːn] **1** *adj* marino(a) **2** *n* marine *mf*, infante *mf* de marina, *Am* fusilero *m* naval

marital [ˈmærɪtəl] *adj* matrimonial; **m. status** estado *m* civil

mark¹ [mɑːk] **1** *n* (**a**) *(left by blow etc)* señal *f*; *(stain)* mancha *f* (**b**) *(sign, token)* señal *f*; *(indication)* indicio *m* (**c**) *(in exam etc)* nota *f* **2** *vt* (**a**) *(stain)* manchar (**b**) *(with tick, cross)* señalar (**c**) *(exam)* corregir; *(student)* dar notas a (**d**) **m. my words** fíjate en lo que te digo
▸ **mark out** *vt sep* (**a**) *(area)* delimitar (**b**) **to m. sb out for** destinar a algn a

mark² [mɑːk] *n (unit of currency)* marco *m*

marked [mɑːkt] *adj (noticeable)* marcado(a), acusado(a)

market [ˈmɑːkɪt] **1** *n* mercado *m*, *CSur* feria *f*, *CAm, Méx* tianguis *m*; **on the m.** en venta; **m. forces** tendencias *fpl* del mercado; **m. price** precio *m* de mercado; **m. research** estudio *m* de mercado **2** *vt (sell)* poner en venta; *(promote)* promocionar

marketing [ˈmɑːkɪtɪŋ] *n* marketing *m*, mercadotecnia *f*

marketplace [ˈmɑːkɪtpleɪs] *n* mercado *m*

marmalade [ˈmɑːməleɪd] *n* mermelada *f (de cítricos)*

marriage [ˈmærɪdʒ] *n (wedding)* boda *f*, *Andes* matrimonio *m*, *RP* casamiento *m*; *(institution, period, relationship)* matrimonio *m*; **m. bureau** agencia *f* matrimonial; **m. certificate** certificado *m* de matrimonio

married [ˈmærɪd] *adj* casado(a); **to be m.** estar *or Am* ser casado(a)

marrow [ˈmærəʊ] *n* (**a**) **(bone) m.**

médula *f* (**b**) *Br* **(vegetable) m.** calabacín *m*

marry [ˈmærɪ] *vt (take in marriage)* casarse con; *(give in marriage)* casar (**to** con); *(unite in marriage)* casar; **to get married** casarse

marsh [mɑːʃ] *n* pantano *m*; **salt m.** marisma *f*

marshal [ˈmɑːʃəl] **1** *n (army officer)* mariscal *m*; *US (police chief)* jefe(a) *m,f* de policía; *(fire chief)* jefe(a) *m,f* de bomberos; *(police officer)* policía *mf*; **2** *vt (pt & pp* **marshalled**, *US* **marshaled**) (**a**) *(people, troops)* dirigir (**b**) *(arguments, thoughts)* poner en orden

martial [ˈmɑːʃəl] *adj* marcial; **m. arts** artes *fpl* marciales

martyr [ˈmɑːtə(r)] **1** *n* mártir *mf* **2** *vt* martirizar

marvel [ˈmɑːvəl] **1** *n* maravilla *f* **2** *vi* **to m. at** maravillarse de

marvellous, *US* **marvelous** [ˈmɑːvələs] *adj* maravilloso(a)

Marxist [ˈmɑːksɪst] *adj & n* marxista *(mf)*

marzipan [ˈmɑːzɪpæn] *n* mazapán *m*

mascara [mæˈskɑːrə] *n* rímel *m*

masculine [ˈmæskjʊlɪn] *adj* masculino(a); *(woman)* hombruna

mash [mæʃ] **1** *n (for animals)* afrecho *m* **2** *vt* **to m. (up)** machacar; **mashed potatoes** puré *m* de *Esp* patatas *or Am* papas

mask [mɑːsk] **1** *n* máscara *f*; *(of doctor, dentist etc)* mascarilla *f* **2** *vt* enmascarar; *Fig (conceal)* ocultar (**from** de)

masochist [ˈmæsəkɪst] *adj & n* masoquista *(mf)*

mason [ˈmeɪsən] *n* (**a**) *(builder)* albañil *m* (**b**) *(freemason)* masón *m*, francmasón *m*

mass¹ [mæs] *n Rel* misa *f*; **to say m.** decir misa

mass² [mæs] **1** *n* (**a**) *(quantity)* masa *f* (**b**) *(large quantity)* montón *m*; *(of people)* multitud *f* (**c**) **the masses** las masas **2** *adj* masivo(a); **m. media** medios *mpl* de comunicación (de masas); **m. production** fabricación *f* en serie

3 *vi (people)* congregarse; *Mil* concentrarse

massacre ['mæsəkə(r)] **1** *n* masacre *f* **2** *vt* masacrar

massage ['mæsɑːʒ, mə'sɑːdʒ] **1** *n* masaje *m* **2** *vt* (**a**) dar masajes a (**b**) *Fig (figures)* amañar

massive ['mæsɪv] *adj* enorme; *(heart attack)* grave

mast [mɑːst] *n* (**a**) *Naut* mástil *m* (**b**) *Rad, TV* torre *f*

master ['mɑːstə(r)] **1** *n* (**a**) *(of dog, servant)* amo *m* (**b**) *Br (teacher)* profesor *m* (**c**) *Univ* **m.'s degree** ≃ máster *m* (**d**) *(expert)* maestro *m* **2** *adj* (**a**) **m. copy** original *m*; **m. key** llave *f* maestra (**b**) *(expert)* maestro(a) **3** *vt* (**a**) *(person, situation)* dominar (**b**) *(subject, skill)* llegar a dominar

mastermind ['mɑːstəmaɪnd] **1** *n* *(person)* cerebro *m* **2** *vt* ser el cerebro de

masterpiece ['mɑːstəpiːs] *n* obra *f* maestra

masturbate ['mæstəbeɪt] *vi* masturbarse

mat¹ [mæt] *n (rug)* alfombrilla *f*; *(doormat)* felpudo *m*; *(rush mat)* estera *f*; *Sport* colchoneta *f*

mat² [mæt] *adj* mate

match¹ [mætʃ] *n* fósforo *m*, *Esp* cerilla *f*, *Am* cerillo *m*

match² [mætʃ] **1** *n* (**a**) *Sport* partido *m*; *(in boxing)* combate *m* (**b**) *Fig* **to meet one's m.** *(equal)* encontrar uno la horma de su zapato **2** *vt* (**a**) *(equal, be the equal of)* igualar (**b**) *(be in harmony with)* armonizar; **they are well matched** *(teams)* van iguales; *(couple)* hacen buena pareja (**c**) *(colours, clothes)* hacer juego con; *(pair of socks, gloves)* ser el compañero de **3** *vi (harmonize)* hacer juego

matchbox ['mætʃbɒks] *n* caja *f* de *Esp* cerillas *or Am* cerillos

matching ['mætʃɪŋ] *adj* que hace juego

matchstick ['mætʃstɪk] *n Esp* cerilla *f*, *Am* cerillo *m*

mate [meɪt] **1** *n* (**a**) *(at school, work)* compañero(a) *m,f*, colega *mf*; *Br, Austr Fam (friend)* amigo(a) *m,f*, *Esp* colega *mf*, *Méx* cuate *mf* (**b**) *Zool (male)* macho *m*; *(female)* hembra *f* (**c**) *(assistant)* ayudante *mf* **2** *vi Zool* aparearse

material [mə'tɪərɪəl] **1** *n* (**a**) *(substance)* materia *f* (**b**) *(cloth)* tejido *m*, tela *f* (**c**) **materials** *(ingredients, equipment)* materiales *mpl* **2** *adj* (**a**) substancial (**b**) *(not spiritual)* material

materialize [mə'tɪərɪəlaɪz] *vi* (**a**) *(hopes)* realizarse; *(plan, idea)* concretarse (**b**) *(show up)* presentarse

maternal [mə'tɜːnəl] *adj* maternal; *(uncle etc)* materno(a)

maternity [mə'tɜːnɪtɪ] *n* maternidad *f*; **m. dress** vestido *m* premamá; **m. hospital** maternidad *f*

math [mæθ] *n US* = **maths**

mathematical [mæθə'mætɪkəl] *adj* matemático(a)

mathematics [mæθə'mætɪks] *n sing* matemáticas *fpl*

maths [mæθs] *n sing Br Fam* matemáticas *fpl*

matinée ['mætɪneɪ] *n Cin* sesión *f* de tarde; *Th* función *f* de tarde

matrimony ['mætrɪmənɪ] *n* matrimonio *m*; *(married life)* vida *f* conyugal

matter ['mætə(r)] **1** *n* (**a**) *(affair, question)* asunto *m*; **as a m. of fact** en realidad (**b**) *(problem)* **what's the m.?** ¿qué pasa? (**c**) **no m. what he does** haga lo que haga; **no m. where you go** dondequiera que vayas; **no m. how** como sea (**d**) *(substance)* materia *f*, sustancia *f* (**e**) *(content)* contenido *m*; *(subject)* tema *m* **2** *vi* importar; **it doesn't m.** no importa, da igual

matter-of-fact ['mætərəv'fækt] *adj* *(person)* práctico(a); *(account)* realista; *(style)* prosaico(a)

mattress ['mætrɪs] *n* colchón *f*

mature [mə'tʃʊə(r)] **1** *adj* maduro(a); *Fin* vencido(a) **2** *vi* madurar; *Fin* vencer **3** *vt* madurar

maximum ['mæksɪməm] **1** n (pl **maxima**) máximo m **2** adj máximo(a)

May [meɪ] n mayo m

may [meɪ] v aux (pt **might**)

> En el inglés hablado, y en el escrito en estilo coloquial, la forma negativa **might not** se transforma en **mightn't**. La forma **might have** se transforma en **might've**

(**a**) *(expressing possibility)* poder, ser posible; **come what m.** pase lo que pase; **he m.** or **might come** puede que venga; **you m.** or **might as well stay** más vale que te quedes (**b**) *(permission)* poder; **m. I?** ¿me permite?; **you m. smoke** pueden fumar (**c**) *(wish)* ojalá (+ subj); **m. you always be happy!** ¡ojalá seas siempre feliz!

maybe ['meɪbi:] adv quizá(s), tal vez

mayonnaise [meɪə'neɪz] n mayonesa f, mahonesa f

mayor [meə(r)] n (man) alcalde m; (woman) alcaldesa f

maze [meɪz] n laberinto m

MBA [embi:'eɪ] n Univ (abbr **Master of Business Administration**) MBA m, máster m en administración de empresas

me [mi:, unstressed mɪ] pers pron (**a**) *(as object)* me; **he gave it to me** me lo dio; **listen to me** escúchame; **she knows me** me conoce (**b**) *(after prep)* mí; **it's for me** es para mí; **with me** conmigo (**c**) *(emphatic)* yo; **it's me** soy yo; **what about ME?** ¿y yo, qué?

meadow ['medəʊ] n prado m, pradera f

meagre, US **meager** ['mi:gə(r)] adj exiguo(a)

meal¹ [mi:l] n (flour) harina f

meal² [mi:l] n (food) comida f

mean¹ [mi:n] vt (pt & pp **meant**) (**a**) *(signify)* significar, querer decir; **what do you m. by that?** ¿qué quieres decir con eso? (**b**) *(intend)* pensar, tener la intención de; **I m. it** (te) lo digo en serio; **she didn't m. to do it** lo hizo sin querer (**c**) *(entail)* suponer (**d**) *(refer to)* referirse a (**e**) *(destine)* destinar (**for** a or para)

mean² [mi:n] adj (**meaner, meanest**) (**a**) *(miserly)* tacaño(a) (**b**) *(unkind)* malo(a); *(petty)* mezquino(a); US (bad-tempered) malhumorado(a); **to be m. to sb** tratar mal a algn (**c**) **it was no m. feat** fue toda una hazaña

mean³ [mi:n] **1** adj (average) medio(a) **2** n (average) promedio m; Math media f

meaning ['mi:nɪŋ] n sentido m, significado m

meaningful ['mi:nɪŋfʊl] adj significativo(a)

meaningless ['mi:nɪŋlɪs] adj sin sentido

means [mi:nz] n (**a**) sing or pl (method) medio m, manera f; **by m. of** por medio de, mediante (**b**) pl (resources, wealth) medios mpl (de vida), recursos mpl (económicos) (**c**) **by all m.!** ¡por supuesto!

meant [ment] pt & pp of **mean¹**

meantime ['mi:ntaɪm] **1** adv mientras tanto **2** n **in the m.** mientras tanto

meanwhile ['mi:nwaɪl] adv mientras tanto

measles ['mi:zəlz] n sing sarampión m

measure ['meʒə(r)] **1** n (**a**) (action, step) medida f (**b**) (ruler) regla f (**c**) **in some m.** hasta cierto punto (**d**) Mus compás m **2** vt (object, area) medir; (person) tomar las medidas de

▶ **measure up** vi **to m. up (to sth)** estar a la altura (de algo)

measurement ['meʒəmənt] n medida f

meat [mi:t] n carne f; Culin **m. pie** empanada f de carne

mechanic [mɪ'kænɪk] n (person) mecánico(a) m,f

mechanical [mɪ'kænɪkəl] adj mecánico(a)

mechanics [mɪ'kænɪks] **1** n sing (science) mecánica f **2** npl (technical aspects) mecanismo m

mechanism ['mekənɪzəm] n mecanismo m

medal ['medəl] n medalla f

medallion [mɪ'dæljən] n medallón m

meddle ['medəl] *vi* entrometerse (**in** en); **to m. with sth** manosear algo

media ['miːdɪə] *npl* medios *mpl* de comunicación; **m. coverage** cobertura periodística

mediate ['miːdɪeɪt] *vi* mediar

mediator ['miːdɪeɪtə(r)] *n* mediador(a) *m,f*

medical ['medɪkəl] **1** *adj (treatment)* médico(a); *(book)* de medicina **2** *n Fam* reconocimiento médico

medication [medɪ'keɪʃən] *n* medicamento *m*, medicina *f*

medicine ['medɪsɪn] *n (science)* medicina *f*; *(drugs etc)* medicamento *m*

medieval [medɪ'iːvəl] *adj* medieval

mediocre [miːdɪ'əʊkə(r)] *adj* mediocre

meditate ['medɪteɪt] *vi* meditar (**on** sobre)

meditation [medɪ'teɪʃən] *n* meditación *f*

Mediterranean [medɪtə'reɪnɪən] **1** *adj* mediterráneo(a) **2** *n* **the M.** el Mediterráneo

medium ['miːdɪəm] **1** *adj (average)* mediano(a); *Br Rad* **m. wave** onda media **2** *n* (**a**) *(pl* **media**) *(means)* medio *m* (**b**) *(pl* **mediums**) *(spiritualist)* médium *mf*

meet [miːt] *(pt & pp* **met**) **1** *vt* (**a**) *(by chance)* encontrar, encontrarse con; *(by arrangement)* reunirse con; *(in formal meeting)* entrevistarse con (**b**) *(get to know)* conocer; **I'd like you to m. my mother** quiero presentarte a mi madre; **the first time I met him** cuando lo conocí (**c**) *(await arrival of)* esperar; *(collect)* ir a buscar (**d**) *(danger)* encontrar; *(opponent)* enfrentarse con (**e**) *(satisfy)* satisfacer; *(obligations)* cumplir con **2** *vi (by chance)* encontrarse; *(by arrangement)* reunirse; *(formal meeting)* entrevistarse; *(get to know each other)* conocerse; *Sport* enfrentarse; *(join)* unirse; *(rivers)* confluir **3** *n (sports event)* encuentro *m*; *(in*

athletics) reunión *f* atlética

▸**meet with** *vt insep (difficulty)* tropezar con; *(loss)* sufrir; *(success)* tener; *esp US (person)* reunirse con

meeting ['miːtɪŋ] *n (chance encounter)* encuentro *m*; *(prearranged)* cita *f*; *(formal)* entrevista *f*; *(of committee etc)* reunión *f*; *(of assembly)* sesión *f*; *(of shareholders)* junta *f*; *(rally)* mitin *m*; *Sport* encuentro *m*; *(of rivers)* confluencia *f*

megaphone ['megəfəʊn] *n* megáfono *m*

mellow ['meləʊ] **1** *adj* maduro(a); *(wine)* añejo(a); *(colour, voice)* suave; *(person)* apacible **2** *vi (fruit)* madurar; *(colour, voice)* suavizarse

melody ['melədɪ] *n* melodía *f*

melon ['melən] *n* melón *m*

melt [melt] **1** *vt (metal)* fundir; *Fig (sb's heart)* ablandar **2** *vi (snow)* derretirse; *(metal)* fundirse; *Fig* ablandarse

▸**melt away** *vi (snow)* derretirse; *Fig (money)* desaparecer; *Fig (confidence)* desvanecerse

▸**melt down** *vt sep (metal)* fundir

member ['membə(r)] *n* miembro *mf*; *(of a society)* socio(a) *m,f*; *(of party, union)* afiliado(a) *m,f*; *US* **M. of Congress** congresista *mf*; *Br* **M. of Parliament** diputado(a) *m,f*

membership ['membəʃɪp] *n (state)* calidad *f* de socio; *(entry)* ingreso *m*; *Pol* afiliación *f*; *(number of members)* número *m* de socios; **m. card** carnet *m* de socio

memento [mə'mentəʊ] *n* recuerdo *m*

memo ['meməʊ] *n (official note)* memorándum *m*; *(personal note)* nota *f*, apunte *m*

memoirs ['memwɑːz] *npl* memorias *fpl*

memorable ['memərəbəl] *adj* memorable

memorial [mɪ'mɔːrɪəl] **1** *adj (plaque etc)* conmemorativo(a) **2** *n* monumento conmemorativo

memorize ['meməraɪz] *vt* memorizar, aprender de memoria

memory ['memərɪ] *n* memoria *f*;

(recollection) recuerdo *m*

men [men] *pl of* **man**

menace ['menɪs] **1** *n (threat)* amenaza *f; (danger)* peligro *m; Fam (person)* pesado(a) *m,f* **2** *vt* amenazar

mend [mend] **1** *vt* reparar, arreglar; *(clothes)* remendar; *(socks etc)* zurcir **2** *vi (ill person)* reponerse **3** *n (patch)* remiendo *m; (darn)* zurcido *m*

menopause ['menəpɔ:z] *n* menopausia *f*

menstruation [menstrʊ'eɪʃən] *n* menstruación *f*

menswear ['menzweə(r)] *n* ropa *f* de caballero *or* hombre

mental ['mentəl] *adj* **(a)** mental; **m. home, m. hospital** hospital psiquiátrico; **m. illness** enfermedad *f* mental **(b)** *Br Fam (mad)* pirado(a), *CSur* rayado(a)

mentality [men'tælɪtɪ] *n* mentalidad *f*

mentally ['mentəlɪ] *adv* mentalmente; **to be m. handicapped** ser un(a) disminuido(a) psíquico(a)

mention ['menʃən] **1** *n* mención *f* **2** *vt* mencionar; **don't m. it!** ¡de nada!

menu ['menju:] *n* **(a)** *(card)* carta *f; (fixed meal)* menú *m*; **today's m.** menú del día **(b)** *Comput* menú *m*

MEP [emi:'pi:] *n (abbr* **Member of the European Parliament)** eurodiputado(a) *m,f*

merchandise ['mɜːtʃəndaɪz] *n* mercancías *fpl*, géneros *mpl*

merchant ['mɜːtʃənt] *n Com, Fin* comerciante *mf; (retailer)* detallista *mf*; **m. bank** banco *m* comercial

merciless ['mɜːsɪlɪs] *adj* despiadado(a)

mercury ['mɜːkjʊrɪ] *n* mercurio *m*

mercy ['mɜːsɪ] *n* misericordia *f*, compasión *f*; **at the m. of** a la merced de; **to have m. on** tener compasión de

mere [mɪə(r)] *adj* mero(a), simple

merely ['mɪəlɪ] *adv* simplemente

merge [mɜːdʒ] **1** *vt (blend)* unir (**with** con); *Com* fusionar **2** *vi* unirse; *(roads)*

empalmar; *Com* fusionarse

merger ['mɜːdʒə(r)] *n Com* fusión *f*

merit ['merɪt] **1** *n (of person)* mérito *m; (of plan etc)* ventaja *f* **2** *vt* merecer, *Am* ameritar

merry ['merɪ] *adj* **(merrier, merriest)** *(happy)* alegre; *Fam (slightly drunk)* alegre, *Esp* piripi; **M. Christmas!** ¡felices Navidades!

merry-go-round ['merɪgəʊraʊnd] *n* tiovivo *m*, carrusel *m*, *RP* calesita *f*

mesh [meʃ] **1** *n Tex* malla *f; Tech* engranaje *m; Fig* red *f* **2** *vt Tech* engranar

mesmerize ['mezməraɪz] *vt* hipnotizar

mess [mes] *n* **(a)** *(confusion)* confusión *f; (disorder)* desorden *m*; **to be in a m.** *(room etc)* estar desordenado(a) **(b)** *(in life, affairs)* lío *m*; **to get into a m.** meterse en un lío **(c)** *(dirt)* suciedad *f* **(d)** *Mil (room)* comedor *m*

▸**mess about, mess around** *Fam* **1** *vt sep* fastidiar **2** *vi (act the fool)* hacer el primo; *(idle)* gandulear; *(kill time)* pasar el rato

▸**mess about with** *vt insep Fam (fiddle with)* manosear; **to m. about with sb** tener un lío con algn

▸**mess up** *vt sep Fam (make untidy)* desordenar; *(dirty)* ensuciar; *(spoil)* estropear

message ['mesɪdʒ] *n (communication)* recado *m; (of story etc)* mensaje *m; Fam* **to get the m.** comprender

messenger ['mesɪndʒə(r)] *n* mensajero(a) *m,f*

messy ['mesɪ] *adj* **(messier, messiest)** *(untidy)* desordenado(a); *(confused)* enredado(a); *(dirty)* sucio(a)

met [met] *pt & pp of* **meet**

metal ['metəl] **1** *n* metal *m* **2** *adj* metálico(a)

metallic [mɪ'tælɪk] *adj* metálico(a); **m. blue** azul metalizado

metaphor ['metəfə(r)] *n* metáfora *f*

meteor ['mi:tɪə(r)] *n* bólido *m*

meter¹ ['mi:tə(r)] *n* contador *m*

meter² ['mi:tər] *n US =* **metre**

method ['meθəd] n método m

methodical [mɪ'θɒdɪkəl] adj metódico(a)

meticulous [mə'tɪkjʊləs] adj meticuloso(a)

metre ['miːtə(r)] n metro m

metric ['metrɪk] adj métrico(a)

Mexican ['meksɪkən] adj & n mejicano(a) (m,f), mexicano(a) (m,f)

Mexico ['meksɪkəʊ] n Méjico, México

mice [maɪs] pl of **mouse**

microchip ['maɪkrəʊtʃɪp] n microplaqueta f, microchip m

microphone ['maɪkrəfəʊn] n micrófono m

microscope ['maɪkrəskəʊp] n microscopio m

microwave ['maɪkrəʊweɪv] n microonda f; **m. (oven)** (horno m) microondas m inv

mid [mɪd] adj **(in) m. afternoon** a media tarde; **(in) m. April** a mediados de abril; **to be in one's m. thirties** tener unos treinta y cinco años

midday 1 n [mɪd'deɪ] mediodía m 2 adj ['mɪddeɪ] de mediodía

middle ['mɪdəl] 1 adj de en medio; **m. age** mediana edad; **the M. Ages** la Edad Media; **the m. class** la clase media 2 n (a) centro m, medio m; **in the m. of** en medio de; **in the m. of winter** en pleno invierno; Fam **in the m. of nowhere** en el quinto pino (b) Fam (waist) cintura f

middle-aged [mɪdəl'eɪdʒd] adj de mediana edad

middle-class [mɪdəl'klɑːs] adj de clase media

midget ['mɪdʒɪt] n enano(a) m,f

midnight ['mɪdnaɪt] n medianoche f

midst [mɪdst] n **in the m. of** en medio de

midway ['mɪdweɪ] adv a medio camino

midweek 1 adv [mɪd'wiːk] entre semana 2 adj ['mɪdwiːk] de entre semana

midwife ['mɪdwaɪf] n comadrona f, partera f

might¹ [maɪt] v aux see **may**

might² [maɪt] n Fml fuerza f, poder m

mighty ['maɪtɪ] 1 adj (**mightier, mightiest**) (strong) fuerte; (powerful) poderoso(a); (great) enorme 2 adv US Fam un montón, Esp cantidad

migraine ['miːgreɪn, 'maɪgreɪn] n jaqueca f

migrant ['maɪgrənt] 1 adj migratorio(a) 2 n (person) emigrante mf; (bird) ave migratoria

migrate [maɪ'greɪt] vi emigrar

mike [maɪk] n Fam micro m

mild [maɪld] adj (person, character) apacible; (climate) templado(a); (punishment) leve; (tobacco, taste) suave

mile [maɪl] n milla f; Fam **miles better** muchísimo mejor

mileage ['maɪlɪdʒ] n kilometraje m

milestone ['maɪlstəʊn] n hito m

militant ['mɪlɪtənt] adj & n militante (mf)

military ['mɪlɪtərɪ] adj militar; **to do one's m. service** hacer el servicio militar

milk [mɪlk] 1 n leche f; **m. chocolate** chocolate m con leche; **m. shake** batido m, Am licuado m 2 vt (a) (cow, goat) ordeñar (b) Fam **they milked him of all his money** le sangraron hasta el último centavo

milky ['mɪlkɪ] adj (**milkier, milkiest**) lechoso(a); (colour) pálido(a); **M. Way** Vía Láctea

mill [mɪl] 1 n (grinder) molino m; (for coffee) molinillo m; (factory) fábrica f; **cotton m.** hilandería f 2 vt moler

▸ **mill about, mill around** vi arremolinarse

milligram(me) ['mɪlɪgræm] n miligramo m

millimetre, US **millimeter** ['mɪlɪmiːtə(r)] n milímetro m

million ['mɪljən] n millón m

millionaire [mɪljə'neə(r)] n millonario(a) m,f

mime [maɪm] 1 n (art) mímica f; (play) pantomima f 2 vt representar con gestos

mimic ['mɪmɪk] **1** *adj & n* mímico(a) *(m,f)* **2** *vt* imitar

mince [mɪns] **1** *n Br (meat) Esp, RP* carne picada, *Am* carne molida; **m. pie** *(containing meat)* = especie de empanada de carne picada; *(containing fruit)* = pastel navideño a base de fruta escarchada, frutos secos y especias **2** *vt Esp, RP* picar, *Am* moler

mincemeat ['mɪnsmiːt] *n (meat)* carne *Esp, RP* picada *or Am* molida; *(fruit)* = relleno a base de fruta escarchada, frutos secos, especias, zumo de limón y grasa animal

mincer ['mɪnsə(r)] *n Esp, RP* picadora *f, Am* moledora *f*

mind [maɪnd] **1** *n* **(a)** *(intellect)* mente *f*; *(brain)* cabeza *f*; **what kind of car do you have in m.?** ¿en qué clase de coche estás pensando?; **to lose one's m.** perder el juicio; **it slipped my m.** lo olvidé por completo **(b)** *(opinion)* **to be in two minds (about sth)** estar indeciso(a) (acerca de algo); **to my m.** a mi parecer **2** *vt* **(a)** *(child)* cuidar; *(house)* vigilar; *(be careful of)* tener cuidado con; **m. the step!** ¡ojo con el escalón!; **m. your own business!** ¡no te metas donde no te llaman! **(b)** *(object to)* tener inconveniente en; **I wouldn't m. a cup of coffee** me vendría bien un café; **never m.** no importa **3** *vi* **(a)** **m. you, he is fifty** ten en cuenta que tiene cincuenta años **(b)** *(object)* importar; **do you m. if I open the window?** ¿le importa que abra la ventana?

minder ['maɪndə(r)] *n* **(a)** *Br Fam (bodyguard)* gorila *m, Méx* guarura *m* **(b) (child** *or* **baby) m.** niñero(a) *mf*

mindless ['maɪndlɪs] *adj (task)* de autómata; *(violence)* injustificable

mine[1] [maɪn] *pos pron (one thing)* (el) mío/(la) mía; *(more than one)*/(los) míos, (las) mías, lo mío; **a friend of m.** un amigo mío; **these gloves are m.** estos guantes son míos; **which is m.?** ¿cuál es el mío?

mine[2] [maɪn] **1** *n* mina *f, Fig* **a m. of information** un pozo de información

2 *vt (coal etc)* extraer; *Mil* minar

mineral ['mɪnərəl] **1** *adj* mineral; **m. water** agua *f* mineral **2** *n* mineral *m*

mingle ['mɪŋgəl] *vi* mezclarse

miniature ['mɪnɪtʃə(r)] **1** *n* miniatura *f* **2** *adj (railway)* en miniatura; *(camera, garden)* diminuto(a)

minimal ['mɪnɪməl] *adj* mínimo(a)

minimum ['mɪnɪməm] **1** *adj* mínimo(a); **m. wage** salario mínimo **2** *n* mínimo *m*

mining ['maɪnɪŋ] **1** *n* minería *f*, explotación *f* de minas; *Mil, Naut* minado *m* **2** *adj* minero(a)

minister ['mɪnɪstə(r)] **1** *n Pol* ministro(a) *m,f*; *Rel* pastor(a) *m,f* **2** *vi* **to m. to sb** atender a algn

ministry ['mɪnɪstrɪ] *n Pol* ministerio *m*; *Rel* sacerdocio *m*

minor ['maɪnə(r)] **1** *adj (lesser)* menor; *(unimportant)* sin importancia; *(role)* secundario(a); *Mus* menor **2** *n Jur* menor *mf* de edad

minority [maɪ'nɒrɪtɪ] *n* minoría *f*; **to be in the m.** ser (la) minoría; *Pol* **m. party** partido minoritario

mint[1] [mɪnt] **1** *n Fin* **the (Royal) M.** ≃ la Casa de la Moneda, *Esp* ≃ la Fábrica Nacional de Moneda y Timbre **2** *vt (coin, words)* acuñar

mint[2] [mɪnt] *n Bot* menta *f*; *(sweet)* pastilla *f* de menta

minus ['maɪnəs] **1** *prep* **5 m. 3** 5 menos 3; **m. 10 degrees** 10 grados bajo cero **2** *adj* negativo(a) **3** *n* **m. (sign)** signo *m* (de) menos

minute[1] ['mɪnɪt] *n* **(a)** minuto *m*; **at the last m.** a última hora; **just a m.** (espera) un momento; **this very m.** ahora mismo **(b) minutes** *(notes)* acta *f*

minute[2] [maɪ'njuːt] *adj (tiny)* diminuto(a); *(examination)* minucioso(a)

miracle ['mɪrəkəl] *n* milagro *m*

miraculous [mɪ'rækjʊləs] *adj* milagroso(a)

mirror ['mɪrə(r)] **1** *n* espejo *m*; *Fig* reflejo *m*; **rear-view m.** retrovisor *m* **2** *vt* reflejar

misbehave [mɪsbɪˈheɪv] *vi* portarse mal

miscalculate [mɪsˈkælkjʊleɪt] *vt & vi* calcular mal

miscarriage [ˈmɪskærɪdʒ] *n Med* aborto *m* (espontáneo); **m. of justice** error *m* judicial

miscellaneous [mɪsɪˈleɪnɪəs] *adj* variado(a); **m. expenses** gastos diversos

mischief [ˈmɪstʃɪf] *n (naughtiness)* travesura *f*; *Fml (evil)* malicia *f*; **to get up to m.** hacer travesuras

mischievous [ˈmɪstʃɪvəs] *adj (naughty)* travieso(a); *(playful)* juguetón(ona); *Fml (wicked)* malicioso(a)

misconduct [mɪsˈkɒndʌkt] *n* mala conducta

misdemeanour, *US* **misdemeanor** [mɪsdɪˈmiːnə(r)] *n (misdeed)* fechoría *f*; *Jur* falta *m*

miser [ˈmaɪzə(r)] *n* avaro(a) *m,f*

miserable [ˈmɪzərəbəl] *adj (sad)* triste; *(unfortunate)* desgraciado(a); *(wretched)* miserable

miserly [ˈmaɪzəlɪ] *adj* avaro(a), tacaño(a)

misery [ˈmɪzərɪ] *n (sadness)* tristeza *f*; *(wretchedness)* desgracia *f*; *(suffering)* sufrimiento *m*; *(poverty)* miseria *f*; *Fam (person)* aguafiestas *mf*

misfit [ˈmɪsfɪt] *n (person)* inadaptado(a) *m,f*

misfortune [mɪsˈfɔːtʃən] *n* desgracia *f*

misgiving [mɪsˈgɪvɪŋ] *n (doubt)* recelo *m*; *(fear)* temor *m*

misguided [mɪsˈgaɪdɪd] *adj* equivocado(a)

mishandle [mɪsˈhændəl] *vt* llevar *or* manejar mal

mishap [ˈmɪshæp] *n* contratiempo *m*

misinform [mɪsɪnˈfɔːm] *vt* informar mal

misinterpret [mɪsɪnˈtɜːprɪt] *vt* interpretar mal

mislay [mɪsˈleɪ] *vt* extraviar

mislead [mɪsˈliːd] *vt* despistar; *(deliberately)* engañar

misleading [mɪsˈliːdɪŋ] *adj (erroneous)* erróneo(a); *(deliberately)* engañoso(a)

mismanagement [mɪsˈmænɪdʒmənt] *n* mala administración *f*

misprint [ˈmɪsprɪnt] *n* errata *f*, error *m* de imprenta

miss¹ [mɪs] *n* señorita *f*

miss² [mɪs] **1** *n (throw etc)* Esp fallo *m*, *Am* falla *f*; *Fam* **to give sth a m.** pasar de algo

2 *vt* **(a)** *(target)* no acertar en; *(shot, penalty)* Esp fallar, *Am* errar **(b)** *(train etc)* perder; *(opportunity)* dejar pasar; **you have missed the point** no has captado la idea **(c)** *(feel lack of)* echar de menos, *esp Am* extrañar; **I m. you** te echo de menos, *esp Am* te extraño **3** *vi (when throwing)* fallar; *(when shooting)* errar

▶ **miss out 1** *vt sep (omit)* saltarse; *(on purpose)* pasar por alto **2** *vt insep* **to m. out on** perderse

missile [ˈmɪsaɪl, *US* ˈmɪsəl] *n Mil* misil *m*; *(object thrown)* proyectil *m*

missing [ˈmɪsɪŋ] *adj (object)* perdido(a); *(person)* desaparecido(a); *(from meeting etc)* ausente; **m. person** desaparecido(a) *m,f*; **three cups are m.** faltan tres tazas

mission [ˈmɪʃən] *n* misión *f*

missionary [ˈmɪʃənərɪ] *n* misionero(a) *m,f*

mist [mɪst] **1** *n* neblina *f*; *(thick)* niebla *f*; *(at sea)* bruma *f* **2** *vi* **to m. over** *or* **up** *(countryside)* cubrirse de neblina; *(window etc)* empañarse

mistake [mɪˈsteɪk] **1** *n* error *m*; **by m.** por equivocación; **I hurt him by m.** le golpeé sin querer; **to make a m.** equivocarse, cometer un error **2** *vt (pt* **mistook**; *pp* **mistaken)** *(meaning)* malentender; **to m. Jack for Bill** confundir a Jack con Bill

mistaken [mɪˈsteɪkən] *adj* equivocado(a), erróneo(a); **you are m.** estás equivocado(a)

mister [ˈmɪstə(r)] *n* señor *m*

mistreat [mɪsˈtriːt] *vt* tratar mal

mistress [ˈmɪstrɪs] *n (of house)* señora

f, ama *f; (lover)* amante *f; Educ (primary school)* maestra *f; (secondary school)* profesora *f*

mistrust [mɪs'trʌst] **1** *n* recelo *m* **2** *vt* desconfiar de

misty ['mɪstɪ] *adj* **(mistier, mistiest)** *(day)* de niebla; *(window etc)* empañado(a)

misunderstand [mɪsʌndə'stænd] *vt & vi* malentender

misunderstanding [mɪsʌndə'stændɪŋ] *n* malentendido *m*; *(disagreement)* desavenencia *f*

misuse 1 *n* [mɪs'juːs] mal uso *m; (of funds)* malversación *f; (of power)* abuso *m* **2** *vt* [mɪs'juːz] emplear mal; *(funds)* malversar; *(power)* abusar de

mitten ['mɪtən] *n* manopla *f; (fingerless)* mitón *m*

mix [mɪks] **1** *n* mezcla *f*
2 *vt* mezclar
3 *vi (blend)* mezclarse **(with** con); *(go well together)* ir bien juntos
▸ **mix up** *vt sep (confuse)* confundir **(with** con); *(papers)* revolver; **to be mixed up in sth** estar involucrado(a) en algo

mixed [mɪkst] *adj (assorted)* surtido(a); *(varied)* variado(a); *(school)* mixto(a); *(feelings)* contradictorio(a)

mixer ['mɪksə(r)] *n* **(a)** *Culin* batidora *f* **(b)** **to be a good m.** *(person)* tener don de gentes

mixture ['mɪkstʃə(r)] *n* mezcla *f*

mix-up ['mɪksʌp] *n Fam* confusión *f,* lío *m*

mm *(abbr* **millimetre(s))** mm

moan [məʊn] **1** *n (groan)* gemido *m,* quejido *m* **2** *vi (groan)* gemir; *(complain)* quejarse **(about** de)

mob [mɒb] **1** *n* multitud *f; (riff-raff)* gentuza *f;* **the m.** el populacho **2** *vt* acosar

mobile ['məʊbaɪl, *US* 'məʊbəl] **1** *adj* móvil; **m. home** caravana *f;* **m. phone** teléfono *m* móvil, *Am* teléfono *m* celular **2** *n* **(a)** *(hanging ornament)* móvil *m* **(b)** *Fam (mobile phone)* móvil *m, Am* celular *m*

mobilize ['məʊbɪlaɪz] *vt* movilizar

mock [mɒk] **1** *adj (sympathy etc)* fingido(a); *(objects)* de imitación
2 *vt (make fun of)* burlarse de
3 *vi* burlarse **(at** de)

mockery ['mɒkərɪ] *n* burla *f*

model ['mɒdəl] **1** *n* modelo *m; (fashion model)* modelo *mf;* **(scale) m.** maqueta *f*
2 *adj (railway)* en miniatura; *(pupil)* ejemplar; *(school)* modelo
3 *vt (clay etc)* modelar; *(clothes)* presentar
4 *vi (make models)* modelar; *(work as model)* trabajar de modelo

modem ['məʊdem] *n Comput* modem *m*

moderate¹ ['mɒdərɪt] **1** *adj* moderado(a); *(reasonable)* razonable; *(average)* regular; *(ability)* mediocre **2** *n Pol* moderado(a) *m,f*

moderate² ['mɒdəreɪt] **1** *vt* moderar **2** *vi* moderarse; *(wind)* calmarse; *(in debate)* arbitrar

moderately ['mɒdərɪtlɪ] *adv* medianamente

moderation [mɒdə'reɪʃən] *n* moderación *f;* **in m.** con moderación

modern ['mɒdən] *adj* moderno(a); *(history)* contemporáneo(a); **m. languages** lenguas modernas

modernize ['mɒdənaɪz] *vt* modernizar

modest ['mɒdɪst] *adj* modesto(a); *(chaste)* púdico(a); *(price)* módico(a); *(success)* discreto(a)

modification [mɒdɪfɪ'keɪʃən] *n* modificación *f*

modify ['mɒdɪfaɪ] *vt* modificar

moist [mɔɪst] *adj* húmedo(a)

moisten ['mɔɪsən] *vt* humedecer

moisture ['mɔɪstʃə(r)] *n* humedad *f*

moisturizer ['mɔɪstʃəraɪzə(r)] *n* crema *f* or leche *f* hidratante

mold¹ [məʊld] *n US* = **mould¹**

mold² [məʊld] *n & vt US* = **mould²**

moldy ['məʊldɪ] *adj US* = **mouldy**

mole¹ [məʊl] *n (beauty spot)* lunar *m*

mole² [məʊl] *n (animal)* topo *m*

molecule ['mɒlɪkjuːl] *n* molécula *f*

molest [mə'lest] *vt* importunar; *(sexually assault)* acosar (sexualmente)

mom [mɒm] *n US Fam* mamá *f*

moment ['məʊmənt] *n* momento *m*; **at the m.** en este momento; **for the m.** de momento; **in a m.** dentro de un momento; **at any m.** de un momento a otro

momentarily ['məʊməntərɪlɪ] *adv* momentáneamente; *US (soon)* dentro de poco

momentum [məʊ'mentəm] *n Phys* momento *m*; *(speed)* velocidad *f*; *Fig* **to gather m.** cobrar velocidad

mommy ['mɒmɪ] *n US Fam* mamá *f*

monarch ['mɒnək] *n* monarca *m*

monarchy ['mɒnəkɪ] *n* monarquía *f*

monastery ['mɒnəstərɪ] *n* monasterio *m*

Monday ['mʌndɪ] *n* lunes *m*

monetary ['mʌnɪtərɪ] *adj* monetario(a)

money ['mʌnɪ] *n* dinero *m*; *(currency)* moneda *f*; **to make m.** ganar dinero

moneylender ['mʌnɪlendə(r)] *n* prestamista *mf*

mongrel ['mʌŋgrəl] *n* perro mestizo

monitor ['mɒnɪtə(r)] **1** *n (screen)* monitor *m*; *Educ* delegado(a) *m,f* **2** *vt (check)* controlar; *(progress, events)* seguir de cerca

monk [mʌŋk] *n* monje *m*

monkey ['mʌŋkɪ] *n* mono *m*; *Br* **m. nut** *Esp* cacahuete *m*, *Am* maní *m*, *CAm, Méx* cacahuate *m*

monologue, *US* **monolog** ['mɒnəlɒg] *n* monólogo *m*

monopolize [mə'nɒpəlaɪz] *vt Fin* monopolizar; *(attention etc)* acaparar

monopoly [mə'nɒpəlɪ] *n* monopolio *m*

monotonous [mə'nɒtənəs] *adj* monótono(a)

monster ['mɒnstə(r)] *n* monstruo *m*

monstrosity [mɒn'strɒsɪtɪ] *n* monstruosidad *f*

monstrous ['mɒnstrəs] *adj (huge)* enorme; *(hideous)* monstruoso(a); *(outrageous)* escandaloso(a)

month [mʌnθ] *n* mes *m*

monthly ['mʌnθlɪ] **1** *adj* mensual; **m. instalment** mensualidad *f* **2** *n (periodical)* revista *f* mensual **3** *adv* mensualmente, cada mes

monument ['mɒnjʊmənt] *n* monumento *m*

moo [mu:] **1** *n* mugido *m* **2** *vi* mugir

mood [mu:d] *n* humor *m*; **to be in a good/bad m.** estar de buen/mal humor; **to be in the m. for (doing) sth** estar de humor para (hacer) algo

moody ['mu:dɪ] *adj* (**moodier, moodiest**) *(changeable)* de humor variable; *(bad-tempered)* malhumorado(a)

moon [mu:n] *n* luna *f*; *Fam* **over the m.** en el séptimo cielo

moonlight ['mu:nlaɪt] *n* luz *f* de la luna

moor¹ [mʊə(r)] *n (heath)* páramo *m*

moor² [mʊə(r)] *vt Naut* amarrar

moose ['mu:s] *n (pl* **moose**) alce *m*

mop [mɒp] **1** *n (for floor)* fregona *f* **2** *vt* fregar

▸ **mop up** *vt sep (liquids)* enjugar; *(enemy forces)* acabar con

mope [məʊp] *vi* **to m. about** *or* **around** andar abatido(a)

moped ['məʊped] *n* ciclomotor *m*, vespa *f*

moral ['mɒrəl] **1** *adj* moral **2** *n* moraleja *f*; **morals** moral *f*, moralidad *f*

morale [mə'rɑ:l] *n* moral *f*, estado *m* de ánimo

morality [mə'rælɪtɪ] *n* moralidad *f*

morbid ['mɔ:bid] *adj Med* mórbido(a); *(mind)* morboso(a)

more [mɔ:(r)] *(comp of* **much, many**) **1** *adj* más; **is there any m. tea?** ¿queda más té?; **I've no m. money** no me queda más dinero; **m. tourists** más turistas **2** *pron* más; **how many m.?** ¿cuántos más?; **many/much m.** muchos(as)/ mucho más; **m. than a hundred** más de cien; **the m. he has, the m. he wants** cuanto más tiene más quiere; **and what is m.** y lo que es más

3 *adv* más; **I won't do it any m.** no lo volveré a hacer; **she doesn't live here any m.** ya no vive aquí; **m. and m. difficult** cada vez más difícil; **m. or less** más o menos

moreover [mɔːˈrəʊvə(r)] *adv* además

morning [ˈmɔːnɪŋ] **1** *n* mañana *f*; *(before dawn)* madrugada *f*; **in the m.** por la mañana; **on Monday mornings** los lunes por la mañana; **tomorrow m.** mañana por la mañana **2** *adj* matutino(a)

Moroccan [məˈrɒkən] *adj & n* marroquí *(mf)*

Morocco [məˈrɒkəʊ] *n* Marruecos

mortal [ˈmɔːtəl] **1** *adj* mortal **2** *n* mortal *mf*

mortgage [ˈmɔːgɪdʒ] **1** *n* hipoteca *f* **2** *vt* hipotecar

mortuary [ˈmɔːtʃʊərɪ] *n* depósito *m* de cadáveres

mosaic [məˈzeɪɪk] *n* mosaico *m*

Moscow [ˈmɒskəʊ, *US* ˈmɒskaʊ] *n* Moscú

Moslem [ˈmɒzləm] *adj & n* musulmán(ana) *(m,f)*

mosque [mɒsk] *n* mezquita *f*

mosquito [mɒsˈkiːtəʊ] *n (pl* **mosquitoes)** mosquito *m, Am* zancudo *m*; **m. net** mosquitero *m*

moss [mɒs] *n* musgo *m*

most [məʊst] **1** *adj (superl of* **much, many)** **(a)** *(greatest in quantity etc)* más; **this house suffered (the) m. damage** esta casa fue la más afectada; **who made (the) m. mistakes?** ¿quién cometió más errores? **(b)** *(the majority of)* la mayoría de, la mayor parte de; **m. people** la mayoría de la gente **2** *pron (greatest part)* la mayor parte; *(greatest number)* lo máximo, lo más; *(the majority of people)* la mayoría; **at the (very) m.** como máximo; **to make the m. of sth** aprovechar algo al máximo **3** *adv (superl of* **much) (a)** más; **the m. intelligent student** el estudiante más inteligente; **what I like m.** lo que más me gusta **(b)** *(very)* muy; **m. of all** sobre todo

mostly [ˈməʊstlɪ] *adv (chiefly)* en su mayor parte; *(generally)* generalmente; *(usually)* normalmente

MOT [eməʊˈtiː] *n Br (abbr* **Ministry of Transport) M. test** inspección técnica de vehículos, *Esp* ≃ ITV, *RP* ≃ VTV *f*

motel [məʊˈtel] *n* motel *m*

moth [mɒθ] *n* mariposa nocturna; **clothes m.** polilla *f*

mother [ˈmʌðə(r)] **1** *n* madre *f*; **M.'s Day** Día *m* de la Madre; **m. tongue** lengua materna **2** *vt* cuidar maternalmente

motherhood [ˈmʌðəhʊd] *n* maternidad *f*

mother-in-law [ˈmʌðərɪnlɔː] *n* suegra *f*

mother-to-be [mʌðətəˈbiː] *n* futura madre

motion [ˈməʊʃən] **1** *n (movement)* movimiento *m*; *(gesture)* ademán *m*; *(proposal)* moción *f* **2** *vt & vi* hacer señas; **to m. (to) sb to do sth** hacer señas a algn para que haga algo

motivate [ˈməʊtɪveɪt] *vt* motivar

motivation [məʊtɪˈveɪʃən] *n* motivación *f*

motive [ˈməʊtɪv] **1** *adj (force)* motriz **2** *n (reason)* motivo *m*; *Jur* móvil *m*

motor [ˈməʊtə(r)] *n (engine)* motor *m*; *Br Fam (car)* coche *m*, *Am* carro *m*, *CSur* auto *m*; **m. racing** carreras *fpl* de coches *or Am* carros *or CSur* autos

motorbike [ˈməʊtəbaɪk] *n Fam* motocicleta *f*, moto *f*

motorboat [ˈməʊtəbəʊt] *n* (lancha) motora *f*

motorcycle [ˈməʊtəsaɪkəl] *n* motocicleta *f*

motorcyclist [ˈməʊtəsaɪklɪst] *n* motociclista *mf*

motorist [ˈməʊtərɪst] *n* automovilista *mf*

motorway [ˈməʊtəweɪ] *n Br* autopista *f*

motto [ˈmɒtəʊ] *n* lema *m*

mould¹ [məʊld] *n (fungus)* moho *m*

mould² [məʊld] **1** *n* molde *m* **2** *vt* moldear; *(clay)* modelar

mouldy ['məʊldɪ] *adj* (**mouldier, mouldiest**) mohoso(a); **to go m.** enmohecerse

mound [maʊnd] *n* montón *m*; *(small hill)* montículo *m*

mount¹ [maʊnt] *n* monte *m*; **M. Everest** (Monte) Everest *m*

▶ **mount up** *vi (accumulate)* acumularse

mount² [maʊnt] **1** *n (horse)* montura *f*; *(support)* soporte *m*, base *f*; *(for photograph)* marco *m*; *(for jewel)* engaste *m*
2 *vt (horse)* subirse *or* montar a; *(campaign)* organizar; *(photograph)* enmarcar; *(jewel)* engastar
3 *vi (go up)* subir; *(get on horse, bike)* montar; *(increase)* subir

mountain ['maʊntɪn] **1** *n* montaña *f*; *Fig (pile)* montón *m* **2** *adj* de montaña, montañés(esa); **m. range** sierra *f*, cordillera *f*

mountaineer [maʊntɪ'nɪə(r)] *n* montañero(a) *m,f*, alpinista *mf*, *Am* andinista *mf*

mountaineering [maʊntɪ'nɪərɪŋ] *n* montañismo *m*, alpinismo *m*, *Am* andinismo *m*

mountainous ['maʊntɪnəs] *adj* montañoso(a)

mourn [mɔːn] *vt & vi* **to m. (for) sb** llorar la muerte de algn

mourning ['mɔːnɪŋ] *n* luto *m*; **in m.** de luto

mouse [maʊs] *n (pl* **mice**) (**a**) *(animal)* ratón *m* (**b**) *Comput Esp* ratón *m*, *Am* mouse *m*

mousse [muːs] *n Culin* mousse *f*; *(for hair)* (**styling**) **m.** espuma *f* (moldeadora)

moustache [mə'stɑːʃ] *n* bigote *m*

mouth 1 *n* [maʊθ] *(pl* **mouths** [maʊðz]) (**a**) boca *f* (**b**) *(of cave etc)* entrada *f*; *(of river)* desembocadura *f* **2** *vt* [maʊð] pronunciar; *(insults)* proferir

mouthful ['maʊθfʊl] *n (of food)* bocado *m*; *(of drink)* sorbo *m*

mouth organ ['maʊθɔːgən] *n* armónica *f*

mouthpiece ['maʊθpiːs] *n Mus*

boquilla *f*; *(of telephone)* micrófono *m*; *Fig (spokesman)* portavoz *m*

mouthwash ['maʊθwɒʃ] *n* elixir *m*, enjuague *m* bucal

movable ['muːvəbəl] *adj* movible, móvil

move [muːv] **1** *n* (**a**) *(movement)* movimiento *m*; **to be on the m.** estar en marcha; **we must make a m.** debemos irnos ya; *Fam* **get a m. on!** ¡date prisa!, *Am* ¡apúrate! (**b**) *(in game)* jugada *f*; *(turn)* turno *m* (**c**) *(course of action)* medida *f* (**d**) *(to new home)* mudanza *f*; *(to new job)* traslado *m*
2 *vt* (**a**) mover; *(furniture etc)* cambiar de sitio; *(transfer)* trasladar; **to m. house** mudarse (de casa) (**b**) *(in game)* mover (**c**) *(motivate)* inducir; *(persuade)* persuadir; **I won't be moved** no me harán cambiar de parecer (**d**) *(affect emotionally)* conmover
3 *vi* (**a**) *(change position)* moverse, desplazarse; *(change house)* mudarse (de casa); *(change post)* trasladarse (**b**) *(train etc)* estar en marcha; **to start moving** ponerse en marcha (**c**) *(leave)* irse, marcharse (**d**) *(in game)* hacer una jugada

▶ **move about 1** *vt sep* cambiar de sitio **2** *vi (be restless)* ir y venir; *(travel)* viajar de un lugar a otro

▶ **move along 1** *vt sep (move forward)* hacer avanzar; *(keep moving)* hacer circular **2** *vi (move forward)* avanzar; *(keep moving)* circular; **m. along!** *(to person on bench)* ¡haz sitio!

▶ **move around** *vt sep & vi* = **move about**

▶ **move away 1** *vt sep* alejar, apartar (**from** de) **2** *vi (move aside)* alejarse, apartarse; *(leave)* irse; *(change house)* mudarse (de casa)

▶ **move back 1** *vt sep (to original place)* volver **2** *vi (withdraw)* retirarse; *(to original place)* volver

▶ **move forward 1** *vt sep* avanzar; *(clock)* adelantar **2** *vi* avanzar, adelantarse

▶ **move in** *vi (into new home)* instalarse

▶ **move off** *vi (go away)* irse,

marcharse; *(train)* salir

▸ **move on** *vi (keep moving)* circular; *(go forward)* avanzar; *(time)* transcurrir

▸ **move out** *vi (leave)* irse, marcharse; *(leave house)* mudarse

▸ **move over** *vi* correrse

▸ **move up** *vi (go up)* subir; *Fig (be promoted)* ser ascendido(a), ascender; *(move along)* correrse, hacer sitio

movement ['mu:vmənt] *n* (a) movimiento *m*; *(gesture)* gesto *m*, ademán *m* (b) *(of goods)* transporte *m*; *(of employees)* traslado *m* (c) *(of goods, capital)* circulación *f*

movie ['mu:vɪ] *n* película *f*; **to go to the movies** ir al cine; **m. star** estrella *f* de cine; *US* **m. theater** cine *m*

moving ['mu:vɪŋ] *adj (that moves)* móvil; *(car etc)* en marcha; *Fig (touching)* conmovedor(a)

mow [məʊ] *vt (pt* **mowed**; *pp* **mown** [məʊn] *or* **mowed**) *(lawn)* cortar; *(corn, wheat)* segar; *Fig* **to m. down** segar

mower ['məʊə(r)] *n* cortacésped *m*

MP [em'pi:] *n Br Pol (abbr* **Member of Parliament)** diputado(a) *m,f*

mph [empi:'eɪtʃ] *(abbr* **miles per hour)** millas *fpl* por hora

Mr ['mɪstə(r)] *(abbr* **Mister)** Sr

Mrs ['mɪsɪz] *(abbr* **Missus)** Sra

Ms [məz] *n* Sra/Srta

> **Ms** es el equivalente femenino de **Mr**, y se utiliza para dirigirse a una mujer sin precisar su estado civil

much [mʌtʃ] *(comp* **more**, *superl* **most**) **1** *adj* mucho(a); **as m. … as** tanto(a) … como; **how m. chocolate?** ¿cuánto chocolate?; **so m.** tanto(a) **2** *adv* mucho; **as m. as** tanto como; **as m. as possible** todo lo posible; **how m.?** ¿cuánto?; **how m. is it?** ¿cuánto es?, ¿cuánto vale?; **m. better** mucho mejor; **m. more** mucho más; **thank you very m.** muchísimas gracias; **too m.** demasiado **3** *pron* mucho; **I thought as m.** lo suponía; **m. of the town was**

destroyed gran parte de la ciudad quedó destruida; **m. remains to be done** queda mucho por hacer

muck [mʌk] *n (dirt)* suciedad *f*; *(mud)* lodo *m*; *Fig* porquería *f*

▸ **muck about**, **muck around** *Br Fam* **1** *vi (idle)* perder el tiempo; *(play the fool)* hacer el tonto **2** *vt sep* **to m. sb about** fastidiar a algn

▸ **muck up** *vt sep (dirty)* ensuciar; *Fig (spoil)* echar a perder

mud [mʌd] *n* lodo *m*, barro *m*; *(thick)* fango *m*; *Fig* **to sling m. at sb** poner a algn por los suelos; **m. flat** marisma *f*

muddle ['mʌdəl] **1** *n* desorden *m*; *Fig (mix-up)* embrollo *m*, lío *m*; **to get into a m.** hacerse un lío **2** *vt* confundir

▸ **muddle through** *vi* arreglárselas, ingeniárselas

▸ **muddle up** *vt sep* confundir

muddy ['mʌdɪ] *adj* (**muddier**, **muddiest**) *(lane)* fangoso(a); *(hands)* cubierto(a) de lodo; *(liquid)* turbio(a)

mudguard ['mʌdgɑ:d] *n Br Esp, RP* guardabarros *m inv, Andes, CAm, Carib* guardafango *m, Méx* salpicadera *f*

muffle ['mʌfəl] *vt (sound)* amortiguar; **to m. (up)** *(person)* abrigar

mug[1] [mʌg] *n (large cup)* tazón *m*; *(beer tankard)* jarra *f*

mug[2] [mʌg] **1** *n Br Fam (gullible person)* bobo(a) *m,f*, primo(a) *m,f, Am* zonzo(a) *m,f*; *(face)* jeta *f* **2** *vt* atracar, asaltar

mugger ['mʌgə(r)] *n* atracador(a) *m,f*

mule [mju:l] *n* mulo(a) *m,f*

multicoloured, *US* **multicolored** ['mʌltɪkʌləd] *adj* multicolor

multimedia [mʌltɪ'mi:dɪə] **1** *n* multimedia *f* **2** *adj* multimedia *inv*

multimillionaire [mʌltɪmɪlɪə'neə(r)] *n* multimillonario(a) *m,f*

multiple ['mʌltɪpəl] **1** *adj* múltiple; **m. sclerosis** esclerosis *f* múltiple **2** *n* múltiplo *m*

multiplication [mʌltɪplɪ'keɪʃən] *n* multiplicación *f*; **m. sign** signo *m* de multiplicar

multiply ['mʌltɪplaɪ] **1** vt multiplicar (**by** por) **2** vi multiplicarse

multistorey [mʌltɪ'stɔːrɪ] adj (building) de varios pisos; **m. car park** estacionamiento m or Esp aparcamiento m or de varias plantas

multitude ['mʌltɪtjuːd] n multitud f, muchedumbre f

mum¹ [mʌm] n Br Fam mamá f

mum² [mʌm] adj **to keep m.** no decir ni pío

mumble ['mʌmbəl] **1** vi hablar entre dientes **2** vt decir entre dientes

mummy¹ ['mʌmɪ] n Br Fam (mother) mamá f

mummy² ['mʌmɪ] n (body) momia f

mumps [mʌmps] n sing paperas fpl

munch [mʌntʃ] vt & vi mascar

municipal [mjuː'nɪsɪpəl] adj municipal

mural ['mjʊərəl] adj & n mural (m)

murder ['mɜːdə(r)] **1** n asesinato m, homicidio m **2** vt asesinar

murderer ['mɜːdərə(r)] n asesino(a) m,f

murky ['mɜːkɪ] adj (murkier, murkiest) oscuro(a); (water) turbio(a)

murmur ['mɜːmə(r)] **1** n murmullo m; (of traffic) ruido m; (complaint) queja f **2** vt & vi murmurar

muscle ['mʌsəl] **1** n músculo m **2** vi Fam **to m. in on sth** entrometerse en asuntos ajenos

muscular ['mʌskjʊlə(r)] adj (pain, tissue) muscular; (person) musculoso(a)

museum [mjuː'zɪəm] n museo m

mushroom ['mʌʃruːm] **1** n hongo m; Esp seta f; (button mushroom) champiñón m **2** vi Fig crecer de la noche a la mañana

music ['mjuːzɪk] n música f; **m. hall** teatro m de variedades; **m. library** fonoteca f

musical ['mjuːzɪkəl] **1** adj musical; **to be m.** estar dotado(a) para la música **2** n musical m

musician [mjuː'zɪʃən] n músico(a) m,f

Muslim ['mʊzlɪm] adj & n musulmán(ana) (m,f)

mussel ['mʌsəl] n mejillón m

must [mʌst] **1** v aux (**a**) (obligation) deber, tener que; **you m. arrive on time** tienes que or debes llegar a la hora (**b**) (probability) deber de; **he m. be ill** debe de estar enfermo **2** n Fam **to be a m.** ser imprescindible

mustache ['mʌstæʃ] n US bigote m

mustard ['mʌstəd] n mostaza f

mustn't ['mʌsənt] = **must not**

musty ['mʌstɪ] adj (mustier, mustiest) que huele a cerrado or a humedad

mute ['mjuːt] **1** adj mudo(a) **2** n (person) mudo(a) m,f; Mus sordina f

mutiny ['mjuːtɪnɪ] **1** n motín m **2** vi amotinarse

mutter ['mʌtə(r)] **1** n (mumble) murmullo m
2 vt murmurar, decir entre dientes
3 vi (angrily) refunfuñar

mutton ['mʌtən] n (carne f de) cordero m

mutual ['mjuːtʃʊəl] adj mutuo(a); (shared) común

mutually ['mjuːtʃʊəlɪ] adv mutuamente

muzzle ['mʌzəl] **1** n (snout) hocico m; (for dog) bozal m; (of gun) boca f **2** vt (dog) abozalar; Fig amordazar

my [maɪ] poss adj mi; **my cousins** mis primos; **my father** mi padre; **one of my friends** un amigo mío; **I washed my hair** me lavé el pelo; **I twisted my ankle** me torcí el tobillo

myself [maɪ'self] pers pron (**a**) (reflexive) me; **I hurt m.** me hice daño (**b**) (alone) yo solo(a); **I was by m.** estaba solo (**c**) (emphatic) yo mismo(a); (**d**) (after prep) mí (mismo(a))

mysterious [mɪ'stɪərɪəs] adj misterioso(a)

mystery ['mɪstərɪ] n misterio m

mystical ['mɪstɪkəl] adj místico(a)

mystify ['mɪstɪfaɪ] vt dejar perplejo(a)

myth [mɪθ] n mito m; **it's a complete m.** es pura fantasía

mythology [mɪ'θɒlədʒɪ] n mitología f

Nn

N, n [en] *n (the letter)* N, n *f*

N *(abbr* **north)** N

nab [næb] *vt Fam (catch)* pescar, *Esp* trincar

nag [næg] **1** *vt* fastidiar, dar la lata a; **to n. sb to do sth** fastidiar *or* dar la lata a algn para que haga algo **2** *vi* quejarse

nail [neɪl] **1** *n* (**a**) *(of finger, toe)* uña *f*; **n. clippers** cortaúñas *m inv*; **n. polish** *or* **varnish** esmalte *m or* laca *f* de uñas (**b**) *(metal)* clavo *m* **2** *vt* (**a**) clavar (**b**) *Fam (catch, trap)* pillar, coger

naïve [naɪˈiːv] *adj* ingenuo(a)

naked [ˈneɪkɪd] *adj* desnudo(a); *(flame)* sin protección; **the n. truth** la pura verdad

name [neɪm] **1** *n* (**a**) nombre *m*; *(surname)* apellido *m*; **what's your n.?** ¿cómo te llamas?; **to call sb names** poner verde a algn (**b**) *(reputation)* reputación *f*; **to make a n. for oneself** hacerse famoso(a) **2** *vt* (**a**) llamar; **to n. sb after** *or US* **for sb** poner a algn el nombre de algn (**b**) *(appoint)* nombrar (**c**) *(refer to)* mencionar

namely [ˈneɪmlɪ] *adv* a saber

nanny [ˈnænɪ] *n* niñera *f*

nap [næp] **1** *n (sleep)* siesta *f*; **to have a n.** echar la *or* una siesta **2** *vi Fig* **to catch sb napping** coger a algn desprevenido(a)

napkin [ˈnæpkɪn] *n* **(table) n.** servilleta *f*

nappy [ˈnæpɪ] *n Br* pañal *m*

narrative [ˈnærətɪv] **1** *n Lit* narrativa *f*; *(story)* narración *f* **2** *adj* narrativo(a)

narrator [nəˈreɪtə(r)] *n* narrador(a) *m,f*

narrow [ˈnærəʊ] **1** *adj* (**a**) *(passage, road etc)* estrecho(a), angosto(a) (**b**)

(restricted) reducido(a); *(sense)* estricto(a); **to have a n. escape** librarse por los pelos **2** *vi* estrecharse

▶ **narrow down 1** *vt sep* reducir, limitar **2** *vi* **to n. down to** reducirse a

narrowly [ˈnærəʊlɪ] *adv* (**a**) *(closely)* de cerca (**b**) *(by a small margin)* por poco

narrow-minded [ˈnærəʊˈmaɪndɪd] *adj* de miras estrechas

nasty [ˈnɑːstɪ] *adj* (**nastier, nastiest**) (**a**) *(person)* desagradable; **to turn n.** *(weather, situation)* ponerse feo(a) (**b**) *(unfriendly)* antipático(a); *(malicious)* malintencionado(a); *Br Fam* **he's a n. piece of work** es un asco de tío (**c**) *(illness, accident)* grave

nation [ˈneɪʃən] *n* nación *f*

national [ˈnæʃnəl] **1** *adj* nacional; **n. anthem** himno *m* nacional; **n. insurance** seguridad *f* social; *Mil* **n. service** servicio *m* militar **2** *n* súbdito(a) *m,f*

nationalist [ˈnæʃnəlɪst] *adj & n* nacionalista *(mf)*

nationality [næʃəˈnælɪtɪ] *n* nacionalidad *f*

nationalize [ˈnæʃnəlaɪz] *vt* nacionalizar

nationwide [ˈneɪʃənwaɪd] *adj* de ámbito nacional

native [ˈneɪtɪv] **1** *adj* (**a**) *(place)* natal; **n. land** patria *f*; **n. language** lengua materna (**b**) *(plant, animal)* originario(a) *(to* de) **2** *n* nativo(a) *m,f*, natural *mf*; *(original inhabitant)* indígena *mf*

NATO, Nato [ˈneɪtəʊ] *n (abbr* **North Atlantic Treaty Organization)** OTAN *f*

natural [ˈnætʃərəl] **1** *adj* (**a**) natural (**b**) *(normal)* normal; **it's only n. that ...** es lógico que ... (**c**) *(born)* nato(a) **2**

n (**a**) **she's a n. for the job** es la persona ideal para el trabajo (**b**) *Mus* becuadro *m*

naturally ['nætʃərəlɪ] *adv* (**a**) *(of course)* naturalmente (**b**) *(by nature)* por naturaleza (**c**) *(in a relaxed manner)* con naturalidad

nature ['neɪtʃə(r)] *n* (**a**) naturaleza *f* (**b**) *(character)* naturaleza *f*, carácter *m*; **by n.** por naturaleza; **human n.** la naturaleza humana (**c**) *(sort, kind)* índole *f*, clase *f*

naught [nɔːt] *n US* = **nought**

naughty ['nɔːtɪ] *adj* (**naughtier, naughtiest**) (**a**) *(child)* travieso(a) (**b**) *(joke, story)* atrevido(a), picante

nausea ['nɔːzɪə] *n Med (sickness)* náusea *f*

nauseating ['nɔːzɪeɪtɪŋ] *adj* nauseabundo(a)

nautical ['nɔːtɪkəl] *adj* náutico(a); **n. mile** milla marítima

naval ['neɪvəl] *adj* naval; **n. officer** oficial *mf* de marina; **n. power** potencia marítima *or* naval

navel ['neɪvəl] *n Anat* ombligo *m*

navigate ['nævɪgeɪt] **1** *vt (river)* navegar por; *Naut (ship)* gobernar **2** *vi* navegar; *(in driving)* indicar la dirección

navy ['neɪvɪ] *n* marina *f*; **n. blue** azul marino

Nazi ['nɑːtsɪ] *adj & n* nazi *(mf)*

NB, nb [en'biː] *(abbr* **nota bene**) N.B.

near [nɪə(r)] **1** *adj (in space)* cercano(a); *(in time)* próximo(a); **in the n. future** en un futuro próximo
2 *adv (in space)* cerca; **that's n. enough** (ya) vale, está bien
3 *prep* cerca de; **n. the end of the film** hacia el final de la película
4 *vt* acercarse a

nearby [nɪə'baɪ] **1** *adj* cercano(a) **2** *adv* cerca

nearly ['nɪəlɪ] *adv* casi; **we haven't n. enough** no alcanza ni con mucho

neat [niːt] *adj* (**a**) *(room, habits etc)* ordenado(a); *(handwriting)* claro(a); *(appearance)* pulcro(a) (**b**) *(idea)* ingenioso(a) (**c**) *(whisky etc)* solo(a) (**d**) *US Fam (fine)* chulísimo(a)

neatly ['niːtlɪ] *adv* (**a**) *(carefully)* cuidadosamente (**b**) *(cleverly)* hábilmente

necessarily [nesɪ'serəlɪ] *adv* necesariamente, por fuerza

necessary ['nesɪsərɪ] **1** *adj* (**a**) *(essential)* necesario(a); **if n.** si es preciso (**b**) *(unavoidable)* inevitable **2** *n* **the n.** lo necesario

necessity [nɪ'sesɪtɪ] *n* (**a**) necesidad *f*; **out of n.** por necesidad (**b**) **necessities** *(articles)* necesidades *fpl*

neck [nek] *n* cuello *m*; *(of animal)* pescuezo *m*; **to stick one's n. out** arriesgarse

necklace ['neklɪs] *n* collar *m*

necktie ['nektaɪ] *n US* corbata *f*

nectarine ['nektəriːn] *n* nectarina *f*

need [niːd] **1** *n* (**a**) necesidad *f*; **there's no n. for you to do that** no hace falta que hagas eso (**b**) *(poverty)* indigencia *f*; **to be in n.** estar necesitado
2 *vt* (**a**) necesitar; **I n. to see him** tengo que verle; *Ironic* **that's all I n.** sólo me faltaba eso (**b**) *(action, solution etc)* requerir, exigir
3 *v aux* tener que, deber; **n. he go?** ¿tiene que ir?; **you needn't wait** no hace falta que esperes

> Cuando se emplea como verbo modal sólo existe una forma, y los auxiliares **do/does** no se usan: **he need only worry about himself**; **need she go?**; **it needn't matter**

needle ['niːdəl] *n* (**a**) *(for sewing, knitting)* aguja *f* (**b**) *Bot* hoja *f*

needlessly ['niːdlɪslɪ] *adv* innecesariamente

needlework ['niːdəlwɜːk] *n (sewing)* costura *f*; *(embroidery)* bordado *m*

needy ['niːdɪ] *adj* (**needier, neediest**) necesitado(a)

negative ['negətɪv] **1** *adj* negativo(a) **2** *n* (**a**) *Ling* negación *f* (**b**) *Phot* negativo *m*

neglect [nɪ'glekt] **1** *vt* (**a**) *(child, duty etc)* descuidar, desatender (**b**) **to n. to do sth** *(omit to do)* no hacer algo **2** *n* dejadez *f*

negligent ['neglɪdʒənt] *adj* negligente, descuidado(a)

negligible ['neglɪdʒɪbəl] *adj* insignificante

negotiate [nɪ'gəʊʃɪeɪt] **1** *vt* (a) *(contract)* negociar (b) *Fig (obstacle)* salvar, franquear **2** *vi* negociar

negotiation [nɪgəʊʃɪ'eɪʃən] *n* negociación *f*

neigh [neɪ] **1** *n* relincho *m* **2** *vi* relinchar

neighbour, *US* **neighbor** ['neɪbə(r)] *n* vecino(a) *m,f*; *Rel* prójimo *m*

neighbourhood, *US* **neighborhood** ['neɪbəhʊd] *n (district)* vecindad *f*, barrio *m*; *(people)* vecindario *m*

neither ['naɪðə(r), 'niːðə(r)] **1** *adj & pron* ninguno de los dos/ninguna de las dos **2** *adv & conj* (a) ni; **n. ... nor** ni ... ni (b) tampoco; **she was not there and n. was her sister** ella no estaba, ni su hermana tampoco

neon ['niːɒn] *n* neón *m*; **n. light** luz *f* de neón

nephew ['nefjuː] *n* sobrino *m*

nerve [nɜːv] *n* (a) *Anat* nervio *m*; **to get on sb's nerves** poner los nervios de punta a algn (b) *(courage)* valor *m* (c) *Fam (cheek)* cara *f*, descaro *m*; **what a n.!** ¡qué cara!

nerve-racking ['nɜːvrækɪŋ] *adj* crispante, exasperante

nervous ['nɜːvəs] *adj* (a) nervioso(a); **n. breakdown** depresión nerviosa (b) *(afraid)* miedoso(a) (c) *(timid)* tímido(a)

nest [nest] **1** *n Orn* nido *m*; *(hen's)* nidal *m*; *(animal's)* madriguera *f*; *Fig* **n. egg** ahorros *mpl* **2** *vi (birds)* anidar

nestle ['nesəl] **1** *vt* recostar **2** *vi (settle comfortably)* acomodarse

net¹ [net] *n* red *f*; *Br* **n. curtains** visillos *mpl*

net² [net] **1** *adj* neto(a); **n. weight** peso neto **2** *vt (earn)* ganar neto

Netherlands ['neðələndz] *npl* **the N.** los Países Bajos

nettle ['netəl] **1** *n Bot* ortiga *f* **2** *vt Fam* irritar

network ['netwɜːk] **1** *n* red *f* **2** *vi (establish contacts)* establecer contactos

neurotic [njʊ'rɒtɪk] *adj & n* neurótico(a) *(m,f)*

neuter ['njuːtə(r)] **1** *adj* neutro(a) **2** *n Ling* neutro *m* **3** *vt (geld)* castrar

neutral ['njuːtrəl] **1** *adj* neutro(a); *Pol* **to remain n.** permanecer neutral **2** *n Aut* punto muerto

neutralize ['njuːtrəlaɪz] *vt* neutralizar

never ['nevə(r)] *adv* nunca, jamás; **n. again** nunca (ja)más; *Fam* **n. mind** da igual, no importa

never-ending ['nevər'endɪŋ] *adj* sin fin, interminable

nevertheless [nevəðə'les] *adv* sin embargo, no obstante

new [njuː] *adj* nuevo(a); **as good as n.** como nuevo; **n. baby** recién nacido *m*; **n. moon** luna nueva; **N. Year** Año Nuevo; **N. Year's Eve** Nochevieja *f*

newborn ['njuːbɔːn] *adj* recién nacido(a)

newcomer ['njuːkʌmə(r)] *n* recién llegado(a) *m,f*; *(to job etc)* nuevo(a) *m,f*

newly ['njuːlɪ] *adv* recién, recientemente

newlywed ['njuːlɪwed] *n* recién casado(a) *m,f*

news [njuːz] *n sing* noticias *fpl*; *(TV programme)* telediario *m*, *Am* noticiero *m*, *Andes, RP* noticioso *m*; **a piece of n.** una noticia; **n. agency** agencia *f* de información; *US* **n. in brief** avance informativo; **n. bulletin** boletín informativo; **n. summary** avance informativo;

newsagent ['njuːzeɪdʒənt] *n Br* vendedor(a) *m,f* de periódicos

newsflash ['njuːzflæʃ] *n* noticia *f* de última hora

newsletter ['njuːzletə(r)] *n* hoja informativa

newspaper ['njuːzpeɪpə(r)] *n* periódico *m*, diario *m*

newsreader ['njuːzriːdə(r)] *n TV, Rad* presentador(a) *m,f* de los informativos

next [nekst] **1** *adj* (**a**) *(in place)* de al lado (**b**) *(in time)* próximo(a); **the n. day** el día siguiente; **n. Friday** el viernes que viene; **n. time** la próxima vez; **the week after n.** dentro de dos semanas (**c**) *(in order)* siguiente, próximo(a); **n. of kin** pariente *m* más cercano
2 *adv* después, luego; **what shall we do n.?** ¿qué hacemos ahora?
3 *prep* **n. to** al lado de, junto a; **n. to nothing** casi nada

NHS [eneit∫'es] *n Br (abbr* **National Health Service**) = la sanidad pública británica

nibble ['nɪbəl] *vt & vi* mordisquear

nice [naɪs] *adj* (**a**) *(person)* simpático(a), *Esp* majo(a), *RP* dulce; *(thing)* agradable; **n. and cool** fresquito(a); **to smell/taste n.** oler/saber bien (**b**) *(nice-looking)* bonito(a), *Am* lindo(a) (**c**) *Ironic* menudo(a)

nicely ['naɪslɪ] *adv* muy bien

niche [niː∫] *n* (**a**) hornacina *f*, nicho *m* (**b**) *Fig* hueco *m*

nick [nɪk] **1** *n* (**a**) *(notch)* muesca *f*; *(cut)* herida pequeña; *Fam* **in the n. of time** en el momento preciso (**b**) *Br Fam (prison)* cárcel *f*, *Esp* trullo *m*, *Andes*, *RP* cana *f*, *Méx* bote *m* **2** *vt Br Fam* (**a**) *(steal)* afanar, *Esp* mangar (**b**) *(arrest)* detener, *Esp* trincar

nickel ['nɪkəl] *n* (**a**) níquel *m* (**b**) *US* moneda *f* de 5 centavos

nickname ['nɪkneɪm] **1** *n* apodo *m* **2** *vt* apodar

niece [niːs] *n* sobrina *f*

night [naɪt] *n* noche *f*; **at n.** de noche; **at twelve o'clock at n.** a las doce de la noche; **last n.** anoche; **n. life** vida nocturna; **n. school** escuela nocturna; **n. shift** turno *m* de noche; *US* **n. stand** *or* **table** mesita *f* or mesilla *f* de noche

nightclub ['naɪtklʌb] *n* sala *f* de fiestas; *(disco)* discoteca *f*

nightdress ['naɪtdres] *n* camisón *m*

nightfall ['naɪtfɔːl] *n* anochecer *m*

nightgown ['naɪtgaʊn] *n* camisón *m*

nightie ['naɪtɪ] *n Fam* camisón *m*

nightingale ['naɪtɪŋgeɪl] *n* ruiseñor *m*

nightmare ['naɪtmeə(r)] *n* pesadilla *f*

night-time ['naɪttaɪm] *n* noche *f*; **at n.** por la noche

nil [nɪl] *n* nada *f*; *Sport* cero *m*; *Br* **two n.** dos a cero

Nile [naɪl] *n* **the N.** el Nilo

nimble ['nɪmbəl] *adj* ágil, rápido(a)

nine [naɪn] *adj & n* nueve *(m inv)*

nineteen [naɪn'tiːn] *adj & n* diecinueve *(m inv)*

ninety ['naɪntɪ] *adj & n* noventa *(m inv)*

ninth [naɪnθ] **1** *adj & n* noveno(a) *(m,f)* **2** *n (fraction)* noveno *m*

nip [nɪp] **1** *vt* (**a**) *(pinch)* pellizcar (**b**) *(bite)* morder; **to n. sth in the bud** cortar algo de raíz **2** *n* (**a**) *(pinch)* pellizco *m* (**b**) *(bite)* mordisco *m*

nipple ['nɪpəl] *n* (**a**) *Anat (female)* pezón *m*; *(male)* tetilla *f* (**b**) *US (on baby's bottle)* tetilla *f*, tetina *f*

nitrogen ['naɪtrədʒən] *n Chem* nitrógeno *m*

no [nəʊ] **1** *adv* no; **come here! – no!** ¡ven aquí! – ¡no!; **no longer** ya no; **no less than** no menos de
2 *adj* ninguno(a); **she has no children** no tiene hijos; **I have no idea** no tengo (ni) idea; **it's no good** *or* **use** no vale la pena; *Aut* **no parking** *(sign)* prohibido aparcar; *Fam* **no way!** ¡ni hablar!
3 *n* no *m*; **to say no** decir que no

nobility [nəʊ'bɪlɪtɪ] *n* nobleza *f*

noble ['nəʊbəl] *adj* noble

nobody ['nəʊbədɪ] **1** *pron* nadie; **there was n. there** no había nadie; **n. else** nadie más **2** *n* nadie *m*; **he's a n.** es un don nadie

nod [nɒd] **1** *n (of greeting)* saludo *m (con la cabeza)*; *(of agreement)* señal *f* de asentimiento
2 *vi (greet)* saludar con la cabeza; *(agree)* asentir con la cabeza
3 *vt* **to n. one's head** inclinar la cabeza
▸ **nod off** *vi* dormirse

noise [nɔɪz] *n* ruido *m*; **to make a n.** hacer ruido

noisy ['nɔɪzɪ] *adj* (**noisier, noisiest**) ruidoso(a)

nominal ['nɒmɪnəl] *adj* nominal; *(payment, rent)* simbólico(a)

nominate ['nɒmɪneɪt] *vt* (**a**) *(propose)* designar, proponer (**b**) *(appoint)* nombrar

nomination [nɒmɪ'neɪʃən] *n* (**a**) *(proposal)* propuesta *f* (**b**) *(appointment)* nombramiento *m*

nondescript [*Br* 'nɒndɪskrɪpt, *US* nɒndɪ'skrɪpt] *adj* indescriptible; *(uninteresting)* soso(a)

none [nʌn] **1** *pron* ninguno(a); **I know n. of them** no conozco a ninguno de ellos; **n. at all** nada en absoluto; **n. other than …** nada menos que … **2** *adv* de ningún modo; **she's n. the worse for it** no se ha visto afectada *or* perjudicada por ello; **n. too soon** a buena hora

nonentity [nɒ'nentɪtɪ] *n (person)* cero *m* a la izquierda

nonetheless [nʌnðə'les] *adv* no obstante, sin embargo

nonexistent [nɒnɪg'zɪstənt] *adj* inexistente

nonfiction [nɒn'fɪkʃən] *n* no ficción *f*

nonsense ['nɒnsəns] *n* tonterías *fpl*, disparates *mpl*; **that's n.** eso es absurdo

nonsmoker [nɒn'sməʊkə(r)] *n* no fumador(a) *m,f*, persona *f* que no fuma

nonstop [nɒn'stɒp] **1** *adj* sin parar; *(train)* directo(a) **2** *adv* sin parar

noodles ['nuːdəlz] *npl Culin* fideos *mpl*

noon [nuːn] *n* mediodía *m*; **at n.** a mediodía

no one ['nəʊwʌn] *pron* nadie; **n. came** no vino nadie

noose [nuːs] *n* lazo *m*; *(hangman's)* soga *f*

nor [nɔː(r)] *conj* ni, ni tampoco; **neither … n.** ni … ni; **neither you n. I** ni tú ni yo; **n. do I** (ni) yo tampoco

norm [nɔːm] *n* norma *f*

normal ['nɔːməl] *adj* normal

normally ['nɔːməlɪ] *adv* normalmente

north [nɔːθ] **1** *n* norte *m*; **the N.** el norte; **N. America** América del Norte, Norteamérica; **N. Korea** Corea del Norte; **N. Pole** Polo *m* Norte **2** *adv* hacia el norte, al norte **3** *adj* del norte; **n. wind** viento *m* del norte

northeast [nɔːθ'iːst] *n* nor(d)este *m*

northerly ['nɔːðəlɪ] *adj* norte, del norte

northern ['nɔːðən] *adj* del norte, septentrional; **n. hemisphere** hemisferio *m* norte; **N. Ireland** Irlanda del Norte

northerner ['nɔːðənə(r)] *n* norteño(a) *m,f*

northward ['nɔːθwəd] *adj & adv* hacia el norte

northwest [nɔːθ'west] *n* noroeste *m*

Norway ['nɔːweɪ] *n* Noruega

Norwegian [nɔː'wiːdʒən] **1** *adj* noruego(a) **2** *n* (**a**) *(person)* noruego(a) *m,f* (**b**) *(language)* noruego *m*

nose [nəʊz] *n* (**a**) nariz *f* (**b**) *(sense of smell)* olfato *m* (**c**) *(of car, plane)* morro *m*

▶**nose about, nose around** *vi* curiosear

nosebleed ['nəʊzbliːd] *n* hemorragia *f* nasal

no-smoking [nəʊ'sməʊkɪŋ] *adj (carriage, area)* de *or* para no fumadores

nostalgic [nɒ'stældʒɪk] *adj* nostálgico(a)

nostril ['nɒstrɪl] *n Anat* orificio *m* nasal

nosy ['nəʊzɪ] *adj* (**nosier, nosiest**) *Fam* entrometido(a)

not [nɒt] *adv* no; **he's n. in today** hoy no está; **n. at all** en absoluto; **thank you – n. at all** gracias – no hay de qué; **n. too well** bastante mal; *Fam* **n. likely!** ¡ni hablar!

En el inglés hablado, y en el escrito en estilo coloquial, **not** se contrae después de verbos modales y auxiliares

notable ['nəʊtəbəl] *adj* notable

notably ['nəʊtəblɪ] *adv* notablemente

notch [nɒtʃ] *n* muesca *f*; *(cut)* corte *m*

▸ **notch up** *vt sep Fig* **to n. up a victory** apuntarse una victoria

note [nəʊt] **1** *n* (**a**) *Mus* nota *f* (**b**) *(on paper)* nota *f* (**c**) **to take n. of** *(notice)* prestar atención a (**d**) *esp Br (banknote)* billete *m* (de banco) (**e**) **notes** apuntes *mpl*; **to take n.** tomar apuntes **2** *vt* (**a**) *(write down)* apuntar, anotar (**b**) *(notice)* notar, fijarse en

notebook ['nəʊtbʊk] *n* cuaderno *m*, libreta *f*; *Comput Esp* ordenador *m or Am* computadora *f* portátil

noted ['nəʊtɪd] *adj* notable, célebre

notepad ['nəʊtpæd] *n* bloc *m* de notas

notepaper ['nəʊtpeɪpə(r)] *n* papel *m* de carta

nothing ['nʌθɪŋ] **1** *n* nada; **I saw n.** no vi nada; **for n.** *(free of charge)* gratis; **it's n.** no es nada; **it's n. to do with you** no tiene nada que ver contigo; **n. else** nada más; *Fam* **n. much** poca cosa **2** *adv* **she looks n. like her sister** no se parece en nada a su hermana

notice ['nəʊtɪs] **1** *n* (**a**) *(warning)* aviso *m*; **he gave a month's n.** presentó la dimisión con un mes de antelación; **at short n.** con poca antelación; **until further n.** hasta nuevo aviso; **without n.** sin previo aviso

(**b**) *(attention)* atención *f*; **to take no n. of sth** no hacer caso de algo, **to take n. of sth** prestar atención a algo

(**c**) *(in newspaper etc)* anuncio *m*

(**d**) *(sign)* letrero *m*, aviso *m*

2 *vt* darse cuenta de, notar

noticeable ['nəʊtɪsəbəl] *adj* que se nota, evidente

noticeboard ['nəʊtɪsbɔːd] *n Br* tablón *m* de anuncios

notification [nəʊtɪfɪ'keɪʃən] *n* aviso *m*

notify ['nəʊtɪfaɪ] *vt* avisar

notion ['nəʊʃən] *n* (**a**) idea *f*, concepto *m* (**b**) *(whim)* capricho *m*

notorious [nəʊ'tɔːrɪəs] *adj Pej* tristemente célebre

nought [nɔːt] *n* cero *m*

noun [naʊn] *n* nombre *m*, sustantivo *m*

nourishment ['nʌrɪʃmənt] *n* alimentación *f*, nutrición *f*

novel[1] ['nɒvəl] *n* novela *f*

novel[2] ['nɒvəl] *adj* original, novedoso(a)

novelist ['nɒvəlɪst] *n* novelista *mf*

novelty ['nɒvəltɪ] *n* novedad *f*

November [nəʊ'vembə(r)] *n* noviembre *m*

novice ['nɒvɪs] *n* (**a**) *(beginner)* novato(a) *m,f*, principiante *mf* (**b**) *Rel* novicio(a) *m,f*

now [naʊ] **1** *adv* (**a**) *(at this moment)* ahora; **just n., right n.** ahora mismo; **from n. on** de ahora en adelante; **n. and then, n. and again** de vez en cuando (**b**) *(for events in past)* entonces (**c**) *(at present, these days)* actualmente, hoy (en) día (**d**) *(not related to time)* **n. (then)** ahora bien; **n., n.!** ¡vamos!, ¡ya está bien!

2 *conj* **n. (that)** ahora que, ya que

3 *n* **until n.** hasta ahora; **he'll be home by n.** ya habrá llegado a casa

nowadays ['naʊədeɪz] *adv* hoy (en) día, actualmente

nowhere ['nəʊweə(r)] *adv* en ninguna parte; **that will get you n.** eso no te servirá de nada; **it's n. near ready** no está preparado, ni mucho menos

nozzle ['nɒzəl] *n* boca *f*, boquilla *f*

nuance ['njuːɑːns] *n* matiz *m*

nuclear ['njuːklɪə(r)] *adj* nuclear; **n. arms** armas *fpl* nucleares; **n. power** energía *f* nuclear; **n. power station** central *f* nuclear

nucleus ['njuːklɪəs] *(pl* **nuclei** ['njuːklɪaɪ]*) n* núcleo *m*

nude [njuːd] **1** *adj* desnudo(a) **2** *n Art, Phot* desnudo *m*; **in the n.** al desnudo

nudge [nʌdʒ] **1** *vt* dar un codazo a **2** *n* codazo *m*

nudist ['njuːdɪst] *adj & n* nudista *(mf)*

nuisance ['njuːsəns] *n* (**a**) molestia *f*, pesadez *f*; **what a n.!** ¡qué lata! (**b**) (person) pesado(a) m,f

null [nʌl] adj nulo(a); **n. and void** nulo y sin valor

numb [nʌm] **1** adj (without feeling) entumecido(a); Fig paralizado(a); **n. with fear** paralizado de miedo **2** vt (with cold) entumecer (de frío); (with anaesthetic) adormecer

number ['nʌmbə(r)] **1** n (**a**) número m; Tel **have you got my n.?** ¿tienes mi (número de) teléfono? (**b**) (quantity) **a n. of people** varias personas (**c**) Br (of car) matrícula f; **n. plate** (placa f de la) matrícula f **2** vt (**a**) (put a number on) numerar (**b**) (count) contar

numeral ['nju:mərəl] n número m, cifra f

numerous ['nju:mərəs] adj numeroso(a)

nun [nʌn] n monja f

nurse [nɜːs] **1** n enfermero(a) m,f **2** vt (**a**) (look after) cuidar, atender (**b**) (baby) acunar (**c**) (suckle) amamantar (**d**) Fig (grudge etc) guardar

nursery ['nɜːsərɪ] n (**a**) (institution) guardería f; **n. school** jardín m de infancia (**b**) (in house) cuarto m de los niños; **n. rhyme** poema m infantil (**c**) (garden centre) vivero m

nursing ['nɜːsɪŋ] n **n. home** Br (where children are born) maternidad f; (for old people, war veterans) residencia f

nut [nʌt] n (**a**) (fruit) fruto seco (**b**) Fam (head) coco m (**c**) Fam (mad person) chiflado(a) m,f, Esp chalado(a) m,f (**d**) Tech tuerca f

nutcase ['nʌtkeɪs] n Fam chiflado(a) m,f, Esp chalado(a) m,f

nutcracker ['nʌtkrækə(r)] n cascanueces m inv

nutmeg ['nʌtmeg] n nuez moscada

nutrition [nju:'trɪʃən] n nutrición f

nutritious [nju:'trɪʃəs] adj nutritivo(a), alimenticio(a)

nuts [nʌts] adj Fam chiflado(a), Esp majara; **to be n.** estar chiflado(a) or majara

nutshell ['nʌtʃel] n cáscara f; Fig **in a n.** en pocas palabras

nylon ['naɪlɒn] **1** n (**a**) nilón m, nailon m (**b**) **nylons** medias fpl de nilón **2** adj de nilón

Oo

O, o [əʊ] *n* (**a**) *(the letter)* O, o *f* (**b**) *Math, Tel* cero *m*

oaf [əʊf] *n* tarugo *m*, zote *m*

oak [əʊk] *n* roble *m*

OAP [əʊeɪ'piː] *n Br* (*abbr* **old age pensioner**) pensionista *mf*, jubilado(a) *m,f*

oar [ɔː(r)] *n* remo *m*

oasis [əʊ'eɪsɪs] *n* (*pl* **oases** [əʊ'eɪsiːz]) oasis *m inv*

oat [əʊt] *n* avena *f*; **rolled oats** copos *mpl* de avena

oath [əʊθ] *n* (*pl* **oaths** [əʊðz]) (**a**) *Jur* juramento *m*; **to take an o.** prestar juramento; (**b**) *(swearword)* palabrota *f*

obedience [ə'biːdɪəns] *n* obediencia *f*

obedient [ə'biːdɪənt] *adj* obediente

obese [əʊ'biːs] *adj* obeso(a)

obey [ə'beɪ] *vt* obedecer; *(law)* cumplir con

obituary [ə'bɪtjʊərɪ] *n* necrología *f*

object[1] ['ɒbdʒɪkt] *n* (**a**) *(thing)* objeto *m* (**b**) *(aim, purpose)* fin *m*, objetivo *m* (**c**) *(obstacle)* inconveniente *m* (**d**) *Ling* complemento *m*

object[2] [əb'dʒekt] *vi* oponerse (**to** a); **do you o. to my smoking?** ¿le molesta que fume?

objection [əb'dʒekʃən] *n* (**a**) objeción *f* (**b**) *(drawback)* inconveniente *m*; **provided there's no o.** si no hay inconveniente

objective [əb'dʒektɪv] **1** *adj* objetivo(a) **2** *n* objetivo *m*

obligation [ɒblɪ'geɪʃən] *n* obligación *f*; **to be under an o. to sb** estarle muy agradecido(a) a algn

obligatory [ɒ'blɪgətərɪ] *adj* obligatorio(a)

oblige [ə'blaɪdʒ] *vt* (**a**) *(compel)* obligar; **I'm obliged to do it** me veo obligado(a) a hacerlo (**b**) *(do a favour for)* hacer un favor a (**c**) **to be obliged** *(grateful)* estar agradecido(a)

obliging [ə'blaɪdʒɪŋ] *adj* solícito(a)

oblique [ə'bliːk] *adj* oblicuo(a), inclinado(a); *Fig* **an o. reference** una alusión indirecta

oblivion [ə'blɪvɪən] *n* olvido *m*; **to sink into o.** caer en el olvido

oblivious [ə'blɪvɪəs] *adj* inconsciente

oblong ['ɒblɒŋ] **1** *adj* oblongo(a) **2** *n* rectángulo *m*

obnoxious [əb'nɒkʃəs] *adj* repugnante

oboe ['əʊbəʊ] *n* oboe *m*

obscene [əb'siːn] *adj* obsceno(a)

obscenity [əb'senɪtɪ] *n* obscenidad *f*

obscure [əb'skjʊə(r)] **1** *adj* (**a**) oscuro(a); *(vague)* vago(a) (**b**) *(author, poet etc)* desconocido(a) **2** *vt (truth)* ocultar

observant [əb'zɜːvənt] *adj* observador(a)

observation [ɒbzə'veɪʃən] *n* observación *f*; *(surveillance)* vigilancia *f*

observe [əb'sɜːv] *vt* (**a**) observar; *(in surveillance)* vigilar (**b**) *(remark)* advertir (**c**) *(obey)* respetar

observer [əb'zɜːvə(r)] *n* observador(a) *m,f*

obsess [əb'ses] *vt* obsesionar; **to be obsessed (with** *or* **by)** estar obsesionado(a) (con)

obsession [əb'seʃən] *n* obsesión *f*

obsolete ['ɒbsəliːt, ɒbsə'liːt] *adj* obsoleto(a)

obstacle ['ɒbstəkəl] *n* obstáculo *m*; *Fig* impedimento *m*; **o. race** carrera *f* de obstáculos

obstinate ['ɒbstɪnɪt] *adj* (**a**) *(person)*

obstinado(a), terco(a) (**b**) *(pain)* persistente

obstruct [əb'strʌkt] *vt* (**a**) obstruir; *(pipe etc)* atascar; *(view)* tapar (**b**) *(hinder)* estorbar; *(progress)* dificultar

obstruction [əb'strʌkʃən] *n* (**a**) obstrucción *f* (**b**) *(hindrance)* obstáculo *m*

obtain [əb'teɪn] *vt* obtener, conseguir

obvious ['ɒbvɪəs] *adj* obvio(a), evidente

obviously ['ɒbvɪəslɪ] *adv* evidentemente; **o.!** ¡claro!, ¡por supuesto!

occasion [ə'keɪʒən] **1** *n* (**a**) ocasión *f*; **on o.** de vez en cuando; **on the o. of** con motivo de (**b**) *(event)* acontecimiento *m* (**c**) *(cause)* motivo *m* **2** *vt Fml* ocasionar

occasional [ə'keɪʒənəl] *adj* esporádico(a), eventual

occasionally [ə'keɪʒənəlɪ] *adv* de vez en cuando

occupant ['ɒkjʊpənt] *n* ocupante *mf*; *(tenant)* inquilino(a) *m,f*

occupation [ɒkjʊ'peɪʃən] *n* (**a**) *(job, profession)* profesión *f*, ocupación *f* (**b**) *(pastime)* pasatiempo *m* (**c**) *(of building, house, country)* ocupación *f*

occupier ['ɒkjʊpaɪə(r)] *n Br* ocupante *mf*; *(tenant)* inquilino(a) *m,f*

occupy ['ɒkjʊpaɪ] *vt* (**a**) *(live in)* ocupar, habitar (**b**) *(time)* pasar; **to o. one's time in doing sth** dedicar su tiempo a hacer algo (**c**) *(building, factory etc in protest)* tomar posesión de

occur [ə'kɜː(r)] *vi* (**a**) *(event)* suceder, acaecer; *(change)* producirse (**b**) *(be found)* encontrarse (**c**) **it occurred to me that ...** se me ocurrió que ...

occurrence [ə'kʌrəns] *n* suceso *m*, incidencia *f*

ocean ['əʊʃən] *n* océano *m*

o'clock [ə'klɒk] *adv* **(it's) one o.** (es) la una; **(it's) two o.** (son) las dos

October [ɒk'təʊbə(r)] *n* octubre *m*

octopus ['ɒktəpəs] *n* pulpo *m*

odd [ɒd] **1** *adj* (**a**) *(strange)* raro(a), extraño(a) (**b**) *(occasional)* esporádico(a); **o. job** trabajillo *m* (**c**) **an o.**

number *(not even)* un impar (**d**) *(unpaired)* desparejado(a); **an o. sock** un calcetín suelto **2** *adv* y pico; **twenty o. people** veinte y pico *or* y tantas personas

oddly ['ɒdlɪ] *adv* extrañamente; **o. enough** por extraño que parezca

odds [ɒdz] *npl* (**a**) *(chances)* probabilidades *fpl*; **the o. are that ...** lo más probable es que ... *(+ subj)* (**b**) *(in betting)* puntos *mpl* de ventaja; **the o. are five to one** las apuestas están cinco a uno (**c**) *Br* **it makes no o.** da lo mismo (**d**) **at o. with sb** *(disagreeing)* reñido(a) con algn (**e**) **o. and ends** *(small things)* cositas *fpl*; *(trinkets)* chucherías *fpl*

odious ['əʊdɪəs] *adj* repugnante

odour, US odor ['əʊdə(r)] *n* olor *m*; *(fragrance)* perfume *m*

of [ɒv, *unstressed* əv] *prep* de; **a friend of mine** un amigo mío; **a bottle of wine** una botella de vino; **a dress (made) of silk** un vestido de seda; **that's very kind of you** es usted muy amable; **there are four of us** somos cuatro; **two of them** dos de ellos; **south of** al sur de; **the 7th of November** el 7 de noviembre

off [ɒf] **1** *prep* de; **she fell o. her horse** se cayó del caballo; **a few kilometres o. the coast** a unos kilómetros de la costa; **I'm o. wine** he perdido el gusto al vino

2 *adv* (**a**) **he turned o. the radio** apagó la radio (**b**) *(absent)* fuera; **I have a day o.** tengo un día libre; **to be o. sick** estar de baja por enfermedad (**c**) *(distant)* **6 miles o.** a 6 millas (**d**) **I'm o. to London** me voy a Londres; (**e**) **10 percent o.** un descuento del 10 por ciento; (**f**) **o. and on** de vez en cuando

3 *adj* (**a**) *(gas etc)* apagado(a); *(water)* cortado(a) (**b**) *(cancelled)* cancelado(a) (**c**) *(low)* bajo(a); *(unsatisfactory)* malo(a); **on the o. chance** por si acaso; **the o. season** la temporada baja (**d**) *(gone bad) (meat, fish)* malo(a), pasado(a); *(milk)* agrio(a)

offence [ə'fens] *n* (**a**) *Jur* delito *m* (**b**)

(insult) ofensa *f*; **to give o.** ofender; **to take o. at sth** ofenderse por algo (**c**) *Mil (attack)* ofensiva *f*

offend [ə'fend] *vt* ofender

offender [ə'fendə(r)] *n (criminal)* delincuente *mf*

offence [ə'fens] *n US* = **offence**

offensive [ə'fensɪv] **1** *adj* (**a**) *(insulting)* ofensivo(a) (**b**) *(repulsive)* repugnante **2** *n Mil* ofensiva *f*; **to be on the o.** estar a la ofensiva

offer ['ɒfə(r)] **1** *vt* (**a**) ofrecer; **to o. to do a job** ofrecerse para hacer un trabajo (**b**) *(propose)* proponer **2** *n* (**a**) oferta *f*; *(proposal)* propuesta *f*; **o. of marriage** proposición *f* de matrimonio (**b**) *Com* **on o.** de oferta

offering ['ɒfərɪŋ] *n* (**a**) ofrecimiento *m* (**b**) *Rel* ofrenda *f*

offhand **1** *adj* ['ɒfhænd] *(abrupt)* brusco(a); *(inconsiderate)* descortés **2** *adv* [ɒf'hænd] **I don't know o.** así sin pensarlo, no lo sé

office ['ɒfɪs] *n* (**a**) *(room)* despacho *m*; *(building)* oficina *f*; *(of lawyer)* despacho, bufete *m*; *US (of doctor, dentist)* consulta *f*; **o. hours** horas *fpl* de oficina (**b**) *Br Pol* ministerio *m* (**c**) *US (federal agency)* agencia *f* gubernamental (**d**) *(position)* cargo *m* (**e**) *Pol* **to be in o.** estar en el poder

officer ['ɒfɪsə(r)] *n* (**a**) *Mil* oficial *mf* (**b**) **(police) o.** agente *mf* de policía (**c**) *(government official)* funcionario(a) *m,f* (**d**) *(of company, society)* director(a) *m,f*

official [ə'fɪʃəl] **1** *adj* oficial **2** *n* funcionario(a) *m,f*

officially [ə'fɪʃəlɪ] *adv* oficialmente

off-licence ['ɒflaɪsəns] *n Br* tienda *f* de bebidas alcohólicas

off-line ['ɒflaɪn] *adj Comput* desconectado(a)

off-peak [ɒf'piːk] *adj (flight)* de temporada baja; *(rate)* de fuera de las horas punta

off-putting ['ɒfpʊtɪŋ] *adj Br Fam* desconcertante

offset [ɒf'set] *vt (pt & pp* **offset)** *(balance out)* compensar

offside **1** *adv* [ɒf'saɪd] *Ftb* fuera de juego **2** *n* ['ɒfsaɪd] *Aut (with left-hand drive)* lado derecho; *(with right-hand drive)* lado izquierdo

offspring ['ɒfsprɪŋ] *n (pl* **offspring)** *(child)* vástago *m*; *(children)* progenitura *f*

often ['ɒfən, 'ɒftən] *adv* a menudo, con frecuencia; **every so o.** de vez en cuando

oh [əʊ] *interj* ¡oh!, ¡ay!; **oh, my God!** ¡Dios mío!

oil [ɔɪl] **1** *n* (**a**) aceite *m*; **o. lamp** lámpara *f* de aceite, quinqué *m*; **o. slick** mancha *f* de aceite; **olive o.** aceite de oliva (**b**) *(petroleum)* petróleo *m*; **o. rig** plataforma petrolera; **o. tanker** petrolero *m* (**c**) *(painting)* pintura *f* al óleo; **o. paint** óleo *m* **2** *vt* engrasar

oilcan ['ɔɪlkæn] *n* aceitera *f*

oilfield ['ɔɪlfiːld] *n* yacimiento petrolífero

oily ['ɔɪlɪ] *adj* **(oilier, oiliest)** aceitoso(a), grasiento(a); *(hair, skin)* graso(a)

ointment ['ɔɪntmənt] *n* ungüento *m*, pomada *f*

O.K., okay [əʊ'keɪ] *Fam* **1** *interj* de acuerdo, *Esp* vale, *Am* ok, *Méx* ándale **2** *adj* bien; **is it O.K. if …?** ¿está bien si …? **3** *vt* dar el visto bueno a

old [əʊld] **1** *adj* (**a**) viejo(a); **an o. man** un anciano; **o. age** vejez *f*; *Br* **o. age pensioner** pensionista *mf*; *Br* **o. boy** *(addressing sb)* antiguo alumno; **o. hand** veterano(a) *m,f*; **good o. John!** ¡el bueno de John! (**b**) **how o. are you?** ¿cuántos años tienes?; **she's five years o.** tiene cinco años (**c**) *(previous)* antiguo(a) **2** *n* **of o.** de antaño

old-fashioned [əʊld'fæʃənd] *adj (outdated)* a la antigua; *(unfashionable)* anticuado(a), pasado(a) de moda

olive ['ɒlɪv] *n* (**a**) *(tree)* olivo *m* (**b**) *(fruit)* aceituna *f*, oliva *f*

Olympic [ə'lɪmpɪk] **1** *adj* olímpico(a); **O. Games** Juegos Olímpicos **2** *npl* **the Olympics** las Olimpiadas

omelette, *US* **omelet** ['ɒmlɪt] *n* tortilla *f*; **Spanish o.** tortilla española *or* de patatas *or Am* papas

omen ['əʊmen] *n* presagio *m*

ominous ['ɒmɪnəs] *adj* de mal agüero

omission [əʊ'mɪʃən] *n* omisión *f*; *Fig* olvido *m*

omit [əʊ'mɪt] *vt* omitir; *(accidentally)* pasar por alto; *(forget)* olvidarse (**to** de)

on [ɒn] **1**, *prep* (**a**) *(location)* sobre, encima de, en; **I hit him on the head** le di un golpe en la cabeza; **it's on the desk** está encima de *or* sobre el escritorio; **hanging on the wall** colgado de la pared; **on page 4** en la página 4
(**b**) *(alongside)* en; **a town on the coast** un pueblo en la costa
(**c**) *(direction)* en, a; **on the right** a la derecha; **on the way** en el camino
(**d**) *(time)* **on 3 April** el 3 de abril; **on a sunny day** un día de sol; **on Monday** el lunes; **on Mondays** los lunes; **on time** a tiempo
(**e**) en; **on TV/the radio** en la tele/radio; **on the phone** al teléfono
(**f**) *(at the time of)* a; **on his arrival** a su llegada; **on learning of this** al conocer esto
(**g**) *(transport)* en/a; **on foot** a pie
(**h**) *(state, process)* en/de; **on holiday/business** de vacaciones/negocios
(**i**) *(regarding)* sobre; **a lecture on numismatics** una conferencia sobre numismática
(**j**) *(against)* contra; **an attack on** un ataque contra
2 *adv* (**a**) *(covering)* encima, puesto; **she had a coat on** llevaba puesto un abrigo
(**b**) *Fam* **have you anything on tonight?** ¿tienes algún plan para esta noche?
(**c**) **and so on** y así sucesivamente; **he talks on and on** habla sin parar; **to work on** seguir trabajando
(**d**) **from that day on** a partir de aquel día; **later on** más tarde
3 *adj Fam* (**a**) **to be on** *(TV, radio, light)* estar encendido(a) *or Am* prendido(a); *(film, play)* estar en cartelera
(**b**) *(definitely planned)* previsto(a); **you're on!** ¡trato hecho! (**c**) *Br Fam*

(acceptable) **that isn't on** eso no está bien

once [wʌns] **1** *adv* (**a**) *(one time)* una vez; **o. a week** una vez por semana; **o. more** una vez más; **o. or twice** un par de veces; *Fig* **o. and for all** de una vez por todas (**b**) *(formerly)* en otro tiempo; **o. (upon a time) there was …** érase una vez … (**c**) **at o.** en seguida, inmediatamente **2** *conj* una vez que *(+ subj)*, en cuanto *(+ subj)*

one [wʌn] **1** *adj* (**a**) un/una; **for o. thing** primero; **you're the o. person who knows** tú eres el único que lo sabe (**b**) *(indefinite)* un/una; **he'll come back o. day** un día volverá
2 *dem pron* **any o.** cualquiera; **that o.** ése/ésa; *(distant)* aquél/aquélla; **this o.** éste/ésta; **the blue ones** los azules/las azules; **the o. on the table** el/la que está encima de la mesa; **the ones that, the ones who** los/las que
3 *indef pron* (**a**) uno(a) *m,f*; **o. at a time** de uno en uno; **o. by o.** uno tras otro (**b**) *(indefinite person)* uno(a) *m,f*; **o. has to fight** hay que luchar; **o. hopes that will never happen** esperemos que no ocurra (**c**) **o. another** el uno al otro; **they love o. another** se aman
4 *n (digit)* uno *m*; **o. hundred/thousand** cien/mil

oneself [wʌn'self] *pron* (**a**) *(reflexive)* uno(a) mismo(a) *m,f*, sí mismo(a) *m,f*; **to talk to o.** hablar para sí (**b**) *(alone)* uno(a) mismo(a) *m,f*; **by o.** solo(a)

one-sided [wʌn'saɪdɪd] *adj (bargain)* desigual; *(judgement)* parcial; *(decision)* unilateral

one-way ['wʌnweɪ] *adj* (**a**) *US (ticket)* de ida (**b**) *(street)* de dirección única

ongoing ['ɒngəʊɪŋ] *adj* (**a**) *(in progress)* en curso, actual (**b**) *(developing)* en desarrollo

onion ['ʌnjən] *n* cebolla *f*

on-line ['ɒnlaɪn] *adj Comput* conectado(a)

onlooker ['ɒnlʊkə(r)] *n* espectador(a) *m,f*

only ['əʊnlɪ] **1** *adj* único(a); **o. son** hijo único

2 *adv* (**a**) solamente, sólo; **staff o.** *(sign)* reservado al personal (**b**) *(not earlier than)* apenas; **he has o. just left** acaba de marcharse hace un momento; **o. yesterday** ayer mismo
3 *conj* pero

onset ['ɒnset] *n (start)* comienzo *m*

onto ['ɒntʊ, *unstressed* 'ɒntə] *prep* sobre, encima de

onward(s) ['ɒnwəd(z)] *adv* a partir de, en adelante; **from this time o.** de ahora en adelante

opaque [əʊ'peɪk] *adj* opaco(a)

open ['əʊpən] **1** *adj* (**a**) abierto(a); **in the o. air** al aire libre; **to be o. with sb** ser sincero(a) con algn; **to keep an o. mind** no tener prejuicios; **I am o. to suggestions** acepto cualquier sugerencia; **o. to criticism** susceptible a la crítica; *Av, Rail* **o. ticket** billete *or Am* boleto abierto (**b**) *(opposition)* manifiesto(a)
2 *vt* (**a**) abrir; **to o. fire** abrir fuego (**b**) *(exhibition etc)* inaugurar; *(negotiations, conversation)* entablar
3 *vi* (**a**) abrir, abrirse; **to o. onto** *(door, window)* dar a (**b**) *(start)* empezar; *Th, Cin* estrenarse
4 *n* **in the o.** al aire libre
▸ **open out 1** *vt sep* abrir, desplegar **2** *vi (flowers)* abrirse; *(view)* extenderse
▸ **open up 1** *vt sep (market etc)* abrir; *(possibilities)* crear **2** *vi* (**a**) abrirse; *Fam* **o. up!** ¡abre la puerta! (**b**) *(start)* empezar

opening ['əʊpənɪŋ] *n* (**a**) *(act)* apertura *f*; **o. night** noche *f* de estreno (**b**) *(beginning)* comienzo *m* (**c**) *(aperture)* abertura *f*; *(gap)* brecha *f* (**d**) *Com* oportunidad *f* (**e**) *(vacancy)* vacante *f*

openly ['əʊpənlɪ] *adv* abiertamente

open-minded [əʊpən'maɪndɪd] *adj* sin prejuicios

opera ['ɒpərə] *n* ópera *f*; **o. house** ópera, teatro *m* de la ópera

operate ['ɒpəreɪt] **1** *vi* (**a**) *(function)* funcionar (**b**) *Med* operar; **to o. on sb for appendicitis** operar a algn de apendicitis **2** *vt* (**a**) *(control)* manejar (**b**) *(business)* dirigir

operation [ɒpə'reɪʃən] *n* (**a**) *(of machine)* funcionamiento *m*; *(by person)* manejo *m* (**b**) *Mil* maniobra *f* (**c**) *Med* operación *f*, intervención quirúrgica; **to undergo an o. for** ser operado(a) de

operator ['ɒpəreɪtə(r)] *n* (**a**) *Ind* operario(a) *m,f* (**b**) *Tel* operador(a) *m,f* (**c**) *(dealer)* negociante *mf*, agente *mf*; **tour o.** agente de viajes

opinion [ə'pɪnjən] *n* opinión *f*; **in my o.** en mi opinión, a mi juicio; **it's a matter of o.** es cuestión de opiniones; **to have a high o. of sb** tener buen concepto de algn; **o. poll** encuesta *f*, sondeo *m*

opponent [ə'pəʊnənt] *n* adversario(a) *m,f*

opportunity [ɒpə'tjuːnɪtɪ] *n* (**a**) oportunidad *f*, ocasión *f* (**b**) *(prospect)* perspectiva *f*

oppose [ə'pəʊz] *vt* oponerse a

opposed [ə'pəʊzd] *adj* opuesto(a); **to be o. to sth** estar en contra de algo; **as o. to** comparado(a) con

opposing [ə'pəʊzɪŋ] *adj* adversario(a)

opposite ['ɒpəzɪt] **1** *adj* (**a**) *(facing)* de enfrente; *(page)* contiguo(a) (**b**) *(contrary)* opuesto(a), contrario(a); **in the o. direction** en dirección contraria
2 *n* **the o.** lo contrario; **quite the o.!** ¡al contrario!
3 *prep* enfrente de, frente a
4 *adv* enfrente

opposition [ɒpə'zɪʃən] *n* (**a**) oposición *f*; **in o. to** en contra de (**b**) *Br Pol* **the O.** la oposición

oppress [ə'pres] *vt* oprimir

oppression [ə'preʃən] *n* opresión *f*

oppressive [ə'presɪv] *adj* opresivo(a); *(atmosphere)* agobiante; *(heat)* sofocante

opt [ɒpt] *vi* optar; **to o. for** optar por; **to o. to do sth** optar por hacer algo
▸ **opt out** *vi* retirarse; **to o. out of doing sth** decidir no hacer algo

optical ['ɒptɪkəl] *adj* óptico(a)

optician [ɒp'tɪʃən] *n* óptico(a) *m,f*

optimism [ˈɒptɪmɪzəm] *n* optimismo *m*

optimist [ˈɒptɪmɪst] *n* optimista *mf*

optimistic [ɒptɪˈmɪstɪk] *adj* optimista

option [ˈɒpʃən] *n* opción *f*; **I have no o.** no tengo más remedio; **to keep one's options open** no comprometerse; **with the o. of** con opción a

optional [ˈɒpʃənəl] *adj* optativo(a), facultativo(a); *Educ* **o. subject** (asignatura *f*) optativa *f*

or [ɔː(r), *unstressed* ə(r)] *conj* **(a)** o; *(before a word beginning with "o" or "ho")* u; **or else** si no, o bien; **whether you like it or not** tanto si te gusta como si no; **either a bun or a piece of cake** (o) una magdalena o un trozo de pastel **(b)** *(with negative)* ni; **he can't read or write** no sabe leer ni escribir

oral [ˈɔːrəl, ˈɒrəl] **1** *adj* oral **2** *n* examen *m* oral

orange [ˈɒrɪndʒ] **1** *n* naranja *f*; **o. juice** *Esp* zumo *m or Am* jugo *m* de naranja **2** *adj* de color naranja

orbit [ˈɔːbɪt] **1** *n* *Astron* órbita *f* **2** *vt* girar alrededor de **3** *vi* girar

orchard [ˈɔːtʃəd] *n* huerto *m*

orchestra [ˈɔːkɪstrə] *n* orquesta *f*; *US (in theatre)* platea *f*

orchid [ˈɔːkɪd] *n* orquídea *f*

ordeal [ɔːˈdiːl] *n* mala experiencia

order [ˈɔːdə(r)] **1** *n* **(a)** *(sequence)* orden *m*; **to put in o.** ordenar **(b)** *(condition)* estado *m*; **out of o.** *(sign)* averiado(a) **(c)** *(peace)* orden *m*; **to restore o.** reestablecer el orden público **(d)** *(command)* orden *f* **(e)** *Com* pedido *m*, encargo *m*; **o. form** hoja *f* de pedido **(f)** *Rel* orden *f* **(g)** **in o. that** para que (+ *subj*), a fin de que (+ *subj*); **in o. to** (+ *infin*) para (+ *infin*), a fin de (+ *infin*) **2** *vt* **(a)** *(command)* ordenar, mandar; **to o. sb to do sth** mandar a algn hacer algo **(b)** *Com* pedir, encargar

orderly [ˈɔːdəlɪ] *adj (tidy etc)* ordenado(a)

ordinance [ˈɔːdɪnəns] *n* *Fml (decree)* ordenanza *f*, decreto *m*

ordinary [ˈɔːdənrɪ] **1** *adj* usual, normal; *(average)* corriente, común; **the o. citizen** el ciudadano de a pie **2** *n* **the o.** lo corriente, lo normal; **out of the o.** fuera de lo común

organ [ˈɔːgən] *n* *Mus, Anat etc* órgano *m*

organic [ɔːˈgænɪk] *adj* orgánico(a); *(farming, food)* biológico(a), ecológico(a)

organism [ˈɔːgənɪzəm] *n* organismo *m*

organization [ɔːgənaɪˈzeɪʃən] *n* organización *f*

organize [ˈɔːgənaɪz] *vt* organizar

organizer [ˈɔːgənaɪzə(r)] *n* organizador(a) *m,f*

orgasm [ˈɔːgæzəm] *n* orgasmo *m*

Oriental [ɔːrɪˈentəl] *adj & n* oriental *(mf)*

orientate [ˈɔːrɪənteɪt] *vt* orientar

origin [ˈɒrɪdʒɪn] *n* origen *m*; **country of o.** país *m* natal *or* de origen

original [əˈrɪdʒɪnəl] **1** *adj* **(a)** original; *(first)* primero(a) **(b)** *(imaginative)* original **2** *n* original *m*

originally [əˈrɪdʒɪnəlɪ] *adv* **(a)** *(at first)* en un principio **(b)** *(with imagination)* con originalidad

originate [əˈrɪdʒɪneɪt] **1** *vt* originar **2** *vi* **to o. from** *or* **in** tener su origen en

ornament [ˈɔːnəmənt] *n* ornamento *m*, adorno *m*

ornamental [ɔːnəˈmentəl] *adj* decorativo(a)

ornate [ɔːˈneɪt] *adj* vistoso(a)

orphan [ˈɔːfən] **1** *n* huérfano(a) *m,f* **2** *vt* **she was orphaned** quedó huérfana

orthodox [ˈɔːθədɒks] *adj* ortodoxo(a)

ostentatious [ɒstenˈteɪʃəs] *adj* ostentoso(a)

ostrich [ˈɒstrɪtʃ] *n* avestruz *f*

other [ˈʌðə(r)] **1** *adj* **(a)** otro(a); **every o. day** cada dos días; **on the o. hand** por otra parte; **o. people have seen it** otros lo han visto; **the o. four** los otros cuatro; **the o. one** el otro/la otra; **the o. thing** lo otro **(b)** **he must be**

somewhere or o. debe de estar en alguna parte
2 *pron* otro(a) *m,f*; **many others** otros muchos; **the others** los otros, los demás; **we see each o. quite often** nos vemos con bastante frecuencia

otherwise ['ʌðəwaɪz] **1** *adv* (**a**) *(if not)* si no (**b**) *(differently)* de otra manera (**c**) *(in other respects)* por lo demás **2** *adj* distinto(a)

ouch [aʊtʃ] *interj (expressing pain)* ¡ay!

ought [ɔːt] *v aux*

En el inglés hablado, y en el escrito en estilo coloquial, la forma negativa **ought not** se transforma en **oughtn't**

(**a**) *(obligation)* deber; **I thought I o. to tell you** creí que debía decírtelo; **she o. to do it** debería hacerlo (**b**) *(vague desirability)* tener que, deber; **you o. to see the exhibition** deberías ver la exposición (**c**) *(expectation)* he o. to pass the exam seguramente aprobará el examen; **that o. to do** con eso bastará

ounce [aʊns] *n* onza *f*

our [aʊə(r)] *pos adj* nuestro(a)

ours [aʊəz] *pos pron (one thing)* (el) nuestro/(la) nuestra; *(more than one)* (los) nuestros/(las) nuestras; **a friend of o.** un amigo nuestro; **these books are ours** estos libros son nuestros; **which is o.?** ¿cuál es el nuestro?

ourselves [aʊə'selvz] *pers pron pl* (**a**) *(reflexive)* nos; **we hurt o.** nos hicimos daño (**b**) *(alone)* nosotros solos/nosotras solas; **we were by o.** estábamos solos (**c**) *(emphatic)* nosotros mismos/nosotras mismas

out [aʊt] **1** *adv* (**a**) *(outside, away)* fuera; **to go o.** salir (**b**) **o. of** *(place, control, danger)* fuera de; **to go o. of the room** salir de la habitación; **o. of date** *(expired)* caducado(a); *(old-fashioned)* pasado(a) de moda (**c**) **o. of** *(cause, motive)* por (**d**) **o. of** *(made from)* de (**e**) **o. of** *(short of, without)* sin (**f**) **o. of** *(among)* entre
2 *adj* (**a**) **the sun is o.** ha salido el sol (**b**) *(unfashionable)* pasado(a) de moda (**c**) *(fire)* apagado(a) (**d**) **she's o.** *(not*

in) ha salido, no está (**e**) *(inaccurate)* equivocado(a); **to be o. in one's calculations** equivocarse en los cálculos (**f**) **before the week is o.** antes de que acabe la semana
3 *prep (out of)* por; **he jumped o. of the window** saltó por la ventana

outbreak ['aʊtbreɪk] *n (of war)* comienzo *m*; *(of disease)* brote *m*; *(of violence)* ola *f*; **at the o. of war** cuando estalló la guerra

outburst ['aʊtbɜːst] *n (of anger)* arrebato *m*; *(of generosity)* arranque *m*

outcast ['aʊtkɑːst] *n* marginado(a) *m,f*

outcome ['aʊtkʌm] *n* resultado *m*

outcry ['aʊtkraɪ] *n* **there was an o.** hubo fuertes protestas

outdated [aʊt'deɪtɪd] *adj* anticuado(a), obsoleto(a)

outdo [aʊt'duː] *(pt* **outdid** [aʊt'dɪd]; *pp* **outdone** [aʊt'dʌn]) *vt* **to o. sb** superar a algn

outdoor ['aʊtdɔː(r)] *adj* (**a**) al aire libre (**b**) *(clothes)* de calle

outdoors [aʊt'dɔːz] *adv* fuera, al aire libre

outer ['aʊtə(r)] *adj* exterior, externo(a)

outfit ['aʊtfɪt] *n* (**a**) *(kit, equipment)* equipo *m* (**b**) *(set of clothes)* conjunto *m* (**c**) *Fam (group)* grupo *m*

outgoing ['aʊtgəʊɪŋ] **1** *adj* (**a**) *(departing)* saliente (**b**) *(sociable)* extrovertido(a) **2** *npl Br* **outgoings** gastos *mpl*

outgrow [aʊt'grəʊ] *(pt* **outgrew** [aʊt'gruː]; *pp* **outgrown** [aʊt'grən]) *vt* **he's outgrowing all his clothes** toda la ropa se le está quedando pequeña; **she'll o. it** se le pasará con la edad

outing ['aʊtɪŋ] *n* excursión *f*

outlaw ['aʊtlɔː] **1** *n* proscrito(a) *m,f* **2** *vt* prohibir

outlay ['aʊtleɪ] *n (pl* **outlays**) *(expense)* desembolso *m*

outlet ['aʊtlet] *n* (**a**) *(opening)* salida *f* (**b**) *(for emotions)* válvula *f* de escape (**c**) *Com* mercado *m*

outline ['aʊtlaɪn] **1** *n* (**a**) *(draft)* bosquejo *m* (**b**) *(outer line)* contorno *m*; *(silhouette)* perfil *m* **2** *vt* (**a**) *(draw* *lines of)* perfilar (**b**) *(summarize)* resumir (**c**) *(describe roughly)* trazar las líneas generales de

outlive [aʊt'lɪv] *vt* sobrevivir a

outlook ['aʊtlʊk] *n* (**a**) *(point of view)* punto *m* de vista (**b**) *(prospect)* perspectiva *f*, *Met* previsión *f*

outnumber [aʊt'nʌmbə(r)] *vt* exceder en número

outpatient ['aʊtpeɪʃənt] *n* paciente externo(a); **outpatients' department** clínica ambulatoria

output ['aʊtpʊt] *n* (**a**) producción *f*; *(of machine)* rendimiento *m* (**b**) *Elec* potencia *f* (**c**) *Comput* salida *f*

outrage ['aʊtreɪdʒ] **1** *n* ultraje *m*; **it's an o.!** ¡es un escándalo! **2** *vt* **to be outraged by sth** indignarse por algo

outrageous [aʊt'reɪdʒəs] *adj* *(behaviour)* escandaloso(a); *(clothes)* extravagante; *(price)* exorbitante

outright 1 *adj* ['aʊtraɪt] *(absolute)* absoluto(a) **2** *adv* [aʊt'raɪt] (**a**) *(completely)* por completo (**b**) *(directly)* directamente, sin reserva (**c**) *(immediately)* en el acto

outset ['aʊtset] *n* comienzo *m*, principio *m*

outside 1 *prep* [aʊt'saɪd, 'aʊtsaɪd] (**a**) fuera de (**b**) *(beyond)* más allá de (**c**) *(other than)* aparte de
2 *adj* ['aʊtsaɪd] (**a**) *(exterior)* exterior, externo(a) (**b**) *(remote)* remoto(a)
3 *adv* [aʊt'saɪd] fuera, afuera
4 *n* [aʊt'saɪd, 'aʊtsaɪd] exterior *m*; **on the o.** por fuera; *Fam* **at the o.** como mucho

outsider [aʊt'saɪdə(r)] *n* (**a**) *(stranger)* extraño(a) *m,f*, forastero(a) *m,f* (**b**) *Pol* = candidato(a) con pocas posibilidades de ganar

outskirts ['aʊtskɜ:ts] *npl* afueras *fpl*

outspoken [aʊt'spəʊkən] *adj* directo(a), abierto(a)

outstanding [aʊt'stændɪŋ] *adj* (**a**) *(exceptional)* destacado(a) (**b**) *(unpaid, unresolved)* pendiente

outstretched [aʊt'stretʃt] *adj* extendido(a)

outward ['aʊtwəd] **1** *adj* (**a**) *(external)*

exterior, externo(a) (**b**) **the o. journey** el viaje de ida **2** *adv* = **outwards**

outwards ['aʊtwədz] *adv* hacia (a)fuera

oval ['əʊvəl] **1** *adj* oval, ovalado(a) **2** *n* óvalo *m*

ovary ['əʊvərɪ] *n* ovario *m*

ovation [əʊ'veɪʃən] *n* ovación *f*

oven ['ʌvən] *n* horno *m*

over ['əʊvə(r)] **1** *prep* (**a**) *(above, on top of)* sobre, encima de, *Am* arriba de (**b**) *(across)* al otro lado de; **the bridge o. the river** el puente que cruza el río (**c**) *(during)* durante (**d**) *(throughout)* por (**e**) *(by the agency of)* por; **o. the phone** por teléfono (**f**) *(more than)* más de; **men o. twenty-five** hombres mayores de veinticinco años; **o. and above** además de (**g**) *(recovered from)* recuperado(a) de
2 *adv* (**a**) **o. here/there** aquí/allí, *Am* acá/allá (**b**) *(throughout)* por; **all o.** por todas partes (**c**) *(more)* más (**d**) *(again)* otra vez; **o. and o. (again)** una y otra vez (**e**) *(in excess)* de más
3 *adj* *(finished)* acabado(a); **it's (all) o.** se acabó

overall 1 *adj* total, global
2 *n Br* **overalls** *(boiler suit)* mono *m* (de trabajo), *Am* overol *m*
3 *adv* [əʊvər'ɔ:l] *(on the whole)* por lo general, en conjunto

overbearing [əʊvə'beərɪŋ] *adj* *(domineering)* dominante; *(important)* significativo(a)

overboard ['əʊvəbɔ:d] *adv* por la borda; **man o.!** ¡hombre al agua!; *Fam* **to go o.** pasarse

overcast ['əʊvəkɑ:st] *adj* nublado(a)

overcharge [əʊvə'tʃɑːdʒ] *vt* (**a**) *(charge too much)* cobrar demasiado (**b**) *(overload)* sobrecargar

overcoat ['əʊvəkəʊt] *n* abrigo *m*

overcome [əʊvə'kʌm] *(pt* **overcame** [əʊvə'keɪm], *pp* **overcome**) *vt* (**a**) *(conquer)* vencer; **o. by grief** deshecho por el dolor (**b**) *(obstacle)* superar

overcrowded [əʊvə'kraʊdɪd] *adj* *(room)* atestado(a) (de gente); *(country)* superpoblado(a)

overdo [əʊvə'duː] *vt* (*pt* **overdid** [əʊvə'dɪd]; *pp* **overdone** [əʊvə'dʌn]) (**a**) *(carry too far)* exagerar; **don't o. it** no te pases (**b**) *Culin* cocer *or* asar demasiado

overdose ['əʊvədəʊs] *n* sobredosis *f*

overdraft ['əʊvədrɑːft] *n* giro *m* en descubierto; *(amount)* saldo *m* deudor

overdraw [əʊvə'drɔː] (*pt* **overdrew** əʊvə'druː], *pp* **overdrawn** [əʊvə'drɔːn]) *vt* **to be overdrawn** tener la cuenta en descubierto

overdue [əʊvə'djuː] *adj* **to be o.** *(person, train)* retrasarse, venir con retraso *or Am* demora; *(bill)* estar sin pagar

overestimate [əʊvər'estɪmeɪt] *vt* sobreestimar

overflow **1** *vi* [əʊvə'fləʊ] *(river)* desbordarse; *(cup etc)* derramarse **2** *n* ['əʊvəfləʊ] *(of river etc)* desbordamiento *m*; **o. pipe** cañería *f* de desagüe

overgrown [əʊvə'grəʊn] *adj* (**a**) *(with grass)* cubierto(a) (de hierba) (**b**) *(in size)* demasiado grande

overhaul **1** *vt* [əʊvə'hɔːl] revisar **2** *n* ['əʊvəhɔːl] revisión *f* y reparación *f*

overhead **1** *adj* ['əʊvəhed] (por) encima de la cabeza; **o. cable** cable aéreo
 2 *adv* [əʊvə'hed] arriba, por encima de la cabeza
 3 *n* ['əʊvəhed] *US* = **overheads**

overheads ['əʊvəhedz] *npl Br* gastos *mpl* generales

overhear [əʊvə'hɪə(r)] (*pt & pp* **overheard** [əʊvə'hɜːd]) *vt* oír por casualidad

overheat [əʊvə'hiːt] *vi* recalentarse

overjoyed [əʊvə'dʒɔɪd] *adj* rebosante de alegría

overlap [əʊvə'læp] *vi* superponerse; *Fig* **our plans o.** nuestros planes coinciden parcialmente

overleaf [əʊvə'liːf] *adv* al dorso

overload **1** *vt* [əʊvə'ləʊd] sobrecargar **2** *n* ['əʊvələʊd] sobrecarga *f*

overlook [əʊvə'lʊk] *vt* (**a**) *(fail to notice)* saltarse (**b**) *(ignore)* no hacer caso de; **we'll o. it this time** esta vez haremos la vista gorda (**c**) *(have a view of)* dar a, tener vista a

overnight **1** *adv* [əʊvə'naɪt] (**a**) *(during the night)* por la noche; **we stayed there o.** pasamos la noche allí (**b**) *(suddenly)* de la noche a la mañana **2** *adj* ['əʊvənaɪt] *(sudden)* repentino(a)

overpowering [əʊvə'paʊərɪŋ] *adj* *(emotion, heat)* tremendo(a), desmesurado(a); *(smell, taste)* fortísimo(a), intensísimo(a)

overpriced [əʊvə'praɪst] *adj* excesivamente caro(a)

overrate [əʊvə'reɪt] *vt* sobreestimar, supervalorar

overreact [əʊvəri'ækt] *vi* reaccionar exageradamente

override [əʊvə'raɪd] (*pt* **overrode** [əʊvə'rəʊd]; *pp* **overridden** [əʊvə'rɪdən]) *vt* (**a**) *(disregard)* hacer caso omiso de (**b**) *(annul, cancel out)* anular (**c**) *(be more important than)* contar más que

overrule [əʊvə'ruːl] *vt* invalidar; *Jur* denegar

overseas **1** *adv* [əʊvə'siːz] en ultramar; **to live o.** vivir en el extranjero **2** *adj* ['əʊvəsiːz] de ultramar; *(person)* extranjero(a); *(trade)* exterior

oversee [əʊvə'siː] (*pt* **oversaw** [əʊvə'sɔː]; *pp* **overseen** [əʊvə'siːn]) *vt* supervisar

overshadow [əʊvə'ʃædəʊ] *vt Fig* eclipsar

oversight ['əʊvəsaɪt] *n* descuido *m*

oversleep [əʊvə'sliːp] (*pt & pp* **overslept** [əʊvə'slept]) *vi* quedarse dormido(a)

overstep [əʊvə'step] *vt Fig* **to o. the mark** pasarse de la raya

overt [əʊ'vɜːt] *adj* patente

overtake [əʊvə'teɪk] (*pt* **overtook** [əʊvə'tʊk]; *pp* **overtaken** [əʊvə'teɪkən]) *vt* (**a**) *Br Aut* adelantar (**b**) *(surpass)* superar a (**c**) *(of night)* sorprender

overthrow [əʊvə'θrəʊ] *vt* (*pt* **overthrew** [əʊvə'θruː]; *pp* **overthrown** [əʊvə'θrəʊn]) *(government)* derribar

overtime ['əʊvətaɪm] n (**a**) (work) horas fpl extra (**b**) US prórroga f

overturn [əʊvə'tɜːn] vt & vi volcar

overweight [əʊvə'weɪt] adj demasiado pesado(a)

overwhelm [əʊvə'welm] vt (**a**) (defeat) aplastar; (overpower) abrumar; **I'm overwhelmed** estoy abrumado (**b**) (with letters, work etc) inundar

overwhelming [əʊvə'welmɪŋ] adj (defeat) aplastante; (desire etc) irresistible

overwork [əʊvə'wɜːk] **1** vi trabajar demasiado **2** vt (person) forzar; (excuse etc) abusar de

owe [əʊ] vt deber

owing ['əʊɪŋ] adj **o. to** debido a, a causa de

owl [aʊl] n (short-eared) **o.** búho m, CAm, Méx tecolote m; (barn) **o.** lechuza f

own [əʊn] **1** adj propio(a); **it's his o. fault** es culpa suya
2 pron (**a**) **my o./your o./his o.** etc lo mío/lo tuyo/lo suyo etc; Fam **to get one's o. back** tomarse la revancha (**b**) **on one's o.** (without help) uno(a) mismo(a); (alone) solo(a)
3 vt poseer, ser dueño(a) de
▶ **own up** vi **to o. up (to sth)** confesar (algo)

owner ['əʊnə(r)] n propietario(a) m,f, dueño(a) m,f

ownership ['əʊnəʃɪp] n propiedad f, posesión f

ox [ɒks] n (pl oxen ['ɒksən]) buey m

oxygen ['ɒksɪdʒən] n oxígeno m; **o. mask** máscara f de oxígeno

oyster ['ɔɪstə(r)] n ostra f

oz (abbr ounce(s)) onza(s) fpl

ozone ['əʊzəʊn] n ozono m; **o. layer** capa f de ozono

Pp

P, p [piː] *n (the letter)* P, p *f*

p (a) *(pl* **pp)** *(abbr* **page)** pág., p **(b)** [piː] *Br Fam (abbr* **penny, pence)** penique(s) *m(pl)*

pa [pɑː] *n US Fam (dad)* papá *m*

pace [peɪs] **1** *n (step)* paso *m; (speed)* ritmo *m;* **to keep p. with** seguir a; *Fig* avanzar al mismo ritmo que; **to set the p.** marcar el paso; *Fig* marcar la pauta **2** *vi* **to p. up and down** ir de un lado a otro

pacemaker ['peɪsmeɪkə(r)] *n Sport* liebre *f; Med* marcapasos *m inv*

Pacific [pə'sɪfɪk] *adj* **the P. (Ocean)** el (océano) Pacífico

pacifier ['pæsɪfaɪə(r)] *n US (for baby)* chupete *m*

pacifist ['pæsɪfɪst] *adj & n* pacifista *(mf)*

pacify ['pæsɪfaɪ] *vt (person)* calmar; *(country)* pacificar

pack¹ [pæk] **1** *n (parcel)* paquete *m; (bundle)* bulto *m; US (of cigarettes)* paquete; *Br (of playing cards)* baraja *f; (of hounds)* jauría *f*
2 *vt* **(a)** *(goods)* embalar, envasar; *(in suitcase)* poner; **to p. one's suitcase** hacer la maleta *or Am* valija; *Fig* marcharse **(b)** *(fill)* atestar **(c)** *(press down)* apretar
3 *vi* **(a)** hacer las maletas; *Fam* **to send sb packing** mandar a paseo a algn **(b)** *(of people)* apiñarse **(into** en)

▸ **pack in** *vt sep Fam (give up)* dejar

▸ **pack off** *vt sep Fam* mandar

▸ **pack up** *Fam* **1** *vt sep (give up)* dejar **2** *vi (stop working)* dejarlo, parar de trabajar; *(machine etc)* estropearse

pack² [pæk] *vt (meeting)* llenar de partidarios

package ['pækɪdʒ] **1** *n* **(a)** *(parcel)* paquete *m; (bundle)* bulto *m* **(b)** *(of proposals etc)* paquete *m; (agreement)* acuerdo *m;* **p. deal** convenio *m* general; **p. tour** viaje *m* todo incluido **2** *vt (goods)* envasar, embalar

packaging ['pækɪdʒɪŋ] *n (for transport, freight)* embalaje *m; (of product)* envasado *m*

packed [pækt] *adj* **(a)** *(crowded)* abarrotado(a) **(b)** **p. lunch** comida *f* preparada de casa *(para excursión, trabajo, colegio)*

packet ['pækɪt] *n* **(a)** *(of tea, cigarettes)* paquete *m; (bag)* bolsa *f* **(b)** *Fam (lot of money)* **to make *or* earn a p.** ganar una millonada *or Méx* un chorro de lana *or RP* una ponchada de guita

packing ['pækɪŋ] *n* embalaje *m;* **p. case** caja *f* de embalar; **to do one's p.** hacer las maletas

pact [pækt] *n* pacto *m*

pad¹ [pæd] **1** *n* **(a)** almohadilla *f; (of paper)* bloc *m*, taco *m* **(b)** **launch p.** plataforma *f* de lanzamiento **(c)** *Fam (flat)* casa *f*, *Esp* choza *f* **2** *vt (chair)* acolchar

▸ **pad out** *vt sep Fig* meter paja en

pad² [pæd] *vi* **to p. about** *or* **around** andar silenciosamente

padded ['pædɪd] *adj (envelope, jacket)* acolchado(a); **p. cell** celda *f* acolchada

padding ['pædɪŋ] *n (material)* relleno *m; Fig (in speech etc)* paja *f*

paddle¹ ['pædəl] **1** *n* **(a)** *(oar)* pala *f;* **p. boat** *or* **steamer** vapor *m* de ruedas **(b)** *US (for table tennis)* pala *f*
2 *vt (boat)* remar con pala en
3 *vi (in boat)* remar con pala

paddle² ['pædəl] *vi* chapotear

paddling pool ['pædlɪŋpuːl] *n (inflatable)* piscina *f or Méx* alberca *f or RP* pileta *f* hinchable; *(in park)* piscina *f*

or Méx alberca *f or RP* pileta *f* para
niños

padlock ['pædlɒk] **1** *n* candado *m* **2** *vt*
cerrar con candado

paediatrician [piːdɪə'trɪʃən] *n* pediatra *mf*

page¹ [peɪdʒ] *n* página *f*

page² [peɪdʒ] **1** *n (servant)* paje *m; (of
knight)* escudero *m; (at club)* botones *m
inv* **2** *vt (call)* avisar por megafonía

pager ['peɪdʒə(r)] *n* buscapersonas *m
inv, Esp* busca *m, Méx* localizador *m,
RP* radiomensaje *m*

paid [peɪd] **1** *adj* pagado(a); *Fig* to put
p. to sth acabar con algo **2** *pt & pp of*
pay

pain [peɪn] **1** *n* (**a**) dolor *m; (grief)*
sufrimiento *m; Fam* he's a p. (in the
neck) es un plomazo *or* pelmazo *or
Méx* sangrón; on p. of death so pena
de muerte (**b**) to take pains over sth
esmerarse en algo **2** *vt (grieve)* dar
pena a

painful ['peɪnfʊl] *adj* doloroso(a);
Fam (very bad) malísimo(a)

painkiller ['peɪnkɪlə(r)] *n* analgésico
m

painless ['peɪnlɪs] *adj* sin dolor; *Fig*
sin dificultades

painstaking ['peɪnzteɪkɪŋ] *adj (person)* concienzudo(a); *(care, research)*
esmerado(a)

paint [peɪnt] **1** *n* pintura *f*
2 *vt* pintar; to p. sth white pintar algo
de blanco
3 *vi* pintar

paintbrush ['peɪntbrʌʃ] *n Art* pincel
m; (for walls) brocha *f*

painter ['peɪntə(r)] *n* pintor(a) *m,f*

painting ['peɪntɪŋ] *n* cuadro *m;
(activity)* pintura *f*

paintwork ['peɪntwɜːk] *n* pintura *f*

pair [peə(r)] *n (of gloves, shoes)* par *m;
(of people, cards)* pareja *f*; a p. of
scissors unas tijeras; a p. of trousers
un pantalón, unos pantalones

pajamas [pə'dʒæməz] *npl US =*
pyjamas

Pakistan [paːkɪ'staːn] *n* Paquistán

Pakistani [paːkɪ'staːnɪ] *adj & n*
paquistaní *(mf)*

pal [pæl] *n Fam* amiguete(a) *m,f, Esp*
colega *mf*

palace ['pælɪs] *n* palacio *m*

pale¹ [peɪl] **1** *adj (skin)* pálido(a);
(colour) claro(a); *(light)* tenue; to turn
p. palidecer **2** *vi* palidecer

pale² [peɪl] *n Fig* to be beyond the p.
ser inaceptable

Palestine ['pælɪstaɪn] *n* Palestina

Palestinian [pælɪ'stɪnɪən] *adj & n*
palestino(a) *(m,f)*

palette ['pælɪt] *n* paleta *f*; p. knife
espátula *f*

palm¹ [paːm] *n (tree)* palmera *f; (leaf)*
palma *f*; date p. palma datilera; P.
Sunday domingo *m* de Ramos

palm² [paːm] *n Anat* palma *f*

▸ **palm off** *vt sep* to p. sth off on sb
colocar *or* endosar algo a algn

pamper ['pæmpə(r)] *vt* mimar, consentir

pamphlet ['pæmflɪt] *n* folleto *m*

pan¹ [pæn] **1** *n* (**a**) *(saucepan)* cazuela
f, cacerola *f* (**b**) *(of scales)* platillo *m* (**c**)
Br (of lavatory) taza *f* **2** *vt Fam (criticize)* vapulear, *Esp* poner por los
suelos

pan² [pæn] *vi Cin* tomar vistas
panorámicas

Panama ['pænəmaː] *n* Panamá; P.
Canal Canal *m* de Panamá

pancake ['pænkeɪk] *n* crepe *f*

panda ['pændə] *n* panda *m; Br* p. car
coche *m or Am* carro *m or CSur* auto *m*
patrulla

pandemonium [pændɪ'məʊnɪəm] *n*
alboroto *m*

pander ['pændə(r)] *vi* to p. to *(person)*
complacer a; *(wishes)* acceder a

pane [peɪn] *n* p. (of glass) hoja *m* de
vidrio *or Esp* cristal

panel ['pænəl] *n* (**a**) *(of wall)* panel *m;
(flat surface)* tabla *f; (of instruments)*
tablero *m; (of ceiling)* artesón *m* (**b**)
(jury) jurado *m; Rad, TV* concursantes
mpl

panic ['pænɪk] **1** *n* pánico *m*; to get

into a p. ponerse histérico(a) **2** *vi* aterrarse

panorama [pænə'rɑːmə] *n* panorama *m*

pansy ['pænzɪ] *n Bot* pensamiento *m*; *Fam Pej* mariquita *m*

pant [pænt] **1** *n* jadeo *m* **2** *vi* jadear

pantomime ['pæntəmaɪm] *n BrTh* = obra de teatro musical para niños basada en un cuento de hadas y representada en Navidad

pantry ['pæntrɪ] *n* despensa *f*

pants [pænts] *npl* (**a**) *Br (men's underwear)* calzoncillos *mpl*, *Chile* fundillos *mpl*, *Col* pantaloncillos *mpl*, *Méx* calzones *mpl*, *Méx* chones *mpl*; *(women's underwear) Esp* bragas *fpl*, *Chile, Col, Méx* calzones *mpl*, *RP* bombacha *f* (**b**) *US (trousers)* pantalones *mpl*

pantyhose ['pæntɪhəʊz] *n US* medias *fpl*, pantis *mpl*

paper ['peɪpə(r)] **1** *n* (**a**) papel *m*; *Fig* **on p.** en teoría; **writing p.** papel de escribir (**b**) *(exam)* examen *m*; *(essay)* trabajo *m* (escrito) (**c**) *Pol* libro *m* (**d**) *(newspaper)* periódico *m*; **the papers** la prensa (**e**) **papers** *(documents)* documentos *mpl* **2** *vt* empapelar

paperback ['peɪpəbæk] *n* libro *m* en rústica

paperclip ['peɪpəklɪp] *n* clip *m*, sujetapapeles *m inv*

paperweight ['peɪpəweɪt] *n* pisapapeles *m inv*

paperwork ['peɪpəwɜːk] *n* papeleo *m*

par [pɑː(r)] *n (parity)* igualdad *f*; *(in golf)* par *m*; *Fig* **it's p. for the course** es lo normal en estos casos; *Fig* **to feel below p.** estar en baja forma

paracetamol [pærə'siːtəmɒl] *n* paracetamol *m*

parachute ['pærəʃuːt] **1** *n* paracaídas *m inv* **2** *vi* **to p. (down)** saltar *or* lanzarse en paracaídas

parade [pə'reɪd] **1** *n* desfile *m*; *Mil* **to be on p.** pasar revista

2 *vt Mil* hacer desfilar; *Fig (flaunt)* hacer alarde de

3 *vi (troops)* pasar revista; *(procession)* desfilar

paradise ['pærədaɪs] *n* paraíso *m*

paradoxical [pærə'dɒksɪkəl] *adj* paradójico(a)

paraffin ['pærəfɪn] *n* parafina *f*; **liquid p.** aceite *m* de parafina; **p. lamp** lámpara *f* de petróleo

paragraph ['pærəgrɑːf] *n* párrafo *m*

paralegal [pærə'liːgəl] *n US* ayudante *mf* de un abogado, *RP* procurador(ora) *m,f*

parallel ['pærəlel] **1** *adj* paralelo(a) (**to** *or* **with** a); *Fig* comparable (**to** *or* **with** a)

2 *n Geog* paralelo *m*; *Geom* paralela *f*; *Fig* paralelo

3 *vt Fig* ser paralelo(a) a

paralyse ['pærəlaɪz] *vt* paralizar

paralysis [pə'rælɪsɪs] *n* parálisis *f*

paralyze ['pærəlaɪz] *vt US* = **paralyse**

paramedic [pærə'medɪk] *n* auxiliar *mf* sanitario(a)

paranoid ['pærənɔɪd] *adj* & *n* paranoico(a) *(m,f)*

paraphrase ['pærəfreɪz] *vt* parafrasear

parasite ['pærəsaɪt] *n* parásito *m*

parasol ['pærəsɒl] *n* sombrilla *f*

parcel ['pɑːsəl] **1** *n* paquete *m*; **p. bomb** paquete bomba **2** *vt* **to p. up** envolver, empaquetar

parched [pɑːtʃt] *adj (land)* reseco(a); *(lips, mouth)* seco(a); *Fig* **to be p.** estar muerto(a) de sed

pardon ['pɑːdən] **1** *n* perdón *m*; *Jur* indulto *m*; **I beg your p.** (Usted) perdone; **(I beg your) p.?** ¿cómo (dice)? **2** *vt* perdonar; *Jur* indultar; **p. me!** ¡Usted perdone!

parents ['peərənts] *npl* padres

Paris ['pærɪs] *n* París

parish ['pærɪʃ] *n* parroquia *f*

Parisian [pə'rɪzɪən] *adj* & *n* parisino(a) *(m,f)*

park [pɑːk] **1** *n* parque *m* **2** *vt* estacionar, *Esp* aparcar

parking ['pɑːkɪŋ] *n* estacionamiento *m*, *Esp* aparcamiento *m*, *Col* parqueadero *m*; **no p.** *(sign)* prohibido estacionar *or Esp* aparcar, estacionamiento prohibido; *US* **p. lot** *Esp* aparcamiento *m*, *RP* playa *f* de estacionamiento, *Col* aparcadero *m*; **p. meter** parquímetro *m*; **p. space** estacionamiento *m*, sitio *m or* hueco *m* para estacionar

parliament ['pɑ:ləmənt] *n* parlamento *m*

parody ['pærədɪ] *n* parodia *f*

parole [pə'rəʊl] *n* *Jur* libertad *f* condicional; **on p.** en libertad bajo palabra

parrot ['pærət] *n* loro *m*, papagayo *m*

parsley ['pɑ:slɪ] *n* perejil *m*

parsnip ['pɑ:snɪp] *n* chirivía *f*

parson ['pɑ:sən] *n* cura *m*

part [pɑ:t] **1** *n* (**a**) parte *f*; *(piece)* trozo *m*; *(episode)* capítulo *m*; *Tech* pieza *f*; **for the most p.** en la mayor parte (**b**) *Cin, Th* papel *m*; **to take p. in sth** participar en algo (**c**) *(place)* lugar *m*; **in these parts** por estos lugares (**d**) **for my p.** por mi parte; **to take sb's p.** tomar partido por algn (**e**) *US (in hair)* raya *f*, *Col, Méx, Ven* carrera *f* **2** *adj (partial)* parcial **3** *adv (partly)* en parte **4** *vt (separate)* separar; **to p. one's hair** hacerse raya *or Col, Méx, Ven* carrera (en el pelo) **5** *vi* separarse; *(say goodbye)* despedirse

▶ **part with** *vt insep* separarse de

partial ['pɑ:ʃəl] *adj* parcial; **to be p. to sth** ser aficionado(a) a algo

participant [pɑ:'tɪsɪpənt] *n* participante *mf*; *(in competition)* concursante *mf*

participate [pɑ:'tɪsɪpeɪt] *vi* participar (**in** en)

participation [pɑ:tɪsɪ'peɪʃən] *n* participación *f*

particular [pə'tɪkjələ(r)] **1** *adj* (**a**) *(special)* particular, especial; **in this p. case** en este caso concreto; **that p. person** esa persona en particular (**b**) *(fussy)* exigente **2** *npl* **particulars** pormenores *mpl*; **to take down sb's particulars** anotar los datos

personales de algn

particularly [pə'tɪkjələlɪ] *adv* particularmente, especialmente

parting ['pɑ:tɪŋ] **1** *n (separation)* separación *f*; *(farewell)* despedida *f*; *Br (in hair)* raya *f*, *Col, Méx, Ven* carrera *f* **2** *adj* de despedida

partition [pɑ:'tɪʃən] **1** *n (wall)* tabique *m*; *(of country)* partición *f* **2** *vt* dividir

partly ['pɑ:tlɪ] *adv* en parte

partner ['pɑ:tnə(r)] **1** *n* compañero(a) *m,f*; *(in dancing, tennis)* pareja *f*; *(husband)* marido *m*; *(wife)* mujer *f*; *Com* socio(a) *m,f* **2** *vt* acompañar

partnership ['pɑ:tnəʃɪp] *n (relationship)* vida *f* en común; *Com* sociedad *f*

partridge ['pɑ:trɪdʒ] *n* perdiz pardilla

part-time ['pɑ:t'taɪm] **1** *adj (work etc)* de tiempo parcial **2** *adv* a tiempo parcial

party ['pɑ:tɪ] **1** *n* (**a**) *(celebration)* fiesta *f* (**b**) *(group)* grupo *m* (**c**) *Pol* partido *m*; **p. political broadcast** espacio *m* electoral **2** *adj* de fiesta

pass [pɑ:s] **1** *n* (**a**) *(of mountain)* desfiladero *m* (**b**) *(permit)* permiso *m*; **bus p.** abono *m* de autobús (**c**) *Sport* pase *m*
2 *vt* (**a**) pasar; *(overtake)* adelantar (**b**) *(exam, law)* aprobar; *Jur* **to p. sentence** dictar sentencia
3 *vi* (**a**) pasar; *(procession)* desfilar; *(car)* adelantar; *(people)* cruzarse; *Sport* hacer un pase; **we passed on the stairs** nos cruzamos en la escalera (**b**) *(in exam)* aprobar

▶ **pass away** *vi Euph* pasar a mejor vida

▶ **pass by 1** *vt sep* pasar de largo **2** *vi* pasar

▶ **pass for** *vt insep* pasar por

▶ **pass off 1** *vt sep* hacer pasar; **to p. oneself off as sth** hacerse pasar por algo **2** *vi (happen)* transcurrir

▶ **pass on 1** *vt sep (hand on)* transmitir **2** *vi Euph* pasar a mejor vida

▶ **pass out** *vi (faint)* desmayarse; *Mil* graduarse

▸**pass over** vt insep (**a**) (aircraft) volar por (**b**) (disregard) pasar por alto

▸**pass up** vt sep Fam (opportunity) renunciar; (offer) rechazar

passable ['pɑːsəbəl] adj (road) transitable; (acceptable) pasable

passage ['pæsɪdʒ] n (**a**) (alleyway) callejón m; (hallway) pasillo m (**b**) (movement) tránsito m; Naut travesía f (**c**) Mus, Lit pasaje m

passenger ['pæsɪndʒə(r)] n pasajero(a) m,f

passer-by [pɑːsɪ'baɪ] n transeúnte mf

passing ['pɑːsɪŋ] **1** n (**a**) (of time) transcurso m; **in p.** de pasada (**b**) (of law) aprobación f **2** adj que pasa; (glance) rápido(a); (thought) pasajero(a)

passion ['pæʃən] n pasión f; **p. fruit** granadilla f

passionate ['pæʃənɪt] adj apasionado(a)

passive ['pæsɪv] adj pasivo(a)

passport ['pɑːspɔːt] n pasaporte m

password ['pɑːswɜːd] n contraseña f

past [pɑːst] **1** n pasado m; **in the p.** en el pasado; **to have a p.** tener antecedentes
2 adj pasado(a); (former) anterior; **in the p. weeks** en las últimas semanas
3 adv por delante; **to run p.** pasar corriendo
4 prep (beyond) más allá de; (more than) más de; **he's p. forty** pasa de los cuarenta (años); **it's five p. ten** son las diez y cinco; Fam **to be p. it** estar muy carroza

pasta ['pæstə] n pasta f, pastas fpl

paste [peɪst] **1** n pasta f; (glue) engrudo m **2** vt (stick) pegar; (put paste on) engomar

pastel ['pæstəl] adj & n pastel (m)

pasteurized ['pæstjəraɪzd] adj pasteurizado(a)

pastime ['pɑːstaɪm] n pasatiempo m

pastor ['pɑːstə(r)] n pastor m

pastry ['peɪstrɪ] n (dough) pasta f; (cake) pastel m, Col, CSur torta f

pasture ['pɑːstʃə(r)] n pasto m

pasty¹ ['pæstɪ] n Culin empanada f, pastel m de carne

pasty² ['peɪstɪ] adj (pastier, pastiest) (complexion) pálido(a)

pat [pæt] **1** n (caress) caricia f; (tap) palmadita f; Fig **to give sb a p. on the back** felicitar a algn **2** vt acariciar; **to p. sb on the back** dar a algn una palmadita en la espalda

patch [pætʃ] n (of material) parche m; Br (of land) terreno m; (of colour, light) mancha f; Br Fam **to be going through a bad p.** estar pasando por una mala racha

▸**patch up** vt sep (wounded person) hacer una cura or Méx, RP curación de urgencia a; **to p. things up** (after argument) limar asperezas

patchwork ['pætʃwɜːk] **1** n labor f de retales **2** adj (quilt etc) hecho(a) con retales distintos

patchy ['pætʃɪ] adj (patchier, patchiest) (colour, performance) desigual; (knowledge) incompleto(a)

patent ['pætənt, Br 'peɪtənt] **1** n Com patente f
2 adj (obvious) patente, evidente
3 vt Com patentar

patently [Br 'peɪtəntlɪ US 'pætəntlɪ] adv **it is p. obvious** está clarísimo

paternal [pə'tɜːnəl] adj paternal; (grandmother etc) paterno(a)

path [pɑːθ] n camino m, sendero m; (route) ruta f; (of missile) trayectoria f

pathetic [pə'θetɪk] adj (pitiful) patético(a); Fam (hopeless) malísimo(a); **she was a p. sight** daba lástima verla

pathway ['pɑːθweɪ] n camino m, sendero m

patience ['peɪʃəns] n (**a**) paciencia f; **to lose one's p. with sb** perder la paciencia con algn (**b**) Br Cards solitario m

patient ['peɪʃənt] **1** adj paciente; **to be p. with sb** tener paciencia con algn **2** n Med paciente mf

patio ['pætɪəʊ] n patio m

patriot ['pætrɪət, 'peɪtrɪət] n patriota mf

patriotic [pætrɪ'ɒtɪk] *adj (person)* patriota; *(speech, act)* patriótico(a)

patrol [pə'trəʊl] **1** *n* patrulla *f*; **p. car** coche *m or Am* carro *m or CSur* auto *m* patrulla **2** *vt* patrullar por

patrolman [pə'trəʊlmən] *n US* policía *m*

patron ['peɪtrən] *n* (**a**) *(of charity)* patrocinador(a) *m,f*; *(of arts)* mecenas *m inv*; **p. saint** (santo(a) *m,f*) patrón(ona) *mf* (**b**) *(customer)* cliente *mf* habitual

patronize ['pætrənaɪz] *vt* (**a**) *(arts)* fomentar; *(shop)* ser cliente habitual de; *(club etc)* frecuentar (**b**) *Pej (person)* tratar con condescendencia

patter¹ ['pætə(r)] **1** *n (of rain)* repiqueteo *m*; *(of feet)* pasito *m* **2** *vi (rain)* repiquetear; *(feet)* hacer ruido sordo

patter² ['pætə(r)] *n Fam* labia *f*; *(of salesman)* discursillo preparado

pattern ['pætən] *n Sewing* patrón *m*; *(design)* dibujo *m*; *(on material)* estampado *m*; *Fig (of behaviour)* modelo *m*

paunch [pɔːntʃ] *n* barriga *f*, panza *f*, *Chile* guata *f*

pause [pɔːz] **1** *n* pausa *f*; *(silence)* silencio *m* **2** *vi* hacer una pausa; *(be silent)* callarse

pave [peɪv] *vt* pavimentar; *(with stones)* empedrar; *Fig* **to p. the way for sb/sth** preparar el terreno para algn/algo

pavement ['peɪvmənt] *n* (**a**) *Br (beside road)* acera *f*, *CSur* vereda *f*, *CAm, Méx* banqueta *f* (**b**) *US (roadway)* calzada *f*

pavilion [pə'vɪljən] *n* pabellón *m*; *Br Sport (changing rooms)* vestuarios *mpl*

paving ['peɪvɪŋ] *n (on road)* pavimento *m*; *(on floor)* enlosado *m*; *(with stones)* empedrado *m*; **p. stone** losa *f*

paw [pɔː] **1** *n (foot)* pata *f*; *(of cat)* garra *f*; *(of lion)* zarpa *f* **2** *vt (of lion)* dar zarpazos a; *Pej (of person)* manosear, sobar

pawn¹ [pɔːn] *n (in chess)* peón *m*; *Fig* **to be sb's p.** ser el juguete de algn

pawn² [pɔːn] *vt* empeñar

pawnbroker ['pɔːnbrəʊkə(r)] *n* prestamista *mf*

pawnshop ['pɔːnʃɒp] *n* casa *f* de empeños

pay [peɪ] *(pt & pp paid)* **1** *n (wages)* paga *f*, sueldo *m*; **p.** *Br* **packet** *or US* **envelope** sobre *m* de la paga; **p. rise** aumento *m* del sueldo; **p. slip** nómina *f* **2** *vt* (**a**) pagar; **to be** *or* **get paid** cobrar (**b**) *(attention)* prestar; *(homage)* rendir; *(visit)* hacer; **to p. sb a compliment** halagar a algn (**c**) *(be profitable for)* compensar **3** *vi* (**a**) pagar; **to p. for sth** pagar (por) algo (**b**) *(be profitable)* ser rentable

▶ **pay back** *vt sep* reembolsar; *Fig* **to p. sb back** vengarse de algn

▶ **pay in** *vt sep (money) Esp* ingresar, *Am* depositar

▶ **pay off 1** *vt sep (debt)* liquidar; *(mortgage)* cancelar **2** *vi (be successful)* dar resultado

▶ **pay out** *vt sep (spend)* gastar (**on** en)

▶ **pay up** *vi* pagar

payable ['peɪəbəl] *adj* pagadero(a)

payment ['peɪmənt] *n* pago *m*; *(of cheque)* cobro *m*; **advance p.** anticipo *m*; **down p.** entrada *f*; **monthly p.** mensualidad *f*

PC ['piː'siː] **1** *n* (**a**) *Br (abbr* **Police Constable**) agente *mf* de policía (**b**) *(abbr* **personal computer**) PC *m* **2** *adj (abbr* **politically correct**) políticamente correcto(a)

PE ['piː'iː] *n Educ (abbr* **physical education**) educación *f* física

pea [piː] *n* guisante *m*, *Am* arveja *f*, *Carib, Méx* chícharo *m*

peace [piːs] *n* paz *f*; *(calm)* tranquilidad *f*; **at** *or* **in p.** en paz; **p. and quiet** tranquilidad; **to make p.** hacer las paces; *(countries)* firmar la paz

peaceful ['piːsfʊl] *adj (demonstration)* pacífico(a); *(place)* tranquilo(a)

peach [piːtʃ] *n* melocotón *m*, *Am* durazno *m*

peacock ['piːkɒk] *n* pavo *m* real

peak [pi:k] *n (of cap)* visera *f; (of mountain)* pico *m; (summit)* cima *f; Fig* cumbre *f;* **p. hours** horas *fpl* punta; **p. period** horas de mayor consumo; **p. season** temporada alta

peal [pi:l] *n (of bells)* repique *m;* **p. of thunder** trueno *m;* **peals of laughter** carcajadas *fpl*

peanut ['pi:nʌt] *n* cacahuete *m, Andes, Carib, RP* maní *m, CAm, Méx* cacahuate *m;* **p. butter** mantequilla *f or* crema *f* de cacahuete *or Andes, Carib, RP* maní *or CAm, Méx* cacahuate

pear [peə(r)] *n* pera *f*

pearl [pɜ:l] *n* perla *f*

peasant ['pezənt] *adj & n* campesino(a) *(m,f)*

pebble ['pebəl] *n* guijarro *m; (small)* china *f*

pecan [*Br* 'pi:kən, *US* pɪ'kæn] *n* pacana *f*

peck [pek] **1** *n (of bird)* picotazo *m; Fam (kiss)* besito *m*
2 *vt (bird)* picotear; *Fam (kiss)* dar un besito a
3 *vi* **to p. at one's food** picar la comida

peckish ['pekɪʃ] *adj Br Fam* **to be p.** tener un poco de hambre *or Esp* gusa

peculiar [pɪ'kju:lɪə(r)] *adj (odd)* extraño(a); *(particular)* característico(a)

pedal ['pedəl] **1** *n* pedal *m* **2** *vi* pedalear

pedantic [pɪ'dæntɪk] *adj* pedante

peddle ['pedəl] *vt & vi Com* vender de puerta en puerta; **to p. drugs** traficar con drogas

pedestal ['pedɪstəl] *n* pedestal *m; Fig* **to put sb on a p.** poner a algn sobre un pedestal

pedestrian [pɪ'destrɪən] **1** *n* peatón(ona) *m,f;* **p. crossing** paso *m* de peatones **2** *adj Pej* prosaico(a)

pediatrician [pi:dɪə'trɪʃən] *n US =* **paediatrician**

pedigree ['pedɪgri:] **1** *n* linaje *m; (family tree)* árbol genealógico; *(of animal)* pedigrí *m* **2** *adj (animal)* de raza

pee [pi:] *Fam* **1** *n* pis *m* **2** *vi* hacer pis

peek [pi:k] **1** *n* ojeada *f* **2** *vi* **to p. at sth** mirar algo a hurtadillas

peel [pi:l] **1** *n* piel *f; (of orange, lemon)* cáscara *f*
2 *vt (fruit)* pelar
3 *vi (paint)* desconcharse; *(wallpaper)* despegarse; *(skin)* pelarse

peeler ['pi:lə(r)] *n* **potato p.** pelapatatas *m inv*

peelings ['pi:lɪŋz] *npl* peladuras *fpl,* mondaduras *fpl*

peep[1] [pi:p] *n (sound)* pío *m*

peep[2] [pi:p] **1** *n (glance)* ojeada *f; (furtive look)* mirada furtiva **2** *vi* **to p. at sth** echar una ojeada a algo; **to p. out from behind sth** dejarse ver detrás de algo

peer[1] [pɪə(r)] *n (equal)* igual *mf; Br (noble)* par *m;* **p. group** grupo parejo

peer[2] [pɪə(r)] *vi* mirar detenidamente; *(shortsightedly)* mirar con ojos de miope

peeved [pi:vd] *adj Fam* fastidiado(a), de mal humor

peg [peg] **1** *n* clavija *f; (for coat, hat)* percha *f* **2** *vt (clothes)* tender; *(prices)* fijar

pejorative [pɪ'dʒɒrətɪv] *adj* peyorativo(a)

pelican ['pelɪkən] *n* pelícano *m; Br* **p. crossing** paso *m* de peatones

pelt[1] [pelt] *n (skin)* pellejo *m*

pelt[2] [pelt] **1** *vt* **to p. sb with sth** tirar algo a algn **2** *vi Fam* **(a) it was pelting (down)** *(raining)* diluviaba, *Esp* caían chuzos de punta **(b) to p. along** *(rush)* correr a toda prisa

pelvis ['pelvɪs] *n* pelvis *f*

pen[1] [pen] **1** *n (for writing)* pluma *f* (estilográfica); *(ballpoint)* bolígrafo *m, Chile* lápiz *m* (de pasta), *Col, Ecuad, Ven* esferográfico *f, Méx* pluma *f, RP* birome *m* **2** *vt* escribir

pen[2] [pen] **1** *n (enclosure)* corral *m; (for sheep)* redil *m; (for children)* corralito *m* **2** *vt* **to p. in** acorralar

penal ['pi:nəl] *adj* penal

penalize ['pi:nəlaɪz] vt castigar; Sport penalizar

penalty ['penəltɪ] n (punishment) pena f; Sport castigo m; Ftb penalti m, Am penal m; **to pay the p. for sth** cargar con las consecuencias de algo; **p. area** área f de castigo

pence [pens] pl of **penny**

pencil ['pensəl] n lápiz m; **p. case** estuche m de lápices; **p. sharpener** sacapuntas m inv

pendant ['pendənt] n colgante m

pending ['pendɪŋ] **1** adj pendiente **2** prep a la espera de; **p. a decision** (until) hasta que se tome una decisión

pendulum ['pendjʊləm] n péndulo m

penetrate ['penɪtreɪt] **1** vt penetrar; Fig adentrarse en **2** vi atravesar; (get inside) penetrar

penguin ['peŋgwɪn] n pingüino m

penicillin [penɪ'sɪlɪn] n penicilina f

peninsula [pɪ'nɪnsjʊlə] n península f

penis ['pi:nɪs] n pene m

penitentiary [penɪ'tenʃərɪ] n US cárcel f, penal m

penknife ['pennaɪf] n navaja f, cortaplumas m inv

penniless ['penɪlɪs] adj **to be p.** estar sin un centavo or Esp duro

penny ['penɪ] n (pl **pennies, pence**) Br penique m; US centavo m

pension ['penʃən] n pensión f; **retirement p.** jubilación f

pensioner ['penʃənə(r)] n jubilado(a) m,f

pent-up ['pentʌp] adj reprimido(a)

penultimate [pɪ'nʌltɪmɪt] adj penúltimo(a)

people ['pi:pəl] npl (a) gente f; (individuals) personas fpl; **many p.** mucha gente; **old p.'s home** asilo m de ancianos; **p. say that …** se dice que …; **some p.** algunas personas (b) (citizens) ciudadanos mpl; (inhabitants) habitantes mpl; **the p.** el pueblo (c) (nation) pueblo m, nación f

pepper ['pepə(r)] **1** n (spice) pimienta f; (vegetable) pimiento m, Méx chile m, RP ají m, Col, Ven pimentón m; **black p.** pimienta negra; Br **p. pot** pimentero m; **red/green p.** pimiento rojo/verde; **p. mill** molinillo m de pimienta **2** vt Fig **peppered with** salpicado(a) de

peppermint ['pepəmɪnt] n menta f; (sweet) pastilla f de menta

per [pɜː(r)] prep por; **five times p. week** cinco veces a la semana; **p. cent** por ciento; **p. day/annum** al or por día/año; **p. capita** per cápita

perceive [pə'siːv] vt (see) percibir

percentage [pə'sentɪdʒ] n porcentaje m

perception [pə'sepʃən] n percepción f

perceptive [pə'septɪv] adj perspicaz

perch¹ [pɜːtʃ] n (fish) perca f

perch² [pɜːtʃ] **1** n (for bird) percha f **2** vi (bird) posarse (**on** en)

percolator ['pɜːkəleɪtə(r)] n cafetera f

perennial [pə'renɪəl] adj Bot perenne

perfect 1 adj ['pɜːfɪkt] perfecto(a); **he's a p. stranger to us** nos es totalmente desconocido; **p. tense** tiempo perfecto **2** vt [pə'fekt] perfeccionar

perfection [pə'fekʃən] n perfección f

perfectly ['pɜːfɪktlɪ] adv perfectamente; (absolutely) completamente

perforation [pɜːfə'reɪʃən] n perforación f; (on stamps etc) perforado m

perform [pə'fɔːm] **1** vt (task) ejecutar, realizar; (piece of music) interpretar; Th representar **2** vi (machine) funcionar; Mus interpretar; Th actuar

performance [pə'fɔːməns] n (of task) ejecución f, realización f; Mus interpretación f; Th representación f; Sport actuación f; (of machine etc) rendimiento m

performer [pə'fɔːmə(r)] n Mus intérprete mf; Th actor m, actriz f

perfume ['pɜːfjuːm] n perfume m

perhaps [pə'hæps, præps] adv tal vez, quizá(s), Am talvez

peril ['perɪl] n (risk) riesgo m; (danger) peligro m

period ['pɪərɪəd] **1** n (a) período m; (stage) etapa f (b) Educ clase f (c) US (full stop) punto m (d) (menstruation) regla f **2** adj (dress, furniture) de época

periodical [pɪərɪ'ɒdɪkəl] **1** adj periódico(a) **2** n revista f

periodically [pɪərɪ'ɒdɪklɪ] adv de vez en cuando

peripheral [pə'rɪfərəl] **1** adj periférico(a) **2** n Comput unidad periférica

perish ['perɪʃ] vi perecer; (material) echarse a perder

perishable ['perɪʃəbəl] adj perecedero(a)

perjury ['pɜːdʒərɪ] n perjurio m

perk [pɜːk] n Br Fam extra m

▸ **perk up** vi (person) animarse; (after illness) reponerse

perm [pɜːm] **1** n permanente f **2** vt **to have one's hair permed** hacerse la permanente

permanent ['pɜːmənənt] adj permanente; (address, job) fijo(a)

permissible [pə'mɪsəbəl] adj admisible

permission [pə'mɪʃən] n permiso m

permissive [pə'mɪsɪv] adj permisivo(a)

permit 1 n ['pɜːmɪt] permiso m; Com licencia f **2** vt [pə'mɪt] **to p. sb to do sth** permitir a algn hacer algo

perpendicular [pɜːpən'dɪkjʊlə(r)] **1** adj perpendicular; (cliff) vertical **2** n perpendicular f

perpetrate ['pɜːpɪtreɪt] vt cometer

perpetrator ['pɜːpɪtreɪtə(r)] n autor(a) m,f

perpetual [pə'petʃʊəl] adj (noise) continuo(a); (arguing) interminable; (snow) perpetuo(a)

perplex [pə'pleks] vt dejar perplejo(a)

persecute ['pɜːsɪkjuːt] vt perseguir; (harass) acosar

persecution [pɜːsɪ'kjuːʃən] n persecución f; (harassment) acoso m

perseverance [pɜːsɪ'vɪərəns] n perseverancia f

persevere [pɜːsɪ'vɪə(r)] vi perseverar

persist [pə'sɪst] vi empeñarse (**in** en)

persistent [pə'sɪstənt] adj (person) perseverante; (smell etc) persistente; (continual) constante

person ['pɜːsən] n (pl **people**) persona f; (individual) individuo m; **in p.** en persona

personal ['pɜːsənəl] (**a**) adj (private) personal; (friend) íntimo(a); **p. computer** ordenador m personal, Am computadora f personal; **p. column** anuncios mpl personales; **p. pronoun** pronombre m personal (**b**) (in person) en persona; **he will make a p. appearance** estará aquí en persona (**c**) Pej (comment etc) indiscreto(a)

personality [pɜːsə'nælɪtɪ] n personalidad f

personally ['pɜːsənəlɪ] adv (for my part) personalmente; (in person) en persona

personify [pɜː'sɒnɪfaɪ] vt personificar, encarnar

personnel [pɜːsə'nel] n personal m

perspective [pə'spektɪv] n perspectiva f

perspire [pə'spaɪə(r)] vi transpirar

persuade [pə'sweɪd] vt persuadir; **to p. sb to do sth** persuadir a algn para que haga algo

persuasion [pə'sweɪʒən] n persuasión f; (opinion, belief) credo m

persuasive [pə'sweɪsɪv] adj persuasivo(a)

pertinent ['pɜːtɪnənt] adj (relevant) pertinente; **p. to** relacionado(a) con, a propósito de

perturbing [pə'tɜːbɪŋ] adj inquietante

Peru [pə'ruː] n Perú

pervade [pɜː'veɪd] vt (of smell) penetrar; (of light) difundirse por; Fig (of influence) extenderse por

perverse [pə'vɜːs] adj (wicked) perverso(a); (contrary) contrario(a) a todo

perversion [Br pə'vɜːʃən, US pər'vɜːrʒən] n (sexual) perversión f; (of justice, truth) desvirtuación f

pervert 1 n ['pɜːvɜːt] Med pervertido(a) m,f (sexual) **2** vt [pə'vɜːt] pervertir; (justice, truth) desvirtuar

pessimism ['pesɪmɪzəm] n pesimismo m

pessimist ['pesɪmɪst] n pesimista mf

pessimistic [pesɪ'mɪstɪk] adj pesimista

pest [pest] n (a) Zool animal nocivo; Bot planta nociva (b) Fam (person) pelma mf; (thing) lata f

pester ['pestə(r)] vt molestar, Esp incordiar

pesticide ['pestɪsaɪd] n pesticida m

pet [pet] 1 n (a) animal doméstico (b) (favourite) preferido(a) m,f; Fam cariño m
2 adj (favourite) preferido(a)
3 vt acariciar
4 vi Fam (sexually) Esp darse or pegarse el lote, Am manosearse

petal ['petəl] n pétalo m

peter ['pi:tə(r)] vi to p. out agotarse

petition [pɪ'tɪʃən] n petición f

petrify ['petrɪfaɪ] vt Literary petrificar; Fig they were petrified se quedaron de piedra

petrol ['petrəl] n Br gasolina f, RP nafta f; **p. can** bidón m de gasolina or RP nafta; **p. pump** surtidor m de gasolina or RP nafta; **p. station** gasolinera f, estación f de servicio, Andes grifo m; **p. tank** depósito m de gasolina, RP tanque m de nafta

petticoat ['petɪkəʊt] n enaguas fpl

petty ['petɪ] adj (**pettier, pettiest**) (trivial) insignificante; (small-minded) mezquino(a); **p. cash** dinero m para gastos pequeños; Naut **p. officer** sargento m de marina

phantom ['fæntəm] adj & n fantasma (m)

pharmacist ['fɑ:məsɪst] n farmacéutico(a) m,f

pharmacy ['fɑ:məsɪ] n farmacia f

phase [feɪz] 1 n fase f 2 vt to p. sth in/out introducir/retirar algo progresivamente

PhD [pi:eɪtʃ'di:] n (abbr Doctor of Philosophy) (person) Doctor(a) m,f en Filosofía

phenomenal [fɪ'nɒmɪnəl] adj fenomenal

phenomenon [fɪ'nɒmɪnən] n (pl phenomena [fɪ'nɒmɪnə]) fenómeno m

Philippines ['fɪlɪpi:nz] npl the P. las (Islas) Filipinas

philosopher [fɪ'lɒsəfə(r)] n filósofo(a) m,f

philosophical [fɪlə'sɒfɪkəl] adj filosófico(a)

philosophy [fɪ'lɒsəfɪ] n filosofía f

phlegm [flem] n flema f

phobia ['fəʊbɪə] n fobia f

phone [fəʊn] n & vt = telephone

phonetic [fə'netɪk] 1 adj fonético(a) 2 n phonetics fonética f

phoney ['fəʊnɪ] 1 adj (phonier, phoniest) (thing) falso(a); (person) farsante 2 n (person) farsante mf

photo ['fəʊtəʊ] n foto f

photocopier ['fəʊtəʊkɒpɪə(r)] n fotocopiadora f

photocopy ['fəʊtəʊkɒpɪ] 1 n fotocopia f 2 vt fotocopiar

photograph ['fəʊtəgræf, 'fəʊtəgrɑ:f] 1 n fotografía f; **black and white/colour p.** fotografía en blanco y negro/en color 2 vt fotografiar

photographer [fə'tɒgrəfə(r)] n fotógrafo(a) m,f

photography [fə'tɒgrəfɪ] n fotografía f

phrase [freɪz] 1 n frase f; **p. book** libro m de frases 2 vt expresar

physical ['fɪzɪkəl] adj físico(a); **p. education** educación física

physician [fɪ'zɪʃən] n médico(a) m,f

physics ['fɪzɪks] n sing física f

physiology [fɪzɪ'ɒlədʒɪ] n fisiología f

physiotherapist [fɪzɪəʊ'θerəpɪst] n fisioterapeuta mf

physique [fɪ'zi:k] n físico m

pianist ['pɪənɪst] n pianista mf

piano [pɪ'ænəʊ] n piano m

pick [pɪk] 1 n (a) (tool) pico m, piqueta f (b) take your p. (choice) elige el que quieras
2 vt (a) (choose) escoger; (team) seleccionar (b) (flowers, fruit) recoger, Esp coger (c) (scratch) hurgar; **to p. one's nose** hurgarse la nariz (d) (lock) forzar

3 *vi* **to p. at one's food** comer sin ganas

▸ **pick off** *vt sep* (**a**) *(remove)* quitar (**b**) *(shoot)* matar uno a uno

▸ **pick on** *vt insep (persecute)* meterse con

▸ **pick out** *vt sep (choose)* elegir; *(distinguish)* distinguir; *(identify)* identificar

▸ **pick up 1** *vt sep* (**a**) *(object on floor)* recoger, *Esp* coger; *(telephone)* descolgar; **to p. oneself up** levantarse; *Fig* reponerse (**b**) *(collect)* recoger; *(shopping, person)* buscar; **to p. up speed** ganar velocidad (**c**) *(acquire)* conseguir; *(learn)* aprender **2** *vi (improve)* mejorarse, ir mejorando; *(prices)* subir

pickaxe, *US* **pickax** ['pɪkæks] *n* piqueta *f*

picket ['pɪkɪt] **1** *n* piquete *m*; **p. line** piquete
 2 *vt* piquetear
 3 *vi* hacer piquete

pickle ['pɪkəl] **1** *n* (**a**) *Br (sauce)* = salsa agridulce a base de trocitos de fruta y verduras (**b**) *Fam (mess)* lío *m*, apuro *m* **2** *vt Culin* conservar en adobo *or* escabeche; **pickled onions** cebollas *fpl* en vinagre

pickpocket ['pɪkpɒkɪt] *n* carterista *mf*

pick-up ['pɪkʌp] *n Br* **p. (arm)** *(on record player)* brazo *m*; **p. (truck)** furgoneta *f*

picnic ['pɪknɪk] **1** *n* comida *f* de campo, picnic *m* **2** *vi* hacer una comida de campo

picture ['pɪktʃə(r)] **1** *n* (**a**) *(painting)* cuadro *m*; *(drawing)* dibujo *m*; *(portrait)* retrato *m*; *(photo)* foto *f*; *(illustration)* ilustración *f*; **p. book** libro ilustrado; **p. postcard** tarjeta *f* postal (**b**) *TV* imagen *f*; *Cin* película *f*; *Br* **to go to the pictures** ir al cine **2** *vt (imagine)* imaginarse

picturesque [pɪktʃə'resk] *adj* pintoresco(a)

pie [paɪ] *n (of fruit)* tarta *f*, pastel *m*; *(of meat, fish)* empanada *f*, pastel, *Col, CSur* torta *f*; *(pasty)* empanadilla *f*

piece [piːs] *n* (**a**) *(of food)* pedazo *m*, trozo *m*; *(of paper)* trozo; *(part)* pieza *f*; **a p. of advice** un consejo; **a p. of news** una noticia; **to break sth into pieces** hacer algo pedazos; *Fig* **to go to pieces** perder el control (de sí mismo) (**b**) *Lit, Mus* obra *f*, pieza *f* (**c**) *(coin)* moneda *f* (**d**) *(in chess)* pieza *f*; *(in draughts)* ficha *f*

▸ **piece together** *vt sep (facts)* reconstruir; *(jigsaw)* hacer

pier [pɪə(r)] *n* embarcadero *m*, muelle *m*; *(promenade)* = paseo de madera que entra en el mar

pierce [pɪəs] *vt* perforar; *(penetrate)* penetrar en

piercing ['pɪəsɪŋ] *adj (sound etc)* penetrante

pig [pɪg] *n* (**a**) *(animal)* cerdo *m* (**b**) *Fam (greedy person)* comilón(ona) *m,f*, glotón(ona) *m,f*, *Am* chacho *m*; *(unpleasant person)* cerdo(a) *m,f*, asqueroso(a) *m,f*, *Am* chancho *m* (**c**) *Fam Pej (policeman) Esp* madero *m*, *Andes* paco *m*, *Méx* tamarindo *m*, *RP* cana *m*

pigeon ['pɪdʒɪn] *n* paloma *f*; *Culin, Sport* pichón *m*

pigeonhole ['pɪdʒɪnhəʊl] *n* casilla *f*

pigment ['pɪgmənt] *n* pigmento *m*

pigtail ['pɪgteɪl] *n* trenza *f*; *(bullfighter's)* coleta *f*

pile¹ [paɪl] **1** *n* montón *m*
 2 *vt* amontonar
 3 *vi Fam* **to p. into** meterse atropelladamente en

▸ **pile up 1** *vt sep (things)* amontonar; *(riches, debts)* acumular **2** *vi* amontonarse

pile² [paɪl] *n (on carpet)* pelo *m*; **thick p.** pelo largo

piles [paɪlz] *npl Med* almorranas *fpl*, hemorroides *fpl*

pile-up ['paɪlʌp] *n Aut* choque *m* en cadena

pilgrim ['pɪlgrɪm] *n* peregrino(a) *m,f*

pilgrimage ['pɪlgrɪmɪdʒ] *n* peregrinación *f*

pill [pɪl] *n* píldora *f*, pastilla *f*; **to be on**

the p. estar tomando la píldora (anticonceptiva)

pillar ['pɪlə(r)] *n* pilar *m*, columna *f*; *Br* **p. box** buzón *m*

pillow ['pɪləʊ] *n* almohada *f*

pillowcase ['pɪləʊkeɪs] *n* funda *f* de almohada

pilot ['paɪlət] **1** *n* piloto *m*
2 *adj (trial)* piloto *inv*; **p. light** piloto *m*; **p. scheme** proyecto piloto
3 *vt* pilotar

pimp [pɪmp] *n* proxeneta *m, Esp* chulo *m, RP* cafiolo *m*

pimple ['pɪmpəl] *n* grano *m*, espinilla *f*

pin [pɪn] **1** *n (for sewing)* alfiler *m; (bolt)* clavija *f; Br (of electric plug)* clavija *f; (in bowling)* bolo *m; (brooch, badge)* pin *m*; **pins and needles** hormigueo *m*
2 *vt (on board)* clavar con chinchetas; *(garment etc)* sujetar con alfileres; **to p. sb against a wall** tener a algn contra una pared; *Fig* **to p. one's hopes on sth** poner sus esperanzas en algo; *Fam* **to p. a crime on sb** endosar un delito a algn

▸ **pin down** *vt sep Fig* **to p. sb down** hacer que algn se comprometa

pinball ['pɪnbɔːl] *n* flipper *m*, máquina *f* de petacos

pincers ['pɪnsəz] *npl (on crab)* pinzas *fpl; (tool)* tenazas *fpl*

pinch [pɪntʃ] **1** *n (nip)* pellizco *m; Fig Br* **at** *or US* **in a p.** en caso de apuro; **a p. of salt** una pizca de sal
2 *vt* pellizcar; *Br Fam (steal)* afanar, *Esp* levantar
3 *vi (shoes)* apretar

pine¹ [paɪn] *n (tree)* pino *m*; **p. cone** piña *f*

pine² [paɪn] *vi* **to p. (away)** consumirse, morirse de pena; **to p. for sth/sb** echar de menos *or* añorar algo/a algn, *Am* extrañar algo/a algn

pineapple ['paɪnæpəl] *n* piña *f, RP* ananá *m*

pink [pɪŋk] **1** *n (colour)* rosa *m; Bot* clavel *m* **2** *adj (colour)* rosa *inv; Pol Fam* rojillo(a)

pinnacle ['pɪnəkəl] *n (of building)* pináculo *m; (of mountain)* cima *f*, pico *m; Fig (of success)* cumbre *f*

pinpoint ['pɪnpɔɪnt] *vt* señalar

pint [paɪnt] *n* pinta *f; Br Fam* **a p. (of beer)** una pinta (de cerveza)

pioneer [paɪə'nɪə(r)] **1** *n (settler)* pionero(a) *m,f; (forerunner)* precursor(a) *m,f* **2** *vt* ser pionero(a) en

pious ['paɪəs] *adj* piadoso(a), devoto(a); *Pej* beato(a)

pip¹ [pɪp] *n (seed)* pepita *f*

pip² [pɪp] *n (sound)* señal *f* (corta); *(on dice)* punto *m*

pipe [paɪp] **1** *n* (**a**) conducto *m*, tubería *f; (of organ)* caramillo *m; Fam* **the pipes** *(bagpipes)* la gaita (**b**) *(for smoking)* pipa *f*; **p. cleaner** limpiapipas *m inv; Fig* **p. dream** sueño *m* imposible **2** *vt (water)* llevar por tubería; *(oil)* transportar por oleoducto; **piped music** hilo *m* musical

▸ **pipe down** *vi Fam* callarse

▸ **pipe up** *vi Fam* hacerse oír

pipeline ['paɪplaɪn] *n* tubería *f*, cañería *f; (for gas)* gasoducto *m; (for oil)* oleoducto *m*

piping ['paɪpɪŋ] **1** *n (for water, gas etc)* tubería *f*, cañería *f* **2** *adj* **p. hot** bien caliente

pirate ['paɪrɪt] *n* pirata *m;* **p. edition** edición *f* pirata; **p. radio** emisora *f* pirata; **p. ship** barco *m* pirata

Pisces ['paɪsiːz] *n* Piscis *m inv*

pissed [pɪst] *adj very Fam* (**a**) *Br (drunk) Esp, Méx* pedo *inv, Col* caído(a), *RP* en pedo (**b**) *US (angry)* cabreado(a)

pistachio [pɪs'tɑːʃɪəʊ] *n (nut)* pistacho *m*

pistol ['pɪstəl] *n* pistola *f*

pit¹ [pɪt] **1** *n* hoyo *m; (large)* hoya *f; (coal mine)* mina *f* de carbón; *Th* platea *f; (in motor racing)* foso *m*, box *m* **2** *vt* **to p. one's wits against sb** medirse con algn

pit² [pɪt] *n (of cherry)* hueso *m*, pipo *m, RP* carozo *m; US (of peach, plum)* hueso, *RP* carozo *m*

pitch [pɪtʃ] **1** *vt* (**a**) *(throw)* lanzar,

arrojar (**b**) *(tent)* armar **2** *n* (**a**) *Mus (of sound)* tono *m* (**b**) *esp Br Sport* campo *m*, cancha *f*

pitcher ['pɪtʃə(r)] *n (container)* cántaro *m*, jarro *m*

pitfall ['pɪtfɔ:l] *n* dificultad *f*, obstáculo *m*

pith [pɪθ] *n (of orange)* piel blanca; *Fig* meollo *m*

pitiful ['pɪtɪfʊl] *adj (producing pity)* lastimoso(a), *(terrible)* lamentable

pitiless ['pɪtɪlɪs] *adj* despiadado(a), implacable

pittance ['pɪtəns] *n* miseria *f*

pity ['pɪtɪ] **1** *n* (**a**) *(compassion)* compasión *f*, piedad *f*; **to take p. on sb** compadecerse de algn (**b**) *(shame)* lástima *f*, pena *f*; **what a p.!** ¡qué pena!, ¡qué lástima! **2** *vt* compadecerse de; **I p. them** me dan pena

pivot ['pɪvət] **1** *n* pivote *m* **2** *vi* girar sobre su eje

pizza ['pi:tsə] *n* pizza *f*; **p. parlour** pizzería *f*

placard ['plækɑ:d] *n* pancarta *f*

place [pleɪs] **1** *n* (**a**) sitio *m*, lugar *m*; **to be in/out of p.** estar en/fuera de su sitio; **to take p.** tener lugar (**b**) *(seat)* sitio *m*; *(on bus)* asiento *m*; *(at university)* plaza *m*; **to change places with sb** intercambiar el sitio con algn; **to take sb's p.** sustituir a algn (**c**) *(position on scale)* posición *f*; *(social position)* rango *m*; **in the first p.** en primer lugar (**d**) *(house)* casa *f*; *(building)* lugar *m*; **we're going to his p.** vamos a su casa

2 *vt* (**a**) poner, colocar; **to p. an order with sb** hacer un pedido a algn (**b**) *(face, person)* recordar; *(in job)* colocar en un empleo

placid ['plæsɪd] *adj* apacible

plague [pleɪg] **1** *n (of insects)* plaga *f*; *Med* peste *f* **2** *vt* **to p. sb with requests** acosar a algn a peticiones

plaice [pleɪs] *n (pl plaice) (fish)* platija *f*

plain [pleɪn] **1** *adj* (**a**) *(clear)* claro(a), evidente; *Fig* **he likes p. speaking** le gusta hablar con franqueza (**b**) *(simple)* sencillo(a); *(chocolate)* amargo(a); *(flour)* sin levadura; **in p. clothes** vestido(a) de paisano; **the p. truth** la verdad lisa y llana (**c**) *(unattractive)* poco atractivo(a) **2** *n* *Geog* llanura *f*, llano *m*

plainly ['pleɪnlɪ] *adv* claramente; *(simply)* sencillamente; **to speak p.** hablar con franqueza

plait [plæt] **1** *n* trenza *f* **2** *vt* trenzar

plan [plæn] **1** *n (scheme)* plan *m*, proyecto *m*; *(drawing)* plano *m*

2 *vt* (**a**) *(for future)* planear, proyectar; *(economy)* planificar (**b**) *(intend)* pensar, tener la intención de; **it wasn't planned** no estaba previsto

3 *vi* hacer planes; **to p. on doing sth** tener la intención de hacer algo

plane¹ [pleɪn] **1** *n* (**a**) *Math* plano *m*; *Fig* nivel *m* (**b**) *Fam Av* avión *m*

2 *adj Geom* plano(a)

3 *vi (glide)* planear

plane² [pleɪn] **1** *n (tool)* cepillo *m* **2** *vt* cepillar

plane³ [pleɪn] *n Bot* **p. (tree)** plátano *m*

planet ['plænɪt] *n* planeta *m*

plank [plæŋk] *n* tabla *f*, tablón *m*

planning ['plænɪŋ] *n* planificación *f*; **family p.** planificación familiar; *Br* **p. permission** licencia *f* de obras

plant¹ [plɑ:nt] **1** *n* planta *f* **2** *vt* *(flowers)* plantar; *(seeds)* sembrar; *(bomb)* colocar

plant² [plɑ:nt] *n (factory)* planta *f*, fábrica *f*; *(machinery)* maquinaria *f*

plantation [plæn'teɪʃən] *n* plantación *f*

plaque [plæk] *n* placa *f*; *(on teeth)* sarro *m*

plaster ['plɑ:stə(r)] **1** *n Constr* yeso *m*; *Med* escayola *f*; *Br* **(sticking) p.** tirita® *f*, *Am* curita *f*; **p. of Paris** yeso mate **2** *vt* *Constr* enyesar; *Fig (cover)* cubrir (**with** de)

plastic ['plæstɪk] **1** *n* plástico *m* **2** *adj* *(cup, bag)* de plástico; **p. surgery** cirugía plástica

plate [pleɪt] **1** *n* (**a**) plato *m* (**b**) *(sheet)* placa *f*; **gold p.** chapa *f* de oro; **p. glass** vidrio cilindrado (**c**) *(in book)* grabado *m*, lámina *f* **2** *vt* chapar

plateau ['plætəʊ] *n* meseta *f*

platform ['plætfɔːm] *n* (**a**) plataforma *f*; *(stage)* estrado *m*; *(at meeting)* tribuna *f* (**b**) *Rail* andén *m*; **p. ticket** billete *m* de andén (**c**) *Pol (programme)* programa *m*

platinum ['plætɪnəm] *n* platino *m*

plausible ['plɔːzəbəl] *adj* plausible

play [pleɪ] **1** *vt* (**a**) *(game)* jugar a; *(team)* jugar contra (**b**) *(instrument, tune)* tocar; **to p. a CD** poner un CD (**c**) *Th (part)* hacer (el papel) de; *(play)* representar; *Fig* **to p. a part in sth** participar en algo

2 *vi* (**a**) *(children)* jugar (**with** con); *(animals)* juguetear (**b**) *Sport* jugar; *Fig* **to p. for time** tratar de ganar tiempo (**c**) *(joke)* bromear (**d**) *Mus* tocar; *(instrument)* sonar

3 *n* (**a**) *Th* obra *f* de teatro (**b**) *Sport* juego *m* (**c**) *Tech & Fig (movement)* juego *m*; **a p. on words** un juego de palabras

▸ **play around** *vi (waste time)* gandulear; *(be unfaithful)* tener líos

▸ **play down** *vt sep* minimizar, quitar importancia a

▸ **play on** *vt insep (take advantage of)* aprovecharse de; *(nerves etc)* exacerbar

▸ **play up 1** *vt sep (annoy)* dar la lata a, fastidiar **2** *vi Br (child, injury etc)* dar guerra

playboy ['pleɪbɔɪ] *n* playboy *m*

player ['pleɪə(r)] *n Sport* jugador(a) *m,f*; *Mus* músico(a) *m,f*; *Th (man)* actor *m*; *(woman)* actriz *f*

playful ['pleɪfʊl] *adj* juguetón(ona)

playground ['pleɪgraʊnd] *n* patio *m* de recreo

playgroup ['pleɪgruːp] *n* jardín *m* de infancia

playing ['pleɪɪŋ] *n* juego *m*; **p. card** carta *f*, naipe *m*; **p. field** campo *m* de deportes

playmate ['pleɪmeɪt] *n* compañero(a) *m,f* de juego

playtime ['pleɪtaɪm] *n (at school)* recreo *m*

playwright ['pleɪraɪt] *n* dramaturgo(a) *m,f*

PLC, plc [piːelˈsiː] *n Br (abbr* **public limited company)** ≃ S.A.

plea [pliː] *n* (**a**) *(request)* petición *f*, súplica *f*, *Am* pedido *m*; *(excuse)* pretexto *m*, disculpa *f* (**b**) *Jur* alegato *m*

plead [pliːd] **1** *vt* (**a**) *Jur & Fig* **to p. sb's cause** defender la causa de algn (**b**) **to p. ignorance** *(give as excuse)* alegar ignorancia **2** *vi* (**a**) *(beg)* rogar, suplicar; **to p. with sb to do sth** suplicar a algn que haga algo (**b**) *Jur* **to p. guilty/not guilty** declararse culpable/inocente

pleasant ['plezənt] *adj* agradable

please [pliːz] **1** *vt (give pleasure to)* agradar, complacer; *(satisfy)* satisfacer; *Fam* **p. yourself** como quieras

2 *vi* complacer; *(give satisfaction)* satisfacer; **easy/hard to p.** poco/muy exigente

3 *adv* por favor; **may I? – p. do** ¿me permite? – desde luego; **p. do not smoke** *(sign)* se ruega no fumar; **yes, p.** sí, por favor

pleased [pliːzd] *adj (happy)* contento(a); *(satisfied)* satisfecho(a); **p. to meet you!** ¡encantado(a)!, ¡mucho gusto!; **to be p. about sth** alegrarse de algo

pleasing ['pliːzɪŋ] *adj (pleasant)* agradable, grato(a); *(satisfactory)* satisfactorio(a)

pleasure ['pleʒə(r)] *n* placer *m*; **it's a p. to talk to him** da gusto hablar con él; **to take great p. in doing sth** disfrutar mucho haciendo algo; **with p.** con mucho gusto

pleat [pliːt] **1** *n* pliegue *m* **2** *vt* hacer pliegues en

pledge [pledʒ] **1** *n* promesa *f*; *(token of love etc)* señal *f*; *(guarantee)* prenda *f* **2** *vt (promise)* prometer; *(pawn)* empeñar

plentiful ['plentɪfʊl] *adj* abundante

plenty ['plentɪ] *n* abundancia *f*; **p. of books** muchos libros; **p. of time** tiempo de sobra; **we've got p.** tenemos de sobra

pliers ['plaɪəz] *npl* alicates *mpl*, tenazas *fpl*

plight [plaɪt] *n* situación *f* grave

plimsolls ['plɪmsəlz] *npl Br* zapatos *mpl* de tenis

plod [plɒd] *vi* andar con paso pesado; *Fig* **to p. on** perseverar; *Fig* **to p. through a report** estudiar laboriosamente un informe

plonk¹ [plɒŋk] *vt esp Br Fam* dejar caer

plonk² [plɒŋk] *n Br Fam (cheap wine)* vino *m* peleón

plot¹ [plɒt] **1** *n* (**a**) *(conspiracy)* complot *m* (**b**) *Th, Lit (story)* argumento *m*, trama *f*
2 *vt* (**a**) *(course, route)* trazar (**b**) *(scheme)* fraguar
3 *vi* conspirar, tramar

plot² [plɒt] *n Agr* terreno *m*; *(for building)* solar *m*; **vegetable p.** campo *m* de hortalizas

plough [plaʊ] **1** *n* arado *m*
2 *vt* arar
3 *vi* **to p. into sth** chocar contra algo

pluck [plʌk] **1** *vt* (**a**) arrancar (**out of** de) (**b**) *(flowers)* coger (**c**) *(chicken)* desplumar (**d**) *(guitar)* puntear **2** *n (courage)* valor *m*, ánimo *m*
▸ **pluck up** *vt sep* **to p. up courage** armarse de valor

plucky ['plʌkɪ] *adj* (**pluckier, pluckiest**) valiente

plug [plʌg] **1** *n* (**a**) *(in bath etc)* tapón *m* (**b**) *Elec* enchufe *m*, clavija *f*; **two-/three-pin p.** clavija bipolar/tripolar **2** *vt* (**a**) *(hole)* tapar (**b**) *Fam (publicize)* dar publicidad a; *(idea etc)* hacer hincapié en
▸ **plug in** *vt sep & vi* enchufar

plughole ['plʌghəʊl] *n* desagüe *m*

plum [plʌm] **1** *n (fruit)* ciruela *f* **2** *adj* a **p. job** *Esp* un chollo *or Méx* churro (de trabajo), *RP* un laburazo

plumb [plʌm] **1** *adv Fam* **p. in the middle** justo en medio; *US* **he's p. crazy** está completamente loco **2** *vt Fig* **to p. the depths** tocar fondo

plumber ['plʌmə(r)] *n* fontanero(a) *m,f, Méx, RP, Ven* plomero(a)

plumbing ['plʌmɪŋ] *n (occupation)* fontanería *f, Méx, RP, Ven* plomería *f; (system)* tuberías *fpl*, cañerías *fpl*

plummet ['plʌmɪt] *vi (bird, plane)* desplomarse, caer en picado *or Am* picada; *Fig (prices)* bajar vertiginosamente; *(morale)* caer a plomo

plump [plʌmp] *adj (person)* relleno(a); *(baby)* rechoncho(a)
▸ **plump down** *vt sep* dejar caer
▸ **plump for** *vt insep* optar por
▸ **plump up** *vt sep (cushions)* ahuecar

plunder ['plʌndə(r)] **1** *vt* saquear **2** *n (action)* saqueo *m*, pillaje *m*; *(loot)* botín *m*

plunge [plʌndʒ] **1** *vt (immerse)* sumergir; *(thrust)* arrojar
2 *vi (dive)* lanzarse, zambullirse; *Fig (fall)* caer, hundirse; *(prices)* desplomarse
3 *n (dive)* zambullida *f; Fig (fall)* desplome *m*; **to take the p.** dar el paso decisivo

plural ['plʊərəl] *adj & n* plural *(m)*

plus [plʌs] **1** *prep* más; **three p. four makes seven** tres más cuatro hacen siete **2** *n Math* signo *m* más; *Fig (advantage)* ventaja *f*

ply [plaɪ] **1** *vt* **to p. one's trade** ejercer su oficio; **to p. sb with drinks** no parar de ofrecer copas a algn **2** *vi (ship)* ir y venir; **to p. for hire** ir en busca de clientes

p.m. [piː'em] *(abbr* **post meridiem)** después del mediodía; **at 2 p.m.** a las dos de la tarde

pneumonia [njuː'məʊnɪə] *n* pulmonía *f*

PO [piː'əʊ] *n (abbr* **Post Office)** oficina *f* de correos; **PO Box** apartado *m* de correos, *CAm, Carib, Méx* casilla *f* postal, *Andes, RP* casilla de correos

poach¹ [pəʊtʃ] *vt* (**a**) **to p. fish/game** pescar/cazar furtivamente (**b**) *Fam Fig (steal)* birlar

poach² [pəʊtʃ] *vt Culin (egg)* escalfar; *(fish)* hervir

pocket ['pɒkɪt] **1** *n* (**a**) bolsillo *m*, *CAm, Méx, Perú* bolsa *f; Fig* **to be £10 in/out of p.** salir ganando/perdiendo 10 libras; **p. money** dinero *m* para gastos (**b**) *(of air)* bolsa *f* (**c**) *(of resistance)* foco *m* **2** *vt (money)* embolsarse

pocketbook ['pɒkɪtbʊk] *n US (wallet)* cartera *f; (handbag) Esp* bolso *m, Col, CSur* cartera *f, Méx* bolsa *f*

poem ['pəʊɪm] *n* poema *m*

poet ['pəʊɪt] *n* poeta *mf*

poetic [pəʊ'etɪk] *adj* poético(a)

poetry ['pəʊɪtrɪ] *n* poesía *f*

poignant ['pɔɪnjənt] *adj* conmovedor(a)

point [pɔɪnt] **1** *n* (**a**) *(sharp end)* punta *f*
(**b**) *(place)* punto *m; Fig* **p. of no return** punto sin retorno
(**c**) *(quality)* **good/bad p.** cualidad buena/mala
(**d**) *(moment)* **at that p.** en aquel momento; **to be on the p. of doing sth** estar a punto de hacer algo
(**e**) *(score)* punto *m*, tanto *m*
(**f**) *(in argument)* punto *m;* **I take your p.** entiendo lo que quieres decir
(**g**) *(purpose)* propósito *m;* **I don't see the p.** no veo el sentido; **there's no p. in going** no merece la pena ir; **to come to the p.** llegar al meollo de la cuestión
(**h**) *(on scale)* punto *m; (in share index)* entero *m;* **six p. three** seis coma tres
(**i**) *Geog* punta *f*
(**j**) **points** *Aut* platinos *mpl; Rail* agujas *fpl*
2 *vt (way etc)* señalar, indicar; **to p. a gun at sb** apuntar a algn con una pistola
3 *vi* señalar, indicar; **to p. at sth/sb** señalar algo/a algn con el dedo
▸**point out** *vt sep* indicar, señalar; *(mention)* hacer resaltar

point-blank ['pɔɪnt'blæŋk] **1** *adj* a quemarropa; *(refusal)* rotundo(a) **2** *adv (shoot)* a quemarropa; *(refuse)* rotundamente

pointed ['pɔɪntɪd] *adj (sharp)* puntiagudo(a); *Fig (comment)* intencionado(a); *(cutting)* mordaz

pointer ['pɔɪntə(r)] *n* (**a**) *(indicator)* indicador *m*, aguja *f; (for map)* puntero *m* (**b**) *(dog)* perro *m* de muestra

pointless ['pɔɪntlɪs] *adj* sin sentido

poise [pɔɪz] **1** *n (bearing)* porte *m; (self-assurance)* aplomo *m* **2** *vt Fig* **to be poised to do sth** estar listo(a) para hacer algo

poison ['pɔɪzən] **1** *n* veneno *m* **2** *vt* envenenar

poisonous ['pɔɪzənəs] *adj (plant, snake)* venenoso(a); *(gas)* tóxico(a); *Fig (rumour)* pernicioso(a)

poke [pəʊk] *vt (with finger or stick)* dar con la punta del dedo/del bastón a; **to p. one's head out** asomar la cabeza; **to p. the fire** atizar el fuego
▸**poke about, poke around** *vi* fisgonear, hurgar
▸**poke out** *vt sep (eye)* sacar

poker[1] ['pəʊkə(r)] *n (for fire)* atizador *m*

poker[2] ['pəʊkə(r)] *n Cards* póquer *m*

Poland ['pəʊlənd] *n* Polonia

polar ['pəʊlə(r)] *adj* polar; **p. bear** oso *m* polar

Pole [pəʊl] *n* polaco(a) *m,f*

pole[1] [pəʊl] *n* palo *m;* **p. vault** salto *m* con pértiga

pole[2] [pəʊl] *n Geog* polo *m; Fig* **to be poles apart** ser polos opuestos

police [pə'liːs] **1** *npl* policía *f;* **p. car** coche *m or Am* carro *or CSur* auto de policía; *Br* **p. constable** policía *m;* **p. force** cuerpo *m* de policía; **p. record** antecedentes *mpl* penales; **p. state** estado *m* policial; **p. station** comisaría *f* **2** *vt* vigilar

policeman [pə'liːsmən] *n* policía *m*

policewoman [pə'liːswʊmən] *n* (mujer *f)* policía *f*

policy ['pɒlɪsɪ] *n Pol* política *f; (of company)* norma *f*, principio *m; Ins* póliza *f* (de seguros)

polio ['pəʊlɪəʊ] *n* poliomielitis *f*

Polish ['pəʊlɪʃ] **1** *adj* polaco(a) **2** *n* (**a**) **the P.** los polacos (**b**) *(language)* polaco *m*

polish ['pɒlɪʃ] **1** *vt* pulir; *(furniture)* encerar; *(shoes)* limpiar; *(silver)* sacar brillo a **2** *n* (**a**) *(for furniture)* cera *f; (for shoes)* betún *m; (for nails)* esmalte *m* (**b**) *(shine)* brillo *m*; *Fig (refinement)* refinamiento *m*

▸ **polish off** *vt sep Fam (work)* despachar; *(food)* zamparse

▸ **polish up** *vt sep Fig* perfeccionar

polite [pə'laɪt] *adj* educado(a)

political [pə'lɪtɪkəl] *adj* político(a)

politician [pɒlɪ'tɪʃən] *n* político(a) *m,f*

politics ['pɒlɪtɪks] *n sing* política *f*

poll [pəʊl] **1** *n* (**a**) votación *f*; **the polls** las elecciones; **to go to the polls** acudir a las urnas (**b**) *(survey)* encuesta *f* **2** *vt (votes)* obtener

pollen ['pɒlən] *n* polen *m*

polling ['pəʊlɪŋ] *n* votación *f*; **p. booth** cabina *f* electoral; **p. station** colegio *m* electoral

pollute [pə'luːt] *vt* contaminar

pollution [pə'luːʃən] *n* contaminación *f*, polución *f*; **environmental p.** contaminación ambiental

polo ['pəʊləʊ] *n Sport* polo *m*; *Br* **p. neck (sweater)** suéter *m or Esp* jersey *m or Col* saco *m or RP* pulóver *m* de cuello alto *or* de cisne

polyester [pɒlɪ'estə(r)] *n* poliéster *m*

polythene ['pɒlɪθiːn] *n Br* polietileno *m*

pompous ['pɒmpəs] *adj (person)* presumido(a); *(speech)* rimbombante

pond [pɒnd] *n* estanque *m*

ponder ['pɒndə(r)] **1** *vt* considerar **2** *vi* **to p. over sth** meditar sobre algo

pong [pɒŋ] *n Br Fam* tufo *m*

pony ['pəʊnɪ] *n* poney *m*

ponytail ['pəʊnɪteɪl] *n* cola *f* de caballo

poodle ['puːdəl] *n* caniche *m*

pool¹ [puːl] *n (of water, oil etc)* charco *m*; *(pond)* estanque *m*; *(in river)* pozo *m*; **(swimming) p.** piscina *f*, *Méx* alberca *f*, *RP* pileta *f*

pool² [puːl] **1** *n* (**a**) *(common fund)* fondo *m* común (**b**) **typing p.** servicio *m* de mecanografía (**c**) *US (snooker)* billar americano (**d**) *Br* **the pools** las quinielas *fpl*, *Arg* el Prode, *Col, CRica* el totogol **2** *vt (funds)* reunir; *(ideas, resources)* juntar

poor [pʊə(r)] **1** *adj* pobre; *(quality)* malo(a); *Fam* **you p. thing!** ¡pobrecito! **2** *npl* **the p.** los pobres

poorly ['pʊəlɪ] **1** *adv (badly)* mal **2** *adj* (**poorlier, poorliest**) *(ill)* mal, malo(a)

pop [pɒp] **1** *vt (burst)* hacer reventar; *(cork)* hacer saltar **2** *vi (burst)* reventar; *(cork)* saltar; *Fam* **I'm just popping over to Ian's** voy un momento a casa de Ian **3** *n* (**a**) *(noise)* pequeña explosión (**b**) *Fam (drink)* gaseosa *f* (**c**) *US Fam (father)* papá *m* (**d**) *Fam Mus* música *f* pop; **p. singer** cantante *mf* pop

▸ **pop in** *vi Fam* entrar un momento, pasar

popcorn ['pɒpkɔːn] *n* palomitas *fpl* de maíz, *RP* pochoclo *m*

Pope [pəʊp] *n* **the P.** el Papa

poplar ['pɒplə(r)] *n* álamo *m*

poppy ['pɒpɪ] *n* amapola *f*

Popsicle® ['pɒpsɪkəl] *n US* polo *m*

popular ['pɒpjʊlə(r)] *adj* popular; *(fashionable)* de moda; *(common)* corriente

popularity [pɒpjʊ'lærɪtɪ] *n* popularidad *f*

populate ['pɒpjʊleɪt] *vt* poblar

population [pɒpjʊ'leɪʃən] *n* población *f*; **the p. explosion** la explosión demográfica

porcelain ['pɔːsəlɪn] *n* porcelana *f*

porch [pɔːtʃ] *n Br (entrance)* zaguán *m*; *US (veranda)* terraza *f*

pore¹ [pɔː(r)] *vi* **to p. over sth** leer *or* estudiar algo detenidamente

pore² [pɔː(r)] *n Anat* poro *m*

pork [pɔːk] *n (carne f de)* cerdo *m or Am* chancho *m*

pornography [pɔː'nɒɡrəfɪ] *n* pornografía *f*

porridge ['pɒrɪdʒ] *n* gachas *fpl* de avena

port¹ [pɔːt] *n (harbour)* puerto *m*; **p. of call** puerto de escala

port² [pɔːt] *n Naut, Av* babor *m*

port³ [pɔːt] *n (wine)* vino *m* de Oporto, oporto *m*

portable ['pɔːtəbəl] *adj* portátil

porter ['pɔːtə(r)] *n (at station)* mozo *m* de equipaje; *esp Br (at hotel)* portero(a) *m,f*, conserje *mf*; *US (on train)* mozo *m*

portfolio [pɔːt'fəʊlɪəʊ] *n (file)* carpeta *f*; *(of artist, politician)* cartera *f*

porthole ['pɔːthəʊl] *n* portilla *f*

portion ['pɔːʃən] *n (part, piece)* parte *f*, porción *f*; *(of food)* ración *f*

▸ **portion out** *vt sep* repartir

portrait ['pɔːtreɪt] *n* retrato *m*

portray [pɔː'treɪ] *vt (paint portrait of)* retratar; *(describe)* describir; *Th* representar

Portugal ['pɔːtjʊgəl] *n* Portugal

Portuguese [pɔːtjʊ'giːz] **1** *adj* portugués(esa) **2** *n (person)* portugués(esa) *m,f*; *(language)* portugués *m*

pose [pəʊz] **1** *vt (problem)* plantear; *(threat)* representar **2** *vi (for painting)* posar; *Pej (behave affectedly)* hacer pose; **to p. as** hacerse pasar por **3** *n (stance)* postura *f*; *Pej (affectation)* pose *f*

posh [pɒʃ] *adj Br Fam* elegante, de lujo; *(person, accent)* Esp pijo(a), Méx fresa, RP (con)cheto(a)

position [pə'zɪʃən] **1** *n* (**a**) *(place)* posición *f*; *(location)* situación *f*; *(rank)* rango *m*; **to be in a p. to do sth** estar en condiciones de hacer algo (**b**) *(opinion)* postura *f* (**c**) *(job)* puesto *m* **2** *vt* colocar

positive ['pɒzɪtɪv] *adj* positivo(a); *(sign)* favorable; *(proof)* incontrovertible; *(sure)* seguro(a); *Fam (absolute)* auténtico(a)

possess [pə'zes] *vt* poseer; *(of fear)* apoderarse de

possession [pə'zeʃən] *n* posesión *f*; **possessions** bienes *mpl*

possessive [pə'zesɪv] *adj* posesivo(a)

possibility [pɒsɪ'bɪlɪtɪ] *n* posibilidad *f*; **possibilities** *(potential)* potencial *m*

possible ['pɒsɪbəl] *adj* posible; **as much as p.** todo lo posible; **as often as p.** cuanto más mejor; **as soon as p.** cuanto antes

possibly ['pɒsɪblɪ] *adv* posiblemente; *(perhaps)* tal vez, quizás; **I can't p. come** no puedo venir de ninguna manera

post¹ [pəʊst] **1** *n (of wood)* poste *m* **2** *vt (affix)* poner, pegar

post² [pəʊst] **1** *n (job)* puesto *m*; *US* **trading p.** factoría *f* **2** *vt Br (assign)* destinar

post³ [pəʊst] *esp Br* **1** *n (mail)* correo *m*; **by p.** por correo; **p. office** oficina *f* de correos; **P. Office Box** apartado *m* de correos **2** *vt (letter)* echar al correo; **to p. sth to sb** mandar algo por correo a algn

postage ['pəʊstɪdʒ] *n* franqueo *m*

postal ['pəʊstəl] *adj* postal, de correos; *Br* **p. code** código *m* postal; *Br* **p. order** giro *m* postal; **p. vote** voto *m* por correo

postbox ['pəʊstbɒks] *n Br* buzón *m* (de correos)

postcard ['pəʊstkɑːd] *n* (tarjeta *f*) postal *f*

postcode ['pəʊstkəʊd] *n Br* código *m* postal

poster ['pəʊstə(r)] *n* póster *m*; *(advertising)* cartel *m*

postgraduate [pəʊst'grædjʊɪt] **1** *n* posgraduado(a) *m,f* **2** *adj* de posgraduado

posthumous ['pɒstjʊməs] *adj* póstumo(a)

postman ['pəʊstmən] *n Br* cartero *m*

postmark ['pəʊstmɑːk] *n* matasellos *m inv*

postmortem [pəʊst'mɔːtəm] *n* autopsia *f*

postpone [pəs'pəʊn] *vt* aplazar

posture ['pɒstʃə(r)] **1** *n* postura *f*; *(affected)* pose *f* **2** *vi* adoptar una pose

pot [pɒt] **1** *n (container)* tarro *m*, pote *m*; *(for cooking)* olla *f*; *(for flowers)* maceta *f*; *Fam* **to go to p.** irse al garete *or* Am al diablo **2** *vt (plant)* poner en una maceta

potato [pə'teɪtəʊ] *n (pl* **potatoes)** patata *f*, Am papa *f*

potent ['pəʊtənt] *adj* potente

potential [pə'tenʃəl] **1** adj potencial, posible **2** n potencial m

pothole ['pɒthəʊl] n Geol cueva f; (in road) bache m

potter[1] ['pɒtə(r)] n alfarero(a) m,f

potter[2] ['pɒtə(r)] vi Br to **p. about** or **around** entretenerse

pottery ['pɒtərɪ] n (craft, place) alfarería f; (objects) cerámica f

potty[1] ['pɒtɪ] adj (**pottier, pottiest**) Br Fam pirado(a), Col corrido(a), CSur rayado(a), Méx zafado(a)

potty[2] ['pɒtɪ] n Fam orinal m

pouch [paʊtʃ] n (**a**) bolsa pequeña; (for ammunition) morral m; (for tobacco) petaca f (**b**) Zool bolsa f abdominal

poultry ['pəʊltrɪ] n (live) aves fpl de corral; (food) pollos mpl

pounce [paʊns] vi to **p. on** abalanzarse encima de

pound[1] [paʊnd] **1** vt (strike) aporrear **2** vi (heart) palpitar; (walk heavily) andar con paso pesado

pound[2] [paʊnd] n (money, weight) libra f

pound[3] [paʊnd] n (for dogs) perrera f; (for cars) depósito m de coches

pour [pɔː(r)] **1** vt echar, verter; to **p. sb a drink** servirle una copa a algn **2** vi correr, fluir; **it's pouring with rain** está lloviendo a cántaros

▸ **pour out** vt sep echar, verter; Fig to **p. one's heart out to sb** desahogarse con algn

pout [paʊt] **1** vi hacer pucheros **2** n puchero m

poverty ['pɒvətɪ] n pobreza f

powder ['paʊdə(r)] **1** n polvo m; **p. compact** polvera f; **p. keg** polvorín m; **p. puff** borla f; **p. room** baño m or Esp servicios mpl or CSur toilette m de señoras **2** vt to **p. one's nose** ponerse polvos en la cara; Euph ir a los servicios or al tocador

powdered ['paʊdəd] adj (milk) en polvo

power ['paʊə(r)] **1** n (**a**) fuerza f; (energy) energía f; Elec **to cut off the p.** cortar la corriente; esp Br **p. point**

enchufe m; **p. station** central or Andes, RP usina f eléctrica (**b**) (ability) poder m (**c**) (authority) poder m; (nation) potencia f; (influence) influencia f; **to be in p.** estar en el poder (**d**) Tech potencia f; (output) rendimiento m **2** vt propulsar, impulsar

powerful ['paʊəfʊl] adj (strong) fuerte; (influential) poderoso(a); (remedy) eficaz; (engine, machine) potente; (emotion) fuerte; (speech) conmovedor(a)

powerless ['paʊəlɪs] adj impotente, ineficaz

PR [piː'ɑː(r)] (abbr **public relations**) relaciones fpl públicas

practical ['præktɪkəl] adj práctico(a); (useful) útil; (sensible) adecuado(a)

practically ['præktɪkəlɪ] adv (almost) casi

practice ['præktɪs] **1** n (**a**) (habit) costumbre f (**b**) (exercise) práctica f; Sport entrenamiento m; Mus ensayo m; **to be out of p.** no estar en forma (**c**) (way of doing sth) práctica f; **in p.** en la práctica; **to put sth into p.** poner algo en práctica (**d**) (of profession) ejercicio m (**e**) (place) (of doctors) consultorio m; (of lawyers) bufete m (**f**) (clients) (of doctors) pacientes mpl; (of lawyers) clientela f **2** vt & vi US = **practise**

practise ['præktɪs] **1** vt practicar; (method) seguir; (principle) poner en práctica; Mus ensayar; (profession) ejercer **2** vi practicar; Sport entrenar; Mus ensayar; (doctor) practicar; (lawyer) ejercer

practitioner [præk'tɪʃənə(r)] n Br Med **general p.** médico(a) m,f de cabecera

pragmatic [præg'mætɪk] adj pragmático(a)

prairie ['preərɪ] n pradera f; US llanura f

praise [preɪz] **1** n alabanza f **2** vt alabar, elogiar

pram [præm] *n Br* cochecito *m* de niño

prank [præŋk] *n* broma *f*; *(of child)* travesura *f*

prawn [prɔːn] *n* gamba *f*, *Am* camarón *m*

pray [preɪ] *vi* rezar, orar

prayer [preə(r)] *n* rezo *m*, oración *f*; *(entreaty)* súplica *f*; **p. book** misal *m*

preach [priːtʃ] *vi* predicar

preacher ['priːtʃə(r)] *n* predicador(a) *m,f*

precarious [prɪ'keərɪəs] *adj* precario(a)

precaution [prɪ'kɔːʃən] *n* precaución *f*

precede [prɪ'siːd] *vt* preceder

precedent ['presɪdənt] *n* precedente *m*

precinct ['priːsɪŋkt] *n* (**a**) *Br (area)* **pedestrian/shopping p.** zona *f* peatonal/comercial (**b**) *US (administrative, police division)* distrito *m*; *(police station)* comisaría *f* (de policía)

precious ['preʃəs] **1** *adj* precioso(a); **p. stones** piedras preciosas **2** *adv Fam* **p. little/few** muy poco/pocos

precipice ['presɪpɪs] *n* precipicio *m*

precipitate 1 *vt* [prɪ'sɪpɪteɪt] precipitar; *Fig* arrojar **2** *adj* [prɪ'sɪpɪtət] precipitado(a)

precise [prɪ'saɪs] *adj* preciso(a), exacto(a); *(meticulous)* meticuloso(a)

precisely [prɪ'saɪslɪ] *adv (exactly)* precisamente, exactamente; **p.!** ¡eso es!, ¡exacto!

precision [prɪ'sɪʒən] *n* precisión *f*

preclude [prɪ'kluːd] *vt* excluir; *(misunderstanding)* evitar

precocious [prɪ'kəʊʃəs] *adj* precoz

preconceived [priːkən'siːvd] *adj* preconcebido(a)

precondition [priːkən'dɪʃən] *n* condición previa

predator ['predətə(r)] *n* depredador *m*

predecessor ['priːdɪsesə(r)] *n* antecesor(a) *m,f*

predicament [prɪ'dɪkəmənt] *n* apuro *m*, aprieto *m*

predict [prɪ'dɪkt] *vt* predecir, pronosticar

predictable [prɪ'dɪktəbəl] *adj* previsible

prediction [prɪ'dɪkʃən] *n* pronóstico *m*

predispose [priːdɪ'spəʊz] *vt* **to be predisposed to doing sth** estar predispuesto(a) a hacer algo

predominant [prɪ'dɒmɪnənt] *adj* predominante

predominate [prɪ'dɒmɪneɪt] *vi* predominar

pre-empt [prɪ'empt] *vt* adelantarse a

preface ['prefɪs] **1** *n* prefacio *m* **2** *vt* prologar

prefect ['priːfekt] *n Br Educ* monitor(a) *m,f*

prefer [prɪ'fɜː(r)] *vt* preferir; **I p. coffee to tea** prefiero el café al té

preferable ['prefərəbəl] *adj* preferible (**to** a)

preference ['prefərəns] *n* preferencia *f*; *(priority)* prioridad *f*; **to give p. to sth** dar prioridad a algo

prefix ['priːfɪks] *n* prefijo *m*

pregnancy ['pregnənsɪ] *n* embarazo *m*

pregnant ['pregnənt] *adj (woman)* embarazada; *(animal)* preñada; *Fig* **a p. pause** una pausa cargada de significado

prehistoric(al) [priːhɪ'stɒrɪk(əl)] *adj* prehistórico(a)

prejudge [priː'dʒʌdʒ] *vt* prejuzgar

prejudice ['predʒʊdɪs] **1** *n (bias)* prejuicio *m*; *(harm)* perjuicio *m* **2** *vt (bias)* predisponer; *(harm)* perjudicar

prejudiced ['predʒʊdɪst] *adj* parcial; **to be p. against/in favour of** estar predispuesto(a) en contra/a favor de

preliminary [prɪ'lɪmɪnərɪ] **1** *adj* preliminar; *Sport (round)* eliminatorio(a) **2** *n* **preliminaries** preliminares *mpl*

prelude ['preljuːd] *n* preludio *m*

premature [premə'tjʊə(r), 'premətjʊə(r)] *adj* prematuro(a)

premeditate [prɪ'medɪteɪt] *vt (crime)* premeditar

premier ['premjə(r)] **1** *n Pol* primer(a) ministro(a) *m,f* **2** *adj* primer, primero(a)

premiere ['premɪeə(r)] *n Cin* estreno *m*

premises ['premɪsɪz] *npl* local *m*; **on the p.** en el local

premium ['priːmɪəm] *n Com, Fin, Ind* prima *f*; **to be at a p.** tener sobreprecio; *Fig* estar muy solicitado(a); *Br* **p. bonds** = bonos numerados emitidos por el Gobierno británico, cuyo comprador entra en un sorteo mensual de premios en metálico

premonition [premə'nɪʃən] *n* presentimiento *m*

preoccupied [priː'ɒkjʊpaɪd] *adj* preocupado(a); **to be p. with sth** preocuparse por algo

prepaid [priː'peɪd] *adj* con el porte pagado

preparation [prepə'reɪʃən] *n* preparación *f*; *(plan)* preparativo *m*

preparatory [prɪ'pærətərɪ] *adj* preparatorio(a), preliminar; **p. school** *Br* = colegio privado para alumnos de entre 7 y 13 años; *US* = escuela secundaria privada

prepare [prɪ'peə(r)] **1** *vt* preparar **2** *vi* prepararse **(for** para); **to p. to do sth** prepararse *or Am* alistarse para hacer algo

prepared [prɪ'peəd] *adj (ready)* preparado(a); **to be p. to do sth** *(willing)* estar dispuesto(a) a hacer algo

preposition [prepə'zɪʃən] *n* preposición *f*

preposterous [prɪ'pɒstərəs] *adj* absurdo(a), ridículo(a)

prerequisite [priː'rekwɪzɪt] *n* condición *f* previa

prerogative [prɪ'rɒgətɪv] *n* prerrogativa *f*

preschool [priː'skuːl] *adj* preescolar

prescribe [prɪ'skraɪb] *vt (set down)* prescribir; *Med* recetar; *Fig (recommend)* recomendar

prescription [prɪ'skrɪpʃən] *n Med* receta *f*

presence ['prezəns] *n* presencia *f*; *(attendance)* asistencia *f*; *Fig* **p. of mind** presencia de ánimo

present¹ ['prezənt] **1** *adj* (**a**) *(in attendance)* presente; *Ling* **p. tense** (tiempo *m*) presente *m*; **to be p. at** estar presente en (**b**) *(current)* actual **2** *n (time)* presente *m*, actualidad *f*; **at p.** actualmente; **for the p.** de momento; **up to the p.** hasta ahora

present² **1** *vt* [prɪ'zent] (**a**) *(give as gift)* regalar; *(medals, prizes etc)* entregar; **to p. sb with sth** obsequiar a algn con algo (**b**) *(report etc)* presentar; *(opportunity)* ofrecer; *(problems)* plantear (**c**) *(introduce) (person, programme)* presentar **2** *n* ['prezənt] *(gift)* regalo *m*; *(formal)* obsequio *m*

presentable [prɪ'zentəbəl] *adj* presentable; **to make oneself p.** arreglarse

presentation [prezən'teɪʃən] *n* (**a**) presentación *f*; **p. ceremony** ceremonia *f* de entrega (**b**) *Rad, TV* representación *f*

present-day ['prezəntdeɪ] *adj* actual, de hoy en día

presenter [prɪ'zentə(r)] *n Rad* locutor(a) *m,f*; *TV* presentador(a) *m,f*

presently ['prezəntlɪ] *adv (soon)* dentro de poco; *US (now)* ahora

preservation [prezə'veɪʃən] *n* conservación *f*

preservative [prɪ'zɜːvətɪv] *n* conservante *m*

preserve [prɪ'zɜːv] **1** *vt* (**a**) *(keep)* mantener (**b**) *Culin* conservar **2** *n* (**a**) *(hunting)* coto *m* (**b**) *Culin* conserva *f*

preside [prɪ'zaɪd] *vi* presidir

presidency ['prezɪdənsɪ] *n* presidencia *f*

president ['prezɪdənt] *n Pol* presidente(a) *m,f*; *US Com* director(a) *m,f*, gerente *mf*

presidential [prezɪ'denʃəl] *adj* presidencial

press [pres] **1** *vt* (**a**) apretar; *(button)* pulsar; *(grapes)* pisar; *(trousers etc)* planchar (**b**) *(urge)* presionar; **to p. sb**

to do sth acosar a algn para que haga algo
2 *vi* (**a**) *(push)* apretar; **to p. against sb/sth** apretarse contra algn/algo; **to p. (down) on sth** hacer presión sobre algo (**b**) *(be urgent)* **time is pressing** el tiempo apremia
3 *n* (**a**) *(machine)* prensa *f*; **to go to p.** *(newspaper)* entrar en prensa (**b**) *Press* **the p.** la prensa; **p. agency** agencia *f* de prensa; **p. conference** rueda *f* de prensa

▸ **press on** *vi* seguir adelante

pressed [prest] *adj* **to be (hard) p. for** andar escaso(a) de; **I'd be hard p. to do it** me costaría mucho hacerlo

pressing ['presɪŋ] *adj* apremiante, urgente

press-up ['presʌp] *n Br* flexión *f* (de brazos)

pressure ['preʃə(r)] *n* presión *f*; *Med, Met* **high/low** altas/bajas presiones; **p. cooker** olla *f* a presión; **p. gauge** manómetro *m*; *Fig* **to bring p. (to bear) on sb** ejercer presión sobre algn

pressurize ['preʃəraɪz] *vt Fig* presionar; **pressurized cabin** cabina presurizada

prestige [pre'stiːʒ] *n* prestigio *m*

prestigious [pres'tɪdʒəs] *adj* prestigioso(a)

presumably [prɪ'zjuːməblɪ] *adv* es de suponer que

presume [prɪ'zjuːm] **1** *vt* suponer, presumir **2** *vi* *(suppose)* suponer; **we p. so/not** suponemos que sí/no

presumption [prɪ'zʌmpʃən] *n* (**a**) *(supposition)* suposición *f* (**b**) *(boldness)* osadía *f*; *(conceit)* presunción *f*

pretence [prɪ'tens] *n* (**a**) *(deception)* fingimiento *m*; **false pretences** estafa *f*; **under the p. of** so pretexto de (**b**) *(claim)* pretensión *f*

pretend [prɪ'tend] **1** *vt (feign)* fingir, aparentar; *(claim)* pretender **2** *vi (feign)* fingir

pretense [prɪ'tens] *n US* = pretence

pretentious [prɪ'tenʃəs] *adj* presuntuoso(a), pretencioso(a)

pretext ['priːtekst] *n* pretexto *m*; **on the p. of** so pretexto de

pretty ['prɪtɪ] **1** *adj* (**prettier, prettiest**) bonito(a), *Am* lindo(a) **2** *adv Fam* bastante; **p. much the same** más o menos lo mismo

prevail [prɪ'veɪl] *vi* (**a**) predominar (**b**) *(win through)* prevalecer (**c**) **to p. upon** *or* **on sb to do sth** *(persuade)* persuadir *or* convencer a algn para que haga algo

prevailing [prɪ'veɪlɪŋ] *adj (wind)* predominante; *(opinion)* general; *(condition, fashion)* actual

prevent [prɪ'vent] *vt* impedir; *(accident)* evitar; *(illness)* prevenir; **to p. sb from doing sth** impedir a algn hacer algo; **to p. sth from happening** evitar que pase algo

prevention [prɪ'venʃən] *n* prevención *f*

preview ['priːvjuː] *n (of film etc)* preestreno *m*

previous ['priːvɪəs] **1** *adj* anterior, previo(a); **p. conviction** antecedente *m* penal **2** *adv* **p. to going** antes de ir

previously ['priːvɪəslɪ] *adv* anteriormente, previamente

prey [preɪ] **1** *n* presa *f*; *Fig* víctima *f* **2** *vi* **to p. on** alimentarse de

price [praɪs] **1** *n* precio *m*; **what p. is that coat?** ¿cuánto cuesta el abrigo?; **p. list** lista *f* de precios; **p. tag** etiqueta *f* **2** *vt (put price on)* poner un precio a; *(value)* valorar

priceless ['praɪslɪs] *adj* que no tiene precio

pricey ['praɪsɪ] *adj Fam* carillo(a)

prick [prɪk] **1** *vt* picar; **to p. one's finger** pincharse el dedo; *Fig* **to p. up one's ears** aguzar el oído **2** *n* (**a**) *(with pin)* pinchazo *m* (**b**) *Vulg (penis) Esp* polla *f*, *Am* verga *f*, *Méx* pito *m*, *RP* pija *f* (**c**) *Vulg (person) Esp* gilipollas *mf inv*, *Am* pendejo(a) *m,f*, *RP* forro *m*

prickly ['prɪklɪ] *adj* (**pricklier, prickliest**) espinoso(a); *Fig (touchy)* enojadizo(a); **p. heat** = sarpullido por causa del calor; **p. pear** higo chumbo, *Am* tuna *f*

pride [praɪd] **1** *n* orgullo *m*; *(arrogance)* soberbia *f*; **to take p. in sth** enorgullecerse de algo **2** *vt* **to p. oneself on** enorgullecerse de

priest [priːst] *n* sacerdote *m*, cura *m*

prim [prɪm] *adj* (**primmer, primmest**) **p. (and proper)** remilgado(a)

primarily ['praɪmərɪlɪ] *adv* ante todo

primary ['praɪmərɪ] **1** *adj* fundamental, principal; **of p. importance** primordial; **p. colour** color primario; **p. education/school** enseñanza/ escuela primaria **2** *n US Pol* (elección *f*) primaria *f*

prime [praɪm] **1** *adj* (**a**) principal; *(major)* primordial; **P. Minister** primer(a) ministro(a) *m,f* (**b**) *(first-rate)* de primera; **p. number** número primo
2 *n* **in the p. of life** en la flor de la vida
3 *vt (pump, engine)* cebar; *(surface)* imprimar; *Fig (prepare)* preparar

primer[1] ['praɪmə(r)] *n (textbook)* cartilla *f*

primer[2] ['praɪmə(r)] *n (paint)* imprimación *f*

primitive ['prɪmɪtɪv] *adj* primitivo(a); *(method, tool)* rudimentario(a)

prince [prɪns] *n* príncipe *m*; **P. Charming** Príncipe Azul

princess [prɪn'ses] *n* princesa *f*

principal ['prɪnsɪpəl] **1** *adj* principal **2** *n Educ* director(a) *m,f*; *Th (in play)* protagonista *mf* principal

principle ['prɪnsɪpəl] *n* principio *m*; **in p.** en principio; **on p.** por principio

print [prɪnt] **1** *vt* (**a**) imprimir; *(publish)* publicar; *Fig* grabar; **printed matter** impresos *mpl* (**b**) *(write)* escribir con letra de imprenta **2** *n* (**a**) *(of hand, foot)* huella *f* (**b**) *(written text)* letra *f*; **out of p.** agotado(a) (**c**) *Tex* estampado *m* (**d**) *Art* grabado *m*; *Phot* copia *f*

▶ **print out** *vt sep Comput* imprimir

printer ['prɪntə(r)] *n (person)* impresor(a) *m,f*; *(machine)* impresora *f*

printing ['prɪntɪŋ] *n (industry)* imprenta *f*; *(process)* impresión *f*; *(print run)* tirada *f*; **p. press** prensa *f*

print-out ['prɪntaʊt] *n Comput* impresión *f*; *(copy)* copia impresa

prior ['praɪə(r)] *adj* previo(a), anterior; **p. to leaving** antes de salir

priority [praɪ'ɒrɪtɪ] *n* prioridad *f*

prison ['prɪzən] *n* cárcel *f*, prisión *f*

prisoner ['prɪzənə(r)] *n* preso(a) *m,f*; **to hold sb p.** detener a algn; **p. of war** prisionero(a) *m,f* de guerra

privacy ['praɪvəsɪ, 'prɪvəsɪ] *n* intimidad *f*

private ['praɪvɪt] **1** *adj* privado(a); *(secretary)* particular; *(matter)* personal; *(letter)* confidencial; **one's p. life** la vida privada de uno; **p.** *(notice)* *(on road)* carretera privada; *(on gate)* propiedad privada; *(on envelope)* confidencial; **p. detective,** *Fam* **p. eye** detective *mf* privado(a); **p. school** escuela privada **2** *n Mil* soldado raso

privately ['praɪvɪtlɪ] *adv* en privado; *(personally)* personalmente

privatize ['praɪvɪtaɪz] *vt* privatizar

privilege ['prɪvɪlɪdʒ] *n* privilegio *m*

privileged ['prɪvɪlɪdʒd] *adj* privilegiado(a)

prize [praɪz] **1** *n* premio *m*
2 *adj (first-class)* de primera (categoría *or* clase)
3 *vt (value)* apreciar, valorar

prizewinner ['praɪzwɪnə(r)] *n* premiado(a) *m,f*

pro[1] [prəʊ] *n* pro *m*; **the pros and cons of an issue** los pros y los contras de una cuestión

pro[2] [prəʊ] *n Fam* profesional *mf*, *Méx* profesionista *mf*

probability [prɒbə'bɪlɪtɪ] *n* probabilidad *f*

probable ['prɒbəbəl] *adj* probable

probably ['prɒbəblɪ] *adv* probablemente

probation [prə'beɪʃən] *n Jur* **to be on p.** estar en libertad condicional; **to be on two months' p.** *(at work)* trabajar dos meses de prueba

probe [prəʊb] **1** *n* sonda *f*; *(investigation)* sondeo *m* **2** *vt Med* sondar; *(investigate)* investigar

▸ **probe into** *vt insep* investigar

problem ['prɒbləm] *n* problema *m*

problematic(al) [prɒblə'mætɪk(əl)] *adj* problemático(a); **it's p.** tiene sus problemas

procedure [prə'si:dʒə(r)] *n* procedimiento *m; (legal, business)* gestión *f,* trámite *m*

proceed [prə'si:d] *vi* seguir, proceder; **to p. to do sth** ponerse a hacer algo; **to p. to the next matter** pasar a la siguiente cuestión

proceedings [prə'si:dɪŋz] *npl (of meeting)* actas *fpl; (measures)* medidas *fpl; Jur* proceso *m*

proceeds ['prəʊsi:dz] *npl* ganancias *fpl*

process ['prəʊses] **1** *n* proceso *m; (method)* método *m,* sistema *m;* **in the p. of** en vías de **2** *vt (information)* tramitar; *(food)* tratar; *Comput* procesar

procession [prə'seʃən] *n* desfile *m; Rel* procesión *f*

processor ['prəʊsesə(r)] *n Comput* procesador *m*

proclaim [prə'kleɪm] *vt* proclamar, declarar

prod [prɒd] *vt (with stick etc)* golpear; *(push)* empujar

prodigy ['prɒdɪdʒɪ] *n* prodigio *m*

produce 1 *vt* [prə'dju:s] **(a)** producir; *Ind* fabricar **(b)** *Th* dirigir; *Rad, TV* realizar; *Cin* producir **(c)** *(give birth to)* dar a luz a **(d)** *(document)* enseñar; *(bring out)* sacar **2** *n* ['prɒdju:s] productos *mpl;* **p. of Spain** producto *m* de España

producer [prə'dju:sə(r)] *n* **(a)** productor(a) *m,f; Ind* fabricante *mf* **(b)** *Th* director(a) *m,f* de escena; *Rad, TV* realizador(a) *m,f; Cin* productor(a) *m,f*

product ['prɒdʌkt] *n* producto *m*

production [prə'dʌkʃən] *n* **(a)** producción *f; Ind* fabricación *f* **(b)** *Th* representación *f; Rad, TV* realización *f; Cin* producción *f;* **p. line** cadena *f* de montaje

productive [prə'dʌktɪv] *adj* productivo(a)

productivity [prɒdʌk'tɪvɪtɪ] *n* productividad *f*

profession [prə'feʃən] *n* profesión *f*

professional [prə'feʃənəl] **1** *adj* profesional; *(soldier)* de profesión; *(polished)* de gran calidad **2** *n* profesional *mf*

professor [prə'fesə(r)] *n Univ Br* catedrático(a) *m,f; US* profesor(a) *m,f*

proficient [prə'fɪʃənt] *adj (in language)* experto(a); *(in skill)* hábil

profile ['prəʊfaɪl] *n* perfil *m;* **in p.** de perfil

profit ['prɒfɪt] **1** *n* **(a)** beneficio *m,* ganancia *f;* **to make a p. on** sacar beneficios de **(b)** *Fml (benefit)* provecho *m* **2** *vi Fig* sacar provecho; **to p. from** aprovecharse de

profitable ['prɒfɪtəbəl] *adj Com* rentable; *Fig (worthwhile)* provecho-so(a)

profound [prə'faʊnd] *adj* profundo(a)

programme ['prəʊgræm] **1** *n* programa *m; (plan)* plan *m* **2** *vt* **(a)** *(plan)* planear, planificar **(b)** *(computer)* programar

programmer ['prəʊgræmə(r)] *n* programador(a) *m,f*

progress 1 *n* ['prəʊgres] progreso *m; (development)* desarrollo *m; Med* mejora *f;* **to make p.** hacer progresos; **in p.** en curso **2** *vi* [prəʊ'gres] avanzar; *(develop)* desarrollar; *(improve)* hacer progresos; *Med* mejorar

progressive [prə'gresɪv] *adj (increasing)* progresivo(a); *Pol* progresista

prohibit [prə'hɪbɪt] *vt* prohibir; **to p. sb from doing sth** prohibir a algn hacer algo

prohibitive [prə'hɪbɪtɪv] *adj* prohibitivo(a)

project 1 *n* ['prɒdʒekt] proyecto *m; (plan)* plan *m; Educ* trabajo *m; US* **(housing) p.** = urbanización con viviendas de protección oficial **2** *vt* [prə'dʒekt] proyectar, planear **3** *vi* [prə'dʒekt] *(stick out)* sobresalir

projector [prə'dʒektə(r)] *n Cin* proyector *m*

prolific [prə'lɪfɪk] *adj* prolífico(a)

prologue ['prəʊlɒg] n prólogo m
prolong [prə'lɒŋ] vt prolongar
prom [prɒm] n Br Fam (seafront) paseo marítimo; Br (concert) = concierto sinfónico en que parte del público está de pie; US (school dance) = baile de fin de curso
promenade [prɒmə'nɑːd] 1 n Br (at seaside) paseo marítimo 2 vi pasearse
prominent ['prɒmɪnənt] adj (standing out) saliente; Fig (important) importante; (famous) eminente
promiscuous [prə'mɪskjʊəs] adj promiscuo(a)
promise ['prɒmɪs] 1 n promesa f; to show p. ser prometedor(a) 2 vt & vi prometer
promising ['prɒmɪsɪŋ] adj prometedor(a)
promote [prə'məʊt] vt ascender; (product) promocionar; (ideas) fomentar; Ftb they've been promoted han subido
promotion [prə'məʊʃən] n (in rank) promoción f, ascenso m; (of product) promoción; (of arts etc) fomento m
prompt ['prɒmpt] 1 adj (quick) rápido(a); (punctual) puntual
2 adv at two o'clock p. a las dos en punto
3 vt (a) (motivate) incitar; to p. sb to do sth instar a algn a hacer algo (b) (actor) apuntar
promptly ['prɒmptlɪ] adv (quickly) rápidamente; (punctually) puntualmente
prone [prəʊn] adj (a) to be p. to do sth ser propenso(a) a hacer algo (b) Fml (face down) boca abajo
pronoun ['prəʊnaʊn] n pronombre m
pronounce [prə'naʊns] 1 vt pronunciar; Fml (declare) declarar 2 vi Fml to p. on sth opinar sobre algo
pronunciation [prənʌnsɪ'eɪʃən] n pronunciación f
proof [pruːf] 1 n prueba f
2 adj (a) (secure) a prueba de (b) this rum is 70 per cent p. este ron tiene 70 grados
3 vt impermeabilizar

prop¹ [prɒp] 1 n (support) puntal m; Fig sostén m 2 vt (support) apoyar; Fig sostener
▶ **prop up** vt sep apoyar
prop² [prɒp] n Fam Th accesorio m
propaganda [prɒpə'gændə] n propaganda f
propel [prə'pel] vt propulsar
propeller [prə'pelə(r)] n hélice f
proper ['prɒpə(r)] adj (a) adecuado(a), correcto(a); the p. time el momento oportuno (b) (real) real, auténtico(a); (actual, exact) propiamente dicho(a) (c) (characteristic) propio(a); Ling p. noun nombre propio
properly ['prɒpəlɪ] adv (suitably, correctly, decently) correctamente; it wasn't p. closed no estaba bien cerrado(a); she refused, quite p. se negó, y con razón
property ['prɒpətɪ] n (a) (quality) propiedad f (b) (possession) propiedad f, posesión f; personal p. bienes mpl; public p. dominio público (c) (estate) finca f
prophecy ['prɒfɪsɪ] n profecía f
prophet ['prɒfɪt] n profeta mf
proportion [prə'pɔːʃən] n proporción f; (part, quantity) parte f; in p. to or with en proporción a
proportional [prə'pɔːʃənəl] adj proporcional (to a); Pol p. representation representación f proporcional
proportionate [prə'pɔːʃənɪt] adj proporcional
proposal [prə'pəʊzəl] n propuesta f; (suggestion) sugerencia f; p. of marriage propuesta de matrimonio
propose [prə'pəʊz] 1 vt proponer; (suggest) sugerir; Fml (intend) tener la intención de 2 vi declararse
proposition [prɒpə'zɪʃən] n propuesta f; Math proposición f
proprietor [prə'praɪətə(r)] n propietario(a) m,f
prose [prəʊz] n Lit prosa f; Educ texto m para traducir
prosecute ['prɒsɪkjuːt] vt procesar
prosecution [prɒsɪ'kjuːʃən] n

(action) proceso *m*, juicio *m*; **the p.** la acusación

prospect 1 *n* ['prɒspekt] *(outlook)* perspectiva *f*; *(hope)* esperanza *f*; **the job has prospects** es un trabajo con porvenir

2 *vt* [prə'spekt] explorar

3 *vi* [prə'spekt] **to p. for gold/oil** buscar oro/petróleo

prospective [prə'spektɪv] *adj (future)* futuro(a); *(possible)* eventual, probable

prospectus [prə'spektəs] *n* prospecto *m*

prosper ['prɒspə(r)] *vi* prosperar

prosperity [prɒ'sperɪtɪ] *n* prosperidad *f*

prosperous ['prɒspərəs] *adj* próspero(a)

prostitute ['prɒstɪtjuːt] *n* prostituta *f*

protagonist [prəʊ'tægənɪst] *n* protagonista *mf*

protect [prə'tekt] *vt* proteger; *(interests etc)* salvaguardar; **to p. sb from sth** proteger a algn de algo

protection [prə'tekʃən] *n* protección *f*

protective [prə'tektɪv] *adj* protector(a)

protein ['prəʊtiːn] *n* proteína *f*

protest 1 *n* ['prəʊtest] protesta *f*; *(complaint)* queja *f*

2 *vt* [prə'test] *US* protestar en contra de

3 *vi* [prə'test] *Br* protestar

Protestant ['prɒtɪstənt] *adj & n* protestante *(mf)*

protester [prə'testə(r)] *n* manifestante *mf*

protracted [prə'træktɪd] *adj* prolongado(a)

proud [praʊd] *adj* orgulloso(a); *(arrogant)* soberbio(a)

prove [pruːv] *vt* (**a**) probar, demostrar; *Math* comprobar; **to p. oneself** dar pruebas de valor (**b**) **it proved to be disastrous** *(turned out)* resultó ser desastroso(a)

proverb ['prɒvɜːb] *n* refrán *m*, proverbio *m*

provide [prə'vaɪd] **1** *vt* proporcionar;

(supplies) suministrar, proveer **2** *vi* proveer; **to p. for sb** mantener a algn

provided [prə'vaɪdɪd] *conj* **p. (that)** con tal de que

providing [prə'vaɪdɪŋ] *conj* = **provided**

province ['prɒvɪns] *n* provincia *f*; *Fig (field of knowledge)* campo *m*

provincial [prə'vɪnʃəl] **1** *adj* provincial; *Pej* provinciano(a) **2** *n Pej (person)* provinciano(a) *m,f*

provision [prə'vɪʒən] *n* provisión *f*; *(supply)* suministro *m*; **provisions** *(food)* provisiones *fpl*, víveres *mpl*

provisional [prə'vɪʒənəl] *adj* provisional

provocative [prə'vɒkətɪv] *adj* provocador(a); *(flirtatious)* provocativo(a)

provoke [prə'vəʊk] *vt* provocar

prowl [praʊl] **1** *n* merodeo *m*; **to be on the p.** merodear, rondar **2** *vi* merodear; *Fam* **to p. about** *or* **around** rondar

proxy ['prɒksɪ] *n Jur (power)* poderes *mpl*; *(person)* apoderado(a) *m,f*; **by p.** por poderes

prudent ['pruːdənt] *adj* prudente

prudish ['pruːdɪʃ] *adj* remilgado(a)

prune¹ [pruːn] *n* ciruela pasa

prune² [pruːn] *vt (roses etc)* podar; *Fig* acortar

pry [praɪ] *vi* curiosear, husmear; **to p. into sb's affairs** meterse en asuntos ajenos

PS, ps [piː'es] *(abbr* **postscript)** P.S., P.D.

pseudonym ['sjuːdənɪm] *n* (p)seudónimo *m*

psychiatric [saɪkɪ'ætrɪk] *adj* psiquiátrico(a)

psychiatrist [saɪ'kaɪətrɪst] *n* psiquiatra *mf*

psychiatry [saɪ'kaɪətrɪ] *n* psiquiatría *f*

psychic ['saɪkɪk] **1** *adj* psíquico(a) **2** *n* médium *mf*

psychoanalysis [saɪkəʊə'nælɪsɪs] *n* psicoanálisis *f*

psychological [saɪkə'lɒdʒɪkəl] adj psicológico(a)

psychologist [saɪ'kɒlədʒɪst] n psicólogo(a) m,f

psychology [saɪ'kɒlədʒɪ] n psicología f

psychopath ['saɪkəʊpæθ] n psicópata mf

PTO, pto [piːtiː'əʊ] (abbr **please turn over**) sigue

pub [pʌb] n Br Fam bar m, pub m

puberty ['pjuːbətɪ] n pubertad f

public ['pʌblɪk] 1 adj público(a); to **make sth p.** hacer público algo; Com to **go p.** (company) salir a Bolsa; **p. company** empresa pública; Br **p. convenience** servicios mpl o Esp aseos mpl públicos; **p. holiday** día f festivo o Am feriado; Br **p. house** pub m, taberna f; Br **p. limited company** sociedad anónima; **p. opinion** opinión pública; Br **p. prosecutor** fiscal m; **p. relations** relaciones públicas; **p. school** Br colegio privado; US colegio público; **p. transport** transporte público
2 n **the p.** el público; **in p.** en público

publication [pʌblɪ'keɪʃən] n publicación f

publicity [pʌ'blɪsɪtɪ] n publicidad f

publicize ['pʌblɪsaɪz] vt (make public) hacer público(a); (advertise) hacer publicidad a

publish ['pʌblɪʃ] vt publicar, editar

publisher ['pʌblɪʃə(r)] n (person) editor(a) m,f; (firm) (casa f) editorial f

pudding ['pʊdɪŋ] n Culin pudín m; Br (dessert) postre m; **Christmas p.** = pudín a base de frutos secos típico de Navidad; **p. basin** cuenco m; **steamed p.** budín m

puddle ['pʌdəl] n charco m

puff [pʌf] 1 n (of wind) racha f; (of smoke) nube f; **p. pastry** pasta f de hojaldre
2 vi (person) jadear, resoplar; (train) echar humo; to **p. on a cigarette** dar chupadas or Esp caladas or Am pitadas a un cigarrillo
3 vt (cigarette) dar una calada a

▸ **puff up** vi hincharse

puke [pjuːk] Fam vi echar la papa, devolver

pull [pʊl] 1 n (a) (act of pulling) tirón m, Am salvo RP jalón m; to **give sth a p.** dar un tirón or Am salvo RP jalón a algo (b) (attraction) atracción f; (influence) enchufe m
2 vt (a) (tug) dar un tirón or Am salvo RP jalón a; to **p. the trigger** apretar el gatillo; to **p. to pieces** hacer pedazos; Fig poner algo por los suelos; Fig to **p. sb's leg** tomar el pelo a algn (b) (draw) tirar, arrastrar (c) (draw out) sacar (d) Fam (people) atraer
3 vi (drag) tirar, Am salvo RP jalar

▸ **pull apart** vt sep desmontar; Fig (criticize) poner por los suelos

▸ **pull down** vt sep (building) derribar

▸ **pull in 1** vt sep (crowds) atraer **2** vi (train) entrar en la estación; (stop) parar

▸ **pull off 1** vt sep Fam (carry out) llevar a cabo **2** vi (vehicle) arrancar

▸ **pull out 1** vt sep (withdraw) retirar **2** vi Aut to **p. out to overtake** salir para adelantar

▸ **pull over** vi (driver) parar en Esp el arcén or Méx el acotamiento or RP la banquina

▸ **pull through** vi reponerse, restablecerse

▸ **pull together** vt sep to **p. oneself together** calmarse

▸ **pull up 1** vt sep (a) (uproot) desarraigar (b) (chair) acercar **2** vi (stop) pararse

pullover ['pʊləʊvə(r)] n suéter m, Esp jersey m, RP pulóver m

pulp [pʌlp] n (of paper, wood) pasta f; (of fruit) pulpa f

pulse¹ [pʌls] n Anat pulso m

pulse² [pʌls] n Bot, Culin legumbre f

pump¹ [pʌmp] 1 n bomba f 2 vt bombear; to **p. sth in/out** meter/sacar algo con una bomba

▸ **pump out** vt sep (empty) vaciar

▸ **pump up** vt sep (tyre) inflar

pump² [pʌmp] n Br (shoe) zapatilla f

pumpkin ['pʌmpkɪn] n calabaza f,

Andes, RP zapallo *m, Col, Carib* ahuyama *f*

pun [pʌn] *n* juego *m* de palabras

punch¹ [pʌntʃ] **1** *n (for making holes)* perforadora *f; (for tickets)* taladradora *f; (for leather etc)* punzón *m* **2** *vt (make hole in)* perforar; *(ticket)* picar; *(leather)* punzar

punch² [pʌntʃ] **1** *n (blow)* puñetazo *m; (in boxing)* pegada *f; Fig* **it lacks p.** le falta fuerza; **p. line** remate *m (de un chiste)* **2** *vt (with fist)* dar un puñetazo a

punch³ [pʌntʃ] *n (drink)* ponche *m*

punctual ['pʌŋktʃʊəl] *adj* puntual

punctuation [pʌŋktjʊˈeɪʃən] *n* puntuación *f*

puncture ['pʌŋktʃə(r)] **1** *n* pinchazo *m, Guat, Méx* ponchadura *f* **2** *vt (tyre)* pinchar, *Guat, Méx* ponchar

pungent ['pʌndʒənt] *adj (smell)* acre; *(taste)* fuerte

punish ['pʌnɪʃ] *vt* castigar

punishment ['pʌnɪʃmənt] *n* castigo *m*

punk [pʌŋk] *n Fam* (**a**) punk *mf;* **p. music** música *f* punk (**b**) *US* mamón *m*

punter ['pʌntə(r)] *n (gambler)* jugador(a) *m,f; (customer)* cliente *mf*

puny ['pjuːnɪ] *adj* (**punier, puniest**) enclenque, endeble

pupil¹ ['pjuːpəl] *n Educ* alumno(a) *m,f*

pupil² ['pjuːpəl] *n Anat* pupila *f*

puppet ['pʌpɪt] *n* títere *m*

puppy ['pʌpɪ] *n* cachorro(a) *m,f,* perrito *m*

purchase ['pɜːtʃɪs] **1** *n* compra *f* **2** *vt* comprar; **purchasing power** poder adquisitivo

purchaser ['pɜːtʃɪsə(r)] *n* comprador(a) *m,f*

pure [pjʊə(r)] *adj* puro(a)

purée ['pjʊəreɪ] *n* puré *m*

purely [pjʊəlɪ] *adv* simplemente

purge [pɜːdʒ] **1** *n* purga *f* **2** *vt* purgar

purify ['pjʊərɪfaɪ] *vt* purificar

puritanical [pjʊərɪˈtænɪkəl] *adj* puritano(a)

purity ['pjʊərɪtɪ] *n* pureza *f*

purple ['pɜːpəl] *adj* morado(a),

purpúreo(a); **to go p. (in the face)** ponerse morado(a)

purpose ['pɜːpəs] *n* (**a**) propósito *m,* intención *f;* **on p.** a propósito (**b**) *(use)* utilidad *f*

purr [pɜː(r)] *vi (cat)* ronronear; *(engine)* zumbar

purse [pɜːs] **1** *n Br (for coins)* monedero *m; US (bag) Esp* bolso *m, Col, CSur* cartera *f, Méx* bolsa *f; (prize money)* premio *m* en metálico **2** *vt* **to p. one's lips** apretarse los labios

pursue [pəˈsjuː] *vt (criminal)* perseguir; *(person)* seguir; *(pleasure)* buscar; *(career)* ejercer

pursuit [pəˈsjuːt] *n (of criminal)* persecución *f; (of animal)* caza *f; (of pleasure)* búsqueda *f; (pastime)* pasatiempo *m*

push [pʊʃ] **1** *n* empujón *m, CAm, Méx* aventón *m; Fig (drive)* brío *m,* dinamismo *m*

2 *vt* (**a**) empujar; *(button)* pulsar, apretar; **to p. one's finger into a hole** meter el dedo en un agujero; *Fig (pressurize)* instar; *(harass)* acosar; *Fam* **to be (hard) pushed for time** estar apurado(a) *or RP* corto de tiempo (**c**) *Fam (product)* promover; **to p. drugs** pasar droga

3 *vi* empujar

▸ **push aside** *vt sep (object)* apartar

▸ **push in** *vi* colarse

▸ **push off** *vi (in boat)* desatracar; *Fam* **p. off!** ¡lárgate!

▸ **push on** *vi (continue)* seguir adelante

▸ **push through** *vt sep* abrirse paso entre

pushchair ['pʊʃtʃeə(r)] *n Br* sillita *f* (de ruedas)

push-up ['pʊʃʌp] *n* flexión *f* (de brazos)

pushy ['pʊʃɪ] *adj* (**pushier, pushiest**) *Fam* agresivo(a)

puss [pʊs], **pussy** ['pʊsɪ] *n Fam* minino *m*

put [pʊt] *(pt & pp* **put**) **1** *vt* (**a**) poner; *(place)* colocar; *(insert)* meter; **to p. to bed** acostar a; **to p. a picture up on the wall** colgar un cuadro en la pared (**b**) *(present)* presentar, exponer; **to p. a question to sb** hacer una pregunta a algn

(**c**) *(express)* expresar, decir; **to p. sth simply** explicar algo de manera sencilla

(**d**) *(estimate)* calcular

(**e**) *(money)* ingresar; *(invest)* invertir

2 *vi Naut* **to p. to sea** zarpar

3 *adv* **to stay p.** quedarse quieto(a)

▶ **put about** *vt sep (rumour)* hacer correr

▶ **put across** *vt sep (idea etc)* comunicar

▶ **put aside** *vt sep (money)* ahorrar; *(time)* reservar

▶ **put away** *vt sep (tidy away)* recoger; *Fam (eat)* zamparse; *(save money)* ahorrar

▶ **put back** *vt sep (postpone)* aplazar; **to p. the clock back** retrasar la hora

▶ **put by** *vt sep (money)* ahorrar

▶ **put down** *vt sep (set down)* dejar; *(suppress)* sofocar; *(humiliate)* humillar; *(criticize)* criticar; *(animal)* provocar la muerte de; *(write down)* apuntar

▶ **put down to** *vt sep* achacar a

▶ **put forward** *vt sep (theory)* exponer; *(proposal)* hacer; **to p. one's name forward for sth** presentarse como candidato(a) para algo

▶ **put in 1** *vt sep (install)* instalar; *(complaint, request)* presentar; *(time)* pasar **2** *vi Naut* hacer escala (**at** en)

▶ **put off** *vt sep (postpone)* aplazar; **to p. sb off doing sth** quitarle *or Am* sacarle a algn las ganas de hacer algo

▶ **put on** *vt sep (clothes)* poner, ponerse; *(show)* montar; *(concert)* dar; *(switch on) (radio)* poner; *(light)* encender, *Am* prender; *(water, gas)* abrir; **to p. on weight** aumentar de peso; **to p. on the brakes** frenar; *Fig* **to p. on a straight face** poner cara de serio(a)

▶ **put out** *vt sep (light, fire)* apagar; *(place outside)* sacar; *(extend) (arm)* extender; *(tongue)* sacar; *(hand)* tender; *(spread) (rumour)* hacer correr; *(annoy)* molestar; *(inconvenience)* incordiar; *(anger)* **to be p. out by sth** enojarse por algo

▶ **put through** *vt sep Tel* **p. me through to Pat, please** póngame con Pat, por favor

▶ **put together** *vt sep (join)* unir, reunir; *(assemble)* armar, montar

▶ **put up** *vt sep (raise)* levantar, subir; *(picture)* colocar; *(curtains)* colgar; *(building)* construir; *(tent)* armar; *(prices)* subir, aumentar; *(accommodate)* alojar, hospedar; **to p. up a fight** ofrecer resistencia

▶ **put up to** *vt sep* **to p. sb up to sth** incitar a algn a hacer algo

▶ **put up with** *vt insep* aguantar, soportar

puzzle ['pʌzəl] **1** *n* rompecabezas *m inv*; *(crossword)* crucigrama *m*; *Fig (mystery)* misterio *m* **2** *vt* dejar perplejo(a); **to be puzzled about sth** no entender algo

▶ **puzzle over** *vt insep* **to p. over sth** dar vueltas a algo (en la cabeza)

PVC [piːviːˈsiː] *n (abbr polyvinyl chloride)* PVC *m*

pyjamas [pəˈdʒɑːməz] *npl* pijama *m*, *Am* piyama *m or f*

pylon ['paɪlən] *n* torre *f* (de conducción eléctrica)

pyramid ['pɪrəmɪd] *n* pirámide *f*

Qq

Q, q [kjuː] *n (the letter)* Q, q *f*

quack [kwæk] **1** *n* (**a**) *(of duck)* graznido *m* (**b**) *Br Fam Pej or Hum (doctor)* matasanos *m inv* **2** *vi* graznar

quadruple [ˈkwɒdrʊpəl, kwɒˈdruːpəl]
1 *n* cuádruplo *m*
2 *adj* cuádruple
3 *vt* cuadruplicar
4 *vi* cuadruplicarse

quaint [kweɪnt] *adj (picturesque)* pintoresco(a); *(original)* singular

quake [kweɪk] **1** *vi* temblar **2** *n Fam* temblor *m* de tierra

Quaker [ˈkweɪkə(r)] *n* cuáquero(a) *m,f*

qualification [kwɒlɪfɪˈkeɪʃən] *n* (**a**) *(ability)* aptitud *f* (**b**) *(requirement)* requisito *m* (**c**) *(diploma etc)* título *m* (**d**) *(reservation)* reserva *f*

qualified [ˈkwɒlɪfaɪd] *adj* (**a**) capacitado(a); **q. teacher** profesor titulado (**b**) **q. approval** *(modified)* aprobación *f* condicional

qualify [ˈkwɒlɪfaɪ] **1** *vt* (**a**) *(entitle)* capacitar (**b**) *(modify)* modificar; *(statement)* matizar; *Ling* calificar **2** *vi* (**a**) **to q. as** *(doctor etc)* sacar el título de; **when did you q.?** ¿cuándo terminaste la carrera? (**b**) *(in competition)* quedar clasificado(a)

quality [ˈkwɒlɪtɪ] *n* (**a**) *(excellence)* calidad *f*; **q. control** control *m* de calidad; *Br* **q. newspapers** prensa *f* no sensacionalista (**b**) *(attribute)* cualidad *f*

quantity [ˈkwɒntɪtɪ] *n* cantidad *f*

quarantine [ˈkwɒrəntiːn] *n* cuarentena *f*

quarrel [ˈkwɒrəl] **1** *n (argument)* riña *f*, pelea *f*; *(disagreement)* desacuerdo *m* **2** *vi (argue)* pelearse, reñir; **to q. with sth** discrepar de algo

quarry¹ [ˈkwɒrɪ] *Min* **1** *n* cantera *f* **2** *vt* extraer

quarry² [ˈkwɒrɪ] *n* presa *f*

quart [kwɔːt] *n (measurement)* = cuarto de galón *(Br = 1,13 l; US = 0,94 l)*

quarter [ˈkwɔːtə(r)] **1** *n* (**a**) cuarto *m*, cuarta parte; **a q. of an hour** un cuarto de hora (**b**) *Br* **it's a q. to three**, *US* **it's a q. of three** son las tres menos cuarto; **it's a q.** *Br* **past** *or US* **after six** son las seis y cuarto (**c**) *US (coin)* cuarto *m* (de dólar) (**d**) *(district)* barrio *m* (**e**) *(of moon)* cuarto *m* (**f**) **quarters** *(lodgings)* alojamiento *m* (**g**) *US Mus* **q. note** negra *f* **2** *vt* (**a**) *(cut into quarters)* dividir en cuartos (**b**) *(accommodate)* alojar

quarterback [ˈkwɔːtəbæk] *n US* quarterback *m*, *Méx* mariscal *m* de campo

quarterfinal [ˈkwɔːtəfaɪnəl] *n Sport* cuarto *m* de final

quarterly [ˈkwɔːtəlɪ] **1** *adj* trimestral **2** *n* publicación *f* trimestral **3** *adv* trimestralmente

quartet(te) [kwɔːˈtet] *n* cuarteto *m*

quartz [kwɔːts] *n* cuarzo *m*; **q. watch** reloj *m* de cuarzo

quash [kwɒʃ] *vt Jur* anular; *(uprising)* aplastar

quay(side) [ˈkiː(saɪd)] *n* muelle *m*

queasy [ˈkwiːzɪ] *adj* (**queasier, queasiest**) **to feel q.** *(ill)* tener náuseas

queen [kwiːn] *n* (**a**) reina *f* (**b**) *Fam Pej* loca *f*, marica *m*

queer [kwɪə(r)] **1** *adj (strange)* extraño(a), raro(a) **2** *n Fam Pej* marica *m*, maricón *m*

quench [kwentʃ] *vt* apagar

query [ˈkwɪərɪ] **1** *n (question)*

pregunta *f* **2** *vt (ask questions about)* preguntar acerca de; *(have doubts about)* poner en duda

quest [kwest] *n Literary* búsqueda *f*

question ['kwestʃən] **1** *n* pregunta *f*; **to ask sb a q.** hacer una pregunta a algn; **he did it without q.** lo hizo sin rechistar; **to call sth into q.** poner algo en duda; **that's out of the q.!** ¡ni hablar!; **q. mark** signo *m* de interrogación; *Fig* interrogante *m* **2** *vt (ask questions of)* hacer preguntas a; *(interrogate)* interrogar; *(query)* poner en duda

questionable ['kwestʃənəbəl] *adj (doubtful)* dudoso(a); *(debatable)* discutible

questionnaire [kwestʃə'neə(r)] *n* cuestionario *m*

queue [kjuː] *Br* **1** *n* cola *f* **2** *vi* **to q. (up)** hacer cola

quiche [kiːʃ] *n* quiche *m or f*

quick [kwɪk] *adj* **(a)** *(fast)* rápido(a); **a q. look** un vistazo; **a q. snack** un bocado; **be q.!** ¡date prisa!, *Am* ¡apúrate! **(b)** *(clever)* espabilado(a); *(wit)* agudo(a) **(c)** **she has a q. temper** se enfada con nada

quicken ['kwɪkən] **1** *vt* acelerar; **to q. one's pace** acelerar el paso **2** *vi (speed up)* acelerarse

quickly ['kwɪklɪ] *adv* rápidamente, de prisa

quid [kwɪd] *n (pl* **quid**) *Br Fam (pound)* libra *f*

quiet ['kwaɪət] **1** *n* **(a)** *(silence)* silencio *m* **(b)** *(calm)* tranquilidad *f* **2** *adj* **(a)** *(silent)* silencioso(a); *(street)* tranquilo(a); **keep q.!** ¡silencio! **(b)** *(calm)* tranquilo(a) **(c)** *(person)* reservado(a) **(d)** *(not showy) (clothes)* sobrio(a); *(colours)* apagado(a) **3** *vt US* calmar **4** *vi US* calmarse

quieten ['kwaɪətən] **1** *vt (silence)* callar; *(calm)* calmar **2** *vi (silence)* callarse; *(calm)* calmarse

▸ **quieten down** *Br* **1** *vt sep* calmar **2** *vi* calmarse

quietly ['kwaɪətlɪ] *adv* **(a)** *(silently)* silenciosamente; **he spoke q.** habló en voz baja **(b)** *(calmly)* tranquilamente **(c)** *(discreetly)* discretamente

quilt [kwɪlt] **1** *n* edredón *m* **2** *vt* acolchar

quip [kwɪp] **1** *n* salida *f*; *(joke)* chiste *m* **2** *vi* bromear

quit [kwɪt] *(pt & pp* **quitted** *or* **quit**) **1** *vt* **(a)** *(leave)* dejar, abandonar **(b)** **q. making that noise!** ¡deja de hacer ese ruido! **2** *vi* **(a)** *(go)* irse; *(give up)* dimitir **(b)** *(cease)* dejar de hacer algo **3** *adj* **let's call it quits** dejémoslo estar

quite [kwaɪt] *adv* **(a)** *(entirely)* totalmente; **she's q. right** tiene toda la razón **(b)** *(rather)* bastante; **q. a while** un buen rato; **that's q. enough!** ¡ya está bien!; **it's q. something** es increíble **(c)** *(exactly)* exactamente; **q. (so)!** ¡en efecto!, ¡exacto!

quiver¹ ['kwɪvə(r)] *vi* temblar

quiver² ['kwɪvə(r)] *n (for arrows)* aljaba *f*, carcaj *m*

quiz [kwɪz] **1** *n Rad, TV* **q. show** concurso *m* **2** *vt* hacer preguntas a

quota ['kwəʊtə] *n* **(a)** *(proportional share)* cuota *f*, parte *f* **(b)** *(prescribed amount, number)* cupo *m*

quotation [kwəʊ'teɪʃən] *n* **(a)** *Lit* cita *f*; **q. marks** comillas *fpl* **(b)** *Fin* cotización *f*

quote [kwəʊt] **1** *vt* **(a)** *(cite)* citar **(b)** *Com* **to q. a price** dar un presupuesto **(c)** *Fin* cotizar **2** *n* **(a)** *Lit* cita *f* **(b)** *Com* presupuesto *m*

Rr

R, r [ɑː(r)] *n (the letter)* R, r *f*

rabbi [ˈræbaɪ] *n* rabí *m*, rabino *m*

rabbit [ˈræbɪt] **1** *n* conejo(a) *m,f*; **r. hutch** conejera *f* **2** *vi Fam* **to r. (on)** enrollarse

rabies [ˈreɪbiːz] *n* rabia *f*

raccoon [rəˈkuːn] *n* mapache *m*

race¹ [reɪs] **1** *n* **(a)** *Sport* carrera *f* **(b)** *Br* **the races** las carreras (de caballos) **2** *vt* **(a)** **I'll r. you!** ¡te echo una carrera! **(b)** *(car, horse)* hacer correr **(c)** *(engine)* acelerar **3** *vi (go quickly)* correr; *(pulse)* acelerarse

race² [reɪs] *n (people)* raza *f*

racecourse [ˈreɪskɔːs] *n Br* hipódromo *m*

racehorse [ˈreɪshɔːs] *n* caballo *m* de carreras

racetrack [ˈreɪstræk] *n (for cars, people, bikes)* pista *f*; *US (for horses)* hipódromo *m*

racial [ˈreɪʃəl] *adj* racial

racing [ˈreɪsɪŋ] **1** *n* carreras *fpl* **2** *adj* de carreras; **r. bicycle** bicicleta *f* de carreras; **r. car** coche *m or Am* carro *m or CSur* auto *m* de carreras

racism [ˈreɪsɪzəm] *n* racismo *m*

racist [ˈreɪsɪst] *adj & n* racista *(mf)*

rack [ræk] **1** *n* **(a)** *(shelf)* estante *m*; *(for clothes)* percha *f*; **luggage r.** portaequipajes *m inv*; **roof r.** baca *f* **(b)** *(for torture)* potro *m* **2** *vt Literary (torment)* atormentar; *Fam Fig* **to r. one's brains** devanarse los sesos

racket¹ [ˈrækɪt] *n* **(a)** *(din)* estruendo *m*, *Esp* jaleo *m* **(b)** *(swindle)* timo *m*; *(shady business)* chanchullo *m*

racket² [ˈrækɪt] *n Sport* raqueta *f*

radar [ˈreɪdɑː(r)] *n* radar *m*

radiant [ˈreɪdɪənt] *adj* radiante, resplandeciente

radiate [ˈreɪdɪeɪt] *vt* irradiar; *Fig* **she radiated happiness** rebosaba de alegría

radiation [reɪdɪˈeɪʃən] *n* radiación *f*

radiator [ˈreɪdɪeɪtə(r)] *n* radiador *m*

radical [ˈrædɪkəl] *adj* radical

radio [ˈreɪdɪəʊ] *n* radio *f*; **on the r.** en *or* por la radio; **r. station** emisora *f* (de radio)

radioactive [reɪdɪəʊˈæktɪv] *adj* radiactivo(a)

radish [ˈrædɪʃ] *n* rábano *m*

radius [ˈreɪdɪəs] *n* radio *m*; **within a r. of** en un radio de

RAF [ɑːreɪˈef] *n Br (abbr* **Royal Air Force)** = fuerzas aéreas británicas

raffle [ˈræfəl] **1** *n* rifa *f* **2** *vt* rifar

raft [rɑːft] *n* balsa *f*

rag [ræg] *n* **(a)** *(torn piece)* harapo *m* **(b)** *(for cleaning)* trapo *m* **(c)** *Fam* **rags** *(clothes)* trapos *mpl* **(d)** *Pej Press* periodicucho *m*

rage [reɪdʒ] **1** *n* **(a)** *(fury)* cólera *f* **(b)** *Fam* **it's all the r.** hace furor **2** *vi* **(a)** *(person)* rabiar, estar furioso(a) **(b)** *Fig (storm, sea)* rugir; *(wind)* bramar

ragged [ˈrægɪd] *adj* **(a)** *(clothes)* hecho(a) jirones **(b)** *(person)* harapiento(a) **(c)** *(edge)* mellado(a) **(d)** *Fig (uneven)* desigual

raid [reɪd] **1** *n Mil* incursión *f*; *(by police)* redada *f*; *(robbery etc)* atraco *m* **2** *vt Mil* hacer una incursión en; *(police)* hacer una redada en; *(rob)* asaltar; *Fam* **to r. the larder** vaciar la despensa

rail [reɪl] *n* **(a)** barra *f* **(b)** *(railing)* baranda *f*, *Esp* barandilla *f* **(c)** *Rail* carril f; **by r.** *(send sth)* por ferrocarril; *(travel)* en tren

railing ['reɪlɪŋ] *n (usu pl)* verja f

railroad ['reɪlrəʊd] *n US* ferrocarril m

railway ['reɪlweɪ] *n Br* ferrocarril m; **r. line, r. track** vía férrea; **r. station** estación f de ferrocarril

rain [reɪn] **1** *n* lluvia f; **in the r.** bajo la lluvia **2** *vi* llover; **it's raining** llueve

rainbow ['reɪnbəʊ] *n* arco m iris

raincoat ['reɪnkəʊt] *n* impermeable m

rainfall ['reɪnfɔːl] *n (falling of rain)* precipitación f; *(amount)* pluviosidad f

rainforest ['reɪnfɒrɪst] *n* selva f tropical

rainy ['reɪnɪ] *adj* **(rainier, rainiest)** lluvioso(a)

raise [reɪz] **1** *n US* aumento m (de sueldo) **2** *vt* **(a)** *(glass)* brindar; *(voice)* subir **(b)** *(prices)* aumentar **(c)** *(money, help)* reunir **(d)** *(issue)* plantear **(e)** *(crops, children)* criar **(f)** *(standards)* mejorar

raisin ['reɪzən] *n* pasa f

rake¹ [reɪk] **1** *n (garden tool)* rastrillo m; *(for fire)* hurgón m **2** *vt (leaves)* rastrillar; *(fire)* hurgar; *(with machine gun)* barrer

rake² [reɪk] *n (dissolute man)* calavera m, libertino m

rally ['rælɪ] **1** *n* **(a)** *(gathering)* reunión f; *Pol* mitin m **(b)** *Aut* rallye m **(c)** *(in tennis)* jugada f
2 *vt (support)* reunir
3 *vi* recuperarse
▸ **rally round** *vi* formar una piña

ram [ræm] **1** *n* **(a)** *Zool* carnero m **(b)** *Tech* maza f **2** *vt* **(a)** *(drive into place)* hincar; *(cram)* embutir; *Fam* **to r. sth home** hacer algo patente **(b)** *(crash into)* chocar con

ramble ['ræmbəl] **1** *n (walk)* caminata f **2** *vi* **(a)** *(walk)* hacer una excursión a pie **(b)** *Fig (digress)* divagar

rambler ['ræmblə(r)] *n* **(a)** *(person)* excursionista mf **(b)** *Bot* rosal m trepador

rambling ['ræmblɪŋ] *adj* **(a)** *(incoherent)* incoherente **(b)** *(house)* laberíntico(a) **(c)** *Bot* trepador(a)

ramp [ræmp] *n* **(a)** rampa f **(b)** *(to plane)* escalerilla f

rampant ['ræmpənt] *adj* incontrolado(a); **corruption is r.** la corrupción está muy extendida

ran [ræn] *pt of* **run**

ranch [rɑːntʃ] *n US* rancho m, hacienda f

rancid ['rænsɪd] *adj* rancio(a)

random ['rændəm] **1** *n* **at r.** al azar **2** *adj* fortuito(a); **r. selection** selección hecha al azar

rang [ræŋ] *pt of* **ring**

range [reɪndʒ] **1** *n* **(a)** *(of mountains)* cordillera f, sierra f **(b)** *US (open land)* pradera f **(c)** *(choice)* surtido m; *(of products)* gama f **(d)** **firing r.** campo m de tiro **(e)** *(of missile)* alcance m; **at close r.** de cerca **(f)** *(cooker)* fogón m, cocina f *or Col, Méx, Ven* estufa f de carbón
2 *vi (extend)* extenderse **(to** hasta); **prices r. from £5 to £20** los precios oscilan entre 5 y 20 libras

rank¹ [ræŋk] **1** *n* **(a)** *Mil (row)* fila f; **the ranks** los soldados rasos **(b)** *(position in army)* graduación f; *(in society)* rango m **(c)** *Br* **(taxi) r.** parada f de taxis
2 *vt (classify)* clasificar
3 *vi (figure)* figurar; **to r. above/ below sb** figurar por encima/debajo de algn; **to r. with** estar al mismo nivel que

rank² [ræŋk] *adj Fml (foul-smelling)* fétido(a)

ransack ['rænsæk] *vt (plunder)* saquear; *(rummage in)* registrar

ransom ['rænsəm] *n* rescate m; **to hold sb to r.** pedir rescate por algn; *Fig* poner a algn entre la espada y la pared

rant [rænt] *vi* vociferar; *Fam* **to r. and rave** pegar gritos

rap [ræp] **1** *n* **(a)** *(blow)* golpe m seco; *(on door)* golpecito m **(b)** *Mus* rap m **2** *vt & vi (knock)* golpear

rape¹ [reɪp] *Jur* **1** *n* violación f **2** *vt* violar

rape² [reɪp] *n Bot* colza f

rapid ['ræpɪd] **1** *adj* rápido(a) **2** *n* **rapids** *(in river)* rápidos *mpl*

rapist ['reɪpɪst] *n* violador(a) *m,f*

rare¹ [reə(r)] *adj* raro(a), poco común

rare² [reə(r)] *adj (steak)* poco hecho(a)

rarely ['reəlɪ] *adv* raras veces

raring ['reərɪŋ] *adj Fam* **to be r. to do sth** morirse de ganas de hacer algo

rarity ['reərɪtɪ] *n* rareza *f*

rascal ['rɑːskəl] *n* granuja *mf*

rash¹ [ræʃ] *n* **(a)** *Med* erupción *f*, sarpullido *m* **(b)** *Fig (of robberies etc)* racha *f*

rash² [ræʃ] *adj (reckless)* impetuoso(a); *(words, actions)* precipitado(a), imprudente

rasher ['ræʃə(r)] *n Br* **r. (of bacon)** loncha *f* de tocino *or Esp* beicon

raspberry ['rɑːzbərɪ] *n* frambuesa *f*

rat [ræt] *n* **(a)** *(animal)* rata *f*; **r. poison** raticida *m* **(b)** *US Fam (informer)* soplón(ona) *m,f*, chivato(a) *m,f*

rate [reɪt] **1** *n* **(a)** *(ratio)* índice *m*, tasa *f*; **at any r.** *(at least)* al menos; *(anyway)* en cualquier caso **(b)** *(cost)* precio *m*; *Fin (of interest, exchange)* tipo *m*, tasa *f* **(c)** **at the r. of** *(speed)* a la velocidad de; *(quantity)* a razón de **(d)** *Br* **(business) rates** impuestos *mpl* municipales *(para empresas)*
2 *vt* **(a)** *(estimate)* estimar **(b)** *(evaluate)* tasar **(c)** *(consider)* considerar

rather ['rɑːðə(r)] *adv* **(a)** *(quite)* más bien, bastante; *(very much so)* muy **(b)** *(more accurately)* mejor dicho; **r. than** *(instead of)* en vez de; *(more than)* más que **(c)** **she would r. stay here** *(prefer to)* prefiere quedarse aquí

ratify ['rætɪfaɪ] *vt* ratificar

rating ['reɪtɪŋ] *n* **(a)** *(valuation)* tasación *f*; *(score)* valoración *f* **(b)** *TV* **(programme) ratings** índice *m* de audiencia **(c)** *Naut* marinero *m* sin graduación

ratio ['reɪʃɪəʊ] *n* razón *f*; **in the r. of** a razón de

ration ['ræʃən] **1** *n* **(a)** *(allowance)* ración *f* **(b)** **rations** víveres *mpl* **2** *vt* racionar

rational ['ræʃənəl] *adj* racional

rationalize ['ræʃənəlaɪz] *vt* racionalizar

rattle ['rætəl] **1** *n* **(a)** *(of train, cart)* traqueteo *m*; *(of metal)* repiqueteo *m*; *(of glass)* tintineo *m* **(b)** *(toy)* sonajero *m*; *(instrument)* carraca *f*
2 *vt* **(a)** *(keys etc)* hacer sonar **(b)** *Fam (unsettle)* poner nervioso(a)
3 *vi* sonar; *(metal)* repiquetear; *(glass)* tintinear

raucous ['rɔːkəs] *adj* estridente

rave [reɪv] **1** *vi* **(a)** *(be delirious)* delirar **(b)** *(be angry)* enfurecerse **(at** con) **(c)** *Fam (show enthusiasm)* entusiasmarse **(about** por) **2** *n Fam* **r. review** crítica *f* muy favorable

raven ['reɪvən] *n* cuervo *m*

ravenous ['rævənəs] *adj* **I'm r.** tengo un hambre que no veo

ravine [rə'viːn] *n* barranco *m*

raving ['reɪvɪŋ] *n Fam* **r. mad** loco(a) de atar

raw [rɔː] *adj* **(a)** *(uncooked)* crudo(a) **(b)** *(not processed)* bruto(a); **r. material** materia prima **(c)** *(emotion)* instintivo(a) **(d)** **r. deal** trato injusto **(e)** *US (inexperienced)* novato(a)

ray¹ [reɪ] *n* rayo *m*; *Fig* **r. of hope** rayo de esperanza

ray² [reɪ] *n (fish)* raya *f*

rayon ['reɪɒn] *n* rayón *m*

razor ['reɪzə(r)] *n (for shaving)* maquinilla *f* de afeitar; **r. blade** hoja *f* de afeitar

Rd *(abbr* **Road)** calle *f*, c/

re [riː] *prep* respecto a, con referencia a

reach [riːtʃ] **1** *vt* **(a)** *(arrive at)* llegar a **(b)** *(contact)* localizar
2 *vi* alcanzar; **to r. for sth** (tratar de) alcanzar algo; **to r. out** extender la mano
3 *n* alcance *m*; **out of r.** fuera del alcance; **within r.** al alcance

react [rɪ'ækt] *vi* reaccionar

reaction [rɪ'ækʃən] *n* reacción *f*

reactionary [rɪ'ækʃənərɪ] *n & adj* reaccionario(a) *(m,f)*

reactor [rɪ'æktə(r)] *n* reactor *m*

read [ri:d] (*pt & pp* **read** [red]) **1** *vt* (**a**) leer (**b**) *Br Univ* estudiar (**c**) *(of dial)* marcar; *(of signpost, text)* decir **2** *vi* leer

▸ **read out** *vt sep* leer en voz alta

readable ['ri:dəbəl] *adj* (**a**) *(interesting)* interesante (**b**) *(legible)* legible

reader ['ri:də(r)] *n* (**a**) lector(a) *m,f* (**b**) *(book)* libro *m* de lectura (**c**) *Br Univ* profesor(a) *m,f* adjunto(a)

readily ['redɪlɪ] *adv* (**a**) *(easily)* fácilmente; **r. available** disponible en el acto (**b**) *(willingly)* de buena gana

reading ['ri:dɪŋ] *n* (**a**) lectura *f* (**b**) *Fig* interpretación *f* (**c**) *(of laws, bill)* presentación *f*

ready ['redɪ] *adj* (**a**) *(prepared)* listo(a), preparado(a); **r., steady, go!** ¡preparados, listos, ya! (**b**) **r. to** *(about to)* a punto de (**c**) *(to hand)* a mano; **r. cash** dinero *m* en efectivo (**d**) *(willing)* dispuesto(a)

ready-made ['redɪ'meɪd] *adj* confeccionado(a); *(food)* preparado(a)

real [rɪəl] *adj* (**a**) real, verdadero(a); *Fam* **for r.** de veras (**b**) *(genuine)* auténtico(a); **r. leather** piel legítima (**c**) *US Com* **r. estate** bienes *mpl* inmuebles; **r. estate agent** agente inmobiliario

realistic [rɪəlɪstɪk] *adj* realista

reality [rɪ'ælɪtɪ] *n* realidad *f*; **in r.** en realidad

realization [rɪəlaɪ'zeɪʃən] *n* (**a**) *(understanding)* comprensión *f* (**b**) *(of plan, assets)* realización *f*

realize ['rɪəlaɪz] *vt* (**a**) *(become aware of)* darse cuenta de (**b**) *(assets, plan)* realizar

really ['rɪəlɪ] *adv* verdaderamente, realmente; **I r. don't know** no lo sé de verdad; **r.?** ¿de veras?

realtor ['rɪəltə(r)] *n US* agente *mf* inmobiliario(a)

reap [ri:p] *vt Agr* cosechar; *Fig* **to r. the benefits** llevarse los beneficios

reappear [rɪə'pɪə(r)] *vi* reaparecer

rear¹ [rɪə(r)] **1** *n* (**a**) *(back part)* parte *f* de atrás (**b**) *Fam (buttocks)* trasero *m* **2** *adj* trasero(a); **r. entrance** puerta *f* de atrás

rear² [rɪə(r)] **1** *vt* (**a**) *(breed, raise)* criar (**b**) *(lift up)* levantar **2** *vi* **to r. up** *(horse)* encabritarse

rearrange [rɪə'reɪndʒ] *vt* (**a**) *(furniture)* colocar de otra manera (**b**) *(appointment)* fijar otra fecha para

rear-view ['rɪəvju:] *adj* **r. mirror** (espejo *m*) retrovisor *m*

reason ['ri:zən] **1** *n* (**a**) motivo *m*, razón *f*; **for no r.** sin razón; **for some r.** por algún motivo (**b**) *(good sense)* razón *f*; **it stands to r.** es lógico; **to listen to r.** atender a razones, *Am* atender razones **2** *vi* (**a**) **to r. with sb** *(argue, work out)* razonar

reasonable ['ri:zənəbəl] *adj* (**a**) *(fair)* razonable (**b**) *(sensible)* sensato(a) (**c**) *(average)* regular

reasonably ['ri:zənəblɪ] *adv* *(fairly)* bastante

reasoning ['ri:zənɪŋ] *n* razonamiento *m*

reassure [ri:ə'ʃuə(r)] *vt* (**a**) *(comfort)* tranquilizar (**b**) *(restore confidence)* dar confianza a

reassuring [ri:ə'ʃuərɪŋ] *adj* consolador(a)

rebate ['ri:beɪt] *n* devolución *f*; **tax r.** devolución fiscal

rebel 1 *adj & n* ['rebəl] rebelde *(mf)* **2** *vi* [rɪ'bel] rebelarse, sublevarse (**against** contra)

rebellion [rɪ'beljən] *n* rebelión *f*

rebound 1 *n* ['ri:baʊnd] *(of ball)* rebote *m*; *Fig* **on the r.** de rebote **2** *vi* [rɪ'baʊnd] *(ball)* rebotar

rebuild [ri:'bɪld] *vt* reconstruir

rebuke [rɪ'bju:k] **1** *n* reproche *m* **2** *vt* reprochar

recall [rɪ'kɔ:l] *vt* (**a**) *(soldiers, products)* hacer volver; *(ambassador)* retirar (**b**) *(remember)* recordar

recap 1 *vt & vi* [ri:'kæp] resumir; **to r. en resumen 2** *n* ['ri:kæp] recapitulación *f*

recede [rɪ'si:d] *vi* retroceder; **to have a receding hairline** tener entradas

receipt [rɪ'si:t] *n* (**a**) *(act)* recepción *f*; **to acknowledge r. of sth** acusar recibo de algo (**b**) *Com (paper)* recibo *m* (**c**) **receipts** *(takings)* recaudación *f*

receive [rɪ'siːv] *vt* (**a**) recibir (**b**) *Jur (stolen goods)* ocultar (**c**) *(welcome)* acoger (**d**) *TV, Rad* captar

receiver [rɪ'siːvə(r)] *n* (**a**) *(person)* receptor(a) *m,f* (**b**) *Jur (of stolen goods)* perista *mf* (**c**) *(of telephone)* auricular *m, RP, Ven* tubo *m*

recent ['riːsənt] *adj* reciente; **in r. years** en los últimos años

recently ['riːsəntlɪ] *adv* hace poco, recientemente

reception [rɪ'sepʃən] *n* (**a**) *(welcome)* recibimiento *m* (**b**) *(party)* recepción *f*; **wedding r.** banquete *m* de boda *or Andes* matrimonio *or RP* casamiento (**c**) **r. (desk)** recepción *f* (**d**) *Rad, TV* recepción *f*

receptionist [rɪ'sepʃənɪst] *n* recepcionista *mf*

receptive [rɪ'septɪv] *adj* receptivo(a)

recess ['riːses, rɪ'ses] *n* (**a**) *(in a wall)* hueco *m* (**b**) *(secret place)* escondrijo *m* (**c**) *US Educ* recreo *m*; *Pol* período *m* de vacaciones

recession [rɪ'seʃən] *n* recesión *f*

recharge [riː'tʃɑːdʒ] *vt (battery)* recargar

recipe ['resɪpɪ] *n Culin* receta *f*; *Fig* fórmula *f*

recipient [rɪ'sɪpɪənt] *n* receptor(a) *m,f*; *(of letter)* destinatario(a) *m,f*

reciprocate [rɪ'sɪprəkeɪt] **1** *vt (favour etc)* devolver **2** *vi* hacer lo mismo

recital [rɪ'saɪtəl] *n* recital *m*

recite [rɪ'saɪt] *vt & vi* recitar

reckless ['reklɪs] *adj (unwise)* imprudente; *(fearless)* temerario(a)

reckon ['rekən] *vt & vi* (**a**) *(calculate)* calcular; *(count)* contar (**b**) *Fam (think)* creer; *(consider)* considerar

▸ **reckon on** *vt insep* contar con

reckoning ['rekənɪŋ] *n* cálculo *m*; **by my r. ...** según mis cálculos ...; *Fig* **day of r.** día *m* del juicio final

reclaim [rɪ'kleɪm] *vt* (**a**) *(recover)* recuperar; *(demand back)* reclamar (**b**)

(marshland etc) convertir

recline [rɪ'klaɪn] *vi* recostarse, reclinarse

recluse [rɪ'kluːs] *n* solitario(a) *m,f*

recognition [rekəg'nɪʃən] *n* reconocimiento *m*; *(appreciation)* apreciación *f*; **changed beyond all r.** irreconocible

recognizable [rekəg'naɪzəbəl] *adj* reconocible

recognize ['rekəgnaɪz] *vt* reconocer

recoil 1 *n* ['riːkɔɪl] *(of gun)* culatazo *m*; *(of spring)* aflojamiento *m* **2** *vi* [rɪ'kɔɪl] (**a**) *(gun)* dar un culatazo; *(spring)* aflojarse (**b**) *(in fear)* espantarse

recollect [rekə'lekt] *vt* recordar

recollection [rekə'lekʃən] *n* recuerdo *m*

recommend [rekə'mend] *vt* recomendar

recommendation [rekəmen'deɪʃən] *n* recomendación *f*

reconcile ['rekənsaɪl] *vt (two people)* reconciliar; *(two ideas)* conciliar; **to r. oneself to** resignarse a

reconsider [riːkən'sɪdə(r)] *vt* reconsiderar

reconstruct [riːkən'strʌkt] *vt* reconstruir

record 1 *n* ['rekɔːd] (**a**) *(account)* relación *f*; *(of meeting)* actas *fpl* (**b**) *(document)* documento *m*; **public records** archivos *mpl* (**c**) *Mus* disco *m*; **r. player** tocadiscos *m inv* (**d**) *Sport* récord *m* **2** *vt* [rɪ'kɔːd] (**a**) *(relate)* hacer constar; *(note down)* apuntar (**b**) *(record, voice)* grabar

recorded [rɪ'kɔːdɪd] *adj Br* **r. delivery** correo certificado; **r. message** mensaje grabado

recorder [rɪ'kɔːdə(r)] *n* (**a**) *(person)* registrador(a) *m,f*; *Jur* magistrado(a) *m,f* (**b**) *Mus* flauta *f*

recording [rɪ'kɔːdɪŋ] *n (registering)* registro *m*; *(recorded music, message etc)* grabación *f*

recount [rɪ'kaʊnt] *vt (tell)* contar

recourse [rɪ'kɔːs] *n* **to have r. to** recurrir a

recover [rɪ'kʌvə(r)] **1** *vt (items, lost*

time) recuperar; *(consciousness)* recobrar **2** *vi (from illness etc)* reponerse

recovery [rɪ'kʌvərɪ] *n* (**a**) *(retrieval)* recuperación *f* (**b**) *(from illness)* restablecimiento *m*

re-create [ri:krɪ'eɪt] *vt* recrear

recreation [rekrɪ'eɪʃən] *n* (**a**) diversión *f* (**b**) *Educ (playtime)* recreo *m*

recrimination [rɪkrɪmɪ'neɪʃən] *n* reproche *m*

recruit [rɪ'kru:t] **1** *n* recluta *m* **2** *vt (soldiers)* reclutar; *(workers)* contratar

rectangle ['rektæŋgəl] *n* rectángulo *m*

rectangular [rek'tæŋgjʊlə(r)] *adj* rectangular

rectify ['rektɪfaɪ] *vt* rectificar

rector ['rektə(r)] *n* (**a**) *Rel* párroco *m* (**b**) *Scot Educ* director(a) *m,f*

recuperate [rɪ'ku:pəreɪt] *vi* reponerse

recur [rɪ'kɜ:(r)] *vi* repetirse

recycle [ri:'saɪkəl] *vt* reciclar

red [red] **1** *adj* (**redder, reddest**) rojo(a); **r. light** semáforo *m* en rojo; **r. wine** vino tinto; **to go r.** ponerse colorado(a); **to have r. hair** ser pelirrojo(a); *Fig* **r. herring** truco *m* para despistar; *Fam* **to roll out the r. carpet for sb** recibir a algn con todos los honores; **R. Cross** Cruz Roja; **R. Indian** piel roja *mf*; **R. Riding Hood** Caperucita Roja; **R. Sea** Mar Rojo; **r. tape** papeleo *m* **2** *n* (**a**) *(colour)* rojo *m* (**b**) *Fin* **to be in the r.** estar en números rojos

redcurrant ['redkʌrənt] *n* grosella roja

redeem [rɪ'di:m] *vt* (**a**) *(regain)* recobrar; *(voucher)* canjear (**b**) *(debt)* amortizar (**c**) *(film, novel etc)* salvar (**d**) *Rel* redimir; *Fig* **to r. oneself** redimirse

red-handed [red'hændɪd] *adj* **he was caught r.** lo *Esp* cogieron *or Am* agarraron con las manos en la masa

redhead ['redhed] *n* pelirrojo(a) *m,f*

red-hot [red'hɒt] *adj* (**a**) candente; **r. news** noticia(s) *f(pl)* de última hora (**b**) *Fam (passionate)* ardiente

redirect [ri:dɪ'rekt] *vt* (**a**) *(funds)* redistribuir (**b**) *(letter)* remitir a la nueva dirección

redo [ri:'du:] *(pt* **redid** [ri:'dɪd], *pp* **redone** [ri:'dʌn]) *vt* rehacer

reduce [rɪ'dju:s] *vt* (**a**) reducir (**b**) *(in rank)* degradar (**c**) *Culin (sauce)* espesar (**d**) *Med* recomponer

reduction [rɪ'dʌkʃən] *n* reducción *f*; *Com (in purchase price)* descuento *m*, rebaja *f*

redundancy [rɪ'dʌndənsɪ] *n Br (dismissal)* despido *m*

redundant [rɪ'dʌndənt] *adj* (**a**) *(superfluous)* redundante (**b**) *Br Ind* **to be made r.** perder el empleo; **to make sb r.** despedir a algn

reed [ri:d] *n* (**a**) *Bot* caña *f* (**b**) *Mus* caramillo *m*

reef [ri:f] *n* arrecife *m*

reek [ri:k] **1** *n* tufo *m* **2** *vi* apestar

reel [ri:l] **1** *n* (**a**) *(spool)* bobina *f*, carrete *m* (**b**) *Scot Mus* danza *f* tradicional **2** *vi (stagger)* tambalearse

ref [ref] *n* (**a**) *Fam Sport* árbitro *m* (**b**) *Com (abbr* **reference**) ref

refectory [rɪ'fektərɪ] *n* refectorio *m*

refer [rɪ'fɜ:(r)] **1** *vt* mandar, enviar; **to r. a matter to a tribunal** remitir un asunto a un tribunal **2** *vi* (**a**) *(allude)* referirse, aludir (**to** a) (**b**) **to r. to** *(consult)* consultar

referee [refə'ri:] **1** *n* (**a**) *Sport* árbitro(a) *m,f* (**b**) *Br (for job application)* garante *mf* **2** *vt Sport* arbitrar

reference ['refərəns] *n* (**a**) referencia *f*; **with r. to** con referencia a; **r. book** libro *m* de consulta; **r. library** biblioteca *f* de consulta (**b**) *Br (from employer)* informe *m*, referencia *f*

referendum [refə'rendəm] *n* referéndum *m*

refill 1 *n* ['ri:fɪl] (**a**) *(replacement)* recambio *m*, carga *f* (**b**) *Fam (drink)* otra copa **2** *vt* [ri:'fɪl] rellenar

refine [rɪ'faɪn] *vt* refinar

refined [rɪ'faɪnd] *adj* refinado(a)

refinement [rɪ'faɪnmənt] *n* refinamiento *m*

reflect [rɪ'flekt] **1** *vt (light, attitude)* reflejar **2** *vi (think)* reflexionar; **to r. on sth** meditar sobre algo

reflection [rɪ'flekʃən] *n* (**a**) *(indication, mirror image)* reflejo *m* (**b**) *(thought)* reflexión *f*; **on r.** pensándolo bien (**c**) *(criticism)* crítica *f*

reflector [rɪ'flektə(r)] *n (of vehicle)* catafaro *m*

reflex ['riːfleks] *n* reflejo *m*

reflexive [rɪ'fleksɪv] *adj* reflexivo(a)

reform [rɪ'fɔːm] **1** *n* reforma *f*; **r. school** reformatorio *m* **2** *vt* reformar

refrain [rɪ'freɪn] **1** *n Mus* estribillo *m*; *Fig* lema *m* **2** *vi* abstenerse (**from** de)

refresh [rɪ'freʃ] *vt* refrescar

refreshing [rɪ'freʃɪŋ] *adj* refrescante; **a r. change** un cambio muy agradable

refreshment [rɪ'freʃmənt] *n* refresco *m*

refrigerator [rɪ'frɪdʒəreɪtə(r)] *n* nevera *f*, frigorífico *m*, *Andes* frigider *m*, *RP* heladera *f*

refuel [riː'fjuːəl] *vi* repostar combustible

refuge ['refjuːdʒ] *n* refugio *m*, cobijo *m*; **to take r.** refugiarse

refugee [refjʊ'dʒiː] *n* refugiado(a) *m,f*

refund 1 *n* ['riːfʌnd] reembolso *m* **2** *vt* [rɪ'fʌnd] reembolsar, devolver

refusal [rɪ'fjuːzəl] *n* negativa *f*; **to have first r. on sth** tener la primera opción en algo

refuse¹ [rɪ'fjuːz] **1** *vt* rechazar; **to r. sb sth** negar algo a algn **2** *vi* negarse

refuse² ['refjuːs] *n* basura *f*; **r. collector** basurero *m*

regain [rɪ'geɪn] *vt* recuperar; *(consciousness)* recobrar

regard [rɪ'gɑːd] **1** *n* (**a**) *(concern)* consideración *f*, respeto *m*; **with r. to** respecto a (**b**) *(esteem)* estima *f* (**c**) **regards** *(good wishes)* saludos *mpl*, *CAm, Col, Ecuad* saludes *fpl*; **give him my regards** dale recuerdos de mi parte **2** *vt* (**a**) *(consider)* considerar (**b**) **as regards** *(regarding)* respecto a

regarding [rɪ'gɑːdɪŋ] *prep* respecto a

regardless [rɪ'gɑːdlɪs] **1** *prep* **r. of** sin tener en cuenta; **r. of the outcome** pase lo que pase **2** *adv* a toda costa

regime [reɪ'ʒiːm] *n* régimen *m*

regiment ['redʒɪmənt] **1** *n* regimiento *m* **2** *vt* regimentar

region ['riːdʒən] *n* (**a**) región *f* (**b**) **in the r. of** aproximadamente

regional ['riːdʒənəl] *adj* regional

register ['redʒɪstə(r)] **1** *n* registro *m* **2** *vt* (**a**) *(record)* registrar (**b**) *(letter)* certificar (**c**) *(show)* mostrar **3** *vi (for course)* inscribirse; *Univ* matricularse

registered ['redʒɪstəd] *adj* certificado(a); *Br* **r. letter** carta certificada; **r. trademark** marca registrada

registration [redʒɪ'streɪʃən] *n* inscripción *f*; *Univ* matrícula *f*; *Br Aut* **r. number** matrícula *f*

registry ['redʒɪstrɪ] *n* registro *m*; **to get married in a r. office** casarse por lo civil; *Br* **r. office** registro civil

regret [rɪ'gret] **1** *n (remorse)* remordimiento *m*; *(sadness)* pesar *m*; **regrets** *(excuses)* excusas *fpl*; **to have no regrets** no arrepentirse de nada **2** *vt* arrepentirse de, lamentar

regrettable [rɪ'gretəbəl] *adj* lamentable

regular ['regjʊlə(r)] **1** *adj* (**a**) regular (**b**) *(usual)* normal (**c**) *(staff)* permanente (**d**) *(frequent)* frecuente (**e**) **r. army** tropas *fpl* regulares (**f**) *US Fam* **a r. guy** un tío legal, *Am* un tipo derecho **2** *n (customer)* cliente *mf* habitual

regularly ['regjʊləlɪ] *adv* con regularidad

regulate ['regjʊleɪt] *vt* regular

regulation [regjʊ'leɪʃən] **1** *n* (**a**) *(control)* regulación *f* (**b**) *(rule)* regla *f* **2** *adj* reglamentario(a)

rehearsal [rɪ'hɜːsəl] *n* ensayo *m*

rehearse [rɪ'hɜːs] *vt & vi* ensayar

reign [reɪn] **1** *n* reinado *m* **2** *vi* reinar

reimburse [riːɪm'bɜːs] *vt* reembolsar

reindeer ['reɪndɪə(r)] *n* reno *m*

reinforce [riːinˈfɔːs] vt *(strengthen)* reforzar; *(support)* apoyar; **reinforced concrete** hormigón *or Am* concreto armado

reinforcement [riːinˈfɔːsmənt] n (a) refuerzo m; *Constr* armazón m (b) *Mil* **reinforcements** refuerzos mpl

reinstate [riːinˈsteit] vt *(to job)* reincorporar

reject 1 n [ˈriːdʒekt] (a) desecho m (b) *Com* **rejects** artículos defectuosos **2** vt [riˈdʒekt] rechazar

rejection [riˈdʒekʃən] n rechazo m

rejoice [riˈdʒɔis] vi regocijarse (**at** or **over** de)

rejuvenate [riˈdʒuːvineit] vt rejuvenecer; *Fig* revitalizar

relapse [riˈlæps] **1** n (a) *Med* recaída f; **to have a r.** sufrir una recaída (b) *(into crime, alcoholism)* reincidencia f **2** vi recaer

relate [riˈleit] **1** vt (a) *(connect)* relacionar (b) *(tell)* relatar **2** vi relacionarse

related [riˈleitid] adj (a) *(linked)* relacionado(a) (**to** con) (b) **to be r. to sb** ser pariente de algn

relation [riˈleiʃən] n (a) *(link)* relación f; **in** or **with r. to** respecto a; **it bears no r. to what we said** no tiene nada que ver con lo que dijimos (b) *(member of family)* pariente(a) m,f

relationship [riˈleiʃənʃip] n (a) *(link)* relación f (b) *(between people)* relaciones fpl; **to have a good/bad r. with sb** llevarse bien/mal con algn

relative [ˈrelətiv] **1** n pariente mf **2** adj relativo(a)

relatively [ˈrelətivli] adv relativamente

relax [riˈlæks] **1** vt *(muscles, rules)* relajar **2** vi relajarse

relaxation [riːlækˈseiʃən] n (a) *(rest)* descanso m, relajación f (b) *(of rules)* relajación f (c) *(pastime)* distracción f

relaxed [riˈlækst] adj relajado(a); *(peaceful)* tranquilo(a)

relaxing [riˈlæksiŋ] adj relajante

relay 1 n [ˈriːlei] (a) relevo m; **r. (race)** carrera f de relevos (b) *Rad, TV*

retransmisión f **2** vt [riˈlei] (a) *(pass on)* difundir (b) *Rad, TV* retransmitir

release [riˈliːs] **1** n (a) *(of prisoner)* liberación f, puesta f en libertad; *(of gas)* escape m (b) *Com* puesta f en venta (c) *Cin* estreno m (d) *(record)* disco m **2** vt (a) *(let go)* soltar; *(prisoner)* poner en libertad; *(gas)* despedir (b) *Com* poner en venta (c) *Cin* estrenar (d) *(record)* editar

relegate [ˈreligeit] vt (a) relegar (b) *Br Ftb* **to be relegated** bajar a una división inferior

relent [riˈlent] vi ceder; *(storm)* aplacarse

relentless [riˈlentlis] adj implacable

relevance [ˈreləvəns] n pertinencia f

relevant [ˈreləvənt] adj pertinente (**to** a); **it is not r.** no viene al caso

reliability [rilaiəˈbiliti] n (a) *(of person)* formalidad f (b) *(of car, machine)* fiabilidad f, *Am* confiabilidad f

reliable [riˈlaiəbəl] adj *(person, machine)* fiable, *Am* confiable; **a r. car** un coche seguro; **a r. source** una fuente fidedigna

relic [ˈrelik] n (a) *Rel* reliquia f (b) *(reminder of past)* vestigio m

relief [riˈliːf] n (a) alivio m (b) *(help)* auxilio m, ayuda f; *US* **to be on r.** cobrar un subsidio (c) *Art, Geog* relieve m

relieve [riˈliːv] vt (a) aliviar; *(monotony)* romper (b) *(take over from)* relevar (c) *Euph* **to r. oneself** hacer sus necesidades (d) **to r. sb of sth** coger algo a algn

religion [riˈlidʒən] n religión f

religious [riˈlidʒəs] adj religioso(a)

relinquish [riˈliŋkwiʃ] vt renunciar a; **to r. one's hold on sth** soltar algo

relish [ˈreliʃ] **1** n (a) *(enjoyment)* deleite m (b) *Culin* condimento m **2** vt agradar

reluctant [riˈlʌktənt] adj reacio(a); **to be r. to do sth** estar poco dispuesto(a) a hacer algo

rely [riˈlai] vi contar (**on** con), confiar (**on** en)

remain [riˈmein] **1** vi (a) *(stay)*

permanecer, quedarse (**b**) *(be left)* quedar; **it remains to be seen** está por ver **2** *npl* **remains** restos *mpl*

remainder [rɪ'meɪndə(r)] *n* resto *m*

remaining [rɪ'meɪnɪŋ] *adj* restante

remark [rɪ'mɑːk] **1** *n* comentario *m* **2** *vt* comentar, observar

remarkable [rɪ'mɑːkəbəl] *adj* extraordinario(a); *(strange)* curioso(a)

remedy ['remɪdɪ] **1** *n* remedio *m* **2** *vt* remediar

remember [rɪ'membə(r)] **1** *vt* (**a**) acordarse de, recordar (**b**) **r. me to your mother** dale recuerdos a tu madre **2** *vi* acordarse, recordar; **I don't r.** no me acuerdo

remind [rɪ'maɪnd] *vt* recordar; **r. me to do it** recuérdame que lo haga; **she reminds me of your sister** me recuerda a tu hermana; **that reminds me** ahora que me acuerdo

reminder [rɪ'maɪndə(r)] *n* recordatorio *m*, aviso *m*

reminisce [remɪ'nɪs] *vi* rememorar

reminiscent [remɪ'nɪsənt] *adj Fml* nostálgico(a); **to be r. of** recordar

remittance [rɪ'mɪtəns] *n* (**a**) *(sending)* envío *m* (**b**) *(payment)* giro *m*, pago *m*

remorse [rɪ'mɔːs] *n* remordimiento *m*

remorseless [rɪ'mɔːslɪs] *adj* despiadado(a)

remote [rɪ'məʊt] *adj* (**a**) *(far away)* remoto(a); **r. control** mando *m* a distancia (**b**) *(isolated)* aislado(a) (**c**) *(possibility)* remoto(a); **I haven't the remotest idea** no tengo la más mínima idea

remotely [rɪ'məʊtlɪ] *adv* (**a**) *(vaguely)* vagamente (**b**) *(distantly)* en lugar aislado

removable [rɪ'muːvəbəl] *adj (detachable)* que se puede quitar

removal [rɪ'muːvəl] *n* (**a**) *(moving house)* mudanza *f*; **r. van** camión *m* de mudanzas (**b**) *(of stain etc)* eliminación *f*

remove [rɪ'muːv] *vt* (**a**) *(move)* quitar, *Am* sacar; **to r. one's make-up** desmaquillarse; **to r. one's name from a list** tachar su nombre de una lista (**b**) *(from office)* despedir

rendezvous ['rɒndɪvuː] **1** *n* (**a**) *(meeting)* cita *f* (**b**) *(place)* lugar *m* de reunión **2** *vi* reunirse

renew [rɪ'njuː] *vt (contract etc)* renovar; *(talks etc)* reanudar; **with renewed vigour** con renovadas fuerzas

renounce [rɪ'naʊns] *vt Fml* renunciar

renovate ['renəveɪt] *vt* renovar, hacer reformas en

renowned [rɪ'naʊnd] *adj* renombrado(a)

rent [rent] **1** *n* (**a**) *(for building, car, TV)* alquiler *m* (**b**) *(for land)* arriendo *m* **2** *vt* (**a**) *(building, car, TV)* alquilar, *Méx* rentar (**b**) *(land)* arrendar

rental ['rentəl] *n (of house etc)* alquiler *m*

reorganize [riː'ɔːgənaɪz] *vt* reorganizar

repair [rɪ'peə(r)] **1** *n* reparación *f*, arreglo *m*; **in good/bad r.** en buen/mal estado **2** *vt* (**a**) arreglar; *(car)* reparar; *(clothes)* remendar (**b**) *(make amends for)* reparar

repay [riː'peɪ] *(pt & pp* **repaid***)* *vt* devolver; **to r. a debt** liquidar una deuda; **to r. a kindness** devolver un favor

repayment [riː'peɪmənt] *n* pago *m*

repeal [rɪ'piːl] *Jur* **1** *n* revocación *f* **2** *vt* revocar

repeat [rɪ'piːt] **1** *vt* repetir; **to r. oneself** repetirse **2** *n (repetition)* repetición *f*; *TV* reposición *f*

repeated [rɪ'piːtɪd] *adj* repetido(a)

repeatedly [rɪ'piːtɪdlɪ] *adv* repetidas veces

repel [rɪ'pel] *vt* (**a**) *(fight off)* repeler (**b**) *(disgust)* repugnar

repellent [rɪ'pelənt] **1** *adj* repelente; **water-r.** impermeable **2** *n* (**insect**) **r.** loción *f*/spray *m* anti-insectos

repent [rɪ'pent] *vt & vi* arrepentirse (de)

repercussion [riːpə'kʌʃən] *n (usu pl)* repercusión *f*

repertoire ['repətwɑː(r)] *n* repertorio *m*

repetition [repɪ'tɪʃən] *n* repetición *f*

repetitive [rɪ'petɪtɪv] *adj* repetitivo(a)

replace [rɪ'pleɪs] *vt* (**a**) *(put back)* volver a poner en su sitio (**b**) *(substitute for)* sustituir, reemplazar

replacement [rɪ'pleɪsmənt] *n* (**a**) *(returning)* reemplazo *m* (**b**) *(person)* sustituto(a) *m,f* (**c**) *(part)* pieza *f* de recambio

replay ['riːpleɪ] *n* repetición *f*

replica ['replɪkə] *n* réplica *f*

reply [rɪ'plaɪ] **1** *n* respuesta *f*, contestación *f* **2** *vi* responder, contestar

report [rɪ'pɔːt] **1** *n* (**a**) informe *m*, *Andes, CAm, Méx, Ven* reporte *m*; *Br* **school r.** informe escolar (**b**) *(piece of news)* noticia *f* (**c**) *Press, Rad, TV* reportaje *m*
2 *vt* (**a**) **it is reported that ...** se dice que ... (**b**) *(tell authorities about)* denunciar (**c**) *Press* hacer un reportaje sobre
3 *vi* (**a**) *(of committee member etc)* hacer un informe (**b**) *Press* hacer un reportaje (**c**) *(for duty etc)* presentarse

reported [rɪ'pɔːtɪd] *adj* **r. speech** estilo indirecto

reporter [rɪ'pɔːtə(r)] *n* periodista *mf*

represent [reprɪ'zent] *vt* representar

representation [reprɪzen'teɪʃən] *n* (**a**) representación *f* (**b**) *Fml* **representations** queja *f*

representative [reprɪ'zentətɪv] **1** *adj* representativo(a) **2** *n* (**a**) representante *mf* (**b**) *US Pol* diputado(a) *m,f*

repress [rɪ'pres] *vt* reprimir, contener

repressive [rɪ'presɪv] *adj* represivo(a)

reprieve [rɪ'priːv] **1** *n* (**a**) *Jur* indulto *m* (**b**) *Fig* alivio *m* **2** *vt Jur* indultar

reprimand ['reprɪmɑːnd] **1** *n* reprimenda *f* **2** *vt* reprender

reprint 1 *n* ['riːprɪnt] reimpresión *f* *vt* [riː'prɪnt] reimprimir

reprisal [rɪ'praɪzəl] *n* represalia *f*

reproach [rɪ'prəʊtʃ] **1** *n* reproche *m*; **beyond r.** intachable **2** *vt* reprochar

reproduce [riːprə'djuːs] **1** *vt* reproducir **2** *vi* reproducirse

reproduction [riːprə'dʌkʃən] *n* reproducción *f*

reptile ['reptaɪl] *n* reptil *m*

republic [rɪ'pʌblɪk] *n* república *f*

republican [rɪ'pʌblɪkən] *adj & n* republicano(a) *(m,f)*; *US Pol* **R. Party** Partido Republicano

repugnant [rɪ'pʌgnənt] *adj* repugnante

repulsive [rɪ'pʌlsɪv] *adj* repulsivo(a)

reputable ['repjʊtəbəl] *adj (company etc)* acreditado(a); *(person, products)* de toda confianza

reputation [repjʊ'teɪʃən] *n* reputación *f*

reputed [rɪ'pjuːtɪd] *adj* supuesto(a); **to be r. to be** ser considerado(a) como

request [rɪ'kwest] **1** *n* petición *f*, solicitud *f*, *Am* pedido *m*; **available on r.** disponible a petición de los interesados; *Br* **r. stop** *(for bus)* parada *f* discrecional **2** *vt* pedir, solicitar

require [rɪ'kwaɪə(r)] *vt* (**a**) *(need)* necesitar, requerir (**b**) *(demand)* exigir

requirement [rɪ'kwaɪəmənt] *n* (**a**) *(need)* necesidad *f* (**b**) *(demand)* requisito *m*

requisite ['rekwɪzɪt] *Fml* **1** *adj* requerido(a) **2** *n* requisito *m*

rescue ['reskjuː] **1** *n* rescate *m*; **r. team** equipo *m* de rescate **2** *vt* rescatar

research [rɪ'sɜːtʃ] **1** *n* investigación *f*; **R. and Development** Investigación más Desarrollo **2** *vt & vi* investigar

researcher [rɪ'sɜːtʃə(r)] *n* investigador(a) *m,f*

resemblance [rɪ'zembləns] *n* semejanza *f*

resemble [rɪ'zembəl] *vt* parecerse a

resent [rɪ'zent] *vt* ofenderse por

resentment [rɪ'zentmənt] *n* resentimiento *m*

reservation [rezə'veɪʃən] *n* reserva *f*, *Am* reservación *f*

reserve [rɪ'zɜːv] **1** *n* (**a**) reserva *f*; **to keep sth in r.** guardar algo de reserva (**b**) *Sport* suplente *mf* (**c**) *Mil* **reserves**

reservas *fpl* **2** *vt* reservar

reserved [rɪˈzɜːvd] *adj* reservado(a)

reservoir [ˈrezəvwɑː(r)] *n* embalse *m*, pantano *m*; *Fig* reserva *f*

reshuffle [riːˈʃʌfəl] *n Pol* remodelación *f*

reside [rɪˈzaɪd] *vi Fml* residir

residence [ˈrezɪdəns] *n Fml (home)* residencia *f; (address)* domicilio *m; (period of time)* permanencia *f*

resident [ˈrezɪdənt] *adj & n* residente *(mf); US Med* = médico que ha cumplido la residencia y prosigue con su especialización; **to be r. in** estar domiciliado(a) en

residential [rezɪˈdenʃəl] *adj* residencial

resign [rɪˈzaɪn] **1** *vt* (**a**) *(give up)* dimitir (**b**) **to r. oneself to sth** resignarse a algo **2** *vi (from job)* dimitir

resignation [rezɪɡˈneɪʃən] *n* (**a**) *(from a job)* dimisión *f* (**b**) *(acceptance)* resignación *f*

resilient [rɪˈzɪlɪənt] *adj (strong)* resistente

resist [rɪˈzɪst] **1** *vt* (**a**) *(not yield to)* resistir (**b**) *(oppose)* oponerse a **2** *vi* resistir

resistance [rɪˈzɪstəns] *n* resistencia *f*

resistant [rɪˈzɪstənt] *adj* **to be r. to sth** *(change, suggestion)* mostrarse remiso(a) a aceptar algo, mostrar resistencia a algo; *(disease)* ser resistente a algo

resit [riːˈsɪt] *vt Br (exam)* volver a presentarse a

resolute [ˈrezəluːt] *adj* resuelto(a), decidido(a)

resolution [rezəˈluːʃən] *n* resolución *f*

resolve [rɪˈzɒlv] **1** *n* resolución *f*
2 *vt* resolver; **to r. to do** resolverse a hacer
3 *vi* resolverse

resort [rɪˈzɔːt] **1** *n* (**a**) *(place)* lugar *m* de vacaciones; **tourist r.** centro turístico (**b**) *(recourse)* recurso *m*; **as a last r.** como último recurso **2** *vi* recurrir (**to** a)

resounding [rɪˈzaʊndɪŋ] *adj* **a r.**

failure un fracaso total; **a r. success** un éxito rotundo

resource [rɪˈsɔːs] *n* recurso *m*

resourceful [rɪˈsɔːsfʊl] *adj* ingenioso(a)

respect [rɪˈspekt] **1** *n* (**a**) *(deference)* respeto *m*; **to pay one's respects to sb** presentar sus respetos a algn (**b**) *(relation, reference)* respecto *m*; **in that r.** a ese respecto; **with r. to** con referencia a **2** *vt* respetar

respectable [rɪˈspektəbəl] *adj* respetable; *(clothes)* decente

respective [rɪˈspektɪv] *adj* respectivo(a)

respond [rɪˈspɒnd] *vi* responder

response [rɪˈspɒns] *n* (**a**) *(reply)* respuesta *f* (**b**) *(reaction)* reacción *f*

responsibility [rɪspɒnsəˈbɪlɪtɪ] *n* responsabilidad *f*

responsible [rɪˈspɒnsəbəl] *adj* responsable (**for** de); **to be r. to sb** tener que dar cuentas a algn

responsive [rɪˈspɒnsɪv] *adj* sensible

rest¹ [rest] **1** *n* (**a**) *(break)* descanso *m*; *US* **r. room** baño *m*, *Esp* servicios *mpl*, *CSur* toilette *m* (**b**) *(peace)* tranquilidad *f*; **at r.** *(object)* inmóvil (**c**) *(support)* apoyo *m*
2 *vt* (**a**) descansar (**b**) *(lean)* apoyar; **to r. a ladder against a wall** apoyar una escalera contra una pared
3 *vi* (**a**) descansar (**b**) *(be calm)* quedarse tranquilo(a) (**c**) **it doesn't r. with me** no depende de mí

rest² [rest] *n* **the r.** *(remainder)* el resto, lo demás; **the r. of the girls** las demás chicas

restaurant [ˈrestərɒnt] *n* restaurante *m*; *Br Rail* **r. car** coche *m* restaurante

restful [ˈrestfʊl] *adj* relajante

restless [ˈrestlɪs] *adj* agitado(a), inquieto(a)

restore [rɪˈstɔː(r)] *vt* (**a**) *(give back)* devolver (**b**) *(re-establish)* restablecer (**c**) *(building etc)* restaurar

restrain [rɪˈstreɪn] *vt* contener; **to r. one's anger** reprimir la cólera; **to r. oneself** contenerse

restrained [rɪˈstreɪnd] *adj (person)*

moderado(a); *(emotion)* contenido(a)

restraint [rɪ'streɪnt] *n* **(a)** *(restriction)* restricción *f*; *(hindrance)* traba *f* **(b)** *(moderation)* moderación *f*

restrict [rɪ'strɪkt] *vt* restringir, limitar

restriction [rɪ'strɪkʃən] *n* restricción *f*, limitación *f*

result [rɪ'zʌlt] **1** *n* **(a)** resultado *m* **(b)** *(consequence)* consecuencia *f*; **as a r. of** como consecuencia de **2** *vi* **(a)** resultar; **to r. from** resultar de **(b) to r. in** causar

resume [rɪ'zjuːm] **1** *vt (journey, work, conversation)* reanudar; *(control)* reasumir **2** *vi* recomenzar

résumé ['rezjʊmeɪ] *n* **(a)** *(summary)* resumen *m* **(b)** *US (curriculum vitae)* currículum (vitae) *m*

resurrection [rezə'rekʃən] *n* resurrección *f*

resuscitate [rɪ'sʌsɪteɪt] *vt* Med reanimar

retail ['riːteɪl] **1** *n* venta *f* al por menor, *Am* menoreo *m*; **r. outlet** punto *m* de venta; **r. price** precio *m* de venta al público; *Br* **r. price index** Índice *m* de Precios al Consumo
  2 *vt* vender al por menor
  3 *vi* venderse al por menor
  4 *adv* al por menor

retailer ['riːteɪlə(r)] *n* detallista *mf*

retain [rɪ'teɪn] *vt* **(a)** *(heat)* conservar; *(personal effects)* guardar **(b)** *(water)* retener **(c)** *(facts, information)* recordar

retaliate [rɪ'tælɪeɪt] *vi* tomar represalias (**against** contra)

retaliation [rɪtælɪ'eɪʃən] *n* represalias *fpl*; **in r.** en represalia

retch [retʃ] *vi* tener náuseas

reticent ['retɪsənt] *adj* reticente

retire [rɪ'taɪə(r)] **1** *vt* jubilar **2** *vi* **(a)** *(stop working)* jubilarse **(b)** *(from race)* retirarse; **to r. for the night** irse a la cama, acostarse

retired [rɪ'taɪəd] *adj* jubilado(a)

retirement [rɪ'taɪəmənt] *n* jubilación *f*

retrace [riː'treɪs] *vt (recall)* reconstruir; **to r. one's steps** volver sobre sus pasos

retract [rɪ'trækt] **1** *vt* **(a)** *(claws)* retraer; *(landing gear)* replegar **(b)** *(statement)* retirar **2** *vi* **(a)** *(claws)* retraerse; *(landing gear)* replegarse **(b)** *Fml* retractarse

retreat [rɪ'triːt] **1** *n* **(a)** *Mil* retirada *f* **(b)** *(shelter)* refugio *m* **(c)** *Rel* retiro *m* **2** *vi* retirarse (**from** de)

retribution [retrɪ'bjuːʃən] *n* represalias *fpl*

retrieve [rɪ'triːv] *vt* **(a)** *(recover)* recuperar; *(of dog)* cobrar; *Comput* recoger **(b)** *(rescue)* salvar

retrospect ['retrəʊspekt] *n* **in r.** retrospectivamente

retrospective [retrəʊ'spektɪv] **1** *adj* retrospectivo(a) **2** *n Art* (exposición *f*) retrospectiva *f*

return [rɪ'tɜːn] **1** *n* **(a)** *(of person)* regreso *m*, vuelta *f*; **by r. of post** a vuelta de correo; **in r. for** a cambio de; **many happy returns!** ¡felicidades!; **r. match** partido *m* de vuelta; *Br* **r. (ticket)** billete *m* de ida y vuelta **(b)** *(of sth borrowed, stolen)* devolución *f* **(c)** *(profit)* beneficio *m*, ganancia *f* **(d)** *(interest)* interés *m*
  2 *vt (give back)* devolver. **r. to sender** *(on envelope)* devuélvase al remitente; **to r. sb's love** corresponder al amor de algn
  3 *vi* **(a)** *(come or go back)* volver, regresar **(b)** *(reappear)* reaparecer

reunion [riː'juːnjən] *n* reunión *f*

reunite [riːjuː'naɪt] *vt* **to be reunited with** *(after separation)* reunirse con

reuse [riː'juːz] *vt* volver a utilizar, reutilizar

reveal [rɪ'viːl] *vt (make known)* revelar; *(show)* dejar ver

revealing [rɪ'viːlɪŋ] *adj* revelador(a)

revel ['revəl] *vi* disfrutar (**in** con); **to r. in doing sth** gozar muchísimo haciendo algo

revelation [revə'leɪʃən] *n* revelación *f*

revenge [rɪ'vendʒ] *n* venganza *f*; **to take r. on sb for sth** vengarse de algo en algn

revenue ['revɪnjuː] *n* renta *f*

reverence ['revərəns] *n* reverencia *f*

reversal [rɪ'vɜːsəl] n (a) (of order) inversión f (b) (of attitude, policy) cambio m total (c) Jur revocación f

reverse [rɪ'vɜːs] 1 adj inverso(a) 2 n (a) quite the r. todo lo contrario (b) (other side) (of cloth) revés m; (of coin) cruz f; (of page) dorso m (c) Aut r. gear marcha f atrás 3 vt (a) (order) invertir (b) (turn round) volver del revés (c) (change) cambiar totalmente (d) Br Tel to r. the charges poner una conferencia a cobro revertido 4 vi Aut dar marcha atrás

revert [rɪ'vɜːt] vi volver (to a)

review [rɪ'vjuː] 1 n (a) (examination) examen m (b) Press crítica f, reseña f (c) (magazine) revista f 2 vt (a) (examine) examinar (b) Mil to r. the troops pasar revista a las tropas (c) (book etc) hacer una crítica de

reviewer [rɪ'vjuːə(r)] n crítico(a) m,f

revise [rɪ'vaɪz] vt (a) (look over) revisar; Br (at school) repasar (b) (change) modificar

revision [rɪ'vɪʒən] n (a) revisión f; Br (at school) repaso m (b) (change) modificación f

revival [rɪ'vaɪvəl] n (a) (of interest) renacimiento m; (of economy, industry) reactivación f; (of a country) resurgimiento m (b) Th reestreno m (c) Med reanimación f

revive [rɪ'vaɪv] 1 vt (a) (interest) renovar; (a law) restablecer; (economy, industry) reactivar; (hopes) despertar (b) Th reestrenar (c) Med reanimar 2 vi (a) (interest, hopes) renacer (b) Med volver en sí

revolt [rɪ'vəʊlt] 1 n rebelión f, sublevación f 2 vi rebelarse, sublevarse 3 vt repugnar, dar asco a

revolting [rɪ'vəʊltɪŋ] adj repugnante

revolution [revə'luːʃən] n revolución f

revolutionary [revə'luːʃənərɪ] adj & n revolucionario(a) (m,f)

revolve [rɪ'vɒlv] 1 vi girar; Fig to r. around girar en torno a 2 vt hacer girar

revolver [rɪ'vɒlvə(r)] n revólver m

revolving [rɪ'vɒlvɪŋ] adj giratorio(a)

revulsion [rɪ'vʌlʃən] n repulsión f

reward [rɪ'wɔːd] 1 n recompensa f 2 vt recompensar

rewarding [rɪ'wɔːdɪŋ] adj provechoso(a)

rewind [riː'waɪnd] (pt & pp rewound [riː'waʊnd]) vt (tape, film) rebobinar

rhetoric ['retərɪk] n retórica f

rhetorical [rɪ'tɒrɪkəl] adj retórico(a)

rheumatism ['ruːmətɪzəm] n reuma m

rhinoceros [raɪ'nɒsərəs] n rinoceronte m

rhubarb ['ruːbɑːb] n ruibarbo m

rhyme [raɪm] 1 n rima f; (poem) poema m 2 vi rimar

rhythm ['rɪðəm] n ritmo m

rib [rɪb] n Anat costilla f; r. cage caja torácica

ribbon ['rɪbən] n cinta f; (in hair etc) lazo m; torn to ribbons hecho(a) jirones

rice [raɪs] n arroz m; r. pudding arroz con leche

rich [rɪtʃ] 1 adj (person, food) rico(a); (soil) fértil; (voice) sonoro(a); (colour) vivo(a) 2 npl the r. los ricos

riches ['rɪtʃɪz] npl riquezas fpl

rid [rɪd] (pt & pp rid) vt librar; to get r. of sth deshacerse de algo; to r. oneself of librarse de

ridden ['rɪdən] pp of ride

riddle¹ ['rɪdəl] n (a) (puzzle) acertijo m, adivinanza f (b) (mystery) enigma m

riddle² ['rɪdəl] vt (with bullets) acribillar

ride [raɪd] (pt rode; pp ridden) 1 n paseo m, vuelta f; a short bus r. un corto trayecto en autobús; Fam to take sb for a r. tomar el pelo a algn 2 vt (bicycle, horse) montar en; can you r. a bicycle? ¿sabes montar or Am andar en bicicleta? 3 vi (a) (on horse) montar or Am andar a caballo (b) (travel) (in bus, train etc) viajar

▶ **ride out** vt sep sobrevivir; to r. out the storm capear el temporal

rider ['raɪdə(r)] *n (of horse) (man)* jinete *m*; *(woman)* amazona *f*; *(of bicycle)* ciclista *mf*; *(of motorbike)* motociclista *mf*

ridge [rɪdʒ] *n (crest of a hill)* cresta *f*; *(hillock)* loma *f*; *(of roof)* caballete *m*; *Met* área *m*

ridicule ['rɪdɪkjuːl] **1** *n* burla *f* **2** *vt* burlarse de

ridiculous [rɪ'dɪkjʊləs] *adj* ridículo(a)

riding ['raɪdɪŋ] *n* equitación *f*; **r. breeches** pantalones *mpl* de montar; **r. school** escuela hípica

rife [raɪf] *adj* abundante; **rumour is r. that …** corre la voz de que …; **to be r. with** abundar en

riffraff ['rɪfræf] *n Fam* chusma *f*, gentuza *f*

rifle¹ ['raɪfəl] *n* fusil *m*, rifle *m*; **r. range** campo *m* de tiro

rifle² ['raɪfəl] *vt* desvalijar

rift [rɪft] *n* (a) *Geol* falla *f* (b) *Fig (in friendship)* ruptura *f*; *Pol (in party)* escisión *f*; *(quarrel)* desavenencia *f*

rig [rɪg] **1** *n* (a) *Naut* aparejo *m* (b) **(oil) r.** *(onshore)* torre *f* de perforación; *(offshore)* plataforma petrolífera **2** *vt Pej* amañar

▸ **rig out** *vt sep Fam* ataviar

▸ **rig up** *vt sep* improvisar, *Esp* apañar

right [raɪt] **1** *adj* (a) *(not left)* derecho(a) (b) *(correct)* correcto(a); *(time)* exacto(a); **to be r.** tener razón **r.?** ¿vale? (c) *(true)* cierto(a) (d) *(suitable)* adecuado(a); **the r. time** el momento oportuno (e) *(proper)* apropiado(a) (f) *Fam (healthy)* bien (g) *Br Fam (complete)* auténtico(a) (h) **r. angle** ángulo recto

2 *n* (a) *(right side)* derecha *f* (b) *(right hand)* mano derecha (c) *Pol* **the R.** la derecha (d) *(lawful claim)* derecho *m*; **in one's own r.** por derecho propio; **r. of way** *(across land)* derecho de paso; *(on roads)* prioridad *f* (e) **r. and wrong** el bien y el mal

3 *adv* (a) *(correctly)* bien; **it's just r.** es justo lo que hace falta (b) **r. away** *(immediately)* en seguida, inmediatamente, *CAm, Méx* ahorita (c) *(to the*

right) a la derecha; **r. and left** a diestro y siniestro (d) *(directly)* directamente; **go r. on** sigue recto; **r. at the top** en todo lo alto; **r. to the end** hasta el final

4 *vt* (a) *(correct)* corregir (b) *(put straight)* enderezar

rightful ['raɪtfʊl] *adj* legítimo(a)

right-hand ['raɪthænd] *adj* derecho(a); **r. drive** conducción *f* por la derecha; **r. side** lado derecho; *Fam* **r. man** brazo derecho

right-handed [raɪt'hændɪd] *adj (person)* que usa la mano derecha; *(tool)* para la mano derecha

rightly ['raɪtlɪ] *adv* debidamente; **and r. so** y con razón

right-wing ['raɪtwɪŋ] *adj* de derechas, derechista

rigid ['rɪdʒɪd] *adj* rígido(a)

rigorous ['rɪgərəs] *adj* riguroso(a)

rim [rɪm] *n (edge)* borde *m*; *(of wheel)* llanta *f*; *(of spectacles)* montura *f*

rind [raɪnd] *n (of fruit, cheese)* corteza *f*

ring¹ [rɪŋ] *(pt* rang; *pp* rung) **1** *n* (a) *(sound of bell)* toque *m*; *(of doorbell, alarm clock)* timbre *m* (b) *Tel* llamada *f*

2 *vt* (a) *(bell)* tocar; *Fig* **it rings a bell** me suena (b) *Br (on phone)* llamar (por teléfono) a, *RP* hablar a

3 *vi* (a) *(bell, phone etc)* sonar (b) **my ears are ringing** tengo un pitido en los oídos (c) *Tel* llamar

▸ **ring back** *vt sep Br Tel* volver a llamar

▸ **ring off** *vi Br Tel* colgar

▸ **ring out** *vi* resonar

▸ **ring up** *vt sep Br Tel* llamar (por teléfono) a, *RP* hablar a

ring² [rɪŋ] **1** *n* (a) *(metal hoop)* aro *m*; **curtain r.** anilla *f*; **r. binder** archivador *m or* carpeta *f* de anillas, *RP* bibliorato *m* (b) *(for finger)* anillo *m*, sortija *f* (c) *(circle)* círculo *m*; *Br* **r. road** carretera *f* de circunvalación (d) *(group of people)* corro *m*; *(of spies)* red *f*; *(of thieves)* banda *f* (e) *(arena)* pista *f*; *(for boxing)* cuadrilátero *m*; *(for bullfights)* ruedo *m* **2** *vt (surround)* rodear

ringing ['rɪŋɪŋ] *n (of bell)* toque *m*, repique *m*; *(in ears)* pitido *m*

ringleader ['rɪŋliːdə(r)] *n* cabecilla *mf*

rink [rɪŋk] *n* pista *f*; **ice r.** pista de hielo

rinse [rɪns] **1** *n* **to give sth a r.** enjuagar *or Esp* aclarar algo **2** *vt (clothes, dishes)* enjuagar, *Esp* aclarar; **to r. one's hands** enjuagarse las manos

riot ['raɪət] **1** *n* (**a**) disturbio *m*, motín *m*; **to run r.** desmandarse; **r. police** policía *f* antidisturbios (**b**) *Fig (of colour)* profusión *f* **2** *vi* amotinarse

rioter ['raɪətə(r)] *n* amotinado(a) *m,f*

rip [rɪp] **1** *n (tear)* rasgón *m* **2** *vt* rasgar, rajar; **to r. one's trousers** rajarse los pantalones **3** *vi* rasgarse, rajarse

▶ **rip off** *vt sep Fam* **to r. sb off** clavar *or Esp* timar a algn

▶ **rip up** *vt sep* hacer pedacitos

ripe [raɪp] *adj* (**a**) maduro(a) (**b**) *(ready)* listo(a); **the time is r.** es el momento oportuno

ripen ['raɪpən] *vt & vi* madurar

rip-off ['rɪpɒf] *n Fam* timo *m*, *Col, RP* cagada *f*

rise [raɪz] **1** *n* (**a**) *(of slope, hill)* cuesta *f* (**b**) *(of waters)* crecida *f* (**c**) *(in prices, temperature)* subida *f*; *Br* (**pay**) **r.** aumento *m* (de sueldo) (**d**) **to give r. to** ocasionar **2** *vi* (*pt* **rose**; *pp* **risen** ['rɪzən]) (**a**) *(land etc)* elevarse (**b**) *(waters)* crecer; *(river)* nacer; *(tide)* subir; *(wind)* levantarse (**c**) *(sun, moon)* salir (**d**) *(voice)* alzarse (**e**) *(in rank)* ascender (**f**) *(prices, temperature)* subir; *(wages)* aumentar (**g**) *(curtain)* subir (**h**) *(from bed)* levantarse (**i**) *(stand up)* levantarse; *Fig (city, building)* erguirse

▶ **rise above** *vt insep* estar por encima de

▶ **rise up** *vi (rebel)* sublevarse

rising ['raɪzɪŋ] **1** *adj (sun)* naciente; *(tide)* creciente; *(prices)* en aumento; **r. damp** humedad *f* **2** *n* (**a**) *(of sun)* salida *f* (**b**) *(rebellion)* levantamiento *m*

risk [rɪsk] **1** *n* riesgo *m*; **at r.** en peligro; **at your own r.** por su cuenta y riesgo;

to take risks arriesgarse **2** *vt* arriesgar; **I'll r. it** correré el riesgo

risky ['rɪskɪ] *adj* (**riskier, riskiest**) arriesgado(a)

rite [raɪt] *n* rito *m*; **the last rites** la extremaunción

ritual ['rɪtjʊəl] *adj & n* ritual *(m)*

rival ['raɪvəl] **1** *adj & n* rival *(mf)* **2** *vt* rivalizar con

rivalry ['raɪvəlrɪ] *n* rivalidad *f*

river ['rɪvə(r)] *n* río *m*; **down/up r.** río abajo/arriba

riveting ['rɪvɪtɪŋ] *adj Fig* fascinante

road [rəʊd] *n* (**a**) carretera *f*; *Br* **A/B r.** carretera nacional/secundaria; **main r.** carretera principal; **r. accident** accidente *m* de tráfico; **r. safety** seguridad *f* vial; **r. sign** señal *f* de tráfico; **r.** *Br* **works** *or US* **work** obras *fpl* (**b**) *(street)* calle *f* (**c**) *(way)* camino *m*

roadblock ['rəʊdblɒk] *n* control *m* policial

roadside ['rəʊdsaɪd] *n* borde *m* de la carretera; **r. restaurant/café** restaurante *m*/cafetería *f* de carretera

roam [rəʊm] **1** *vt* vagar por, rondar **2** *vi* vagar

roar [rɔː(r)] **1** *n (of lion)* rugido *m*; *(of bull, sea, wind)* bramido *m*; *(of crowd)* clamor *m* **2** *vi (lion, crowd)* rugir; *(bull, sea, wind)* bramar; *(crowd)* clamar; *Fig* **to r. with laughter** reírse a carcajadas

roaring ['rɔːrɪŋ] *adj* **a r. success** un éxito clamoroso; **to do a r. trade** hacer un negocio redondo

roast [rəʊst] **1** *adj (meat)* asado(a); **r. beef** rosbif *m* **2** *n Culin* asado *m* **3** *vt (meat)* asar; *(coffee, nuts)* tostar **4** *vi* asarse

rob [rɒb] *vt* robar; *(bank)* atracar

robber ['rɒbə(r)] *n* ladrón(ona) *m,f*; **bank r.** atracador(a) *m,f*

robbery ['rɒbərɪ] *n* robo *m*

robe [rəʊb] *n (ceremonial)* toga *f*, *(dressing gown)* bata *f*

robin ['rɒbɪn] *n* petirrojo *m*

robot ['rəʊbɒt] *n* robot *m*

robust [rəʊˈbʌst] *adj (sturdy)* robusto(a)

rock [rɒk] **1** *n* (**a**) roca *f*; *Fig* **on the rocks** *(marriage)* a punto de fracasar; *(whisky)* con hielo (**b**) *US (stone)* piedra *f* (**c**) *Br (sweet)* **stick of r.** = barra de caramelo de menta que se vende sobre todo en localidades costeras y lleva el nombre del lugar impreso (**d**) *Mus* música *f* rock; **r. and roll** rock and roll *m*
2 *vt* (**a**) *(chair)* mecer; *(baby)* acunar (**b**) *(shake)* hacer temblar; *Fig (shock)* conmover
3 *vi* (**a**) *(move to and fro)* mecerse (**b**) *(shake)* vibrar

rocket [ˈrɒkɪt] **1** *n* cohete *m*; **r. launcher** lanzacohetes *m inv* **2** *vi Fam (prices)* dispararse

rocky [ˈrɒkɪ] *adj* (**rockier, rockiest**) rocoso(a); *Fam Fig (unsteady)* inseguro(a); **the R. Mountains** las Montañas Rocosas

rod [rɒd] *n (of metal)* barra *f*; *(stick)* vara *f*; **fishing r.** caña *f* de pescar

rode [rəʊd] *pt of* **ride**

rodent [ˈrəʊdənt] *n* roedor *m*

rogue [rəʊg] *n* granuja *m*

role, rôle [rəʊl] *n* papel *m*; **to play a r.** desempeñar un papel

roll [rəʊl] **1** *n* (**a**) *(of paper, film)* rollo *m* (**b**) *(bread)* panecillo *m*, *Méx* bolillo *m* (**c**) *(list of names)* lista *f*, nómina *f* (**d**) *(of drum)* redoble *m*; *(of thunder)* fragor *m*
2 *vt* (**a**) *(ball)* hacer rodar (**b**) *(cigarette)* liar (**c**) *(push)* empujar
3 *vi* (**a**) *(ball)* rodar (**b**) *(animal)* revolcarse (**c**) *(ship)* balancearse (**d**) *(drum)* redoblar; *(thunder)* retumbar
► **roll about, roll around** *vi* rodar (de acá para allá)
► **roll by** *vi (years)* pasar
► **roll in** *vi Fam* (**a**) *(arrive)* llegar (**b**) *(money)* llegar a raudales
► **roll over** *vi* dar una vuelta
► **roll up 1** *vt sep* enrollar; *(blinds)* subir; **to r. up one's sleeves** (ar)remangarse **2** *vi Fam (arrive)* llegar

roller [ˈrəʊlə(r)] *n* (**a**) *Tech* rodillo *m*; **r.**
blades patines *mpl* en línea; **r. coaster** montaña rusa; **r. skates** patines *mpl* (de ruedas) (**b**) *(large wave)* ola *f* grande (**c**) *(for hair)* rulo *m*, *Chile* tubo *m*, *RP* rulero *m*

ROM [rɒm] *n Comput (abbr* **read-only memory**) ROM *f*

Roman [ˈrəʊmən] *adj & n* romano(a) *(m,f)*; **R. Catholic** católico(a) *m,f* (romano(a)); **R. law** derecho romano; **R. numerals** números romanos

romance [rəʊˈmæns] **1** *n* (**a**) *(tale)* novela romántica (**b**) *(love affair)* aventura amorosa (**c**) *(romantic quality)* lo romántico **2** *vi* fantasear

Romania [rəˈmeɪnɪə] *n* Rumanía

Romanian [rəˈmeɪnɪən] **1** *adj* rumano(a) **2** *n (person)* rumano(a) *m,f*, *(language)* rumano *m*

romantic [rəʊˈmæntɪk] *adj & n* romántico(a) *(m,f)*

romp [rɒmp] **1** *n* jugueteo *m* **2** *vi* juguetear

rompers [ˈrɒmpəz] *npl* pelele *m*

roof [ru:f] **1** *n* (**a**) *(of building)* tejado *m*; *Fam Fig* **to go through the r.** *(prices)* estar por las nubes; *(with anger)* subirse por las paredes (**b**) *Aut* techo *m*; **r. rack** baca *f* (**c**) *(of mouth)* cielo *m* **2** *vt* techar

rooftop [ˈru:ftɒp] *n* tejado *m*; *Fig* **to shout sth from the rooftops** proclamar algo a los cuatro vientos

room [ru:m] *n* (**a**) *(in house)* habitación *f*, cuarto *m*; *(in hotel)* habitación *f*; *(bedroom)* dormitorio *m*, *Am* cuarto *m*, *CAm, Col, Méx* recámara *f*; **single r.** habitación individual; **r. service** servicio *m* de habitaciones (**b**) *(space)* sitio *m*, espacio *m*, *Am* lugar *m*, *Andes* campo *m*; **to make r. (for sb)** hacer sitio *or Am* lugar *or Andes* campo (para *or* a algn)

roommate [ˈru:mmeɪt] *n* compañero(a) *m,f* de habitación

roomy [ˈru:mɪ] *adj* (**roomier, roomiest**) amplio(a)

roost [ru:st] **1** *n* palo *m*, percha *f*; *(hen)* **r.** gallinero *m*; *Fig* **to rule the r.** llevar la batuta **2** *vi* posarse

rooster ['ruːstə(r)] *n esp US* gallo *m*

root¹ [ruːt] **1** *n* raíz *f*; **to take r.** echar raíces
  2 *vt* arraigar
  3 *vi* arraigar
► **root out, root up** *vt sep* arrancar de raíz

root² [ruːt] *vi (search)* buscar; **to r. about** *or* **around for sth** hurgar en busca de algo

root³ [ruːt] *vi Fam* **to r. for a team** animar a un equipo

rope [rəʊp] **1** *n* **(a)** *(thin)* cuerda *f*; *(thick)* soga *f*; *Naut* cabo *m* **(b)** *Fam Fig* **to know the ropes** estar al tanto
  2 *vt (package)* atar; *(climbers)* encordar
► **rope in** *vt sep Fam* enganchar
► **rope off** *vt sep* acordonar

rosary ['rəʊzərɪ] *n* rosario *m*

rose¹ [rəʊz] *pt of* **rise**

rose² [rəʊz] *n* **(a)** *Bot* rosa *f*; **r. bed** rosaleda *f*; **r. bush** rosal *m* **(b)** *(colour)* rosa *m* **(c)** *(of watering can)* alcachofa *f*

rosette [rəʊˈzet] *n (of ribbons)* escarapela *f*

roster ['rɒstə(r)] *n* lista *f*

rosy ['rəʊzɪ] *adj* **(rosier, rosiest) (a)** *(complexion)* sonrosado(a) **(b)** *Fig (future)* prometedor(a)

rot [rɒt] **1** *n* **(a)** *(decay)* putrefacción *f*; **dry r.** putrefacción de la madera **(b)** *Br Fam (nonsense)* sandeces *fpl*, *Am* pendejadas *fpl* **2** *vt* pudrir
► **rot away** *vi* pudrirse

rota ['rəʊtə] *n Br* lista *f*

rotate [rəʊˈteɪt] **1** *vt* **(a)** *(revolve)* hacer girar **(b)** *(jobs, crops)* alternar
  2 *vi (revolve)* girar

rotation [rəʊˈteɪʃən] *n* rotación *f*

rotten ['rɒtən] *adj* **(a)** *(decayed)* podrido(a); *(tooth)* picado(a) **(b)** *Fam (very bad)* malísimo(a); *Fam* **I feel r.** me siento *Esp* fatal *or Am* pésimo

rough [rʌf] **1** *adj* **(a)** *(surface, skin)* áspero(a); *(terrain)* accidentado(a); *(sea)* agitado(a); *(weather)* tempestuoso(a) **(b)** *(violent)* violento(a) **(c)** *(wine)* áspero(a) **(d)** *Fam* **to feel r.** encontrarse fatal **(e)** *(approximate)* aproximado(a); **r. draft** borrador *m* **(f)** *(harsh)* severo(a)
  2 *adv* duramente; *Fam Fig* **to sleep r.** dormir a la intemperie *or Am* al raso
  3 *vt Fam* **we had to r. it** nos las arreglamos *or Esp* apañamos como pudimos

roughen ['rʌfən] *vt* poner áspero(a)

roughly ['rʌflɪ] *adv* **(a)** *(crudely)* toscamente **(b)** *(clumsily)* torpemente **(c)** *(not gently)* bruscamente **(d)** *(approximately)* aproximadamente

round [raʊnd] **1** *adj* redondo(a); **r. trip** viaje *m* de ida y vuelta
  2 *n* **(a)** *(series)* serie *f*; **r. of talks** ronda *f* de negociaciones **(b)** *(of ammunition)* cartucho *m*; *(salvo)* salva *f* **(c)** *(of drinks)* ronda *f*, *Am* vuelta *f* **(d)** *(in golf)* partido *m* **(e)** *(in boxing)* round *m* **(f)** *(in a competition)* eliminatoria *f*
  3 *adv* **all year r.** durante todo el año; **to invite sb r.** invitar a algn a casa
  4 *prep* alrededor de; **r. here** por aquí; **it's just r. the corner** está a la vuelta de la esquina, *RP* queda a la vuelta
  5 *vt (turn)* dar la vuelta a
► **round off** *vt sep* acabar, concluir
► **round on** *vt insep (attack)* atacar
► **round up** *vt sep (cattle)* acorralar, rodear; *(people)* reunir

roundabout ['raʊndəbaʊt] **1** *n Br* **(a)** *(merry-go-round)* tiovivo *m*, carrusel *m*, *RP* calesita *f* **(b)** *(for cars)* rotonda *f*, *Esp* glorieta *f* **2** *adj* indirecto(a)

rounders ['raʊndəz] *n Br* = juego parecido al béisbol

rouse [raʊz] *vt* despertar; *(stir up)* suscitar

route [ruːt] **1** *n* **(a)** ruta *f*; *(of bus)* línea *f*; *Naut* derrota *f*; *Fig* camino *m*; **r. map** mapa *m* de carreteras **(b)** *US* **R.** ≃ carretera *f* nacional **2** *vt* encaminar

routine [ruːˈtiːn] **1** *n* **(a)** rutina *f* **(b)** *Th* número *m* **2** *adj* rutinario(a)

row¹ [rəʊ] *n* fila *f*, hilera *f*; *US* **r. house** casa *f* adosada; *Fig* **three times in a r.** tres veces seguidas

row² [rəʊ] *vt & vi (in a boat)* remar

row³ [raʊ] **1** *n* **(a)** *(quarrel)* pelea *f*, bronca *f* **(b)** *(noise)* jaleo *m*; *(protest)* escándalo *m* **2** *vi* pelearse

rowdy ['raʊdɪ] **1** *adj* (**rowdier, rowdiest**) (**a**) *(noisy)* ruidoso(a); *(disorderly)* alborotador(a) (**b**) *(quarrelsome)* camorrista **2** *n* camorrista *mf*

rowing ['rəʊɪŋ] *n* remo *m*; *esp Br* **r. boat** bote *m* de remos

royal ['rɔɪəl] **1** *adj* real; **r. blue** azul marino; **the R. Family** la Familia Real **2** *npl* **the Royals** los miembros de la Familia Real

royalty ['rɔɪəltɪ] *n* (**a**) *(royal persons)* miembro(s) *m(pl)* de la Familia Real (**b**) **royalties** derechos *mpl* de autor

rub [rʌb] **1** *n* **to give sth a r.** frotar algo **2** *vt* frotar; *(hard)* restregar; *(massage)* friccionar **3** *vi* rozar (**against** contra)

▸ **rub down** *vt sep* rotar; *(horse)* almohazar; *(surface)* raspar

▸ **rub in** *vt sep* (**a**) *(cream etc)* frotar con (**b**) *Fam* **don't r. it in** no me lo refriegues

▸ **rub off 1** *vt sep (erase)* borrar **2** *vi Fig* **to r. off on sb** influir en algn

▸ **rub out** *vt sep* borrar

rubber¹ ['rʌbə(r)] *n* (**a**) *(substance)* goma *f*, *Am* hule *m*; **r. band** goma; **r. stamp** tampón *m* (**b**) *Br (eraser)* goma *f* (de borrar) (**c**) *Fam (condom)* goma *f*, *Méx* impermeable *m*, *RP* forro *m*

rubber² ['rʌbə(r)] *n (in bridge)* rubber *m*

rubbish ['rʌbɪʃ] *n* (**a**) *Br (refuse)* basura *f*; *Br* **r. bin** cubo *m* or *Am* bote *m* de la basura; **r. dump** *or* **tip** vertedero *m* (**b**) *Fam (worthless thing)* birria *f* (**c**) *Fam (nonsense)* tonterías *fpl*

rubble ['rʌbəl] *n* escombros *mpl*

ruby ['ruːbɪ] *n* rubí *m*

rucksack ['rʌksæk] *n* mochila *f*

rudder ['rʌdə(r)] *n* timón *m*

rude [ruːd] *adj* (**a**) *(impolite)* maleducado(a); *(foul-mouthed)* grosero(a); **don't be r. to your mother** no le faltes al respeto a tu madre (**b**) *(abrupt)* **a r. awakening** un despertar repentino

rug [rʌg] *n* alfombra *f*, alfombrilla *f*

rugby ['rʌgbɪ] *n* rugby *m*; **r. league** rugby a trece; **r. union** rugby a quince

rugged ['rʌgɪd] *adj* (**a**) *(terrain)* accidentado(a) (**b**) *(features)* marcado(a) (**c**) *(character)* vigoroso(a)

ruin ['ruːɪn] **1** *n* (**a**) ruina *f* (**b**) **ruins** ruinas *fpl*, restos *mpl*; **in ruins** en ruinas **2** *vt* arruinar; *(spoil)* estropear

ruined ['ruːɪnd] *adj (building)* en ruinas

rule [ruːl] **1** *n* (**a**) regla *f*, norma *f*; **to work to r.** hacer una huelga de celo; **as a r.** por regla general (**b**) *(government)* dominio *m*; *(of monarch)* reinado *m*; **r. of law** imperio *m* de la ley **2** *vt & vi (govern)* gobernar; *(of monarch)* reinar; *(decide)* decidir; *(decree)* decretar (**c**) *(draw)* tirar

▸ **rule out** *vt sep* descartar

ruler ['ruːlə(r)] *n* (**a**) dirigente *mf*; *(monarch)* soberano(a) *m,f* (**b**) *(for measuring)* regla *f*

ruling ['ruːlɪŋ] **1** *adj (in charge)* dirigente; *Fig (predominant)* predominante; **the r. party** el partido en el poder **2** *n Jur* fallo *m*

rum [rʌm] *n* ron *m*

Rumania [ruːˈmeɪnɪə] *n* = **Romania**

rumble ['rʌmbəl] **1** *n* (**a**) ruido sordo; *(of thunder)* estruendo *m* (**b**) *(of stomach)* ruido *m* **2** *vi* (**a**) hacer un ruido sordo; *(thunder)* retumbar (**b**) *(stomach etc)* hacer ruidos

rummage ['rʌmɪdʒ] *vi* revolver (**through** en); *US* **r. sale** *(in store)* = venta de productos discontinuados o sin salida en un almacén; *(for charity)* rastrillo benéfico

rumour, *US* **rumor** ['ruːmə(r)] **1** *n* rumor *m*; **r. has it that ...** se dice que ... **2** *vt* **it is rumoured that** se rumorea que

rump [rʌmp] *n (of animal)* ancas *fpl*; *Fam Hum (of person)* trasero *m*; **r. steak** filete *m* de lomo

run [rʌn] *(pt* **ran**; *pp* **run**) **1** *n* (**a**) carrera *f*; **on the r.** fugado(a); **to go for a r.** hacer footing; *Fig* **in the long r.** a largo plazo (**b**) *(trip)* paseo *m*, vuelta *f* (**c**) *(sequence)* serie *f* (**d**) *(in stocking)* carrera *f*

2 *vt* **(a)** correr; **to r. a race** correr en una carrera **(b)** *(drive)* llevar **(c)** *(house, business)* llevar; *(company)* dirigir; *(organize)* organizar **(d)** *(fingers)* pasar **(e)** *Comput* **to r. a program** ejecutar un programa

3 *vi* **(a)** correr **(b)** *(colour)* desteñirse **(c)** *(water, river)* correr; **to leave the tap running** dejar el grifo abierto; *Fam* **your nose is running** se te caen los mocos **(d)** *(machine)* funcionar **(on** con**)** **(e)** *Pol* **to r. for president** presentarse como candidato a la presidencia **(f)** *(range)* oscilar **(between** entre**)** **(g)** **shyness runs in the family** la timidez le viene de familia

▸ **run about** *vi* corretear

▸ **run across** *vt insep (meet)* tropezar con

▸ **run away** *vi* fugarse; *(horse)* desbocarse

▸ **run down 1** *vt insep (stairs)* bajar corriendo

  2 *vt sep* **(a)** *(in car)* atropellar **(b)** *(criticize)* criticar

  3 *vi (battery)* agotarse; *(clock)* pararse

▸ **run in** *vt sep Aut* rodar

▸ **run into** *vt insep* **(a)** *(room)* entrar corriendo en **(b)** *(people, problems)* tropezar con **(c)** *(crash into)* chocar contra

▸ **run off 1** *vt sep (print)* tirar **2** *vi* escaparse

▸ **run on 1** *vt sep Typ* enlazar **2** *vi (meeting)* continuar

▸ **run out** *vi* **(a)** *(exit)* salir corriendo **(b)** *(come to an end)* agotarse; *(of contract)* vencer; **to r. out of** quedarse sin

▸ **run over 1** *vt sep (in car)* atropellar

  2 *vt insep (rehearse)* ensayar

  3 *vi (overflow)* rebosar

▸ **run through** *vt insep* **(a)** *(of river)* pasar por **(b)** *(read quickly)* echar un vistazo a **(c)** *(rehearse)* ensayar

▸ **run up** *vt sep* **(a)** *(flag)* izar **(b)** *(debts)* acumular

▸ **run up against** *vt insep* tropezar con

runaway ['rʌnəweɪ] **1** *n* fugitivo(a) *m,f* **2** *adj (person)* huido(a); *(horse)* desbocado(a); *(vehicle)* incontrolado(a); *(inflation)* galopante; *(success)* clamoroso(a)

rung[^1] [rʌŋ] *pp of* **ring**[^1]

rung[^2] [rʌŋ] *n (of ladder)* escalón *m*, peldaño *m*

runner ['rʌnə(r)] *n* **(a)** *(person)* corredor(a) *m,f* **(b)** *Br* **r. bean** *Esp* judía *f* verde, *Bol, RP* chaucha *f*, *Méx* ejote *m*

runner-up [rʌnər'ʌp] *n* subcampeón(ona) *m,f*

running ['rʌnɪŋ] **1** *n* **(a)** **he likes r.** le gusta correr; *Fig* **to be in the r. for sth** tener posibilidades de conseguir algo **(b)** *(of company)* dirección *f* **(c)** *(of machine)* funcionamiento *m* **2** *adj* **(a)** **r. commentary** comentario *m* en directo; **r. costs** costos *mpl* de mantenimiento; *Pol* **r. mate** candidato *m* a la vicepresidencia; **r. water** agua *f* corriente **(b)** **three weeks r.** tres semanas seguidas

runny ['rʌnɪ] *adj* (**runnier, runniest**) blando(a); *(egg)* crudo(a); *(butter)* derretido(a); *(nose)* que moquea

runway ['rʌnweɪ] *n Av* pista *f* (de aterrizaje y despegue *or Am* decolaje)

rupture ['rʌptʃə(r)] **1** *n* **(a)** *Med* hernia *f* **(b)** *Fig* ruptura *f* **2** *vt* **(a)** **to r. oneself** herniarse **(b)** *(break)* romper

rural ['rʊərəl] *adj* rural

ruse [ruːz] *n* ardid *m*, astucia *f*

rush[^1] [rʌʃ] *n Bot* junco *m*

rush[^2] [rʌʃ] **1** *n* **(a)** *(hurry)* prisa *f*, *Am* apuro *m*; **the r. hour** *Esp* la hora punta, *Am* la hora pico **(b)** *(demand)* demanda *f*

  2 *vt* **(a)** *(task)* hacer de prisa; *(person)* meter prisa a; **to r. sb to hospital** llevar a algn urgentemente al hospital **(b)** *(attack)* abalanzarse sobre; *Mil* tomar por asalto

  3 *vi (go quickly)* precipitarse

▸ **rush about** *vi* correr de un lado a otro

▸ **rush into** *vt insep Fig* **to r. into sth** hacer algo sin pensarlo bien

[^1]: 1
[^2]: 2

► **rush off** *vi* irse corriendo

rusk [rʌsk] *n* = galleta dura para niños

Russia ['rʌʃə] *n* Rusia

Russian ['rʌʃən] **1** *adj* ruso(a) **2** *n* (**a**) *(person)* ruso(a) *m,f* (**b**) *(language)* ruso *m*

rust [rʌst] **1** *n* (**a**) *(substance)* herrumbre *f* (**b**) *(colour)* pardo rojizo
2 *vt* oxidar
3 *vi* oxidarse

rustic ['rʌstɪk] *adj* rústico(a)

rustle ['rʌsəl] **1** *n* crujido *m*
2 *vt (papers etc)* hacer crujir
3 *vi (steal cattle)* robar ganado

rusty ['rʌstɪ] *adj* (**rustier, rustiest**) oxidado(a); *Fam Fig* **my French is a bit r.** tengo el francés un poco oxidado

rut [rʌt] *n* (**a**) *(furrow)* surco *m*; *(groove)* ranura *f* (**b**) *Fig* **to be in a r.** ser esclavo de la rutina (**c**) *Zool* celo *m*

ruthless ['ruːθlɪs] *adj* despiadado(a)

RV [ɑːˈviː] *n US (abbr* **recreational vehicle**) autocaravana *f*, casa *f or* coche *m* caravana

rye [raɪ] *n* centeno *m*; **r. bread** pan *m* de centeno; **r. grass** ballica *f*; *US* **r. (whiskey)** whisky *m* de centeno

Ss

S, s [es] *n (the letter)* S, s *f*

S *(abbr* **south)** S

sabotage ['sæbətɑːʒ] **1** *n* sabotaje *m*
2 *vt* sabotear

sack [sæk] **1** *n* **(a)** *(bag)* saco *m* **(b)**
Fam **to get the s.** ser despedido(a);
Fam **to give sb the s.** despedir a algn
2 *vt* **(a)** *Fam* despedir **(b)** *Mil* saquear

sacred ['seɪkrɪd] *adj* sagrado(a)

sacrifice ['sækrɪfaɪs] **1** *n* sacrificio *m*
2 *vt* sacrificar

sad [sæd] *adj* **(sadder, saddest)** triste;
how s.! ¡qué pena!

sadden ['sædən] *vt* entristecer

saddle ['sædəl] **1** *n (for horse)* silla *f* (de
montar); *(of bicycle etc)* sillín *m* **2** *vt*
(horse) ensillar; *Fam* **to s. sb with sth**
encajar *or Esp, Méx* encasquetar algo a
algn

sadistic [sə'dɪstɪk] *adj* sádico(a)

sadly ['sædlɪ] *adv (to reply, smile)*
tristemente; **s., this is so** así es, por
desgracia

sadness ['sædnɪs] *n* tristeza *f*

safari [sə'fɑːrɪ] *n* safari *m*; **s. park**
reserva *f*

safe [seɪf] **1** *adj* **(a)** *(unharmed)*
ileso(a); *(out of danger)* a salvo; **s. and
sound** sano(a) y salvo(a) **(b)** *(not
dangerous)* inocuo(a) **(c)** *(secure, sure)*
seguro(a) **(d)** *(driver)* prudente **2** *n*
(for money etc) caja *f* fuerte

safeguard ['seɪfgɑːd] **1** *n (protection)*
salvaguarda *f*; *(guarantee)* garantía *f*
2 *vt* proteger, salvaguardar

safely ['seɪflɪ] *adv* **(a)** con toda
seguridad **(b) to arrive s.** llegar sin
incidentes

safety ['seɪftɪ] *n* seguridad *f*; **s. first!**
¡la seguridad ante todo!; **s. belt**
cinturón *m* de seguridad; **s. net** red *f*

de protección; **s. pin** imperdible *m*,
Am alfiler *m* de gancho, *CAm, Méx*
seguro *m*

sag [sæg] *vi* **(a)** *(roof)* hundirse; *(wall)*
pandear; *(wood, iron)* combarse;
(flesh) colgar **(b)** *Fig (spirits)* flaquear

saga ['sɑːgə] *n (story)* saga *f*; *Fig* **a s. of
corruption** una historia interminable
de corrupción

Sagittarius [sædʒɪ'teərɪəs] *n* Sagitario *m*

Sahara [sə'hɑːrə] *n* **the S.** el Sahara

said [sed] **1** *adj* dicho(a) **2** *pt & pp of*
say

sail [seɪl] **1** *n* **(a)** *(canvas)* vela *f*; **to set
s.** zarpar **(b)** *(trip)* paseo *m* en barco
2 *vt (ship)* gobernar; *Literary* navegar
3 *vi* **(a)** ir en barco **(b)** *(set sail)* zarpar

▸ **sail through** *vt insep Fam* **he sailed
through university** en la universidad
todo le fue sobre ruedas

sailboat ['seɪlbəʊt] *n US* velero *m*

sailing ['seɪlɪŋ] *n* navegación *f*;
(yachting) vela *f*; *Fam* **it's all plain s.**
es todo coser y cantar; *Br* **s. boat**
(barco *m*) velero *m*; **s. ship** barco *m* de
vela

sailor ['seɪlə(r)] *n* marinero *m*

saint [seɪnt] *n* santo(a) *m,f*; *(before all
masculine names except those beginning*
Do *or* **To)** San; *(before feminine names)*
Santa; **S. Dominic** Santo Domingo; **S.
Helen** Santa Elena; **S. John** San Juan;
All Saints' Day Día *m* de Todos los
Santos

sake [seɪk] *n* **for the s. of** por (el bien
de); **for your own s.** por tu propio bien

salad ['sæləd] *n* ensalada *f*; **potato s.**
ensalada de patatas *or Am* papas; **s.
bowl** ensaladera *f*; *Br* **s. cream** salsa *f*
tipo mahonesa; **s. dressing** aderezo *m*
or Esp aliño *m* para la ensalada

salami [sə'lɑːmɪ] n salami m, Am salame m

salary ['sælərɪ] n salario m, sueldo m

sale [seɪl] n (a) venta f; for or on s. en venta; **sales department** departamento m comercial; **sales manager** jefe(a) m,f de ventas; **sales tax** impuesto m de venta (b) (at low prices) rebajas fpl

salesclerk ['seɪlzklɜːrk] n US dependiente(a) m,f

salesman ['seɪlzmən] n (a) vendedor m; (in shop) dependiente m (b) (commercial traveller) representante m

saleswoman ['seɪlzwʊmən] n (a) vendedora f; (in shop) dependienta f (b) (commercial traveller) representante f

salmon ['sæmən] **1** n salmón m **2** adj (de color) salmón

salon ['sælɒn] n salón m

saloon [sə'luːn] n (a) (on ship) cámara f (b) US (bar) taberna f, bar m; Br **s. (bar)** bar de lujo (c) Br (car) turismo m

salt [sɔːlt] **1** n sal f; Fig **to take sth with a pinch of s.** creer algo con reservas; **bath salts** sales de baño; **smelling salts** sales aromáticas

2 adj salado(a)

3 vt (a) (cure) salar (b) (add salt to) echar sal a

saltcellar ['sɔːltselə(r)], US **saltshaker** ['sɔːltʃeɪkər] n salero m

salty ['sɔːltɪ] adj (**saltier, saltiest**) salado(a)

salute [sə'luːt] **1** n (greeting) saludo m **2** vt (a) Mil saludar (b) Fig (achievement etc) aplaudir

3 vi Mil saludar

salvage ['sælvɪdʒ] **1** n (a) (of ship etc) salvamento m, rescate m (b) (objects recovered) objetos recuperados (c) Jur derecho m de salvamento **2** vt (from ship etc) rescatar

salvation [sæl'veɪʃən] n salvación f; **S. Army** Ejército m de Salvación

same [seɪm] **1** adj mismo(a); **at that very s. moment** en ese mismísimo momento; **at the s. time** (simultaneously) al mismo tiempo; (however)

sin embargo; **in the s. way** del mismo modo; **the two cars are the s.** los dos coches son iguales

2 pron **the s.** el mismo/la misma/lo mismo; Fam **the s. here** lo mismo digo yo; Fam **the s. to you!** ¡igualmente!

3 adv del mismo modo, igual; **all the s., just the s.** sin embargo, aun así; **it's all the s. to me** (a mí) me da igual or lo mismo

sample ['sɑːmpəl] **1** n muestra f **2** vt (wines) catar; (dish) probar

sanction ['sæŋkʃən] **1** n (a) (authorization) permiso m (b) (penalty) sanción f (c) Pol **sanctions** sanciones fpl **2** vt sancionar

sanctuary ['sæŋktjʊərɪ] n (a) Rel santuario m (b) Pol asilo m (c) (for birds, animals) reserva f

sand [sænd] **1** n arena f; **s. castle** castillo m de arena; **s. dune** duna f **2** vt **to s. (down)** lijar

sandal ['sændəl] n sandalia f, Andes, CAm ojota f, Méx guarache f

sandwich ['sænwɪdʒ, 'sænwɪtʃ] **1** n (with sliced bread) sándwich m; (with French bread) Esp bocadillo m, Am sándwich m, CSur sánduiche m, Méx torta f; Educ **s. course** curso teórico-práctico **2** vt intercalar; **it was sandwiched between two lorries** quedó encajonado entre dos camiones

sandy ['sændɪ] adj (**sandier, sandiest**) (a) (earth, beach) arenoso(a) (b) (hair) rubio(a) rojizo(a)

sane [seɪn] adj (not mad) cuerdo(a); (sensible) sensato(a)

sang [sæŋ] pt of **sing**

sanitary ['sænɪtərɪ] adj sanitario(a); (hygienic) higiénico(a); **s.** Br **towel** or US **napkin** compresa f, Am toalla f higiénica

sanitation [sænɪ'teɪʃən] n sanidad f (pública); (plumbing) sistema m de saneamiento

sanity ['sænɪtɪ] n cordura f, juicio m; (good sense) sensatez f

sank [sæŋk] pt of **sink**

sap¹ [sæp] n Bot savia f

sap² [sæp] *vt (undermine)* minar; *Fig* agotar

sapphire ['sæfaɪə(r)] *n* zafiro *m*

sarcastic [sɑ:'kæstɪk] *adj* sarcástico(a)

sardine [sɑ:'di:n] *n* sardina *f*

Sardinia [sɑ:'dɪnɪə] *n* Cerdeña

sat [sæt] *pt & pp of* **sit**

satchel ['sætʃəl] *n* cartera *f* de colegial

satellite ['sætəlaɪt] *n* satélite *m*; **s. dish (aerial)** antena parabólica

satin ['sætɪn] *n* satén *m*; **s. finish** (acabado *m*) satinado *m*

satire ['sætaɪə(r)] *n* sátira *f*

satirical [sə'tɪrɪkəl] *adj* satírico(a)

satisfaction [sætɪs'fækʃən] *n* satisfacción *f*

satisfactory [sætɪs'fæktərɪ] *adj* satisfactorio(a)

satisfy ['sætɪsfaɪ] *vt* **(a)** satisfacer **(b)** *(fulfil)* cumplir con **(c)** *(convince)* convencer

satisfying ['sætɪsfaɪɪŋ] *adj* satisfactorio(a); *(pleasing)* agradable; *(meal)* que llena

saturate ['sætʃəreɪt] *vt* saturar **(with** de)

Saturday ['sætədɪ] *n* sábado *m*

sauce [sɔ:s] *n* **(a)** salsa *f* **(b)** *Br Fam (impudence)* descaro *m*

saucepan ['sɔ:spən] *n* cacerola *f*; *(large)* olla *f*

saucer ['sɔ:sə(r)] *n* platillo *m*

Saudi Arabia ['saʊdɪə'reɪbɪə] *n* Arabia Saudí

sauna ['sɔ:nə] *n* sauna *f*, *Am* sauna *m* or *f*

saunter ['sɔ:ntə(r)] **1** *n* paseo *m* **2** *vi* pasearse

sausage ['sɒsɪdʒ] *n (raw)* salchicha *f*; *(cured)* salchichón *m*; *(spicy)* chorizo *m*; *Fam* **s. dog** perro *m* salchicha; *Br* **s. roll** empanada *f* de carne

savage ['sævɪdʒ] **1** *adj* **(a)** *(ferocious)* feroz; *(cruel)* cruel; *(violent)* salvaje **(b)** *(primitive)* salvaje
2 *n* salvaje *mf*
3 *vt (attack)* embestir; *Fig (criticize)* criticar despiadadamente

save [seɪv] **1** *vt* **(a)** *(rescue)* salvar, rescatar; *Fig* **to s. face** salvar las apariencias **(b)** *(put by)* guardar; *(money, energy, time)* ahorrar; *(food)* almacenar; **it saved him a lot of trouble** le evitó muchos problemas
2 *vi* **(a)** **to s. (up)** ahorrar **(b)** **to s. on paper** *(economize)* ahorrar papel
3 *n Ftb* parada *f*
4 *prep Literary* salvo, excepto

saving ['seɪvɪŋ] *n* **(a)** *(of time, money)* ahorro *m* **(b)** **savings** ahorros *mpl*; **savings account** cuenta *f* de ahorros

saviour, *US* **savior** ['seɪvjə(r)] *n* salvador(a) *m,f*

savour, *US* **savor** ['seɪvə(r)] **1** *n* sabor *m*, gusto *m* **2** *vi* saborear

savoury, *US* **savory** ['seɪvərɪ] *adj (tasty)* sabroso(a); *(salted)* salado(a); *(spicy)* picante

saw¹ [sɔ:] *(pt* sawed; *pp* sawed *or* sawn [sɔ:n]) **1** *n (tool)* sierra *f* **2** *vt & vi* serrar

▶ **saw up** *vt sep* serrar **(into** en)

saw² [sɔ:] *pt of* **see**

sawdust ['sɔ:dʌst] *n* **(a)** serrín *m*

saxophone ['sæksəfəʊn] *n* saxofón *m*

say [seɪ] **1** *vt (pt & pp* said**)** **(a)** decir; **it goes without saying that ...** huelga decir que ...; **it is said that ...** se dice que ...; **not to s. ...** por no decir ...; **that is to s.** es decir; **to s. yes/no** decir que sí/no; *Fam* **I s.!** ¡oigal; **what does the sign s.?** ¿qué pone en el letrero? **(b)** *(think)* pensar **(c)** **shall we s. Friday then?** ¿quedamos el viernes, pues?
2 *n* **I have no s. in the matter** no tengo ni voz ni voto en el asunto; **to have one's s.** dar su opinión

saying ['seɪɪŋ] *n* refrán *m*, dicho *m*

scab [skæb] *n* **(a)** *Med* costra *f* **(b)** *Fam* esquirol *mf*, *Am* rompehuelgas *mf inv*

scaffolding ['skæfəldɪŋ] *n Constr* andamio

scald [skɔ:ld] **1** *n* escaldadura *f* **2** *vt* escaldar

scale¹ [skeɪl] *n (of fish, on skin)* escama *f*, *(in boiler)* incrustaciones *fpl*

▶ **scale down** *vt sep (drawing)* reducir

a escala; *(production)* reducir

scale² [skeɪl] **1** *n* (**a**) escala *f*; **on a large s.** a gran escala; **to s.** a escala; **s. model** maqueta *f* (**b**) *(extent)* alcance *m* (**c**) *Mus* escala *f* **2** *vt (climb)* escalar

scales [skeɪlz] *npl* **(pair of) s.** *(shop, kitchen)* balanza *f*; *(bathroom)* báscula *f*

scalp [skælp] **1** *n* cuero cabelludo **2** *vt* arrancar el cuero cabelludo a

scamper ['skæmpə(r)] *vi* corretear

scampi ['skæmpɪ] *n* gambas empanadas

scan [skæn] **1** *vt* (**a**) *(scrutinize)* escrutar; *(horizon)* otear (**b**) *(glance at)* ojear (**c**) *(of radar)* explorar **2** *n Med* exploración ultrasónica; *(in gynaecology etc)* ecografía *f*

scandal ['skændəl] *n* (**a**) escándalo *m*; **what a s.!** ¡qué vergüenza! (**b**) *(gossip)* chismorreo *m*, *Esp* cotilleo *m*

scandalous ['skændələs] *adj* escandaloso(a)

Scandinavia [skændɪ'neɪvɪə] *n* Escandinavia

Scandinavian [skændɪ'neɪvɪən] *adj & n* escandinavo(a) *(m,f)*

scanner ['skænə(r)] *n Med, Comput* escáner *m*

scanty ['skæntɪ] *adj* (**scantier, scantiest**) escaso(a); *(meal)* insuficiente; *(clothes)* ligero(a)

scapegoat ['skeɪpɡəʊt] *n* chivo expiatorio

scar [skɑː(r)] *n* cicatriz *f*

scarce [skeəs] *adj* escaso(a); *Fig* **to make oneself s.** largarse

scarcely ['skeəslɪ] *adv* apenas

scare [skeə(r)] **1** *n (fright)* susto *m*; *(widespread alarm)* pánico *m*; **bomb s.** amenaza *f* de bomba **2** *vt* asustar, espantar; *Fam* **to be scared stiff** estar muerto(a) de miedo

▸**scare away, scare off** *vt sep* ahuyentar

scarf [skɑːf] *n (pl* **scarfs** *or* **scarves** [skɑːvz]) *(long, woollen)* bufanda *f*; *(square)* pañuelo *m*; *(silk)* fular *m*

scarlet ['skɑːlɪt] **1** *adj* escarlata **2** *n* escarlata *f*; **s. fever** escarlatina *f*

scary ['skeərɪ] *adj Fam (noise, situation)* aterrador(a), espantoso(a); *(film, book)* de miedo

scathing ['skeɪðɪŋ] *adj* mordaz, cáustico(a)

scatter ['skætə(r)] **1** *vt* (**a**) *(papers etc)* esparcir, desparramar (**b**) *(crowd)* dispersar **2** *vi* dispersarse

scavenger ['skævɪndʒə(r)] *n* (**a**) *(person)* rebuscador(a) *m,f*, trapero *m* (**b**) *(animal)* animal *m* carroñero

scenario [sɪ'nɑːrɪəʊ] *n* (**a**) *Cin* guión *m* (**b**) *(situation)* situación *f* hipotética

scene [siːn] *n* (**a**) *Th, Cin, TV* escena *f* (**b**) *(place)* lugar *m*, escenario *m* (**c**) **to make a s.** *(fuss)* hacer una escena, *Esp* montar un número

scenery ['siːnərɪ] *n* (**a**) *(landscape)* paisaje *m* (**b**) *Th* decorado *m*

scenic ['siːnɪk] *adj (picturesque)* pintoresco(a)

scent [sent] **1** *n* (**a**) *(smell)* olor *m*; *(of food)* aroma *m* (**b**) *(perfume)* perfume *m* (**c**) *(in hunting)* pista *f* **2** *vt* (add perfume to) perfumar; *(smell)* olfatear; *Fig* presentir

sceptic ['skeptɪk] *n* escéptico(a) *m,f*

sceptical ['skeptɪkəl] *adj* escéptico(a)

schedule ['ʃedjuːl, *US* 'skedʒʊəl] **1** *n* (**a**) *(plan, agenda)* programa *m*; *(timetable)* horario *m*; **on s.** a la hora (prevista); **to be behind s.** llevar retraso (**b**) *(list)* lista *f*; *(inventory)* inventario *m* **2** *vt (plan)* programar, fijar

scheduled ['ʃedjuːld, *US* 'skedʒʊəld] *adj* previsto(a), fijo(a); **s. flight** vuelo regular

scheme [skiːm] **1** *n* (**a**) *(plan)* plan *m*; *(project)* proyecto *m*; *(idea)* idea *f*; **colour s.** combinación *f* de colores (**b**) *(plot)* intriga *f*; *(trick)* ardid *m* **2** *vi (plot)* tramar, intrigar

schizophrenic [skɪtsəʊ'frenɪk] *adj & n* esquizofrénico(a) *(m,f)*

schmuck [ʃmʌk] *n US Fam* lelo(a) *m,f*

scholar ['skɒlə(r)] *n (learned person)* erudito(a) *m,f*; *(pupil)* alumno(a) *m,f*

scholarly ['skɒləlɪ] *adj* erudito(a)

scholarship ['skɒləʃɪp] *n* (**a**)

(learning) erudición *f* (**b**) *(grant)* beca *f*;
s. holder becario(a) *m,f*

school [sku:l] **1** *n* (**a**) *(for children) (up to 14)* colegio *m*, escuela *f*; *(from 14 to 18)* instituto *m*; **s. friend** amigo(a) *m,f* del colegio; **s. year** año *m* escolar (**b**) *US (university)* universidad *f* (**c**) *(university department)* facultad *f* (**d**) *(group of artists)* escuela *f* **2** *vt (teach)* enseñar; *(train)* formar

schoolboy ['sku:lbɔɪ] *n* alumno *m*

schoolchild ['sku:ltʃaɪld] *n* alumno(a) *m,f*

schoolgirl ['sku:lgɜ:l] *n* alumna *f*

schoolteacher ['sku:lti:tʃə(r)] *n* profesor(a) *m,f*; *(primary school)* maestro(a) *m,f*

science ['saɪəns] *n* ciencia *f*; *(school subject)* ciencias; **s. fiction** cienciaficción *f*

scientific [saɪən'tɪfɪk] *adj* científico(a)

scientist ['saɪəntɪst] *n* científico(a) *m,f*

scissors ['sɪzəz] *npl* tijeras *fpl*; **a pair of s.** unas tijeras

scoff¹ [skɒf] *vi (mock)* mofarse (**at** de)

scoff² [skɒf] *vt Br Fam (eat)* zamparse

scold [skəʊld] *vt* regañar, reñir

scone [skəʊn, skɒn] *n* bollo *m*, pastelito *m*

scoop [sku:p] *n* (**a**) *(for flour)* pala *f*; *(for ice cream)* cucharón *m*; *(amount)* palada *f*, cucharada *f* (**b**) *Press* exclusiva *f*

▶ **scoop out** *vt sep (flour etc)* sacar con pala; *(water) (from boat)* achicar

▶ **scoop up** *vt sep* recoger

scooter ['sku:tə(r)] *n (child's)* patinete *m*; *(adult's)* Vespa® *f*

scope [skəʊp] *n* (**a**) *(range)* alcance *m*; *(of undertaking)* ámbito *m* (**b**) *(freedom)* libertad *f*

scorch [skɔ:tʃ] *vt (singe)* chamuscar

scorching ['skɔ:tʃɪŋ] *adj Fam* abrasador(a)

score [skɔ:(r)] **1** *n* (**a**) *Sport* tanteo *m*; *Cards, Golf* puntuación *f*; *(result)* resultado *m* (**b**) **on that s.** a ese

respecto (**c**) *(twenty)* veintena *f* (**d**) *Mus (of opera)* partitura *f*; *(of film)* música *f*

2 *vt* (**a**) *(goal)* marcar; *(points)* conseguir (**b**) *(wood)* hacer una muesca en; *(paper)* rayar

3 *vi* (**a**) *Sport* marcar un tanto; *Ftb* marcar un gol (**b**) *Fam* ligar (**with** con)

▶ **score out** *vt sep (word etc)* tachar

scoreboard ['skɔ:bɔ:d] *n* marcador *m*

scorn [skɔ:n] **1** *n* desprecio *m* **2** *vt* despreciar

scornful ['skɔ:nfʊl] *adj* desdeñoso(a)

Scorpio ['skɔ:pɪəʊ] *n* Escorpio *m*, Escorpión *m*

scorpion ['skɔ:pɪən] *n* alacrán *m*, escorpión *m*

Scot [skɒt] *n* escocés(esa) *m,f*

Scotch [skɒtʃ] **1** *adj* escocés(esa); *US* **S. tape®** cinta adhesiva, *Esp* celo® *m*, *CAm, Méx* Durex® *m* **2** *n (whisky)* whisky *m* escocés

Scotland ['skɒtlənd] *n* Escocia

Scotsman ['skɒtsmən] *n* escocés *m*

Scotswoman ['skɒtswʊmən] *n* escocesa *f*

Scottish ['skɒtɪʃ] *adj* escocés(esa)

scoundrel ['skaʊndrəl] *n* sinvergüenza *mf*, canalla *m*

scour¹ [skaʊə(r)] *vt (clean)* fregar, restregar

scour² [skaʊə(r)] *vt (search) (countryside)* rastrear; *(building)* registrar

scout [skaʊt] **1** *n Mil* explorador(a) *m,f*; *Sport, Cin* cazatalentos *m inv*; **boy s.** boy *m* scout **2** *vi Mil* reconocer el terreno; **to s. around for sth** andar en busca de algo

scowl [skaʊl] **1** *vi* fruncir el ceño; **to s. at sb** mirar a algn con ceño **2** *n* ceño *m*

scram [skræm] *(pt & pp* **scrammed***) vi Fam* largarse, *Esp, RP* pirarse; **s.!** ¡largo!

scramble ['skræmbəl] **1** *vi* trepar; **to s. for** pelearse por; **to s. up a tree** trepar a un árbol

2 *vt* (**a**) *Culin* **scrambled eggs** huevos revueltos (**b**) *Rad, Tel (message)* codificar; *(broadcast)* interferir

3 *n (climb)* subida *f; Fig* **it's going to be a s.** *(rush)* va a ser muy apresurado

scrap¹ [skræp] **1** *n* **(a)** *(small piece)* pedazo *m;* **there isn't a s. of truth in it** no tiene ni un ápice de verdad; **s. (metal)** chatarra *f;* **s. dealer** *or* **merchant** chatarrero(a) *m,f;* **s. paper** papel *m* de borrador; **s. yard** *(for cars)* cementerio *m* de coches **(b)** **scraps** restos *mpl; (of food)* sobras *fpl* **2** *vt (discard)* desechar; *Fig (idea)* descartar

scrap² [skræp] *Fam* **1** *n (fight)* pelea *f* **2** *vi* pelearse **(with** con)

scrapbook ['skræpbʊk] *n* álbum *m* de recortes

scrape [skreɪp] **1** *vt (paint, wood)* raspar; *(knee)* arañarse, hacerse un rasguño en

2 *vi (make noise)* chirriar; *(rub)* rozar
3 *n Fam (trouble)* lío *m*

▸ **scrape through** *vi Fam (exam)* aprobar por los pelos

▸ **scrape together** *vt sep* reunir a duras penas

scratch [skrætʃ] **1** *n* **(a)** *(on skin, paintwork)* arañazo *m; (on record)* raya *f* **(b)** *(noise)* chirrido *m* **(c)** *Fig* **to be up to s.** dar la talla; *Fig* **to start from s.** partir de cero

2 *adj* **s. team** equipo improvisado
3 *vt* **(a)** *(with nail, claw)* arañar, rasguñar; *(paintwork)* rayar **(b)** *(to relieve itching)* rascarse

scratchcard ['skrætʃkɑːd] *n* tarjeta *f* de rasca y gana, boleto *m* de lotería instantánea, *Am* raspadito *m*

scream [skriːm] **1** *n* chillido *m;* **screams of laughter** carcajadas *fpl*
2 *vt (insults etc)* gritar
3 *vi* chillar; **to s. at sb** chillar a algn

screech [skriːtʃ] **1** *n (of person)* chillido *m; (of tyres, brakes)* chirrido *m* **2** *vi (person)* chillar; *(tyres)* chirriar

screen [skriːn] **1** *n* **(a)** *(movable partition)* biombo *m* **(b)** *Fig* cortina *f* **(c)** *Cin, TV & Comput* pantalla *f* **2** *vt* **(a)** *(protect)* proteger; *(conceal)* tapar **(b)** *(candidates)* seleccionar **(c)** *(show) (film)* proyectar; *(for first time)* estrenar **(d)** *Med* examinar

screw [skruː] **1** *n* **(a)** tornillo *m* **(b)** *(propeller)* hélice *f* **2** *vt* **(a)** atornillar; **to s. sth down** *or* **in** *or* **on** fijar algo con tornillos **(b)** *Vulg Esp* follar, *Am* coger

▸ **screw up** *vt sep* **(a)** *(piece of paper)* arrugar; *(one's face)* torcer **(b)** *very Fam (ruin)* joder

screwdriver ['skruːdraɪvə(r)] *n* destornillador *m, Am* desatornillador *m*

scribble ['skrɪbəl] **1** *n* garabatos *mpl*
2 *vt (message etc)* garabatear
3 *vi* hacer garabatos

script [skrɪpt] *n* **(a)** *(writing)* escritura *f; (handwriting)* letra *f; Typ* letra cursiva **(b)** *(in exam)* escrito *m* **(c)** *Cin* guión *m*

scroll [skrəʊl] *n* rollo *m* de pergamino

scrounge [skraʊndʒ] *Fam* **1** *vi* gorrear, *Esp* gorronear; **to s. (around)** for buscar; **to s. off sb** vivir a costa de algn **2** *vt* gorrear, *Esp* gorronear

scrub¹ [skrʌb] *n (undergrowth)* maleza *f*

scrub² [skrʌb] **1** *vt* **(a)** frotar **(b)** *Fam (cancel)* borrar **2** *n (cleaning)* fregado *m*

scruff [skrʌf] *n* pescuezo *m,* cogote *m*

scruffy ['skrʌfɪ] *adj* **(scruffier, scruffiest)** *Fam* desaliñado(a)

scrum [skrʌm] *n* melé *f, Am* scrum *f;* **s. half** medio (de) melé *mf*

scrupulous ['skruːpjʊləs] *adj* escrupuloso(a)

scrutinize ['skruːtɪnaɪz] *vt* escudriñar

scuba diving ['skuːbədaɪvɪŋ] *n* buceo *m or* submarinismo *m* con botellas de oxígeno

scuffle ['skʌfəl] **1** *n* pelea *f* **2** *vi* pelearse **(with** con)

sculptor ['skʌlptə(r)] *n* escultor(a) *m,f*

sculpture ['skʌlptʃə(r)] *n* escultura *f*

scum [skʌm] *n* **(a)** *(on liquid)* espuma *f* **(b)** *Fig* escoria *f*

scurry ['skʌrɪ] *vi (run)* corretear; *(hurry)* apresurarse; **to s. away** *or* **off** escabullirse

sea [siː] *n* mar *m or f;* **by the s.** a orillas del mar; **out at s.** en alta mar; **to go by s.** ir en barco; **to put to s.** zarpar; *Fig* **to be all at s.** estar desorientado(a); **s.**

breeze brisa marina; *Fig* **s. change** metamorfosis *f*; **s. level** nivel *m* del mar; **s. lion** león marino; **s. water** agua *f* de mar

seafood ['si:fu:d] *n* marisco *m*, *Am* mariscos *mpl*

seafront ['si:frʌnt] *n* paseo marítimo

seagull ['si:gʌl] *n* gaviota *f*

seal¹ [si:l] *n* *Zool* foca *f*

seal² [si:l] **1** *n* (**a**) *(official stamp)* sello *m* (**b**) *(airtight closure)* cierre hermético; *(on bottle)* precinto *m* **2** *vt* (**a**) *(with official stamp)* sellar; *(with wax)* lacrar (**b**) *(close)* cerrar; *(make airtight)* cerrar herméticamente (**c**) *(determine)* **this sealed his fate** esto decidió su destino

► **seal off** *vt sep (pipe etc)* cerrar; *(area)* acordonar

seam [si:m] *n* (**a**) *Sewing* costura *f*; *Tech* juntura *f*; *Fam* **to be bursting at the seams** *(room)* rebosar de gente (**b**) *Geol*, *Min* veta *f*, filón *m*

search [sɜ:tʃ] **1** *vt (files etc)* buscar en; *(building, suitcase)* registrar; *(person)* cachear; *(one's conscience)* examinar **2** *vi* buscar; **to s. through** registrar **3** *n* búsqueda *f*; *(of building etc)* registro *m*; *(of person)* cacheo *m*; **in s. of** en busca de; *Comput* **s. engine** motor *m* de búsqueda; **s. party** equipo *m* de salvamento; **s. warrant** orden *f* de registro

searchlight ['sɜ:tʃlaɪt] *n* reflector *m*

seashell ['si:ʃel] *n* concha marina

seashore ['si:ʃɔ:(r)] *n (beach)* playa *f*

seasick ['si:sɪk] *adj* mareado(a); **to get s.** marearse

seaside ['si:saɪd] *n* playa *f*, costa *f*; **s. resort** lugar turístico de veraneo; **s. town** pueblo costero

season¹ ['si:zən] *n* época *f*; *(of year)* estación *f*; *(for sport etc)* temporada *f*; **the busy s.** la temporada alta; **the rainy s.** la estación de lluvias; **in s.** *(fruit)* en sazón; *(animal)* en celo; *Br* **s. ticket** abono *m*

season² ['si:zən] *vt Culin* sazonar

seasonal ['si:zənəl] *adj* estacional

seasoning ['si:zənɪŋ] *n* condimento *m*, aderezo *m*

seat [si:t] **1** *n* (**a**) asiento *m*; *(place)* plaza *f*; *Cin*, *Th* localidad *f*; **to take a s.** sentarse; *Aut* **s. belt** cinturón *m* de seguridad (**b**) *Parl* escaño *m* **2** *vt* (**a**) *(guests etc)* sentar (**b**) *(accommodate)* tener cabida para

seating ['si:tɪŋ] *n* asientos *mpl*

seaweed ['si:wi:d] *n* alga *f* (marina)

secluded [sɪ'klu:dɪd] *adj* retirado(a), apartado(a)

second¹ ['sekənd] **1** *adj* segundo(a); **every s. day** cada dos días; **it's the s. highest mountain** es la segunda montaña más alta; **on s. thought(s)** … pensándolo bien …; **to have s. thoughts about sth** dudar de algo; **to settle for s. best** conformarse con lo que hay **2** *n* (**a**) *(in series)* segundo(a) *m*,*f*; **Charles the S.** Carlos Segundo; **the s. of October** el dos de octubre (**b**) *Aut (gear)* segunda *f* (**c**) *Com* **seconds** artículos defectuosos **3** *vt (motion)* apoyar **4** *adv* **to come s.** terminar en segundo lugar

second² ['sekənd] *n (time)* segundo *m*; *Fam* **in a s.** enseguida; *Fam* **just a s.!** ¡un momentito!; **s. hand** *(of watch, clock)* segundero *m*

secondary ['sekəndərɪ] *adj* secundario(a); *Br* **s. school** escuela secundaria

second-class ['sekənd'klɑ:s] **1** *adj Br (ticket, carriage)* de segunda (clase) **2** *adv* **to travel s.** viajar en segunda

second-hand ['sekənd'hænd] *adj & adv* de segunda mano

secondly ['sekəndlɪ] *adv* en segundo lugar

second-rate ['sekənd'reɪt] *adj* de segunda categoría

secrecy ['si:krəsɪ] *n* secreto *m*; **in s.** en secreto

secret ['si:krɪt] **1** *adj* secreto(a); **to keep sth s.** mantener algo en secreto; **s. ballot** votación secreta **2** *n* secreto *m*; *Fig* clave *f*; **in s.** en secreto; **to keep a s.** guardar un secreto

secretarial [sekrɪˈteərɪəl] *adj* de secretario(a)

secretary [ˈsekrətrɪ] *n* secretario(a) *m,f*; **S. of State** *Br* ministro(a) *m,f* con cartera; *US* ministro(a) *m,f* de Asuntos Exteriores

secretive [ˈsiːkrɪtɪv] *adj* reservado(a)

secretly [ˈsiːkrɪtlɪ] *adv* en secreto

sect [sekt] *n* secta *f*

section [ˈsekʃən] *n* (**a**) *(part)* sección *f*, parte *f*; *(of law)* artículo *m*; *(of community)* sector *m*; *(of orchestra, department)* sección (**b**) *(cut)* corte *m*

sector [ˈsektə(r)] *n* sector *m*

secular [ˈsekjʊlə(r)] *adj (school, teaching)* laico(a); *(music, art)* profano(a); *(priest)* seglar, secular

secure [sɪˈkjʊə(r)] **1** *adj* seguro(a); *(window, door)* bien cerrado(a); *(ladder etc)* firme **2** *vt* (**a**) *(make safe)* asegurar (**b**) *(fix) (rope, knot)* sujetar, fijar; *(object to floor)* afianzar; *(window, door)* cerrar bien (**c**) *(obtain)* conseguir, obtener

security [sɪˈkjʊərɪtɪ] *n* (**a**) seguridad *f* (**b**) *Fin (for loan)* fianza *f* (**c**) *Fin* **securities** valores *mpl*

sedan [sɪˈdæn] *n* (**a**) *Hist* **s. chair** silla *f* de manos (**b**) *US Aut* turismo *m*

sedative [ˈsedətɪv] *adj & n* sedante *(m)*

seduce [sɪˈdjuːs] *vt* seducir

seductive [sɪˈdʌktɪv] *adj* seductor(a)

see[1] [siː] *(pt* **saw***; pp* **seen***) vt & vi* (**a**) ver; **let's s.** a ver; **s. page 10** véase la página 10; **to s. the world** recorrer el mundo; **s. you (later)/soon!** ¡hasta luego/pronto! (**b**) *(meet with)* ver, tener cita con; **they are seeing each other** *(couple)* salen juntos (**c**) *(understand)* entender; **as far as I can s.** por lo visto; **I s.** ya veo (**d**) **to s. sb home** acompañar a algn a casa

▶ **see about** *vt insep (deal with)* ocuparse de

▶ **see off** *vt sep (say goodbye to)* despedirse de

▶ **see out** *vt sep* (**a**) *(show out)* acompañar hasta la puerta (**b**) *(survive)* sobrevivir

▶ **see through** **1** *vt insep Fam* **to s. through sb** verle el plumero a algn **2** *vt sep* (**a**) **I'll s. you through** puedes contar con mi ayuda; **£20 should s. me through** con 20 libras me las apaño (**b**) **to s. sth through** *(carry out)* llevar algo a cabo

▶ **see to** *vt insep (deal with)* ocuparse de

see[2] [siː] *n Rel* sede *f*; **the Holy S.** la Santa Sede

seed [siːd] **1** *n* (**a**) *Bot* semilla *f*; *(of fruit)* pepita *f*; **to go to s.** *(plant)* granar; *Fig (person)* descuidarse (**b**) *(in tennis) (player)* cabeza *mf* de serie **2** *vt* (**a**) *(sow with seed)* sembrar (**b**) *(grapes)* despepitar (**c**) *(in tennis)* preseleccionar

seedy [ˈsiːdɪ] *adj* (**seedier, seediest**) *Fam (bar etc)* sórdido(a); *(clothes)* raído(a); *(appearance)* desaseado(a)

seeing [ˈsiːɪŋ] *conj* **s. that** visto que, dado que

seek [siːk] *(pt & pp* **sought***)* **1** *vt* (**a**) *(look for)* buscar (**b**) *(advice, help)* solicitar **2** *vt* buscar; **to s. to do sth** procurar hacer algo

▶ **seek after** *vt insep* buscar; **much sought after** *(person)* muy solicitado(a); *(thing)* muy cotizado(a)

seem [siːm] *vi* parecer; **I s. to remember his name was Colin** creo recordar que su nombre era Colin; **it seems to me that** me parece que; **so it seems** eso parece

seemingly [ˈsiːmɪŋlɪ] *adv* aparentemente, según parece

seen [siːn] *pp of* **see**

seep [siːp] *vi* **to s. through/into/out** filtrarse por/en/de

seesaw [ˈsiːsɔː] **1** *n* balancín *m*, subibaja *m* **2** *vi* (**a**) columpiarse, balancearse (**b**) *Fig* vacilar, oscilar

see-through [ˈsiːθruː] *adj* transparente

segment [ˈsegmənt] *n* segmento *m*; *(of orange)* gajo *m*

segregate [ˈsegrɪgeɪt] *vt* segregar (**from** de)

segregation [segrɪˈgeɪʃən] *n* segregación *f*

seize [siːz] vt (grab) agarrar, Esp coger; Jur (property, drugs) incautar; (assets) secuestrar; (territory) tomar; (arrest) detener; **to s. an opportunity** aprovechar una ocasión; **to s. power** hacerse con el poder

▸ **seize on** vt insep (chance) agarrar; (idea) aferrarse a

▸ **seize up** vi agarrotarse

seizure [ˈsiːʒə(r)] n (a) Jur (of property, drugs) incautación f; (of newspaper) secuestro m; (arrest) detención f (b) Med ataque m (de apoplejía)

seldom [ˈseldəm] adv rara vez, raramente

select [sɪˈlekt] **1** vt (thing) escoger, elegir; (team) seleccionar **2** adj selecto(a)

selection [sɪˈlekʃən] n (choosing) elección f; (people or things chosen) selección f; (range) surtido m

selective [sɪˈlektɪv] adj selectivo(a)

self [self] n (pl **selves**) uno(a) mismo(a), sí mismo(a); **the s.** (in psychology) el yo

self-addressed envelope [ˈselfəˈdrestˈenvələʊp] n sobre m dirigido a uno mismo

self-assured [selfəˈʃʊəd] adj seguro(a) de sí mismo(a)

self-catering [selfˈkeɪtərɪŋ] adj sin servicio de comida

self-centred, US **self-centered** [selfˈsentəd] adj egocéntrico(a)

self-confidence [selfˈkɒnfɪdəns] n confianza f en sí mismo(a)

self-confident [selfˈkɒnfɪdənt] adj seguro(a) de sí mismo(a)

self-conscious [selfˈkɒnʃəs] adj cohibido(a)

self-control [selfkənˈtrəʊl] n autocontrol m

self-defence, US **self-defense** [selfdɪˈfens] n autodefensa f

self-discipline [selfˈdɪsɪplɪn] n autodisciplina f

self-employed [selfɪmˈplɔɪd] adj (worker) autónomo(a)

self-esteem [selfɪˈstiːm] n amor propio, autoestima f

self-evident [selfˈevɪdənt] adj evidente, patente

self-indulgent [selfɪnˈdʌldʒənt] adj inmoderado(a)

self-interest [selfˈɪntrɪst] n egoísmo m

selfish [ˈselfɪʃ] adj egoísta

selfishness [ˈselfɪʃnɪs] n egoísmo m

selfless [ˈselflɪs] adj desinteresado(a)

self-pity [selfˈpɪtɪ] n autocompasión f

self-portrait [selfˈpɔːtreɪt] n autorretrato m

self-raising [ˈselfreɪzɪŋ] adj **s. flour** Esp harina f con levadura, Am harina f con polvos de hornear, RP harina f leudante

self-respect [selfrɪˈspekt] n amor propio, dignidad f

self-righteous [selfˈraɪtʃəs] adj santurrón(ona)

self-rising [ˈselfraɪzɪŋ] n US = **self-raising**

self-sacrifice [ˈselfˈsækrɪfaɪs] n abnegación f

self-satisfied [selfˈsætɪsfaɪd] adj satisfecho(a) de sí mismo(a)

self-service [selfˈsɜːvɪs] **1** n (in shop etc) autoservicio m **2** adj de autoservicio

self-taught [selfˈtɔːt] adj autodidacta

sell [sel] (pt & pp **sold**) **1** vt vender **2** vi venderse; **this record is selling well** este disco se vende bien **3** n **hard/soft s.** (in advertising) publicidad agresiva/discreta

▸ **sell off** vt sep vender; (goods) liquidar

▸ **sell out 1** vi **to s. out to the enemy** claudicar ante el enemigo **2** vt sep Com **we're sold out of sugar** se nos ha agotado el azúcar; Th **sold out** (sign) agotadas las localidades

sell-by date [ˈselbaɪdeɪt] n Com fecha f límite de venta

seller [ˈselə(r)] n vendedor(a) m,f

Sellotape® [ˈseləteɪp] **1** n Br cinta adhesiva, Esp celo m, CAm, Méx Durex® m **2** vt pegar or fijar con celo

semen ['si:men] *n* semen *m*

semester [sɪ'mestə(r)] *n* semestre *m*

semi- ['semɪ] *prefix* semi-

semicircle ['semɪsɜ:kəl] *n* semicírculo *m*

semicolon [semɪ'kəʊlən] *n* punto y coma *m*

semidetached [semɪdɪ'tætʃt] *Br* **1** *adj* adosado(a) **2** *n* chalé adosado, casa adosada

semifinal [semɪ'faɪnəl] *n* semifinal *f*

seminar ['semɪnɑ:(r)] *n* seminario *m*

semolina [semə'li:nə] *n* sémola *f*

senate ['senɪt] *n* (a) *Pol* senado *m* (b) *Univ* claustro *m*

senator ['senətə(r)] *n* senador(a) *m,f*

send [send] (*pt & pp* **sent**) **1** *vt* (a) *(letter)* enviar, mandar; *(radio signal)* transmitir; *(rocket, ball)* lanzar; **he was sent to prison** lo mandaron a la cárcel; **to s. sth flying** tirar algo (b) **to s. sb mad** *(cause to become)* volver loco(a) a algn **2** *vi* **to s. for sb** mandar llamar a algn; **to s. for sth** encargar algo

▸ **send away 1** *vt sep (dismiss)* despedir **2** *vi* **to s. away for sth** escribir pidiendo algo

▸ **send back** *vt sep (goods etc)* devolver; *(person)* hacer volver

▸ **send in** *vt sep (application etc)* mandar; *(troops)* enviar

▸ **send off** *vt sep* (a) *(letter etc)* enviar; *(goods)* despachar (b) *Ftb (player)* expulsar

▸ **send on** *vt sep (luggage) (ahead)* facturar; *(later)* mandar (más tarde)

▸ **send out** *vt sep* (a) *(person)* echar (b) *(invitations)* enviar (c) *(emit)* emitir

▸ **send up** *vt sep* (a) hacer subir; *(rocket)* lanzar; *(smoke)* echar (b) *Br Fam (parody)* parodiar, remedar

sender ['sendə(r)] *n* remitente *mf*

senile ['si:naɪl] *adj* senil

senior ['si:njə(r)] **1** *adj* (a) *(in age)* mayor; **William Armstrong S.** William Armstrong padre; **s. citizen** jubilado(a) *m,f* (b) *(in rank)* superior; *(with longer service)* más antiguo(a);

Mil **s. officer** oficial *mf* de alta graduación **2** *n* (a) **she's three years my s.** *(in age)* me lleva tres años (b) *US Educ* estudiante *mf* del último curso

sensation [sen'seɪʃən] *n* sensación *f*; **to be a s.** ser un éxito; **to cause a s.** causar sensación

sensational [sen'seɪʃənəl] *adj (marvellous)* sensacional; *(exaggerated)* sensacionalista

sense [sens] **1** *n* (a) *(faculty)* sentido *m*; *(feeling)* sensación *f*; **s. of direction/humour** sentido *m* de la orientación/del humor (b) *(wisdom)* sentido *m* común, juicio *m*; **common s.** sentido común; *(meaning)* sentido *m*; *(of word)* significado *m*; **in a s.** en cierto sentido; **it doesn't make s.** no tiene sentido (d) **to come to one's senses** recobrar el juicio **2** *vi* sentir, percatarse de

senseless ['senslɪs] *adj* (a) *(absurd)* insensato(a), absurdo(a) (b) *(unconscious)* sin conocimiento

sensibility [sensɪ'bɪlɪtɪ] *n* (a) *(sensitivity)* sensibilidad *f* (b) **sensibilities** susceptibilidad *f*

sensible ['sensɪbəl] *adj* (a) *(wise)* sensato(a) (b) *(choice)* acertado(a) (c) *(clothes, shoes)* práctico(a), cómodo(a)

sensitive ['sensɪtɪv] *adj* (a) *(person)* sensible; *(touchy)* susceptible (b) *(skin)* delicado(a); *(document)* confidencial

sensitivity [sensɪ'tɪvɪtɪ] *n* sensibilidad *f*

sensual ['sensjʊəl] *adj* sensual

sensuous ['sensjʊəs] *adj* sensual

sent [sent] *pt & pp of* **send**

sentence ['sentəns] **1** *n* (a) *frase f*; *Ling* oración *f* (b) *Jur* sentencia *f*; **to pass s. on sb** imponer una pena a algn; **life s.** cadena perpetua **2** *vt Jur* condenar

sentiment ['sentɪmənt] *n* (a) *(sentimentality)* sensiblería *f* (b) *(feeling)* sentimiento *m* (c) *(opinion)* opinión *f*

sentimental [sentɪ'mentəl] *adj* sentimental

separate 1 *vt* ['sepəreɪt] separar

(**from** de); *(divide)* dividir (**into** en); *(distinguish)* distinguir

2 *vi* ['sepəreɪt] separarse

3 *adj* ['sepərɪt] separado(a); *(different)* distinto(a); *(entrance)* particular

4 *npl* **separates** ['sepərɪts] *(clothes)* piezas *fpl*

separately ['sepərətlɪ] *adv* por separado

separation [sepə'reɪʃən] *n* separación *f*

September [sep'tembə(r)] *n* se(p)-tiembre *m*

septic ['septɪk] *adj* séptico(a); **to become s.** *(wound)* infectarse; **s. tank** fosa séptica

sequel ['si:kwəl] *n* secuela *f*; *(of film etc)* continuación *f*

sequence ['si:kwəns] *n* (**a**) *(order)* secuencia *f*, orden *m* (**b**) *(series)* serie *f*, sucesión *f*; *Cin* **film s.** secuencia *f*

serenade [serɪ'neɪd] *n* serenata *f*

serene [sɪ'ri:n] *adj* sereno(a), tranquilo(a)

sergeant ['sɑ:dʒənt] *n Mil* sargento *mf*; *(of police)* ≃ oficial *mf* de policía; **s. major** sargento *mf* mayor

serial ['sɪərɪəl] *n* (**a**) *Rad, TV* serial *m*; *(soap opera)* radionovela *f*, telenovela *f* (**b**) **s. number** número *m* de serie

serialize ['sɪərɪəlaɪz] *vt* *(in newspaper, magazine)* publicar por entregas; *(on TV)* emitir en forma de serial

series ['sɪəri:z] *n* *(pl* **series***)* serie *f*; *(of books)* colección *f*; *(of concerts, lectures)* ciclo *m*

serious ['sɪərɪəs] *adj* (**a**) *(solemn, earnest)* serio(a); **I am s.** hablo en serio (**b**) *(causing concern)* grave

seriously ['sɪərɪəslɪ] *adv* (**a**) *(in earnest)* en serio (**b**) *(dangerously, severely)* gravemente

sermon ['sɜ:mən] *n* sermón *m*

servant ['sɜ:vənt] *n* *(domestic)* criado(a) *m,f*; *Fig* servidor(a) *m,f*

serve [sɜ:v] **1** *vt* (**a**) servir (**b**) *(customer)* atender a (**c**) *(in tennis)* servir (**d**) **it serves him right** bien merecido lo tiene

2 *vi* (**a**) servir; **to s. on a committee** ser miembro de una comisión (**b**) *(in tennis)* servir

3 *n* *(in tennis)* servicio *m*

▶**serve out, serve up** *vt sep* servir

server ['sɜ:və(r)] *n Comput* servidor *m*

service ['sɜ:vɪs] **1** *n* (**a**) servicio *m*; **at your s.!** ¡a sus órdenes!; **s. (charge) included** servicio incluido; **s. area** área *m* de servicio; **s. industry** sector *m* de servicios; **s. station** estación *f* de servicio (**b**) *Mil* **the Services** las Fuerzas Armadas (**c**) *(maintenance)* revisión *f* (**d**) *Rel* oficio *m*; *(mass)* misa *f* (**e**) *(in tennis)* servicio *m*

2 *vt (car, machine)* revisar

serviceman ['sɜ:vɪsmən] *n* militar *m*

serviette [sɜ:vɪ'et] *n Br* servilleta *f*

servile ['sɜ:vaɪl] *adj* servil

serving ['sɜ:vɪŋ] *n* *(portion)* ración *f*; **s. spoon** cuchara *f* de servir

session ['seʃən] *n* (**a**) sesión *f*; **to be in s.** estar reunido(a); *(Parliament, court)* celebrar una sesión (**b**) *Educ (academic year)* año académico

set¹ [set] *(pt & pp* **set***)* **1** *vt* (**a**) *(put, place)* poner, colocar; *(trap)* poner (**for** para); **the novel is s. in Moscow** la novela se desarrolla en Moscú; **to s. fire to sth** prender fuego a algo; **to s. sb free** poner en libertad a algn

(**b**) *(time, price)* fijar; *(record)* establecer; **to s. one's watch** poner el reloj en hora

(**c**) *(bone)* encajar

(**d**) *(arrange)* arreglar; **he s. the words to music** puso música a la letra; **to s. the table** poner la mesa

(**e**) *(exam, homework)* poner; *(example)* dar; *(precedent)* sentar

2 *vi* (**a**) *(sun, moon)* ponerse (**b**) *(jelly, jam)* cuajar; *(cement)* fraguar; *(bone)* encajarse (**c**) **to s. to** *(begin)* ponerse a

3 *n* *(stage)* *Cin* plató *m*; *Th* escenario *m*; *(scenery)* decorado *m*

4 *adj* (**a**) *(task, idea)* fijo(a); *(date, time)* señalado(a); *(opinion)* inflexible; **s. phrase** frase hecha; **to be s. on doing sth** estar empeñado(a) en hacer algo (**b**) *(ready)* listo(a)

▶**set about** *vt insep* (**a**) *(begin)* empezar (**b**) *(attack)* agredir

▶**set aside** vt sep (time, money) reservar; (differences) dejar de lado

▶**set back** vt sep (a) (delay) retrasar; (hinder) entorpecer (b) Fam (cost) costar

▶**set down** vt sep (luggage etc) dejar (en el suelo); Br (passengers) dejar

▶**set in** vi (winter, rain) comenzar; **panic s. in** cundió el pánico

▶**set off 1** vi (depart) salir **2** vt sep (a) (bomb) hacer estallar; (burglar alarm) hacer sonar; (reaction) desencadenar (b) (enhance) hacer resaltar

▶**set out 1** vi (a) (depart) salir; **to s. out for ...** partir hacia ... (b) **to s. out to do sth** proponerse hacer algo **2** vt sep (arrange) disponer; (present) presentar

▶**set up 1** vt sep (a) (position) colocar; (statue, camp) levantar; (tent, stall) montar (b) (business etc) establecer; Fam montar; (committee) constituir; Fam **you've been s. up!** ¡te han timado! **2** vi establecerse

set² [set] n (a) (series) serie f; (of golf clubs etc) juego m; (of tools) estuche m; (of books) colección f; (of teeth) dentadura f; **chess s.** juego de ajedrez; **s. of cutlery** cubertería f (b) (of people) grupo m; Pej (clique) camarilla f (c) Math conjunto m (d) (in tennis) set m (e) TV **s.** televisor m

setback ['setbæk] n revés m, contratiempo m

settee [se'ti:] n sofá m

setting ['setɪŋ] n (a) (background) marco m; (of novel, film) escenario m (b) (of jewel) engaste m

settle ['setəl] **1** vt (a) (put in position) colocar (b) (decide on) acordar; (date, price) fijar; (problem) resolver; (differences) arreglar (c) (debt) pagar (d) (nerves) calmar; (stomach) asentar (e) (establish) (person) instalar
2 vi (a) (bird, insect) posarse; (dust) depositarse; (liquid) asentarse; **to s. into an armchair** acomodarse en un sillón (b) (put down roots) afincarse; (in a colony) asentarse (c) (child, nerves) calmarse (d) (pay) pagar; **to s.**

out of court llegar a un acuerdo amistoso

▶**settle down** vi (a) (put down roots) instalarse; (marry) casarse (b) **to s. down to work** ponerse a trabajar (c) (child) calmarse; (situation) normalizarse

▶**settle for** vt insep conformarse con

▶**settle in** vi (move in) instalarse; (become adapted) adaptarse

▶**settle with** vt sep (pay debt to) ajustar cuentas con

settlement ['setəlmənt] n (a) (agreement) acuerdo m (b) (of debt) pago m (c) (colony) asentamiento m; (village) poblado m

settler ['setlə(r)] n colono m

setup ['setʌp] n (system) sistema m; (situation) situación f; Fam montaje m

seven ['sevən] adj & n siete (m inv)

seventeen [sevən'ti:n] adj & n diecisiete (m inv), diez y siete (m inv)

seventeenth [sevən'ti:nθ] **1** adj & n decimoséptimo(a) (m,f) **2** n (fraction) decimoséptima parte

seventh ['sevənθ] **1** adj & n séptimo(a) (m,f) **2** n (fraction) séptimo m

seventy ['sevəntɪ] adj & n setenta (m inv)

sever ['sevə(r)] vt (cut) cortar; Fig (relations) romper

several ['sevərəl] **1** adj (a) (more than a few) varios(as) (b) (different) distintos(as) **2** pron algunos(as)

severe [sɪ'vɪə(r)] adj severo(a); (climate, blow) duro(a); (illness, loss) grave; (pain) intenso(a)

sew [səʊ] (pt sewed; pp sewed or sewn) vt & vi coser

▶**sew up** vt sep (stitch together) coser; (mend) remendar

sewage ['su:ɪdʒ] n aguas fpl residuales

sewer ['su:ə(r)] n alcantarilla f, cloaca f

sewing ['səʊɪŋ] n costura f; **s. machine** máquina f de coser

sewn [səʊn] pp of **sew**

sex [seks] n sexo m; **s. education**

educación *f* sexual; **to have s. with sb** tener relaciones sexuales con algn; **s. appeal** sex-appeal *m*

sexist ['seksɪst] *adj & n* sexista *(mf)*

sexual ['seksjʊəl] *adj* sexual

sexuality [seksjʊ'ælɪtɪ] *n* sexualidad *f*

sexy ['seksɪ] *adj* (**sexier, sexiest**) *Fam* sexi, erótico(a)

shack [ʃæk] *n* casucha *f*, *Esp* chabola *f*, *CSur, Ven* rancho *m*

shade [ʃeɪd] **1** *n* (**a**) *(shadow)* sombra *f*; **in the s.** a la sombra (**b**) *(eyeshade)* visera *f*; *(lampshade)* pantalla *f*; *US (blind)* persiana *f* (**c**) *(of colour)* tono *m*, matiz *m*; *Fig (of meaning)* matiz *f*; *Fam* **shades** gafas *fpl* or *Am* anteojos *mpl* de sol **2** *vt (from sun)* proteger contra el sol

shadow ['ʃædəʊ] **1** *n* (**a**) *(shade)* sombra *f* (**b**) *Br* **the S. Cabinet** el gabinete de la oposición **2** *vt Fig* seguir la pista a

shady ['ʃeɪdɪ] *adj* (**shadier, shadiest**) *(place)* a la sombra; *(suspicious) (person)* sospechoso(a); *(deal)* turbio(a)

shaft [ʃɑːft] *n* (**a**) *(of tool, golf club)* mango *m* (**b**) *Tech* eje *m* (**c**) *(of mine)* pozo *m*; *(of lift, elevator)* hueco *m* (**d**) *(beam of light)* rayo *m*

shaggy ['ʃægɪ] *adj* (**shaggier, shaggiest**) *(hairy)* peludo(a); *(long-haired)* melenudo(a); *(beard)* desgreñado(a)

shake [ʃeɪk] *(pt* **shook***; pp* **shaken**) **1** *n* sacudida *f*

2 *vt (carpet etc)* sacudir; *(bottle)* agitar; *(dice)* mover; *(building)* hacer temblar; **the news shook him** la noticia le conmocionó; **to s. hands with sb** estrechar la mano a algn; **to s. one's head** negar con la cabeza

3 *vi (person, building)* temblar; **to s. with cold** tiritar de frío

▶ **shake off** *vt sep* (**a**) *(dust etc)* sacudirse (**b**) *Fig (bad habit)* librarse de; *(cough, cold)* quitarse or *Am* de encima; *(pursuer)* dar esquinazo a

▶ **shake up** *vt sep Fig (shock)* trastornar; *(reorganize)* reorganizar

shaken ['ʃeɪkən] *pp of* **shake**

shaky ['ʃeɪkɪ] *adj* (**shakier, shakiest**) *(hand, voice)* tembloroso(a); *(step)* inseguro(a); *(handwriting)* temblón(ona)

shall [ʃæl, *unstressed* ʃəl] *v aux*

En el inglés hablado, y en el escrito en estilo coloquial, el verbo **shall** se contrae de manera que **I/you/he** *etc* **shall** se transforman en **I'll/you'll/he'll** *etc*. La forma negativa **shall not** se transforma en **shan't**

(**a**) *(used to form future tense) (first person only)* **I s.** *or* **I'll buy it** lo compraré; **I s. not** *or* **I shan't say anything** no diré nada (**b**) *(used to form questions) (usu first person)* **s. I close the door?** ¿cierro la puerta?; **s. I mend it for you?** ¿quieres que te lo repare?; **s. we go?** ¿nos vamos? (**c**) *(emphatic, command, threat) (all persons)* **we s. overcome** venceremos; **you s. leave immediately** te irás enseguida

shallow ['ʃæləʊ] *adj* poco profundo(a); *Fig* superficial

sham [ʃæm] **1** *adj* falso(a); *(illness etc)* fingido(a)

2 *n* (**a**) *(pretence)* engaño *m*, farsa *f* (**b**) *(person)* fantoche *m*

3 *vt* fingir, simular

4 *vi* fingir

shambles ['ʃæmbəlz] *n sing* confusión *f*; **the performance was a s.** la función fue un desastre

shame [ʃeɪm] **1** *n* (**a**) vergüenza *f*; *Am salvo RP* pena *f*; **to put to s.** *(far outdo)* eclipsar, sobrepasar (**b**) *(pity)* pena *f*, lástima *f*; **what a s.!** ¡qué pena!, ¡qué lástima! **2** *vt* avergonzar, *Am salvo RP* apenar; *(disgrace)* deshonrar

shameful ['ʃeɪmfʊl] *adj* vergonzoso(a)

shameless ['ʃeɪmlɪs] *adj* desvergonzado(a)

shampoo [ʃæm'puː] **1** *n* champú *m* **2** *vt* lavar con champú; **to s. one's hair** lavarse el pelo

shan't [ʃɑːnt] = **shall not**

shape [ʃeɪp] **1** *n* (**a**) forma *f*; *(shadow)* silueta *m*; **to take s.** tomar forma (**b**) in

good/bad s. *(condition)* en buen/mal estado; **to be in good s.** *(health)* estar en forma

2 *vt* dar forma a; *(clay)* modelar; *(stone)* tallar; *(character)* formar; *(destiny)* determinar; **star-shaped** con forma de estrella

3 *vi (also* **s. up***)* tomar forma; **to s. up well** *(events)* tomar buen cariz; *(person)* hacer progresos

shapeless ['ʃeɪplɪs] *adj* amorfo(a), informe

shapely ['ʃeɪplɪ] *adj* (**shapelier, shapeliest**) escultural

share ['ʃeə(r)] **1** *n* (**a**) *(portion)* parte *f* (**b**) *Fin* acción *f*; **s. index** índice *m* de la Bolsa; **s. prices** cotizaciones *fpl*

2 *vt* (**a**) *(divide)* dividir (**b**) *(have in common)* compartir

3 *vi* compartir

▸ **share out** *vt sep* repartir

shareholder ['ʃeəhəʊldə(r)] *n* accionista *mf*

shark [ʃɑːk] *n* (**a**) *(fish)* tiburón *m* (**b**) *Fam (swindler)* estafador(a) *m,f*; **loan s.** usurero(a) *m,f*

sharp [ʃɑːp] **1** *adj* (**a**) *(razor, knife)* afilado(a), *Am* filoso(a); *(needle, pencil)* puntiagudo(a) (**b**) *(bend)* cerrado(a) (**c**) *(contrast)* marcado(a) (**d**) *(clever)* listo(a); *(quick-witted)* avispado(a); *(cunning)* astuto(a) (**e**) *(pain, cry)* agudo(a) (**f**) *(sour)* acre (**g**) *(temper)* arisco(a); *(tone)* seco(a) (**h**) *Mus* sostenido(a)

2 *adv* **at two o'clock s.** *(exactly)* a las dos en punto

3 *n Mus* sostenido *m*

sharpen ['ʃɑːpən] *vt* (**a**) *(knife)* afilar; *(pencil)* sacar punta a (**b**) *Fig (desire, intelligence)* agudizar

sharply ['ʃɑːplɪ] *adv* (**a**) *(abruptly)* bruscamente (**b**) *(clearly)* marcadamente

shat [ʃæt] *pt & pp of* **shit**

shatter ['ʃætə(r)] **1** *vt* hacer añicos; *(nerves)* destrozar; *(hopes)* frustrar **2** *vi* hacerse añicos

shattered ['ʃætəd] *adj Fam* **to be s.** *(stunned)* quedarse destrozado(a); *Br*

(exhausted) estar rendido(a), *Méx* estar camotes

shave [ʃeɪv] *(pt* **shaved***; pp* **shaved** *or* **shaven** ['ʃeɪvən]*)* **1** *n* afeitado *m*; **to have a s.** afeitarse; *Fig* **to have a close s.** escaparse por los pelos

2 *vt (person)* afeitar; *(wood)* cepillar

3 *vi* afeitarse

shaver ['ʃeɪvə(r)] *n* (**electric**) **s.** máquina *f* de afeitar

shaving ['ʃeɪvɪŋ] *n* (**a**) *(of wood)* viruta *f* (**b**) **s. brush** brocha *f* de afeitar; **s. cream** crema *f* de afeitar; **s. foam** espuma *f* de afeitar

shawl [ʃɔːl] *n* chal *m*, *Am* rebozo *m*

she [ʃiː] *pers pron* ella *(usually omitted in Spanish, except for contrast)*

sheaf [ʃiːf] *n (pl* **sheaves***) Agr* gavilla *f*; *(of arrows)* haz *m*; *(of papers, banknotes)* fajo *m*

shear [ʃɪə(r)] *(pt* **sheared***; pp* **shorn** *or* **sheared***)* **1** *vt (sheep)* esquilar; **to s. off** cortar **2** *vi* esquilar ovejas

sheath [ʃiːθ] *n* (**a**) *(for sword)* vaina *f*; *(for knife, scissors)* funda *f* (**b**) *(contraceptive)* preservativo *m*

shed¹ [ʃed] *n (in garden)* cobertizo *m*; *(for cattle)* establo *m*; *(in factory)* nave *f*, *Andes, Carib, RP* galpón *m*

shed² [ʃed] *(pt & pp* **shed***) vt* (**a**) *(clothes)* despojarse de; *(unwanted thing)* deshacerse de; **the snake s. its skin** la serpiente mudó de piel (**b**) *(blood, tears)* derramar

sheep [ʃiːp] *n (pl* **sheep***)* oveja *f*

sheepdog ['ʃiːpdɒg] *n* perro *m* pastor

sheepish ['ʃiːpɪʃ] *adj* avergonzado(a)

sheepskin ['ʃiːpskɪn] *n* piel *f* de carnero

sheer [ʃɪə(r)] *adj* (**a**) *(utter)* total, puro(a) (**b**) *(cliff)* escarpado(a); *(drop)* vertical (**c**) *(stockings, cloth)* fino(a)

sheet [ʃiːt] *n* (**a**) *(on bed)* sábana *f* (**b**) *(of paper)* hoja *f*; *(of tin, glass, plastic)* lámina *f*; *(of ice)* capa *f*

shelf [ʃelf] *n (pl* **shelves***) (on bookcase)* estante *m*; *(in cupboard)* tabla *f*; **shelves** estantería *f*

shell [ʃel] **1** *n* (**a**) *(of egg, nut)* cáscara *f*; *(of pea)* vaina *f*; *(of tortoise etc)* caparazón *m*; *(of snail etc)* concha *f* (**b**) *(of building)* armazón *m* (**c**) *(mortar etc)* obús *m*, proyectil *m*; *(cartridge)* cartucho *m*; **s. shock** neurosis *f* de guerra **2** *vt* (**a**) *(peas)* desvainar; *(nuts)* pelar (**b**) *Mil* bombardear

shellfish ['ʃelfɪʃ] *n* (*pl* **shellfish**) marisco *m*, mariscos *mpl*

shelter ['ʃeltə(r)] **1** *n* (**a**) *(protection)* abrigo *m*, amparo *m*; **to take s. (from)** refugiarse (de) (**b**) *(place)* refugio *m*; *(for homeless)* asilo *m*; **bus s.** marquesina *f*
 2 *vt* (**a**) *(protect)* abrigar, proteger (**b**) *(take into one's home)* ocultar
 3 *vi* refugiarse

sheltered ['ʃeltəd] *adj (place)* abrigado(a); **to lead a s. life** vivir apartado(a) del mundo

shelve [ʃelv] *vt Fig (postpone)* dar carpetazo a

shelving ['ʃelvɪŋ] *n* estanterías *fpl*

shepherd ['ʃepəd] **1** *n* pastor *m*; **s.'s pie** = pastel de carne picada con puré de patatas *or Am* papas **2** *vt Fig* **to s. sb in** hacer entrar a algn

sheriff ['ʃerɪf] *n Br* = representante de la Corona; *Scot* ≃ juez *mf* de primera instancia; *US* sheriff *m*

sherry ['ʃerɪ] *n* jerez *m*

shield [ʃiːld] **1** *n* (**a**) escudo *m*; *(of policeman)* placa *f* (**b**) *(on machinery)* blindaje *m* **2** *vt* proteger (**from** de)

shift [ʃɪft] **1** *n* (**a**) *(change)* cambio *m*; *US Aut* (**gear**) **s.** cambio de velocidades (**b**) *(period of work, group of workers)* turno *m*; **to be on the day s.** hacer el turno de día
 2 *vt (change)* cambiar; *(move)* cambiar de sitio, trasladar
 3 *vi (move)* moverse; *(change place)* cambiar de sitio; *(opinion)* cambiar; *(wind)* cambiar de dirección

shiftwork ['ʃɪftwɜːk] *n* trabajo *m* por turnos

shifty ['ʃɪftɪ] *adj* (**shiftier, shiftiest**) *(look)* furtivo(a); *(person)* sospecho-so(a)

shimmer ['ʃɪmə(r)] **1** *vi* relucir; *(shine)* brillar **2** *n* luz trémula, reflejo

trémulo; *(shining)* brillo *m*

shin [ʃɪn] *n* espinilla *f*, *RP* canilla *f*; **s. pad** espinillera *f*, *RP* canillera *f*

shine [ʃaɪn] (*pt & pp* **shone**) **1** *vi* (**a**) *(light)* brillar; *(metal)* relucir (**b**) *Fig (excel)* sobresalir (**at** en)
 2 *vt* (**a**) *(lamp)* dirigir (**b**) *(pt & pp* **shined**) *(polish)* sacar brillo a; *(shoes)* limpiar
 3 *n* brillo *m*, lustre *m*

shiny ['ʃaɪnɪ] *adj* (**shinier, shiniest**) brillante

ship [ʃɪp] **1** *n* barco *m*, buque *m* **2** *vt* (**a**) *(take on board)* embarcar (**b**) *(transport)* transportar (en barco); *(send)* enviar, mandar

shipment ['ʃɪpmənt] *n* (**a**) *(act)* transporte *m* (**b**) *(load)* consignación *f*, envío *m*

shipping ['ʃɪpɪŋ] *n* (**a**) *(ships)* barcos *mpl*; **s. lane** vía *f* de navegación (**b**) *(loading)* embarque *m*; *(transporting)* transporte *m* (en barco); **s. company** compañía naviera

shipwreck ['ʃɪprek] **1** *n* naufragio *m* **2** *vt* **to be shipwrecked** naufragar

shipyard ['ʃɪpjɑːd] *n* astillero *m*

shirk [ʃɜːk] **1** *vt (duty)* faltar a; *(problem)* eludir **2** *vi* gandulear

shirt [ʃɜːt] *n* camisa *f*; **in s. sleeves** en mangas de camisa; *Fam* **keep your s. on!** ¡no te sulfures!

shit [ʃɪt] *Vulg* **1** *n (excrement)* mierda *f*; *(mess)* porquería *f*, mierda *f*; **to** *Br* **have** *or US* **take a s.** cagar **2** *vt* (*pt & pp* **shitted** *or* **shat**) **to s. oneself** *(defecate)* cagarse (encima); *(be scared)* cagarse *or Esp* jiñarse de miedo

shiver ['ʃɪvə(r)] **1** *vi (with cold)* tiritar; *(with fear)* temblar, estremecerse **2** *n* *(with cold, fear)* escalofrío *m*

shoal [ʃəʊl] *n (of fish)* banco *m*

shock [ʃɒk] **1** *n* (**a**) *(jolt)* choque *m*; **s. absorber** amortiguador *m*; **s. wave** onda expansiva (**b**) *(upset)* conmoción *f*; *(scare)* susto *m* (**c**) *Med* shock *m* **2** *vt* *(upset)* conmover; *(startle)* sobresaltar; *(scandalize)* escandalizar

shocking ['ʃɒkɪŋ] *adj* (**a**) *(causing horror)* espantoso(a); *Fam (very bad)* horroroso(a) (**b**) *(disgraceful)* escandaloso(a) (**c**) **s. pink** rosa chillón

shoddy ['ʃɒdɪ] *adj* (**shoddier, shoddiest**) *(goods)* de mala calidad; *(work)* chapucero(a)

shoe [ʃuː] **1** *n* (**a**) zapato *m*; *(for horse)* herradura *f*; **brake s.** zapata *f*; **s. polish** betún *m*; **s. repair (shop)** remiendo *m* de zapatos; **s. shop,** *US* **s. store** zapatería *f* (**b**) **shoes** calzado *m* **2** *vt* (*pt & pp* **shod** [ʃɒd]) *(horse)* herrar

shoelace ['ʃuːleɪs] *n* cordón *m* (de zapatos)

shone [ʃɒn, *US* ʃəʊn] *pt & pp of* **shine**

shoo [ʃuː] **1** *interj* ¡fuera! **2** *vt* to **s. (away)** espantar

shook [ʃʊk] *pt of* **shake**

shoot [ʃuːt] (*pt & pp* **shot**) **1** *n Bot* retoño *m*; *(of vine)* sarmiento *m*
2 *vt* (**a**) pegar un tiro a; *(kill)* matar; *(execute)* fusilar; *(hunt)* cazar; **to s. dead** matar a tiros (**b**) *(missile, glance)* lanzar; *(bullet, ball)* disparar (**c**) *(film)* rodar, filmar; *Phot* fotografiar
3 *vi* (**a**) *(with gun)* disparar (**at sb** a algn); **to s. at a target** tirar al blanco; *Ftb* **to s. at the goal** chutar a puerta (**b**) **to s. past** *or* **by** pasar flechado(a)
▶ **shoot down** *vt sep (aircraft)* derribar
▶ **shoot out** *vi (person)* salir disparado(a); *(water)* brotar; *(flames)* salir
▶ **shoot up** *vi* (**a**) *(flames)* salir; *(water)* brotar; *(prices)* dispararse (**b**) *Fam (inject drugs)* pincharse, *Esp* chutarse

shooting ['ʃuːtɪŋ] **1** *n* (**a**) *(shots)* tiros *mpl*; *(murder)* asesinato *m*; *(hunting)* caza *f*; **s. star** estrella *f* fugaz (**b**) *(of film)* rodaje *m* **2** *adj (pain)* punzante

shop [ʃɒp] **1** *n* (**a**) tienda *f*; *(large store)* almacén *m*; **s. assistant** dependiente(a) *m,f*; **s. window** escaparate *m*, *Am* vidriera *f*, *Am* vitrina *f* (**b**) *(workshop)* taller *m*; **s. floor** *(place)* planta *f*; *(workers)* obreros *mpl*; **s. steward** enlace *mf* sindical **2** *vi* hacer compras; **to go shopping** ir de compras

shopkeeper ['ʃɒpkiːpə(r)] *n* tendero(a) *m,f*

shoplifter ['ʃɒplɪftə(r)] *n* ladrón(ona) *m,f*(de tiendas)

shopper ['ʃɒpə(r)] *n* comprador(a) *m,f*

shopping ['ʃɒpɪŋ] *n (purchases)* compra *fpl*, *Am* compras *fpl*; **s. bag/ basket** bolsa *f*/cesta *f* de la compra; **s. centre** *or* **precinct** centro *m* comercial

shore [ʃɔː(r)] *n (of sea, lake)* orilla *f*; *US (beach)* playa *f*; *(coast)* costa *f*; **to go on s.** desembarcar

short [ʃɔːt] **1** *adj* (**a**) *(physically)* corto(a); *(person)* bajo(a), *Méx* chaparro(a), *RP* petiso(a); **in the s. term** a corto plazo; **s. circuit** cortocircuito *m*; **s. cut** atajo *m*; **s. story** relato corto, cuento *m*; **s. wave** onda corta (**b**) *(brief)* corto(a), breve; **"Bob" is s. for "Robert"** "Bob" es el diminutivo de "Robert"; **in s.** en pocas palabras (**c**) **to be s. of breath** faltarle a uno la respiración; **to be s. of food** andar escaso(a) de comida
2 *adv* (**a**) **to pull up s.** pararse en seco (**b**) **to cut s.** *(holiday)* interrumpir; *(meeting)* suspender; **we're running s. of coffee** se nos está acabando el café (**c**) **s. of** *(except)* excepto, menos

shortage ['ʃɔːtɪdʒ] *n* escasez *f*

shortbread ['ʃɔːtbred] *n* mantecado *m*

short-circuit [ʃɔːt'sɜːkɪt] **1** *vt* provocar un cortocircuito en **2** *vi* tener un cortocircuito

shortcomings ['ʃɔːtkʌmɪŋz] *npl* defectos *mpl*

shorten ['ʃɔːtən] *vt (skirt, visit)* acortar; *(word)* abreviar; *(text)* resumir

shorthand ['ʃɔːthænd] *n* taquigrafía *f*; *Br* **s. typist** taquimecanógrafo(a) *m,f*

shortly ['ʃɔːtlɪ] *adv (soon)* dentro de poco; **s. after** poco después

shorts [ʃɔːts] *npl* (**a**) pantalones *mpl* cortos; **a pair of s.** un pantalón corto (**b**) *US (underpants)* calzoncillos *mpl*

short-sighted [ʃɔːt'saɪtɪd] *adj (person)* miope; *Fig (plan etc)* sin visión de futuro.

short-term ['ʃɔːttɜːm] *adj* a corto plazo

shot¹ [ʃɒt] *n* (**a**) *(act, sound)* tiro *m*,

disparo *m* (**b**) *(pellets)* perdigones *mpl* (**c**) *(person)* tirador(a) *m,f* (**d**) *Ftb (kick)* tiro *m* (a puerta); *(in billiards, cricket, golf)* golpe *m* (**e**) *(attempt)* tentativa *f*; **to have a s. at sth** intentar hacer algo (**f**) *(injection)* inyección *f*; *Fam* pinchazo *m* (**g**) *(drink)* trago *m* (**h**) *Phot* foto *f*; *Cin* toma *f*

shot² [ʃɒt] *pt & pp of* **shoot**

shotgun [ˈʃɒtgʌn] *n* escopeta *f*

should [ʃʊd, *unstressed* ʃəd] *v aux*

En el inglés hablado, y en el escrito en estilo coloquial, la forma negativa **should not** se transforma en **shouldn't**

(**a**) *(duty)* deber; **all employees s. wear helmets** todos los empleados deben llevar casco; **he s. have been an architect** debería haber sido arquitecto (**b**) *(probability)* deber de; **he s. have finished by now** ya debe de haber acabado; **this s. be interesting** esto promete ser interesante (**c**) *(conditional use)* **if anything strange s. happen** si pasara algo raro (**d**) **I s. like to ask a question** quisiera hacer una pregunta

shoulder [ˈʃəʊldə(r)] **1** *n* (**a**) hombro *m*; **s. blade** omóplato *m*; **s. strap** *(of garment)* tirante *m*, *CSur* bretel *m*; *(of bag)* correa *f*; *Br Aut* **hard s.** arcén *m*, *Andes* berma *f*, *Méx* acotamiento *m*, *RP* banquina *f*, *Ven* hombrillo *m* (**b**) *Culin* paletilla *f* (**c**) *US Aut* arcén *m*, *Andes* berma *f*, *Méx* acotamiento *m*, *RP* banquina *f*, *Ven* hombrillo *m* **2** *vt Fig (responsibilities)* cargar con

shout [ʃaʊt] **1** *n* grito *m*
2 *vt* gritar
3 *vi* gritar; **to s. at sb** gritar a algn
▶ **shout down** *vt sep* abuchear

shouting [ˈʃaʊtɪŋ] *n* gritos *mpl*, vocerío *m*

shove [ʃʌv] **1** *n Fam* empujón *m*
2 *vt* empujar; **to s. sth into one's pocket** meterse algo en el bolsillo a empellones
3 *vi* empujar; *(jostle)* dar empellones
▶ **shove off** *vi Fam* largarse

▶ **shove up** *vi Fam (move along)* correrse

shovel [ˈʃʌvəl] **1** *n* pala *f*; **mechanical s.** excavadora *f* **2** *vt* mover con pala *or* a paladas

show [ʃəʊ] *(pt* **showed**; *pp* **shown** *or* **showed**) **1** *vt* (**a**) *(ticket etc)* mostrar; *(painting etc)* exponer; *(film)* poner (**b**) *(display)* demostrar (**c**) *(explain)* explicar (**d**) *(temperature, way etc)* indicar (**e**) *(prove)* demostrar (**f**) *(conduct)* llevar; **to s. sb in** hacer pasar a algn; **to s. sb to the door** acompañar a algn hasta la puerta
2 *vi (be visible)* notarse
3 *n* (**a**) *(display)* demostración *f* (**b**) *(outward appearance)* apariencia *f* (**c**) *(exhibition)* exposición *f*; **on s.** expuesto(a) (**d**) *Th (entertainment)* espectáculo *m*; *(performance)* función *f*; *Rad, TV* programa *m*; **s. business** *or Fam* **biz** el mundo del espectáculo
▶ **show off 1** *vt sep* (**a**) *(highlight)* hacer resaltar (**b**) *Fam (flaunt)* hacer alarde de **2** *vi Fam* farolear
▶ **show up 1** *vt sep* (**a**) *(reveal)* sacar a luz; *(highlight)* hacer resaltar (**b**) *Fam (embarrass)* dejar en evidencia **2** *vi* (**a**) *(stand out)* destacarse (**b**) *Fam (arrive)* aparecer

showdown [ˈʃəʊdaʊn] *n* enfrentamiento *m*

shower [ˈʃaʊə(r)] **1** *n* (**a**) *(rain)* chubasco *m*, chaparrón *m* (**b**) *Fig (of stones, insults)* lluvia *f* (**c**) *(bath)* ducha *f*, *Col, Méx, Ven* regadera *f*; **to have a s.** ducharse
2 *vt* (**a**) *(spray)* rociar (**b**) *Fig* **to s. gifts/praise on sb** colmar a algn de regalos/elogios
3 *vi* ducharse

showery [ˈʃaʊərɪ] *adj* lluvioso(a)

shown [ʃəʊn] *pp of* **show**

show-off [ˈʃəʊɒf] *n Fam* fanfarrón(ona) *m,f*, *Esp* fantasma *mf*

showy [ˈʃəʊɪ] *adj* llamativo(a)

shrank [ʃræŋk] *pt of* **shrink**

shred [ʃred] **1** *n* triza *f*; *(of cloth)* jirón *m*; *(of paper)* tira *f* **2** *vt (paper)* hacer trizas; *(vegetables)* rallar

shrewd [ʃruːd] adj astuto(a); (clear-sighted) perspicaz; (wise) sabio(a); (decision) acertado(a)

shriek [ʃriːk] 1 n chillido m; **shrieks of laughter** carcajadas fpl 2 vi chillar

shrill [ʃrɪl] adj agudo(a), estridente

shrimp [ʃrɪmp] n Br camarón m, quisquilla f; US (prawn) gamba f

shrine [ʃraɪn] n (tomb) sepulcro m; (chapel) capilla f; (holy place) lugar sagrado

shrink [ʃrɪŋk] (pt shrank; pp shrunk) 1 vt encoger
2 vi (a) (clothes) encoger(se) (b) (savings) disminuir (c) **to s. (back)** echarse atrás; **to s. from doing sth** no tener valor para hacer algo
3 n Fam (psychiatrist) psiquiatra mf

shrivel [ʃrɪvəl] 1 vt **to s. (up)** encoger; (plant) secar; (skin) arrugar 2 vi encogerse; (plant) secarse; (skin) arrugarse

shroud [ʃraʊd] 1 n Rel sudario m 2 vt Fig envolver

shrub [ʃrʌb] n arbusto m

shrug [ʃrʌg] 1 vt **to s. one's shoulders** encogerse de hombros
2 vi encogerse de hombros
3 n encogimiento m de hombros
▸ **shrug off** vt sep no dejarse desanimar por

shrunk [ʃrʌŋk] pp of **shrink**

shrunken [ʃrʌŋkən] adj encogido(a)

shudder [ʃʌdə(r)] 1 n (a) escalofrío m, estremecimiento m (b) (of machinery) sacudida f 2 vi (a) (person) estremecerse (b) (machinery) dar sacudidas

shuffle [ʃʌfəl] 1 vt (a) (feet) arrastrar (b) (papers etc) revolver; (cards) barajar 2 vi (a) (walk) andar arrastrando los pies (b) Cards barajar

shun [ʃʌn] vt (person) esquivar; (responsibility) rehuir

shut [ʃʌt] (pt & pp shut) 1 vt cerrar
2 vi cerrarse
3 adj cerrado(a)
▸ **shut down** 1 vt sep (factory) cerrar
2 vi (factory) cerrar
▸ **shut off** vt sep (gas, water etc) cortar

▸ **shut out** vt sep (a) (lock out) dejar fuera a (b) (exclude) excluir

▸ **shut up** vt sep (a) (close) cerrar (b) (imprison) encerrar (c) Fam (silence) callar 2 vi Fam (keep quiet) callarse

shutter [ʃʌtə(r)] n (a) (on window) contraventana f, postigo m (b) Phot obturador m

shuttle [ʃʌtəl] 1 n (a) (in weaving) lanzadera f (b) Av puente aéreo; **(space) s.** transbordador m espacial 2 vi ir y venir

shy [ʃaɪ] 1 adj (shyer, shyest or shier, shiest) (timid) tímido(a), Am salvo RP penoso(a); (reserved) reservado(a) 2 vi (horse) espantarse (at de); Fig **to s. away from doing sth** negarse a hacer algo

Sicily [ˈsɪsɪlɪ] n Sicilia

sick [sɪk] adj (a) (ill) enfermo(a); **s. leave** baja f por enfermedad; **s. pay** subsidio m de enfermedad (b) **to feel s.** (about to vomit) tener ganas de devolver; **to be s.** devolver (c) Fam (fed up) harto(a) (d) Fam (mind, joke) morboso(a); **s. humour** humor negro

sicken [sɪkən] 1 vt (make ill) poner enfermo; (revolt) dar asco a 2 vi (fall ill) enfermar

sickening [sɪkənɪŋ] adj nauseabundo(a); (revolting) repugnante; (horrifying) escalofriante

sickly [sɪklɪ] adj (sicklier, sickliest) (a) (person) enfermizo(a) (b) (taste) empalagoso(a) (c) (smile) forzado(a)

sickness [sɪknɪs] n (a) (illness) enfermedad f (b) (nausea) náuseas fpl

side [saɪd] 1 n (a) lado m; (of coin etc) cara f; (of hill) ladera f
(b) (of body) costado m; (of animal) ijar m; **by my s.** a mi lado; **s. by s.** juntos
(c) (edge) borde m; (of lake, river) orilla f
(d) Fig (aspect) aspecto m
(e) (team) equipo m; Pol partido m; **she's on our s.** está de nuestro lado; **to take sides with sb** ponerse de parte de algn; **s. effect** efecto secundario; **s. entrance** entrada f

lateral; **s. street** calle *f* lateral

2 *vi* **to s. with sb** ponerse de parte de algn

sideboard ['saɪdbɔːd] *n* aparador *m*

sideburns ['saɪdbɜːnz], *Br* **sideboards** ['saɪdbɔːdz] *npl* patillas *fpl*

sidelight ['saɪdlaɪt] *n Aut* luz *f* lateral, piloto *m*

sideline ['saɪdlaɪn] *n* (**a**) *Sport* línea *f* de banda (**b**) *Com (product)* línea suplementaria; *(job)* empleo suplementario

sidestep ['saɪdstep] *vt (issue)* esquivar

sidetrack ['saɪdtræk] *vt Fig (person)* despistar

sidewalk ['saɪdwɔːk] *n US* acera *f,* *CSur* vereda *f, CAm, Méx* banqueta *f*

sideways ['saɪdweɪz] **1** *adj (movement)* lateral; *(look)* de reojo **2** *adv* de lado

siding ['saɪdɪŋ] *n (on railway)* apartadero *m; (connected at only one end to main track)* vía *f* muerta

siege [siːdʒ] *n* sitio *m*, cerco *m*; **to lay s. to** sitiar

sieve [sɪv] **1** *n (fine)* tamiz *m; (coarse)* criba *f* **2** *vt (fine)* tamizar; *(coarse)* cribar

sift [sɪft] *vt (sieve)* tamizar; *Fig* **to s. through** examinar cuidadosamente

sigh [saɪ] **1** *vi* suspirar **2** *n* suspiro *m*

sight [saɪt] **1** *n* (**a**) *(faculty)* vista *f;* **at first s.** a primera vista; **to catch s. of** divisar; **to know by s.** conocer de vista; **to lose s. of sth/sb** perder algo/a algn de vista (**b**) *(range of vision)* vista *f;* **within s.** a la vista; **to come into s.** aparecer (**c**) *(spectacle)* espectáculo *m* (**d**) *(on gun)* mira *f; Fig* **to set one's sights on** tener la mira puesta en (**e**) **the sights** *(of city)* los lugares de interés

2 *vt* ver; *(land)* divisar

sightseeing ['saɪtsiːɪŋ] *n* turismo *m;* **to go s.** hacer turismo

sign [saɪn] **1** *n* (**a**) *(symbol)* signo *m* (**b**) *(gesture)* gesto *m; (signal)* señal *f* (**c**) *(indication)* señal *f; (trace)* rastro *m,* huella *f* (**d**) *(notice)* anuncio *m; (board)* letrero *m*

2 *vt* (**a**) *(letter etc)* firmar (**b**) *Ftb* fichar

3 *vi* firmar

▸ **sign on** *vi Br (worker)* firmar un contrato; *Br Fam* = registrarse para recibir el seguro de desempleo, *Esp* apuntarse al paro; *(regularly)* ir a firmar *or Esp* sellar

▸ **sign up 1** *vt sep (soldier)* reclutar; *(worker)* contratar **2** *vi (soldier)* alistarse; *(worker)* firmar un contrato

signal ['sɪgnəl] **1** *n* señal *f; Rad, TV* sintonía *f; Rail* **s. box** garita *f* de señales

2 *vt* (**a**) *(message)* transmitir por señales (**b**) *(direction etc)* indicar

3 *vi (with hands)* hacer señales; *(in car)* señalar

signature ['sɪgnɪtʃə(r)] *n (name)* firma *f; Rad, TV* **s. tune** sintonía *f*

significance [sɪg'nɪfɪkəns] *n* *(meaning)* significado *m; (importance)* importancia *f*

significant [sɪg'nɪfɪkənt] *adj* *(meaningful)* significativo(a); *(important)* importante

significantly [sɪg'nɪfɪkəntlɪ] *adv* *(markedly)* sensiblemente

signify ['sɪgnɪfaɪ] *vt* (**a**) *(mean)* significar (**b**) *(show, make known)* indicar

signpost ['saɪnpəʊst] *n* poste *m* indicador

silence ['saɪləns] **1** *n* silencio *m* **2** *vt* acallar; *(engine)* silenciar

silent ['saɪlənt] *adj* silencioso(a); *(not talkative)* callado(a); *(film)* mudo(a); **be s.!** ¡cállate!; **to remain s.** guardar silencio

silently ['saɪləntlɪ] *adv* silenciosamente

silhouette [sɪluːˈet] *n* silueta *f*

silicon ['sɪlɪkən] *n* silicio *m;* **s. chip** chip *m* (de silicio)

silk [sɪlk] **1** *n* seda *f* **2** *adj* de seda

silky ['sɪlkɪ] *adj* (**silkier, silkiest**) *(cloth)* sedoso(a); *(voice etc)* aterciopelado(a)

sill [sɪl] *n (of window)* alféizar *m*

silly ['sɪlɪ] *adj* (**sillier, silliest**) tonto(a)

silver ['sɪlvə(r)] **1** *n* (**a**) *(metal)* plata *f* (**b**) *Br (coins)* monedas *fpl* plateadas *(de entre 5 y 50 peniques)* (**c**) *(tableware)* vajilla *f* de plata **2** *adj* de plata; **s. foil** *(tinfoil)* papel *m* de aluminio; *Br* **s. paper** papel de plata; **s. wedding** bodas *fpl* de plata

silver-plated [sɪlvə'pleɪtɪd] *adj* plateado(a)

similar ['sɪmɪlə(r)] *adj* parecido(a), semejante (**to** a); **to be s.** parecerse

similarity [sɪmɪ'lærɪtɪ] *n* semejanza *f*

similarly ['sɪmɪlǝlɪ] *adv* (**a**) *(as well)* igualmente (**b**) *(likewise)* del mismo modo, asimismo

simmer ['sɪmǝ(r)] **1** *vt* cocer a fuego lento **2** *vi* cocerse a fuego lento

► **simmer down** *vi Fam* calmarse

simple ['sɪmpǝl] *adj* (**a**) sencillo(a); **s. interest** interés *m* simple (**b**) *(natural)* natural (**c**) *(foolish)* simple; *(naïve)* ingenuo(a); *(dim)* de pocas luces

simplicity [sɪm'plɪsɪtɪ] *n* (**a**) sencillez *f* (**b**) *(naïveté)* ingenuidad *f*

simplify ['sɪmplɪfaɪ] *vt* simplificar

simply ['sɪmplɪ] *adv* (**a**) *(plainly)* sencillamente (**b**) *(only)* simplemente, sólo

simulate ['sɪmjʊleɪt] *vt* simular

simultaneous [sɪmǝl'teɪnɪǝs] *adj* simultáneo(a)

sin [sɪn] **1** *n* pecado *m* **2** *vi* pecar

since [sɪns] **1** *adv* (**ever**) **s.** desde entonces; **long s.** hace mucho tiempo; **it has s. come out that …** desde entonces se ha sabido que … **2** *prep* desde; **she has been living here s. 1975** vive aquí desde 1975 **3** *conj* (**a**) *(time)* desde que; **how long is it s. you last saw him?** ¿cuánto tiempo hace que lo viste por última vez? (**b**) *(because, as)* ya que, puesto que

sincere [sɪn'sɪǝ(r)] *adj* sincero(a)

sincerely [sɪn'sɪǝlɪ] *adv* sinceramente; **Yours s.** *(in letter)* le saluda atentamente

sincerity [sɪn'serɪtɪ] *n* sinceridad *f*

sinful ['sɪnfʊl] *adj (person)* pecador(a); *(act, thought)* pecaminoso(a); *Fig (waste etc)* escandaloso(a)

sing [sɪŋ] *(pt sang; pp sung)* **1** *vt* cantar **2** *vi (person, bird)* cantar; *(kettle, bullets)* silbar

singe [sɪndʒ] *vt* chamuscar

singer ['sɪŋǝ(r)] *n* cantante *mf*

singing ['sɪŋɪŋ] *n (art)* canto *m*; *(songs)* canciones *fpl*; *(of kettle)* silbido *m*

single ['sɪŋgǝl] **1** *adj* (**a**) *(solitary)* solo(a) (**b**) *(only one)* único(a) (**c**) *(not double)* sencillo(a); **s. bed/room** cama *f*/habitación *f* individual (**d**) *(unmarried)* soltero(a) **2** *n* (**a**) *Br Rail* billete *m or Am* boleto *m or Am* pasaje *m* sencillo *or* de ida (**b**) *(record)* single *m* (**c**) *Sport* **singles** individuales *mpl*

► **single out** *vt sep (choose)* escoger; *(distinguish)* distinguir

single-handed ['sɪŋgǝl'hændɪd] *adj & adv* sin ayuda

single-minded ['sɪŋgǝl'maɪndɪd] *adj* resuelto(a)

singly ['sɪŋglɪ] *adv (individually)* por separado; *(one by one)* uno por uno

singular ['sɪŋgjʊlǝ(r)] **1** *adj* (**a**) *Ling* singular (**b**) *Fml (outstanding)* excepcional (**c**) *Fml (unique)* único(a) **2** *n Ling* singular *m*

sinister ['sɪnɪstǝ(r)] *adj* siniestro(a)

sink¹ [sɪŋk] *n (in kitchen)* fregadero *m*; *(in bathroom)* lavabo *m, Am* lavamanos *m inv*

sink² [sɪŋk] *(pt sank; pp sunk)* **1** *vt* (**a**) *(ship)* hundir, echar a pique; *Fig (hopes)* acabar con (**b**) *(hole, well)* cavar; *(post, knife, teeth)* hincar **2** *vi* (**a**) *(ship)* hundirse (**b**) *Fig* **my heart sank** se me cayó el alma a los pies (**c**) *(sun)* ponerse (**d**) **to s. to one's knees** hincarse de rodillas

► **sink in** *vi (penetrate)* penetrar; *Fig* **it hasn't sunk in yet** todavía no me he/se ha/*etc* hecho a la idea

sinner ['sɪnǝ(r)] *n* pecador(a) *m,f*

sinus ['saɪnǝs] *n* seno *m* (nasal)

sip [sɪp] **1** *n* sorbo *m* **2** *vt* sorber, beber a sorbos

siphon ['saɪfǝn] *n* sifón *m*

► **siphon off** *vt sep (liquid)* sacar con sifón; *Fig (funds, traffic)* desviar

sir [sɜː(r)] *n Fml* (**a**) señor *m*; **yes, s.** sí, señor (**b**) *(title)* sir; **S. Walter Raleigh** Sir Walter Raleigh

siren ['saɪrən] *n* sirena *f*

sister ['sɪstə(r)] *n* (**a**) *(relation)* hermana *f* (**b**) *Br Med* enfermera *f* jefe (**c**) *Rel* hermana *f*; *(before name)* sor

sister-in-law ['sɪstərɪnlɔː] *n* cuñada *f*

sit [sɪt] *(pt & pp* **sat**) **1** *vt* (**a**) *(child etc)* sentar (**in/on** en) (**b**) *Br (exam)* presentarse a **2** *vi* (**a**) *(action)* sentarse (**b**) *(be seated)* estar sentado(a) (**c**) *(object)* estar; *(be situated)* hallarse; *(person)* quedarse (**d**) *(assembly)* reunirse

▸ **sit back** *vi* recostarse

▸ **sit down** *vi* sentarse

▸ **sit in on** *vt insep* asistir sin participar a

▸ **sit out** *vt sep* aguantar hasta el final

▸ **sit through** *vt insep* aguantar

▸ **sit up** *vi* (**a**) incorporarse (**b**) *(stay up late)* quedarse levantado(a)

site [saɪt] **1** *n* (**a**) *(area)* lugar *m*; **building s.** solar *m*; *(under construction)* obra *f* (**b**) *(location)* situación *f*; **nuclear testing s.** zona *f* de pruebas nucleares **2** *vt* situar

sitting ['sɪtɪŋ] **1** *n* *(of committee)* sesión *f*; *(in canteen)* turno *m* **2** *adj Br* **s. room** sala *f* de estar

situated ['sɪtjʊeɪtɪd] *adj* situado(a), ubicado(a)

situation [sɪtjʊ'eɪʃən] *n* (**a**) situación *f* (**b**) *(job)* puesto *m*; *Br* **situations vacant** *(in newspaper)* ofertas de trabajo

six [sɪks] *adj & n* seis *(m inv)*

sixteen [sɪks'tiːn] *adj & n* dieciséis *(m inv)*, diez y seis *(m inv)*

sixteenth [sɪks'tiːnθ] **1** *adj & n* decimosexto(a) *(m,f)* **2** *n (fraction)* dieciseisavo *m*

sixth [sɪksθ] **1** *adj* sexto(a); *Br Educ* **the s. form** = últimos dos cursos del bachillerato británico previos a los estudios superiores; *Br Educ* **s. former** = estudiante de los dos últimos cursos del bachillerato británico **2** *n* (**a**) *(in series)* sexto(a) *m,f* (**b**) *(fraction)* sexto *m*, sexta parte

sixty ['sɪkstɪ] *adj & n* sesenta *(m inv)*

size [saɪz] *n* tamaño *m*; *(of garment)* talla *f*; *(of shoes)* número *m*; *(of person)* estatura *f*; *(scope)* alcance *m*; **what s. do you take?** *(garment)* ¿qué talla tienes?; *(shoes)* ¿qué número calzas?

▸ **size up** *vt sep (person)* juzgar; *(situation, problem)* evaluar

sizzle ['sɪzəl] *vi* chisporrotear

skate[1] [skeɪt] **1** *n* patín *m* **2** *vi* patinar

skate[2] [skeɪt] *n (fish)* raya *f*

skateboard ['skeɪtbɔːd] *n* monopatín *m*, *RP* skate *m*

skater ['skeɪtə(r)] *n* patinador(a) *m,f*

skating ['skeɪtɪŋ] *n* patinaje *m*; **s. rink** pista *f* de patinaje

skeleton ['skelɪtən] **1** *n* (**a**) esqueleto *m* (**b**) *(of building)* armazón *m* (**c**) *(outline)* esquema *m* **2** *adj (staff, service)* reducido(a); **s. key** llave maestra

skeptic ['skeptɪk] *n US =* **sceptic**

skeptical ['skeptɪkal] *adj US =* **sceptical**

sketch [sketʃ] **1** *n* (**a**) *(preliminary drawing)* bosquejo *m*, esbozo *m*; *(drawing)* dibujo *m*; *(outline)* esquema *m*; *(rough draft)* boceto *m* (**b**) *Th, TV* sketch *m* **2** *vt (draw)* dibujar; *(preliminary drawing)* bosquejar, esbozar

sketchy ['sketʃɪ] *adj* (**sketchier**, **sketchiest**) *(incomplete)* incompleto(a); *(not detailed)* vago(a)

skewer ['skjʊə(r)] *n* pincho *m*, broqueta *f*

ski [skiː] **1** *n* esquí *m* **2** *adj* de esquí; **s. boots** botas *fpl* de esquiar; **s. jump** *(action)* salto *m* con esquís; **s. lift** telesquí *m*; *(with seats)* telesilla *f*; **s. pants** pantalón *m* de esquiar; **s. resort** estación *f* de esquí; **s. stick** *or* **pole** bastón *m* de esquiar **3** *vi* esquiar; **to go skiing** ir a esquiar

skid [skɪd] **1** *n* patinazo *m* **2** *vi* patinar

skier ['skiːə(r)] *n* esquiador(a) *m,f*

skiing ['skiːɪŋ] *n* esquí *m*

skilful ['skɪlfʊl] *adj* hábil, diestro(a)

skill [skɪl] *n* (**a**) *(ability)* habilidad *f*,

destreza f; *(talent)* don m (**b**) *(technique)* técnica f

skilled [skɪld] adj (**a**) *(dextrous)* hábil, diestro(a); *(expert)* experto(a) (**b**) *(worker)* cualificado(a)

skillful ['skɪlfʊl] adj US = skilful

skim [skɪm] **1** vt (**a**) *(milk)* Esp quitar la nata a, Am sacar la crema a; **skimmed milk** leche desnatada (**b**) *(brush against)* rozar; **to s. the ground** *(bird, plane)* volar a ras de suelo **2** vi Fig **to s. through a book** hojear un libro

skimpy ['skɪmpɪ] adj (**skimpier, skimpiest**) *(shorts)* muy corto(a); *(meal)* escaso(a)

skin [skɪn] **1** n (**a**) *(of person)* piel f; *(of face)* cutis m; *(complexion)* tez f (**b**) *(of fruit)* piel f; *(of lemon)* cáscara f; *(peeling)* mondadura f (**c**) *(of sausage)* pellejo m **2** vt (**a**) *(animal)* despellejar (**b**) *(graze)* arañar

skinny ['skɪnɪ] adj (**skinnier, skinniest**) Fam flaco(a)

skip¹ [skɪp] **1** n *(jump)* salto m, brinco m

2 vi *(jump)* saltar, brincar; *(with rope)* saltar a la cuerda or Esp comba; Fig **to s. over sth** saltarse algo

3 vt Fig saltarse

skip² [skɪp] n Br *(for rubbish)* contenedor m

skirt [skɜːt] **1** n falda f, CSur pollera f **2** vt *(town etc)* rodear; *(coast)* bordear; Fig *(problem)* esquivar

skittle ['skɪtəl] n (**a**) *(pin)* bolo m (**b**) **skittles** *(game)* (juego m de los) bolos mpl, boliche m

skull [skʌl] n Anat cráneo m; Fam calavera f

skunk [skʌŋk] n mofeta f

sky [skaɪ] n cielo m; **s. blue** azul m celeste

skydiving ['skaɪdaɪvɪŋ] n caída f libre (en paracaídas)

skylight ['skaɪlaɪt] n tragaluz m, claraboya f

skyline ['skaɪlaɪn] n *(of city)* perfil m

skyscraper ['skaɪskreɪpə(r)] n rascacielos m inv

slack [slæk] **1** adj (**a**) *(not taut)* flojo(a)

(**b**) *(lax)* descuidado(a); *(lazy)* vago(a) (**c**) *(market)* flojo(a); **business is s.** hay poco negocio **2** n *(in rope)* parte floja

slacken ['slækən] **1** vt (**a**) *(rope)* aflojar (**b**) *(speed)* reducir **2** vi (**a**) *(rope)* aflojarse; *(wind)* amainar (**b**) *(trade)* aflojar

▸ **slacken off** vi disminuirse

slam [slæm] **1** n *(of door)* portazo m

2 vt *(bang)* cerrar de golpe; **to s. sth down on the table** soltar algo sobre la mesa de un palmetazo; **to s. the door** dar un portazo; **to s. on the brakes** dar un frenazo

3 vi *(door)* cerrarse de golpe

slander ['slɑːndə(r)] **1** n difamación f, calumnia f **2** vt difamar, calumniar

slang [slæŋ] n argot m

slant [slɑːnt] **1** n (**a**) inclinación f; *(slope)* pendiente f (**b**) Fig *(point of view)* punto m de vista

2 vt Fig *(problem etc)* enfocar subjetivamente

3 vi inclinarse

slap [slæp] **1** n palmada f; *(in face)* bofetada f

2 adv Fam **he ran s. into the fence** se dio de lleno contra la valla; **s. in the middle of …** justo en medio de …

3 vt pegar con la mano; *(hit in face)* dar una bofetada a; **to s. sb on the back** dar a algn una palmada en la espalda

slapdash ['slæpdæʃ] adj Fam descuidado(a); *(work)* chapucero(a)

slapstick ['slæpstɪk] n bufonadas fpl, payasadas fpl

slash [slæʃ] **1** n Fam Typ barra oblicua

2 vt (**a**) *(with knife)* acuchillar; *(with sword)* dar un tajo a (**b**) Fig *(prices)* rebajar

slate [sleɪt] **1** n pizarra f; Fig **to wipe the s. clean** hacer borrón y cuenta nueva **2** vt Fam vapulear, Esp poner por los suelos, Méx viborear

slaughter ['slɔːtə(r)] **1** n *(of animals)* matanza f; *(of people)* carnicería f **2** vt *(animals)* matar; *(people)* matar brutalmente; *(in large numbers)* masacrar

slave [sleɪv] **1** n esclavo(a) m,f; **s. trade** trata f de esclavos **2** vi **to**

s. (away) dar el callo

slavery ['sleɪvərɪ] n esclavitud f

sleazy ['sliːzɪ] adj (**sleazier, sleaziest**) sórdido(a)

sledge [sledʒ] n Br trineo m

sledgehammer ['sledʒhæmə(r)] n almádena f

sleek [sliːk] adj (hair) lustroso(a); (appearance) impecable

sleep [sliːp] **1** n sueño m; **to go to s.** dormirse; Fig **to send to s.** (hacer) dormir; **my foot has gone to s.** se me ha dormido el pie **2** vi (pt & pp **slept**) dormir; **to s. like a log** dormir como un lirón

▸ **sleep in** vi Br (oversleep) quedarse dormido(a); (have a lie-in) quedarse en la cama

▸ **sleep with** vt insep Fam **to s. with sb** acostarse con algn

sleeper ['sliːpə(r)] n (**a**) (person) durmiente mf; **to be a heavy s.** tener el sueño pesado (**b**) Br Rail (on track) traviesa f (**c**) Rail (coach) coche-cama m; (berth) litera f

sleeping ['sliːpɪŋ] adj **s. bag** saco m de dormir, Col, Méx sleeping m (bag), RP bolsa f de dormir; **S. Beauty** la Bella Durmiente; **s. car** coche-cama m; Br Com **s. partner** socio(a) m,f comanditario(a); **s. pill** somnífero m

sleepy ['sliːpɪ] adj (**sleepier, sleepiest**) soñoliento(a); **to be** or **feel s.** tener sueño

sleet [sliːt] **1** n aguanieve f **2** vi **it's sleeting** cae aguanieve

sleeve [sliːv] n (of garment) manga f; (of record) funda f

sleigh [sleɪ] n trineo m; **s. bell** cascabel m

slender ['slendə(r)] adj (**a**) (thin) delgado(a) (**b**) Fig (hope, chance) remoto(a)

slept [slept] pt & pp of **sleep**

slice [slaɪs] **1** n (**a**) (of bread) rebanada f; (of ham) loncha f; (of beef etc) tajada f; (of lemon etc) rodaja f; (of cake) trozo m (**b**) (utensil) pala f **2** vt (food) cortar a rebanadas/lonchas/tajadas/rodajas; (divide) partir

slick [slɪk] **1** adj (**a**) (programme, show) logrado(a) (**b**) (skilful) hábil, mañoso(a) **2** n (oil) **s.** marea negra

slide [slaɪd] (pt & pp **slid** [slɪd]) **1** n (**a**) (act) resbalón m (**b**) (in prices etc) baja f (**c**) (in playground) tobogán m (**d**) Phot diapositiva f; **s. projector** proyector m de diapositivas (**e**) Br (for hair) pasador m

2 vt deslizar; (furniture) correr

3 vi (on purpose) deslizarse; (slip) resbalar

sliding ['slaɪdɪŋ] adj (door, window) corredizo(a); Fin **s. scale** escala f móvil

slight [slaɪt] **1** adj (**a**) (small) pequeño(a); **not in the slightest** en absoluto (**b**) (build) menudo(a); (slim) delgado(a); (frail) delicado(a) (**c**) (trivial) leve

2 n (affront) desaire m

3 vt (**a**) (scorn) despreciar (**b**) (snub) desairar

slightly ['slaɪtlɪ] adv (a little) ligeramente, algo

slim [slɪm] **1** adj (**slimmer, slimmest**) (**a**) (person) delgado(a) (**b**) Fig (resources) escaso(a); (hope, chance) remoto(a) **2** vi adelgazar

slime [slaɪm] n (mud) lodo m, cieno m; (of snail) baba f

slimy ['slaɪmɪ] adj (**slimier, slimiest**) (**a**) (muddy) lodoso(a); (snail) baboso(a) (**b**) Fig (person) zalamero(a)

sling [slɪŋ] **1** n (**a**) (catapult) honda f; (child's) tirador m (**b**) Med cabestrillo m **2** vt (pt & pp **slung**) (throw) tirar

slip [slɪp] **1** n (**a**) (slide) resbalón m (**b**) (mistake) error m; (moral) desliz m; **a s. of the tongue** un lapsus linguae (**c**) (of paper) trocito m

2 vi (**a**) (slide) resbalar (**b**) Med dislocarse; **slipped disc** vértebra dislocada (**c**) (move quickly) ir de prisa (**d**) (standards etc) deteriorarse

3 vt (**a**) (slide) dar a escondidas (**b**) **it slipped my memory** se me fue de la cabeza

▸ **slip away** vi (person) escabullirse

▸ **slip off** vt sep (clothes) quitarse rápidamente

▸ **slip on** *vt sep (clothes)* ponerse rápidamente

▸ **slip out** *vi* (a) *(leave)* salir (b) *Fig* **the secret slipped out** se le escapó el secreto

▸ **slip up** *vi Fam (blunder)* cometer un desliz

slipper ['slɪpə(r)] *n* zapatilla *f*

slippery ['slɪpərɪ] *adj* resbaladizo(a)

slit [slɪt] **1** *n (opening)* hendidura *f*, *(cut)* corte *m*, raja *f* **2** *vt (pt & pp* **slit)** cortar, rajar

slob [slɒb] *n Fam (untidy person)* cerdo(a) *m,f*, *Esp* guarro(a) *m,f*; *(lazy person)* dejado(a) *m,f*, tirado(a) *m,f*

slog [slɒg] *Fam* **1** *n* **it was a bit of a s.** fue un aburrimiento *or Esp* tostonazo (de trabajo); **it's a long s.** *(walk)* hay un buen trecho *or Esp* una buena tirada **2** *vi (work hard)* trabajar como un/una negro(a), *Esp* dar el callo

slogan ['sləʊgən] *n* (e)slogan *m*, lema *m*

slop [slɒp] **1** *vi* **to s. (over)** derramarse; **to s. about** chapotear **2** *vt* derramar

slope [sləʊp] **1** *n (incline)* cuesta *f*, pendiente *f*; *(up)* subida *f*; *(down)* bajada *f*; *(of mountain)* ladera *f*; *(of roof)* vertiente *f* **2** *vi* inclinarse; **to s. up/down** subir/bajar en pendiente

▸ **slope off** *vi Br Fam* escabullirse

sloping ['sləʊpɪŋ] *adj* inclinado(a)

sloppy ['slɒpɪ] *adj* **(sloppier, sloppiest)** *Fam* descuidado(a); *(work)* chapucero(a); *(appearance)* desaliñado(a)

slot [slɒt] **1** *n* (a) *(for coin)* ranura *f*; *(opening)* rendija *f*; **s. machine** *(for gambling)* (máquina *f*) tragaperras *f inv*; *(vending machine)* distribuidor automático (b) *Rad, TV* espacio *m* **2** *vt (place)* meter; *(put in)* introducir **3** *vi* **to s. in** *or* **together** encajar

slouch [slaʊtʃ] *vi* andar *or* sentarse con los hombros caídos

slow [sləʊ] **1** *adj* (a) lento(a); **in s. motion** a cámara lenta; **to be s. to do sth** tardar *or Am* demorar en hacer algo (b) *(clock)* atrasado(a) (c) *(stupid)*

lento(a), torpe **2** *adv* despacio, lentamente **3** *vt (car)* reducir la marcha de; *(progress)* retrasar **4** *vi* **to s. down** *or* **up** ir más despacio; *(in car)* reducir la velocidad

slowly ['sləʊlɪ] *adv* despacio, lentamente

slug [slʌg] **1** *n* (a) *Zool* babosa *f* (b) *US Fam (bullet)* posta *f* (c) *Fam (blow)* porrazo *m* **2** *vt Fam (hit)* aporrear

sluggish ['slʌgɪʃ] *adj* (a) *(river, engine)* lento(a); *Com* flojo(a) (b) *(lazy)* perezoso(a)

slum [slʌm] *n (district)* barrio *m* bajo; *(on outskirts)* arrabal *m*, suburbio *m*; *(house)* tugurio *m*

slump [slʌmp] **1** *n* (a) *(drop in sales etc)* bajón *m* (b) *(economic depression)* crisis económica *f* **2** *vi* (a) *(sales etc)* caer de repente; *(prices)* desplomarse; *(the economy)* hundirse; *Fig (morale)* hundirse (b) *(fall)* caer

slung [slʌŋ] *pt & pp of* **sling**

slur [slɜː(r)] **1** *n (stigma)* mancha *f*; *(slanderous remark)* calumnia *f* **2** *vt (word)* tragarse

slush [slʌʃ] *n* (a) *(melting snow)* nieve medio fundida (b) *Fam* sentimentalismo *m* (c) *US Fam* **s. fund** fondos *mpl* para corrupción *or Esp* corruptelas

slut [slʌt] *n very Fam Pej* (a) *(untidy woman)* marrana *f*, *Esp* guarra *f* (b) *(whore)* fulana *f*

sly [slaɪ] *adj* **(slyer, slyest** *or* **slier, sliest)** (a) *(cunning)* astuto(a) (b) *(secretive)* furtivo(a) (c) *(mischievous)* travieso(a) (d) *(underhand)* malicioso(a)

smack¹ [smæk] **1** *n* (a) *(slap)* bofetada *f* (b) *(sharp sound)* ruido sonoro **2** *vt* (a) *(slap)* dar una bofetada a (b) *(hit)* golpear; *Fig* **to s. one's lips** relamerse

smack² [smæk] *vi Fig* **to s. of** oler a

small [smɔːl] **1** *adj* (a) pequeño(a), *Am* chico(a); *Fig* **s. print** letra pequeña (b) *(in height)* bajo(a) (c) *(scant)* escaso(a); **s. change** cambio *m*, suelto *m*, *Am* vuelto *m* (d) *(minor)* insignificante; **s. businessmen** pequeños comerciantes; **s. talk** charloteo *m* **(e)** *(increase)* ligero(a) **2** *n* **s. of the back** región *f* lumbar

small-minded [smɔːlˈmaɪndɪd] *adj* mezquino(a)

smallpox [ˈsmɔːlpɒks] *n* viruela *f*

smart [smɑːt] **1** *adj* **(a)** *(elegant)* elegante **(b)** *(clever)* listo(a), inteligente; *Fam* **s. alec(k)** sabelotodo *mf*, listillo(a) *m,f*, *Méx*, *RP* vivo(a) *m,f*; **(c)** *(quick)* rápido(a); *(pace)* ligero(a) **2** *vi* **(a)** *(sting)* picar, escocer **(b)** *Fig* sufrir

smarten [ˈsmɑːtən] **1** *vt* **to s. (up)** arreglar **2** *vi* **to s. (oneself) up** arreglarse

smartly [ˈsmɑːtlɪ] *adv* **(a)** *(elegantly)* elegantemente **(b)** *(quickly)* rápidamente, con rapidez

smash [smæʃ] **1** *n* **(a)** *(loud noise)* estrépito *m*; *(collision)* choque violento **(b)** *(in tennis)* smash *m* **2** *vt* **(a)** *(break)* romper; *(shatter)* hacer pedazos; *(crush)* aplastar **(b)** *(destroy)* destrozar; *(defeat)* aplastar **(c)** *(record)* fulminar **3** *vi* *(break)* romperse; *(shatter)* hacerse pedazos; *(crash)* estrellarse; *(in tennis)* hacer un mate

▸ **smash up** *vt sep Fam (car)* hacer pedazos; *(place)* destrozar

smashing [ˈsmæʃɪŋ] *adj Br Fam* genial, *Méx* padre, *RP* bárbaro(a)

smattering [ˈsmætərɪŋ] *n* **he had a s. of French** hablaba un poquito de francés

smear [smɪə(r)] **1** *n* **(a)** *(smudge)* mancha *f*; **s. (test)** citología *f* **(b)** *Fig (defamation)* calumnia *f* **2** *vt* **(a)** *(butter etc) untar; (grease)* embadurnar **(b)** *(make dirty)* manchar **(c)** *Fig (defame)* calumniar, difamar

smell [smel] *(pt & pp* **smelled** *or* **smelt)** **1** *n* **(a)** *(sense)* olfato *m* **(b)** *(odour)* olor *m* **2** *vt* oler; *Fig* olfatear **3** *vi* oler **(of** a); **it smells good/like lavender** huele bien/a lavanda; **he smelt of whisky** olía a whisky

smelly [ˈsmelɪ] *adj* **(smellier, smelliest)** *Fam* maloliente, apestoso(a)

smelt[1] [smelt] *vt (ore)* fundir

smelt[2] [smelt] *pt & pp of* **smell**

smile [smaɪl] **1** *n* sonrisa *f* **2** *vi* sonreír; **to s. at sb** sonreír a algn; **to s. at sth** reírse de algo

smirk [smɜːk] **1** *n (conceited)* sonrisa satisfecha; *(foolish)* sonrisa boba **2** *vi (conceitedly)* sonreír con satisfacción; *(foolishly)* sonreír bobamente

smoke [sməʊk] **1** *n* humo *m*; **s. bomb** bomba *f* de humo; **s. screen** cortina *f* de humo **2** *vi* fumar; *(chimney etc)* echar humo **3** *vt* **(a)** *(tobacco)* fumar; **to s. a pipe** fumar en pipa **(b)** *(fish, meat)* ahumar

smoker [ˈsməʊkə(r)] *n* **(a)** *(person)* fumador(a) *m,f* **(b)** *Rail* vagón *m* de fumadores

smoky [ˈsməʊkɪ] *adj* **(smokier, smokiest)** **(a)** *(chimney)* humeante; *(room)* lleno(a) de humo; *(atmosphere)* cargado(a) (de humo); *(taste)* ahumado(a) **(b)** *(colour)* ahumado(a)

smooth [smuːð] **1** *adj* **(a)** *(surface)* liso(a); *(skin)* suave; *(road)* llano(a) **(b)** *(beer, wine)* suave **(c)** *(flowing)* fluido(a) **(d)** *(flight)* tranquilo(a); *(transition)* sin problemas **(e)** *Pej (slick)* zalamero(a) **2** *vt* **(a)** *(hair etc)* alisar **(b)** *(plane down)* limar

▸ **smooth out** *vt sep (creases)* alisar; *Fig (difficulties)* allanar; *(problems)* resolver

▸ **smooth over** *vt sep Fig* **to s. things over** limar asperezas

smoothly [ˈsmuːðlɪ] *adv* sobre ruedas

smother [ˈsmʌðə(r)] *vt* **(a)** *(asphyxiate)* asfixiar; *(suffocate)* sofocar **(b)** *Fig (cover)* cubrir **(with** de)

smoulder [ˈsməʊldə(r)] *vi (fire)* arder sin llama; *Fig (passions)* arder; **smouldering hatred** odio latente

smudge [smʌdʒ] **1** *n (stain)* mancha *f*; *(of ink)* borrón *m* **2** *vt* manchar; *(piece of writing)* emborronar

smug [smʌg] *adj* **(smugger, smuggest)** engreído(a)

smuggle [ˈsmʌgəl] *vt* pasar de contrabando

smuggler [ˈsmʌglə(r)] *n* contrabandista *mf*

smuggling [ˈsmʌgəlɪŋ] *n* contrabando *m*

snack [snæk] *n* tentempié *m*, *Esp* piscolabis *m inv*, *Méx* botana *f*; **s. bar** cafetería *f*

snag [snæg] **1** *n (difficulty)* pega *f*, problemilla *m* **2** *vt (clothing)* enganchar

snail [sneɪl] *n* caracol *m*

snake [sneɪk] *n (big)* serpiente *f*; *(small)* culebra *f*

snap [snæp] **1** *n* (a) *(noise)* ruido seco; *(of branch, fingers)* chasquido *m* (b) *(bite)* mordisco *m* (c) *Phot (foto f)* instantánea *f*
2 *adj (sudden)* repentino(a)
3 *vt* (a) *(branch etc)* partir (en dos) (b) *(make noise)* **to s. one's fingers** chasquear los dedos; **to s. sth shut** cerrar algo de golpe (c) *Phot* sacar una foto de
4 *vi* (a) *(break)* romperse (b) *(make noise)* hacer un ruido seco (c) *(whip)* chasquear; **to s. shut** cerrarse de golpe (d) **to s. at sb** *(dog)* intentar morder a algn; *Fam (person)* hablar en mal tono a algn
▸ **snap off 1** *vt sep (branch etc)* arrancar **2** *vi (branch etc)* separarse
▸ **snap up** *vt sep Fam* **to s. up a bargain** llevarse una ganga

snarl¹ [snɑːl] **1** *n* gruñido *m* **2** *vi* gruñir

snarl² [snɑːl] **1** *n (in wool)* maraña *f* **2** *vt* **to s. (up)** *(wool)* enmarañar; *(traffic)* atascar; *(plans)* enredar

snatch [snætʃ] **1** *n* (a) *Fam (theft)* robo *m*; **bag s.** tirón *m* (b) *(fragment)* fragmentos *mpl*
2 *vt* (a) *(grab)* arrebatar (b) *Fam (steal)* robar; *(kidnap)* secuestrar
3 *vi* **to s. at sth** intentar agarrar *or Esp* coger algo

sneak [sniːk] *(pt & pp* **sneaked** *or US* **snuck)* **1** *n Br Fam Esp* chivato(a) *m,f*, *Méx* hocicón(ona) *m,f*, *RP* buchón(ona) *m,f*
2 *vt* **to s. sth out of a place** sacar algo de un lugar a escondidas
3 *vi* (a) **to s. off** escabullirse; **to s. in/**

out entrar/salir a hurtadillas (b) *Fam* **to s. on sb** *(tell tales)* ir con cuentos, *Esp* chivarse

sneaker [ˈsniːkə(r)] *n US* playera *f*

sneer [snɪə(r)] *vi* **to s. at** hacer un gesto de desprecio a

sneeze [sniːz] **1** *n* estornudo *m* **2** *vi* estornudar

sniff [snɪf] **1** *n (by person)* aspiración *f*; *(by dog)* husmeo *m*
2 *vt (flower etc)* oler; *(suspiciously)* husmear; *(snuff etc)* aspirar; *(glue)* esnifar
3 *vi* aspirar por la nariz

snigger [ˈsnɪgə(r)] **1** *n* risa disimulada **2** *vi* reír disimuladamente; **to s. at sth** burlarse de algo

snip [snɪp] **1** *n* (a) *(cut)* tijeretada *f*; *(small piece)* recorte *m* (b) *Br Fam (bargain)* *Esp* chollo *m*, *Am* regalo *m* **2** *vt* cortar a tijeretazos

snivel [ˈsnɪvəl] *vi* lloriquear

snob [snɒb] *n* (e)snob *mf*

snobbish [ˈsnɒbɪʃ] *adj* (e)snob

snooker [ˈsnuːkə(r)] *n* snooker *m*, billar *m* ruso

snoop [snuːp] *vi* fisgonear, *Esp* fisgar

snooze [snuːz] *Fam* **1** *n Esp* siestecilla *f*, *Am* siesta *f* **2** *vi* echarse una *Esp* siestecilla *or Am* siesta

snore [snɔː(r)] **1** *n* ronquido *m* **2** *vi* roncar

snoring [ˈsnɔːrɪŋ] *n* ronquidos *mpl*

snorkel [ˈsnɔːkəl] *n (of swimmer)* tubo *m* de respiración; *(of submarine)* esnórquel *m*

snort [snɔːt] **1** *n* resoplido *m* **2** *vi* resoplar

snot [snɒt] *n Fam* mocos *mpl*

snout [snaʊt] *n (of animal, gun etc)* morro *m*

snow [snəʊ] **1** *n* nieve *f*; **s. shower** nevada *f*
2 *vi* nevar; **it's snowing** está nevando
3 *vt Fig* **to be snowed under with work** estar agobiado(a) de trabajo

snowball [ˈsnəʊbɔːl] **1** *n* bola *f* de nieve **2** *vi Fig* aumentar rápidamente

snowdrop [ˈsnəʊdrɒp] *n* campanilla *f* de invierno

snowflake ['snəʊfleɪk] n copo m de nieve

snowman ['snəʊmæn] n hombre m de nieve

snowplough, US **snowplow** ['snəʊplaʊ] n quitanieves m inv

snowshoe ['snəʊʃuː] n raqueta f (de nieve)

snowstorm ['snəʊstɔːm] n nevasca f

snub [snʌb] **1** n (of person) desaire m; (of offer) rechazo m **2** vt (person) desairar; (offer) rechazar

snuck [snʌk] US pt & pp of **sneak**

snug [snʌg] adj (**snugger, snuggest**) (**a**) (cosy) cómodo(a) (**b**) (tightfitting) ajustado(a)

snuggle ['snʌgəl] vi to s. down in bed acurrucarse en la cama; to s. up to sb arrimarse a algn

so [səʊ] **1** adv (**a**) (to such an extent) tanto; **he was so tired that ...** estaba tan cansado que ...; **it's so long since ...** hace tanto tiempo que ...; Fam **so long!** ¡hasta luego!
(**b**) (degree) tanto; **a week or so** una semana más o menos; **we loved her so (much)** la queríamos tanto; Fam **he's ever so handsome!** ¡es tan guapo!
(**c**) (thus, in this way) así, de esta manera; **and so on, and so forth** y así sucesivamente; **if so** en este caso; **I think/hope so** creo/espero que sí; **I told you so** ya te lo dije; **so far** hasta ahora or allí; **so they say** eso dicen
(**d**) (also) **I'm going to Spain – so am I** voy a España – yo también **2** conj (**a**) (expresses result) así que; **so you like England, do you?** ¿así que te gusta Inglaterra, pues?; Fam **so what?** ¿y qué? (**b**) (expresses purpose) para que; **I'll put the key here so (that) everyone can see it** pongo la llave aquí para que todos la vean

soak [səʊk] **1** vt (washing, food) remojar; (cotton, wool) empapar (**in** en) **2** vi (washing, food) estar en remojo
▸ **soak in** vi penetrar
▸ **soak up** vt sep absorber

soaking ['səʊkɪŋ] adj (object) empapado(a); (person) calado(a) hasta los huesos

soap [səʊp] **1** n (**a**) jabón m; **s. flakes** jabón en escamas; **s. powder** jabón en polvo (**b**) TV **s. opera** culebrón m **2** vt enjabonar

soapsuds ['səʊpsʌdz] npl espuma f (de jabón)

soar [sɔː(r)] vi (bird, plane) remontar el vuelo; Fig (skyscraper) elevarse; (hopes, prices) aumentar

sob [sɒb] **1** n sollozo m **2** vi sollozar

sober ['səʊbə(r)] adj (not drunk, moderate) sobrio(a); (sensible) sensato(a); (serious) serio(a); (colour) discreto(a)
▸ **sober up** vi **he sobered up** se le pasó la borrachera

soccer ['sɒkə(r)] n fútbol m

sociable ['səʊʃəbəl] adj (gregarious) sociable; (friendly) amistoso(a)

social ['səʊʃəl] adj social; **s. class** clase f social; **s. climber** arribista mf; **S. Democratic** socialdemócrata; US **s. insurance** seguro m social; **s. security** seguridad f social; **the s. services** los servicios sociales; **s. work** asistencia f social; **s. worker** asistente(a) m,f social

socialist ['səʊʃəlɪst] adj & n socialista (mf)

socialize ['səʊʃəlaɪz] **1** vi alternar, mezclarse con la gente **2** vt socializar

society [sə'saɪətɪ] **1** n (**a**) sociedad f; **the consumer s.** la sociedad de consumo; **(high) s.** la alta sociedad (**b**) (club) asociación f (**c**) (companionship) compañía f **2** adj de sociedad; **s. column** ecos mpl de sociedad

sociology [səʊsɪ'ɒlədʒɪ] n sociología f

sock [sɒk] n calcetín m, CSur zoquete m

socket ['sɒkɪt] n (**a**) (of eye) cuenca f (**b**) Elec enchufe m

soda ['səʊdə] n (**a**) Chem sosa f; **baking s.** bicarbonato sódico (**b**) **s. water** soda f (**c**) US (fizzy drink) gaseosa f

sofa [ˈsəʊfə] n sofá m; **s. bed** sofá cama

soft [sɒft] adj (**a**) (not hard) blando(a); **s. drinks** refrescos mpl; **s. drugs** drogas blandas; **s. toy** muñeco m de peluche (**b**) (skin, colour, hair, light, music) suave; (breeze, steps) ligero(a) (**c**) (lenient) permisivo(a) (**d**) (voice) bajo(a)

softball [ˈsɒftbɔːl] n = juego parecido al béisbol jugado en un campo más pequeño y con una pelota más blanda

soften [ˈsɒfən] **1** vt (leather, heart) ablandar; (skin) suavizar; Fig (blow) amortiguar **2** vi (leather, heart) ablandarse; (skin) suavizarse

softly [ˈsɒftlɪ] adv (gently) suavemente; (quietly) silenciosamente

software [ˈsɒftweə(r)] n Comput software m; **s. package** paquete m

soggy [ˈsɒgɪ] adj (**soggier, soggiest**) empapado(a); (bread) pastoso(a)

soil [sɔɪl] **1** n (earth) tierra f **2** vt (dirty) ensuciar; Fig (reputation) manchar

solar [ˈsəʊlə(r)] adj solar

sold [səʊld] pt & pp of **sell**

soldier [ˈsəʊldʒə(r)] n soldado m; (officer) militar m; **toy s.** soldadito m de plomo

▸ **soldier on** vi Fig continuar contra viento y marea

sole¹ [səʊl] n (of foot) planta f; (of shoe, sock) suela f

sole² [səʊl] n (fish) lenguado m

sole³ [səʊl] adj (only) único(a)

solely [ˈsəʊllɪ] adv únicamente

solemn [ˈsɒləm] adj solemne

solicitor [səˈlɪsɪtə(r)] n abogado(a) m,f; (for wills) notario(a) m,f

solid [ˈsɒlɪd] **1** adj (**a**) (not liquid) sólido(a); (firm) firme (**b**) (not hollow, pure) (metal) macizo(a) (**c**) (of strong material) resistente **2** n sólido m

solidarity [sɒlɪˈdærɪtɪ] n solidaridad f

solitary [ˈsɒlɪtərɪ] adj (**a**) (alone) solitario(a); (secluded) apartado(a) (**b**) (only) solo(a)

solitude [ˈsɒlɪtjuːd] n soledad f

solo [ˈsəʊləʊ] n solo m

soloist [ˈsəʊləʊɪst] n solista mf

soluble [ˈsɒljʊbəl] adj soluble

solution [səˈluːʃən] n solución f

solve [sɒlv] vt resolver, solucionar

solvent [ˈsɒlvənt] adj & n solvente (m)

sombre, US **somber** [ˈsɒmbə(r)] adj (dark) sombrío(a); (gloomy) lúgubre; (pessimistic) pesimista

some [sʌm] **1** adj (**a**) (with plural nouns) unos(as), algunos(as); (several) varios(as); (a few) unos(as) cuantos(as); **there were s. roses** había unas rosas; **s. more peas** más guisantes

(**b**) (with singular nouns) algún/alguna; (a little) un poco de; **there's s. wine left** queda un poco de vino; **would you like s. coffee?** ¿quiere café?

(**c**) (certain) cierto(a), alguno(a); **to s. extent** hasta cierto punto; **s. people say that ...** algunas personas dicen que ...

(**d**) (unspecified) algún/alguna; **for s. reason or other** por una razón o por otra; **s. day** algún día

(**e**) (quite a lot of) bastante; **s. years ago** hace algunos años

2 pron (**a**) (people) algunos(as), unos(as); **s. go by bus and s. by train** unos van en autobús y otros en tren (**b**) (objects) algunos(as); (a few) unos(as) cuantos(as); (a little) algo, un poco; (certain ones) algunos(as)

3 adv **s. thirty cars** unos treinta coches

somebody [ˈsʌmbədɪ] pron alguien; **s. else** otro(a)

somehow [ˈsʌmhaʊ] adv (**a**) (in some way) de alguna forma (**b**) (for some reason) por alguna razón

someone [ˈsʌmwʌn] pron = **somebody**

someplace [ˈsʌmpleɪs] adv US = **somewhere**

somersault [ˈsʌməsɔːlt] **1** n voltereta f; (by acrobat etc) salto m mortal; (by car) vuelta f de campana **2** vi dar volteretas; (acrobat etc) dar un salto mortal; (car) dar una vuelta de campana

something [ˈsʌmθɪŋ] pron & n algo;

s. to eat/drink algo de comer/beber; **are you drunk or s.?** ¿estás borracho o qué?; **s. must be done** hay que hacer algo; **she has a certain s.** tiene un no sé qué; **is s. the matter?** ¿le pasa algo?; **s. else** otra cosa; **s. of the kind** algo por el estilo

sometime ['sʌmtaɪm] *adv* algún día; **s. last week** un día de la semana pasada; **s. next year** durante el año que viene

sometimes ['sʌmtaɪmz] *adv* a veces, de vez en cuando

somewhat ['sʌmwɒt] *adv Fml* algo, un tanto

somewhere ['sʌmweə(r)] *adv* (a) *(in some place)* en alguna parte; *(to some place)* a alguna parte; **s. else** *(in some other place)* en otra parte; *(to some other place)* a otra parte; **s. or other** no sé dónde (b) **s. in the region of** *(approximately)* más o menos

son [sʌn] *n* hijo *m*; **eldest/youngest s.** hijo mayor/menor

song [sɒŋ] *n* canción *f*; *(of bird)* canto *m*

son-in-law ['sʌnɪnlɔ:] *n* yerno *m*

soon [su:n] *adv* (a) *(within a short time)* pronto, dentro de poco; *(quickly)* rápidamente; **s. after midnight** poco después de medianoche; **s. afterwards** poco después (b) **as s. as I arrived** en cuanto llegué; **as s. as possible** cuanto antes (c) *(preference)* **I would just as s. stay at home** prefiero quedarme en casa

soot [sʊt] *n* hollín *m*

soothe [su:ð] *vt (calm)* tranquilizar; *(pain)* aliviar

sophisticated [sə'fɪstɪkeɪtɪd] *adj* sofisticado(a)

sopping ['sɒpɪŋ] *adj Fam* **s. (wet)** como una sopa

soppy ['sɒpɪ] *adj* (**soppier, soppiest**) *Fam* sensiblero(a), *Esp* ñoño(a)

soprano [sə'prɑːnəʊ] *n* soprano *mf*

sordid ['sɔ:dɪd] *adj* sórdido(a)

sore [sɔ:(r)] **1** *adj* (a) dolorido(a); **to have a s. throat** tener dolor de garganta (b) *Fam (annoyed) esp Esp*

enfadado(a), enojado(a) (**about** por); **to feel s. about sth** estar resentido(a) por algo **2** *n* llaga *f*

sorrow ['sɒrəʊ] *n* pena *f*, dolor *m*

sorry ['sɒrɪ] **1** *adj* (**sorrier, sorriest**) (a) **I feel very s. for her** me da mucha pena (b) *(pitiful)* triste (c) **to be s. (about sth)** sentir (algo); **I'm s. I'm late** siento llegar tarde **2** *interj* (a) *(apology)* ¡perdón! (b) *Br (for repetition)* ¿cómo?

sort [sɔ:t] **1** *n* (a) *(kind)* clase *f*, tipo *m*; *(brand)* marca *f*; **it's a s. of teapot** es una especie de tetera (b) **he is a musician of sorts** tiene algo de músico; **there's an office of sorts** hay una especie de despacho (c) **s. of** en cierto modo **2** *vt (classify)* clasificar

▸ **sort out** *vt sep* (a) *(classify)* clasificar; *(put in order)* ordenar (b) *(problem)* arreglar, solucionar

so-so ['səʊsəʊ] *adv Fam* así así, regular

sought [sɔ:t] *pt & pp of* **seek**

soul [səʊl] *n* (a) alma *f* (b) **he's a good s.** *(person)* es muy buena persona (c) *Mus (música f)* soul *m*

sound¹ [saʊnd] **1** *n* sonido *m*; *(noise)* ruido *m*; **s. effects** efectos sonoros **2** *vt (bell, trumpet)* tocar; **to s. the alarm** dar la señal de alarma **3** *vi* (a) *(trumpet, bell, alarm)* sonar (b) *(give an impression)* parecer; **it sounds interesting** parece interesante

▸ **sound out** *vt sep* sondear

sound² [saʊnd] **1** *adj* (a) *(healthy)* sano(a); *(in good condition)* en buen estado (b) *(safe, dependable)* seguro(a); *(correct)* acertado(a); *(logical)* lógico(a) (c) *(basis etc)* sólido(a) (d) *(sleep)* profundo(a) **2** *adv* **to be s. asleep** estar profundamente dormido(a)

sound³ [saʊnd] *vt Naut, Med* sondar

sound⁴ [saʊnd] *n Geog* estrecho *m*

soundly ['saʊndlɪ] *adv* (a) *(logically)* razonablemente (b) *(solidly)* sólidamente (c) **to sleep s.** dormir profundamente

soundproof ['saʊndpruːf] *adj* insonorizado(a)

soundtrack ['saʊndtræk] *n* banda sonora

soup [suːp] *n* sopa *f*; *(thin, clear)* caldo *m*; *Fam* **in the s.** en un apuro; **s. dish** plato hondo; **s. spoon** cuchara *f* sopera

sour [saʊə(r)] *adj* (a) *(fruit, wine)* agrio(a); *(milk)* cortado(a); **to go s.** *(milk)* cortarse; *(wine)* agriarse; *Fig (situation)* empeorar (b) *Fig (person)* amargado(a)

source [sɔːs] *n* fuente *f*; *(of infection)* foco *m*

south [saʊθ] **1** *n* sur *m*; **in the s. of England** en el sur de Inglaterra; **to the s. of York** al sur de York
2 *adj* del sur; **S. Africa** Sudáfrica; **S. African** sudafricano(a) *(m,f)*; **S. Korea** Corea del Sur; **S. Pole** Polo *m* Sur
3 *adv (location)* al sur; *(direction)* hacia el sur

southeast [saʊθ'iːst] **1** *n* sudeste *m* **2** *adv (location)* al sudeste; *(direction)* hacia el sudeste

southern ['sʌðən] *adj* del sur, meridional; **S. Europe** Europa del Sur; **the s. hemisphere** el hemisferio sur

southerner ['sʌðənə(r)] *n* sureño(a) *m,f*

southward ['saʊθwəd] *adj & adv* hacia el sur

southwest [saʊθ'west] **1** *n* suroeste *m* **2** *adj* suroeste
3 *adv (location)* al suroeste; *(direction)* hacia el suroeste

souvenir [suːvə'nɪə(r)] *n* recuerdo *m*, souvenir *m*

sovereign ['sɒvrɪn] **1** *n* (a) *(monarch)* soberano(a) *m,f* (b) *Hist (coin)* soberano *m* **2** *adj* soberano(a)

sovereignty ['sɒvrəntɪ] *n* soberanía *f*

sow¹ [səʊ] *vt (pt* sowed; *pp* sowed *or* sown [səʊn]) sembrar

sow² [saʊ] *n Zool* cerda *f*, puerca *f*, *Am* chancha *f*

soya ['sɔɪə] *n* soja *f*; **s. bean** semilla *f* de soja

space [speɪs] **1** *n* (a) espacio *m*; **s. age** era *f* espacial; **s. shuttle** transbordador *m* espacial; **s. station** estación *f* espacial (b) *(room)* sitio *m*; **in a confined s.** en un espacio reducido
2 *vt (also s. out)* espaciar, separar

spaceship ['speɪsʃɪp] *n* nave *f* espacial

spacious ['speɪʃəs] *adj* espacioso(a), amplio(a)

spade¹ [speɪd] *n (for digging)* pala *f*

spade² [speɪd] *n Cards* pica *f*

spaghetti [spə'getɪ] *n* espaguetis *mpl*

Spain [speɪn] *n* España

span [spæn] **1** *n (of wing)* envergadura *f*; *(of hand)* palmo *m*; *(of arch)* luz *f*; *(of road)* tramo *m*; *(of time)* lapso *m*; **life s.** vida *f*
2 *vt (river etc)* extenderse sobre, atravesar; *(period of time etc)* abarcar
3 *pt of* spin

Spaniard ['spænjəd] *n* español(a) *m,f*

Spanish ['spænɪʃ] **1** *adj* español(a) **2** *n* (a) **the S.** los españoles (b) *(language)* español *m*, castellano *m*

spank [spæŋk] *vt* zurrar

spanner ['spænə(r)] *n Br* llave *f* plana *(herramienta)*; *Fam* **to throw a s. in the works** estropear los planes

spare [speə(r)] **1** *vt* (a) *(do without)* prescindir de; **I can't s. the time** no tengo tiempo (b) *(begrudge)* escatimar (c) *(show mercy to)* perdonar (d) **s. me the details** ahórrate los detalles
2 *adj (left over)* sobrante; *(surplus)* de sobra, de más; **s. part** (pieza *f* de) recambio *m*; **s. room** cuarto *m* de los invitados; **s. wheel** rueda *f* de recambio *or RP* auxilio, *Méx* llanta *f* de refacción
3 *n Aut* (pieza *f* de) recambio *m*

sparingly ['speərɪŋlɪ] *adv* en poca cantidad

spark [spɑːk] **1** *n* chispa *f*; *Aut* **s. plug** bujía *f* **2** *vi* echar chispas
▸ **spark off** *vt sep* desatar

sparkle ['spɑːkəl] **1** *vi (diamond, glass)* centellear, destellar; *(eyes)* brillar **2** *n (of diamond, glass)* centelleo *m*, destello *m*; *(of eyes)* brillo *m*

sparkling ['spɑːklɪŋ] *adj* (a)

(diamond, glass) centelleante; *(eyes)* brillante; **s. wine** vino espumoso **(b)** *Fig (person, conversation)* vivaz

sparrow ['spærəʊ] *n* gorrión *m*

sparse [spɑːs] *adj (thin)* escaso(a); *(scattered)* esparcido(a); *(hair)* ralo(a)

spasm ['spæzəm] *n* **(a)** *Med* espasmo *m*; *(of coughing)* acceso *m* **(b)** *(of anger, activity)* arrebato *m*

spat [spæt] *pt & pp of* **spit¹**

spate [speɪt] *n* **(a)** *(of letters)* avalancha *f*; *(of words)* torrente *m*; *(of accidents)* racha *f* **(b)** *Br (river)* desbordamiento *m*; **to be in full s.** estar crecido(a)

spatter ['spætə(r)] *vt* salpicar (**with** de)

speak [spiːk] *(pt* **spoke**; *pp* **spoken) 1** *vt* **(a)** *(utter)* decir; **to s. the truth** decir la verdad **(b)** *(language)* hablar **2** *vi* **(a)** *(gen)* hablar, *esp Am* conversar, *Méx* platicar; **roughly speaking** a grandes rasgos; **so to s.** por así decirlo; **speaking of ...** a propósito de ...; **to s. to sb** hablar *or esp Am* conversar *or Méx* platicar con algn **(b)** *(make a speech)* pronunciar un discurso; *(take the floor)* tomar la palabra **(c)** *Tel* hablar; **speaking!** ¡al habla!; **who's speaking, please?** ¿de parte de quién?

▶ **speak for** *vt insep (person, group)* hablar en nombre de; **it speaks for itself** es evidente

▶ **speak out** *vi* **to s. out against sth** denunciar algo

▶ **speak up** *vi* hablar más fuerte; *Fig* **to s. up for sb** intervenir a favor de algn

speaker ['spiːkə(r)] *n* **(a)** *(in dialogue)* interlocutor(a) *m,f*; *(at conference)* conferenciante *mf*, *Am* conferencista *mf*; **(public) s.** orador(a) *m,f* **(b)** *(of language)* hablante *mf* **(c)** *(loudspeaker)* altavoz *m*, *Am* altoparlante *m*, *Méx* bocina *f*

spear [spɪə(r)] *n* lanza *f*; *(javelin)* jabalina *f*; *(harpoon)* arpón *m*

special ['speʃəl] **1** *adj* especial; *(specific)* específico(a); *(exceptional)* extraordinario(a); **s. delivery** envío *m* urgente; **s. effects** efectos *mpl* especiales **2** *n Rad, TV* programa *m* especial

specialist ['speʃəlɪst] *n* especialista *mf*

speciality [speʃɪ'ælɪtɪ] *n esp Br* especialidad *f*

specialize ['speʃəlaɪz] *vi* especializarse (**in** en)

specially ['speʃəlɪ] *adv (specifically)* especialmente; *(on purpose)* a propósito

specialty ['speʃəltɪ] *n US* = **speciality**

species ['spiːʃiːz] *n (pl* **species)** especie *f*

specific [spɪ'sɪfɪk] *adj* específico(a); *(definite)* concreto(a); *(precise)* preciso(a); **to be s.** concretar

specifically [spɪ'sɪfɪklɪ] *adv (exactly)* específicamente; *(expressly)* expresamente; *(namely)* en concreto

specifications [spesɪfɪ'keɪʃənz] *npl (of machine)* especificaciones *fpl or* características *fpl* técnicas

specify ['spesɪfaɪ] *vt* especificar, precisar

specimen ['spesɪmɪn] *n (sample)* muestra *f*; *(example)* ejemplar *m*; **urine/tissue s.** espécimen de orina/tejido

speck [spek] *n (of dust)* mota *f*; *(stain)* manchita *f*; *(small trace)* pizca *f*

specs [speks] *npl Fam (spectacles)* gafas *fpl*, *Am* lentes *mpl*, *Am* anteojos *mpl*

spectacle ['spektəkəl] *n* **(a)** *(display)* espectáculo *m* **(b)** **spectacles** *(glasses)* gafas *fpl*, *Am* lentes *mpl*, *Am* anteojos *mpl*

spectacular [spek'tækjʊlə(r)] **1** *adj* espectacular, impresionante **2** *n Cin, TV* (gran) espectáculo *m*

spectator [spek'teɪtə(r)] *n* espectador(a) *m,f*

spectre, *US* **specter** ['spektə(r)] *n* espectro *m*, fantasma *m*

spectrum ['spektrəm] *n* espectro *m*

speculate ['spekjʊleɪt] *vi* especular

speculation [spekjʊ'leɪʃən] *n* especulación *f*

sped [sped] *pt & pp of* **speed**

speech [spi:tʃ] *n* (**a**) *(faculty)* habla *f*; *(pronunciation)* pronunciación *f*; **freedom of s.** libertad *f* de expresión (**b**) *(address)* discurso *m*; **to give a s.** pronunciar un discurso (**c**) *Ling* **part of s.** parte *f* de la oración

speechless ['spi:tʃlɪs] *adj* mudo(a), boquiabierto(a)

speed [spi:d] **1** *n* velocidad *f*; *(rapidity)* rapidez *f*; **at top s.** a toda velocidad; **s. limit** límite *m* de velocidad **2** *vi* (**a**) *(pt & pp* **sped**) *(go fast)* ir corriendo; *(hurry)* apresurarse; **to s. along** *(car etc)* ir a toda velocidad; **to s. past** pasar volando (**b**) *(pt & pp* **speeded**) *(exceed speed limit)* conducir con exceso de velocidad

▸ **speed up 1** *vt sep* acelerar; *(person)* meter prisa a **2** *vi (person)* darse prisa, *Am* apurarse

speedboat ['spi:dbəʊt] *n* lancha rápida

speedometer [spɪ'dɒmɪtə(r)] *n* velocímetro *m*

speedy ['spi:dɪ] *adj* (**speedier**, **speediest**) veloz, rápido(a)

spell¹ [spel] *(pt & pp* **spelt** *or* **spelled**) **1** *vt (letter by letter)* deletrear; *Fig (denote)* significar; **how do you s. your name?** ¿cómo se escribe su nombre? **2** *vi* **she can't s.** comete faltas de ortografía

▸ **spell out** *vt sep Fig* explicar con detalle

spell² [spel] *n (magical)* hechizo *m*, encanto *m*

spell³ [spel] *n* (**a**) *(period)* período *m*; *(short period)* rato *m*; *Met* **cold s.** ola *f* de frío (**b**) *(shift)* turno *m*

spell-checker ['speltʃekə(r)] *n Comput* corrector *m* ortográfico

spelling ['spelɪŋ] *n* ortografía *f*

spelt [spelt] *pt & pp of* **spell**

spend [spend] *(pt & pp* **spent**) *vt* (**a**) *(money)* gastar (**on** en) (**b**) *(time)* pasar; **to s. time on sth** dedicar tiempo a algo

spending ['spendɪŋ] *n* gastos *mpl*; **s. money** dinero *m* de bolsillo; **s. power** poder adquisitivo

spent [spent] **1** *adj* gastado(a) **2** *pt & pp of* **spend**

sperm [spɜ:m] *n* esperma *m*; **s. bank** banco *m* de esperma; **s. whale** cachalote *m*

sphere [sfɪə(r)] *n* esfera *f*

spice [spaɪs] **1** *n* (**a**) especia *f* (**b**) *Fig* sal *f* **2** *vt* (**a**) *Culin* sazonar (**b**) **to s. (up)** *(story etc)* salpimentar

spicy ['spaɪsɪ] *adj* (**spicier**, **spiciest**) (**a**) *Culin* sazonado(a); *(hot)* picante (**b**) *Fig (story etc)* picante

spider ['spaɪdə(r)] *n* araña *f*; *Br* **s.'s** *or US* **s. web** telaraña *f*

spike¹ [spaɪk] *n (sharp point)* punta *f*; *(metal rod)* pincho *m*; *(on railing)* barrote *m*; *Sport (on shoes)* clavo *m*

spike² [spaɪk] *n Bot* espiga *f*

spiky ['spaɪkɪ] *adj* (**spikier**, **spikiest**) puntiagudo(a); *(hairstyle)* de punta

spill [spɪl] *(pt & pp* **spilled** *or* **spilt** [spɪlt]) **1** *vt* derramar **2** *vi (liquid)* derramarse

▸ **spill over** *vi* desbordarse

spin [spɪn] *(pt* **span** *or* **spun**; *pp* **spun**) **1** *vt* (**a**) *(wheel etc)* hacer girar; *(washing)* centrifugar (**b**) *(cotton, wool)* hilar; *(spider's web)* tejer **2** *vi (wheel etc)* girar; *Av* caer en barrena; *Aut* patinar **3** *n* (**a**) *(turn)* vuelta *f*, giro *m* (**b**) *Sport* efecto *m* (**c**) *Br* **to go for a s.** *(ride)* dar una vuelta (**d**) *Pol* **s. doctor** asesor(a) *m,f* político(a) *(para dar buena prensa a un partido o político)*

spinach ['spɪnɪtʃ] *n* espinacas *fpl*

spin-dryer [spɪn'draɪə(r)] *n* secador centrífugo

spine [spaɪn] *n* (**a**) *Anat* columna *f* vertebral, espinazo *m*; *(of book)* lomo *m* (**b**) *Zool* púa *f*; *Bot* espina *f*

spinster ['spɪnstə(r)] *n* soltera *f*

spiral ['spaɪərəl] **1** *n* espiral *f* **2** *adj* en espiral; **s. staircase** escalera *f* de caracol

spire ['spaɪə(r)] *n (of church)* aguja *f*

spirit¹ ['spɪrɪt] n (**a**) (soul) espíritu m, alma f; (ghost) fantasma m (**b**) (attitude) espíritu m; (mood) humor m (**c**) (courage) valor m; (liveliness) ánimo m; (vitality) vigor m (**d**) **spirits** (mood) humor m; **to be in good spirits** estar de buen humor

spirit² ['spɪrɪt] n (**a**) Chem alcohol m; **s. level** nivel m de aire (**b**) **spirits** (alcoholic drinks) licores mpl

spiritual ['spɪrɪtjʊəl] adj espiritual

spit¹ [spɪt] (pt & pp **spat**) **1** vt escupir **2** vi escupir; Fam **he's the spitting image of his father** es el vivo retrato de su padre
3 n (saliva) saliva f

spit² [spɪt] n Culin asador m

spite [spaɪt] **1** n (**a**) (ill will) rencor m, ojeriza f (**b**) **in s. of** a pesar de, pese a; **in s. of the fact that** a pesar de que, pese a que **2** vt (annoy) fastidiar

spiteful ['spaɪtfʊl] adj (person) rencoroso(a); (remark) malévolo(a); (tongue) viperino(a)

splash [splæʃ] **1** vt salpicar **2** vi (**a**) **to s. (about)** (in water) chapotear (**b**) (water etc) salpicar **3** n (**a**) (noise) chapoteo m (**b**) (spray) salpicadura f; Fig (of colour) mancha f
▸ **splash out** vi Fam tirar la casa por la ventana

splendid ['splendɪd] adj espléndido(a)

splendour, US splendor ['splendə(r)] n esplendor m

splint [splɪnt] n tablilla f

splinter ['splɪntə(r)] **1** n (wood) astilla f; (bone, stone) esquirla f; (glass) fragmento m; **s. group** grupo m disidente **2** vi (**a**) (wood etc) astillarse (**b**) Pol escindirse

split [splɪt] (pt & pp **split**) **1** n (crack) grieta f, hendidura f; (tear) desgarrón m; Fig (division) cisma m; Pol escisión f **2** adj partido(a); **in a s. second** en una fracción de segundo **3** vt (**a**) (crack) agrietar; (cut) partir; (tear) rajar; (atom) desintegrar (**b**) (divide) dividir (**c**) (share out) repartir (**d**) Pol escindir

4 vi (**a**) (crack) agrietarse; (into two parts) partirse; (garment) rajarse (**b**) (divide) dividirse (**c**) Pol escindirse
▸ **split up 1** vt sep (break up) partir; (divide up) dividir; (share out) repartir **2** vi (couple) separarse

spoil [spɔɪl] (pt & pp **spoiled** or **spoilt**) **1** vt (**a**) (ruin) estropear, echar a perder (**b**) (child) mimar a; **to be spoilt for choice** tener demasiadas cosas para elegir **2** vi (food) estropearse

spoilt [spɔɪlt] **1** adj (**a**) (food, merchandise) estropeado(a) (**b**) (child) mimado(a) **2** pt & pp of **spoil**

spoke¹ [spəʊk] pt of **speak**

spoke² [spəʊk] n (of wheel) radio m, rayo m

spoken ['spəʊkən] pp of **speak**

spokesman ['spəʊksmən] n portavoz m

spokeswoman ['spəʊkswʊmən] n portavoz f

sponge [spʌndʒ] **1** n esponja f; Fig **to throw in the s.** arrojar la toalla; Br **s. cake** bizcocho m **2** vt (wash) lavar con esponja **3** vi Fam vivir de gorra
▸ **sponge off, sponge on** vt insep vivir a costa de

sponger ['spʌndʒə(r)] n Fam gorrero(a) m,f, Esp, Méx gorrón(ona) m,f, RP garronero(a) m,f

sponsor ['spɒnsə(r)] **1** vt patrocinar; Fin avalar; (support) respaldar **2** n patrocinador(a) m,f; Fin avalador(a) m,f

sponsorship ['spɒnsəʃɪp] n patrocinio m; Fin aval m; (support) respaldo m

spontaneous [spɒn'teɪnɪəs] adj espontáneo(a)

spooky ['spu:kɪ] adj (spookier, spookiest) Fam espeluznante

spoon [spu:n] **1** n cuchara f; (small) cucharita f **2** vt sacar con cuchara; (serve) servir con cuchara

spoonful ['spu:nfʊl] n cucharada f

sport [spɔ:t] **1** n (**a**) deporte m (**b**) Fam **he's a good s.** es buena persona; **be a s.!** ¡sé amable! **2** vt (display) lucir

sports [spɔːts] *adj* **s. car** coche *m* or *Am* carro *m* or *CSur* auto *m* deportivo; **s. centre** polideportivo *m*; *Br* **s. jacket** chaqueta *f* or *Am* saco *m* de sport

sportsman ['spɔːtsmən] *n* deportista *m*

sportswoman ['spɔːtswʊmən] *n* deportista *f*

spot [spɒt] **1** *n* (**a**) *(dot)* punto *m*; *(on fabric)* lunar *m* (**b**) *(stain)* mancha *f* (**c**) *(pimple)* grano *m* (**d**) *(place)* sitio *m*, lugar *m*; **on the s.** *(person)* allí, presente; **to be in a tight s.** estar en un apuro; **to put sb on the s.** poner a algn en un aprieto (**e**) *Br Fam (small amount) (of rain, wine)* gota *f*; **a s. of bother** una problemilla **2** *vt (notice)* darse cuenta de, notar; *(see)* ver

spotless ['spɒtlɪs] *adj (very clean)* impecable; *Fig (reputation etc)* intachable

spotlight ['spɒtlaɪt] *n* foco *m*; *Aut* faro *m* auxiliar; *Fig* **to be in the s.** ser objeto de la atención pública

spotty ['spɒtɪ] *adj* (**spottier, spottiest**) *Pej* con granos

spouse [spaʊs] *n* cónyuge *mf*

spout [spaʊt] **1** *n (of jug)* pico *m*; *(of teapot)* pitorro *m*
2 *vt Fam (nonsense)* soltar
3 *vi* **to s. out/up** *(liquid)* brotar

sprain [spreɪn] **1** *n* esguince *m* **2** *vt* torcer; **to s. one's ankle** torcerse el tobillo

sprang [spræŋ] *pt of* **spring²**

spray¹ [spreɪ] **1** *n* (**a**) *(of water)* rociada *f*; *(from sea)* espuma *f*; *(from aerosol)* pulverización *f* (**b**) *(aerosol)* spray *m*; *(for plants)* pulverizador *m*; **s. can** aerosol *m* **2** *vt (water)* rociar; *(insecticide, perfume)* pulverizar

spray² [spreɪ] *n (of flowers)* ramita *f*

spread [spred] *(pt & pp* **spread**) **1** *n* (**a**) extensión *f*; *(of ideas)* difusión *f*; *(of disease, fire)* propagación *f*; *(of terrorism)* generalización *f* (**b**) *(for bread)* pasta *f*; **cheese s.** queso *m* para untar (**c**) *Fam (large meal)* banquetazo *m*
2 *vt* (**a**) *(unfold)* desplegar; *(lay out)*

extender (**b**) *(butter etc)* untar (**c**) *(news)* difundir; *(rumour)* hacer correr; *(disease, fire)* propagar; *(panic)* sembrar
3 *vi* (**a**) *(stretch out)* extenderse; *(unfold)* desplegarse (**b**) *(news)* difundirse; *(rumour)* correr; *(disease)* propagarse

spreadsheet ['spredʃiːt] *n Comput* hoja *f* de cálculo

spree [spriː] *n* juerga *f*; **to go on a s.** ir de juerga

spring¹ [sprɪŋ] **1** *n (season)* primavera *f* **2** *adj* primaveral; **s. onion** cebolleta *f*, *RP* cebolla *f* de verdeo; **s. roll** rollo *m* de primavera, *RP* arrollado *m* de primavera

spring² [sprɪŋ] *(pt* **sprang**; *pp* **sprung**) **1** *n* (**a**) *(of water)* manantial *m*, fuente *f* (**b**) *(of watch etc)* resorte *m*; *(of mattress)* muelle *m*; *Aut* ballesta *f*
2 *vi* (**a**) *(jump)* saltar; **the lid sprang open** la tapa se abrió de golpe (**b**) *(appear)* aparecer (de repente)
3 *vt* (**a**) **to s. a leak** hacer agua (**b**) *Fig (news, surprise)* dar de golpe

▸ **spring up** *vi* aparecer; *(plants)* brotar; *(buildings)* elevarse; *(problems)* surgir

springboard ['sprɪŋbɔːd] *n* trampolín *m*

springtime ['sprɪŋtaɪm] *n* primavera *f*

sprinkle ['sprɪŋkəl] *vt (with water)* rociar (**with** de); *(with sugar)* espolvorear (**with** de)

sprint [sprɪnt] **1** *n* esprint *m* **2** *vi* esprintar

sprout [spraʊt] **1** *vi (bud)* brotar; *Fig* crecer rápidamente **2** *n* (**Brussels**) **sprouts** coles *fpl* or *CSur* repollitos *mpl* de Bruselas

spruce [spruːs] *adj* pulcro(a)

▸ **spruce up** *vt sep* acicalar

sprung [sprʌŋ] *pp of* **spring²**

spun [spʌn] *pt & pp of* **spin**

spur [spɜː(r)] **1** *n* (**a**) espuela *f* (**b**) *Fig (stimulus)* acicate *m*; **on the s. of the moment** sin pensarlo **2** *vt* (**a**) *(horse)* espolear (**b**) *Fig* incitar

spurt [spɜːt] **1** n (a) (of liquid) chorro m (b) Fig (of activity etc) racha f; (effort) esfuerzo m **2** vi (a) (liquid) chorrear (b) (make an effort) hacer un último esfuerzo; (accelerate) acelerar

spy [spaɪ] **1** n espía mf **2** vt Fml (see) divisar **3** vi espiar (**on** a)

spying ['spaɪɪŋ] n espionaje m

squabble ['skwɒbəl] **1** n riña f, pelea f **2** vi reñir, pelearse (**over** or **about** por)

squad [skwɒd] n Mil pelotón m; (of police) brigada f; Sport equipo m; **drugs s.** brigada antidroga

squalid ['skwɒlɪd] adj (very dirty) asqueroso(a); (poor) miserable; (motive) vil

squalor ['skwɒlə(r)] n (dirtiness) mugre f; (poverty) miseria f

squander ['skwɒndə(r)] vt (money) derrochar, despilfarrar; (time) desperdiciar

square [skweə(r)] **1** n (a) cuadro m; (on chessboard, crossword) casilla f (b) (in town) plaza f (c) Math cuadrado m **2** adj (a) (in shape) cuadrado(a) (b) Math (metre, root) cuadrado(a) (c) **a s. meal** una buena comida (d) (old-fashioned) carroza; (conservative) carca **3** vt (a) Math elevar al cuadrado (b) (settle) arreglar **4** vi (agree) cuadrar (**with** con)

squash¹ [skwɒʃ] **1** n Br (drink) **orange/lemon** (bebida f a base de) concentrado m de naranja/limón **2** vt (crush) aplastar **3** vi aplastarse

squash² [skwɒʃ] n Sport squash m

squash³ [skwɒʃ] n US (vegetable) calabacín m

squat [skwɒt] **1** adj (person) rechoncho(a) **2** vi (a) (crouch) agacharse, sentarse en cuclillas (b) (in building) ocupar ilegalmente **3** n Br (illegally occupied dwelling) casa f ocupada (ilegalmente)

squawk [skwɔːk] **1** n graznido m **2** vi graznar

squeak [skwiːk] **1** n (of mouse) chillido m; (of hinge, wheel) chirrido m; (of shoes) crujido m **2** vi (mouse) chillar; (hinge, wheel) chirriar, rechinar; (shoes) crujir

squeal [skwiːl] **1** n (of animal, person) chillido m **2** vi (a) (animal, person) chillar (b) Fam (inform) chivarse

squeamish ['skwiːmɪʃ] adj muy sensible

squeeze [skwiːz] **1** vt apretar; (lemon etc) exprimir; (sponge) estrujar; **to s. paste out of a tube** sacar pasta de un tubo apretando **2** vi **to s. in** apretujarse **3** n (a) (pressure) estrujón m; **a s. of lemon** unas gotas de limón (b) (of hand) apretón m; (hug) abrazo m; (crush) apiñamiento m; **credit s.** reducción f de créditos

squid [skwɪd] n calamar m; (small) chipirón m

squint [skwɪnt] **1** n (a) bizquera f; **to have a s.** ser bizco(a) (b) Br (quick look) ojeada f, vistazo m **2** vi (a) ser bizco(a) (b) **to s. at sth** (glance) echar un vistazo a algo; (with eyes half-closed) mirar algo con los ojos entrecerrados

squirm [skwɜːm] vi retorcerse; (with embarrassment) ruborizarse, avergonzarse, Am apenarse

squirrel ['skwɪrəl] n ardilla f

squirt [skwɜːt] **1** n (of liquid) chorro m **2** vt lanzar a chorro **3** vi **to s. out** salir a chorros

St (a) (abbr **Saint**) S./Sto./Sta. (b) (abbr **Street**) c/

stab [stæb] **1** n (with knife) puñalada f; (of pain) punzada f **2** vt apuñalar

stability [stə'bɪlɪtɪ] n estabilidad f

stabilize ['steɪbɪlaɪz] **1** vt estabilizar **2** vi estabilizarse

stable¹ ['steɪbəl] adj estable

stable² ['steɪbəl] n cuadra f, caballeriza f

stack [stæk] **1** n (pile) montón m; Fam **he's got stacks of money** está forrado **2** vt (pile up) amontonar, apilar; Fig **the odds are stacked**

against us todo está en contra nuestra

stadium ['steɪdɪəm] *n* estadio *m*

staff [stɑːf] **1** *n* (**a**) *(personnel)* personal *m*; *Mil* estado *m* mayor; **s. meeting** claustro *m*; *Br* **s. nurse** enfermera cualificada (**b**) *(stick)* bastón *m*; *(of shepherd)* cayado *m* **2** *vt* proveer de personal

stag [stæg] *n* ciervo *m*, venado *m*; *Fam* **s. party** despedida *f* de soltero

stage [steɪdʒ] **1** *n* (**a**) *(platform)* plataforma *f* (**b**) *(in theatre)* escenario *m*; **s. door** entrada *f* de artistas; **s. fright** miedo escénico; **s. manager** director(a) *m,f* de escena (**c**) *(phase) (of development, journey, rocket)* etapa *f*; *(of road, pipeline)* tramo *m*; **at this s. of the negotiations** a estas alturas de las negociaciones; **in stages** por etapas **2** *vt* (**a**) *(play)* poner en escena, montar (**b**) *(arrange)* organizar; *(carry out)* llevar a cabo

stagger ['stægə(r)] **1** *vi* tambalearse **2** *vt* (**a**) *(amaze)* asombrar (**b**) *(hours, work)* escalonar

stagnant ['stægnənt] *adj* estancado(a)

stain [steɪn] **1** *n* (**a**) mancha *f*; **s. remover** quitamanchas *m inv* (**b**) *(dye)* tinte *m* **2** *vt* (**a**) manchar (**b**) *(dye)* teñir **3** *vi* mancharse

stained [steɪnd] *adj* **s. glass window** vidriera *f* de colores

stainless ['steɪnlɪs] *adj (steel)* inoxidable

stair [steə(r)] *n* escalón *m*, peldaño *m*; **stairs** escalera *f*

staircase ['steəkeɪs] *n* escalera *f*

stake¹ [steɪk] **1** *n (stick)* estaca *f*; *(for plant)* rodrigón *m*; *(post)* poste *m* **2** *vt* **to s. (out)** cercar con estacas

stake² [steɪk] **1** *n* (**a**) *(bet)* apuesta *f*; **the issue at s.** el tema en cuestión; **to be at s.** *(at risk)* estar en juego (**b**) *(investment)* interés *m* **2** *vt (bet)* apostar; *(invest)* invertir; **to s. a claim to sth** reivindicar algo

stale [steɪl] *adj (food)* pasado(a); *(bread)* duro(a)

stalemate ['steɪlmeɪt] *n (in chess)* tablas *fpl*; *Fig* **to reach s.** llegar a un punto muerto

stalk¹ [stɔːk] *n (of plant)* tallo *m*; *(of fruit)* rabo *m*

stalk² [stɔːk] **1** *vt (of hunter)* cazar al acecho; *(of animal)* acechar **2** *vi* **he stalked out of the room** salió *esp Esp* enfadado *or esp Am* enojado de la habitación

stall¹ [stɔːl] **1** *n* (**a**) *(in market)* puesto *m*; *(at fair)* caseta *f* (**b**) *(stable)* establo *m*; *(stable compartment)* casilla *f* de establo (**c**) *Br Cin, Th* **the stalls** el patio de butacas
2 *vt (hold off)* retener
3 *vi Aut* pararse, *Esp* calarse; *Av* perder velocidad

stall² [stɔːl] *vi* **to s. (for time)** intentar ganar tiempo

stamina ['stæmɪnə] *n* resistencia *f*

stammer ['stæmə(r)] **1** *n* tartamudeo *m* **2** *vi* tartamudear

stamp [stæmp] **1** *n* (**a**) *(postage stamp)* sello *m*, *Am* estampilla *f*, *CAm, Méx* timbre *m*; **s. collector** filatelista *mf*; *Br* **duty** *or US* **tax** póliza *f*, = impuesto de transmisiones patrimoniales (**b**) *(rubber stamp)* tampón *m*; *(for metals)* cuño *m* (**c**) *(with foot)* patada *f*
2 *vt* (**a**) *(with postage stamp)* poner el sello a; *Br* **stamped addressed envelope**, *US* **self-addressed stamped envelope** sobre franqueado con la dirección del remitente (**b**) *(with rubber stamp)* sellar (**c**) **to s. one's feet** patear; *(in dancing)* zapatear
3 *vi* patear

▶ **stamp out** *vt sep Fig (racism etc)* acabar con; *(rebellion)* sofocar

stampede [stæm'piːd] **1** *n* estampida *f*; *Fig (rush)* desbandada *f* **2** *vi* desbandarse; *Fig (rush)* precipitarse

stance [stæns] *n* postura *f*

stand [stænd] *(pt & pp* **stood**) **1** *n* (**a**) *(position)* posición *f*, postura *f*; **to make a s.** resistir (**b**) *(of lamp, sculpture)* pie *m* (**c**) *(market stall)* puesto *m*; *(at fair)* caseta *f*; *(at exhibition)* stand *m* (**d**) *(platform)* plataforma *f*; *(in stadium)* gradas *fpl*,

Esp graderío *m*; *US (witness box)* estrado *m*

2 *vt* (**a**) *(place)* poner, colocar (**b**) *(tolerate)* aguantar, soportar

3 *vi* (**a**) *(be upright)* estar de pie *or Am* parado(a); *(get up)* levantarse; *(remain upright)* quedarse de pie *or Am* parado(a); **s. still!** ¡estáte quieto(a)! (**b**) *(be situated)* estar, encontrarse (**c**) *(remain valid)* seguir vigente (**d**) **as things s.** tal como están las cosas (**e**) *Pol* presentarse

▸**stand back** *vi (allow sb to pass)* abrir paso

▸**stand by 1** *vi* (**a**) *(do nothing)* quedarse sin hacer nada (**b**) *(be ready)* estar listo(a) **2** *vt insep (person)* apoyar a; *(promise)* cumplir con; *(decision)* atenerse a

▸**stand down** *vi Fig* retirarse

▸**stand for** *vt insep* (**a**) *(mean)* significar (**b**) *(represent)* representar (**c**) *(tolerate)* aguantar

▸**stand in** *vi* sustituir

▸**stand in for** *vt insep* sustituir

▸**stand out** *vi (mountain etc)* destacarse (**against** contra); *Fig (person)* destacar

▸**stand up** *vi (get up)* ponerse de pie, *Am* pararse; *(be standing)* estar de pie; *Fig* **it will s. up to wear and tear** es muy resistente; *Fig* **to s. up for sb** defender a algn; *Fig* **to s. up to sb** hacer frente a algn

standard ['stændəd] **1** *n* (**a**) *(level)* nivel *m*; **s. of living** nivel de vida (**b**) *(criterion)* criterio *m* (**c**) *(norm)* norma *f*, estándar *m* **2** *adj* normal, estándar; **s. lamp** lámpara *f* de pie

standardize ['stændədaɪz] *vt* normalizar

standby ['stændbaɪ] *n* (**a**) *(thing)* recurso *m* (**b**) *(person)* suplente *mf*; **to be on s.** *Mil* estar de retén; *Av* estar en la lista de espera; **s. ticket** billete *m* sin reserva

stand-in ['stændɪn] *n* suplente *mf*; *Cin* doble *mf*

standing ['stændɪŋ] **1** *adj* (**a**) *(not sitting)* de pie; *(upright)* recto(a); **to**

give sb a s. ovation ovacionar a algn de pie; **there was s. room only** no quedaban asientos (**b**) *(committee)* permanente; *(invitation)* permanente; *Br* **s. order** pago fijo **2** *n* (**a**) *(social position)* rango *m* (**b**) *(duration)* duración *f*; *(in job)* antigüedad *f*

standpoint ['stændpɔɪnt] *n* punto *m* de vista

standstill ['stændstɪl] *n* **at a s.** *(car, traffic)* parado(a); *(industry)* paralizado(a); **to come to a s.** *(car, traffic)* pararse; *(industry)* paralizarse

stank [stæŋk] *pt of* **stink**

staple¹ ['steɪpəl] **1** *n (fastener)* grapa *f*, *Chile* corchete *m*, *RP* ganchito *m* **2** *vt* grapar

staple² ['steɪpəl] **1** *adj (food)* básico(a); *(product)* de primera necesidad **2** *n (food)* alimento básico

stapler ['steɪpələ(r)] *n* grapadora *f*, *Am* engrapadora *f*, *Chile* corchetera *f*, *RP* abrochadora *f*

star [stɑː(r)] **1** *n* estrella *f*
2 *adj* estelar
3 *vt Cin* tener como protagonista a
4 *vi Cin* **to s. in a movie** protagonizar una película

starboard ['stɑːbəd] *n* estribor *m*

starch [stɑːtʃ] **1** *n* almidón *m* **2** *vt* almidonar

stare [steə(r)] **1** *n* mirada fija **2** *vi* mirar fijamente

stark [stɑːk] *adj (landscape)* desolado(a); *(décor)* austero(a); **the s. truth** la dura realidad; **s. poverty** la miseria

start [stɑːt] **1** *n* (**a**) *(beginning)* principio *m*, comienzo *m*; *(of race)* salida *f*; **for a s.** para empezar; **from the s.** desde el principio; **to make a fresh s.** volver a empezar (**b**) *(advantage)* ventaja *f* (**c**) *(jump)* sobresalto *m*

2 *vt* (**a**) *(begin)* empezar, comenzar; **to s. doing sth** empezar a hacer algo (**b**) *(cause)* causar, provocar (**c**) *(found)* fundar; **to s. a business** montar un negocio (**d**) *(set in motion)* arrancar

3 *vi* (**a**) *(begin)* empezar, comenzar;

(engine) arrancar; **starting from Monday** a partir del lunes (**b**) *(take fright)* asustarse, sobresaltarse

▸ **start off** *vi* (**a**) *(begin)* empezar, comenzar; **to s. off by/with** empezar por/con (**b**) *(leave)* salir, ponerse en camino

▸ **start up** 1 *vt sep (engine)* arrancar 2 *vi* empezar; *(car)* arrancar

starter ['stɑːtə(r)] *n* (**a**) *Sport (official)* juez *mf* de salida; *(competitor)* competidor(a) *m,f* (**b**) *Aut* motor *m* de arranque (**c**) *Culin* entrada *f*

starting ['stɑːtɪŋ] *n* **s. block** taco *m* de salida; **s. point** punto *m* de partida; **s. post** línea *f* de salida

startle ['stɑːtəl] *vt* asustar

starvation [stɑːˈveɪʃən] *n* hambre *f*

starve [stɑːv] 1 *vt* privar de comida; *Fig* **he was starved of affection** fue privado de cariño 2 *vi* pasar hambre; **to s. to death** morirse de hambre

state [steɪt] 1 *n* (**a**) estado *m*; **s. of emergency** estado de emergencia; **s. of mind** estado de ánimo; **to be in no fit s. to do sth** no estar en condiciones de hacer algo (**b**) **the States** los Estados Unidos; *US* **s. highway** ≃ carretera *f* nacional; *US* **S. Department** Departamento *m* de Estado, = Ministerio de Asuntos *or Am* Relaciones Exteriores estadounidense

2 *adj* (**a**) *Pol* estatal; **s. education** enseñanza pública; **s. ownership** propiedad *f* del Estado (**b**) *(ceremonial)* de gala; **s. visit** visita *f* oficial

3 *vt* declarar, afirmar; *(case)* exponer; *(problem)* plantear

statement ['steɪtmənt] *n* (**a**) declaración *f*; **official s.** comunicado *m* oficial; *Jur* **to make a s.** prestar declaración (**b**) *Fin* estado *m* de cuenta; **monthly s.** balance *m* mensual

statesman ['steɪtsmən] *n* estadista *m*

static ['stætɪk] 1 *adj* estático(a) 2 *n Rad* ruido *m*

station ['steɪʃən] 1 *n* (**a**) estación *f*; *US* **s. wagon** camioneta *f* (**b**) *(position)* puesto *m* (**c**) *(social standing)*

rango *m* 2 *vt (place)* colocar; *Mil* apostar

stationary ['steɪʃənərɪ] *adj (not moving)* inmóvil; *(unchanging)* estacionario(a)

stationer ['steɪʃənə(r)] *n* papelero(a) *m,f*; **s.'s (shop)** papelería *f*

stationery ['steɪʃənərɪ] *n (paper)* papel *m* de escribir; *(pens, ink etc)* artículos *mpl* de escritorio

statistic [stəˈtɪstɪk] *n* estadística *f*

statue ['stætjuː] *n* estatua *f*

stature ['stætʃə(r)] *n (physical build)* estatura *f*; *(reputation)* talla *f*, estatura *f*

status ['steɪtəs] *n* estado *m*; **social s.** estatus *m*; **s. symbol** signo *m* de prestigio; **s. quo** status quo *m*

stave [steɪv] *n Mus* pentagrama *m*

▸ **stave off** *vt sep (repel)* rechazar; *(avoid)* evitar; *(delay)* aplazar

stay¹ [steɪ] 1 *n Esp, Méx* estancia *f, Am* estadía *f*

2 *vi* (**a**) *(remain)* quedarse, permanecer (**b**) *(reside temporarily)* alojarse; **she's staying with us for a few days** ha venido a pasar unos días con nosotros

3 *vt Fig* **to s. the course** aguantar hasta el final; **staying power** resistencia *f*

▸ **stay in** *vi* quedarse en casa

▸ **stay on** *vi* quedarse

▸ **stay out** *vi* **to s. out all night** no volver a casa en toda la noche

▸ **stay up** *vi* no acostarse

stay² [steɪ] *n (rope)* estay *m*, viento *m*

steadily ['stedɪlɪ] *adv (improve)* constantemente; *(walk)* con paso seguro; *(gaze)* fijamente; *(rain, work)* sin parar

steady ['stedɪ] 1 *adj* (**steadier, steadiest**) firme, seguro(a); *(gaze)* fijo(a); *(prices)* estable; *(demand, speed)* constante; *(pace)* regular; *(worker)* aplicado(a); **s. job** empleo fijo

2 *vt (table etc)* estabilizar; *(nerves)* calmar

3 *vi (market)* estabilizarse

steak [steɪk] *n* filete *m*, bistec *m, RP* bife *m*

steal [sti:l] (*pt* **stole**; *pp* **stolen**) **1** *vt* robar; **to s. a glance at sth** echar una mirada furtiva a algo; **to s. the show** llevarse todos los aplausos **2** *vi* (**a**) *(rob)* robar (**b**) *(move quietly)* moverse con sigilo; **to s. away** escabullirse

stealthy ['stelθɪ] *adj* (**stealthier**, **stealthiest**) sigiloso(a), furtivo(a)

steam [sti:m] **1** *n* vapor *m*; *Fam* **to let off s.** desahogarse; **s. engine** máquina *f* de vapor
2 *vt* Culin cocer al vapor
3 *vi* *(give off steam)* echar vapor; *(bowl of soup etc)* humear
▸ **steam up** *vi* *(window etc)* empañarse

steamer ['sti:mə(r)] *n* Naut vapor *m*

steel [sti:l] **1** *n* acero *m*; **s. industry** industria siderúrgica **2** *vt* Fig **to s. oneself to do sth** armarse de valor para hacer algo

steep¹ [sti:p] *adj* *(hill etc)* empinado(a); *Fig (price, increase)* excesivo(a)

steep² [sti:p] *vt* *(washing)* remojar; *(food)* poner en remojo

steeple ['sti:pəl] *n* aguja *f*

steer [stɪə(r)] **1** *vt* dirigir; *(car)* conducir, *Am* manejar; *(ship)* gobernar **2** *vi* *(car)* conducir, *Am* manejar; *Fig* **to s. clear of sth** evitar algo

steering ['stɪərɪŋ] *n* dirección *f*; **assisted s.** dirección asistida; **s. wheel** volante *m*, *Andes* timón *m*

stem [stem] **1** *n* (**a**) *(of plant)* tallo *m*; *(of glass)* pie *m*; *(of pipe)* tubo *m* (**b**) *(of word)* raíz *f*
2 *vi* **to s. from** derivarse de
3 *vt* *(blood)* restañar; *(flood, attack)* contener

stench [stentʃ] *n* hedor *m*

step [step] **1** *n* (**a**) *(of plant)* paso *m*; *(sound)* pisada *f*; **s. by s.** poco a poco (**b**) *(measure)* medida *f*; **a s. in the right direction** un paso acertado (**c**) *(stair)* peldaño *m*, escalón *m* (**d**) **steps** escalera *f* **2** *vi* dar un paso; **s. this way, please** haga el favor de pasar por aquí; **to s. aside** apartarse
▸ **step down** *vi* dimitir

▸ **step forward** *vi* *(volunteer)* ofrecerse
▸ **step in** *vi* intervenir
▸ **step up** *vt sep* aumentar

stepdaughter ['stepdɔ:tə(r)] *n* hijastra *f*

stepfather ['stepfɑ:ðə(r)] *n* padrastro *m*

stepladder ['steplædə(r)] *n* escalera *f* de tijera

stepmother ['stepmʌðə(r)] *n* madrastra *f*

stepson ['stepsʌn] *n* hijastro *m*

stereo ['sterɪəʊ] **1** *n* estéreo *m* **2** *adj* estereo(fónico(a))

stereotype ['sterɪətaɪp] *n* estereotipo *m*

sterile ['steraɪl] *adj* *(barren)* estéril

sterilize ['sterɪlaɪz] *vt* esterilizar

sterling ['stɜːlɪŋ] **1** *n* libras *fpl* esterlinas; **s. silver** plata *f* de ley; **the pound s.** la libra esterlina **2** *adj* *(person, quality)* excelente

stern¹ [stɜːn] *adj* *(severe)* severo(a)

stern² [stɜːn] *n* Naut popa *f*

steroid ['sterɔɪd] *n* esteroide *m*

stethoscope ['steθəskəʊp] *n* estetoscopio *m*

stew [stju:] **1** *n* estofado *m*, cocido *m* **2** *vt* *(meat)* guisar, estofar; *(fruit)* cocer

steward ['stjʊəd] *n* *(on estate)* administrador *m*; *(on ship)* camarero *m*; *(on plane)* auxiliar *m* de vuelo

stewardess ['stjʊədɪs] *n* *(on ship)* camarera *f*; *(on plane)* auxiliar *f* de vuelo, azafata *f*, *Am* aeromoza *f*

stick¹ [stɪk] *n* (**a**) palo *m*; *(walking stick)* bastón *m*; *(of dynamite)* cartucho *m*; *Br Fam* **to give sb s.** dar caña a algn (**b**) *Fam* **to live in the sticks** vivir en el quinto infierno *or Esp* pino

stick² [stɪk] (*pt & pp* **stuck**) **1** *vt* (**a**) *(push)* meter; *(knife)* clavar; **he stuck his head out of the window** asomó la cabeza por la ventana (**b**) *Fam (put)* meter (**c**) *(with glue etc)* pegar (**d**) *Fam (tolerate)* soportar, aguantar **2** *vi* (**a**) *(become attached)* pegarse (**b**) *(window, drawer)* atrancarse; *(machine* *part)* encasquillarse

▸ **stick at** *vt insep* perseverar en

▸ **stick by** *vt insep (friend)* ser fiel a; *(promise)* cumplir con

▸ **stick out 1** *vi (project)* sobresalir; *(be noticeable)* resaltar **2** *vt sep (tongue)* sacar; *Fig* **to s. one's neck out** jugarse el tipo

▸ **stick to** *vt insep (principles)* atenerse a

▸ **stick up 1** *vi (project)* sobresalir; *(hair)* ponerse de punta **2** *vt sep* (a) *(poster)* fijar (b) *(hand etc)* levantar

▸ **stick up for** *vt insep* defender

sticker ['stɪkə(r)] *n (label)* etiqueta adhesiva; *(with slogan)* pegatina *f*

sticky ['stɪkɪ] *adj* (**stickier, stickiest**) pegajoso(a); *(label)* engomado(a); *(weather)* bochornoso(a); *Fam (situation)* difícil

stiff [stɪf] **1** *adj* (a) rígido(a), tieso(a); *(collar, lock)* duro(a); *(joint)* entumecido(a); *(machine part)* atascado(a); **to have a s. neck** tener tortícolis (b) *Fig (test)* difícil; *(punishment)* severo(a); *(price)* excesivo(a); *(drink)* fuerte; *(person) (unnatural)* estirado(a) **2** *n Fam (corpse)* fiambre *m*

stiffen ['stɪfən] **1** *vt (fabric)* reforzar; *(collar)* almidonar; *Fig (resistance)* fortalecer **2** *vi (person)* ponerse tieso(a); *(joints)* entumecerse; *Fig (resistance)* fortalecerse

stifle ['staɪfəl] **1** *vt* sofocar; *(yawn)* reprimir **2** *vi* ahogarse, sofocarse

stigma ['stɪgmə] *n* estigma *m*

still [stɪl] **1** *adv* (a) *(up to this time)* todavía, aún, *Am* siempre (b) *(with comp adj & adv) (even)* aún; **s. colder** aún más frío (c) *(nonetheless)* no obstante, con todo (d) *(however)* sin embargo (e) *(motionless)* quieto; **to stand s.** no moverse **2** *adj (calm)* tranquilo(a); *(peaceful)* sosegado(a); *(silent)* silencioso(a); *(motionless)* inmóvil; *Art* **s. life** naturaleza muerta

stilted ['stɪltɪd] *adj* afectado(a)

stimulant ['stɪmjʊlənt] *n* estimulante *m*

stimulate ['stɪmjʊleɪt] *vt* estimular

stimulus ['stɪmjʊləs] *n (pl* **stimuli** ['stɪmjʊlaɪ]*)* estímulo *m*; *Fig* incentivo *m*

sting [stɪŋ] *(pt & pp* **stung**) **1** *n (part of bee, wasp)* aguijón *m*; *(wound)* picadura *f*; *(burning)* escozor *m*; *Fig (of remorse)* punzada *f*; *Fig (of remark)* sarcasmo *m*

2 *vt* picar; *Fig (conscience)* remorder; *Fig (remark)* herir en lo vivo

3 *vi* picar

stingy ['stɪndʒɪ] *adj* (**stingier, stingiest**) *Fam (person)* tacaño(a); *(amount)* escaso(a); **to be s. with** escatimar

stink [stɪŋk] **1** *n* peste *m*, hedor *m* **2** *vi* (*pt* **stank** *or* **stunk**; *pp* **stunk**) apestar, heder (**of** a)

stipulate ['stɪpjʊleɪt] *vt* estipular

stir [stɜ:(r)] **1** *n Fig* revuelo *m*

2 *vt* (a) *(liquid)* remover (b) *(move)* agitar (c) *Fig (curiosity, interest)* despertar; *(anger)* provocar

3 *vi (move)* rebullirse

▸ **stir up** *vt sep Fig (memories, curiosity)* despertar; *(passions)* excitar; *(anger)* provocar; *(revolt)* fomentar

stirrup ['stɪrəp] *n* estribo *m*

stitch [stɪtʃ] **1** *n* (a) *Sewing* puntada *f*; *(in knitting)* punto *m*; *Med* punto (de sutura); *Fam* **we were in stitches** nos tronchábamos de risa (b) *(pain)* punzada *f* **2** *vt Sewing* coser; *Med* suturar, dar puntos a

stock [stɒk] **1** *n* (a) *(supply)* reserva *f*; *Com (goods)* existencias *fpl*, stock *m*; *(selection)* surtido *m*; **out of s.** agotado(a); **to have sth in s.** tener existencias de algo; *Fig* **to take s. of** evaluar (b) *Fin* capital *m* social; **stocks and shares** acciones *fpl*, valores *mpl*; **S. Exchange** Bolsa *f* (de valores); **s. market** bolsa (c) *Culin* caldo *m*; **s. cube** cubito *m* de caldo (d) *(descent)* estirpe *f*

2 *adj (excuse, response)* de siempre; *(phrase)* gastado(a)

3 *vt* (a) *(have in stock)* tener existencias de (b) *(provide)* abastecer, surtir (**with** de); *(cupboard)* llenar (**with** de)

▸ **stock up** *vi* abastecerse (**on** *or* **with** de)

stockbroker ['stɒkbrəʊkə(r)] *n* corredor(a) *m,f* de Bolsa

stockpile ['stɒkpaɪl] **1** *n* reservas *fpl* **2** *vt* almacenar; *(accumulate)* acumular

stocky ['stɒkɪ] *adj* (**stockier, stockiest**) *(squat)* rechoncho(a); *(heavily built)* fornido(a)

stodgy ['stɒdʒɪ] *adj* (**stodgier, stodgiest**) *(food)* indigesto(a); *Fig (book, person)* pesado(a)

stole¹ [stəʊl] *pt of* **steal**

stole² [stəʊl] *n* estola *f*

stolen ['stəʊlən] *pp of* **steal**

stomach ['stʌmək] **1** *n* estómago *m*; **s. ache** dolor *m* de estómago; **s. upset** trastorno gástrico **2** *vt Fig* aguantar

stone [stəʊn] **1** *n* **(a)** piedra *f*; *(on grave)* lápida *f* **(b)** *(of fruit)* hueso *m*, *RP* carozo *m* **(c)** *Br (weight)* = 6,348 kg **2** *adj* de piedra

stone-cold [stəʊn'kəʊld] *adj* helado(a)

stoned [stəʊnd] *adj Fam (drugged)* colocado(a); *(drunk)* como una cuba

stone-deaf [stəʊn'def] *adj* sordo(a) como una tapia

stony ['stəʊnɪ] *adj* (**stonier, stoniest**) *(ground)* pedregoso(a); *Fig (look, silence)* glacial

stood [stʊd] *pt & pp of* **stand**

stool [stu:l] *n* **(a)** *(seat)* taburete *m* **(b)** *Med* heces *fpl*

stoop [stu:p] *vi* **(a)** *(have a stoop)* andar encorvado(a) **(b)** *(bend)* **to s. down** inclinarse, agacharse **(c)** *Fig* **to s. to** rebajarse a; **he wouldn't s. so low** no se rebajaría tanto

stop [stɒp] **1** *n* **(a)** *(halt)* parada *f*, alto *m*; **to come to a s.** pararse; **to put a s. to sth** poner fin a algo **(b)** *(break)* pausa *f*; *(for refuelling etc)* escala *f* **(c)** *(for bus, tram)* parada *f* **(d)** *(punctuation mark)* punto *m* **2** *vt* **(a)** *(conversation)* interrumpir; *(pain, abuse etc)* poner fin a **(b)** *(payments)* suspender; *(cheque)* anular **(c)** **to s. doing sth** dejar de hacer algo; **s. it!** ¡basta ya! **(d)** *(prevent)* evitar; **to s. sb from doing sth** impedir a algn hacer algo

3 *vi* **(a)** *(person, moving vehicle)* pararse, detenerse **(b)** *(cease)* acabarse, terminar

▸ **stop by** *vi Fam* visitar

▸ **stop off** *vi* pararse un rato

▸ **stop over** *vi (spend the night)* pasar la noche; *(for refuelling etc)* hacer escala

▸ **stop up** *vt sep (hole)* tapar

stopover ['stɒpəʊvə(r)] *n* parada *f*; *Av* escala *f*

stoppage ['stɒpɪdʒ] *n* **(a)** *(of game, payments)* suspensión *f*; *(of work)* paro *m*; *(strike)* huelga *f*; *(deduction)* deducción *f* **(b)** *(blockage)* obstrucción *f*

stopper ['stɒpə(r)] *n* tapón *m*

stopwatch ['stɒpwɒtʃ] *n* cronómetro *m*

storage ['stɔ:rɪdʒ] *n* almacenaje *m*, almacenamiento *m*; **s. battery** acumulador *m*; **s. heater** placa acumuladora

store [stɔ:(r)] **1** *n* **(a)** *(stock)* provisión *f* **(b)** **stores** víveres *mpl* **(c)** *(warehouse)* almacén *m* **(d)** *esp US (shop)* tienda *f*; **department s.** gran almacén *m* **2** *vt* **(a)** *(furniture, computer data)* almacenar; *(keep)* guardar **(b)** **to s. (up)** acumular

storekeeper ['stɔ:ki:pə(r)] *n US* tendero(a) *m,f*

storeroom ['stɔ:ru:m] *n* despensa *f*

storey ['stɔ:rɪ] *n* piso *m*

stork [stɔ:k] *n* cigüeña *f*

storm [stɔ:m] **1** *n* tormenta *f*; *(with wind)* vendaval *m*; *Fig (uproar)* revuelo *m*; *Fig* **she has taken New York by s.** ha cautivado a todo Nueva York **2** *vt* tomar por asalto **3** *vi (with rage)* echar pestes

stormy ['stɔ:mɪ] *adj* (**stormier, stormiest**) *(weather)* tormentoso(a); *Fig (discussion)* acalorado(a); *(relationship)* tempestuoso(a)

story¹ ['stɔ:rɪ] *n* historia *f*; *(tale, account)* relato *m*; *(article)* artículo *m*; *(plot)* trama *f*; *(joke)* chiste *m*; *(rumour)* rumor *m*; **it's a long s.** sería largo de contar; **tall s.** cuento chino

story² ['stɔ:rɪ] *n US* = **storey**

stout [staʊt] **1** *adj* (**a**) *(fat)* gordo(a), corpulento(a) (**b**) *(strong)* fuerte (**c**) *(brave)* valiente; *(determined)* firme **2** *n (beer)* cerveza negra

stove [stəʊv] *n* (**a**) *(for heating)* estufa *f* (**b**) *(cooker)* cocina *f*, *Col*, *Méx*, *Ven* estufa *f*

stow [stəʊ] *vt* (**a**) *(cargo)* estibar (**b**) *(put away)* guardar

▸ **stow away** *vi (on ship, plane)* viajar de polizón

stowaway ['stəʊəweɪ] *n* polizón *mf*

straight [streɪt] **1** *adj* (**a**) *(not bent)* recto(a), derecho(a); *(hair)* liso(a) (**b**) *(honest)* honrado(a); *(answer)* sincero(a); *(refusal)* rotundo(a) **2** *adv* (**a**) *(in a straight line)* en línea recta (**b**) *(directly)* directamente, derecho; **keep s. ahead** sigue todo recto (**c**) **s. away** en seguida

straighten ['streɪtən] *vt (sth bent)* enderezar, poner derecho(a); *(tie, picture)* poner bien; *(hair)* alisar

▸ **straighten out** *vt sep (problem)* resolver

straightforward [streɪt'fɔːwəd] *adj* (**a**) *(honest)* honrado(a); *(sincere)* franco(a) (**b**) *Br (simple)* sencillo(a)

strain¹ [streɪn] **1** *vt* (**a**) *(rope etc)* estirar; *Fig* crear tensiones en (**b**) *Med* torcer(se); *(eyes, voice)* forzar; *(heart)* cansar (**c**) *(liquid)* filtrar; *(vegetables, tea)* colar **2** *vi (pull)* tirar (**at** de) **3** *n* (**a**) tensión *f*; *(effort)* esfuerzo *m* (**b**) *(exhaustion)* agotamiento *m* (**c**) *Med* torcedura *f* (**d**) *Mus* **strains** son *m*

strain² [streɪn] *n* (**a**) *(breed)* raza *f* (**b**) *(streak)* vena *f*

strained ['streɪnd] *adj* (**a**) *(muscle)* torcido(a); *(eyes)* cansado(a); *(voice)* forzado(a) (**b**) *(atmosphere)* tenso(a)

strainer ['streɪnə(r)] *n* colador *m*

strait [streɪt] *n* (**a**) *Geog* estrecho *m* (**b**) *(usu pl) (difficulty)* aprieto *m*; **in dire straits** en un gran aprieto

strand¹ [strænd] *vt Fig (person)* abandonar; **to leave stranded** dejar plantado(a)

strand² [strænd] *n (of thread)* hebra *f*; *(of hair)* pelo *m*

strange [streɪndʒ] *adj* (**a**) *(unknown)* desconocido(a); *(unfamiliar)* nuevo(a) (**b**) *(odd)* raro(a), extraño(a)

stranger ['streɪndʒə(r)] *n (unknown person)* desconocido(a) *m,f*; *(outsider)* forastero(a) *m,f*

strangle ['stræŋgəl] *vt* estrangular

strap [stræp] **1** *n (of leather)* correa *f*; *(on bag)* bandolera *f*; *(on dress, bra)* tirante *m*, *Am* bretel *m* **2** *vt* atar con correa

strategic [strə'tiːdʒɪk] *adj* estratégico(a)

strategy ['strætɪdʒɪ] *n* estrategia *f*

straw [strɔː] *n* (**a**) *(line)* raya *f*; *Fig* **to clutch at straws** agarrarse a un clavo ardiente; *Fam* **that's the last s.!** ¡eso ya es el colmo! (**b**) *(for drinking)* pajita *f*, *Méx* popote *m*

strawberry ['strɔːbərɪ] *n* fresa *f*, *CSur* frutilla *f*

stray [streɪ] **1** *vi (from path)* desviarse; *(get lost)* extraviarse **2** *n* animal extraviado **3** *adj (bullet)* perdido(a); *(animal)* callejero(a)

streak [striːk] **1** *n* (**a**) *(line)* raya *f*; **s. of lightning** rayo *m* (**b**) *(in hair)* reflejo *m* (**c**) *Fig (of genius etc)* vena *f*; *Fig (of luck)* racha *f* **2** *vt* rayar (**with** de) **3** *vi* **to s. past** pasar como un rayo

stream [striːm] **1** *n* (**a**) *(brook)* arroyo *m*, riachuelo *m* (**b**) *(of water, air)* flujo *m*; *(of blood)* chorro *m*; *(of light)* raudal *m* (**c**) *(of people)* oleada *f* **2** *vi* (**a**) *(liquid)* correr (**b**) **to s. in/out/past** *(people etc)* entrar/salir/pasar en tropel

streamer ['striːmə(r)] *n (paper ribbon)* serpentina *f*

streamlined ['striːmlaɪnd] *adj* (**a**) *(car)* aerodinámico(a) (**b**) *(system, method)* racionalizado(a)

street [striːt] *n* calle *f*; **the man in the s.** el hombre de la calle; **s. map, s. plan** (plano *m*) callejero *m*

streetcar ['striːtkɑː(r)] *n US* tranvía *m*

strength [streŋθ] *n* (**a**) fuerza *f*; *(of*

rope etc) resistencia *f*; *(of emotion, colour)* intensidad *f*; *(of alcohol)* graduación *f* (**b**) *(power)* poder *m* (**c**) *(ability)* punto *m* fuerte

strengthen ['streŋθən] **1** *vt* (**a**) reforzar; *(character)* fortalecer (**b**) *(intensify)* intensificar **2** *vi* (**a**) *(gen)* reforzarse (**b**) *(intensify)* intensificarse

strenuous ['strenjʊəs] *adj* (**a**) *(denial)* enérgico(a); *(effort, life)* intenso(a) (**b**) *(exhausting)* fatigoso(a), cansado(a)

stress [stres] **1** *n* (**a**) *Tech* tensión *f* (**b**) *Med* estrés *m* (**c**) *(emphasis)* hincapié *m*; *(on word)* acento *m* **2** *vt (emphasize)* subrayar; *(word)* acentuar

stressful ['stresfʊl] *adj* estresante

stretch [stretʃ] **1** *vt (elastic)* estirar; *(wings)* desplegar

2 *vi (elastic)* estirarse; *Fig* **my money won't s. to it** mi dinero no me llegará para eso

3 *n* (**a**) *(length)* trecho *m*, tramo *m* (**b**) *(of land)* extensión *f*; *(of time)* intervalo *m*

▸ **stretch out 1** *vt sep (arm, hand)* alargar; *(legs)* estirar **2** *vi* (**a**) *(person)* estirarse (**b**) *(countryside, years etc)* extenderse

stretcher ['stretʃə(r)] *n* camilla *f*

stricken ['strɪkən] *adj (with grief)* afligido(a); *(with illness)* aquejado(a); *(by disaster etc)* afectado(a); *(damaged)* dañado(a)

strict [strɪkt] *adj* (**a**) estricto(a) (**b**) *(absolute)* absoluto(a)

strictly ['strɪktlɪ] *adv* (**a**) *(categorically)* terminantemente (**b**) *(precisely)* estrictamente; **s. speaking** en sentido estricto

stride [straɪd] **1** *n* zancada *f*, tranco *m*; *Fig (progress)* progresos *mpl* **2** *vi (pt* **strode**; *pp* **stridden** ['strɪdən]) **to s. (along)** andar a zancadas

strike [straɪk] *(pt & pp* **struck**) **1** *vt* (**a**) *(hit)* pegar, golpear (**b**) *(collide with)* chocar contra; *(of bullet, lightning)* alcanzar (**c**) *(match)* encender, *Am* prender (**d**) **the clock struck three** el reloj dio las tres (**e**) *(oil, gold)* descubrir (**f**) *(impress)* impresionar; **it strikes**

me ... me parece ...

2 *vi* (**a**) *(attack)* atacar; *(disaster)* sobrevenir (**b**) *(clock)* dar la hora (**c**) *(workers)* declararse en huelga

3 *n* (**a**) *(by workers)* huelga *f*; **to call a s.** convocar una huelga (**b**) *Mil* ataque *m*

▸ **strike back** *vi* devolver el golpe

▸ **strike down** *vt sep* fulminar, abatir

▸ **strike out 1** *vt sep (cross out)* tachar **2** *vi* **to s. out at sb** arremeter contra algn

▸ **strike up** *vt insep* (**a**) *(friendship)* trabar; *(conversation)* entablar (**b**) *(tune)* empezar a tocar

striker ['straɪkə(r)] *n* (**a**) *(worker)* huelguista *mf* (**b**) *Fam Ftb* marcador(a) *m,f*

striking ['straɪkɪŋ] *adj (eye-catching)* llamativo(a); *(noticeable)* notable; *(impressive)* impresionante

string [strɪŋ] **1** *n* (**a**) *(cord)* cuerda *f*; *Fig* **to pull strings for sb** enchufar a algn; **s. bean** judía *f* verde, *Bol, RP* chaucha *f*, *CAm* ejote *m*, *Col, Cuba* habichuela *f*, *Chile* poroto *m* verde, *Ven* vainita *f* (**b**) *(of events)* cadena *f*; *(of lies)* sarta *f* (**c**) *(of racket, guitar)* cuerda *f*; *Mus* **the strings** los instrumentos de cuerda

2 *vt (pt & pp* **strung**) (**a**) *(beads)* ensartar (**b**) *(racket etc)* encordar (**c**) *(beans)* quitar la hebra a

stringed [strɪŋd] *adj (instrument)* de cuerda

stringent ['strɪndʒənt] *adj* severo(a), estricto(a)

strip¹ [strɪp] **1** *vt* (**a**) *(person)* desnudar; *(bed)* quitar la ropa de; *(paint)* rascar, quitar, *Am* sacar (**b**) *Tech* **to s. (down)** desmontar **2** *vi (undress)* desnudarse; *(perform striptease)* hacer un striptease

▸ **strip off 1** *vt sep* quitar, *Am* sacar **2** *vi (undress)* desnudarse

strip² [strɪp] *n* tira *f*; *(of land)* franja *f*; *(of metal)* fleje *m*; *Br* **football s.** indumentaria *f*; **s. cartoon** historieta *f*; **s. lighting** alumbrado *m* fluorescente; **to tear sb off a s.** echar una bronca a algn

stripe [straɪp] n raya f; Mil galón m

striped [straɪpt] adj rayado(a), a rayas

strive [straɪv] (pt **strove**; pp **striven** ['strɪvən]) vi **to s. to do sth** esforzarse por hacer algo

strode [strəʊd] pt of **stride**

stroke [strəʊk] 1 n (a) **a s. of luck** un golpe de suerte (b) (of pen) trazo m; (of brush) pincelada f (c) (caress) caricia f (d) Med apoplejía f 2 vt acariciar

stroll [strəʊl] 1 vi dar un paseo 2 n paseo m

stroller ['strəʊlə(r)] n US (for baby) cochecito m

strong [strɒŋ] 1 adj (a) fuerte (b) (durable) sólido(a) (c) (firm, resolute) firme (d) (colour) intenso(a); (light) brillante 2 adv fuerte; **to be going s.** (business) ir fuerte; (elderly person) conservarse bien

strove [strəʊv] pt of **strive**

struck [strʌk] pt & pp of **strike**

structure ['strʌktʃə(r)] n estructura f; (constructed thing) construcción f; (building) edificio m

struggle ['strʌgəl] 1 vi luchar 2 n lucha f; (physical fight) pelea f

strung [strʌŋ] pt & pp of **string**

strut [strʌt] vi pavonearse

stub [stʌb] 1 n (of cigarette) colilla f; (of pencil) cabo m; (of cheque) matriz f 2 vt (a) (strike) golpear (b) **to s. (out)** apagar

stubble ['stʌbəl] n (in field) rastrojo m; (on chin) barba f de tres días

stubborn ['stʌbən] adj (a) terco(a), testarudo(a) (b) (stain) difícil (c) (refusal) rotundo(a)

stuck [stʌk] pt & pp of **stick²**

stuck-up [stʌk'ʌp] adj Fam creído(a)

stud¹ [stʌd] 1 n (on clothing) tachón m; (on football boots) Esp taco m, RP tapón m; (on shirt) botonadura f 2 vt (decorate) tachonar (**with** de); Fig (dot, cover) salpicar (**with** de)

stud² [stʌd] n (horse) semental m

student ['stjuːdənt] n estudiante mf; **s. teacher** profesor(a) m,f en prácticas

studio ['stjuːdɪəʊ] n TV, Cin estudio m;

(artist's) taller m; **s. (apartment** or Br **flat)** estudio

studious ['stjuːdɪəs] adj estudioso(a)

study ['stʌdɪ] 1 vt estudiar; (facts etc) examinar, investigar; (behaviour) observar

2 vi estudiar; **to s. to be a doctor** estudiar para médico

3 n (a) estudio m; **s. group** grupo m de trabajo (b) (room) despacho m, estudio m

stuff [stʌf] 1 vt (a) (container) llenar (**with** de); Culin rellenar (**with** con or de); (animal) disecar (b) (cram) atiborrar (**with** de) 2 n Fam (a) (substance) cosa f (b) (things) cosas fpl

stuffing ['stʌfɪŋ] n Culin relleno m

stuffy ['stʌfɪ] adj (**stuffier, stuffiest**) (a) (room) mal ventilado(a); (atmosphere) cargado(a) (b) (pompous) estirado(a); (narrow-minded) de miras estrechas

stumble ['stʌmbəl] vi tropezar, dar un traspié; Fig **to s. across** or **on** or **upon** tropezar or dar con

stump [stʌmp] 1 n (a) (of pencil) cabo m; (of tree) tocón m; (of arm, leg) muñón m (b) (in cricket) estaca f 2 vt (puzzle) confundir; **to be stumped** estar perplejo(a)

stun [stʌn] vt (of blow) aturdir; Fig (of news etc) sorprender

stung [stʌŋ] pt & pp of **sting**

stunk [stʌŋk] pt & pp of **stink**

stunning ['stʌnɪŋ] adj (blow) duro(a); (news) sorprendente; Fam (woman, outfit) fenomenal

stunt¹ [stʌnt] vt (growth) atrofiar

stunt² [stʌnt] n (a) Av acrobacia f (b) **publicity s.** truco publicitario (c) Cin escena peligrosa; **s. man** doble m

stupid ['stjuːpɪd] adj estúpido(a), imbécil

stupidity [stjuːˈpɪdɪtɪ] n estupidez f

sturdy ['stɜːdɪ] adj (**sturdier, sturdiest**) robusto(a), fuerte; (resistance) enérgico(a)

stutter ['stʌtə(r)] 1 vi tartamudear 2 n tartamudeo m

sty [staɪ] n (pen) pocilga f

style [staɪl] **1** n (**a**) estilo m; (of dress) modelo m (**b**) (fashion) moda f (**c**) **to live in s.** (elegance) vivir a lo grande **2** vt (hair) marcar

stylish ['staɪlɪʃ] adj con estilo

sub- [sʌb] prefix sub-

subconscious [sʌb'kɒnʃəs] **1** adj subconsciente **2** n **the s.** el subconsciente

subdue [səb'djuː] vt (**a**) (nation, people) sojuzgar (**b**) (feelings) dominar (**c**) (colour, light) atenuar

subject 1 n ['sʌbdʒɪkt] (**a**) (citizen) súbdito m (**b**) (topic) tema m; **s. matter** materia f; (contents) contenido m (**c**) Educ asignatura f (**d**) Ling sujeto m
2 adj ['sʌbdʒɪkt] **s. to** (law, tax) sujeto(a) a; (conditional upon) previo(a) **3** vt [səb'dʒekt] someter

subjective [səb'dʒektɪv] adj subjetivo(a)

subjunctive [səb'dʒʌŋktɪv] **1** adj subjuntivo(a) **2** n subjuntivo m

sublime [sə'blaɪm] adj sublime

submarine ['sʌbməriːn] n submarino m

submerge [səb'mɜːdʒ] vt sumergir; (flood) inundar; Fig **submerged in ...** sumido(a) en ...

submissive [səb'mɪsɪv] adj sumiso(a)

submit [səb'mɪt] **1** vt (**a**) (present) presentar (**b**) (subject) someter (**to** a) **2** vi (surrender) rendirse

subordinate [sə'bɔːdɪnɪt] adj & n subordinado(a) (m,f)

subscribe [səb'skraɪb] vi (magazine) suscribirse (**to** a); (opinion, theory) adherirse (**to** a)

subscriber [səb'skraɪbə(r)] n abonado(a) m,f

subscription [səb'skrɪpʃən] n (to magazine) suscripción f; (to club) cuota f

subsequent ['sʌbsɪkwənt] adj subsiguiente

subside [səb'saɪd] vi (land) hundirse; (floodwater) bajar; (wind, anger) amainar

subsidence [səb'saɪdəns] n (of land) hundimiento m; (of floodwater) bajada f; (of wind) amaine m

subsidiary [sʌb'sɪdɪərɪ] **1** adj (role) secundario(a) **2** n Com sucursal f, filial f

subsidize ['sʌbsɪdaɪz] vt subvencionar

subsidy ['sʌbsɪdɪ] n subvención f

substance ['sʌbstəns] n (**a**) sustancia f (**b**) (essence) esencia f (**c**) **a woman of s.** (wealth) una mujer acaudalada

substantial [səb'stænʃəl] adj (**a**) (solid) sólido(a) (**b**) (sum, loss) importante; (difference, improvement) notable; (meal) abundante

substitute ['sʌbstɪtjuːt] **1** vt sustituir; **to s. X for Y** sustituir X por Y **2** n (person) suplente mf; (thing) sucedáneo m

substitution [sʌbstɪ'tjuːʃən] n sustitución f; Sport sustitución f, cambio m

subtitle ['sʌbtaɪtəl] n subtítulo m

subtle ['sʌtəl] adj sutil; (taste) delicado(a); (remark) ingenioso(a); (irony) fino(a)

subtotal ['sʌbtəʊtəl] n subtotal m

subtract [səb'trækt] vt restar

subtraction [səb'trækʃən] n resta f

suburb ['sʌbɜːb] n barrio periférico; **the suburbs** las afueras

suburban [sə'bɜːbən] adj suburbano(a)

suburbia [sə'bɜːbɪə] n barrios residenciales periféricos

subversive [səb'vɜːsɪv] adj & n subversivo(a) (m,f)

subway ['sʌbweɪ] n (**a**) Br (underpass) paso subterráneo (**b**) US (underground railway) metro m, RP subte m

succeed [sək'siːd] **1** vi (**a**) (person) tener éxito; (plan) salir bien; **to s. in doing sth** conseguir hacer algo (**b**) (follow after) suceder; **to s. to** (throne) suceder a **2** vt (monarch) suceder a

success [sək'ses] n éxito m

successful [sək'sesful] adj de éxito, exitoso(a); (business) próspero(a);

(marriage) feliz; **to be s. in doing sth** lograr hacer algo

successfully [sək'sesfʊlɪ] *adv* con éxito

succession [sək'seʃən] *n* sucesión *f*, serie *f*; **in s.** sucesivamente

successive [sək'sesɪv] *adj* sucesivo(a), consecutivo(a)

successor [sək'sesə(r)] *n* sucesor(a) *m,f*

succumb [sə'kʌm] *vi* sucumbir (**to** a)

such [sʌtʃ] **1** *adj* (**a**) *(of that sort)* tal, semejante; **artists s. as Monet** artistas como Monet; **at s. and s. a time** a tal hora; **in s. a way that** de tal manera que (**b**) *(so much, so great)* tanto(a); **he's always in s. a hurry** siempre anda con tanta prisa; **she was in s. pain** sufría tanto **2** *adv (so very)* tan; **it's s. a long time ago** hace tanto tiempo; **she's s. a clever woman** es una mujer tan inteligente; **s. a lot of books** tantos libros; **we had s. good weather** hizo un tiempo tan bueno

suck [sʌk] **1** *vt (by pump)* aspirar; *(liquid)* sorber; *(lollipop, blood)* chupar **2** *vi (person)* chupar; *(baby)* mamar

▶ **suck in** *vt sep (of whirlpool)* tragar

suckle ['sʌkəl] *vt (mother)* amamantar

suction ['sʌkʃən] *n* succión *f*

sudden ['sʌdən] *adj* (**a**) *(hurried)* súbito(a), repentino(a) (**b**) *(unexpected)* imprevisto(a) (**c**) *(abrupt)* brusco(a); **all of a s.** de repente

suddenly ['sʌdənlɪ] *adv* de repente

suds [sʌdz] *npl* espuma *f* de jabón, jabonaduras *fpl*

sue [su:, sju:] *Jur* **1** *vt* demandar **2** *vi* presentar una demanda; **to s. for divorce** solicitar el divorcio

suede [sweɪd] *n* ante *m*, gamuza *f*; *(for gloves)* cabritilla *f*

suffer ['sʌfə(r)] **1** *vt* (**a**) sufrir (**b**) *(tolerate)* aguantar, soportar **2** *vi* sufrir; **to s. from** sufrir de

sufferer ['sʌfərə(r)] *n Med* enfermo(a) *m,f*

suffering ['sʌfərɪŋ] *n (affliction)* sufrimiento *m*; *(pain, torment)* dolor *m*

sufficient [sə'fɪʃənt] *adj* suficiente, bastante

sufficiently [sə'fɪʃəntlɪ] *adv* suficientemente, bastante

suffix ['sʌfɪks] *n Ling* sufijo *m*

suffocate ['sʌfəkeɪt] **1** *vt* asfixiar **2** *vi* asfixiarse

sugar ['ʃʊgə(r)] **1** *n* azúcar *m or f*; **s. beet** remolacha *f* (azucarera), *Méx* betabel *m* (azucarero); **s. bowl** azucarero *m*; **s. cane** caña *f* de azúcar **2** *vt* azucarar, echar azúcar a

suggest [sə'dʒest] *vt* (**a**) *(propose)* sugerir (**b**) *(advise)* aconsejar (**c**) *(indicate, imply)* indicar

suggestion [sə'dʒestʃən] *n* (**a**) *(proposal)* sugerencia *f* (**b**) *(trace)* sombra *f*; *(small amount)* toque *m*

suggestive [sə'dʒestɪv] *adj* (**a**) *(reminiscent, thought-provoking)* sugerente (**b**) *(remark)* insinuante

suicide ['sju:ɪsaɪd] *n* suicidio *m*

suit [su:t, sju:t] **1** *n* (**a**) *(clothes)* traje *m*, *Andes, RP* terno *m* (**b**) *Jur* pleito *m* (**c**) *Cards* palo *m* **2** *vt* (**a**) *(be convenient to)* convenir a, venir bien a (**b**) *(be right, appropriate for)* ir bien a; **red really suits you** el rojo te favorece mucho; **they are well suited** están hechos el uno para el otro (**c**) *(please)* **s. yourself!** ¡como quieras!

suitable ['sju:təbəl] *adj (convenient)* conveniente; *(appropriate)* adecuado(a); **the most s. woman for the job** la mujer más indicada para el puesto

suitcase ['su:tkeɪs] *n* maleta *f*, *Méx* petaca *f*, *RP* valija *f*

suite [swi:t] *n* (**a**) *(of furniture)* juego *m* (**b**) *(of hotel rooms, music)* suite *f*

sulk [sʌlk] *vi* enfurruñarse

sullen ['sʌlən] *adj* hosco(à); *(sky)* plomizo(a)

sultana [sʌl'tɑ:nə] *n esp Br (raisin)* pasa *f* de Esmirna

sum [sʌm] *n* (**a**) *(arithmetic problem, amount)* suma *f* (**b**) *(total amount)* total *m*; *(of money)* importe *m*

▶ **sum up 1** *vt sep* resumir **2** *vi* resumir; **to s. up ...** en resumidas cuentas ...

summarize ['sʌmərɑɪz] *vt & vi* resumir

summary ['sʌmərɪ] **1** *n* resumen *m* **2** *adj* sumario(a)

summer ['sʌmə(r)] **1** *n* verano *m* **2** *adj (holiday etc)* de verano; *(weather)* veraniego(a); *(resort)* de veraneo

summertime ['sʌmətɑɪm] *n* verano *m*

summit ['sʌmɪt] *n* (**a**) *(of mountain)* cima *f*, cumbre *f* (**b**) *Pol* **s. (meeting)** cumbre *f*

summon ['sʌmən] *vt* (**a**) *(meeting, person)* convocar (**b**) *(aid)* pedir (**c**) *Jur* citar

▸ **summon up** *vt sep (resources)* reunir; **to s. up one's courage** armarse de valor

summons ['sʌmənz] **1** *n sing* (**a**) *(call)* llamada *f*, llamamiento *m* (**b**) *Jur* citación *f* judicial **2** *vt Jur* citar

sumptuous ['sʌmptjʊəs] *adj* suntuoso(a)

sun [sʌn] **1** *n* sol *m* **2** *vt* **to s. oneself** tomar el sol

sunbathe ['sʌnbeɪð] *vi* tomar el sol

sunburn ['sʌnbɜːn] *n (burn)* quemadura *f* de sol

sunburnt ['sʌnbɜːnt] *adj (burnt)* quemado(a) por el sol; *(tanned)* bronceado(a)

Sunday ['sʌndɪ] *n* domingo *m inv*; **S. newspaper** periódico *m* del domingo; **S. school** catequesis *f*

sundial ['sʌndɑɪəl] *n* reloj *m* de sol

sunflower ['sʌnflaʊə(r)] *n* girasol *m*

sung [sʌŋ] *pp of* **sing**

sunglasses ['sʌnglɑːsɪz] *npl* gafas *fpl* *or Am* anteojos de sol

sunk [sʌŋk] *pp of* **sink²**

sunlamp ['sʌnlæmp] *n* lámpara *f* solar

sunlight ['sʌnlɑɪt] *n* sol *m*, luz *f* del sol

sunny ['sʌnɪ] *adj* (**sunnier, sunniest**) (**a**) *(day)* de sol; *(place)* soleado(a); **it is s.** hace sol (**b**) *Fig (smile, disposition)* alegre; *(future)* prometedor(a)

sunrise ['sʌnrɑɪz] *n* salida *f* del sol

sunroof ['sʌnruːf] *n* *Aut* techo corredizo

sunset ['sʌnset] *n* puesta *f* del sol

sunshade ['sʌnʃeɪd] *n* sombrilla *f*

sunshine ['sʌnʃɑɪn] *n* sol *m*, luz *f* del sol

sunstroke ['sʌnstrəʊk] *n* insolación *f*

suntan ['sʌntæn] *n* bronceado *m*; **s. oil** crema protectora; **s. lotion** (aceite *m*) bronceador *m*

super ['suːpə(r)] *adj Fam* genial, *Am* salvo *RP* chévere, *Méx* padre, *RP* bárbaro(a)

super- ['suːpə(r)] *prefix* super-, sobre-

superb [sʊ'pɜːb] *adj* espléndido(a)

superficial [suːpə'fɪʃəl] *adj* superficial

superfluous [suː'pɜːfluəs] *adj* sobrante, superfluo(a); **to be s.** sobrar

superintendent [suːpərɪn'tendənt] *n* (**a**) *(police officer) (in UK)* comisario(a) *m,f*; *(in US)* comisario(a) *m,f* jefe (**b**) *US (of apartment building)* portero(a) *m,f*

superior [suː'pɪərɪə(r)] **1** *adj* (**a**) superior (**b**) *(haughty)* altivo(a) **2** *n* superior(a) *m,f*

superiority [suːpɪərɪ'ɒrɪtɪ] *n* superioridad *f*

superlative [suː'pɜːlətɪv] **1** *adj* superlativo(a) **2** *n Ling* superlativo *m*

supermarket ['suːpəmɑːkɪt] *n* supermercado *m*

supernatural [suːpə'nætʃərəl] **1** *adj* sobrenatural **2** *n* **the s.** lo sobrenatural

superpower ['suːpəpaʊə(r)] *n Pol* superpotencia *f*

supersonic [suːpə'sɒnɪk] *adj* supersónico(a)

superstition [suːpə'stɪʃən] *n* superstición *f*

superstitious [suːpə'stɪʃəs] *adj* supersticioso(a)

supervise ['suːpəvɑɪz] *vt* supervisar; *(watch over)* vigilar

supervisor ['suːpəvɑɪzə(r)] *n* supervisor(a) *m,f*

supper ['sʌpə(r)] *n* cena *f*; **to have s.** cenar

supple ['sʌpəl] *adj* flexible

supplement 1 n ['sʌplɪmənt] suplemento m **2** vt ['sʌplɪment] complementar

supplementary [sʌplɪ'mentərɪ] adj adicional

supplier [sə'plaɪə(r)] n suministrador(a) m,f; Com proveedor(a) m,f

supply [sə'plaɪ] **1** n (a) suministro m; Com provisión f; (stock) surtido m; **s. and demand** oferta f y demanda (b) **supplies** (food) víveres mpl; Mil pertrechos mpl **2** vt (a) (provide) suministrar (b) (with provisions) aprovisionar (c) (information) facilitar (d) Com surtir

support [sə'pɔːt] **1** n (a) (moral) apoyo m (b) (funding) ayuda económica **2** vt (a) (weight etc) sostener (b) Fig (back) apoyar; (substantiate) respaldar (c) Sport ser (hincha) de (d) (sustain) mantener; (feed) alimentar

supporter [sə'pɔːtə(r)] n Pol partidario(a) m,f; Sport hincha mf

supportive [sə'pɔːtɪv] adj **he was s.** apoyó mucho, fue muy comprensivo

suppose [sə'pəʊz] vt suponer; (presume) creer; **I s. not/so** supongo que no/sí; **you're not supposed to smoke in here** no está permitido fumar aquí dentro; **you're supposed to be in bed** deberías estar acostado(a) ya

suppress [sə'pres] vt suprimir; (feelings, laugh etc) contener; (news, truth) callar; (revolt) sofocar

supreme [sʊ'priːm] adj supremo(a); **with s. indifference** con total indiferencia; US Jur **S. Court** Tribunal m Supremo, Am Corte f Suprema

surcharge ['sɜːtʃɑːdʒ] n recargo m

sure [ʃʊə(r)] **1** adj (a) seguro(a); **I'm s. (that) ...** estoy seguro(a) de que ...; **make s. that it's ready** asegúrate de que esté listo; **s. of oneself** seguro(a) de sí mismo (b) Fam **s. thing!** ¡claro!; US **it s. is cold** qué frío que hace **2** adv (a) (of course) claro (b) (certainly) seguro (c) **s. enough** efectivamente

surely ['ʃʊəlɪ] adv (without a doubt)

sin duda; **s. not!** ¡no puede ser!

surf [sɜːf] **1** n (waves) oleaje m; (foam) espuma f
2 vt Comput **to s. the Net** navegar por Internet
3 vi Sport hacer surf

surface ['sɜːfɪs] **1** n superficie f; (of road) firme m
2 adj superficial; **s. area** área f de la superficie; **by s. mail** por vía terrestre or marítima
3 vt (road) revestir
4 vi (submarine etc) salir a la superficie; Fam (wake up) levantarse

surfboard ['sɜːfbɔːd] n tabla f de surf

surfing ['sɜːfɪŋ] n surf m, surfing m

surge [sɜːdʒ] **1** n (a) (growth) alza f (b) (of sea, sympathy) oleada f; Fig (of anger, energy) arranque m **2** vi **to s. forward** (people) avanzar en tropel

surgeon ['sɜːdʒən] n cirujano(a) m,f

surgery ['sɜːdʒərɪ] n (a) (operation) cirugía f (b) Br (consulting room) consultorio m; **s. hours** horas fpl de consulta

surgical ['sɜːdʒɪkəl] adj quirúrgico(a); **s. spirit** alcohol m de 90°

surly ['sɜːlɪ] adj (**surlier, surliest**) (bad-tempered) hosco(a), malhumorado(a); (rude) maleducado(a)

surname ['sɜːneɪm] n apellido m

surpass [sɜː'pɑːs] vt superar

surplus ['sɜːpləs] **1** n (of goods) excedente m; (of budget) superávit m
2 adj excedente

surprise [sə'praɪz] **1** n sorpresa f; **to take sb by s.** Esp coger or Am agarrar desprevenido(a) a algn
2 adj (visit) inesperado(a); **s. attack** ataque m sorpresa
3 vt (astonish) sorprender; **I'm not surprised that ...** no me extraña que ...

surprising [sə'praɪzɪŋ] adj sorprendente

surrender [sə'rendə(r)] **1** n Mil rendición f; (of weapons) entrega f; Ins rescate m
2 vt Mil rendir; (right) renunciar a
3 vi (give in) rendirse

surrogate ['sʌrəgɪt] *n Fml* substituto(a) *m,f*; **s. mother** madre *f* de alquiler

surround [sə'raʊnd] **1** *n* marco *m*, borde *m* **2** *vt* rodear

surrounding [sə'raʊndɪŋ] **1** *adj* circundante **2** *npl* **surroundings** *(of place)* alrededores *mpl*, cercanías *fpl*

surveillance [sɜ:'veɪləns] *n* vigilancia *f*

survey 1 *n* ['sɜ:veɪ] **(a)** *(of building)* inspección *f*; *(of land)* reconocimiento *m* **(b)** *(of trends etc)* encuesta *f* **(c)** *(overall view)* panorama *m* **2** *vt* [sə'veɪ] **(a)** *(building)* inspeccionar; *(land)* medir **(b)** *(trends etc)* hacer una encuesta sobre **(c)** *(look at)* contemplar

surveyor [sə'veɪə(r)] *n* agrimensor(a) *m,f*; **quantity s.** aparejador(a) *m,f*

survival [sə'vaɪvəl] *n* supervivencia *f*

survive [sə'vaɪv] **1** *vi* sobrevivir; *(remain)* perdurar **2** *vt* sobrevivir a

survivor [sə'vaɪvə(r)] *n* superviviente *mf*

susceptible [sə'septəbəl] *adj (to attack)* susceptible **(to** a); *(to illness)* propenso(a) **(to** a)

suspect 1 *adj* ['sʌspekt] *(dubious)* sospechoso(a)
2 *n* ['sʌspekt] sospechoso(a) *m,f*
3 *vt* [sə'spekt] **(a)** *(person)* sospechar **(of** de); *(plot, motives)* recelar de **(b)** *(think likely)* imaginar, creer

suspend [sə'spend] *vt* suspender; *(pupil)* expulsar por un tiempo

suspense [sə'spens] *n (uncertainty)* incertidumbre *f*; *(in movie)* Esp suspense *m*, Am suspenso *m*; **to keep sb in s.** mantener a algn en la incertidumbre

suspicion [sə'spɪʃən] *n* **(a)** sospecha *f*; *(mistrust)* recelo *m*; *(doubt)* duda *f* **(b)** *(trace)* pizca *f*

suspicious [sə'spɪʃəs] *adj* **(a)** *(arousing suspicion)* sospechoso(a) **(b)** *(distrustful)* receloso(a); **to be s. of sb** desconfiar de algn

sustain [sə'steɪn] *vt* **(a)** sostener **(b)** *(nourish)* sustentar **(c)** *Jur (objection)* admitir **(d)** *(injury etc)* sufrir

swagger ['swægə(r)] **1** *n* pavoneo *m* **2** *vi* pavonearse

swallow¹ ['swɒləʊ] **1** *n (of drink, food)* trago *m*
2 *vt* **(a)** *(drink, food)* tragar **(b)** *Fig (believe)* tragarse
3 *vi* tragar

▸ **swallow up** *vt sep Fig* **(a)** *(engulf)* tragar **(b)** *(eat up)* consumir

swallow² ['swɒləʊ] *n Orn* golondrina *f*

swam [swæm] *pt of* **swim**

swamp [swɒmp] **1** *n* ciénaga *f* **2** *vt* **(a)** *(boat)* hundir **(b)** *Fig* inundar **(with** or **by** de)

swan [swɒn] **1** *n* cisne *m* **2** *vi Fam* **to s. around** pavonearse; **to s. around doing nothing** hacer el vago

swap [swɒp] **1** *n Fam* intercambio *m* **2** *vt* cambiar

▸ **swap round, swap over** *vt sep (switch)* cambiar

swarm [swɔ:m] **1** *n* enjambre *m*, **2** *vi (bees)* enjambrar; *Fig* **Neath was swarming with tourists** Neath estaba lleno de turistas

swat [swɒt] *vt* aplastar

sway [sweɪ] **1** *n* **(a)** *(movement)* balanceo *m* **(b)** **to hold s. over sb** dominar a algn
2 *vi* **(a)** *(swing)* balancearse, mecerse **(b)** *(totter)* tambalearse
3 *vt Fig (persuade)* convencer

swear [sweə(r)] *(pt* swore; *pp* sworn*)*
1 *vt (vow)* jurar; **to s. an oath** prestar juramento **2** *vi* **(a)** *(formally)* jurar, prestar juramento **(b)** *(curse)* soltar tacos, decir palabrotas; *(blaspheme)* jurar; **to s. at sb** echar pestes contra algn

swearword ['sweəwɜ:d] *n* palabrota *f*

sweat [swet] **1** *n (perspiration)* sudor *m*; *Fam (hard work)* trabajo duro
2 *vi (perspire)* sudar; *Fig (work hard)* sudar la gota gorda
3 *vt Fam* **to s. it out** aguantar

sweater ['swetə(r)] *n* suéter *m*, *Esp* jersey *m*, *RP* pulóver *m*

sweatshirt ['swetʃɜ:t] *n* sudadera *f*, *Col, RP* buzo *m*

Swede [swi:d] *n (person)* sueco(a) *m,f*

Sweden ['swiːdən] *n* Suecia

Swedish ['swiːdɪʃ] **1** *adj* sueco(a) **2** *n* (**a**) *(language)* sueco *m* (**b**) **the S.** los suecos

sweep [swiːp] *(pt & pp swept)* **1** *n* (**a**) *(with broom)* barrido *m, Am* barrida *f* (**b**) *(chimney)* **s.** deshollinador(a) *m,f* **2** *vt (floor etc)* barrer **3** *vi* (**a**) *(with broom)* barrer (**b**) **to s. in/out/past** entrar/salir/pasar rápidamente

► **sweep aside** *vt sep* apartar bruscamente; *Fig (objections)* rechazar

► **sweep away** *vt sep* (**a**) *(dust)* barrer (**b**) *(of storm)* arrastrar

► **sweep up** *vi* barrer

sweeping ['swiːpɪŋ] *adj* (**a**) *(broad)* amplio(a); **a s. statement** una declaración demasiado general (**b**) *(victory)* aplastante (**c**) *(reforms, changes etc)* radical

sweet [swiːt] **1** *adj* (**a**) dulce; *(sugary)* azucarado(a); **to have a s. tooth** ser goloso(a); **s. pea** guisante *m* de olor; **s. shop** confitería *f* (**b**) *(pleasant)* agradable; *(smell)* fragante; *(sound)* melodioso(a) (**c**) *(person, animal)* encantador(a) **2** *n* (**a**) *Br (confectionery)* dulce *m*; **(boiled) s.** caramelo *m* (**b**) *(dessert)* postre *m*

sweetcorn ['swiːtkɔːn] *n* maíz tierno, *Andes, RP* choclo *m, Méx* elote *m*

sweeten ['swiːtən] *vt* (**a**) *(tea etc)* azucarar (**b**) *Fig (temper)* aplacar; **to s. the pill** suavizar el golpe

sweetheart ['swiːthɑːt] *n* (**a**) *(boyfriend)* novio *m*; *(girlfriend)* novia *f* (**b**) *(dear, love)* cariño *m*, amor *m*

swell [swel] **1** *n (of sea)* marejada *f*, oleaje *m* **2** *adj US Fam* genial, *Méx* padre, *RP* bárbaro(a) **3** *vt (pt* **swelled***; pp* **swollen**) *(part of body)* hincharse; *(river)* subir

► **swell up** *vi* hincharse

swelling ['swelɪŋ] *n* hinchazón *f; Med* tumefacción *f*

swept [swept] *pt & pp of* **sweep**

swerve [swɜːv] **1** *n* (**a**) *(by car)* viraje *m* (**b**) *Sport (by player)* regate *m* **2** *vi*

(**a**) *(car)* dar un viraje brusco (**b**) *Sport (player)* dar un regate

swift [swɪft] **1** *adj* rápido(a), veloz **2** *n Orn* vencejo *m* (común)

► **swill out** *vt sep* enjuagar, *Esp* aclarar

swim [swɪm] *(pt* **swam***; pp* **swum**) **1** *vi* nadar; **to go swimming** ir a nadar; *Fam* **my head is swimming** la cabeza me da vueltas **2** *vt (the Channel)* pasar a nado **3** *n* baño *m*; **to go for a s.** ir a nadar *or* bañarse

swimmer ['swɪmə(r)] *n* nadador(a) *m,f*

swimming ['swɪmɪŋ] *n* natación *f;* **s. cap** gorro *m* de baño; **s. costume** traje *m* de baño, bañador *m, Ecuad, Perú, RP* malla *f;* **s. pool** piscina *f, Méx* alberca *f, RP* pileta *f;* **s. trunks** *Esp* bañador *m (de hombre), Ecuad, Perú, RP* malla *f (de hombre)*

swindle ['swɪndəl] **1** *n* estafa *f* **2** *vt* estafar

swindler ['swɪndlə(r)] *n* estafador(a) *m,f*

swine [swaɪn] *n* (**a**) *(pl* **swine***) (pig)* cerdo *m*, puerco *m, Am* chancho *m* (**b**) *(pl* **swines***) Fam (person)* canalla *mf*, cochino(a) *m,f*

swing [swɪŋ] *(pt & pp* **swung**) **1** *n* (**a**) balanceo *m*, vaivén *m; Fig (in votes etc)* viraje *m* (**b**) *(in golf)* swing *m* (**c**) *(plaything)* columpio *m* (**d**) *(rhythm)* ritmo *m*; **in full s.** en plena marcha **2** *vi* (**a**) *(move to and fro)* balancearse; *(arms, legs)* menearse; *(on swing)* columpiarse (**b**) *(turn)* girar; **he swung round** dio media vuelta **3** *vt (cause to move to and fro)* balancear; *(arms, legs)* menear

swipe [swaɪp] **1** *n* golpe *m* **2** *vt* (**a**) *(hit)* dar un tortazo a (**b**) *Fam (steal)* afanar, birlar

swirl [swɜːl] **1** *n* remolino *m*; *(of cream, smoke)* voluta *f* **2** *vi* arremolinarse

Swiss [swɪs] **1** *adj* suizo(a) **2** *n* (*pl* **Swiss***) (person)* suizo(a) *m,f;* **the S.** los suizos

switch [swɪtʃ] **1** *n* (**a**) *Elec* interruptor *m* (**b**) *(changeover)* cambio repentino;

(exchange) intercambio *m* (**c**) *US Rail* agujas *fpl* **2** *vt* (**a**) *(jobs, direction)* cambiar de (**b**) *(allegiance)* cambiar (**to** por); *(attention)* desviar (**to** hacia)

▸ **switch off** *vt sep* apagar

▸ **switch on** *vt sep* encender, *Am* prender

▸ **switch over** *vi* cambiar (**to** a)

switchboard ['swɪtʃbɔːd] *n* centralita *f*, *Am* conmutador *m*

Switzerland ['swɪtsələnd] *n* Suiza

swivel ['swɪvəl] **1** *n* **s. chair** silla giratoria **2** *vt & vi* girar

swollen ['swəʊlən] **1** *adj (ankle, face)* hinchado(a); *(river, lake)* crecido(a) **2** *pp of* **swell**

swoop [swuːp] **1** *n* (**a**) *(of bird)* calada *f*, *(of plane)* (vuelo *m* en) picado (**b**) *(by police)* redada *f* **2** *vi* (**a**) *(plane, bird)* volar en picado *or Am* picada (**b**) *(police)* hacer una redada

swop [swɒp] *n & vt* = **swap**

sword [sɔːd] *n* espada *f*

swore [swɔː(r)] *pt of* **swear**

sworn [swɔːn] **1** *adj* jurado(a) **2** *pp of* **swear**

swot [swɒt] *vi Br Fam* matarse estudiando, *Esp* empollar, *RP* tragar (**for** para)

swum [swʌm] *pp of* **swim**

swung [swʌŋ] *pt & pp of* **swing**

sycamore ['sɪkəmɔː(r)] *n* (**a**) *Br* sicomoro *m* (**b**) *US (plane tree)* plátano *m*

syllable ['sɪləbəl] *n* sílaba *f*

syllabus ['sɪləbəs] *n* programa *m* de estudios

symbol ['sɪmbəl] *n* símbolo *m*

symbolic [sɪm'bɒlɪk] *adj* simbólico(a)

symmetry ['sɪmɪtrɪ] *n* simetría *f*

sympathetic [sɪmpə'θetɪk] *adj* (**a**) *(showing pity)* compasivo(a) (**b**) *(understanding)* comprensivo(a); *(kind)* amable

sympathize ['sɪmpəθaɪz] *vi* (**a**) *(show pity)* compadecerse (**with** de) (**b**) *(understand)* comprender

sympathy ['sɪmpəθɪ] *n* (**a**) *(pity)* compasión *f* (**b**) *(condolences)* pésame *m*; **letter of s.** pésame; **to express one's s.** dar el pésame (**c**) *(understanding)* comprensión *f*

symphony ['sɪmfənɪ] *n* sinfonía *f*

symptom ['sɪmptəm] *n* síntoma *m*

synagogue ['sɪnəgɒg] *n* sinagoga *f*

synchronize ['sɪŋkrənaɪz] *vt* sincronizar

syndicate ['sɪndɪkɪt] *n* corporación *f*; **newspaper s.** sindicato periodístico

syndrome ['sɪndrəʊm] *n* síndrome *m*

synonym ['sɪnənɪm] *n* sinónimo *m*

synonymous [sɪ'nɒnɪməs] *adj* sinónimo(a) (**with** de)

synthetic [sɪn'θetɪk] *adj* sintético(a)

syringe [sɪ'rɪndʒ] *n* jeringa *f*, jeringuilla *f*

syrup ['sɪrəp] *n* jarabe *m*, almíbar *m*

system ['sɪstəm] *n* sistema *m*; *Fam* **the s.** el orden establecido; *Comput* **systems analyst** analista *mf* de sistemas

systematic [sɪstɪ'mætɪk] *adj* sistemático(a)

Tt

T, t [tiː] *n (the letter)* T, t *f*

ta [tɑː] *interj Br Fam* gracias

tab [tæb] *n* (**a**) *(flap)* lengüeta *f*; *(label)* etiqueta *f*; *Fam* **to keep tabs on sb** vigilar a algn (**b**) *US Fam (bill)* cuenta *f*

table ['teɪbəl] **1** *n* (**a**) mesa *f*; **to lay** or **set the t.** poner la mesa; **t. lamp** lámpara *f* de mesa; **t. mat** salvamanteles *m inv*; **t. tennis** ping-pong® *m*, tenis *m* de mesa; **t. wine** vino *m* de mesa (**b**) *(of figures)* tabla *f*, cuadro *m*; **t. of contents** índice *m* de materias **2** *vt (motion, proposal) Br* presentar; *US* posponer

tablecloth ['teɪbəlklɒθ] *n* mantel *m*

tablespoon ['teɪbəlspuːn] *n* cucharón *m*

tablespoonful ['teɪbəlspuːnfʊl] *n* cucharada *f* grande

tablet ['tæblɪt] *n* (**a**) *Med* pastilla *f* (**b**) *(of stone)* lápida *f*

tabloid ['tæblɔɪd] *n* periódico *m* de pequeño formato; **t. press** prensa sensacionalista

taboo [tə'buː] *adj & n* tabú *(m)*

tack [tæk] **1** *n* (**a**) *(small nail)* tachuela *f* (**b**) *Sewing* hilván *m* (**c**) *Naut* amura *f*; *(distance)* bordada *f*; *Fig* **to change t.** cambiar de rumbo
  2 *vt* (**a**) **to t. sth down** clavar algo con tachuelas (**b**) *Sewing* hilvanar
  3 *vi Naut* virar de bordo

▶ **tack on** *vt sep (add)* añadir

tackle ['tækəl] **1** *n* (**a**) *(equipment)* aparejos *mpl*; **fishing t.** aparejos de pescar (**b**) *(challenge) (in football)* entrada *f*; *(in rugby, American football)* placaje *m*, *Am* tackle *m* **2** *vt* agarrar; *(task)* emprender; *(problem)* abordar; *(in football)* entrar a; *(in rugby, American football)* hacer un placaje a, *Am* tacklear

tacky¹ ['tækɪ] *adj* (**tackier, tackiest**) pegajoso(a)

tacky² ['tækɪ] *adj Fam (tasteless)* chabacano(a), ordinario(a)

tact [tækt] *n* tacto *m*, diplomacia *f*

tactful ['tæktfʊl] *adj* diplomático(a)

tactic ['tæktɪk] *n* táctica *f*; **tactics** táctica *f*

tactical ['tæktɪkəl] *adj* táctico(a)

tactless ['tæktlɪs] *adj (person)* poco diplomático(a); *(question)* indiscreto(a)

tag [tæg] *n* (**a**) *(label)* etiqueta *f* (**b**) *(saying)* coletilla *f*

▶ **tag along** *vi Fam* pegarse

▶ **tag on** *vt sep (add to end)* añadir

tail [teɪl] **1** *n* (**a**) cola *f*; **t. end** cola (**b**) *(of shirt)* faldón *m*; **to wear tails** ir de frac; **t. coat** frac *m* (**c**) **tails** *(of coin)* cruz *f*, *Andes, Ven* sello *m*, *Méx* sol *m*, *RP* ceca *f* **2** *vt Fam (follow)* seguir de cerca

▶ **tail away, tail off** *vi* desvanecerse

tailback ['teɪlbæk] *n Br* caravana *f*

tail-light ['teɪllaɪt] *n Aut* faro *m* trasero

tailor ['teɪlə(r)] **1** *n* sastre *m*; **t.'s (shop)** sastrería *f* **2** *vt (suit)* confeccionar; *Fig* adaptar

take [teɪk] *(pt* **took**; *pp* **taken**) *vt* (**a**) tomar, coger, *Am* agarrar; **to t. an opportunity** aprovechar una oportunidad; **to t. hold of sth** agarrar algo; **to t. sth from one's pocket** sacarse algo del bolsillo; **t. your time!** ¡tómate el tiempo que quieras!; **to t. a bath** bañarse; **to t. care (of oneself)** cuidarse; **is this seat taken?** ¿está ocupado este asiento?; **to t. a decision** tomar una decisión; **to t. a liking/dislike to sb** tomar cariño/ antipatía a algn; **to t. a photograph**

sacar una fotografía; **t. the first road on the left** coja la primera a la izquierda; **to t. the train** coger el tren
(**b**) *(accept)* aceptar
(**c**) *(win)* ganar; *(prize)* llevarse
(**d**) *(eat, drink)* tomar; **to t. drugs** drogarse
(**e**) **she's taking (a degree in) law** estudia derecho; **to t. an exam (in …)** examinarse (de …)
(**f**) *(person to a place)* llevar
(**g**) *(endure)* aguantar
(**h**) *(consider)* considerar
(**i**) **I t. it that …** supongo que …
(**j**) *(require)* requerir; **it takes an hour to get there** se tarda una hora en llegar hasta allí
(**k**) **to be taken ill** enfermar
▸ **take after** *vt insep* parecerse a
▸ **take apart** *vt sep (machine)* desmontar
▸ **take away** *vt sep* (**a**) *(carry off)* llevarse (**b**) **to t. sth away from sb** quitar *or Am* sacar algo a algn (**c**) *Math* restar
▸ **take back** *vt sep* (**a**) *(give back)* devolver; *(receive back)* recuperar (**b**) *(withdraw)* retractarse
▸ **take down** *vt sep* (**a**) *(lower)* bajar (**b**) *(demolish)* derribar (**c**) *(write)* apuntar
▸ **take in** *vt sep* (**a**) *(shelter, lodge)* alojar, acoger (**b**) *Sewing* meter (**c**) *(include)* abarcar (**d**) *(understand)* entender (**e**) *(deceive)* engañar
▸ **take off** **1** *vt sep* (**a**) quitar, *Am* sacar; **he took off his jacket** se quitó *or Am* se sacó la chaqueta (**b**) *(lead or carry away)* llevarse (**c**) *(deduct)* descontar (**d**) *(imitate)* imitar burlonamente **2** *vi (plane)* despegar, *Am* decolar
▸ **take on** *vt sep* (**a**) *(undertake)* encargarse de (**b**) *(acquire)* tomar (**c**) *(employ)* contratar (**d**) *(compete with)* competir con
▸ **take out** *vt sep* sacar, quitar; **he's taking me out to dinner** me ha invitado a cenar fuera
▸ **take over** **1** *vt sep Com, Pol* tomar

posesión de **2** *vi* **to t. over from sb** relevar a algn
▸ **take to** *vt insep (become fond of)* coger cariño a; **to t. to drink** darse a la bebida
▸ **take up** *vt sep* (**a**) *Sewing* acortar (**b**) *(accept)* aceptar; *(adopt)* adoptar (**c**) **I've taken up the piano/French** he empezado a tocar el piano/a aprender francés (**d**) *(occupy)* ocupar

takeaway ['teɪkəweɪ] *Br* **1** *n (food)* comida *f* para llevar; *(restaurant)* restaurante *m* que vende comida para llevar **2** *adj (food)* para llevar

taken ['teɪkən] *pp of* **take**

takeoff ['teɪkɒf] *n* (**a**) *(plane, economy)* despegue *m, Am* decolaje *m* (**b**) *(imitation)* imitación burlona

takeover ['teɪkəʊvə(r)] *n Com* absorción *f; military* **t.** golpe *m* militar; **t. bid** oferta pública de adquisición, OPA *f*

takings ['teɪkɪŋz] *npl Br Com* recaudación *f*

talc [tælk] *n* talco *m*

tale [teɪl] *n* cuento *m*; **to tell tales** contar chismes

talent ['tælənt] *n* talento *m*

talented ['tæləntɪd] *adj* dotado(a)

talk [tɔːk] **1** *vi* hablar, *CAm, Méx* platicar; *(chat)* charlar; *(gossip)* chismorrear
2 *vt* **to t. nonsense** decir tonterías; **to t. sense** hablar con sentido común; **to t. shop** hablar del trabajo
3 *n* (**a**) *(conversation)* conversación *f, CAm, Méx* plática *f* (**b**) *(words)* palabras *fpl*; **he's all t.** no hace más que hablar (**c**) *(rumour)* rumor *m*; *(gossip)* chismes *mpl* (**d**) *(lecture)* charla *f*
▸ **talk into** *vt sep* **to t. sb into sth** convencer a algn para que haga algo
▸ **talk out of** *vt sep* **to t. sb out of sth** disuadir a algn de que haga algo
▸ **talk over** *vt sep* discutir

talkative ['tɔːkətɪv] *adj* hablador(a)

tall [tɔːl] *adj* alto(a); **a tree 10 m t.** un árbol de 10 m (de alto); **how t. are you?** ¿cuánto mides?; *Fig* **that's a t.**

order eso es mucho pedir

tally ['tælɪ] **1** *vi* **to t. with sth** corresponderse con algo **2** *n Com* apunte *m*; **to keep a t. of** llevar la cuenta de

tambourine [tæmbə'riːn] *n* pandereta *f*

tame [teɪm] **1** *adj* (**a**) *(animal)* domado(a); *(by nature)* manso(a); *(person)* dócil (**b**) *(style)* soso(a) **2** *vt* domar

tamper ['tæmpə(r)] *vi* **to t. with** *(text)* adulterar; *(records, an entry)* falsificar; *(lock)* intentar forzar

tampon ['tæmpɒn] *n* tampón *m*

tan [tæn] **1** *n* (**a**) *(colour)* marrón rojizo (**b**) *(of skin)* bronceado *m*, *Esp* moreno *m*
  2 *adj (colour)* marrón rojizo
  3 *vt* (**a**) *(leather)* curtir (**b**) *(skin)* broncear
  4 *vi* ponerse moreno(a)

tangerine [tændʒə'riːn] *n* clementina *f*

tangible ['tændʒəbəl] *adj* tangible

tangle ['tæŋgəl] *n (of thread)* maraña *f*; *Fig* lío *m*; *Fig* **to get into a t.** hacerse un lío

tangled ['tæŋgəld] *adj* enredado(a), enmarañado(a)

tank [tæŋk] *n* (**a**) *(container)* depósito *m* (**b**) *Mil* tanque *m*

tanker ['tæŋkə(r)] *n Naut* tanque *m*; *(for oil)* petrolero *m*; *Aut* camión *m* cisterna

tantrum ['tæntrəm] *n* rabieta *f*

tap¹ [tæp] **1** *vt* golpear suavemente; *(with hand)* dar una palmadita a
  2 *vi* **to t. at the door** llamar suavemente a la puerta
  3 *n* golpecito *m*; **t. dancing** claqué *m*

tap² [tæp] *n Br (for water)* grifo *m*, *Chile, Col, Méx* llave *f*, *RP* canilla *f*; *Fig* **funds on t.** fondos *mpl* disponibles

tape [teɪp] **1** *n* (**a**) *(cinta f*; **sticky t.** cinta adhesiva; **t. measure** cinta métrica (**b**) *(for recording)* cinta *f* (magnetofónica); **t. recorder** magnetófono *m*, cassette *m*; **t. recording** grabación *f* **2** *vt* (**a**) pegar (con cinta adhesiva); *Fig* **I've got him/it taped**

lo tengo controlado (**b**) *(record)* grabar (en cinta)

taper ['teɪpə(r)] **1** *vi* estrecharse; *(to a point)* afilarse **2** *n (candle)* vela *f*
  ▸ **taper off** *vi* ir disminuyendo

tapestry ['tæpɪstrɪ] *n* tapiz *m*

tar [tɑː(r)] *n* alquitrán *m*

target ['tɑːgɪt] *n* (**a**) *(object aimed at)* blanco *m*; **t. practice** tiro *m* al blanco (**b**) *(purpose)* meta *f*

tariff ['tærɪf] *n* tarifa *f*, arancel *m*

tarmac® ['tɑːmæk] **1** *n* (**a**) *(substance)* alquitrán *m* (**b**) *Av* pista *f* de aterrizaje **2** *vt* alquitranar

tarnish ['tɑːnɪʃ] *vt* deslustrar

tart¹ [tɑːt] *n Br Culin* tarta *f*

tart² [tɑːt] *adj (taste)* ácido(a), agrio(a)

tart³ [tɑːt] *Fam* **1** *n* fulana *f*, *Méx* piruja *f*
  2 *vt Br* **to t. oneself up** emperifollarse

tartan ['tɑːtən] *n* tartán *m*

task [tɑːsk] *n* tarea *f*; **to take sb to t.** reprender a algn; *Mil* **t. force** destacamento *m* (de fuerzas)

taste [teɪst] **1** *n* (**a**) *(sense)* gusto *m*; *(flavour)* sabor *m*; **it has a burnt t.** sabe a quemado (**b**) *(sample) (of food)* bocado *m*; *(of drink)* trago *m* (**c**) *(liking)* afición *f*; **to have a t. for sth** gustarle a uno algo (**d**) **in bad t.** de mal gusto; **to have (good) t.** tener (buen) gusto
  2 *vt (sample)* probar
  3 *vi* **to t. of sth** saber a algo

tasteful ['teɪstfʊl] *adj* de buen gusto

tasteless ['teɪstlɪs] *adj* (**a**) *(food)* soso(a) (**b**) *(in bad taste)* de mal gusto

tasty ['teɪstɪ] *adj* (**tastier, tastiest**) sabroso(a)

tatters ['tætəz] *npl* **in t.** hecho(a) jirones

tattoo¹ [tæ'tuː] *n Mil* retreta *f*

tattoo² [tæ'tuː] **1** *vt* tatuar **2** *n (mark)* tatuaje *m*

tatty ['tætɪ] *adj* (**tattier, tattiest**) *Fam* ajado(a), *Esp* sobado(a)

taught [tɔːt] *pt & pp of* **teach**

taunt [tɔːnt] **1** *vt* **to t. sb with sth** echar algo en cara a algn **2** *n* pulla *f*

Taurus ['tɔːrəs] *n* Tauro *m*

taut [tɔːt] *adj* tenso(a), tirante

tax [tæks] **1** *n* impuesto *m*; **t. free** exento(a) de impuestos; **t. collector** recaudador(a) *m,f* (de impuestos); **t. evasion** evasión *f* fiscal; **t. return** declaración *f* de renta **2** *vt* (**a**) gravar (**b**) *(patience etc)* poner a prueba

taxable ['tæksəbəl] *adj* imponible

taxation [tæk'seɪʃən] *n* impuestos *mpl*

taxi ['tæksɪ] **1** *n* taxi *m*; **t. driver** taxista *mf*; **t.** *Br* **rank** *or US* **stand** parada *f* de taxis **2** *vi (aircraft)* rodar por la pista

taxpayer ['tækspeɪə(r)] *n* contribuyente *mf*

tea [tiː] *n* (**a**) té *m*; **t. bag** bolsita *f* de té; **t. break** descanso *m*; *Br* **t. cosy** cubretetera *f*; **t. leaf** hoja *f* de té; **t. service** *or* **set** juego *m* de té; **t. towel** trapo *m* *or* paño *m* (de cocina), *RP* repasador *m* (**b**) *(snack)* merienda *f*; **(high) t.** merienda-cena *f*

teach [tiːtʃ] *(pt & pp* **taught**) **1** *vt* enseñar; *(subject)* dar clases de; **to t. sb (how) to do sth** enseñar a algn a hacer algo; *US* **to t. school** ser profesor(a) **2** *vi* dar clases, ser profesor(a)

teacher ['tiːtʃə(r)] *n* profesor(a) *m,f*; *(in primary school)* maestro(a) *m,f*

teaching ['tiːtʃɪŋ] *n* enseñanza *f*

teacup ['tiːkʌp] *n* taza *f* de té

team [tiːm] *n* equipo *m*; *(of oxen)* yunta *f*

teamwork ['tiːmwɜːk] *n* trabajo *m* en equipo

teapot ['tiːpɒt] *n* tetera *f*

tear¹ [tɪə(r)] *n* lágrima *f*; **to be in tears** estar llorando; **t. gas** gas lacrimógeno

tear² [teə(r)] *(pt* **tore**; *pp* **torn**) **1** *vt* (**a**) rajar, desgarrar (**b**) **to t. sth out of sb's hands** arrancarle algo de las manos a algn
  2 *vi* (**a**) *(cloth)* rajarse (**b**) **to t. along** ir a toda velocidad
  3 *n* desgarrón *m*; *(in clothes)* rasgón *m*

▸ **tear down** *vt sep* derribar

▸ **tear off** *vt sep* arrancar

▸ **tear out** *vt sep* arrancar

▸ **tear up** *vt sep* (**a**) romper, hacer pedazos (**b**) *(uproot)* arrancar de raíz

tearoom ['tiːruːm] *n Br* = **teashop**

tease [tiːz] **1** *vt* tomar el pelo a **2** *n* bromista *mf*

teashop ['tiːʃɒp] *n Br* salón *m* de té

teaspoon ['tiːspuːn] *n* cucharilla *f*

teaspoonful ['tiːspuːnfʊl] *n* cucharadita *f*

teatime ['tiːtaɪm] *n esp Br* hora *f* del té

technical ['teknɪkəl] *adj* técnico(a); *Br* **t. college** instituto *m* de formación profesional

technician [tek'nɪʃən] *n* técnico(a) *m,f*

technique [tek'niːk] *n* técnica *f*

technological [teknə'lɒdʒɪkəl] *adj* tecnológico(a)

technology [tek'nɒlədʒɪ] *n* tecnología *f*

tedious ['tiːdɪəs] *adj* tedioso(a), aburrido(a)

teem [tiːm] *vi* **to t. with** rebosar de; *Fam* **it was teeming down** llovía a cántaros

teenage ['tiːneɪdʒ] *adj* adolescente

teenager ['tiːneɪdʒə(r)] *n* adolescente *mf*

teens [tiːnz] *npl* adolescencia *f*

teeshirt ['tiːʃɜːt] *n* camiseta *f*, *Méx* playera, *RP* remera *f*

teeth [tiːθ] *pl of* **tooth**

teethe [tiːð] *vi* echar los dientes

teetotaller [tiː'təʊtələ(r)] *n* abstemio(a) *m,f*

telecommunications ['telɪkəmjuːnɪ'keɪʃənz] *n sing* telecomunicaciones *fpl*

telegram ['telɪgræm] *n* telegrama *m*

telegraph ['telɪgrɑːf] **1** *n* telégrafo *m*; **t. pole** poste telegráfico **2** *vt & vi* telegrafiar

telephone ['telɪfəʊn] **1** *n* teléfono *m*; **t. banking** telebanca *f*; *Br* **t. booth** *or* **box** cabina *f* (telefónica); **t. call** llamada telefónica, *Am* llamado telefónico; **t. directory** guía telefónica, *Am* directorio *m* de teléfonos; **t. number** número *m* de teléfono **2** *vt* telefonear, llamar por teléfono a, *Am* hablar por teléfono a

telescope ['telɪskəʊp] **1** *n* telescopio *m*

2 *vi* plegarse (como un catalejo)

3 *vt* plegar

televise ['telɪvaɪz] *vt* televisar

television ['telɪvɪʒən] *n* televisión *f*; **t. programme** programa *m* de televisión; **t. (set)** televisor *m*

telex ['teleks] **1** *n* télex *m* **2** *vt* enviar por télex

tell [tel] (*pt & pp* **told**) **1** *vt* (a) *(say)* decir; *(relate)* contar; *(inform)* comunicar; **to t. lies** mentir; **to t. sb about sth** contarle algo a algn (b) *(order)* mandar; **to t. sb to do sth** decir a algn que haga algo (c) *(distinguish)* distinguir; **to know how to t. the time** saber decir la hora

2 *vi* (a) *(reveal)* reflejar (b) **who can t.?** *(know)* ¿quién sabe? (c) *(have effect)* notarse; **the pressure is telling on her** está acusando la presión

▸ **tell off** *vt sep Fam (scold)* **to t. sb off (for)** echar una reprimenda *or Esp* bronca a algn (por)

telltale ['telteɪl] *n* acusica *mf*, *Esp* chivato(a) *m,f*; **t. signs** señales reveladoras

telly ['telɪ] *n Br Fam* **the t.** la tele

temper ['tempə(r)] **1** *n* (a) *(mood)* humor *m*; **to keep one's t.** no perder la calma; **to lose one's t.** perder los estribos (b) *(temperament)* **to have a bad t.** tener (mal) genio **2** *vt (in metallurgy)* templar; *Fig* suavizar

temperament ['tempərəmənt] *n* temperamento *m*

temperate ['tempərɪt] *adj* (a) mesurado(a) (b) *(climate)* templado(a)

temperature ['temprɪtʃə(r)] *n* temperatura *f*; **to have a t.** tener fiebre

temple¹ ['tempəl] *n Archit* templo *m*

temple² ['tempəl] *n Anat* sien *f*

tempo ['tempəʊ] *n* tempo *m*

temporary ['tempərərɪ] *adj* temporal, *Am* temporario(a); *(office, arrangement, repairs)* provisional, *Am* temporario(a)

tempt [tempt] *vt* tentar; **to t. providence** tentar la suerte; **to t. sb to do sth** incitar a algn a hacer algo

temptation [temp'teɪʃən] *n* tentación *f*

tempting ['temptɪŋ] *adj* tentador(a)

ten [ten] *adj & n* diez *(m inv)*

tenacious [tɪ'neɪʃəs] *adj* tenaz

tenancy ['tenənsɪ] *n (of house)* alquiler *m*; *(of land)* arrendamiento *m*

tenant ['tenənt] *n (of house)* inquilino(a) *m,f*; *(of farm)* arrendatario(a) *m,f*

tend¹ [tend] *vi (be inclined)* tender, tener tendencia (**to** a)

tend² [tend] *vt (care for)* cuidar

tendency ['tendənsɪ] *n* tendencia *f*

tender¹ ['tendə(r)] *adj (affectionate)* cariñoso(a); *(compassionate)* compasivo(a); *(meat)* tierno(a)

tender² ['tendə(r)] **1** *vt* ofrecer; **to t. one's resignation** presentar la dimisión

2 *vi Com* **to t. for** sacar a concurso

3 *n* (a) *Com* oferta *f* (b) **legal t.** moneda *f* de curso legal

tenement ['tenɪmənt] *n* **t. (building)** bloque *m* de apartamentos *or Esp* pisos *or Arg* departamentos

tennis ['tenɪs] *n* tenis *m*; **t. ball** pelota *f* de tenis; **t. court** pista *f* de tenis; **t. player** tenista *mf*; **t. racket** raqueta *f* de tenis; **t. shoe** zapatilla *f* de tenis

tenor ['tenə(r)] *n Mus* tenor *m*

tense¹ [tens] *adj* tenso(a)

tense² [tens] *n Ling* tiempo *m*

tension ['tenʃən] *n* tensión *f*

tent [tent] *n* tienda *f* de campaña, *Am* carpa *f*; **t. peg** estaca *f*

tentative ['tentətɪv] *adj* (a) *(not definite)* de prueba (b) *(hesitant)* indeciso(a)

tenth [tenθ] **1** *adj & n* décimo(a) *(m,f)* **2** *n (fraction)* décimo *m*

tenuous ['tenjʊəs] *adj* (a) tenue (b) *(argument)* flojo(a)

tepid ['tepɪd] *adj* tibio(a)

term [tɜːm] **1** *n* (a) *(period)* período *m*; *Educ* trimestre *m*; **t. of office** mandato *m*, legislatura *f*; **in the long/short t.** a largo/corto plazo (**b**) *(word)* término *m*; *Fig* **in terms of money** en cuanto al dinero (**c**) **terms** *(conditions)* condiciones *fpl*; **to come to terms with** hacerse a la idea de (**d**) **to be on good/bad terms with sb** tener buenas/malas relaciones con algn **2** *vt* calificar de

terminal ['tɜ:mɪnəl] **1** *adj* terminal; **t. cancer** cáncer incurable **2** *n* terminal *f*

terminate ['tɜ:mɪneɪt] **1** *vt* terminar; **to t. a pregnancy** abortar **2** *vi* terminarse

terminus ['tɜ:mɪnəs] *n (pl* **termini** [tɛ:mɪnaɪ]) terminal *m*

terrace ['terəs] *n* (**a**) *Agr* bancal *m* (**b**) *Br (of houses)* hilera *f* de casas (**c**) *(patio)* terraza *f* (**d**) *Br Ftb* **the terraces** las gradas

terrain [tə'reɪn] *n* terreno *m*

terrestrial [tɪ'restrɪəl] *adj* terrestre

terrible ['terəbəl] *adj* horrible, terrible

terribly ['terəblɪ] *adv* tremendamente mal, *Esp* fatal

terrier ['terɪə(r)] *n* terrier *m*

terrific [tə'rɪfɪk] *adj* (**a**) *Fam (excellent)* estupendo, genial (**b**) *(extreme)* tremendo(a)

terrify ['terɪfaɪ] *vt* aterrorizar

terrifying ['terɪfaɪɪŋ] *adj* aterrador(a)

territory ['terɪtərɪ] *n* territorio *m*

terror ['terə(r)] *n* terror *m*

terrorism ['terərɪzəm] *n* terrorismo *m*

terrorist ['terərɪst] *adj & n* terrorista *(mf)*

terrorize ['terəraɪz] *vt* aterrorizar

test [test] **1** *vt* probar, someter a una prueba; *(analyse)* analizar; *Med* hacer un análisis de **2** *n* prueba *f*, examen *m*; **t. match** partido *m* internacional; **t. pilot** piloto *m* de pruebas; **t. tube** probeta *f*; **t.-tube baby** niño *m* probeta

testament ['testəmənt] *n* testamento *m*; **Old/New T.** Antiguo/Nuevo Testamento

testicle ['testɪkəl] *n* testículo *m*

testify ['testɪfaɪ] **1** *vt* declarar **2** *vi Fig* **to t. to sth** atestiguar algo

testimony ['testɪmənɪ] *n* testimonio *m*, declaración *f*

tetanus ['tetənəs] *n* tétano(s) *m inv*

tether ['teðə(r)] **1** *n* ronzal *m*; *Fig* **to be at the end of one's t.** estar hasta la coronilla **2** *vt (animal)* atar

text [tekst] **1** *n* texto *m* **2** *vt (send text message to)* enviar un mensaje de texto a

textbook ['tekstbʊk] *n* libro *m* de texto

textile ['tekstaɪl] **1** *n* tejido *m* **2** *adj* textil

texture ['tekstʃə(r)] *n* textura *f*

Thames [temz] *n* **the T.** el Támesis

than [ðæn, *unstressed* ðən] *conj* que; *(with numbers)* de; **he's older t. me** es mayor que yo; **I have more/less t. you** tengo más/menos que tú; **more interesting t. we thought** más interesante de lo que creíamos; **more t. once** más de una vez; **more t. ten people** más de diez personas

thank [θæŋk] *vt* agradecer a; **t. you** gracias

thankful ['θæŋkfʊl] *adj* agradecido(a)

thanks [θæŋks] *npl* gracias *fpl*; **no t.** no gracias; **many t.** muchas gracias; **t. for phoning** gracias por llamar; **t. to** gracias a

Thanksgiving [θæŋks'gɪvɪŋ] *n US* **T. Day** Día *m* de Acción de Gracias

that [ðæt, *unstressed* ðət] **1** *dem pron (pl* **those**) (**a**) ése *m*, ésa *f*; *(further away)* aquél *m*, aquélla *f*; **this one is new but t. is old** éste es nuevo pero ése es viejo

(**b**) *(indefinite)* eso; *(remote)* aquello; **after t.** después de eso; **like t.** así; **t.'s right** eso es; **t.'s where I live** allí vivo yo; **what's t.?** ¿qué es eso?; **who's t.?** ¿quién es?

(**c**) *(with relative)* el/la; **all those I saw** todos los que vi

2 *dem adj (pl* **those**) *(masculine)* ese; *(feminine)* esa; *(further away) (masculine)* aquel; *(feminine)* aquella; **at t. time** en aquella época; **t. book** ese/aquel libro; **t. one** ése/aquél

3 *rel pron* (**a**) *(subject, direct object)*

que; **all (t.) you said** todo lo que dijiste; **the letter (t.) I sent you** la carta que te envié (**b**) *(governed by preposition)* que, el/la que, los/las que, el/la cual, los/las cuales; **the car (t.) they came in** el coche en el que vinieron (**c**) *(when)* que, en que; **the moment (t.) you arrived** el momento en que llegaste

El pronombre relativo **that** puede omitirse salvo cuando es sujeto de la oración subordinada

4 *conj* que; **he said (t.) he would come** dijo que vendría

La conjunción **that** se puede omitir cuando introduce una oración subordinada

5 *adv* así de, tanto, tan; **I don't think it can be t. old** no creo que sea tan viejo; **we haven't got t. much money** no tenemos tanto dinero

thatched [θætʃt] *adj* cubierto(a) con paja; **t. cottage** casita *f* con techo de paja; **t. roof** techo *m* de paja

thaw [θɔ:] **1** *vt (snow)* derretir; *(food, freezer)* descongelar
2 *vi* descongelarse; *(snow)* derretirse
3 *n* deshielo *m*

the [ðə, *before vowel sound* ðɪ, *emphatic* ði:] **1** *def art* (**a**) el/la; *pl* los/las; **at/to t.** al/a la; *pl* a los/a las; **of or from t.** del/de la; *pl* de los/de las; **t. Alps** los Alpes (**b**) *(omitted)* **George t. Sixth** Jorge Sexto (**c**) **by t. day** al día; **by t. dozen** a docenas (**d**) *(with adjectives used as nouns)* **t. elderly** los ancianos
2 *adv* **t. more t. merrier** cuantos más mejor; **t. sooner t. better** cuanto antes mejor

theatre, *US* **theater** [ˈθɪətə(r)] *n* teatro *m*
theatrical [θɪˈætrɪkəl] *adj* teatral
theft [θeft] *n* robo *m*; **petty t.** hurto *m*
their [ðeə(r)] *poss adj (one thing)* su; *(various things)* sus
theirs [ðeəz] *poss pron* (el) suyo/(la) suya; *pl* (los) suyos/(las) suyas
them [ðem, *unstressed* ðəm] *pers pron*

pl (**a**) *(direct object)* los/las; *(indirect object)* les; **I know t.** los/las conozco; **I shall tell t. so** se lo diré (a ellos/ellas); **it's t.!** ¡son ellos!; **speak to t.** hábleles (**b**) *(with preposition)* ellos/ellas; **walk in front of t.** camine delante de ellos; **they took the keys away with t.** se llevaron las llaves; **both of t., the two of t.** los dos; **neither of t.** ninguno de los dos; **none of t.** ninguno de ellos

theme [θi:m] *n* tema *m*; **t. tune** sintonía *f*

themselves [ðəmˈselvz] *pers pron pl (as subject)* ellos mismos/ellas mismas; *(as direct or indirect object)* se; *(after a preposition)* sí mismos/sí mismas; **they did it by t.** lo hicieron ellos solos

then [ðen] **1** *adv* (**a**) *(at that time)* entonces; **since t.** desde entonces; **there and t.** en el acto; **till t.** hasta entonces (**b**) *(next, afterwards)* luego (**c**) *(anyway)* de todas formas (**d**) *(in that case)* entonces; **go t.** pues vete
2 *conj* entonces
3 *adj* **the t. president** el entonces presidente

theoretic(al) [θɪəˈretɪk(əl)] *adj* teórico(a)

theory [ˈθɪərɪ] *n* teoría *f*

therapeutic [θerəˈpju:tɪk] *adj also Fig* terapéutico(a)

therapy [ˈθerəpɪ] *n* terapia *f*

there [ðeə(r), *unstressed* ðə(r)] **1** *adv* (**a**) *(indicating place)* allí, allá; *(nearer speaker)* ahí; **here and t.** acá y allá; **in t.** ahí dentro; **is Peter t.?** ¿está Peter? (**b**) *(emphatic)* **that man t.** aquel hombre (**c**) *(unstressed)* **t. is …/t. are …** hay …; **t. were six of us** éramos seis (**d**) *(in respect)* **t.'s the difficulty** ahí está la dificultad
2 *interj* **so t.!** ¡eal!; **t., t.** bien, bien

thereabouts [ˈðeərəbauts], *US* **thereabout** [ˈðeərəbaut] *adv* **in Cambridge or t.** en Cambridge o por allí cerca; **at four o'clock or t.** a las cuatro o así

thereby [ˈðeəbaɪ] *adv* por eso *or* ello

therefore ['ðeəfɔː(r)] *adv* por lo tanto, por eso

thermometer [θə'mɒmɪtə(r)] *n* termómetro *m*

Thermos® ['θɜːməs] *n* T. **(flask)** termo *m*

thermostat ['θɜːməstæt] *n* termostato *m*

these [ðiːz] **1** *dem adj pl* estos(as) **2** *dem pron pl* éstos(as); *see* **this**

thesis ['θiːsɪs] *n* (*pl* **theses** ['θiːsiːz]) tesis *f inv*

they [ðeɪ] *pron pl* **(a)** ellos/ellas *(usually omitted in Spanish, except for contrast)*; **t. are dancing** están bailando; **t. are rich** son ricos **(b)** *(stressed)* **t. alone** ellos solos; **t. themselves told me** me lo dijeron ellos mismos **(c)** *(with relative)* los/las **(d)** *(indefinite)* **that's what t. say** eso es lo que se dice; **t. say that ...** se dice que ...

thick [θɪk] **1** *adj* **(a)** *(book etc)* grueso(a); **a wall 2 m t.** un muro de 2 m de espesor **(b)** *(dense)* espeso(a) **(c)** *Fam (stupid)* tonto(a)
2 *adv* densamente
3 *n* **to be in the t. of it** estar metido(a) de lleno

thicken ['θɪkən] **1** *vt* espesar **2** *vi* espesarse; *Fig (plot)* complicarse

thickness ['θɪknɪs] *n* (*of wall etc*) espesor *m*; *(of wire, lips)* grueso *m*; *(of liquid, woodland)* espesura *f*

thief [θiːf] *n* (*pl* **thieves** [θiːvz]) ladrón(ona) *m,f*

thigh [θaɪ] *n* muslo *m*

thimble ['θɪmbəl] *n* dedal *m*

thin [θɪn] **1** *adj* **(thinner, thinnest)** **(a)** delgado(a); **a t. slice** una loncha fina **(b)** *(hair, vegetation)* ralo(a); *(liquid)* claro(a); *(population)* escaso(a) **(c)** *Fig (voice)* débil; **a t. excuse** un pobre pretexto **2** *vt* **to t. (down)** *(paint)* diluir

thing [θɪŋ] *n* **(a)** cosa *f*; **my things** *(clothing)* mi ropa *f*; *(possessions)* mis cosas *fpl*; **for one t.** en primer lugar; **the t. is ...** resulta que ...; **what with one t. and another** entre unas cosas y

otras; **as things are** tal como están las cosas **(b)** **poor little t.!** ¡pobrecito(a)!

think [θɪŋk] (*pt & pp* **thought**) **1.** *vt* **(a)** *(believe)* pensar, creer; **I t. so/not** creo que sí/no **(b)** **I thought as much** yo me lo imaginaba
2 *vi* **(a)** pensar (**of** *or* **about** en); **give me time to t.** dame tiempo para reflexionar; **to t. ahead** prevenir **(b)** *(have as opinion)* opinar, pensar; **to t. highly of sb** apreciar a algn; **what do you t.?** ¿a ti qué te parece? **(c)** **just t.!** ¡imagínate!

▸**think out** *vt sep* meditar; **a carefully thought-out answer** una respuesta razonada

▸**think over** *vt sep* reflexionar; **we'll have to t. it over** lo tendremos que pensar

▸**think up** *vt sep* imaginar, idear

thinly ['θɪnlɪ] *adv* poco, ligeramente

third [θɜːd] **1** *adj* tercero(a); *(before masculine singular noun)* tercer; **(on) the t. of March** el tres de marzo; **the T. World** el Tercer Mundo; **t. party insurance** seguro *m* a terceros **2** *n* **(a)** *(in series)* tercero(a) *m,f* **(b)** *(fraction)* tercio *m*, tercera parte

thirdly ['θɜːdlɪ] *adv* en tercer lugar

thirst [θɜːst] *n* sed *f*

thirsty ['θɜːstɪ] *adj* **(thirstier, thirstiest)** sediento(a); **to be t.** tener sed

thirteen [θɜː'tiːn] *adj & n* trece (*m inv*)

thirteenth [θɜː'tiːnθ] **1** *adj & n* decimotercero(a) *(m,f)* **2** *n (fraction)* decimotercera parte

thirtieth ['θɜːtɪɪθ] **1** *adj & n* trigésimo(a) *(m,f)* **2** *n (fraction)* trigésima parte

thirty ['θɜːtɪ] *adj & n* treinta *(m inv)*

this [ðɪs] **1** *dem adj* (*pl* **these**) *(masculine)* este; *(feminine)* esta; **t. book/these books** este libro/estos libros; **t. one** éste/ésta
2 *dem pron* (*pl* **these**) **(a)** *(indefinite)* esto; **it was like t.** fue así **(b)** *(place)* **t. is where we met** fue aquí donde nos conocimos **(c)** *(time)* **it should have come before t.** debería haber llegado ya **(d)** *(specific person or thing)* éste *m*,

ésta *f*; **I prefer these to those** me gustan más éstos que aquéllos; *(introduction)* **t. is Mr Álvarez** le presento al Sr. Álvarez

3 *adv* **he got t. far** llegó hasta aquí; **t. small/big** así de pequeño/grande

thistle ['θɪsəl] *n* cardo *m*

thorn [θɔ:n] *n* espina *f*

thorough ['θʌrə] *adj (careful)* minucioso(a); *(work)* concienzudo(a); *(knowledge)* profundo(a); **to carry out a t. enquiry into a matter** investigar a fondo un asunto

thoroughfare ['θʌrəfeə(r)] *n (road)* carretera *f*; *(street)* calle *f*

thoroughly ['θʌrəlɪ] *adv (carefully)* a fondo; *(wholly)* completamente

those [ðəʊz] **1** *dem pron pl* ésos(as); *(remote)* aquéllos(as); **t. who** los que/ las que **2** *dem adj pl* esos(as); *(remote)* aquellos(as); *see* **that**

though [ðəʊ] **1** *conj* (a) aunque; **strange t. it may seem** por (muy) extraño que parezca (b) **as t.** como si; **it looks as t. he's gone** parece que se ha ido **2** *adv* sin embargo

thought [θɔ:t] **1** *n* (a) *(act of thinking)* pensamiento *m*; **what a tempting t.!** ¡qué idea más tentadora! (b) *(reflection)* reflexión *f* (c) **it's the t. that counts** *(intention)* lo que cuenta es la intención **2** *pt & pp of* **think**

thoughtful ['θɔ:tfʊl] *adj (pensive)* pensativo(a); *(considerate)* atento(a)

thoughtless ['θɔ:tlɪs] *adj (person)* desconsiderado(a); *(action)* irreflexivo(a)

thousand ['θaʊzənd] *adj & n* mil *(m)*; **thousands of people** miles de personas

thrash [θræʃ] **1** *vt* dar una paliza a **2** *vi* **to t. about** *or* **around** agitarse

▸ **thrash out** *vt sep* discutir a fondo

thrashing ['θræʃɪŋ] *n (beating, defeat)* paliza *f*

thread [θred] **1** *n* (a) *(hilo m;* **length of t.** hebra *f* (b) *(of screw)* rosca *f* **2** *vt* (a) *(needle)* enhebrar (b) **to t. one's way (through)** colarse (por)

threat [θret] *n* amenaza *f*

threaten ['θretən] *vt* amenazar; **to t. to do sth** amenazar con hacer algo

threatening ['θretənɪŋ] *adj* amenazador(a)

three [θri:] *adj & n* tres *(m inv)*

threshold ['θreʃəʊld] *n* umbral *m*; *Fig* **to be on the t. of** estar a las puertas *or* en los umbrales de

threw [θru:] *pt of* **throw**

thrifty ['θrɪftɪ] *adj* (**thriftier, thriftiest**) económico(a), ahorrador(a)

thrill [θrɪl] **1** *n* (a) *(excitement)* emoción *f* (b) *(quiver)* estremecimiento *m* **2** *vt (excite)* emocionar; *(audience)* entusiasmar

thriller ['θrɪlə(r)] *n* thriller *m*

thrilling ['θrɪlɪŋ] *adj* emocionante

thrive [θraɪv] *(pt thrived or throve; pp thrived or thriven ['θrɪvən])* *vi* (a) *(person)* rebosar de salud (b) *Fig (business)* prosperar; **he thrives on it** le viene de maravilla

thriving ['θraɪvɪŋ] *adj Fig* próspero(a)

throat [θrəʊt] *n* garganta *f*

throb [θrɒb] **1** *n (of heart)* latido *m*; *(of machine)* zumbido *m* **2** *vi (heart)* latir; *(machine)* zumbar; **my head is throbbing** me va a estallar la cabeza

throne [θrəʊn] *n* trono *m*

throttle ['θrɒtəl] **1** *n* **t. (valve)** *(of engine)* válvula reguladora **2** *vt (person)* estrangular

▸ **throttle back** *vt sep (engine)* desacelerar

through [θru:] **1** *prep* (a) *(place)* a través de, por; **to look t. the window** mirar por la ventana (b) *(time)* a lo largo de; **all t. his life** durante toda su vida; *US* **Tuesday t. Thursday** desde el martes hasta el jueves inclusive (c) *(by means of)* por, mediante; **I learnt of it t. Jack** me enteré por Jack (d) *(because of)* a *or* por causa de; **t. ignorance** por ignorancia

2 *adj* **a t. train** un tren directo; **t. traffic** tránsito *m*

3 *adv* (a) *(from one side to the other)* de un lado a otro; **to let sb t.** dejar pasar a algn; *Fig* **socialist/French t. and t.**

socialista/francés por los cuatro costados (**b**) **I'm t. with him** he terminado con él (**c**) *Tel* **to get t. to sb** comunicar con algn

throughout [θruːˈaʊt] **1** *prep* por todo(a); **t. the year** durante todo el año **2** *adv* *(place)* en todas partes; *(time)* todo el tiempo

throw [θrəʊ] **1** *vt* *(pt* **threw**; *pp* **thrown**) (**a**) tirar, *Am* aventar; *(to the ground)* derribar; *(rider)* desmontar; *Fig* **he threw a fit** le dio un ataque; *Fig* **to t. a party** dar una fiesta (**b**) *(disconcert)* desconcertar **2** *n* tiro *m*, lanzamiento *m*; *(in wrestling)* derribo *m*

▸ **throw away** *vt sep* *(rubbish)* tirar, *Am* botar; *(money)* malgastar; *(opportunity)* perder

▸ **throw in** *vt sep* (**a**) tirar; *Sport* sacar de banda; *Fig* **to t. in the towel** arrojar la toalla (**b**) *(include)* añadir; *(in deal)* incluir (gratis)

▸ **throw off** *vt sep* *(person, thing)* deshacerse de; *(clothes)* quitarse

▸ **throw out** *vt sep* *(rubbish)* tirar; *(person)* echar

▸ **throw up 1** *vt sep* (**a**) lanzar al aire (**b**) *Constr* construir rápidamente **2** *vi* *Fam* vomitar, devolver

thrown [θrəʊn] *pp of* **throw**

thrush [θrʌʃ] *n Orn* tordo *m*, zorzal *m*

thrust [θrʌst] **1** *vt* *(pt & pp* **thrust**) empujar con fuerza; **he t. a letter into my hand** me puso una carta violentamente en la mano **2** *n* *(push)* empujón *m*; *Av, Phys* empuje *m*

thud [θʌd] *n* ruido sordo

thug [θʌg] *n* *(lout)* gamberro *m*; *(criminal)* criminal *m*

thumb [θʌm] **1** *n* pulgar *m* **2** *vt* (**a**) manosear (**b**) **to t. a lift** hacer autostop, *CAm, Méx, Perú* pedir aventón

▸ **thumb through** *vt insep* *(book)* hojear

thump [θʌmp] **1** *n* (**a**) *(sound)* ruido sordo (**b**) *(blow)* golpazo *m*; *Fam* torta *f* **2** *vt* golpear **3** *vi* (**a**) **to t. on the table** golpear la

mesa (**b**) *(heart)* latir ruidosamente

thunder [ˈθʌndə(r)] **1** *n* trueno *m*; **t. of applause** estruendo *m* de aplausos **2** *vi* tronar

thunderstorm [ˈθʌndəstɔːm] *n* tormenta *f*

Thursday [ˈθɜːzdɪ] *n* jueves *m*

thus [ðʌs] *adv* así, de esta manera; **and t. …** así que …

thyme [taɪm] *n* tomillo *m*

tic [tɪk] *n* tic *m*

tick¹ [tɪk] **1** *n* (**a**) *(sound)* tic-tac *m* (**b**) *Br Fam* **I'll do it in a t.** ahora mismo lo hago (**c**) *(mark)* marca *f* de visto bueno **2** *vi* hacer tic-tac **3** *vt* marcar

▸ **tick off** *vt sep* (**a**) *(mark)* marcar (**b**) *Br Fam (reprimand)* regañar

▸ **tick over** *vi Aut* funcionar al ralentí

tick² [tɪk] *n* *(insect)* garrapata *f*

ticket [ˈtɪkɪt] *n* (**a**) *(for train, plane, lottery)* billete *m*, *Am* boleto *m*; *(for theatre, cinema)* entrada *f*, *Col, Méx* boleto; **t. collector** revisor(a) *m,f*; **t. office** taquilla *f*, *Am* boletería *f* (**b**) *(receipt)* recibo *m* (**c**) *(label)* etiqueta *f* (**d**) *Aut* multa *f*

tickle [ˈtɪkəl] **1** *vt* hacer cosquillas a **2** *vi* hacer cosquillas **3** *n* cosquillas *fpl*

ticklish [ˈtɪklɪʃ] *adj* **to be t.** tener cosquillas

tick-tack-toe [tɪktækˈtəʊ] *n US* tres en raya *m*

tide [taɪd] *n* (**a**) marea *f*; **high/low t.** marea alta/baja (**b**) *Fig (of events)* curso *m*; **the t. has turned** han cambiado las cosas; **to go against the t.** ir contra corriente

tidy [ˈtaɪdɪ] **1** *adj* (**tidier, tidiest**) (**a**) *(room, habits)* ordenado(a) (**b**) *(appearance)* arreglado(a) **2** *vt* arreglar; **to t. away** poner en su sitio **3** *vi* **to t. (up)** ordenar las cosas

tie [taɪ] **1** *vt* *(shoelaces etc)* atar; **to t. a knot** hacer un nudo **2** *vi Sport* empatar (**with** con) **3** *n* (**a**) *(bond)* lazo *m*, vínculo *m* (**b**) *Fig (hindrance)* atadura *f* (**c**) *(clothing)* corbata *f* (**d**) *Sport (match)* partido *m*; *(draw)* empate *m*

▶ **tie down** *vt sep* sujetar; *Fig* **to be tied down** estar atado(a); *Fig* **to t. sb down to a promise** obligar a algn a cumplir una promesa

▶ **tie up** *vt sep* (**a**) *(parcel, dog)* atar (**b**) *(deal)* concluir (**c**) *(capital)* inmovilizar; *Fig* **I'm tied up just now** de momento estoy muy ocupado(a)

tier [tɪə(r)] *n (of seats)* fila *f*; *(in stadium)* grada *f*; **four-t. cake** pastel *m* de cuatro pisos

tiger ['taɪgə(r)] *n* tigre *m*

tight [taɪt] **1** *adj* (**a**) apretado(a); *(clothing)* ajustado(a); *(seal)* hermético(a); **my shoes are too t.** me aprietan los zapatos (**b**) *(scarce)* escaso(a); **money's a bit t.** estamos escasos de dinero (**c**) *(mean)* agarrado(a) (**d**) *Fam (drunk)* alegre, *Esp* piripi

2 *adv* estrechamente; *(seal)* herméticamente; **hold t.** agárrate fuerte; **shut t.** bien cerrado(a); **to sit t.** no moverse de su sitio

tighten ['taɪtən] **1** *vt (screw)* apretar, *(rope)* tensar; *Fig* **to t. (up) restrictions** intensificar las restricciones **2** *vi* apretarse; *(cable)* tensarse

tightrope ['taɪtrəʊp] *n* cuerda floja *f*; **t. walker** funámbulo(a) *m,f*

tights [taɪts] *npl (woollen)* leotardos *mpl*, *Col* medias *fpl* veladas, *RP* cancanes *mpl*; *Br (nylon, silk)* medias *fpl*, pantis *mpl*

tile [taɪl] **1** *n (of roof)* teja *f*; *(glazed)* azulejo *m*; *(for floor)* baldosa *f* **2** *vt (roof)* tejar; *(wall)* poner azulejos en, *Esp* alicatar; *(floor)* embaldosar

till¹ [tɪl] *n (for cash)* caja *f*

till² [tɪl] *vt (field)* labrar, cultivar

till³ [tɪl] **1** *prep* hasta; **from morning t. night** de la mañana a la noche; **t. then** hasta entonces **2** *conj* hasta que

tilt [tɪlt] **1** *n* (**a**) *(angle)* inclinación *f* (**b**) **(at) full t.** *(speed)* a toda velocidad **2** *vi* **to t. over** volcarse; **to t. (up)** inclinarse

3 *vt* inclinar

timber ['tɪmbə(r)] *n (wood)* madera *f*

(de construcción); *(trees)* árboles *mpl*; **(piece of) t.** viga *f*

time [taɪm] **1** *n* (**a**) tiempo *m*; **all the t.** todo el tiempo; **I haven't seen him for a long t.** hace mucho (tiempo) que no lo veo; **in a short t.** en poco tiempo; **in no t.** en un abrir y cerrar de ojos; **in t. a tiempo; in three weeks' t.** dentro de tres semanas; **to take one's t. over sth** hacer algo con calma; **t. bomb** bomba *f* de relojería; **t. limit** límite *m* de tiempo; *(for payment etc)* plazo *m*; **t. zone** huso horario

(**b**) *(era)* época *f*, tiempos *mpl*; **to be behind the times** tener ideas anticuadas

(**c**) *(point in time)* momento *m*; **at that t.** (en aquel) entonces; **at the same t.** al mismo tiempo; **at times** a veces; **from t. to t.** de vez en cuando

(**d**) *(time of day)* hora *f*; **on t.** puntualmente; **what's the t.?** ¿qué hora es?

(**e**) **t. of year** época *f* del año

(**f**) **to have a good/bad t.** pasarlo bien/mal

(**g**) *(occasion)* vez *f*; **four at a t.** cuatro a la vez; **next t.** la próxima vez; **t. after t.** una y otra vez

(**h**) *(in multiplication)* **three times four** tres (multiplicado) por cuatro; **four times as big** cuatro veces más grande

(**i**) *Mus* compás *m*; **in t.** al compás **2** *vt* (**a**) *(speech)* calcular la duración de; *Sport (race)* cronometrar (**b**) *(choose the time of)* escoger el momento oportuno para

timely ['taɪmlɪ] *adj* (**timelier, timeliest**) oportuno(a)

timer ['taɪmə(r)] *n (device)* temporizador *m*

timetable ['taɪmteɪbəl] *n* horario *m*

timid ['tɪmɪd] *adj* tímido(a)

timing ['taɪmɪŋ] *n* (**a**) *(timeliness)* oportunidad *f*; *(coordination)* coordinación *f*; **your t. was wrong** no calculaste bien (**b**) *Sport* cronometraje *m*

tin [tɪn] **1** *n* (**a**) *(metal)* estaño *m*; **t. plate** hojalata *f* (**b**) *esp Br (container)* lata *f*, *Am* tarro *m* **2** *vt* enlatar; **tinned food** conservas *fpl*

tinfoil ['tɪnfɔɪl] *n* papel *m* de estaño

tinge [tɪndʒ] **1** *n* tinte *m*, matiz *m* **2** *vt* teñir

tingle ['tɪŋgəl] *vi* **my feet are tingling** siento un hormigueo en los pies

tinker ['tɪŋkə(r)] **1** *n Pej* calderero(a) *mf* **2** *vi* **stop tinkering with the radio** deja de toquetear la radio

tinkle ['tɪŋkəl] *vi* tintinear

tinsel ['tɪnsəl] *n* oropel *m*

tint [tɪnt] **1** *n* tinte *m*, matiz *m* **2** *vt* teñir; **to t. one's hair** teñirse el pelo

tiny ['taɪnɪ] *adj* (**tinier, tiniest**) pequeñito(a); **a t. bit** un poquitín

tip¹ [tɪp] **1** *n* (*end*) punta *f*; (*of cigarette*) colilla *f*; **it's on the t. of my tongue** lo tengo en la punta de la lengua **2** *vt* poner cantera a; **tipped with steel** con punta de acero

▸ **tip off** *vt sep* (*police*) dar el chivatazo a

▸ **tip over 1** *vt sep* volcar **2** *vi* volcarse

tip² [tɪp] **1** *n* (**a**) (*gratuity*) propina *f* (**b**) (*advice*) consejo *m* (**c**) *Sport* (*racing*) pronóstico *m* **2** *vt* (**a**) dar una propina a (**b**) *Sport* pronosticar

tip³ [tɪp] **1** *n Br* **rubbish t.** vertedero *m* **2** *vt* inclinar; *Br* (*rubbish*) verter **3** *vi* **to t. (up)** ladearse; (*cart*) bascular

tipsy ['tɪpsɪ] *adj* (**tipsier, tipsiest**) contentillo(a)

tiptoe ['tɪptəʊ] **1** *vi* caminar *or Esp* andar de puntillas; **to t. in/out** entrar/salir de puntillas **2** *n* **on t.** de puntillas

tire¹ [taɪə(r)] *n US* = **tyre**

tire² [taɪə(r)] **1** *vt* cansar; **to t. sb out** agotar a algn **2** *vi* cansarse; **to t. of doing sth** cansarse de hacer algo

tired ['taɪəd] *adj* cansado(a); **t. out** rendido(a); **to be t.** estar cansado(a); **to be t. of sth** estar harto(a) de algo

tiredness ['taɪədnɪs] *n* (*fatigue*) cansancio *m*, fatiga *f*

tireless ['taɪəlɪs] *adj* incansable

tiresome ['taɪəsəm] *adj* pesado(a)

tiring ['taɪərɪŋ] *adj* agotador(a)

tissue ['tɪʃuː, 'tɪsjuː] *n* (**a**) *Biol* tejido *m* (**b**) *Tex* tisú *m*; **t. paper** papel *m* de seda (**c**) (*handkerchief*) pañuelo *m* de papel, kleenex® *m*

titbit ['tɪtbɪt] *n* tentempié *m*, refrigerio *m*

title ['taɪtəl] *n* (**a**) título *m*; *Cin* **credit titles** ficha técnica; **t. page** portada *f*; **t. role** papel *m* principal (**b**) *Jur* título *m*

titter ['tɪtə(r)] **1** *vi* reírse nerviosamente; (*foolishly*) reírse tontamente **2** *n* risa ahogada; (*foolish*) risilla tonta

to [tuː, *unstressed before vowels* tʊ, *before consonants* tə] **1** *prep* (**a**) (*with place*) a; (*expressing direction*) hacia; **he went to France/Japan** fue a Francia/Japón; **I'm going to Mary's** voy a casa de Mary; **it is 30 miles to London** Londres está a 30 millas; **the train to Madrid** el tren de Madrid; **to the east** hacia el este; **to the right** a la derecha

(**b**) (*time*) a; **from two to four** de dos a cuatro; *Br* **it's ten to (six)** son (las seis) menos diez, *Am* salvo *RP* faltan diez (para las seis)

(**c**) (*as far as*) hasta; **accurate to a millimetre** exacto(a) hasta el milímetro

(**d**) (*with indirect object*) **he gave it to his cousin** se lo dio a su primo

(**e**) (*towards a person*) **he was very kind to me** se portó muy bien conmigo

(**f**) (*of*) de; **adviser to the president** consejero *m* del presidente

(**g**) **to come to sb's assistance** acudir en ayuda de algn; **to everyone's surprise** para sorpresa de todos

(**h**) **to the best of my knowledge** que yo sepa

(**i**) (*compared to*) **that's nothing to what I've seen** eso no es nada en comparación con lo que he visto yo

(**j**) (*in proportion*) **one house to the square kilometre** una casa por kilómetro cuadrado; **six votes to four** seis votos contra cuatro

2 *with infin* (**a**) *with simple infinitives* **to** *is not translated but is shown by the verb endings;* **to buy** comprar; **to come** venir (**b**) *(in order to)* para; *(with verbs of motion or purpose)* a, por; **he did it to help me** lo hizo para ayudarme; **he stopped to talk** se detuvo a hablar

(**c**) *various verbs followed by dependent infinitives take particular prepositions* (a, de, en, por, con, para *etc*) *and others take no preposition; see the entry of the verb in question*

(**d**) *(with adj and infin)* a, de; **difficult to do** difícil de hacer; **too hot to drink** demasiado caliente para bebérselo

(**e**) *(with noun and infin)* **the first to complain** el primero en quejarse; **to have a great deal to do** tener mucho que hacer

(**f**) *(with verbs of ordering, wishing etc)* **he asked me to do it** me pidió que lo hiciera

(**g**) *(replacing infin)* **go if you want to** váyase si quiere

3 *adv* **to go to and fro** ir y venir; **to push the door to** encajar la puerta

toad [təʊd] *n* sapo *m*

toadstool ['təʊdstuːl] *n Esp* seta *f* venenosa, *Am* hongo *m* (venenoso)

toast¹ [təʊst] *Culin* **1** *n* pan tostado; **a slice of t.** una tostada **2** *vt* tostar

toast² [təʊst] **1** *n (drink)* brindis *m inv*; **to drink a t. to** brindar por **2** *vt* brindar por

toaster ['təʊstə(r)] *n* tostador *m* (de pan)

tobacco [tə'bækəʊ] *n* tabaco *m*

tobacconist [tə'bækənɪst] *n Br* estanquero(a) *m,f*; *Br* **t.'s (shop)** estanco *m*, *CSur* quiosco *m*, *Méx* estanquillo *m*

toboggan [tə'bɒgən] *n* tobogán *m*

today [tə'deɪ] **1** *n* hoy *m* **2** *adv* hoy; *(nowadays)* hoy en día; **a week t.** justo dentro de una semana

toddler ['tɒdlə(r)] *n* niño(a) *m,f* que empieza a andar; **the toddlers** los pequeñitos

toe [təʊ] **1** *n* dedo *m* del pie; **big t.** dedo gordo **2** *vt* **to t. the line** conformarse

toffee ['tɒfɪ] *n* caramelo *m*

together [tə'geðə(r)] *adv* junto, juntos(as); **all t.** todos juntos; **t. with** junto con; **to bring t.** reunir

toil [tɔɪl] **1** *n* trabajo duro **2** *vi* afanarse, trabajar (duro); **to t. up a hill** subir penosamente una cuesta

toilet ['tɔɪlɪt] *n* (**a**) *Br (in house)* cuarto *m* de baño, retrete *m*; *(in public place)* baño(s) *m(pl)*, *Esp* servicio(s) *m(pl)*, *CSur* toilette *f*; **t. paper** *or* **tissue** papel higiénico; **t. roll** rollo *m* de papel higiénico (**b**) *(washing etc)* aseo *m* (personal); **t. bag** neceser *m*; **t. soap** jabón *m* de tocador

toiletries ['tɔɪlɪtrɪz] *npl* artículos *mpl* de aseo

token ['təʊkən] **1** *n* (**a**) *(sign)* señal *f*; **as a t. of respect** en señal de respeto (**b**) *Com* vale *m*; **book t.** vale para comprar libros **2** *adj* simbólico(a)

told [təʊld] *pt & pp of* **tell**

tolerable ['tɒlərəbəl] *adj* tolerable

tolerance ['tɒlərəns] *n* tolerancia *f*

tolerant ['tɒlərənt] *adj* tolerante

tolerate ['tɒləreɪt] *vt* tolerar

toll¹ [təʊl] **1** *vt* tocar **2** *vi* doblar

toll² [təʊl] *n* (**a**) *(charge)* peaje *m*, *Méx* cuota *f* (**b**) *(loss)* pérdidas *fpl*; **the death t.** el número de víctimas mortales

tomato [tə'mɑːtəʊ, *US* tə'meɪtəʊ] *n (pl* **tomatoes)** tomate *m*, *Méx* jitomate *m*

tomb [tuːm] *n* tumba *f*, sepulcro *m*

tombstone ['tuːmstəʊn] *n* lápida *f* sepulcral

tomorrow [tə'mɒrəʊ] **1** *n* mañana *m*; **the day after t.** pasado mañana; **t. night** mañana por la noche **2** *adv* mañana; **see you t.!** ¡hasta mañana!; **t. week** dentro de ocho días a partir de mañana

ton [tʌn] *n* tonelada *f*; *Fam* **tons of** montones de

tone [təʊn] **1** *n* tono *m* **2** *vi* **to t. (in) with sth** armonizar con algo

▶ **tone down** *vt sep* atenuar

tongs [tɒŋz] *npl (for sugar, hair)* tenacillas *fpl*; **(fire) t.** tenazas *fpl*

tongue [tʌŋ] *n* (**a**) lengua *f*, *Fig* **to say sth t. in cheek** decir algo con la boca pequeña; *Fig* **t. twister** trabalenguas *m inv* (**b**) *(of shoe)* lengüeta *f*; *(of bell)* badajo *m*

tonic ['tɒnɪk] **1** *n* (**a**) *Med* tónico *m* (**b**) *(drink)* tónica *f* **2** *adj* tónico(a)

tonight [tə'naɪt] *adv & n* esta noche

tonne [tʌn] *n* = **ton**

tonsil ['tɒnsəl] *n* amígdala *f*; **to have one's tonsils out** ser operado(a) de las amígdalas

tonsillitis [tɒnsɪ'laɪtɪs] *n* amigdalitis *f*

too [tuː] *adv* (**a**) *(besides)* además (**b**) *(also)* también (**c**) *(excessively)* demasiado; **t. much money** demasiado dinero; **£10 t. much** 10 libras de más; **t. frequently** con demasiada frecuencia; **t. old** demasiado viejo

took [tʊk] *pt of* **take**

tool [tuːl] *n (utensil)* herramienta *f*

tooth [tuːθ] *n (pl* **teeth**) (**a**) diente *m*; *(molar)* muela *f*; *Fig* **to fight t. and nail** luchar a brazo partido (**b**) *(of saw)* diente *m*; *(of comb)* púa *f*

toothache ['tuːθeɪk] *n* dolor *m* de muelas

toothbrush ['tuːθbrʌʃ] *n* cepillo *m* de dientes

toothpaste ['tuːθpeɪst] *n* pasta dentífrica

top¹ [tɒp] **1** *n* (**a**) *(upper part)* parte *f* de arriba; *(of hill)* cumbre *f*, cima *f*; *(of tree)* copa *f*; **from t. to bottom** de arriba abajo; **on t. of** encima de; *Fig* **on t. of it all …** para colmo …; **t. hat** sombrero *m* de copa (**b**) *(surface)* superficie *f* (**c**) *(of list etc)* cabeza *f* (**d**) *(of bottle etc)* tapa *f*, tapón *m* (**e**) *(garment)* camiseta *f* (**f**) *(best)* lo mejor

2 *adj* (**a**) *(part)* superior, de arriba; **the t. floor** el último piso (**b**) *(highest)* más alto(a); *Br Aut* **t. gear** directa *f* (**c**) *(best)* mejor

3 *vt* (**a**) *(place on top of)* coronar; *Fig* **and to t. it all** y para colmo (**b**) *Th* **to t. the bill** encabezar el reparto

▸ **top up** *vt sep* llenar hasta el tope; **to t. up the petrol tank** llenar el depósito

top² [tɒp] *n (toy)* peonza *f*

topic ['tɒpɪk] *n* tema *m*

topical ['tɒpɪkəl] *adj* de actualidad

topple ['tɒpəl] **1** *vi (building)* venirse abajo; **to t. (over)** volcarse **2** *vt* volcar; *Fig (government)* derrocar

top-secret ['tɒp'siːkrɪt] *adj* de alto secreto

topsy-turvy ['tɒpsɪ'tɜːvɪ] *adj & adv* al revés; *(in confusion)* en desorden, patas arriba

torch [tɔːtʃ] *n Br (electric)* linterna *f*

tore [tɔː(r)] *pt of* **tear²**

torment 1 *vt* [tɔː'ment] atormentar **2** *n* ['tɔːment] tormento *m*, suplicio *m*

torn [tɔːn] *pp of* **tear²**

tornado [tɔː'neɪdəʊ] *n* tornado *m*

torpedo [tɔː'piːdəʊ] *n* torpedo *m*

torrent ['tɒrənt] *n* torrente *m*

tortoise ['tɔːtəs] *n* tortuga *f* (de tierra)

tortuous ['tɔːtjʊəs] *adj (path)* tortuoso(a); *(explanation)* enrevesado(a)

torture ['tɔːtʃə(r)] **1** *vt* torturar; *Fig* atormentar **2** *n* tortura *f*; *Fig* tormento *m*

Tory ['tɔːrɪ] *adj & n Br Pol* conservador(a) *(m,f)*

toss [tɒs] **1** *vt* (**a**) *(ball)* tirar; **to t. a coin** echar a cara o cruz, *Méx* echar a águila o sol, *RP* echar a cara o seca (**b**) *(throw about)* sacudir

2 *vi* (**a**) **to t. about** agitarse; **to t. and turn** dar vueltas en la cama (**b**) *Sport* **to t. (up)** sortear

3 *n* (**a**) *(of ball)* lanzamiento *m*; *(of coin)* sorteo *m* (a cara o cruz) (**b**) *(of head)* sacudida *f*

tot¹ [tɒt] *n* (**a**) **(tiny) t.** *(child)* nene(a) *m,f* (**b**) *(of whisky etc)* trago *m*

tot² [tɒt] *vt Br* **to t. up** sumar

total ['təʊtəl] **1** *n* total *m*; *(in bill)* importe *m*; **grand t.** suma *f* total

2 *adj* total

3 *vt* sumar

4 *vi* **to t. up to** ascender a

totally ['təʊtəlɪ] *adv* totalmente

totter ['tɒtə(r)] *vi* tambalearse

touch [tʌtʃ] **1** *vt* (**a**) tocar; *Fig* **to t. on a subject** tocar un tema (**b**) *(equal)* igualar (**c**) *(move)* conmover

2 *vi* tocarse

3 *n* (**a**) toque *m* (**b**) *(sense of touch)* tacto *m* (**c**) *(contact)* contacto *m*; **to be/get/keep in t. with sb** estar/ponerse/mantenerse en contacto con algn (**d**) *(small amount)* pizca *f*

▸ **touch down** *vi (plane)* aterrizar

▸ **touch off** *vt sep* desencadenar

▸ **touch up** *vt sep (picture)* retocar

touchdown ['tʌtʃdaʊn] *n* (**a**) *(of plane)* aterrizaje *m*; *(of space capsule)* amerizaje *m* (**b**) *(in American football)* ensayo *m*

touched [tʌtʃt] *adj* (**a**) *(moved)* emocionado(a) (**b**) *Fam (crazy) Esp* tocado(a) del ala, *Am* zafado(a)

touching ['tʌtʃɪŋ] *adj* conmovedor(a)

touchy ['tʌtʃɪ] *adj* (**touchier, touchiest**) *Fam (person)* susceptible; *(subject)* delicado(a)

tough [tʌf] **1** *adj (material, competitor etc)* fuerte, resistente; *(test, criminal, meat)* duro(a); *(punishment)* severo(a); *(problem)* difícil **2** *n (person)* matón *m*

toughen ['tʌfən] *vt* endurecer

toupee ['tu:peɪ] *n* tupé *m*

tour [tʊə(r)] **1** *n* (**a**) *(journey)* viaje *m*; **package t.** viaje organizado (**b**) *(of monument etc)* visita *f*; *(of city)* recorrido turístico (**c**) *Sport, Th* gira *f*; **on t.** de gira

2 *vt* (**a**) *(country)* viajar por (**b**) *(building)* visitar (**c**) *Th* estar de gira en

3 *vi* estar de viaje

tourism ['tʊərɪzəm] *n* turismo *m*

tourist ['tʊərɪst] *n* turista *mf*; **t. centre** centro *m* de información turística; *Av* **t. class** clase *f* turista

tournament ['tʊənəmənt] *n* torneo *m*

tout [taʊt] **1** *vt Com* tratar de vender; *Br (tickets)* revender

2 *vi* = salir a la caza y captura de compradores

3 *n Com* gancho *m*

tow [təʊ] **1** *n* **to take a car in t.** remolcar un coche; *US* **t. truck** grúa *f* **2** *vt* remolcar

towards [tə'wɔ:dz, tɔ:dz] *prep* (**a**) *(direction, time)* hacia (**b**) *(with regard to)* hacia, (para) con; **our duty t. others** nuestro deber para con los demás; **what is your attitude t. religion?** ¿cuál es su actitud respecto a la religión?

towel ['taʊəl] **1** *n* toalla *f*; **hand t.** toallita *f*; **t.** *Br* **rail** *or US* **bar** toallero *m* **2** *vi* **to t. dry** secar con una toalla

tower ['taʊə(r)] **1** *n* torre *f* **2** *vi* **to t. over** *or* **above sth** dominar algo

town [taʊn] *n* ciudad *f*; *(small)* pueblo *m*; **to go into t.** ir al centro; *Fam* **to go to t.** tirar la casa por la ventana; *Br* **t. council** ayuntamiento *m*; **t. councillor** concejal(a) *m,f*; **t. hall** ayuntamiento *m*; **t. planning** urbanismo *m*

toxic ['tɒksɪk] *adj* tóxico(a)

toy [tɔɪ] **1** *n* juguete *m* **2** *vi* **to t. with an idea** acariciar una idea; **to t. with one's food** comer sin gana

trace [treɪs] **1** *n* (**a**) *(sign)* indicio *m*, vestigio *m* (**b**) *(tracks)* huella(s) *f(pl)* **2** *vt* (**a**) *(drawing)* calcar (**b**) *(plan)* bosquejar (**c**) *(locate)* seguir la pista de

tracing ['treɪsɪŋ] *n* **t. paper** papel *m* de calco

track [træk] **1** *n* (**a**) *(trail)* huellas *fpl*, pista *f*; **to keep/lose t. of sb** no perder/perder de vista a algn (**b**) *(pathway)* camino *m*; **to be on the right/wrong t.** ir por el buen/mal camino

(**c**) *Sport* pista *f*; *(for motor racing)* circuito *m*; *Fig* **t. record** historial *m* (**d**) *Rail* vía *f*; *Fig* **he has a one-t. mind** tiene una única obsesión (**e**) *(on record, CD)* canción *f* (**f**) *US Educ* = cada una de las divisiones del alumnado en grupos por niveles de aptitud

2 *vt* seguir la pista de; *(with radar)* seguir la trayectoria de

▸ **track down** *vt sep (locate)* localizar

tracksuit ['træksu:t] *n Esp* chándal *m*, *Méx* pants *m*, *RP* jogging *m*

tractor ['træktə(r)] *n* tractor *m*

trade [treɪd] **1** *n* (**a**) *(profession)* oficio *m*; **by t.** de oficio (**b**) *Com* comercio *m*; **it's good for t.** es bueno para los negocios; **the building t.** (la industria de) la construcción; **t. name** nombre *m* comercial; **t. union** sindicato *m*; **t. unionist** sindicalista *mf*

2 *vi* comerciar (**in** en)

3 *vt* **to t. sth for sth** trocar algo por algo

▸ **trade in** *vt sep* dar como entrada

trademark ['treɪdmɑːk] *n* marca *f* (de fábrica); **registered t.** marca registrada

trader ['treɪdə(r)] *n* comerciante *mf*

tradesman ['treɪdzmən] *n (shop-keeper)* tendero *m*

trading ['treɪdɪŋ] *n* comercio *m*; *Br* **t. estate** polígono *m* industrial

tradition [trə'dɪʃən] *n* tradición *f*

traditional [trə'dɪʃənəl] *adj* tradicional

traffic ['træfɪk] **1** *n* (a) tráfico *m*, circulación *f*; *US* **t. circle** rotonda *f*; **t. island** isleta *f*; **t. jam** atasco *m*; **t. lights** semáforo *m*; *Br* **t. warden** ≃ guardia *mf* urbano(a) (b) *(trade)* tráfico *m* **2** *vi* (*pt & pp* **trafficked**) **to t. in drugs** traficar con droga

trafficker ['træfɪkə(r)] *n* traficante *mf*

tragedy ['trædʒɪdɪ] *n* tragedia *f*

tragic ['trædʒɪk] *adj* trágico(a)

trail [treɪl] **1** *vt* (a) *(drag)* arrastrar (b) *(follow)* rastrear

2 *vi* (a) *(drag)* arrastrarse (b) **to t. behind** rezagarse

3 *n* (a) *(track)* pista *f*, rastro *m* (b) *(path)* senda *f*, camino *m* (c) *(of smoke)* estela *f*

trailer ['treɪlə(r)] *n* (a) *Aut* remolque *m* (b) *US Aut (caravan)* caravana *f* (c) *Cin* trailer *m*, avance *m*

train [treɪn] **1** *n* (a) *Rail* tren *m* (b) *(of vehicles)* convoy *m*; *(of followers)* séquito *m*; *(of events)* serie *f* (c) *(of dress)* cola *f*

2 *vt* (a) *(teach)* formar; *Sport* entrenar; *(animal)* amaestrar; *(voice etc)* educar (b) *(gun)* apuntar (**on** a); *(camera)* enfocar (**on** a)

3 *vi* prepararse; *Sport* entrenarse

trainee [treɪ'niː] *n* aprendiz(a) *m,f*

trainer ['treɪnə(r)] *n* (a) *Sport* entrenador(a) *m,f*; *(of dogs)* amaestrador(a) *m,f*; *(of lions)* domador(a) *m,f* (b) *Br* **trainers** *(shoes)* zapatillas *fpl* de deporte

training ['treɪnɪŋ] *n (instruction)* formación *f*; *Sport* entrenamiento *m*; *(of animals)* amaestramiento *m*; *(of lions)* doma *f*; **to go into t.** empezar el entrenamiento; **vocational t.** formación profesional

trait [treɪt] *n* rasgo *m*

traitor ['treɪtə(r)] *n* traidor(a) *m,f*

tram [træm], **tramcar** ['træmkɑː(r)] *n Br* tranvía *m*

tramp [træmp] **1** *vi* (a) *(travel on foot)* caminar (b) *(walk heavily)* andar con pasos pesados **2** *n (person)* vagabundo(a) *m,f*; *Pej* **she's a t.** es una fulana *or Méx* reventada

trample ['træmpəl] *vt* **to t. down the grass** pisotear la hierba; **to t. sth underfoot** pisotear algo

trampoline ['træmpəliːn] *n* cama elástica

trance [trɑːns] *n* trance *m*

tranquillizer ['træŋkwɪlaɪzə(r)] *n* tranquilizante *m*

transaction [træn'zækʃən] *n (pro-cedure)* tramitación *f*; *(deal)* transacción *f*

transatlantic [trænzət'læntɪk] *adj* transatlántico(a)

transcend [træn'send] *vt* trascender

transfer 1 *vt* [træns'fɜː(r)] trasladar; *(funds)* trasferir; *Jur* ceder; *Ftb* traspasar; *US Rail* hacer transbordo **2** *n* ['trænsfɜː(r)] (a) *(of funds)* trasferencia *f*; *Jur* cesión *f*; *Ftb* traspaso *m* (b) *(picture, design)* calcomanía *f* (c) *US Rail* transbordo *m*

transform [træns'fɔːm] *vt* trasformar

transformation [trænsfə'meɪʃən] *n* trasformación *f*

transformer [træns'fɔːmə(r)] *n Elec* transformador *m*

transfusion [træns'fjuːʒən] *n Med* transfusión *f* (de sangre)

transit ['trænzɪt] *n* tránsito *m*; **in t.** de tránsito

transition [træn'zɪʃən] *n* transición *f*

transitive ['trænzɪtɪv] *adj* transitivo(a)

translate [træns'leɪt] *vt* traducir

translation [træns'leɪʃən] *n* traducción *f*

translator [træns'leɪtə(r)] *n* traductor(a) *m,f*

transmission [trænz'mɪʃən] *n* transmisión *f*

transmit [trænz'mɪt] *vt* transmitir

transmitter [trænz'mɪtə(r)] *n* Rad *(set)* transmisor *m*; Rad, TV *(station)* emisora *f*

transparent [træns'pærənt] *adj* transparente

transpire [træn'spaɪə(r)] *vi (happen)* ocurrir; **it transpired that …** ocurrió que …

transplant 1 *vt* [træns'plɑːnt] trasplantar **2** *n* ['trænsplɑːnt] trasplante *m*

transport 1 *vt* [træns'pɔːt] transportar **2** *n* ['trænspɔːt] transporte *m*; **t. aircraft/ship** avión *m*/buque *m* de transporte; Br **t. café** bar *m* de carretera

transvestite [trænz'vestaɪt] *n* Fam travestido(a) *m,f,* Esp travestí *mf*

trap [træp] **1** *n* trampa *f*; **t. door** trampilla *f;* Th escotillón *m* **2** *vt* atrapar

trash [træʃ] *n (inferior goods)* bazofia *f;* US *(rubbish)* basura *f;* Fig **to talk a lot of t.** decir tonterías; US **t. can** cubo *m* de la basura

trashy ['træʃɪ] *adj* **(trashier, trashiest)** Fam de pacotilla, Esp cutre, Méx gacho(a)

traumatic [trɔ:'mætɪk] *adj* traumático(a)

travel ['trævəl] **1** *vi* (a) viajar; **to t. through** recorrer (b) *(vehicle, electric current)* ir; Fig *(news)* propagarse **2** *vt* recorrer **3** *n* viajar *m*; **t. agency** agencia *f* de viajes

traveller, US **traveler** ['trævələ(r)] *n* viajero(a) *m,f;* **t.'s** Br **cheque** or US **check** cheque *m* de viaje

travelling, US **traveling** ['trævəlɪŋ] **1** *adj (salesman)* ambulante **2** *n* viajes *mpl,* (el) viajar *m;* **I'm fond of t.** me gusta viajar; **t. expenses** gastos *mpl* de viaje

travesty ['trævɪstɪ] *n* parodia *f* burda

tray [treɪ] *n (for food)* bandeja *f; (for letters)* cesta *f (para la correspondencia)*

treacherous ['tretʃərəs] *adj* (a) *(person)* traidor(a); *(action)* traicionero(a) (b) *(dangerous)* peligroso(a)

treachery ['tretʃərɪ] *n* traición *f*

treacle ['tri:kəl] *n* Br melaza *f*

tread [tred] *(pt* **trod;** *pp* **trod** or **trodden) 1** *vi* pisar; **to t. on** pisar **2** *vt* (a) *(step on)* pisar (b) **to t. water** mantenerse a flote verticalmente **3** *n* (a) *(step)* paso *m; (sound)* ruido *m* de pasos (b) *(of tyre)* banda *f* de rodadura

treason ['tri:zən] *n* traición *f*

treasure ['treʒə(r)] **1** *n* tesoro *m* **2** *vt (keep)* guardar como oro en paño; *(value)* apreciar muchísimo

treasurer ['treʒərə(r)] *n* tesorero(a) *m,f*

treat [tri:t] **1** *n* (a) *(present)* regalo *m* (b) *(pleasure)* placer *m* **2** *vt* (a) tratar; **to t. badly** maltratar (b) *(regard)* considerar (c) **he treated them to dinner** les invitó a cenar

treatment ['tri:tmənt] *n* (a) *(of person)* trato *m* (b) *(of subject, of patient)* tratamiento *m*

treaty ['tri:tɪ] *n* tratado *m*

treble ['trebəl] **1** *adj* (a) *(triple)* triple (b) Mus **t. clef** clave *f* de sol; **t. voice** voz *f* triple **2** *vt* triplicar **3** *vi* triplicarse

tree [tri:] *n* árbol *m;* **apple/cherry t.** manzano *m*/cerezo *m*

trek [trek] **1** *n (journey)* viaje *m* (largo y difícil); Fam *(walk)* caminata *f* **2** *vi* hacer un viaje largo y difícil; Fam *(walk)* ir caminando

tremble ['trembəl] *vi* temblar, estremecerse

tremendous [trɪ'mendəs] *adj (huge)* enorme; *(success)* arrollador(a); *(shock* *etc)* tremendo(a); *Fam (marvellous)* estupendo(a)

trench [trentʃ] *n* (**a**) *(ditch)* zanja *f*; *Mil* trinchera *f* (**b**) **t. coat** trinchera *f*

trend [trend] **1** *n (tendency)* tendencia *f*; *(fashion)* moda *f* **2** *vi* tender (**to** or **towards** hacia)

trendy ['trendɪ] *adj* (**trendier, trendiest**) *Fam (person)* modernillo(a) *m,f*, *RP* modernoso(a) *m,f*; *(clothes)* a la última

trespass ['trespəs] *vi* entrar sin autorización

trial ['traɪəl] *n* (**a**) *Jur* proceso *m*, juicio *m* (**b**) *(test)* prueba *f*; **on t.** a prueba; **by t. and error** a fuerza de equivocarse (**c**) **trials** *(competition)* concurso *m* (**d**) **trials** *(suffering)* sufrimiento *m*; **trials and tribulations** tribulaciones *fpl*

triangle ['traɪæŋgəl] *n* triángulo *m*

triangular [traɪˈæŋgjʊlə(r)] *adj* triangular

tribe [traɪb] *n* tribu *f*

tribunal [traɪˈbjuːnəl] *n* tribunal *m*

tribute ['trɪbjuːt] *n* (**a**) *(payment)* tributo *m* (**b**) *(mark of respect)* homenaje *m*; **to pay t. to** rendir homenaje a

trick [trɪk] **1** *n* (**a**) *(ruse)* ardid *m*; *(dishonest)* engaño *m*; *(in question)* trampa *f* (**b**) *(practical joke)* broma *f*; **to play a t. on sb** gastarle una broma a algn; *(malicious)* jugar una mala pasada a algn (**c**) *(of magic, knack)* truco *m* (**d**) *Cards* baza *f* **2** *vt* engañar; **to t. sb out of sth** quitar or *Am* sacarle algo a algn a base de engaños

trickle ['trɪkəl] **1** *vi* discurrir; *(water)* gotear **2** *n* hilo *m*

tricky ['trɪkɪ] *adj* (**trickier, trickiest**) *(person)* astuto(a); *(situation, mechanism)* delicado(a)

tricycle ['traɪsɪkəl] *n* triciclo *m*

trifle ['traɪfəl] **1** *n* (**a**) *(insignificant thing)* bagatela *f* (**b**) *Br Culin* = postre de bizcocho, gelatina, frutas y *Esp* nata or *Am* crema de leche **2** *vi* **to t. with** tomar a la ligera

trifling ['traɪflɪŋ] *adj* insignificante, trivial

trigger ['trɪgə(r)] **1** *n (of gun)* gatillo *m*; *(of mechanism)* disparador *m* **2** *vt* **to t. (off)** desencadenar

trilogy ['trɪlədʒɪ] *n* trilogía *f*

trim [trɪm] **1** *adj* (**trimmer, trimmest**) *(neat)* aseado(a) **2** *vt* (**a**) *(cut)* recortar; *Fig (expenses)* disminuir (**b**) *(decorate)* adornar **3** *n* (**a**) *(condition)* estado *m*; *Naut* asiento *m* (**b**) *(cut)* recorte *m*

trinket ['trɪŋkɪt] *n* baratija *f*

trio ['triːəʊ] *n* trío *m*

trip [trɪp] **1** *n* (**a**) *(journey)* viaje *m*; *(excursion)* excursión *f*; **to go on a t.** ir de excursión (**b**) *Fam* **to be on a t.** *(on drugs)* estar colocado(a) **2** *vi* (**a**) **to t. (up)** *(stumble)* tropezar (**over** con); *Fig (err)* equivocarse (**b**) **to t. along** ir con paso ligero **3** *vt* **to t. sb (up)** poner la zancadilla a algn; *Fig* coger or pillar a algn

triple ['trɪpəl] **1** *adj* triple **2** *vt* triplicar **3** *vi* triplicarse

triplet ['trɪplɪt] *n* trillizo(a) *m,f*

triplicate ['trɪplɪkɪt] *adj* **in t.** por triplicado

tripod ['traɪpɒd] *n* trípode *m*

triumph ['traɪəmf] **1** *n* triunfo *m* **2** *vi* triunfar

triumphant [traɪˈʌmfənt] *adj* triunfante

trivial ['trɪvɪəl] *adj* trivial, banal

trod [trɒd] *pt & pp of* **tread**

trodden ['trɒdən] *pp of* **tread**

trolley ['trɒlɪ] *n Br* carro *m*

trombone [trɒmˈbəʊn] *n* trombón *m*

troop [truːp] **1** *n* (**a**) *(of people)* grupo *m* (**b**) *Mil* **troops** tropas *fpl* **2** *vi* **to t. in/out/off** entrar/salir/marcharse en tropel

trooper ['truːpə(r)] *n* (**a**) *(soldier)* soldado *m* *(de caballería o división acorazada)* (**b**) *US (policeman)* policía *mf*

trophy ['trəʊfɪ] *n* trofeo *m*

tropic ['trɒpɪk] *n* trópico *m*

tropical ['trɒpɪkəl] *adj* tropical

trot [trɒt] **1** *vi* trotar **2** *n* trote *m*; **to go at a t.** ir al trote; *Br Fam* **on the t.** *(in succession)* seguidos(as)

trouble ['trʌbəl] **1** *n* (a) *(misfortune)* desgracia *f* (b) *(problems)* problemas *mpl*; **to be in t.** estar en un lío; **to cause sb t.** ocasionar problemas a algn; **to get sb out of t.** sacar a algn de un apuro; **the t. is that ...** lo que pasa es que ... (c) *(effort)* esfuerzo *m*; **it's no t.** no es ninguna molestia; **it's not worth the t.** no merece la pena; **to take the t. to do sth** molestarse en hacer algo (d) *(conflict)* conflicto *m* (e) *Med* enfermedad *f*; **to have liver t.** tener problemas de hígado **2** *vt* (a) *(affect)* afligir; *(worry)* preocupar; **that doesn't t. him at all** eso le tiene sin cuidado (b) *(bother)* molestar **3** *vi* molestarse

troublemaker ['trʌbəlmeɪkə(r)] *n* alborotador(a) *m,f*

troublesome ['trʌbəlsəm] *adj* molesto(a)

trough [trɒf] *n* (a) **(drinking) t.** abrevadero *m*; **(feeding) t.** pesebre *m* (b) *(of wave)* seno *m* (c) *Geog, Met* depresión *f*

trousers ['trauzəz] *npl* pantalón *m*, pantalones *mpl*

trout [traut] *n* trucha *f*

trowel ['trauəl] *n* (a) *(builder's)* palustre *m* (b) *(for gardening)* desplantador *m*

truant ['tru:ənt] *n Br* **to play t.** faltar a clase, *Esp* hacer novillos, *Méx* irse de pinta

truce [tru:s] *n* tregua *f*

truck¹ [trʌk] *n* (a) *Br Rail* vagón *m* (b) *Aut* camión *m*; **t. driver** camionero(a) *m,f, CAm, Méx* trailero(a) *m,f*

truck² [trʌk] *n* (a) **to have no t. with** no estar dispuesto a tolerar (b) *US* verduras *fpl*; **t. farm** huerta *f*; **t. farmer** hortelano(a) *m,f*; **t. farming** cultivo *m* de hortalizas

trucker ['trʌkə(r)] *n US (lorry driver)* camionero(a) *m,f, CAm, Méx* trailero(a) *m,f*

trudge [trʌdʒ] *vi* caminar con dificultad

true [tru:] *adj* **(truer, truest)** (a) verdadero(a); **it's t. that ...** es verdad que ...; **to come t.** cumplirse, hacerse realidad (b) *(faithful)* fiel (c) *(aim)* acertado(a)

truly ['tru:lɪ] *adv* (a) de verdad; **really and t.?** ¿de veras? (b) *(faithfully)* fielmente; **yours t.** atentamente

trump [trʌmp] *Cards* **1** *n* triunfo *m* **2** *vt* fallar

trumpet ['trʌmpɪt] *n* trompeta *f*

truncheon ['trʌntʃən] *n Br* porra *f (de policía)*

trunk [trʌŋk] *n* (a) *(of tree, body)* tronco *m* (b) *(of elephant)* trompa *f* (c) *(luggage)* baúl *m* (d) *Br Tel* **t. call** llamada *f or Am* llamado *m* de larga distancia, *Esp* conferencia *f*; **t. road** carretera *f* principal (e) *US (of car)* maletero *m, CAm, Méx* cajuela *f, RP* baúl *m*

trust [trʌst] **1** *n* (a) confianza *f*; **breach of t.** abuso *m* de confianza (b) *Jur* fideicomiso *m* (c) *Fin* trust *m* **2** *vt* (a) *(hope)* esperar (b) *(rely upon)* fiarse de; **to t. sb with sth** confiar algo a algn **3** *vi* confiar (**in** en)

trusted ['trʌstɪd] *adj* de fiar

trustworthy ['trʌstwɜːðɪ] *adj (person)* de confianza, *Am* confiable; *(information)* fidedigno(a), *Am* confiable

truth [tru:θ] *n* verdad *f*; **to tell the t.** decir la verdad

truthful ['tru:θfʊl] *adj (person)* veraz, sincero(a); *(testimony)* verídico(a)

try [traɪ] *(pt & pp* **tried)** **1** *vt* (a) *(attempt)* intentar; **to t. to do sth** tratar de *or* intentar hacer algo (b) *(test)* probar, ensayar; **to t. sb's patience** poner a prueba la paciencia de algn (c) *Jur* juzgar **2** *vi* intentar **3** *n* (a) *(attempt)* tentativa *f*, intento *m* (b) *Sport* ensayo *m*

▸ **try on** *vt sep (dress)* probarse

▸ **try out** *vt sep* probar

trying ['traɪɪŋ] *adj (person)* molesto(a), pesado(a); **to have a t. time** pasar un mal rato

T-shirt ['tiːʃɜːt] *n* camiseta *f*, *Méx* playera, *RP* remera *f*

tub [tʌb] *n* (**a**) *(container)* tina *f*, cuba *f* (**b**) *(bath)* bañera *f*, *Am* tina *f*, *Am* bañadera *f*

tuba ['tjuːbə] *n* tuba *f*

tube [tjuːb] *n* (**a**) tubo *m*; *Anat* conducto *m*; *(of bicycle)* cámara *f* (de aire) (**b**) *Br Fam* **the t.** *(underground)* el metro, *RP* el subte

tuberculosis [tjʊbɜːkjʊ'ləʊsɪs] *n* tuberculosis *f*

tuck [tʌk] **1** *vt* **to t. sb in** arropar a algn; **to t. one's shirt into one's trousers** meterse la camisa por dentro (de los pantalones) **2** *n Sewing* pliegue *m*

▸ **tuck in** *vi Fam* devorar

Tuesday ['tjuːzdɪ] *n* martes *m*

tuft [tʌft] *n (of hair)* mechón *m*

tug [tʌg] **1** *vt (pull at)* tirar de; *(haul along)* arrastrar; *Naut* remolcar **2** *n* (**a**) *(pull)* tirón *m*; **t. of war** *(game)* lucha *f* de la cuerda; *Fig* lucha encarnizada (**b**) *Naut* remolcador *m*

tuition [tjuː'ɪʃən] *n* instrucción *f*; **private t.** clases *fpl* particulares; **t. fees** honorarios *mpl*

tulip ['tjuːlɪp] *n* tulipán *m*

tumble ['tʌmbəl] **1** *vi (person)* caerse; *(acrobat)* dar volteretas; *(building)* venirse abajo **2** *vt* volcar **3** *n* (**a**) caída *f* (**b**) **t. dryer** secadora *f*

tumbler ['tʌmblə(r)] *n* vaso *m*

tummy ['tʌmɪ] *n Fam* barriga *f*, *Chile* guata *f*

tumour, *US* **tumor** ['tjuːmə(r)] *n* tumor *m*

tuna ['tjuːnə] *n* atún *m*, bonito *m*

tune [tjuːn] **1** *n* (**a**) *(melody)* melodía *f*; *Fig* **to change one's t.** cambiar de tono (**b**) *Mus* tono *m*; **in/out of t.** afinado/

desafinado; **to sing out of t.** desafinar **2** *vt Mus* afinar **3** *vi Rad, TV* **to t. in to a station** sintonizar una emisora

▸ **tune up** *vi* afinar los instrumentos

tuner ['tjuːnə(r)] (**a**) *(of pianos)* afinador(a) *m,f* (**b**) *Rad, TV (knob)* sintonizador *m*

Tunisia [tjuː'nɪzɪə] *n* Túnez

tunnel ['tʌnəl] **1** *n* túnel *m*; *Min* galería *f* **2** *vt* **to t. through** abrir un túnel a través de

turban ['tɜːbən] *n* turbante *m*

turbulent ['tɜːbjʊlənt] *adj* turbulento(a)

turf [tɜːf] *n* (**a**) *(grass)* césped *m*; *(peat)* turba *f* (**b**) *Br* **t. accountant** *(in horse racing)* corredor(a) *m,f* de apuestas

▸ **turf out** *vt sep Br Fam* **to t. sb out** poner a algn de patitas en la calle

Turk [tɜːk] *n* turco(a) *m,f*

Turkey ['tɜːkɪ] *n* Turquía

turkey ['tɜːkɪ] *n* pavo *m*, *Méx* guajolote *m*

Turkish ['tɜːkɪʃ] **1** *adj* turco(a) **2** *n (language)* turco *m*

turmoil ['tɜːmɔɪl] *n* confusión *f*

turn [tɜːn] **1** *vt* (**a**) volver; *(rotate)* girar, hacer girar; **to t. sth inside out** volver algo del revés; **to t. a page** volver una hoja; **to t. one's head/gaze** volver la cabeza/mirada (**towards** hacia); **to t. the corner** doblar *or Am* voltear la esquina (**b**) *(change)* transformar (**into** en) (**c**) *(on lathe)* tornear

2 *vi* (**a**) *(rotate)* girar (**b**) *(turn round)* volverse, dar la vuelta; **to t. to sb** volverse hacia algn; *Fig (for help)* acudir a algn; **to t. upside down** volcarse; *Fig* **to t. on sb** volverse contra algn (**c**) *(become)* volverse; **the milk has turned sour** la leche se ha cortado

3 *n* (**a**) *(of wheel)* vuelta *f*; **done to a t.** *(meat)* en su punto

(**b**) *(change of direction)* cambio *m* de dirección; *(in road)* curva *f*; **left/right t.** giro *m* a la izquierda/derecha; *US Aut* **t. signal** intermitente *m*, *Col, Ecuad, Méx* direccional *m o f* (**c**) **to do sb a good t.** hacer un favor a algn

(**d**) *Med* ataque *m*

(**e**) *(in game, queue)* turno *m*, vez *f*; **it's your t.** te toca a ti; **to take turns (at doing sth)**, *Br* **to take it in turns to do sth** turnarse para hacer algo

(**f**) *Th* número *m*

(**g**) **t. of phrase** giro *m*

▸ **turn aside 1** *vt sep* desviar **2** *vi* desviarse

▸ **turn away 1** *vt sep (person)* rechazar **2** *vi* volver la cabeza

▸ **turn back 1** *vt sep (person)* hacer retroceder; *(clock)* retrasar **2** *vi* volverse

▸ **turn down** *vt sep* (**a**) *(gas, radio etc)* bajar (**b**) *(reject)* rechazar (**c**) *(fold)* doblar

▸ **turn in** *Fam* **1** *vt sep (person)* entregar a la policía **2** *vi* acostarse

▸ **turn off 1** *vt sep (electricity)* desconectar; *(gas, light)* apagar; *(water)* cerrar **2** *vi* desviarse

▸ **turn on** *vt sep (electricity)* encender; *Am* prender; *(tap, gas)* abrir; *(machine)* poner en marcha; *Fam* **it turns me on** me excita

▸ **turn out 1** *vt sep* (**a**) *(extinguish)* apagar (**b**) *(eject)* echar; *(empty)* vaciar (**c**) *(produce)* producir **2** *vi* (**a**) *(attend)* asistir (**b**) **it turns out that ...** resulta que ...; **things have turned out well** las cosas han salido bien

▸ **turn over 1** *vt sep (turn upside down)* poner al revés; *(page)* dar la vuelta a **2** *vi* volverse

▸ **turn round 1** *vt sep* volver **2** *vi (rotate)* girar, dar vueltas

▸ **turn up 1** *vt sep* (**a**) *(collar)* levantar; **to t. up one's shirt sleeves** arremangarse; **turned-up nose** nariz respingona (**b**) *Rad, TV* subir **2** *vi* (**a**) *Fig* **something is sure to t. up** algo saldrá (**b**) *(arrive)* llegar, presentarse (**c**) *(attend)* asistir

turning ['tɜːnɪŋ] *n* (**a**) *Fig* **t. point** punto decisivo (**b**) *(in road)* salida *f*

turnip ['tɜːnɪp] *n* nabo *m*

turnout ['tɜːnaʊt] *n* asistencia *f*

turnover ['tɜːnəʊvə(r)] *n Com (sales)* facturación *f*; *(of goods)* movimiento *m*

turnpike ['tɜːnpaɪk] *n US* autopista *f* de peaje

turntable ['tɜːnteɪbəl] *n (for record)* plato *m* (giratorio)

turn-up ['tɜːnʌp] *n Br (of trousers)* vuelta *f*

turquoise ['tɜːkwɔɪz] **1** *n (colour, stone)* turquesa *f* **2** *adj* **t. (blue)** azul turquesa

turret ['tʌrɪt] *n* torrecilla *f*

turtle ['tɜːtəl] *n Br* tortuga *f*; *US (tortoise)* tortuga *f*

tusk [tʌsk] *n* colmillo *m*

tussle ['tʌsəl] *n* pelea *f*, lucha *f*

tutor ['tjuːtə(r)] *n Br Univ* tutor(a) *m,f*; **private t.** profesor(a) *m,f* particular

tutorial [tjuː'tɔːrɪəl] *n Br Univ* tutoría *f*, seminario *m*

tuxedo [tʌk'siːdəʊ] *n US* smoking *m*

TV [tiː'viː] *n (abbr* **television**) televisión *f*

tweezers ['twiːzəz] *npl* pinzas *fpl*

twelfth [twelfθ] **1** *adj & n* duodécimo(a) *(m,f)* **2** *n (fraction)* duodécimo *m*

twelve [twelv] *adj & n* doce *(m inv)*

twentieth ['twentɪɪθ] **1** *adj & n* vigésimo(a) *(m,f)* **2** *n (fraction)* vigésimo *m*

twenty ['twentɪ] *adj & n* veinte *(m inv)*

twice [twaɪs] *adv* dos veces; **he's t. as old as I am** tiene el doble de años que yo

twiddle ['twɪdəl] **1** *vt* dar vueltas a; **to t. one's thumbs** estar mano sobre mano **2** *vi* **to t. with sth** juguetear con algo

twig¹ [twɪg] *n* ramilla *f*

twig² [twɪg] *vi Br Fam* darse cuenta

twilight ['twaɪlaɪt] *n* crepúsculo *m*

twin [twɪn] **1** *n* mellizo(a) *m,f*; **identical twins** gemelos (idénticos); **t. brother/sister** hermano gemelo/ hermana gemela; **t. beds** camas *fpl* gemelas **2** *vt* hermanar

twine [twaɪn] **1** *n* bramante *m* **2** *vt* entretejer

3 *vi* **to t. round sth** enroscarse alrededor de algo

twinge [twɪndʒ] *n (of pain)* punzada *f*; *Fig* **t. of conscience** remordimiento *m*

twinkle ['twɪŋkəl] *vi (stars)* centellear; *(eyes)* brillar

twirl [twɜːl] **1** *vt* girar rápidamente **2** *vi (spin)* girar rápidamente; *(dancer)* piruetear **3** *n (movement)* giro rápido; *(of dancer)* pirueta *f*

twist [twɪst] **1** *vt* torcer; *(sense)* tergiversar; **to t. one's ankle** torcerse el tobillo **2** *vi (smoke)* formar volutas; *(path)* serpentear **3** *n* **(a)** *(of yarn)* torzal *m* **(b)** *(movement)* torsión *f*; *Med* torcedura *f* **(c)** *(in road)* vuelta *f* **(d)** *(dance)* twist *m*

twit [twɪt] *n Br Fam* lerdo(a) *m,f*, *Esp* memo(a) *m,f*

twitch [twɪtʃ] **1** *vt* dar un tirón a **2** *vi* crisparse; **his face twitches** tiene un tic en la cara

twitter ['twɪtə(r)] **1** *vi* gorjear **2** *n* gorjeo *m*

two [tuː] **1** *adj* dos *inv*; *Fig* **to be in** or **of t. minds about sth** estar indeciso(a) respecto a algo **2** *n* dos *m inv*; *Fig* **to put t. and t. together** atar cabos

two-faced ['tuː'feɪst] *adj* hipócrita

twofold ['tuːfəʊld] *adj* doble

tycoon [taɪ'kuːn] *n* magnate *m*

type [taɪp] **1** *n* **(a)** *(kind)* tipo *m*, clase *f*; *(brand)* marca *f*; *(of car)* modelo *m* **(b)** *Typ* carácter *m*; *(print)* caracteres *mpl* **2** *vt & vi (with typewriter)* escribir a máquina; *(with word processor)* escribir en *Esp* el ordenador *or Am* la computadora

typewriter ['taɪpraɪtə(r)] *n* máquina *f* de escribir

typhoid ['taɪfɔɪd] *n* **t. (fever)** fiebre tifoidea

typhoon [taɪ'fuːn] *n* tifón *m*

typical ['tɪpɪkəl] *adj* típico(a)

typing ['taɪpɪŋ] *n* mecanografía *f*

typist ['taɪpɪst] *n* mecanógrafo(a) *m,f*

tyrant ['taɪrənt] *n* tirano(a) *m,f*

tyre [taɪə(r)] *n* neumático *m*, *Am* llanta *f*; **t. pressure** presión *f* de los neumáticos

Uu

U, u [juː] *n (the letter)* U, u *f*

U [juː] *adj (film)* ≃ (apta) para todos los públicos

ugh [ʌx] *interj* ¡uf!, ¡puf!

ugly [ˈʌglɪ] *adj* (**uglier, ugliest**) feo(a); *(situation)* desagradable; *Fig* **u. duckling** patito feo

UK [juːˈkeɪ] *n (abbr* **United Kingdom)** Reino *m* Unido

ulcer [ˈʌlsə(r)] *n (sore)* llaga *f*; *(internal)* úlcera *f*

ultimate [ˈʌltɪmɪt] *adj* (**a**) *(final)* último(a); *(aim)* final (**b**) *(basic)* esencial

ultimately [ˈʌltɪmɪtlɪ] *adv* (**a**) *(finally)* finalmente (**b**) *(basically)* en el fondo

ultimatum [ʌltɪˈmeɪtəm] *n* ultimátum *m*

ultraviolet [ʌltrəˈvaɪəlɪt] *adj* ultravioleta

umbrella [ʌmˈbrelə] *n* paraguas *m inv*, *Col* sombrilla *f*

umpire [ˈʌmpaɪə(r)] **1** *n* árbitro *m* **2** *vt* arbitrar

umpteen [ʌmpˈtiːn] *adj Fam* muchísimos(as), la tira de

umpteenth [ʌmpˈtiːnθ] *adj* enésimo(a)

UN [juːˈen] *n (abbr* **United Nations (Organization))** ONU *f*

unable [ʌnˈeɪbəl] *adj* incapaz; **to be u. to do sth/anything** no poder hacer algo/nada

unacceptable [ʌnəkˈseptəbəl] *adj* inaceptable

unaccompanied [ʌnəˈkʌmpənɪd] *adj* solo(a)

unaccustomed [ʌnəˈkʌstəmd] *adj* **he's u. to this climate** no está muy acostumbrado a este clima

unanimous [juːˈnænɪməs] *adj* unánime

unarmed [ʌnˈɑːmd] *adj* desarmado(a)

unassuming [ʌnəˈsjuːmɪŋ] *adj* sin pretensiones

unattainable [ʌnəˈteɪnəbəl] *adj* inalcanzable

unattended [ʌnəˈtendɪd] *adj (counter etc)* desatendido(a); **to leave a child u.** dejar a un niño solo

unattractive [ʌnəˈtræktɪv] *adj* poco atractivo(a)

unauthorized [ʌnˈɔːθəraɪzd] *adj* (**a**) *(person)* no autorizado(a) (**b**) *(trade etc)* ilícito(a), ilegal

unavailable [ʌnəˈveɪləbəl] *adj* **to be u.** no estar disponible

unavoidable [ʌnəˈvɔɪdəbəl] *adj* inevitable; *(accident)* imprevisible

unaware [ʌnəˈweə(r)] *adj* **to be u. of sth** ignorar algo

unawares [ʌnəˈweəz] *adv* (**a**) *(unexpectedly)* desprevenido(a) (**b**) *(without knowing)* inconscientemente

unbalanced [ʌnˈbælənst] *adj* desequilibrado(a)

unbearable [ʌnˈbeərəbəl] *adj* insoportable

unbeatable [ʌnˈbiːtəbəl] *adj (team)* invencible; *(price, quality)* inmejorable

unbelievable [ʌnbɪˈliːvəbəl] *adj* increíble

unbia(s)sed [ʌnˈbaɪəst] *adj* imparcial

unblock [ʌnˈblɒk] *vt (sink, pipe)* desatascar

unborn [ʌnˈbɔːn] *adj* sin nacer, nonato(a)

unbreakable [ʌnˈbreɪkəbəl] *adj* irrompible; *Fig* inquebrantable

unbroken [ʌnˈbrəʊkən] *adj* (**a**) *(whole)* intacto(a) (**b**) *(uninterrupted)* continuo(a) (**c**) *(record)* imbatido(a)

unbutton [ʌn'bʌtən] *vt* desabrochar

uncanny [ʌn'kænɪ] *adj* misterioso(a), extraño(a)

uncertain [ʌn'sɜːtən] *adj* (**a**) *(not certain)* incierto(a); *(doubtful)* dudoso(a); **in no u. terms** claramente (**b**) *(hesitant)* indeciso(a)

uncertainty [ʌn'sɜːtəntɪ] *n* incertidumbre *f*

unchanged [ʌn'tʃeɪndʒd] *adj* igual

uncle ['ʌŋkəl] *n* tío *m*

unclear [ʌn'klɪə(r)] *adj* poco claro(a)

uncomfortable [ʌn'kʌmftəbəl] *adj* incómodo(a); **to make things u. for** complicarle la vida a

uncommon [ʌn'kɒmən] *adj* (**a**) *(rare)* poco común; *(unusual)* extraordinario(a) (**b**) *(excessive)* excesivo(a)

uncompromising [ʌn'kɒmprəmaɪzɪŋ] *adj* intransigente; **u. honesty** sinceridad absoluta

unconditional [ʌnkən'dɪʃənəl] *adj* incondicional; **u. refusal** negativa rotunda

unconnected [ʌnkə'nektɪd] *adj* no relacionado(a)

unconscious [ʌn'kɒnʃəs] **1** *adj* (**a**) inconsciente (**of** de) (**b**) *(unintentional)* involuntario(a) **2** *n* **the u.** el inconsciente

unconstitutional [ʌnkɒnstɪ'tjuːʃənəl] *adj* inconstitucional, anticonstitucional

uncontrollable [ʌnkən'trəʊləbəl] *adj* incontrolable; *(desire)* irresistible

unconventional [ʌnkən'venʃənəl] *adj* poco convencional, original

uncooperative [ʌnkəʊ'ɒpərətɪv] *adj* poco cooperativo(a)

uncouth [ʌn'kuːθ] *adj (rude)* grosero(a)

uncover [ʌn'kʌvə(r)] *vt* destapar; *Fig* descubrir

undecided [ʌndɪ'saɪdɪd] *adj* (**a**) *(person)* indeciso(a) (**b**) *(issue)* pendiente; **it's still u.** está aún por decidir

undeniable [ʌndɪ'naɪəbəl] *adj* innegable

under ['ʌndə(r)] **1** *prep* (**a**) debajo de, bajo, *Am* abajo de; **u. the sun** bajo el sol

(**b**) *(less than)* menos de; **incomes u. £1,000** ingresos inferiores a 1.000 libras; **u. age** menor de edad

(**c**) *(of rank)* de rango inferior a

(**d**) **u. Caesar** bajo César

(**e**) *(subject to)* bajo; **u. arrest** detenido(a); **u. cover** a cubierto; **u. the circumstances** dadas las circunstancias; *Fig* **I was u. the impression that …** tenía la impresión de que …

(**f**) *(according to)* según, conforme a

2 *adv* abajo, debajo

undercharge [ʌndə'tʃɑːdʒ] *vt* cobrar menos de lo debido

underclothes ['ʌndəkləʊðz] *npl* ropa *f* interior

undercover [ʌndə'kʌvə(r)] *adj* secreto(a)

undercut [ʌndə'kʌt] *(pt & pp* **undercut***)* *vt Com* vender más barato que

underdeveloped [ʌndədɪ'veləpt] *adj* subdesarrollado(a)

underdog ['ʌndədɒg] *n* desvalido(a) *m,f*

underestimate [ʌndər'estɪmeɪt] *vt* infravalorar

underfoot [ʌndə'fʊt] *adv* en el suelo

undergo [ʌndə'gəʊ] *(pt* **underwent***; pp* **undergone** [ʌndə'gɒn]*)* *vt* experimentar; *(change)* sufrir; *(test etc)* pasar por

undergraduate [ʌndə'grædjʊɪt] *n* estudiante *mf* universitario(a)

underground 1 *adj* ['ʌndəgraʊnd] subterráneo(a); *Fig* clandestino(a)

2 *n* ['ʌndəgraʊnd] (**a**) *Pol* movimiento clandestino (**b**) *Br* **the u.** *(train)* el metro, *RP* el subte

3 *adv* [ʌndə'graʊnd] *Fig* **to go u.** pasar a la clandestinidad

undergrowth ['ʌndəgrəʊθ] *n* maleza *f*

underhand 1 *adj* ['ʌndəhænd] *(method)* ilícito(a); *(person)* solapado(a) **2** *adv* [ʌndə'hænd] bajo cuerda

underline [ʌndə'laɪn] *vt* subrayar

underlying [ʌndə'laɪɪŋ] *adj (basic)* fundamental

undermine [ʌndə'maɪn] *vt* socavar, minar

underneath [ʌndə'niːθ] **1** *prep* debajo de, bajo **2** *adv* abajo, debajo **3** *adj* de abajo **4** *n* parte *f* inferior

underpaid [ʌndə'peɪd] *adj* mal pagado(a)

underpants ['ʌndəpænts] *npl* calzoncillos *mpl*, *Chile* fundillos *mpl*, *Méx* calzones *mpl*

underpass ['ʌndəpɑːs] *n* paso subterráneo

underprivileged [ʌndə'prɪvɪlɪdʒd] **1** *adj* desfavorecido(a) **2** *npl* the u. los menos favorecidos

underrate [ʌndə'reɪt] *vt* subestimar, infravalorar

underside ['ʌndəsaɪd] *n* parte *f* inferior

understand [ʌndə'stænd] (*pt & pp* **understood**) *vt & vi* (a) *(comprehend)* entender, comprender; **do I make myself understood?** ¿me explico? (b) *(assume, believe)* entender; **she gave me to u. that ...** me dio a entender que ... (c) *(hear)* tener entendido (d) **to u. one another** entenderse

understandable [ʌndə'stændəbəl] *adj* comprensible

understanding [ʌndə'stændɪŋ] **1** *n* (a) *(intellectual grasp)* entendimiento *m*, comprensión *f* (b) *(interpretation)* intepretación *f* (c) *(agreement)* acuerdo *m* (d) **on the u. that ...** a condición de que ... **2** *adj* comprensivo(a)

understatement [ʌndə'steɪtmənt] *n* **to make an u.** minimizar, subestimar; **to say that the boy is rather clever is an u.** decir que el chico es bastante listo es quedarse corto

understood [ʌndə'stʊd] **1** *adj* (a) **I wish it to be u. that ...** que conste que ... (b) *(agreed on)* convenido(a) (c)

(implied) sobreentendido(a) **2** *pt & pp* of **understand**

undertake [ʌndə'teɪk] (*pt* **undertook**; *pp* **undertaken** [ʌndə'teɪkən]) *vt* (a) *(responsibility)* asumir; *(task, job)* encargarse de (b) *(promise)* comprometerse a

undertaker ['ʌndəteɪkə(r)] *n* empresario(a) *m,f* de pompas fúnebres; **u.'s** funeraria *f*

undertaking [ʌndə'teɪkɪŋ] *n* (a) *(task)* empresa *f* (b) *(promise)* compromiso *m*

undertone ['ʌndətəʊn] *n* **in an u.** en voz baja

undertook [ʌndə'tʊk] *pt of* **undertake**

underwater [ʌndə'wɔːtə(r)] **1** *adj* submarino(a) **2** *adv* bajo el agua

underwear ['ʌndəweə(r)] *n* ropa *f* interior

underwent [ʌndə'went] *pt of* **undergo**

undesirable [ʌndɪ'zaɪrəbəl] *adj & n* indeseable *(mf)*

undiscovered [ʌndɪ'skʌvəd] *adj* sin descubrir

undisputed [ʌndɪ'spjuːtɪd] *adj (unchallenged)* incontestable; *(unquestionable)* indiscutible

undo [ʌn'duː] (*pt* **undid**; *pp* **undone**) *vt* (a) deshacer; *(button)* desabrochar (b) *(put right)* enmendar

undoing [ʌn'duːɪŋ] *n* perdición *f*

undone¹ [ʌn'dʌn] *adj (unfinished)* inacabado(a)

undone² [ʌn'dʌn] **1** *adj (knot etc)* deshecho(a); **to come u.** *(shoelace)* desatarse; *(button, blouse)* desabrocharse; *(necklace etc)* soltarse **2** *pp of* **undo**

undoubted [ʌn'daʊtɪd] *adj* indudable

undress [ʌn'dres] **1** *vt* desnudar **2** *vi* desnudarse

undue [ʌn'djuː] (a) *adj (excessive)* excesivo(a) (b) *(improper)* indebido(a)

unduly [ʌn'djuːlɪ] *adv* excesivamente

unearthly [ʌn'ɜːθlɪ] *adj* (a) *(being)*

sobrenatural (**b**) *Fam (din)* espantoso(a); **at an u. hour** a una hora intempestiva

uneasy [ʌn'iːzɪ] *adj* (**a**) *(worried)* preocupado(a); *(disturbing)* inquietante (**b**) *(uncomfortable)* incómodo(a)

uneconomic(al) [ʌniːkəˈnɒmɪk(əl)] *adj* poco económico(a)

uneducated [ʌnˈedjʊkeɪtɪd] *adj* inculto(a)

unemployed [ʌnɪmˈplɔɪd] **1** *adj* desempleado(a), *Esp* parado(a), *Am* desocupado(a); **to be u.** estar desempleado(a) *or Esp* en (el) paro *or Am* desocupado(a) **2** *npl* **the u.** los desempleados, *Esp* los parados, *Am* los desocupados

unemployment [ʌnɪmˈplɔɪmənt] *n* desempleo *m*, *Esp* paro *m*, *Am* desocupación *f*; **u. benefit**, *US* **u. compensation** subsidio *m* de desempleo *or Am* de desocupación

unequal [ʌnˈiːkwəl] *adj* desigual

uneven [ʌnˈiːvən] *adj* (**a**) *(not level)* desigual; *(bumpy)* accidentado(a) (**b**) *(variable)* irregular

uneventful [ʌnɪˈventfʊl] *adj* sin acontecimientos

unexpected [ʌnɪkˈspektɪd] *adj* *(unhoped for)* inesperado(a); *(event)* imprevisto(a)

unexplained [ʌnɪksˈpleɪnd] *adj* inexplicado(a)

unfair [ʌnˈfeə(r)] *adj* injusto(a); *Sport* sucio(a)

unfaithful [ʌnˈfeɪθʊl] *adj* *(friend)* desleal; *(husband, wife)* infiel

unfamiliar [ʌnfəˈmɪljə(r)] *adj* *(unknown)* desconocido(a); *(not conversant)* no familiarizado(a) *(with* con)

unfashionable [ʌnˈfæʃənəbəl] *adj* pasado(a) de moda; *(ideas etc)* poco popular

unfasten [ʌnˈfɑːsən] *vt* *(knot)* desatar; *(clothing, belt)* desabrochar

unfavourable, *US* **unfavorable** [ʌnˈfeɪvərəbəl] *adj* desfavorable; *(criticism)* adverso(a); *(winds)* contrario(a)

unfinished [ʌnˈfɪnɪʃt] *adj* inacabado(a); **u. business** un asunto pendiente

unfit [ʌnˈfɪt] *adj* (**a**) *(thing)* inadecuado(a); *(person)* no apto(a) (**for** para) (**b**) *(incompetent)* incompetente (**c**) *(physically)* incapacitado(a); **to be u.** no estar en forma

unfold [ʌnˈfəʊld] **1** *vt* (**a**) *(sheet)* desdoblar; *(newspaper)* abrir (**b**) *(plan, secret)* revelar **2** *vi* (**a**) *(open up)* abrirse; *(landscape)* extenderse (**b**) *(plot)* desarrollarse (**c**) *(secret)* descubrirse

unforeseeable [ʌnfəˈsiːəbəl] *adj* imprevisible

unforeseen [ʌnfɔːˈsiːn] *adj* imprevisto(a)

unforgettable [ʌnfəˈgetəbəl] *adj* inolvidable

unforgivable [ʌnfəˈgɪvəbəl] *adj* imperdonable

unfortunate [ʌnˈfɔːtʃənɪt] *adj (person, event)* desgraciado(a); *(remark)* desafortunado(a); **how u.!** ¡qué mala suerte!

unfortunately [ʌnˈfɔːtʃənɪtlɪ] *adv* desgraciadamente, por desgracia

unfounded [ʌnˈfaʊndɪd] *adj* infundado(a)

unfriendly [ʌnˈfrendlɪ] *adj* (**unfriendlier, unfriendliest**) antipático(a), poco amistoso(a)

unfulfilled [ʌnfʊlˈfɪld] *adj* **to feel u.** sentirse insatisfecho(a)

unfurnished [ʌnˈfɜːnɪʃt] *adj* sin amueblar

ungainly [ʌnˈgeɪnlɪ] *adj* *(gait)* desgarbado(a)

ungrateful [ʌnˈgreɪtfʊl] *adj (person)* desagradecido(a); *(task)* ingrato(a)

unhappy [ʌnˈhæpɪ] *adj* (**unhappier, unhappiest**) (**a**) *(sad)* triste (**b**) *(wretched)* desgraciado(a), infeliz; *(unfortunate)* desafortunado(a)

unharmed [ʌnˈhɑːmd] *adj* ileso(a), indemne

unhealthy [ʌnˈhelθɪ] *adj* (**unhealthier, unhealthiest**) (**a**) *(ill)* enfermizo(a) (**b**) *(unwholesome)* malsano(a)

unhelpful [ʌnˈhelpfʊl] *adj (person)* poco servicial; *(criticism, advice)* poco constructivo(a)

unhurt [ʌn'hɜːt] *adj* ileso(a), indemne

unhygienic [ʌnhaɪ'dʒiːnɪk] *adj* anti-higiénico(a)

uniform ['juːnɪfɔːm] *adj & n* uniforme *(m)*

unify ['juːnɪfaɪ] *vt* unificar

unilateral [juːnɪ'lætərəl] *adj* unilateral

unimaginative [ʌnɪ'mædʒɪnətɪv] *adj* **to be u.** *(person)* tener poca imaginación; *(book, choice)* ser muy poco original, no tener originalidad

unimportant [ʌnɪm'pɔːtənt] *adj* poco importante

uninhabited [ʌnɪn'hæbɪtɪd] *adj* despoblado(a)

uninhibited [ʌnɪn'hɪbɪtɪd] *adj* sin inhibición

uninspiring [ʌnɪn'spaɪərɪŋ] *adj* que no inspira

unintelligible [ʌnɪn'telɪdʒəbəl] *adj* ininteligible, incomprensible

unintentional [ʌnɪn'tenʃənəl] *adj* involuntario(a)

uninterested [ʌn'ɪntərestɪd] *adj* poco interesado(a)

uninteresting [ʌn'ɪntrɪstɪŋ] *adj* poco interesante

uninterrupted [ʌnɪntə'rʌptɪd] *adj* ininterrumpido(a)

union ['juːnjən] **1** *n* (a) unión *f* (b) *(organization)* sindicato *m* (c) *US* **the U.** los Estados Unidos; *Br* **U. Jack** bandera *f* del Reino Unido **2** *adj* sindical

unique [juː'niːk] *adj* único(a)

unison ['juːnɪsən] *n Mus* unisonancia *f*; *Fig (harmony)* armonía *f*; **in u.** al unísono

unit ['juːnɪt] *n* (a) unidad *f*; **monetary u.** unidad monetaria; *Br Fin* **u. trust** sociedad *f* de inversiones (b) *(piece of furniture)* módulo *m*; **kitchen u.** mueble *m* de cocina (c) *Tech* grupo *m* (d) *(department)* servicio *m* (e) *(team)* equipo *m*

unite [juː'naɪt] **1** *vt* unir **2** *vi* unirse

unity ['juːnɪtɪ] *n* unidad *f*; *(harmony)* armonía *f*

universal [juːnɪ'vɜːsəl] *adj* universal

universe ['juːnɪvɜːs] *n* universo *m*

university [juːnɪ'vɜːsɪtɪ] **1** *n* universidad *f* **2** *adj* universitario(a)

unjust [ʌn'dʒʌst] *adj* injusto(a)

unkind [ʌn'kaɪnd] *adj (not nice)* poco amable; *(cruel)* despiadado(a)

unknowingly [ʌn'nəʊɪŋlɪ] *adv* inconscientemente, inadvertidamente

unknown [ʌn'nəʊn] **1** *adj* desconocido(a); **u. quantity** incógnita *f* **2** *n* **the u.** lo desconocido

unlawful [ʌn'lɔːfʊl] *adj (not legal)* ilegal

unleaded [ʌn'ledɪd] *adj* **u.** *Br* **petrol** or *US* **gasoline** gasolina *f* or *RP* nafta *f* sin plomo

unleash [ʌn'liːʃ] *vt* (a) *(dog)* soltar (b) *Fig (release)* liberar; *(provoke)* desencadenar

unless [ʌn'les] *conj* a menos que, a no ser que

unlike [ʌn'laɪk] **1** *adj* diferente, distinto(a) **2** *prep* a diferencia de

unlikely [ʌn'laɪklɪ] *adj* (a) *(improbable)* poco probable (b) *(unusual)* raro(a)

unlimited [ʌn'lɪmɪtɪd] *adj* ilimitado(a)

unload [ʌn'ləʊd] *vt & vi* descargar

unlock [ʌn'lɒk] *vt* abrir (con llave)

unlucky [ʌn'lʌkɪ] *adj* (**unluckier, unluckiest**) *(unfortunate)* desgraciado(a); **to be u.** *(person)* tener mala suerte; *(thing)* traer mala suerte

unmade [ʌn'meɪd] *adj (bed)* deshecho(a), sin hacer

unmanageable [ʌn'mænɪdʒəbəl] *adj (people)* ingobernable; *(child, hair)* incontrolable

unmarried [ʌn'mærɪd] *adj* soltero(a)

unmistakable [ʌnmɪs'teɪkəbəl] *adj* inconfundible

unmoved [ʌn'muːvd] *adv* **to watch/listen u.** observar/escuchar impertérrito(a)

unnatural [ʌn'nætʃərəl] *adj* (a) *(against nature)* antinatural; *(abnormal)* anormal (b) *(affected)* afectado(a)

unnecessary [ʌn'nesɪsərɪ] *adj* innecesario(a), inútil; **it's u. to add that ...** sobra añadir que ...

unnoticed [ʌn'nəʊtɪst] *adj* desapercibido(a); **to let sth pass u.** pasar algo por alto

unoccupied [ʌn'ɒkjʊpaɪd] *adj (house)* desocupado(a); *(seat)* libre

unofficial [ʌnə'fɪʃəl] *adj* no oficial; *Ind* **u. strike** huelga *f* no apoyada por los sindicatos

unorthodox [ʌn'ɔ:θədɒks] *adj* **(a)** *(behaviour etc)* poco ortodoxo(a) **(b)** *Rel* heterodoxo(a)

unpack [ʌn'pæk] **1** *vt (boxes)* desembalar; *(suitcase)* deshacer, *Am* desempacar **2** *vi* deshacer la(s) maleta(s)

unpaid [ʌn'peɪd] *adj* **(a)** *(work, volunteer)* no retribuido(a) **(b)** *(bill, debt)* impagado(a)

unparalleled [ʌn'pærəleld] *adj* **(a)** *(in quality)* incomparable **(b)** *(without precedent)* sin precedente

unpleasant [ʌn'plezənt] *adj* desagradable **(to** con)

unplug [ʌn'plʌg] *vt* desenchufar

unpopular [ʌn'pɒpjʊlə(r)] *adj* impopular; **to make oneself u.** ganarse la antipatía de todos

unprecedented [ʌn'presɪdentɪd] *adj* sin precedente

unpredictable [ʌnprɪ'dɪktəbəl] *adj* imprevisible

unprepared [ʌnprɪ'peəd] *adj (speech etc)* improvisado(a); *(person)* desprevenido(a)

unprofessional [ʌnprə'feʃənəl] *adj (unethical)* poco profesional; *(substandard)* de aficionado(a)

unpublished [ʌn'pʌblɪʃt] *adj* inédito(a)

unqualified [ʌn'kwɒlɪfaɪd] *adj* **(a)** *(without qualification)* sin título; *(incompetent)* incompetente **(b)** *(unconditional)* incondicional; *(denial)* rotundo(a); *(endorsement)* sin reserva; *(success)* total

unquestionable [ʌn'kwestʃənəbəl] *adj* indiscutible

unravel [ʌn'rævəl] **1** *vt* desenmarañar **2** *vi* desenmarañarse

unrealistic [ʌnrɪə'lɪstɪk] *adj* poco realista

unreasonable [ʌn'ri:zənəbəl] *adj* poco razonable; *(demands)* desmedido(a); *(prices)* exorbitante; *(hour)* inoportuno(a)

unrecognizable [ʌnrekəg'naɪzəbl] *adj* irreconocible

unrelated [ʌnrɪ'leɪtɪd] *adj (not connected)* no relacionado(a)

unrelenting [ʌnrɪ'lentɪŋ] *adj (behaviour)* implacable; *(struggle)* encarnizado(a)

unreliable [ʌnrɪ'laɪəbəl] *adj* **(a)** *(person)* de poca confianza **(b)** *(information)* que no es de fiar; *(machine)* poco fiable

unrepentant [ʌnrɪ'pentənt] *adj* impenitente

unrest [ʌn'rest] *n (social etc)* malestar *m*; **political u.** agitación política

unroll [ʌn'rəʊl] *vt* desenrollar

unruly [ʌn'ru:lɪ] *adj* **(unrulier, unruliest)** **(a)** *(child)* revoltoso(a) **(b)** *(hair)* rebelde

unsafe [ʌn'seɪf] *adj (dangerous)* peligroso(a); *(risky)* inseguro(a); **to feel u.** sentirse expuesto(a)

unsaid [ʌn'sed] *adj* **it's better left u.** más vale no decir nada; **much was left u.** quedó mucho por decir

unsatisfactory [ʌnsætɪs'fæktərɪ] *adj* insatisfactorio(a); **it's most u.** deja mucho que desear

unscrew [ʌn'skru:] *vt* destornillar

unscrupulous [ʌn'skru:pjʊləs] *adj* sin escrúpulos

unseemly [ʌn'si:mlɪ] *adj* impropio(a)

unseen [ʌn'si:n] **1** *adj* invisible; *(unnoticed)* inadvertido(a) **2** *n Br Educ* = texto no trabajado en clase

unselfish [ʌn'selfɪʃ] *adj* desinteresado(a)

unsettle [ʌn'setəl] *vt* perturbar

unshaven [ʌn'ʃeɪvən] *adj* sin afeitar

unsightly [ʌn'saɪtlɪ] *adj* feo(a), desagradable

unskilled [ʌn'skɪld] *adj (worker)* no

cualificado(a); *(work)* no especializado(a)

unsociable [ʌnˈsəʊʃəbəl] *adj* insociable, huraño(a)

unsophisticated [ʌnsəˈfɪstɪkeɪtɪd] *adj* (**a**) *(naïve)* ingenuo(a) (**b**) *(simple)* poco sofisticado(a)

unspeakable [ʌnˈspiːkəbəl] *adj* (**a**) indecible (**b**) *Fig (evil)* atroz

unstable [ʌnˈsteɪbəl] *adj* inestable

unsteady [ʌnˈstedɪ] *adj (not firm)* inestable; *(table, chair)* cojo(a); *(hand, voice)* tembloroso(a)

unstuck [ʌnˈstʌk] *adj* **to come u.** despegarse; *Fig* venirse abajo

unsuccessful [ʌnsəkˈsesfʊl] *adj* (**a**) *(fruitless)* fracasado(a); *(useless)* vano(a) (**b**) *(businessman etc)* fracasado(a); *(candidate)* derrotado(a); **to be u. at sth** no tener éxito con algo

unsuitable [ʌnˈsuːtəbəl] *adj* (**a**) *(person)* no apto(a) (**b**) *(thing)* inadecuado(a); *(remark)* inoportuno(a); *(time)* inconveniente

unsuited [ʌnˈsuːtɪd] *adj* (**a**) *(person)* no apto(a); *(thing)* impropio(a) (**to** para) (**b**) *(incompatible)* incompatible

unsure [ʌnˈʃʊə(r)] *adj* poco seguro(a)

untangle [ʌnˈtæŋgəl] *vt* desenredar, desenmarañar

unthinkable [ʌnˈθɪŋkəbəl] *adj* impensable, inconcebible

untidy [ʌnˈtaɪdɪ] *adj* (**untidier, untidiest**) *(room, person)* desordenado(a); *(hair)* despeinado(a); *(appearance)* desaseado(a)

untie [ʌnˈtaɪ] *vt* desatar; *(free)* soltar

until [ʌnˈtɪl] **1** *conj* hasta que; **she worked u. she collapsed** trabajó hasta desfallecer; **u. she gets back** hasta que vuelva **2** *prep* hasta; **u. now** hasta ahora; **u. ten o'clock** hasta las diez; **not u. Monday** hasta el lunes no

untold [ʌnˈtəʊld] *adj* (**a**) *(indescribable)* indecible (**b**) *Fig (loss, wealth)* incalculable (**c**) *(not told)* sin contar

untoward [ʌntəˈwɔːd] *adj* (**a**) *(unfortunate)* desafortunado(a) (**b**) *(adverse)* adverso(a)

untrue [ʌnˈtruː] *adj* (**a**) *(false)* falso(a)

(**b**) *(unfaithful)* infiel (**c**) *(inexact)* inexacto(a)

untruthful [ʌnˈtruːθfʊl] *adj (person)* embustero(a), mentiroso(a); *(story, reply)* falso(a)

unused [ʌnˈjuːzd] *adj* (**a**) *(car)* sin usar; *(flat etc)* sin estrenar; *(stamp)* sin matar (**b**) *(not in use)* que ya no se utiliza (**c**) [ʌnˈjuːst] *(unaccustomed)* desacostumbrado(a) (**to** a)

unusual [ʌnˈjuːʒʊəl] *adj (rare)* insólito(a), poco común; *(original)* original; *(exceptional)* excepcional

unusually [ʌnˈjuːʒʊəlɪ] *adv* excepcionalmente

unveil [ʌnˈveɪl] *vt* descubrir

unwanted [ʌnˈwɒntɪd] *adj (attentions, baby)* no deseado(a); *(clothes, trinkets)* desechado(a)

unwarranted [ʌnˈwɒrəntɪd] *adj* injustificado(a); *(remark)* gratuito(a)

unwelcome [ʌnˈwelkəm] *adj (visitor)* molesto(a); *(visit)* inoportuno(a); *Fig (news etc)* desagradable

unwell [ʌnˈwel] *adj* malo(a), indispuesto(a)

unwieldy [ʌnˈwiːldɪ] *adj (difficult to handle)* poco manejable; *(clumsy)* torpe

unwilling [ʌnˈwɪlɪŋ] *adj* **to be u. to do sth** no estar dispuesto a hacer algo

unwind [ʌnˈwaɪnd] *(pt & pp* **unwound**) **1** *vt* desenrollar **2** *vi* (**a**) desenrollarse (**b**) *(relax)* relajarse

unwise [ʌnˈwaɪz] *adj* imprudente, desaconsejable

unwitting [ʌnˈwɪtɪŋ] *adj* involuntario(a)

unworthy [ʌnˈwɜːðɪ] *adj* indigno(a)

unwound [ʌnˈwaʊnd] *pt & pp of* **unwind**

unwrap [ʌnˈræp] *vt (gift)* desenvolver; *(package)* deshacer

unzip [ʌnˈzɪp] *(pt & pp* **unzipped**) *vt* abrir la cremallera *or Am* el cierre de

up [ʌp] **1** *prep* (**a**) *(movement)* **to climb up the mountain** escalar la montaña; **to walk up the street** caminar *or Esp* andar por la calle (**b**) *(position)* en lo alto de; **further up the street** más adelante (en la misma calle); **halfway up the ladder** a mitad de la escalera

2 *adv* (**a**) *(upwards)* arriba, hacia arriba; *(position)* arriba; **from £10 up** de 10 libras para arriba; **halfway up** a medio camino; **right up (to the top)** hasta arriba (del todo); **this side up** *(sign)* este lado hacia arriba

(**b**) **the moon is up** ha salido la luna

(**c**) *(towards)* hacia; **to come** *or* **go up to sb** acercarse a algn; **to walk up and down** ir de un lado a otro

(**d**) *(in, to)* **he's up in Yorkshire** está en Yorkshire

(**e**) **it's up for discussion** se está discutiendo; **up for sale** en venta

(**f**) *Fam* **something's up** pasa algo; **what's up (with you)?** ¿qué pasa (contigo)?

(**g**) **up to** *(as far as, until)* hasta; **I can spend up to £5** puedo gastar un máximo de 5 libras; **up to here** hasta aquí; **up to now** hasta ahora

(**h**) **to be up to** *(depend on)* depender de; *(be capable of)* estar a la altura de

(**i**) **he's up to sth** está tramando algo

3 *adj* (**a**) *(out of bed)* levantado(a) (**b**) *(finished)* terminado(a); **time's up** (ya) es la hora

4 *vt Fam* aumentar

5 *n Fig* **ups and downs** altibajos *mpl*

upbringing ['ʌpbrɪŋɪŋ] *n* educación *f*

update [ʌp'deɪt] *vt* actualizar, poner al día

upgrade 1 *vt* [ʌp'greɪd] (**a**) *(promote)* ascender (**b**) *(improve)* mejorar la calidad de (**c**) *Comput (software, hardware)* actualizar **2** *n* ['ʌpgreɪd] *Comput* actualización *f*

upheaval [ʌp'hiːvəl] *n* trastorno *m*

uphill 1 *adj* ['ʌphɪl] ascendente; *Fig* arduo(a) **2** *adv* [ʌp'hɪl] cuesta arriba

uphold [ʌp'həʊld] *(pt & pp* **upheld** [ʌp'held]) *vt* sostener

upholstery [ʌp'həʊlstərɪ] *n* tapizado *m*, tapicería *f*

upkeep ['ʌpkiːp] *n* mantenimiento *m*

upon [ə'pɒn] *prep Fml* en, sobre; **once u. a time …** érase una vez …; **u. my word** (mi) palabra de honor

upper ['ʌpə(r)] **1** *adj* (**a**) *(position)* superior; **u. storey** piso de arriba; *Fig* **to have the u. hand** llevar la delantera (**b**) *(in rank)* alto(a); **the u. class** la clase alta; **the U. House** la Cámara Alta **2** *n (of shoe)* pala *f*

uppermost ['ʌpəməʊst] *adj* más alto(a); *Fig* **it was u. in my mind** era lo que me preocupaba más

upright ['ʌpraɪt] **1** *adj* (**a**) *(vertical)* vertical (**b**) *(honest)* honrado(a)

2 *adv* derecho

3 *n Ftb (post)* poste *m*

uprising ['ʌpraɪzɪŋ] *n* sublevación *f*

uproar ['ʌprɔː(r)] *n* tumulto *m*, alboroto *m*

uproot [ʌp'ruːt] *vt (plant)* arrancar de raíz

upset 1 *vt* [ʌp'set] *(pt & pp* **upset**) (**a**) *(overturn)* volcar; *(spill)* derramar (**b**) *(shock)* trastornar; *(worry)* preocupar; *(displease)* disgustar (**c**) *(spoil)* desbaratar (**d**) *(make ill)* sentar mal a

2 *adj* [ʌp'set] *(shocked)* alterado(a); *(displeased)* disgustado(a); **to have an u. stomach** sentirse mal del estómago **3** *n* ['ʌpset] (**a**) *(reversal)* revés *m* (**b**) *Sport* resultado inesperado

upshot ['ʌpʃɒt] *n* resultado *m*

upside ['ʌpsaɪd] *n* **u. down** al revés

upstairs [ʌp'steəz] **1** *adv* al piso de arriba; **she lives u.** vive en el piso de arriba **2** *n* piso *m* de arriba

uptight [ʌp'taɪt] *adj Fam* nervioso(a)

uptown ['ʌptaʊn] *n US* zona *f* residencial

upward ['ʌpwəd] *adj* ascendente

upward(s) ['ʌpwəd(z)] *adv* hacia arriba; **from ten (years) u.** a partir de los diez años; *Fam* **u. of** algo más de

urban ['ɜːbən] *adj* urbano(a)

urge [ɜːdʒ] **1** *vt* (**a**) instar; *(plead)* exhortar (**b**) *(advocate)* preconizar; **to u. that sth should be done** insistir en que se haga algo **2** *n* impulso *m*

▸ **urge on** *vt sep* animar a

urgency ['ɜːdʒənsɪ] *n* urgencia *f*

urgent ['ɜːdʒənt] *adj* urgente; *(need, tone)* apremiante

urinate ['jʊərɪneɪt] *vi* orinar

urine [ˈjʊərɪn] *n* orina *f*

urn [ɜːn] *n* (**a**) urna *f* (**b**) **tea u.** tetera *f* grande

us [ʌs, *unstressed* əs] *pers pron* (**a**) *(as object)* nos; **let's forget it** olvidémoslo (**b**) *(after prep)* nosotros(as); **both of us** nosotros dos; **he's one of us** es de los nuestros (**c**) *(after verb to be)* nosotros(as); **she wouldn't believe it was us** no creía que fuéramos nosotros (**d**) *Fam* me; **give us a kiss!** ¡dame un beso!

USA [juːesˈeɪ] *n (abbr* **United States of America**) EE.UU. *mpl*

usage [ˈjuːsɪdʒ] *n* (**a**) *(habit, custom)* costumbre *f* (**b**) *Ling* uso *m*

use 1 *vt* [juːz] (**a**) emplear, utilizar; **what is it used for?** ¿para qué sirve?; **to u. force** hacer uso de la fuerza (**b**) *(consume)* consumir, gastar (**c**) *(take unfair advantage of)* aprovecharse de **2** *v aux* **used to** [ˈjuːstə] soler, acostumbrar; **where did you u. to live?** ¿dónde vivías (antes)?

> Como verbo auxiliar, aparece siempre en la forma **used to**. Se traduce al español por el verbo principal en pretérito imperfecto, o por el pretérito imperfecto de **soler** más infinitivo

3 *n* [juːs] (**a**) uso *m*, empleo *m*; *(handling)* manejo *m*; **directions for u.** modo de empleo; **in u.** en uso; **not in u.** *(on lift)* no funciona; **to make (good) u. of sth** aprovechar algo; **to put to good u.** sacar partido de (**b**) *(application)* aplicación *f* (**c**) *(usefulness)* utilidad *f*; **what's the u.?** ¿para qué?; *Fam* **it's no u. crying** no sirve de nada llorar; **to be of u.** servir

▸ **use up** *vt sep* acabar

use-by date [ˈjuːzbaɪdeɪt] *n Com* fecha *f* de caducidad

used *adj* (**a**) [juːzd] *(second-hand)* usado(a) (**b**) [juːst] **to be u. to** estar acostumbrado(a) a

useful [ˈjuːsfʊl] *adj* útil; *(practical)* práctico(a); *Br* **to come in u.** venir bien

useless [ˈjuːslɪs] *adj* inútil

user [ˈjuːzə(r)] *n* (**a**) usuario(a) *m,f* (**b**) *Fam (of drugs)* drogadicto(a) *m,f*

user-friendly [juːzəˈfrendlɪ] *adj also Comput* de fácil manejo

usual [ˈjuːʒʊəl] **1** *adj* corriente, normal; **as u.** como siempre; **at the u. hour** a la hora habitual; **earlier than u.** más pronto que de costumbre **2** *n* lo habitual; **out of the u.** fuera de lo común

usually [ˈjuːʒʊəlɪ] *adv* normalmente

usurp [juːˈzɜːp] *vt* usurpar

utensil [juːˈtensəl] *n* utensilio *m*; **kitchen utensils** batería *f* de cocina

utility [juːˈtɪlɪtɪ] *n* (**a**) utilidad *f*; **u. room** cuarto *m* de planchar; *(for storage)* trascocina *f* (**b**) **(public) u.** empresa *f* de servicio público

utilize [ˈjuːtɪlaɪz] *vt* utilizar

utmost [ˈʌtməʊst] **1** *adj* sumo(a); **of the u. importance** de suma importancia **2** *n* máximo *m*; **to do** *or* **try one's u.** hacer todo lo posible; **to the u.** al máximo, a más no poder

utter¹ [ˈʌtə(r)] *vt (words)* pronunciar; *(sigh)* dar; *(cry, threat)* lanzar

utter² [ˈʌtə(r)] *adj* total, completo(a)

utterly [ˈʌtəlɪ] *adv* completamente, totalmente

U-turn [ˈjuːtɜːn] *n* cambio *m* de sentido; *Pol* giro *m* de 180 grados

Vv

V, v [viː] *n (the letter)* V, v *f*

V *(abbr* **volt(s))** V

vacancy [ˈveɪkənsɪ] *n* (**a**) *(job)* vacante *f* (**b**) *(room)* habitación *f* libre; **no vacancies** *(sign)* completo

vacant [ˈveɪkənt] *adj* (**a**) *(empty)* vacío(a) (**b**) *(job)* vacante; *Br* **situations v.** *(in newspaper)* ofertas de trabajo (**c**) *(free, not in use)* libre

vacate [vəˈkeɪt] *vt (flat)* desalojar

vacation [vəˈkeɪʃən] **1** *n Br Univ, US* vacaciones *fpl;* **on v.** de vacaciones **2** *vi US* pasar las vacaciones (**in/at** en)

vaccinate [ˈvæksɪneɪt] *vt* vacunar

vaccination [væksɪˈneɪʃən] *n Med* vacunación *f*

vaccine [ˈvæksiːn] *n* vacuna *f*

vacuum [ˈvækjʊəm] **1** *n* vacío *m;* **v. cleaner** aspiradora *f; Br* **v. flask** termo *m* **2** *vt (carpet, room)* pasar la aspiradora por

vagina [vəˈdʒaɪnə] *n* vagina *f*

vague [veɪg] *adj (imprecise)* vago(a), impreciso(a); *(indistinct)* borroso(a)

vain [veɪn] *adj* (**a**) *(proud)* vanidoso(a), presumido(a) (**b**) *(hopeless)* vano(a); **in v.** en vano

valentine [ˈvæləntaɪn] *n* (**a**) *(card)* = tarjeta que se manda el Día de los Enamorados (**b**) *(sweetheart)* novio(a) *m,f*

valid [ˈvælɪd] *adj* válido(a); **no longer v.** caducado(a)

validate [ˈvælɪdeɪt] *vt* validar

valley [ˈvælɪ] *n* valle *m*

valuable [ˈvæljʊəbəl] **1** *adj* valioso(a), de valor **2** *npl* **valuables** objetos *mpl* de valor

valuation [væljʊˈeɪʃən] *n* (**a**) *(act)* valoración *f* (**b**) *(price)* valor *m*

value [ˈvæljuː] **1** *n* valor *m;* **to get good v. for money** sacarle jugo al dinero; *Br* **v.-added tax** impuesto *m* sobre el valor añadido *or Am* agregado **2** *vt* valorar

valve [vælv] *n* (**a**) *Anat, Tech* válvula *f* (**b**) *Rad* lámpara *f*

van [væn] *n* (**a**) *Aut* furgoneta *f* (**b**) *Br Rail* furgón *m*

vandal [ˈvændəl] *n* vándalo(a) *m,f, Esp* gamberro(a) *m,f*

vandalism [ˈvændəlɪzəm] *n* vandalismo *m, Esp* gamberrismo *m*

vandalize [ˈvændəlaɪz] *vt* destruir, destrozar

vanilla [vəˈnɪlə] *n* vainilla *f*

vanish [ˈvænɪʃ] *vi* desaparecer

vanity [ˈvænɪtɪ] *n* vanidad *f;* **v. bag** *or* **case** neceser *m*

vapour [ˈveɪpə(r)] *n* vapor *m; (on windowpane)* vaho *m;* **v. trail** estela *f* de humo

variable [ˈveərɪəbəl] *adj & n* variable *(f)*

variant [ˈveərɪənt] *n* variante *f*

variation [veərɪˈeɪʃən] *n* variación *f*

varied [ˈveərɪd] *adj* variado(a), diverso(a)

variety [vəˈraɪɪtɪ] *n* (**a**) *(diversity)* variedad *f; (assortment)* surtido *m;* **for a v. of reasons** por razones diversas (**b**) **v. show** espectáculo *m* de variedades

various [ˈveərɪəs] *adj* diversos(as), varios(as)

varnish [ˈvɑːnɪʃ] **1** *n* barniz *m; Br* **nail v.** esmalte *m* de uñas **2** *vt* barnizar; *Br (nails)* esmaltar

vary [ˈveərɪ] *vi* variar; **prices v. from £2 to £4** los precios oscilan entre 2 y 4 libras; **to v. in size** variar de tamaño

vase [*Br* vɑːz, *US* veɪs] *n* jarrón *m*

vast [vɑːst] *adj* vasto(a); *(majority)* inmenso(a)

VAT [viːeɪˈtiː, væt] *n Br (abbr* **value-added tax)** IVA *m*

vat [væt] *n* cuba *f*, tina *f*

Vatican [ˈvætɪkən] *n* **the V.** el Vaticano

vault¹ [vɔːlt] *n* bóveda *f*; *(for wine)* bodega *f*; *(tomb)* cripta *f*; *(of bank)* cámara acorazada, *Am* bóveda *f* de seguridad

vault² [vɔːlt] **1** *vt & vi* saltar **2** *n* salto *m*

VCR [viːsiːˈɑː(r)] *n (abbr* **video cassette recorder)** (aparato *m* de) vídeo *m* o *Am* video *m*

VDU [viːdiːˈjuː] *n (abbr* **visual display unit)** monitor *m*

veal [viːl] *n* ternera *f*

veer [vɪə(r)] *vi (ship)* virar; *(car)* girar

vegan [ˈviːgən] *n* vegetariano(a) *m,f,* = vegetariano estricto que no come ningún producto de origen animal

vegetable [ˈvedʒtəbəl] *n (food)* verdura *f*, hortaliza *f*; **v. garden** huerta *f*, huerto *m*

vegetarian [vedʒɪˈteərɪən] *adj & n* vegetariano(a) *(m,f)*

vegetation [vedʒɪˈteɪʃən] *n* vegetación *f*

vehicle [ˈviːɪkəl] *n* vehículo *m*

veil [veɪl] **1** *n* velo *m* **2** *vt* velar

vein [veɪn] *n* vena *f*

velvet [ˈvelvɪt] *n* terciopelo *m*

vending [ˈvendɪŋ] *n* **v. machine** máquina expendedora

vendor [ˈvendɔː(r)] *n* vendedor(a) *m,f*

veneer [vɪˈnɪə(r)] *n (a) (covering)* chapa *f* **(b)** *Fig* apariencia *f*

vengeance [ˈvendʒəns] *n* venganza *f*; *Fam* **it was raining with a v.** llovía con ganas

venison [ˈvenɪsən] *n* carne *f* de venado

venom [ˈvenəm] *n* veneno *m*

vent [vent] **1** *n (a) (opening)* abertura *f*, orificio *m*; *(grille)* rejilla *f* de ventilación; **air v.** respiradero *m* **(b)** *(of volcano)* chimenea *f* **2** *vt Fig (feelings)* descargar

ventilate [ˈventɪleɪt] *vt* ventilar

ventilation [ventɪˈleɪʃən] *n* ventilación *f*

ventriloquist [venˈtrɪləkwɪst] *n* ventrílocuo(a) *m,f*

venture [ˈventʃə(r)] **1** *vt* arriesgar, aventurar; **he didn't v. to ask** no se atrevió a preguntarlo **2** *vi* arriesgarse; **to v. out of doors** atreverse a salir **3** *n* empresa arriesgada, aventura *f*; *Com* **business/joint v.** empresa comercial/colectiva

venue [ˈvenjuː] *n (a) (meeting place)* lugar *m* de reunión **(b)** *(for concert etc)* local *m*

veranda(h) [vəˈrændə] *n* porche *m*, terraza *f*

verb [vɜːb] *n* verbo *m*

verbal [ˈvɜːbəl] *adj* verbal

verdict [ˈvɜːdɪkt] *n (a) Jur* veredicto *m*, fallo *m* **(b)** *(opinion)* opinión *f*, juicio *m*

verge [vɜːdʒ] **1** *n (a) (margin)* borde *m*; *Fig* **on the v. of** al borde de; *Fig* **to be on the v. of doing sth** estar a punto de hacer algo **(b)** *Br (of road)* arcén *m*, *Andes* berma *f*, *Méx* acotamiento *m*, *RP* banquina *f*, *Ven* hombrillo *m* **2** *vi* rayar (**on** en)

verify [ˈverɪfaɪ] *vt* verificar, comprobar

vermin [ˈvɜːmɪn] *npl (a) (animals)* bichos *mpl*, sabandijas *fpl* **(b)** *Fig* gentuza *f*

versatile [ˈvɜːsətaɪl] *adj (person)* polifacético(a); *(object)* versátil

verse [vɜːs] *n (a) (stanza)* estrofa *f* **(b)** *(poetry)* versos *mpl*, poesía *f* **(c)** *(of song)* copla *f* **(d)** *(of Bible)* versículo *m*

versed [vɜːst] *adj* **to be (well) v. in** ser (muy) versado en

version [ˈvɜːʃən, ˈvɜːʒən] *n (a)* versión *f*; **stage v.** adaptación *f* teatral **(b)** *Aut* modelo *m*

versus [ˈvɜːsəs] *prep* contra

vertical [ˈvɜːtɪkəl] *adj & n* vertical *(f)*

very [ˈverɪ] **1** *adv (a) (extremely)* muy; **to be v. hungry** tener mucha hambre; **v. much** muchísimo; **v. well** muy bien **(b)** *(emphatic)* **at the v. latest** como máximo; **at the v. least** como mínimo; **the v. first/last** el primero/último de todos; **the v. same day** el mismo día **2** *adj* (**a**) **at the v. end/beginning** al final/principio de todo (**b**) *(precise)* **at this v. moment** en este mismo momento; **her v. words** sus palabras exactas (**c**) *(mere)* **the v. thought of it!** ¡sólo con pensarlo!

vessel ['vesəl] *n* (**a**) *(container)* vasija *f* (**b**) *Naut* buque *m*, nave *f* (**c**) *Anat, Bot* vaso *m*

vest [vest] **1** *n* (**a**) *Br (undershirt)* camiseta *f* de tirantes *or Am* breteles (**b**) *US* chaleco *m* **2** *vt Jur* **by the power vested in me ...** por los poderes que se me han conferido ...

vested ['vestɪd] *adj Jur, Fin* **v. interests** derechos adquiridos; *Fig* intereses *mpl* personales

vestige ['vestɪdʒ] *n* vestigio *m*

vet [vet] **1** *n* veterinario(a) *m,f* **2** *vt Br* someter a investigación, examinar

veteran ['vetərən] *n* (**a**) veterano(a) *m,f* (**b**) *US* **(war) v.** ex combatiente *mf*

veto ['vi:təʊ] **1** *n* (*pl* **vetoes**) veto *m* **2** *vt Pol* vetar; *(suggestion etc)* descartar

via ['vaɪə] *prep* por, vía

viable ['vaɪəbəl] *adj* viable, factible

viaduct ['vaɪədʌkt] *n* viaducto *m*

vibrant ['vaɪbrənt] *adj* (**a**) *(sound)* vibrante (**b**) *Fig (personality)* vital; *(city)* animado(a)

vibrate [vaɪ'breɪt] *vi* vibrar (**with** de)

vibration [vaɪ'breɪʃən] *n* vibración *f*

vicar ['vɪkə(r)] *n* párroco *m*

vice¹ [vaɪs] *n* vicio *m*

vice² [vaɪs] *n Br (tool)* torno *m* de banco

vice- [vaɪs] *prefix* vice-; **v.-chancellor** rector(a) *m,f*; **v.-president** vicepresidente(a) *m,f*

vice versa [vaɪsɪ'vɜːsə] *adv* viceversa

vicious ['vɪʃəs] *adj (violent)* violento(a); *(malicious)* malintencionado(a); *(cruel)* cruel; **v. circle** círculo vicioso

victim ['vɪktɪm] *n* víctima *f*

victimize ['vɪktɪmaɪz] *vt* perseguir, tratar injustamente

victorious [vɪk'tɔːrɪəs] *adj* victorioso(a)

victory ['vɪktərɪ] *n* victoria *f*

video ['vɪdɪəʊ] *n* vídeo *m*, *Am* video *m*; **v. camera** cámara *f* de vídeo *or Am* video; **v. cassette** cinta *f* de vídeo *or Am* video; **v. game** videojuego *m*; **v. (cassette) recorder** (aparato *m* de) vídeo *m or Am* video; **v. tape** cinta *f* de vídeo *or Am* video

video-tape ['vɪdɪəʊteɪp] *vt* grabar (en vídeo *or Am* video)

vie [vaɪ] *vi* competir (**against** *or* **with** con)

view [vjuː] **1** *n* (**a**) *(sight)* vista *f*, panorama *m*; **on v.** a la vista; **to come into v.** aparecer; *Fig* **in v. of the fact that ...** dado que ... (**b**) *(opinion)* opinión *f*; **point of v.** punto *m* de vista (**c**) *(aim)* fin *m*; **with a v. to** con la intención de **2** *vt* (**a**) *(look at)* mirar; *(house etc)* visitar (**b**) *(consider)* contemplar; *(topic, problem)* enfocar

viewer ['vjuːə(r)] *n* (**a**) *TV* televidente *mf* (**b**) *Phot* visionador *m*

viewfinder ['vjuːfaɪndə(r)] *n* visor *m*

viewpoint ['vjuːpɔɪnt] *n* punto *m* de vista

vigilant ['vɪdʒɪlənt] *adj* alerta

vigorous ['vɪgərəs] *adj* vigoroso(a), enérgico(a)

vile [vaɪl] *adj* (**a**) *(evil)* vil, infame (**b**) *(disgusting)* repugnante (**c**) *Fam (awful)* horrible

villa ['vɪlə] *n* (**a**) *(in country)* casa *f* de campo (**b**) *Br* chalet *m*

village ['vɪlɪdʒ] *n* *(small)* aldea *f*; *(larger)* pueblo *m*

villager ['vɪlɪdʒə(r)] *n* aldeano(a) *m,f*

villain ['vɪlən] *n* villano(a) *m,f*; *Cin, Th* malo(a) *m,f*

vindicate ['vɪndɪkeɪt] *vt* justificar, vindicar

vindictive [vɪn'dɪktɪv] *adj* vengativo(a)

vine [vaɪn] *n* vid *f*; *(climbing)* parra *f*

vinegar ['vɪnɪgə(r)] *n* vinagre *m*

vineyard ['vɪnjəd] *n* viña *f*, viñedo *m*

vintage ['vɪntɪdʒ] **1** n (**a**) *(crop, year)* cosecha f (**b**) *(season)* vendimia f (**c**) *(era)* era f **2** *adj* (**a**) *(wine)* añejo(a) (**b**) *(classic)* clásico(a); **v. car** coche m de época

violate ['vaɪəleɪt] *vt* violar

violence ['vaɪələns] n violencia f

violent ['vaɪələnt] *adj* (**a**) violento(a) (**b**) *(intense)* intenso(a)

violet ['vaɪəlɪt] **1** n (**a**) *Bot* violeta f (**b**) *(colour)* violeta m **2** *adj* violeta

violin [vaɪə'lɪn] n violín m

violinist [vaɪə'lɪnɪst] n violinista mf

VIP [viːaɪ'piː] n *Fam* (*abbr* **very important person**) personaje m muy importante

viper ['vaɪpə(r)] n víbora f

virgin ['vɜːdʒɪn] **1** n virgen f; **the V. Mary** la Virgen María; **to be a v.** ser virgen **2** *adj* virgen

Virgo ['vɜːgəʊ] n virgo m

virile ['vɪraɪl] *adj* viril

virtual ['vɜːtjʊəl] *adj* virtual; *Comput* **v. reality** realidad f virtual

virtually ['vɜːtjʊəlɪ] *adv (almost)* prácticamente

virtue ['vɜːtjuː] n virtud f; **by v. of** en virtud de

virtuous ['vɜːtjʊəs] *adj* virtuoso(a)

virus ['vaɪrəs] n virus m *inv*; *Comput* **v. check** detección m de virus

visa ['viːzə] n visado m, *Am* visa f

visibility [vɪzɪ'bɪlɪtɪ] n visibilidad f

visible ['vɪzɪbəl] *adj* visible

vision ['vɪʒən] n (**a**) visión f (**b**) *(eyesight)* vista f

visit ['vɪzɪt] **1** *vt* (**a**) *(person)* visitar, hacer una visita a (**b**) *(place)* visitar, ir a **2** n visita f; **to pay sb a v.** hacerle una visita a algn

visitor ['vɪzɪtə(r)] n (**a**) *(guest)* invitado(a) m,f; **we've got visitors** tenemos visita (**b**) *(in hotel)* cliente(a) m,f (**c**) *(tourist)* turista mf

visor ['vaɪzə(r)] n visera f

visual ['vɪʒʊəl] *adj* visual; **v. aids** medios mpl visuales

visualize ['vɪʒʊəlaɪz] *vt* (**a**) *(imagine)* imaginar(se) (**b**) *(foresee)* prever

vital ['vaɪtəl] *adj* (**a**) *(lively)* enérgico(a) (**b**) *(essential)* fundamental (**c**) *(decisive)* decisivo(a); *Fam* **v. statistics** medidas fpl del cuerpo de la mujer (**d**) *Med (function, sign)* vital

vitality [vaɪ'tælɪtɪ] n vitalidad f

vitamin ['vɪtəmɪn, *US* 'vaɪtəmɪn] n vitamina f

vivacious [vɪ'veɪʃəs] *adj* vivaz

vivid ['vɪvɪd] *adj* (**a**) *(bright, lively)* vivo(a), intenso(a) (**b**) *(graphic)* gráfico(a)

vocabulary [və'kæbjʊlərɪ] n vocabulario m

vocal ['vəʊkəl] *adj* vocal; **v. cords** cuerdas fpl vocales

vocation [vəʊ'keɪʃən] n vocación f

vocational [vəʊ'keɪʃənəl] *adj* profesional; **v. training** formación f profesional

vociferous [vəʊ'sɪfərəs] *adj* (**a**) *(protest)* enérgico(a) (**b**) *(noisy)* clamoroso(a)

vodka ['vɒdkə] n vodka m

vogue [vəʊg] n boga f, moda f; **in v.** de moda

voice [vɔɪs] **1** n voz f; **to lose one's v.** quedarse afónico; *Fig* **at the top of one's v.** a voz en grito; *Comput* **v. mail** buzón m de voz **2** *vt* (**a**) *(express)* manifestar (**b**) *Ling* sonorizar

void [vɔɪd] **1** *adj* (**a**) **v. of** sin (**b**) *Jur* nulo(a), inválido(a) **2** n vacío m

volatile ['vɒlətaɪl] *adj* volátil

volcano [vɒl'keɪnəʊ] n (*pl* **volcanoes**) volcán m

volley ['vɒlɪ] **1** n (**a**) *(of shots)* descarga f (**b**) *Fig (of stones, insults)* lluvia f (**c**) *(in tennis, football)* volea f **2** *vt (in tennis, football)* volear

volleyball ['vɒlɪbɔːl] n voleibol m

volt [vəʊlt] n voltio m

voltage ['vəʊltɪdʒ] n voltaje m

volume ['vɒljuːm] n (**a**) volumen m (**b**) *(book)* volumen m, tomo m; *Fig* **to speak volumes** decirlo todo

voluntary ['vɒləntərɪ] *adj* voluntario(a); **v. organization** organización benéfica

volunteer [vɒlən'tɪə(r)] **1** *n* voluntario(a) *m,f*
2 *vt (help etc)* ofrecer
3 *vi* (**a**) ofrecerse (**for** para) (**b**) *Mil* alistarse como voluntario

vomit ['vɒmɪt] **1** *vt & vi* vomitar **2** *n* vómito *m*

vote [vəʊt] **1** *n* voto *m; (voting)* votación *f;* **v. of confidence** voto de confianza; **to take a v. on sth** someter algo a votacíon; **to have the v.** tener derecho al voto
2 *vt* (**a**) votar (**b**) *(elect)* elegir (**c**) *Fam* proponer
3 *vi* votar; **to v. for sb** votar a algn

voter ['vəʊtə(r)] *n* votante *mf*

voting ['vəʊtɪŋ] *n* votación *f*

vouch [vaʊtʃ] *vi* **to v. for sth/sb** responder de algo/por algn

voucher ['vaʊtʃə(r)] *n Br* vale *m*

vow [vaʊ] **1** *n* voto *m* **2** *vt* jurar

vowel ['vaʊəl] *n* vocal *f*

voyage ['vɔɪɪdʒ] *n* viaje *m; (crossing)* travesía *f;* **to go on a v.** hacer un viaje (en barco)

vulgar ['vʌlgə(r)] *adj (coarse)* vulgar, ordinario(a); *(in poor taste)* de mal gusto

vulnerable ['vʌlnərəbəl] *adj* vulnerable

vulture ['vʌltʃə(r)] *n* buitre *m*

Ww

W, w [ˈdʌbəlju:] n *(the letter)* W, w f

W (**a**) *(abbr* **west)** O (**b**) *(abbr* **watt(s))** W

wad [wɒd] n *(of paper)* taco m; *(of cotton wool)* bolita f; *(of banknotes)* fajo m

waddle [ˈwɒdəl] vi caminar or andar como un pato

wade [weɪd] vi caminar por el agua; **to w. across a river** vadear un río

▶ **wade through** vt insep hacer con dificultad; **I'm wading through the book** me cuesta mucho terminar el libro

wafer [ˈweɪfə(r)] n barquillo m; *Rel* hostia f

waffle¹ [ˈwɒfəl] n *(food)* Esp gofre m, Am wafle m

waffle² [ˈwɒfəl] Br Fam **1** vi meter mucha paja; **to w. on** parlotear **2** n paja f

waft [wɑːft, wɒft] **1** vt llevar por el aire **2** vi flotar (por or en el aire)

wag [wæg] **1** vt menear **2** vi *(tail)* menearse

wage [weɪdʒ] **1** n *(also* **wages)** salario m, sueldo m; **w. earner** asalariado(a) m,f; **w. freeze** congelación f salarial **2** vt *(campaign)* realizar (**against** contra); **to w. war (on)** hacer la guerra (a)

wager [ˈweɪdʒə(r)] **1** n apuesta f **2** vt apostar

waggle [ˈwægəl] **1** vt menear **2** vi menearse

wa(g)gon [ˈwægən] n *(horse-drawn)* carro m; Br Rail vagón m

wail [weɪl] **1** n lamento m, gemido m **2** vi *(person)* lamentar, gemir

waist [weɪst] n Anat cintura f; Sewing talle m

waistcoat [ˈweɪstkəʊt] n Br chaleco m

wait [weɪt] **1** n espera f; *(delay)* demora f; **to lie in w.** estar al acecho **2** vi (**a**) esperar, aguardar; **I can't w. to see her** me muero de ganas de verla; **while you w.** en el acto; **to keep sb waiting** hacer esperar a algn (**b**) Br **to w. at table** servir la mesa

▶ **wait about, wait around** vi esperar

▶ **wait on** vt insep servir

waiter [ˈweɪtə(r)] n camarero m, Andes, RP mozo m, Chile, Ven mesonero m, Col, Guat, Méx, Salv mesero m

waiting [ˈweɪtɪŋ] n **no w.** *(sign)* prohibido aparcar; **w. list** lista f de espera; **w. room** sala f de espera

waitress [ˈweɪtrɪs] n camarera f, Andes, RP moza f, Chile, Ven mesonera f, Col, Guat, Méx, Salv mesera f

wake¹ [weɪk] *(pt* **woke;** *pp* **woken) 1** vt **to w. sb (up)** despertar a algn

2 vi **to w. (up)** despertar(se)

3 n *(for dead)* velatorio m, Am velorio m

wake² [weɪk] n *(in water)* estela f; Fig **in the w. of** tras

Wales [weɪlz] n (el país de) Gales

walk [wɔːk] **1** n (**a**) *(long)* caminata m; *(short)* paseo m; **to go for a w.** dar un paseo; **to take the dog for a w.** sacar a pasear al perro (**b**) *(gait)* andares mpl, modo m de caminar or Esp andar (**c**) **people from all walks of life** gente f de toda condición

2 vt (**a**) **we walked her home** la acompañamos a casa (**b**) *(dog)* pasear

3 vi (**a**) caminar, Esp andar (**b**) *(go on foot)* ir andando

▶ **walk away** vi irse (caminando or Esp andando); Fig **to w. away with a prize** llevarse un premio

▶ **walk into** vt insep (**a**) *(place)* entrar

en; *Fig (trap)* caer en (**b**) *(bump into)* chocarse contra

▸ **walk out** *vi* salir; *Ind* declararse en huelga; **to w. out on sb** abandonar a algn

▸ **walk up** *vi* **to w. up to sb** abordar a algn

walker ['wɔːkə(r)] *n* paseante *mf*; *Sport* marchador(a) *m,f*

walking ['wɔːkɪŋ] **1** *n* caminar *m*, *Esp* andar *m*; *(hiking)* excursionismo *m* **2** *adj* **at w. pace** a paso de marcha; **w. shoes** zapatos *mpl* de andar; **w. stick** bastón *m*

Walkman® ['wɔːkmən] *n* (*pl* **Walkmans**) walkman® *m*

wall [wɔːl] *n* (**a**) *(freestanding, exterior)* muro *m*; *Fig* **to have one's back to the w.** estar entre la espada y la pared; **garden w.** tapia *f* (**b**) *(interior)* pared *f* (**c**) *Ftb* barrera *f*

▸ **wall up** *vt sep (door, fireplace)* tabicar

wallet ['wɒlɪt] *n* cartera *f*

wallpaper ['wɔːlpeɪpə(r)] **1** *n* papel pintado **2** *vt* empapelar

walnut ['wɔːlnʌt] *n* nuez *f*; *(tree, wood)* nogal *m*

walrus ['wɔːlrəs] *n* morsa *f*

waltz [wɔːls] **1** *n* vals *m* **2** *vi* bailar un vals

wand [wɒnd] *n* (**magic**) **w.** varita *f* (mágica)

wander ['wɒndə(r)] **1** *vt* **to w. the streets** vagar por las calles **2** *vi* (**a**) *(aimlessly)* vagar, errar; **to w. about** deambular; **to w. in/out** entrar/salir sin prisas (**b**) *(stray)* desviarse; *(mind)* divagar

wangle ['wæŋgəl] *vt Fam* agenciarse

want [wɒnt] **1** *n* (**a**) *(lack)* falta *f*; **for w. of** por falta de (**b**) *(poverty)* miseria *f* **2** *vt* (**a**) *(desire)* querer, desear; **to w. to do sth** querer hacer algo (**b**) *Fam (need)* necesitar; **the grass wants cutting** hace falta cortar el césped (**c**) *(seek)* buscar; **you're wanted on the phone** te llaman al teléfono

▸ **want for** *vt insep* carecer de; **to w.**

for nothing tenerlo todo

wanted ['wɒntɪd] *adj (on police poster)* se busca; **w., a good cook** *(advertisement)* se necesita buen cocinero

war [wɔː(r)] *n* guerra *f*; **to be at w. (with)** estar en guerra (con); *Fig* **to declare/wage w. on** declarar/hacer la guerra a; **w. crime** crimen *m* de guerra

ward [wɔːd] *n* (**a**) *(of hospital)* sala *f* (**b**) *Jur* pupilo(a) *m,f*; **w. of court** pupilo(a) bajo tutela judicial (**c**) *Br Pol* distrito *m* electoral

▸ **ward off** *vt sep (blow)* parar, desviar; *(attack)* rechazar; *(danger)* evitar; *(illness)* prevenir

warden ['wɔːdən] *n* (**a**) *(of institution, hostel)* guardián(ana) *m,f*; **game w.** guardia *m* de coto (**b**) *US (of prison)* director(a) *m,f*, alcaide(esa) *m,f*

wardrobe ['wɔːdrəʊb] *n* (**a**) armario *m*, ropero *m* (**b**) *(clothes)* guardarropa *m* (**c**) *Th* vestuario *m*

warehouse ['weəhaʊs] *n* almacén *m*

wares [weəz] *npl* mercancías *fpl*

warfare ['wɔːfeə(r)] *n* guerra *f*

warm [wɔːm] **1** *adj* (**a**) *(water)* tibio(a); *(hands)* caliente; *(climate)* cálido(a); **a w. day** un día de calor; **I am w.** tengo calor; **it is (very) w. today** hoy hace (mucho) calor; **w. clothing** ropa *f* de abrigo (**b**) *(welcome, applause)* cálido(a)

2 *vt* calentar; *Fig* alegrar

3 *vi* calentarse; **to w. to sb** cogerle simpatía a algn

▸ **warm up 1** *vt sep* (**a**) calentar; *(soup)* (re)calentar (**b**) *(audience)* animar **2** *vi* (**a**) calentarse; *(food)* (re)calentarse; *(person)* entrar en calor (**b**) *(athlete)* hacer ejercicios de calentamiento (**c**) *Fig (audience, party)* animarse

warmth [wɔːmθ] *n* *(heat)* calor *m*; *Fig* cordialidad *f*

warn [wɔːn] *vt* avisar (**of** de), advertir (**about/against** sobre/contra); **he warned me not to go** me advirtió que no fuera; **to w. sb that** advertir a algn que

warning ['wɔ:nɪŋ] **1** *adj* **w. light** piloto *m*; **w. sign** señal *f* de aviso **2** *n* (**a**) *(of danger)* advertencia *f*, aviso *m* (**b**) *(replacing punishment)* amonestación *f* (**c**) *(notice)* aviso *m*; **without w.** sin previo aviso

warp [wɔ:p] **1** *vt* (**a**) *(wood)* alabear, combar (**b**) *Fig (mind)* pervertir **2** *vi* alabearse, combarse

warrant ['wɒrənt] **1** *n* (**a**) *Jur* orden *f* judicial; **death w.** sentencia *f* de muerte (**b**) *(authorization note)* cédula *f*; *Com* bono *m* **2** *vt* (**a**) *(justify)* justificar (**b**) *(guarantee)* garantizar

warranty ['wɒrəntɪ] *n Com* garantía *f*

warren ['wɒrən] *n* conejera *f*; *Fig* laberinto *m*

warrior ['wɒrɪə(r)] *n* guerrero(a) *m,f*

wart [wɔ:t] *n* verruga *f*

wartime ['wɔ:taɪm] *n* tiempos *mpl* de guerra

wary ['weərɪ] *adj* (**warier, wariest**) cauteloso(a); **to be w. of doing sth** dudar en hacer algo; **to be w. of sb/sth** recelar de algn/algo

was [wɒz] *pt of* **be**

wash [wɒʃ] **1** *n* (**a**) lavado *m*; **to have a w.** lavarse (**b**) *(of ship)* estela *f*; *(sound)* chapoteo *m*

2 *vt* (**a**) lavar; *(dishes)* fregar; **to w. one's hair** lavarse el pelo (**b**) *(of sea, river)* arrastrar

3 *vi* (**a**) *(person)* lavarse; *(do the laundry)* hacer la colada (**b**) *(lap)* batir

▸ **wash away** *vt sep (of sea)* llevarse; *(traces)* borrar

▸ **wash off** *vi* lavar, quitar *or Am* sacar lavando

▸ **wash out 1** *vt sep* (**a**) *(stain)* quitar lavando (**b**) *(bottle)* enjuagar **2** *vi* quitarse lavando

▸ **wash up 1** *vt sep Br (dishes)* fregar **2** *vi* (**a**) *Br* fregar los platos (**b**) *US* lavarse rápidamente

washable ['wɒʃəbəl] *adj* lavable

washbasin ['wɒʃbeɪsən], *US* **washbowl** ['wɒʃbəʊl] *n* lavabo *m*, *Am* lavamanos *m inv*

washcloth ['wɒʃklɒθ] *n US* manopla *f*

washer ['wɒʃə(r)] *n (on tap)* zapata *f*, junta *f*

washing ['wɒʃɪŋ] *n (action)* lavado *m*; *(of clothes)* colada *f*; (**dirty**) **w.** ropa sucia; **to do the w.** hacer la colada; **w. line** tendedero *m*; **w. machine** lavadora *f*, *RP* lavarropas *m inv*; **w. powder** detergente *m*

washing-up [wɒʃɪŋ'ʌp] *n Br* (**a**) *(action)* fregado *m*; **w. bowl** palangana *f or Esp* barreño *m* para lavar los platos; **w. liquid** (detergente *m*) lavavajillas *m inv* (**b**) *(dishes)* platos *mpl* (para fregar)

wasp [wɒsp] *n* avispa *f*

waste [weɪst] **1** *adj* (**a**) *(unwanted)* desechado(a); **w. products** productos *mpl* de desecho (**b**) *(ground)* baldío(a) **2** *n* (**a**) *(unnecessary use)* desperdicio *m*; *(of resources, effort, money)* derroche *m*; *(of time)* pérdida *f*; **to go to w.** echarse a perder (**b**) *(leftovers)* desperdicios *mpl*; *(rubbish)* basura *f*; **radioactive w.** desechos *mpl* radiactivos; *Br* **w. disposal unit** trituradora *f* (de desperdicios); **w. pipe** tubo *m* de desagüe

3 *vt (squander)* desperdiciar, malgastar; *(resources)* derrochar; *(money)* despilfarrar; *(time)* perder

▸ **waste away** *vi* consumirse

wasteful ['weɪstfʊl] *adj* derrochador(a)

wastepaper [weɪst'peɪpə(r)] *n* **w. basket** *or* **bin** papelera *f*, *Méx* bote *m*

watch [wɒtʃ] **1** *n* (**a**) *(lookout)* vigilancia *f*; **to keep a close w. on sth/sb** vigilar algo/a algn muy atentamente (**b**) *Mil (body)* guardia *f*; *(individual)* centinela *m*; **to be on w.** estar de guardia (**c**) *(timepiece)* reloj *m* **2** *vt* (**a**) *(observe)* mirar, observar (**b**) *(keep an eye on)* vigilar; *(with suspicion)* acechar (**c**) *(be careful of)* tener cuidado con; *Fig* **to w. one's step** ir con pies de plomo

3 *vi (look)* mirar, observar; **w. out!** ¡cuidado!

▸ **watch out for** *vt insep (be careful of)* tener cuidado con

watchdog ['wɒtʃdɒg] *n* perro *m* guardián; *Fig* guardián(ana) *m,f*

watchful ['wɒtʃfʊl] *adj* vigilante

watchstrap ['wɒtʃstræp] *n Br* correa *f* (de reloj)

water ['wɔːtə(r)] **1** *n* (**a**) agua *f*; **w. bottle** cantimplora *f*; **w. lily** nenúfar *m*; **w. main** conducción *f* de aguas; **w. polo** water polo *m*; **w. sports** deportes acuáticos; **w. tank** depósito *m* de agua (**b**) **to pass w.** orinar
2 *vt (plants)* regar
3 *vi* **my eyes are watering** me lloran los ojos; **it made my mouth w.** se me hizo la boca agua

▸ **water down** *vt sep (drink)* aguar

watercolour, *US* **watercolor** ['wɔːtəkʌlə(r)] *n* acuarela *f*

watercress ['wɔːtəkres] *n* berro *m*

waterfall ['wɔːtəfɔːl] *n* cascada *f*; *(very big)* catarata *f*

watering ['wɔːtərɪŋ] *n (of plants)* riego *m*; **w. can** regadera *f*; **w. place** abrevadero *m*

watermelon ['wɔːtəmelən] *n* sandía *f*

waterproof ['wɔːtəpruːf] **1** *adj (material)* impermeable; *(watch)* sumergible **2** *n (coat)* impermeable *m*

watertight ['wɔːtətaɪt] *adj* hermético(a)

watery ['wɔːtərɪ] *adj* (**a**) *(soup)* aguado(a); *(coffee)* flojo(a) (**b**) *(eyes)* lacrimoso(a) (**c**) *(pale)* pálido(a)

watt [wɒt] *n* vatio *m*

wave [weɪv] **1** *n* (**a**) *(at sea)* ola *f* (**b**) *(in hair)* & *Rad* onda *f* (**c**) *Fig (of anger, strikes etc)* oleada *f* (**d**) *(gesture)* saludo *m* con la mano
2 *vt* (**a**) agitar; *(brandish)* blandir (**b**) *(hair)* ondular
3 *vi* (**a**) agitar el brazo; **she waved (to me)** *(greeting)* me saludó con la mano; *(goodbye)* se despidió (de mí) con la mano; *(signal)* me hizo señas con la mano (**b**) *(flag)* ondear; *(corn)* ondular

wavelength ['weɪvleŋθ] *n* longitud *f* de onda

waver ['weɪvə(r)] *vi (hesitate)* vacilar (**between** entre); *(voice)* temblar; *(courage)* flaquear

wavy ['weɪvɪ] *adj* (**wavier, waviest**) ondulado(a)

wax¹ [wæks] **1** *n* cera *f* **2** *vt* encerar

wax² [wæks] *vi* (**a**) *(moon)* crecer (**b**) **to w. lyrical** exaltarse

way [weɪ] **1** *n* (**a**) *(route)* camino *m*; *(road)* vía *f*, camino; **on the w. here** de camino hacia aquí; **out of the w.** apartado(a); **to ask the w.** preguntar el camino; **to go the wrong w.** ir por el camino equivocado; **to lose one's w.** perderse; **which is the w. to the station?** ¿por dónde se va a la estación?; **w. in** entrada *f*; **w. out** salida *f*; **on the w. back** en el viaje de regreso; **on the w. up/down** en la subida/bajada; **you're in the w.** estás estorbando; **(get) out of the w.!** ¡quítate de en medio!; **there's a wall in the w.** hay un muro en medio; **to give w.** ceder; *Aut* ceder el paso
(**b**) *(direction)* dirección *f*; **which w. did he go?** ¿por dónde se fue?; **that w.** por allá
(**c**) *(distance)* distancia *f*; **a long w. off** lejos; *Fig* **we've come a long w.** hemos hecho grandes progresos
(**d**) **to get under w.** *(travellers, work)* ponerse en marcha; *(meeting, match)* empezar
(**e**) *(means, method)* método *m*, manera *f*; **I'll do it my w.** lo haré a mi manera
(**f**) *(manner)* modo *m*, manera *f*; **in a friendly w.** de modo amistoso; *Fam* **no w.!** ¡ni hablar!; **she has a w. with children** tiene un don para los niños; **either w.** en cualquier caso; **in a w.** en cierto sentido
(**g**) *(custom)* hábito *m*, costumbre *f*; **to be set in one's ways** tener costumbres arraigadas
(**h**) *(state)* estado *m*; **leave it the w. it is** déjalo tal como está; **he is in a bad w.** está bastante mal
(**i**) **by the w.** a propósito
2 *adv Fam* mucho, muy; **w. back in 1940** allá en 1940

wayward ['weɪwəd] *adj* rebelde; *(capricious)* caprichoso(a)

WC [dʌblju:'si:] *n (abbr* **water closet**) váter *m*, WC *m*

we [wi:] *pers pron* nosotros(as) *(usually omitted in Spanish, except for contrast)*

weak [wi:k] *adj* débil; *(argument, excuse)* pobre; *(team, piece of work, tea)* flojo(a)

weaken ['wi:kən] **1** *vt* debilitar; *(argument)* quitar fuerza a **2** *vi* (**a**) debilitarse (**b**) *(concede ground)* ceder

weakness ['wi:knɪs] *n* debilidad *f*; *(character flaw)* punto flaco

wealth [welθ] *n* riqueza *f*; *Fig* abundancia *f*

wealthy ['welθɪ] *adj* (**wealthier**, **wealthiest**) rico(a)

weapon ['wepən] *n* arma *f*

wear [weə(r)] *(pt* wore; *pp* worn) **1** *vt* (**a**) *(clothes)* llevar puesto, vestir; *(shoes)* llevar puestos, calzar; **he wears glasses** lleva gafas; **to w. black** vestirse de negro (**b**) *(erode)* desgastar
2 *vi* **to w. (thin/smooth)** desgastarse (con el roce)
3 *n* (**a**) ropa *f*; **leisure w.** ropa de sport (**b**) *(use) (clothes)* uso *m* (**c**) *(deterioration)* desgaste *m*; **normal w. and tear** desgaste natural
▸ **wear away 1** *vt sep* erosionar **2** *vi* *(stone etc)* erosionarse; *(inscription)* borrarse
▸ **wear down 1** *vt sep* *(heels)* desgastar; *Fig* **to w. sb down** vencer la resistencia de algn **2** *vi* desgastarse
▸ **wear off** *vi* *(effect, pain)* pasar, desaparecer
▸ **wear out 1** *vt sep* gastar; *Fig* agotar **2** *vi* gastarse

weary ['wɪərɪ] **1** *adj* (**wearier**, **weariest**) (**a**) *(tired)* cansado(a) (**b**) *(fed up)* harto(a)
2 *vt* cansar
3 *vi* cansarse (**of** de)

weather ['weðə(r)] **1** *n* tiempo *m*; **the w. is fine** hace buen tiempo; *Fig* **to feel under the w.** no encontrarse bien; **w. chart** mapa meteorológico; **w. forecast** parte meteorológico **2** *vt* *Fig (crisis)* aguantar; *Fig* **to w. the storm** capear el temporal

weave [wi:v] *(pt* wove; *pp* woven) **1** *n* tejido *m*
2 *vt* (**a**) *Tex* tejer (**b**) *(intertwine)* entretejer (**c**) *(intrigues)* tramar
3 *vi* *(person, road)* zigzaguear

web [web] *n* (**a**) *(of spider)* telaraña *f* (**b**) *(of lies)* sarta *f* (**c**) *Comput* **the W.** la Web; **w. page** página *f* web; **w. site** sitio *m* web

wed [wed] *(pt & pp* wed *or* wedded) *vt Literary* casarse con

wedding ['wedɪŋ] *n* boda *f*, *Andes* matrimonio *m*, *RP* casamiento *m*; **w. cake** tarta *f or* pastel *m* de boda; **w. day** día *m* de la boda; **w. dress** traje *m* de novia; **w. present** regalo *m* de boda; **w. ring** alianza *f*

wedge [wedʒ] **1** *n* (**a**) cuña *f*; *(for table leg)* calce *m* (**b**) *(of cake, cheese)* trozo *m* grande **2** *vt* calzar; **to be wedged tight** *(object)* estar completamente atrancado(a)

Wednesday ['wenzdɪ] *n* miércoles *m*

wee¹ [wi:] *adj esp Scot* pequeñito(a)

wee² [wi:] *Br Fam* **1** *n* pipí *m* **2** *vi* hacer pipí

weed [wi:d] **1** *n Bot* mala hierba
2 *vt* (**a**) *(garden)* escardar (**b**) *Fig* **to w. out** eliminar
3 *vi* escardar

weedkiller ['wi:dkɪlə(r)] *n* herbicida *m*

week [wi:k] *n* semana *f*; **a w. (ago) today/yesterday** hoy hace/ayer hizo una semana; **a w. today** justo dentro de una semana; **last/next w.** la semana pasada/que viene; **once a w.** una vez por semana; **w. in, w. out** semana tras semana

weekday ['wi:kdeɪ] *n* día *m* laborable

weekend [wi:k'end] *n* fin *m* de semana

weekly ['wi:klɪ] **1** *adj* semanal
2 *adv* semanalmente; **twice w.** dos veces por semana
3 *n Press* semanario *m*

weep [wi:p] *(pt & pp* wept) **1** *vi* llorar; **to w. for sb** llorar la muerte de algn **2** *vt (tears)* derramar

weigh [weɪ] **1** *vt* (**a**) pesar (**b**) *Fig*

(consider) ponderar (**c**) **to w. anchor** levar anclas **2** *vi* (**a**) pesar (**b**) *Fig (influence)* influir

▸ **weigh down** *vt sep* sobrecargar

▸ **weigh in** *vi* (**a**) *Sport* pesarse (**b**) *Fam (join in)* intervenir

▸ **weigh up** *vt sep (matter)* evaluar; *(person)* formar una opinión sobre; **to w. up the pros and cons** sopesar los pros y los contras

weight [weɪt] *n* (**a**) peso *m*; **to lose w.** adelgazar; **to put on w.** subir de peso (**b**) *(of clock, scales)* pesa *f* (**c**) *Fig* **that's a w. off my mind** eso me quita *or Am* saca un peso de encima

weightlifting ['weɪtlɪftɪŋ] *n* halterofilia *f*, levantamiento *m* de pesos

weighty ['weɪtɪ] *adj* (**weightier**, **weightiest**) pesado(a); *Fig (problem, matter)* importante, grave; *(argument)* de peso

weird [wɪəd] *adj* raro(a), extraño(a)

welcome ['welkəm] **1** *adj (person)* bienvenido(a); *(news)* grato(a); *(change)* oportuno(a); **to make sb w.** acoger a algn calurosamente; **you're w.!** ¡no hay de qué!
2 *n (greeting)* bienvenida *f*
3 *vt* acoger; *(more formally)* darle la bienvenida a; *(news)* acoger con agrado; *(decision)* aplaudir

welfare ['welfeə(r)] *n* (**a**) *(well-being)* bienestar *m*; **animal/child w.** protección *f* de animales/de menores; **w. work** asistencia *f* social; **w. worker** asistente *mf* social (**b**) *US (social security)* seguridad *f* social

well¹ [wel] *n* (**a**) pozo *m* (**b**) *(of staircase, lift)* hueco *m* (**c**) *(of court, hall)* hemiciclo *m*

▸ **well up** *vi* brotar

well² [wel] **1** *adj* (**a**) *(healthy)* bien; **to get w.** reponerse (**b**) *(satisfactory)* bien; **all is w.** todo va bien; **it's just as w.** menos mal
2 *adv* (**better, best**) (**a**) *(properly)* bien; **he has done w. (for himself)** ha prosperado; **she did w. in the exam** el examen le fue bien; **w. done!** ¡muy bien!

(**b**) *(thoroughly)* bien; *Culin* **w. done** muy hecho(a)
(**c**) **he's w. over thirty** tiene treinta años bien cumplidos; **w. after six o'clock** mucho después de las seis
(**d**) *(easily, with good reason)* **he couldn't very w. say no** difícilmente podía decir que no; **I may w. do that** puede que haga eso
(**e**) **as w.** también; **as w. as** así como; **children as w. as adults** tanto niños como adultos
3 *interj* (**a**) *(surprise)* ¡bueno!, ¡vaya!; **w. I never!** ¡no me digas! (**b**) *(agreement, interrogation, resignation)* bueno; **very w.** bueno; **w.?** ¿y bien? (**c**) *(doubt)* pues; **w., I don't know** pues no sé (**d**) *(resumption)* **w., as I was saying** pues (bien), como iba diciendo

well-behaved ['welbɪheɪvd] *adj (child)* formal, educado(a)

well-being ['welbiːɪŋ] *n* bienestar *m*

well-built ['welbɪlt] *adj (building etc)* de construcción sólida; *(person)* fornido(a)

well-informed ['welɪnfɔːmd] *adj* bien informado(a)

wellingtons ['welɪŋtənz] *npl Br* botas *fpl* de agua *or* goma *or Méx, Ven* caucho

well-known ['welnəʊn] *adj* (bien) conocido(a)

well-meaning [wel'miːnɪŋ] *adj* bien intencionado(a)

well-off [wel'ɒf] *adj (rich)* acomodado(a)

well-to-do [weltə'duː] *adj* acomodado(a)

Welsh [welʃ] **1** *adj* galés(esa); **W. rarebit** = tostada con queso fundido **2** *n* (**a**) *(language)* galés *m* (**b**) **the W.** los galeses

Welshman ['welʃmən] *n* galés *m*

Welshwoman ['welʃwʊmən] *n* galesa *f*

went [went] *pt of* **go**

wept [wept] *pt & pp of* **weep**

were [wɜː(r), *unstressed* wə(r)] *pt of* **be**

west [west] **1** *n* oeste *m*, occidente *m*; **in/to the w.** al oeste; *Pol* **the W.** los países occidentales

2 *adj* del oeste, occidental; **the W. Indies** las Antillas; **W. Indian** antillano(a)

3 *adv* al oeste, hacia el oeste

western ['westən] **1** *adj* del oeste, occidental; **W. Europe** Europa Occidental **2** *n Cin* western *m*, película *f* del oeste

westward ['westwəd] *adj* **in a w. direction** hacia el oeste

westwards ['westwədz] *adv* hacia el oeste

wet [wet] **1** *adj* (**wetter, wettest**) (**a**) mojado(a); *(slightly)* húmedo(a); *Fig* **w. blanket** aguafiestas *mf inv*; **w. paint** *(sign)* recién pintado; **w. through** *(person)* calado(a) hasta los huesos; *(thing)* empapado(a) (**b**) *(rainy)* lluvioso(a) (**c**) *Br Fam (person)* soso(a) **2** *vt* (*pt & pp* **wet**) mojar; **to w. oneself** orinarse

whack [wæk] **1** *vt (hit hard)* dar un porrazo *or Méx* madrazo a **2** *n* (**a**) *(blow)* porrazo *m*, *Méx* madrazo *m* (**b**) *Fam (share)* parte *f*, porción *f*

whale [weɪl] *n* ballena *f*

what [wɒt, *unstressed* wət] **1** *adj* (**a**) *(direct question)* qué; **w. (sort of) bird is that?** ¿qué tipo de ave es ésa?; **w. good is that?** ¿para qué sirve eso? (**b**) *(indirect question)* qué; **ask her w. colour she likes** pregúntale qué color le gusta
2 *pron* (**a**) *(direct question)* qué; **w. about your father?** ¿y tu padre (qué)?; **w. about going tomorrow?** ¿qué te parece si vamos mañana?; **w. did it cost?** ¿cuánto costó?; **w. did you do that for?** ¿por qué hiciste eso?; **w. (did you say)?** ¿cómo?; **w. is happening?** ¿qué pasa?; **w. is it?** *(definition)* ¿qué es?; *(what's the matter)* ¿qué pasa?; **w.'s this for?** ¿para qué sirve esto?
(**b**) *(indirect question)* qué, lo que; **he asked me w. I thought** me preguntó lo que pensaba; **I didn't know w. to say** no sabía qué decir
(**c**) **guess w.!** ¿sabes qué?; **it's just w. I need** es exactamente lo que necesito
(**d**) *(in exclamations)* **w. a goal!** ¡qué

or vaya golazo!; **w. a lovely picture!** ¡qué cuadro más bonito!

3 *interj (surprise, indignation)* ¡cómo!; **w., no dessert!** ¿cómo, no hay postre?

whatever [wɒt'evə(r), *unstressed* wət'evə(r)] **1** *adj* (**a**) *(any)* cualquiera que; **at w. time you like** a la hora que quieras; **of w. colour** no importa de qué color (**b**) *(with negative)* **nothing w.** nada en absoluto
2 *pron* (**a**) *(what)* **w. happened?** ¿qué pasó? (**b**) *(anything, all that)* (todo) lo que; **do w. you like** haz lo que quieras (**c**) *(no matter what)* **don't tell him, w. you do** no se te ocurra decírselo; **w. (else) you find** cualquier (otra) cosa que encuentres

whatsoever [wɒtsəʊ'evə(r)] *adj* **anything w.** cualquier cosa; **nothing w.** nada en absoluto

wheat [wiːt] *n* trigo *m*; **w. germ** germen *m* de trigo

wheedle ['wiːdəl] *vt* **to w. sb into doing sth** engatusar a algn para que haga algo; **to w. sth out of sb** sonsacar algo a algn halagándole

wheel [wiːl] **1** *n* rueda *f*
2 *vt (bicycle)* empujar
3 *vi* (**a**) *(bird)* revolotear (**b**) **to w. round** girar sobre los talones

wheelbarrow ['wiːlbærəʊ] *n* carretilla *f*

wheelchair ['wiːltʃeə(r)] *n* silla *f* de ruedas

wheeze [wiːz] *vi* respirar con dificultad, resollar

when [wen] **1** *adv* (**a**) *(direct question)* cuándo; **since w.?** ¿desde cuándo?; **w. did he arrive?** ¿cuándo llegó? (**b**) *(indirect question)* cuándo; **tell me w. to go** dime cuándo debo irme (**c**) *(on which)* cuando, en que; **the days w. I work** los días en que trabajo
2 *conj* (**a**) cuando; **I'll tell you w. she comes** se lo diré cuando llegue (**b**) *(whenever)* cuando (**c**) *(given that, if)* si (**d**) *(although)* aunque

whenever [wen'evə(r)] **1** *conj (when)* cuando; *(every time)* siempre que **2** *adv* **w. that might be** sea cuando sea

where [weə(r)] *adv* (**a**) *(direct question)* dónde; *(direction)* adónde; **w. are you going?** ¿adónde vas?; **w. did we go wrong?** ¿en qué nos equivocamos?; **w. do you come from?** ¿de dónde es usted?
(**b**) *(indirect question)* dónde; *(direction)* adónde; **tell me w. you went** dime adónde fuiste
(**c**) *(at, in which)* donde; *(direction)* adonde, a donde
(**d**) *(when)* cuando

whereabouts 1 *adv* [weərə'baʊts] **w. do you live?** ¿por dónde vives? **2** *n* ['weərəbaʊts] paradero *m*

whereas [weər'æz] *conj* (**a**) *(but, while)* mientras que (**b**) *Jur* considerando que

whereby [weə'baɪ] *adv* por el/la/lo cual

wherever [weər'evə(r)] **1** *conj* dondequiera que; **I'll find him w. he is** le encontraré dondequiera que esté; **sit w. you like** siéntate donde quieras **2** *adv (direct question)* adónde

whether ['weðə(r)] *conj* (**a**) *(if)* si; **I don't know w. it is true** no sé si es verdad; **I doubt w. he'll win** dudo que gane (**b**) **w. he comes or not** venga o no

which [wɪtʃ] **1** *adj* (**a**) *(direct question)* qué; **w. colour do you prefer?** ¿qué color prefieres?; **w. one?** ¿cuál?; **w. way?** ¿por dónde? (**b**) *(indirect question)* qué; **tell me w. dress you like** dime qué vestido te gusta (**c**) **by w. time** y para entonces; **in w. case** en cuyo caso
2 *pron* (**a**) *(direct question)* cuál/cuáles; **w. of you did it?** ¿quién de vosotros lo hizo?
(**b**) *(indirect question)* cuál/cuáles; **I don't know w. I'd rather have** no sé cuál prefiero
(**c**) *(defining relative)* que; *(after preposition)* que, el/la cual, los/las cuales, el/la que, los/las que; **here are the books (w.) I have read** aquí están los libros que he leído; **the accident (w.) I told you about** el accidente del que te hablé; **the car in w. he was**

travelling el coche en (el) que viajaba; **this is the one (w.) I like** éste es el que me gusta
(**d**) *(non-defining relative)* el/la cual, los/las cuales; **I played three sets, all of w. I lost** jugué tres sets, todos los cuales perdí
(**e**) *(referring to a clause)* lo cual, lo que; **he won, w. made me very happy** ganó, lo cual *or* lo que me alegró mucho

whichever [wɪtʃ'evə(r)] **1** *adj* el/la que, cualquiera que; **I'll take w. books you don't want** tomaré los libros que no quieras **2** *pron* el/la que

while [waɪl] **1** *n* (**a**) *(length of time)* rato *m*, tiempo *m*; **in a little w.** dentro de poco; **once in a w.** de vez en cuando (**b**) **it's not worth your w. staying** no merece la pena que te quedes **2** *conj* (**a**) *(time)* mientras; **he fell asleep w. driving** se durmió mientras conducía (**b**) *(although)* aunque (**c**) *(whereas)* mientras que
▸ **while away** *vt sep* **to w. away the time** pasar el rato

whilst [waɪlst] *conj Br* = **while**

whim [wɪm] *n* capricho *m*, antojo *m*

whimper ['wɪmpə(r)] **1** *n* quejido *m* **2** *vi* lloriquear

whine [waɪn] *vi* (**a**) *(child)* lloriquear; *(with pain)* dar quejidos (**b**) *(complain)* quejarse (**c**) *(engine)* chirriar

whip [wɪp] **1** *n* (**a**) *(for punishment)* látigo *m*; *(for riding)* fusta *f* (**b**) *Br Pol* = oficial encargado(a) de la disciplina de un partido **2** *vt* (**a**) *(as punishment)* azotar; *(horse)* fustigar (**b**) *Culin* batir; **whipped cream** *Esp* nata montada, *Am* crema batida (**c**) *Fam (steal)* mangar
▸ **whip away** *vt sep* arrebatar
▸ **whip up** *vt sep (passions, enthusiasm)* avivar; *(support)* incrementar

whirl [wɜ:l] **1** *n* giro *m*; *Fig* torbellino *m* **2** *vt* **to w. sth round** dar vueltas a *or* hacer girar algo **3** *vi* **to w. round** girar con rapidez; *(leaves etc)* arremolinarse

whirlpool ['wɜ:lpu:l] *n* remolino *m*

whirlwind ['wɜ:lwɪnd] *n* torbellino *m*

whirr [wɜ:(r)] *vi* zumbar, runrunear

whisk [wɪsk] **1** *n* Culin batidor *m*; *(electric)* batidora *f* **2** *vt* Culin batir

▶ **whisk away, whisk off** *vt sep* quitar bruscamente, llevarse de repente

whiskers ['wɪskəz] *npl* (of person) patillas *fpl*; (of cat) bigotes *mpl*

whisky, US **whiskey** ['wɪskɪ] *n* whisky *m*

whisper ['wɪspə(r)] **1** *n* (a) *(sound)* susurro *m* (b) *(rumour)* rumor *m*
  2 *vt* decir en voz baja
  3 *vi* susurrar

whistle ['wɪsəl] **1** *n* (a) *(instrument)* pito *m* (b) *(sound)* silbido *m*, pitido *m*
  2 *vt (tune)* silbar
  3 *vi (person, kettle, wind)* silbar; *(train)* pitar

white [waɪt] **1** *adj* blanco(a); **to go w.** *(face)* palidecer; *(hair)* encanecer; **w. coffee** café *m* con leche; **w. hair** pelo cano; *Fig* **a w. lie** una mentira piadosa; **w. sauce** bechamel *f. Col, CSur* salsa *f* blanca
  2 *n* (a) *(colour, person, of eye)* blanco *m* (b) *(of egg)* clara *f*

whitewash ['waɪtwɒʃ] **1** *n* (a) cal *f* (b) *Fig (cover-up)* encubrimiento *m* (c) *Fig (defeat)* paliza *f* **2** *vt* (a) *(wall)* enjalbegar, blanquear (b) *Fig* encubrir

whiz(z) [wɪz] *vi* (a) *(sound)* silbar (b) **to w. past** pasar volando; *Fam* **w. kid** joven *mf* dinámico(a) y emprendedor(a)

who [hu:] *pron* (a) *(direct question)* quién/quiénes; **w. are they?** ¿quiénes son?; **w. is it?** ¿quién es? (b) *(indirect question)* quién; **I don't know w. did it** no sé quién lo hizo (c) *(defining relative)* que; **those w. don't know** los que no saben (d) *(non-defining relative)* quien/quienes, el/la cual, los/las cuales; **Elena's mother, w. is very rich …** la madre de Elena, la cual es muy rica …

whoever [hu:'evə(r)] *pron* (a) quienquiera que; **give it to w. you like** dáselo a quien quieras; **w. said that is a fool** el que dijo eso es un tonto; **w. you are** quienquiera que seas (b) *(direct question)* **w. told you that?** ¿quién te dijo eso?

whole [həʊl] **1** *adj* (a) *(entire)* entero(a), íntegro(a); **a w. week** una semana entera; **he took the w. lot** se los llevó todos (b) *(in one piece)* intacto(a) **2** *n* (a) *(single unit)* todo *m*, conjunto *m*; **as a w.** en su totalidad (b) *(all)* totalidad *f*; **the w. of London** todo Londres (c) **on the w.** en general

wholemeal ['həʊlmi:l] *adj Br* integral

wholesale ['həʊlseɪl] *Com* **1** *n* compraventa *f* al por mayor, *Am* mayoreo *m*
  2 *adj* al por mayor; *Fig* total
  3 *adv* al por mayor; *Fig* en su totalidad

wholesome ['həʊlsəm] *adj* sano(a)

wholly ['həʊllɪ] *adv* enteramente, completamente

whom [hu:m] *pron Fml* (a) *(direct question) (accusative)* a quién; **w. did you talk to?** ¿con quién hablaste?; *(after preposition)* **of/from w.?** ¿de quién?; **to w. are you referring?** ¿a quién te refieres? (b) *rel (accusative)* que, a quien/a quienes; **those w. I have seen** aquéllos a quienes he visto (c) *rel (after preposition)* quien/quienes, el/la cual, los/las cuales; **my brothers, both of w. are miners** mis hermanos, que son mineros los dos

> En la actualidad, sólo aparece en contextos formales. **Whom** se puede sustituir por **who** en todos los casos salvo cuando va después de preposición

whooping cough ['hu:pɪŋkɒf] *n* tos ferina

whore [hɔ:(r)] *n very Fam Pej* puta *f*

whose [hu:z] **1** *pron* (a) *(direct question)* de quién/de quiénes; **w. are these gloves?** ¿de quién son estos guantes?; **w. is this?** ¿de quién es esto? (b) *(indirect question)* de quién/de quiénes; **I don't know w. these coats are** no sé de quién son estos abrigos (c) *rel* cuyo(s)/cuya(s); **the man w.**

children we saw el hombre a cuyos hijos vimos
2 *adj* **w. car/house is this?** ¿de quién es este coche/esta casa?

why [waɪ] **1** *adv* por qué; *(for what purpose)* para qué; **w. did you do that?** ¿por qué hiciste eso?; **w. not go to bed?** ¿por qué no te acuestas?; **I don't know w. he did it** no sé por qué lo hizo
2 *interj* **(a)** *(fancy that!)* ¡toma!, ¡vaya!; **w., it's David!** ¡si es David! **(b)** *(protest, assertion)* sí, vamos

wick [wɪk] *n* mecha *f*

wicked ['wɪkɪd] *adj* **(a)** malvado(a) **(b)** *Fam* malísimo(a); *(temper)* de perros

wicker ['wɪkə(r)] **1** *n* mimbre *m* **2** *adj* de mimbre

wicket ['wɪkɪt] *n (in cricket) (stumps)* palos *mpl*

wide [waɪd] **1** *adj* **(a)** *(road, trousers)* ancho(a); *(gap, interval)* grande; **it is 10 m w.** tiene 10 m de ancho **(b)** *(area, knowledge, support, range)* amplio(a); **w. interests** intereses muy diversos **(c)** *(off target)* desviado(a)
2 *adv* **to open one's eyes w.** abrir los ojos de par en par; **w. awake** completamente despierto(a); **w. open** abierto(a) de par en par

widely ['waɪdlɪ] *adv (travel etc)* extensamente; *(believed)* generalmente; **he is w. known** es muy conocido

widen ['waɪdən] **1** *vt* ensanchar; *(interests)* ampliar **2** *vi* ensancharse

widespread ['waɪdspred] *adj (unrest, belief)* general; *(damage)* extenso(a); **to become w.** generalizarse

widow ['wɪdəʊ] *n* viuda *f*

widower ['wɪdəʊə(r)] *n* viudo *m*

width [wɪdθ] *n* **(a)** anchura *f* **(b)** *(of material, swimming pool)* ancho *m*

wield [wi:ld] *vt (weapon)* blandir; *Fig (power)* ejercer

wife [waɪf] *n (pl* **wives)** mujer *f,* esposa *f*

wig [wɪg] *n* peluca *f*

wiggle ['wɪgəl] **1** *vt (finger etc)* menear; **to w. one's hips** contonearse
2 *vi* menearse

wild [waɪld] **1** *adj* **(a)** *(animal, tribe)* salvaje; **w. beast** fiera *f*
(b) *(plant)* silvestre
(c) *(landscape)* agreste; **the W. West** el Salvaje Oeste
(d) *(temperament, behaviour)* alocado(a); *(appearance)* desordenado(a); *(passions etc)* desenfrenado(a); *(laughter, thoughts)* loco(a); *(applause)* fervoroso(a); *Fam Fig* **she is w. about him/about tennis** está loca por él/por el tenis
2 *adv Fig* **to run w.** *(children)* desmandarse
3 *n* **in the w.** en el estado salvaje

wilderness ['wɪldənɪs] *n* desierto *m*

wildlife ['waɪldlaɪf] *n* fauna *f;* **w. park** parque *m* natural

wildly ['waɪldlɪ] *adv* **(a)** *(rush round etc)* como un(a) loco(a); *(shoot)* sin apuntar; *(hit out)* a tontas y a locas **(b)** **w. enthusiastic** loco(a) de entusiasmo; **w. inaccurate** totalmente erróneo(a)

wilful, *US* **wilfull** ['wɪlfʊl] *adj* **(a)** *(stubborn)* terco(a) **(b)** *Jur* premeditado(a)

will¹ [wɪl] **1** *n* **(a)** voluntad *f;* **good/ill w.** buena/mala voluntad; **of my own free w.** por mi propia voluntad **(b)** *Jur (testament)* testamento *m*; **to make one's w.** hacer testamento **2** *vt* **fate willed that …** el destino quiso que …

will² [wɪl] *v aux*

En el inglés hablado, y en el escrito en estilo coloquial, el verbo **will** se contrae de manera que **I/you/he** *etc* **will** se transforman en **I'll, you'll, he'll** *etc.* La forma negativa **will not** se transforma en **won't**

(a) *(future) (esp 2nd & 3rd person)* **they'll come** vendrán; **w. he be there? – yes, he w.** ¿estará allí? – sí(, estará); **you'll tell him, won't you?** se lo dirás, ¿verdad?; **she won't do it** no lo hará
(b) *(command)* **you w. be here at eleven!** ¡debes estar aquí a las once!
(c) *(future perfect)* **they'll have**

finished by tomorrow habrán terminado para mañana

(**d**) *(willingness)* **I won't have it!** ¡no lo permito!; **won't you sit down?** ¿quiere sentarse?

(**e**) *(custom)* **accidents w. happen** siempre habrá accidentes

(**f**) *(persistence)* **if you w. go out without a coat ...** si te empeñas en salir sin abrigo ...

willing ['wɪlɪŋ] *adj (obliging)* complaciente; **to be w. to do sth** estar dispuesto(a) a hacer algo

willingly ['wɪlɪŋlɪ] *adv* de buena gana

willingness ['wɪlɪŋnɪs] *n* buena voluntad

willpower ['wɪlpaʊə(r)] *n* (fuerza f de) voluntad f

wilt [wɪlt] *vi* marchitarse

win [wɪn] *(pt & pp* won) **1** *n* victoria f **2** *vt* (**a**) ganar; *(prize)* llevarse; *(victory)* conseguir (**b**) *Fig (sympathy, friendship)* ganarse; *(praise)* cosechar; **to w. sb's love** conquistar a algn **3** *vi* ganar

▸ **win back** *vt sep* recuperar

▸ **win over** *vt sep (to cause, idea)* atraer (**to** a); *(voters, support)* ganarse

▸ **win through** *vi* conseguir triunfar

wince [wɪns] *vi* tener un rictus de dolor

winch [wɪntʃ] *n* cigüeña f, torno m

wind¹ [wɪnd] **1** *n* (**a**) viento m; *Fig* **to get w. of sth** olerse algo; **w. farm** parque eólico (**b**) *(breath)* aliento m; **to get one's second w.** recobrar el aliento (**c**) *Med* flato m, gases mpl (**d**) **w. instrument** instrumento m de viento **2** *vt* **to be winded** quedarse sin aliento

wind² [waɪnd] *(pt & pp* wound) **1** *vt* (**a**) *(on to a reel)* enrollar (**b**) **to w. on/ back** *(film, tape)* avanzar/rebobinar (**c**) *(clock)* dar cuerda a **2** *vi (road, river)* serpentear

▸ **wind down 1** *vt sep (window)* bajar **2** *vi Fam (person)* relajarse

▸ **wind up 1** *vt sep* (**a**) *(roll up)* enrollar (**b**) *(business etc)* cerrar; *(debate)*

clausurar (**c**) *(clock)* dar cuerda a **2** *vi (meeting)* terminar

windfall ['wɪndfɔːl] *n Fig* ganancia inesperada

winding ['waɪndɪŋ] *adj (road, river)* sinuoso(a); *(staircase)* de caracol

windmill ['wɪndmɪl] *n* molino m (de viento)

window ['wɪndəʊ] *n* ventana f; *(of vehicle, ticket office etc)* ventanilla f; **(shop) w.** escaparate m, *Am* vidriera f, *Chile, Col, Méx* vitrina f; **to clean the windows** limpiar los cristales; **w. box** jardinera f; **w. cleaner** limpiacristales mf inv

windowpane ['wɪndəʊpeɪn] *n* vidrio m or *Esp* cristal m (de ventana)

window-shopping ['wɪndəʊʃɒpɪŋ] *n* **to go w.** ir a mirar escaparates

windowsill ['wɪndəʊsɪl] *n* alféizar m

windscreen ['wɪndskriːn], *US* **windshield** ['wɪndʃiːld] *n* parabrisas m inv; **w. wiper** limpiaparabrisas m inv

windsurfing ['wɪndsɜːfɪŋ] *n* **to go w.** ir a hacer windsurf or tabla a vela

windy ['wɪndɪ] *adj* (**windier, windiest**) *(weather)* ventoso(a); *(place)* desprotegido(a) del viento; **it is very w. today** hoy hace mucho viento

wine [waɪn] *n* vino m; **w. cellar** bodega f; **w. list** lista f de vinos; **w. merchant** vinatero(a) m,f; **w. tasting** cata f de vinos; **w. vinegar** vinagre m de vino

wineglass ['waɪnɡlɑːs] *n* copa f (para vino)

wing [wɪŋ] *n* (**a**) *Orn, Av* ala f (**b**) *(of building)* ala f (**c**) *Br Aut* aleta f; **w. mirror** retrovisor m externo (**d**) *Th* **(in the) wings** (entre) bastidores mpl (**e**) *Ftb* banda f (**f**) *Pol* ala f; **the left w.** la izquierda

wink [wɪŋk] **1** *n* guiño m **2** *vi* (**a**) *(person)* guiñar (el ojo) (**b**) *(light)* parpadear

winner ['wɪnə(r)] *n* ganador(a) m,f

winning ['wɪnɪŋ] *adj (person, team)* ganador(a); *(number)* premiado(a); *(goal)* decisivo(a); **w. post** meta f

winter ['wɪntə(r)] **1** *n* invierno m

2 *adj* de invierno; **w. sports** deportes *mpl* de invierno

3 *vi* invernar

wipe [waɪp] *vt* limpiar; **to w. one's brow** enjugarse la frente; **to w. one's feet/nose** limpiarse los pies/las narices

▸ **wipe away** *vt sep (tear)* enjugar

▸ **wipe off** *vt sep* quitar frotando; **to w. sth off the blackboard/the tape** borrar algo de la pizarra/de la cinta

▸ **wipe out** *vt sep* **(a)** *(erase)* borrar **(b)** *(army)* aniquilar; *(species etc)* exterminar

▸ **wipe up** *vt sep* limpiar

wiper ['waɪpə(r)] *n* Aut limpiaparabrisas *m inv*

wire [waɪə(r)] **1** *n* **(a)** alambre *m*; *Elec* cable *m*; *Tel* hilo; **w. cutters** cizalla *f* **(b)** *(telegram)* telegrama *m* **2** *vt* **(a)** **to w. (up) a house** poner la instalación eléctrica de una casa; **to w. (up) an appliance to the mains** conectar un aparato a la toma eléctrica **(b)** *(information)* enviar por telegrama

wiring ['waɪərɪŋ] *n* *(network)* cableado *m*; *(action)* instalación *f* del cableado

wisdom ['wɪzdəm] *n* **(a)** *(learning)* sabiduría *f*, saber *m* **(b)** *(good sense) (of person)* cordura *f*; *(of action)* sensatez *f* **(c)** **w. tooth** muela *f* del juicio

wise [waɪz] *adj* **(a)** sabio(a); **a w. man** un sabio **(b)** *(remark)* juicioso(a); *(decision)* acertado(a); **it would be w. to keep quiet** sería prudente callarse

wish [wɪʃ] **1** *n* **(a)** *(desire)* deseo *m* **(for** de); **to make a w.** pedir un deseo **(b)** **best wishes** felicitaciones *fpl*; **give your mother my best wishes** salude a su madre de mi parte; **with best wishes, Peter** *(at end of letter)* saludos cordiales, Peter

2 *vt* **(a)** *(want)* querer, desear; **I w. I could stay longer** me gustaría poder quedarme más tiempo; **I w. you had told me!** ¡ojalá me lo hubieras dicho! **(b)** **to w. sb goodnight** darle las buenas noches a algn; **to w. sb well**

desearle a algn mucha suerte

3 *vi (want)* desear; **as you w.** como quieras; **to w. for sth** desear algo

wishful ['wɪʃfʊl] *adj* **it's w. thinking** es hacerse ilusiones

wisp [wɪsp] *n (of wool, hair)* mechón *m*; *(of smoke)* voluta *f*

wistful ['wɪstfʊl] *adj* melancólico(a)

wit [wɪt] *n* **(a)** *(intelligence) (often pl)* inteligencia *f*; *Fig* **to be at one's wits' end** estar para volverse loco(a); *Fam Fig* **to have one's wits about one** ser despabilado(a) **(b)** *(humour)* ingenio *m*

witch [wɪtʃ] *n* bruja *f*; *Fig* **w. hunt** caza *f* de brujas

with [wɪð, wɪθ] *prep* con; **do you have any money w. you?** ¿traes dinero?; **the man w. the glasses** el hombre de las gafas; **he went w. me/you** fue conmigo/contigo; **w. all his faults, I admire him** le admiro con todos sus defectos; **w. your permission** con su permiso; **we're all w. you** *(support)* todos estamos contigo; **you're not w. me, are you?** *(understand)* no me entiendes, ¿verdad?; **to fill a vase w. water** llenar un jarrón de agua; **it is made w. butter** está hecho con mantequilla; **to be paralysed w. fear** estar paralizado(a) de miedo

withdraw [wɪð'drɔ:] *(pt* **withdrew**; *pp* **withdrawn) 1** *vt* **(a)** retirar, sacar; **to w. money from the bank** sacar dinero del banco **(b)** *(go back on)* retirar; *(statement)* retractarse de; *(plan, claim)* renunciar a **2** *vi* **(a)** retirarse **(b)** *(drop out)* renunciar

withdrawal [wɪð'drɔ:əl] *n* retirada *f*; *(of statement)* retractación *f*; *(of complaint, plan)* renuncia *f*; **w. symptoms** síndrome *m* de abstinencia

withdrawn [wɪð'drɔ:n] **1** *adj* *(person)* introvertido(a) **2** *pp of* withdraw

withdrew [wɪð'dru:] *pt of* withdraw

withhold [wɪð'həʊld] *(pt & pp* **withheld** [wɪð'held]) *vt (money)* retener; *(decision)* aplazar; *(consent)* negar; *(information)* ocultar

within [wɪ'ðɪn] **1** prep (**a**) *(inside)* dentro de (**b**) *(range)* **the house is w. walking distance** se puede ir andando a la casa; **situated w. 5 km of the town** situado(a) a menos de 5 km de la ciudad; **w. sight of the sea** con vistas al mar (**c**) *(time)* **they arrived w. a few days of each other** llegaron con pocos días de diferencia; **w. the next five years** durante los cinco próximos años

2 adv dentro; **from w.** desde dentro

without [wɪ'ðaʊt] prep sin; **he did it w. my knowing** lo hizo sin que lo supiera yo; *Fig* **to do** or **go w. sth** *(voluntarily)* prescindir de algo; *(forcibly)* pasar(se) sin algo

withstand [wɪð'stænd] *(pt & pp* **withstood** [wɪð'stʊd]) vt resistir a; *(pain)* aguantar

witness ['wɪtnɪs] **1** n (**a**) *(person)* testigo mf; **w. box**, *US* **w. stand** barra f de los testigos (**b**) *(evidence)* **to bear w. to sth** dar fe de algo **2** vt (**a**) *(see)* presenciar, ser testigo de (**b**) *Fig (notice)* notar (**c**) *Jur* **to w. a document** firmar un documento como testigo

witty ['wɪtɪ] adj (**wittier, wittiest**) ingenioso(a), agudo(a)

wives [waɪvz] pl of **wife**

wizard ['wɪzəd] n hechicero m, mago m

wobble ['wɒbəl] vi *(table, ladder etc)* tambalearse; *(jelly)* temblar

wobbly ['wɒblɪ] adj *(chair, table)* cojo(a); *(shelf, ladder)* tambaleante

woe [wəʊ] n *Literary* infortunio m; **w. betide you if I catch you!** ¡ay de ti si te cojo!

woke [wəʊk] pt of **wake**

woken ['wəʊkən] pp of **wake**

wolf [wʊlf] n *(pl* **wolves** [wʊlvz]) lobo m; *Fig* **a w. in sheep's clothing** un lobo con piel de cordero

woman ['wʊmən] n *(pl* **women**) mujer f; **old w.** vieja f; *Fam* **women's libber** feminista mf; *Fam* **women's lib** movimiento m feminista; **women's rights** derechos mpl de la mujer

womb [wu:m] n matriz f, útero m

women ['wɪmɪn] pl of **woman**

won [wʌn] pt & pp of **win**

wonder ['wʌndə(r)] **1** n (**a**) *(miracle)* milagro m; **no w. he hasn't come** no es de extrañar que no haya venido (**b**) *(amazement)* admiración f, asombro m **2** vt (**a**) *(be surprised)* sorprenderse (**b**) *(ask oneself)* preguntarse; **I w. why** ¿por qué será? **3** vi (**a**) *(marvel)* maravillarse; **to w. at sth** admirarse de algo (**b**) *(reflect)* **it makes you w.** te da que pensar

wonderful ['wʌndəfʊl] adj maravilloso(a)

won't [wəʊnt] = **will not**

wood [wʊd] n (**a**) *(forest)* bosque m (**b**) *(material)* madera f; *(for fire)* leña f

wooden ['wʊdən] adj (**a**) de madera; **w. spoon/leg** cuchara f/pata f de palo (**b**) *Fig (acting)* sin expresión

woodwork ['wʊdwɜːk] n (**a**) *(craft)* carpintería f (**b**) *(of building)* maderaje m

woodworm ['wʊdwɜːm] n carcoma f

wool [wʊl] **1** n lana f; *Fig* **to pull the w. over sb's eyes** embaucar or dar el pego a algn **2** adj de lana

woollen, *US* **woolen** ['wʊlən] **1** adj (**a**) de lana (**b**) *(industry)* lanero(a) **2** npl **woollens** géneros mpl de lana or de punto

word [wɜːd] **1** n (**a**) *(spoken, written)* palabra f; **in other words ...** es decir ..., o sea ...; *Fig* **a w. of advice** un consejo; *Fig* **I'd like a w. with you** quiero hablar contigo un momento; *Fig* **she didn't say it in so many words** no lo dijo de modo tan explícito; **in the words of the poet ...** como dice el poeta ...; *Fig* **w. for w.** palabra por palabra; **w. processing** tratamiento m de textos; **w. processor** procesador m de textos

(**b**) *Fig (message)* mensaje m; **by w. of mouth** de palabra; **is there any w. from him?** ¿hay noticias de él?; **to send w.** mandar recado

(**c**) *Fig (promise)* palabra f; **he's a man of his w.** es hombre de palabra

2 *vt (express)* formular; **a badly worded letter** una carta mal redactada

wording ['wɜ:dɪŋ] *n* expresión *f*; **I changed the w. slightly** cambié algunas palabras

wordy ['wɜ:dɪ] *adj* verboso(a)

wore [wɔ:(r)] *pt of* **wear**

work [wɜ:k] **1** *n* (**a**) trabajo *m*; **his w. in the field of physics** su labor en el campo de la física; **it's hard w.** cuesta trabajo

 (**b**) *(employment)* trabajo *m*, empleo *m*; **to be out of w.** no tener trabajo, *Esp* estar parado(a)

 (**c**) *(action)* obra *f*, acción *f*; **keep up the good w.!** ¡que siga así!

 (**d**) **a w. of art** una obra de arte

 (**e**) **works** *(construction)* obras *fpl*; **public works** obras (públicas)

 (**f**) **works** *(machinery)* mecanismo *m*

 (**g**) *Br* **works** *(factory)* fábrica *f*

2 *vt* (**a**) *(drive)* hacer trabajar; **to w. one's way up in a firm** trabajarse el ascenso en una empresa (**b**) *(machine)* manejar (**c**) *(miracles, changes)* operar, hacer (**d**) *(land)* cultivar (**e**) *(wood, metal etc)* trabajar

3 *vi* (**a**) trabajar (**on** *or* **at** en); **to w. as a gardener** trabajar de jardinero (**b**) *(machine)* funcionar; **it works on gas** funciona con gas (**c**) *(drug)* surtir efecto; *(system)* funcionar bien; *(plan, trick)* salir bien (**d**) *(operate)* obrar; **to w. loose** soltarse; **we have no data to w. on** no tenemos datos en que basarnos

▸ **work off** *vt sep (fat)* eliminar trabajando; *(anger)* desahogar

▸ **work out 1** *vt sep* (**a**) *(plan)* idear; *(itinerary)* planear; *(details)* desarrollar (**b**) *(problem)* solucionar; *(solution)* encontrar; *(amount)* calcular; **I can't w. out how he did it** no me explico cómo lo hizo **2** *vi* (**a**) **things didn't w. out for her** las cosas no le salieron bien (**b**) **it works out at five each** sale a cinco cada uno (**c**) *Sport* hacer ejercicio

▸ **work through** *vi* penetrar (**to** hasta)

▸ **work up** *vt sep (excite)* acalorar; **to get worked up** excitarse

workaholic [wɜ:kə'hɒlɪk] *n Fam* adicto(a) *m,f* al trabajo

worker ['wɜ:kə(r)] *n* trabajador(a) *m,f*; *(manual)* obrero(a) *m,f*

workforce ['wɜ:kfɔ:s] *n* mano *f* de obra

working ['wɜ:kɪŋ] **1** *adj* (**a**) *(population, capital)* activo(a); **w. class** clase obrera; **w. man** obrero *m* (**b**) *(clothes, conditions, hours)* de trabajo; **w. day** día *m* laborable; *(number of hours)* jornada *f* laboral (**c**) **it is in w. order** funciona (**d**) *(majority)* suficiente; **w. knowledge** conocimientos básicos

 2 *n* **workings** *(mechanics)* funcionamiento *m*; *Min* explotación *f*

workload ['wɜ:kləʊd] *n* cantidad *f* de trabajo

workman ['wɜ:kmən] *n (manual)* obrero *m*

workmanship ['wɜ:kmənʃɪp] *n (appearance)* acabado *m*; *(skill)* habilidad *f*, arte *m*; **a fine piece of w.** un trabajo excelente

workshop ['wɜ:kʃɒp] *n* taller *m*

world [wɜ:ld] *n* mundo *m*; **the best in the w.** el mejor del mundo; *Ftb* **the W. Cup** los Mundiales; **w. record** récord *m* mundial; **w. war** guerra *f* mundial

worldly ['wɜ:ldlɪ] *adj* mundano(a)

worldwide ['wɜ:ldwaɪd] *adj* mundial

worm [wɜ:m] **1** *n* (**a**) gusano *m*; **(earth) w.** lombriz *f* (**b**) *Med* **worms** lombrices *fpl* **2** *vt* **to w. a secret out of sb** sonsacarle un secreto a algn

worn [wɔ:n] **1** *adj* gastado(a), usado(a) **2** *pp of* **wear**

worn-out ['wɔ:naʊt] *adj (thing)* gastado(a); *(person)* rendido(a), agotado(a)

worried ['wʌrɪd] *adj* inquieto(a), preocupado(a)

worry ['wʌrɪ] **1** *vt* (**a**) preocupar, inquietar; **it doesn't w. me** me trae sin cuidado (**b**) *(pester)* molestar

 2 *vi* preocuparse (**about** por); **don't w.** no te preocupes

3 *n (state)* inquietud *f*; *(cause)* preocupación *f*

worrying ['wʌriiŋ] *adj* inquietante, preocupante

worse [wɜːs] **1** *adj (comp of bad)* peor; **he gets w. and w.** va de mal en peor; **to get w.** empeorar; *Fam* **w. luck!** ¡mala suerte!

2 *n* **a change for the w.** un empeoramiento; *Fig* **to take a turn for the w.** empeorar

3 *adv (comp of badly)* peor; **w. than ever** peor que nunca

worsen ['wɜːsən] *vt & vi* empeorar

worship ['wɜːʃɪp] **1** *vt* adorar **2** *n* **(a)** adoración *f* **(b)** *(ceremony)* culto *m* **(c)** *Br* **his W. the Mayor** el señor alcalde; *Jur* **Your W.** señoría

worst [wɜːst] **1** *adj (superl of bad)* peor; **the w. part about it is that …** lo peor es que …

2 *n* **(a)** *(person)* el/la peor, los/las peores **(b)** **the w. of the storm is over** ya ha pasado lo peor de la tormenta

3 *adv (superl of badly)* peor; *Fig* **to come off w.** salir perdiendo

worth [wɜːθ] **1** *adj* **(a)** **to be w. £3** valer 3 libras; **a house w. £50,000** una casa que vale 50.000 libras **(b)** *(deserving of)* merecedor(a) de; **a book w. reading** un libro que merece la pena leer; **for what it's w.** por si sirve de algo; **it's w. your while, it's w. it** vale *or* merece la pena; **it's w. mentioning** es digno de mención **2** *n* **(a)** *(in money)* valor *m*; **£5 w. of petrol** gasolina por valor de 5 libras **(b)** *(of person)* valía *f*

worthless ['wɜːθlɪs] *adj* sin valor; *(person)* despreciable

worthwhile [wɜːθ'waɪl] *adj* valioso(a), que vale la pena

worthy ['wɜːðɪ] *adj* **(worthier, worthiest)** **(a)** *(deserving)* digno(a) **(of** de); *(winner, cause)* justo(a) **(b)** *(citizen)* respetable; *(effort, motives, action)* loable

would [wʊd, *unstressed* wəd] *v aux*

En el inglés hablado, y en el escrito en estilo coloquial, el verbo **would** se contrae de manera que **I/you/he** *etc* **would** se transforman en **I'd, you'd, he'd** *etc.* La forma negativa **would not** se transforma en **wouldn't**

(a) *(conditional)* **I w. go if I had time** iría si tuviera tiempo; **he w. have won but for that** habría ganado si no hubiera sido por eso

(b) *(reported speech)* **he said that he w. come** dijo que vendría

(c) *(willingness)* **the car wouldn't start** el coche no arrancaba; **w. you do me a favour?** ¿me haces un favor?

(d) *(wishing)* **I'd rather go home** preferiría ir a casa; **w. you like a cigarette?** ¿quiere un cigarrillo?

(e) *(custom)* **we w. go for walks** solíamos dar un paseo

wound¹ [waʊnd] *pt & pp of* **wind²**

wound² [wuːnd] **1** *n* herida *f* **2** *vt* herir

wove [wəʊv] *pt of* **weave**

woven ['wəʊvən] *pp of* **weave**

wow [waʊ] *Fam interj* ¡hala!, *RP* ¡uau!

wrap [ræp] **1** *vt* **to w. (up)** envolver; **he wrapped his arms around her** la estrechó entre sus brazos

2 *vi Fam* **w. up well** abrígate

3 *n (shawl)* chal *m*; *(cape)* capa *f*

wrapper ['ræpə(r)] *n (of sweet)* envoltorio *m*; *(of book)* sobrecubierta *f*

wrapping ['ræpɪŋ] *n* **w. paper** papel *m* de envolver

wreath [riːθ] *n (pl* **wreaths** [riːðz, riːθs])* *(of flowers)* corona *f*; **laurel w.** corona de laurel

wreck [rek] **1** *n* **(a)** *Naut* naufragio *m*; *(ship)* barco naufragado **(b)** *(of car, plane)* restos *mpl*; *(of building)* ruinas *fpl* **(c)** *Fig (person)* ruina *f* **2** *vt* **(a)** *(ship)* hacer naufragar **(b)** *(car, machine)* destrozar **(c)** *Fig (health, life)* arruinar; *(plans, hopes)* desbaratar; *(chances)* echar a perder

wreckage ['rekɪdʒ] *n (of ship, car, plane)* restos *mpl*; *(of building)* ruinas *fpl*

wrench [rentʃ] **1** *n* **(a)** *(pull)* tirón *m*

(b) *Med* torcedura *f* (c) *(tool) Br* llave inglesa; *US* llave **2** *vt* **to w. oneself free** soltarse de un tirón; **to w. sth off sb** arrebatarle algo a algn; **to w. sth off/open** quitar/abrir algo de un tirón

wrestle ['resəl] *vi* luchar

wrestler ['reslə(r)] *n* luchador(a) *m,f*

wrestling ['reslɪŋ] *n* lucha *f*

wretched ['retʃɪd] *adj* (a) desdichado(a); *(conditions)* deplorable; *Fam (bad, poor)* horrible (b) **I feel w.** *(ill)* me siento fatal (c) *(contemptible)* despreciable (d) *Fam (damned)* maldito(a), condenado(a)

wriggle ['rɪgəl] **1** *vt* menear **2** *vi* **to w. (about)** *(worm)* serpentear; *(restless child)* moverse nerviosamente; **to w. free** escapar deslizándose

wring [rɪŋ] *(pt & pp* wrung) *vt* (a) *(clothes)* escurrir; *(hands)* retorcer (b) *Fig (extract)* arrancar, sacar

wrinkle ['rɪŋkəl] **1** *n* arruga *f* **2** *vt* arrugar **3** *vi* arrugarse

wrist [rɪst] *n* muñeca *f*

wristwatch ['rɪstwɒtʃ] *n* reloj *m* de pulsera

write [raɪt] *(pt* wrote; *pp* written) **1** *vt* escribir; *(article)* redactar; *(cheque)* extender **2** *vi* escribir (**about** sobre); **to w. for a paper** colaborar en un periódico

▸ **write back** *vi* contestar

▸ **write down** *vt sep* poner por escrito; *(note)* apuntar

▸ **write in** *vi* escribir

▸ **write off 1** *vt sep (debt)* condonar; *(car)* destrozar **2** *vi* **to w. off for sth** pedir algo por escrito

▸ **write out** *vt sep (cheque, recipe)* extender

▸ **write up** *vt sep (notes)* redactar; *(diary, journal)* poner al día

writer ['raɪtə(r)] *n (by profession)*

escritor(a) *m,f; (of book, letter)* autor(a) *m,f*

writing ['raɪtɪŋ] *n* (a) *(script)* escritura *f; (handwriting)* letra *f;* **in w.** por escrito (b) **writings** escritos *mpl* (c) *(action)* escritura *f;* **w. desk** escritorio *m*

written ['rɪtən] *pp of* **write**

wrong [rɒŋ] **1** *adj* (a) *(person)* equivocado(a); **to be w.** no tener razón; **you're w. in thinking that ...** te equivocas si piensas que ...

(b) *(answer, way)* incorrecto(a), equivocado(a); **my watch is w.** mi reloj anda mal; **to go the w. way** equivocarse de camino; *Tel* **I've got the w. number** me he confundido de número (c) *(unsuitable)* impropio(a), inadecuado(a); *(time)* inoportuno(a); **to say the w. thing** decir algo inoportuno (d) *(immoral etc)* malo(a); **what's w. with smoking?** ¿qué tiene de malo fumar?

(e) **something's w.** hay algo que no está bien; **what's w. (with you)?** ¿qué (te) pasa?

2 *adv* mal, incorrectamente; **to get it w.** equivocarse; *Fam* **to go w.** *(plan)* fallar, salir mal

3 *n* (a) *(evil, bad action)* mal *m* (b) *(injustice)* injusticia *f; (offence)* agravio *m;* **the rights and wrongs of a matter** lo justo y lo injusto de un asunto (c) **to be in the w.** *(be to blame)* tener la culpa

4 *vt (treat unfairly)* ser injusto(a) con; *(offend)* agraviar

wrongly ['rɒŋlɪ] *adv* (a) *(incorrectly)* incorrectamente (b) *(mistakenly)* equivocadamente (c) *(unjustly)* injustamente

wrote [rəʊt] *pt of* **write**

wrung [rʌŋ] *pt & pp of* **wring**

wry [raɪ] *adj* (**wrier, wriest** *or* **wryer, wryest**) sardónico(a)

Xx

X, x [eks] *n (the letter)* X, x *f*

xenophobia [zenə'fəʊbɪə] *n* xenofobia *f*

Xerox® ['zɪərɒks] **1** *n* fotocopia *f*, xerocopia *f* **2** *vt* fotocopiar

Xmas ['krɪsməs, 'eksməs] *n (abbr Christmas)* Navidad *f*

X-ray ['eksreɪ] **1** *n (radiation)* rayo *m* X; *(picture)* radiografía *f*; **to have an X.** hacerse una radiografía **2** *vt* radiografiar

xylophone ['zaɪləfəʊn] *n* xilófono *m*, xilofón *m*

Yy

Y, y [waɪ] *n (the letter)* Y, y *f*

yacht [jɒt] *n* yate *m*; **y. club** club náutico

yard¹ [jɑːd] *n (measure)* yarda *f (aprox 0,914 m)*

yard² [jɑːd] *n* patio *m*; *US* jardín *m*

yarn [jɑːn] *n* **(a)** *Sewing* hilo *m* **(b)** *(story)* historia *f*, cuento *m*; **to spin a y.** *(lie)* inventarse una historia

yawn [jɔːn] **1** *vi* bostezar **2** *n* bostezo *m*

year [jɪə(r)] *n* **(a)** año *m*; **all y. round** durante todo el año; **last y.** el año pasado; **next y.** el año que viene; **y. in, y. out** año tras año; **I'm ten years old** tengo diez años **(b)** *Educ* curso *m*; **first-y. student** estudiante *mf* de primero

yearly ['jɪəlɪ] **1** *adj* anual **2** *adv* anualmente, cada año

yearn [jɜːn] *vi* **to y. for sth** anhelar algo

yeast [jiːst] *n* levadura *f*

yell [jel] **1** *vi* gritar **2** *n* grito *m*, alarido *m*

yellow ['jeləʊ] **1** *adj* amarillo(a); *Tel* **Y. Pages**® páginas amarillas **2** *n* amarillo *m*

yes [jes] **1** *adv* sí; **you said y.** dijiste que sí **2** *n* sí *m*

yesterday ['jestədeɪ] *adv & n* ayer *m*; **the day before y.** anteayer; **y. morning** ayer por la mañana

yet [jet] **1** *adv* **(a)** **not y.** aún no, todavía no; **as y.** hasta ahora; **I haven't eaten y.** no he comido todavía **(b)** *(in questions)* ya; **has he arrived y.?** ¿ha venido ya? **(c)** *(even)* más; **y. again** otra vez; **y. more** todavía más **(d)** *(eventually)* todavía, aún; **he'll win y.** todavía puede ganar **2** *conj* sin embargo

yield [jiːld] **1** *n* **(a)** rendimiento *m* **(b)** *Agr* cosecha *f* **(c)** *Fin* beneficio *m* **2** *vt* producir; *Agr* dar; *(money)* producir **3** *vi* **(a)** *(surrender, break)* ceder **(b)** *US Aut* ceder el paso

yoga ['jəʊgə] *n* yoga *m*

yog(h)urt ['jɒgət] *n* yogur *m*

yolk [jəʊk] *n* yema *f*

you [juː, *unstressed* jʊ] *pers pron*

In Spanish, the formal form **usted** takes a third person singular verb and **ustedes** takes a third person plural verb. In many Latin American countries, **ustedes** is the standard form of the second person plural and is not considered formal

pron (**a**) *(subject) (usually omitted in Spanish, except for contrast) (singular)* tú, *esp RP* vos, *Fml* usted; *(pl) Esp* vosotros(as), *Am or Fml* ustedes; **have you got it?** *(singular)* ¿lo tienes tú?, *Fml* ¿lo tiene usted?; *(pl) Esp* ¿lo tenéis vosotros?, *Am or Fml* ¿lo tienen ustedes?

(**b**) *(direct object) (singular)* te, *Fml* lo(la); *(pl) Esp* os, *Am or Fml* los(las); **I can understand your son but not you** *(singular)* a tu hijo lo entiendo, pero a ti no, *Fml* a su hijo lo entiendo, pero a usted no; *(pl) Esp* a vuestro hijo lo entiendo, pero a vosotros no, *Am or Fml* a su hijo lo entiendo, pero a ustedes no

(**c**) *(indirect object) (singular)* te, *Fml* le; *(pl) Esp* os, *Am or Fml* les; **I gave y. the book** *(singular)* te di el libro, *Fml* le di el libro; *(pl) Esp* os di el libro, *Am or Fml* les di el libro; **I told y.** *(singular)* te lo dije, *Fml* se lo dije; *(pl) Esp* os lo dije, *Am or Fml* se lo dije

(**d**) *(after preposition) (singular)* ti, *Fml* usted; *(pl) Esp* vosotros(as), *Am or Fml* ustedes

(**e**) *(impers)* **y. don't do that kind of thing** esas cosas no se hacen

young [jʌŋ] **1** *adj (age)* joven; *(brother etc)* pequeño(a); **y. lady** señorita *f*; **y. man** joven *m* **2** *npl* (**a**) *(people)* **the y.** los jóvenes, la juventud (**b**) *(animals)* crías *fpl*

youngster [ˈjʌŋstə(r)] *n* muchacho(a) *m,f*

your [jɔ:(r), *unstressed* jə(r)] *poss adj* (**a**) *(of one person)* tu, *Fml* su; **y. house** tu/su casa; **y. books** tus/sus libros

(**b**) *(of more than one person) Esp* vuestro(a), *Am or Fml* su; **y. house** *Esp* vuestra casa, *Am or Fml* su casa; **y. books** *Esp* vuestros libros, *Am or Fml* sus libros

(**c**) *(for parts of body, clothes) (translated by definite article)* **did you hit y. head?** ¿te has *or Fml* se ha dado un golpe en la cabeza?

(**d**) *(impersonal)* **smoking is bad for y. health** el tabaco perjudica la salud

yours [jɔ:z] *poss pron*

In Spanish, the forms **tuyo(a)**, **suyo(a)** and **vuestro(a)** require a definite article in the singular and in the plural when they are the subject of the phrase

(**a**) *(of one person) (singular)* tuyo(a) *m,f*, *Fml* suyo(a) *m,f*; *(pl)* tuyos(as) *m,fpl*, *Fml* suyos(as) *m,fpl*; **my house is big but y. is bigger** mi casa es grande, pero la tuya/suya es mayor; **this book is y.** este libro es tuyo/suyo; **these books are y.** estos libros son tuyos/suyos; **y. (sincerely/faithfully)** atentamente

(**b**) *(of more than one person) (singular) Esp* vuestro(a), *Am or Fml* suyo(a); *(pl) Esp* vuestros(as), *Am or Fml* suyos(as); **this book is y.** este libro es vuestro/suyo; **these books are y.** estos libros son vuestros/suyos

yourself [jɔ:ˈself] *pron* (**a**) *(reflexive)* te, *Fml* se; **have you hurt y.?** ¿te has hecho daño?, *Fml* ¿se ha hecho daño? (**b**) *(emphatic)* tú mismo *m*, tú misma *f*, *Fml* usted mismo *m*, usted misma *f*; **you told me y.** me lo dijiste tú mismo, *Fml* me lo dijo usted mismo; (**c**) *(after preposition)* ti, *Fml* usted; **did you do this by y.?** ¿lo has hecho tú solo?, *Fml* ¿lo ha hecho usted solo?; **do you live by y.?** ¿vives solo?, *Fml* ¿vive solo?

yourselves [jɔ:ˈselvz] *pron* (**a**) *(reflexive) Esp* os, *Am or Fml* se; **have you hurt y.?** *Esp* ¿os habéis hecho daño?, *Am or Fml* ¿se han hecho daño? (**b**) *(emphatic) Esp* vosotros mismos(as), *Am or Fml* ustedes mismos(as); **did you do all the work y.?** *Esp* ¿habéis hecho todo el trabajo vosotros solos?, *Am or Fml* ¿han hecho todo el trabajo ustedes solos?

(**c**) *(after preposition) Esp* vosotros(as), *Am or Fml* ustedes; **did you do this by y.?** *Esp* ¿lo habéis hecho vosotros solos?, *Am or Fml* ¿lo han hecho ustedes solos?; **did you buy it for y.?**

Esp ¿os lo habéis comprado para vosotros?, *Am or Fml* ¿se lo han comprado para ustedes?

youth [ju:θ] *n* (**a**) juventud *f* (**b**) *(young man)* joven *m*; **y. club** club *m*

juvenil; **y. hostel** albergue *m* juvenil

youthful ['ju:θfʊl] *adj* juvenil, joven

yuppie ['jʌpɪ] *n* yupi *mf*; **a y. restaurant** un restaurante de yupis

Zz

Z, z [zed, *US* zi:] *n (the letter)* Z, z *f*

zany ['zeɪnɪ] *adj* (**zanier, zaniest**) *Fam* (**a**) *(mad)* *Esp* chiflado(a), *Am* zafado(a), *RP* rayado(a) (**b**) *(eccentric)* estrafalario(a)

zeal [zi:l] *n (enthusiasm)* entusiasmo *m*

zealous ['zeləs] *adj (enthusiastic)* entusiasta

zebra ['zi:brə, 'zebrə] *n* cebra *f*; *Br* **z. crossing** paso *m* de cebra

zero ['zɪərəʊ] *n* cero *m*; **z. hour** hora *f* cero

zest [zest] *n (eagerness)* entusiasmo *m*

zigzag ['zɪgzæg] **1** *n* zigzag *m* **2** *vi* zigzaguear

zinc [zɪŋk] *n* cinc *m*, zinc *m*

zip [zɪp] **1** *n* (**a**) *Br* **z. (fastener)** cremallera *f*, *Am* cierre *m* (**b**) *Fam* brío *m*; *US* **z. code** código *m* postal **2** *vi* cerrarse con cremallera

▶**zip by** *vi* pasar como un rayo

▶**zip up** *vt sep* cerrar la cremallera *or Am* el cierre de; **to z. sb up** cerrar la cremallera *or Am* el cierre a algn

zipper ['zɪpə(r)] *n US* cremallera *f*, *Am* cierre *m*

zit [zɪt] *n Fam* grano *m*

zodiac ['zəʊdɪæk] *n* zodiaco *m*, zodíaco *m*

zone [zəʊn] **1** *n* zona *f* **2** *vt* dividir en zonas

zoo [zu:] *n* zoo *m*

zoom [zu:m] **1** *n* (**a**) *(buzz)* zumbido *m* (**b**) **z. lens** zoom *m*, teleobjetivo *m* **2** *vi* (**a**) *(buzz)* zumbar (**b**) **to z. past** pasar volando

▶**zoom in** *vi (camera)* acercarse rápidamente

zucchini [zu:'ki:nɪ] *n US* calabacín *m*, *CSur* zapallito *m*

Supplement

Spanish Verb Conjugations

Models for regular verbs

TOMAR to take

INDICATIVE

PRESENT	FUTURE	CONDITIONAL
1. tomo	tomaré	tomaría
2. tomas	tomarás	tomarías
3. toma	tomará	tomaría
1. tomamos	tomaremos	tomaríamos
2. tomáis	tomaréis	tomaríais
3. toman	tomarán	tomarían

IMPERFECT	PRETERITE	PERFECT
1. tomaba	tomé	he tomado
2. tomabas	tomaste	has tomado
3. tomaba	tomó	ha tomado
1. tomábamos	tomamos	hemos tomado
2. tomabais	tomasteis	habéis tomado
3. tomaban	tomaron	han tomado

FUTURE PERFECT	CONDITIONAL PERFECT	PLUPERFECT
1. habré tomado	habría tomado	había tomado
2. habrás tomado	habrías tomado	habías tomado
3. habrá tomado	habría tomado	había tomado
1. habremos tomado	habríamos tomado	habíamos tomado
2. habréis tomado	habríais tomado	habíais tomado
3. habrán tomado	habrían tomado	habían tomado

SUBJUNCTIVE

PRESENT	IMPERFECT	PERFECT/PLUPERFECT
1. tome	tom-ara/ase	haya/hubiera* tomado
2. tomes	tom-aras/ases	hayas/hubieras tomado
3. tome	tom-ara/ase	haya/hubiera tomado

* the alternative form 'hubiese' etc is also possible.

1. tomemos	tom-áramos/ásemos	hayamos/hubiéramos tomado
2. toméis	tom-arais/aseis	hayáis/hubierais tomado
3. tomen	tom-aran/asen	hayan/hubieran tomado

IMPERATIVE	INFINITIVE	PARTICIPLE
(tú) toma	**PRESENT**	**PRESENT**
(Vd) tome	tomar	tomando
(nosotros) tomemos		
(vosotros) tomad	**PERFECT**	**PAST**
(Vds) tomen	haber tomado	tomado

COMER to eat

INDICATIVE

PRESENT	FUTURE	CONDITIONAL
1. como	comeré	comería
2. comes	comerás	comerías
3. come	comerá	comería
1. comemos	comeremos	comeríamos
2. coméis	comeréis	comeríais
3. comen	comerán	comerían

IMPERFECT	PRETERITE	PERFECT
1. comía	comí	he comido
2. comías	comiste	has comido
3. comía	comió	ha comido
1. comíamos	comimos	hemos comido
2. comíais	comisteis	habéis comido
3. comían	comieron	han comido

FUTURE PERFECT	CONDITIONAL PERFECT	PLUPERFECT
1. habré comido	habría comido	había comido
2. habrás comido	habrías comido	habías comido
3. habrá comido	habría comido	había comido
1. habremos comido	habríamos comido	habíamos comido
2. habréis comido	habríais comido	habíais comido
3. habrán comido	habrían comido	habían comido

SUBJUNCTIVE

PRESENT	IMPERFECT	PERFECT/PLUPERFECT
1. coma	com-iera/iese	haya/hubiera* comido
2. comas	com-ieras/ieses	hayas/hubieras comido
3. coma	com-iera/iese	haya/hubiera comido
1. comamos	com-iéramos/iésemos	hayamos/hubiéramos comido
2. comáis	com-ierais/ieseis	hayáis/hubierais comido
3. coman	com-ieran/iesen	hayan/hubieran comido

* the alternative form 'hubiese' etc is also possible

IMPERATIVE	INFINITIVE	PARTICIPLE
(tú) come	**PRESENT**	**PRESENT**
(Vd) coma	comer	comiendo
(nosotros) comamos		
(vosotros) comed	**PERFECT**	**PAST**
(Vds) coman	haber comido	comido

PARTIR to leave

INDICATIVE

PRESENT	FUTURE	CONDITIONAL
1. parto	partiré	partiría
2. partes	partirás	partirías
3. parte	partirá	partiría
1. partimos	partiremos	partiríamos
2. partís	partiréis	partiríais
3. parten	partirán	partirían

IMPERFECT	PRETERITE	PERFECT
1. partía	partí	he partido
2. partías	partiste	has partido
3. partía	partió	ha partido
1. partíamos	partimos	hemos partido
2. partíais	partisteis	habéis partido
3. partían	partieron	han partido

FUTURE PERFECT	CONDITIONAL PERFECT	PLUPERFECT
1. habré partido	habría partido	había partido
2. habrás partido	habrías partido	habías partido
3. habrá partido	habría partido	había partido
1. habremos partido	habríamos partido	habíamos partido
2. habréis partido	habríais partido	habíais partido
3. habrán partido	habrían partido	habían partido

SUBJUNCTIVE

PRESENT	IMPERFECT	PERFECT/PLUPERFECT
parta	parti-era/ese	haya/hubiera* partido
partas	parti-eras/eses	hayas/hubieras partido
parta	parti-era/ese	haya/hubiera partido
partamos	parti-éramos/ésemos	hayamos/hubiéramos partido
partáis	parti-erais/eseis	hayáis/hubierais partido
partan	parti-eran/esen	hayan/hubieran partido

* the alternative form 'hubiese' etc is also possible

IMPERATIVE

(tú) parte
(Vd) parta
(nosotros) partamos
(vosotros) partid
(Vds) partan

INFINITIVE

PRESENT
partir

PERFECT
haber partido

PARTICIPLE

PRESENT
partiendo

PAST
partido

Models for irregular verbs

[1] pensar PRES pienso, piensas, piensa, pensamos, pensáis, piensan; **PRES SUBJ** piense, pienses, piense, pensemos, penséis, piensen; **IMPERAT** piensa, piense, pensemos, pensad, piensen

[2] contar PRES cuento, cuentas, cuenta, contamos, contáis, cuentan; **PRES SUBJ** cuente, cuentes, cuente, contemos, contéis, cuenten; **IMPERAT** cuenta, cuente, contemos, contad, cuenten

[3] perder PRES pierdo, pierdes, pierde, perdemos, perdéis, pierden; **PRES SUBJ** pierda, pierdas, pierda, perdamos, perdáis, pierdan; **IMPERAT** pierde, pierda, perdamos, perded, pierdan

[4] morder PRES muerdo, muerdes, muerde, mordemos, mordéis, muerden; **PRES SUBJ** muerda, muerdas, muerda, mordamos, mordáis, muerdan; **IMPERAT** muerde, muerda, mordamos, morded, muerdan

[5] sentir PRES siento, sientes, siente, sentimos, sentís, sienten; **PRES SUBJ** sienta, sientas, sienta, sintamos, sintáis, sientan; **PRES P** sintiendo; **IMPERAT** siente, sienta, sintamos, sentid, sientan

[6] vestir PRES visto, vistes, viste, vestimos, vestís, visten; **PRES SUBJ** vista, vistas, vista, vistamos, vistáis, vistan; **PRES P** vistiendo; **IMPERAT** viste, vista, vistamos, vestid, vistan

[7] dormir PRES duermo, duermes, duerme, dormimos, dormís, duermen; **PRES SUBJ** duerma, duermas, duerma, durmamos, durmáis, duerman; **PRES P** durmiendo; **IMPERAT** duerme, duerma, durmamos, dormid, duerman

[8] andar PRET anduve, anduviste, anduvo, anduvimos, anduvisteis, anduvieron; **IMPERF SUBJ** anduviera/anduviese

[9] caber PRES quepo, cabes, cabe, cabemos, cabéis, caben; **PRES SUBJ** quepa, quepas, quepa, quepamos, quepáis, quepan; **FUT** cabré; **COND** cabría; **PRET** cupe, cupiste, cupo, cupimos, cupisteis, cupieron; **IMPERF SUBJ** cupiera/cupiese; **IMPERAT** cabe, quepa, quepamos, cabed, quepan

[10] conducir PRES conduzco, conduces, conduce, conducimos, conducís, conducen; **PRES SUBJ** conduzca, conduzcas, conduzca, conduzcamos, conduzcáis, conduzcan; **PRET** conduje, condujiste, condujo, condujimos, condujisteis, condujeron; **IMPERF SUBJ** condujera/condujese; **IMPERAT** conduce, conduzca, conduzcamos, conducid, conduzcan

[11] dar PRES doy, das, da, damos, dais, dan; **PRES SUBJ** dé, des, dé, demos, deis, den; **PRET** di, diste, dio, dimos, disteis, dieron; **IMPERF SUBJ** diera/diese; **IMPERAT** da, dé, demos, dad, den

[12] decir PRES digo, dices, dice, decimos, decís, dicen; **PRES SUBJ** diga, digas, diga, digamos, digáis, digan; **FUT** diré; **COND** diría; **PRET** dije, dijiste, dijo, dijimos, dijisteis, dijeron; **IMPERF SUBJ** dijera/dijese; **PRES P** diciendo; **PP** dicho; **IMPERAT** di, diga, digamos, decid, digan

[13] ESTAR to be

INDICATIVE

PRESENT	FUTURE	CONDITIONAL
1. estoy	estaré	estaría
2. estás	estarás	estarías
3. está	estará	estaría
1. estamos	estaremos	estaríamos
2. estáis	estaréis	estaríais
3. están	estarán	estarían

IMPERFECT	PRETERITE	PERFECT
1. estaba	estuve	he estado
2. estabas	estuviste	has estado
3. estaba	estuvo	ha estado
1. estábamos	estuvimos	hemos estado
2. estabais	estuvisteis	habéis estado
3. estaban	estuvieron	han estado

FUTURE PERFECT	CONDITIONAL PERFECT	PLUPERFECT
1. habré estado	habría estado	había estado
2. habrás estado	habrías estado	habías estado
3. habrá estado	habría estado	había estado
1. habremos estado	habríamos estado	habíamos estado
2. habréis estado	habríais estado	habíais estado
3. habrán estado	habrían estado	habían estado

SUBJUNCTIVE

PRESENT	IMPERFECT	PERFECT/PLUPERFECT
1. esté	estuv-iera/iese	haya/hubiera* estado
2. estés	estuv-ieras/ieses	hayas/hubieras estado
3. esté	estuv-iera/iese	haya/hubiera estado
1. estemos	estuv-iéramos/iésemos	hayamos/hubiéramos estado
2. estéis	estuv-ierais/ieseis	hayáis/hubierais estado
3. estén	estuv-ieran/iesen	hayan/hubieran estado

IMPERATIVE

(tú) está
(Vd) esté
(nosotros) estemos
(vosotros) estad
(Vds) estén

INFINITIVE

PRESENT
estar

PERFECT
haber estado

PARTICIPLE

PRESENT
estando

PAST
estado

* the alternative form 'hubiese' etc is also possible

[14] HABER to have (*auxiliary*)

INDICATIVE

PRESENT	FUTURE	CONDITIONAL
1. he	habré	habría
2. has	habrás	habrías
3. ha/hay*	habrá	habría
1. hemos	habremos	habríamos
2. habéis	habréis	habríais
3. han	habrán	habrían

IMPERFECT	PRETERITE	PERFECT
1. había	hube	
2. habías	hubiste	
3. había	hubo	ha habido*
1. habíamos	hubimos	
2. habíais	hubisteis	
3. habían	hubieron	

FUTURE PERFECT	CONDITIONAL PERFECT	PLUPERFECT
1.		
2.		
3. habrá habido*	habría habido*	había habido*
1.		
2.		
3.		

SUBJUNCTIVE

PRESENT	IMPERFECT	PERFECT/PLUPERFECT
1. haya	hub-iera/iese	
2. hayas	hub-ieras/ieses	
3. haya	hub-iera/iese	haya/hubiera** habido*
1. hayamos	hub-iéramos/iésemos	
2. hayáis	hub-ierais/ieseis	
3. hayan	hub-ieran/iesen	

INFINITIVE

PRESENT
haber
PERFECT
haber habido*

PARTICIPLE

PRESENT
habiendo
PAST
habido

* 'haber' is an auxiliary verb used with the participle of another verb to form compound tenses (eg he bebido – I have drunk). 'Hay' means 'there is/are' and all third person singular forms in their respective tenses have this meaning. The forms highlighted with an asterisk are used only for this latter construction.

** the alternative form 'hubiese' is also possible.

[15] hacer PRES hago, haces, hace, hacemos, hacéis, hacen; **PRES SUBJ** haga, hagas, haga, hagamos, hagáis, hagan; **FUT** haré; **COND** haría; **PRET** hice, hiciste, hizo, hicimos, hicisteis, hicieron; **IMPERF SUBJ** hiciera/hiciese; **PP** hecho; **IMPERAT** haz, haga, hagamos, haced, hagan

[16] ir PRES voy, vas, va, vamos, vais, van; **PRES SUBJ** vaya, vayas, vaya, vayamos, vayáis, vayan; **IMPERF** iba, ibas, iba, íbamos, ibais, iban; **PRET** fui, fuiste, fue, fuimos, fuisteis, fueron; **IMPERF SUBJ** fuera/fuese; **PRES P** yendo; **IMPERAT** ve, vaya, vamos, id, vayan

[17] oír PRES oigo, oyes, oye, oímos, oís, oyen; **PRES SUBJ** oiga, oigas, oiga, oigamos, oigáis, oigan; **PRET** oí, oiste, oyó, oímos, oísteis, oyeron; **IMPERF SUBJ** oyera/oyese; **PRES P** oyendo; **PP** oído; **IMPERAT** oye, oiga, oigamos, oíd, oigan

[18] poder PRES puedo, puedes, puede, podemos, podéis, pueden; **PRES SUBJ** pueda, puedas, pueda, podamos, podáis, puedan; **FUT** podré; **COND** podría; **PRET** pude, pudiste, pudo, pudimos, pudisteis, pudieron; **IMPERF SUBJ** pudiera/pudiese; **PRES P** pudiendo; **IMPERAT** puede, pueda, podamos, poded, puedan

[19] poner PRES pongo, pones, pone, ponemos, ponéis, ponen; **PRES SUBJ** ponga, pongas, ponga, pongamos, pongáis, pongan; **FUT** pondré; **PRET** puse, pusiste, puso, pusimos, pusisteis, pusieron; **IMPERF SUBJ** pusiera/pusiese; **PP** puesto; **IMPERAT** pon, ponga, pongamos, poned, pongan

[20] querer PRES quiero, quieres, quiere, queremos, queréis, quieren; **PRES SUBJ** quiera, quieras, quiera, queramos, queráis, quieran; **FUT** querré; **COND** querría; **PRET** quise, quisiste, quiso, quisimos, quisisteis, quisieron; **IMPERF SUBJ** quisiera/quisiese; **IMPERAT** quiere, quiera, queramos, quered, quieran

[21] saber PRES sé, sabes, sabe, sabemos, sabéis, saben; **PRES SUBJ** sepa, sepas, sepa, sepamos, sepáis, sepan; **FUT** sabré; **COND** sabría; **PRET** supe, supiste, supo, supimos, supisteis, supieron; **IMPERF SUBJ** supiera/supiese; **IMPERAT** sabe, sepa, sepamos, sabed, sepan

[22] salir PRES salgo, sales, sale, salimos, salís, salen; **PRES SUBJ** salga, salgas, salga, salgamos, salgáis, salgan; **FUT** saldré; **COND** saldría; **IMPERAT** sal, salga, salgamos, salid, salgan

[23] ser PRES soy, eres, es, somos, sois, son; **PRES SUBJ** sea, seas, sea, seamos, seáis, sean; **IMPERF** era, eras, era, éramos, erais, eran; **PRET** fui, fuiste, fue, fuimos, fuisteis, fueron; **IMPERF SUBJ** fuera/fuese; **IMPERAT** sé, sea, seamos, sed, sean

[24] tener PRES tengo, tienes, tiene, tenemos, tenéis, tienen; **PRES SUBJ** tenga, tengas, tenga, tengamos, tengáis, tengan; **FUT** tendré; **COND** tendría; **PRET** tuve, tuviste, tuvo, tuvimos, tuvisteis, tuvieron; **IMPERF SUBJ** tuviera/tuviese; **IMPERAT** ten, tenga, tengamos, tened, tengan

[25] traer PRES traigo, traes, trae, traemos, traéis, traen; **PRES SUBJ** traiga, traigas, traiga, traigamos, traigáis, traigan; **PRET** traje, trajiste, trajo, trajimos, trajisteis, trajeron; **IMPERF SUBJ** trajera/trajese; **IMPERAT** trae, traiga, traigamos, traed, traigan

[26] valer PRES valgo, vales, vale, valemos, valéis, valen; **PRES SUBJ** valga, valgas, valga, valgamos, valgáis, valgan; **FUT** valdré; **COND** valdría; **IMPERAT** vale, valga, valemos, valed, valgan

[27] venir PRES vengo, vienes, viene, venimos, venís, vienen; **PRES SUBJ** venga, vengas, venga, vengamos, vengáis, vengan; **FUT** vendré; **COND** vendría; **PRET** vine, viniste, vino, vinimos, vinisteis, vinieron; **IMPERF SUBJ** viniera/viniese; **PRES P** viniendo; **IMPERAT** ven, venga, vengamos, venid, vengan

[28] ver PRES veo, ves, ve, vemos, veis, ven; **PRES SUBJ** vea, veas, vea, veamos, veáis, vean; **IMPERF** veía, veías, veía, veíamos, veíais, veían; **PRET** vi, viste, vio, vimos, visteis, vieron; **IMPERF SUBJ** viera/viese; **IMPERAT** ve, vea, veamos, ved, vean

[29] desviar PRES desvío, desvías, desvía, desviamos, desviáis, desvían; **PRES SUBJ** desvíe, desvíes, desvíe, desviemos, desviéis, desvíen; **IMPERAT** desvía, desvíe, desviemos, desviéis, desvíen

[30] continuar PRES continúo, continúas, continúa, continuamos, continuáis, continúan; **PRES SUBJ** continúe, continúes, continúe, continuemos, continuéis, continúen; **IMPERAT** continúa, continúe, continuemos, continuad, continúen

[31] adquirir PRES adquiero, adquieres, adquiere, adquirimos, adquirís, adquieren; **PRES SUBJ** adquiera, adquieras, adquiera, adquiramos, adquiráis, adquieran; **IMPERAT** adquiere, adquiera, adquiramos, adquirid, adquieran

[32] jugar PRES juego, juegas, juega, jugamos, jugáis, juegan; **PRES SUBJ** juegue, juegues, juegue, juguemos, juguéis, jueguen; **IMPERAT** juega, juegue, juguemos, jugad, jueguen

[33] agradecer PRES agradezco, agradeces, agradece, agradecemos, agradecéis, agradecen; **PRES SUBJ** agradezca, agradezcas, agradezca, agradezcamos, agradezcáis, agradezcan; **IMPERAT** agradece, agradezca, agradezcamos, agradeced, agradezcan

[34] conocer PRES conozco, conoces, conoce, conocemos, conocéis, conocen; **PRES SUBJ** conozca, conozcas, conozca, conozcamos, conozcáis, conozcan; **IMPERAT** conoce, conozca, conozcamos, conoced, conozcan

[35] lucir PRES luzco, luces, luce, lucimos, lucís, lucen; **PRES SUBJ** luzca, luzcas, luzca, luzcamos, luzcáis, luzcan; **IMPERAT** luce, luzca, luzcamos, lucid, luzcan

[36] leer PRET leí, leíste, leyó, leímos, leísteis, leyeron; **IMPERF SUBJ** leyera/leyese; **PRES P** leyendo; **PP** leído; **IMPERAT** lee, lea, leamos, leed, lean

[37] huir PRES huyo, huyes, huye, huimos, huís, huyen; **PRES SUBJ** huya, huyas, huya, huyamos, huyáis, huyan; **PRET** huí, huiste, huyó, huimos, huisteis, huyeron; **IMPERF SUBJ** huyera/huyese; **PRES P** huyendo; **PP** huido; **IMPERAT** huye, huya, huyamos, huid, huyan

[38] roer PRES roo/roigo/royo, roes, roe, roemos, roéis, roen; **PRES SUBJ** roa/roiga/roya, roas, roa, roamos, roáis, roan; **PRET** roí, roíste, royó, roímos, roísteis, royeron; **IMPERF SUBJ** royera/royese; **PRES P** royendo; **PP** roído; **IMPERAT** roe, roa, roamos, roed, roan

[39] caer PRES caigo, caes, cae, caemos, caéis, caen; **PRES SUBJ** caiga, caigas, caiga, caigamos, caigáis, caigan; **PRES P** cayendo; **PP** caído; **IMPERAT** cae, caiga, caigamos, caed, caigan

[40] cazar PRET cacé, cazaste, cazó, cazamos, cazasteis, cazaron; **PRES SUBJ** cace, caces, cace, cacemos, cacéis, cacen

[41] cocer PRES cuezo, cueces, cuece, cocemos, cocéis, cuecen; **PRES SUBJ** cueza, cuezas, cueza, cozamos, cozáis, cuezan; **IMPERAT** cuece, cueza, cozamos, coced, cuezan

[42] llegar PRET llegué, llegaste, llegó, llegamos, llegasteis, llegaron; **PRES SUBJ** llegue, llegues, llegue, lleguemos, lleguéis, lleguen

[43] cambiar PRES cambio, cambias, cambia, cambiamos, cambiáis, cambian; **PRES SUBJ** cambie, cambies, cambie, cambiemos, cambiéis, cambien; **IMPERAT** cambia, cambie, cambiemos, cambiad, cambien

[44] sacar PRET saqué, sacaste, sacó, sacamos, sacasteis, sacaron; **PRES SUBJ** saque, saques, saque, saquemos, saquéis, saquen; **IMPERAT** saca, saque, saquemos, sacad, saquen

[45] averiguar PRET averigüé, averiguaste, averiguó, averiguamos, averiguasteis, averiguaron; **PRES SUBJ** averigüe, averigües, averigüe, averigüemos, averigüéis, averigüen; **IMPERAT** averigua, averigüe, averigüemos, averiguad, averigüen

[46] asir PRES asgo, ases, ase, asimos, asís, asen; **PRES SUBJ** asga, asgas, asga, asgamos, asgáis, asgan; **IMPERAT** ase, asga, asgamos, asid, asgan

[47] adecuar PRES adecuo/adecúo, adecuas/adecúas, adecua/adecúa, adecuamos, adecuáis, adecuan/adecúan; **PRES SUBJ** adecue/adecúe, adecues/adecúes, adecue/adecúe, adecuemos, adecuéis, adecuen/adecúen; **IMPERAT** adecua/adecúa, adecue/adecúe, adecuemos, adecuad, adecuen/adecúen

[48] delinquir PRES delinco, delinques, delinque, delinquimos, delinquís, delinquen; **PRES SUBJ** delinca, delincas, delinca, delincamos, delincáis, delincan; **IMPERAT** delinque, delinca, delincamos, delinquid, delincan

[49] mecer PRES mezo, meces, mece, mecemos, mecéis, mecen; **PRES SUBJ** meza, mezas, meza, mezamos, mezáis, mezan; **IMPERAT** mece, meza, mezamos, meced, mezan

[50] errar PRES yerro, yerras, yerra, erramos, erráis, yerran; **PRES SUBJ** yerre, yerres, yerre, erremos, erréis, yerren; **IMPERAT** yerra, yerre, erremos, errad, yerren

[51] comenzar PRES comienzo, comienzas, comienza, comenzamos, comenzáis, comienzan; **PRES SUBJ** comience, comiences, comience, comencemos, comencéis, comiencen; **IMPERAT** comienza, comience, comencemos, comenzad, comiencen

[52] zurcir PRES zurzo, zurces, zurce, zurcimos, zurcís, zurcen; **PRES SUBJ** zurza, zurzas, zurza, zurzamos, zurzáis, zurzan; **IMPERAT** zurce, zurza, zurzamos, zurcid, zurzan

[53] proteger PRES protejo, proteges, protege, protegemos, protegéis, protegen; **PRES SUBJ** proteja, protejas, proteja, protejamos, protejáis, protejan; **IMPERAT** protege, proteja, protejamos, proteged, protejan

[54] discernir PRES discierno, disciernes, discierne, discernimos, discernís, disciernen; **PRES SUBJ** discierna, disciernas, discierna, discernamos, discernáis, disciernan; **IMPERAT** discierne, discierna, discernamos, discernid, disciernan

[55] erguir PRES irgo/yergo, irgues/yergues, irgue/yergue, erguimos, erguís, irguen/yerguen; **PRET** erguí, erguiste, irguió, erguimos, erguisteis, irguieron; **PRES SUBJ** irga/yerga, irgas/yergas, irga/yerga, irgamos/yergamos, irgáis/yergáis, irgan/yergan; **IMPERF SUBJ** irguiera/irguiese; **IMPERAT** irgue/yergue, irga/yerga, irgamos/yergamos, erguid, irgan/yergan

[56] reír PRES río, ríes, ríe, reímos, reís, ríen; **PRET** reí, reíste, rió, reímos, reísteis, rieron; **PRES SUBJ** ría, rías, ría, riamos, riáis, rían; **IMPERF SUBJ** riera/riese; **IMPERAT** ríe, ría, riamos, reíd, rían

[57] dirigir PRES dirijo, diriges, dirige, dirigimos, dirigís, dirigen; **PRES SUBJ** dirija, dirijas, dirija, dirijamos, dirijáis, dirijan; **IMPERAT** dirige, dirija, dirijamos, dirigid, dirijan

[58] regir PRES rijo, riges, rige, regimos, regís, rigen; **PRES SUBJ** rija, rijas, rija, rijamos, rijáis, rijan; **IMPERAT** rige, rija, rijamos, regid, rijan

[59] distinguir PRES distingo, distingues, distingue, distinguimos, distinguís, distinguen; **PRES SUBJ** distinga, distingas, distinga, distingamos, distingáis, distingan; **IMPERAT** distingue, distinga, distingamos, distinguid, distingan

[60] nacer PRES nazco, naces, nace, nacemos, nacéis, nacen; **PRES SUBJ** nazca, nazcas, nazca, nazcamos, nazcáis, nazcan; **IMPERAT** nace, nazca, nazcamos, naced, nazcan

[61] yacer PRES yazco/yazgo/yago, yaces, yace, yacemos, yacéis, yacen; **PRES SUBJ** yazca/yazga/yaga; **IMPERAT** yace/yaz, yazca/yazga/yaga, yazcamos/yazgamos/ yagamos, yaced, yazcan/yazgan/yagan

[62] argüir PRES arguyo, arguyes, arguye, argüimos, argüís, arguyen; **PRET** argüí, argüiste, arguyó, argüimos, argüisteis, arguyeron; **PRES SUBJ** arguya, arguyas, arguya, arguyamos, arguyáis, arguyan; **IMPERF SUBJ** arguyera/arguyese; **IMPERAT** arguye, arguya, arguyamos, argüid, arguyan

[63] avergonzar PRES avergüenzo, avergüenzas, avergüenza, avergonzamos, avergonzáis, avergüenzan; **PRET** avergoncé, avergonzaste, avergonzó, avergonzamos, avergonzasteis, avergonzaron; **PRES SUBJ** avergüence, avergüences, avergüence, avergoncemos, avergoncéis, avergüencen; **IMPERAT** avergüenza, avergüence, avergoncemos, avergonzad, avergüencen

[64] trocar PRES trueco, truecas, trueca, trocamos, trocáis, truecan; **PRET** troqué, trocaste, trocó, trocamos, trocasteis, trocaron; **PRES SUBJ** trueque, trueques, trueque, troquemos, troquéis, truequen; **IMPERAT** trueca, trueque, troquemos, trocad, truequen

[65] oler PRES huelo, hueles, huele, olemos, oléis, huelen; **PRES SUBJ** huela, huelas, huela, olamos, oláis, huelan; **IMPERAT** huele, huela, olamos, oled, huelan

Verbos irregulares ingleses

INFINITIVE	PAST SIMPLE	PAST PARTICIPLE
arise	arose	arisen
awake	awoke	awoken
be	was, were	been
bear	bore	borne
beat	beat	beaten
become	became	become
begin	began	begun
bend	bent	bent
bet	bet, betted	bet, betted
bid (offer)	bid	bid
bind	bound	bound
bite	bit	bitten
bleed	bled	bled
blow	blew	blown
break	broke	broken
breed	bred	bred
bring	brought	brought
broadcast	broadcast	broadcast
build	built	built
burn	burnt, burned	burnt, burned
burst	burst	burst
buy	bought	bought
cast	cast	cast
catch	caught	caught
choose	chose	chosen
cling	clung	clung
come	came	come
cost	cost	cost
creep	crept	crept
cut	cut	cut
deal	dealt	dealt
dig	dug	dug
dive	dove	dived
do	did	done
draw	drew	drawn
dream	dreamt, dreamed	dreamt, dreamed
drink	drank	drunk
drive	drove	driven
eat	ate	eaten
fall	fell	fallen
feed	fed	fed
feel	felt	felt
fight	fought	fought
find	found	found
flee	fled	fled

INFINITIVE	PAST SIMPLE	PAST PARTICIPLE
fling	flung	flung
fly	flew	flown
forbid	forbad(e)	forbidden
forecast	forecast	forecast
foresee	foresaw	foreseen
forget	forgot	forgotten
forgive	forgave	forgiven
freeze	froze	frozen
get	got	gotten
give	gave	given
go	went	gone
grind	ground	ground
grow	grew	grown
hang	hung, hanged	hung, hanged
have	had	had
hear	heard	heard
hide	hid	hidden
hit	hit	hit
hold	held	held
hurt	hurt	hurt
keep	kept	kept
kneel	knelt	knelt
know	knew	known
lay	laid	laid
lead	led	led
lean	leant, leaned	leant, leaned
leap	leapt, leaped	leapt, leaped
learn	learnt, learned	learnt, learned
leave	left	left
lend	lent	lent
let	let	let
lie	lay	lain
light	lit, lighted	lit, lighted
lose	lost	lost
make	made	made
mean	meant	meant
meet	met	met
mislay	mislaid	mislaid
mislead	misled	misled
mistake	mistood	mistaken
misunderstand	misunderstood	misunderstood
mow	mowed	mown, mowed
outdo	outdid	outdone
overcome	overcame	overcome
overdo	overdid	overdone
overtake	overtook	overtaken
pay	paid	paid
put	put	put
quit	quit	quit
read	read	read
redo	redid	redone

INFINITIVE	PAST SIMPLE	PAST PARTICIPLE
rend	rent	rent
rewind	rewound	rewound
ride	rode	ridden
ring	rang	rung
rise	rose	risen
run	ran	run
saw	sawed	sawn, sawed
say	said	said
see	saw	seen
seek	sought	sought
sell	sold	sold
send	sent	sent
set	set	set
sew	sewed	sewn, sewed
shake	shook	shaken
shear	sheared	shorn, sheared
shed	shed	shed
shine	shone	shone
shoot	shot	shot
show	showed	shown, showed
shrink	shrank, shrunk	shrunk
shut	shut	shut
sing	sang	sung
sink	sank	sunk
sit	sat	sat
sleep	slept	slept
slide	slid	slid
sling	slung	slung
slink	slunk	slunk
slit	slit	slit
smell	smelt, smelled	smelt, smelled
sneak	sneaked, *US* snuck	sneaked, *US* snuck
sow	sowed	sown, sowed
speak	spoke	spoken
speed	sped, speeded	sped, speeded
spell	spelt, spelled	spelt, spelled
spend	spent	spent
spill	spilt, spilled	spilt, spilled
spin	spun	spun
spit	spat	spat
split	split	split
spoil	spoilt, spoiled	spoilt, spoiled
spread	spread	spread
spring	sprang	sprung
stand	stood	stood
steal	stole	stolen
stick	stuck	stuck
sting	stung	stung
stink	stank	stunk
stride	strode	stridden
strike	struck	struck

INFINITIVE	PAST SIMPLE	PAST PARTICIPLE
string	strung	strung
strive	strove	striven
swear	swore	sworn
sweep	swept	swept
swell	swelled	swollen
swim	swam	swum
swing	swung	swung
take	took	taken
teach	taught	taught
tear	tore	torn
tell	told	told
think	thought	thought
thrive	thrived, throve	thrived, thriven
throw	threw	thrown
thrust	thrust	thrust
tread	trod	trodden
undergo	underwent	undergone
understand	understood	understood
undertake	undertook	undertaken
undo	undid	undone
upset	upset	upset
wake	woke	woken
wear	wore	worn
weave	wove	woven
weep	wept	wept
wet	wet	wet
win	won	won
wind	wound	wound
withdraw	withdrew	withdrawn
withhold	withheld	withheld
wring	wrung	wrung
write	wrote	written

Conversation Guide
I. The Basics

Spanish has two separate sets of words to translate "you", "your", "yours", and "yourself". **Tú, te, tu/tus,** and **el tuyo** etc all correspond to the **tú** form of the verb, used when speaking to one person you know well (such as a friend or relative) or to someone younger (in parts of South America and in most of Central America, the pronoun **vos** is used in these informal contexts). **Usted, suyo/suyos,** and **el suyo** etc correspond to the **usted** form of the verb, and are used when speaking to one person you do not know well. If in doubt as to whether to call someone **tú** or **usted,** it is always safer to use the **usted** form. A Spanish-speaking person may invite you to use the less formal **tú** form by saying, "Puedes tutearme". All translations in this guide use formal **usted,** except in those examples where the context clearly indicates an informal situation.

Ustedes, suyo/suyos, and **el suyo** etc correspond to the **ustedes** form of the verb, and are used when speaking to more than one person. **Ustedes** is both formal and informal use in Latin America, but only formal in Spain. When speaking informally to more than one person in Spain, **vosotros, vuestro/vuestros,** and **el vuestro** etc are used, with the corresponding **vosotros** form of the verb.

good evening buenas noches	**OK** OK
good morning/afternoon buenos días/buenas tardes	**please** por favor
	see you later hasta luego
good night buenas noches	**see you on Monday** hasta el lunes
goodbye adiós	**see you soon** hasta pronto
hello hola	**see you tomorrow** hasta mañana
hi hola	**thank you** gracias
no no	**yes** sí
no, thank you no, gracias	**yes, please** sí, por favor

1) Meeting someone you know

How are you?
¿Cómo está?

Very good, thank you. And you?
Muy bien, gracias. ¿Y usted?

Hi, how are you doing?
Hola, ¿cómo le va?

Fine, and you?
Bien, ¿y a usted?

Good evening, how are you?
Buenas noches, ¿cómo le va?

Not too bad.
Bien.

Not very well, I have the flu.
No demasiado bien, tengo gripe or (*Méx*) gripa.

How are your parents/children?　　**They're doing well, thanks.**
¿Cómo están tus papás/hijos?　　　　Están bien, gracias.

2) Introducing yourself and meeting people you don't know

Name:

What's your name?　　　　　　　**My name is John.**
¿Cómo se llama?　　　　　　　　　　Me llamo John.

Let me introduce you to my brother Steve. And this is my cousin Rachel.
Le presento a mi hermano Steve. Y ella es mi prima Rachel.

Hi, I'm Peter, Anna's colleague.
Hola, yo soy Peter, un compañero de Anna.

I'm sorry, I've forgotten your name.
Discúlpeme, no me acuerdo de su nombre.

Pleased to meet you.
Encantado de conocerla.

Age:

How old are you?　　　　　　　　**I'm 12/24/45 years old.**
¿Qué edad tiene?　　　　　　　　　　Tengo doce/veinticuatro/cuarenta y
　　　　　　　　　　　　　　　　　　cinco años.

What's your date of birth?　　　　**I was born in 19 ...**
¿Cuál es su fecha de nacimiento?　　Nací en mil novecientos ...

Nationality:

What country are you from?　　　　**I'm from the United States.**
¿De qué país es usted?　　　　　　　Soy de Estados Unidos.

What's your nationality?　　　　　**I'm American.**
¿Cuál es su nacionalidad?　　　　　　Soy estadounidense.

Where do you live?　　　　　　　　**I live in New York.**
¿Dónde vive?　　　　　　　　　　　　Vivo en Nueva York.

I come from a little rural town in Montana.
Soy de un pueblito rural de Montana.

Occupation:

What do you do?　　　　　　　　　**I'm still in high school.**
¿A qué te dedicas?　　　　　　　　　Todavía estoy en la secundaria.

I'm a student/a teacher/a doctor.　**I'm retired.**
Soy estudiante/profesor/médico.　　Soy/Estoy jubilado.

I work in a bank.
Trabajo en un banco.

I work in the export department of a computer hardware company.
Trabajo en el departamento de exportaciones de una empresa de informática.

Family:

Do you have any brothers and sisters?
¿Tiene hermanos?

I have two brothers and one sister.
Tengo dos hermanos y una hermana.

I'm an only child.
Soy hijo único.

I have an older brother.
Tengo un hermano mayor.

I have a younger sister.
Tengo una hermana menor.

I have two little sisters.
Tengo dos hermanitas.

Are you married?
¿Es casado?

I'm single/separated/divorced.
Soy soltero/separado/divorciado.

Do you have any children?
¿Tiene hijos?

I have one son/daughter.
Tengo un hijo/una hija.

3) Likes and dislikes

I like skiing/swimming/playing basketball.
Me gusta esquiar/nadar/jugar al básquetbol.

I'm fond of classical music.
Me gusta (mucho) la música clásica.

I love movies.
Me encanta ir al cine.

I like/love playing chess/pool.
Me gusta/Me encanta jugar al ajedrez/al billar.

What's your favorite band/book?
¿Cuál es tu grupo/libro favorito?

I prefer reading/shopping.
Prefiero leer/ir de compras.

I prefer coffee to tea.
Prefiero el café al té.

I prefer football to basketball.
Prefiero el fútbol americano al básquetbol.

Did you enjoy the movie?
¿Te gustó la película?

I really liked it/didn't like it.
Me gustó mucho/No me gustó.

I liked/didn't like the ending.
Me gustó/No me gustó el final.

I don't like going to the opera.
No me gusta ir a la ópera.

I don't like that at all.
No me gusta nada.

I hate cheese.
Odio el queso.

I can't stand this kind of music.
No soporto este tipo de música.

This book is (really) awful.
Este libro es (realmente) horrible.

4) Expressing surprise and interest

No, you're kidding! Are you sure?
¡No puede ser! ¿Estás seguro?

Really?
¿En serio?

You're kidding?
¡Estás bromeando!

Are you pulling my leg?
¿Me estás tomando el pelo?

What a coincidence/a surprise!
¡Qué coincidencia/sorpresa!

Really? I'm a doctor too!
¿En serio? ¡Yo también soy médico!

That's strange.
¡Qué raro!

It's really interesting/fascinating/ amazing.
Es realmente interesante/fascinante/ increíble.

5) Expressing disappointment

What a shame!
¡Qué lástima!

It's too bad it's raining.
Es una lástima que esté lloviendo. (subjuntivo)

What a pity he couldn't come!
¡Qué lástima que no haya podido venir! (subjuntivo)

The concert has been canceled, how disappointing!
El concierto se canceló. ¡Qué lástima!

6) Saying thank you and expressing gratitude

Thank you.
Gracias.

Thank you very much.
Muchas gracias.

Thank you, that's really nice.
Gracias, es muy amable.

Thank you, but you shouldn't have!
Gracias, ¡no se hubiera molestado!

It's very kind of you.
Muy amable.

I'd like that very much.
Me gustaría mucho.

Thanks for your help/for helping me.
Gracias por su ayuda/por ayudarme.

To which the other person may reply:

De nada.
You're welcome.

Por favor, no hay de qué.
Please, don't mention it.

7) Apologizing

Sorry, it was an accident!
¡Perdón, no fue a propósito!

I'm (really) sorry.
Lo siento (de verdad).

I'm sorry I'm late.
Discúlpeme por el atraso.

I'm sorry to bother you, but ...
Disculpe que lo moleste, pero ...

I apologize.
Discúlpeme.

Excuse me.
Perdón.

Sorry for interrupting the conversation.
Perdón por interrumpir la conversación.

Sorry, it's my fault.
Perdón, es mi culpa.

I'm sorry but it's not my fault.
Discúlpeme, pero no es mi culpa.

I'm afraid I won't be able to come.
Temo que no podré ir.

That's very kind of you but unfortunately I'm not free that day.
Es muy amable de su parte pero lamentablemente voy a estar ocupado
  ese día.

To which the other person may reply:

No es nada.
It doesn't matter.

No se preocupe.
Don't worry about it.

8) Congratulations and compliments

Congratulations!
¡Felicitaciones!

I wish you lots of happiness.
Les deseo lo mejor.

I'm very happy for you!
¡Me alegro por usted!

It's great/wonderful/beautiful!
¡Es excelente/maravilloso/hermoso!

It was very good/delicious.
Estaba muy rico/delicioso.

I had a great time.
Me divertí mucho.

The party was a big success.
La fiesta fue un éxito.

9) Making suggestions and expressing desires

Do you want to go?
¿Quiere ir?

**Would you like to go to a
  restaurant?**
¿Le gustaría ir a un restaurante?

How about going to the museum?
¿Y si vamos al museo?

How about a pizza?
¿Qué tal una pizza?

I think we should meet at seven.
Podríamos encontrarnos a las siete.

Let's meet outside the restaurant.
Nos vemos en la puerta del
  restaurante.

I want to go back to the apartment.
Quiero volver al apartamento.

**I don't want to go to the swimming
  pool.**
No quiero ir a la alberca.

I feel like going to the movies.
Quiero ir al cine.

I don't feel like watching TV.
No tengo ganas de mirar televisión.

I wouldn't mind going to the theater.
Me gustaría ir al teatro.

I'd rather stay at home/do something else.
Preferiría quedarme en casa/hacer alguna otra cosa.

I'd like to go to Spain next year.
Me gustaría ir a España el año que viene.

I wish I was on vacation.
Ojalá estuviera de vacaciones.

I don't mind.
Me da lo mismo.

I have no preference.
No tengo preferencia.

10) Making requests

Can we have more bread, please?
¿Podría traernos más pan, por favor?

Could you please make a little less noise?
¿Podría hacer un poco menos de ruido?

Could I have a glass of water?
¿Podría traerme un vaso de agua?

Could I make a phone call?
¿Puedo hacer una llamada?

Can I open the window?
¿Puedo abrir la ventana?

Could you lend me ...?
¿Podría prestarme ...?

Can I borrow ...?
¿Podría prestarme ...?

Would it be possible to go?
¿Se puede ir?

Do you mind if I smoke?
¿Le molesta si fumo?

Would you be able to give me a ride?
¿Podría llevarme?

11) Expressing an opinion

What do you think?
¿Qué le parece?

What's your opinion?
¿Qué opina?

I think/I don't think that's a very good idea.
Creo que es una muy buena idea./No creo que sea muy buena idea.

I think we should go.
Creo que deberíamos ir.

I think she's very pretty.
Me parece muy bonita.

In my opinion, he shouldn't have said that.
En mi opinión, no debió haber dicho eso.

I agree/don't agree with you.
Estoy/No estoy de acuerdo con usted.

I've changed my mind.
Cambié de opinión.

I'm sure they'll win.
Estoy seguro de que van a ganar.

I totally agree with him.	**I disagree.**
Estoy totalmente de acuerdo con él.	No estoy de acuerdo.
You're (absolutely) right.	**No, not at all/absolutely not.**
Tiene (toda la) razón.	No, en absoluto.
Of course not!	**You're mistaken.**
¡Por supuesto que no!	Se equivoca.
You're wrong.	**That's true/not true.**
Está equivocado.	Es verdad./No es verdad.
Nonsense!	
¡Qué disparate!	

12) Having problems understanding Spanish

Could you speak more slowly?	**Can you repeat that, please?**
¿Podría hablar más despacio?	¿Podría repetir, por favor?
I don't understand this expression.	**I understand a little.**
No entiendo esta expresión.	Entiendo un poquito.
I don't understand a word of that.	**I didn't understand.**
No entiendo ni una palabra.	No entendí.

I can understand Spanish but I can't speak it.
Entiendo español, pero no sé hablarlo.

I speak hardly any Spanish.	**I have trouble understanding/**
Casi no hablo español.	**speaking.**
	Me cuesta entender/hablar.
Do you speak English?	**Pardon?/What?/Eh?**
¿Habla inglés?	¿Perdón?/¿Qué?/¿Eh?
What's it called?	**How do you say … in Spanish?**
¿Cómo se llama esto?	¿Cómo se dice … en español?
How do you spell it/pronounce it?	**Could you write it down?**
¿Cómo se escribe/pronuncia?	¿Podría escribírmelo?
What does it mean?	**What's that?**
¿Qué quiere decir?	¿Qué es eso?
What's happening?	
¿Qué pasa?	

II. Vacations in Mexico

1) Traveling and using public transportation

Traveling by plane:

Where is the Mexicana check-in desk?
¿En dónde está la ventanilla de Mexicana?

What time does boarding start?
¿A qué hora es el abordaje?

I'd like to confirm my return flight.
Quisiera confirmar mi vuelo de
  regreso.

I'd like a window seat/an aisle seat.
Quisiera un asiento en la ventana/
  el pasillo.

One of my suitcases is missing.
Me falta una maleta.

I'd like to report the loss of my luggage/my hand luggage.
Quisiera reportar la pérdida de mis maletas/mi maleta de mano.

The plane was two hours late and I've missed my connection.
El avión se atrasó dos horas y perdí la conexión.

Traveling by train:

I'd like to reserve a ticket, please.
Quisiera reservar un pasaje, por favor.

What are the reduced fares?
¿Cuáles son las tarifas rebajadas?

How much is a ticket to ...?
¿Cuánto cuesta el pasaje a ...?

Are there any tickets left for ...?
¿Quedan pasajes a ...?

No smoking (section), please.
Sección de no fumar, por favor.

Do you have a timetable, please?
¿Tiene los horarios, por favor?

When is the next train to Los Mochis?
¿A qué hora sale el próximo tren a
  Los Mochis?

Is there an earlier/a later one?
¿Hay alguno más temprano/tarde?

What platform does the train for ...
  leave from?
¿De qué plataforma sale el tren a ...?

I've missed the last train.
Perdí el último tren.

On the subway:

Where can I buy tickets?
¿Dónde puedo comprar boletos?

Does this line go to Chapultepec?
¿Esta línea para en Chapultepec?

Can I have a map of the subway?
¿Podría darme un mapa del metro?

What time is the last subway train?
¿A qué hora pasa el último metro?

Which line do I take to get to ...?
¿Qué línea tengo que tomar para
  ir a ...?

Traveling by bus:

Where can I get a bus to ...?
¿Dónde puedo tomar el camión a ...?

Is this the right stop for ...?
¿Es esta la parada del camión ...?

Does the bus for the airport leave from here?
¿El camión al aeropuerto sale de aquí?

Where is the bus station?
¿Dónde está la central camionera?

Renting a car:

I'd like to rent a car for a week.
Quisiera rentar un carro por una semana.

How much is the deposit?
¿Cuánto es el depósito?

I'd like to take out comprehensive insurance.
Quisiera contratar un seguro cobertura total.

I'd like an automatic/a stickshift.
Quisiera un carro automático/con cambios.

On the road:

Where can I find a gas station/a repair shop?
¿Dónde hay una gasolinería/un taller de reparaciones?

I've broken down.
Tengo una falla mecánica.

I have a flat tire. Where can I park?
Se me ponchó una llanta. ¿Dónde puedo estacionarme?

It won't start; the battery's dead.
No arranca, se descargó la batería.

I have a problem with the brakes/ the light indicators.
Tengo un problema con los frenos/ las luces.

Taking a cab:

I'd like to reserve a taxi for 8 o'clock.
Quisiera reservar un taxi para las 8 en punto.

Is this cab for hire?
¿Está libre?

How much will it cost to go to the airport?
¿Cuánto costaría ir hasta al aeropuerto?

I'd like to go to the train station.
Quisiera ir a la estación de trenes.

Could you take me to this address, please?
¿Podría llevarme a esta dirección, por favor?

You can drop me off here, thanks.
Déjeme aquí, por favor.

Asking for directions:

Excuse me, where is ..., please?
Perdón, ¿dónde queda ..., por favor?

I'm looking for ...
Estoy buscando ...

Could you tell me how to get to ...?
¿Podría decirme cómo llego a ...?

I'm lost.
Estoy perdido.

Which way is it to ...?
¿Cuál es el camino para llegar a ...?

Is it far/near?
¿Está lejos/cerca?

How can I get to the station?
¿Cómo llego a la estación?

Can you show me the way?
¿Podría mostrarme el camino?

Could you show me on the map?
¿Podría mostrármelo en el mapa?

Understanding the person you asked for help:

Es la segunda calle a la derecha/
  a la izquierda.
**It's the second street on the right/
  on the left.**

Tome la próxima salida.
Take the next exit.

Siga derecho hasta el semáforo.
Keep going straight on until you get to the (traffic) lights.

2) Renting accommodations

Staying in a hotel or a B&B:

Do you have any rooms available?
¿Tiene alguna habitación libre?

It's for a couple and two children.
Es para un matrimonio y dos niños.

I'd like to reserve a room for tomorrow night, please.
Quisiera reservar una habitación para mañana en la noche, por favor.

I've reserved three single/double rooms over the phone, in the name of ...
Reservé por teléfono tres habitaciones para una persona/dobles, a
  nombre de ...

Would it be possible to stay another night/to add an extra bed?
¿Podríamos quedarnos otra noche/agregar una cama?

Can I see the room?
¿Puedo ver la habitación?

**How much is a room with its own
  bathroom?**
¿Cuánto cuesta una habitación con
  baño privado?

Do you take credit cards?
¿Aceptan tarjetas de crédito?

**We're planning to stay for two
  nights.**
Pensamos quedarnos dos noches.

Is breakfast included?
¿El desayuno está incluido?

The key for room 12, please.
La llave de la habitación doce,
  por favor.

The outlet for razors isn't working.
El enchufe para la afeitadora no
  funciona.

We don't have towels/toilet paper.
No tenemos toallas/papel higiénico.

Could you wake me up at seven o'clock?
¿Podría despertarme a las siete en punto?

Understanding the receptionist:

No, lo siento, no tenemos lugar.
No, I'm sorry, we're full.

¿Podría llenar esta forma?
Could you fill out this form?

El check-out es al mediodía.
Check-out time is noon.

El desayuno se sirve entre las siete y media y las nueve.
Breakfast is served between 7:30 and 9.

Renting an apartment or a bungalow:

I'm looking for something to rent close to the center of town
Estoy buscando departamento para rentar cerca del centro.

Is it completely furnished?
¿Está totalmente amueblado?

Is there a washing machine?
¿Hay lavadora?

Where do I pick up/leave the keys?
¿Dónde entrego/retiro las llaves?

Where is the electricity meter?
¿Dónde está el contador de la luz?

Where do I take the garbage out?
¿Dónde se saca la basura?

Are there any spare ...?
¿Hay ... de recambio?

I'm sorry, I can't find/I've broken the ...
Lo siento, no encuentro/se me rompió el ...

There's no hot water.
No hay agua caliente.

Camping:

Is there a campsite near here?
¿Hay algún lugar para acampar aquí cerca?

I'd like a space for one tent for two days.
Quiero un lugar para una tienda de campaña por dos días.

We want to rent a trailer.
Queremos rentar una casa rodante.

Where are the showers?
¿Dónde quedan las regaderas?

Is there a swimming pool/a night club/a tennis court in the campsite?
¿Hay alberca/discoteca/cancha de tenis en el campamento?

How much is it a day/per person/per tent?
¿Cuánto cuesta por día/persona/tienda de campaña?

3) Visiting

I'd like some information on ...
Quisiera información sobre ...

What is there to see/visit in the area?
¿Qué hay para ver/visitar en la región?

Is it open on Sundays?
¿Está abierto los domingos?

Is it free?
¿Es gratis?

How much does it cost to get in?
¿Cuánto cuesta la entrada?

Are there any discounts for young people?
¿Hay descuento para jóvenes?

How long does the tour last?
¿Cuánto dura la visita?

When is the next guided tour?
¿A qué hora es la próxima visita guiada?

Is this ticket valid for the exhibition too?
¿El boleto también sirve para la exposición?

Are there many hiking paths here?
¿Hay muchos senderos para caminatas por aquí?

4) Inquiring about the weather for the next few days

Do you know what the weather's going to be like this weekend?
¿Sabe cómo va a estar el tiempo el fin de semana?

What's the weather forecast for tomorrow?
¿Cuál es el pronóstico del tiempo para mañana?

Understanding the answer:

Han anunciado lluvias/tormentas.
They've forecast rain/storms.

Va a llover/nevar.
It's going to rain/to snow.

Va a hacer frío/calor/un calor sofocante.
It's going to be cold/hot/stiflingly hot.

Parece que va a estar bonito mañana.
The weather should be good tomorrow.

Lamentablemente prevén mal tiempo.
I'm afraid they're forecasting bad weather.

Va a haber neblina/heladas.
It's going to be foggy/icy.

Va a estar soleado, igual que hoy.
It will be sunny, like today.

Va a haber viento/mucho viento.
It's going to be windy/very windy.

Va a hacer 30° C a la sombra/ menos 2.
It's going to be 86° F in the shade/ minus 2.

Va a refrescar/entibiar.
It's going to get colder/warmer.

III. Going out

1) Going for a drink

Do you want to go for a drink?
¿Quiere ir a tomar una copa?

Let's go for a coffee.
Vamos a tomar un café.

Excuse me, please!
 (to call the waiter)
¡Disculpe!

What are you having?
¿Qué va a tomar?

I'll buy you a drink. What would you like?
Lo invito con una copa. ¿Qué quiere tomar?

It's on me!
¡Yo invito!

Could I have a beer?
Una cerveza, por favor.

I'd like a glass of dry white wine.
Quisiera un vaso de vino blanco seco.

I'll have a Coke® with/without ice, please.
Voy a tomar una Coca-Cola® con/sin hielo, por favor.

A coffee and a glass of water, please.
Un café y un vaso de agua, por favor.

Something non-alcoholic.
Algo sin alcohol.

I'll have the same.
Lo mismo para mí.

I'll have the same again.
Voy a tomar otra vez lo mismo.

To your health!
¡Salud!

Could you bring me an ashtray?
¿Podría traerme un cenicero?

We can go to a club afterwards.
Podemos ir a una discoteca después.

2) Going to the restaurant

Reserving a table:

Hello, I'd like to reserve a table for two for tomorrow night, around 8 o'clock.
Hola, quisiera reservar una mesa para dos, para mañana en la noche, alrededor de las ocho.

I've reserved a table in the name of …
Tengo una mesa reservada a nombre de …

A table for four, please.
Una mesa para cuatro, por favor.

You don't have a table available before then?
¿No tiene ninguna mesa libre más temprano?

Understanding the waiter:

¿Para qué hora?
For what time?

¿A las ocho y media le queda bien?
Would 8:30 suit you?

Buenos días, ¿van a comer?
Hello, will you be eating?

¿Para cuántas personas?
For how many people?

¿Tiene reserva? ¿A nombre de quién?
**Have you reserved a table?
What's the name?**

¿Fumar o no fumar?
Smoking or no-smoking?

Ordering food:

Could you bring me the menu/the wine list/the dessert menu, please?
¿Me podría traer la carta/la carta de vinos/la carta de postres, por favor?

What do you recommend?
¿Qué nos recomienda?

Do you have vegetarian dishes?
¿Tiene platos vegetarianos?

What's today's special?
¿Cuál es la especialidad de hoy?

I'll take that, then.
Voy a pedir eso entonces.

We'll both have the set menu.
Plato del día para los dos.

Where is the restroom, please?
¿Dónde es el tocador, por favor?

This isn't what I ordered, I asked for ...
Esto no es lo que pedí, yo había pedido ...

Could we have another jug of water/some more bread, please?
¿Podría traernos otra jarra de agua/un poco más de pan, por favor?

Understanding the waiter:

¿Ya eligieron?
Are you ready to order?

¿Y para beber?
And what would you like to drink?

¿Quieren algún postre?
Would you like a dessert?

¡Buen provecho!
Enjoy your meal!

Commenting on the food:

It's delicious.
Está delicioso.

It was really good.
Estaba muy rico.

It's very greasy/too spicy.
Está demasiado grasoso/picante.

It doesn't have enough salt.
Le falta sal.

Asking for the check:

Could I have the check, please?
La cuenta, por favor.

I think there's a mistake in the check.
Creo que hay un error en la cuenta.

Is the tip included?
¿Está incluida la propina?

We're all paying together.
Vamos a pagar todo junto.

3) Arranging to meet someone

What are you doing tonight?
¿Qué planes tiene para esta noche?

Do you have anything planned?
¿Tiene planes para esta noche?

How about going to the movies?
¿Qué te parece si vamos al cine?

When do you want to meet? And where?
¿A qué hora nos encontramos? ¿Y en dónde?

We can meet in front of the movie theater.
Podemos encontrarnos en la puerta del cine.

I'll meet you later, I need to stop by the hotel first.
Los veré más tarde, necesito hacer una parada en el hotel primero.

4) Going to see movies, shows, and concerts

I'd like three tickets for ...
Quisiera tres entradas para ...

Are there any discounts for students?
¿Hay descuento para estudiantes?

What time does the program/movie start?
¿A qué hora es la función/la película?

How long is the movie?
¿Cuánto dura la película?

Is the movie in the original language?
¿Esta película está en versión original?

It's out next week.
Se estrena la semana que viene.

I'd like to go to a show.
Me gustaría ir a ver un espectáculo.

Do we have to reserve in advance?
¿Hay que reservar con anticipación?

Do we have good seats?
¿Tenemos buenas localidades?

Will we be able to see the stage?
¿Se ve bien el escenario?

Are there any free/open-air concerts?
¿Hay conciertos gratis/al aire libre?

What kind of music is it?
¿Qué tipo de música es?

Understanding the clerk in the box office:

No hay más entradas para esta función.
This showing is sold out.

Las entradas están agotadas hasta ...
It's sold out until ...

El espectáculo dura una hora y media, incluyendo el intervalo.
The performance lasts for an hour and a half, including the intermission.

IV. Stores, Banks, and Post Offices

1) Buying food

Is there a supermarket/market nearby?
¿Hay algún supermercado/mercado por aquí cerca?

Where can I find a grocery store that stays open late?
¿Dónde puedo encontrar una tienda que esté abierta hasta tarde?

I'm looking for the frozen foods/dairy products aisle.
Busco la sección de productos congelados/lácteos.

I'd like five slices of ham/a little piece of that cheese.
Quisiera cinco rebanadas de jamón/un pedacito de ese queso.

It's for four people.
Es para cuatro personas.

A kilo of potatoes, please.
Un kilo de papas, por favor.

A little more/less, please.
Un poco más/menos, por favor.

Could I taste it?
¿Puedo probarlo?

That's everything, thanks.
Nada más, gracias.

Could I have a (plastic) bag?
¿Podría darme una bolsa (de plástico)?

Paying:

Where can I pay?
¿Dónde se paga?

How much do I owe you?
¿Cuánto le debo?

Can I pay by Visa®?
¿Puedo pagar con tarjeta Visa®?

I'll pay cash.
Voy a pagar en efectivo.

You've made a mistake with my change.
Se equivocó con el cambio.

Sorry, I don't have any change.
Lo siento, no tengo cambio.

Could you give me change, please?
¿Podría darme cambio, por favor?

Could I have a receipt?
¿Podría darme un recibo?

Understanding the clerk:

¿Algo más?
Is there anything else?

¿Cómo va a pagar?
How would you like to pay?

¿No tiene nada de cambio?
Don't you have any change?

Puede marcar su clave.
You can type in your number.

2) Buying clothes

I'm looking for the men's/children's department.
Busco la sección de hombres/niños.

I'd like a jacket/a pair of pants/a shirt.
Quisiera una chaqueta/un pantalón/una camisa.

No thanks, I'm only looking.
No gracias, sólo estoy mirando.

Where are the dressing rooms?
¿Dónde quedan los probadores?

I'd like to try on the one in the window.
Quisiera probarme el que está en la vidriera.

I take a size 8.
Calzo del número ocho en Estados Unidos.

Can I try it on?
¿Puedo probármelo?

It's too small/large.
Es demasiado pequeño/grande.

Do you have it in another color/in red?
¿Lo tiene en otro color/en rojo?

I need a bigger/smaller size.
Necesito una talla más grande/más pequeña.

The skirt is too short/long.
La falda es demasiado corta/larga.

Yes, that's fine, I'll take them.
Sí, está bien, me los llevo.

I'll think about it.
Voy a pensarlo.

Understanding the clerk:

¿Buenos días, qué se les ofrece?
Hello, can I help you?

¿Qué es lo que buscan?
Are you looking for something?

¿Qué talla usa?
What's your size?

Sólo lo tenemos en azul o negro.
We only have it in blue or black.

No nos queda ninguno en esa talla.
We don't have any left in this size.

Le queda bien.
It really suits/fits you.

Podemos encargarlo/ajustarlo.
We can order it/do alterations.

3) Buying presents and souvenirs

I'm looking for a present to take back.
Busco un regalo para llevar a casa.

It's for a little four-year-old girl.
Es para una niñita de cuatro años.

I'd like something easy to transport.
Quisiera algo fácil de transportar.

Does it keep well?
¿Se conserva bien?

It's a present; can you gift-wrap it for me?
Es para regalar; ¿podría envolvérmelo?

4) Going to the bank

Are banks open on Saturdays?
¿Los bancos abren los sábados?

I'm looking for an ATM.
Estoy buscando un cajero automático.

Where can I change money?
¿Dónde puedo cambiar dinero?

I'd like to change $80.
Quisiera cambiar ochenta dólares.

What commission do you charge?
¿Cuánto es la comisión?

Can I have $300 in cash?
¿Podría darme trescientos dólares en efectivo?

I'd like to transfer some money.
Quisiera hacer un giro.

I'm waiting for a money order.
Estoy esperando una orden de pago.

The ATM has swallowed my card.
El cajero automático se tragó mi tarjeta.

I'd like to report the loss of my credit cards.
Quisiera informar el extravío de mis tarjetas de crédito.

5) Going to the post office

Is there a mailbox near here?
¿Hay un buzón cerca de aquí?

Where can I find a post office?
¿Dónde puedo encontrar una oficina de correos?

Is the post office open on Saturdays?
¿El correo está abierto los sábados?

What time does the post office close?
¿A qué hora cierra el correo?

I'd like five stamps for the United States.
Quisiera cinco estampillas para Estados Unidos.

I'd like to send this letter/postcard/ package to New York.
Quisiera enviar esta carta/postal/ este paquete a Nueva York.

I'd like to send it by registered mail.
Quisiera enviarla certificada.

How much is a stamp for Spain?
¿Cuánto cuesta una estampilla para España?

How long will it take to get there?
¿Cuánto tiempo tarda en llegar?

Where can I buy envelopes?
¿Dónde puedo comprar sobres?

Is there any mail for me?
¿Hay correo para mí?

Did I receive any mail?
¿Llegó algo para mí en el correo?

V. Expressions of time

1) The date

Note that in Spanish, months and days are masculine and do not have a capital letter. Cardinal numbers (e.g. *dos*, *tres*, etc.) are used for the dates of the month except the first.

What's today's date? ¿Qué fecha es hoy?	**What day is it today?** ¿Qué día es hoy?
It's Tuesday, May first. Es martes primero de mayo.	**It's November second/third, 2005.** Es dos/tres de noviembre de 2005.
Today is September fifteenth. Hoy es quince de septiembre.	**I was born in 1962/1985.** Nací en 1962/1985.
I wrote to you on March twenty-second. Le escribí el veintidós de marzo.	**This store is open on Sunday mornings.** Esta tienda abre los domingos en la mañana.

I've been there before, several years ago. I think it was in 1996.
Estuve ahí hace unos años. Creo que fue en 1996.

I spent a month in Spain a few years ago.
Pasé un mes en España hace algunos años.

I came last year at the same time/in 2002.
Estuve aquí el año pasado, en la misma época/en 2002.

Understanding:

Fue construido a mediados del siglo XVII.
It was built in the middle of the 17th century.

Sale cada dos semanas/dos veces por mes.
It comes out once every two weeks/twice a month.

La gente sale sobre todo el fin de semana, pero muy poco entre semana.
People go out mainly on the weekend, but very rarely during the week.

¿Hasta cuándo se queda?
How long are you staying?

¿Se va dentro de dos días?
Are you leaving in two days?

Tómelo tres veces por día/hora.
Take it three times a day/an hour.

2) The time

The 24-hour clock is commonly used in Spanish (e.g. 2:35 p.m. = 14h35 = *tres menos veincitinco* or *catorce treinta y cinco*). In Mexico it is commonly said: *veinticinco para las tres* or *dos y treinta y cinco*.

I'm on time/early/late.
Estoy a tiempo/adelantado/atrasado.

It's very early/late.
Es muy temprano/tarde.

Excuse me, do you have the time, please?
Disculpe, ¿me dice la hora, por favor?

What time is it?
¿Qué hora es?

It's three o'clock exactly.
Son las tres en punto.

It's almost one o'clock.
Es casi la una.

It's ten after one/ten to one.
Es la una y diez/una menos diez, (*Méx*) diez para la una.

It's a quarter after one/to one.
Es la una y cuarto/una menos cuarto, (*Méx*) cuarto para la una.

It's one-thirty.
Es la una y media.

It's noon/midnight.
Son las doce del mediodía/de la noche.

It's eleven-forty.
Son las once cuarenta.

It's twenty after twelve.
Son las doce y veinte.

I arrived around two o'clock.
Llegué alrededor de las dos en punto.

It's two (o'clock) in the afternoon.
Son las dos de la tarde.

I have an appointment at 8 a.m./ 8 p.m.
Tengo una cita a las ocho de la mañana/a ocho de la noche.

It was eight (o'clock) in the morning/ in the evening.
Eran las ocho de la mañana/de la noche.

Are you free in the morning? Does 10:30 suit you?
¿Está libre en la mañana? ¿Le viene bien a las diez y media?

I've been waiting for two hours/ since 3 p.m.
Hace dos horas que estoy esperando./ Estoy esperando desde las tres de la tarde.

I waited for twenty minutes.
Esperé veinte minutos.

The train was fifteen minutes late.
El tren llegó quince minutos tarde.

I got home an hour ago.
Volví a casa hace una hora.

Do you want to meet in half an hour?
¿Nos encontramos dentro de media hora?

I'll be back in a quarter of an hour.
Vuelvo dentro de quince minutos.

It lasts for around three quarters of an hour/an hour and a half.
Dura alrededor de tres cuartos de hora/de una hora y media.

There's a three-hour time difference between ... and ...
Hay tres horas de diferencia entre ... y ...

I don't have time to take a nap in the afternoon.
No tengo tiempo de dormir la siesta.

I'm in a hurry, come on, hurry up!
Estoy apurado, vamos, ¡apúrese!

VI. Using the telephone

When giving their telephone numbers, Spanish-speakers say the first three numbers together and the rest, two by two: 409 37 58: cuatrocientos nueve, treinta y siete, cincuenta y ocho. In large cities (due to the many digits in phone numbers), Mexicans say the telephone numbers two by two. When it comes to cellphones, which start with 044, people usually say: *cero cuarenta y cuatro*, and after that, the numbers are said two by two.

1) Calling from a pay phone

Where can I buy a phone card?
¿Dónde puedo comprar una tarjeta de teléfono/telefónica?

Do you know if there's a card-/coin-operated pay phone near here?
¿Sabe si hay un teléfono público de tarjeta/monedas por aquí?

Could you give me change of ... to make a phone call?
¿Podría darme cambio de ...? Es para hacer una llamada.

I'd like to make a collect call.
Quisiera hacer una llamada por cobrar.

2) Asking for information from the operator or switchboard

Could you put me through to information, please?
¿Podría comunicarme con información, por favor?

I'm trying to get a number in Monterrey.
Estoy intentando conseguir un número en Monterrey.

Could you give me the number for ..., please?
¿Podría darme el número de ..., por favor?

What's the country code for Chile?
¿Cuál es el código de Chile?

How do I get an outside line?
¿Cómo hago una llamada al exterior?

3) Answering the telephone

When the phone is ringing:

I'll get it!
¡Yo contesto!

Can you get it, please?
¿Puedes contestar, por favor?

When you pick up the phone:

Hello?
¿Bueno?

Hello, Helen Smith speaking
Hola, habla Helen Smith.

4) Confirming you are the person to whom the caller wishes to speak

Yes, it's me.
Sí, soy yo.

This is he/she.
Es él/ella mismo(a).

How can I help you?
¿En qué puedo servirle?

What can I do for you?
¿Qué puedo hacer por usted?

5) Asking to speak to someone

Hi María. This is Sharon here. Is Pedro there?
Buenos días María. Habla Sharon. ¿Está Pedro por ahí?

Can/could I speak to Esteban, please? It's David.
¿Puedo/podría hablar con Esteban, por favor? De parte de David.

To which the other person may reply

Un momento, por favor. Voy a buscarlo.
Just a moment, please. I'll get him for you.

No corte, se lo paso.
Hold on, I'll just hand you over to him.

Lo siento, pero no está aquí en este momento.
I'm sorry but he's not in right now.

Ha salido. Estará de vuelta en media hora.
He's gone out. He'll be back in half an hour.

6) Asking to speak to someone in a company or institution

Hello, I'd like to speak to Mr. Flores, this is Tim Clark.
Hola, quisiera hablar con el señor Flores, de parte de Tim Clark.

Could you put me through to the sales manager, please?
¿Podría comunicarme con el gerente de ventas, por favor?

Could you put me through to extension 321, please?
¿Podría comunicarme a la extensión trescientos veintiuno.

Phrases used by a receptionist or secretary taking a call

Mudanzas García, buen día/buenas tardes.
Good morning/afternoon, Mudanzas García.

¿De parte de quién?
Who's calling?/Who should I say is calling?

No corte, ya le paso.   Da ocupado.
One moment, I'll put you through.   **The line's busy.**

No contestan.   Le diré que llamó.
There's no answer.   **I'll tell him you called.**

Está en otra llamada, ¿quiere esperar?   Lo siento, está en reunión/
He's on another call, would you like   de vacaciones.
  to hold?   **I'm sorry, he's in a meeting/**
                                           on vacation.

¿Quiere que le dé algún mensaje?   ¿Quiere dejarle un mensaje?
Would you like me to give him a   **Would you like to leave a message?**
  message?

7) Leaving a message for someone

Just tell him I called, thanks. I'll try again later.
Sólo dígale que llamé, gracias. Volveré a intentarlo más tarde.

Could you tell her that I called? Thank you.
¿Podría decirle que llamé? Gracias.

Could you tell him I'll call back later? Do you know when I'll be able to
  reach him/when he'll be back?
¿Podría decirle que volveré a llamar más tarde? ¿Sabe cuándo puedo
  encontrarlo/cuándo estará de vuelta?

Could you ask her to call me back today? She can reach me at ...
¿Podría pedirle que me llame hoy? Me encuentra en el ...

Do you have a pen and paper?   **My name is ... and my phone**
¿Tiene papel y lápiz?   **number is ...**
                                         Mi nombre es ... y mi número es ...

8) Stating the reason for one's call

Hi Jorge, it's James. I just wanted to know if you had any plans for this
  evening.
Hola Jorge, habla James. Sólo quería saber si tenías planes para esta noche.

Hello, Lucía? It's me, Peter. Are you free to go to the movies on Saturday?
Hola, ¿Lucía? Soy yo, Peter. ¿Estás libre para ir al cine el sábado?

Hello, is this Mr. Tapia? ... Hi. This is Frank Simpson. I'm calling about the ad in ...
Hola, ¿es la casa del señor Tapia? ... Buen día. Me llamo Frank Simpson. Lo llamo por el aviso publicado en ...

I'm calling to inform you that I still haven't received my itemized phone bill.
Lo llamo para informarle que todavía no he recibido la factura de teléfono detallada.

I'm just calling to let you know I'll be a bit late.
Lo llamo para avisarle que voy a llegar un poquito atrasado.

I'd like to make an appointment for next Monday.
Quisiera hacer una cita para el próximo lunes.

9) Understanding recorded messages

● *On someone's answering machine:*

Hola. Usted se ha comunicado con Rafael y Gracia. No estamos en casa en este momento, pero puede dejar un mensaje y lo llamaremos en cuanto volvamos.
Hello, you've reached Rafael and Gracia. We're not available right now, but please leave us a message and we'll return your call as soon as we can.

Por favor, deje su mensaje después de la señal.
Please leave a message after the tone.

● *When you are asked to follow instructions:*

Apriete la tecla numeral/asterisco.
Press the hash/star key.

● *If you are put through to an answering machine, the usual recorded message while waiting is:*

Por favor espere mientras conectamos su llamada.
Please hold while we connect your call.

● *If you have to leave a message, you will hear the following standard set of sentences:*

Usted se ha comunicado con ... No podemos responder a su llamado. Por favor, deje su nombre y número de teléfono después de la señal y lo llamaremos lo antes posible. Gracias.
You've reached... We're unable to take your call right now. Please leave your name and number after the beep and we'll get back to you as soon as we can. Thank you.

● *If you have dialed a number that doesn't exist, you will hear:*

El número que usted marcó no existe.
The number you have dialed has not been recognized.

10) Leaving a message on an answering machine

Hi, it's Kate. I see you're not at home. Oh well … I'll call back later. Bye!
Hola, habla Kate. Por lo visto no estás en casa. Bueno … volveré a llamar más tarde. Bye.

Hello, it's me again. It's just to tell you there are some traffic delays, but I see you've already left. Too bad.
Hola, soy yo otra vez. Sólo quería decirte que hay varios embotellamientos en el camino. Pero por lo visto ya has salido. Qué pena.

Hello, it's David McLean here. Can you contact me on my cell phone whenever you get this message? The number's 07712 745 792. Thank you.
Buen día, habla David McLean. ¿Podría por favor llamarme al celular cuando reciba este mensaje? Mi número es cero setenta y siete, doce, setenta y cuatro, cincuenta y siete, noventa y dos. Gracias.

Hello, this is Kim Thomas from Double Page bookstore. I'm calling to tell you that the book you ordered has arrived.
Buen día, habla Kim Thomas de la librería Double Page. Llamo para decirle que el libro que encargó ya ha llegado.

11) Ending the conversation

Thank you, goodbye.
Gracias, adiós.

Thanks a lot. Bye.
Gracias. Bye.

Thanks for your help, bye.
Gracias por tu ayuda, bye.

Thank you for calling.
Gracias por llamar.

Sorry, but I've got to hang up. My mom needs the phone. Can I call you back later?
Disculpa, pero tengo que cortar. Mi madre precisa el teléfono. ¿Te puedo llamar más tarde?

I've got to go.
Tengo que cortar.

We'll talk soon, OK?
Nos hablamos pronto, ¿ok?

We'll talk again, OK?
Nos hablamos, ¿ok?

12) Cell phones

Do you have a cellphone number?
¿Tiene un número de celular?

I've run out of minutes.
Se me terminaron los minutos.

The signal's very bad.
La señal es muy mala.

I can't get any reception here.
No capto llamadas aquí.

Do you know where I can get a new phone card for my cellphone?
¿Sabe dónde puedo comprar una tarjeta para mi celular?

Can I plug my cellphone in here to recharge it? The battery's dead.
¿Puedo conectar mi celular aquí para recargarlo? Estoy sin batería.

Is there an outlet so that I can recharge my cellphone?
¿Hay un enchufe por aquí, para recargar mi celular?

Did you get my text message?   I forgot my charger.
¿Ha recibido mi mensaje?   Me olvidé del cargador.

13) Problems

I'm sorry, I must have dialed the wrong number.
Perdón, debo haber marcado el número equivocado.

Sorry to have bothered you.
Siento haberlo molestado.

You've dialed the wrong number.   You've got the wrong number.
Marcó un número equivocado.   Se equivocó de número.

Could you say that again more slowly?
¿Podría repetir lo que dijo, pero más despacio?

I can barely hear you. Could you speak up?
Lo oigo muy mal. ¿Podría hablar más fuerte?

I'm sorry, I didn't really understand. Could you spell it?
Discúlpeme, no entendí bien. ¿Cómo se deletrea?

Hello, can you hear me?   We got cut off.
Hola, ¿me oye?   Se cortó.

Hold on, we're going to be cut off, I need to put some more change in.
Espera, se va a cortar, tengo que poner más monedas.

I can't reach him.   I keep getting a busy signal.
No logro comunicarme.   Da siempre ocupado.

I don't have many minutes left on my card.
No me quedan muchos minutos en la tarjeta.

Spanish–English

Aa

a *prep*

> **a** combines with the article **el** to form the contraction **al** (e.g. **al centro** to the centre)

(**a**) *(dirección)* to; **ir a Colombia** to go to Colombia; **llegar a Valencia** to arrive in Valencia; **subir al tren** to get on the train; **vete a casa** go home

(**b**) *(lugar)* at, on; **a la derecha** on the right; **a la entrada** at the entrance; **a lo lejos** in the distance; **a mi lado** at *o* by my side, next to me; **al sol** in the sun; **a la mesa** at (the) table

(**c**) *(tiempo)* at; **a las doce** at twelve o'clock; **a los sesenta años** at the age of sixty; **a los tres meses/la media hora** three months/half an hour later; **al principio** at first

(**d**) *(distancia)* away; **a 100 km de aquí** 100 km from here

(**e**) *(manera)* **a la inglesa** (in the) English fashion *o* manner *o* style; **escrito a máquina** typed, type-written; **a mano** by hand

(**f**) *(proporción)* **a 90 km por hora** at 90 km an hour; **a dos euros el kilo** two euros a kilo; **tres veces a la semana** three times a week

(**g**) *Dep* **ganar cuatro a dos** to win four (to) two

(**h**) *(complemento indirecto)* to; *(procedencia)* from; **díselo a Javier** tell Javier; **te lo di a ti** I gave it to you; **saludé a tu tía** I said hello to your aunt

(**i**) *Fam* **ir a por algn/algo** to go and fetch sb/sth

(**j**) *(verbo + a + infinitivo)* to; **aprender a nadar** to learn (how) to swim; **fueron a ayudarle** they went to help him

(**k**) *(nombre + a + infinitivo)* **distancia a recorrer** distance to be covered

(**l**) **a no ser por …** if it were not for …; **a no ser que** unless; **a ver** let's see; **¡a comer!** lunch/dinner, *etc* is ready!

abad *nm* abbot

abadía *nf* abbey

abajeño, -a *nm,f Am* lowlander

abajo 1 *adv* (**a**) *(en una casa)* downstairs; **el piso de a.** the downstairs flat (**b**) *(dirección)* down, downwards; **ahí/aquí a.** down there/here; **la parte de a.** the bottom (part); **más a.** further down; **hacia a.** down, downwards; **calle a.** down the street; **echar algo a.** to knock sth down; **venirse a.** *(edificio)* to fall down; *Fig (proyecto)* to fall through

2 *interj* **¡a. la censura!** down with censorship!

abalear *vt Andes, CAm, Ven* to shoot at

abandonado, -a *adj* (**a**) abandoned; **tiene a su familia muy abandonada** he takes absolutely no interest in his family (**b**) *(desaseado)* untidy, unkempt

abandonar 1 *vt* (**a**) *(lugar)* to leave, to quit; *(persona, cosa)* to abandon; *(proyecto, plan)* to give up (**b**) *Dep (carrera)* to drop out of **2 abandonarse** *vpr* to let oneself go

abandono *nm* (**a**) *(acción)* abandoning, desertion (**b**) *(de proyecto, idea)* giving up (**c**) *(descuido)* neglect

abanicarse *vpr* to fan oneself

abanico *nm* (**a**) fan (**b**) *(gama)* range; **un amplio a. de posibilidades** a wide range of possibilities

abarcar [44] *vt (incluir)* to cover

abarrotado, -a *adj* packed, crammed (**de** with)

abarrotería *nf CAm, Méx* grocer's (shop), grocery store

abarrotero, -a *nm,f CAm, Méx* grocer

abarrotes *nmpl Andes, CAm, Méx* (**a**) *(mercancías)* groceries (**b**) **tienda de a.** grocer's (shop), grocery store

abastecer [33] **1** *vt* to supply **2 abastecerse** *vpr* **abastecerse de** to be supplied with

abatible *adj* folding, collapsible; **asiento a.** reclining seat

abatido, -a *adj* downcast

abatir 1 *vt* (**a**) *(derribar)* to knock down, to pull down (**b**) *(matar)* to kill; **a. a tiros** to shoot down (**c**) *(desanimar)* to depress, to dishearten **2 abatirse** *vpr (desanimarse)* to lose heart, to become depressed

abdicar [44] *vt & vi* to abdicate

abdomen *nm* abdomen

abdominales *nmpl* sit-ups

abecedario *nm* alphabet

abeja *nf* bee; **a. reina** queen bee

abejorro *nm* bumblebee

aberración *nf* aberration

abertura *nf (hueco)* opening, gap; *(grieta)* crack, slit

abeto *nm Bot* fir (tree); **a. rojo** spruce

abierto, -a *adj* (**a**) open; *(grifo)* (turned) on; **a. de par en par** wide open (**b**) *(persona)* open-minded

abismo *nm* abyss; *Fig* **al borde del a.** on the brink of ruin; *Fig* **entre ellos media un a.** they are worlds apart

ablandar 1 *vt* to soften **2 ablandarse** *vpr* (**a**) to soften, to go soft (**b**) *Fig (persona)* to mellow

abofetear *vt* to slap

abogado, -a *nm,f Br* lawyer, *US* attorney; *(en tribunal supremo)* lawyer, *Br* barrister; **a. de oficio** legal aid lawyer; **a. defensor** counsel for the defence; **a. del diablo** devil's advocate; **a. laboralista** union lawyer

abolición *nf* abolition

abolir *vt defect* to abolish

abollar *vt* to dent

abonado, -a 1 *nm,f (a revista)* subscriber; *(a teléfono, de gas)* customer **2** *adj Fin (pagado)* paid; **a. en cuenta** credited

abonar 1 *vt* (**a**) *Agr* to fertilize (**b**)

(pagar) to pay (for) (**c**) *(subscribir)* to subscribe **2 abonarse** *vpr* to subscribe (**a** to)

abonero, -a *nm,f Méx* hawker, street trader

abono *nm* (**a**) *Agr (producto)* fertilizer; *(estiércol)* manure (**b**) *(pago)* payment (**c**) *(a revista etc)* subscription; *(billete)* season ticket (**d**) *Méx (plazo)* instalment; **pagar en abonos** to pay by instalments

abordar *vt (persona)* to approach; *(barco)* to board; **a. un asunto** to tackle a subject

aborrecer [33] *vt* to detest, to loathe

abortar 1 *vi (involuntariamente)* to miscarry, to have a miscarriage; *(intencionadamente)* to abort, to have an abortion **2** *vt* to abort

aborto *nm* miscarriage; *(provocado)* abortion

abrasador, -a *adj* scorching

abrasar 1 *vt & vi* to scorch **2 abrasarse** *vpr* to burn

abrazadera *nf* clamp

abrazar [40] **1** *vt* to embrace, to hug; *Fig (doctrina)* to embrace **2 abrazarse** *vpr* **abrazarse a algn** to embrace sb; **se abrazaron** they embraced each other

abrazo *nm* embrace, hug; **un a., abrazos** *(en carta)* best wishes

abrebotellas *nm inv* bottle opener

abrecartas *nm inv* letter-opener, paperknife

abrelatas *nm inv* can opener, *Br* tin-opener

abreviar [43] **1** *vt* to shorten; *(texto)* to abridge; *(palabra)* to abbreviate **2** *vi* to be quick o brief; **para a.** to cut a long story short

abreviatura *nf* abbreviation

abridor *nm (de latas, botellas)* (can-)opener, *Br* (tin-)opener

abrigar [42] *vt* (**a**) to keep warm; **esta chaqueta abriga mucho** this cardigan is very warm (**b**) *(proteger)* to protect, to shelter (**c**) *(esperanza)* to cherish; *(duda)* to have, to harbour

abrigo *nm* (**a**) *(prenda)* coat, overcoat;

ropa de a. warm clothes (b) al a. de protected o sheltered from

abril *nm* April

abrillantador *nm* polish

abrillantar *vt* to polish

abrir¹ *nm* en un a. y cerrar de ojos in the twinkling of an eye

abrir² (*pp* abierto) 1 *vi* to open 2 *vt* (a) to open; *(cremallera)* to undo (b) *(gas, grifo)* to turn on (c) *Jur* a. (un) expediente to start proceedings 3 abrirse *vpr* (a) to open; *Fig* abrirse paso to make one's way (b) *Fam* ¡me abro! I'm off!

abrochar *vt*, **abrocharse** *vpr* (*botones*) to do up; *(camisa)* to button (up); *(cinturón)* to fasten; *(zapatos)* to tie up; *(cremallera)* to do up

abrumador, -a *adj* overwhelming

abrumar *vt* to overwhelm, to crush; tantos problemas me abruman all these problems are getting on top of me

abrupto, -a *adj* (a) *(terreno)* steep, abrupt (b) *Fig* abrupt, sudden

ábside *nm Arquit* apse

absolución *nf* (a) *Rel* absolution (b) *Jur* acquittal

absolutamente *adv* absolutely, completely; a. nada nothing at all

absoluto, -a *adj* absolute; en a. not at all, by no means

absolver [4] (*pp* absuelto) *vt* (a) *Rel* to absolve (b) *Jur* to acquit

absorbente *adj* (a) *(papel)* absorbent (b) *Fig* absorbing, engrossing

absorber *vt* to absorb

absorto, -a *adj* absorbed, engrossed (en in)

abstemio, -a 1 *adj* teetotal, abstemious 2 *nm,f* teetotaller

abstención *nf* abstention

abstenerse [24] *vpr* to abstain (de from); *(privarse)* to refrain (de from)

abstinencia *nf* abstinence; síndrome de a. withdrawal symptoms

abstracto, -a *adj* abstract

absuelto, -a *pp de* absolver

absurdo, -a 1 *adj* absurd 2 *nm* absurdity, absurd thing

abuelo *nm* (a) grandfather; *Fam* grandad, grandpa; *Fig* old man (b) abuelos grandparents

abultado, -a *adj* bulky, big

abultar 1 *vi* to be bulky; abulta mucho it takes up a lot of space 2 *vt* to exaggerate

abundancia *nf* abundance, plenty; *Fig* nadar en la a. to be rolling in money

abundante *adj* abundant, plentiful

aburrido, -a *adj* (a) ser a. to be boring (b) estar a. to be bored; estar a. de *(harto)* to be tired of

aburrimiento *nm* boredom; ¡qué a.! how boring!, what a bore!

aburrir 1 *vt* to bore 2 aburrirse *vpr* to get bored; aburrirse como una ostra to be bored stiff

abusado, -a *adj Méx Fam* smart, sharp

abusar *vi* (a) *(propasarse)* to go too far (b) a. de *(situación, persona)* to take (unfair) advantage of; *(poder, amabilidad)* to abuse; a. de la bebida/del tabaco to drink/smoke too much o to excess; *Jur* a. de un niño/una mujer to abuse a child/woman

abusivo, -a *adj (precio)* exorbitant

abuso *nm* abuse

a. C. (*abr* antes de Cristo) BC

a/c (*abr* a cuenta) on account

acá *adv* (a) *(lugar)* here, over here; más a. nearer; ¡ven a.! come here! (b) de entonces a. since then

acabar 1 *vt* to finish (off); *(completar)* to complete 2 *vi* (a) to finish, to end; a. bien to have a happy ending; a. con algo *(terminarlo)* to finish sth; *(romperlo)* to break sth (b) a. de ... to have just ...; acaba de entrar he has just come in; no acaba de convencerme I'm not quite convinced (c) acabaron casándose o por casarse they ended up getting married 3 acabarse *vpr* to finish, to come to an end; se nos acabó la gasolina we ran out of *Br* petrol o *US* gas; *Fam* ¡se acabó! that's that!

academia *nf* academy; **a. de idiomas** language school

académico, -a *adj & nm,f* academic

acalorado, -a *adj* (**a**) hot (**b**) *Fig (excitado)* worked up, excited; *(debate etc)* heated, angry

acalorarse *vpr* (**a**) to get warm *o* hot (**b**) *Fig* to get excited *o* worked up

acampada *nf* camping; **ir de a.** to go camping; **zona de a.** camp site, *US* campground

acampanado, -a *adj* bell-shaped; *(prendas)* flared

acampar *vi* to camp

acantilado *nm* cliff

acaparar *vt* (**a**) *(productos)* to hoard; *(el mercado)* to corner (**b**) *Fig* to monopolize

acápite *nm* (**a**) *Am (párrafo)* paragraph (**b**) *CAm (título)* title

acariciar [43] *vt* to caress; *(pelo, animal)* to stroke; *(esperanza)* to cherish

acaso *adv* perhaps, maybe; **¿a. no le lo dije?** did I not tell you, by any chance?; **por si a.** just in case; **si a. viene …** if he should come …

acatarrarse *vpr* to catch a cold

acaudalado, -a *adj* rich, wealthy

acceder *vi* **a. a** *(consentir)* to accede to, to consent to; *(tener acceso)* to gain admittance to; *Informát* to access

accesible *adj* accessible; *(persona)* approachable

acceso *nm* (**a**) *(entrada)* access, entry; *Informát* **a. al azar, a. directo** random access; *Univ* **prueba de a.** entrance examination; **a. a Internet** Internet access (**b**) *(carretera)* approach, access (**c**) *Med & Fig* fit

accesorio, -a *adj & nm* accessory

accidentado, -a **1** *adj (terreno)* uneven, hilly; *(viaje, vida)* eventful **2** *nm,f* casualty, accident victim

accidental *adj* accidental; **un encuentro a.** a chance meeting

accidente *nm* (**a**) accident; **por a.** by chance; **a. laboral** industrial accident (**b**) *Geog* **accidentes geográficos** geographical features

acción *nf* (**a**) action; *(acto)* act; **poner en a.** to put into action; **ponerse en a.** to go into action; **campo de a.** field of action; **película de a.** adventure movie *o Br* film (**b**) *Fin* share

acechar *vt* to lie in wait for; **un grave peligro nos acecha** great danger awaits us

aceite *nm* oil; **a. de girasol/maíz/ oliva** sunflower/corn/olive oil

aceitoso, -a *adj* oily

aceituna *nf* olive; **a. rellena** stuffed olive

acelerador *nm Aut* accelerator

acelerar *vt* to accelerate

acelga *nf* chard

acento *nm* (**a**) accent; *(de palabra)* stress (**b**) *(énfasis)* stress, emphasis

acentuar [30] **1** *vt* (**a**) to stress (**b**) *Fig* to emphasize, to stress **2 acentuarse** *vpr Fig* to become more pronounced *o* noticeable

aceptable *adj* acceptable

aceptación *nf* (**a**) acceptance (**b**) **tener poca a.** to have little success, not to be popular

aceptar *vt* to accept

acequia *nf* irrigation ditch *o* channel

acera *nf Br* pavement, *US* sidewalk; *Fam Pey* **ser de la a. de enfrente** to be gay *o* queer

acerca *adv* **a. de** about

acercamiento *nm* bringing together, coming together; *Pol* rapprochement

acercar [44] **1** *vt* to bring near *o* nearer, to bring (over); *Fig* to bring together; **¿te acerco a casa?** can I give you a *Br* lift *o US* ride home? **2 acercarse** *vpr* (**a**) **acercarse (a)** to approach (**b**) *(ir)* to go; *(venir)* to come

acero *nm* steel; **a. inoxidable** stainless steel

acertado, -a *adj* (**a**) *(solución)* right, correct; *(decisión)* wise (**b**) **no estuviste muy a. al decir eso** it wasn't very wise of you to say that

acertar [1] **1** *vt (pregunta)* to get right; *(adivinar)* to guess correctly; **a. las**

quinielas to win the pools **2** *vi* to be right; **acertó con la calle que buscaba** she found the street she was looking for

acertijo *nm* riddle

achinado, -a *adj* (**a**) *(ojos)* slanting (**b**) *RP (aindiado)* Indian-looking

acholado, -a *adj Bol, Chile, Perú Pey (mestizo) (físicamente)* Indian-looking; *(culturalmente)* = who has adopted Indian ways

ácido, -a 1 *adj (sabor)* sharp, tart; *Quím* acidic; *Fig (tono)* harsh **2** *nm Quím* acid

acierto *nm (buena decisión)* good choice o idea; **con gran a.** very wisely

aclamar *vt* to acclaim

aclarar 1 *vt* (**a**) *(explicar)* to clarify, to explain; *(color)* to lighten, to make lighter (**b**) *Esp (enjuagar)* to rinse **2** *v impers Met* to clear (up) **3 aclararse** *vpr* (**a**) *(decidirse)* to make up one's mind; *(entender)* to understand (**b**) *Met* to clear (up)

aclimatación *nf Br* acclimatization, *US* acclimation

aclimatar 1 *vt Br* to acclimatize, *US* to acclimate (**a** to) **2 aclimatarse** *vpr Fig* **aclimatarse a algo** to get used to sth

acogedor, -a *adj* cosy, warm

acoger [53] **1** *vt* (**a**) *(recibir)* to receive; *(a invitado)* to welcome (**b**) *(persona desvalida)* to take in **2 acogerse** *vpr Fig* **acogerse a** to take refuge in; *(amnistía)* to avail oneself of; **acogerse a la ley** to have recourse to the law

acogida *nf* reception, welcome

acomodado, -a *adj* well-off, well-to-do

acomodador, -a *nm,f* usher, *f* usherette

acomodar 1 *vt* (**a**) *(alojar)* to lodge, to accommodate (**b**) *(en cine etc)* to find a place for **2 acomodarse** *vpr* (**a**) *(adaptarse)* to adapt

acompañamiento *nm Culin, Mús* accompaniment

acompañante 1 *nmf* companion **2** *adj* accompanying

acompañar *vt* (**a**) to accompany; **le acompañó hasta la puerta** she saw him to the door; **me acompañó al médico** he came with me to see the doctor; **¿te acompaño a casa?** can I walk you home?; *Fml* **le acompaño en el sentimiento** my condolences (**b**) *(adjuntar)* to enclose

acomplejado, -a *adj* **estar a.** to have a complex (**por** about)

acondicionado, -a *adj* **aire a.** air conditioning

acondicionador *nm* conditioner

acondicionar *vt* to prepare, to set up; *(mejorar)* to improve; *(cabello)* to condition

aconsejable *adj* advisable

aconsejar *vt* to advise

acontecer [33] *v impers* to happen, to take place

acontecimiento *nm* event

acoplar 1 *vt* (**a**) to fit (together), to join (**b**) *Téc* to couple, to connect **2 acoplarse** *vpr (nave espacial)* to dock

acordado, -a *adj* agreed; **según lo a.** as agreed

acordar [2] **1** *vt* to agree; *(decidir)* to decide **2 acordarse** *vpr* to remember; **no me acuerdo (de Silvia)** I can't remember (Silvia)

acorde 1 *adj* in agreement **2** *nm Mús* chord

acordeón *nm* (**a**) *(instrument)* accordion (**b**) *Col, Méx Fam (en examen)* crib

acortar *vt* to shorten; **a. distancias** to cut down the distance

acosar *vt* to harass; *Fig* **a. a algn a preguntas** to bombard sb with questions

acoso *nm* harassment; **a. sexual** sexual harassment

acostar [2] **1** *vt* to put to bed **2 acostarse** *vpr* (**a**) to go to bed (**b**) *Fam* **acostarse con algn** to sleep with sb, to go to bed with sb

acostumbrar 1 *vi* **a. a** *(soler)* to be in the habit of **2** *vt* **a. a algn a algo** *(habituar)* to get sb used to sth

3 acostumbrarse *vpr (habituarse)* **acostumbrarse a algo** to get used to sth

acotamiento *nm Méx (arcén) Br* hard shoulder, *US* shoulder

acreditado *adj* (**a**) *(médico, abogado)* distinguished; *(marca)* reputable (**b**) *(embajador, representante)* accredited

acreditar *vt* (**a**) to be a credit to (**b**) *(probar)* to prove (**c**) *(embajador)* to accredit (**d**) *Fin* to credit

acrílico, -a *adj* acrylic

acriollarse *vpr Am* to adopt local ways

acrobacia *nf* acrobatics *sing*

acróbata *nmf* acrobat

acta *nf* (**a**) *(de reunión)* minutes, record (**b**) *(certificado)* certificate, official document; **a. notarial** affidavit; **A. Única (Europea)** Single European Act

Takes the masculine articles **el** and **un**

actitud *nf* attitude

activar *vt* (**a**) to activate (**b**) *(avivar)* to liven up

actividad *nf* activity

activo, -a 1 *adj* active; **en a.** on active service **2** *nm Fin* assets

acto *nm* (**a**) act, action; **a. sexual** sexual intercourse; **en el a.** at once; **a. seguido** immediately afterwards; *Mil* **en a. de servicio** in action; **hacer a. de presencia** to put in an appearance (**b**) *(ceremonia)* ceremony (**c**) *Teatro* act

actor *nm* actor

actriz *nf* actress

actuación *nf* (**a**) performance (**b**) *(intervención)* intervention, action

actual *adj* current, present; *(al día)* up-to-date; **un tema muy a.** a very topical subject

actualidad *nf* (**a**) present time; **en la a.** at present; **estar de a.** to be fashionable; **temas de a.** topical subjects (**b**) *(hechos)* current affairs

actualizar [40] *vt* to update, to bring up to date; *Informát (software, hardware)* to upgrade

actualmente *adv (hoy en día)* nowadays, these days; *(ahora)* at the moment, at present

actuar [30] *vi* (**a**) to act; **a. como** *o* **de** to act as (**b**) *Cin, Teatro* to perform, to act

acuarela *nf* watercolour

Acuario *nm* Aquarium

acuático, -a *adj* aquatic; **esquí a.** water-skiing

acudir *vi (ir)* to go; *(venir)* to come, to arrive; **nadie acudió en su ayuda** nobody came to help him; **no sé dónde a.** I don't know where to turn

acueducto *nm* aqueduct

acuerdo *nm* agreement; **¡de a.!** all right!, O.K.!; **de a. con** in accordance with; **de común a.** by common consent; **estar de a. en algo** to agree on sth; **ponerse de a.** to agree; **a. marco** framework agreement

acumulación *nf* accumulation

acumular 1 *vt* to accumulate **2 acumularse** *vpr* (**a**) to accumulate, to build up (**b**) *(gente)* to crowd

acupuntura *nf* acupuncture

acusación *nf* (**a**) accusation (**b**) *Jur* charge

acusado, -a 1 *nm,f* accused, defendant **2** *adj (marcado)* marked, noticeable

acusar 1 *vt* (**a**) to accuse (**de** of); *Jur* to charge (**de** with) (**b**) *(golpe etc)* to feel; *Fig* **su cara acusaba el cansancio** his face showed his exhaustion (**c**) *Com* **a. recibo** to acknowledge receipt **2 acusarse** *vpr* (**a**) *(acentuarse)* to become more pronounced (**b**) *Fig (notarse)* to show

acústica *nf* acoustics *sing*

adaptación *nf* adaptation

adaptador *nm* adapter

adaptar 1 *vt* (**a**) to adapt (**b**) *(ajustar)* to adjust **2 adaptarse** *vpr* to adapt oneself (**a** to)

adecuado, -a *adj* appropriate, suitable

adecuar [47] *vt* to adapt

a. de J.C. *(abr* **antes de Jesucristo)** BC

adelantado, -a *adj* (**a**) advanced; *(desarrollado)* developed; *(precoz)* precocious (**b**) *(reloj)* fast (**c**) **pagar por a.** to pay in advance

adelantamiento *nm* overtaking; **hacer un a.** to overtake

adelantar 1 *vt* (**a**) to move *o* bring forward; *(reloj)* to put forward; *Fig* to advance (**b**) *Aut* to overtake (**c**) *(fecha)* to bring forward; *Fig* **a. (los) acontecimientos** to get ahead of oneself 2 *vi* (**a**) to advance (**b**) *(progresar)* to make progress (**c**) *(reloj)* to be fast 3 **adelantarse** *vpr* (**a**) *(ir delante)* to go ahead (**b**) *(reloj)* to gain, to be fast (**c**) **el verano se ha adelantado** we are having an early summer

adelante 1 *adv* forward; **más a.** *(lugar)* further on; *(tiempo)* later; **seguir a.** to keep going, to carry on; **llevar a. un plan** to carry out a plan 2 *interj* **¡a.!** come in!

adelanto *nm* (**a**) advance; *(progreso)* progress (**b**) **el reloj lleva diez minutos de a.** the watch is ten minutes fast (**c**) *(de dinero)* advance payment

adelgazar [40] *vi* to slim, to lose weight

además *adv* moreover, furthermore; **a., no lo he visto nunca** what's more, I've never seen him; **a. de él** besides him

adentro 1 *adv (dentro)* inside; **mar a.** out to sea; **tierra a.** inland 2 *nmpl* **decir algo para sus adentros** to say sth to oneself

adherente *adj* adhesive, sticky

adherir [5] 1 *vt* to stick on 2 **adherirse** *vpr* **adherirse a** to adhere to; *(partido)* to join

adhesión *nf* adhesion; *(a partido)* joining; *(a teoría)* adherence

adhesivo, -a *adj & nm* adhesive

adicción *nf* addiction; **crear a.** to be addictive

adición *nf* addition

adicional *adj* additional

adicto, -a 1 *nm,f* addict 2 *adj* addicted (**a** to)

adiós 1 *interj* goodbye; *Fam* bye-bye; *(al cruzarse)* hello 2 *nm* goodbye

adivinanza *nf* riddle, puzzle

adivinar *vt* to guess; **a. el pensamiento de algn** to read sb's mind

adivino, -a *nm,f* fortune-teller

adjetivo, -a 1 *nm* adjective 2 *adj* adjectival

adjuntar *vt* to enclose

administración *nf* (**a**) *(gobierno)* **la A.** *Br* the Government, *US* the Administration; *Pol* **a. central** central government; **a. pública** civil service (**b**) *(de empresa)* administration, management (**c**) *(oficina)* (branch) office

administrar 1 *vt* (**a**) to administer (**b**) *(dirigir)* to run, to manage 2 **administrarse** *vpr* to manage one's own money

administrativo, -a 1 *adj* administrative 2 *nm,f (funcionario)* official

admiración *nf* (**a**) admiration; **causar a.** to impress (**b**) *Ling Br* exclamation mark, *US* exclamation point

admirar 1 *vt* (**a**) to admire (**b**) *(sorprender)* to amaze, to astonish 2 **admirarse** *vpr* to be amazed, to be astonished

admisible *adj* admissible, acceptable

admitir *vt* (**a**) to admit, to let in (**b**) *(aceptar)* to accept; **no se admiten cheques** *(en letrero)* no cheques accepted (**c**) *(tolerar)* to allow (**d**) *(reconocer)* to admit, to acknowledge; **admito que mentí** I admit that I lied

admón. *(abr* **administración)** admin.

adobe *nm* adobe

adolescencia *nf* adolescence

adolescente *adj & nmf* adolescent

adonde *adv* where

adónde *adv interr* where (to)?

adopción *nf* adoption

adoptar *vt* to adopt

adoptivo, -a *adj (hijo)* adopted; *(padres)* adoptive; *Fig* **país a.** country of adoption

adoquín *nm* cobble, paving stone

adorable *adj* adorable

adoración *nf* adoration; **sentir a.**

por algn to worship sb

adorar *vt* (**a**) *Rel* to worship (**b**) *Fig* to adore

adornar *vt* to adorn, to decorate

adorno *nm* decoration, adornment; **de a.** decorative

adosado, -a *adj* adjacent; *(casa)* semidetached

adquirir [31] *vt* to acquire; *(comprar)* to purchase

adquisición *nf* acquisition; *(compra)* buy, purchase

adquisitivo, -a *adj* **poder a.** purchasing power

adrede *adv* deliberately, on purpose

aduana *nf* customs

aduanero, -a **1** *adj* customs **2** *nm,f* customs officer

adulterio *nm* adultery

adúltero, -a **1** *adj* adulterous **2** *nm,f* *(hombre)* adulterer; *(mujer)* adulteress

adulto, -a *adj & nm,f* adult

adverbio *nm* adverb

adversario, -a **1** *nm,f* adversary, opponent **2** *adj* opposing

adverso, -a *adj* adverse

advertencia *nf* warning

advertir [5] *vt* (**a**) to warn; *(informar)* to inform, to advise; *Fam* **te advierto que yo tampoco lo vi** mind you, I didn't see it either (**b**) *(notar)* to realize, to notice

aéreo, -a *adj* (**a**) aerial (**b**) *Av* air; **tráfico a.** air traffic; *Com* **por vía aérea** by air

aeróbic *nm* aerobics *sing*

aeromodelismo *nm* aeroplane modelling

aeromozo, -a *nm,f Am* air steward, *f* air hostess

aeronave *nf* airship

aeropuerto *nm* airport

aerosol *nm* aerosol

afán *nm* (**a**) *(esfuerzo)* effort (**b**) *(celo)* zeal

afanador, -a *nm,f* (**a**) *Méx (empleado)* (office) cleaner (**b**) *Méx, RP Fam (ladrón)* crook, thief

afección *nf* disease

afectado, -a *adj* affected

afectar *vt* **a. a** to affect; **le afectó mucho** she was deeply affected; **afecta a todos** it concerns all of us

afectivo *adj (emocional)* emotional; **tener problemas afectivos** to have emotional problems

afecto *nm* affection; **tomarle a. a algn** to become fond of sb

afectuoso, -a *adj* affectionate

afeitado *nm* shave

afeitar *vt*, **afeitarse** *vpr* to shave

afeminado, -a *adj* effeminate

afiche *nm Am* poster

afición *nf* (**a**) liking; **tiene a. por la música** he is fond of music (**b**) *Dep* **la a.** the fans

aficionado, -a **1** *nm,f* (**a**) enthusiast; **un a. a la música** a music lover (**b**) *(no profesional)* amateur **2** *adj* (**a**) keen, fond; **ser a. a algo** to be fond of sth (**b**) *(no profesional)* amateur

aficionarse *vpr* to become fond (**a** of), to take a liking (**a** to)

afilado, -a *adj* sharp

afilar *vt* to sharpen

afiliado, -a *nm,f* member

afiliarse [43] *vpr* to become a member

afín *adj (semejante)* kindred, similar; *(relacionado)* related

afinar *vt* (**a**) *(puntería)* to sharpen (**b**) *(instrumento)* to tune

afinidad *nf* affinity

afirmación *nf* affirmation; **afirmaciones** *(declaración)* statement

afirmar (**a**) *vt (aseverar)* to state, to declare (**b**) *(afianzar)* to strengthen, to reinforce

afirmativo, -a *adj* affirmative; **en caso a. ...** if the answer is yes ...

afligir [57] **1** *vt* to afflict **2** **afligirse** *vpr* to grieve, to be distressed

aflojar **1** *vt* to loosen

2 *vi (viento etc)* to weaken, to grow weak

3 **aflojarse** *vpr* to come o work loose; *(rueda)* to go down

afluencia *nf* inflow, influx; **gran a. de**

público great numbers of people

afluente *nm* tributary

afónico, -a *adj* **estar a.** to have lost one's voice

aforo *nm (capacidad)* seating capacity

afortunadamente *adv* fortunately, luckily

afortunado, -a *adj* fortunate; **las Islas Afortunadas** the Canaries

África *n* Africa

africano, -a *adj & nm,f* African

afrodisíaco, -a *adj & nm* aphrodisiac

afrutado, -a *adj* fruity

afuera 1 *adv* outside; **la parte de a.** the outside; **más a.** further out; **salir a.** to come *o* go out **2** *nfpl* **afueras** outskirts

agachar 1 *vt* to lower **2 agacharse** *vpr* to duck

agarrar 1 *vt* (**a**) to grasp, to seize; **agárralo fuerte** hold it tight (**b**) *Am (tomar)* to take; **a. un taxi** to take a taxi (**c**) *Fam (pillar)* to catch; **a. una borrachera** to get drunk *o* pissed **2 agarrarse** *vpr* to hold on; **agarraos bien** hold tight

agencia *nf* agency; *(sucursal)* branch; **a. de viajes** travel agency; **a. de seguros** insurance agency; **a. inmobiliaria** *Br* estate agent's, *US* real estate office

agenda *nf* diary

agente *nmf* agent; **a. de policía** *(hombre)* policeman; *(mujer)* policewoman; **a. de bolsa** stockbroker; **a. de seguros** insurance broker

ágil *adj* agile

agilidad *nf* agility

agitación *nf (intranquilidad)* restlessness; *(social, político)* unrest

agitado, -a *adj* agitated; *(persona)* anxious; *(mar)* rough; **una vida muy agitada** a very hectic life

agitar 1 *vt (botella)* to shake; *(multitud)* to agitate **2 agitarse** *vpr (persona)* to become agitated; *(mar)* to become rough

agnóstico, -a *adj & nm,f* agnostic

agobiado, -a *adj Fig* **a. de pro-**

blemas snowed under with problems; *Fig* **a. de trabajo** up to one's eyes in work

agobiar [43] **1** *vt* to overwhelm **2 agobiarse** *vpr (con problemas)* to be over-anxious; *(por el calor)* to suffocate

agosto *nm* August; *Fam* **hacer su a.** to make a packet

agotado, -a *adj* (**a**) *(cansado)* exhausted, worn out (**b**) *Com* sold out; *(existencias)* exhausted; *(libro)* out of print

agotador, -a *adj* exhausting

agotamiento *nm* exhaustion

agotar 1 *vt* (**a**) *(cansar)* to exhaust, to wear out (**b**) *(acabar)* to exhaust, to use up (completely) **2 agotarse** *vpr* (**a**) *(acabarse)* to run out, to be used up; *Com* to be sold out (**b**) *(persona)* to become exhausted *o* tired out

agradable *adj* pleasant

agradar *vi* to please; **no me agrada** I don't like it

agradecer [33] *vt* (**a**) *(dar las gracias)* to thank for; **les agradezco su atención** (I) thank you for your attention; **te lo agradezco mucho** thank you very much (**b**) *(estar agradecido)* to be grateful to; **te agradecería que vinieras** I'd be grateful if you'd come (**c**) *(uso impers)* **siempre se agradece un descanso** a rest is always welcome

agradecido, -a *adj* grateful; **le estoy muy a.** I am very grateful to you

agradecimiento *nm* gratitude

agredir *vt* defect to assault

agregado, -a 1 *adj Educ* **profesor a.** *(escuela)* secondary school teacher; *Univ* assistant teacher **2** *nm,f Pol* attaché

agregar [42] **1** *vt* (**a**) *(añadir)* to add (**b**) *(destinar)* to appoint **2 agregarse** *vpr* **agregarse a** to join

agresión *nf* aggression

agresivo, -a *adj* aggressive

agresor, -a 1 *nm,f* aggressor, attacker **2** *adj* attacking

agreste *adj (abrupto, rocoso)* rough, rugged; *Fig (basto, rudo)* coarse, uncouth

agrícola *adj* agricultural

agricultor, -a *nm,f* farmer

agricultura *nf* agriculture; **a. biológica** *o* **ecológica** organic farming

agridulce *adj* bittersweet

agringarse [42] *vpr Am Pey* = to become like a North American or European

agrio, -a 1 *adj* sour **2** *nmpl* **agrios** citrus fruits

agrupación *nf* association

agrupar 1 *vt* to group **2 agruparse** *vpr* (**a**) *(congregarse)* to group together, to form a group (**b**) *(asociarse)* to associate

agua *nf* water; **a. potable** drinking water; **a. corriente/del grifo** running/tap water; **a. dulce/salada** fresh/salt water; **a. mineral sin/con gas** still/fizzy *o* sparkling mineral water; **a. de colonia** (eau de) cologne; *Fig* **estar con el a. al cuello** to be up to one's neck in it; **aguas jurisdiccionales** territorial waters; **aguas residuales** sewage

Takes the masculine articles **el** and **un**

aguacate *nm* *(árbol)* avocado; *(fruto)* avocado (pear)

aguacero *nm* shower, downpour

aguafiestas *nmf inv* spoilsport, wet blanket

aguamala *nf Carib, Col, Ecuad, Méx* jellyfish

aguamiel *nm o nf* (**a**) *Am (bebida)* = water mixed with honey or cane syrup (**b**) *Carib, Méx (jugo)* maguey juice

aguanieve *nf* sleet

aguantar 1 *vt* (**a**) *(soportar)* to tolerate; **no lo aguanto más** I can't stand it any longer (**b**) *(sostener)* to support, to hold; **aguanta esto** hold this (**c**) **aguanta la respiración** hold your breath **2 aguantarse** *vpr* (**a**) *(contenerse)* to keep back; *(lágrimas)* to hold back; **no pude aguantarme la risa** I couldn't help laughing (**b**) *(resignarse)* to resign oneself

aguardar 1 *vt* to await **2** *vi* to wait

aguardiente *nm* liquor, brandy

aguarrás *nm* turpentine

aguatero,-a *nm,f Am* water seller

aguaviva *nf RP* jellyfish

agudeza *nf* (**a**) sharpness; *(del dolor)* acuteness (**b**) *Fig (ingenio)* witticism, witty saying

agudo, -a *adj (dolor)* acute; *(voz)* high-pitched; *(sonido)* treble, high; *Fig (ingenioso)* witty; *Fig (sentido)* sharp, keen

águila *nf* (**a**) eagle; **á. real** golden eagle; (**b**) *Méx (de moneda)* heads; **¿á. o sol?** heads or tails?

Takes the masculine articles **el** and **un**

aguinaldo *nm* = tip given at Christmas, *Br* Christmas box; **pedir el a.** to go carol singing

agüita *nf Chile* (herbal) tea

aguja *nf* (**a**) needle; *(de reloj)* hand; *(de tocadiscos)* stylus (**b**) *Arquit* spire (**c**) *Ferroc* point, *US* switch

agujerear *vt* to make holes in

agujero *nm* (**a**) hole; **a. negro** black hole (**b**) *Econ* deficit, shortfall

agujetas *nfpl* (**a**) *Esp (en los músculos)* stiffness; **tener a.** to be stiff (**b**) *Méx* shoelaces

ahí *adv* there; **a. está** there he/she/it is; **ve por a.** go that way; **está por a.** it's over there; **setenta o por a.** seventy or thereabouts; **de a.** hence

ahijado, -a *nm,f* godchild; *(niño)* godson; *(niña)* goddaughter; **ahijados** godchildren

ahogado, -a 1 *adj* (**a**) *(en líquido)* drowned; **morir a.** to drown (**b**) *(asfixiado)* suffocated **2** *nm,f* drowned person

ahogar [42] **1** *vt* (**a**) *(en líquido)* to drown (**b**) *(asfixiar)* to suffocate **2 ahogarse** *vpr* (**a**) *(en líquido)* to drown, to be drowned; *Fig* **ahogarse en un vaso de agua** to make a mountain out of a molehill (**b**) *(asfixiarse)* to suffocate (**c**) *(motor)* to be flooded

ahora 1 *adv* (**a**) *(en este momento)* now; **a. mismo** right now; **de a. en**

adelante from now on; **por a.** for the time being (**b**) **a. voy** I'm coming; **a. vuelvo** I'll be back in a minute (**c**) **hasta a.** *(hasta el momento)* until now, so far; *(hasta luego)* see you later **2** *conj* **a. bien** *(sin embargo)* however; *(y bueno)* well then

ahorcar [44] **1** *vt* to hang **2 ahorcarse** *vpr* to hang oneself

ahorita, ahoritica *adv Am salvo RP Fam* (**a**) *(en el presente)* (right) now; **a. voy** I'm just coming (**b**) *(pronto)* in a second (**c**) *(hace poco)* just now, a few minutes ago

ahorrar 1 *vt* to save **2 ahorrarse** *vpr* **ahórrate los comentarios** keep your comments to yourself

ahorro *nm* (**a**) saving; **a. energético** energy saving (**b**) **ahorros** savings; *Fin* **caja de ahorros** savings bank

ahuecar [44] *vt* (**a**) to hollow out; *Fam* **a. el ala** to clear off, to beat it (**b**) *(voz)* to deepen

ahuevado, -a *adj CAm, Ecuad, Perú Fam (tonto)* **estar a. con algo** to be bowled over by sth

ahumado, -a *adj (cristal, jamón)* smoked; *(bacon)* smoky; **salmón a.** smoked salmon

airbag [ˈerβaɣ, airˈβaɣ] *nm (pl* **airbags)** airbag

aire *nm* (**a**) air; **a. acondicionado** air conditioning; **al a.** *(hacia arriba)* into the air; *(al descubierto)* uncovered; **al a. libre** in the open air; **en el a.** *(pendiente)* in the air; *Rad* on the air; **saltar por los aires** to blow up; **tomar el a.** to get some fresh air; **necesito un cambio de aires** I need a change of scene
(**b**) *(viento)* wind; **hace a.** it's windy
(**c**) *(aspecto)* air, appearance
(**d**) **él va a su a.** he goes his own sweet way
(**e**) **darse aires** to put on airs

airear *vt (ropa, lugar)* to air; *Fig (asunto)* to publicize

airoso, -a *adj* graceful, elegant; *Fig* **salir a. de una situación** to come out of a situation with flying colours

aislado, -a *adj* (**a**) isolated (**b**) *Téc* insulated

aislamiento *nm* (**a**) isolation (**b**) *Téc* insulation

aislante 1 *adj* **cinta a.** insulating tape **2** *nm* insulator

aislar *vt* (**a**) to isolate (**b**) *Téc* to insulate

ajedrez *nm* (**a**) *(juego)* chess (**b**) *(piezas y tablero)* chess set

ajeno, -a *adj* belonging to other people; **los bienes ajenos** other people's goods; **por causas ajenas a nuestra voluntad** for reasons beyond our control

ajetreo *nm* activity, hard work, bustle

ají *nm (pl* **ajís** o **ajíes)** *Andes, RP* (**a**) *(pimiento)* chilli (pepper) (**b**) *(salsa)* = sauce made from oil, vinegar, garlic and chilli

ajiaco *nm* (**a**) *Andes, Carib (estofado)* = chilli-based stew (**b**) *Méx (estofado con ajo)* = tripe stew flavoured with garlic

ajillo *nm Culin* **al a.** fried with garlic

ajo *nm* garlic; **cabeza/diente de a.** head/clove of garlic; *Fam* **estar en el a.** to be in on it

ajuar *nm (de novia)* trousseau

ajustado, -a *adj* tight

ajustar *vt* (**a**) to adjust (**b**) *(apretar)* to tighten (**c**) *Fin (cuenta)* to settle; *Fig* **ajustarle las cuentas a algn** to settle a score with sb

al *(contracción de* **a** + **el)** (**a**) *ver* **a** (**b**) *(+ infinitivo)* **al salir** on leaving; **está al caer** it's about to happen; **al parecer** apparently

ala 1 *nf* (**a**) wing; *Fig* **cortarle las alas a algn** to clip sb's wings (**b**) *(de sombrero)* brim **2** *nmf Dep* winger

> Takes the masculine articles **el** and **un**

alabanza *nf* praise

alabar *vt* to praise

alabastro *nm* alabaster

alacena *nf (food)* cupboard

alambrar *vt* to fence with wire

alambre *nm* wire; **a. de púas** barbed wire

alameda *nf* (**a**) poplar grove (**b**) *(paseo)* avenue, boulevard

álamo *nm* poplar

alardear *vi* to brag, to boast; **a. de rico** *o* **de riqueza** to flaunt one's wealth

alargar [42] **1** *vt* (**a**) to lengthen; *(estirar)* to stretch; **ella alargó la mano para cogerlo** she stretched out her hand to get it (**b**) *(prolongar)* to prolong, to extend (**c**) *(dar)* to pass, to hand over; **alárgame ese jersey** can you pass me that sweater?
  2 alargarse *vpr* (**a**) to get longer (**b**) *(prolongarse)* to go on (**c**) **¿puedes alargarme a casa?** can you give me a lift home?

alarma *nf* alarm; **la a. saltó** the alarm went off; **falsa a.** false alarm; **señal de a.** alarm (signal)

alarmante *adj* alarming

alarmar 1 *vt* to alarm **2 alarmarse** *vpr* to be alarmed

alba *nf* dawn, daybreak

> Takes the masculine articles **el** and **un**

albañil *nm* bricklayer

albarán *nm Esp Com* delivery note, despatch note

albaricoque *nm Esp* apricot

albatros *nm inv* albatross

albedrío *nm* will; **libre a.** free will

alberca *nf* (**a**) *(depósito)* water tank (**b**) *Col, Méx (piscina)* swimming pool

albergar [42] **1** *vt (alojar)* to house, to accommodate; *Fig (sentimientos)* to cherish, to harbour **2 albergarse** *vpr* to stay

albergue *nm* hostel; **a. juvenil** youth hostel

albóndiga *nf* meatball

albornoz *nm* bathrobe

alborotado, -a *adj* (**a**) worked up, agitated (**b**) *(desordenado)* untidy, messy (**c**) *(mar)* rough; *(tiempo)* stormy

alborotar 1 *vt* (**a**) *(agitar)* to agitate, to work up (**b**) *(desordenar)* to make untidy, to turn upside down
  2 *vi* to kick up a racket
  3 alborotarse *vpr* (**a**) to get excited *o* worked up (**b**) *(mar)* to get rough;

(tiempo) to get stormy

alboroto *nm* (**a**) *(jaleo)* din, racket (**b**) *(desorden)* disturbance, uproar

albufera *nf* lagoon

álbum *nm* album

alcachofa *nf* (**a**) *Bot* artichoke (**b**) *Esp (de regadera)* rose, sprinkler; *(de ducha)* shower head

alcalde *nm* mayor

alcaldía *nf* (**a**) *(cargo)* mayorship (**b**) *(oficina)* mayor's office

alcalino, -a *adj* alkaline

alcance *nm* (**a**) reach; **al a. de cualquiera** within everybody's reach; **dar a. a** to catch up with; **fuera del a. de los niños** out of the reach of children (**b**) *Fig* scope; *(de noticia)* importance

alcanfor *nm* camphor

alcantarilla *nf* sewer; *(boca)* drain

alcanzar [40] **1** *vt* (**a**) to reach; *(persona)* to catch up with; **la producción alcanza dos mil unidades** production is up to two thousand units (**b**) **alcánzame la sal** *(pasar)* pass me the salt (**c**) *(conseguir)* to attain, to achieve
  2 *vi (ser suficiente)* to be sufficient; **con un kilo no alcanza para todos** one kilo won't be enough for all of us

alcaparra *nf (fruto)* caper; *(planta)* caper bush

alcaucil *nm RP* artichoke

alcayata *nf* hook

alcázar *nm* (**a**) *(fortaleza)* fortress, citadel (**b**) *(castillo)* castle, palace

alcoba *nf* bedroom

alcohol *nm* alcohol

alcohólico, -a *adj & nm,f* alcoholic

alcoholismo *nm* alcoholism

alcoholizado, -a *adj & nm,f* alcoholic

alcoholizarse *vpr* to become an alcoholic

alcornoque *nm* cork oak

aldea *nf* village

aldeano, -a 1 *adj* village **2** *nm,f* villager

alebrestarse *vpr* (**a**) *Méx (alborotarse, entusiasmarse)* to get excited (**b**) *Méx, Ven (rebelarse, indisciplinarse)* to rebel (**c**) *Col (ponerse nervioso)* to get nervous

alegrar 1 *vt* (**a**) *(complacer)* to make happy o glad; **me alegra que se lo hayas dicho** I am glad you told her (**b**) *Fig (avivar)* to enliven, to brighten up **2 alegrarse** *vpr* to be glad, to be happy; **me alegro de verte** I am pleased to see you; **me alegro por ti** I am happy for you

alegre *adj* (**a**) *(contento)* happy, glad (**b**) *(color)* bright; *(música)* lively; *(lugar)* pleasant, cheerful (**c**) *Fig (borracho)* tipsy, merry

alegremente *adv (con alegría)* happily, joyfully; *(irreflexivamente)* blithely

alegría *nf* joy, happiness

alejar 1 *vt* to move further away **2 alejarse** *vpr* to go away, to move away; **no te alejes de mí** keep close to me

alemán, -ana 1 *adj & nm,f* German **2** *nm (idioma)* German

Alemania *n* Germany; **A. del Este/Oeste** East/West Germany; **A. Occidental/Oriental** West/East Germany

alergia *nf* allergy

alérgico, -a *adj* allergic

alero *nm* eaves

alerta *nf & adj* alert; **estar en estado de a.** to be (on the) alert

aleta *nf (de pez)* fin; *(de foca, de nadador)* flipper

alevín *nm (pescado)* young fish; *Fig (principiante)* beginner

alfabético, -a *adj* alphabetic

alfabetización *nf* teaching to read and write; **campaña de a.** literacy campaign

alfabetizar *vt (personas)* to teach to read and write

alfabeto *nm* alphabet

alfarero, -a *nm,f* potter

alférez *nm* second lieutenant

alfil *nm* bishop

alfiler *nm* pin; *(broche)* pin, brooch; *(de corbata)* tiepin; *(para tender)* peg; *Andes, RP, Ven* **a. de gancho**

(imperdible) safety pin

alfombra *nf* rug; *(moqueta)* carpet

alfombrilla *nf* rug, mat

alga *nf* alga; *(marina)* seaweed

> Takes the masculine articles **el** and **un**

álgebra *nf* algebra

> Takes the masculine articles **el** and **un**

algo 1 *pron indef* (**a**) *(afirmativo)* something; *(interrogativo)* anything; **a. así** something like that; **¿a. más?** anything else?; **por a. será** there must be a reason for it; *Fam* **a. es a.** it's better than nothing (**b**) *(cantidad indeterminada)* some; **¿queda a. de pastel?** is there any cake left? **2** *adv (un poco)* quite, somewhat; **se siente a. mejor** she's feeling a bit better

algodón *nm* cotton; **a. (hidrófilo)** *Br* cotton wool, *US* absorbent cotton; **a. de azúcar** *Br* candy floss, *US* cotton candy

alguien *pron indef (afirmativo)* somebody, someone; *(interrogativo)* anybody, anyone

alguno, -a 1 *adj* (**a**) *(delante de nombre) (afirmativo)* some; *(interrogativo)* any; **algunos días** some days; **algunas veces** some times; **¿has tomado alguna medicina?** have you taken any medicine?; **¿le has visto alguna vez?** have you ever seen him? (**b**) *(después de nombre)* not at all; **no vino persona alguna** nobody came

> **algún** is used instead of **alguno** before masculine singular nouns (e.g. **algún día** some day)

2 *pron indef* (**a**) someone, somebody; **a. dirá que ...** someone might say that ...; **a. que otro** some (**b**) **algunos, -as** some (people)

alhaja *nf* jewel

aliado, -a 1 *adj* allied **2** *nm,f* **los Aliados** the Allies

alianza *nf* (**a**) *(pacto)* alliance (**b**) *(anillo)* wedding ring

aliarse [29] *vpr* to become allies, to form an alliance

alicates *nmpl* pliers

aliciente *nm* (**a**) *(atractivo)* lure, charm (**b**) *(incentivo)* incentive

aliento *nm* (**a**) breath; **sin a.** breathless (**b**) *(ánimo)* encouragement

aligerar 1 *vt (acelerar)* to speed up; **a. el paso** to quicken one's pace **2** *vi Fam* **¡aligera!** hurry up!

alijo *nm* haul; **un a. de drogas** a consignment of drugs

alimentación *nf (comida)* food; *(acción)* feeding; *Téc* supply

alimentar 1 *vt* (**a**) *(dar alimento)* to feed; *(ser nutritivo)* to be nutritious (**b**) *Fig (sentimientos)* to nourish (**c**) *Informát* to feed; *Téc* to supply **2 alimentarse** *vpr* **alimentarse con** *o* **de** to live on

alimenticio, -a *adj* nutritious; **productos alimenticios** food products, foodstuffs; **valor a.** nutritional value

alimento *nm* (**a**) *(comida)* food (**b**) *Fig* **tiene poco a.** it is not very nourishing

alinear 1 *vt* to align, to line up **2 alinearse** *vpr* to line up

aliñar *vt* to season, to flavour; *(ensalada)* to dress

aliño *nm* seasoning, dressing

alioli *nm* garlic mayonnaise

aliscafo, alíscafo *nm RP* hydrofoil

alistar 1 *vt Mil* to recruit, enlist **2 alistarse** *vpr* (**a**) *Mil* to enlist, to enrol (**b**) *Am (prepararse)* to get ready

aliviar [43] **1** *vt (dolor)* to soothe, to relieve; *(carga)* to lighten, to make lighter **2 aliviarse** *vpr (dolor)* to diminish, to get better

alivio *nm* relief

allá *adv* (**a**) *(lugar alejado)* there, over there; **a. abajo/arriba** down/up there; **¡a. voy!** here I go!; **más a.** further on; **más a. de** beyond; **el más a.** the beyond (**b**) *(tiempo)* **a. por los años veinte** back in the twenties (**c**) **a. tú** that's your problem

allegado, -a 1 *adj* close **2** *nm,f* close friend

allí *adv* there, over there; **a. abajo/arriba** down/up there; **de a. para acá** back and forth; **por a.** *(movimiento)* that way; *(posición)* over there

alma *nf* soul; **no había ni un a.** there was not a soul

> Takes the masculine articles **el** and **un**

almacén *nm* (**a**) *(local)* warehouse; *(habitación)* storeroom (**b**) *Com* **(grandes) almacenes** department store *sing* (**c**) *Andes, RP (de alimentos)* grocer's (shop), grocery store (**d**) *CAm (de ropa)* clothes shop

almacenar *vt* to store

almanaque *nm* calendar

almeja *nf* clam; *muy Fam* pussy

almendra *nf* almond; **a. garapiñada** sugared almond

almendrado 1 *adj* almond-shaped; **ojos almendrados** almond eyes **2** *nm Culin* almond paste

almendro *nm* almond tree

almíbar *nm* syrup

almidón *nm* starch

almidonado, -a 1 *adj* starched **2** *nm* starching

almidonar *vt* to starch

almirante *nm* admiral

almohada *nf* pillow; *Fam* **consultarlo con la a.** to sleep on it

almohadilla *nf* (small) cushion

almorrana *nf Fam* pile

almorzar [2] **1** *vi* to have lunch **2** *vt* to have for lunch

almuerzo *nm* lunch

aló *interj Andes, Carib (al teléfono)* hello!

alocado, -a *adj* thoughtless, rash

alojamiento *nm* accommodation; **dar a.** to accommodate

alojar 1 *vt* to accommodate **2 alojarse** *vpr* to stay

alondra *nf* lark; **a. común** skylark

alpargata *nf* canvas sandal, espadrille

Alpes *npl* **los A.** the Alps

alpinismo *nm* mountaineering, climbing

alpinista *nmf* mountaineer, climber

alpino, -a *adj* Alpine; **esquí a.** downhill skiing

alpiste (**a**) *(planta)* canary grass (**b**) *(semilla)* birdseed

alquilar *vt* to hire; *(pisos, casas)* to rent; **se alquila** *(en letrero)* to let

alquiler *nm* (**a**) *(de pisos, casas)* renting; **a. de coches** *Br* car hire, *US* car rental; **de a.** *(pisos, casas)* to let, rented; *(coche)* for hire; *(televisión)* for rent (**b**) *(precio)* hire, rental; *(de pisos, casas)* rent

alquitrán *nm* tar

alrededor **1** *adv (lugar)* round, around; **mira a.** look around; **a. de la mesa** round the table; **a. de las dos** around two o'clock; **a. de quince** about fifteen **2** *nmpl* **alrededores** surrounding area; **en los alrededores de Murcia** in the area round Murcia

alta *nf* **dar de** *o* **el a.** *(a un enfermo)* to discharge from hospital

> Takes the masculine articles **el** and **un**

altar *nm* altar

altavoz *nm* loudspeaker

alteración *nf* (**a**) *(cambio)* alteration (**b**) *(alboroto)* quarrel, row; **a. del orden público** disturbance of the peace (**c**) *(excitación)* agitation

alterar **1** *vt* to alter, to change; **a. el orden público** to disturb the peace **2 alterarse** *vpr* (**a**) *(cambiar)* to change (**b**) *(inquietarse)* to be upset (**c**) *(alimentos)* to go off

altercado *nm* quarrel, argument

alternar **1** *vt* to alternate

   2 *vi (rela-cionarse)* to meet people, to socialize

   3 alternarse *vpr* to alternate

alternativa *nf* alternative

alterno, -a *adj* alternate; **días alternos** alternate days

alteza *nf* Highness; **Su A. Real** His/Her Royal Highness

altibajos *nmpl Fig* ups and downs

altillo *nm* (**a**) *(desván)* attic, loft (**b**) *Esp (armario)* = small storage cupboard above head height, usually above another cupboard

altiplano *nm* high plateau

altitud *nf* altitude

altivo, -a *adj* arrogant, haughty

alto¹, -a 1 *adj (persona, árbol, edificio)* tall; *(montaña, techo, presión)* high; *(sonido)* loud; *Fig (precio, tecnología)* high; *(tono)* high-pitched; **los pisos altos** the top floors; **en lo a.** at the top; **alta sociedad** high society; **clase alta** upper class; **en voz alta** aloud, in a loud voice; **a altas horas de la noche** late at night

   2 *adv* (**a**) high, high up (**b**) *(sonar, hablar etc)* loud, loudly; **pon la radio más alta** turn the radio up; **¡habla más a.!** speak up!

   3 *nm* (**a**) *(altura)* height; **¿cuánto tiene de a.?** how tall/high is it?; *Fig* **por todo lo a.** in a grand way (**b**) *(elevación)* hill

alto² *nm* (a**) *(interrupción)* stop, break (**b**) *Mil* halt; **dar el a.** to order to halt; **un a. el fuego** a cease-fire

altoparlante *nm Am* loudspeaker

altramuz *nm* lupin

altruismo *nm* altruism

altruista 1 *adj* altruistic **2** *nmf* altruist

altura *nf* (**a**) height; **de 10 m de a.** 10 m high (**b**) *(nivel)* level; **a la misma a.** on the same level; *Geog* on the same latitude; **a la a. del cine** by the cinema; *Fig* **estar a la a. de las circunstancias** to meet the challenge; *Fig* **no está a su a.** he does not measure up to him; *Fig* **a estas alturas** at this stage (**c**) *Rel* **alturas** heaven

alubia *nf* bean

alucinación *nf* hallucination

alucinar 1 *vt* to hallucinate; *Fig (encantar)* to fascinate **2** *vi Fam* to be amazed, to be spaced out

alud *nm* avalanche

aludido, -a *adj Fig* **darse por a.** to take it personally

aludir *vi* to allude to, to mention

alumbrado, -a 1 *adj* lit **2** *nm Elec* lighting; **a. público** street lighting

alumbrar 1 *vt (iluminar)* to light, to illuminate **2** *vi (parir)* to give birth

aluminio *nm Br* aluminium, *US* aluminum

alumno, -a *nm,f* (**a**) *(de colegio)* pupil; **a. externo** day pupil; **a. interno**

boarder (**b**) *Univ* student

alusión *nf* allusion, mention

alverja *nf Am* pea

alza *nf* (**a**) rise; **en a.** rising; **jugar al a.** *(bolsa)* to bull the market (**b**) *Mil* sight

Takes the masculine articles **el** and **un**

alzar [40] **1** *vt* to raise, to lift; **a. el vuelo** to take off; **a. los ojos/la vista** to look up; **álzate el cuello** turn your collar up **2 alzarse** *vpr* (**a**) *(levantarse)* to get up, to rise (**b**) *(rebelarse)* to rise, to rebel (**c**) **alzarse con la victoria** to win, to be victorious

a.m. *adv* a.m.

amabilidad *nf* kindness; *Fml* **tenga la a. de esperar** would you be so kind as to wait?

amable *adj* kind, nice; *Fml* **¿sería usted tan a. de ayudarme?** would you be so kind as to help me?

amaestrado *adj (animal)* trained; *(en circo)* performing

amaestrar *vt* to train; *(domar)* to tame

amamantar *vt* to breast-feed; *Zool* to suckle

amancay *nm Andes* golden hurricane lily

amanecer [33] **1** *v impers* to dawn; **¿a qué hora amanece?** when does it get light?; **amaneció lluvioso** it was rainy at daybreak **2** *vi* **amanecimos en Finlandia** we were in Finland at daybreak; **amaneció muy enfermo** he woke up feeling very ill **3** *nm* dawn, daybreak; **al a.** at dawn

amanerado, -a *adj* mannered, affected

amansar *vt* (**a**) to tame (**b**) *Fig (apaciguar)* to tame, to calm

amante *nmf* lover; **a. del arte** art lover

amapola *nf* poppy

amar 1 *vt* to love **2 amarse** *vpr* to love each other

amargado, -a 1 *adj (rencoroso)* embittered, bitter; *Fam (agobiado)* pissed off; **estoy a. con los exámenes** I'm pissed off with the exams **2** *nm,f* bitter person

amargar [42] **1** *vt* to make bitter; *Fig* to embitter, to sour **2 amargarse** *vpr Fig* to become embittered o bitter; **no te amargues por eso** don't let that make you bitter

amargo, -a *adj* bitter

amarillear 1 *vt* to turn yellow **2** *vi* to (turn) yellow

amarillo, -a *adj & nm* yellow; **prensa amarilla** gutter press

amarilloso, -a *adj Col, Méx, Ven* yellowish

amarrar *vt Náut* to moor, to tie up; *(atar)* to tie (up), to bind

amarre *nm Náut* mooring

amarrete, -a *adj Andes, RP Fam* mean, tight

amasar *vt* (**a**) *Culin* to knead (**b**) *Fig (fortuna)* to amass

amasiato *nm CAm, Chile, Méx (concubinato)* cohabitation, common-law marriage

amasio, -a *nm,f CAm, Méx* live-in lover, common-law partner

amateur [amaˈter] *adj & nmf (pl amateurs)* amateur

amazona *nf* (**a**) *(jinete)* horsewoman (**b**) *(en mitología)* Amazon

Amazonas *n* **el A.** the Amazon

amazónico, -a *adj* Amazonian

ámbar *nm* amber

ambición *nf* ambition

ambicioso, -a 1 *adj* ambitious **2** *nm,f* ambitious person

ambientador *nm* air freshener

ambiental *adj* environmental

ambiente 1 *nm* (**a**) *(gen)* environment; *Fig (medio)* environment, milieu (**b**) *Andes, RP (habitación)* room **2** *adj* environmental; **temperatura a.** room temperature

ambigüedad *nf* ambiguity

ambiguo, -a *adj* ambiguous

ámbito *nm* field, sphere; **empresa de a. nacional** nationwide company

ambos, -as *adj pl Fml* both; **por a. lados** on both sides

ambulancia *nf* ambulance

ambulante *adj* travelling, mobile; **biblioteca a.** mobile library

ambulatorio *nm* surgery, clinic

amén[1] *nm* amen

amén[2] *adv* **a. de** in addition to

amenaza *nf* threat

amenazar [40] *vt* to threaten; **a. de muerte a algn** to threaten to kill sb

amenizar [40] *vt* to liven up

ameno, -a *adj* entertaining

América *n* America; **A. Central/del Norte/del Sur** Central/North/South America

americana *nf (prenda)* jacket

americano, -a *adj & nm,f* American

ameritar *vt Am* to deserve

ametralladora *nf* machine gun

ametrallar *vt* to machine-gun

amígdala *nf* tonsil

amigo, -a 1 *nm,f* friend; **hacerse a. de** to make friends with; **hacerse amigos** to become friends; **son muy amigos** they are very good friends **2** *adj (aficionado)* fond (**de** of)

amistad *nf* (a) friendship (b) amistades friends

amnesia *nf* amnesia

amnistía *nf* amnesty

amo *nm* (a) *(dueño)* owner (b) *(señor)* master

amodorrarse *vpr* to get drowsy

amoldar 1 *vt* to adapt, to adjust **2** amoldarse *vpr* to adapt oneself

amoniaco, amoníaco *nm* ammonia

amontonar 1 *vt* to pile up, to heap up **2** amontonarse *vpr* to pile up, to heap up; *(gente)* to crowd together

amor *nm* love; **hacer el a.** to make love; **a. propio** self-esteem; **¡por el a. de Dios!** for God's sake!

amordazar [40] *vt (perro)* to muzzle; *(persona)* to gag

amoroso, -a *adj* loving, affectionate

amortiguador *nm Aut* shock absorber

amortiguar [45] *vt (golpe)* to cushion; *(ruido)* to muffle; *(luz)* to subdue

amparar 1 *vt* to protect **2** ampararse *vpr* to seek refuge

amparo *nm* protection, shelter; **al a. de la ley** under the protection of the law

ampliación *nf* enlargement; *(de plazo, casa)* extension

ampliar [29] *vt* to enlarge; *(casa, plazo)* to extend

amplificador *nm* amplifier

amplio, -a *adj* large, roomy; *(ancho)* wide, broad; **en el sentido más a. de la palabra** in the broadest sense of the word

amplitud *nf* (a) spaciousness; **a. de miras** broad-mindedness (b) *(de espacio)* room, space (c) *Fís* amplitude

ampolla *nf* (a) *Med* blister; *Fig* **levantar ampollas** to raise people's hackles (b) *(de medicina)* ampoule

amueblado, -a *adj (piso)* furnished

amueblar *vt* to furnish

amuermar *vt Esp Fam (aburrir)* to bore

amuleto *nm* amulet; **a. de la suerte** lucky charm

amurallar *vt* to wall, to fortify

analfabetismo *nm* illiteracy

analfabeto, -a *nm,f* illiterate

analgésico, -a *adj & nm* analgesic

análisis *nm inv* analysis; **a. de sangre** blood test

analítico, -a *adj* analytical

analizar [40] *vt* to analyse

analogía *nf* analogy

análogo, -a *adj* analogous, similar

ananá *nm*, **ananás** *nm inv* pineapple

anaranjado, -a *adj & nm* orange

anarquía *nf* anarchy

anárquico, -a *adj* anarchic

anarquista *adj & nmf* anarchist

anatomía *nf* anatomy

anatómico, -a *adj* anatomical

anca *nf* haunch; **ancas de rana** frogs' legs

Takes the masculine articles **el** and **un**

ancho, -a 1 *adj* wide, broad; **a lo a.** breadthwise; **te está muy a.** it's too big for you

2 *nm* (**a**) *(anchura)* width, breadth; **2 m de a.** 2 m wide; **¿qué a. tiene?** how wide is it? (**b**) *Cost* width

3 *nfpl Esp Fam* **a mis** *o* **tus anchas** at ease, comfortable

anchoa *nf* anchovy

anchura *nf* width, breadth

anciano, -a 1 *adj* very old **2** *nm,f* old person; **los ancianos** old people

ancla *nf* anchor

Takes the masculine articles **el** and **un**

ándale *interj CAm, Méx Fam* come on!

Andalucía *n* Andalusia

andaluz, -a *adj & nm,f* Andalusian

andamio *nm* scaffold

andar¹ *nm* **a.** *o* **andares** *nmpl* walk, gait

andar² [8] **1** *vi* (**a**) *esp Esp (caminar)* to walk (**b**) *(coche etc)* to move; **este coche anda despacio** this car goes very slowly (**c**) *(funcionar)* to work; **esto no anda** this doesn't work (**d**) *Fam* **anda por los cuarenta** he's about forty; **anda siempre diciendo que ...** he's always saying that ...; **¿cómo andamos de tiempo?** how are we off for time?; **tu bolso debe a. por ahí** your bag must be over there somewhere

2 *vt (recorrer)* to walk

ándele *interj CAm, Méx Fam* come on!

andén *nm* (**a**) *(en estación)* platform (**b**) *Andes, CAm (acera) Br* pavement, *US* sidewalk (**c**) *Andes (bancal de tierra)* terrace

Andes *nmpl* Andes

andinismo *nm Am* mountaineering, mountain climbing

andinista *nmf Am* mountaineer, mountain climber

andino, -a *adj & nm,f* Andean

anécdota *nf* anecdote

anecdótico, -a *adj* anecdotal

anemia *nf* anaemia

anémico, -a 1 *adj* anaemic **2** *nm,f* anaemia sufferer

anestesia *nf* anaesthesia

anestesista *nmf* anaesthetist

anexo, -a 1 *adj* attached, joined (**a** to) **2** *nm* appendix

anfetamina *nf* amphetamine

anfibio, -a 1 *adj* amphibious **2** *nm* amphibian

anfiteatro *nm* (**a**) amphitheatre (**b**) *Cin, Teatro* gallery

anfitrión, -ona *nm,f* host, *f* hostess

ángel *nm* (**a**) angel; **á. de la guarda** guardian angel (**b**) *Am (micrófono)* hand-held microphone

angelical, angélico, -a *adj* angelic

angina *nf* angina; **tener anginas** to have tonsillitis; *Med* **a. de pecho** angina pectoris

anglosajón, -ona *adj & nm,f* Anglo-Saxon

anguila *nf* eel; **a. de mar** conger eel

angula *nf* elver

angular *adj* angular; *Fot* (**objetivo**) **gran a.** wide-angle lens; **piedra a.** cornerstone

ángulo *nm* angle; *(rincón)* corner

angustia *nf* anguish

angustiado, -a *adj* anguished, distressed

angustiar [43] *vt* to distress

angustioso, -a *adj* distressing

anhelar *vt* to long for, to yearn for

anhelo *nm* longing, yearning

anidar *vi* to nest

anilla *nf* ring; **carpeta de anillas** ring-binder

anillo *nm* ring; **a. de boda** wedding ring

ánima *nf* soul

Takes the masculine articles **el** and **un**

animación *nf (diversión)* entertainment

animado, -a *adj (fiesta etc)* lively

animal 1 *nm* animal; *Fig (basto)* brute; *(necio)* dunce **2** *adj* animal

animar 1 *vt* (**a**) *(alentar)* to encourage (**b**) *(alegrar) (persona)* to cheer up; *(fiesta, bar)* to liven up, to brighten up **2 animarse** *vpr* (**a**) *(persona)* to cheer up; *(fiesta, reunión)* to brighten up (**b**) **¿te animas a venir?** do you fancy coming along?

ánimo *nm* (**a**) *(espíritu)* spirit; **estado de á.** frame o state of mind (**b**) **con á. de** *(intención)* with the intention of (**c**) *(valor, coraje)* courage; **dar ánimos a** to encourage; **¡á.!** cheer up!

aniñado, -a *adj* childlike; *Pey* childish

aniquilar *vt* to annihilate

anís *nm* (**a**) *(bebida)* anisette (**b**) *(grano)* aniseed

aniversario *nm* anniversary

ano *nm* anus

anoche *adv* last night; *(por la tarde)* yesterday evening; **antes de a.** the night before last

anochecer [33] **1** *v impers* to get dark; **cuando anochece** at nightfall, at dusk **2** *vi* to be somewhere at dusk; **anochecimos en Cuenca** we were in Cuenca at dusk **3** *nm* nightfall, dusk

anomalía *nf* anomaly

anómalo, -a *adj* anomalous

anonimato *nm* anonymity; **permanecer en el a.** to remain anonymous o nameless

anónimo, -a 1 *adj* (**a**) *(desconocido)* anonymous (**b**) *Com* **sociedad anónima** public liability company, *US* incorporated company **2** *nm (carta)* anonymous letter

anorak *nm* (*pl* **anoraks**) anorak

anorexia *nf* anorexia

anotar 1 *vt* (**a**) to annotate (**b**) *(apuntar)* to take down, to make a note of **2 anotarse** *vpr RP (en curso)* to enrol (**en** for); *(para actividad)* to sign up (**en** for)

ansia *nf* (**a**) *(deseo)* longing, yearning (**b**) *(ansiedad)* anxiety (**c**) *Med* sick feeling

| Takes the masculine articles **el** and **un** |

ansiedad *nf* anxiety; **con a.** anxiously

ansioso, -a *adj* (**a**) *(deseoso)* eager (**por** for) (**b**) *(avaricioso)* greedy

antártico, -a 1 *adj* Antarctic **2** *nm* **el A.** the Antarctic

ante¹ *nm* (**a**) *Zool* elk, moose (**b**) *(piel)* suede

ante² *prep* (**a**) before, in the presence of; *Jur* **a. notario** in the presence of a notary; **a. todo** most of all (**b**) *(en vista de)* faced with, in view of; **a. la crisis energética** faced with the energy crisis

anteanoche *adv* the night before last

anteayer *adv* the day before yesterday

antebrazo *nm* forearm

antecedente 1 *adj* previous **2** *nm* antecedent **3** *nmpl* (**a**) **antecedentes** *(historial)* record; *Jur* **antecedentes penales** criminal record (**b**) *Fig* **poner en antecedentes** to put in the picture

anteceder *vt* to precede, to go before

antecesor, -a *nm,f* (**a**) *(en un cargo)* predecessor (**b**) *(antepasado)* ancestor

antelación *nf* notice; **con poca a.** at short notice; **con un mes de a.** a month beforehand, with a month's notice

antemano *adv* **de a.** beforehand, in advance

antena *nf* (**a**) *Rad, TV* aerial; **a. parabólica** satellite dish; **en a.** on the air (**b**) *Zool* antenna, feeler

anteojo *nm* (**a**) telescope (**b**) **anteojos** *(binoculares)* binoculars; *Am (gafas)* spectacles, glasses

antepasado, -a *nm,f* ancestor

antepenúltimo, -a *adj* antepenultimate; **el capítulo a.** the last chapter but two

anterior *adj* (**a**) previous; **el día a.** the day before (**b**) *(delantero)* front; **parte a.** front part

antes *adv* (**a**) *(tiempo)* before; **a. de las tres** before three o'clock; **mucho a.** long before; **la noche a.** the night before; **cuanto a.** as soon as possible (**b**) *(antaño)* in the past; **a. llovía más** it used to rain more in the past (**c**) *(lugar)* before; **a. del semáforo** before the traffic lights (**d**) **a. prefiero hacerlo yo** I'd rather do it myself; **a. (bien)** on the contrary

antesala *nf* antechamber, anteroom; *Fig* **en la a. de** on the eve of

antiabortista 1 *adj* anti-abortion,

pro-life **2** *nmf* anti-abortion *o* pro-life campaigner

antiarrugas *adj inv* anti-wrinkle

antibiótico, -a *adj & nm* antibiotic

anticiclón *nm* anticyclone, high pressure area

anticipado, -a *adj* brought forward; **elecciones anticipadas** early elections; **gracias anticipadas** thanks in advance; *Com* **por a.** in advance

anticipar 1 *vt (acontecimiento)* to bring forward; *(dinero)* to pay in advance; **no anticipemos acontecimientos** we'll cross that bridge when we come to it

2 anticiparse *vpr* **(a)** *(adelantarse)* to beat to it; **iba a decírtelo, pero él se me anticipó** I was going to tell you, but he beat me to it **(b)** *(llegar pronto)* to arrive early; *Fig* **anticiparse a su tiempo** to be ahead of one's time

anticipo *nm (adelanto)* advance; **pedir un a.** to ask for an advance (on one's wages)

anticonceptivo, -a *adj & nm* contraceptive

anticuado, -a *adj* antiquated

anticuario, -a *nm,f* antique dealer

anticucho *nm Andes (brocheta)* kebab

anticuerpo *nm* antibody

antidepresivo, -a 1 *adj* antidepressant **2** *nm* antidepressant (drug)

antier *adv Am Fam* the day before yesterday

antifaz *nm* mask

antiguamente *adv (hace mucho)* long ago; *(previamente)* formerly

antigüedad *nf* **(a)** *(período histórico)* antiquity; **en la a.** in olden days, in former times **(b)** *(en cargo)* seniority **(c)** **tienda de antigüedades** antique shop

antiguo, -a *adj* **(a)** old, ancient **(b)** *(pasado de moda)* old-fashioned **(c)** *(en cargo)* senior **(d)** *(anterior)* former

antihistamínico, -a *adj & nm* antihistamine

antiinflamatorio, -a 1 *adj* anti-

inflammatory **2** *nm* anti-inflammatory drug

Antillas *nfpl* **las A.** the West Indies, the Antilles

antílope *nm* antelope

antipatía *nf* antipathy, dislike; **tener a. a** to dislike

antipático, -a *adj* unpleasant; **Pedro me es a.** I don't like Pedro

antirrobo 1 *adj inv* antitheft; **alarma a.** burglar alarm; *(para coche)* car alarm **2** *nm (para coche)* car alarm; *(para casa)* burglar alarm

antiséptico, -a *adj & nm* antiseptic

antojitos *nmpl Ecuad, Méx* snacks, appetizers

antojo *nm* **(a)** *(capricho)* whim, caprice; *(de embarazada)* craving; **a su a.** in one's own way, as one pleases **(b)** *(en la piel)* birthmark

antología *nf* anthology

antónimo *nm* antonym

antorcha *nf* torch

antro *nm* dump, hole; *Fig* **a. de perdición** den of vice

anual *adj* annual; **ingresos anuales** yearly income

anuario *nm* yearbook

anular¹ *nm* ring finger

anular² ** *vt* **(a) *Com (pedido)* to cancel; *Dep (gol)* to disallow; *(matrimonio)* to annul; *Jur (ley)* to repeal **(b)** *Informát* to delete

anunciar [43] **1** *vt* **(a)** *(producto etc)* to advertise **(b)** *(avisar)* to announce **2 anunciarse** *vpr* to advertise oneself; **anunciarse en un periódico** to put an advert in a newspaper

anuncio *nm* **(a)** *(comercial)* advertisement, advert, ad **(b)** *(aviso)* announcement **(c)** *(cartel)* notice, poster

anzuelo *nm* (fish) hook

añadidura *nf* addition; **por a.** besides, on top of everything else

añadir *vt* to add **(a** to**)**

añicos *nmpl* smithereens; **hacer a.** to smash to smithereens

año *nm* **(a)** year; **el a. pasado** last

year; **el a. que viene** next year; **hace años** a long time ago, years ago; **los años noventa** the nineties; **todo el a.** all the year (round); **a. luz** light year (**b**) **¿cuántos años tienes?** how old are you?; **tiene seis años** he's six years old; **entrado en años** getting on

añoranza *nf* longing, yearning

añorar *vt (pasado)* to long for, to yearn for; *(país)* to feel homesick for, to miss

aorta *nf Anat* aorta

apache *adj & nmf* Apache

apachurrar *vt Fam* to squash, to crush

apacible *adj* mild, calm

apadrinar *vt* (**a**) *(en bautizo)* to act as godfather to; *(en boda)* to be best man for (**b**) *(artista)* to sponsor

apagado, -a *adj* (**a**) *(luz, cigarro)* out (**b**) *(color)* dull; *(voz)* sad; *(mirada)* expressionless, lifeless; *(carácter, persona)* spiritless

apagar [42] *vt (fuego)* to put out; *(luz, tele etc)* to turn off, to switch off; *(color)* to soften; *(sed)* to quench

apagón *nm* power cut, blackout

apaisado, -a *adj* (**a**) oblong (**b**) *(papel)* landscape

apalabrar *vt (concertar)* to make a verbal agreement on

apalancado, -a *adj Esp Fam* **se pasó la tarde a. delante del televisor** he spent the afternoon lounging in front of the television

apañado, -a *adj Fam (hábil, mañoso)* clever, resourceful; **estar a.** to have had it; **¡estamos apañados!** we've had it!

apañar 1 *vt* to mend, to fix **2** **apañarse** *vpr Esp (arreglarse)* to cope, to manage; **apañárselas (para hacer algo)** to manage (to do sth)

apapachar *vt Méx Fam (mimar)* to cuddle; *(consentir)* to spoil

apapacho *nm Méx Fam (mimo)* cuddle

aparador *nm (mueble)* sideboard; *(de tienda)* shop window

aparato *nm* (**a**) *(piece of)* apparatus; *(dispositivo)* device; *(instrumento)* instrument; **a. de radio/televisión** radio/television set; **a. digestivo** digestive system; **a. eléctrico** thunder and lightning (**b**) *Tel* **¿quién está al a.?** who's speaking? (**c**) *(ostentación)* display

aparcamiento *nm Esp (parking) Br* car park, *US* parking lot; *(hueco)* parking place

aparcar [44] *vt Esp* to park

aparecer [33] **1** *vi* (**a**) to appear; **no aparece en mi lista** he is not on my list (**b**) to turn up, to show up; **¿apareció el dinero?** did the money turn up?; **no apareció nadie** nobody turned up **2** **aparecerse** *vpr* to appear

aparejador, -a *nm,f* quantity surveyor

aparejar *vt* (**a**) *(caballo)* to harness (**b**) *(emparejar)* to pair off

aparejo *nm* (**a**) *(equipo)* equipment (**b**) *(de caballo)* harness

aparentar 1 *vt* (**a**) *(fingir)* to affect (**b**) *(tener aspecto)* to look; **no aparenta esa edad** she doesn't look that age **2** *vi* to show off

aparente *adj* (**a**) apparent; **sin motivo a.** for no apparent reason (**b**) *Fam (conveniente)* suitable

aparición *nf* (**a**) appearance (**b**) *(visión)* apparition

apariencia *nf* appearance; **en a.** apparently; *Fig* **guardar las apariencias** to keep up appearances

apartado, -a 1 *adj (lugar)* remote, isolated; **mantente a. de él** keep away from him **2** *nm* (**a**) *(párrafo)* section, paragraph (**b**) **a. de correos** Post Office Box

apartamento *nm esp Am (en edificio) Br* flat, *US* apartment; *Esp (más pequeño)* apartment

apartar 1 *vt* (**a**) *(alejar)* to move away, to remove; **a. la mirada** to look away (**b**) *(guardar)* to put aside **2** *vi* **¡aparta!** move out of the way! **3** **apartarse** *vpr (alejarse)* to move over, to move away; **apártate de en medio** move out of the way

aparte 1 *adv* (**a**) aside; **ponlo a.** put it

aside; **modestia/bromas a.** modesty/ joking apart (**b**) **eso hay que pagarlo a.** *(separadamente)* you have to pay for that separately (**c**) **a. de eso** *(además)* besides that; *(excepto)* apart from that (**d**) **eso es caso a.** that's completely different **2** *nm* (**a**) *Teatro* aside (**b**) *Ling* **punto y a.** full stop, new paragraph

apasionado, -a 1 *adj* passionate; **a. de la música** very fond of music **2** *nm,f* enthusiast

apasionante *adj* exciting

apasionar *vt* to excite, to thrill; **le apasiona el jazz** he is mad about jazz

apdo. *(abr* **apartado)** PO Box

apechugar [42] *vi* **a. con** to shoulder

apego *nm* love, affection; **tener a. a** to be attached to

apellidarse *vpr* to have as a surname, to be called

apellido *nm* surname; **a. de soltera** maiden name

apenado, -a *adj* (**a**) *(entristecido)* sad (**b**) *Am salvo RP (avergonzado)* embarrassed; **está muy a. por lo que hizo** he's very embarrassed about what he did

apenar 1 *vt* to sadden **2 apenarse** *vpr* (**a**) *(entristecerse)* to be saddened (**b**) *Am salvo RP (avergonzarse)* to be embarrassed

apenas *adv* (**a**) *(casi no)* hardly, scarcely; **a. come** he hardly eats anything; **a. (si) hay nieve** there is hardly any snow (**b**) *(tan pronto como)* scarcely; **a. llegó, sonó el teléfono** no sooner had he arrived than the phone rang

apéndice *nm* appendix

apendicitis *nf inv* appendicitis

aperitivo *nm (bebida)* apéritif; *(comida)* appetizer

apertura *nf* (**a**) *(comienzo)* opening (**b**) *Pol* liberalization

apestar 1 *vi* to stink (**a** of) **2** *vt* to infect with the plague

apetecer [33] *vi Esp* **¿qué te apetece para cenar?** what would you like for supper?; **¿te apetece ir al cine?** do you fancy going to the cinema?

apetecible *adj* tempting, inviting

apetito *nm* appetite; **tengo mucho a.** I'm really hungry

apetitoso, -a *adj* appetizing, tempting; *(comida)* delicious, tasty

apicultura *nf* beekeeping, apiculture

apiñado, -a *adj (apretado)* packed, crammed

apiñarse *vpr* to crowd together

apio *nm* celery

apisonadora *nf* roadroller, steam-roller

aplanar *vt* to level

aplastar *vt* (**a**) to flatten, to squash (**b**) *Fig (vencer)* to crush

aplaudir *vt* (**a**) to clap, to applaud (**b**) *Fig* to applaud

aplauso *nm* applause

aplazar [40] *vt* to postpone, to adjourn; *Fin (pago)* to defer

aplicación *nf* application

aplicado, -a *adj* hard-working

aplicar [44] **1** *vt* to apply **2 aplicarse** *vpr* (**a**) *(esforzarse)* to apply oneself, to work hard (**b**) *(norma, ley)* to apply, to be applicable

aplique *nm* wall light, wall lamp

aplomo *nm* aplomb

apoderarse *vpr* to take possession (**de** of), to seize; *Fig* **el miedo se apoderó de ella** she was seized by fear

apodo *nm* nickname

apogeo *nm* height; **estar en pleno a.** *(fama etc)* to be at its height

aportación *nf* contribution

aportar 1 *vt* to contribute **2** *vi Náut* to reach port

aposta *adv Esp* on purpose, intentionally

apostar¹ [2] **1** *vt* to bet; **te apuesto una cena a que no viene** I bet you a dinner that he won't come
2 *vi* to bet (**por** on); **a. a los caballos** to bet on horses; **apuesto a que sí viene** I bet she will come
3 apostarse *vpr* to bet; **me apuesto lo que quieras** I bet you anything

apostar² *vt (situar)* to post, to station

apóstol *nm* apostle

apóstrofo *nm* apostrophe

apoyar 1 *vt* (**a**) to lean (**b**) *(causa)* to support **2 apoyarse** *vpr* (**a**) **apoyarse en** to lean on; **apóyate en mi brazo** take my arm (**b**) **apoyarse en** *(opinión)* to be based on, to rest on

apoyo *nm* support

apreciable *adj* appreciable, noticeable

apreciación *nf* appreciation

apreciado, -a *adj (querido)* esteemed, highly regarded

apreciar [43] **1** *vt* (**a**) to appreciate (**b**) *(percibir)* to notice, to see **2 apreciarse** *vpr* to be noticeable

aprecio *nm* regard, esteem; **tener a. a algn** to be fond of sb

apremiar [43] *vi* to be urgent; **el tiempo apremia** time is at a premium

aprender *vt* to learn; **así aprenderás** that'll teach you

aprendiz, -a *nm,f* apprentice, trainee

aprendizaje *nm* (**a**) learning (**b**) *(instrucción)* apprenticeship, traineeship

aprensión *nf* apprehension

aprensivo, -a *adj* apprehensive

apresurado, -a *adj (persona)* in a hurry; *(cosa)* hurried

apresurar 1 *vt (paso etc)* to speed up **2 apresurarse** *vpr* to hurry up

apretado, -a *adj* (**a**) *(ropa, cordón)* tight; **íbamos todos apretados en el coche** we were all squashed together in the car (**b**) *(día, agenda)* busy

apretar [1] **1** *vt (botón)* to press; *(nudo, tornillo)* to tighten; **a. el gatillo** to pull the trigger; **me aprietan las botas** these boots are too tight for me

2 *vi* **apretaba el calor** it was really hot

3 apretarse *vpr* to squeeze together, to cram together; *Fig* **apretarse el cinturón** to tighten one's belt

apretujar 1 *vt* to squeeze, to crush **2 apretujarse** *vpr* to squeeze together, to cram together

aprisa *adv* quickly

aprobado *nm Educ* pass

aprobar [2] *vt* (**a**) *(autorizar)* to approve (**b**) *(estar de acuerdo con)* to approve of (**c**) *Educ* to pass (**d**) *Pol (ley)* to pass

aprontar 1 *vt (preparar)* to quickly prepare *o* get ready **2 aprontarse** *vpr RP (prepararse)* to get ready

apropiado, -a *adj* suitable, appropriate

apropiarse [43] *vpr* to appropriate

aprovechado, -a *adj* (**a**) **mal a.** *(recurso, tiempo)* wasted; **bien a.** put to good use (**b**) *(espacio)* well-planned (**c**) *(egoísta)* self-seeking

aprovechar 1 *vt* (**a**) to make good use of, to make the most of; **aprovechamos bien la tarde** we've done lots of things this afternoon (**b**) *(recursos etc)* to take advantage of; **a. la ocasión** to seize the opportunity

2 *vi* **¡que aproveche!** enjoy your meal!, bon appétit!

3 aprovecharse *vpr* to use to one's advantage, to take advantage; **aprovecharse de algn** to take advantage of sb; **aprovecharse de algo** to make the most of sth

aproximación *nf* (**a**) approximation (**b**) *(en lotería)* consolation prize

aproximadamente *adv* approximately, roughly

aproximar 1 *vt* to bring *o* put nearer **2 aproximarse** *vpr* **aproximarse (a)** to approach

apto, -a *adj* (**a**) *(apropiado)* suitable, appropriate; *Cin* **a. para todos los públicos** *Br* U, *US* G (**b**) *(capacitado)* capable, able (**c**) *Educ* passed

apuesta *nf* bet, wager

apuesto, -a *adj* good-looking; *(hombre)* handsome

apunado, -a *adj Andes* **estar a.** to have altitude sickness

apunarse *vpr Andes* to get altitude sickness

apuntador, -a *nm,f Teatro* prompter

apuntar *vt* (**a**) *(con arma)* to aim (**b**) *(señalar)* to point out (**c**) *(anotar)* to note down, to make a note of (**d**) *(indicar)* to indicate, to suggest; **todo**

parece a. a ... everything seems to point to ...

2 *vi* **cuando apunta el día** when day breaks

3 apuntarse *vpr* (**a**) *(en una lista)* to put one's name down (**b**) *Fam* **¿te apuntas?** are you game?; **me apunto** count me in

apunte *nm (usu pl)* note; **tomar apuntes** to take notes

apuñalar *vt* to stab

apurar 1 *vt* (**a**) *(terminar)* to finish off, to end (**b**) *(preocupar)* to worry **2 apurarse** *vpr* (**a**) *Esp, Méx (preocuparse)* to worry, to get worried; **no te apures** don't worry (**b**) *(darse prisa)* to rush, to hurry, to pester; **apúrate** get a move on

apuro *nm* (**a**) *(situación difícil)* tight spot, fix, jam; **estar en un a.** to be in a tight spot (**b**) *(escasez de dinero)* hardship; **pasar apuros** to be hard up (**c**) *(vergüenza)* embarrassment; **¡qué a.!** how embarrassing!

aquel, -ella *(pl* **aquellos, -ellas)** *adj dem* (**a**) that; **a. niño** that boy (**b**) **aquellos, -as** those; **aquellas niñas** those girls

aquél, -élla *(pl* **aquéllos, -éllas)** *pron dem m,f* (**a**) that one; *(el anterior)* the former; **aquél/aquélla ... éste/ésta** the former ... the latter (**b**) **todo a. que** anyone who, whoever (**c**) **aquéllos, -as** those; *(los anteriores)* the former

Note that **aquél** and its various forms can be written without an accent when there is no risk of confusion with the adjective

aquello *pron neut m* that, it

aquellos, -as *adj dem pl ver* **aquel**

aquéllos, -as *pron dem m,fpl ver* **aquél, -élla**

aquí *adv* (**a**) *(lugar)* here; **a. arriba/ fuera** up/out here; **a. está** here it is; **a. mismo** right here; **de a. para allá** up and down, to and fro; **hasta a.** this far; **por a., por favor** this way please; **está por a.** it's around here somewhere (**b**) *(tiempo)* **de a. en adelante** from now

on; **de a. a junio** between now and June; **hasta a.** up till now

árabe 1 *adj (de Arabia)* Arab

2 *nmf (persona)* Arab

3 *nm (idioma)* Arabic

Arabia *n* Arabia; **A. Saudí** Saudi Arabia

arado *nm* plough

arandela *nf Téc* washer; *(anilla)* ring

araña *nf* (**a**) spider (**b**) *(lámpara)* chandelier

arañar *vt* to scratch

arañazo *nm* scratch

arar *vt* to plough

arbitrar *vt* (**a**) to arbitrate (**b**) *Dep* to referee; *Ten* to umpire

árbitro, -a *nm,f* (**a**) *Dep* referee; *(de tenis)* umpire (**b**) *(mediador)* arbitrator

árbol *nm* (**a**) *Bot* tree (**b**) *Téc* shaft (**c**) *Náut* mast (**d**) *(gráfico)* tree (diagram); **á. genealógico** family o genealogical tree

arbusto *nm* bush, shrub

arca *nf* (**a**) chest (**b**) *(para caudales)* strongbox, safe; **arcas públicas** Treasury

Takes the masculine articles **el** and **un**

arcada *nf* (**a**) arcade; *(de puente)* arch (**b**) *(náusea)* retching

arcaico, -a *adj* archaic

arcángel *nm* archangel

arcén *nm Esp (en carretera) Br* hard shoulder, *US* shoulder

archipiélago *nm* archipelago

archivador *nm* filing cabinet

archivar *vt* (**a**) *(documento etc)* to file (away) (**b**) *(caso, asunto)* to shelve (**c**) *Informát* to save

archivo *nm* (**a**) file (**b**) *(archivador)* filing cabinet (**c**) **archivos** archives (**d**) *Informát* file; **a. adjunto** attachment

arcilla *nf* clay

arco *nm* (**a**) *Arquit* arch (**b**) *Mat, Elec* arc (**c**) *(de violín)* bow (**d**) *(para flechas)* bow; **tiro con a.** archery (**e**) **a. iris** rainbow (**f**) *esp Am Dep (portería)* goal, goalmouth

arder *vi* to burn; *Fam* **la conversación**

está que arde the conversation is really heating up; **Juan está que arde** Juan is really fuming

ardiente *adj* (**a**) *(encendido)* burning; **capilla a.** chapel of rest (**b**) *Fig (fervoroso)* eager

ardilla *nf* squirrel

área *nf* (**a**) area; *Dep* penalty area (**b**) *(medida)* are *(100 square metres)*

Takes the masculine articles **el** and **un**

arena *nf* (**a**) sand; **playa de a.** sandy beach (**b**) *Taurom* bullring

arenoso, -a *adj* sandy

arenque *nm* herring; *Culin* **a. ahumado** kipper

arepa *nf Carib, Col* = pancake made of maize flour

arete *nm Andes, Méx (pendiente)* earring; *Esp (en forma de aro)* hoop earring

Argelia *n* Algeria

Argentina *n* Argentina

argentino, -a *adj & nm,f* Argentinian, Argentine

argolla *nf* (**a**) *(aro)* (large) ring (**b**) *Andes, Méx (alianza)* wedding ring (**c**) *Carib (pendiente)* hoop earring

argot (*pl* **argots**) *nm (popular)* slang; *(técnico)* jargon

argüende *nm Méx Fam* (**a**) *(chisme)* gossip (**b**) *(fiesta)* party, *Br* rave-up

argüir [62] *vt* (**a**) *(deducir)* to deduce (**b**) *(argumentar)* to argue

argumentar 1 *vt (alegar)* to argue **2** *vi (discutir)* to argue

argumento *nm* (**a**) *Lit, Teatro (trama)* plot (**b**) *(razonamiento)* argument

aria *nf (de ópera)* aria

árido, -a *adj* arid; *Fig* dry

Aries *nm* Aries

arista *nf* edge

aristocracia *nf* aristocracy

aristócrata *nmf* aristocrat

aritmética *nf* arithmetic

arlequín *nm* harlequin

arma *nf* weapon; **a. blanca** knife; **a. de fuego** firearm; **a. homicida** murder weapon; **a. nuclear** nuclear weapon;

Fig **a. de doble filo** double-edged sword

Takes the masculine articles **el** and **un**

armada *nf* navy

armadillo *nm* armadillo

armadura *nf* (**a**) *(armazón)* frame (**b**) *Hist* suit of armour

armamento *nm* armaments; **a. nuclear** nuclear weapons

armar 1 *vt* (**a**) *(tropa, soldado)* to arm (**b**) *(piezas)* to fit o put together, to assemble (**c**) *Fam* **armaron un escándalo** they created a scandal **2 armarse** *vpr* to arm oneself; *Fig* **armarse de paciencia** to summon up one's patience; *Fig* **armarse de valor** to pluck up courage; *Fam* **se armó la gorda** all hell broke loose

armario *nm (para ropa)* wardrobe; *(de cocina)* cupboard; **a. empotrado** built-in wardrobe o cupboard

armazón *nm* frame; *(de madera)* timberwork; *Arquit* shell

armisticio *nm* armistice

armonía *nf* harmony

armónica *nf* harmonica, mouth organ

armonizar [40] *vt & vi* to harmonize

aro *nm* (**a**) *(gen)* hoop; *Fam* **pasar por el a.** to knuckle under (**b**) *Am (pendiente)* earring; *(en forma de aro)* hoop earring (**c**) *Ven (alianza)* wedding ring (**d**) *Col (montura)* rim (**e**) *Bol (anillo)* ring

aroma *nm* aroma; *(de vino)* bouquet

arpa *nf* harp

Takes the masculine articles **el** and **un**

arqueología *nf* archaeology

arqueólogo, -a *nm,f* archaeologist

arquero, -a *nm,f* (**a**) *(tirador)* archer (**b**) *Am (portero de fútbol)* goalkeeper

arquitecto, -a *nm,f* architect

arquitectónico, -a *adj* architectural

arquitectura *nf* architecture

arraigar [42] *vi* to take root

arrancar [44] **1** *vt* (**a**) *(planta)* to uproot, to pull up; **a. de raíz** to uproot (**b**) *(extraer)* to pull o tear off o out; *(diente, pelo)* to pull out; *Fig (confesión* *etc)* to extract; **arranca una hoja del cuaderno** tear a page out of the notebook (**c**) *(coche, motor)* to start; *Informát* to boot

2 *vi* (**a**) *Aut, Téc* to start; *Informát* to boot (up) (**b**) *(empezar)* to begin; **a. a llorar** to burst out crying

arranque *nm* (**a**) *Aut, Téc* starting (**b**) *(comienzo)* start (**c**) *Fam (arrebato)* outburst, fit

arrastrar 1 *vt* to pull (along), to drag (along); **vas arrastrando el vestido** your dress is trailing on the ground; **lo arrastró la corriente** he was swept away by the current **2 arrastrarse** *vpr* to drag oneself; *Fig (humillarse)* to crawl

arrastre *nm* (**a**) pulling, dragging; *Esp Fam* **estar para el a.** to have had it (**b**) **(pesca de) a.** trawling (**c**) *RP Fam* **tener a.** to have a lot of influence

arrebatar 1 *vt (coger)* to snatch, to seize; *Fig (cautivar)* to captivate, to fascinate **2 arrebatarse** *vpr (enfurecerse)* to become furious; *(exaltarse)* to get carried away

arrebato *nm* outburst, fit

arreglar 1 *vt* (**a**) to arrange; *(problema)* to sort out; *(habitación)* to tidy; *(papeles)* to put in order (**b**) *(reparar)* to repair, to fix (**c**) *(vestir)* to get ready **2 arreglarse** *vpr* (**a**) *(vestirse)* to get ready (**b**) *Fam* **arreglárselas** to manage (**c**) *(reconciliarse)* to make up

arreglo *nm* (**a**) arrangement; *(acuerdo)* compromise (**b**) *(reparación)* repair; **no tiene a.** it is beyond repair; *Fam* **¡no tienes a.!** you're hopeless! (**c**) *Fml* **con a. a** in accordance with

arrendatario, -a *nm,f* leaseholder, lessee; *(inquilino)* tenant

arreos *nmpl* (**a**) *(de caballería)* harness, trappings (**b**) *(adornos)* adornments

arrepentirse [5] *vpr* **a. de** to regret; *Rel* to repent

arrestar *vt* to arrest, to detain; *(encarcelar)* to put in prison

arriba 1 *adv* up; *(encima)* on the top; **ahí a.** up there; **de a. abajo** from top

to bottom; *Fam* **mirar a algn de a. abajo** to look sb up and down; **desde a.** from above; **hacia a.** upwards; **de un millón para a.** from one million upwards; **más a.** higher up, further up; **a. del todo** right on *o* at the top; **la parte de a.** the top (part); **vive a.** he lives upstairs; **véase más a.** see above **2** *interj* get up!, up you get!; **¡a. la República!** long live the Republic!; **¡a. las manos!** hands up!

3 *prep Am* **a. (de)** on top of

arribeño, -a *Am* **1** *adj* highland **2** *nm,f* highlander

arriesgado, -a *adj* (**a**) *(peligroso)* risky (**b**) *(temerario)* fearless, daring

arriesgar [42] **1** *vt* to risk **2 arriesgarse** *vpr* to risk; **se arriesga demasiado** he's taking too many risks

arrimar 1 *vt* to move closer, to bring near *o* nearer; *Fam* **a. el hombro** to lend a hand **2 arrimarse** *vpr* to move *o* get close, to come near *o* nearer

arroba *nm Informát* at, @ sign

arrodillarse *vpr* to kneel down

arrogancia *nf* arrogance

arrogante *adj* arrogant

arrojar 1 *vt* (**a**) *(tirar)* to throw, to fling (**b**) *Com (saldo)* to show **2 arrojarse** *vpr* to throw oneself, to fling oneself

arroyo *nm* brook, stream

arroz *nm* rice; **a. con leche** rice pudding

arruga *nf (en la piel)* wrinkle; *(en la ropa)* crease

arrugar [42] **1** *vt (piel)* to wrinkle; *(ropa)* to crease; *(papel)* to crumple (up) **2 arrugarse** *vpr (piel)* to wrinkle; *(ropa)* to crease

arruinar 1 *vt* to ruin **2 arruinarse** *vpr* to be ruined

arsenal *nm* (**a**) *Esp (de barcos)* shipyard (**b**) *(de armas)* arsenal

arsénico *nm* arsenic

arte *nm o nf* (**a**) art; **bellas artes** fine arts; *Fam* **por amor al a.** for the love of it (**b**) *(habilidad)* skill

Takes the masculine articles **el** and **un**

artefacto *nm* device; **a. explosivo** explosive device

arteria *nf* artery; *(carretera)* highway

artesanal *adj* handmade

artesanía *nf* (**a**) *(cualidad)* craftsmanship (**b**) *(objetos)* crafts, handicrafts

artesano, -a **1** *nm,f* craftsman, *f* craftswoman **2** *adj* handmade

ártico, -a **1** *adj* arctic; **el océano Á.** the Arctic Ocean **2** *nm* **el Á.** the Arctic

articulación *nf* (**a**) *Anat* joint, articulation (**b**) *Téc* joint

articulado, -a *adj (tren etc)* articulated

articular *vt* to articulate

articulista *nmf* feature writer

artículo *nm* article; **a. de fondo** leader (article)

artificial *adj* artificial; *Tex* man-made *o* synthetic

artificio *nm* (**a**) artifice; **fuego de a.** firework (**b**) *(artimaña)* ruse

artista *nmf* artist; **a. de cine** movie *o* *Br* film star

artístico, -a *adj* artistic

arveja *nf RP* pea

arzobispo *nm* archbishop

as *nm* ace

asa *nf* handle

Takes the masculine articles **el** and **un**

asado, -a **1** *adj Culin* roast; **pollo a.** roast chicken; *Fig* **a. de calor** roasting, boiling hot **2** *nm Culin* roast; *Col, CSur (barbacoa)* barbecue

asador *nm* (**a**) *(aparato)* roaster (**b**) *(restaurante)* grill, grillroom

asalariado, -a **1** *adj* salaried **2** *nm,f* wage earner, salaried worker

asaltar *vt* to assault, to attack; *(banco)* to rob; *Fig* to assail

asalto *nm* (**a**) assault, attack; **a. a un banco** bank robbery (**b**) *(en boxeo)* round

asamblea *nf* meeting; **a. general** general meeting

asar **1** *vt* to roast **2** **asarse** *vpr Fig* to be roasting, to be boiling hot

ascendencia *nf* ancestry, ancestors; **de a. escocesa** of Scottish descent

ascendente **1** *adj* rising **2** *nm (en astrología)* ascendant

ascender [3] **1** *vt (en un cargo)* to promote **2** *vi* (**a**) to move upward; *(temperatura)* to rise; **la factura asciende a ...** the bill adds up to ... (**b**) *(al trono)* to ascend (**c**) *(de categoría)* to be promoted

ascendiente *nmf* ancestor

ascenso *nm* promotion; *(subida)* rise

ascensor *nm Br* lift, *US* elevator

asco *nm* disgust, repugnance; **me da a.** it makes me (feel) sick; **¡qué a.!** how disgusting *o* revolting!

ascua *nf* ember; *Fig* **en ascuas** on tenterhooks

Takes the masculine articles **el** and **un**

aseado, -a *adj* tidy, neat

asear **1** *vt* to clean, to tidy up **2** **asearse** *vpr* to wash, to get washed

asegurado, -a *adj* (**a**) insured (**b**) *(indudable)* secure

asegurar **1** *vt* (**a**) to insure (**b**) *(garantizar)* **me aseguró que ...** he assured me that ...; **a. el éxito de un proyecto** to ensure the success of a project (**c**) *(cuerda)* to fasten **2** **asegurarse** *vpr* (**a**) to make sure; **asegurarse de que ...** to make sure that ... (**b**) *Seg* to insure oneself

asentir [5] *vi* to assent, to agree; **a. con la cabeza** to nod

aseo *nm* (**a**) *(limpieza)* cleanliness, tidiness (**b**) *Esp (habitación)* bathroom; **aseos** *Br* toilets, *US* restroom

aséptico, -a *adj Med* aseptic; *Fig (indiferente)* detached

asequible *adj* affordable; *(comprensible)* easy to understand; *(alcanzable)* attainable

asesinar *vt* to murder; *(rey, ministro)* to assassinate

asesinato *nm* murder; *(de rey, ministro)* assassination

asesino, -a **1** *adj* murderous **2** *nm,f* killer; *(hombre)* murderer; *(mujer)* murderess; *Pol* assassin

asesor, -a **1** *nm,f* adviser; **a. fiscal** tax adviser **2** *adj* advisory

asesorar 1 *vt* (**a**) to advise, to give (professional) advice to (**b**) *Com* to act as consultant to **2 asesorarse** *vpr* to consult

asesoría *nf* consultant's office

asfaltado, -a 1 *adj* asphalt **2** *nm* *(acción)* asphalting, surfacing; *(asfalto)* asphalt, (road) surface

asfaltar *vt* to asphalt, to surface

asfalto *nm* asphalt

asfixia *nf* asphyxiation, suffocation

asfixiante *adj* asphyxiating, suffocating; *Fam* **hace un calor a.** it's stifling

asfixiar [43] *vt*, **asfixiarse** *vpr* to asphyxiate, to suffocate

así *adv* (**a**) *(de esta manera)* like this *o* that, this way, thus; **ponlo a.** put it this way; **a. de grande/alto** this big/tall; **algo a.** something like this *o* that; **¿no es a.?** isn't that so *o* right?; **a. a.** so-so (**b**) **a las seis o a.** around six o'clock; **diez años o a.** ten years more or less (**c**) **a. como** as well as (**d**) **aun a.** and despite that (**e**) **a. pues** so; **a. que ...** so ...

Asia *n* Asia; **A. Menor** Asia Minor

asiático, -a *adj & nm,f* Asian

asiento *nm* (**a**) seat; **a. trasero/ delantero** back/front seat; **tome a.** take a seat (**b**) *(poso)* sediment (**c**) *Fin* entry

asignatura *nf* subject; **a. pendiente** failed subject

asilado, -a *nm,f* refugee

asilo *nm* asylum; **a. de ancianos** old people's home; *Pol* **a. político** political asylum

asimilación *nf* assimilation

asimilar *vt* to assimilate

asir [46] **1** *vt* to grasp, to take hold of **2 asirse** *vpr también Fig* to cling (**a** to)

asistencia *nf* (**a**) *(presencia)* attendance; **falta de a.** absence (**b**) **a. médica/técnica** medical/technical assistance (**c**) *(público)* audience, public

asistente *nmf* (**a**) *(ayudante)* assistant, helper; **a. social** social worker

(**b**) *(presente)* person present; **los asistentes** *(el público)* the audience

asistir 1 *vt* to assist, to help **2** *vi* **a. (a)** to attend, to be present (at)

asma *nf* asthma

> Takes the masculine articles **el** and **un**

asmático, -a *adj & nm,f* asthmatic

asno *nm* donkey, ass

asociación *nf* association

asociar [43] **1** *vt* to associate **2 asociarse** *vpr* (**a**) to be associated (**b**) *Com* to become partners

asolar [2] *vt* to devastate, to destroy

asomar 1 *vt* to put out, to stick out; **asomó la cabeza por la ventana** he put his head out of the window **2** *vi* to appear **3 asomarse** *vpr* (**a**) to lean out; **asomarse a la ventana** to lean out of the window (**b**) *(entrar)* to pop in; *(salir)* to pop out

asombrar 1 *vt* to amaze, to astonish **2 asombrarse** *vpr* to be astonished; **asombrarse de algo** to be amazed at sth

asombro *nm* amazement, astonishment

asorocharse *vpr Andes* (**a**) *(por la altitud)* to get altitude sickness (**b**) *(sonrojarse)* to blush

aspa *nf* (**a**) *(de molino)* arm; *(de ventilador)* blade (**b**) *(cruz)* cross

> Takes the masculine articles **el** and **un**

aspecto *nm* (**a**) look, appearance (**b**) *(de un asunto)* aspect

aspereza *nf* roughness; *Fig* **limar asperezas** to smooth things over

áspero, -a *adj* rough; *Fig (carácter)* surly

aspiradora *nf* vacuum cleaner, *Br* Hoover®

aspirar 1 *vt* (**a**) *(respirar)* to inhale, to breathe in (**b**) *Téc (absorber)* to suck in, to draw in **2** *vi Fig* **a. a algo** to aspire after sth

aspirina *nf* aspirin

asquear *vt* to disgust, to make sick

asquerosidad *nf* filthy *o* revolting thing; **¡que a.!** how revolting!

asqueroso, -a 1 *adj (sucio)* filthy; *(desagradable)* revolting, disgusting **2** *nm,f* filthy o revolting person

asta *nf* (**a**) *(de bandera)* staff, pole; **a media a.** at half-mast (**b**) *Zool (cuerno)* horn

Takes the masculine articles **el** and **un**

asterisco *nm* asterisk

astillero *nm* shipyard

astro *nm* star

astrología *nf* astrology

astrólogo, -a *nm,f* astrologer

astronauta *nmf* astronaut

astronomía *nf* astronomy

astronómico, -a *adj* astronomical

astrónomo, -a *nm,f* astronomer

astuto, -a *adj* astute, shrewd

asumir *vt* to assume

asunto *nm* (**a**) subject; **no es a. tuyo** it's none of your business (**b**) **Asuntos Exteriores** Foreign Affairs

asustar 1 *vt* to frighten, to scare **2 asustarse** *vpr* to be frightened, to be scared

atacar [44] *vt* to attack, to assault; *Fig* **me ataca los nervios** he gets on my nerves

atajo *nm* (**a**) *(camino corto, medio rápido)* short cut (**b**) *Esp Pey (panda)* bunch

ataque *nm* (**a**) attack, assault; **a. aéreo** air raid (**b**) *Med* fit; **a. cardíaco** o **al corazón** heart attack; **a. de nervios/tos** fit of hysterics/coughing

atar 1 *vt* (**a**) to tie; *Fig* **a. cabos** to put two and two together; *Fam* **loco de a.** as mad as a hatter (**b**) *Fig* to tie down **2 atarse** *vpr Fig* to get tied up; **átate los zapatos** do your shoes up

atardecer [33] **1** *v impers* to get o grow dark **2** *nm* evening, dusk

atareado, -a *adj* busy

atasco *nm* traffic jam

ataúd *nm* coffin

ate *nm Méx* quince jelly

ateísmo *nm* atheism

atención 1 *nf* attention; **llamar la a.** to attract attention; **prestar/poner a.** to pay attention (**a** to) **2** *interj* attention!

atender [3] **1** *vt* to attend to; *(petición)* to agree to **2** *vi (alumno)* to pay attention (**a** to)

atentado *nm* attack; **a. terrorista** terrorist attack

atentamente *adv* **le saluda a.** *(en carta)* yours sincerely o faithfully

atento, -a *adj* (**a**) attentive; **estar a. a** to be mindful o aware of (**b**) *(amable)* thoughtful, considerate; **atentos saludos de** *(en carta)* yours faithfully

ateo, -a 1 *adj* atheistic **2** *nm,f* atheist

aterrizaje *nm Av* landing; **a. forzoso** forced landing

aterrizar [40] *vi* to land

aterrorizar [40] **1** *vt* to terrify; *Mil, Pol* to terrorize **2 aterrorizarse** *vpr* to be terrified

atestado¹, -a *adj* packed, crammed; **estaba a. de gente** it was full of people

atestado² *nm Jur* affidavit, statement; **atestados** testimonials

atestiguar [45] *vt* (**a**) *Jur* to testify to (**b**) *Fig* to vouch for

ático *nm (piso)* = attic *Br* flat o *US* apartment, usually with a roof terrace; *(desván)* attic

atinar *vi* to get it right; **a. a hacer algo** to succeed in doing sth; **a. al blanco** to hit the target; **atinó con la solución** he found the solution

atingencia *nf* (**a**) *Am, CAm, Chile, Méx (relación)* connection (**b**) *Chile, Méx (adecuación)* appropriateness; **la Cámara está estudiando la a. de esa ley** the House is investigating whether the law is appropriate o acceptable (**c**) *Méx (tino)* good sense

atípico, -a *adj* atypical

atizar [40] *vt* (**a**) *(fuego)* to poke, to stir (**b**) *(sospechas, discordias)* to fan (**c**) *Esp (persona)* **me atizó bien fuerte** *(un golpe)* he hit me really hard; *(una paliza)* he gave me a good hiding

atlántico, -a 1 *adj* Atlantic **2** *nm* **el** *(océano)* **A.** the Atlantic (Ocean)

atlas *nm inv* atlas

atleta *nmf* athlete

atlético, -a *adj* athletic

atletismo *nm* athletics *sing*

atmósfera *nf* atmosphere

atmosférico, -a *adj* atmospheric

atole, atol *nm CAm, Méx* = thick hot drink made of corn meal

atolondrar 1 *vt* to confuse, to bewilder **2 atolondrarse** *vpr* to be confused, to be bewildered

atómico, -a *adj* atomic

átomo *nm* atom

atónito, -a *adj* amazed, astonished

atontado, -a *adj* (**a**) *(tonto)* silly, foolish (**b**) *(aturdido)* bewildered, amazed

atorarse *vpr* (**a**) *(atragantarse)* to choke (**con** on) (**b**) *Am (atascarse)* to get stuck (**c**) *Am (meterse en un lío)* to get into a mess

atorón *nm Méx* traffic jam

atorrante *adj RP Fam (holgazán)* lazy

atracador, -a *nm,f (de banco)* (bank) robber; *(en la calle)* attacker, mugger

atracar [44] **1** *vt* to hold up; *(persona)* to rob

2 *vi Náut* to come alongside, to tie up

3 atracarse *vpr (de comida)* to stuff oneself (**de** with), to gorge oneself (**de** on)

atracción *nf* attraction; **parque de atracciones** funfair

atraco *nm* hold-up, robbery; **a. a mano armada** armed robbery

atractivo, -a 1 *adj* attractive, appealing **2** *nm* attraction, appeal

atraer [25] *vt* to attract

atragantarse *vpr* to choke (**con** on), to swallow the wrong way; *Fig* **esa chica se me ha atragantado** I can't stand that girl

atrapar *vt* to catch

atrás *adv* (**a**) *(lugar)* at the back, behind; **hacia/para a.** backwards; **puerta de a.** back *o* rear door; *Fig* **echarse a.** to back out (**b**) *(tiempo)* previously, in the past, ago; **un año a.** a year ago; **venir de muy a.** to go *o* date back a long time

atrasado, -a *adj* late, slow; *(pago)* overdue; *(reloj)* slow; *(país)* backward; *Prensa* **número a.** back number

atrasar 1 *vt* to put back

2 *vi (reloj)* to be slow

3 atrasarse *vpr* (**a**) to remain *o* stay behind, to lag behind (**b**) *(tren)* to be late

atraso *nm* (**a**) delay (**b**) *(de país)* backwardness (**c**) *Fin* **atrasos** arrears

atravesar [1] **1** *vt* (**a**) *(calle)* to cross (**b**) *(muro)* to pierce, to go through (**c**) *(poner a través)* to lay across, to put across, to put crosswise **2 atravesarse** *vpr* to get in the way; *Fig* **se me ha atravesado Luis** I can't stand Luis

atreverse *vpr* to dare; **a. a hacer algo** to dare to do sth

atrevido, -a *adj* (**a**) *(osado)* daring, bold (**b**) *(insolente)* insolent, impudent (**c**) *(ropa etc)* daring, risqué

atribución *nf* (**a**) *(imputación)* attribution (**b**) *(competencia)* responsibility, duty

atribuir [37] **1** *vt* to attribute, to ascribe **2 atribuirse** *vpr* to assume

atributo *nm* attribute

atrio *nm* (**a**) *(pórtico)* portico (**b**) *(patio interior)* atrium

atropellar *vt* to knock down, to run over

atropello *nm* (**a**) *Aut* knocking down, running over (**b**) *(abuso)* abuse

ATS *nmf Esp (abr* **ayudante técnico sanitario***)* qualified nurse

atún *nm* tuna, tunny

audaz *adj* audacious, bold

audiencia *nf* (**a**) *(público)* audience; *TV, Rad* **horas de máxima a.** prime time; **índice de a.** viewing figures, ratings (**b**) *(entrevista)* audience (**c**) *Jur* court hearing

audiovisual *adj* audio-visual

auditivo, -a 1 *adj* auditory; **comprensión auditiva** listening comprehension **2** *nm* receiver

auditor *nm Fin* auditor

auditoría *nf Fin* (**a**) *(profesión)* auditing (**b**) *(despacho)* auditor's,

auditing company (**c**) *(balance)* audit;
a. externa/interna external/internal
audit

auditorio *nm* (**a**) *(público)* audience
(**b**) *(sala)* auditorium, hall

auge *nm* peak; *Econ* boom; *Fig* **estar
en a.** to be thriving *o* booming

aula *nf (en colegio)* classroom; *Univ*
lecture room; **a. magna** amphitheatre

Takes the masculine articles **el** and **un**

aullar *vt* to howl, to yell

aullido *nm* howl, yell

aumentar 1 *vt* to increase; *(precios)*
to put up; *(producción)* to step up; *Fot*
to enlarge; *Opt* to magnify
  2 *vi (precios)* to go up, to rise; *(valor)*
to appreciate
  3 aumentarse *vpr* to increase, to be
on the increase

aumento *nm* increase; *Opt* mag-
nification; **a. de precios** rise in prices;
ir en a. to be on the increase

aun *adv* even; **a. así** even so, even then;
a. más even more

aún *adv* still; *(en negativas)* yet; **a. está
aquí** he's still here; **ella no ha venido
a.** she hasn't come yet

aunque *conj* although, though; *(enfático)* even if, even though; **a. no
vengas** even if you don't come

aureola *nf* halo

auricular *nm* (**a**) *Tel* receiver (**b**)
auriculares earphones, headphones

ausencia *nf* absence

ausente 1 *adj* absent **2** *nmf* absentee

austeridad *nf* austerity

austero, -a *adj* austere

Australia *n* Australia

australiano, -a *adj & nm,f* Australian

Austria *n* Austria

austríaco, -a *adj & nm,f* Austrian

autenticidad *nf* authenticity

auténtico, -a *adj* authentic

auto[1] *nm esp CSur (coche)* car

auto[2] *nm Jur* decree, writ; **autos**
(pleito) papers, documents

autobiografía *nf* autobiography

autobús *nm* bus

autocar *nm Esp* bus, *Br* coach

autocontrol *nm* self-control

autóctono, -a *adj* indigenous

autoescuela *nf* driving school, school
of motoring

autógrafo *nm* autograph

automático, -a *adj* automatic

automóvil *nm Br* car, *US* automobile

automovilismo *nm* motoring

automovilista *nmf* motorist

autonomía *nf* (**a**) autonomy (**b**)
(región) autonomous region

autonómico, -a *adj* autonomous,
self-governing; **elecciones autonó-
micas** elections for the autonomous
parliament; **televisión autonómica**
regional television

autónomo, -a *adj* autonomous

autopista *nf Br* motorway, *US*
freeway; *Informát* **autopista de la
información** information superhigh-
way

autopsia *nf* autopsy, postmortem

autor, -a *nm,f* author, *f* authoress; *(de
crimen)* perpetrator

autoría *nf (de obra)* authorship; *(de
crimen)* perpetration

autoridad *nf* authority

autoritario, -a *adj* authoritarian

autorización *nf* authorization; **dar a.
a algn (para hacer algo)** to authorize
sb (to do sth)

autorizado, -a *adj* authoritative,
official

autorizar [40] *vt* to authorize

autorretrato *nm* self-portrait

autoservicio *nm* self-service; *(supermercado)* supermarket

autostop *nm* hitch-hiking; **hacer a.** to
hitch-hike

autostopista *nmf* hitch-hiker

autosuficiente *adj* self-sufficient

autovía *nf Br* dual carriageway, *US*
divided highway

auxiliar [43] **1** *adj & nmf* auxiliary,
assistant **2** *vt* to help, to assist

auxilio *nm* help, assistance; **primeros
auxilios** first aid

auyama *nf Carib, Col* pumpkin

Av. *nf* (*abr* **Avenida**) Ave

aval *nm Com, Fin* endorsement

avalancha *nf* avalanche

avalar *vt* to guarantee, to endorse

avance *nm* (**a**) advance (**b**) *Fin* advance payment (**c**) *TV* a. **informativo** news summary, *US* news in brief

avanzado, -a *adj* advanced; **de avanzada edad** advanced in years

avanzar [40] *vt* to advance

avaricioso, -a *adj* greedy

avaro, -a 1 *adj* avaricious, miserly **2** *nm,f* miser

Avda. = **Av.**

AVE *nf* (*abr* **Alta Velocidad Española**) High Speed Train

ave *nf* bird; **aves de corral** poultry; **a. de rapiña** bird of prey

Takes the masculine articles **el** and **un**

avellana *nf* hazelnut

avellano *nm* hazelnut tree

avena *nf* oats

avenida *nf* avenue

aventar [1] **1** *vt* (**a**) *Agr* to winnow (**b**) *(el fuego)* to fan (**c**) *Andes, CAm, Méx Fam (tirar)* to throw; **le aventé una bofetada** I slapped him (**d**) *CAm, Méx, Perú (empujar)* to push, to shove **2 aventarse** *vpr Méx* (**a**) *(tirarse)* to throw oneself (**b**) *(atreverse)* **aventarse a hacer algo** to dare to do sth

aventón *nm CAm, Méx, Perú* **dar a. a algn** to give sb a ride; **pedir a.** to hitch a ride

aventura *nf* (**a**) adventure (**b**) *(amorosa)* (love) affair

aventurarse *vpr* to venture

aventurero, -a *adj* adventurous

avergonzado, -a *adj* ashamed

avergonzar [63] **1** *vt* to shame **2 avergonzarse** *vpr* to be ashamed (**de** of)

avería *nf* breakdown

averiado, -a *adj* out of order; *(coche)* broken down

averiar [29] **1** *vt* to break **2 averiarse**

vpr (estropearse) to malfunction, to go wrong; *(coche)* to break down

averiguar [45] *vt* to ascertain

aversión *nf* aversion

avestruz *nm* ostrich

aviación *nf* (**a**) aviation; **accidente de a.** plane crash; **a. civil** civil aviation (**b**) *Mil* air force

aviador, -a *nm,f* aviator, flier; *Mil (piloto)* air force pilot

avión¹ *nm* aircraft, *Br* aeroplane, *US* airplane; **viajar en a.** to fly, to go by plane; **por a.** *(en carta)* airmail

avión² *nm Orn* martin

avioneta *nf* light aircraft *o* plane

avisar *vt* (**a**) *(informar)* to inform; **avísame cuando hayas acabado** let me know when you finish (**b**) *(advertir)* to warn; **ya te avisé** I warned you (**c**) *(llamar)* to call for; **a. a la policía** to notify the police; **a. al médico** to send for the doctor

aviso *nm* (**a**) notice; *(advertencia)* warning; *(nota)* note; **hasta nuevo a.** until further notice; **sin previo a.** without notice (**b**) **estar sobre a.** to know what's going on, be in on it (**c**) *Am (anuncio)* advertisement; **a. clasificado** classified advertisement

avispa *nf* wasp

avituallamiento *nm* provisioning

avituallar *vt* to provide with food

axila *nf* armpit, axilla

ay *interj (dolor)* ouch!

ayer 1 *adv* yesterday; **a. por la mañana/por la tarde** yesterday morning/afternoon; **a. por la noche** last night; **antes de a.** the day before yesterday **2** *nm* **el a.** yesteryear

ayuda *nf* help, assistance; **ir en a. de algn** to come to sb's assistance; **a. al desarrollo** development aid

ayudante *nmf* assistant; *Med* **a. técnico-sanitario** nurse

ayudar 1 *vt* to help; **¿en qué puedo ayudarle?** (how) can I help you? **2 ayudarse** *vpr* (**a**) *(unos a otros)* to help (**b**) **ayudarse de** to use, to make use of

ayunar *vi* to fast

ayuntamiento *nm (institución) Br* town council, *US* city council; *(edificio) Br* town hall, *US* city hall

azada *nf* hoe

azafata *nf* (**a**) *Av* air stewardess, *Br* air hostess (**b**) *(de congresos)* stewardess; *(de concurso)* hostess

azafate *nm CAm, Carib, Méx, Perú* tray

azafrán *nm* saffron

azar *nm* chance; **por a.** by chance; **al a.** at random; **juegos de a.** games of chance; **los azares de la vida** the ups and downs of life

azotea *nf* flat roof

azúcar *nm o nf* sugar

azucarado, -a *adj* sweetened

azucarera *nf (fábrica)* sugar refinery; *(recipiente)* sugar bowl

azucena *nf* white lily

azufre *nm* sulphur

azul *adj & nm* blue; **a. celeste** sky blue; **a. marino** navy blue; **a. turquesa** turquoise; **sangre a.** blue blood

azulado, -a *adj* bluish

azulejo *nm* (glazed) tile

Bb

baba *nf* dribble; *Fig* **se le caía la b.** he was delighted

babero *nm* bib

babor *nm Náut* port, port side

babosa *nf* slug

babosada *nf CAm, Méx Fam (disparate)* daft thing; **¡no digas babosadas!** don't talk *Br* rubbish *o US* bull!

baboso, -a *Fam* **1** *adj* (**a**) *(despreciable)* slimy (**b**) *Am (tonto)* daft, stupid **2** *nm,f* (**a**) *(persona despreciable)* creep (**b**) *Am (tonto)* twit, idiot

baca *nf Aut* roof rack

bacalao *nm (pez)* cod

bacán 1 *adj Cuba, Perú* cool, wicked **2** *nm Cuba* toff; **como un b.** like a real gentleman

bachillerato *nm* = academically orientated Spanish secondary school course for pupils aged 14-17

bacon *nm Esp* bacon

bádminton *nm* badminton

bafle, baffle ['bafle] *nm* loudspeaker

bahía *nf* bay

bailar *vt & vi* to dance; *Fig* **b. al son que le tocan** to toe the line; *Fam* **¡que me quiten lo baila(d)o!** but at least I had a good time!

bailarín, -ina *nm,f* dancer; *(clásico)* ballet dancer

baile *nm* (**a**) *(danza)* dance (**b**) *(fiesta popular)* dance; *(formal)* ball; **b. de disfraces** fancy dress ball

baja *nf* (**a**) *(descenso)* drop, fall; *Fin* **jugar a la b.** to bear the market (**b**) *(cese)* **dar de b. a algn** *(en una empresa)* to lay sb off; *(en un club, sindicato)* to expel sb; **darse de b. (de)** *(dimitir)* to resign (from); *(salirse)* to drop out (of)

(**c**) *(permiso) (por enfermedad)* sick leave; **estar/darse de b.** to be on/take sick leave; **b. por maternidad** maternity leave

(**d**) *Mil* loss, casualty; **bajas civiles** civilian casualties

bajada *nf* (**a**) *(descenso)* descent (**b**) *(cuesta)* slope (**c**) **b. de bandera** *(de taxi)* minimum fare

bajar 1 *vt* (**a**) to come/go down; **b. la escalera** to come/go downstairs (**b**) *(descender)* to bring/get/take down; *(volumen)* to turn down; *(voz, telón)* to lower; *(precios etc)* to reduce, to cut; *(persiana)* to let down; *(cabeza)* to bow *o* lower

2 *vi* (**a**) to go/come down (**b**) *(apearse)* to get off; *(de un coche)* to get out (**de** of) (**c**) *(disminuir)* to fall, to drop

3 bajarse *vpr* (**a**) to come/go down (**b**) *(apearse)* to get off; *(de un coche)* to get out (**de** of)

bajativo *nm Andes, RP (licor)* digestive liqueur; *(tisana)* herbal tea

bajial *nm Méx, Perú* lowland

bajío *nm* (**a**) sandbank (**b**) *(terreno bajo)* lowland

bajo, -a 1 *adj* low; *(persona)* short; *(sonido)* faint, soft; **en voz baja** in a low voice; **planta baja** ground floor; **de baja calidad** of poor quality; **la clase baja** the lower class

2 *nm* (**a**) *Mús* bass (**b**) *(planta baja) (piso) Br* ground floor flat, *US* first floor apartment

3 *adv* low; *(hablar)* quietly

4 *prep* under, underneath; **b. cero** below zero **b. tierra** underground; **b. la lluvia** in the rain

bala *nf* bullet; *Fig* **como una b.** like a shot

balacear *vt Am* to shoot

balacera *nf Am* shoot-out

balada *nf* ballad

balance *nm* (**a**) *Fin* balance sheet; *Fig* **hacer b. de una situación** to take stock of a situation (**b**) *(resultado)* outcome

balanceo *nm* (**a**) rocking, swinging; *(de barco, avión)* rolling; (**b**) *Am Aut* wheel balance

balancín *nm* (**a**) *(mecedora)* rocking chair; *(en el jardín)* swing hammock (**b**) *(columpio)* seesaw

balanza *nf* scales; *Fig* **estar en la b.** to be in the balance *o* in danger; **b. comercial** balance of trade; **b. de pagos** balance of payments

balar *vi* to bleat

balcón *nm* balcony

balde¹ *nm* pail, bucket

balde² *loc adv* (**a**) **de b.** *(gratis)* free (**b**) **en b.** *(en vano)* in vain

baldosa *nf* (ceramic) floor tile; *(para pavimentar)* flagstone, paving stone

balear 1 *vt Am (disparar)* to shoot **2** *adj* Balearic

Baleares *npl* **las (Islas) B.** the Balearic Islands

baleo *nm Am* shoot-out

balido *nm* bleating, bleat

ballena *nf* whale

ballet [ba'le] *nm (pl* **ballets**) ballet

balneario *nm* spa, health resort

balón *nm* (**a**) ball, football; *Fig* **b. de oxígeno** boost (**b**) *(bombona)* gas cylinder

baloncesto *nm* basketball

balonmano *nm* handball

balonvolea *nm* volleyball

balsa *nf* (**a**) *Náut* raft (**b**) *Fig* **como una b. de aceite** very quiet

bálsamo *nm* balsam, balm

bambú *nm (pl* **bambúes** *o* **bambús**) bamboo

banana *nf* banana

banca *nf* (**a**) *(asiento)* bench (**b**) *Com, Fin* (the) banks; *(actividad)* banking; **b. electrónica** electronic banking (**c**) *(en juegos)* bank

banco *nm* (**a**) bench (**b**) *Com, Fin* bank (**c**) **b. de arena** sandbank (**d**) *(de peces)* shoal, school (**e**) *Geol* layer

banda *nf* (**a**) *Mús* band (**b**) *Cin* **b. sonora** sound track (**c**) *(de pájaros)* flock (**d**) *(cinta)* sash (**e**) *(lado)* side; *Ftb* **línea de b.** touchline; **saque de b.** throw-in

bandeja *nf* tray; *Fig* **servir algo a algn en b.** to hand sth to sb on a plate

bandera *nf* flag; **b. azul** *(en playa)* blue flag

banderilla *nf* (**a**) *Taurom* banderilla, = barbed dart thrust into bull's back (**b**) *Esp (aperitivo)* = hors d'œuvre of pickles and olives on a cocktail stick

banderín *nf* pennant, small flag

bandido *nm* bandit, outlaw

bando¹ *nm* (**a**) *Jur (edicto)* edict, proclamation (**b**) **bandos** banns

bando² *nm* faction, side; **pasarse al otro b.** to go over to the other side, to change side

banjo ['banjo] *nm* banjo

banquero, -a *nm,f* banker

banqueta *nf* (**a**) *(asiento)* stool (**b**) *(para los pies)* foot-stool (**c**) *CAm, Méx (acera) Br* pavement, *US* sidewalk

banquina *nf RP (arcén) Br* hard shoulder, *US* shoulder

bañadera *nf* (**a**) *Arg (bañera)* bath (**b**) *RP (vehículo)* = old-fashioned school bus

bañado *nm Bol, RP (terreno)* marshy area

bañador *nm Esp (de mujer)* swimsuit; *(de hombre)* swimming trunks

bañar 1 *vt* (**a**) to bath (**b**) *(cubrir)* to coat, cover; **b. en oro** to goldplate **2 bañarse** *vpr (en baño)* to have *o* take a bath; *(en mar, piscina)* to go for a swim; *Am (ducharse)* to have a shower

bañera *nf* bath, bathtub

bañista *nmf* bather, swimmer

baño *nm* (**a**) bath; **tomar un b.** to have *o* take a bath; *Fig* **darse un b. de sol** to sunbathe; **b. de sangre** bloodbath (**b**) *(de oro etc)* coat; *(de chocolate etc)* coating, covering (**c**) *(cuarto de aseo)* bathroom; *(servicios) Br* toilet, *US* bathroom

bar *nm* bar, pub

baraja *nf Br* pack *o US* deck (of cards)

barajar *vt (cartas)* to shuffle; *Fig (nombres, cifras)* to juggle with

baranda, *Esp* **barandilla** *nf (de escalera)* handrail, banister; *(de balcón)* handrail

baratija *nf* trinket, knick-knack

barato, -a 1 *adj* cheap **2** *adv* cheaply

barba *nf* (**a**) *Anat* chin (**b**) *(pelo)* beard; *Esp* **2 euros por b.** 2 euros a head

barbacoa *nf* barbecue

barbaridad *nf* (**a**) atrocity (**b**) *(disparate)* piece of nonsense; **no digas barbaridades** don't talk nonsense (**c**) **una b.** a lot; **costar una b.** to cost a fortune

barbarie *nf* savagery, cruelty

bárbaro, -a 1 *adj* (**a**) *Hist* barbarian (**b**) *(cruel)* barbaric, barbarous (**c**) *Fam (enorme)* massive (**d**) *RP Fam (estupendo)* tremendous, terrific **2** *nm,f Hist* barbarian

barbería *nf* barber's (shop)

barbero *nm* barber

barbilla *nf* chin

barbudo, -a *adj* with a heavy beard

barca *nf* small boat

barcaza *nf* lighter

Barcelona *n* Barcelona

barcelonés, -esa 1 *adj* of/from Barcelona **2** *nm,f* person from Barcelona

barco *nm* boat, ship; **b. de pasajeros** liner; **b. de vapor** steamer

barítono *nm* baritone

barman *(pl* **barmans)** *nm* barman

barniz *nm* (**a**) *(en madera)* varnish; *(en cerámica)* glaze (**b**) *Fig* veneer

barnizado, -a *adj (madera)* varnished; *(cerámica)* glazed

barnizar [40] *vt (madera)* to varnish; *(cerámica)* to glaze

barómetro *nm* barometer

barquillo *nm* wafer

barra *nf* (**a**) bar; **b. de pan** French loaf,

baguette; **b. de labios** lipstick (**b**) *(mostrador)* bar; **b. americana** = bar where hostesses chat with clients (**c**) *Dep* **b. fija** horizontal bar; **barras paralelas** parallel bars (**d**) *Andes, RP Fam (de amigos)* gang; **b. brava** = group of violent soccer supporters

barraca *nf* (**a**) *(caseta)* shack, hut (**b**) *(en Valencia y Murcia)* thatched farmhouse

barranco *nm (despeñadero)* cliff, precipice; *(torrentera)* gully, ravine

barrendero, -a *nm,f* sweeper, street sweeper

barreño *nm Esp* washing-up bowl

barrer 1 *vt* to sweep **2** *vi (en elecciones)* to win by a landslide

barrera *nf* barrier

barriada *nf* (**a**) *(barrio popular)* neighbourhood, area (**b**) *Am (barrio de chabolas)* shanty town

barriga *nf* belly; *Fam* tummy

barril *nm* barrel; **cerveza de b.** draught beer

barrio *nm* area, district, *US* neighborhood; **del b.** local; **el B. Gótico** the Gothic Quarter; **b. chino** *(de chinos)* Chinatown; *Esp (de prostitución)* red-light district; **barrios bajos** slums

barro *nm* (**a**) *(lodo)* mud (**b**) *(arcilla)* clay; **objetos de b.** earthenware

barroco, -a *adj* baroque

bártulos *nmpl Fam* things, bits and pieces

barullo *nm (alboroto)* row, din; *(confusión)* confusion

basar 1 *vt* to base (**en** on) **2 basarse** *vpr (teoría, película)* **basarse en** to be based on; **¿en qué te basas para decir eso?** what grounds do you have for saying that?

basca *nf Esp Fam* people, crowd

báscula *nf* scales; *(para camiones)* weighbridge

base *nf* (**a**) base; **sueldo b.** minimum wage; *Informát* **b. de datos** database (**b**) *(de argumento, teoría)* basis; **en b. a** on the basis of; **a b. de estudiar** by studying; **a b. de productos naturales** using natural products (**c**) *(de* *partido)* grass roots; **miembro de b.** rank and file member (**d**) *(nociones)* grounding

básico, -a *adj* basic

basta *interj* that's enough!; **¡b. de chistes/tonterías!** that's enough jokes/ of this nonsense!

bastante 1 *adj* (**a**) *(suficiente)* enough; **b. tiempo/comida** enough time/food; **bastantes platos** enough plates (**b**) *(abundante)* quite a lot of; **hace b. calor/frío** it's quite hot/cold; **bastantes amigos** quite a lot of friends **2** *adv* (**a**) *(suficiente)* enough; **con esto hay b.** that is enough; **no soy lo b. rico (como) para …** I am not rich enough to … (**b**) *(considerablemente)* fairly, quite; **me gusta b.** I quite like it; **vamos b. al cine** we go to the cinema quite *o* fairly often

bastar 1 *vi* to be sufficient *o* enough, to suffice; **basta con tres** three will be enough; **¡basta de tonterías!** enough of this nonsense!; **basta con tocarlo para que se abra** you only have to touch it and it opens; **¡basta (ya)!** that's enough!, that will do! **2 bastarse** *vpr* **bastarse a sí mismo** to be self-sufficient, to rely only on oneself

bastardo, -a *adj & nm,f* bastard

bastidor *nm* (**a**) *(armazón)* frame (**b**) *Teatro* **bastidores** wings; *Fig* **entre bastidores** behind the scenes

basto, -a *adj (cosa)* rough, coarse; *(persona)* coarse, uncouth

bastón *nm* stick, walking stick

basura *nf Br* rubbish, *US* garbage, *US* trash

basurero *nm* (**a**) *(persona) Br* dustman, *US* garbage man (**b**) *(lugar) Br* rubbish tip *o* dump, *US* garbage dump

bata *nf (para casa)* dressing gown; *(de médico etc)* white coat; *(de científico)* lab coat

batacazo *nm* (**a**) *(golpe)* bump, bang; **los resultados representan un nuevo b. para el partido** the results are another blow for the party (**b**) *CSur Fam (triunfo inesperado)* surprise victory

batalla *nf* battle; **librar b.** to do *o* join battle; **b. campal** pitched battle

batería 1 *nf*(**a**) battery (**b**) *Mús* drums (**c**) **b. de cocina** pots and pans, set of pans **2** *nmf* drummer

batido, -a 1 *adj* (**a**) *Culin* whipped (**b**) *Dep* **tierra batida** clay **2** *nm* milk shake

batidora *nf (eléctrica)* mixer

batín *nm* short dressing gown

batir 1 *vt* (**a**) to beat (**b**) *(huevo)* to beat; *(nata)* to whip, to whisk (**c**) *(récord)* to break (**d**) *(en caza)* to beat **2 batirse** *vpr* to fight

batuta *nf Mús* baton; *Fig* **llevar la b.** to be in charge

baúl *nm* (**a**) *(cofre)* trunk (**b**) *Arg, Col (maletero) Br* boot, *US* trunk

bautismo *nm* baptism, christening

bautizar [40] *vt* to baptize, to christen; *(vino)* to water down

bautizo *nm* baptism, christening

baya *nf* berry

bayeta *nf* floorcloth

bayoneta *nf* bayonet

bazar *nm* bazaar

be *nf*(**a**) *Esp (letra)* = name of the letter b (**b**) *Am* **be alta** *o* **grande** *o* **larga** b *(to distinguish from "v")*

beato, -a *adj (piadoso)* devout; *Pey* prudish, sanctimonious

bebe, -a *nm,f Andes, RP* baby

bebé *nm* baby; **b. probeta** test-tube baby

beber *vt & vi* to drink

bebida *nf* drink; **darse a la b.** to take to drink

bebido, -a *adj* drunk

beca *nf* grant

becario, -a *nm,f* grant holder

becerro *nm* calf

bechamel *nf* bechamel; **salsa b.** bechamel sauce, white sauce

bedel *nm* beadle

begonia *nf* begonia

beige *adj & nm inv* beige

béisbol *nm* baseball

belén *nm* nativity scene, crib

belga *adj & nmf* Belgian

Bélgica *n* Belgium

bélico, -a *adj* warlike, bellicose; *(preparativos etc)* war; **material b.** armaments

belleza *nf* beauty

bello, -a *adj* beautiful

bellota *nf Bot* acorn; *Fig* **animal de b.** blockhead

bencina *nf Chile (gasolina) Br* petrol, *US* gas

bencinera *nf Chile Br* petrol station, *US* gas station

bendecir [12] *vt* to bless; **b. la mesa** to say grace; **¡Dios te bendiga!** God bless you!

bendición *nf* blessing

bendito, -a 1 *adj* blessed; *(maldito)* damned **2** *nm,f (bonachón)* good sort, kind soul; *(tontorrón)* simple soul

beneficencia *nf* beneficence, charity

beneficiar [43] **1** *vt* to benefit **2** **beneficiarse** *vpr* **beneficiarse de** *o* **con algo** to profit from *o* by sth

beneficio *nm* (a) *Com, Fin* profit (b) *(bien)* benefit; **en b. propio** in one's own interest; **un concierto a b. de ...** a concert in aid of ...

benéfico, -a *adj* charitable

benevolencia *nf* benevolence

benevolente, benévolo, -a *adj* benevolent

bengala *nf* flare

berberecho *nm* (common) cockle

berenjena *nf Br* aubergine, *US* eggplant

berma *nf Andes (arcén) Br* hard shoulder, *US* shoulder

Bermudas *nfpl* **las (Islas) B.** Bermuda

bermudas *nmpl o nfpl* Bermuda shorts

berrinche *nm Fam* tantrum

berza *nf* cabbage

besar 1 *vt* to kiss **2 besarse** *vpr* to kiss

beso *nm* kiss

bestia 1 *nf* beast, animal; **b. de carga** beast of burden

    2 *nmf Fam Fig* brute, beast

3 *adj Fig* brutish, boorish; **a lo b.** rudely

besugo *nm* (a) *(pez)* sea bream (b) *Esp (persona)* idiot, half-wit

betabel *nf Méx Br* beetroot, *US* beet

betarraga *nf Andes Br* beetroot, *US* beet

betún *nm (para el calzado)* shoe polish; *Quím* bitumen

biberón *nm* baby's bottle, feeding bottle

Biblia *nf* Bible

bibliografía *nf* bibliography

bibliorato *nm RP* lever arch file

biblioteca *nf* (a) *(institución)* library; **b. ambulante** mobile library (b) *Chile, Perú, RP (mueble)* bookcase

bibliotecario, -a *nm,f* librarian

bicarbonato *nm* bicarbonate; **b. sódico** bicarbonate of soda

bíceps *nm inv* biceps

bicho *nm* (a) *bug, insect;* **¿qué b. le ha picado?** *Br* what's up with him?, *US* what's eating him? (b) *Taurom* bull (c) *Fam* **todo b. viviente** every living soul; **un b. raro** a weirdo, an oddball

bici *nf Fam* bike

bicicleta *nf* bicycle; **montar en b.** to ride a bicycle

bicolor *adj* two-coloured; *Pol* **gobierno b.** two-party government

bidé *nm* bidet

bidón *nm* drum

bien¹ 1 *adv* (a) *(correctamente)* well; **habla b. (el) inglés** she speaks English well; **responder b.** to answer correctly; **hiciste b. en decírmelo** you were right to tell me; **las cosas le van b.** things are going well for him; **¡b.!** good!, great!; **¡muy b.!** excellent, first class!; **¡qué b.!** great!, fantastic! (b) *(de salud)* well; **sentirse/encontrarse/estar b.** to feel well (c) **vivir b.** to be comfortably off; **¡está b.!** *(¡de acuerdo!)* fine!, all right!; **¡ya está b.!** that's (quite) enough!; **aquí se está muy b.** it's really nice here; **esta falda te sienta b.** this skirt suits you; *Fam* **ese libro está muy**

b. that book is very good
(**d**) *(intensificador)* very, quite; **b. temprano** very early, nice and early; **b. caliente** pretty hot; **b. es verdad que …** it's quite clear that …
(**e**) **más b.** rather, a little
(**f**) **b. podía haberme avisado** she might have let me know
2 *conj* **ahora b.** now, now then; **o b.** or, or else; **b. … o b. …** either … or …; **no b.** as soon as; **no b. llegó …** no sooner had she arrived than …; **si b.** although, even if
3 *adj inv* **la gente b.** the wealthy, the upper classes

bien² *nm* (**a**) *(bondad)* good; **el b. y el mal** good and evil; **un hombre/familia de b.** a good man/family (**b**) *(bienestar)* **por el b. de** for the good of; **lo hace por tu b.** he does it for your sake (**c**) **bienes** goods; **bienes de equipo** capital goods; **bienes inmuebles** real estate, *US* real property; **bienes de consumo** consumer goods

bienal *nf* biennial exhibition

bienestar *nm (personal)* well-being, contentment; *(comodidad)* ease, comfort; **la sociedad del b.** the affluent society

bienvenida *nf* welcome; **dar la b. a algn** to welcome sb

bienvenido, -a *adj* welcome

bife *nm Andes, RP* (**a**) *(bistec)* steak (**b**) *(bofetada)* slap

bifocal *adj* bifocal; **gafas bifocales** bifocals

bigote *nm (de persona)* moustache; *(de animal) (usu pl)* whiskers

bigotudo, -a *adj* with a big moustache

bigudí *nm (pl* **bigudís** *o* **bigudíes)** curler

bilingüe *adj* bilingual

billar *nm* (**a**) *(juego)* billiards *sing*; **b. americano** pool; **b. ruso** snooker (**b**) *(mesa)* billiard table

billete *nm* (**a**) *Esp (transporte)* ticket; **b. de ida** *(en avión)* one-way (ticket); **b. de ida y vuelta** *Br* return (ticket), *US* round-trip (ticket) (**b**) *(de banco) Br* note, *US* bill; **un b. de cinco euros** a five euro note

billetera *nf*, **billetero** *nm* wallet, *US* billfold

billón *nm* trillion

bingo *nm* (**a**) *(juego)* bingo (**b**) *(sala)* bingo hall

biodegradable *adj* biodegradable

biografía *nf* biography

biográfico, -a *adj* biographical

biología *nf* biology

biopsia *nf* biopsy

bioquímica *nf* biochemistry

biquini *nm* bikini

birlar *vt Fam* to pinch, *Br* to nick

birome *nf RP* Biro®, ballpoint (pen)

birra *nf Fam* beer, *US* brew

birria *nf Fam* rubbish

bisabuelo *nm* great-grandfather; **bisabuelos** great-grandparents

bisexual *adj & nmf* bisexual

bisnieto, -a *nm,f* great-grandson, *f* great-granddaughter; **mis bisnietos** my great-grandchildren

bisonte *nm* bison, American buffalo

bistec *nm (pl* **bistecs)** steak

bisturí *nm (pl* **bisturíes)** scalpel

bisutería *nf* imitation jewellery

bit *nm (pl* **bits)** *Informát* bit

bíter *nm* bitters

bizco, -a 1 *adj* cross-eyed **2** *nm,f* cross-eyed person

bizcocho *nm* sponge cake

blanca *nf Esp* **estar sin b.** to be flat broke

blanco¹, -a 1 *adj* white; *(tez)* fair **2** *nm,f (hombre)* white man; *(mujer)* white woman; **los blancos** whites

blanco² *nm* (**a**) *(color)* white (**b**) *(hueco)* blank; **dejó la hoja en b.** he left the page blank; **votos en b.** blank votes; *Fig* **pasar la noche en b.** to have a sleepless night; **me quedé en b.** my mind went blank (**c**) *(diana)* target; **dar en el b.** to hit the target; *Fig* **ser el b. de todas las miradas** to be the centre of attention

blando, -a *adj* soft

blanquear *vt* (**a**) to whiten (**b**) *(encalar)* to whitewash (**c**) *(dinero)* to launder

blanquillo *nm* (**a**) *CAm, Méx (huevo)* egg (**b**) *Andes (melocotón)* white peach

blindado, -a *adj Mil* armoured, armour-plated; *(antibalas)* bullet-proof; **coche b.** bullet-proof car; **puerta blindada** reinforced door, security door

blindar *vt* to armour-plate

bloc *(pl* **blocs**) *nm* pad; **b. de notas** notepad

bloque *nm* (**a**) block; **en b.** en bloc; **b. de pisos** *Br* (block of) flats, *US* apartment block (**b**) *Pol* bloc; **el b. comunista** the Communist Bloc

bloquear *vt* (**a**) to block (**b**) *Mil* to blockade

bloqueo *nm* blockade; *Dep* block

blúmer *nm (pl* **blúmers** o **blúmeres**) *CAm, Carib* panties, *Br* knickers

blusa *nf* blouse

bluyín *nm*, **bluyines** *nmpl Andes, Ven* jeans

bobada *nf* nonsense; **decir bobadas** to talk nonsense

bobina *nf* (**a**) reel (**b**) *Elec* coil

bobo, -a 1 *adj (tonto)* stupid, silly; *(ingenuo)* naïve **2** *nm,f* fool

boca *nf* (**a**) mouth; **b. abajo** face downward; **b. arriba** face upward; *Fam* **¡cierra la b.!** shut up!; *Fam* **con la b. abierta** open-mouthed; *Fam* **se le hizo la b. agua** his mouth watered; **el b. a b.** kiss of life, mouth-to-mouth resuscitation (**b**) **b. del metro** *Br* tube o underground entrance, *US* subway entrance; **b. de riego** hydrant

bocacalle *nf* entrance to a street

bocadillo *nm* (**a**) *Esp (con pan)* filled roll *(made with a baguette)*; **un b. de jamón/tortilla** a ham/an omelette sandwich (**b**) *(de cómic)* balloon

bocado *nm* (**a**) *(mordedura)* bite (**b**) *(de caballo)* bit

bocata *nm Esp Fam* filled roll *(made with a baguette)*

boceto *nm Arte* sketch, outline; *(esquema)* outline, plan

bochorno *nm* (**a**) *(tiempo)* sultry o close weather; *(calor sofocante)* stifling heat (**b**) *Fig (vergüenza)* shame, embarrassment

bochornoso, -a *adj* (**a**) *(tiempo)* sultry, close, muggy; *(calor)* stifling (**b**) *Fig (vergonzoso)* shameful, embarrassing

bocina *nf* horn; **tocar la b.** to blow o sound one's horn

bocón, -ona *nm,f Am Fam (bocazas)* **ser b.** to be a bigmouth o blabbermouth

boda *nf* wedding, marriage; **bodas de plata** silver wedding

bodega *nf* (**a**) wine cellar; *(tienda)* wine shop (**b**) *Náut* hold (**c**) *Méx (almacén)* warehouse (**d**) *CAm, Carib (colmado)* small grocery store

bodegón *nm* still life

bodrio *nm Fam* **un b.** *Br* rubbish, *US* trash

bofetada *nf*, **bofetón** *nm* slap on the face; **dar una b.** o **un b. a algn** to slap sb's face

bogavante *nm* lobster

bohemio, -a 1 *adj* (**a**) *(aspecto, vida, barrio)* bohemian (**b**) *(de Bohemia)* Bohemian **2** *nm,f* (**a**) *(artista, vividor)* bohemian (**b**) *(de Bohemia)* Bohemian

bohío *nm Carib* hut, cabin

boicot *nm (pl* **boicots**) boycott

boicotear *vt* to boycott

bóiler *nm Méx* boiler

boina *nf* beret

bola *nf* (**a**) ball; *(canica)* marble; **b. de nieve** snowball; **no dar pie con b.** to be unable to do anything right (**b**) *Fam (mentira)* fib, lie; **meter bolas** to tell fibs (**c**) *(rumor)* rumour; **corre la b. por ahí de que te has echado novio** they say you've got yourself a boyfriend

bolear *vt Méx (sacar brillo)* to shine, to polish

bolera *nf* bowling alley

bolería *nf Méx* shoeshine store

bolero *nm* bolero

boleta *nf* (**a**) *Cuba, Méx, RP (para*

votar) ballot, voting slip (**b**) *CSur (comprobante) (de venta, de depósito bancario)* receipt (**c**) *CAm, CSur (multa)* parking ticket (**d**) *Méx (de calificaciones) Br* (school) report, *US* report card

boletería *nf Am (de cine, teatro)* box office; *(de estación)* ticket office

boletero, -a *nm,f Am* box office attendant

boletín *nm* bulletin; **B. Oficial del Estado** Official Gazette

boleto *nm* (**a**) *(de lotería, rifa)* ticket (**b**) *Am (para transporte)* ticket (**c**) *Col, Méx (para espectáculo)* ticket

boli *nm Esp Fam* pen, Biro®

boliche *nm* (**a**) *(juego)* bowling (**b**) *(bola)* jack (**c**) *(lugar)* bowling alley (**d**) *CSur Fam (bar)* cheap bar; *(tienda)* small-town store

bolígrafo *nm* ballpoint (pen), *Br* Biro®

bolillo *nm* (**a**) *(en costura)* bobbin (**b**) *Méx (panecillo)* bread roll

bolita *nf CSur (bola)* marble; **jugar a las bolitas** to play marbles

Bolivia *n* Bolivia

boliviano, -a *adj & nm,f* Bolivian

bollería *nf* (**a**) *(tienda)* cake shop (**b**) *(productos)* cakes

bollo *nm* (**a**) *Culin* bun, bread roll (**b**) *(abolladura)* dent

bolo¹ *nm (pieza)* skittle, pin; **bolos** *(juego)* (ten-pin) bowling

bolo², -a *nm,f CAm Fam (borracho)* boozer

bolsa¹ *nf* bag; *Méx (de mano) Br* handbag, *US* purse; *Av* **b. de aire** air pocket; **b. de deportes** sports bag; **b. de la compra** shopping bag; **b. de viaje** travel bag

bolsa² *nf Fin* Stock Exchange; **jugar a la b.** to play the market

bolsillo *nm (en prenda)* pocket; **de b.** pocket, pocket-size; **libro de b.** paperback; **lo pagó de su b.** he paid for it out of his own pocket

bolso *nm* (**a**) *Esp (de mujer) Br* handbag, *US* purse (**b**) *(de viaje)* bag

boludear *vi RP Fam* (**a**) *(hacer tonterías)* to mess about (**b**) *(decir tonterías)* to talk rubbish (**c**) *(perder el tiempo)* to waste one's time

boludo, -a *nm,f RP Fam (estúpido) Br* prat, *US* jerk

bomba¹ *nf* pump; *Chile, Ecuad, Ven (gasolinera) Br* petrol station, *US* gas station; **b. de aire** air pump; **b. de incendios** fire engine; *Chile, Ecuad, Ven* **b. (de gasolina)** *(surtidor) Br* petrol pump, *US* gas pump

bomba² *nf* bomb; **b. atómica/de hidrógeno/de neutrones** atomic/hydrogen/neutron bomb; **b. de relojería** time bomb; **b. fétida** stink bomb; *Fam* **noticia b.** shattering piece of news; *Esp Fam* **pasarlo b.** to have a whale of a time

bombacha *nf RP (braga) Br* knickers, *US* panties; **bombachas** *(pantalones)* = loose trousers worn by cowboys

bombardear *vt* to bomb, to shell; **b. a algn a preguntas** to bombard sb with questions

bombardeo *nm* bombing, bombardment

bombero, -a *nm,f* (**a**) *(de incendios)* firefighter; *(hombre)* fireman; *(mujer)* firewoman; **cuerpo de bomberos** *Br* fire brigade, *US* fire department; **parque de bomberos** fire station (**b**) *Ven (de gasolinera) Br* petrol-pump *o US* gas-pump attendant

bombilla *nf Esp* (light) bulb

bombillo *nm CAm, Carib, Col, Méx* (light) bulb

bombita *nf RP* light bulb

bombo *nm* (**a**) *Mús* bass drum; *Fig* **a b. y platillo(s)** with a great song and dance; *Fam* **darse b.** to blow one's own trumpet (**b**) *(de sorteo)* lottery drum

bombón *nm* chocolate

bombona *nf* cylinder; **b. de butano** butane gas cylinder

bonanza *nf* (**a**) *Náut (tiempo)* fair weather; *(mar)* calm at sea (**b**) *Fig (prosperidad)* prosperity

bondad *nf* goodness; *Fml* **tenga la b. de esperar** please be so kind as to wait

bondadoso, -a *adj* kind, good-natured

boniato *nm Esp, Cuba, Urug* sweet potato

bonificación *nf* bonus

bonificar [44] *vt Com* to give a bonus to

bonito¹, -a *adj* pretty, nice

bonito² *nm* tuna

bono *nm* (a) *(vale)* voucher (b) *Fin* bond, debenture; **bonos del tesoro** *o* **del Estado** Treasury bonds

bonobús *nm Esp* = multiple-journey bus ticket

bonoloto *nm* = Spanish state-run lottery

bonsái *nm* bonsai

boñiga *nf* cowpat

boquerón *nm* anchovy

boquete *nm* hole

boquilla *nf* (a) *(de cigarro)* tip; *(de pipa)* mouthpiece; **decir algo de b.** to pay lip service· to sth (b) *Mús* mouthpiece (c) *(orificio)* opening

borda *nf Náut* gunwale; **arrojar** *o* **echar por la b.** to throw overboard; **fuera b.** *(motor)* outboard motor

bordado, -a 1 *adj* embroidered; *Esp* **el examen me salió b.** I made a good job of that exam **2** *nm* embroidery

bordar *vt* (a) to embroider (b) *Fig* to do excellently

borde¹ *nm (de mesa, camino)* edge; *Cost* hem, edge; *(de vasija)* rim, brim; **al b. de** on the brink of, on the verge of; **al b. del mar** at the seaside

borde² *Esp Fam* **1** *adj (antipático)* **ser b.** to be *Br* a ratbag *o US* an s.o.b. **2** *nmf (antipático) Br* ratbag, *US* s.o.b., stroppy person

bordear *vt* to go round the edge of, to skirt

bordillo *nm Br* kerb, *US* curb

bordo *nm* **a b.** on board; **subir a b.** to go on board

bordó *adj inv RP* burgundy

borla *nf* tassel

borra *nf* (a) *(pelusa)* fluff (b) *(poso)* sediment, dregs

borrachera *nf (embriaguez)* drunkenness; **agarrarse** *o* **cogerse una b.** to get drunk

borracho, -a 1 *adj* (a) *(bebido)* drunk; **estar b.** to be drunk (b) *(bizcocho)* with rum **2** *nm,f* drunkard, drunk

borrador *nm* (a) *(escrito)* rough copy, first draft (b) *(croquis)* rough *o* preliminary sketch (c) *(para pizarra)* board duster

borrar 1 *vt* (a) *(con goma) Br* to rub out, *US* to erase; *(pizarra)* to clean (b) *Informát* to delete **2 borrarse** *vpr (de un club etc)* to drop out, to withdraw

borrasca *nf* area of low pressure

borrón *nm* blot, smudge

borroso, -a *adj* blurred; **veo b.** I can't see clearly, everything's blurred

bosque *nm* wood

bostezar [40] *vi* to yawn

bostezo *nm* yawn

bota *nf* (a) *(de vino)* boot; *Fig* **ponerse las botas** to make a killing (b) *(de vino)* wineskin

botana *nf Méx* snack, appetizer

botánica *nf* botany

botar 1 *vi* (a) *Esp (saltar)* to jump (b) *(pelota)* to bounce **2** *vt* (a) *(barco)* to launch (b) *(pelota)* to bounce (c) *Am salvo RP (tirar)* to throw away; **bótalo a la basura** throw it away

bote *nm* (a) *(envase) (tarro)* jar; *Esp (lata)* tin, can; *(de champú, pastillas)* bottle; *Am* **b. de la basura** *Br* rubbish bin, *US* garbage can; **b. de humo** smoke canister

(b) *(barca)* boat; **b. salvavidas** lifeboat; **b. de remos** rowing boat

(c) *(propinas)* tips; **para el b.** as a tip

(d) *(salto)* jump; **dar botes** *(saltar)* to jump up and down; *(tren, coche)* to bump up and down; **pegar un b.** *(de susto)* to jump, to give a start

(e) *(de pelota)* bounce; **dar botes** to bounce

(f) *(expresiones) Esp* **chupar del b.** to feather one's nest; *Esp* **tener en el b. a algn** to have sb eating out of one's hand

botella *nf* (a) bottle (b) *Cuba (auto-*

estop) **dar b. a algn** to give sb a ride *o esp Br* lift; **hacer b.** to hitch-hike

botellín *nm* small bottle

botijo *nm* earthenware pitcher *(with spout and handle)*

botín¹ *nm (de un robo)* loot, booty

botín² *nm (calzado)* ankle boot

botiquín *nm* (**a**) medicine chest *o* cabinet; *(portátil)* first-aid kit (**b**) *(enfermería)* first-aid post

botón *nm* button; **pulsar el b.** to press the button; **b. de muestra** sample

bouquet [bu'ke] *nm (pl* **bouquets)** bouquet

boutique [bu'tik] *nf* boutique

bóveda *nf* vault

bovino, -a *adj* bovine; **ganado b.** cattle

box *nm* (**a**) *(de caballo)* stall (**b**) *(de coches)* pit (**c**) *Am (boxeo)* boxing

boxear *vi* to box

boxeo *nm* boxing

boya *nf* (**a**) *Náut* buoy (**b**) *(corcho)* float

bozal *nm* (**a**) *(para perro)* muzzle (**b**) *Am (cabestro)* halter

braga *nf Esp Br* knickers, *US* panties

bragueta *nf (de pantalón etc) Br* flies, *US* zipper

bramar *vi* to low, to bellow

brandy *nm (pl* **brandies)** brandy

brasa *nf* ember, red-hot coal; **a la b.** barbecued

brasero *nm* brazier

brasier *nm Carib, Col, Méx* bra

Brasil *n* Brazil

brasileño, -a, *RP* **brasilero, -a** *adj & nm,f* Brazilian

bravo, -a 1 *adj* (**a**) *(valiente)* brave, courageous (**b**) *(feroz)* fierce, ferocious; **un toro b.** a fighting bull (**c**) *(mar)* rough, stormy **2** *interj* well done!, bravo!

braza *nf* (**a**) *(medida)* fathom (**b**) *Esp (en natación)* breaststroke; **nadar a b.** to do the breaststroke

brazalete *nm* (**a**) *(insignia)* armband (**b**) *(pulsera)* bracelet

brazo *nm* arm; *(de animal)* foreleg; *(de sillón, tocadiscos)* arm; **en brazos** in one's arms; **ir del b.** to walk arm in arm; *Fig* **con los brazos abiertos** with open arms; *Fig* **no dar su b. a torcer** not to give in, stand firm; **b. de gitano** *Br* Swiss roll, *US* jelly roll

brebaje *nm* concoction, brew

brecha *nf (en muro)* opening, gap; *Mil & Fig* breach; *Fig* **estar siempre en la b.** to be always in the thick of things

brécol *nm* broccoli

bretel *nm CSur* strap; **un vestido sin breteles** a strapless dress

breva *nf* (**a**) *(fruta)* early fig (**b**) *Esp Fam* **¡no caerá esa b.!** some chance (of that happening)!

breve *adj* brief; **en b., en breves momentos** shortly, soon; **en breves palabras** in short

brevedad *nf* briefness; *(concisión)* brevity; **con la mayor b. posible** as soon as possible

brevet *nm Chile (de avión)* pilot's licence; *Bol, Ecuad, Perú (de automóvil) Br* driving licence, *US* driver's license; *RP (de velero)* sailor's licence

brezo *nm* heather

bricolaje *nm Br* DIY, do-it-yourself, *US* home improvement

brida *nf* (**a**) *(rienda)* rein, bridle (**b**) *Téc* flange

brigada 1 *nf* (**a**) *Mil* brigade (**b**) *(de policías)* squad; **b. antiterrorista** anti-terrorist squad **2** *nm Mil* sergeant major

brillante 1 *adj* brilliant **2** *nm* diamond

brillantina *nf* brilliantine

brillar *vi (resplandecer)* to shine; *(ojos, joyas)* to sparkle; *(lentejuelas etc)* to glitter; **b. por su ausencia** to be conspicuous by one's absence

brillo *nm (resplandor)* shine; *(del sol, de la luna)* brightness; *(de lentejuelas etc)* glittering; *(del cabello, tela)* sheen; *(de color)* brilliance; *(de pantalla)* brightness; *(de zapatos)* shine; **sacar b. a** to shine, to polish

brilloso, -a *adj Am* shining

brindar 1 *vi* to drink a toast; **b. por algn/algo** to drink to sb/sth

2 *vt* (**a**) *(oportunidad)* to offer, to provide (**b**) *Taurom* to dedicate (**a** to)
3 brindarse *vpr* to offer (**a** to), to volunteer (**a** to)

brindis *nm inv* (**a**) toast (**b**) *Taurom* dedication (of the bull)

brío *nm* energy

brisa *nf* breeze; **b. marina** sea breeze

británico, -a 1 *adj* British; **las Islas Británicas** the British Isles **2** *nm,f* Briton; **los británicos** the British

brizna *nf (de hierba)* blade; *(de carne)* string

broca *nf Téc* bit

brocha *nf (para pintar)* paintbrush; **b. de afeitar** shaving brush

broche *nm* (**a**) *(joya)* brooch; *Fig* **poner el b. de oro** to finish with a flourish (**b**) *(de vestido)* fastener

brocheta *nf Culin* shish kebab; *(aguja)* skewer

broma *nf (chiste)* joke; **bromas aparte** joking apart; **en b.** as a joke; **¡ni en b.!** not on your life!; **b. pesada** practical joke; **gastar una b.** to play a joke

bromear *vi* to joke

bromista 1 *adj* fond of joking *o* playing jokes **2** *nmf* joker, prankster

bronca *nf (a)* *(jaleo)* row; **armar (una) b.** to kick up a row (**b**) *Esp (crítica)* scolding, telling-off; **echar una b. a algn** to bawl sb out (**c**) *RP Fam (rabia)* **me da b.** it hacks me off; **el jefe le tiene b.** the boss can't stand him

bronce *nm* bronze

bronceado, -a 1 *adj* suntanned, tanned **2** *nm* suntan, tan

bronceador, -a 1 *adj* **leche bronceadora** suntan cream **2** *nm* suntan cream *o* lotion

broncearse *vpr* to get a tan *o* a suntan

bronquio *nm* bronchial tube

bronquitis *nf inv* bronchitis

brotar *vi (planta)* to sprout; *(agua)* to spring, to gush; *(lágrimas)* to well up; *(epidemia)* to break out

brote *nm* (**a**) *Bot (renuevo)* bud, shoot; *(de agua)* gushing (**b**) *(de epidemia, violencia)* outbreak

bruja *nf* witch, sorceress

brujería *nf* witchcraft, sorcery

brujo, -a 1 *nm* wizard, sorcerer **2** *adj Méx Fam* broke; **estar b.** to be broke

brújula *nf* compass

brusco, -a *adj* (**a**) *(persona)* brusque, abrupt (**b**) *(repentino)* sudden, sharp

brusquedad *nf* brusqueness, abruptness

brutal *adj* brutal

brutalidad *nf* brutality

bruto, -a 1 *adj* (**a**) *(necio)* stupid, thick; *(grosero)* coarse, uncouth (**b**) *Fin* gross; **peso b.** gross weight (**c**) **un diamante en b.** an uncut diamond **2** *nm,f* blockhead, brute

bucear *vi* to swim under water

buche *nm* maw; *(de ave)* craw; *Fam (estómago)* belly, stomach

bucle *nm* curl, ringlet

bucólico, -a *adj* (**a**) *(campestre)* **un paisaje b.** a charmingly rural landscape (**b**) *Lit* bucolic

bueno, -a

> **buen** is used instead of **bueno** before masculine singular nouns (e.g. **buen hombre** good man). The comparative form of **bueno** is **mejor** (better), and the superlative form is **el mejor** (masculine) or **la mejor** (feminine) (the best)

1 *adj* (**a**) good; **un alumno muy b.** a very good pupil; **una buena película** a good movie *o Br* film
(**b**) *(amable) (con* **ser***)* good, kind; **el b. de Carlos** good old Carlos; **es muy buena persona** he's a very kind soul
(**c**) *(sano) (con* **estar***)* well, in good health
(**d**) *(tiempo)* good; **hoy hace buen tiempo** it's fine today; **mañana hará b.** it will be fine *o* a nice day tomorrow
(**e**) *(conveniente)* good; **no es b. comer tanto** it's not good for you to eat so much
(**f**) *(considerable)* considerable; **un buen número de** a good number of
(**g**) *(grande)* good, big; **un buen trozo**

de pastel a nice *o* good big piece of cake

(**h**) *Fam (atractivo)* gorgeous, sexy; **Rosa está muy buena** Rosa's a bit of all right!; **una tía buena** a good-looking girl

(**i**) *Irón* fine, real, proper; **¡en buen lío te has metido!** that's a fine mess you've got yourself into!

(**j**) **¡buenas!** *(saludos)* hello!

(**k**) *(locuciones)* **de buenas a primeras** suddenly, all at once; **por las buenas** willingly; *Irón* **¡buena la has hecho!** that's done it!; **un susto de los buenos** a real fright; *Irón* **¡estaría b.!** I should jolly well hope not!; *Irón* **librarse de una buena** to get off scot-free

2 *interj* (**a**) *(vale)* all right, OK

(**b**) *(expresa sorpresa)* hey!

(**c**) *Col, Méx (al teléfono)* hello

buey *nm (pl* **bueyes)** ox, bullock

búfalo, -a *nm,f* buffalo

bufanda *nf* scarf

bufé *nm* buffet; **b. libre** self-service buffet meal

bufete *nm (despacho de abogado)* lawyer's office

buffet *nm (pl* **buffets)** = **bufé**

buhardilla *nf* attic, garret

búho *nm* owl; **b. real** eagle owl

buitre *nm* vulture

bujía *nf* (**a**) *Aut* spark plug (**b**) *Fís* candlepower

bula *nf (documento)* (papal) bull

bulbo *nm* bulb

bulerías *nfpl* = popular Andalusian song and dance

bulevar *nm* boulevard

Bulgaria *n* Bulgaria

búlgaro, -a *adj & nm,f* Bulgarian

bulín *nm RP Fam (picadero)* bachelor pad

bulla *nf Fam* (**a**) *(ruido)* racket, uproar; **armar b.** to kick up a racket (**b**) *Esp (prisa)* **meter b. a algn** to hurry sb up

bullicio *nm (de ciudad, mercado)* hustle and bustle; *(de multitud)* hubbub

bullicioso, -a 1 *adj* (**a**) *(agitado)* *(reunión, multitud)* noisy; *(calle, mercado)* busy, bustling (**b**) *(inquieto)* rowdy, boisterous **2** *nm,f* boisterous person

bulto *nm* (**a**) *(cosa indistinta)* shape, form (**b**) *(maleta, caja)* piece of luggage (**c**) *Med* lump (**d**) **hacer mucho b.** to be very bulky; *Fam* **escurrir el b.** to pass the buck

bumerán *nm* boomerang

bungalow [bunga'lo] *nm (pl* **bungalows)** bungalow

búnker *nm* (**a**) *(refugio)* bunker (**b**) *Esp Pol* reactionary forces

buñuelo *nm* doughnut

BUP *nm (abr* **Bachillerato Unificado Polivalente)** = formerly, academically orientated Spanish secondary school course for pupils aged 14-17

buque *nm* ship; **b. de guerra** warship; **b. de pasajeros** liner, passenger ship; **b. insignia** flagship

burbuja *nf* bubble; **hacer burbujas** to bubble, make bubbles

burdel *nm* brothel

burgués, -esa *adj & nm,f* bourgeois

burguesía *nf* bourgeoisie

burla *nf* gibe, jeer; **hacer b. de algo/algn** to make fun of sth/sb; **hacer b. a algn** to stick one's tongue out at sb

burlar 1 *vt* (**a**) *(engañar)* to deceive (**b**) *(eludir)* to dodge, to evade **2 burlarse** *vpr* to make fun (**de** of), to laugh (**de** at)

buró *nm* (**a**) *Pol* executive committee (**b**) *(escritorio)* bureau, desk (**c**) *Méx (mesa de noche)* bedside table

burrada *nf (comentario)* stupid *o* foolish remark; *(hecho)* stupid *o* foolish act

burro, -a 1 *nm,f* (**a**) donkey, ass; *Fam Fig* **bajarse del b.** to climb *o* back down (**b**) *Fam (estúpido)* dimwit, blockhead (**c**) **b. de carga** dogsbody, drudge **2** *adj Fam* (**a**) *(necio)* stupid, dumb (**b**) *(obstinado)* stubborn

buscador, -a 1 *nm,f (en general)* hunter; **b. de oro** gold prospector **2** *nm Informát (en Internet)* search engine

buscar [44] **1** *vt* (**a**) to look *o* search for; **b. una palabra en el diccionario** to look up a word in the dictionary (**b**) **ir a b. algo** to go and get sth, to fetch sth; **fue a buscarme a la estación** she picked me up at the station

2 buscarse *vpr Fam* **buscarse la vida** to try and earn one's living; *Fam* **te la estás buscando** you're asking for it; **se busca** *(en anuncios)* wanted

buseta *nf Col, CRica, Ecuad, Ven* minibus

busto *nm* bust

butaca *nf* (**a**) *(sillón)* armchair, easy chair (**b**) *Cin, Teatro* seat; **b. de platea** *o* **patio** seat in the stalls

butano *nm* butane; **(gas) b.** butane gas

butifarra *nf* sausage

buzo *nm* (**a**) *(persona)* diver (**b**) *Arg (sudadera)* sweatshirt (**c**) *Col, Urug (jersey)* sweater, *Br* jumper

buzón *nm* post box, *Br* letter box, *US* mailbox; *Informát (de correo electrónico)* (electronic) mailbox; **echar una carta al b.** to *Br* post *o US* mail a letter; **b. de voz** voice mail

Cc

c/ (**a**) (*abr* **calle**) St; Rd (**b**) (*abr* **cargo**) cargo, freight (**c**) (*abr* **cuenta**) a/c

cabal 1 *adj* (**a**) (*exacto*) exact, precise (**b**) (*honesto*) honest, upright **2** *nmpl Fam* **no está en sus cabales** he's not in his right mind

cabalgar [42] *vt & vi* to ride

cabalgata *nf* cavalcade; **la c. de los Reyes Magos** the procession of the Three Wise Men

caballa *nf* mackerel

caballería *nf* (**a**) (*cabalgadura*) mount, steed (**b**) *Mil* cavalry

caballero *nm* (**a**) gentleman; **¿qué desea, c.?** can I help you, sir?; **ropa de c.** menswear (**b**) *Hist* knight (**c**) **caballeros** (*en letrero*) gents

caballete *nm* (**a**) (*de pintor*) easel (**b**) *Téc* trestle (**c**) (*de nariz*) bridge

caballito *nm* (**a**) **c. de mar** seahorse (**b**) **caballitos** merry-go-round, *US* carousel

caballo *nm* (**a**) horse; **a c.** on horseback; **montar a c.** to ride; *Fig* **a c. entre ...** halfway between ... (**b**) *Téc* **c. de vapor** horsepower (**c**) (*pieza de ajedrez*) knight (**d**) *Naipes* queen (**e**) *Fam* (*heroína*) horse, smack

cabaña *nf* cabin

cabaret *nm* (*pl* **cabarets**) cabaret

cabecear *vi* to nod **2** *vt Dep* to head

cabecera *nf* (**a**) (*de fila, mesa*) head; (*de cama*) headboard (**b**) *Esp* (*de texto*) heading; (*de periódico*) masthead

cabecilla *nmf* leader

cabellera *nf* head of hair

cabello *nm* (**a**) hair (**b**) *Culin* **c. de ángel** = sweet made of gourd and syrup

caber [9] *vi* (**a**) to fit, to be (able to be) contained; **cabe en el maletero** it fits in the boot; **¿cabemos todos?** is there room for all of us?; **en este coche/jarro caben ...** this car/jug holds ...; **no cabe por la puerta** it won't go through the door; **no me cabe en la cabeza** I can't understand it; **no cabe duda** there is no doubt; **cabe la posibilidad de que ...** there is a possibility *o* chance that ...; **no está mal dentro de lo que cabe** it isn't bad, under the circumstances

(**b**) **cabe señalar que ...** we should point out that ...

(**c**) *Mat* **doce entre cuatro caben a tres** four into twelve goes three (times)

cabestrillo *nm* sling

cabeza 1 *nf* head; **en c.** in the lead; **por c.** a head, per person; *Fig* **a la c. de** at the front *o* top of; *Fig* **estar mal de la c.** to be a mental case; **c. de turco** scapegoat; **el** *o* **la c. de familia** the head of the family **2** *nm* **c. rapada** skinhead

cabezada *nf* (**a**) (*golpe*) butt, blow on the head (**b**) *Fam* **echar una c.** to have a snooze; **dar cabezadas** to nod

cabida *nf* capacity; **dar c. a** to leave room for

cabina *nf* cabin; **c. telefónica** (*con puerta*) *Br* phone box, *US* phone booth

cabinero, -a *nm,f Col* flight attendant

cable *nm* cable; *Fam* **echarle un c. a algn** to give sb a hand

cabo *nm* (**a**) (*extremo*) end; **al c. de** after; **de c. a rabo** from start to finish (**b**) *Mil* corporal; (*policía*) sergeant (**c**) *Náut* rope, cable; *Fig* **atar cabos** to put two and two together; *Fig* **no dejar ningún c. suelto** to leave no loose ends (**d**) *Geog* cape; **Ciudad del C.** Cape Town; **C. Verde** Cape Verde

cabra *nf* goat; *Fam* **estar como**

una c. to be off one's head

cabré *indic fut de* **caber**

cabrear *muy Fam* **1** *vt* to make angry, *Br* to piss off **2 cabrearse** *vpr* to get *Br* pissed off *o US* pissed

cabreo *nm muy Fam* rage, fit; **agarrar** *o Esp* **coger un c.** to get really *Br* narked *o US* pissed

cabrito *nm Zool* kid

cabro, -a *nm,f Chile Fam* kid

cabrón, -ona *nm,f Vulg* bastard, *f* bitch, *US* asshole

cabronada *nf muy Fam* dirty trick

cabuya *nf* (a) *(planta)* agave (b) *(fibra)* hemp fibre (c) *CAm, Col, Ven (cuerda)* rope

caca *nf Fam Br* poo, *US* poop

cacahuete, *CAm, Méx* **cacahuate** *nm* peanut, *US* groundnut

cacao *nm* (a) *Bot* cacao (b) *(polvo, bebida)* cocoa (c) *Fam (lío)* mess

cacarear 1 *vi (gallina)* to cluck **2** *vt Fig* to boast about

cacería *nf* (a) *(actividad)* hunting, shooting (b) *(partida)* hunt, shoot

cacerola *nf* saucepan

cachalote *nm* sperm whale

cacharro *nm* (a) earthenware pot *o* jar (b) *Fam (cosa)* thing, piece of junk (c) **cacharros** *(de cocina)* pots and pans

cachear *vt* to frisk, to search

cachemir *nm,* **cachemira** *nf* cashmere

cachetada *nf* slap

cachete *nm* (a) *(bofetada)* slap (b) *Am (mejilla)* cheek

cachila *nf RP (automóvil)* vintage car

cachimba *nf* (a) *(pipa)* pipe (b) *RP (pozo)* well

cachivache *nm Fam* thing, knick-knack

cacho¹ *nm Fam (pedazo)* bit, piece; *Esp* **¡c. tonto!** you idiot!

cacho² *nm* (a) *Andes, Ven (asta)* horn (b) *Andes, Guat, Ven (cuento)* story; **no me vengan a contar cachos, que sé lo que pasó** don't start telling me stories, I know what happened (c) *Andes, Guat, Ven (burla)* joke

cachondearse *vpr Esp Fam* **c. de algn** to make a fool out of sb, *Br* to take the mickey out of sb

cachondeo *nm Esp Fam* **ser un c.** to be a laugh; **tomarse algo a c.** to take sth as a joke

cachondo, -a *adj* (a) *Esp, Méx muy Fam (sexualmente)* **estar c.** to be randy; **ponerse c.** to get randy *o* turned on (b) *Esp Fam (divertido)* **ser c.** to be funny

cachorro, -a *nm,f (de perro)* pup, puppy; *(de gato)* kitten; *(de otros animales)* cub, baby

cacique *nm (jefe)* local boss

cacto *nm,* **cactus** *nm inv Bot* cactus

cada *adj (de dos)* each; *(de varios)* each, every; **c. día** every day; **c. dos días** every second day; **c. vez más** more and more; **¿c. cuánto?** how often?; **c. dos por tres** every other minute; **cuatro de c. diez** four out of (every) ten; **¡tienes c. cosa!** you come out with some fine ideas!

cadáver *nm (de persona)* corpse, (dead) body; *(de animal)* body, carcass; **ingresar c.** to be dead on arrival

cadena *nf* (a) chain; *(correa de perro)* lead, leash (b) *TV* channel (c) *Ind* line; **c. de montaje** assembly line; **trabajo en c.** assembly line work (d) *Geog* **c. montañosa** mountain range (e) *Jur* **c. perpetua** life imprisonment (f) *Aut* **cadenas** tyre chains

cadencia *nf* rhythm; *Mús* cadenza

cadera *nf* hip

cadete 1 *nm (en ejército)* cadet; **2** *nm,f RP (chico de los recados)* office junior

caducar [44] *vi* to expire

caducidad *nf* expiry; **fecha de c.** *(en alimento, medicamento)* use-by date

caduco, -a *adj* (a) *Bot* deciduous (b) *(anticuado)* out-of-date

caer [39] **1** *vi* (a) to fall; **dejar c.** to drop; *Fig* **está al c.** *(llegar)* he'll arrive any minute now; *(ocurrir)* it's on the way (b) *(fecha)* to be; **su cumpleaños cae en sábado** his birthday falls on a Saturday (c) *(entender)* to understand, to see; **ya caigo** I get it; **no caí** I didn't twig (**d**) *Esp (estar, quedar)* **cae cerca de aquí** it's not far from here (**e**) **me cae bien/mal** I like/don't like her

2 caerse *vpr* to fall (down); **me caí de la moto** I fell off the motorbike; **se le cayó el pañuelo** she dropped her handkerchief

café *nm* (**a**) coffee; **c. con leche** white coffe; *Esp* **c. solo,** *Andes, Ven* **c. tinto** black coffee (**b**) *(cafetería)* café

cafeína *nf* caffeine

cafetera *nf* coffee-maker

cafetería *nf* snack bar, coffee bar; *Ferroc* buffet car

cafiche *nm Andes Fam (proxeneta)* pimp

cagar [42] *Fam* **1** *vi* to shit, to crap **2 cagarse** *vpr* to crap oneself; **cagarse de miedo** to be shit-scared

caída *nf* (**a**) fall; *(de pelo, diente)* loss (**b**) *(de precios)* drop (**c**) *Pol* downfall, collapse

caído, -a 1 *adj* fallen **2** *nmpl* **los caídos** the fallen

caimán *nm* alligator

caja *nf* (**a**) box; **c. fuerte** safe; *Fam (TV)* **la c. tonta** the box, *Br* the telly, *US* the boob tube (**b**) *(de leche etc)* carton (**c**) *(de embalaje)* crate, case; **una c. de cerveza** a crate of beer (**d**) *Fin (en tienda)* cash desk; *(en banco)* cashier's desk (**e**) *Aut* **c. de cambios** gearbox (**f**) *Esp (entidad financiera)* **c. de ahorros** savings bank (**g**) *(féretro)* coffin

cajero, -a *nm,f* cashier; **c. automático** cash point, cash dispenser

cajetilla *nf* packet, pack

cajón *nm* (**a**) *(en un mueble)* drawer; *Fig* **c. de sastre** jumble; *Fam* **de c.** obvious, self-evident (**b**) *(caja grande)* crate, chest

cajuela *nf CAm, Méx (maletero) Br* boot, *US* trunk

cal¹ *nf* lime; *Fig* **a c. y canto** hermetically; *Fam* **una de c. y otra de arena** six of one and half a dozen of the other

cal² *(abr* **caloría)** cal

cala *nf* (**a**) *Geog* creek, cove (**b**) *Náut* hold

calabacín *nm Bot* (**a**) *(pequeño) Br* courgette, *US* zucchini (**b**) *(grande) Br* marrow, *US* squash

calabaza *nf* pumpkin, gourd

calabozo *nm* (**a**) *(prisión)* jail, prison (**b**) *(celda)* cell

calada *nf Esp Fam (de cigarrillo)* drag, puff

calamar *nm* squid *inv;* *Culin* **calamares a la romana** squid fried in batter

calambre *nm* (**a**) *Elec (descarga)* electric shock; **ese cable da c.** that wire is live (**b**) *(en músculo)* cramp

calamidad *nf* calamity

calar 1 *vt* (**a**) *(mojar)* to soak, to drench (**b**) *(agujerear)* to pierce, to penetrate **2** *vi* (**a**) *(prenda)* to let in water (**b**) *Náut* to draw **3 calarse** *vpr* (**a**) *(prenda, techo)* to let in water; *(mojarse)* to get soaked (**b**) *(el sombrero)* to pull down (**c**) *Esp (motor)* to stall

calavera 1 *nf* (**a**) *(cráneo)* skull (**b**) *Méx Aut* **calaveras** tail lights **2** *nm* tearaway

calcar [44] *vt* (**a**) *(un dibujo)* to trace (**b**) *Fig (imitar)* to copy, to imitate

calcetín *nm* sock

calcio *nm* calcium

calcomanía *nf* transfer

calculador, -a *adj también Fig* calculating

calculadora *nf* calculator

calcular *vt* (**a**) *Mat* to calculate (**b**) *(evaluar)* to (make an) estimate (**c**) *(suponer)* to figure, to guess

cálculo *nm* (**a**) calculation; **según mis cálculos** by my reckoning (**b**) *Med* gallstone (**c**) *Mat* calculus

caldear *vt* to heat up

caldera *nf* (**a**) *(industrial)* boiler; *(olla)* cauldron (**b**) *Urug (hervidor)* kettle

calderilla *nf* small change

caldo *nm* stock, broth; **c. de cultivo** culture medium; *Fig* breeding ground

calefacción *nf* heating; **c. central** central heating

calefaccionar *vt CSur (calentar)* to heat (up), to warm (up)

calefactor *nm* heater

calefón *nm CSur (calentador)* water heater

calendario *nm* calendar

calentador *nm* heater

calentamiento *nm Dep* warm-up

calentar [1] **1** *vt* (**a**) *(agua, horno)* to heat; *(comida, habitación)* to warm up; *Fig* **no me calientes la cabeza** don't bug me (**b**) *Fam (pegar)* to smack (**c**) *Fam (excitar)* to arouse (sexually), to turn on **2 calentarse** *vpr* (**a**) to get hot *o* warm, to heat up (**b**) *Fig* **se calentaron los ánimos** people became very excited

calesita *nf RP* merry-go-round, *US* carousel

calibrar *vt* to gauge, to bore

calibre *nm* (**a**) *(de arma)* calibre (**b**) *Fig (importancia)* importance

calidad *nf* (**a**) quality; **de primera c.** first-class; **un vino de c.** good-quality wine (**b**) **en c. de** as

cálido, -a *adj* warm; **una cálida acogida** a warm welcome

caliente *adj* (**a**) hot (**b**) *Fig (debate)* heated; **en c.** in the heat of the moment (**c**) *Fam (cachondo)* hot, randy

calificación *nf* (**a**) qualification (**b**) *Educ Br* mark, *US* grade

calificar [44] *vt* (**a**) to describe (**de** as); **le calificó de inmoral** he called him immoral (**b**) *(examen)* to mark, to grade

caligrafía *nf* calligraphy; *(modo de escribir)* handwriting

cáliz *nm* chalice

callado, -a *adj* quiet; **te lo tenías muy c.** you were keeping that quiet

callar 1 *vi* (**a**) *(dejar de hablar)* to stop talking; **¡calla!** be quiet!, *Fam* shut up! (**b**) *(no hablar)* to keep quiet, to say nothing

2 *vt (noticia)* not to mention, to keep to oneself

3 callarse *vpr* to stop talking, to be quiet; **¡cállate!** shut up!

calle *nf* (**a**) street, road; **c. de dirección única** one-way street; **c. mayor** *Br* high street, *US* main street; **el hombre de la c.** the man in the street (**b**) *Esp Dep* lane

calleja *nf* narrow street

callejero, -a 1 *nm (mapa)* street directory **2** *adj* street; **gato c.** alley cat

callejón *nm* back alley *o* street; **c. sin salida** cul-de-sac, dead end

callejuela *nf* narrow street, lane

callo *nm* (**a**) *Med* callus, corn; *Fam* **dar el c.** to slog (**b**) *Esp Culin* **callos** tripe

calma *nf* (**a**) calm; **¡c.!** calm down!; **en c.** calm; **tómatelo con c.** take it easy (**b**) *Met* calm weather; **c. chicha** dead calm

calmante *nm* painkiller

calmar 1 *vt (persona)* to calm (down); *(dolor)* to soothe, to relieve **2 calmarse** *vpr* (**a**) *(persona)* to calm down (**b**) *(dolor, viento)* to ease off

calor *nm* (**a**) heat; **hace c.** it's hot; **tengo c.** I'm hot; **entrar en c.** to warm up (**b**) *Fig (afecto)* warmth

caloría *nf* calorie

calote *nm RP Fam* swindle

calumnia *nf* (**a**) calumny (**b**) *Jur* slander

calumniar [43] *vt* (**a**) to calumniate (**b**) *Jur* to slander

calumnioso, -a *adj (de palabra)* slanderous; *(por escrito)* libellous

caluroso, -a *adj* hot; *(acogida etc)* warm

calva *nf* bald patch

calvario *nm (vía crucis)* Calvary, Stations of the Cross; *Fig (sufrimiento)* ordeal

calvicie *nf* baldness

calvo, -a 1 *adj* bald; **ni tanto ni tan c.** neither one extreme nor the other **2** *nm* bald man

calzada *nf* road (surface), *US* pavement

calzado *nm* shoes, footwear

calzador *nm* shoehorn

calzar [40] **1** *vt* (**a**) *(poner calzado)* to put shoes on; **¿qué número calzas?** what size do you take? (**b**) *(mueble)* to wedge **2 calzarse los zapatos** to put on one's shoes

calzón *nm* (**a**) *Esp Dep* shorts (**b**) *Andes, Méx, RP (bragas)* panties, *Br* knickers; **un c., unos calzones** a pair of panties *o Br* knickers (**c**) *Bol, Méx* **calzones** *(calzoncillos) Br* underpants, *US* shorts

calzoncillos *nmpl (slip)* briefs, *Br* (under)pants, *US* shorts; *(bóxer)* boxer shorts

calzoneta *nm CAm* swimming trunks

cama *nf* bed; **estar en** *o* **guardar c.** to be confined to bed; **hacer la c.** to make the bed; **irse a la c.** to go to bed; **c. doble/individual** double/single bed; **c. turca** couch

camaleón *nm* chameleon

cámara 1 *nf* (**a**) *(aparato)* camera; **a c. lenta** in slow motion (**b**) *Pol* Chamber, House; **C. Alta/Baja** Upper/Lower House (**c**) *Aut* inner tube (**d**) *(habitación)* room, chamber; **c. de gas** gas chamber; **c. frigorífica** cold-storage room; **música de c.** chamber music **2** *nmf* cameraman, *f* camerawoman

camarada *nmf* comrade

camarero, -a *nm,f* (**a**) *(de restaurante)* waiter, *f* waitress; *(tras la barra)* barman, *f* barmaid (**b**) *(de avión)* flight attendant

camarón *nm Br* shrimp, *US* prawn

camarote *nm* cabin

camastro *nm* ramshackle bed

camba *Bol Fam* **1** *adj* of/from the forested lowland region of Bolivia **2** *nmf* person from the forested lowland region of Bolivia

cambalache *nm RP (tienda)* junk shop

cambiar [43] **1** *vt* (**a**) to change; **c. algo de sitio** to move sth (**b**) *(intercambiar)* to swap, to exchange (**c**) *(dinero)* to change

2 *vi* to change; **c. de casa** to move (house); **c. de idea** to change one's mind; **c. de trabajo** to get another job; **c. de velocidad** to change gear

3 cambiarse *vpr* (**a**) *(de ropa)* to change (clothes) (**b**) *(de casa)* to move (house)

cambio *nm* (**a**) change; *(de impresiones)* exchange; **c. de planes** change of plans; **un c. en la opinión** **pública** a shift in public opinion; *Fig* **a c. de** in exchange for; **en c.** on the other hand (**b**) *(dinero)* change; **¿tienes c. de cinco euros?** have you got change for five euros? (**c**) *Fin (de divisas)* exchange; *(de acciones)* price (**d**) *Aut* gear change; **c. automático** automatic transmission

cambur *nm Ven (plátano)* banana

camello, -a 1 *nm,f* camel **2** *nm Fam (traficante de drogas)* (drug) pusher

camellón *nm Col, Méx (en avenida) Br* central reservation, *US* median (strip)

camembert ['kamember] *nm (pl* **camemberts)** camembert

camerino *nm* dressing room

camilla *nf* (**a**) stretcher (**b**) **mesa c.** = small round table under which a heater is placed

camillero, -a *nm,f* stretcher-bearer

caminante *nmf* walker

caminar 1 *vi* to walk **2** *vt* to cover, to travel; **caminaron 10 km** they walked for 10 km

caminata *nf* long walk

camino *nm* (**a**) *(ruta)* route, way; **ir c. de** to be going to; **ponerse en c.** to set off; *Fig* **ir por buen/mal c.** to be on the right/wrong track; **abrirse c.** to break through; **a medio c.** half-way; **en el c. a, de c. a** on the way to; **estar en c.** to be on the way; **nos coge** *o* **pilla de c.** it is on the way (**b**) *(vía)* path, track (**c**) *(modo)* way

camión *nm* (**a**) truck, *Br* lorry; **c. cisterna** tanker; **c. de la basura** *Br* dustcart, *US* garbage truck; **c. frigorífico** refrigerated truck (**b**) *CAm, Méx (autobús)* bus

camionero, -a *nm,f Br* lorry driver, *US* trucker

camioneta *nf* van

camisa *nf* shirt; **en mangas de c.** in one's shirtsleeves; **c. de fuerza** straitjacket

camisería *nf (tienda)* shirt shop, outfitter's

camiseta *nf* (**a**) *(ropa interior) Br* vest, *US* undershirt (**b**) *(de manga corta)* T-shirt (**c**) *Dep (de tirantes)* vest; *(con* *mangas*) shirt; **sudar la c.** to run oneself into the ground

camisola *nf* (**a**) *(prenda interior)* camisole (**b**) *Dep* sports shirt

camisón *nm* nightdress, *Fam* nightie

camomila *nf* camomile

camorra *nf Fam* trouble

camote *nm* (**a**) *Andes, CAm, Méx (batata)* sweet potato; *(bulbo)* tuber, bulb (**b**) *Méx Fam (complicación)* mess; **meterse en un c.** to get into a mess *o* pickle

campamento *nm* camp

campana *nf* bell; **pantalones de campana** bell-bottom trousers

campanario *nm* belfry, bell tower

campaña *nf* (**a**) campaign; **c. electoral** election campaign; **c. publicitaria** advertising campaign (**b**) *Mil* campaign; **hospital/ambulancia de c.** field hospital/ambulance (**c**) *RP (campo)* countryside

campechano, -a *adj* unpretentious

campeón, -ona *nm,f* champion; **c. mundial** world champion

campeonato *nm* championship; **un tonto de c.** an utter idiot

campera *nf* (**a**) *Esp (bota)* cowboy boot (**b**) *RP (chaqueta)* jacket

campesino, -a *nm,f* countryman, *f* countrywoman

campestre *adj* rural

cámping *nm* (*pl* **cámpings**) campsite, *US* campground; **hacer** *o* **ir de c.** to go camping

campista *nmf* camper

campo *nm* (**a**) country, countryside; **a c. través** cross-country; **trabaja (en) el c.** he works (on) the land; **trabajo de c.** fieldwork (**b**) *(parcela)* field (**c**) *Fís, Fot* field (**d**) *(ámbito)* field; **c. de acción** field of action; *Mil* **c. de batalla** battlefield; **c. de concentración** concentration camp (**e**) *Esp Dep (de fútbol)* pitch; *(de golf)* course (**f**) *RP (hacienda)* farm, ranch (**g**) *Andes (sitio)* room, space

campus *nm inv* campus

camuflar *vt* to camouflage

cana *nf (gris)* grey hair; *(blanca)* white hair; **tener canas** to have grey hair; *Fam* **echar una c. al aire** to let one's hair down

Canadá *n* Canada

canadiense *adj & nmf* Canadian

canal *nf* (**a**) *(artificial)* canal; *(natural)* channel; **C. de la Mancha** English Channel (**b**) *TV, Elec, Informát* channel

canalla **1** *nm* swine, rotter **2** *nf* riffraff, mob

canapé *nm* (**a**) *Culin* canapé (**b**) *(sofá)* couch, sofa

Canarias *nfpl* **las (islas) C.** the Canary Islands, the Canaries

canario, -a 1 *adj & nm,f* Canarian **2** *nm Orn* canary

canasta *nf* basket

canastilla *nf* small basket; *(de un bebé)* layette

cancán *nm* frilly petticoat; *RP* **cancanes** *(leotardos) Br* tights, *US* pantyhose *(plural)*

cancela *nf* wrought-iron gate

cancelación *nf* cancellation

cancelar *vt* (**a**) *(acto etc)* to cancel (**b**) *(deuda)* to pay off (**c**) *Chile, Ven (compra)* to pay for

Cáncer *nm* Cancer

cáncer *nm* cancer; **c. de pulmón/ mama** lung/breast cancer

cancerígeno, -a *adj* carcinogenic

cancha *nf Dep* court

canciller *nm* chancellor

cancillería *nf (de asuntos exteriores)* foreign ministry

canción *nf* song

cancionero *nm* songbook

candado *nm* padlock

candela *nf* fire

candelabro *nm* candelabrum

candidato, -a *nm,f* candidate; *(a un puesto)* applicant

candidatura *nf* (**a**) *(lista)* list of candidates (**b**) **presentar su c.** to submit one's application

candil *nm* oil lamp; *Méx (candelabro)* chandelier

candilejas *nfpl Teatro* footlights

canela *nf* cinnamon

canelones *nmpl Culin* cannelloni

cangrejo *nm (de mar)* crab; *(de río)* freshwater crayfish

canguro 1 *nm* kangaroo **2** *nmf Esp Fam* baby-sitter

caníbal *adj & nmf* cannibal

canica *nf* marble

canijo, -a *adj Fam* puny, weak

canilla *nf* (a) *Fam (espinilla)* shinbone (b) *RP (grifo) Br* tap, *US* faucet (c) *Méx (fuerza)* strength

canillera *nf Am (temblor de piernas)* **tenía c.** his legs were trembling *o* shaking

canillita *nm RP* newspaper vendor

canje *nm* exchange

canjeable *adj* exchangeable

canjear *vt* to exchange

canoa *nf* canoe

canon *nm* (a) canon, norm (b) *Mús, Rel* canon (c) *Com* royalty

canónico, -a *adj* canonical; *Jur* **derecho c.** canon law

canoso, -a *adj (de pelo blanco)* white-haired; *(de pelo gris)* grey-haired; *(pelo)* white, grey

cansado, -a *adj* (a) *(agotado)* tired, weary; **estar c.** to be tired (b) **ser c.** *(pesado)* to be boring *o* tiresome

cansador, -a *adj Andes, RP (que cansa)* tiring; *(que aburre)* boring

cansancio *nm* tiredness, weariness; *Fam* **estoy muerto de c.** I'm on my last legs

cansar 1 *vt* to tire **2** *vi* to be tiring **3 cansarse** *vpr* to get tired; **se cansó de esperar** he got fed up (with) waiting

cantábrico, -a *adj* Cantabrian; **Mar C.** Bay of Biscay

cantaleta *nf Am* **la misma c.** the same old story

cantante 1 *nmf* singer **2** *adj* singing; **llevar la voz c.** to rule the roost

cantaor, -a *nm,f* flamenco singer

cantar¹ *vt & vi* (a) *Mús* to sing; *Fig* **en menos que canta un gallo** in a flash (b) *Fam (confesar)* to sing, to spill the beans (c) *Esp muy Fam (apestar)* to stink

cantar² *nm Lit* song; *Fam* **¡eso es otro c.!** that's a totally different thing!

cántaro *nm* pitcher; *Fig* **llover a cántaros** to rain cats and dogs

cantautor, -a *nm,f* singer-songwriter

cante *nm* (a) *(canto)* singing; **c. hondo, c. jondo** flamenco (b) *Esp Fam* **dar el c.** to attract attention

cantegril *nm Urug* shanty town

cantera *nf* (a) *(de piedra)* quarry (b) *Fig Ftb* young players

cantero *nm* (a) *(masón)* stonemason (b) *Cuba, RP (parterre)* flowerbed

cantidad 1 *nf* quantity; *(de dinero)* amount, sum; **en c.** a lot; *Fam* **c. de gente** thousands of people **2** *adv Esp Fam* a lot; **me gusta c.** I really like it a lot

cantimplora *nf* water bottle

cantina *nf* canteen

canto¹ *nm* (a) *(arte)* singing (b) *(canción)* song

canto² *nm (borde)* edge; **de c.** on its side

canto³ *nm (guijarro)* pebble, stone; **c. rodado** *(grande)* boulder; *(pequeño)* pebble

canturrear *vi* to hum, to croon

caña *nf* (a) *Esp (de cerveza)* small glass of beer (b) *Bot (tallo)* reed; *(tallo)* cane, stem; **c. de azúcar** sugar cane (c) *(de pescar)* rod (d) *Fam* **darle c. al coche** to go at full speed (e) *Andes, Cuba, RP (aguardiente)* caña, = type of rum made using sugar cane spirit

cáñamo *nm* hemp

cañaveral *nm* reedbed

cañería *nf* (piece of) piping; **cañerías** plumbing

cañero, -a *nm,f Am (trabajador)* sugar plantation worker; *(propietario)* sugar plantation owner

caño *nm (tubo)* tube; *(tubería)* pipe

cañón *nm* (a) cannon; *Fig* **estar siempre al pie del c.** to be always ready for a fight (b) *(de fusil)* barrel (c) *Geog* canyon

cañonazo *nm* gunshot

caoba *nf* mahogany

caos *nm inv* chaos

caótico, -a *adj* chaotic

capa *nf* (**a**) *(prenda)* cloak, cape; **de c. caída** low-spirited (**b**) *(de pintura)* layer, coat; *Culin* coating (**c**) *Geol* stratum, layer

capacidad *nf* (**a**) *(cabida)* capacity (**b**) *(aptitud)* capacity, ability

caparazón *nm* shell

capataz, -a *nm,f* foreman, *f* forewoman

capaz **1** *adj* capable, able; **ser c. de hacer algo** *(tener la habilidad de)* to be able to do sth; *(atreverse a)* to dare to do sth; **si se entera es c. de despedirle** if he finds out he could quite easily sack him **2** *adv* *Andes, RP Fam (tal vez)* maybe

capazo *nm* large wicker basket

capellán *nm* chaplain

capicúa *adj* **número c.** reversible number; **palabra c.** palindrome

capilar *adj* hair; **loción c.** hair lotion

capilla *nf* chapel; **c. ardiente** chapel of rest

capital **1** *nf* capital

2 *nm Fin* capital; **c. activo** *o* **social** working *o* share capital

3 *adj* capital, main; **de importancia c.** of capital importance; **pena c.** capital punishment

capitalismo *nm* capitalism

capitalista *adj & nmf* capitalist

capitán, -ana *nm,f* captain; **c. general** *Br* field marshal, *US* general of the army

capitanía *nf Mil* (**a**) *(empleo)* captaincy (**b**) *(oficina)* military headquarters; **c. general** Captaincy General

capitel *nm Arquit* capital

capítulo *nm* (**a**) *(de libro)* chapter (**b**) *Fig* **dentro del c. de …** *(tema)* under the heading of …

capó *nm Aut Br* bonnet, *US* hood

capón *nm* rap on the head with the knuckles

capota *nf Aut Br* convertible roof, *US* convertible top

capote *nm* (**a**) *Taurom* cape (**b**) *Mil* greatcoat

capricho *nm* (**a**) *(antojo)* whim, caprice (**b**) *Mús* caprice, capriccio

caprichoso, -a *adj* whimsical

Capricornio *nm* Capricorn

cápsula *nf* capsule

captar *vt* (**a**) *(ondas)* to receive, to pick up (**b**) *(comprender)* to understand, to grasp (**c**) *(interés etc)* to attract

capturar *vt* *(criminal)* to capture; *(cazar, pescar)* to catch; *Mil* to seize

capucha *nf* hood

capuchino *nm* *(café)* cappuccino

capullo **1** *nm* (**a**) *(de insecto)* cocoon (**b**) *(de flor)* bud (**c**) *Esp Vulg (glande)* head **2** *nm,f Esp muy Fam (persona despreciable)* jerk, *Br* dickhead

cara **1** *nf* (**a**) face; **c. a c.** face to face; **c. a la pared** facing the wall; **poner mala c.** to pull a long face; **tener buena/ mala c.** to look good/bad; *Fig* **c. de circunstancias** serious look; *Fig* **dar la c.** to face the consequences (of one's acts); *Fig* **dar la c. por algn** to stand up for sb; *Fig* **(de) c. a** with a view to; *Fig* **echarle a algn algo en c.** to reproach sb for sth

(**b**) *(lado)* side; *(de moneda)* right side; **¿c. o cruz?** heads or tails?; **echar algo a c. o cruz** to toss (a coin) for sth, *US* to flip (a coin) for sth

(**c**) *Fam (desfachatez)* cheek, nerve; **¡qué c. (más dura) tienes!** what a cheek you've got!

2 *nm Fam (desvergonzado)* cheeky person

carabela *nf* caravel

carabina *nf* (**a**) *(arma)* carbine, rifle (**b**) *(persona)* chaperon

carabinero *nm* (**a**) *(marisco)* scarlet shrimp, = type of large red prawn (**b**) *Chile (policía)* military policeman

caracol **1** *nm* (**a**) *(de tierra)* snail; *Am* shell (**b**) *(rizo)* kiss-curl **2** *interj* **¡caracoles!** good heavens!

caracola *nf* conch

caracolada *nf Culin* = stew made with snails

carácter *nm* (*pl* **caracteres**) (**a**)

(temperamento) character; **de mucho c.** with a strong character; **tener buen/mal c.** to be good-natured/bad-tempered (**b**) *Fig (índole)* nature; **con c. de invitado** as a guest (**c**) *Impr* character

característica *nf* characteristic

característico, -a *adj* characteristic

caracterizar [40] *vt* to characterize

caradura *nmf Fam* cheeky devil; **¡qué c. eres!** you're so cheeky!

carajillo *nm Fam* = coffee with a dash of brandy

caramba *interj Fam (sorpresa)* good heavens!, *Br* blimey!, *US* jeez!; *(enfado)* for heaven's sake!

carambola *nf Br* cannon, *US* carom

caramelo *nm* (**a**) *(dulce) Br* (boiled) sweet, *US* candy (**b**) *(azúcar quemado)* caramel; *Culin* **a punto de c.** syrupy

caraota *nf Ven* bean

carátula *nf* (**a**) *(cubierta)* cover (**b**) *(máscara)* mask

caravana *nf* (**a**) *(vehículo) Br* caravan, *US* trailer (**b**) *(de tráfico) Br* tailback, *US* backup (**c**) *Urug (aro, pendiente)* earring

caray *interj (sorpresa)* good heavens!, *Br* blimey!, *US* jeez!; *(enfado)* for heaven's sake!

carbón *nm* coal; **c. vegetal** charcoal; **c. mineral** coal

carboncillo *nm* charcoal

carbono *nm* carbon

carburador *nm* carburettor

carburante *nm* fuel

carcajada *nf* guffaw

cárcel *nf* prison, jail

carcoma *nf* woodworm

cardenal *nm* (**a**) *Rel* cardinal (**b**) *Med* bruise

cardiaco, -a, cardíaco, -a 1 *adj* cardiac, heart; **ataque c.** heart attack **2** *nm,f* person with a heart condition

cardinal *adj* cardinal; **punto/número c.** cardinal point/number

cardiólogo, -a *nm,f* cardiologist

cardo *nm (con espinas)* thistle

carecer [33] *vi* **c. de** to lack

carencia *nf* lack (**de** of)

careta *nf* mask; **c. antigás** gas mask

carey *nm* tortoiseshell

carga *nf* (**a**) *(acción)* loading (**b**) *(cosa cargada)* load; *(de avión, barco)* cargo, freight; *Fig* **c. afectiva** emotional content (**c**) *Fin (gasto)* debit; **c. fiscal** tax charge (**d**) *Fig (obligación)* burden (**e**) *Mil, Elec* charge

cargado, -a *adj* (**a**) loaded (**b**) *(bebida)* strong; **un café c.** a strong coffee (**c**) *(ambiente)* heavy; **atmósfera cargada** stuffy atmosphere (**d**) *Fig* burdened; **c. de deudas** up to one's eyes in debt (**e**) *Elec* charged

cargador *nm* (**a**) *(de arma)* chamber (**b**) *(persona)* loader; **c. de muelle** docker, stevedore (**c**) *(de baterías)* charger

cargar [42] **1** *vt* (**a**) to load; *(mechero, pluma)* to fill; *(batería)* to charge; *Fig* **c. las culpas a algn** to put the blame on sb (**b**) *Com* to charge; **cárguelo a mi cuenta** charge it to my account **2** *vi* (**a**) **c. con** *(llevar)* to carry; *Fig* **c. con la responsabilidad** to take the responsibility; *Fig* **c. con las consecuencias** to suffer the consequences (**b**) *Mil* **c. contra** to charge **3 cargarse** *vpr* (**a**) *Esp Fam* **te la vas a cargar** you're asking for trouble and you're going to get it (**b**) *Fam (estropear)* to smash, to ruin (**c**) *Fam (matar)* to kill, to bump off

cargo *nm* (**a**) *(puesto)* post, position; **alto c.** *(puesto)* top job, high ranking position; *(persona)* top person (**b**) **estar al c. de** to be in charge of; **correr a c. de** *(gastos)* to be met by; **hacerse c. de** to take charge of; **hazte c. de mi situación** please try to understand my situation (**c**) *Fin* charge, debit; **con c. a mi cuenta** charged to my account (**d**) *Jur* charge, accusation

cargosear *vt CSur* to annoy, to pester

cargoso, -a *adj CSur* annoying

cariado, -a *adj* decayed

Caribe 1 *adj* **el mar C.** the Caribbean (Sea) **2** *nm* **el C.** *(mar)* the Caribbean

(Sea); *(región)* the Caribbean

caribeño, -a 1 *adj* Caribbean **2** *nm,f* person from the Caribbean

caricatura *nf* caricature

caricia *nf* caress, stroke

caridad *nf* charity

caries *nf inv* decay, caries

cariño *nm* (**a**) *(amor)* affection; **coger/ tener c. a algo/algn** to grow/to be fond of sth/sb; **con c.** *(en carta)* love (**b**) *(apelativo)* dear, love, *US* honey (**c**) *(abrazo)* cuddle

cariñoso, -a *adj* loving, affectionate

carisma *nm* charisma

caritativo, -a *adj* charitable

cariz *nm* look

carmín *nm* (**de color**) **c.** carmine; **c. (de labios)** lipstick

carnal *adj* (**a**) *(de carne)* carnal (**b**) *(pariente)* first; **primo c.** first cousin

carnaval *nm* carnival

carne *nf* (**a**) flesh; *Fam* **ser de c. y hueso** to be only human; *Fig* **c. de cañón** cannon fodder; **c. de gallina** goosepimples; **c. viva** raw flesh (**b**) *(alimento)* meat; **c. de cerdo/corde- ro/ternera/vaca** pork/lamb/veal/beef (**c**) *(de fruta)* pulp

carné *nm* card; **c. de conducir** *Br* driving licence, *US* driver's license; **c. de identidad** identity card

carnear *vt* (**a**) *Andes, RP (sacrificar)* to slaughter, to butcher (**b**) *Chile (engañar)* to deceive, to take in

carnero *nm* ram; *Culin* mutton

carnicería *nf* (**a**) butcher's (shop) (**b**) *Fig (masacre)* slaughter

carnicero, -a *nm,f* butcher

carnitas *nfpl Méx* = small pieces of braised pork

caro, -a 1 *adj* expensive, dear **2** *adv* **salir c.** to cost a lot; **te costará c.** *(amenaza)* you'll pay dearly for this

carozo *nm RP (de fruta, aceituna)* stone, *US* pit

carpa *nf* (**a**) *(pez)* carp (**b**) *(de circo)* big top; *(en parque, la calle)* marquee (**c**) *Am (de tienda de campaña)* tent

carpeta *nf* file, folder

carpintería *nf* (**a**) *(oficio)* carpentry; **c. metálica** metalwork (**b**) *(taller)* carpenter's (shop)

carpintero, -a *nm,f* carpenter

carrera *nf* (**a**) run; **a la c.** in a hurry (**b**) *(competición)* race; **c. contra reloj** race against the clock; **c. de coches** rally, meeting; **echar una c. a algn** to race sb; **c. de armamentos** arms race (**c**) *(estudios)* university course; **hacer la c. de derecho/físicas** to study law/ physics (at university) (**d**) *(profesión)* career, profession (**e**) *(en medias) Br* ladder, *US* run

carrerilla *nf* **tomar** *o Esp* **coger c.** to take a run; **decir algo de c.** to reel sth off

carreta *nf* cart

carrete *nm (de hilo)* reel; *(de película)* spool; *(de cable)* coil

carretera *nf* road; **c. de acceso** access road; *(en autopista)* slip road; **c. de circunvalación** *Br* ring road, *US* beltway; **c. comarcal** minor road; *Méx* **c. de cuota** toll road; **c. nacional** *Br* ≃ A road, *US* ≃ state highway

carretero, -a *adj Am* road; **un accidente c.** a road accident

carretilla *nf* wheelbarrow

carril *nm* (**a**) *Ferroc* rail (**b**) *Aut* lane

carriola *nf* (**a**) *(cama)* truckle bed (**b**) *Méx (coche de bebé) Br* pram, *US* baby carriage

carrito *nm* trolley, *US* cart

carro *nm* (**a**) *(carreta)* cart; *Fam* **¡para el c.!** hang on a minute! (**b**) *Mil* **c. de combate** tank (**c**) *(de máquina de escribir)* carriage (**d**) *Am salvo RP (automóvil)* car (**e**) *Méx (vagón)* car; **c. comedor** dining car

carrocería *nf Aut* bodywork

carromato *nm (carro)* wagon

carroña *nf* carrion

carroza 1 *nf* (**a**) *(coche de caballos)* coach, carriage (**b**) *(de carnaval)* float **2** *nmf Fam* old fogey

carruaje *nm* carriage, coach

carrusel *nm (tiovivo)* merry-go- round, *US* carousel

carta *nf* (**a**) *(escrito)* letter (**b**) *(menú)* menu; **a la c.** à la carte; **c. de vinos** wine list (**c**) *Naipes* card; **echar las cartas a algn** to tell sb's fortune (**d**) *Geog (mapa)* chart (**e**) *Fig* **tomar cartas en un asunto** to take part in an affair

cartabón *nm* set square

cartearse *vpr* to correspond (**con** with), to exchange letters (**con** with)

cartel *nm* poster; **pegar/fijar carteles** to put *o* stick up bills

cartelera *nf* billboard, *Br* hoarding; *Prensa* **c. de espectáculos** entertainments section *o* page

cartera *nf* (**a**) *(de bolsillo)* wallet, *US* billfold (**b**) *(para documentos)* briefcase; *(de colegial)* satchel, schoolbag (**c**) *Pol (ministerio)* portfolio (**d**) *Com* portfolio; **c. de pedidos** order book (**e**) *Andes, RP (bolso) Br* handbag, *US* purse

carterista *nm* pickpocket

cartero, -a *nm,f Br* postman, *f* postwoman, *US* mailman, *f* mailwoman

cartilla *nf* (**a**) *(libreta)* book; **c. de ahorros** savings book (**b**) *(libro)* first reader; *Fam* **leerle la c. a algn** to tell sb off

cartón *nm* (**a**) *(material)* card, cardboard; **c. piedra** papier mâché (**b**) *(de cigarrillos)* carton

cartucho *nm* (**a**) *(de balas)* cartridge (**b**) *(de papel)* cone

cartulina *nf* card

casa *nf* (**a**) *(edificio)* house; **c. de huéspedes** *Br* guesthouse, *US* rooming house; **c. de socorro** first-aid post (**b**) *(hogar)* home; **vete a c.** go home; **en c. de Daniel** at Daniel's; **de andar por c.** everyday (**c**) *(empresa)* company, firm; **c. matriz/principal** head/central office

casadero, -a *adj* of marrying age

casado, -a 1 *adj* married **2** *nm,f* married person; **los recién casados** the newlyweds

casamiento *nm* marriage; *(boda)* wedding

casar¹ 1 *vt* to marry **2** *vi* to match, to go

o fit together **3 casarse** *vpr* to marry, to get married; **casarse por la iglesia/ por lo civil** to get married in church/ in a registry office

casar² *vt Jur* to annul, to quash

cascabel *nm* bell

cascada *nf* waterfall, cascade

cascado, -a *adj* (**a**) *Esp Fam (estropeado)* bust, *Br* clapped-out; *(persona, ropa)* worn-out (**b**) *(ronco)* rasping

cascanueces *nm inv* nutcracker

cascar [44] **1** *vt* (**a**) to crack (**b**) *Fam* **cascarla** to kick the bucket, to snuff it **2** *vi Esp Fam (hablar)* to witter on **3 cascarse** *vpr* to crack

cáscara *nf* shell; *(de fruta)* skin, peel; *(de grano)* husk

casco *nm* (**a**) *(para la cabeza)* helmet (**b**) *(de caballo)* hoof (**c**) *Esp, Méx (envase)* empty bottle (**d**) **c. urbano** city centre (**e**) *(de barco)* hull (**f**) **cascos** *(auriculares)* headphones

caserío *nm* country house

casero, -a 1 *adj* (**a**) *(hecho en casa)* home-made (**b**) *(persona)* home-loving **2** *nm,f (dueño)* landlord, *f* landlady

caseta *nf* hut, booth; *(de feria, exposición)* stand, stall; *Méx* **c. de cobro** tollbooth; *Méx* **c. telefónica** phone box, *US* phone booth

casete 1 *nm (magnetófono)* cassette player *o* recorder **2** *nf (cinta)* cassette (tape)

casi *adv* almost, nearly; **c. mil personas** almost one thousand people; **c. ni me acuerdo** I can hardly remember it; **c. nunca** hardly ever; **c. nadie** hardly anyone; **c. me caigo** I almost fell

casilla *nf* (**a**) *(de caja, armario)* compartment; *(para cartas)* pigeonhole; *Andes, RP* **c. de correos** PO Box; *CAm, Carib, Méx* **c. postal** PO Box (**b**) *(recuadro)* box (**c**) *Fig* **sacar a algn de sus casillas** to drive sb mad

casillero *nm* pigeonholes

casino *nm* casino

caso *nm* case; **el c. es que …** the fact *o*

thing is that ...; **el c. Mattei** the Mattei affair; **(en) c. contrario** otherwise; **en c. de necesidad** if need be; **en cualquier c.** in any case; **en el mejor/ peor de los casos** at best/worst; **en ese c.** in such a case; **en todo c.** in any case; **en un c. extremo, en último c.** as a last resort; **hacer c. a** o **de algn** to pay attention to sb; **hacer c. omiso de** to take no notice of; **no venir al c.** to be beside the point; **pongamos por c.** let's say

caspa *nf* dandruff

casquete *nm* (**a**) *(de bala)* case, shell (**b**) *Geog* **c. polar** polar cap

casquillo *nm (de bala)* case

casta *nf* (**a**) *(linaje)* lineage, descent (**b**) *(animales)* breed; **de c.** thoroughbred, purebred (**c**) *(división social)* caste

castaña *nf* chestnut; *Fig* **sacarle a algn las castañas del fuego** to save sb's bacon

castaño, -a 1 *adj* chestnut-brown; *(pelo, ojos)* brown, dark **2** *nm Bot* chestnut

castañuela *nf* castanet

castellano, -a 1 *adj & nm,f* Castilian **2** *nm (idioma)* Spanish, Castilian

castidad *nf* chastity

castigar [42] *vt* (**a**) to punish (**b**) *(dañar)* to harm, to ruin (**c**) *Jur, Dep* to penalize

castigo *nm* punishment; *Jur* penalty; *Dep* **área de c.** penalty area

castillo *nm* castle

castizo, -a *adj* pure, authentic

casto, -a *adj* chaste

castor *nm* beaver

castrar *vt* to castrate

casualidad *nf* chance, coincidence; **de** o **por c.** by chance; **dio la c. que ...** it so happened that ...; **¿tienes un lápiz, por c.?** do you happen to have a pencil?; **¡que c.!** what a coincidence!

catacumbas *nfpl* catacombs

catalán, -ana 1 *adj & nm,f* Català **2** *nm (idioma)* Catalan

catálogo *nm* catalogue

Cataluña *n* Catalonia

catamarán *nm* catamaran

catar *vt* to taste

catarata *nf* (**a**) waterfall (**b**) *Med* cataract

catarro *nm* (common) cold

catástrofe *nf* catastrophe

catastrófico, -a *adj* catastrophic

catear *vt* (**a**) *Esp Fam (suspender)* to fail, *US* to flunk (**b**) *Am (casa)* to search

catecismo *nm* catechism

cátedra *nf* (professorial) chair; **le han dado la c.** they have appointed him professor

catedral *nf* cathedral

catedrático, -a *nm,f Educ* (**a**) *Univ* professor (**b**) *(de instituto)* head of department

categoría *nf* category; *Fig* class; **de c.** *(persona)* important; *(vino etc)* quality

catequesis *nf inv* catechism lesson, ≃ Sunday school

cateto, -a *nm,f Pey* yokel, bumpkin

catire, -a *adj Carib (rubio)* blond, *f* blonde

catolicismo *nm* Catholicism

católico, -a *adj & nm,f* Catholic

catorce *adj & nm inv* fourteen

catre *nm Fam* camp bed, *US* cot

cauce *nm* (**a**) *(de un río)* bed (**b**) *Fig (canal)* channel; **cauces oficiales** official channels

caucho *nm* (**a**) *(sustancia)* rubber (**b**) *Ven (impermeable) Br* mac, *US* slicker (**c**) *Ven (neumático)* tyre

caudal *nm* (**a**) *(de un río)* flow (**b**) *(riqueza)* wealth, riches

caudaloso, -a *adj (río)* plentiful

caudillo *nm* leader, head

causa *nf* (**a**) cause; **a** o **por c. de** because of (**b**) *(ideal)* cause (**c**) *Jur (caso)* case; *(juicio)* trial

causante 1 *adj* causal, causing **2** *nmf* **el c. del incendio** the person who caused the fire

causar *vt* to cause, to bring about; **me causa un gran placer** it gives me great pleasure; **c. buena/mala impresión** to make a good/bad impression

cáustico, -a *adj* caustic

cautela *nf* caution

cautivador, -a 1 *adj* captivating, enchanting **2** *nm,f* charmer

cautivar *vt* (**a**) to capture, to take prisoner (**b**) *Fig (fascinar)* to captivate

cautiverio *nm*, **cautividad** *nf* captivity

cautivo, -a *adj & nm,f* captive

cauto, -a *adj* cautious, wary

cava 1 *nf (bodega)* wine cellar **2** *nm (vino espumoso)* cava, champagne

cavar *vt* to dig

caverna *nf* cave; **hombre de las cavernas** caveman

caviar *nm* caviar

cavidad *nf* cavity

cavilar *vt* to ponder

caza 1 *nf* (**a**) hunting; **ir de c.** to go hunting; **c. furtiva** poaching (**b**) *(animales)* game; **c. mayor/menor** big/small game (**c**) *Fig (persecución)* hunt; **c. de brujas** witch hunt **2** *nm Av* fighter, fighter plane

cazabe *nm Am* cassava bread

cazador, -a *nm,f* hunter; **c. furtivo** poacher

cazadora *nf* (waist-length) jacket

cazar [40] *vt* to hunt; *Fam* **cazarlas al vuelo** to be quick on the uptake

cazo *nm* (**a**) *(cacerola)* saucepan (**b**) *(cucharón)* ladle

cazuela *nf* saucepan; *(guiso)* casserole, stew; **a la c.** stewed

cazurro, -a 1 *adj (bruto)* stupid **2** *nm,f (bruto)* idiot, fool

c/c *(abr* **cuenta corriente)** c/a

CD *nm (pl* **CDs)** *(abr* **compact disc)** CD; **CD interactivo** interactive CD

CD-ROM ['θeðe'rrom] *nm (pl* **CD-ROMs)** CD-ROM

cebar 1 *vt* (**a**) *(animal)* to fatten; *(persona)* to feed up (**b**) *(anzuelo)* to bait (**c**) *(fuego, caldera)* to stoke, to fuel; *(máquina, arma)* to prime (**d**) *RP (mate)* to prepare, to brew **2 cebarse** *vpr* **cebarse con** *(ensañarse)* to delight in tormenting

cebo *nm* bait

cebolla *nf* onion

cebolleta *nf Br* spring onion, *US* scallion

cebra *nf* zebra; **paso de c.** *Br* zebra crossing, *US* crosswalk

cecear *vi* to lisp

ceder 1 *vt* to give, to hand over; *Aut* **c. el paso** to give way **2** *vi* (**a**) *(cuerda, cable)* to give way (**b**) *(lluvia, calor)* to diminish, to slacken (**c**) *(consentir)* to give in

cedro *nm* cedar

cédula *nf* (**a**) document, certificate; *Am* **c. de identidad** identity card (**b**) *Com, Fin* bond, certificate, warrant

cegato, -a *Fam* **1** *adj* short-sighted **2** *nm,f* short-sighted person

ceguera *nf* blindness

ceja *nf* eyebrow

celda *nf* cell; **c. de castigo** punishment cell

celebración *nf* (**a**) *(festejo)* celebration (**b**) *(de juicio etc)* holding

celebrar 1 *vt* (**a**) to celebrate; **celebro que todo saliera bien** I'm glad everything went well (**b**) *(reunión, juicio, elecciones)* to hold (**c**) *(triunfo)* to laud **2 celebrarse** *vpr* to take place, to be held

célebre *adj* famous, well-known

celebridad *nf* (**a**) celebrity, fame (**b**) *(persona)* celebrity

celeste 1 *adj* (**a**) *(de cielo)* celestial (**b**) *(color)* sky-blue **2** *nm* sky blue

celestial *adj* celestial, heavenly

celo *nm* (**a**) *(esmero)* zeal (**b**) **en c.** *(macho)* in rut; *(hembra) Br* on heat, *US* in heat (**c**) *(celos)* jealousy; **tener celos (de algn)** to be jealous (of sb)

celofán *nm* cellophane®

celoso, -a *adj* (**a**) jealous (**b**) *(cumplidor)* conscientious

célula *nf* cell

celular 1 *adj* (**a**) cellular (**b**) **coche c.** police van (**c**) *Am* **teléfono c.** mobile phone, cellphone **2** *nm Am* mobile (phone), cellphone

celulitis *nf inv* cellulitis

cementerio *nm* cemetery, graveyard; **c. de coches** scrapyard

cemento *nm* cement; **c. armado** reinforced cement

cena *nf* evening meal; *(antes de acostarse)* supper; **la Última C.** the Last Supper

cenar 1 *vi* to have supper o dinner **2** *vt* to have for supper o dinner

cencerro *nm* cowbell

cenefa *nf (de ropa)* edging, trimming; *(de suelo, techo)* ornamental border, frieze

cenicero *nm* ashtray

ceniza *nf* ash

censar *vt* to take a census of

censo *nm* census; *Esp* **c. electoral** electoral roll

censor *nm* censor

censura *nf* (a) censorship (b) *Pol* **moción de c.** vote of no confidence

censurar *vt* (a) *(libro, película)* to censor (b) *(criticar)* to censure, to criticize

centena *nf* hundred; **una c. de ...** a hundred ...

centenar *nm* hundred; **un c. de ...** a hundred ...; **a centenares** by the hundred

centenario *nm* centenary, hundredth anniversary

centeno *nm* rye

centésimo, -a *adj & nm,f* hundredth

centígrado, -a *adj* centigrade

centímetro *nm* centimetre

céntimo *nm* cent

centinela *nm* sentry

centollo *nm* spider crab

centrado, -a *adj* (a) centred (b) *(equilibrado)* balanced

central 1 *adj* central **2** *nf* (a) *Elec* **c. nuclear/térmica** nuclear/coal-fired power station (b) *(oficina principal)* head office

centralismo *nm* centralism

centralita *nf Tel* switchboard

centrar 1 *vt* (a) to centre (b) *(esfuerzos, atención)* to concentrate, to centre (**en** on) **2** **centrarse** *vpr* (a) to be centred o based (b) **centrarse en** *(concentrarse)* to concentrate on

céntrico, -a *adj* centrally situated; **zona céntrica** centrally situated area

centrifugar [42] *vt* to centrifuge; *(ropa)* to spin-dry

centro *nm* (a) middle, centre; **c. de la ciudad** town o city centre (b) *(establecimiento)* institution, centre; **c. comercial** shopping centre o *US* mall

Centroamérica *n* Central America

centuria *nf* century

ceñido, -a *adj* tight-fitting, clinging

ceñirse [6] *vpr* (a) *(atenerse, limitarse)* to limit oneself, to stick (**a** to); **c. al tema** to keep to the subject (b) **c. a** *(prenda)* to cling to

ceño *nm* scowl, frown; **con el c. fruncido** frowning

cepa *nf* (a) *(de vid)* vine (b) *Fig* **vasco de pura c.** *(origen)* Basque through and through

cepillar 1 *vt* (a) to brush (b) *(en carpintería)* to plane (down) (c) *Fam (robar)* to pinch **2** **cepillarse** *vpr* (a) *(con cepillo)* to brush (b) *Fam (matar)* to do in (c) *muy Fam* to lay

cepillo *nm* brush; *(en carpintería)* plane; **c. de dientes** toothbrush; **c. del pelo** hairbrush

cepo *nm* (a) *(para cazar)* trap (b) *Aut* clamp

cera *nf* wax; *(de abeja)* beeswax

cerámica *nf* ceramics *sing*

ceramista *nmf* potter

cerca¹ *adv* (a) near, close; **ven más c.** come closer; **ya estamos c.** we are almost there (b) **c. de** *(al lado de)* near, close to; **el colegio está c. de mi casa** the school is near my house (c) **c. de** *(casi)* nearly, around; **c. de cien personas** about one hundred people (d) **de c.** closely; **lo vi muy de c.** I saw it close up

cerca² *nf* fence, wall

cercanía *nf* (a) proximity, nearness (b) **cercanías** outskirts, suburbs; **(tren de) cercanías** suburban train

cercano, -a *adj* nearby; **el C. Oriente** the Near East

cercar [44] *vt* (a) *(tapiar)* to fence, to

enclose (**b**) *(rodear)* to surround

cerco *nm* (**a**) circle, ring (**b**) *Mil (sitio)* siege; **poner c. (a una ciudad)** to besiege (a town)

cerda *nf* (**a**) *Zool* sow (**b**) *(pelo)* bristle; **cepillo de c.** bristle brush

cerdo *nm* (**a**) pig (**b**) *(carne)* pork (**c**) *Fam* pig, arsehole

cereal *nm* cereal

cerebro *nm* brain; *Fig (inteligencia)* brains

ceremonia *nf* ceremony

ceremonioso, -a *adj* ceremonious, formal; *Pey* pompous, stiff

cereza *nf* cherry

cerezo *nm* cherry tree

cerilla *nf Esp* match

cerillo *nm CAm, Ecuad, Méx* match

cero *nm* zero; *Dep Br* nil, *US* zero; *Fig* **partir de c.** to start from scratch; *Fig* **ser un c. a la izquierda** to be useless o a good-for-nothing

cerquillo *nm Am Br* fringe, *US* bangs

cerrado, -a *adj* (**a**) closed, shut; **a puerta cerrada** behind closed doors (**b**) *(reservado)* reserved; *(intransigente)* uncompromising, unyielding; *Fam (torpe)* thick; *(acento)* broad; *(curva)* tight, sharp (**c**) *(barba)* bushy

cerradura *nf* lock

cerrajería *nf* (**a**) *(oficio)* locksmithery (**b**) *(local)* locksmith's (shop)

cerrajero, -a *nm,f* locksmith

cerrar [1] **1** *vt* to shut, to close; *(grifo, gas)* to turn off; *(luz)* to turn off, to switch off; *(cremallera)* to do up; *(negocio)* to close down; *(cuenta)* to close; *(carta)* to seal; *(puños)* to clench; **c. con llave** to lock; **c. el paso a algn** to block sb's way; *Fam* **c. el pico** to shut one's trap

2 *vi* to close, to shut

3 cerrarse *vpr* to close, to shut; *Fam* **cerrarse en banda** to stick to one's guns

cerro *nm* hill

cerrojo *nm* bolt; **echar el c. (de una puerta)** to bolt (a door)

certamen *nm* competition, contest

certeza *nf* certainty; **saber (algo) con c.** to be certain (of sth); **tener la c. de que …** to be sure o certain that …

certidumbre *nf* certainty

certificado, -a 1 *adj* (**a**) certified (**b**) *(correo)* registered **2** *nm* certificate

certificar [44] *vt* (**a**) to certify (**b**) *(carta)* to register

cervecería *nf* (**a**) *(bar)* pub, bar (**b**) *(fábrica)* brewery

cerveza *nf* beer; **c. de barril** draught beer; **c. dorada** o **ligera** lager; **c. negra** stout

cesante *adj (destituido)* dismissed, sacked; *CSur, Méx (parado)* unemployed

cesar 1 *vi* **c. (de)** to stop, to cease; **sin c.** incessantly **2** *vt (empleado)* to dismiss, *Br* to sack

cesárea *nf* Caesarean (section)

cese *nm* (**a**) cessation, suspension (**b**) *(despido)* dismissal

cesión *nf* cession, transfer; *Jur* **c. de bienes** surrender of property

césped *nm* lawn, grass

cesta *nf* basket; **c. de Navidad** Christmas hamper

cesto *nm* basket

cetro *nm* sceptre

chabacano, -a 1 *adj* cheap **2** *nm Méx (fruto)* apricot; *(árbol)* apricot tree

chabola *nf Esp* shack; **barrio de chabolas** shanty town

chacarero, -a *nm,f Andes, RP* farmer

chacha *nf* maid

cháchara *nf Fam* small talk, chinwag; **estar de c.** to have a yap

chacolí *nm* = light wine from the Basque Country

chacra *nf Andes, RP* farm

chafar *vt* (**a**) *Fam (plan etc)* to ruin, to spoil (**b**) *(aplastar)* to squash, to flatten

chal *nm* shawl

chalado, -a *adj Fam* crazy, nuts (**por** about)

chalé *nm* villa

chaleco *nm Br* waistcoat, *US* vest; *(de punto)* sleeveless pullover; **c. antibalas** bullet-proof vest; **c. salvavidas** life jacket

chalet = chalé

chalupa nf (a) *(embarcación)* boat, launch (b) *Méx (torta)* = small tortilla with a raised rim to contain a filling

chamaco, -a nm,f *Méx Fam* (a) *(muchacho)* kid (b) *(pareja)* boyfriend, f girlfriend

chamba nf *CAm, Méx, Perú, Ven Fam (trabajo)* job

chambón, -ona nm,f *Am Fam* sloppy o shoddy worker

champa nf *CAm (tienda de campaña)* tent

champán, champaña nm o nf champagne

champiñón nm mushroom

champú nm (pl **champús** o **champúes**) shampoo

chamuscado, -a adj *(pelo, plumas)* singed; *(tela, papel)* scorched; *(tostada)* burnt

chamuscar [44] vt to singe, to scorch

chamusquina nf singeing, scorching; *Fam* **esto me huele a c.** there's something fishy going on here

chance 1 nm o nf *Am* opportunity **2** adv *Méx* maybe

chanchada nf *Am* (a) *(porquería)* **¡no hagas chanchadas!** stop that, don't be disgusting! (b) *Fam (jugarreta)* dirty trick

chancho, -a nm,f *Am* pig, f sow

chancla nf *Br* flip-flop, *US, Austr* thong

chanclo nm *(zueco)* clog; *(de goma)* overshoe, galosh

chándal nm (pl **chandals**) *Esp* tracksuit

changa nf *Bol, RP (trabajo temporal)* odd job

changador nm *RP (cargador)* porter

changarro nm *Méx (tienda)* small shop; *(puesto)* stand

chantaje nm blackmail; **hacer c. a algn** to blackmail sb

chantajista nmf blackmailer

chapa nf (a) *(de metal)* sheet; *(de madera)* panel-board (b) *(tapón)* bottle top, cap (c) *(de adorno)* badge

(d) *RP (de matrícula)* *Br* number plate, *US* license plate (e) *Col, Cuba, Méx (cerradura)* lock

chapado, -a adj *(metal)* plated; **c. en oro** gold-plated; *Fig* **c. a la antigua** old-fashioned

chapar 1 vt *(recubrir)* *(con metal)* to plate; *(con madera)* to veneer **2** vi *Esp muy Fam (cerrar)* to shut, to close

chaparrón nm downpour, heavy shower

chapopote nm *Carib, Méx* bitumen, pitch

chapucería nf botch (job)

chapucero, -a adj *(trabajo)* slapdash, shoddy; *(persona)* bungling

chapulín nm *CAm, Méx (saltamontes)* grasshopper

chapuza nf (a) *(trabajo mal hecho)* shoddy piece of work (b) *(trabajo ocasional)* odd job

chaqué nm morning coat

chaqueta nf jacket; *Pol* **cambiar de c.** to change sides

chaquetilla nf short jacket

chaquetón nm heavy jacket, short coat

charca nf pond, pool

charco nm puddle

charcutería nf delicatessen

charla nf *(conversación)* talk, chat; *(conferencia)* informal lecture o address; *Informát* chat

charlar vi to talk, to chat; *Informát* to chat

charlatán, -ana 1 adj *(parlanchín)* talkative; *(chismoso)* gossipy **2** nm,f (a) *(parlanchín)* chatterbox; *(chismoso)* gossip; *(bocazas)* bigmouth (b) *(embaucador)* trickster, charmer

charol nm (a) *(piel)* patent leather; **zapatos de c.** patent leather shoes (b) *Andes (bandeja)* tray

charola nf *Bol, CAm, Méx* tray

charque, charqui nm *Andes, RP* jerked o salted beef

charro, -a 1 adj (a) *Esp (salmantino)* Salamancan (b) *(recargado)* gaudy, showy (c) *Méx (líder sindical)* = in league with the bosses **2** *nm,f* (**a**) *Esp (salmantino)* Salamancan (**b**) *Méx (jinete)* horseman, *f* horsewoman

chárter *adj inv* (**vuelo**) **c.** charter (flight)

chasca *nf Andes (greña)* mop of hair

chasco *nm Fam* disappointment; **llevarse un c.** to be disappointed

chasis *nm inv* chassis

chatarra *nf* scrap (metal), scrap iron; *Fam* junk

chatarrero, -a *nm,f* scrap (metal) dealer

chato, -a 1 *adj* (**a**) *(nariz)* snub; *(persona)* snub-nosed (**b**) *(objeto)* flat, flattened (**c**) *PRico, RP Fam (sin ambiciones)* commonplace; **una vida chata** a humdrum existence **2** *nm Esp Fam* = small glass of wine

chau *interj Bol, CSur, Perú Fam* bye!, see you!

chaucha 1 *adj RP Fam* dull, boring **2** *nf* (**a**) *Bol, RP* green bean (**b**) *Andes (patata)* early potato

chaveta *nf* (**a**) *(clavija)* cotter pin (**b**) *Fam (cabeza)* nut, head; **perder la c.** *(volverse loco)* to go off one's rocker (**c**) *Andes (navaja)* penknife

chavo, -a *Fam* **1** *nm,f Méx* (**a**) *(chico)* guy; *(chica)* girl (**b**) *(novio)* boyfriend; *(novia)* girlfriend **2** *nm (dinero)* **no tener un c.** to be broke

che *interj RP Fam* **¿qué hacés, c.?, ¿cómo andás, c.?** hey, how's it going, then?; **c., ¡vení para acá!** hey, over here, you!

Checoslovaquia *n* Czechoslovakia

chef [tʃef] *nm (pl* **chefs**) chef

chele, -a *CAm* **1** *adj (rubio)* blond, *f* blonde; *(de piel blanca)* fair-skinned **2** *nmf (rubio)* blond, *f* blonde; *(de piel blanca)* fair-skinned person

cheque *nm Br* cheque, *US* check; **c. al portador** cheque payable to bearer; **c. de viaje** *o* (**de**) **viajero** traveller's cheque

chequeo *nm Med* checkup; *Aut* service

chequera *nf Br* chequebook, *US* checkbook

chévere *adj Am salvo RP Fam* great, fantastic

chic *adj inv* chic, elegant

chicha¹ *nf* (**a**) *Esp Fam (para comer)* meat (**b**) *Esp Fam (de persona)* flesh; **tiene pocas chichas** *(está flaco)* he's as thin as a rake (**c**) *(bebida alcohólica)* = alcoholic drink made from fermented maize (**d**) *(bebida refrescante)* = thick, sweet drink made from rice, condensed milk and vanilla

chicha² *adj inv Náut* **calma c.** dead calm

chícharo *nm CAm, Méx* pea

chicharra *nf* (**a**) *(insecto)* cicada (**b**) *Méx (timbre)* electric buzzer

chiche *nm* (**a**) *Andes, RP Fam (juguete)* toy (**b**) *Andes, RP (adorno)* delicate ornament (**c**) *CAm, Méx muy Fam (pecho)* tit

chichón *nm* bump, lump

chicle *nm* chewing gum

chico, -a 1 *nm,f (muchacho)* boy, lad; *(muchacha)* girl **2** *adj* small, little

chicote *nm Am* whip

chiflado, -a *adj Fam* mad, crazy (**por** about)

chiflar *vt* (**a**) *(silbar)* to hiss (at), to boo (at) (**b**) *Fam* **le chiflan las motos** he's really into motorbikes

chiflido *nm* whistling

chigüín, -a *nm CAm Fam* kid

chilango, -a *Méx Fam* **1** *adj* of/from Mexico City **2** *nm,f* person from Mexico City

Chile *n* Chile

chileno, -a *adj & nm,f* Chilean

chillar *vi (persona)* to scream, to shriek; *(ratón)* to squeak; *(frenos)* to screech, to squeal; *(puerta)* to creak, to squeak

chillido *nm (de persona)* scream, shriek; *(de ratón)* squeak; *(de frenos)* screech, squeal; *(de puerta)* creaking, squeaking

chillón, -ona *adj* (**a**) *(voz)* shrill, high-pitched; *(sonido)* harsh, strident (**b**) *(color)* loud, gaudy

chilpotle *nm Méx* = smoked or

pickled jalapeño chile

chimbo, -a *adj Col, Ven Fam* (a) *(de mala calidad)* crap, useless (b) *(complicado)* screwed-up

chimenea *nf* (a) *(hogar abierto)* fireplace, hearth (b) *(conducto)* chimney; *(de barco)* funnel, stack

chimichurri *nm RP* = barbecue sauce made from garlic, parsley, oregano and vinegar

chimpancé *nm* chimpanzee

China *n* China

china *nf* (a) pebble, small stone; *Fam* **tocarle a uno la c.** to get the short straw (b) *Fam (droga)* deal

chinampa *nf Méx* = man-made island for growing flowers, fruit and vegetables, in Xochimilco near Mexico City

chinche *nf* bedbug; *Fam* **caer como chinches** to drop like flies

chincheta *nf Br* drawing pin, *US* thumbtack

chinchín *interj* cheers!, (to) your (good) health!

chinchulín *nm*, **chinchulines** *nmpl Andes, RP (plato)* = piece of sheep or cow intestine, plaited and then roasted

chingado, -a *adj Esp, Méx muy Fam (estropeado)* bust, *Br* knackered

chingana *nf Andes Fam* = cheap bar or café

chingar [42] **1** *vt* (a) *Esp, Méx muy Fam (estropear)* to bust, *Br* to knacker (b) *Esp, Méx muy Fam (molestar)* **c. a algn** to piss sb off, to get up sb's nose (c) *Esp, Méx Vulg (copular)* to fuck; *Méx* **¡chinga tu madre!** fuck you!
2 *vi Esp, Méx Vulg (copular)* to screw, to fuck
3 chingarse *vpr Méx muy Fam (estropearse)* to pack in, to conk out

chino¹ *nm (piedrecita)* pebble, stone

chino², -a *adj* (a) *(de China)* Chinese; *Fam* **eso me suena a c.** it's all Greek to me (b) *Am (mestizo)* of mixed ancestry (c) *(rizado)* curly

chip *nm (pl* **chips**) *Informát* chip

chipirón *nm* baby squid

chiqueo *nm Méx Fam* show of affection; **hacerle chiqueos a algn** to kiss and cuddle sb

chirimoya *nf* custard apple

chiripá *nm (pl* **chiripaes**) *Bol, CSur* = garment worn by gauchos over trousers

chisme *nm* (a) *(habladuría)* piece of gossip (b) *Fam (trasto)* knick-knack; *(cosa)* thing

chismoso, -a 1 *adj* gossipy **2** *nm,f* gossip

chispa *nf* (a) spark; **echar chispas** to fume (b) *Fam (un poco)* bit, tiny amount (c) *Fam (agudeza)* wit, sparkle; *(viveza)* liveliness

chiste *nm* joke; **contar un c.** to tell a joke; **c. verde** blue joke, dirty joke

chistorra *nf* = type of cured pork sausage typical of Aragon and Navarre

chistoso, -a *adj (persona)* funny, witty; *(anécdota)* funny, amusing

chivarse *vpr Esp Fam (niños)* to tell, *Br* to split *(de* on); *(delincuentes)* to squeal, *Br* to grass *(de* on)

chivatazo *nm Esp Fam* tip-off; **dar el c.** to squeal, *Br* to grass

chivato, -a 1 *nm,f Esp Fam (delator) Br* grass, *US* rat; *(acusica)* telltale **2** *nm* (a) *(luz)* warning light (b) *(alarma)* alarm bell (c) *Ven Fam (pez gordo)* big cheese

chivito *nm* (a) *Arg (carne)* roast kid (b) *Urug* steak sandwich *(containing cheese and salad)*

chocar [44] **1** *vi* (a) *(topar)* to crash, to collide; **c. con** *o* **contra** to run into, to collide with (b) *(en discusión)* to clash **2** *vt* (a) *(topar)* to knock; *(la mano)* to shake; *Fam* **¡chócala!, ¡choca esos cinco!** shake (on it)!, put it there! (b) *(sorprender)* to surprise

chocho, -a 1 *adj (senil)* senile; **viejo c.** old dodderer **2** *nm* (a) *(altramuz)* lupin (b) *Esp, Méx Vulg (vulva) Br* fanny, *US* beaver

choclo *nm Andes, RP* maize, *US* corn

chocolate *nm* (a) chocolate; **c. con leche** milk chocolate (b) *Esp Fam (droga)* dope

chocolatería *nf* (**a**) *(fábrica)* chocolate factory (**b**) *(establecimiento)* = café where drinking chocolate is served

chocolatina *nf* bar of chocolate, chocolate bar

chófer *Esp,* **chofer** *Am nm* chauffeur

chollo *nm Esp Fam (ganga)* bargain

chomba *nf* (**a**) *Arg* polo shirt (**b**) *Chile, Perú (suéter)* sweater

chompa *nf Andes* sweater, pullover

chompipe *nm CAm, Méx* turkey

chongo *nm Méx* (**a**) *(moño)* bun (**b**) **chongos zamoranos** *(dulce)* = Mexican dessert made from milk curds, served in syrup

chonta *nf CAm, Perú* = type of palm tree

chop, chopp *nm (pl* **chops, chopps**) *CSur* (**a**) *(jarra)* beer mug (**b**) *(cerveza)* (mug of) beer

chopo *nm* poplar

choque *nm* (**a**) impact; *(de coches etc)* crash, collision; **c. frontal** head-on collision; **c. múltiple** pile-up (**b**) *Fig (contienda)* clash

chorizo *nm* (**a**) chorizo, highly-seasoned pork sausage (**b**) *Esp Fam (ladrón)* thief

choro *nm Andes* mussel

chorrada *nf Esp Fam* **decir una c.** to say something stupid; **chorradas** *Br* rubbish, *US* garbage

chorrear *vi* to drip, to trickle; *Fam* **c. de sudor** to pour with sweat; *Fam* **tengo el abrigo chorreando** my coat is dripping wet

chorro *nm* (**a**) *(de agua etc)* spurt; *(muy fino)* trickle; **salir a chorros** to gush forth (**b**) *Téc* jet (**c**) *Fig* stream, flood

choto *nm,f* (**a**) *(cabrito)* kid, young goat; *Fam* **estar como una chota** to be crazy, to be off one's rocker (**b**) *(ternero)* calf

choza *nf* hut, shack

christmas *nm inv* Christmas card

chubasco *nm* heavy shower, downpour

chubasquero *nm* raincoat, *Br* mac

chúcaro, -a *adj Andes, CAm, RP* (**a**) *(animal)* wild (**b**) *Fam (persona)* **ser c.** to be shy o withdrawn

chuchería *nf Fam Br* sweet, *US* candy

chucho *nm Fam* (**a**) *(perro)* mutt, dog (**b**) *RP (susto)* fright; **un c. de frío** a shiver

chueco, -a 1 *adj Am (torcido)* twisted; *(patizambo)* bowlegged; *Méx, Ven Fam (cojo)* lame **2** *nm,f Am (patizambo)* bowlegged person; *Méx, Ven Fam (cojo)* lame person

chufa *nf* groundnut

chuleta *nf* (**a**) *(de carne)* chop; **c. de cerdo** pork chop (**b**) *Esp, Ven Fam (en exámenes)* crib note

chullo *nm Andes* woollen cap

chulo, -a *Fam* **1** *nm,f Esp* show-off **2** *nm (proxeneta)* pimp **3** *adj Esp, Méx Fam (bonito)* cool, *Br* top, *US* neat

chumbera *nf* prickly pear cactus

chuño *nm Andes, RP* potato starch

chupachups® *nm inv Esp* lollipop

chupado, -a *adj* (**a**) *(flaco)* skinny, thin (**b**) *Fam* **está c.** it's dead easy

chupamedias *nmf inv Andes, RP, Ven Fam* toady

chupar 1 *vt* (**a**) to suck (**b**) *(lamer)* to lick (**c**) *(absorber)* to soak up, to absorb **2** *vi* to suck **3 chuparse** *vpr* (**a**) **está para chuparse los dedos** it's really mouthwatering (**b**) *Esp Fam* to put up with; **nos chupamos toda la película** we sat through the whole film

chupe *nm* (**a**) *Andes, Arg (comida)* stew (**b**) *Méx, RP Fam (bebida)* booze

chupete *nm Br* dummy, *US* pacifier

chupito *nm* shot

churrasco *nm* barbecued meat

churrería *nf* fritter shop

churro *nm* (**a**) = dough formed into sticks or rings, fried in oil and covered in sugar (**b**) *Fam (chapuza)* mess

chusma *nf* rabble, mob

chutar 1 *vi* (**a**) *Dep (a gol)* to shoot (**b**) *Esp Fam (funcionar)* to work; **¡y vas que chutas!** and then you're well away! **2 chutarse** *vpr Esp Fam* *(drogas)* to shoot up

chute *nm* (a) *Dep* shot (b) *Esp Fam (drogas)* fix

Cía., cía. *(abr* **compañía)** Co

cibercafé *nm Informát* Internet cafe, cybercafe

cicatriz *nf* scar

cicatrizar [40] *vt & vi Med* to heal

ciclismo *nm* cycling

ciclista 1 *adj* cycling **2** *nmf* cyclist

ciclo *nm* cycle; *(de conferencias etc)* course, series

ciclomotor *nm* moped

ciclón *nm* cyclone

ciego, -a 1 *adj* (a) *(invidente)* blind; **a ciegas** blindly (b) *Esp Fam (borracho)* blind drunk, *Br* pissed; *(de droga)* stoned **2** *nm,f* blind person; **los ciegos** the blind

cielo *nm* (a) sky (b) *Rel* heaven; *Fig* **caído del c.** *(oportuno)* heaven-sent; *(inesperado)* out of the blue; **¡c. santo!** good heavens! (c) *Arquit* **c. raso** ceiling (d) **c. de la boca** roof of the mouth

ciempiés *nm inv* centipede

cien *adj & nm inv* hundred; **c. libras** a *o* one hundred pounds; **c. por c.** one hundred percent

ciencia *nf* (a) science; *Fig* **saber algo a c. cierta** to know sth for certain; **c. ficción** science fiction; **c. infusa** intuition; **ciencias ocultas** the occult (b) *(conocimiento)* knowledge

científico, -a 1 *adj* scientific **2** *nm,f* scientist

cientista *nmf CSur* **c. social** social scientist

ciento *adj* hundred; **c. tres** one hundred and three; **por c.** percent

cierre *nm* (a) *(acción)* closing, shutting; *(de fábrica)* shutdown; *TV* close-down; **c. patronal** lockout (b) *(de bolso)* clasp; *(de puerta)* catch; *(prenda)* fastener; **c. de seguridad** safety lock; **c. centralizado** central locking (c) *Andes, Méx, RP (cremallera) Br* zip (fastener), *US* zipper; *Andes, Méx* **c. relámpago** *Br* zip (fastener), *US* zipper

cierto, -a 1 *adj* (a) *(verdadero)* true; *(seguro)* certain; **estar en lo c.** to be right; **lo c. es que ...** the fact is that ...; **por c.** by the way (b) *(algún)* certain; **ciertas personas** certain *o* some people **2** *adv* certainly

ciervo, -a *nm,f* deer; *(macho)* stag; *(hembra)* doe, hind

cifra *nf* (a) *(número)* figure, number (b) *(código)* cipher, code

cigala *nf* Norway lobster, scampi

cigarra *nf* cicada

cigarrillo *nm* cigarette

cigarro *nm* (a) *(puro)* cigar (b) *(cigarrillo)* cigarette

cigüeña *nf* (a) *Orn* stork (b) *Téc* crank

cilindrada *nf Aut* cylinder capacity

cilíndrico, -a *adj* cylindrical

cilindro *nm* cylinder

cima *nf* summit

cimientos *nmpl* foundations; **echar** *o* **poner los c.** to lay the foundations

cinco *adj & nm inv* five

cincuenta *adj & nm inv* fifty

cine *nm* (a) *(local)* cinema, *US* movie theater (b) *(arte)* cinema; **c. mudo** silent movies *o Br* films; **c. sonoro** talking pictures, talkies

cineasta *nmf* movie maker *o* director, *Br* film maker *o* director

cinematografía *nf* cinematography, *Br* film-making

cinematográfico, -a *adj* movie, *Br* film; **la industria cinematográfica** the movie *o Br* film industry

cínico, -a 1 *adj* shameless **2** *nm,f* shameless person; **es un c.** he's shameless, he has no shame

cinismo *nm* shamelessness

cinta *nf* (a) *(tira)* band, strip; *(para adornar)* ribbon; *Cost* braid, edging (b) *Téc, Mús* tape; **c. adhesiva/aislante** adhesive/insulating tape; **c. de vídeo** video tape; **c. transportadora** conveyor belt (c) *Cin* movie, *Br* film

cintura *nf* waist

cinturón *nm* belt; *Fig* **apretarse el c.** to tighten one's belt; **c. de seguridad** safety belt; *Am* **c. de miseria** = slum or shanty town area round a large city

cipote¹ *nm* (**a**) *Fam (bobo)* dimwit, moron (**b**) *Vulg (pene)* prick, cock

cipote², -a *nm,f CAm* kid

ciprés *nm* cypress

circo *nm* circus

circuito *nm* circuit

circulación *nf* (**a**) circulation (**b**) *Aut (tráfico)* traffic

circular 1 *adj & nf* circular **2** *vi (moverse)* to circulate; *(líquido)* to flow; *(tren, autobús)* to run; *Fig (rumor)* to go round; **circule por la izquierda** *(en letrero)* keep to the left

círculo *nm* circle; *Fig* **c. vicioso** vicious circle

circunferencia *nf* circumference

circunscribir *vt* (**a**) *(limitar)* to restrict, to confine (**b**) *Geom* to circumscribe

circunscrito, -a *adj* circumscribed

circunstancia *nf* circumstance; **en estas circunstancias ...** under the circumstances ...

circunstancial *adj* circumstantial

cirio *nm* wax candle

cirrosis *nf inv* cirrhosis

ciruela *nf* plum; **c. claudia** greengage; **c. pasa** prune

ciruelo *nm* plum tree

cirugía *nf* surgery; **c. estética** *o* **plástica** plastic surgery

cirujano, -a *nm,f* surgeon

cisma *nm* (**a**) *Rel* schism (**b**) *Pol* split

cisne *nm* swan

cisterna *nf* cistern, tank

cita *nf* (**a**) appointment; **darse c.** to come together (**b**) *(amorosa)* date (**c**) *(mención)* quotation

citación *nf Jur* citation, summons *sing*

citar 1 *vt* (**a**) *(dar cita)* to arrange to meet, to make an appointment with (**b**) *(mencionar)* to quote (**c**) *Jur* to summons **2 citarse** *vpr* to arrange to meet, to make a date (**con** with)

cítrico, -a 1 *adj* citric, citrus **2** *nmpl* **cítricos** citrus fruits

ciudad *nf* town; *(capital)* city; *Méx* **c. perdida** shanty town

ciudadanía *nf* citizenship

ciudadano, -a 1 *nm,f* citizen; **el c. de a pie** the man in the street **2** *adj* civic

cívico, -a *adj* civic

civil 1 *adj* (**a**) civil; **matrimonio c.** civil marriage (**b**) *Mil* civilian **2** *nm* member of the Guardia Civil

civilización *nf* civilization

civilizado, -a *adj* civilized

civismo *nm* (**a**) *(urbanidad)* public-spiritedness (**b**) *(cortesía)* civility

cl *(abr* **centilitro)** cl

clan *nm* clan

clara *nf* (**a**) *(de huevo)* white (**b**) *Esp Fam (bebida)* shandy

claraboya *nf* skylight

clarear *vi* (**a**) *(amanecer)* to dawn (**b**) *(despejar)* to clear up (**c**) *(transparentar)* to wear thin, to become transparent

claridad *nf* (**a**) *(luz)* light, brightness (**b**) *(inteligibilidad)* clarity; **con c.** clearly

clarinete *nm* clarinet

clarividencia *nf* far-sightedness, perception

claro, -a 1 *adj* (**a**) clear; **dejar algo c.** to make sth clear (**b**) *(líquido, salsa)* thin (**c**) *(color)* light

2 *interj* of course!; **¡c. que no!** of course not!; **¡c. que sí!** certainly!

3 *nm* (**a**) *(espacio)* gap, space; *(en un bosque)* clearing (**b**) *Met* bright spell

4 *adv* clearly

clase *nf* (**a**) *(grupo)* class; **c. alta/media** upper/middle class; **clases pasivas** pensioners; **primera/segunda c.** first/second class (**b**) *(tipo)* kind, sort; **toda c. de ...** all kinds of ... (**c**) *Educ (curso)* class; *(aula)* classroom; **c. particular** private class *o* lesson (**d**) *(estilo)* class; **tener c.** to have class

clásico, -a 1 *adj* classical; *(típico)* classic; *(en el vestir)* classic **2** *nm* classic

clasificación *nf* (**a**) classification; *Dep* league table (**b**) *(para campeonato, concurso)* qualification

clasificador, -a 1 *adj* classifying **2**

nm (mueble) filing cabinet

clasificar [44] **1** *vt* to classify, to class **2 clasificarse** *vpr Dep* to qualify

claudicar [44] *vi* to give in

claustro *nm* (**a**) *Arquit* cloister (**b**) *(reunión)* ≃ staff meeting, *US* faculty meeting

claustrofobia *nf* claustrophobia

cláusula *nf* clause

clausura *nf* (**a**) *(cierre)* closure; **ceremonia de c.** closing ceremony (**b**) *Rel* enclosure

clausurar *vt* to close

clavadista *nmf CAm, Méx* diver

clavado, -a *adj* (**a**) *(con clavos)* nailed (**b**) *(a la medida)* just right (**c**) *(parecido)* almost identical; **ser c. a algn** to be the spitting image of sb

clavar 1 *vt* (**a**) to nail; *(clavo)* to bang *o* hammer in; *(estaca)* to drive in (**b**) *Fam (timar)* to sting *o* fleece **2 clavarse** *vpr* **clavarse una astilla** to get a splinter

clave 1 *nf* key; **la palabra c.** the key word **2** *nm* harpsichord

clavel *nm* carnation

clavícula *nf* collarbone

clavija *nf Téc* jack

clavo *nm* (**a**) nail; *Fig* **dar en el c.** to hit the nail on the head (**b**) *Bot* clove

claxon *nm* horn; **tocar el c.** to sound the horn

cleptomanía *nf* kleptomania

clericó *nm RP* = drink made of white wine and fruit

clérigo *nm* priest

clero *nm* clergy

clic *nm* (*pl* **clics**) *Informát* click; **hacer c.** to click; **hacer doble c.** to double-click

cliché *nm* (**a**) *Fig (tópico)* cliché (**b**) *Fot* negative (**c**) *Impr* plate

click = **clic**

cliente *nmf* customer, client

clima *nm* climate

climático, -a *adj* climatic

climatizado, -a *adj* air-conditioned

climatología *nf* (**a**) *(tiempo)* climate (**b**) *(ciencia)* climatology

clímax *nm inv* climax

clínica *nf* clinic

clínico, -a *adj* clinical

clip *nm* (*pl* **clips**) clip

cloaca *nf* sewer, drain

cloro *nm* chlorine

clorofila *nf* chlorophyll

clóset *nm* (*pl* **clósets**) *Am* fitted cupboard, *US* closet

club *nm* (*pl* **clubs** *o* **clubes**) club; **c. náutico** yacht club

cm (*abr* **centímetro(s)**) cm

coacción *nf* coercion

coaccionar *vt* to coerce

coartada *nf* alibi

coba *nf Esp, Méx Fam (halago)* flattery; **dar c. a algn** *(adular)* to suck up *o* crawl to sb; *(aplacar)* to soft-soap sb

cobarde 1 *adj* cowardly **2** *nmf* coward

cobardía *nf* cowardice

cobertizo *nm* shed, shack

cobija *nf Am (manta)* blanket

cobijar 1 *vt* to shelter **2 cobijarse** *vpr* to take shelter

cobra *nf* cobra

cobrador, -a *nm,f* (**a**) *(de autobús)* conductor, *f* conductress (**b**) *(de luz, agua etc)* collector

cobrar 1 *vt* (**a**) *(dinero)* to charge; *(cheque)* to cash; *(salario)* to earn; **¿me cobra?** how much is that? (**b**) *Fig (fuerza)* to gain, to get; **c. ánimos** to take courage *o* heart; **c. importancia** to become important

2 *vi Fam* to catch it

3 cobrarse *vpr* **¿se cobra?** *(al pagar)* how much is that?

cobre *nm* copper

cobro *nm* *(pago)* collecting; *(de cheque)* cashing; *Tel* **llamada a c. revertido** *Br* reverse-charge call, *US* collect call

coca *nf* (**a**) *Bot* coca (**b**) *Fam (droga)* cocaine, coke

cocaína *nf* cocaine

cocainómano, -a *nm,f* cocaine addict

cocalero, -a *Bol, Perú* **1** *adj* **región cocalera** coca-producing area; **productor c.** coca farmer *o* producer

2 *nm,f* coca farmer *o* producer

cocción *nf* cooking; *(en agua)* boiling; *(en horno)* baking

cocear *vi* to kick

cocer [41] **1** *vt* to cook; *(hervir)* to boil; *(hornear)* to bake
2 *vi (hervir)* to boil
3 cocerse *vpr* (**a**) *(comida)* to cook; *(hervir)* to boil; *(hornear)* to bake (**b**) *(tramarse)* to be going on

cochayuyo *nm Chile, Perú* seaweed

coche *nm* (**a**) car, *US* automobile; **en c.** by car; **c. de carreras** racing car; **c. de bomberos** fire engine, *US* fire truck; **c. fúnebre** hearse (**b**) *Ferroc* coach, *Br* carriage, *US* car; **c. cama** sleeping car, sleeper (**c**) *(de caballos)* carriage

cochinillo *nm* suckling pig

cochino, -a 1 *nm,f* (**a**) pig, *f* sow (**b**) *Fam (persona)* filthy person, pig **2** *adj (sucio)* filthy, disgusting

cocido *nm* stew

cocina *nf* (**a**) kitchen (**b**) *(aparato)* cooker, stove; **c. eléctrica/de gas** electric/gas cooker (**c**) *(arte)* cooking; **c. casera** home cooking; **c. española** Spanish cooking *o* cuisine

cocinar *vt & vi* to cook

cocinero, -a *nm,f* cook

coco[1] *nm* coconut; *Fam (cabeza)* nut; **comerle el c. a algn** to brainwash sb; **comerse el c.** to get obsessed

coco[2] *nm Fam (fantasma)* bogeyman

cocodrilo *nm* crocodile

cocoliche *nm RP Fam* = pidgin Spanish spoken by Italian immigrants

cocotero *nm* coconut palm

cóctel *nm* cocktail; **c. Molotov** Molotov cocktail

coctelera *nf* cocktail shaker

codazo *nm* (**a**) *(señal)* nudge with one's elbow (**b**) *(golpe)* blow with one's elbow

codiciar [43] *vt* to covet

codificado, -a *adj (emisión de TV)* scrambled

código *nm* code; **c. de circulación** highway code; **c. postal** *Br* postcode, postal code, *US* zip code

codo *nm* elbow; *Fig* **c. con c.** side by side; *Fam* **hablar por los codos** to talk nonstop

codorniz *nf* quail

coeficiente *nm* (**a**) coefficient (**b**) *(grado)* rate; **c. intelectual** intelligence quotient

coetáneo, -a *adj & nm,f* contemporary

coexistencia *nf* coexistence

coexistir *vi* to coexist

cofia *nf* bonnet

cofradía *nf* *(hermandad)* brotherhood; *(asociación)* association

cofre *nm* *(arca)* trunk, chest; *(para joyas)* box, casket

coger [53] **1** *vt* (**a**) to take; *(del suelo)* to pick (up); *(fruta, flores)* to pick; *(asir)* to seize, take hold of; *(bus, tren)* to take, catch; *(pelota, ladrón, resfriado)* to catch; *(entender)* to grasp; *(costumbre)* to pick up; *(velocidad, fuerza)* to gather; *(atropellar)* to run over, knock down (**b**) *Am Vulg* to screw, to fuck
2 *vi Fam* **cogió y se fue** he upped and left
3 cogerse *vpr (agarrarse)* to hold on

cogida *nf* goring

cogollo *nm (de lechuga)* heart

cogote *nm Esp* nape *o* back of the neck

cohabitar *vi* to live together, to cohabit

coherencia *nf* coherence

coherente *adj* coherent

cohete *nm* rocket; **c. espacial** space rocket

COI *nm Dep (abr* **Comité Olímpico Internacional**) IOC

coima *nf Andes, RP Fam* bribe, *Br* backhander

coincidencia *nf* coincidence

coincidir *vi* (**a**) to coincide (**b**) *(concordar)* to agree; **todos coincidieron en señalar que** everyone agreed that (**c**) *(encontrarse)* to meet by chance

coito *nm* coitus, intercourse

cojear *vi (persona)* to limp, to hobble; *(mueble)* to wobble

cojín *nm* cushion

cojo, -a 1 *adj (persona)* lame; *(mueble)* rickety **2** *nm,f* lame person

cojón *nm Esp Vulg* ball; **de cojones** *(estupendo) Br* bloody *o US* goddamn brilliant; *(pésimo) Br* bloody *o US* goddamn awful

cojonudo, -a *adj Esp muy Fam Br* bloody *o US* goddamn brilliant

cojudez *nf Andes muy Fam* **¡qué c.!** *(acto)* what a *Br* bloody *o US* goddamn stupid thing to do!; *(dicho)* what a *Br* bloody *o US* goddamn stupid thing to say!

cojudo, -a *adj Andes muy Fam Br* bloody *o US* goddamn stupid

col *nf* cabbage; **c. de Bruselas** Brussels sprout

cola *nf* **(a)** *(de animal)* tail; *(de vestido)* train; *(de pelo)* ponytail; **a la c.** at the back *o* rear; **c. traer c.** to have consequences **(b)** *(fila) Br* queue, *US* line; **hacer c.** *Br* to queue (up), *US* to stand in line **(c)** *(pegamento)* glue

colaboración *nf* **(a)** collaboration **(b)** *Prensa* contribution

colaborador, -a 1 *nm,f* **(a)** collaborator **(b)** *Prensa* contributor **2** *adj* collaborating

colaborar *vi* to collaborate, to co-operate

colada *nf Esp* wash, laundry; **hacer la c.** to do the washing *o* laundry

colado, -a *adj* **(a)** *(líquido)* strained **(b)** *Fam (enamorado)* **estar c. por algn** to have a crush on sb

colador *nm* colander, sieve; *(de té, café)* strainer

colar [2] **1** *vt* **(a)** *(líquido)* to strain, to filter **(b)** *(por agujero)* to slip **2** *vi Fam* **esa mentira no cuela** that lie won't wash **3** **colarse** *vpr* **(a)** to slip in; *(a fiesta)* to gatecrash; *(en una cola) Br* to jump the queue, *US* to cut in line **(b)** *Fam (pasarse)* to go too far

colcha *nf* bedspread

colchón *nm* mattress

colchoneta *nf* air bed

colección *nf* collection

coleccionar *vt* to collect

coleccionista *nmf* collector

colecta *nf* collection

colectivo, -a 1 *adj* collective **2** *nm* **(a)** *(asociación)* association **(b)** *Andes (taxi)* collective taxi *(with a fixed rate and travelling a fixed route)* **(c)** *Arg, Bol (autobús)* bus

colega *nmf* **(a)** *(compañero profesional)* colleague, *US* co-worker **(b)** *Esp Fam (amigo)* pal, *Br* mate, *US* buddy

colegiado, -a *nm,f Dep* referee

colegial, -a 1 *adj (escolar)* school **2** *nm,f (alumno)* schoolboy; *(alumna)* schoolgirl; **los colegiales** the schoolchildren

colegio *nm* **(a)** *(escuela)* school; **c. privado** private school, *Br* public *o* independent school **(b)** *(profesional)* association, college; **c. de abogados** the Bar; *Pol* **c. electoral** electoral college **(c)** *Esp* **c. mayor** hall of residence

cólera¹ *nf* anger, rage

cólera² *nm Med* cholera

colérico, -a *adj* furious

colesterol *nm* cholesterol

coleta *nf* pigtail, ponytail; *Fig* **cortarse la c.** to retire

colgador *nm (percha)* hanger, coathanger; *(gancho)* hook

colgar [2] **1** *vt* **(a)** to hang (up); *(colada)* to hang (out) **(b)** *(ahorcar)* to hang **2** *vi* **(a)** to hang **(de** from); *Fig* **c. de un hilo** to hang by a thread **(b)** *Tel* to hang up **3** **colgarse** *vpr (ahorcarse)* to hang oneself

coliflor *nf* cauliflower

colilla *nf (cigarette)* end *o* butt

colimba *nf Arg Fam* military service

colina *nf* hill

colirio *nm* eye-drops

colitis *nf* colitis

colla *Bol* **1** *adj* of/from the altiplano **2** *nmf* = indigenous person from the altiplano

collage *nm* collage

collar *nm* **(a)** *(adorno)* necklace **(b)** *(de perro)* collar

collarín nm surgical collar

colmado, -a adj full, filled; (cucharada) heaped

colmar vt (**a**) to fill (right up); (vaso, copa) to fill to the brim; Fig to shower (**de** with) (**b**) (ambiciones) to fulfil, to satisfy

colmena nf beehive

colmillo nm eye o canine tooth; Zool (de carnívoro) fang; (de jabalí, elefante) tusk

colmo nm height; **el c. de** the height of; **¡eso es el c.!** that's the last straw!; **para c.** to top it all

colocación nf (**a**) (acto) positioning (**b**) (disposición) layout (**c**) (empleo) job, employment

colocado, -a adj (**a**) (empleado) employed (**b**) Fam (drogado) high

colocar [44] **1** vt (**a**) to place, to put (**b**) Fin (invertir) to invest (**c**) (emplear) to give work to **2 colocarse** vpr (**a**) (situarse) to put oneself (**b**) (emplearse) to take a job (**de** as) (**c**) Fam (drogarse) to get high

Colombia n Colombia

colombiano, -a adj & nm,f Colombian

colonia¹ nf colony; (campamento) summer camp; Méx (barrio) district

colonia² nf (perfume) cologne

colonización nf colonization

colonizar [40] vt to colonize

colono nm settler, colonist

coloquial adj colloquial

coloquio nm discussion, colloquium

color nm colour; Cin, Fot **en c.** in colour; **de colores** multicoloured; **persona de c.** coloured person

colorado, -a 1 adj red; **ponerse c.** to blush **2** nm red

colorante nm colouring

colorete nm rouge

colorido nm colour

colosal adj colossal

columna nf column; Anat **c. vertebral** vertebral column, spinal column

columpiar [43] **1** vt to swing **2 columpiarse** vpr to swing

columpio nm swing

coma¹ nf (**a**) Ling, Mús comma (**b**) Mat point; **tres c. cinco** three point five

coma² nm Med coma

comadre nf (**a**) (madrina) = godmother of one's child, or mother of one's godchild (**b**) Fam (amiga) Br mate, US buddy

comadreja nf weasel

comadrona nf midwife

comal nm CAm, Méx = flat clay or metal dish used for baking "tortillas"

comandante nm (**a**) Mil commander, commanding officer (**b**) Av captain

comando nm (**a**) Mil commando (**b**) Informát command

comarca nf region

comba nf Esp (**a**) (juego) skipping; **jugar a la c.** Br to skip, US to jump rope (**b**) (cuerda) Br skipping rope, US jump rope

combate nm combat; (en boxeo) fight; Mil battle; **fuera de c.** out for the count; (eliminado) out of action

combatir 1 vt to combat **2** vi **c. contra** to fight against

combinación nf (**a**) combination (**b**) (prenda) slip

combinado, -a 1 adj combined **2** nm (**a**) (cóctel) cocktail (**b**) Dep line-up

combinar vt, **combinarse** vpr to combine

combustible 1 nm fuel **2** adj combustible

combustión nf combustion

comecocos nm inv (**a**) Fam (para convencer) **este panfleto es un c.** this pamphlet is designed to brainwash you (**b**) Fam (cosa difícil de comprender) mind-bending problem o puzzle (**c**) (juego) pac-man®

comedia nf comedy

comediante, -a nm,f (hombre) actor; (mujer) actress

comedor nm dining room

comensal nmf companion at table

comentar vt **c. algo con algn** to talk sth over with sb; **me han comentado que …** I've been told that …

comentario *nm* (a) comment, remark; *(crítica)* commentary; **sin c.** no comment (b) **comentarios** *(cotilleos)* gossip

comentarista *nmf* commentator

comenzar [51] *vt & vi* to begin, to start; **comenzó a llover** it started raining *o* to rain; **comenzó diciendo que ...** he started by saying that ...

comer 1 *vt* (a) *(alimentos)* to eat (b) *(en juegos)* to take, to capture **2** *vi* *(ingerir alimentos)* to eat; *Esp, Méx (al mediodía)* to have lunch; **dar de c. a algn** to feed sb **3 comerse** *vpr* (a) to eat (b) *Fig (saltarse)* to skip

comercial *adj* commercial

comercializar [40] *vt* to market

comerciante *nmf* merchant

comerciar [43] *vi* to trade; **comercia con oro** he trades in gold

comercio *nm* (a) commerce, trade; **c. exterior** foreign trade; *Informát* **c. electrónico** e-commerce; **c. justo** fair trade (b) *(tienda)* shop

comestible 1 *adj* edible **2** *nmpl* **comestibles** food, foodstuff(s); **tienda de comestibles** grocer's shop, *US* grocery store

cometa 1 *nm Astron* comet **2** *nf (juguete)* kite

cometer *vt (error, falta)* to make; *(delito, crimen)* to commit

cometido *nm* (a) *(tarea)* task, assignment (b) *(deber)* duty; **cumplir su c.** to do one's duty

cómic *nm (pl* **cómics)** comic

comicios *nmpl* elections

cómico, -a 1 *adj* (a) comical, funny (b) *Teatro* **actor c.** comedian **2** *nm,f* comic; *(hombre)* comedian; *(mujer)* comedienne

comida *nf* (a) *(alimento)* food (b) *(almuerzo, cena)* meal; *Esp, Méx (al mediodía)* lunch

comienzo *nm* beginning, start; **a comienzos de** at the beginning of; **dar c. (a algo)** to begin *o* start (sth)

comillas *nfpl* inverted commas; **entre c.** in inverted commas

comilón, -ona 1 *adj* greedy, gluttonous **2** *nm,f* big eater, glutton

comilona *nf Fam* blowout, *Br* slap-up meal

comino *nm* cumin, cummin; *Fam* **me importa un c.** I don't give a damn (about it)

comisaría *nf* police station, *US* precinct, *US* station house

comisario *nm* (a) *(de policía) Br* superintendent, *US* captain (b) *(delegado)* commissioner; **c. europeo** European Commissioner

comisión *nf* (a) *Com (retribución)* commission; **a** *o* **con c.** on a commission basis (b) *(comité)* committee; **la C. Europea** the European Commission

comisura *nf* corner *(of mouth, eyes)*

comité *nm* committee

comitiva *nf* suite, retinue

como 1 *adv* (a) *(manera)* **me gusta c. cantas** I like the way you sing; **dilo c. quieras** say it however you like

(b) *(comparación)* like; **habla c. su padre** he talks like his father; **blanco c. la nieve** as white as snow

(c) *(según)* as; **c. decíamos ayer** as we were saying yesterday

(d) *(en calidad de)* as; **c. presidente** as president; **lo compré c. recuerdo** I bought it as a souvenir

(e) *(aproximadamente)* about; **c. unos diez** about ten

2 *conj* (a) *Esp (+ subjuntivo) (si)* if; **c. no estudies vas a suspender** if you don't study hard, you'll fail

(b) *(porque)* as, since; **c. no venías me marché** as you didn't come, I left

(c) **c. si** as if; **c. si nada** *o* **tal cosa** as if nothing had happened

cómo 1 *adv* (a) **¿c.?** *(¿perdón?)* what? (b) *(interrogativo)* how?; **¿c. estás?** how are you?; **¿c. lo sabes?** how do you know?; **¿c. es de grande/ancho?** how big/wide is it?; *Esp* **¿a c. están los tomates?** how much are the tomatoes?; **¿c. es que no viniste a la fiesta?** *(por qué)* how come you didn't come to the party? (c) *(exclamativo)* how!; **¡c. has crecido!** you've really

grown a lot!; **¡c. no!** but of course!
2 *nm* **el c. y el porqué** the whys and wherefores

cómoda *nf* chest of drawers

comodidad *nf* (**a**) comfort (**b**) *(conveniencia)* convenience

comodín *nm Naipes* joker

cómodo, -a *adj* (**a**) comfortable; **ponerse c.** to make oneself comfortable (**b**) *(útil)* handy, convenient

comodón, -ona 1 *adj (amante de la comodidad)* comfort-loving; *(vago)* laid-back; **no seas c.** don't be so lazy **2** *nm,f (amante de la comodidad)* comfort-lover; *(vago)* laid-back person

compa *nmf Fam* pal, *Br* mate, *US* buddy

compacto, -a *adj* compact; **disco c.** compact disc

compadecer [33] **1** *vt* to feel sorry for, to pity **2 compadecerse** *vpr* to have *o* take pity (**de** on)

compadre *nm* (**a**) *(padrino)* = godfather of one's child, or father of one's godchild (**b**) *Fam (amigo) Br* mate, *US* buddy

compadrear *vi RP* to brag, to boast

compadreo *nm (amistad)* friendship

compaginar *vt* to combine

compañerismo *nm* companionship, comradeship

compañero, -a *nm,f* companion; **c. de colegio** school friend; *Esp* **c. de piso** *Br* flatmate, *US* roommate

compañía *nf* company; **hacer c. (a algn)** to keep (sb) company; **c. de seguros/de teatro** insurance/theatre company

comparación *nf* comparison; **en c.** comparatively; **en c. con** compared to; **sin c.** beyond compare

comparar *vt* to compare (**con** with)

comparsa *nf* band of revellers

compartimento, compartimiento *nm* compartment; **c. de primera/segunda clase** first-/second-class compartment

compartir *vt* to share

compás *nm* (**a**) *Téc* (pair of) compasses (**b**) *Náut* compass (**c**) *Mús (división)* time; *(intervalo)* beat; *(ritmo)* rhythm; **c. de espera** *Mús* bar rest; *Fig (pausa)* delay; **al c. de** in time to

compasión *nf* compassion, pity; **tener c. (de algn)** to feel sorry (for sb)

compasivo, -a *adj* compassionate

compatible *adj* compatible

compatriota *nmf* compatriot; fellow countryman, *f* fellow countrywoman

compenetrarse *vpr* to understand each other *o* one another

compensación *nf* compensation

compensar 1 *vt (pérdida, error)* to make up for; *(indemnizar)* to compensate (for) **2** *vi* to be worthwhile; **este trabajo no compensa** this job's not worth my while

competencia *nf* (**a**) *(rivalidad, empresas rivales)* competition (**b**) *(capacidad)* competence (**c**) *(incumbencia)* field, province; **no es de mi c.** it's not up to me

competente *adj* competent

competición *nf* competition, contest

competir [6] *vi* to compete (**con/en/por** with *o* against/in/for)

competitivo, -a *adj* competitive

complacer [60] **1** *vt* to please; *Fml* **me complace presentarles a …** it gives me great pleasure to introduce to you … **2 complacerse** *vpr* to delight (**en** in), to take pleasure (**en** in)

complaciente *adj* obliging

complejidad *nf* complexity

complejo, -a *adj & nm* complex

complementar 1 *vt* to complement **2 complementarse** *vpr* to complement (each other), to be complementary to (each other)

complementario, -a *adj* complementary

complemento *nm* complement; *Ling* object

completamente *adv* completely

completar *vt* to complete

completo, -a *adj* (**a**) *(terminado)* complete; **por c.** completely (**b**) *(lleno)* full; **al c.** full up to capacity

complexión *nf* build; **de c. fuerte** well-built

complicación *nf* complication

complicado, -a *adj* (**a**) *(complejo)* complicated (**b**) *(implicado)* involved

complicar [44] **1** *vt* (**a**) to complicate (**b**) **c. en** *(involucrar)* to involve in **2 complicarse** *vpr* to get complicated; **complicarse la vida** to make life difficult for oneself

cómplice *nmf* accomplice

complot *nm* (*pl* **complots**) conspiracy, plot

componente 1 *adj* component **2** *nm* (**a**) *(pieza)* component; *(ingrediente)* ingredient (**b**) *(persona)* member

componer [19] (*pp* **compuesto**) **1** *vt* (**a**) *(formar)* to compose, to make up (**b**) *Mús, Lit* to compose (**c**) *(reparar)* to mend, to repair **2 componerse** *vpr* (**a**) **componerse de** *(consistir)* to be made up of, to consist of (**b**) *(arreglarse)* to dress up (**c**) *Fam* **componérselas** to manage

comportamiento *nm* behaviour

comportar 1 *vt* to entail, to involve **2 comportarse** *vpr* to behave; **comportarse mal** to misbehave

composición *nf* composition

compositor, -a *nm,f* composer

compostura *nf* composure

compota *nf* compote

compra *nf* *(acción)* buying; *(cosa comprada)* purchase, buy; **hace** *Esp* **la c.** *o Am* **las compras** to do the shopping; **ir de compras** to go shopping

comprador, -a *nm,f* purchaser, buyer

comprar *vt* (**a**) to buy (**b**) *Fig (sobornar)* to bribe, to buy off

comprender *vt* (**a**) *(entender)* to understand; **se comprende** it's understandable (**b**) *(contener)* to comprise, to include

comprensible *adj* understandable

comprensión *nf* understanding

comprensivo, -a *adj* understanding

compresa *nf* (**a**) *(para mujer)* sanitary

Br towel *o US* napkin (**b**) *Med* compress

compresor, -a 1 *adj* compressing **2** *nm* compressor

comprimido, -a 1 *nm Farm* tablet **2** *adj* compressed; **escopeta de aire c.** air rifle

comprimir *vt* to compress

comprobación *nf* checking

comprobar [2] *vt* to check

comprometer 1 *vt* (**a**) *(arriesgar)* to compromise, to jeopardize (**b**) *(obligar)* to compel, to force **2 comprometerse** *vpr* (**a**) **comprometerse a hacer algo** to undertake to do sth (**b**) *(novios)* to become engaged

comprometido, -a *adj* (**a**) *(situación)* difficult (**b**) *(para casarse)* engaged

compromiso *nm* (**a**) *(obligación)* obligation, commitment; **sin c.** without obligation; **por c.** out of a sense of duty (**b**) **poner (a algn) en un c.** to put (sb) in a difficult *o* embarrassing situation (**c**) *(acuerdo)* agreement; *Fml* **c. matrimonial** engagement; **soltero y sin c.** single and unattached

compuerta *nf* floodgate, sluicegate

compuesto, -a 1 *adj* (**a**) compound (**b**) **c. de** composed of **2** *nm* compound

compungido, -a *adj* *(arrepentido)* remorseful; *(triste)* sorrowful, sad

comulgar [42] *vi* (**a**) to receive Holy Communion (**b**) *Fig* **no comulgo con sus ideas** I don't share his ideas

común 1 *adj* (**a**) common; **de c. acuerdo** by common consent; **hacer algo en c.** to do sth jointly; **poco c.** unusual; **por lo c.** generally (**b**) *(compartido)* shared, communal; **amigos comunes** mutual friends **2** *nm Br Pol* **los Comunes** the Commons

comuna *nf* (**a**) *(colectividad)* commune (**b**) *Am (municipalidad)* municipality

comunero, -a *nm,f Perú, Méx (indígena)* = member of an indigenous village community

comunicación *nf* (**a**) communication; **ponerse en c. (con algn)** to get in touch (with sb) (**b**) *(comunicado)* communication; **c. oficial** communiqué (**c**) *Tel* connection; **se nos cortó la c.** we were cut off (**d**) *(unión)* link, connection

comunicado, -a 1 *adj* **una zona bien comunicada** a well-served zone; **dos ciudades bien comunicadas** two towns with good connections (between them) **2** *nm* communiqué; **c. de prensa** press release

comunicar [44] **1** *vt* to communicate; **comuníquenoslo lo antes posible** let us know as soon as possible

2 *vi* (**a**) to communicate (**b**) *Esp Tel Br* to be engaged, *US* to be busy; **está comunicando** it's *Br* engaged *o US* busy **3 comunicarse** *vpr* to communicate

comunicativo, -a *adj* communicative

comunidad *nf* community; **C. Europea** European Community; **C. de Estados Independientes** Commonwealth of Independent States

comunión *nf* communion

comunismo *nm* communism

comunista *adj & nmf* communist

comunitario, -a *adj* (**a**) of *o* relating to the community (**b**) *(de UE)* of *o* relating to the EU; **la política agraria comunitaria** the common agricultural policy

con *prep* (**a**) with; **córtalo c. las tijeras** cut it with the scissors; **voy cómodo c. este jersey** I'm comfortable in this sweater

(**b**) *(compañía)* with; **vine c. mi hermana** I came with my sister

(**c**) **c. ese frío/niebla** in that cold/fog; **estar c. (la) gripe** to have the flu

(**d**) *(contenido)* with; **una bolsa c. dinero** a bag (full) of money

(**e**) *(relación)* to; **habló c. todos** he spoke to everybody; **sé amable c. ella** be nice to her

(**f**) *(+ infinitivo)* **c. llamar será suficiente** it will be enough just to phone

(**g**) *(+ que + subjuntivo)* **bastará c. que lo esboces** a general idea will do

(**h**) **c. tal (de) que ...** provided that ...; **c. todo (y eso)** even so

conato *nm* attempt; **c. de asesinato** attempted murder

cóncavo, -a *adj* concave

concebir [6] **1** *vt* (**a**) *(plan, hijo)* to conceive (**b**) *(entender)* to understand **2** *vi* *(mujer)* to become pregnant, to conceive

conceder *vt* to grant; *(premio)* to award

concejal, -a *nm,f* town councillor

concentración *nf* concentration; *(de manifestantes)* gathering; *(de coches, motos)* rally; *(de equipo)* base

concentrado *nm* concentrate

concentrar 1 *vt* to concentrate **2 concentrarse** *vpr* (**a**) *(mentalmente)* to concentrate (**en** on) (**b**) *(reunirse)* to gather

concepción *nf* conception

concepto *nm* (**a**) *(idea)* concept; **tener buen/mal c. de** to have a good/a bad opinion of; **bajo** *o* **por ningún c.** under no circumstances (**b**) **en c. de** under the heading of (**c**) *(en factura)* item

concernir [54] *v impers* (**a**) *(afectar)* to concern; **en lo que a mí concierne** as far as I am concerned; **en lo que concierne a** with regard/respect to (**b**) *(corresponder)* to be up to

concertación *nf* compromise, agreement

concertar [1] **1** *vt* (**a**) *(cita)* to arrange; *(precio)* to agree on; *(acuerdo)* to reach (**b**) *(una acción etc)* to plan, to co-ordinate **2** *vi* to agree, to tally

concesión *nf* (**a**) concession (**b**) *(de un premio, contrato)* awarding

concesionario, -a *nm,f* dealer

concha *nf* (**a**) *Zool (caparazón)* shell; *(carey)* tortoiseshell (**b**) *Andes, RP (vulva) Vulg* cunt (**c**) *Ven (de árbol)* bark; *(de fruta)* peel, rind; *(de pan)* crust; *(de huevo)* shell

concheto, -a *RP Fam* **1** *adj* posh **2** *nm,f* rich kid

conchudo, -a *nm,f* (**a**) *Andes, Méx, Ven Fam (desfachatado)* **ser un c.** to be shameless, *Br* to have a brass neck (**b**) *Andes, Méx, Ven Fam (cómodo)* lazybones, layabout (**c**) *Perú, RP muy Fam* jerk, *Br* dickhead

conciencia *nf* (**a**) conscience; **tener la c. tranquila** to have a clear conscience (**b**) *(conocimiento)* consciousness, awareness; **a c.** conscientiously; **tener/tomar c. (de algo)** to be/to become aware (of sth)

concienciar [43], *Am* **concientizar** [40] **1** *vt* to make aware (**de** of) **2 concienciarse,** *Am* **concientizarse** *vpr* to become aware (**de** of)

concienzudo, -a *adj* conscientious

concierto *nm* (**a**) *Mús* concert; *(composición)* concerto (**b**) *(acuerdo)* agreement

conciliación *nf* *(en un litigio)* reconciliation; *(en un conflicto laboral)* conciliation

conciliar [43] *vt* to reconcile; **c. el sueño** to get to sleep

concisión *nf* conciseness

conciso, -a *adj* concise

concluir [37] *vt* to conclude

conclusión *nf* conclusion; **sacar una c.** to draw a conclusion

concordancia *nf también Ling* agreement

concordar [2] **1** *vi* to agree; **esto no concuerda con lo que dijo ayer** this doesn't fit in with what he said yesterday **2** *vt* to bring into agreement

concordia *nf* concord

concretar *vt (precisar)* to specify, to state explicitly; *(fecha, hora)* to fix

concreto, -a 1 *adj* (**a**) *(preciso, real)* concrete (**b**) *(particular)* specific; **en c.** specifically; **en el caso c. de …** in the specific case of … **2** *nm Am* concrete

concubina *nf* concubine

concurrencia *nf* (**a**) *(de dos cosas)* concurrence (**b**) *(público)* audience

concurrente 1 *adj* concurrent **2** *nmf* person present

concurrido, -a *adj* crowded, busy

concursante *nmf* (**a**) contestant, competitor (**b**) *(para un empleo)* candidate

concursar *vi* to compete, to take part

concurso *nm* (**a**) *(competición)* competition; *(de belleza etc)* contest; *TV* quiz show; **presentar (una obra) a c.** to invite tenders (for a piece of work) (**b**) *Fml (ayuda)* help

condado *nm (territorio)* county

condal *adj* of o relating to a count; **la Ciudad C.** Barcelona

conde *nm* count

condecoración *nf* decoration

condena *nf* (**a**) *Jur* sentence (**b**) *(desaprobación)* condemnation, disapproval

condenado, -a 1 *adj* (**a**) *Jur* convicted; **c. a muerte** condemned to death (**b**) *Rel & Fam* damned; **c. al fracaso** doomed to failure **2** *nm,f* (**a**) *Jur* convicted person; *(a muerte)* condemned person (**b**) *Rel* damned person

condenar 1 *vt* (**a**) *Jur* to convict, to find guilty; **c. a algn a muerte** to condemn sb to death (**b**) *(desaprobar)* to condemn **2 condenarse** *vpr Rel* to be damned

condensación *nf* condensation

condensar *vt,* **condensarse** *vpr* to condense

condición *nf* (**a**) condition; **en buenas/malas condiciones** in good/bad condition; **condiciones de trabajo** working conditions; **con la c. de que …** on the condition that … (**b**) *(manera de ser)* nature, character (**c**) **en su c. de director** *(calidad)* in his capacity as director

condicional *adj* conditional

condimentar *vt* to season, to flavour

condimento *nm* seasoning, flavouring

condominio *nm Am (edificio) Br* block of flats, *US* condominium

conducción *nf* (**a**) *Esp (de vehículo)* driving (**b**) *(por tubería)* piping; *(por cable)* wiring

conducir [10] **1** *vt (coche)* to drive; *(electricidad)* to conduct **2** *vi Aut* to drive; **permiso de c.** *Br* driving licence, *US* driver's license (**b**) *(camino,* *actitud)* to lead; **eso no conduce a nada** this leads nowhere

conducta *nf* behaviour, conduct; **mala c.** misbehaviour, misconduct

conducto *nm* (**a**) *(tubería)* pipe; *Fig* **por conductos oficiales** through official channels (**b**) *Anat* duct, canal

conductor, -a 1 *nm,f Aut* driver **2** *nm Elec* conductor

conectar *vt* (**a**) to connect up (**b**) *Elec* to plug in, to switch on

conejera *nf (madriguera)* (rabbit) warren; *(conejar)* rabbit hutch

conejo *nm* rabbit

conexión *nf* connection

confección *nf* (**a**) *Cost* dressmaking, tailoring (**b**) *(de un plan etc)* making, making up

confederación *nf* confederation

conferencia *nf* (**a**) lecture; **dar una c. (sobre algo)** to give a lecture (on sth) (**b**) **c. de prensa** press conference (**c**) *Tel* long-distance call

conferenciante *nmf* lecturer

confesar [1] **1** *vt* to confess, to admit; *(crimen)* to own up to; *Rel (pecados)* to confess **2** *vi Jur* to own up **3 confesarse** *vpr* to confess; **c. culpable** to admit one's guilt; *Rel* to go to confession

confesión *nf* confession, admission; *Rel* confession

confesionario *nm Rel* confessional

confesor *nm* confessor

confeti *nm* (*pl* **confetis**) confetti

confiado, -a *adj* (**a**) *(seguro)* self-confident (**b**) *(crédulo)* gullible, unsuspecting

confianza *nf* (**a**) *(seguridad)* confidence; **tener c. en uno mismo** to be self-confident (**b**) **de c.** reliable (**c**) **tener c. con algn** to be on intimate terms with sb; **con toda c.** in all confidence; **tomarse (demasiadas) confianzas** to take liberties

confiar [29] **1** *vt (entregar)* to entrust; *(información, secreto)* to confide **2** *vi* **c. en** to trust; **confío en ella** I

trust her; **no confíes en su ayuda** don't count on his help **3 confiarse** *vpr* to confide (**en** *o* **a** in); **confiarse demasiado** to be over-confident

confidencia *nf* confidence

confidencial *adj* confidential

confidente, -a *nm,f* (**a**) *(hombre)* confidant; *(mujer)* confidante (**b**) *(de la policía)* informer

configuración *nf también Informát* configuration

configurar *vt* to shape, to form

confirmación *nf* confirmation

confirmar *vt* to confirm; **la excepción confirma la regla** the exception proves the rule

confiscar [44] *vt* to confiscate

confitado, -a *adj* candied; **frutas confitadas** crystallized fruit

confite *nm Br* sweet, *US* candy

confitería *nf* (**a**) *(tienda)* confectioner's (**b**) *RP (café)* café

confitura *nf* preserve, jam

conflictivo, -a *adj (asunto)* controversial; *(época)* unsettled; **niño c.** problem child

conflicto *nm* conflict; **c. laboral** industrial dispute

confluencia *nf* confluence

confluir [37] *vi* to converge; *(caminos, ríos)* to meet, to come together

conformar 1 *vt* to shape **2 conformarse** *vpr* to resign oneself, to be content

conforme 1 *adj* (**a**) *(satisfecho)* satisfied; **c. agreed**, all right; **no estoy c.** I don't agree (**b**) **c. a** in accordance *o* keeping with **2** *conj* (**a**) *(según, como)* as; **c. lo vi/lo oí** as I saw/heard it (**b**) *(a medida que)* as; **la policía los detenía c. iban saliendo** the police were arresting them as they came out

conformidad *nf* (**a**) approval, consent (**b**) **en c. con** in conformity with

conformismo *nm* conformity

conformista *adj & nmf* conformist

confort *nm* (*pl* **conforts**) comfort;

todo c. *(en anuncio)* all mod cons

confortable *adj* comfortable

confrontación *nf* (a) *(enfrentamiento)* confrontation (b) *(comparación)* contrast

confundir 1 *vt* (a) to confuse (**con** with); **c. a una persona con otra** to mistake somebody for somebody else (b) *(persona)* to mislead (c) *(turbar)* to confound

2 confundirse *vpr* (a) *(equivocarse)* to be mistaken; *Tel* **se ha confundido** you've got the wrong number (b) *(mezclarse)* to mingle; **se confundió entre el gentío** he disappeared into the crowd

confusión *nf* confusion

confuso, -a *adj* (a) confused; *(formas, recuerdo)* blurred, vague (b) *(mezclado)* mixed up

congelación *nf* (a) freezing (b) *Fin* freeze; **c. salarial** wage freeze (c) *Med* frostbite

congelado, -a 1 *adj* frozen; *Med* frostbitten **2** *nmpl* **congelados** frozen food

congelador *nm* freezer

congelar 1 *vt* to freeze **2 congelarse** *vpr* (a) to freeze; *Fam* **me estoy congelando** I'm freezing (b) *Med* to get *o* become frostbitten

congeniar [43] *vi* to get on (**con** with)

congénito, -a *adj* congenital

congestión *nf* congestion; *Med* **c. cerebral** stroke

conglomerado *nm* conglomerate

congregar [42] *vt*, **congregarse** *vpr* to congregate, to assemble

congresista *nmf* member of a congress

congreso *nm* congress, conference; *Pol* **C. de los Diputados** = lower house of Spanish Parliament, *Br* ≃ House of Commons, *US* ≃ House of Representatives

conjetura *nf* conjecture; **por c.** by guesswork

conjugación *nf* conjugation

conjugar [42] *vt* to conjugate; *Fig* *(planes, opiniones)* to combine

conjunción *nf* conjunction

conjuntivitis *nf inv* conjunctivitis

conjunto, -a 1 *nm* (a) *(grupo)* collection, group (b) *(todo)* whole; **de c.** overall; **en c.** on the whole (c) *Mús (pop)* group, band (d) *(prenda)* outfit, ensemble (e) *Mat* set (f) *Dep* team **2** *adj* joint

conmemoración *nf* commemoration

conmemorar *vt* to commemorate

conmigo *pron pers* with me; **vino c.** he came with me; **él habló c.** he talked to me

conmoción *nf* commotion, shock; **c. cerebral** concussion

conmover [4] *vt* to touch, to move

conmutador *nm* (a) *Elec* switch (b) *Am Tel* switchboard

cono *nm* cone; **C. Sur** = Chile, Argentina, Paraguay and Uruguay

conocer [34] **1** *vt* (a) to know; **dar (algo/algn) a c.** to make (sth/sb) known (b) *(a una persona)* to meet (c) *(reconocer)* to recognize; **te conocí por la voz** I recognized you by your voice **2 conocerse** *vpr (dos personas)* to know each other; *(por primera vez)* to meet

conocido, -a 1 *adj* known; *(famoso)* well-known **2** *nm,f* acquaintance

conocimiento *nm* (a) knowledge; **con c. de causa** with full knowledge of the facts (b) *(conciencia)* consciousness; **perder/recobrar el c.** to lose/regain consciousness (c) **conocimientos** knowledge

conque *conj* so

conquista *nf* conquest

conquistador, -a *nm,f* conqueror

conquistar *vt (país, ciudad)* to conquer; *Fig (puesto, título)* to win; *(a una persona)* to win over

consagrado, -a *adj* (a) *Rel* consecrated (b) *(dedicado)* dedicated (c) *(reconocido)* recognized, established

consagrar 1 *vt* (a) *Rel* to consecrate (b) *(artista)* to confirm (c) *(tiempo,* *vida)* to devote **2 consagrarse** *vpr* **(a)** **consagrarse a** *(dedicarse)* to devote oneself to, to dedicate oneself to **(b)** *(lograr fama)* to establish oneself

consciente *adj* **(a)** conscious, aware; **ser c. de algo** to be aware of sth **(b)** *Med* conscious

conscripto *nm Andes, Arg* conscript

consecuencia *nf* **(a)** consequence; **a** *o* **como c. de** as a consequence *o* result of; **en c.** therefore; **tener** *o* **traer (malas) consecuencias** to have (ill) effects; **sacar como** *o* **en c.** to come to a conclusion **(b)** *(coherencia)* consistency; **actuar en c.** to be consistent

consecuente *adj* consistent

consecutivo, -a *adj* consecutive; **tres días consecutivos** three days in a row

conseguir [6] *vt* **(a)** to get, to obtain; *(objetivo)* to achieve **(b)** **conseguí terminar** I managed to finish

consejo *nm* **(a)** *(recomendación)* advice; **un c.** a piece of advice **(b)** *(junta)* council; **c. de ministros** cabinet; *(reunión)* cabinet meeting; **c. de administración** board of directors; **c. de guerra** court martial

consenso *nm* consensus

consentido, -a *adj* spoiled

consentir [5] **1** *vt* **(a)** *(tolerar)* to allow, to permit; **no consientas que haga eso** don't allow him to do that **(b)** *(mimar)* to spoil **2** *vi* to consent; **c. en** to agree to

conserje *nm (de colegio, ministerio)* doorman, *Br* porter; *(de bloque de viviendas)* *Br* caretaker, *US* superintendent, *US* supervisor

conserjería *nf (de colegio, ministerio)* porter's lodge; *(de bloque de viviendas)* *Br* caretaker's office, *US* superintendent's *o* supervisor's office

conserva *nf* canned food, *Br* tinned food

conservador, -a 1 *adj & nm,f* conservative; *Pol* Conservative **2** *nm (de museo)* curator

conservante *nm* preservative

conservar 1 *vt* to conserve, to preserve; *(mantener)* to keep up, to maintain; *(alimentos)* to preserve **2 conservarse** *vpr* **(a)** *(tradición etc)* to survive **(b) conservarse bien** *(persona)* to age well

conservatorio *nm* conservatory

considerable *adj* considerable

consideración *nf* **(a)** consideration; **tomar algo en c.** to take sth into account **(b)** *(respeto)* regard **(c) de c.** important, considerable; **herido de c.** seriously injured

considerar *vt* to consider; **lo considero imposible** I think it's impossible

consigna *nf* **(a)** *(para maletas)* *Br* left-luggage office, *US* checkroom **(b)** *Mil* orders, instructions

consigo¹ *pron pers* **(a)** *(tercera persona) (hombre)* with him; *(mujer)* with her; *(cosa, animal)* with it; *(plural)* with them; *(usted)* with you **(b) hablar c. mismo** to speak to oneself

consigo² *indic pres de* **conseguir**

consiguiente *adj* resulting, consequent; **por c.** therefore, consequently

consistencia *nf* **(a)** consistency **(b)** *(de argumento)* soundness

consistente *adj* **(a)** *(firme)* firm, solid **(b)** *(teoría)* sound **(c) c. en** consisting of

consistir *vi* to consist **(en** of); **el secreto consiste en tener paciencia** the secret lies in being patient

consistorio *nm* town *o US* city council

consola *nf* console table; *Informát* console

consolar [2] **1** *vt* to console, to comfort **2 consolarse** *vpr* to console oneself, to take comfort **(con** from)

consolidación *nf* consolidation

consolidar *vt*, **consolidarse** *vpr* to consolidate

consomé *nm* clear soup, consommé

consonante *adj & nf* consonant

consorcio *nm* consortium

consorte 1 *adj* **príncipe c.** prince consort **2** *nmf (cónyuge)* partner, spouse

conspiración *nf* conspiracy, plot

conspirar *vi* to conspire, to plot

constancia *nf* (**a**) constancy, perseverance (**b**) *(testimonio)* proof, evidence; **dejar c. de algo** to put sth on record

constante 1 *adj* constant; *(persona)* steadfast **2** *nf* constant feature; *Mat* constant

constantemente *adv* constantly

constar *vi* (**a**) *(figurar)* to figure, to be included (**en** in); **c. en acta** to be on record (**b**) **me consta que ...** I am absolutely certain that ... (**c**) **c. de** to be made up of, to consist of

constelación *nf* constellation

constipado, -a 1 *adj* **estar c.** to have a cold *o* a chill **2** *nm* cold, chill

constiparse *vpr* to catch a cold *o* a chill

constitución *nf* constitution

constitucional *adj* constitutional

constituir [37] **1** *vt* (**a**) *(formar)* to constitute; **estar constituido por** to consist of (**b**) *(suponer)* to represent (**c**) *(fundar)* to constitute, to set up **2** **constituirse** *vpr* **constituirse en** to set oneself up as

construcción *nf* (**a**) construction; *(sector)* the building industry; **en c.** under construction (**b**) *(edificio)* building

constructivo, -a *adj* constructive

constructor, -a 1 *nm,f* builder **2** *adj* **empresa constructora** builders, construction company

construir [37] *vt* to build, to manufacture

consuelo *nm* consolation

cónsul *nmf* consul

consulado *nm* consulate

consulta *nf* (**a**) consultation; **obra de c.** reference book (**b**) *(despacho de médico) Br* surgery, *US* office; **horas de c.** surgery hours

consultar *vt* to consult, to seek advice (**con** from); *(libro)* to look up

consultorio *nm* (**a**) *(de un médico) Br* surgery, *US* office; (**b**) *Prensa* problem page, advice column

consumición *nf* (**a**) consumption (**b**) *(bebida)* drink

consumidor, -a 1 *nm,f* consumer **2** *adj* consuming

consumir 1 *vt* to consume **2** **consumirse** *vpr (al hervir)* to boil away; *Fig (persona)* to waste away

consumismo *nm* consumerism

consumo *nm* consumption; **bienes de c.** consumer goods; **sociedad de c.** consumer society

contabilidad *nf Com* (**a**) *(profesión)* accountancy (**b**) *(de empresa, sociedad)* accounting, bookkeeping

contable *nmf Esp* accountant

contacto *nm* contact; *Aut* ignition; **perder el c.** to lose touch; **ponerse en c.** to get in touch

contador, -a 1 *nm,f Am (persona)* accountant; **c. público** *Br* chartered accountant, *US* certified public accountant **2** *nm (aparato)* meter; **c. de agua** water meter

contagiar [43] **1** *vt Med* to pass on **2** **contagiarse** *vpr* (**a**) *(persona)* to get infected (**b**) *(enfermedad)* to be contagious

contagio *nm* contagion

contagioso, -a *adj* contagious; *Fam (risa)* infectious

container *nm (pl* **containers**) *(para mercancías)* container

contaminación *nf* contamination; *(del aire)* pollution

contaminado, -a *adj (alimento)* contaminated; *(medio ambiente)* polluted

contaminar *vt* to contaminate; *(aire, agua)* to pollute

contar [2] **1** *vt* (**a**) *(sumar)* to count (**b**) *(narrar)* to tell **2** *vi* (**a**) to count (**b**) **c. con** *(confiar en)* to count on; *(tener)* to have **3** **contarse** *vpr Fam* **¿qué te cuentas?** how's it going?

contemplación *nf* (**a**) *(meditación)* contemplation (**b**) *(consideración)* **contemplaciones** consideration; **tratar a algn sin contemplaciones** not to take sb's feelings into account; **nos echaron sin contemplaciones** they threw us out unceremoniously

contemplar *vt* to contemplate; *(considerar)* to consider; *(estipular)* to stipulate

contemporáneo, -a *adj & nm,f* contemporary

contenedor *nm* container

contener [24] **1** *vt* (a) to contain (b) *(pasiones etc)* to restrain, to hold back **2 contenerse** *vpr* to control oneself, to hold (oneself) back

contenido *nm* content, contents

contentar 1 *vt* (a) *(satisfacer)* to please (b) *(alegrar)* to cheer up **2 contentarse** *vpr* (a) *(conformarse)* to make do (**con** with), to be satisfied (**con** with) (b) *(alegrarse)* to cheer up

contento, -a *adj* happy, pleased (**con** with)

contestación *nf* answer; **dar c.** to answer

contestador *nm* **c. automático** answering machine

contestar *vt* (a) to answer (b) *Fam (replicar)* to answer back

contexto *nm* context

contigo *pron pers* with you

contiguo, -a *adj* contiguous (**a** to), adjoining

continental *adj* continental

continente *nm* (a) *Geog* continent (b) *(compostura)* countenance

continuación *nf* continuation; **a c.** next

continuamente *adv* continuously

continuar [30] *vt & vi* to continue, to carry on (with); **continúa en Francia** he's still in France; **continuará** to be continued

continuo, -a 1 *adj* (a) continuous; *Aut* **línea continua** solid white line (b) *(reiterado)* continual, constant **2** *nm* continuum

contorno *nm* (a) outline (b) **contornos** surroundings, environment

contra 1 *prep* against; **en c. de** against **2** *nm* **los pros y los contras** the pros and cons

contrabajo *nm* double bass

contrabandista *nmf* smuggler; **c. de armas** gunrunner

contrabando *nm* smuggling; **c. de armas** gunrunning; **pasar algo de c.** to smuggle sth in

contracorriente 1 *nf* crosscurrent **2** *adv* **ir (a) c.** to go against the tide

contradecir [12] *(pp* **contradicho)** *vt* to contradict

contradicción *nf* contradiction

contradictorio, -a *adj* contradictory

contraer [25] **1** *vt* to contract; **c. matrimonio con algn** to marry sb **2 contraerse** *vpr* to contract

contraindicado, -a *adj* **está c. beber alcohol durante el embarazo** alcohol should be avoided during pregnancy

contralor *nm Am (en institución, empresa)* comptroller

contraloría *nf Am (oficina)* comptroller's office

contraluz *nm* view against the light; **a c.** against the light

contrapartida *nf* en **c.** in return

contrapelo: a contrapelo *loc adv (acariciar)* the wrong way; **su intervención iba a c. del resto** his remarks went against the general opinion; **vivir a c.** to have an unconventional lifestyle

contrapeso *nm* counterweight

contrariar [29] *vt* (a) *(oponerse a)* to oppose, to go against (b) *(disgustar)* to upset

contrario, -a 1 *adj* (a) opposite; **lo c. de** the opposite of; **en el lado/sentido c.** on the other side/in the other direction; **al c., por el c.** on the contrary; **de lo c.** otherwise; **todo lo c.** quite the opposite (b) *(perjudicial)* contrary (**a** to) **2** *nm,f* opponent, rival **3** *nf* **llevar la contraria** to be contrary

contraseña *nf* password

contrastar *vt* to contrast (**con** with)

contraste *nm* (a) contrast (b) *(en oro, plata)* hallmark

contratar *vt* to hire, to engage

contratiempo *nm* setback, hitch

contrato *nm* contract; **c. de trabajo** work contract; **c. de alquiler** lease, leasing agreement; **c. basura** short-term contract with poor conditions

contribuir [37] **1** *vt* to contribute (**a** to) **2** *vi* (**a**) to contribute (**b**) *(pagar impuestos)* to pay taxes

contrincante *nmf* rival, opponent

control *nm* (**a**) control; **c. a distancia** remote control (**b**) *(inspección)* check; *(de policía etc)* checkpoint

controlar **1** *vt* (**a**) to control (**b**) *(comprobar)* to check **2 controlarse** *vpr* to control oneself

contusión *nf* contusion, bruise

conuco *nm Carib (parcela)* small plot of land

convalidar *vt* to validate; *(documento)* to ratify

convencer [49] *vt* to convince; **c. a algn de algo** to convince sb about sth

convención *nf* convention

convencional *adj* conventional

conveniente *adj* (**a**) *(oportuno)* convenient; *(aconsejable)* advisable (**b**) *(precio)* good, fair

convenio *nm* agreement; **c. laboral** agreement on salary and conditions

convenir [27] *vt & vi* (**a**) *(acordar)* to agree; **c. una fecha** to agree on a date; **sueldo a c.** salary negotiable; **c. en** (**b**) *(ser oportuno)* to suit, to be good for; **conviene recordar que …** it's as well to remember that …

convento *nm (de monjas)* convent; *(de monjes)* monastery

conversación *nf* conversation

conversada *nf Am Fam* chat

conversar *vi* to converse, to talk

convertir [54] **1** *vt* to change, to convert **2 convertirse** *vpr* (**a**) **convertirse en** to turn into, to become (**b**) *Rel* to be converted (**a** to)

convicción *nf* conviction; **tengo la c. de que …** I am convinced that …

convidado, -a *adj & nm,f* guest

convidar *vt* to invite

convincente *adj* convincing

convite *nm* reception

convivencia *nf* life together; *Fig* coexistence

convivir *vi* to live together; *Fig* to coexist (**con** with)

convocar [44] *vt* to summon; *(reunión, elecciones)* to call

convocatoria *nf* (**a**) *(a huelga etc)* call (**b**) *Educ* diet

convulsión *nf Med* convulsion; *(agitación social)* upheaval

cónyuge *nmf* spouse; **cónyuges** married couple, husband and wife

coña *nf Esp muy Fam* **está de c.** she's just pissing around

coñac *nm (pl* **coñacs)** brandy, cognac

coñazo *nm Esp muy Fam* pain, drag; **dar el c.** to be a real pain

coño *esp Esp Vulg* **1** *nm* cunt, twat **2** *interj (enfado)* for fuck's sake!

cooperar *vi* to co-operate (**con** with)

cooperativa *nf* co-operative

coordinación *nf* co-ordination

coordinar *vt* to co-ordinate

copa *nf* (**a**) glass; **tomar una c.** to have a drink (**b**) *(de árbol)* top (**c**) *Dep* cup (**d**) *Naipes* **copas** hearts

copeo *nm Fam* boozing; **ir de c.** to go out boozing

copetín *nm RP (bebida)* aperitif; *(comida)* appetizer

copia *nf* copy; *Informát* **c. de seguridad** backup; *Informát* **hacer una c. de seguridad de algo** to back up sth

copiar [43] *vt* to copy

copiloto *nm Av* co-pilot; *Aut* co-driver

copioso, -a *adj* abundant, copious

copla *nf* verse, couplet

copo *nm* flake; *(de nieve)* snowflake; **copos de maíz** cornflakes

coquetear *vi* to flirt (**con** with)

coqueto, -a **1** *adj* coquettish **2** *nm,f* flirt

coraje *nm* (**a**) *(valor)* courage (**b**) *(ira)* anger, annoyance; *Fig* **dar c. a algn** to infuriate sb; **¡qué c.!** how maddening!

coral¹ *nm Zool* coral

coral² *nf Mús* choral, chorale

coraza *nf* armour; *Fig* protection

corazón *nm* (**a**) heart; *Fig* **de (todo) c.** in all sincerity; *Fig* **tener buen c.** to be kind-hearted (**b**) *(parte central)* heart; *(de fruta)* core (**c**) *Naipes* **corazones** hearts

corbata *nf* tie, *US* necktie; **con c.** wearing a tie

corchea *nf Mús Br* quaver, *US* eighth note

corchete *nm* (**a**) *Impr* square bracket (**b**) *Cost* hook and eye

corcho *nm* cork; *(de pesca)* float

cordel *nm* rope, cord

cordero, -a *nm,f* lamb

cordial *adj* cordial, warm

cordillera *nf* mountain chain *o* range

cordón *nm* string; *(de zapatos)* shoelace; *Anat* **c. umbilical** umbilical cord; **c. policial** police cordon; *CSur, Cuba (de la vereda) Br* kerb, *US* curb

Corea *n* Korea; **C. del Norte/Sur** North/South Korea

coreografía *nf* choreography

corista **1** *nmf (en coro)* chorus singer **2** *nf (en cabaret)* chorus girl

cornada *nf Taurom* goring

cornamenta *nf* (**a**) *(de toro)* horns; *(de ciervo)* antlers (**b**) *Fam Fig (de marido engañado)* cuckold's horns

córnea *nf* cornea

corneja *nf* crow

córner *nm* (*pl* **córners**) *Dep* corner (kick); **sacar un c.** to take a corner

cornete *nm* (**a**) *Anat* turbinate bone (**b**) *(helado)* cornet, cone

cornisa *nf* cornice

coro *nm Mús* choir; *Teatro* chorus; *Fig* **a c.** all together

corona *nf* (**a**) crown (**b**) *(de flores etc)* wreath, garland; **c. funeraria** funeral wreath

coronar *vt* to crown

coronel *nm* colonel

coronilla *nf* crown of the head; *Fam* **estar hasta la c. (de)** to be fed up (with)

corpiño *nm (vestido)* bodice; *Arg (sostén)* bra

corporal *adj* corporal; **castigo c.** corporal punishment; **olor c.** body odour, BO

corpulento, -a *adj* corpulent, stout

corpus *nm* corpus

corral *nm* farmyard, *US* corral; *(de casa)* courtyard

correa *nf* (**a**) *(tira)* strap; *(de reloj)* watchstrap; *(de pantalón)* belt; *(de perro)* lead, leash (**b**) *Téc* belt

corrección *nf* (**a**) *(rectificación)* correction (**b**) *(urbanidad)* courtesy, politeness

correcto, -a *adj* (**a**) *(sin errores)* correct (**b**) *(educado)* polite, courteous (**con to); *(conducta)* proper

corredor, -a *nm,f* (**a**) *Dep* runner (**b**) *Fin* **c. de bolsa** stockbroker

corregir [58] **1** *vt* to correct **2 corregirse** *vpr* to mend one's ways

correo *nm* (**a**) *Br* post, *US* mail; **echar algo al c.** to *Br* post *o US* mail sth; **por c.** by *Br* post *o US* mail; **c. aéreo** airmail; **c. certificado** registered *Br* post *o US* mail; *Informát* **c. electrónico** electronic mail, e-mail; *Informát* **me envió un c. (electrónico)** *(un mensaje)* she e-mailed me, she sent me an e-mail (**b**) *Esp* **Correos** *(institución)* the post office

correr **1** *vi* (**a**) to run; *(coche)* to go fast; *(conductor)* to drive fast; *(viento)* to blow; *Fig* **no corras, habla más despacio** don't rush, speak slower; **c. prisa** to be urgent (**b**) **c. con los gastos** to foot the bill; **corre a mi cargo** I'll take care of it

2 *vt* (**a**) *(cortina)* to draw; *(cerrojo)* to close; *(aventura etc)* to have; **c. el riesgo** *o* **peligro** to run the risk (**b**) *(mover)* to pull up, to draw up

3 correrse *vpr* (**a**) *(moverse)* to move over (**b**) *Fam* **correrse una juerga** to go on a spree (**c**) *Andes, Esp muy Fam (tener un orgasmo)* to come

correspondencia *nf* (**a**) correspondence (**b**) *Ferroc* connection

corresponder **1** *vi* (**a**) to correspond

(**a** to; **con** with) (**b**) *(incumbir)* to concern, to be incumbent upon; **esta tarea te corresponde a ti** it's your job to do this (**c**) *(pertenecer)* to belong; **me dieron lo que me correspondía** they gave me my share **2 corresponderse** *vpr* (**a**) *(ajustarse)* to correspond (**b**) *(dos cosas)* to tally; **no se corresponde con la descripción** it does not match the description (**c**) *(dos personas)* to love each other

correspondiente *adj* corresponding (**a** to)

corresponsal *nmf* correspondent

corrida *nf* **c. (de toros)** bullfight

corriente 1 *adj* (**a**) *(común)* common (**b**) *(agua)* running (**c**) *(mes, año)* current, present; **el diez del c.** the tenth of this month (**d**) *Fin (cuenta)* current (**e**) **estar al c.** to be up to date **2** *nf* (**a**) current, stream; *Fig* **ir o navegar contra c.** to go against the tide; *Fam* **seguirle o llevarle la c. a algn** to humour sb; *Elec* **c. eléctrica** (electric) current (**b**) *(de aire) Br* draught, *US* draft (**c**) *(tendencia)* trend, current

corro *nm* (**a**) circle, ring (**b**) *(juego)* ring-a-ring-a-roses

corromper 1 *vt* (**a**) *(pudrir)* to turn bad, to rot (**b**) *(pervertir)* to corrupt, to pervert **2 corromperse** *vpr* (**a**) *(pudrirse)* to go bad, to rot (**b**) *(pervertirse)* to become corrupted

corrupción *nf* (**a**) *(putrefacción)* rot, decay (**b**) *Fig* corruption; *Jur* **c. de menores** corruption of minors

corsé *nm* corset

corsetería *nf* ladies' underwear shop

cortacésped *nm o nf* lawnmower

cortado, -a 1 *adj* (**a**) cut (up) (**b**) *(leche)* sour (**c**) *(labios)* chapped (**d**) *Fam (tímido)* shy **2** *nm* small coffee with a dash of milk

cortante *adj* (**a**) *(afilado)* sharp (**b**) *Fig (tajante) (frase, estilo)* cutting; *(viento)* biting; *(frío)* bitter

cortar 1 *vt* (**a**) to cut; *(carne)* to carve; *(árbol)* to cut down; *Fam* **c. por lo sano** to take drastic measures; *Fam* **cortó**

con su novio she split up with her boyfriend (**b**) *(piel)* to chap, to crack (**c**) *(luz, teléfono)* to cut off (**d**) *(paso, carretera)* to block **2 cortarse** *vpr* (**a**) *(herirse)* to cut oneself (**b**) **cortarse el pelo** to have one's hair cut (**c**) *(leche etc)* to curdle (**d**) *Tel* **se cortó la comunicación** we were cut off (**e**) *Fam (aturdirse)* to become all shy

cortaúñas *nm inv* nail clippers

corte¹ *nm* (**a**) cut; **c. de pelo** haircut; *TV* **c. publicitario** commercial break; **c. de mangas** ≃ V-sign (**b**) *(sección)* section; **c. transversal** cross-section (**c**) *Fam* rebuff; **dar un c. a algn** to cut sb dead

corte² *nf* (**a**) *(real)* court (**b**) *Esp* **las Cortes** (Spanish) Parliament

cortés *adj* *(pl* **corteses)** courteous, polite

cortesía *nf* courtesy, politeness

corteza *nf* *(de árbol)* bark; *(de queso)* rind; *(de pan)* crust

cortijo *nm* Andalusian farm *o* farmhouse

cortina *nf* curtain; **c. de humo** smoke screen

corto, -a 1 *adj* (**a**) *(distancia, tiempo)* short; *Fam* **c. de luces** dim-witted; **c. de vista** short-sighted; *Aut* **luz corta** dipped headlights (**b**) *Fam* **quedarse c.** *(calcular mal)* to underestimate (**c**) *(apocado)* timid, shy **2** *nm* *Cin* short (movie *o* *Br* film)

cortometraje *nm* short (movie *o* *Br* film)

cosa *nf* (**a**) thing; **no he visto c. igual** I've never seen anything like it; **no ser gran c.** not to be up to much (**b**) *(asunto)* matter, business; **eso es c. tuya** that's your business *o* affair; **eso es otra c.** that's different (**c**) **hace c. de una hora** about an hour ago

coscorrón *nm* knock *o* blow on the head

cosecha *nf* (**a**) *Agr* harvest, crop (**b**) *(año del vino)* vintage

cosechar *vt* to harvest, to gather (in)

coser *vt* (**a**) to sew; *Fam* **es c. y cantar**

it's a piece of cake (**b**) *Med* to stitch up

cosmopolita *adj & nmf* cosmopolitan

cosmos *nm inv* cosmos

coso *nm* (**a**) *Taurom* bullring (**b**) *CSur Fam (objeto)* whatnot, thing; **¿para qué sirve ese c.?** *(en aparato)* what's this thing o thingumajig for?

cosquillas *nfpl* tickling; **hacer c. a algn** to tickle sb; **tener c.** to be ticklish

cosquilleo *nm* tickling

costa¹ *nf* coast; *(litoral)* coastline; *(playa)* beach, seaside

costa² *nf* **a c. de** at the expense of; **a toda c.** at all costs, at any price; **vive a c. mía** he lives off me

costado *nm* side; **de c.** sideways; **es catalana por los cuatro costados** she's Catalan through and through

costanera *nf CSur* promenade

costar [2] *vi* (**a**) to cost; **¿cuánto cuesta?** how much is it?; **c. barato/caro** to be cheap/expensive (**b**) *Fig* **te va a c. caro** you'll pay dearly for this; **c. trabajo** o **mucho** to be hard; **me cuesta hablar francés** I find it difficult to speak French; **cueste lo que cueste** at any cost

Costa Rica *n* Costa Rica

costarricense *adj & nmf*, **costarriqueño, -a** *adj & nm,f* Costa Rican

coste *nm Esp* cost; **a precio de c.** (at) cost price; **c. de la vida** cost of living

costero, -a 1 *adj* coastal; **ciudad costera** seaside town **2** *nf Méx* promenade

costilla *nf* (**a**) *Anat* rib (**b**) *Culin* cutlet

costo¹ *nm* cost

costo² *nm Esp Fam (hachís)* dope, shit, stuff

costoso, -a *adj* costly, expensive

costra *nf* crust; *Med* scab

costumbre *nf* (**a**) *(hábito)* habit; **como de c.** as usual; **tengo la c. de levantarme temprano** I usually get up early; **tenía la c. de ...** he used to ... (**b**) *(tradición)* custom

costura *nf* (**a**) sewing (**b**) *(confección)* dressmaking; **alta c.** haute couture (**c**) *(línea de puntadas)* seam

costurera *nf* seamstress

costurero *nm* sewing basket

cota *nf Geog* height above sea level; *Fig* rating

cotejar *vt* to compare

cotidiano, -a *adj* daily; **vida cotidiana** everyday life

cotilla *nmf Esp Fam* busybody, gossip

cotilleo *nm Esp Fam* gossip

cotillón *nm* = party on New Year's Eve or 5th of January

cotización *nf* (**a**) *Fin* (market) price, quotation (**b**) *(cuota)* membership fees, subscription

cotizar [40] **1** *vt Fin* to quote
2 *vi* to pay national insurance
3 **cotizarse** *vpr Fin* **cotizarse a** to sell at

coto *nm* (**a**) enclosure, reserve; **c. de caza** game reserve (**b**) **poner c. a** to put a stop to

cotorra *nf* parrot; *Fig (persona)* chatterbox

country *nm (pl* **countries**) *Arg* = luxury suburban housing development

coyuntura *nf* (**a**) *Anat* articulation, joint (**b**) *Fig (circunstancia)* juncture; **la c. económica** the economic situation

coz *nf* kick; **dar una c.** to kick

cráneo *nm* cranium, skull

cráter *nm* crater

creación *nf* creation

creador, -a *nm,f* creator

crear *vt* to create

creatividad *nf* creativity

creativo, -a *adj* creative

crecer [33] *vi* (**a**) to grow; **c. en importancia** to become more important (**b**) *(al tricotar)* to increase

crecimiento *nm* growth

credencial *adj* credential; **(cartas) credenciales** credentials

crédito *nm* (**a**) *Com, Fin* credit (**b**) *(confianza)* belief; **dar c. a** to believe

credo *nm* creed

creencia *nf* belief

creer [36] **1** *vt* (**a**) to believe (**b**)

(pensar) to think; **creo que no** I don't think so; **creo que sí** I think so; **ya lo creo** I should think so

2 *vi* to believe; **c. en** to believe in

3 creerse *vpr* **(a)** to consider oneself to be; **¿qué te has creído?** what o who do you think you are? **(b) no me lo creo** I can't believe it

creído, -a 1 *adj* arrogant, vain **2** *nm,f* bighead

crema *nf* cream

cremallera *nf Br* zip (fastener), *US* zipper

crepe *nm* crêpe, pancake

cresta *nf* (a) crest; *(de gallo)* comb **(b)** *(de punk)* mohican

cretino, -a 1 *adj* stupid, cretinous **2** *nm,f* cretin

creyente *nmf* believer

cría *nf* **(a)** *(cachorro)* young **(b)** *(crianza)* breeding, raising

criadero *nm* nursery

criadilla *nf Culin* bull's testicle

criado, -a 1 *adj* **mal c.** spoilt **2** *nm,f* servant

crianza *nf (de animales)* breeding; *Fig* **vinos de c.** vintage wines

criar [29] *vt* **(a)** *(animales)* to breed, to raise; *(niños)* to bring up, to rear **(b)** *(producir)* to have, to grow

criatura *nf* **(a)** (living) creature **(b)** *(crío)* baby, child

crimen *nm* murder; **c. de guerra** war crime

criminal *nmf & adj* criminal

crío, -a 1 *nm Fam* kid **2** *adj* babyish

criollo, -a *adj & nm,f* Creole

críquet *nm* cricket

crisis *nf inv* **(a)** crisis **(b)** *(ataque)* fit, attack; **c. nerviosa** nervous breakdown

cristal *nm* **(a)** crystal; **c. de roca** rock crystal **(b)** *Esp (vidrio)* glass; *(de gafas)* lens; *(de ventana)* (window) pane

cristalería *nf (conjunto)* glassware; *(vasos)* glasses

cristalino, -a *adj* crystal clear

cristianismo *nm* Christianity

cristiano, -a *adj & nm,f* Christian

Cristo *nm* Christ

criterio *nm* **(a)** *(pauta)* criterion **(b)** *(opinión)* opinion **(c)** *(discernimiento)* discretion; **lo dejo a tu c.** I'll leave it up to you

crítica *nf* **(a)** criticism **(b)** *Prensa* review; **tener buena c.** to get good reviews **(c)** *(conjunto de críticos)* critics

criticar [44] **1** *vt* to criticize **2** *vi* *(murmurar)* to gossip

crítico, -a 1 *adj* critical **2** *nm,f* critic

croar *vi* to croak

croissant [krwa'san] *nm* *(pl* **croissants**) croissant

croissantería [krwasante'ria] *nf* = shop selling filled croissants

crol *nm* crawl

cromo *nm* **(a)** *(metal)* chromium, chrome **(b)** *Esp (estampa)* picture card

crónica *nf* **(a)** account, chronicle **(b)** *Prensa* feature, article

cronometrar *vt* to time

cronómetro *nm* stopwatch

croqueta *nf* croquette

croquis *nm inv* sketch

cross *nm inv Dep (carrera)* cross-country race; *(deporte)* cross-country (running)

cruce *nm* **(a)** crossing; *(de carreteras)* crossroads; *(de razas)* crossbreeding **(b)** *Tel* crossed line

crucero *nm Náut* cruise; *(barco)* cruiser

crucial *adj* crucial

crucifijo *nm* crucifix

crucigrama *nm* crossword (puzzle)

crudo, -a 1 *adj* **(a)** raw; *(comida)* underdone; *Fam Fig* **lo veo muy c.** it doesn't look too good **(b)** *(clima)* harsh **(c)** *(color)* cream **2** *nm (petróleo)* crude

cruel *adj* cruel

crueldad *nf* cruelty; *Fig (del clima)* severity

crujido *nm (de puerta)* creak, creaking; *(de dientes)* grinding

crujiente *adj* crunchy

crustáceo *nm* crustacean

cruz *nf* (a) cross; **C. Roja** Red Cross; **c.**

gamada swastika (**b**) **¿cara o c.?** ≃ heads or tails?

cruza *nf Am* cross, crossbreed

cruzada *nf* crusade

cruzar [40] **1** *vt* (**a**) to cross (**b**) *(palabras, miradas)* to exchange (**c**) *(animal, planta)* to cross, to crossbreed **2** *vi (atravesar)* to cross **3 cruzarse** *vpr* to cross; **cruzarse con algn** to pass sb

cta. *Com* (*abr* **cuenta**) a/c

cta. cte. *Com* (*abr* **cuenta corriente**) c/a

cte. (*abr* **corriente**) inst.

cuaderno *nm* notebook

cuadra *nf* (**a**) *(establo)* stable (**b**) *Am (en calle)* block (**c**) *Perú (recibidor)* reception room

cuadrado, -a 1 *adj* (**a**) *Geom* square (**b**) *(complexión física)* broad, stocky (**c**) *Fig (mente)* rigid **2** *nm* (**a**) *Geom* square (**b**) *Mat* square; **elevar (un número) al c.** to square (a number)

cuadrar 1 *vt* (**a**) *Mat* to square (**b**) *Andes (aparcar)* to park **2** *vi (coincidir)* to square, agree (**con** with); *(sumas, cifras)* to tally **3 cuadrarse** *vpr (soldado)* to stand to attention

cuadriculado, -a *adj* **papel c.** square paper

cuadrilla *nf (equipo)* gang, team; *Mil* squad; *Taurom* bullfighter's team

cuadro *nm* (**a**) *Geom* square; **tela a cuadros** checked cloth (**b**) *Arte* painting, picture (**c**) *Teatro* scene (**d**) *Elec, Téc* panel; **c. de mandos** control panel (**e**) *(gráfico)* chart, graph

cuajada *nf* curd

cual 1 *pron rel (precedido de artículo)* (**a**) *(persona) (sujeto)* who; *(objeto)* whom (**b**) *(cosa)* which **2** *pron* (**a**) **tal c.** exactly as (**b**) *Literario (comparativo)* such as, like

cuál 1 *pron interr* which (one)?, what?; **¿c. quieres?** which one do you want? **2** *adj interr* which **3** *loc adv* **a c. más tonto** each more stupid than the other

cualidad *nf* quality

cualificado, -a *adj* qualified

cualquier *adj indef* any; **c. cosa** anything; **en c. momento** at any moment *o* time

cualquiera (*pl* **cualesquiera**) **1** *adj indef* (**a**) *(indefinido)* any; **un profesor c.** any teacher (**b**) *(corriente)* ordinary

> Note that **cualquier** is used before singular nouns (e.g. **cualquier hombre** any man)

2 *pron indef* (**a**) *(persona)* anybody; **c. te lo puede decir** anybody can tell you (**b**) *(cosa, animal)* anyone (**c**) **c. que sea** whatever it is **3** *nmf Fig* **ser un c.** to be a nobody; **es una c.** she's a tart

cuando 1 *adv (de tiempo)* when; **c. más** at the most; **c. menos** at least; **de c. en c., de vez en c.** from time to time **2** *conj* (**a**) *(temporal)* when; **c. quieras** whenever you want; **c. vengas** when you come (**b**) *(condicional) (si)* if (**c**) *(concesiva) (aunque)* (**aun**) **c.** even if **3** *prep* during, at the time of; **c. la guerra** during the war; **c. niño** as a child

cuándo *adv interr* when?; **¿desde c.?** since when?; **¿para c. lo quieres?** when do you want it for?

cuantía *nf* quantity, amount

cuanto, -a 1 *adj* all; **gasta c. dinero gana** he spends all the money *o* as much as he earns; **unas cuantas niñas** a few girls **2** *pron rel* as much as; **coma c. quiera** eat as much as you want; **regala todo c. tiene** he gives away everything he's got **3** *pron indef pl* **unos cuantos** a few **4** *adv* (**a**) *(tiempo)* **c. antes** as soon as possible; **en c.** as soon as (**b**) *(cantidad)* **c. más … más** the more … the more; **c. más lo miro, más me gusta** the more I look at it, the more I like it; **cuantas más personas (haya) mejor** the more the merrier (**c**) **en c. a** with respect to, regarding; **en c. a Juan** as for Juan, as far as Juan is concerned

cuánto, -a 1 *adj & pron interr (sing)* how much?; *(pl)* how many?; **¿cuántas**

veces? how many times?; **¿c. es?** how much is it? **2** *adv* how, how much; **¡cuánta gente hay!** what a lot of people there are!

cuarenta *adj & nm inv* forty; *Fam* **cantarle a algn las c.** to give sb a piece of one's mind

cuaresma *nf* Lent

cuartel *nm Mil* barracks; **c. general** headquarters; *Fig* **no dar c.** to give no quarter

cuartelazo *nm* military uprising, revolt

cuarteto *nm* quartet

cuartilla *nf* sheet of paper

cuarto, -a 1 *nm* (**a**) *(habitación)* room; **c. de baño** bathroom; **c. de estar** living room (**b**) *(cuarta parte)* quarter; **c. de hora** quarter of an hour; *Dep* **cuartos de final** quarter finals (**c**) *Fam* **cuartos** *(dinero)* dough, money **2** *adj & nm,f* fourth

cuarzo *nm* quartz

cuate *nmf CAm, Ecuad, Méx Fam* (**a**) *(amigo)* pal, *US* buddy (**b**) *(persona)* *(hombre)* guy, *Br* bloke; *(mujer)* woman

cuatro 1 *adj & nm inv* four **2** *nm Fam* a few; **cayeron c. gotas** it rained a little bit

cuatrocientos, -as *adj & nm* four hundred

Cuba *n* Cuba

cubalibre *nm* rum/gin and coke

cubano, -a *adj & nm,f* Cuban

cubertería *nf* cutlery

cubeta *nf (cuba pequeña)* bucket, pail; *(de barómetro)* bulb; *Fot* tray

cúbico, -a *adj* cubic; *Mat* **raíz cúbica** cube root

cubierta *nf* (**a**) cover (**b**) *(de rueda)* tyre (**c**) *Náut* deck (**d**) *(techo)* roof

cubierto, -a 1 *adj* (**a**) covered; *(piscina)* indoors; *(cielo)* overcast (**b**) *(trabajo, plaza)* filled **2** *nm* (**a**) *(en la mesa)* place setting (**b**) **cubiertos** cutlery

cubito *nm* little cube; **c. de hielo** ice cube

cúbito *nm Anat* ulna

cubo *nm* (**a**) bucket; **c. de la basura** *Br* rubbish bin, *US* garbage can (**b**) *Mat* cube (**c**) *(de rueda)* hub

cubrir *(pp* **cubierto**) **1** *vt* to cover **2** **cubrirse** *vpr (cielo)* to become overcast

cucaracha *nf* cockroach

cuchara *nf* spoon

cucharada *nf* spoonful; **c. rasa/ colmada** level/heaped spoonful

cucharilla *nf* teaspoon; **c. de café** coffee spoon

cucharón *nm* ladle

cuchilla *nf* blade; **c. de afeitar** razor blade

cuchillo *nm* knife

cuclillas *nfpl* **en c.** squatting; **ponerse en c.** to squat (down)

cucurucho *nm* (**a**) *(para helado)* cornet (**b**) *(de papel)* paper cone

cuello *nm* (**a**) *(de persona, animal, botella)* neck (**b**) *(de prendas)* collar

cuenca *nf* (**a**) *Geog* basin (**b**) *(de los ojos)* socket

cuenco *nm* earthenware bowl

cuenta *nf* (**a**) *(factura)* bill; *(en restaurante) Br* bill, *US* check; (**b**) *Fin (de banco)* account; **c. corriente** *Br* current account, *US* checking account (**c**) *(cálculo)* count; **hacer cuentas** to do sums; **c. atrás** countdown (**d**) *(de collar)* bead (**e**) *Informát* account; **c. de correo (electrónico)** e-mail account (**f**) *(locuciones)* **caer en la c., darse c.** to realize; **dar c.** to report; **tener en c.** to take into account; **más sillas de la c.** too many chairs; **en resumidas cuentas** in short; **pedir cuentas** to ask for an explanation; **trabajar por c. propia** to be self-employed

cuentagotas *nm inv* dropper

cuentakilómetros *nm inv (distancia) Br* $\simeq$ mileometer, *US* $\simeq$ odometer; *(velocidad)* speedometer

cuento *nm* story; *Lit* short story; **contar un c.** to tell a story; *Fig* **eso no viene a c.** that's beside the point; **c. chino** tall story; **c. de hadas** fairy story

cuerda *nf* (**a**) *(cordel)* rope; *Fig* **bajo**

c. dishonestly; **c. floja** tightrope; **cuerdas vocales** vocal cords (**b**) *(de instrumento)* string (**c**) *(del reloj)* spring; **dar c. al reloj** to wind up a watch

cueriza *nf Andes Fam* beating, leathering

cuerno *nm* horn; *(de ciervo)* antler; *Fam* **¡vete al c.!** get lost!; *Fam* **ponerle cuernos a algn** to be unfaithful to sb

cuero *nm* (**a**) leather; **chaqueta de c.** leather jacket (**b**) **c. cabelludo** scalp; *Fam* **en cueros (vivos)** (stark) naked

cuerpo *nm* (**a**) body; **de c. entero** full-length; *Fig* **tomar c.** to take shape (**b**) *(cadáver)* corpse; **de c. presente** lying in state (**c**) *(parte)* section, part (**d**) *(grupo)* corps, force; **c. de bomberos** *Br* fire brigade, *US* fire department; **c. diplomático** diplomatic corps

cuervo *nm* raven

cuesta 1 *nf* slope; **c. abajo** downhill; **c. arriba** uphill 2 *loc adv* **a cuestas** on one's back o shoulders

cuestión *nf* (**a**) *(asunto)* matter, question; **es c. de vida o muerte** it's a matter of life or death; **en c. de unas horas** in just a few hours (**b**) *(pregunta)* question

cuestionario *nm* questionnaire

cueva *nf* cave

cuico, -a *nm,f Méx Fam* cop

cuidado 1 *nm* (**a**) care; **con c.** carefully; **tener c.** to be careful; **estar al c. de** *(cosa)* to be in charge of; *(persona)* to look after; **me trae sin c.** I couldn't care less (**b**) *Med* **cuidados intensivos** intensive care 2 *interj* look out!, watch out!; **¡c. con lo que dices!** watch what you say!; **¡c. con el escalón!** mind the step!

cuidadoso, -a *adj* careful

cuidar 1 *vt* to care for, to look after; **c. de que todo salga bien** to make sure that everything goes all right; **c. los detalles** to pay attention to details 2 **cuidarse** *vpr* **cuídate** look after yourself

cuitlacoche *nm CAm, Méx* corn smut, = edible fungus which grows on maize

culata *nf* (**a**) *(de arma)* butt (**b**) *Aut* cylinder head

culebra *nf* snake

culebrón *nm Esp Fam* soap opera

culo *nm* (**a**) *Am Fam (nalgas) Br* bum, *US* butt; *Esp Vulg* **¡vete a tomar por c.!** fuck off! (**b**) *(de recipiente)* bottom

culpa *nf* (**a**) blame; **echar la c. a algn** to put the blame on sb; **fue c. mía** it was my fault; **por tu c.** because of you (**b**) *(culpabilidad)* guilt

culpabilidad *nf* guilt, culpability

culpable 1 *nmf* offender, culprit 2 *adj* guilty; *Jur* **declararse c.** to plead guilty

culpar *vt* to blame; **c. a algn de un delito** to accuse sb of an offence

cultivar *vt* (**a**) to cultivate (**b**) *Biol* to culture

cultivo *nm* (**a**) cultivation; *(planta)* crop (**b**) *Biol* culture

culto, -a 1 *adj* educated; *(palabra)* learned 2 *nm* cult; *Rel* worship

cultura *nf* culture

cultural *adj* cultural

culturismo *nm* body building

cumbre *nf* (**a**) *(de montaña)* summit, top; **(conferencia) c.** summit conference (**b**) *Fig (culminación)* pinnacle

cumpleaños *nm inv* birthday; **¡feliz c.!** happy birthday!

cumplido, -a 1 *adj* (**a**) completed; *(plazo)* expired; **misión cumplida** mission accomplished (**b**) *(cortés)* polite 2 *nm* compliment

cumplir 1 *vt* (**a**) to carry out, to fulfil; *(deseo)* to fulfil; *(promesa)* to keep; *(sentencia)* to serve (**b**) **ayer cumplí veinte años** I was twenty (years old) yesterday

2 *vi* (**a**) *(plazo)* to expire, to end (**b**) **c. con el deber** to do one's duty

3 **cumplirse** *vpr* (**a**) *(deseo, sueño)* to be fulfilled, to come true (**b**) *(plazo)* to expire

cúmulo *nm* pile, load

cuna *nf* (**a**) cot (**b**) *Fig (origen)* cradle

cundir *vi* (**a**) *(propagarse)* to spread (**b**) *Esp (dar de sí) (comida, reservas)* to go a long way; *(trabajo, estudio)* to go well; **me cundió mucho el tiempo** I got a lot done

cuneta *nf (de la carretera)* gutter; **quedarse en la c.** to be left behind

cuña *nf* (**a**) *(pieza)* wedge; **c. publicitaria** commercial break (**b**) *Andes, RP Fam (enchufe)* **tener c.** to have friends in high places

cuñado, -a *nm,f (hombre)* brother-in-law; *(mujer)* sister-in-law

cuota *nf* (**a**) *(de club etc)* membership fees *pl*, dues *pl* (**b**) *Am (plazo)* instalment; **comprar en cuotas** to buy on *Br* hire purchase *o US* an installment plan (**c**) *(porción)* quota, share (**d**) *Méx (importe)* toll; **autopista de c.** toll motorway, *US* turnpike

cuplé *nm* popular song

cupo *nm* ceiling; *Mil* **excedente de c.** exempt from military service

cupón *nm* coupon, voucher

cúpula *nf* dome, cupola; *(líderes)* leadership

cura 1 *nm Rel* priest **2** *nf Med* cure; *Fig* **no tiene c.** there's no remedy

curandero, -a *nm,f* quack

curar 1 *vt* (**a**) *(sanar)* to cure; *(herida)* to dress; *(enfermedad)* to treat (**b**) *(carne, pescado)* to cure
2 *vi (sanar)* to recover, to get well; *(herida)* to heal up
3 curarse *vpr* to recover, to get well; *(herida)* to heal up; **c. en salud** to make sure

curcuncho, -a *adj Andes Fam* hunchbacked

curiosidad *nf* curiosity; **tener c. de** to be curious about

curioso, -a 1 *adj* (**a**) *(indiscreto)* curious, inquisitive (**b**) *(extraño)* strange,

odd; **lo c. es que ...** the strange thing is that ... (**c**) *(limpio)* neat, tidy **2** *nm,f* (**a**) *(mirón)* onlooker (**b**) *(chismoso)* nosy-parker, busybody

curita *nf Am (para heridas) Br* (sticking)plaster, *US* Band-aid®

currante *Esp Fam* **1** *adj* hard-working **2** *nmf* worker

currar *vi Esp Fam* to work

currículum (vitae) [ku'rrikulum ('bite)] *nm (pl* **currícula** *o* **currículums (vitae)**) curriculum vitae, *Br* CV, *US* résumé

curro *nm Esp Fam* work

curry *nm* curry; **pollo al c.** chicken curry

cursi *adj (vestido, canción)* tacky, *Br* naff; *(modales, persona)* affected

cursillo *nm* short course; **c. de reciclaje** refresher course

curso *nm* (**a**) *(año académico)* year; *(clase)* class (**b**) *Fig* **año/mes en c.** current year/month; **en el c. de** during (**c**) *(de acontecimientos, río)* course (**d**) *Fin* **moneda de c. legal** legal tender

cursor *nm* cursor

curtiembre *nf Andes, RP* tannery

curva *nf* (**a**) curve (**b**) *(en carretera)* bend; **c. cerrada** sharp bend

curvado, -a *adj (forma)* curved; *(espalda)* bent

custodia *nf* custody

cutis *nm inv* complexion

cutre *adj Esp Fam (sórdido)* shabby, dingy

cuyo, -a *pron rel & pos (de persona)* whose; *(de cosa)* of which; **en c. caso** in which case

Dd

D. (*abr* **don**) Mr

dado¹, -a *adj* (**a**) given; **en un momento d.** at a certain point (**b**) **ser d. a** to be given to (**c**) **d. que** since, given that

dado² *nm* die, dice

daga *nf* dagger

dalia *nf* dahlia

dama *nf* (**a**) *(señora)* lady (**b**) *(en damas)* king (**c**) **damas** *(juego)* Br draughts, US checkers

damasco *nm* (**a**) *(tela)* damask (**b**) *Andes, RP (albaricoque)* apricot

danés, -esa 1 *adj* Danish **2** *nm,f (persona)* Dane **3** *nm* (**a**) *(idioma)* Danish (**b**) **gran d.** *(perro)* Great Dane

danza *nf* dancing; *(baile)* dance

danzar [40] *vt & vi* to dance

dañar *vt (cosa)* to damage; *(persona)* to hurt, to harm

dañino, -a *adj* harmful, damaging (**para** to)

daño *nm (a cosa)* damage; *(a persona) (físico)* hurt; *(perjuicio)* harm; **se hizo d. en la pierna** he hurt his leg; *Jur* **daños y perjuicios** (legal) damages

dar [11] **1** *vt* (**a**) to give; *(recado, recuerdos)* to pass on, to give; *(noticia)* to tell

(**b**) *(mano de pintura, cera)* to apply, to put on

(**c**) *(película)* to show, to screen; *(fiesta)* to throw, to give

(**d**) *(cosecha)* to produce, to yield; *(fruto, flores)* to bear; *(beneficio, interés)* to give, to yield

(**e**) *(bofetada etc)* to deal; **d. a algn en la cabeza** to hit sb on the head

(**f**) **dale a la luz** switch the light on; **d. la mano a algn** to shake hands with sb; **d. los buenos días/las buenas noches a algn** to say good morning/

good evening to sb; **me da lo mismo, me da igual** it's all the same to me; **¿qué más da?** what difference does it make?

(**g**) *(hora)* to strike; **ya han dado las nueve** it's gone nine (o'clock)

(**h**) **d. de comer a** to feed

(**i**) **d. a conocer** *(noticia)* to release; **d. a entender a algn que …** to give sb to understand that …

(**j**) **d. por** *(considerar)* to assume, to consider; **lo dieron por muerto** he was assumed dead, he was given up for dead; **d. por descontado/sabido** to take for granted, to assume

2 *vi* (**a**) **me dio un ataque de tos/risa** I had a coughing fit/an attack of the giggles

(**b**) **d. a** *(ventana, habitación)* to look out onto, to overlook; *(puerta)* to open onto, to lead to

(**c**) **d. con** *(persona)* to come across; **d. con la solución** to hit upon the solution

(**d**) **d. de sí** *(ropa)* to stretch, to give

(**e**) **d. en** to hit; **el sol me daba en los ojos** the sun was (shining) in my eyes

(**f**) **d. para** to be enough o sufficient for; **el presupuesto no da para más** the budget will not stretch any further

(**g**) **le dio por nadar** he took it into his head to go swimming

(**h**) **d. que hablar** to set people talking; **el suceso dio que pensar** the incident gave people food for thought

3 **darse** *vpr* (**a**) **se dio un caso extraño** something strange happened

(**b**) *(hallarse)* to be found, to exist

(**c**) **darse a** to take to; **se dio a la bebida** he took to drink

(**d**) **darse con** o **contra** to bump o crash into

(**e**) **dárselas de** to consider oneself

(**f**) **darse por satisfecho** to feel satisfied; **darse por vencido** to give in

(**g**) **se le da bien/mal el francés** she's good/bad at French

dardo *nm* dart

dátil *nm* date

dato *nm* (**a**) piece of information; **datos personales** personal details (**b**) *Informát* **datos** data

d.C. (*abr* **después de Cristo**) AD

dcha. (*abr* **derecha**) rt.

de *prep*

> **de** combines with the article **el** to form the contraction **del** (e.g. **del hombre** of the man)

(**a**) *(pertenencia)* of; **el título de la novela** the title of the novel; **el coche/hermano de Sofía** Sofía's car/brother; **las bicicletas de los niños** the boys' bicycles

(**b**) *(procedencia)* from; **de Madrid a Valencia** from Madrid to Valencia; **soy de Palencia** I'm from *o* I come from Palencia

(**c**) *(descripción)* **el niño de ojos azules** the boy with blue eyes; **el señor de la chaqueta** the man in the jacket; **un reloj de oro** a gold watch; **un joven de veinte años** a young man of twenty

(**d**) *(contenido)* of; **un saco de patatas** a sack of potatoes

(**e**) *(oficio)* as; **trabaja de secretaria** she's working as a secretary

(**f**) *(acerca de)* about; **curso de informática** computer course

(**g**) *(tiempo)* **a las tres de la tarde** at three in the afternoon; **de día** by day; **de noche** at night; **de lunes a jueves** from Monday to Thursday; **de pequeño** as a child; **de año en año** year in year out

(**h**) *(precio)* at; **patatas de 30 céntimos el kilo** potatoes at 30 cents a kilo

(**i**) **una avenida de 3 km** an avenue 3 km long; **una botella de litro** a litre bottle

(**j**) *(con superlativo)* in; **el más largo de España** the longest in Spain

(**k**) *(causa)* with, because of; **llorar de alegría** to cry with joy; **morir de hambre** to die of hunger

(**l**) *(condicional)* **de haber llegado antes** if he had arrived before; **de no ser así** if that wasn't *o* weren't the case

debajo *adv* underneath, below; **el mío es el de d.** mine is the one below; **está d. de la mesa** it's under the table; **por d. de lo normal** below normal; **salió por d. del coche** he came out from under the car

debate *nm* debate

debatir 1 *vt* to debate **2 debatirse** *vpr* to struggle; **debatirse entre la vida y la muerte** to fight for one's life

deber¹ *nm* (**a**) duty; **cumplir con su d.** to do one's duty (**b**) *Educ* **deberes** homework

deber² **1** *vt* *(dinero, explicación)* to owe **2** *vi* (**a**) *(obligación)* must; **debe (de) comer** he must eat; **la factura debe pagarse mañana** the bill must be paid tomorrow

(**b**) *(consejo)* **deberías visitar a tus padres** you ought to visit your parents; **no debiste hacerlo** you shouldn't have done it

(**c**) *(suposición)* **deben de estar fuera** they must be out

3 deberse *vpr* **deberse a** to be due to; **esto se debe a la falta de agua** this is due to lack of water

debido, -a *adj* (**a**) due; **a su d. tiempo** in due course; **con el d. respeto** with due respect (**b**) *(adecuado)* proper; **más de lo d.** too much; **tomaron las debidas precauciones** they took the proper precautions; **como es d.** properly (**c**) **d. a** because of, due to; **d. a que** because of the fact that

débil *adj* weak; *(luz)* dim; **punto d.** weak spot

debilidad *nf* weakness; *Fig* **tener d. por** *(persona)* to have a soft spot for; *(cosa)* to have a weakness for

debilitar 1 *vt* to weaken, to debilitate **2 debilitarse** *vpr* to weaken, to grow weak

debut *nm* (*pl* **debuts**) début, debut

década *nf* decade; **en la d. de los noventa** during the nineties

decadencia *nf* decadence

decadente *adj & nmf* decadent

decaer [39] *vi* to deteriorate

decaído, -a *adj* down

decano, -a *nm,f Univ* dean

decena *nf* (about) ten; **una d. de veces** (about) ten times; **por decenas** in tens

decente *adj* decent; *(decoroso)* modest

decepción *nf* disappointment

decepcionar *vt* to disappoint

decidido, -a *adj* determined, resolute

decidir 1 *vt & vi* to decide 2 **decidirse** *vpr* to make up one's mind; **decidirse a hacer algo** to make up one's mind to do sth; **decidirse por algo** to decide on sth

decimal *adj & nm* decimal; **el sistema métrico d.** the decimal system

décimo, -a 1 *adj & nm,f* tenth 2 *nm* (**a**) *(parte)* tenth (**b**) *(billete de lotería)* tenth part of a lottery ticket

decir¹ *nm* saying

decir² [12] (*pp* **dicho**) 1 *vt* (**a**) to say; **dice que no quiere venir** he says he doesn't want to come

(**b**) **d. una mentira/la verdad** to tell a lie/the truth

(**c**) *Esp* **¿diga?, ¿dígame?** *(al teléfono)* hello?

(**d**) **¿qué me dices del nuevo jefe?** what do you think of the new boss?

(**e**) *(sugerir)* to mean; **¿qué te dice el cuadro?** what does the picture mean to you?; **esta película no me dice nada** this film doesn't appeal to me

(**f**) **querer d.** to mean

(**g**) *(locuciones)* **es d.** that is (to say); **por así decirlo** as it were, so to speak; **digamos** let's say; **digo yo** in my opinion; **el qué dirán** what people say; **ni que d. tiene** needless to say; **¡no me digas!** really!; *Esp* **¡y que lo digas!** you can say that again!

2 **decirse** *vpr* **¿cómo se dice "mesa" en inglés?** how do you say "mesa" in English?; **se dice que ...** they say that ...

decisión *nf* (**a**) decision; **tomar una d.** to take o make a decision (**b**) *(resolución)* determination; **con d.** decisively

declaración *nf* (**a**) declaration; **d. de (la) renta** tax declaration o return (**b**) *(afirmación)* statement; **hacer declaraciones** to comment (**c**) *Jur* **prestar d.** to give evidence

declarado, -a *adj (manifiesto)* open, professed; **es un homosexual d.** he is openly gay; **hay un odio d. entre ellos** there is open hostility between them

declarar 1 *vt* (**a**) to declare; **d. la guerra a** to declare war on (**b**) *(afirmar)* to state (**c**) *Jur* **d. culpable/inocente a algn** to find sb guilty/not guilty

2 *vi* (**a**) to declare (**b**) *Jur* to testify

3 **declararse** *vpr* (**a**) **declararse a favor/en contra de** to declare oneself in favour of/against; **declararse en huelga** to go on strike; **declararse a algn** to declare one's love for sb (**b**) *(guerra, incendio)* to start, to break out (**c**) *Jur* **declararse culpable** to plead guilty

declinar *vt & vi* to decline

decolaje *nm Am* take-off

decolar *vi Am* to take off

decoración *nf* decoration

decorado *nm* scenery, set

decorar *vt* to decorate

decretar *vt* to decree

decreto *nm* decree; **d.-ley** decree, *Br* order in council

dedal *nm* thimble

dedicación *nf* dedication

dedicar [44] 1 *vt* to dedicate; *(tiempo, esfuerzos)* to devote (**a** to) 2 **dedicarse** *vpr* **¿a qué se dedica Vd.?** what do you do for a living?; **los fines de semana ella se dedica a pescar** at weekends she spends her time fishing

dedo *nm (de la mano)* finger; *(del pie)* toe; **d. anular/corazón/índice/meñique** ring/middle/index/little finger; **d. pulgar, d. gordo** thumb; **hacer d.** to hitch-hike; *Fig* **elegir a algn a d.** to handpick sb

deducción *nf* deduction

deducir [10] **1** *vt* (**a**) to deduce, to infer (**b**) *Com* to deduct **2 deducirse** *vpr* **de aquí se deduce que ...** from this it follows that ...

defecar [44] *vi* to defecate

defecto *nm* defect, fault; **d. físico** physical defect

defender [3] **1** *vt* to defend (**de** from); **d. del frío/viento** to shelter from the cold/wind **2 defenderse** *vpr* (**a**) to defend oneself (**b**) *Fam* **se defiende en francés** he can get by in French

defensa **1** *nf* defence; **en d. propia, en legítima d.** in self-defence; **salir en d. de algn** to come out in defence of sb **2** *nm Dep* defender, back

defensor, -a *nm,f* defender; **abogado d.** counsel for the defence; *Esp* **defensor del pueblo** ombudsman

deficiencia *nf* deficiency, shortcoming; **d. mental** mental deficiency; **d. renal** kidney failure

deficiente **1** *adj* deficient **2** *nmf* **d. mental** mentally retarded person **3** *nm Educ* fail

déficit *nm* (*pl* **déficits**) deficit; (*carencia*) shortage

definición *nf* definition; **por d.** by definition

definir *vt* to define

definitivo, -a *adj* definitive; **en definitiva** in short

deformación *nf* deformation

deformar **1** *vt* to deform, to put out of shape; (*cara*) to disfigure; *Fig (la verdad, una imagen)* to distort **2 deformarse** *vpr* to go out of shape, to become distorted

defraudar *vt* (**a**) (*decepcionar*) to disappoint (**b**) (*al fisco*) to defraud, to cheat; **d. a Hacienda** to evade taxes

defunción *nf Fml* decease, demise

degenerado, -a *adj & nm,f* degenerate

degenerar *vi* to degenerate

degustación *nf* tasting

dejadez *nf* slovenliness

dejar **1** *vt* (**a**) to leave; **déjame en paz** leave me alone (**b**) *Esp* (*prestar*) **d. algo a algn** to lend sb sth, to lend sth to sb (**c**) (*abandonar*) to give up; **dejé el tabaco y la bebida** I gave up smoking and drinking (**d**) (*permitir*) to let, to allow; **d. entrar/salir** to let in/out; **d. caer** to drop (**e**) (*omitir*) to leave out, to omit (**f**) (+ *adj*) to make; **d. triste** to make sad; **d. preocupado/sorprendido** to worry/surprise (**g**) (*posponer*) **dejaron el viaje para el verano** they put the trip off until the summer **2** *v aux* **d. de** (+ *infinitivo*) to stop, to give up; **dejó de fumar el año pasado** he gave up smoking last year; **no deja de llamarme** she's always phoning me up **3 dejarse** *vpr* (**a**) **me he dejado las llaves dentro** I've left the keys inside (**b**) (*locuciones*) **dejarse barba** to grow a beard; **dejarse caer** to flop down; **dejarse llevar por** to be influenced by

del (*contracción de* **de** + **el**) *ver* **de**

delantal *nm* apron

delante *adv* (**a**) in front; **la entrada de d.** the front entrance (**b**) **d. de** in front of; (*en serie*) ahead of (**c**) **por d.** in front; **se lo lleva todo por d.** he destroys everything in his path; **tiene toda la vida por d.** he has his whole life ahead of him

delantera *nf* (**a**) (*ventaja*) lead; **tomar la d.** take the lead (**b**) *Ftb* forward line, forwards

delantero, -a **1** *adj* front **2** *nm Ftb* forward; **d. centro** centre forward

delatar *vt* (**a**) to inform against (**b**) *Fig* to give away

delegación *nf* (**a**) (*acto, delegados*) delegation (**b**) (*sucursal*) local office; *Esp* **D. del Gobierno** = office representing central government in each province; *Esp* **D. de Hacienda** = head tax office (*in each province*) (**c**) *Chile, Ecuad, Méx (distrito municipal)* municipal district

delegado, -a *nm,f* (**a**) delegate; **d. de Hacienda** chief tax inspector (**b**) *Com* representative

delegar [42] *vt* to delegate (**en** to)

deletrear *vt* to spell (out)

delfín *nm* dolphin

delgado, -a *adj* slim; *(capa)* fine

deliberado, -a *adj* deliberate

deliberar *vi* to deliberate (on), to consider

delicadeza *nf* (**a**) *(finura)* delicacy, daintiness (**b**) *(tacto)* tactfulness; **falta de d.** tactlessness

delicado, -a *adj* (**a**) delicate (**b**) *(exigente)* fussy, hard to please (**c**) *(sensible)* hypersensitive

delicia *nf* delight; **hacer las delicias de algn** to delight sb

delicioso, -a *adj (comida)* delicious; *(agradable)* delightful

delincuencia *nf* delinquency

delincuente *adj & nmf* delinquent; **d. juvenil** juvenile delinquent

delinquir [48] *vi* to commit a crime

delirante *adj* delirious

delirar *vi* to be delirious

delirio *nm* delirium; **delirios de grandeza** delusions of grandeur

delito *nm* crime, offence

delta *nm* delta; **ala d.** hang-glider

demanda *nf* (**a**) *Jur* lawsuit (**b**) *Com* demand

demandar *vt* to sue

demás 1 *adj* **los/las d.** the rest of; **la d. gente** the rest of the people **2** *pron* **lo/los/las d.** the rest; **por lo d.** otherwise, apart from that; **y d.** etcetera

demasiado, -a 1 *adj (singular)* too much; *(plural)* too many; **hay demasiada comida** there is too much food; **quieres demasiadas cosas** you want too many things **2** *adv* too (much); **es d. grande/caro** it is too big/dear; **fumas/trabajas d.** you smoke/work too much

demencia *nf* dementia, insanity

demente 1 *adj* insane, mad **2** *nmf* mental patient

democracia *nf* democracy

demócrata 1 *adj* democratic **2** *nmf* democrat

democrático, -a *adj* democratic

demoledor, -a *adj Fig* devastating

demoler [4] *vt* to demolish

demonio *nm* devil, demon; *Fam* **¿cómo/dónde demonios …?** how/ where the hell …?; *Fam* **¡demonio(s)!** hell!, damn!; *Fam* **¡d. de niño!** you little devil!

demora *nf* delay

demorar 1 *vt* (**a**) *(retrasar)* to delay, hold up (**b**) *(tardar)* **demoraron 3 días en pintar la casa** it took them three days to paint the house
2 *vi Am (tardar)* **¡no demores!** don't be late!; **este quitamanchas demora en actuar** this stain remover takes a while to work
3 demorarse *vpr* (**a**) *(retrasarse)* to be delayed, be held up (**b**) *(detenerse)* to dally (**c**) *esp Am (tardar)* to be late; **no se demoren** don't be late

demostración *nf* demonstration; **una d. de fuerza/afecto** a show of strength, affection

demostrar [2] *vt* (**a**) *(mostrar)* to show, to demonstrate (**b**) *(evidenciar)* to prove

denominación *nf* denomination; **d. de origen** *(vinos)* = guarantee of region of origin

densidad *nf* density; **d. de población** population density

denso, -a *adj* dense

dentadura *nf* teeth, set of teeth; **d. postiza** false teeth, dentures

dentífrico, -a 1 *adj* **pasta/crema dentífrica** toothpaste **2** *nm* toothpaste

dentista *nmf* dentist

dentro *adv* (**a**) *(en el interior)* inside; **aquí d.** in here; **por d.** (on the) inside; **por d. está triste** deep down (inside) he feels sad (**b**) **d. de** *(lugar)* inside (**c**) **d. de poco** shortly, soon; **d. de un mes** in a month's time; **d. de lo que cabe** all things considered

denunciante *nmf* = person who reports a crime

denunciar [43] *vt* (**a**) *(delito)* to report

(**a** to) (**b**) *(criticar)* to denounce

departamento *nm* (**a**) department (**b**) *Ferroc* compartment (**c**) *(territorial)* province, district (**d**) *Arg (piso) Br* flat, *US* apartment

dependencia *nf* (**a**) dependence (**de** on) (**b**) **dependencias** premises

depender *vi* to depend (**de** on); *(económicamente)* to be dependent (**de** on)

dependiente 1 *adj* dependent (**de** on) **2** *nm Br* shop *or* sales assistant, *US* salesclerk

depilar *vt* to remove the hair from; *(cejas)* to pluck

depilatorio, -a *adj & nm* depilatory; **crema depilatoria** hair-remover, hair-removing cream

deporte *nm* sport; **hacer d.** to practise sports; **d. de aventura** adventure sport

deportista 1 *nmf (hombre)* sportsman; *(mujer)* sportswoman **2** *adj* sporty

deportivo, -a 1 *adj* sports; **club/ chaqueta d.** sports club/jacket **2** *nm Aut* sports car

depositar 1 *vt* (**a**) *Fin* to deposit (**b**) *(colocar)* to place, to put **2** **depositarse** *vpr* to settle

depósito *nm* (**a**) *Fin* deposit; **en d.** on deposit (**b**) *(de agua, gasolina)* tank (**c**) **d. de basuras** rubbish tip *o* dump; **d. de cadáveres** mortuary, morgue

depresión *nf* depression; **d. nerviosa** nervous breakdown

depresivo, -a *adj* depressive

deprimido, -a *adj* depressed

deprimir 1 *vt* to depress **2** **deprimirse** *vpr* to get depressed

deprisa *adv* quickly

depuradora *nf* purifier

depurar *vt* (**a**) *(agua)* to purify (**b**) *(partido)* to purge (**c**) *(estilo)* to refine

derecha *nf* (**a**) *(mano)* right hand (**b**) *(lugar)* right, right-hand side; **a la d.** to *o* on the right, on the right-hand side (**c**) *Pol* **la d.** the right; *Esp* **ser de derechas** to be right-wing

derecho, -a 1 *adj* (**a**) *(de la derecha)* right (**b**) *(recto)* upright, straight

2 *nm* (**a**) *(privilegio)* right; **derechos civiles/humanos** civil/human rights; **tener d. a** to be entitled to, to have the right to; **estar en su d.** to be within one's rights; **no hay d.** it's not fair (**b**) *Jur* law; **d. penal/político** criminal/ constitutional law (**c**) *Com* **derechos** duties; **derechos de autor** royalties; **derechos de matrícula** enrolment fees

3 *adv* **siga todo d.** go straight ahead

derivar 1 *vt* to divert; *(conversación)* to steer

2 *vi* (**a**) to drift (**b**) **d. de** to derive from **3** **derivarse** *vpr* (**a**) **derivarse de** *(proceder)* to result *o* stem from (**b**) **derivarse de** *Ling* to be derived from

dermoprotector *adj* skin-protecting

derramar 1 *vt* to spill; *(lágrimas)* to shed **2** **derramarse** *vpr* to spill

derrame *nm Med* discharge; **d. cerebral** brain haemorrhage

derrapar *vi* to skid

derretir [6] *vt*, **derretirse** *vpr* to melt; *(hielo, nieve)* to thaw

derribar *vt* (**a**) *(edificio)* to pull down, to knock down (**b**) *(avión)* to shoot down (**c**) *(gobierno)* to bring down

derrochar *vt* to waste, to squander

derroche *nm* (**a**) *(de dinero, energía)* waste, squandering (**b**) *(abundancia)* profusion, abundance

derrota *nf* (**a**) defeat (**b**) *Náut* (ship's) course

derrotar *vt* to defeat, to beat

derrumbar 1 *vt (edificio)* to knock down, to pull down **2** **derrumbarse** *vpr* to collapse, to fall down; *(techo)* to fall in, to cave in

desabrochar 1 *vt* to undo **2** **desabrocharse** *vpr* (**a**) **desabróchate la camisa** undo your shirt (**b**) *(prenda)* to come undone

desacreditar *vt* (**a**) *(desprestigiar)* to discredit, to bring into discredit (**b**) *(criticar)* to disparage

desacuerdo *nm* disagreement

desafiar [29] *vt* to challenge

desafinar 1 *vi* to sing out of tune; *(instrumento)* to play out of tune **2** *vt* to put out of tune **3 desafinarse** *vpr* to go out of tune

desafío *nm* challenge

desafortunado, -a *adj* unlucky, unfortunate

desagradable *adj* unpleasant, disagreeable

desagradecido, -a 1 *adj* ungrateful **2** *nm,f* ungrateful person

desagüe *nm (vaciado)* drain; *(cañería)* waste pipe, drainpipe

desahogarse [42] *vpr* to let off steam; **se desahogó de su depresión** he got his depression out of his system

desaire *nm* slight, rebuff

desajuste *nm* upset; **d. económico** economic imbalance; **un d. de horarios** clashing timetables

desaliñado, -a *adj* scruffy, untidy

desalojar *vt* (a) *(inquilino)* to evict; *(público)* to move on; *(lugar)* to evacuate (b) *(abandonar)* to move out of, to abandon

desamparado, -a 1 *adj (persona)* helpless, unprotected; *(lugar)* abandoned, forsaken **2** *nm,f* helpless o abandoned person

desangrarse *vpr* to lose (a lot of) blood

desanimar 1 *vt* to discourage, to dishearten **2 desanimarse** *vpr* to lose heart, to get discouraged

desaparecer [33] *vi* to disappear

desaparecido, -a 1 *adj* missing **2** *nm,f* missing person

desaparición *nf* disappearance

desapercibido, -a *adj* (a) *(inadvertido)* unnoticed; **pasar d.** to go unnoticed (b) *(desprevenido)* unprepared

desaprovechar *vt (dinero, tiempo)* to waste; **d. una ocasión** to fail to make the most of an opportunity

desarmador *nm Méx (herramienta)* screwdriver

desarrollado, -a *adj* developed; **país**

d. developed country

desarrollar 1 *vt* to develop **2 desarrollarse** *vpr* (a) *(persona, enfermedad)* to develop (b) *(tener lugar)* to take place

desarrollo *nm* development; **países en vías de d.** developing countries

desasosiego *nm* restlessness, uneasiness

desastre *nm* disaster; **eres un d.** you're just hopeless

desatar 1 *vt* to untie, to undo; *(provocar)* to unleash **2 desatarse** *vpr* (a) *(zapato, cordón)* to come undone (b) *(tormenta)* to break; *(pasión)* to run wild

desatino *nm* blunder

desatornillar *vt* to unscrew

desavenencia *nf* disagreement

desayunar 1 *vi* to have breakfast; *Fml* to breakfast **2** *vt* to have for breakfast

desayuno *nm* breakfast

desbarajuste *nm* confusion, disorder

desbaratar *vt* to ruin, to wreck; *(jersey)* to unravel

desbolado, -a *RP Fam* **1** *adj* messy, untidy **2** *nm,f* untidy person

desbolarse *vpr RP Fam* to undress, to strip

desbole *nm RP Fam* mess, chaos

desbordar 1 *vt* to overflow; *Fig* to overwhelm **2** *vi* to overflow (**de** with) **3 desbordarse** *vpr* to overflow, to flood

descabellado, -a *adj* crazy, wild

descafeinado, -a *adj* (a) *(café)* decaffeinated (b) *Fig* watered-down, diluted

descalificar [44] *vt* to disqualify

descalzarse [40] *vpr* to take one's shoes off

descalzo, -a *adj* barefoot

descampado *nm* waste ground

descansar *vi* (a) to rest, to have a rest; *(corto tiempo)* to take a break (b) *Euf* **que en paz descanse** may he/she rest in peace

descansillo *nm* landing

descanso *nm* (**a**) rest, break; **un día de d.** a day off (**b**) *(en cine)* intermission; *(en teatro)* Br interval, US intermission; *Dep* half-time, interval (**c**) *(alivio)* relief (**d**) *(rellano)* landing

descapotable *adj & nm* convertible

descarado, -a 1 *adj* (**a**) *(insolente)* cheeky, insolent; *(desvergonzado)* shameless (**b**) *Esp Fam* **d. que sí/no** *(por supuesto)* of course/course not **2** *nm,f* cheeky person

descarga *nf* (**a**) unloading (**b**) *Elec, Mil* discharge

descargar [42] **1** *vt* (**a**) to unload (**b**) *Elec* to discharge (**c**) *(disparar)* to fire; *(golpe)* to deal
2 *vi (tormenta)* to burst
3 descargarse *vpr (batería)* to go flat

descaro *nm* cheek, nerve; **¡qué d.!** what a cheek!

descarrilar *vi* to go off the rails, to be derailed

descartar 1 *vt* to rule out **2 descartarse** *vpr Naipes* to discard cards; **me descarté de un cinco** I got rid of a five

descendencia *nf* descendants; **morir sin d.** to die without issue

descender [3] **1** *vi* (**a**) *(temperatura, nivel)* to fall, to drop (**b**) **d. de** to descend from **2** *vt* to lower

descendiente *nmf* descendant

descenso *nm* (**a**) descent; *(de temperatura)* fall, drop (**b**) *Dep* relegation

descifrar *vt* to decipher; *(mensaje)* to decode; *(misterio)* to solve; *(motivos, causas)* to figure out

descolgar [2] **1** *vt (teléfono)* to pick up; *(cuadro, cortinas)* to take down **2 descolgarse** *vpr* to let oneself down, to slide down

descolorido, -a *adj* faded

descomponer [19] *(pp* **descompuesto) 1** *vt* (**a**) to break down (**b**) *(corromper)* to rot, to decompose **2 descomponerse** *vpr* (**a**) *(corromperse)* to rot, to decompose (**b**) *(ponerse nervioso)* to lose one's cool (**c**) *Am (tiempo atmosférico)* to turn nasty

descomposición *nf* (**a**) *(de carne)* decomposition, rotting; *(de país)* disintegration (**b**) *Quím* breakdown (**c**) *Esp (diarrea)* diarrhoea

descompostura *nf* (**a**) *Am (malestar)* unpleasant o nasty turn (**b**) *Méx, RP (avería)* breakdown

descompuesto, -a *adj* (**a**) *(podrido)* rotten, decomposed (**b**) *(furioso)* furious

desconcertante *adj* disconcerting

desconcertar [1] **1** *vt* to disconcert **2 desconcertarse** *vpr* to be bewildered, to be puzzled

desconfianza *nf* distrust, mistrust

desconfiar [29] *vi* **d. (de)** to distrust, to mistrust

descongelar *vt (nevera)* to defrost; *(créditos)* to unfreeze

descongestionar *vt* to clear

desconocer [34] *vt* not to know, to be unaware of

desconocido, -a 1 *adj* unknown; *(irreconocible)* unrecognizable
2 *nm* **lo d.** the unknown
3 *nm,f* stranger

desconocimiento *nm* ignorance, lack of knowledge

desconsiderado, -a 1 *adj* inconsiderate, thoughtless **2** *nm,f* inconsiderate o thoughtless person

desconsolado, -a *adj* disconsolate, grief-stricken

desconsuelo *nm* grief, sorrow

descontar [2] *vt* (**a**) to deduct (**b**) *Dep (tiempo)* to add on

descrédito *nm* disrepute, discredit

describir *(pp* **descrito)** *vt* to describe

descripción *nf* description

descrito, -a *pp de* **describir**

descuartizar [40] *vt* to cut up, to cut into pieces

descubierto, -a 1 *adj* open, uncovered; **a cielo d.** in the open **2** *nm* (**a**) *Fin* overdraft (**b**) **al d.** in the open; **poner al d.** to uncover, to bring out into the open

descubrimiento *nm* discovery

descubrir *(pp* **descubierto)** *vt* to

discover; *(conspiración)* to uncover; *(placa)* to unveil

descuento *nm* discount

descuidado, -a *adj* (**a**) *(desaseado)* untidy, neglected (**b**) *(negligente)* careless, negligent (**c**) *(desprevenido)* off one's guard

descuidar 1 *vt* to neglect, to overlook **2** *vi* **descuida, voy yo** don't worry, I'll go

3 descuidarse *vpr (despistarse)* to be careless; **como te descuides, llegarás tarde** if you don't watch out, you'll be late

descuido *nm* (**a**) oversight, mistake; **por d.** inadvertently, by mistake (**b**) *(negligencia)* negligence, carelessness

desde *adv* (**a**) *(tiempo)* since; **d. ahora** from now on; **d. el lunes/entonces** since Monday/then; **espero d. hace media hora** I've been waiting for half an hour; **no lo he visto d. hace un año** I haven't seen him for a year (**b**) *(lugar)* from; **d. arriba/abajo** from above/below (**c**) **d. luego** of course (**d**) **d. que** ever since; **d. que lo conozco** ever since I've known him

desdén *nm* disdain

desdentado, -a *adj* toothless

desdicha *nf* misfortune; **por d.** unfortunately

desdoblar *vt* to unfold

desear *vt* (**a**) to desire; **deja mucho que d.** it leaves a lot to be desired (**b**) *(querer)* to want; **¿qué desea?** can I help you?; **estoy deseando que vengas** I'm looking forward to your coming (**c**) **te deseo buena suerte/feliz Navidad** I wish you good luck/a merry Christmas

desechable *adj* disposable, throwaway

desechar *vt* (**a**) *(tirar)* to discard, to throw out *o* away (**b**) *(oferta)* to turn down, to refuse; *(idea, proyecto)* to drop, to discard

desecho *nm* (**a**) *(objeto usado)* unwanted object; **material de d.** *(residuos)* waste products (**b**) *(escoria)* dregs; **desechos** *(basura)* *Br* rubbish,

US garbage, *US* trash; *(residuos)* waste products

desembarcar [44] **1** *vt (mercancías)* to unload; *(personas)* to disembark **2** *vi* to disembark

desembocadura *nf* mouth

desembocar [44] *vi* **d. en** *(río)* to flow into; *(calle, situación)* to lead to

desempeñar *vt* (**a**) *(cargo)* to hold, to occupy; *(función)* to fulfil; *(papel)* to play (**b**) *(recuperar)* to redeem

desempleo *nm* unemployment; **cobrar el d.** to be on the dole

desencadenar 1 *vt* (**a**) to unchain (**b**) *(provocar)* to unleash **2 desencadenarse** *vpr* (**a**) *(prisionero)* to break loose; *(viento, pasión)* to rage (**b**) *(conflicto)* to start, to break out

desencajar 1 *vt (pieza)* to knock out; *(hueso)* to dislocate **2 desencajarse** *vpr* (**a**) *(pieza)* to come out; *(hueso)* to become dislocated (**b**) *(cara)* to become distorted

desencanto *nm* disenchantment

desenchufar *vt* to unplug

desenfadado, -a *adj* carefree, free and easy

desenfrenado, -a *adj* frantic, uncontrolled; *(vicio, pasión)* unbridled

desengañar 1 *vt* **d. a algn** to open sb's eyes **2 desengañarse** *vpr* (**a**) to be disappointed (**b**) *Fam* **¡desengáñate!** get real!

desengaño *nm* disappointment; **llevarse** *o* **sufrir un d. con algo** to be disappointed in sth

desenlace *nm* (**a**) result, outcome; **un feliz d.** a happy ending (**b**) *Cin, Teatro* ending, dénouement

desenmascarar *vt* to unmask

desenredar *vt* to untangle, to disentangle

desentenderse [3] *vpr* **se desentendió de mi problema** he didn't want to have anything to do with my problem

desenvolver [4] (*pp* **desenvuelto**) **1** *vt* to unwrap **2 desenvolverse** *vpr* (**a**) *(persona)* to manage, to cope (**b**) *(hecho)* to develop

desenvuelto, -a *adj* relaxed

deseo *nm* wish; *(sexual)* desire; **formular un d.** to make a wish

desequilibrado, -a 1 *adj* unbalanced **2** *nm,f* unbalanced person

desesperación *nf (desesperanza)* despair; *(exasperación)* desperation

desesperar 1 *vt* to drive to despair; *(exasperar)* to exasperate **2 desesperarse** *vpr* to despair

desestatización *nf Am* privatization, sell-off

desestatizar *vt Am* to privatize, to sell off

desfachatez *nf* cheek, nerve

desfallecer [33] *vi* (a) *(debilitarse)* to feel faint; *(desmayarse)* to faint (b) *(desanimarse)* to lose heart

desfigurar *vt (cara)* to disfigure; *(verdad)* to distort

desfiladero *nm* narrow pass

desfile *nm Mil* parade, march-past; **d. de modas** fashion show

desgana *nf* (a) *(inapetencia)* lack of appetite (b) *(apatía)* apathy, indifference; **con d.** reluctantly, unwillingly

desgastar 1 *vt* to wear out **2 desgastarse** *vpr (consumirse)* to wear out; *(persona)* to wear oneself out

desgracia *nf* (a) misfortune; **por d.** unfortunately (b) *(deshonor)* disgrace (c) **desgracias personales** loss of life

desgraciadamente *adv* unfortunately

desgraciado, -a 1 *adj* unfortunate; *(infeliz)* unhappy **2** *nm,f* unfortunate person; **un pobre d.** a poor devil

desgreñado, -a *adj* dishevelled

deshacer [15] *(pp* **deshecho) 1** *vt* (a) *(paquete)* to undo; *(maleta)* to unpack (b) *(plan)* to destroy, to ruin (c) *(acuerdo)* to break off (d) *(disolver)* to dissolve; *(derretir)* to melt

2 deshacerse *vpr* (a) to come undone o untied (b) **deshacerse de algn/algo** to get rid of sb/sth (c) *(afligirse)* to go to pieces; **deshacerse en lágrimas** to cry one's eyes out (d) *(disolverse)* to dissolve; *(derretirse)* to melt (e) *(niebla)* to fade away, to disappear

deshecho, -a *adj* (a) *(cama)* unmade; *(maleta)* unpacked; *(paquete)* unwrapped (b) *(roto)* broken, smashed (c) *(disuelto)* dissolved; *(derretido)* melted (d) *(abatido)* devastated, shattered (e) *(cansado)* exhausted, tired out

desheredar *vt* to disinherit

deshidratar *vt* to dehydrate

deshielo *nm* thaw

deshonesto, -a *adj* (a) dishonest (b) *(indecente)* indecent, improper

deshonor *nm*, **deshonra** *nf* dishonour

deshuesar *vt (carne)* to bone; *(fruto) Br* to stone, *US* to pit

desierto, -a 1 *nm* desert **2** *adj* (a) *(deshabitado)* uninhabited (b) *(vacío)* empty, deserted (c) *(premio)* void

designar *vt* (a) to designate (b) *(fecha, lugar)* to fix

desigual *adj* (a) uneven (b) *(lucha)* unequal (c) *(carácter)* changeable

desigualdad *nf* (a) inequality (b) *(del terreno)* unevenness

desilusión *nf* disappointment, disillusionment

desilusionar *vt* to disappoint, to disillusion

desinfectante *adj & nm* disinfectant

desinfectar *vt* to disinfect

desinflar 1 *vt* to deflate; *(rueda)* to let down **2 desinflarse** *vpr* to go flat

desintegración *nf* disintegration

desinterés *nm* (a) *(indiferencia)* lack of interest, apathy (b) *(generosidad)* unselfishness

desinteresado, -a *adj* selfless, unselfish

desistir *vi* to desist

deslave *nm* landslide *(caused by flooding or rain)*

desliz *nm* mistake, slip; **cometer** o **tener un d.** to slip up

deslizar [40] **1** *vi* to slide **2 deslizarse** *vpr* (a) *(patinar)* to slide (b) *(fluir)* to flow

deslumbrar *vt* to dazzle

desmadrarse *vpr Esp Fam* to go wild

desmaquillador, -a 1 *nm* make-up remover **2** *adj* **leche desmaquilladora** cleansing cream

desmaquillarse *vpr* to remove one's make-up

desmayarse *vpr* to faint

desmayo *nm* faint, fainting fit; **tener un d.** to faint

desmentir [5] *vt* to deny

desmesurado, -a *adj* excessive

desmontar 1 *vt* (**a**) *(desarmar)* to take to pieces, to dismantle (**b**) *(allanar)* to level **2** *vi* **d. (de)** to dismount, to get off

desmoralizar [40] *vt* to demoralize

desnatado, -a *adj (leche)* skimmed

desnivel *nm (en el terreno)* drop, difference in height

desnudar 1 *vt* to undress **2 desnudarse** *vpr* to get undressed

desnudo, -a 1 *adj* naked, nude **2** *nm Arte* nude

desnutrición *nf* malnutrition

desobedecer [33] *vt* to disobey

desobediente 1 *adj* disobedient **2** *nmf* disobedient person

desodorante *adj & nm* deodorant

desorden *nm* untidiness, mess; **¡qué d.!** what a mess!; **d. público** civil disorder

desordenar *vt* to make untidy, to mess up

desorganización *nf* disorganization

desorientar 1 *vt* to disorientate **2 desorientarse** *vpr* to lose one's sense of direction, to lose one's bearings; *Fig* to become disorientated

despachar *vt* (**a**) *(asunto)* to get through (**b**) *(correo)* to send, dispatch (**c**) *(en tienda)* to serve (**d**) *Fam (despedir)* to send packing, sack (**e**) *Am (facturar)* to check in

despacho *nm* (**a**) *(oficina)* office; *(en casa)* study (**b**) *(venta)* sale (**c**) *(comunicación)* dispatch

despacio *adv* (**a**) *(lentamente)* slowly (**b**) *(en voz baja)* quietly

despampanante *adj Fam* stunning

desparpajo *nm* self-assurance; **con d.** in a carefree manner

despecho *nm* spite; **por d.** out of spite

despectivo, -a *adj* derogatory, disparaging

despedida *nf* farewell, goodbye; **d. de soltera** hen party *o* night; **d. de soltero** stag party *o* night, *US* bachelor party

despedir [6] **1** *vt* (**a**) *(empleado)* to fire, *Br* to sack (**b**) *(decir adiós)* to see off, to say goodbye to (**c**) *(olor, humo etc)* to give off **2 despedirse** *vpr* (**a**) *(decir adiós)* to say goodbye (**de** to) (**b**) *Fig* to forget, to give up; **ya puedes despedirte del coche** you can say goodbye to the car

despegar [42] **1** *vt* to take off, to detach
2 *vi Av* to take off
3 despegarse *vpr* to come unstuck

despegue *nm* take-off

despeinar 1 *vt (pelo)* to ruffle; **d. a algn** to mess up sb's hair **2 despeinarse** *vpr* to get one's hair messed up

despejado, -a *adj* clear; *(cielo)* cloudless

despejar 1 *vt* to clear; *(misterio, dudas)* to clear up **2 despejarse** *vpr* (**a**) *(cielo)* to clear (**b**) *(persona)* to clear one's head

despensa *nf* pantry, larder

despeñadero *nm* cliff, precipice

desperdiciar [43] *vt* to waste; *(oportunidad)* to throw away

desperdicio *nm* (**a**) *(acto)* waste (**b**) **desperdicios** *(basura)* rubbish; *(desechos)* scraps, leftovers

desperezarse [40] *vpr* to stretch (oneself)

desperfecto *nm* (**a**) *(defecto)* flaw, imperfection (**b**) *(daño)* damage

despertador *nm* alarm clock

despertar [1] **1** *vt* to wake (up), to awaken; *Fig (sentimiento etc)* to arouse **2 despertarse** *vpr* to wake (up)

despido *nm* dismissal, sacking

despierto, -a *adj* (**a**) *(desvelado)*

awake (**b**) *(vivo)* quick, sharp

despiole *nm RP Fam* rumpus, shindy

despistado, -a 1 *adj* (**a**) *(olvidadizo)* scatterbrained (**b**) *(confuso)* confused **2** *nm,f* scatterbrain

despistar 1 *vt* (**a**) *(hacer perder la pista a)* to lose, to throw off one's scent (**b**) *Fig* to mislead **2 despistarse** *vpr* (**a**) *(perderse)* to get lost (**b**) *(distraerse)* to switch off

despiste *nm* (**a**) *(cualidad)* absent-mindedness (**b**) *(error)* slip-up

desplazar [40] **1** *vt* to displace **2 desplazarse** *vpr* to travel

desplegar [1] **1** *vt* (**a**) to open (out), to spread (out) (**b**) *(energías etc)* to use, to deploy **2 desplegarse** *vpr* (**a**) *(abrirse)* to open (out), to spread (out) (**b**) *Mil* to deploy

desplomarse *vpr* to collapse; *(precios)* to slump, to fall sharply

despojo *nm* (**a**) stripping (**b**) **despojos** leftovers, scraps

despreciar [43] *vt* (**a**) *(desdeñar)* to scorn, to despise (**b**) *(rechazar)* to reject, to spurn

desprecio *nm* (**a**) *(desdén)* scorn, disdain (**b**) *(desaire)* slight, snub

desprender 1 *vt* (**a**) *(separar)* to remove, to detach (**b**) *(olor, humo etc)* to give off **2 desprenderse** *vpr* (**a**) *(soltarse)* to come off *o* away (**b**) **desprenderse de** to rid oneself of, to free oneself from (**c**) **de aquí se desprende que ...** it can be deduced from this that ...

desprendimiento *nm* (**a**) loosening, detachment; **d. de tierras** landslide (**b**) *Fig (generosidad)* generosity, unselfishness

despreocuparse *vpr* (**a**) *(tranquilizarse)* to stop worrying (**b**) *(desentenderse)* to be unconcerned, to be indifferent (**de** to)

desprevenido, -a *adj* unprepared; **coger** *o* **pillar a algn d.** to catch sb unawares

desprolijo, -a *adj RP (casa)* messy, untidy; *(cuaderno)* untidy; *(persona)* unkempt, dishevelled

desproporcionado, -a *adj* disproportionate

después *adv* (**a**) afterwards, later; *(entonces)* then; *(seguidamente)* next; **una semana d.** a week later; **poco d.** soon after (**b**) *(lugar)* next (**c**) **d. de** after; **d. de la guerra** after the war; **mi calle está d. de la tuya** my street is the one after yours; **d. de cenar** after eating; **d. de todo** after all (**d**) **d. de que** after; **d. de que viniera** after he came

destacar [44] **1** *vt Fig* to emphasize, to stress

2 *vi* to stand out

3 destacarse *vpr* to stand out

destajo *nm* piecework; **trabajar a d.** to do piecework

destapador *nm Am* bottle opener

destapar 1 *vt* to take the lid off; *(botella)* to open; *Fig (asunto)* to uncover; *RP (caño)* to unblock **2 destaparse** *vpr* to get uncovered

destello *nm* flash, sparkle

destemplado, -a *adj* (**a**) *(voz, gesto)* sharp, snappy; **con cajas destempladas** rudely, brusquely (**b**) *(tiempo)* unpleasant (**c**) *(enfermo)* indisposed, out of sorts (**d**) *Mús* out of tune, discordant

desteñir [6] **1** *vt & vi* to discolour **2 desteñirse** *vpr* to lose colour, to fade

desterrar [1] *vt* to exile

destierro *nm* exile

destilación *nf* distillation

destilar *vt* to distil

destilería *nf* distillery

destinar *vt* (**a**) *(dinero etc)* to set aside, to assign (**b**) *(empleado)* to appoint

destinatario, -a *nm,f* (**a**) *(de carta)* addressee (**b**) *(de mercancías)* consignee

destino *nm* (**a**) *(rumbo)* destination; **el avión con d. a Bilbao** the plane to Bilbao (**b**) *(sino)* fate, fortune (**c**) *(de empleo)* post

destornillador *nm* screwdriver

destornillar *vt* to unscrew

destrozar [40] *vt* (**a**) *(destruir)* to

destroy; *(rasgar)* to tear to shreds *o* pieces (**b**) *(afligir)* to shatter; *(vida, reputación)* to ruin

destrucción *nf* destruction

destruir [37] *vt* to destroy

desubicado, -a *nm,f Andes, RP* **es un d.** he has no idea of how to behave

desuso *nm* disuse; **caer en d.** to fall into disuse; **en d.** obsolete, outdated

desvalijar *vt (robar)* to clean out, to rob; *(casa, tienda)* to burgle

desván *nm* attic, loft

desvanecimiento *nm (desmayo)* fainting fit

desvariar [29] *vi* to talk nonsense

desvelar 1 *vt* to keep awake **2 desvelarse** *vpr* (**a**) *(despabilarse)* to stay awake (**b**) *(desvivirse)* to devote oneself (**por** to) (**c**) *CAm, Méx (quedarse despierto)* to stay up *o* awake

desventaja *nf* (**a**) disadvantage; **estar en d.** to be at a disadvantage (**b**) *(inconveniente)* drawback

desvergonzado, -a 1 *adj* (**a**) *(indecente)* shameless (**b**) *(descarado)* insolent **2** *nm,f* (**a**) *(sinvergüenza)* shameless person (**b**) *(fresco)* insolent *o* cheeky person

desvestir [6] **1** *vt* to undress **2 desvestirse** *vpr* to undress (oneself)

desviar [29] **1** *vt (río, carretera)* to divert; *(golpe, conversación)* to deflect; **d. la mirada** to look away **2 desviarse** *vpr* to go off course; *(coche)* to turn off; *Fig* **desviarse del tema** to digress

desvío *nm Br* diversion, *US* detour

detallar *vt* to give the details of

detalle *nm* (**a**) detail; **entrar en detalles** to go into details (**b**) *(delicadeza)* nice thought, nicety; **¡qué d.!** how nice!, how sweet! (**c**) *(toque decorativo)* touch, ornament

detallista 1 *adj* perfectionist **2** *nmf Com* retailer

detectar *vt* to detect

detective *nmf* detective; **d. privado** private detective *o* eye

detener [24] **1** *vt* (**a**) to stop, to halt (**b**)

Jur (arrestar) to arrest, to detain **2 detenerse** *vpr* to stop

detenido, -a 1 *adj* (**a**) *(parado)* standing still, stopped (**b**) *(arrestado)* detained (**c**) *(minucioso)* detailed, thorough **2** *nm,f* detainee, person under arrest

detergente *adj & nm* detergent

determinación *nf* (**a**) determination; **con d.** determinedly (**b**) *(decisión)* decision

determinado, -a *adj* (**a**) *(preciso)* definite, precise (**b**) *(resuelto)* decisive, resolute (**c**) *Ling* definite

determinante *adj* decisive

determinar 1 *vt* (**a**) *(fecha etc)* to fix, to set (**b**) *(decidir)* to decide on (**c**) *(condicionar)* to determine (**d**) *(ocasionar)* to bring about **2 determinarse** *vpr* to make up one's mind to

detestable *adj* detestable, repulsive

detestar *vt* to detest, to hate

detrás *adv* (**a**) behind, on *o* at the back (**de** of) (**b**) **d. de** behind

deuda *nf* debt; **estoy en d. contigo** *(monetaria)* I am in debt to you; *(moral)* I am indebted to you; **d. del Estado** public debt; **d. pública** *Br* national debt, *US* public debt

devaluación *nf* devaluation

devaluar [30] *vt* to devalue

devoción *nf* (**a**) *Rel* devoutness (**b**) *(al trabajo etc)* devotion; *Fam* **Juan no es santo de mi d.** Juan isn't really my cup of tea

devolución *nf* (**a**) giving back, return; *Com* refund, repayment (**b**) *Jur* devolution

devolver [4] (*pp* **devuelto**) **1** *vt* to give back, to return; *(dinero)* to refund **2** *vi (vomitar)* to vomit, to throw *o* bring up **3 devolverse** *vpr Am salvo RP* to come back

devorar *vt* to devour

devoto, -a 1 *adj* pious, devout **2** *nm,f* (**a**) *Rel* pious person (**b**) *(seguidor)* devotee

devuelto, -a *pp de* **devolver**

DGT *nf* (*abr* **Dirección General de Tráfico**) = government department responsible for road transport

di (**a**) *pt indef de* **dar** (**b**) *imperat de* **decir**

día *nm* day; **¿qué d. es hoy?** what's the date today?; **d. a d.** day by day; **de d.** by day; **durante el d.** during the daytime; **de un d. para otro** overnight; **un d. sí y otro no** every other day; **pan del d.** fresh bread; **hoy (en) d.** nowadays; **el d. de mañana** in the future; *Fig* **estar al d.** to be up to date; *Fig* **poner al d.** to bring up to date; **d. festivo** holiday; **d. laborable** working day; **d. libre** free day, day off; **es de d.** it is daylight; **hace buen/mal d.** it's a nice/bad day, the weather is nice/bad today

diabetes *nf inv* diabetes

diabético, -a *adj & nm,f* diabetic

diablo *nm* devil; *Fam* **¡al d. con …!** to hell with …!; *Fam* **vete al d.** get lost; *Fam* **¿qué/cómo diablos …?** what/ how the hell …?

diablura *nf* mischief

diabólico, -a *adj* (**a**) *(del diablo)* diabolic (**b**) *(muy malo, difícil)* diabolical

diadema *nf* tiara

diagnosticar [44] *vt* to diagnose

diagnóstico *nm* diagnosis

dialecto *nm* dialect

diálogo *nm* dialogue

diamante *nm* diamond

diana *nf* (**a**) *Mil* reveille (**b**) *(blanco)* bull's eye

diapositiva *nf* slide

diariero, -a *nm,f* *Andes, RP* newspaper seller

diario, -a 1 *nm* (**a**) *Prensa* (daily) newspaper (**b**) *(memorias)* diary; *Náut* **d. de a bordo, d. de navegación** logbook **2** *adj* daily; **a d.** daily, every day

diarrea *nf* diarrhoea

dibujar *vt* to draw

dibujo *nm* (**a**) drawing; **dibujos animados** cartoons (**b**) *(arte)* drawing; **d. artístico** artistic drawing; **d.**

lineal draughtsmanship

diccionario *nm* dictionary; **buscar** *o* **mirar una palabra en el d.** to look up a word in the dictionary

dicha *nf* happiness

dicho, -a *adj* (**a**) said; **mejor d.** or rather; **d. de otro modo** to put it another way; **d. sea de paso** let it be said in passing; **d. y hecho** no sooner said than done (**b**) **dicha persona** *(mencionado)* the above-mentioned person

diciembre *nm* December

dictado *nm* dictation; *Fig* **dictados** dictates

dictador, -a *nm,f* dictator

dictadura *nf* dictatorship

dictamen *nm* *(juicio)* ruling; *(informe)* report

dictar *vt* (**a**) to dictate (**b**) *(ley)* to enact; *(sentencia)* to pass

dictatorial *adj* dictatorial

diecinueve *adj & nm inv* nineteen

dieciocho *adj & nm inv* eighteen

dieciséis *adj & nm inv* sixteen

diecisiete *adj & nm inv* seventeen

diente *nm* tooth; *Téc* cog; *(de ajo)* clove; **d. de leche** milk tooth; **dientes postizos** false teeth; *Fig* **hablar entre dientes** to mumble; *Fig* **poner los dientes largos a algn** to make sb green with envy

diera *subj imperf de* **dar**

diéresis *nf inv* diaeresis

diesel *adj & nm* diesel

diestro, -a 1 *adj* (**a**) *(hábil)* skilful, clever (**b**) *Esp* **a d. y siniestro** right, left and centre **2** *nm* *Taurom* bullfighter, matador

dieta *nf* (**a**) diet; **estar a d.** to be on a diet (**b**) **dietas** expense *o* subsistence allowance

dietética *nf* dietetics *sing*

diez *adj & nm inv* ten

diferencia *nf* difference; **a d. de** unlike

diferenciar [43] **1** *vt* to differentiate, to distinguish (**entre** between) **2** **diferenciarse** *vpr* to differ (**de** from), to be different (**de** from o *US* **than**)

diferente 1 *adj* different (**de** from o *US* than) **2** *adv* differently

diferido, -a *adj TV* **en d.** recorded

diferir [5] **1** *vt (posponer)* to postpone, to put off **2** *vi (diferenciarse)* to differ, to be different; **d. de algn en algo** to differ from sb in sth

difícil *adj* difficult, hard; **d. de creer/ hacer** difficult to believe/do; **es d. que venga** it is unlikely that she'll come

dificultad *nf* difficulty; *(aprieto)* trouble, problem

difundir *vt*, **difundirse** *vpr* to spread

difunto, -a 1 *adj* late, deceased **2** *nm,f* deceased

difusión *nf* **(a)** *(de noticia)* spreading; **tener gran d.** to be widely broadcast **(b)** *Rad, TV* broadcasting

digerir [5] *vt* to digest; *Fig* to assimilate

digestión *nf* digestion; **corte de d.** sudden indigestion

digitador, -a *nm,f Am* keyboarder

digital *adj* digital; **huellas digitales** fingerprints; **tocadiscos d.** CD player

digitar *vt Am (teclear)* to key, to type

dígito *nm* digit

dignarse *vpr* **d. (a)** to deign to, to condescend to

dignidad *nf* dignity

digno, -a *adj* **(a)** *(merecedor)* worthy; **d. de admiración** worthy of admiration; **d. de mención/verse** worth mentioning/seeing **(b)** *(decoroso)* decent, good

digo *indic pres de* **decir**

dilema *nm* dilemma

diligente *adj* diligent

diluviar [43] *v impers* to pour with rain

diluvio *nm* flood; **el D. (Universal)** the Flood

dimensión *nf* **(a)** dimension, size; **de gran d.** very large **(b)** *Fig (importancia)* importance

diminuto, -a *adj* minute, tiny

dimitir *vi* to resign (**de** from); **d. de un**

cargo to give in o tender one's resignation

Dinamarca *n* Denmark

dinámico, -a *adj* dynamic

dinamita *nf* dynamite

dinastía *nf* dynasty

dinero *nm* money; **d. contante (y sonante)** cash; **d. efectivo** o **en metálico** cash; **gente de d.** wealthy people

dinosaurio *nm* dinosaur

diócesis *nf inv* diocese

dios *nm* god; **¡D. mío!** my God!; **¡por D.!** for goodness sake!; **a la buena de D.** any old how; **hacer algo como D. manda** to do sth properly; *Fam* **ni d.** nobody; *Fam* **todo d.** everybody

diploma *nm* diploma

diplomacia *nf* diplomacy

diplomado, -a 1 *adj* qualified **2** *nm,f* holder of a diploma

diplomarse *vpr* to graduate

diplomático, -a 1 *adj* diplomatic; **cuerpo d.** diplomatic corps **2** *nm,f* diplomat

diplomatura *nf Educ* ≃ diploma, = qualification obtained after three years of university study

diptongo *nm* diphthong

diputación *nf Esp* **d. provincial** = governing body of each province, ≃ county council

diputado, -a *nm,f Br* ≃ Member of Parliament, MP, *US* ≃ representative

dique *nm* dike

dirección *nf* **(a)** direction; *Aut (en letrero)* **d. prohibida** no entry; **calle de d. única** one-way street **(b)** *(señas)* address; *Informát* **d. de correo electrónico** e-mail address **(c)** *Cin, Teatro* direction **(d)** *(destino)* destination **(e)** *Aut, Téc* steering **(f)** *(dirigentes)* management; *(cargo)* directorship; *(de un partido)* leadership; *(de un colegio)* headship

direccional *nm* o *nf Col, Ecuad, Méx Br* indicator, *US* turn signal

directa *nf Aut* top gear

directo, -a adj direct; *TV, Rad* **en d.** live

director, -a nm,f *(de empresa)* director; *(de hotel, banco)* manager; *(de colegio)* Br headmaster, f headmistress, US principal; *(de periódico)* editor; **d. de cine** movie o Br film director; **d. de orquesta** conductor; **d. gerente** managing director

directorio nm Informát directory; Am salvo RP **d. telefónico** telephone directory

dirigente **1** adj leading; **clase d.** ruling class **2** nmf leader

dirigir [57] **1** vt to direct; *(empresa)* to manage; *(negocio, colegio)* to run; *(orquesta)* to conduct; *(partido)* to lead; *(periódico)* to edit; *(coche, barco)* to steer; **d. la palabra a algn** to speak to sb

2 dirigirse vpr (a) **dirigirse a** o **hacia** to go to, to make one's way towards (b) *(escribir)* to write; **diríjase al apartado de correos 42** write to PO Box 42 (c) *(hablar)* to speak

discar vt Andes, RP to dial

discernir [54] vt to discern, to distinguish; **d. algo de algo** to distinguish sth from sth

disciplina nf discipline

discípulo, -a nm,f disciple

disco nm (a) disc; **d. de freno** brake disc (b) Mús record; **d. compacto** compact disc (c) Informát disk; **d. duro** o **fijo/flexible** hard/floppy disk (d) Dep discus (e) Tel dial

discoteca nf (a) *(lugar)* discotheque (b) *(colección)* record collection

discreción nf (a) discretion (b) **a d.** at will

discrepancia nf *(desacuerdo)* disagreement; *(diferencia)* discrepancy

discreto, -a adj (a) discreet (b) *(mediocre)* average

discriminación nf discrimination

discriminar vt (a) to discriminate against (b) Fml *(diferenciar)* to discriminate between, to distinguish

disculpa nf excuse; **dar disculpas** to make excuses; **pedir disculpas a**

algn to apologize to sb

disculpar **1** vt to excuse **2 disculparse** vpr to apologize (**por** for)

discurrir vi (a) *(reflexionar)* to think (b) Fig *(transcurrir)* to pass, to go by (c) Fml *(río)* to wander

discurso nm speech; **dar** o **pronunciar un d.** to make a speech

discusión nf argument

discutible adj debatable

discutir **1** vi to argue (**de** about) **2** vt to discuss, to talk about

disecar [44] vt (a) *(animal)* to stuff (b) *(planta)* to dry

diseñador, -a nm,f designer; **d. gráfico** graphic designer

diseñar vt to design

diseño nm design; **d. de interiores** interior design

disfraz nm disguise; *(para fiesta)* fancy dress; **fiesta de disfraces** fancy dress party

disfrazar [40] **1** vt to disguise **2 disfrazarse** vpr to disguise oneself; **disfrazarse de pirata** to dress up as a pirate

disfrutar **1** vi (a) *(gozar)* to enjoy oneself (b) *(poseer)* **d. (de)** to enjoy **2** vt to enjoy

disgustar **1** vt to upset **2 disgustarse** vpr (a) *(molestarse)* to get upset, to be annoyed (b) *(dos amigos)* to quarrel

disgusto nm (a) *(preocupación)* annoyance; **llevarse un d.** to get upset; **dar un d. a algn** to upset sb (b) *(desgracia)* trouble; **a d.** unwillingly; **sentirse** o **estar a d.** to feel ill at ease (c) *(desavenencia)* fall-out, disagreement

disidente adj & nmf dissident

disimular vt to conceal, to hide

disminución nf decrease

disminuir [37] **1** vt to reduce **2** vi to diminish

disolvente adj & nm solvent

disolver [4] *(pp* **disuelto**) vt to dissolve

disparar **1** vt *(pistola etc)* to fire; *(flecha, balón)* to shoot; **d. a algn** to shoot at sb **2 dispararse** *vpr* (**a**) *(arma)* to go off, to fire (**b**) *(precios)* to rocket

disparate *nm* (**a**) *(dicho)* nonsense; **decir disparates** to talk nonsense (**b**) *(acto)* foolish act

disparo *nm* shot; *Dep* **d. a puerta** shot

dispensar *vt* (**a**) *(disculpar)* to pardon, to forgive (**b**) *(eximir)* to exempt

dispersar 1 *vt* to disperse; *(esparcir)* to scatter **2 dispersarse** *vpr* to disperse

disponer [19] (*pp* **dispuesto**) **1** *vt* (**a**) *(arreglar)* to arrange, to set out (**b**) *(ordenar)* to order

  2 *vi* **d. de** to have at one's disposal

  3 disponerse *vpr* to prepare, to get ready

disponible *adj* available

disposición *nf* (**a**) *(uso)* disposal; **a su d.** at your disposal *o* service (**b**) *(colocación)* arrangement, layout (**c**) **no estar en d. de** not to be prepared to (**d**) *(orden)* order, law

dispositivo *nm* device

dispuesto, -a *adj* (**a**) *(ordenado)* arranged (**b**) *(a punto)* ready (**c**) *(decidido)* determined; **no estar d. a** not to be prepared to (**d**) **según lo d. por la ley** in accordance with what the law stipulates

disputa *nf (discusión)* argument; *(contienda)* contest

disputar 1 *vt* (**a**) *(premio)* to compete for (**b**) *Dep (partido)* to play **2 disputarse** *vpr* *(premio)* to compete for

disquete *nm Informát* diskette, floppy disk

disquetera *nf Informát* disk drive

distancia *nf* distance; **a d.** from a distance

distanciar [43] **1** *vt* to separate **2 distanciarse** *vpr* to become separated; *(de otra persona)* to distance oneself

distante *adj* distant, far-off

distinción *nf* distinction; **a d. de** unlike; **sin d. de** irrespective of

distinguido, -a *adj* distinguished

distinguir [59] **1** *vt* (**a**) *(diferenciar)* to distinguish (**b**) *(reconocer)* to recognize (**c**) *(honrar)* to honour

  2 *vi (diferenciar)* to discriminate

  3 distinguirse *vpr* to distinguish oneself

distintivo, -a 1 *adj* distinctive, distinguishing **2** *nm* distinctive sign *o* mark

distinto, -a *adj* different

distracción *nf* (**a**) entertainment; *(pasatiempo)* pastime, hobby (**b**) *(descuido)* distraction, absent-mindedness

distraer [25] **1** *vt* (**a**) *(atención)* to distract (**b**) *(divertir)* to entertain, to amuse **2 distraerse** *vpr* (**a**) *(divertirse)* to amuse oneself (**b**) *(abstraerse)* to let one's mind wander

distraído, -a *adj* (**a**) *(divertido)* entertaining (**b**) *(abstraído)* absent-minded

distribución *nf* (**a**) distribution (**b**) *(disposición)* layout

distribuir [37] *vt* to distribute; *(trabajo)* to share out

distrito *nm* district; **d. postal** postal district

disturbio *nm* riot, disturbance

disuelto, -a *pp de* **disolver**

diurno, -a *adj* daytime

diva *nf Mús* diva, prima donna

diván *nm* divan, couch

diversidad *nf* diversity

diversión *nf* fun

diverso, -a *adj* different; **diversos** several, various

divertido, -a *adj* amusing, funny

divertir [5] **1** *vt* to amuse, to entertain **2 divertirse** *vpr* to enjoy oneself, to have a good time; **¡que te diviertas!** enjoy yourself!, have fun!

dividir 1 *vt* to divide (**en** into); *Mat* **15 dividido entre 3** 15 divided by 3 **2 dividirse** *vpr* to divide, to split up

divino, -a *adj* divine

divisa *nf* (**a**) *(emblema)* symbol, emblem (**b**) *Com* **divisas** foreign currency

divisar *vt* to make out, to discern

división *nf* division

divorciado, -a 1 *adj* divorced **2** *nm,f* divorcé, *f* divorcée

divorciar [43] **1** *vt* to divorce **2 divorciarse** *vpr* to get divorced; **se divorció de él** she divorced him, she got a divorce from him

divorcio *nm* divorce

divulgar [42] *vt* to disclose; *Rad, TV* to broadcast

dizque *adv Andes, Carib, Méx Fam* apparently

DNI *nm* (*abr* **Documento Nacional de Identidad**) Identity Card, ID card

dobladillo *nm* (*de traje, vestido*) hem; (*de pantalón*) *Br* turn-up, *US* cuff

doblaje *nm Cin* dubbing

doblar 1 *vt* (**a**) to double; **me dobla la edad** he is twice as old as I am (**b**) (*plegar*) to fold *o* turn up (**c**) (*torcer*) to bend (**d**) (*la esquina*) to go round (**e**) (*película*) to dub
2 *vi* (**a**) (*girar*) to turn; **d. a la derecha/izquierda** to turn right/left (**b**) (*campanas*) to toll
3 doblarse *vpr* (**a**) (*plegarse*) to fold (**b**) (*torcerse*) to bend

doble 1 *adj* double; **arma de d. filo** double-edged weapon **2** *nm* (**a**) double; **gana el d. que tú** she earns twice as much as you do (**b**) *Dep* **dobles** doubles

doce *adj & nm inv* twelve

docena *nf* dozen

docente *adj* teaching; **centro d.** educational centre

dócil *adj* docile

doctor, -a *nm,f* doctor

doctorado *nm Univ* doctorate, PhD

doctorarse *vpr* to get one's doctorate (**en** in)

doctrina *nf* doctrine

documentación *nf* documentation; (*DNI, de conducir etc*) papers

documental *adj & nm* documentary

documento *nm* document; **d. nacional de identidad** identity card

dogma *nm* dogma

dogmático, -a *adj & nm,f* dogmatic

dólar *nm* dollar

doler [4] **1** *vi* to hurt, to ache; **me duele la cabeza** I've got a headache; **me duele la mano** my hand is sore **2 dolerse** *vpr* to be sorry *o* sad

dolor *nm* (**a**) *Med* pain; **d. de cabeza** headache; **d. de muelas** toothache (**b**) (*pena*) grief, sorrow

doloroso, -a *adj* painful

domador, -a *nm,f* (*de animales salvajes*) tamer; (*de caballos*) breaker; **d. de leones** lion tamer

domar *vt* to tame; (*caballo*) to break in

domesticar [44] *vt* to domesticate; (*animal*) to tame

doméstico, -a *adj* domestic; **animal d.** pet

domicilio *nm* home, residence; (*señas*) address; **sin d. fijo** of no fixed abode; **d. fiscal** registered office

dominante *adj* (**a**) dominant (**b**) (*déspota*) domineering

dominar 1 *vt* (**a**) to dominate, to rule (**b**) (*situación*) to control; (*idioma*) to speak very well; (*asunto*) to master; (*paisaje etc*) to overlook
2 *vi* (**a**) to dominate (**b**) (*resaltar*) to stand out
3 dominarse *vpr* to control oneself

domingo *nm inv* Sunday; **D. de Resurrección** *o* **Pascua** Easter Sunday

dominguero, -a *nm,f Fam* (*excursionista*) weekend tripper; (*conductor*) weekend driver

dominical 1 *adj* Sunday **2** *nm* (*suplemento*) Sunday supplement

dominio *nm* (**a**) (*poder*) control; (*de un idioma*) command; **d. de sí mismo** self-control (**b**) (*ámbito*) scope, sphere; **ser del d. público** to be public knowledge (**c**) (*territorio*) dominion (**d**) *Informát* domain

dominó, dómino *nm* dominoes

don¹ *nm* (**a**) (*habilidad*) gift, talent; **tener el d. de** to have a knack for; **tener d. de gentes** to get on well with people (**b**) (*regalo*) present, gift

don² *nm* **Señor D. José García** Mr José Garcia; **D. Fulano de Tal** Mr So-and-So; **un d. nadie** a nobody

donante *nmf* donor; *Med* **d. de sangre** blood donor

donativo *nm* donation

donde *adv rel* where; **a** *o* **en d.** where; **de** *o* **desde d.** from where; **está d. lo dejaste** it is where you left it; *Fam* **está d. su tía** he's at his aunt's

> **donde** combines with the preposition **a** to form **adonde** when following a noun, a pronoun or an adverb expressing location (e.g. **el sitio adonde vamos** the place where we're going; **es allí adonde iban** that's where they were going)

dónde *adv interr* where?; **¿de d. eres?** where are you from?; **¿por d. se va a la playa?** which way is it to the beach?

> **dónde** can combine with the preposition **a** to form **adónde** (e.g. **¿adónde vamos?** where are we going?)

dónut® *nm* (*pl* **dónuts**) doughnut

dopaje *nm Dep* drug-taking

dopar 1 *vt* (*caballo etc*) to dope **2 doparse** *vpr* to take drugs

doping *nm* (*pl* **dopings**) *Dep* drug-taking

dorado, -a 1 *adj* golden **2** *nm Téc* gilding

dormilón, -ona 1 *adj Fam* sleepy-headed
 2 *nm,f* sleepyhead
 3 *nf Ven* nightdress

dormir [7] **1** *vi* to sleep; **tener ganas de d.** to feel sleepy;
 2 *vt* **d. la siesta** to have an afternoon nap
 3 dormirse *vpr* to fall asleep; **se me ha dormido el brazo** my arm has gone to sleep

dormitorio *nm* (**a**) (*de una casa*) bedroom (**b**) (*de colegio, residencia*) dormitory; **ciudad d.** dormitory town

dorsal 1 *adj* **espina d.** spine **2** *nm Dep* number

dorso *nm* back; **instrucciones al d.** instructions over; **véase al d.** see overleaf

dos *adj & nm inv* two; **los d.** both;

nosotros/vosotros d. both of us/you; *Fam* **cada d. por tres** every other minute; *Fam* **en un d. por tres** in a flash

doscientos, -as *adj & nm* two hundred

dosis *nf inv* dose

dotado, -a *adj* (**a**) (*persona*) gifted (**b**) (*equipado*) equipped; **d. de** provided with

dotar *vt* **d. de** to provide with

doy *indic pres de* **dar**

Dr. (*abr* **doctor**) Dr

Dra. (*abr* **doctora**) Dr

dragón *nm* dragon

drama *nm* drama

dramático, -a *adj* dramatic

dramaturgo, -a *nm,f* playwright, dramatist

droga *nf* drug; **d. blanda/dura** soft/hard drug

drogadicción *nf* drug addiction

drogadicto, -a *nm,f* drug addict

droguería *nf Esp* = shop selling paint, cleaning materials, etc

dto. (*abr* **descuento**) discount

dual *adj* dual

ducha *nf* shower; **darse/tomar una d.** to take/have a shower

ducharse *vpr* to shower, to have *o* take a shower

duda *nf* doubt; **sin d.** without a doubt; **no cabe d.** (there is) no doubt; **poner algo en d.** to question sth; **sacar a algn de dudas** to dispel sb's doubts

dudar 1 *vi* (**a**) to doubt (**b**) (*vacilar*) to hesitate (**en** to); **dudaba entre ir o quedarme** I hesitated whether to go *o* to stay (**c**) **d. de algn** (*desconfiar*) to suspect sb **2** *vt* to doubt

duelo¹ *nm* (*combate*) duel

duelo² *nm* (*luto*) mourning

duende *nm* (**a**) (*espíritu*) goblin, elf (**b**) (*encanto*) magic, charm

dueño *nm* owner; (*de casa etc*) landlord; *Fig* **ser d. de sí mismo** to be self-possessed

dulce 1 *adj* (**a**) (*sabor*) sweet (**b**) (*carácter, voz*) gentle (**c**) (*metal*) soft (**d**) **agua d.** fresh water **2** *nm* (**a**) *Culin (pastel)* cake (**b**) *(caramelo) Br* sweet, *US* candy

dulzura *nf* (**a**) sweetness (**b**) *Fig* gentleness, softness

duna *nf* dune

dúo *nm* duet

dúplex *nm* (**a**) *(piso)* duplex, duplex apartment (**b**) *Tel* link-up

duplicar [44] **1** *vt* to duplicate; *(cifras)* to double **2 duplicarse** *vpr* to double

duración *nf* duration, length; **disco de larga d.** long-playing record

durante *prep* during; **d. el día** during the day; **d. todo el día** all day long; **viví en La Coruña d. un año** I lived in La Coruña for a year

durar *vi* (**a**) to last (**b**) *(ropa, calzado)* to wear well, to last

durazno *nm (fruto)* peach; *(árbol)* peach tree

Durex® *nm Méx Br* Sellotape®, *US* Scotch® tape

dureza *nf* (**a**) hardness; *(severidad)* harshness, severity (**b**) *(callosidad)* corn

duro, -a 1 *adj* (**a**) hard; *Dep* **juego d.** rough play (**b**) *(resistente)* tough; *(severo)* hard (**c**) *(clima)* harsh **2** *nm Esp Antes (moneda)* 5-peseta coin **3** *adv* hard; **trabajar d.** to work hard

DVD *nm (abr* **Disco Versátil Digital)** DVD

Ee

e *conj* and

> **e** is used instead of **y** in front of words beginning with "i" or "hi" (e.g. **apoyo e interés** support and interest; **corazón e hígado** heart and liver)

ébano *nm* ebony

ebrio, -a *adj* inebriated; **e. de dicha** drunk with joy

ebullición *nf* boiling; **punto de e.** boiling point

echar 1 *vt* (**a**) *(lanzar)* to throw; *Fig* **e. una mano** to give a hand; *Fig* **e. una mirada/una ojeada** to have a look/a quick look *o* glance

(**b**) *(carta)* to post, *US* to mail; *(vino, agua)* to pour; **e. sal al estofado** to put salt in the stew; **e. gasolina al coche** to put *Br* petrol *o US* gas in the car

(**c**) *(expulsar)* to throw out; *(despedir)* to fire, *Br* to sack

(**d**) *(humo, olor etc)* to give off

(**e**) *Fam (película)* to show

(**f**) **le echó 37 años** he reckoned she was about 37

(**g**) **e. de menos** *o* **en falta** to miss

(**h**) **e. abajo** *(edificio)* to demolish

2 *vi* (+ **a** + *infinitivo*) *(empezar)* to begin to; **echó a correr** he ran off

3 echarse *vpr* (**a**) *(tumbarse)* to lie down; *(lanzarse)* to throw oneself

(**b**) **échate a un lado** stand aside; *Fig* **echarse atrás** to get cold feet

(**c**) *Fam* **echarse novio/novia** to get a boyfriend/girlfriend

(**d**) (+ **a** + *infinitivo*) *(empezar)* to begin to; **echarse a llorar** to burst into tears; **echarse a reír** to burst out laughing; **echarse a perder** *(comida)* to go bad

eclesiástico, -a 1 *adj* ecclesiastical **2** *nm* clergyman

eclipse *nm* eclipse

eco *nm* echo; *Fig* **hacerse e. de una noticia** to publish an item of news; **tener e.** to arouse interest

ecología *nf* ecology

ecológico, -a *adj* ecological; *(alimentos)* organic; *(detergente)* environmentally-friendly

economía *nf* (**a**) economy; **con e.** economically (**b**) *(ciencia)* economics *sing*

económico, -a *adj* (**a**) economic (**b**) *(barato)* economical, inexpensive (**c**) *(persona)* thrifty

economista *nmf* economist

ecosistema *nm* ecosystem

ecuación *nf* equation

Ecuador *n* Ecuador

ecuador *nm Geog* equator

ecuatoriano, -a *adj & nm,f* Ecuadorian

edad *nf* age; **¿qué e. tienes?** how old are you?; **la tercera e.** senior citizens; **E. Media** Middle Ages

edición *nf* (**a**) *(publicación)* publication; *(de sellos)* issue (**b**) *(conjunto de ejemplares)* edition

edificante *adj* edifying

edificar [44] *vt* to build

edificio *nm* building

editar *vt* (**a**) *(libro, periódico)* to publish; *(disco)* to release (**b**) *Informát* to edit

editor, -a 1 *adj* publishing **2** *nm,f* publisher

editorial 1 *adj* publishing **2** *nf* publisher, publishing house **3** *nm Prensa* editorial, leader article

edredón *nm* eiderdown, *Br* duvet

educación *nf* (**a**) education; **e. física** physical education (**b**) *(formación)* upbringing (**c**) **buena/mala e.** *(modales)* good/bad manners; **falta de e.** bad manners

educado, -a *adj* polite

educar [44] *vt (hijos)* to raise; *(alumnos)* to educate; *(la voz)* to train

educativo, -a *adj* educational; **sistema e.** education system

EE.UU. *(abr* **Estados Unidos)** USA

efectivo, -a 1 *adj* effective; **hacer algo e.** to carry sth out; *Fin* **hacer e. un cheque** to cash a cheque **2** *nm* (**a**) *Fin* **en e.** in cash (**b**) *Mil* **efectivos** forces

efecto *nm* (**a**) *(resultado)* effect; **efectos especiales/sonoros** special/ sound effects; **efectos personales** personal belongings *o* effects; **a efectos de …** for the purposes of …; **en e.** quite!, yes indeed! (**b**) *(impresión)* impression; **causar** *o* **hacer e.** to make an impression (**c**) *Dep* spin

efectuar [30] *vt* to carry out; *(viaje)* to make; *Com (pedido)* to place

eficacia *nf (de persona)* efficiency; *(de remedio etc)* effectiveness

eficaz *adj (persona)* efficient; *(remedio, medida etc)* effective

eficiente *adj* efficient

EGB *nf Educ (abr* **Enseñanza General Básica)** = formerly, stage of Spanish education system for pupils aged 6-14

Egipto *n* Egypt

egoísmo *nm* egoism, selfishness

egoísta 1 *adj* ego(t)istic, selfish **2** *nmf* ego(t)ist, selfish person

egresar *vi Am (de escuela)* to leave school after completing one's studies, *US* to graduate; *(de universidad)* to graduate

egreso *nm Am (de universidad)* graduation

ej. *(abr* **ejemplo)** example, ex.

eje *nm* (**a**) *Téc (de rueda)* axle; *(de máquina)* shaft (**b**) *Mat* axis (**c**) *Hist* **el E.** the Axis

ejecución *nf* (**a**) *(de orden)* carrying out (**b**) *(ajusticiamiento)* execution (**c**) *Mús* performance

ejecutar *vt* (**a**) *(orden)* to carry out (**b**) *(ajusticiar)* to execute (**c**) *Mús* to perform, to play (**d**) *Informát* to run

ejecutivo, -a 1 *adj* executive; *Pol* **el poder e.** the government **2** *nm* executive

ejemplar 1 *nm* (**a**) *(de libro)* copy; *(de revista, periódico)* number, issue (**b**) *(espécimen)* specimen **2** *adj* exemplary, model

ejemplo *nm* example; **por e.** for example; **dar e.** to set an example

ejercer [49] **1** *vt* (**a**) *(profesión etc)* to practise (**b**) *(influencia)* to exert (**c**) **e. el derecho de/a …** to exercise one's right to … **2** *vi* to practise (**de** as)

ejercicio *nm* (**a**) *(de profesión)* practice; **hacer e.** to take *o* do exercise (**b**) *Fin* tax year; **e. económico** financial *o* fiscal year

ejército *nm* army

ejote *nm CAm, Méx* green bean

el *(f* **la,** *mpl* **los,** *fpl* **las)** **1** *art def m* (**a**) the (**b**) *(no se traduce)* **el Sr. García** Mr García; **el hambre/destino** hunger/ fate (**c**) *(con partes del cuerpo, prendas de vestir)* **me he cortado el dedo** I've cut my finger; **métetelo en el bolsillo** put it in your pocket (**d**) *(con días de la semana)* **el lunes** on Monday

> **el** is used instead of **la** before feminine nouns which are stressed on the first syllable and begin with "a" or "ha" (e.g. **el agua, el hacha**). Note that **el** combines with the prepositions **a** and **de** to produce the contracted forms **al** and **del**

2 *pron* (**a**) the one; **el de las once** the eleven o'clock one; **el que tienes en la mano** the one you've got in your hand; **el que quieras** whichever one you want (**b**) *(no se traduce)* **el de tu amigo** your friend's

él *pron pers* (**a**) *(sujeto) (persona)* he; *(animal, cosa)* it (**b**) *(complemento) (persona)* him; *(animal, cosa)* it

> Usually omitted in Spanish as a subject except for emphasis or contrast

elaborar *vt* (**a**) *(producto)* to manufacture, to produce (**b**) *(teoría)* to develop

elasticidad *nf* elasticity; *Fig* flexibility

elástico, -a *adj & nm* elastic

elección *nf* choice; *Pol* **elecciones** election

electricidad *nf* electricity

electricista *nmf* electrician

eléctrico, -a *adj* electric

electrocutar *vt* to electrocute

electrodoméstico *nm* (domestic) electrical appliance

electrónica *nf* electronics *sing*

electrónico, -a *adj* electronic

elefante *nm* elephant

elegancia *nf* elegance

elegante *adj* elegant

elegir [58] *vt* (**a**) to choose (**b**) *Pol* to elect

elemental *adj* (**a**) *(fundamental)* basic, fundamental (**b**) *(simple)* elementary

elemento *nm* (**a**) element (**b**) *(componente)* component, part (**c**) *Esp Fam (persona)* Br chap, US guy; **un e. de cuidado** a bad lot (**d**) **elementos** elements; *(fundamentos)* rudiments

elevación *nf* elevation; **e. de precios** rise in prices; **e. del terreno** rise in the ground

elevado, -a *adj* (**a**) high; *(edificio)* tall (**b**) *(pensamiento etc)* lofty, noble

elevador *nm* (**a**) *(montacargas)* hoist (**b**) *Méx (ascensor)* Br lift, US elevator

elevar 1 *vt* to raise 2 **elevarse** *vpr* (**a**) *(subir)* to rise; *(edificio)* to stand (**b**) **elevarse a** *(cantidad)* to amount o come to

eliminación *nf* elimination

eliminar *vt* to eliminate

élite *nf* elite, élite

ella *pron pers f* (**a**) *(sujeto)* she; *(animal, cosa)* it, she (**b**) *(complemento)* her; *(animal, cosa)* it, her

Usually omitted in Spanish as a subject except for emphasis or contrast

ello *pron pers neut* it; **por e.** for that reason

ellos *pron pers mpl* (**a**) *(sujeto)* they (**b**) *(complemento)* them

Usually omitted in Spanish as a subject except for emphasis or contrast

elocuencia *nf* eloquence

elocuente *adj* eloquent; **los hechos son elocuentes** the facts speak for themselves

elogiar [43] *vt* to praise

elogio *nm* praise

elote *nm* *CAm, Méx (mazorca)* corncob, ear of maize o US corn; *(granos)* sweetcorn, US corn

eludir *vt* to avoid

e-mail ['imeil] *nm* (*pl* **e-mails**) e-mail

emancipar 1 *vt* to emancipate 2 **emanciparse** *vpr* to become emancipated

embajada *nf* embassy

embajador, -a *nm,f* ambassador

embalar *vt* to pack

embalsamar *vt* to embalm

embalse *nm* dam, reservoir

embarazada 1 *adj* pregnant; **dejar e.** to get pregnant 2 *nf* pregnant woman, expectant mother

embarazo *nm* (**a**) *(preñez)* pregnancy (**b**) *(obstáculo)* obstacle (**c**) *(turbación)* embarrassment

embarcación *nf* (**a**) *(nave)* boat, craft (**b**) *(embarco)* embarkation

embarcadero *nm* quay

embarcar [44] 1 *vt* to ship 2 *vi* to embark, to go on board 3 **embarcarse** *vpr* (**a**) *Náut* **embarcarse (en)** to go on board; *Av* to board (**b**) **embarcarse en un proyecto** to embark on a project

embargar [42] *vt* (**a**) *Jur* to seize, to impound (**b**) *Fig* **le embarga la emoción** he's overwhelmed with joy

embargo *nm* (**a**) *Jur* seizure of property (**b**) *Com, Pol* embargo (**c**) **sin e.** however, nevertheless

embarque *nm* *(de persona)* boarding;

(de mercancías) loading; **tarjeta de e.** boarding card

embestir [6] *vt* (**a**) *Taurom* to charge (**b**) *(atacar)* to attack

emblema *nm* emblem

emborrachar *vt*, **emborracharse** *vpr* to get drunk

emboscada *nf* ambush; **tender una e.** to lay an ambush

embotellado *nm* bottling

embotellamiento *nm Aut* traffic jam

embotellar *vt* (**a**) to bottle (**b**) *(tráfico)* to block

embrague *nm* clutch

embrión *nm* embryo

embrujar *vt también Fig* to bewitch

embudo *nm* funnel

embustero, -a *nm,f* cheater, liar

embutido *nm* sausage

emergencia *nf* emergency; **salida de e.** emergency exit; **en caso de e.** in an emergency

emigración *nf* emigration; *(de pájaros)* migration

emigrante *adj & nmf* emigrant

emigrar *vi* to emigrate; *(pájaros)* to migrate

eminente *adj* eminent

emisión *nf* (**a**) emission (**b**) *(de bonos, sellos)* issue (**c**) *Rad, TV* broadcasting

emisora *nf (de radio)* radio station

emitir *vt* (**a**) to emit; *(luz, calor)* to give off (**b**) *(opinión, juicio)* to express (**c**) *Rad, TV* to transmit (**d**) *(bonos, sellos)* to issue

emoción *nf* (**a**) emotion (**b**) *(excitación)* excitement; **¡qué e.!** how exciting!

emocionado, -a *adj* deeply moved *o* touched

emocionante *adj* (**a**) *(conmovedor)* moving, touching (**b**) *(excitante)* exciting, thrilling

emocionar 1 *vt* (**a**) *(conmover)* to move, to touch (**b**) *(excitar)* to thrill **2 emocionarse** *vpr* (**a**) *(conmoverse)* to be moved (**b**) *(excitarse)* to get excited

empacar [44] *vt* (**a**) *(mercancías)* to pack (**b**) *Am* to annoy

empacho *nm (de comida)* indigestion, upset stomach; *Fig* surfeit

empalmar 1 *vt (tubos, cables)* to connect, to join **2 empalmarse** *vpr Esp Vulg* to get a hard-on

empanada *nf* pie

empanadilla *nf* pasty

empañar *vt*, **empañarse** *vpr (cristales)* to steam up

empapado, -a *adj* soaked

empapar 1 *vt* (**a**) *(mojar)* to soak (**b**) *(absorber)* to soak up **2 empaparse** *vpr* (**a**) *(persona)* to get soaked (**b**) *Fam Fig* **empaparse (de)** to take in

empapelar *vt* to paper, to wallpaper

empaquetar *vt* to pack

empastar *vt (diente)* to fill

empaste *nm (de diente)* filling

empatar 1 *vi (en competición)* to tie; *(en partido)* to draw **2** *vt* (**a**) *Dep* **e. el partido** to equalize (**b**) *Andes, Ven (enlazar, empalmar)* to join, to link

empate *nm Dep* draw, tie

empeñar 1 *vt* to pawn **2 empeñarse** *vpr* (**a**) *(insistir)* to insist (**en** on), to be determined (**en** to) (**b**) *(endeudarse)* to get into debt

empeño *nm* (**a**) *(insistencia)* insistence; **poner e. en algo** to put a lot of effort into sth (**b**) *(deuda)* pledge; **casa de empeños** pawnshop

empeorar 1 *vi* to deteriorate, to worsen

2 *vt* to make worse

3 empeorarse *vpr* to deteriorate, to worsen

emperador *nm* emperor

empezar [51] *vt & vi (a hacer algo)* to begin; *(algo)* to start, to commence

empinado, -a *adj (cuesta)* steep

empleado, -a *nm,f* employee; *(de oficina, banco)* clerk; **empleada del hogar** servant, maid

emplear *vt* (**a**) *(usar)* to use; *(contratar)* to employ (**b**) *(dinero, tiempo)* to spend

empleo *nm* (**a**) *(oficio)* job; *Pol* employment (**b**) *(uso)* use; **modo de e.** instructions for use

emplomar *vt RP (diente)* to fill

empotrado, -a *adj* fitted

emprender *vt* to undertake; *Fam* **emprenderla con algn** to pick on sb

empresa *nf* (a) *Com, Ind* firm, company; **e. punto com** dot com (company); **e. de trabajo temporal** temping agency (b) *Pol* **la libre e.** free enterprise (c) *(tarea)* undertaking

empresario, -a *nm,f* (a) *(hombre, mujer de negocios)* businessman, *f* businesswoman (b) *(patrón)* employer

empujar *vt* to push, to shove

empujón *nm* push, shove; **dar empujones** to push and shove

en *prep* (a) *(posición)* in, on, at; **en Madrid/Bolivia** in Madrid/Bolivia; **en la mesa** on the table; **en el bolso** in the bag; **en casa/el trabajo** at home/work (b) *(movimiento)* into; **entró en el cuarto** he went into the room (c) *(tiempo)* in, on, at; **en 1940** in 1940; **en verano** in summer; *Am* **en la mañana/tarde** in the morning/afternoon; *Am* **en la noche** at night; **cae en martes** it falls on a Tuesday; **en ese momento** at that moment (d) *(transporte)* by, in; **en coche/tren** by car/train; **en avión** by air (e) *(modo)* **en español** in Spanish; **en broma** jokingly; **en serio** seriously (f) *(reducción, aumento)* by; **los precios aumentaron en un diez por ciento** the prices went up by ten percent (g) *(tema, materia)* **experto en política** expert in politics (h) *(división, separación)* in; **lo dividió en tres partes** he divided it in three (i) *(con infinitivo)* **la conocí en el andar** I recognized her by her walk; **ser sobrio en el vestir** to dress simply

enaguas *nfpl* underskirt, petticoat

enamorado, -a 1 *adj* in love **2** *nm,f* person in love

enamorar 1 *vt* to win the heart of **2 enamorarse** *vpr* to fall in love (**de** with)

enano, -a *adj & nm,f* dwarf

encabezar [40] *vt* (a) *(carta, lista)* to head; *(periódico)* to lead (b) *(rebelión, carrera, movimiento)* to lead

encadenar *vt* to chain

encajar 1 *vt* (a) *(ajustar)* to insert; **e. la puerta** to push the door to (b) *Fam (asimilar)* to take (c) *(comentario)* to get in; **e. un golpe a algn** to land sb a blow **2** *vi* (a) *(ajustarse)* to fit (b) *Fig* **e. con** to fit (in) with, to square with

encaje *nm* lace

encalar *vt* to whitewash

encamotarse *vpr Andes, CAm Fam* to fall in love

encantado, -a *adj* (a) *(contento)* delighted; **e. de conocerle** pleased to meet you (b) *(embrujado)* enchanted

encantador, -a 1 *adj* charming, delightful **2** *nm,f* magician

encantar *vt (hechizar)* to bewitch, to cast a spell on; *Fig* **me encanta nadar** I love swimming

encanto *nm* (a) *(atractivo)* charm; **ser un e.** to be charming (b) *(hechizo)* spell

encapotado, -a *adj* overcast

encapricharse *vpr* (a) *(obstinarse)* **e. con algo/hacer algo** to set one's mind on sth/doing sth (b) *Esp (sentirse atraído)* **e. de algn** to become infatuated with sb; **e. de algo** to take a real liking to sth

encaramarse *vpr* to climb up

encarar 1 *vt* to face, to confront **2 encararse** *vpr* **encararse con** to face up to

encarcelar *vt* to imprison, to jail

encarecer [33] **1** *vt* to put up the price of **2 encarecerse** *vpr* to go up (in price)

encargado, -a 1 *nm,f Com* manager, *f* manager, manageress; *(responsable)* person in charge **2** *adj* in charge

encargar [42] **1** *vt* (a) to put in charge of, to entrust with (b) *Com (mercancías)* to order, to place an order for; *(encuesta)* to commission **2 encargarse** *vpr* **encargarse de** to see to, to deal with

encargo *nm* (a) *(pedido)* order; *Esp* **hecho de e.** tailor-made (b) *(recado)* errand (c) *(tarea)* job, assignment

encariñarse *vpr* **e. con** to become fond of, to get attached to

encarnado, -a *adj (rojo)* red

encausar *vt* to prosecute

encendedor *nm* lighter

encender [3] **1** *vt* (**a**) *(luz, radio, tele)* to switch on, to put on; *(cigarro, vela, fuego)* to light; *(cerilla)* to strike, to light (**b**) *Fig* to inflame, to stir up **2** **encenderse** *vpr* (**a**) *(fuego)* to catch; *(luz)* to go o come on (**b**) *(cara)* to blush, to go red

encendido *nm* ignition

encerado *nm (pizarra) Br* blackboard, *US* chalkboard

encerrar [1] **1** *vt* (**a**) to shut in; *(con llave)* to lock in (**b**) *Fig (contener)* to contain, to include **2** **encerrarse** *vpr* to shut oneself up o in; *(con llave)* to lock oneself in

encestar *vi Dep* to score (a basket)

enchilarse *vpr Méx Fam* to get angry

enchinar *vt Méx* to curl

enchufar *vt* (**a**) *Elec* to plug in (**b**) *(unir)* to join, to connect (**c**) *Fam (para un trabajo)* to pull strings for

enchufe *nm* (**a**) *Elec (hembra)* socket; *(macho)* plug (**b**) *Fam* contact

encía *nf* gum

enciclopedia *nf* encyclopedia

encierro *nm Pol (protesta)* sit-in

encima *adv* (**a**) on top; *(arriba)* above; *(en el aire)* overhead; **déjalo e.** put it on top; **¿llevas cambio e.?** do you have any change on you?; *Fig* **quitarse algo de e.** to get rid of sth; **ahí e.** up there (**b**) *(además)* besides (**c**) **e. de** *(sobre)* on; *(en el aire)* above; *Fig (además)* besides; **e. de la mesa** on the table (**d**) **por e.** above; *Fig* **por e. de sus posibilidades** beyond his abilities; **leer un libro por e.** to skip through a book

encimera *nf Esp (de cocina)* worktop

encina *nf* holm oak

encinta *adj* pregnant

encoger [53] **1** *vi (contraerse)* to contract; *(prenda)* to shrink **2** *vt* to contract; *(prenda)* to shrink

3 **encogerse** *vpr (contraerse)* to contract; *(prenda)* to shrink; **encogerse de hombros** to shrug (one's shoulders)

encolar *vt (papel)* to paste; *(madera)* to glue

encolerizar [40] **1** *vt* to infuriate, to anger **2** **encolerizarse** *vpr* to become furious

encomienda *nf* (**a**) assignment, mission (**b**) *(paquete postal)* parcel

encontrar [2] **1** *vt* (**a**) *(hallar)* to find; **no lo encuentro** I can't find it; **lo encuentro muy agradable** I find it very pleasant (**b**) *(dar con)* to meet; *(problema)* to run into, to come up against **2** **encontrarse** *vpr* (**a**) *(persona)* to meet (**b**) *(sentirse)* to feel, to be; **encontrarse a gusto** to feel comfortable (**c**) *(estar)* to be

encrucijada *nf* crossroads

encuadernar *vt* to bind

encuadre *nm Cin, TV* framing

encubierto, -a *adj (secreto)* hidden; *(operación)* covert

encubrir *vt* to conceal

encuentro *nm* (**a**) encounter, meeting (**b**) *Dep* meeting, match; **e. amistoso** friendly (match)

encuesta *nf* (**a**) *(sondeo)* (opinion) poll, survey (**b**) *(investigación)* investigation, inquiry

encuestador, -a *nm,f* pollster

enderezar [40] **1** *vt (poner derecho)* to straighten out; *(poner vertical)* to set upright **2** **enderezarse** *vpr* to straighten up

endeudarse *vpr* to get into debt

endiñar *vt Esp Fam* **e. algo a algn** *(golpe)* to land o deal sb sth; *(tarea)* to lumber sb with sth

endivia *nf* endive

endrogarse [42] *vpr Chile, Méx, Perú (endeudarse)* to get into debt

enemigo, -a 1 *adj* enemy; **soy e. de la bebida** I'm against drink **2** *nm,f* enemy

energía *nf* energy; **e. hidráulica/ nuclear** hydro-electric/nuclear power;

Fig **e. vital** vitality

enérgico, -a *adj* energetic; *(decisión)* firm; *(tono)* emphatic

enero *nm* January

enfadado, -a *adj esp Esp (enojado)* angry; *(molesto)* annoyed; **estamos enfadados** we've fallen out with each other

enfadar *esp Esp* **1** *vt* to make angry *o* annoyed **2 enfadarse** *vpr* **(a)** to get angry **(con** with) **(b)** *(dos personas)* to fall out

enfado *nm esp Esp* anger; *(desavenencia)* fall-out

enfermar *vi*, **enfermarse** *vpr* to become *o* fall ill, to be taken ill

enfermedad *nf* illness; *(contagiosa)* disease

enfermería *nf* infirmary

enfermero, -a *nm,f (mujer)* nurse; *(hombre)* (male) nurse

enfermizo, -a *adj* unhealthy, sickly

enfermo, -a 1 *adj* ill; **caer e.** to be taken ill; *Fam* **esa gente me pone e.** those people make me sick **2** *nm,f* ill person; *(paciente)* patient

enfocar [44] *vt* **(a)** *(imagen)* to focus; *(persona)* to focus on **(b)** *(tema)* to approach **(c)** *(con linterna)* to shine a light on

enfoque *nm* **(a)** focus; *(acción)* focusing **(b)** *(de un tema)* approach

enfrentamiento *nm* clash

enfrentar 1 *vt* **(a)** *(situación, peligro)* to confront **(b)** *(enemistar)* to set at odds **2 enfrentarse** *vpr* **(a) enfrentarse con** *o* **a** to face up to, to confront **(b)** *Dep* **enfrentarse (a)** *(rival)* to meet

enfrente *adv* **(a)** opposite, facing; **la casa de e.** the house opposite *o* across the road **(b) e. de** opposite (to); facing; **e. del colegio** opposite the school

enfriamiento *nm* **(a)** *(proceso)* cooling **(b)** *Med (catarro)* cold, chill

enfriar [29] **1** *vt* to cool (down), to chill **2** *vi* to cool down **3 enfriarse** *vpr* **(a)** to get *o* go cold **(b)** *(resfriarse)* to get *o* catch a cold **(c)** *Fig (pasión)* to cool down

enganchar 1 *vt* **(a)** to hook; *Ferroc* to couple **(b)** *Fam (pillar)* to nab **2 engancharse** *vpr* to get caught *o* hooked; *Fam (a la droga)* to get hooked

enganche *nm (gancho)* hook; *Ferroc* coupling

engañar 1 *vt* to deceive, to mislead; *(estafar)* to cheat, to trick; *(mentir a)* to lie to; *(al marido, a la mujer)* to be unfaithful to **2 engañarse** *vpr* to deceive oneself

engaño *nm* **(a)** deceit; *(estafa)* fraud, swindle; *(mentira)* lie **(b)** *(error)* mistake, misunderstanding

engañoso, -a *adj (palabras)* deceitful; *(apariencias)* deceptive; *(consejo)* misleading

engendrar *vt* **(a)** *Biol* to engender **(b)** *Fig* to give rise to, to cause

englobar *vt* to include

engordar 1 *vt* to fatten (up), to make fat **2** *vi* **(a)** to put on weight, to get fat; **he engordado 3 kilos** I've put on 3 kilos **(b)** *(comida, bebida)* to be fattening

engranaje *nm* **(a)** *Téc* gearing **(b)** *Fig* machinery

engrapadora *nf Am* stapler

engrapar *vt Am* to staple

engrasar *vt* **(a)** *(lubricar)* to lubricate, to oil **(b)** *(manchar)* to make greasy, to stain with grease

engreído, -a *adj* vain, conceited

enhorabuena *nf* congratulations; **dar la e. a algn** to congratulate sb

enigma *nm* enigma

enjabonar *vt* to soap

enjuagar [42] *vt* to rinse

enlace *nm* **(a)** *(unión)* link, connection; **e. químico** chemical bond **(b)** *Ferroc* connection **(c)** *(casamiento)* marriage **(d)** *(persona)* liaison officer; *Esp* **e. sindical** shop steward

enlazar [40] *vt & vi* to link, to connect **(con** with)

enlosar *vt* to tile

enmendar [1] **1** *vt (corregir)* to correct, to put right; *Jur* to amend **2 enmendarse** *vpr (persona)* to reform, to mend one's ways

enmienda *nf* correction; *Jur, Pol* amendment

enmudecer [33] *vi (callar)* to fall silent; *Fig* to be dumbstruck

enojado, -a *adj (irritado)* angry; *(molesto)* annoyed;

enojar *esp Am* **1** *vt* to anger, to annoy **2 enojarse** *vpr* to get angry, to lose one's temper

enojo *nm esp Am* anger, annoyance

enorme *adj* enormous

enredadera *nf* climbing plant, creeper

enredar 1 *vt* (**a**) *(pelo)* to entangle, to tangle up (**b**) *Fig (asunto)* to confuse, to complicate (**c**) *Fig (implicar)* to involve (**en** in) (**d**) *(confundir)* to mix up

2 enredarse *vpr* (**a**) *(pelo)* to get entangled, to get tangled (up) *o* in a tangle (**b**) *Fig (asunto)* to get complicated *o* confused (**c**) *Fig* **enredarse con** *(involucrarse)* to get involved with (**d**) *(confundirse)* to get mixed up

enredo *nm* (**a**) *(maraña)* tangle (**b**) *Fig (lío)* muddle, mess

enriquecer [33] **1** *vt* to make rich; *Fig* to enrich **2 enriquecerse** *vpr* to get *o* become rich, to prosper; *Fig* to become enriched

enrojecer [33] **1** *vt* to redden, to turn red **2** *vi (ruborizarse)* to blush **3 enrojecerse** *vpr* to blush

enrollar 1 *vt* to roll up; *(cable)* to coil; *(hilo)* to wind up **2 enrollarse** *vpr* (**a**) *Fam (hablar)* to chatter, to go on and on (**b**) *Fam* **enrollarse con algn** *(tener relaciones)* to have an affair with sb

ensaimada *nf* = kind of spiral pastry from Majorca

ensalada *nf* salad

ensaladera *nf* salad bowl

ensaladilla *nf Esp* **e. rusa** Russian salad

ensanchar 1 *vt* to enlarge, to widen; *Cost* to let out **2 ensancharse** *vpr* to get wider

ensayar *vt* to test, to try out; *Teatro* to rehearse; *Mús* to practise

ensayo *nm* (**a**) *(prueba)* test, trial (**b**) *Teatro* rehearsal; **e. general** dress rehearsal (**c**) *(escrito)* essay

enseguida, en seguida *adv (inmediatamente)* at once, straight away; *(poco después)* in a minute, soon; **e. voy** I'll be right there

ensenada *nf* inlet, cove

enseñanza *nf* (**a**) *(educación)* education (**b**) *(de idioma etc)* teaching (**c**) **enseñanzas** teachings

enseñar *vt* (**a**) to teach; **e. a algn a hacer algo** to teach sb how to do sth (**b**) *(mostrar)* to show; *(señalar)* to point out

enseres *nmpl (bártulos)* belongings, goods; *(de trabajo)* tools

ensopar *vt Andes, RP, Ven Fam* to soak

ensuciar [43] **1** *vt* (**a**) to get dirty (**b**) *Fig (reputación)* to harm, to damage **2 ensuciarse** *vpr* to get dirty

ente *nm* (**a**) *(institución)* organization, body; **e. público** public service organization (**b**) *(ser)* being

entender [3] **1** *vt (comprender)* to understand; **a mi e.** to my way of thinking; **dar a algn a e. que ...** to give sb to understand that ...

2 *vi* (**a**) *(comprender)* to understand (**b**) **e. de** *(saber)* to know about

3 entenderse *vpr* (**a**) *(comprenderse)* to be understood, to be meant (**b**) *Fam* **entenderse (bien) con** to get on (well) with

entendido, -a 1 *nm,f* expert **2** *adj* **tengo e. que ...** I understand that ...

enterar 1 *vt* to inform (**de** about *o* of) **2 enterarse** *vpr* to find out; **me he enterado de que ...** I understand ...; **ni me enteré** I didn't even realize it

entero, -a 1 *adj* (**a**) *(completo)* entire, whole; **por e.** completely (**b**) *Fig (íntegro)* honest, upright (**c**) *Fig (firme)* strong **2** *nm* (**a**) *Mat* whole number (**b**) *Fin* point

enterrar [1] *vt* to bury

entidad *nf* organization; **e. comercial** company, firm

entierro *nm* (**a**) burial (**b**) *(ceremonia)* funeral

entlo. *(abr* entresuelo) mezzanine

entonces *adv* then; **por aquel e.** at that time; **el e. ministro** the then minister

entrada *nf* (**a**) entrance (**b**) *(billete)* ticket; *(recaudación)* takings (**c**) **de e.** for a start (**d**) *Culin* entrée (**e**) *Com* entry; **e. de capital** capital inflow (**f**) *Esp (pago inicial)* down payment, deposit (**g**) *Com* **entradas** *(ingresos)* receipts, takings (**h**) *(en la frente)* receding hairline

entrante 1 *adj* coming; **el mes e.** next month; **el ministro e.** the incoming minister **2** *nm Esp* starter

entrañable *adj* (**a**) *(lugar)* intimate, close (**b**) *(persona)* affectionate, warm-hearted

entrañas *nfpl* bowels

entrar 1 *vi* (**a**) to come in, to go in, to enter; *Fig* **no me entran las matemáticas** I can't get the hang of maths (**b**) *(encajar)* to fit (**c**) **el año que entra** next year, the coming year (**d**) *(venir)* to come over; **me entró dolor de cabeza** I got a headache; **me entraron ganas de reír** I felt like laughing
  2 *vt* (**a**) to introduce (**b**) *Informát* to enter

entre *prep* (**a**) *(dos)* between (**b**) *(más de dos)* among(st)

entreabierto, -a *adj (ojos etc)* half-open; *(puerta)* ajar

entreacto *nm* interval, intermission

entrecejo *nm* space between the eyebrows; **fruncir el e.** to frown, to knit one's brow

entrecot *nm* (*pl* **entrecots** *o* **entrecotes**) fillet steak

entrega *nf* (**a**) *(de productos)* delivery; *(de premios)* presentation (**b**) *(fascículo)* part, instalment (**c**) *(devoción)* selflessness

entregar [42] **1** *vt* to hand over; *(deberes etc)* to give in, to hand in; *Com* to deliver **2 entregarse** *vpr* (**a**) *(rendirse)* to give in, to surrender (**b**) **entregarse a** to devote oneself to; *Pey* to indulge in

entrelazar [40] *vt,* **entrelazarse** *vpr* to entwine

entremeses *nmpl Culin* hors d'oeuvres

entrenador, -a *nm,f* trainer, coach

entrenamiento *nm* training

entrenar *vi,* **entrenarse** *vpr* to train

entrepierna *nf* crotch, crutch

entresuelo *nm* mezzanine

entretanto 1 *adv* meanwhile **2** *nm* **en el e.** in the meantime

entretención *nf Chile* entertainment

entretener [24] **1** *vt* (**a**) *(divertir)* to entertain, to amuse (**b**) *(retrasar)* to delay; *(detener)* to hold up, to detain **2 entretenerse** *vpr* (**a**) *(distraerse)* to amuse oneself, to while away the time (**b**) *(retrasarse)* to be delayed, to be held up

entretenido, -a *adj* enjoyable, entertaining

entretenimiento *nm* entertainment, amusement

entretiempo 1 *nm CSur* half-time **2 de entretiempo** *loc adj* **ropa de e.** spring/autumn clothes

entrever [28] *vt* to glimpse, to catch sight of; *Fig* **dejó e. que …** she hinted that …

entreverar *CSur* **1** *vt* to mix **2 entreverarse** *vpr* to get tangled

entrevero *nm CSur* tangle, mess

entrevista *nf* interview

entrevistador, -a *nm,f* interviewer

entrevistar 1 *vt* to interview **2 entrevistarse** *vpr* **entrevistarse con algn** to have an interview with sb

entristecer [33] **1** *vt* to sadden, to make sad **2 entristecerse** *vpr* to be sad **(por** about)

entrometerse *vpr* to meddle, to interfere **(en** in)

entusiasmar 1 *vt* to fill with enthusiasm **2 entusiasmarse** *vpr* to get excited *o* enthusiastic **(con** about)

entusiasmo *nm* enthusiasm; **con e.** enthusiastically

entusiasta 1 *adj* enthusiastic, keen **(de** on) **2** *nmf* enthusiast

envasar *vt (embotellar)* to bottle; *(empaquetar)* to pack; *(enlatar)* to can, to tin

envase *nm* (**a**) *(acto)* packing; *(de botella)* bottling; *(de lata)* canning (**b**) *(recipiente)* container (**c**) *(botella vacía)* empty

envejecer [33] **1** *vi* to grow old **2** *vt* to age

envenenamiento *nm* poisoning

envenenar *vt* to poison

envergadura *nf* (**a**) *(importancia)* importance, scope; **de gran e.** large-scale (**b**) *(de pájaro, avión)* span, wingspan; *Náut* breadth (of sail)

enviar [29] *vt* to send

envidia *nf* envy; **tener e. de algn** to envy sb

envidiar [43] *vt* to envy; **no tener nada que e.** to be in no way inferior (**a** to)

envidioso, -a *adj* envious

envío *nm* sending; *(remesa)* consignment; *(paquete)* parcel; **gastos de e.** postage and packing; **e. contra reembolso** cash on delivery

enviudar *vi (hombre)* to become a widower, to lose one's wife; *(mujer)* to become a widow, to lose one's husband

envolver [4] *(pp* **envuelto**) **1** *vt* (**a**) *(con papel)* to wrap (**b**) *(cubrir)* to envelop (**c**) *(en complot, etc)* to involve (**en** in) **2 envolverse** *vpr* (**a**) to wrap oneself up (**en** in) (**b**) *(implicarse)* to become involved (**en** in)

enyesar *vt* to plaster; *Med* to put in plaster

epidemia *nf* epidemic

epidermis *nf inv Anat* epidermis

episodio *nm* episode

época *nf* time; *Hist* period, epoch; *Agr* season; **en esta é. del año** at this time of the year; **hacer é.** to be a landmark; **mueble de é.** period furniture

equilibrado, -a *adj* (**a**) *(igualado)* balanced (**b**) *(sensato)* sensible

equilibrar *vt* to balance

equilibrio *nm* balance

equilibrista *nmf* tightrope walker

equipaje *nm Br* luggage, *US* baggage; **hacer el e.** to pack, to do the packing

equipar *vt* to equip, to furnish (**con** *o* **de** with)

equipo *nm* (**a**) *(de expertos, jugadores)* team (**b**) *(aparatos)* equipment; **e. de alta fidelidad** hi-fi stereo system (**c**) *(ropas)* outfit

equitación *nf* horse *o US* horseback riding

equivalente *adj* equivalent

equivaler [26] *vi* to be equivalent (**a** to)

equivocación *nf* error, mistake

equivocado, -a *adj* mistaken, wrong

equivocar [44] **1** *vt* to mix up **2 equivocarse** *vpr* to make a mistake; *Tel* **se equivocó de número** he dialled the wrong number; **se equivocó de fecha** he got the wrong date

era¹ *nf (época)* era, age

era² *nf Agr* threshing floor

era³ *pt indef de* **ser**

eres *indic pres de* **ser**

erguido, -a *adj* upright

erguir [55] **1** *vt* to raise **2 erguirse** *vpr* to rise up

erizo *nm* hedgehog; **e. marino** *o* **de mar** sea urchin

ermita *nf* hermitage

erótico, -a *adj* erotic

erotismo *nm* eroticism

errante *adj* wandering

errar [50] **1** *vt* to miss, to get wrong **2** *vi* (**a**) *(vagar)* to wander, to roam (**b**) *(fallar)* to err

erróneo, -a *adj* erroneous, wrong

error *nm* error, mistake; *Informát* bug; **por e.** by mistake, in error; *Impr* **e. de imprenta** misprint; **caer en un e.** to make a mistake

eructar *vi* to belch, to burp

eructo *nm* belch, burp

erudito, -a **1** *adj* erudite, learned **2** *nm,f* scholar

erupción *nf* (**a**) *(de volcán)* eruption (**b**) *(en la piel)* rash

es *indic pres de* **ser**

esbelto, -a *adj* slender

esbozo *nm* sketch, outline, rough draft

escabeche *nm* brine

escabechina *nf Fam (destrozo)* destruction

escala *nf* (**a**) scale; *(de colores)* range; **e. musical** scale; **en gran e.** on a large scale (**b**) *(parada) Náut* port of call; *Av* stopover; **hacer e. en** to call in at, to stop over in (**c**) *(escalera)* ladder, stepladder

escalador, -a *nm,f* climber, mountaineer

escalar *vt* to climb, to scale

escalera *nf* (**a**) stair; **e. de incendios** fire escape; **e. mecánica** escalator; **e. de caracol** spiral staircase (**b**) *(escala)* ladder (**c**) *Naipes* run

escalerilla *nf (de piscina)* steps; *Náut* gangway; *Av* (boarding) ramp

escalofrío *nm* shiver; **me dio un e.** it gave me the shivers

escalón *nm* step; **e. lateral** *(en letrero)* ramp

escalope *nm* escalope

escama *nf Zool* scale; *(de jabón)* flake

escampar *vi* to stop raining, to clear up

escandalizar [40] **1** *vt* to scandalize, to shock **2 escandalizarse** *vpr* to be shocked (**de** at o by)

escándalo *nm* (**a**) *(alboroto)* racket, din; **armar un e.** to kick up a fuss (**b**) *(desvergüenza)* scandal

escaño *nm (parlamentario)* seat

escapar 1 *vi* to escape, to run away **2 escaparse** *vpr* (**a**) to escape, to run away; **se me escapó de las manos** it slipped out of my hands; **se me escapó el tren** I missed the train (**b**) *(gas etc)* to leak, to escape

escaparate *nm* shop window

escape *nm* (**a**) *(de gas etc)* leak, escape (**b**) *Téc* exhaust; **tubo de e.** exhaust (pipe) (**c**) *(huida)* escape; *(escapatoria)* way out

escarabajo *nm* beetle

escarbar *vt* (**a**) *(suelo)* to scratch; *(fuego)* to poke (**b**) *Fig* to inquire

into, to investigate

escarcha *nf* hoarfrost, frost

escarmentar [1] *vi* to learn one's lesson

escarola *nf* curly endive

escasear *vi* to be scarce

escasez *nf* scarcity

escaso, -a *adj* scarce; *(dinero)* tight; *(conocimientos)* scant; **e. de dinero** short of money

escayola *nf* (**a**) plaster of Paris, stucco (**b**) *Med* plaster

escayolar *vt Med* to put in plaster

escena *nf* (**a**) scene (**b**) *(escenario)* stage; **poner en e.** to stage

escenario *nm* (**a**) *Teatro* stage (**b**) *(entorno)* scenario; *(de crimen)* scene; *(de película)* setting

escepticismo *nm* scepticism

escéptico, -a *adj & nm,f* sceptic

esclavitud *nf* slavery

esclavo, -a *adj & nm,f* slave

esclusa *nf* lock, sluicegate

escoba *nf* brush, broom

escobilla *nf* brush

escocer [41] **1** *vi* to sting, to smart **2 escocerse** *vpr (piel)* to chafe

escocés, -esa 1 *adj* Scottish, Scots; **falda escocesa** kilt **2** *nm,f* Scotsman, *f* Scotswoman

Escocia *n* Scotland

escoger [53] *vt* to choose

escolar 1 *adj (curso, año)* school **2** *nmf (niño)* schoolboy; *(niña)* schoolgirl

escolaridad *nf* schooling

escollo *nm* reef; *Fig* pitfall

escolta *nf* escort

escombros *nmpl* rubbish, debris

esconder 1 *vt* to hide (**de** from), to conceal (**de** from) **2 esconderse** *vpr* to hide (**de** from)

escondidas *adv* **a e.** secretly

escondite *nm* (**a**) *(lugar)* hiding place, hide-out (**b**) *(juego)* hide-and-seek

escopeta *nf* shotgun; **e. de aire comprimido** air gun; **e. de cañones recortados** *Br* sawn-off shotgun, *US* sawed-off shotgun

Escorpio *nm* Scorpio

escorpión *nm* scorpion

escotado, -a *adj* low-cut

escote *nm* low neckline

escotilla *nf* hatch, hatchway

escribir (*pp* escrito) **1** *vt* to write; **e. a mano** to write in longhand; **e. a máquina** to type **2 escribirse** *vpr* (**a**) *(dos personas)* to write to each other, to correspond (**b**) **se escribe con h** it is spelt with an h

escrito, -a 1 *adj* written; **e. a mano** handwritten, in longhand; **por e.** in writing **2** *nm* writing

escritor, -a *nm,f* writer

escritorio *nm* (**a**) *(mueble)* writing desk, bureau; *(oficina)* office (**b**) *Informát* desktop

escritura *nf* (**a**) *Jur* deed, document; **e. de propiedad** title deed (**b**) *Rel* **Sagradas Escrituras** Holy Scriptures

escrúpulo *nm* (**a**) scruple; **una persona sin escrúpulos** an unscrupulous person (**b**) *(esmero)* care (**c**) **me da e.** *(asco)* it makes me feel squeamish

escuadra *nf* (**a**) *(instrumento)* square (**b**) *Mil* squad; *Náut* squadron; *Dep* team; *(de coches)* fleet

escuchar 1 *vt* to listen to; *(oír)* to hear **2** *vi* to listen; *(oír)* to hear

escudo *nm* (**a**) *(arma defensiva)* shield (**b**) *(blasón)* coat of arms

escuela *nf* school; **e. de bellas artes** art school; **e. de conducir/de idiomas** driving/language school

esculcar [44] *vt Méx* to search

esculpir *vt* to sculpt; *(madera)* to carve; *(metal)* to engrave

escultor, -a *nm,f* sculptor, *f* sculptress; *(de madera)* woodcarver; *(de metales)* engraver

escultura *nf* sculpture

escupir 1 *vi* to spit **2** *vt* to spit out

escurrir 1 *vt (plato, vaso)* to drain; *(ropa)* to wring out; **e. el bulto** to wriggle out **2 escurrirse** *vpr* (**a**) *(platos etc)* to drip (**b**) *(escaparse)* to run *o* slip away (**c**) *(resbalarse)* to slip

ese, -a (*pl* esos, -as) *adj dem* (**a**) that

(**b**) **esos, -as** those

ése, -a (*pl* ésos, -as) *pron dem m,f* (**a**) that one (**b**) **ésos, -as** those (ones); *Fam* **¡ni por ésas!** no way!; *Fam* **¡no me vengas con ésas!** come off it!

> Note that **ése** and its various forms can be written without an accent when there is no risk of confusion with the adjective

esencia *nf* essence

esencial *adj* essential; **lo e.** the main thing

esfera *nf* (**a**) sphere; *Fig* sphere, field (**b**) *(de reloj de pulsera)* dial; *(de reloj de pared)* face

esférico, -a 1 *adj* spherical **2** *nm (balón)* ball

esforzarse [2] *vpr* to make an effort (**por** to)

esfuerzo *nm* effort

esfumarse *vpr Fam* to beat it

esgrima *nf Dep* fencing

esguince *nm* sprain

eslabón *nm* link

eslalon *nm* (*pl* eslalons) *Dep* slalom; **e. gigante** giant slalom

eslip *nm* (*pl* eslips) men's briefs, underpants

Eslovaquia *n* Slovakia

esmalte *nm* enamel; *(de uñas)* nail polish *o* varnish

esmeralda *nf* emerald

esmerarse *vpr* to be careful; *(esforzarse)* to go to great lengths

esmero *nm* great care

esmoquin *nm Br* dinner jacket, *US* tuxedo

esnob (*pl* esnobs) **1** *adj (persona)* snobbish; *(restaurante etc)* posh **2** *nmf* snob

eso *pron neut* that; **¡e. es!** that's it!; **por e.** that's why; *Fam* **a e. de las diez** around ten; *Fam* **e. de las Navidades sale muy caro** this whole Christmas thing costs a fortune

esos, -as *adj dem pl ver* ese, -a

espacial *adj* spatial, spacial; **nave e.** spaceship

espacio *nm* (**a**) space; *(de tiempo)* length; **a doble e.** double-spaced (**b**) *Rad, TV* programme

espacioso, -a *adj* spacious, roomy

espada 1 *nf* (**a**) sword; **estar entre la e. y la pared** to be between the devil and the deep blue sea; **pez e.** swordfish (**b**) *Naipes* spade **2** *nm Taurom* matador

espaguetis *nmpl* spaghetti

espalda *nf* (**a**) *Anat* back; **espaldas** back; **a espaldas de algn** behind sb's back; **por la e.** from behind; **volver la e. a algn** to turn one's back on sb; *Fam* **e. mojada** wetback (**b**) *(en natación)* backstroke

espantapájaros *nm inv* scarecrow

espanto *nm* fright; *Fam* **de e.** dreadful, shocking

espantoso, -a *adj* dreadful

España *n* Spain

español, -a 1 *adj* Spanish **2** *nm,f* Spaniard; **los españoles** the Spanish **3** *nm (idioma)* Spanish

esparadrapo *nm Br* (sticking) plaster, *US* Band-aid®

esparcir [52] **1** *vt (papeles, semillas)* to scatter; *Fig (rumor)* to spread **2 esparcirse** *vpr* (**a**) to be scattered (**b**) *(relajarse)* to relax

espárrago *nm* asparagus

espasmo *nm* spasm

espátula *nf Culin* spatula; *Arte* palette knife; *Téc* stripping knife; *(de albañil)* trowel

especia *nf* spice

especial *adj* special; **en e.** especially; **e. para ...** suitable for ...

especialidad *nf* speciality, *US* specialty; *Educ* main subject

especialista *nmf* specialist

especializarse [40] *vpr* to specialize (**en** in)

especialmente *adv (exclusivamente)* specially; *(muy)* especially

especie *nf* (**a**) *Biol* species *inv* (**b**) *(clase)* kind; **una e. de salsa** a kind of sauce (**c**) *Com* **en e.** in kind

especificar [44] *vt* to specify

específico, -a *adj* specific; **peso e.** specific gravity

espectáculo *nm* (**a**) *(escena)* spectacle, sight; *Fam* **dar un e.** to make a spectacle of oneself (**b**) *Teatro, Cin, TV* show; **montar un e.** to put on a show

espectador, -a *nm,f Dep* spectator; *(de accidente)* onlooker; *Teatro, Cin* member of the audience; **los espectadores** the audience; *TV* the viewers

especulación *nf* speculation; **e. del suelo** land speculation

espejismo *nm* mirage

espejo *nm* mirror; *Aut* **e. retrovisor** rear-view mirror

espera *nf* wait; **en e. de ...** waiting for ...; **a la e. de** expecting; **sala de e.** waiting room

esperanza *nf* hope; **tener la e. puesta en algo** to have one's hopes pinned on sth; **e. de vida** life expectancy; **en estado de buena e.** expecting, pregnant

esperar 1 *vi* (**a**) *(aguardar)* to wait (**b**) *(tener esperanza de)* to hope **2** *vt* (**a**) *(aguardar)* to wait for; **espero a mi hermano** I'm waiting for my brother (**b**) *(tener esperanza de)* to hope for; **espero que sí** I hope so; **espero que vengas** I hope you'll come (**c**) *(estar a la espera de)* to expect; **te esperábamos ayer** we were expecting you yesterday (**d**) *Fig (bebé)* to expect

esperma *nm* sperm

espeso, -a *adj (bosque, niebla)* dense; *(líquido)* thick; *(masa)* stiff

espesor *nm* thickness; **3 m de e.** 3 m thick

espía *nmf* spy

espiar [29] **1** *vi* to spy **2** *vt* to spy on

espiga *nf* (**a**) *(de trigo)* ear (**b**) *Téc* pin

espina *nf* (**a**) *Bot* thorn (**b**) *(de pescado)* bone (**c**) *Anat* **e. dorsal** spinal column, spine (**d**) *Fig* **ése me da mala e.** there's something fishy about that one

espinaca *nf* spinach

espinilla *nf* (**a**) *Anat* shin (**b**) *(en la piel)* spot

espionaje *nm* spying, espionage; **novela de e.** spy story

espiral *adj & nf* spiral

espirar *vi* to breathe out, to exhale

espiritismo *nm* spiritualism

espíritu *nm* (**a**) spirit; **e. deportivo** sportsmanship (**b**) *Rel (alma)* soul; **el E. Santo** the Holy Ghost

espiritual *adj* spiritual

espléndido, -a *adj* (**a**) *(magnífico)* splendid (**b**) *(generoso)* lavish, generous

esplendor *nm* splendour

espliego *nm* lavender

esponja *nf* sponge

esponjoso, -a *adj* spongy; *(bizcocho)* light

espontaneidad *nf* spontaneity; **con e.** naturally

espontáneo, -a **1** *adj* spontaneous **2** *nm Taurom* = spectator who spontaneously joins in the bullfight

esposas *nfpl* handcuffs

esposo, -a *nm,f* husband, *f* wife

espray *nm* spray

esprint *nm (pl* **esprints**) sprint

esprínter *nmf* sprinter

espuma *nf* foam; *(de olas)* surf; *(de cerveza)* froth, head; *(de jabón)* lather; **e. de afeitar** shaving foam

esquela *nf Esp* funeral notice *(in newspaper)*

esqueleto *nm* (**a**) skeleton (**b**) *Constr* framework

esquema *nm* diagram

esquematizar *vt* (**a**) *(en forma de gráfico)* to draw a diagram of (**b**) *(resumir)* to outline

esquí *nm (pl* **esquíes** *o* **esquís**) (**a**) *(objeto)* ski (**b**) *(deporte)* skiing; **e. acuático** waterskiing

esquiador, -a *nm,f* skier

esquiar [29] *vi* to ski

esquilar *vt* to shear

esquimal *adj & nmf* Eskimo

esquina *nf* corner; *Dep* **saque de e.** corner (kick)

esquivar *vt (a una persona)* to avoid; *(un golpe)* to dodge

estabilidad *nf* stability

estable *adj* stable

establecer [33] **1** *vt* to establish; *(fundar)* to set up, to found; *(récord)* to set **2 establecerse** *vpr* to settle

establecimiento *nm* establishment

establo *nm* cow shed

estaca *nf* stake, post; *(de tienda de campaña)* peg

estación *nf* (**a**) station; **e. de servicio** service station; **e. de esquí** ski resort (**b**) *(del año)* season

estacionamiento *nm Aut (acción)* parking; *(lugar) Br* car park, *US* parking lot

estacionar *vt,* **estacionarse** *vpr Aut* to park

estada *nf* stay

estadía *nf Am* stay; **planeó una e. de tres días en Lima** he planned a three-day stop in Lima

estadio *nm* (**a**) *Dep* stadium (**b**) *(fase)* stage

estadística *nf* statistics *sing;* **una e.** a statistic

estado *nm* (**a**) *Pol* state (**b**) *(situación)* state, condition; **en buen e.** in good condition; **e. de salud** condition, state of health; **e. de excepción** state of emergency; **estar en e.** to be pregnant; **e. civil** marital status (**c**) *Mil* **e. mayor** general staff (**d**) *(país, división territorial)* state; **Estados Unidos de América** United States of America

estadounidense **1** *adj* American **2** *nmf* American

estafa *nf* swindle

estafador, -a *nm,f* swindler

estafar *vt* to swindle

estalactita *nf* stalactite

estalagmita *nf* stalagmite

estallar *vi* (**a**) to burst; *(bomba)* to explode, to go off; *(guerra)* to break out (**b**) *Fig (de cólera etc)* to explode; **e. en sollozos** to burst into tears

estallido *nm* explosion; *(de guerra)* outbreak

estambre *nm Bot* stamen

estamento *nm Hist* estate; *Fig (grupo)* group

estampado, -a 1 *adj (tela)* printed **2** *nm* (**a**) *(tela)* print (**b**) *(proceso)* printing

estampida *nf* (**a**) *(estampido)* bang (**b**) *(carrera rápida)* stampede; **de e.** suddenly

estampilla *nf Am* (postage) stamp

estancado, -a *adj (agua)* stagnant; *Fig* static, at a standstill; **quedarse e.** to get stuck *o* bogged down

estancar [44] **1** *vt* (**a**) *(agua)* to hold back (**b**) *Fig (asunto)* to block; *(negociaciones)* to bring to a standstill **2 estancarse** *vpr* to stagnate; *Fig* to get bogged down

estancia *nf* (**a**) *Esp, Méx (tiempo)* stay (**b**) *(habitación)* room (**c**) *CSur (hacienda)* ranch, farm

estanciero, -a *nm,f CSur* ranch owner, rancher

estanco, -a 1 *nm Esp* tobacconist's **2** *adj* watertight

estándar *adj & nm* standard

estanque *nm* pool, pond

estante *nm* shelf; *(para libros)* bookcase

estantería *nf* shelves, shelving

estaño *nm* tin

estar [13] **1** *vi* (**a**) to be; **está en la playa** he is at the beach; **e. en casa** to be in, to be at home; **estamos en Caracas** we are in Caracas; **¿está tu madre?** is your mother in?; **¿cómo estás?** how are you?; **los precios están bajos** prices are low

(**b**) *(+ adj)* to be; **está cansado/ enfermo** he's tired/ill; **está vacío** it's empty

(**c**) *(+ adv)* to be; **está bien/mal** it's all right/wrong; **e. mal de dinero** he's short of money; **estará listo enseguida** it'll be ready in a minute

(**d**) *(+ ger)* to be; **está escribiendo** she is writing; **estaba comiendo** he was eating

(**e**) *(+ a + fecha)* to be; **¿a cuántos estamos?** what's the date (today)?;

estamos a 2 de noviembre it is the 2nd of November

(**f**) *(+ precio)* to be at; **están a dos euros el kilo** they're two euros a kilo

(**g**) *(locuciones)* **e. al caer** to be just round the corner; **¿estamos?** OK?

(**h**) *(+ de)* **e. de paseo** to be out for a walk; **e. de vacaciones/viaje** to be (away) on holiday/a trip; **estoy de jefe hoy** I'm the boss today

(**i**) *(+ para)* **estará para las seis** it will be finished by six; **hoy no estoy para bromas** I'm in no mood for jokes today

(**j**) *(+ por)* **está por hacer** it has still to be done; **eso está por ver** it remains to be seen; **estoy por esperar** *(a favor de)* I'm for waiting

(**k**) *(+ con)* to have; **e. con la gripe** to have the flu, to be down with flu; **estoy con Jaime** *(de acuerdo con)* I agree with Jaime

(**l**) *(+ sin)* to have no; **e. sin luz/agua** to have no light/water

(**m**) *(+ que)* **está que se duerme** he is nearly asleep; *Fam* **está que rabia** he's hopping mad

2 estarse *vpr* **¡estáte quieto!** keep still!, stop fidgeting!

estárter *nm* (*pl* **estárters**) choke

estatal *adj* state; **enseñanza e.** state education

estático, -a *adj* static

estatua *nf* statue

estatura *nf* (**a**) height; **¿cuál es tu e.?** how tall are you? (**b**) *(renombre)* stature

estatus *nm inv* status; **e. quo** status quo

estatuto *nm inv Jur* statute; *(de ciudad)* by-law; *(de empresa etc)* rules

este¹ 1 *adj* eastern; *(dirección)* easterly **2** *nm* east; **al e. de** to the east of

este², -a *(pl* **estos, -as)** *adj dem* (**a**) this (**b**) **estos, -as** these

éste, -a *(pl* **éstos, -as)** *pron dem m,f* (**a**) this one; **aquél ... é.** the former ... the latter (**b**) **éstos, -as** these (ones); **aquéllos ... é.** the former ... the latter

Note that **éste** and its various forms can be written without an accent when there is no risk of confusion with the adjective

estera *nf* rush mat

estéreo *nm & adj* stereo

estéril *adj* (**a**) sterile (**b**) *Fig (esfuerzo)* futile

esterilizar [40] *vt* to sterilize

esternón *nm* sternum, breastbone

estero *nm* (**a**) *(pantano) Am* marsh, swamp (**b**) *Ven (charca)* puddle, pool (**c**) *Chile (arroyo)* stream

estética *nf* aesthetics *sing*

estibador *nm* docker, stevedore

estiércol *nm* manure, dung

estilo *nm* (**a**) style; *(modo)* manner, fashion; **algo por el e.** something like that; **e. de vida** way of life (**b**) *(en natación)* stroke (**c**) *Ling* **e. directo/indirecto** direct/indirect speech

estilográfica *nf* (**pluma**) **e.** fountain pen

estima *nf* esteem, respect

estimación *nf* (**a**) *(estima)* esteem, respect (**b**) *(valoración)* evaluation; *(cálculo aproximado)* estimate

estimado, -a *adj* esteemed, respected; **E. Señor** *(en carta)* Dear Sir

estimulante 1 *adj* stimulating **2** *nm* stimulant

estimular *vt* (**a**) to stimulate (**b**) *Fig* to encourage

estímulo *nm* *Biol, Fís* stimulus; *Fig* encouragement

estirado, -a *adj Fig* stiff

estirar 1 *vt* to stretch; *Fig (dinero)* to spin out; *Fig* **e. la pata** to kick the bucket **2 estirarse** *vpr* to stretch

estirpe *nf* stock, pedigree

esto *pron neut* this, this thing, this matter; *Fam* **e. de la fiesta** this business about the party

estofado *nm* stew

estoicismo *nm* stoicism

estoico, -a 1 *adj* stoical **2** *nm,f* stoic

estómago *nm* stomach; **dolor de e.** stomach ache

estorbar 1 *vt* (**a**) *(dificultar)* to hinder, to get in the way of (**b**) *(molestar)* to disturb **2** *vi* to be in the way

estorbo *nm* (**a**) *(obstáculo)* obstruction, obstacle (**b**) *(molestia)* nuisance

estornudar *vi* to sneeze

estornudo *nm* sneeze

estos, -as *adj dem pl ver* **este, -a**

éstos, -as *pron dem m,fpl ver* **éste, -a**

estoy *indic pres de* **estar**

estrafalario, -a *adj Fam* outlandish

estrangulador, -a *nm,f* strangler

estrangular *vt* to strangle; *Med* to strangulate

estratega *nmf* strategist

estrategia *nf* strategy

estratégico, -a *adj* strategic

estrechar 1 *vt* (**a**) to make narrow (**b**) *(mano)* to shake; *(lazos de amistad)* to tighten; **me estrechó entre sus brazos** he hugged me **2 estrecharse** *vpr* to narrow, to become narrower

estrecho, -a 1 *adj* (**a**) narrow; *(ropa, zapato)* tight; *(amistad, relación)* close, intimate (**b**) *Fig* **e. de miras** narrow-minded **2** *nm Geog* strait, straits

estrella *nf* star; **e. de cine** movie *o Br* film star; *Zool* **e. de mar** starfish; **e. fugaz** shooting star

estrellar 1 *vt Fam* to smash **2 estrellarse** *vpr (morir)* to die in a car crash; *Aut, Av* **estrellarse contra** *(chocar)* to crash into

estremecer [33] *vt,* **estremecerse** *vpr* to shake

estrenar *vt* (**a**) to use for the first time; *(ropa)* to wear for the first time (**b**) *Teatro, Cin* to premiere

estreno *nm Teatro* first performance; *Cin* premiere

estreñimiento *nm* constipation

estrepitoso, -a *adj* deafening; *Fig (fracaso)* spectacular

estrés *nm* stress

estría *nf* (**a**) *(en la piel)* stretch mark (**b**) *Arquit* flute, fluting

estribillo *nm (en canción)* chorus; *(en poema)* refrain

estribo *nm* (**a**) stirrup; *Fig* **perder los estribos** to lose one's temper, to lose one's head (**b**) *Arquit* buttress; *(de puente)* pier, support

estribor *nm* starboard

estricto, -a *adj* strict

estrofa *nf* verse

estropajo *nm* scourer

estropeado, -a (**a**) *adj (averiado)* broken (**b**) *(dañado)* damaged (**c**) *(echado a perder)* ruined, spoiled

estropear 1 *vt (averiar)* to break; *(dañar)* to damage; *(echar a perder)* to ruin, to spoil **2 estropearse** *vpr (máquina)* to break down; *(comida)* to go off, to spoil

estructura *nf* structure; *(armazón)* frame, framework

estuario *nm* estuary

estuche *nm* case; *(para lápices)* pencil case

estudiante *nmf* student

estudiar [43] *vt & vi* to study

estudio *nm* (**a**) study; *(encuesta)* survey; *Com* **e. de mercado** market research (**b**) *(sala)* studio; **e. cinematográfico/de grabación** film/recording studio (**c**) *(apartamento)* studio *Br* flat *o US* apartment (**d**) **estudios** studies

estudioso, -a 1 *adj* studious **2** *nm,f* specialist

estufa *nf (calentador)* heater, *Br* fire; *Méx (cocina)* stove

estupefacto, -a *adj* astounded, flabbergasted

estupendo, -a *adj* super, marvellous; **¡e.!** great!

estupidez *nf* stupidity

estúpido, -a 1 *adj* stupid **2** *nm,f* idiot

etapa *nf* stage; **por etapas** in stages

etarra *nmf* = member of ETA

etc. *(abr* **etcétera***)* etc

etcétera *adv* etcetera

eternidad *nf* eternity; *Fam* **una e. ages**

eterno, -a *adj* eternal

ética *nf* ethic; *(ciencia)* ethics *sing*

ético, -a *adj* ethical

etimología *nf* etymology

etiqueta *nf* (**a**) *(de producto)* label (**b**) *(ceremonia)* etiquette; **de e.** formal

étnico, -a *adj* ethnic

eucalipto *nm* eucalyptus

eucaristía *nf* eucharist

eufemismo *nm* euphemism

eufórico, -a *adj* euphoric

euro *nm (moneda)* euro

Europa *n* Europe

europeo, -a *adj & nm,f* European

Euskadi *n* the Basque Country

euskera *adj & nm* Basque

eutanasia *nf* euthanasia

evacuación *nf* evacuation

evacuar [47] *vt* to evacuate

evadir 1 *vt (respuesta, peligro, impuestos)* to avoid; *(responsabilidad)* to shirk **2 evadirse** *vpr* to escape

evaluación *nf* evaluation; *Educ* assessment; **e. continua** continuous assessment

evaluar [30] *vt* to evaluate, to assess

evangelio *nm* gospel

evangelización *nf* evangelization, evangelizing

evaporar 1 *vt* to evaporate **2 evaporarse** *vpr* to evaporate; *Fig* to vanish

evasión *nf (fuga)* escape; *Fig* evasion; **e. fiscal** *o* **de impuestos** tax evasion

eventual *adj* (**a**) *(posible)* possible; *(gastos)* incidental (**b**) *(trabajo, obrero)* casual, temporary

eventualidad *nf* contingency

evidencia *nf* obviousness; **poner a algn en e.** to show sb up

evidente *adj* obvious

evidentemente *adv* obviously

evitar *vt* to avoid; *(prevenir)* to prevent; *(desastre)* to avert

evocar [44] *vt (traer a la memoria)* to evoke; *(acordarse de)* to recall

evolución *nf* evolution; *(desarrollo)* development

evolucionar *vi* to develop; *Biol* to evolve; **el enfermo evoluciona favorablemente** the patient is improving

exactamente *adv* exactly, precisely

exactitud *nf* accuracy; **con e.** precisely

exacto, -a *adj* exact; **¡e.!** precisely!; **para ser e.** to be precise

exageración *nf* exaggeration

exagerado, -a *adj* exaggerated; *(excesivo)* excessive

exagerar 1 *vt* to exaggerate **2** *vi* to overdo it

exaltar 1 *vt (ensalzar)* to praise, to extol **2 exaltarse** *vpr (acalorarse)* to get overexcited, to get carried away

examen *nm* examination, exam; *Esp* **e. de conducir** driving test; *Am* **e. de manejar** driving test; *Med* **e. médico** checkup

examinar 1 *vt* to examine **2 examinarse** *vpr Esp* to take *o* sit an examination

excavación *nf* excavation; *(en arqueología)* dig

excavadora *nf* digger

excavar *vt* to excavate, to dig

excedencia *nf Esp* leave (of absence)

exceder 1 *vt* to exceed, to surpass **2 excederse** *vpr* to go too far

excelencia *nf* (**a**) excellence; **por e.** par excellence (**b**) *(título)* **Su E.** His/Her Excellency

excelente *adj* excellent

excentricidad *nf* eccentricity

excéntrico, -a *adj* eccentric

excepción *nf* exception; **a e. de** with the exception of, except for; **de e.** exceptional; *Pol* **estado de e.** state of emergency

excepcional *adj* exceptional

excepto *adv* except (for), apart from

excesivo, -a *adj* excessive

exceso *nm* excess; **en e.** in excess, excessively; **e. de equipaje** excess baggage; **e. de velocidad** speeding

excitar 1 *vt* to excite **2 excitarse** *vpr* to get excited

exclamación *nf* exclamation

excluir [37] *vt* to exclude; *(rechazar)* to reject

exclusiva *nf Prensa* exclusive; *Com* sole right

exclusivo, -a *adj* exclusive

excursión *nf* excursion

excusa *nf (pretexto)* excuse; *(disculpa)* apology

excusar 1 *vt* (**a**) *(justificar)* to excuse (**b**) *(eximir)* to exempt (**de** from) **2 excusarse** *vpr (disculparse)* to apologize

exento, -a *adj* exempt, free (**de** from)

exhaustivo, -a *adj* exhaustive

exhibición *nf* exhibition

exhibir 1 *vt* (**a**) *(mostrar)* to exhibit, to display (**b**) *(lucir)* to show off **2 exhibirse** *vpr* to show off, to make an exhibition of oneself

exigencia *nf* (**a**) demand (**b**) *(requisito)* requirement

exigente *adj* demanding, exacting

exigir [57] *vt* to demand

exilar 1 *vt* to exile **2 exilarse** *vpr* to go into exile

exiliar [43] = **exilar**

exilio *nm* exile

existencia *nf* (**a**) *(vida)* existence (**b**) *Com* **existencias** stock, stocks

existir *vi* to exist, to be (in existence)

éxito *nm* success; **con é.** successfully; **tener é.** to be successful

exitoso, -a *adj* successful

exótico, -a *adj* exotic

expedición *nf* expedition

expediente *nm* (**a**) *(informe)* dossier, record; *(ficha)* file; *Educ* **e. académico** academic record, *US* transcript; **abrirle e. a algn** *(título)* to place sb under enquiry (**b**) *Jur* proceedings, action

expedir [6] *vt* (**a**) *(carta)* to send, to dispatch (**b**) *(pasaporte etc)* to issue

expendedor, -a 1 *nm,f* seller **2** *nm* **e. automático** vending machine

expensas *nfpl* **a e. de** at the expense of

experiencia *nf* (**a**) experience; **por e.** from experience (**b**) *(experimento)* experiment

experimentado, -a *adj* experienced

experimental *adj* experimental

experimentar 1 *vi* to experiment **2** *vt* to undergo; *(aumento)* to show; *(pérdida)* to suffer; *(sensación)* to experience, to feel; *Med* **e. una mejoría** to improve, to make progress

experimento *nm* experiment

experto, -a *nm,f* expert

expirar *vi* to expire

explicación *nf* explanation

explicar [44] **1** *vt* to explain **2 explicarse** *vpr (persona)* to explain (oneself); **no me lo explico** I can't understand it

explícito, -a *adj* explicit

explorador, -a *nm,f* (**a**) *(persona)* explorer (**b**) *Med* probe; *Téc* scanner

explorar *vt* to explore; *Med (internamente)* to explore; *(externamente)* to examine; *Téc* to scan; *Mil* to reconnoitre

explosión *nf* explosion, blast; **hacer e.** to explode; **motor de e.** internal combustion engine; **e. demográfica** population explosion

explosivo, -a *adj & nm* explosive

explotación *nf* (**a**) *(abuso)* exploitation (**b**) *(uso)* exploitation, working; *Agr* cultivation (of land); *(granja)* farm

explotar 1 *vi (bomba)* to explode, to go off **2** *vt* (**a**) *(aprovechar)* to exploit; *(recursos)* to tap; *(tierra)* to cultivate (**b**) *(abusar de)* to exploit

exponente *nmf* exponent

exponer [19] *(pp* **expuesto)** **1** *vt* (**a**) *(mostrar)* to exhibit, to display (**b**) *(explicar)* to expound, to put forward (**c**) *(arriesgar)* to expose **2 exponerse** *vpr* to expose oneself (**a** to); **te expones a perder el trabajo** you run the risk of losing your job

exportación *nf* export

exportar *vt* to export

exposición *nf* (**a**) *Arte* exhibition; **e. universal** international exposition *o* exhibition, *US* world's fair; **sala de exposiciones** gallery (**b**) *(de hechos, ideas)* exposé (**c**) *Fot* exposure

expositor, -a 1 *adj* exponent **2** *nm,f (en feria)* exhibitor; *(de teoría)* exponent

exprés *adj* express; **(olla) e.** pressure cooker; **(café) e.** espresso (coffee)

expresar 1 *vt* to express; *(manifestar)* to state **2 expresarse** *vpr* to express oneself

expresión *nf* expression; **la mínima e.** the bare minimum

expresivo, -a *adj* expressive

expreso, -a 1 *adj* express; **con el fin e. de** with the express purpose of **2** *nm Ferroc* express (train) **3** *adv* on purpose, deliberately

exprimidor *nm* squeezer, juicer

exprimir *vt (limón)* to squeeze; *(zumo)* to squeeze out; *Fig (persona)* to exploit, to bleed dry

expuesto, -a *adj* (**a**) *(sin protección)* exposed; **estar e. a** to be exposed to (**b**) *(peligroso)* risky, dangerous (**c**) *(exhibido)* on display, on show

expulsar *vt* (**a**) to expel, to throw out; *Dep (jugador)* to send off (**b**) *(gas etc)* to belch out

expulsión *nf* expulsion; *Dep* sending-off

exquisitez *nf* (**a**) *(cualidad)* exquisiteness (**b**) *(cosa)* exquisite thing; *(comida)* delicacy

exquisito, -a *adj* exquisite; *(comida)* delicious; *(gusto)* refined

éxtasis *nm inv* ecstasy

extender [3] **1** *vt* (**a**) to extend; *(agrandar)* to enlarge (**b**) *(mantel, mapa)* to spread (out), to open (out); *(mano, brazo)* to stretch (out) (**c**) *(crema, mantequilla)* to spread (**d**) *(cheque)* to make out; *(documento)* to draw up; *(certificado)* to issue **2 extenderse** *vpr* (**a**) *(en el tiempo)* to extend, to last (**b**) *(en el espacio)* to spread out, to stretch (**c**) *(rumor, noticia)* to spread, to extend (**d**) *Fig (hablar demasiado)* to go on

extensión *nf (de libro etc)* length; *(de cuerpo)* size; *(de terreno)* area, expanse; *(edificio anexo)* extension; **en toda la e. de la palabra** in every sense of the word; **por e.** by extension

extenso, -a *adj (terreno)* extensive; *(libro, película)* long

exterior 1 *adj* (**a**) *(de fuera)* outer; *(puerta)* outside (**b**) *(política, deuda)* foreign; *Pol* **Ministerio de Asuntos Exteriores** Ministry of Foreign Affairs, *Br* ≃ Foreign Office, *US* ≃ State

Department **2** *nm* (**a**) *(parte de fuera)* exterior, outside (**b**) *(extranjero)* abroad (**c**) **exteriores** *C in* location

exterminar *vt* to exterminate

externo, -a 1 *adj* external; *Farm* **de uso e.** for external use only **2** *nm,f Educ* day pupil

extinguir [59] **1** *vt (fuego)* to extinguish, to put out; *(raza)* to wipe out **2 extinguirse** *vpr (fuego)* to go out; *(especie)* to become extinct, to die out

extintor *nm Esp* fire extinguisher

extirpar *vt* (**a**) *Med* to remove (**b**) *Fig* to eradicate, to stamp out

extra 1 *adj* (**a**) *(suplementario)* extra; **horas e.** overtime; **paga e.** bonus (**b**) *(superior)* top-quality
2 *nm* extra
3 *nmf Cin, Teatro* extra

extracción *nf* (**a**) extraction (**b**) *(en lotería)* draw

extracto *nm* (**a**) extract; **e. de fresa** strawberry extract; **e. de regaliz** liquorice; *Fin* **e. de cuenta** statement of account (**b**) *(resumen)* summary

extractor *nm* extractor

extradición *nf* extradition

extraer [25] *vt* to extract, to take out

extranjero, -a 1 *adj* foreign
2 *nm,f* foreigner
3 *nm* abroad; **en el e.** abroad

extrañar 1 *vt* (**a**) *(sorprender)* to surprise; **no es de e.** it's hardly surprising (**b**) *(echar de menos)* to miss **2 extrañarse** *vpr* **extrañarse de** to be surprised at

extrañeza *nf* (**a**) *(sorpresa)* surprise, astonishment (**b**) *(singularidad)* strangeness

extraño, -a 1 *adj* strange; *Med* **cuerpo e.** foreign body **2** *nm,f* stranger

extraordinario, -a *adj* extraordinary; *Prensa* **edición extraordinaria** special edition

extraterrestre *nmf* alien

extravagante *adj* odd, outlandish

extraviar [29] **1** *vt* to mislay, to lose **2 extraviarse** *vpr* to be missing, to get mislaid

extremar 1 *vt* **e. la prudencia** to be extremely careful **2 extremarse** *vpr* to take great pains, to do one's utmost

extremaunción *nf* extreme unction

extremidad *nf* (**a**) *(extremo)* end, tip (**b**) *Anat (miembro)* limb, extremity

extremista *adj & nmf* extremist

extremo, -a 1 *nm (de calle, cable)* end; *(máximo)* extreme; **en e.** very much; **en último e.** as a last resort
2 *nm,f (en fútbol)* winger; **e. derecha/izquierda** outside right/left
3 *adj* extreme; **E. Oriente** Far East

extrovertido, -a *adj & nm,f* extrovert

Ff

fabada *nf* = stew of beans, pork sausage and bacon

fábrica *nf* factory; **marca de f.** trademark; **precio de f.** factory *o* ex-works price

fabricante *nmf* manufacturer

fabricar [44] *vt* (a) *Ind* to manufacture (b) *Fig (mentiras etc)* to fabricate

fábula *nf* fable

fabuloso, -a *adj* fabulous

faceta *nf* facet

facha 1 *nf* (a) *(aspecto)* look (b) *(mamarracho)* mess; **vas hecho una f.** you look a mess **2** *nmf Esp Fam Pey (fascista)* fascist

fachada *nf* façade

fácil *adj* (a) easy; **f. de comprender** easy to understand (b) *(probable)* likely, probable; **es f. que ...** it's (quite) likely that ...

facilidad *nf* (a) *(sencillez)* easiness (b) *(soltura)* ease (c) *(servicio)* facility; **dar facilidades** to make things easy; *Com* **facilidades de pago** easy terms (d) **f. para los idiomas** gift for languages

facilitar *vt (proporcionar)* to provide, to supply (a with)

factor *nm* (a) factor (b) *Ferroc* luggage clerk

factura *nf* (a) *Com* invoice (b) *Arg (repostería)* cakes and pastries

facturación *nf* (a) *Com* invoicing (b) *(de equipajes) (en aeropuerto)* check-in; *(en estación)* registration

facturar *vt* (a) *Com* to invoice (b) *(en aeropuerto)* to check in; *(en estación)* to register

facultad *nf* faculty; **facultades mentales** faculties

faena *nf* (a) *(tarea)* task (b) *Fam (mala pasada)* dirty trick (c) *Taurom* performance

fainá *nf Urug (plato)* = baked dough made from chickpea flour, served with pizza

faisán *nm* pheasant

faja *nf* (a) *(corsé)* girdle, corset (b) *(banda)* sash (c) *(de terreno)* strip

fajo *nm (de ropa etc)* bundle; *(de billetes)* wad

falange *nf* (a) *Anat, Mil* phalanx (b) *Pol* **la F. (Española)** the Falange

falda *nf* (a) *(prenda)* skirt; **f. pantalón** culottes (b) *(de montaña)* slope, hillside (c) *(de mesa)* cover (d) *(regazo)* lap

falencia *nf* (a) *Am Com (bancarrota)* bankruptcy (b) *CSur (error)* fault

falla *nf* (a) *(defecto)* defect, fault; **este cajón tiene una f.** there's something wrong with this drawer (b) *Am (error)* mistake; **un trabajo lleno de fallas** a piece of work full of mistakes (c) *Geol* fault

fallar¹ 1 *vi Jur* to rule **2** *vt (premio)* to award

fallar² 1 *vi* to fail; **le falló la puntería** he missed his aim; *Fig* **no me falles** don't let me down **2** *vt* to miss

fallecer [33] *vi Fml* to pass away, to die

fallo¹ *nm Esp* (a) *(error)* mistake; **f. humano** human error (b) *(del corazón, de los frenos)* failure

fallo² *nm* (a) *Jur* judgement, sentence (b) *(en concurso)* awarding

falluto, -a *RP Fam* **1** *adj* phoney, hypocritical **2** *nm,f* hypocrite

falsedad *nf* (a) falseness, *(doblez)* hypocrisy (b) *(mentira)* falsehood

falsete *nm* falsetto; **voz de f.** falsetto voice

falsificar [44] *vt* to falsify; *(cuadro,*

firma, moneda) to forge

falso, -a *adj* (a) false; **dar un paso en f.** *(tropezar)* to trip, to stumble; *Fig* to make a blunder; **jurar en f.** to commit perjury (b) *(persona)* insincere

falta *nf* (a) *(carencia)* lack; **por f. de** for want o lack of; **sin f.** without fail; **f. de educación** bad manners

(b) *(escasez)* shortage

(c) *(ausencia)* absence; **echar algo/a algn en f.** to miss sth/sb

(d) *(error)* mistake; *(defecto)* fault, defect; **f. de ortografía** spelling mistake; **sacar faltas a algo/a algn** to find fault with sth/sb

(e) *Jur* misdemeanour

(f) *(en fútbol)* foul; *(en tenis)* fault

(g) **hacer f.** to be necessary; **(nos) hace f. una escalera** we need a ladder; **harán f. dos personas para mover el piano** it'll take two people to move the piano; **no hace f. que ...** there is no need for ...

faltante *Am nm* deficit

faltar *vi* (a) *(no estar)* to be missing; **¿quién falta?** who is missing?

(b) *(escasear)* to be lacking o needed; **le falta confianza en sí mismo** he lacks confidence in himself; **¡lo que me faltaba!** that's all I needed!; **¡no faltaría o faltaba más!** *(por supuesto)* (but) of course!

(c) *(quedar)* to be left; **¿cuántos kilómetros faltan para Managua?** how many kilometres is it to Managua?; **ya falta poco para las vacaciones** it won't be long now till the holidays; **faltó poco para que me cayera** I very nearly fell

(d) **f. a su palabra/promesa** to break one's word/promise; **f. al respeto a algn** to treat sb with disrespect

fama *nf* (a) fame, renown; **de f. mundial** world-famous (b) *(reputación)* reputation

familia *nf* family; **estar en f.** to be among friends; **f. numerosa** large family

familiar 1 *adj* (a) *(de la familia)* family; **empresa f.** family business (b) *(conocido)* familiar **2** *nmf* relation, relative

familiarizarse [40] *vpr* **f. con** to familiarize oneself with

famoso, -a 1 *adj* famous **2** *nm* famous person

fanatismo *nm* fanaticism

fandango *nm (baile)* fandango

fanfarrón, -ona *Fam* **1** *adj* boastful **2** *nm,f* show-off

fantasía *nf* fantasy; **joya de f.** imitation jewellery

fantasma *nm* (a) *(espectro)* ghost (b) *Esp Fam (fanfarrón)* braggart, show-off

fantástico, -a *adj* fantastic

farmacéutico, -a 1 *adj* pharmaceutical **2** *nm,f* pharmacist, *Br* chemist, *US* druggist

farmacia *nf* (a) *(tienda)* pharmacy, *Br* chemist's (shop), *US* drugstore (b) *(ciencia)* pharmacology

faro *nm* (a) *(torre)* lighthouse (b) *(de coche)* headlight, headlamp

farol *nm* (a) lantern; *(en la calle)* streetlight, streetlamp (b) *Fam (fanfarronada)* bragging; **tirarse un f.** to brag (c) *(en naipes)* bluff

farola *nf* streetlight, streetlamp

farolillo *nm Fig* **ser el f. rojo** to bring up the rear

farsa *nf* farce

farsante *nmf* fake, impostor

fascismo *nm* fascism

fascista *adj & nmf* fascist

fase *nf* (a) *(etapa)* phase, stage (b) *Elec, Fís* phase

fastidiar [43] **1** *vt* (a) *(molestar)* to annoy, to bother; *Fam* **¡no fastidies!** you're kidding! (b) *Esp Fam (estropear)* to damage, to ruin; *(planes)* to spoil

2 fastidiarse *vpr Esp* (a) *(aguantarse)* to put up with it, to resign oneself; **que se fastidie** that's his tough luck (b) *Fam (estropearse)* to get damaged, to break down (c) **me he fastidiado el tobillo** I've hurt my ankle

fastidio *nm* nuisance

fatal 1 *adj* (a) *Esp Fam (muy malo)* terrible, awful (b) *(mortal)* deadly, fatal (c) *(inexorable)* fateful, inevitable **2** *adv*

Esp Fam awfully, terribly; **lo pasó f.** he had a rotten time

fatalidad *nf* (**a**) *(destino)* fate (**b**) *(desgracia)* misfortune

fatiga *nf* (**a**) *(cansancio)* fatigue (**b**) **fatigas** *(dificultades)* troubles, difficulties

fatigar [42] **1** *vt* to tire, to weary **2 fatigarse** *vpr* to tire, to become tired

fauna *nf* fauna

favor *nm* favour; **por f.** please; **¿puedes hacerme un f.?** can you do me a favour?; **estar a f. de** to be in favour of; **haga el f. de sentarse** please sit down

favorable *adj* favourable; **f. a** in favour of

favorecer [33] *vt* (**a**) to favour (**b**) *(sentar bien)* to flatter

favorito, -a *adj & nm,f* favourite

fax *nm* (**a**) *(aparato)* fax (machine); **mandar algo por f.** to fax sth (**b**) *(documento)* fax

fayuquero, -a *nm,f Méx Fam* dealer in contraband

fe *nf* (**a**) faith; **de buena/mala fe** with good/dishonest intentions (**b**) *(certificado)* certificate; **fe de bautismo/ matrimonio** baptism/marriage certificate (**c**) *Impr* **fe de erratas** errata

fealdad *nf* ugliness

febrero *nm* February

fecha *nf* (**a**) date; **f. límite** *o* **tope** deadline; **f. de caducidad** sell-by date; **hasta la f.** so far; **en f. próxima** at an early date (**b**) **fechas** *(época)* time; **el año pasado por estas fechas** this time last year

fechar *vt* to date

fecundo, -a *adj* fertile

federación *nf* federation

felicidad *nf* happiness; **(muchas) felicidades** *(en cumpleaños)* many happy returns

felicitación *nf* **tarjeta de f.** greetings card

felicitar *vt* to congratulate (**por** on); **¡te felicito!** congratulations!

feligrés, -esa *nm,f* parishioner

feliz *adj* (**a**) *(contento)* happy; **¡felices Navidades!** Happy *o* Merry Christmas! (**b**) *(decisión etc)* fortunate

felpudo *nm* mat, doormat

femenino, -a *adj* feminine; *(equipo, ropa)* women's; **el sexo f.** the female sex, women

feminismo *nm* feminism

feminista *adj & nmf* feminist

fémur *nm* femur

fenomenal 1 *adj* (**a**) phenomenal (**b**) *Fam (fantástico)* great, terrific **2** *adv Fam* wonderfully, marvellously; **lo pasamos f.** we had a fantastic time

fenómeno, -a 1 *nm* (**a**) phenomenon (**b**) *(prodigio)* genius (**c**) *(monstruo)* freak

2 *adj Fam* fantastic, terrific

3 *interj* fantastic!, terrific!

feo, -a 1 *adj* ugly; *(asunto etc)* nasty **2** *nm Fam* **hacerle un f. a algn** to offend sb

féretro *nm* coffin

feria *nf* fair; **f. de muestras/del libro** trade/book fair

feriado, -a *Am* **1** *adj* **día f.** (public) holiday **2** *nm* (public) holiday

fermentación *nf* fermentation

feroz *adj* fierce, ferocious; **el lobo f.** the big bad wolf

ferretería *nf Br* ironmonger's (shop), *US* hardware store

ferrocarril *nm Br* railway, *US* railroad

ferroviario, -a *adj* rail(way), *US* railroad

ferry *nm* ferry

fértil *adj* fertile

fertilidad *nf* fertility

festival *nm* festival

festividad *nf* festivity

festivo, -a 1 *adj* (**a**) *(ambiente etc)* festive (**b**) **día f.** holiday **2** *nm* holiday

feta *nf RP* slice

feto *nm* foetus

fiaca *nf Méx, CSur Fam (pereza)* laziness; **¡qué fiaca tener que ponerme a planchar!** what a pain *o Br* fag having to do the ironing!

fiambre *nm* (**a**) *Culin Br* cold meat, *US*

cold cut (**b**) *Fam (cadáver)* stiff, corpse

fiambrera *nf* lunchbox

fianza *nf (depósito)* deposit; *Jur* bail; **en libertad bajo f.** on bail

fiar [29] **1** *vt* (**a**) *(avalar)* to guarantee (**b**) *(vender sin cobrar)* to sell on credit **2 fiarse** *vpr* **fiarse (de)** to trust

fibra *nf* fibre; *(de madera)* grain; **f. de vidrio** fibreglass

ficción *nf* fiction

ficha *nf* (**a**) *(tarjeta)* filing card; **f. técnica** specifications, technical data; *Cin* credits (**b**) *(en juegos)* counter; *(de ajedrez)* piece, man; *(de dominó)* domino

fichar 1 *vt* (**a**) to put on file (**b**) *Dep* to sign up **2** *vi* (**a**) *(en el trabajo) (al entrar)* to clock in; *US* to punch in; *(al salir)* to clock out *o* off, *US* to punch out (**b**) *Dep* to sign

fichero *nm* card index

ficticio, -a *adj* fictitious

fidelidad *nf* faithfulness; **alta f.** high fidelity, hi-fi

fideo *nm* noodle

fiebre *nf* fever; **tener f.** to have a temperature

fiel 1 *adj* (**a**) *(leal)* faithful, loyal (**b**) *(exacto)* accurate, exact **2** *nm* (**a**) *(de balanza)* needle, pointer (**b**) *Rel* **los fieles** the congregation

fieltro *nm* felt

fiera *nf* (**a**) wild animal; *Fam* **estaba hecho una f.** he was hopping mad (**b**) *Taurom* bull

fiero, -a *adj (salvaje)* wild; *(feroz)* fierce, ferocious

fierro *nm Am (hierro)* iron

fiesta *nf* (**a**) *(entre amigos)* party (**b**) **día de f.** holiday (**c**) *Rel* feast; **f. de guardar** holiday of obligation (**d**) *(festividad)* celebration, festivity

figura *nf* figure

figurar 1 *vi (en lista)* to figure **2 figurarse** *vpr* (**a**) to imagine, to suppose; **ya me lo figuraba** I thought as much (**b**) **¡figúrate!, ¡figúrese!** just imagine!

figurativo, -a *adj Arte* figurative

figurín *nm* fashion sketch; *Fig* **ir** *o* **estar hecho un f.** to be dressed up to the nines

fijador *nm* (**a**) *(gomina)* gel (**b**) *Fot* fixative

fijar 1 *vt* to fix; **prohibido f. carteles** *(en letrero)* post no bills **2 fijarse** *vpr* (**a**) *(darse cuenta)* to notice (**b**) *(poner atención)* to pay attention, to watch

fijo, -a *adj* (**a**) fixed; **sin domicilio f.** of no fixed abode (**b**) *(trabajo)* steady

fila *nf* (**a**) file; **en f. india** in single file; **poner en f.** to line up (**b**) *(de cine, teatro)* row (**c**) *Mil* **filas** ranks; **llamar a algn a filas** to call sb up; **¡rompan filas!** fall out!, dismiss!

filatelia *nf* philately, stamp collecting

filete *nm (de carne, pescado)* fillet

filiación *nf Pol* affiliation

filial 1 *adj* (**a**) *(de hijos)* filial (**b**) *Com* subsidiary **2** *nf Com* subsidiary

Filipinas *npl* **(las) F.** (the) Philippines

filmar *vt* to film, to shoot

filoso, -a *adj Am* sharp

filosofar *vi* to philosophize

filosofía *nf* philosophy; *Fig* **con f.** philosophically

filósofo, -a *nm,f* philosopher

filtrar 1 *vt* (**a**) to filter (**b**) *(información)* to leak **2 filtrarse** *vpr* (**a**) *(líquido)* to seep (**b**) *(información)* to leak out

filtro *nm* filter

filudo *adj Andes* sharp

fin *nm* (**a**) *(final)* end; **dar** *o* **poner f. a** to put an end to; **llegar** *o* **tocar a su f.** to come to an end; **en f.** anyway; **¡por** *o* **al f.!** at last!; **f. de semana** weekend; **al f. y al cabo** when all's said and done (**b**) *(objetivo)* purpose, aim; **a f. de** in order to, so as to; **a f. de que** in order that, so that; **con el f. de** with the intention of

final 1 *adj* final

2 *nm* end; **al f.** in the end; **f. de línea** terminal; **f. feliz** happy ending; **a finales de octubre** at the end of October

3 *nf Dep* final

finalidad *nf* purpose, aim

finalista 1 *nmf* finalist 2 *adj* in the final

finalizar [40] *vt & vi* to end, to finish

financiación *nf* financing

financiar [43] *vt* to finance

financista *nmf Am* financier

finanzas *nfpl* finances

finca *nf (inmueble)* property; *(de campo)* country house

fingir [57] 1 *vt* to feign 2 **fingirse** *vpr* to pretend to be

finlandés, -esa 1 *adj* Finnish 2 *nm,f (persona)* Finn 3 *nm (idioma)* Finnish

Finlandia *n* Finland

fino, -a 1 *adj* (a) *(hilo, capa)* fine (b) *(flaco)* thin (c) *(educado)* refined, polite (d) *(oído)* sharp, acute; *(olfato)* keen (e) *(humor, ironía)* subtle 2 *nm (vino)* = type of dry sherry

fiordo *nm Geog* fiord

firma *nf* (a) signature (b) *(empresa)* firm, company

firmar *vt* to sign

firme 1 *adj* (a) firm; *Fig* **mantenerse f.** to hold one's ground; **tierra f.** terra firma (b) *Mil* **¡firmes!** attention! 2 *nm (de carretera)* road surface 3 *adv* hard

firmemente *adv* firmly

firmeza *nf* firmness

fiscal 1 *adj* fiscal 2 *nmf Jur Br* ≃ public prosecutor, *US* ≃ district attorney

fiscalía *nf Jur (cargo) Br* ≃ post of public prosecutor, *US* ≃ post of district attorney; *(oficina) Br* ≃ public prosecutor's office, *US* ≃ district attorney's office

física *nf* physics *sing*

físico, -a 1 *adj* physical 2 *nm,f (profesión)* physicist 3 *nm* physique

fisioterapeuta *nmf* physiotherapist

fisonomía *nf* physiognomy

fisonomista *nmf Fam* **ser buen/mal f.** to be good/no good at remembering faces

flaco, -a 1 *adj* (a) *(delgado)* skinny (b) *Fig* **punto f.** weak spot 2 *nm,f Am Fam (como apelativo)* **¿cómo estás, flaca?** hey, how are you doing?

flamante *adj* (a) **nuevecito f.** *(nuevo)* brand-new (b) *(vistoso)* splendid, brilliant

flamenco, -a 1 *adj* (a) *Mús* flamenco (b) *(de Flandes)* Flemish 2 *nm* (a) *Mús* flamenco (b) *Orn* flamingo (c) *(idioma)* Flemish

flan *nm* crème caramel

flaqueza *nf* weakness

flash [flaʃ, flas] *nm (pl* **flashes)** *Fot* flash

flato *nm Esp* **tener f.** to have a stitch

flauta *nf* flute; **f. dulce** recorder

flecha *nf* arrow

fleco *nm* fringe

flemón *nm* gumboil, abscess

flequillo *nm Br* fringe, *US* bangs

flexibilidad *nf* flexibility

flexible *adj* flexible

flexión *nf* (a) *Ling* inflection (b) **flexiones de brazo** push-ups, *Br* press-ups

flojear *vi (ventas etc)* to fall off, go down; *(piernas)* to weaken, grow weak; *(memoria)* to fail; *Andes Fam (holgazanear)* to laze about o around

flojera *nf Fam* weakness, faintness

flojo, -a *adj* (a) *(tornillo, cuerda etc)* loose, slack (b) *(perezoso)* lazy, idle; *(examen, trabajo, resultado)* poor

flor *nf* (a) flower; **en f.** in blossom; *Fig* **en la f. de la vida** in the prime of life; *Fig* **la f. y nata** the cream (of society) (b) **a f. de piel** skin-deep

flora *nf* flora

florecer [33] *vi* (a) *(plantas)* to flower (b) *Fig (negocio)* to flourish, to thrive

florero *nm* vase

florido, -a *adj* (a) *(con flores)* flowery (b) *(estilo)* florid

florista *nmf* florist

floristería *nf* florist's (shop)

flota *nf* fleet

flotador *nm* (a) *(de pesca)* float (b) *(para nadar)* rubber ring

flotar *vi* to float

flote *nm* floating; **a f.** afloat; **sacar a f. un negocio** to put a business on a sound footing

fluido, -a 1 *adj* fluid; *(estilo etc)* fluent **2** *nm* fluid; **f. eléctrico** current

fluir [37] *vi* to flow

flúor *nm* fluorine

FM *nf* (*abr* **Frecuencia Modulada**) FM

foca *nf* seal

foco *nm* (**a**) *Elec* spotlight, floodlight (**b**) *(de ideas, revolución etc)* centre, focal point (**c**) *Am (de vehículo)* (car) headlight; *(farola)* streetlight (**d**) *Andes, Méx (bombilla)* light bulb

foie-gras [fwa'ɣras] *nm inv* (pâté de) foie-gras

folclore *nm* folklore

folclórico, -a 1 *adj* traditional, popular **2** *nm,f Esp* = singer of traditional Spanish songs

fólder *nm Andes, CAm, Méx (carpeta)* folder

folio *nm* sheet of paper

folklórico, -a = **folclórico**

follaje *nm* foliage

follar *vi & vt Esp muy Fam* to lay, *Br* to shag

folleto *nm* leaflet; *(turístico)* brochure

follón *nm Esp Fam* (**a**) *(discusión)* row (**b**) *(lío)* mess; **me hice un f. con las listas** I got into a real muddle o mess with the lists

fomentar *vt* to promote

fonda *nf* inn

fondo¹ *nm* (**a**) *(parte más baja)* bottom; **a f.** thoroughly; **tocar f.** *Náut* to touch bottom; *Fig* to reach rock bottom; *Fig* **en el f. es bueno** deep down he's kind; **doble f.** false bottom (**b**) *(de habitación)* back; *(de pasillo)* end (**c**) *(segundo término)* background; **música de f.** background music (**d**) *Dep* **corredor de f.** long-distance runner; **esquí de f.** cross-country skiing

fondo² *nm Fin* fund; **cheque sin fondos** bad cheque; *Fam* **f. común** kitty

fono *nm Am Fam* phone

fontanero, -a *nm,f* plumber

footing *nm* jogging; **hacer f.** to go jogging

forastero, -a *nm,f* outsider, stranger

forense 1 *adj* forensic **2** *nmf* (**médico**) **f.** forensic surgeon

forestal *adj* forest; **repoblación f.** reafforestation

forfait [for'fait, for'fe] *nm* (*pl* **forfaits**) (**a**) *(para esquiar)* ski pass (**b**) *Dep* default

forjar *vt* (*metal*) to forge; *Fig* to create, to make

forma *nf* (**a**) form, shape; **en f. de L** L-shaped (**b**) *(manera)* way; **de esta f.** in this way; **de f. que** so that; **de todas formas** anyway, in any case; **no hubo f. de convencerla** there was no way we could convince her; **f. de pago** method of payment (**c**) *Dep* form; **estar en f.** to be on form; **estar en baja f.** to be off form (**d**) **formas** *(modales)* manners

formación *nf* (**a**) formation (**b**) *(educación)* upbringing (**c**) *(enseñanza)* training; **f. profesional** vocational training

formal *adj* (**a**) formal (**b**) *(serio)* serious, serious-minded (**c**) *(fiable)* reliable, dependable

formalidad *nf* (**a**) formality (**b**) *(seriedad)* seriousness (**c**) *(fiabilidad)* reliability (**d**) **formalidades** *(trámites)* formalities

formar 1 *vt* (**a**) to form; **f. parte de algo** to be a part of sth (**b**) *(educar)* to bring up; *(enseñar)* to educate, to train **2 formarse** *vpr* (**a**) to be formed, to form; **se formó un charco** a puddle formed; **formarse una impresión de algo** to get an impression of sth (**b**) *(educarse)* to be educated o trained

formidable *adj* (**a**) *(estupendo)* wonderful, terrific (**b**) *(espantoso)* formidable

fórmula *nf* formula; *Aut* **f. uno** formula one

formular *vt* (*quejas, peticiones*) to make; *(deseo)* to express; *(pregunta)* to ask; *(una teoría)* to formulate

formulario *nm* form

forofo, -a *nm,f Esp Fam* fan, supporter

forrar 1 *vt (por dentro)* to line; *(por fuera)* to cover **2 forrarse** *vpr Fam (de dinero)* to make a packet

forro *nm* (**a**) *(por dentro)* lining; *(por fuera)* cover, case (**b**) *RP Fam (preservativo)* rubber

fortaleza *nf* (**a**) strength; *(de espíritu)* fortitude (**b**) *Mil* fortress, stronghold

fortuna *nf* (**a**) *(destino)* fortune, fate (**b**) *(suerte)* luck; **por f.** fortunately (**c**) *(capital)* fortune

forzado, -a *adj* forced; **a marchas forzadas** at a brisk pace; **trabajos forzados** hard labour

forzar [2] *vt* (**a**) *(obligar)* to force; **f. a algn a hacer algo** to force sb to do sth (**b**) *(puerta, candado)* to force, to break open

forzosamente *adv* necessarily

fósforo *nm (cerilla)* match

fósil *adj & nm* fossil

foso *nm* (**a**) *(hoyo)* pit (**b**) *(de fortificación)* moat (**c**) *(en garage)* inspection pit

foto *nf Fam* photo; **sacar/echar una f.** to take a photo

fotocopia *nf* photocopy

fotocopiadora *nf* photocopier

fotocopiar [43] *vt* to photocopy

fotografía *nf* (**a**) photograph; **echar** *o* **hacer** *o* **sacar fotografías** to take photographs (**b**) *(arte)* photography

fotografiar [29] *vt* to photograph, to take a photograph of

fotográfico, -a *adj* photographic

fotógrafo, -a *nm,f* photographer

fotomatón *nm* passport photo machine

FP *nf Educ* (*abr* **Formación Profesional**) vocational training

fra. (*abr* **factura**) inv

fracasar *vi* to fail

fracaso *nm* failure

fracción *nf* (**a**) fraction (**b**) *Pol* faction

fraccionamiento *nm Méx (urbanización)* housing estate

fractura *nf* fracture

fragancia *nf* fragrance

frágil *adj* (**a**) *(quebradizo)* fragile (**b**) *(débil)* frail

fragmento *nm* fragment; *(de novela etc)* passage

fraile *nm* friar, monk

frambuesa *nf* raspberry

francamente *adv* frankly

francés, -esa 1 *adj* French; *Culin* **tortilla francesa** plain omelette **2** *nm,f* Frenchman, *f* Frenchwoman **3** *nm (idioma)* French

Francia *n* France

franco, -a 1 *adj* (**a**) *(persona)* frank (**b**) *Com* **f. a bordo** free on board; **f. fábrica** ex-works; **puerto f.** free port (**c**) *CSur, Méx (día)* **me dieron el día f.** they gave me the day off **2** *nm Antes (moneda)* franc

francotirador, -a *nm,f* sniper

franela *nf* (**a**) *(tejido)* flannel (**b**) *Bol, Col, Ven (camiseta) (interior) Br* vest, *US* undershirt; *(exterior)* T-shirt (**c**) *Bol, Col, Ven (sudadera)* sweatshirt

franja *nf* *(de terreno)* strip; *(de bandera)* stripe; *Cost* fringe, border

franqueo *nm* postage

frasco *nm* small bottle, flask

frase *nf (oración)* sentence; *(expresión)* phrase; **f. hecha** set phrase *o* expression

fraternal *adj* brotherly, fraternal

fraternidad *nf* brotherhood, fraternity

fraude *nm* fraud; **f. fiscal** tax evasion

fray *nm Rel* brother

frazada *nf Am* blanket

frecuencia *nf* frequency; **con f.** frequently, often

frecuente *adj* frequent

fregadero *nm Esp, Méx* (kitchen) sink

fregado¹ *nm* (**a**) *(lavado)* washing (**b**) *Fam (follón)* racket

fregado², -a *adj Andes, Méx, Ven Fam* (**a**) *(persona) (ser)* annoying; **mi vecino es muy f.** my neighbour's a real pain (**b**) *(persona) (estar)* **perdí las llaves, ¡estoy fregada!** I've lost my keys, I've had it! (**c**) *(objeto) (roto)* bust

fregar [1] *vt* (**a**) *(lavar)* to wash; *(suelo)* to mop (**b**) *Andes, Méx, Ven Fam (molestar)* to annoy, irritate (**c**) *Andes, Méx, Ven Fam (estropear)* to bust, to break

fregón, -ona *adj Col, Ecuad, Méx (molesto)* annoying

fregona *nf Esp* mop

freír [56] *(pp* **frito)** 1 *vt* to fry 2 **freírse** *vpr* to fry; *Fig* **freírse de calor** to be roasting

frenar *vt* to brake; *Fig (inflación etc)* to slow down; *(impulsos)* to restrain

frenazo *nm* sudden braking; **dar un f.** to jam on the brakes

frenético, -a *adj* frantic

freno *nm* (**a**) brake; **pisar/soltar el f.** to press/release the brake; **f. de disco/tambor** disc/drum brake; **f. de mano** *Br* handbrake, *US* emergency brake (**b**) *(de caballería)* bit (**c**) *Fig* curb, check; **poner f. a algo** to curb sth

frente 1 *nm* front; **al f. de** at the head of; **chocar de f.** to crash head on; **hacer f. a algo** to face sth, to stand up to sth 2 *nf Anat* forehead; **f. a f.** face to face 3 *adv* **f. a** in front of, opposite

fresa *nf* (**a**) *Esp, CAm, Carib, Méx (planta, fruto)* strawberry (**b**) *Téc* milling cutter

fresco, -a 1 *adj* (**a**) *(frío)* cool (**b**) *(comida, fruta)* fresh (**c**) *(reciente)* fresh, new (**d**) *(caradura)* cheeky, forward, *US* fresh; **se quedó tan f.** he didn't bat an eyelid; **¡qué f.!** what a nerve! 2 *nm* (**a**) *(frescor)* fresh air, cool air; **al f.** in a cool place; **hace f.** it's chilly (**b**) *Arte* fresco

fresno *nm* ash tree

fresón *nm* (large) strawberry

frigider *nm Andes* refrigerator, *Br* fridge, *US* icebox

frigorífico, -a 1 *nm Esp Br* refrigerator, *Br* fridge, *US* icebox 2 *adj* **cámara frigorífica** cold store

frijol, fríjol *nm Am salvo RP* bean

frío, -a 1 *adj* (**a**) cold (**b**) *(indiferente)* cold, cool, indifferent; **su comentario me dejó f.** her remark left me cold 2 *nm* cold; **hace f.** it's cold

friolento, -a *adj Am* sensitive to the cold

fritada *nf* fry-up, dish of fried food

fritanga *nf* (**a**) *Esp (comida frita)* fry-up; (**b**) *Am Pey (comida grasienta)* greasy food

frito, -a 1 *adj* (**a**) *Culin* fried (**b**) *Fam* exasperated, fed up; **me tienes f.** I'm sick to death of you 2 *nm* **fritos** fried food

fritura *nf* fry-up, dish of fried food

frívolo, -a *adj* frivolous

frondoso, -a *adj* leafy, luxuriant

frontera *nf* frontier

fronterizo, -a *adj* frontier, border; **países fronterizos** neighbouring countries

frontón *nm Dep* pelota

frotar 1 *vt* to rub 2 **frotarse** *vpr* to rub; **frotarse las manos** to rub one's hands together

fruncir [52] *vt* (**a**) *Cost* to gather (**b**) *(labios)* to purse, to pucker; **f. el ceño** to frown, to knit one's brow

frustración *nf* frustration

frustrar 1 *vt* to frustrate; *(defraudar)* to disappoint 2 **frustrarse** *vpr* (**a**) *(esperanza)* to fail, to go awry (**b**) *(persona)* to be frustrated *o* disappointed

fruta *nf* fruit; **f. del tiempo** fresh fruit

frutal 1 *adj* fruit; **árbol f.** fruit tree 2 *nm* fruit tree

frutería *nf* fruit shop

frutero, -a 1 *nm,f* fruit seller, *Br* fruiterer 2 *nm* fruit dish *o* bowl

frutilla *nf Bol, CSur, Ecuad* strawberry

fruto *nm* fruit; **frutos secos** nuts; **dar f.** to bear fruit; *Fig (dar buen resultado)* to be fruitful; **sacar f. de algo** to profit from sth

fuego *nm* (**a**) fire; **fuegos artificiales** fireworks (**b**) *(lumbre)* light; **¿me da f., por favor?** have you got a light, please? (**c**) *Culin* **a f. lento** on a low flame; *(al horno)* in a slow oven

fuelle *nm (para soplar)* bellows

fuente *nf* (**a**) fountain; *Chile, Col, Méx, Ven* **f. de soda** *(cafetería)* = café or counter selling ice cream, soft drinks etc, *US* soda fountain *(serving soft drinks and alcohol)* (**b**) *(recipiente)* dish, serving dish (**c**) *(de información)* source

fuera[1] *adv* (**a**) outside, out; **quédate f.** stay outside; **sal f.** go out; **desde f.** from (the) outside; **por f.** on the outside; **la puerta de f.** the outer door (**b**) **f. de** out of; **f. de serie** extraordinary; *Fig* **estar f. de sí** to be beside oneself (**c**) *Dep* **el equipo de f.** the away team; **jugar f.** to play away; **f. de juego** offside

fuera[2] **1** *subj imperf de* **ir 2** *subj imperf de* **ser**

fuerte 1 *adj* strong; *(dolor)* severe; *(sonido)* loud; *(comida)* heavy; **el plato f.** the main course; *Fig* the most important event **2** *nm* (**a**) *(fortaleza)* fort (**b**) *(punto fuerte)* forte, strong point **3** *adv* **¡abrázame f.!** hold me tight!; **comer f.** to eat a lot; **¡habla más f.!** speak up!; **¡pégale f.!** hit him hard!

fuerza *nf* (**a**) *(fortaleza)* strength; *Fig* **a f. de** by dint of (**b**) *(violencia)* force; **a la f.** *(por obligación)* of necessity; *(con violencia)* by force; **por f.** of necessity; **f. mayor** force majeure (**c**) *Fís* force (**d**) *(cuerpo)* force; **las fuerzas del orden** the forces of law and order; **f. aérea** air force; **fuerzas armadas** armed forces

fuese 1 *subj imperf de* **ir 2** *subj imperf de* **ser**

fuete *nm Am salvo RP* whip

fuga *nf* (**a**) *(huida)* escape; **darse a la f.** to take flight (**b**) *(de gas etc)* leak

fugarse [42] *vpr* to escape; **f. de casa** to run away from home

fugaz *adj* fleeting, brief

fugitivo, -a *nm,f* fugitive

fui 1 *pt indef de* **ir 2** *pt indef de* **ser**

fulana *nf* whore, tart

fulano, -a *nm,f* so-and-so; *(hombre)* what's-his-name; *(mujer)* what's-hername; **Doña Fulana de tal** Mrs So-and-so

fulminante *adj (cese)* summary; *(muerte, enfermedad)* sudden; *(mirada)* withering

fumador, -a *nm,f* smoker; **los no fumadores** nonsmokers

fumar 1 *vt & vi* to smoke; **no f.** *(en letrero)* no smoking **2 fumarse** *vpr* to smoke; **fumarse un cigarro** to smoke a cigarette

función *nf* (**a**) function; **en f. de** according to (**b**) *(cargo)* duties; **entrar en funciones** to take up one's duties; **presidente en funciones** acting president (**c**) *Cin, Teatro* performance

funcionar *vi* to work; **no funciona** *(en letrero)* out of order

funcionario, -a *nm,f* civil servant; **f. público** public official

funda *nf* cover; *(de gafas etc)* case; *(de espada)* sheath; **f. de almohada** pillowcase

fundación *nf* foundation

fundador, -a *nm,f* founder

fundamental *adj* fundamental

fundamento *nm* basis, grounds; **sin f.** unfounded

fundar 1 *vt* (**a**) *(empresa)* to found (**b**) *(teoría)* to base, to found **2 fundarse** *vpr* (**a**) *(empresa)* to be founded (**b**) *(teoría)* to be based (**en** on)

fundición *nf* (**a**) *(de metales)* smelting (**b**) *(fábrica)* foundry

fundir 1 *vt* (**a**) to melt; *(bombilla, plomos)* to blow (**b**) *(unir)* to unite, join **2 fundirse** *vpr* (**a**) *(derretirse)* to melt (**b**) *(bombilla, plomos)* to blow (**c**) *(unirse)* to merge (**d**) *Am Fam (arruinarse)* to go bust

funeral *nm* funeral

fungir *vi Méx, Perú* to act, to serve (**de** o **como** as)

funicular *nm* funicular (railway)

furgón *nm Aut* van

furgoneta *nf* van

furia *nf* fury; **ponerse hecho una f.** to become furious, to fly into a rage

furioso, -a *adj* furious; **ponerse f.** to become furious

furor *nm* fury, rage; *Fig* **hacer f.** to be all the rage

fusible *nm* fuse

fusil *nm* gun, rifle

fusilar *vt* to shoot, to execute

fusión *nf* (**a**) *(de metales)* fusion; *(del hielo)* thawing, melting; **punto de f.** melting point (**b**) *Com* merger

fustán *nm Am* petticoat

fútbol *nm* soccer, *Br* football

futbolín *nm Esp Br* table football, *US* foosball

futbolista *nmf* soccer *o Br* football player, *Br* footballer

futuro,-a 1 *adj* future **2** *nm* future; **en un f. próximo** in the near future; *CSur, Méx* **a f.** in the future

Gg

g (*abr* **gramo**) g

gabán *nm* overcoat

gabardina *nf (prenda)* raincoat

gabinete *nm* (**a**) *(despacho)* study; **g. de abogados** lawyers' office (**b**) *Pol* cabinet

gafas *nfpl* glasses, spectacles; **g. de sol** sunglasses

gafe *Esp Fam* **1** *adj* jinxed; **ser g.** to be jinxed **2** *nmf* jinxed person

gafete *nm Méx* badge

gaita *nf* bagpipes

gala *nf* (**a**) *(vestido)* full dress; **de g.** dressed up; *(ciudad)* decked out (**b**) *Esp (espectáculo)* gala; **hacer g. de** to glory in (**c**) **galas** finery

galán *nm* (**a**) handsome young man; *Hum* ladies' man (**b**) *Teatro* leading man

galaxia *nf* galaxy

galería *nf* (**a**) *Arquit* covered balcony (**b**) *(museo)* art gallery (**c**) *Teatro* gallery, gods

Gales *n* (**el país de**) **G.** Wales

galés, -esa **1** *adj* Welsh
2 *nm,f* Welshman, *f* Welshwoman; **los galeses** the Welsh
3 *nm (idioma)* Welsh

Galicia *n* Galicia

gallego, -a **1** *adj* (**a**) Galician (**b**) *CSur, Cuba Fam* = sometimes pejorative term used to refer to a Spanish person
2 *nm,f* (**a**) Galician, native of Galicia (**b**) *CSur, Cuba Fam* = sometimes pejorative term used to refer to a Spaniard, especially an immigrant
3 *nm (idioma)* Galician

galleta *nf* (**a**) *Culin Br* biscuit, *US* cookie (**b**) *Esp Fam (cachete)* slap

gallina **1** *nf* hen **2** *nmf Fam* coward, chicken

gallinero *nm* (**a**) hen run (**b**) *Teatro* **el g.** the gods

gallo *nm* (**a**) cock, rooster; *Fam Fig* **en menos que un canto de g.** before you could say Jack Robinson (**b**) *Fam Mús* off-key note

galopar *vi* to gallop

galope *nm* gallop; **a g. tendido** flat out

galpón *nm Andes, Carib, RP* shed

gama *nf* range; *Mús* scale

gamba *nf* prawn, *US* shrimp

gamberro, -a *Esp* **1** *nm,f* hooligan, lout, *Br* yob **2** *adj* loutish

gamonal *nm Andes, CAm, Ven* (**a**) *(cacique)* village, chief (**b**) *(caudillo)* cacique, local political boss

gamuza *nf* (**a**) *Zool* chamois (**b**) *(trapo)* chamois o shammy leather

gana *nf* (**a**) *(deseo)* wish (**de** for); **de buena g.** willingly; **de mala g.** reluctantly; *Fam* **no me da la g.** I don't feel like it (**b**) **tener ganas de (hacer) algo** to feel like (doing) sth; **quedarse con las ganas** not to manage (**c**) *(apetito)* appetite; **comer con ganas** to eat heartily

ganadería *nf* (**a**) *(crianza)* livestock farming (**b**) *(conjunto de ganado)* livestock

ganadero, -a *nm,f* livestock farmer

ganado *nm* (**a**) livestock (**b**) *Fam Fig (gente)* crowd

ganador, -a **1** *adj* winning **2** *nm,f* winner

ganancia *nf* profit

ganar **1** *vt* (**a**) *(sueldo)* to earn (**b**) *(victoria)* to win (**c**) *(aventajar)* to beat (**d**) *(alcanzar)* to reach **2 ganarse** *vpr* (**a**) to earn; **ganarse el pan** to earn one's daily bread (**b**) *(merecer)* to deserve; **se lo ha ganado** he deserves it

ganchillo nm crochet work

gancho nm (**a**) hook (**b**) Fam Fig (gracia, atractivo) charm (**c**) Andes, CAm, Méx (horquilla) hairpin (**d**) Andes, CAm, Méx, Ven (percha) hanger (**e**) Col, Ven (pinza) Br (clothes) peg, US clothes pin

gandul, -a nm,f loafer

ganga nf bargain

ganso, -a 1 nm,f (**a**) goose; (macho) gander (**b**) Fam dolt **2** adj Fam ginormous; **pasta gansa** bread, dough

gánster nm (pl **gánsters** o **gánsteres**) gangster

garabato nm scrawl

garaje nm garage

garantía nf (**a**) guarantee (**b**) Jur (fianza) bond, security

garbanzo nm chickpea

garfio nm hook, grappling iron

garganta nf (**a**) throat (**b**) (desfiladero) narrow pass

gargantilla nf short necklace

gárgaras nfpl gargling sing; Fam ¡**vete a hacer g.!** get lost!

garra nf (**a**) Zool claw; (de ave) talon (**b**) Fig (fuerza) force; **tener g.** to be compelling

garrafa nf carafe

garrapata nf tick

garúa nf Andes, RP, Ven drizzle

gas nm (**a**) gas; Esp **g. ciudad** town gas; **gases (nocivos)** fumes; **g. de escape** exhaust fumes (**b**) (en bebida) fizz; **agua con g.** fizzy water (**c**) Med **gases** flatulence

gasa nf gauze

gaseosa nf (**a**) Esp, Arg (bebida transparente) pop, Br lemonade (**b**) CAm, RP (refresco con gas) fizzy drink, US soda

gaseoso, -a adj (estado) gaseous; (bebida) fizzy

gasfitero, -a nm,f Ecuad plumber

gasóleo, gasoil nm diesel oil

gasolina nf Br petrol, US gas, US gasoline

gasolinera, Méx **gasolinería** nf Br petrol o US gas station

gastar 1 vt (**a**) (consumir) (dinero, tiempo) to spend; (gasolina, electricidad) to consume (**b**) Fig (malgastar) to waste (**c**) Esp (ropa) to wear; ¿**qué número gastas?** what size do you take? (**d**) **g. una broma a algn** to play a practical joke on sb **2 gastarse** vpr (**a**) (zapatos etc) to wear out (**b**) (gasolina etc) to run out

gasto nm expenditure; **gastos** expenses; **gastos de viaje** travelling expenses

gastritis nf inv Med gastritis

gastronomía nf gastronomy

gastronómico nf gastronomy

gatear vi (**a**) to crawl (**b**) (trepar) to climb

gatillo nm (de armas) trigger; **apretar el g.** to pull the trigger

gato nm (**a**) cat (**b**) Aut, Téc jack

gauchada nf CSur favour

gaucho, -a 1 adj RP Fam (servicial) helpful, obliging **2** nm,f gaucho

gaveta nf drawer

gavilán nm Orn sparrowhawk

gaviota nf seagull

gazpacho nm Culin gazpacho

gel nm gel; **g. (de ducha)** shower gel

gelatina nf (de carne) gelatine; (de fruta) Br jelly, US Jell-O®

gemelo, -a 1 adj & nm,f (identical) twin **2 gemelos** nmpl (**a**) (de camisa) cufflinks (**b**) (anteojos) binoculars

gemido nm groan

Géminis nm Gemini

gemir [6] vi to groan

generación nf generation

generador nm Elec generator

general 1 adj general; **por lo** o **en g.** in general, generally; **2** nm Mil, Rel general

generalizar [40] **1** vt (**a**) to generalize (**b**) (extender) to spread **2 generalizarse** vpr to become widespread o common

generalmente adv generally

generar *vt* to generate

género *nm* (**a**) *(clase)* kind, sort (**b**) *Arte, Lit* genre (**c**) *(mercancía)* article (**d**) *Ling* gender (**e**) *Biol* genus; **el g. humano** mankind

generosidad *nf* generosity

generoso, -a *adj* (**a**) generous (**con** to) (**b**) *(vino)* full-bodied

genial *adj* great, *Br* brilliant

genio *nm* (**a**) *(carácter)* temperament; *(mal carácter)* temper; **estar de mal g.** to be in a bad mood (**b**) *(facultad)* genius

genital 1 *adj* genital **2 genitales** *nmpl* genitals

gente *nf* (**a**) people *sing* (**b**) *(familia)* folks *sing*

gentil *adj* (**a**) *(amable)* kind (**b**) *(pagano)* pagan

gentileza *nf* kindness; *Fml* **por g. de** by courtesy of

genuino, -a *adj* *(puro)* genuine; *(verdadero)* authentic

geografía *nf* geography

geometría *nf* geometry

geométrico, -a *adj* geometric

geranio *nm* geranium

gerente *nmf* manager

germen *nm también Fig* germ

gestión *nf* (**a**) *(administración)* management (**b**) **gestiones** *(negociaciones)* negotiations; *(trámites)* formalities

gestionar *vt* to take steps to acquire o obtain; *(negociar)* to negotiate

gesto *nm* (**a**) *(mueca)* face (**b**) *(con las manos)* gesture

gestor, -a *nm,f* = person who carries out dealings with public bodies on behalf of private customers or companies, combining the roles of solicitor and accountant

gestoría *nf* = office of a "gestor"

Gibraltar *n* Gibraltar; **el peñón de G.** the Rock of Gibraltar

gibraltareño, -a 1 *adj* of/from Gibraltar **2** *nm,f* Gibraltarian

gigante, -a 1 *nm,f* giant **2** *adj* giant, enormous

gigantesco, -a *adj* gigantic

gil, -a *nm,f CSur Fam* jerk, *Br* twit

gimnasia *nf* gymnastics

gimnasio *nm* gymnasium

gimnasta *nmf* gymnast

ginebra *nf* *(bebida)* gin

ginecólogo, -a *nm,f* gynaecologist

gin-tonic, gintonic [jin'tonik] *nm* (*pl* **gin-tonics, gintonics**) gin and tonic

gira *nf Teatro, Mús* tour

girar 1 *vi* (**a**) *(dar vueltas)* to spin (**b**) **g. a la derecha/izquierda** to turn right/ left **2** *vt Fin* (**a**) *(expedir)* to draw (**b**) *(dinero)* to transfer

girasol *nm* sunflower

giro *nm* (**a**) *(vuelta)* turn (**b**) *(de acontecimientos)* direction (**c**) *(frase)* turn of phrase (**d**) *Fin* draft; **g. telegráfico** money order; **g. postal** postal o money order

gis *nm Méx* chalk

gitano, -a *adj & nm,f* gypsy, gipsy

glaciar *nm* glacier

glándula *nf* gland

global *adj* comprehensive; **precio g.** all-inclusive price

globo *nm* (**a**) balloon (**b**) *(esfera)* globe (**c**) *(lámpara)* globe, glass lampshade

glóbulo *nm* globule

gloria *nf* (**a**) *(fama)* glory (**b**) *Rel* heaven; *Fam Fig* **estar en la g.** to be in seventh heaven (**c**) *Fam (delicia)* delight

glorieta *nf* (**a**) *(plazoleta)* small square (**b**) *Esp (rotonda) Br* roundabout, *US* traffic circle (**c**) *(en un jardín)* arbour

glorioso, -a *adj* glorious

glotón, -ona 1 *adj* greedy **2** *nm,f* glutton

glucosa *nf Quím* glucose

gobernador, -a *nm,f* governor

gobernante *adj* ruling

gobernar [1] **1** *vt* to govern; *(un país)* to rule **2** *vi Náut* to steer

gobiernista *Andes, Méx* **1** *adj* government **2** *nmf* government supporter

gobierno nm (**a**) Pol government (**b**) (mando) running (**c**) Náut steering (**d**) Náut (timón) rudder

goce nm enjoyment

godo, -a 1 adj Gothic **2** nm,f Hist Goth

gofio nm Andes, Carib, RP (harina) roasted maize o US corn meal

gol nm goal

goleador, -a nm,f goal scorer

golf nm golf; **palo de g.** golf club

golfo¹, -a 1 nm (gamberro) lout, Br yob; (pillo) rogue, wide boy **2** nf Fam Pey tart

golfo² nm Geog gulf; **el g. Pérsico** the Persian Gulf

golondrina nf swallow

golosina nf Br sweet, US candy

goloso, -a adj sweet-toothed

golpe nm (**a**) blow; (llamada) knock; (puñetazo) punch; **de g.** all of a sudden; **g. de estado** coup d'état; **g. de suerte** stroke of luck; **no dar ni g.** not to lift a finger (**b**) Aut bump (**c**) (desgracia) blow; **un duro g.** a great blow (**d**) (de humor) witticism

golpear vt to hit; (con el puño) to punch; (puerta, cabeza) to bang

golpiza nf Am beating

goma nf (**a**) rubber; **g. de pegar** glue; **g. de borrar** eraser, Br rubber (**b**) (elástica) rubber o Br elastic band (**c**) Cuba, CSur (neumático) tyre (**d**) Fam (preservativo) rubber

gomería nf CSur tyre centre

gomero nm CSur (planta) rubber plant

gomina nf hair cream

góndola nf (**a**) (embarcación) gondola (**b**) Perú (autobús interurbano) (intercity) bus (**c**) Bol (autobús urbano) city bus (**d**) (en supermercado) gondola

gordo, -a 1 adj (**a**) (carnoso) fat (**b**) (grueso) thick (**c**) (importante) big; **me cae g.** I can't stand him; **de g.** in a big way

2 nm,f (**a**) fat person; Fam fatty (**b**) Am Fam (como apelativo) ¿**cómo estás, g.?** how's it going, big man?

3 nm **el g.** (de lotería) the jackpot

gordura nf fatness

gorila nm (**a**) (animal) gorilla (**b**) Esp Fig (en discoteca etc) bouncer

gorjear vi (ave) to chirp

gorjeo nm chirping

gorra nf cap; (con visera) peaked cap; Esp, Méx Fam **de g.** for free

gorrión nm sparrow

gorro nm (**a**) cap (**b**) Fam **estar hasta el g. (de)** to be up to here (with)

gota nf (**a**) drop; (de sudor) bead; **g. a g.** drop by drop; **ni g.** not a bit (**b**) Med gout

gotera nf leak

gótico, -a adj Gothic

gozar [40] **1** vt to enjoy **2** vi (disfrutar) **g. (de)** to enjoy

gozo nm pleasure

grabación nf recording

grabado nm (**a**) (arte) engraving (**b**) (dibujo) drawing

grabar vt (**a**) (sonidos, imágenes) to record (**b**) Informát to save (**c**) Arte to engrave

gracia nf (**a**) (atractivo) grace (**b**) (chiste) joke; **hacer** o **tener g.** to be funny (**c**) (indulto) pardon

gracioso, -a 1 adj (**a**) (divertido) funny (**b**) (garboso) graceful **2** nm,f Teatro comic character

grada nf (**a**) (peldaño) step (**b**) **gradas** (en estadio) terraces

graderío nm Esp (gradas) Teatro rows; Dep terraces

gradiente 1 nm gradient **2** nf CSur, Ecuad gradient, slope

grado nm (**a**) (unidad) degree (**b**) Mil rank (**c**) **de buen g.** willingly, gladly

graduación nf (**a**) grading (**b**) Mil rank

graduado, -a nm,f graduate

gradual adj gradual

gradualmente adv gradually

graduar [30] **1** vt (**a**) Educ to confer a degree on (**b**) Mil to confer a rank on, to commission (**c**) (regular) to regulate **2** **graduarse** vpr (**a**) Educ, Mil to graduate (**b**) **graduarse la vista** to have one's eyes tested

graffiti *nm* piece of graffiti

grafía *nf* written symbol

gráfico, -a 1 *adj* graphic; **diseño g.** graphic design **2** *nm* graph

gragea *nf Med* pill

grajo, -a 1 *nm,f Orn* rook **2** *nm Andes, Carib Fam (olor)* BO, body odour

gramática *nf* grammar

gramatical *adj* grammatical

gramo *nm* gram, gramme

gran = grande

granada *nf* (a) *(fruto)* pomegranate (b) *Mil* grenade

granate 1 *adj inv (color)* maroon **2** *nm (color)* maroon

grande *adj* (a) *(tamaño)* big, large; *Fig (persona)* great; **Gran Bretaña** Great Britain (b) *(cantidad)* large; **vivir a lo g.** to live in style; *Fig* **pasarlo en g.** to have a great time

> **gran** is used instead of **grande** before masculine singular nouns (e.g. **gran hombre** great man)

grandeza *nf* (a) *(importancia)* greatness (b) *(grandiosidad)* grandeur; **delirios de g.** delusions of grandeur

grandioso, -a *adj* grandiose

granel *nm* **a g.** *(sin envase)* loose; *(en gran cantidad)* in bulk; *(en abundancia)* in abundance; **vender/comprar vino a g.** to sell/buy wine from the barrel

granero *nm Agr* granary

granito *nm* granite

granizada *nf* hailstorm

granizado *nm* = drink of flavoured crushed ice

granizar [40] *v impers* to hail

granja *nf* farm

granjero, -a *nm,f* farmer

grano *nm* (a) grain; *(de café)* bean; **ir al g.** to get to the point (b) *(espinilla)* spot

granuja *nm* (a) *(pilluelo)* ragamuffin (b) *(estafador)* con-man

grapa *nf* (a) staple (b) *Constr* cramp (c) *CSur (bebida)* grappa

grapadora *nf* stapler

grapar *vt* to staple

grasa *nf* grease

grasiento, -a *adj* greasy

graso, -a *adj (pelo)* greasy; *(materia)* fatty

gratificar [44] *vt* (a) *(satisfacer)* to gratify (b) *(recompensar)* to reward

gratinado *adj Culin* au gratin

gratinar *vt Culin* to cook au gratin

gratis *adj inv & adv* free

gratitud *nf* gratitude

grato, -a *adj* pleasant

gratuito, -a *adj* (a) *(de balde)* free (of charge) (b) *(arbitrario)* gratuitous

grave *adj* (a) *(importante)* serious (b) *(muy enfermo)* seriously ill (c) *(voz, nota)* low

gravedad *nf* (a) *(seriedad, importancia)* seriousness (b) *Fís* gravity

gravilla *nf* chippings

Grecia *n* Greece

gremio *nm* (a) *Hist* guild (b) *(profesión)* profession, trade

greña *nf* lock of entangled hair; *Fam* **andar a la g.** to squabble

griego, -a *adj & nm,f* Greek

grieta *nf* crack; *(en la piel)* chap

grifero, -a *nm,f Perú Br* petrol pump attendant, *US* gas pump attendant

grifo *nm* (a) *Esp (llave) Br* tap, *US* faucet (b) *Perú (gasolinera) Br* petrol station, *US* gas station

grill [gril] *nm (pl* **grills)** grill

grillo *nm* cricket

gringo, -a *Fam* **1** *adj* (a) *(estadounidense)* gringo, American (b) *Am (extranjero)* gringo, foreign **2** *nm,f* (a) *(estadounidense)* gringo, American (b) *Am (extranjero)* gringo, foreigner *(from a non-Spanish speaking country)*

gripa *nf Col, Méx* flu

gripe *nf* flu

gris *adj & nm* grey

gritar *vt & vi* to shout

grito *nm* shout; **a voz en g.** at the top of one's voice

grosella *nf (fruto)* redcurrant; **g. negra** blackcurrant; **g. silvestre** gooseberry

grosería *nf* (**a**) *(ordinariez)* rude word *o* expression (**b**) *(rusticidad)* rudeness

grosero, -a *adj* *(tosco)* coarse; *(maleducado)* rude

grosor *nm* thickness

grotesco, -a *adj* grotesque

grúa *nf* (**a**) *Constr* crane (**b**) *Aut Br* breakdown van *o* truck, *US* tow truck

grueso, -a 1 *adj* thick; *(persona)* stout **2** *nm (parte principal)* bulk

grumo *nm* lump; *(de leche)* curd

gruñido *nm* grunt

gruñir *vi* to grunt

grupa *nf* hindquarters

grupo *nm* (**a**) group; *Informát* **g. de noticias** newsgroup (**b**) *Téc* unit, set

gruta *nf* cave

guaca *nf* (**a**) *Am (sepultura)* = pre-Columbian Indian tomb (**b**) *Am (tesoro)* hidden treasure (**c**) *CRica, Cuba (hucha)* moneybox

guacal *nm* (**a**) *CAm, Méx (calabaza)* gourd (**b**) *Carib, Col, Méx (jaula)* cage

guacamol, guacamole *nm* guacamole, avocado dip

guachafita *nf Col, Ven Fam* racket, uproar

guachimán *nm Am* night watchman

guacho, -a *adj & nm,f Andes, RP* (**a**) *muy Fam (persona huérfana)* orphan (**b**) *Fam (sinvergüenza)* bastard, swine

guaco *nm Am (cerámica)* = pottery object found in pre-Columbian Indian tomb

guagua *nf* (**a**) *Andes (niño)* baby (**b**) *Cuba, PRico, RDom* bus

guajiro, -a *nm,f* (**a**) *Cuba Fam (campesino)* peasant (**b**) *(de Guajira)* person from Guajira *(Colombia, Venezuela)*

guajolote *nm CAm, Méx* (**a**) *(pavo)* turkey (**b**) *(tonto)* fool, idiot

guampa *nf Bol, CSur* horn

guanajo *nm Carib* turkey

guante *nm* glove

guantera *nf Aut* glove compartment

guapo, -a *adj* (**a**) *esp Esp (atractivo)* good-looking; *(hombre)* handsome; *(mujer)* pretty (**b**) *Am (valiente)* gutsy;

ser g. to have guts

guaraca *nf Am* sling

guarache *nm Méx (sandalia)* = crude sandal with a sole made from a tyre

guarangada *nf Bol, CSur* rude remark

guarango, -a *adj Bol, CSur* rude

guardabarros *nm inv Esp, Bol, RP (de vehículo) Br* mudguard, *US* fender

guardacoches *nmf inv* parking attendant

guardaespaldas *nmf inv* bodyguard

guardafango *nm inv Andes, CAm, Carib (de automóvil, bicicleta) Br* mudguard, *US* fender

guardameta *nmf Dep* goalkeeper

guardapolvo *nm* overalls

guardar 1 *vt* (**a**) *(conservar)* to keep (**b**) *(un secreto)* to keep; **g. silencio** to remain silent; **g. cama** to stay in bed (**c**) *(poner en un sitio)* to put away (**d**) *(reservar)* to keep (**e**) *Informát* to save **2 guardarse** *vpr* **guardarse de hacer algo** *(abstenerse)* to be careful not to do sth; **guardársela a algn** to have it in for sb

guardarropa *nm* (**a**) *(cuarto)* cloakroom (**b**) *(armario)* wardrobe

guardería *nf* **g. infantil** nursery (school)

guardia 1 *nf* (**a**) *(vigilancia)* watch (**b**) **la G. Civil** the civil guard (**c**) *(turno de servicio)* duty; *Mil* guard duty; **de g.** on duty; **farmacia de g.** duty chemist **2** *nmf* policeman, *f* policewoman

guardián, -ana *nm,f (de persona)* guardian; *(de finca)* keeper

guarida *nf (de animal)* lair; *(refugio)* hide-out

guarnición *nf* (**a**) *Culin* garnish (**b**) *Mil* garrison

guarro, -a *Esp* **1** *adj* filthy **2** *nm,f* pig

guarura *nm Méx Fam* bodyguard

guasa *nf* mockery

guasca *nf Chile, Perú* whip

guaso, -a *adj* (**a**) *Chile (campesino)* peasant (**b**) *Andes, RP* **ser un g.** *(grosero)* to be crude *o* coarse; *(maleducado)* to be rude

guata *nf* (**a**) *(relleno)* padding (**b**) *Andes Fam (barriga)* belly

Guatemala *n* (**a**) *(país)* Guatemala (**b**) *(ciudad)* Guatemala City

guatemalteco, -a *adj & nm,f* Guatemalan

guayaba *nf (fruta)* guava

güero, -a *adj Méx Fam* blond, *f* blonde, fair-haired

guerra *nf* war; **en g.** at war; **g. bacteriológica** germ warfare; **g. civil/fría/mundial/nuclear** civil/cold/world/nuclear war; *Fam* **dar g.** to be a real nuisance

guerrero, -a 1 *nm,f* warrior **2** *adj* warlike

guerrilla *nf* (**a**) *(partida armada)* guerrilla force *o* band (**b**) *(lucha)* guerrilla warfare

guerrillero, -a 1 *adj* guerrilla; **ataque g.** guerrilla attack **2** *nm,f* guerrilla

güevón = **huevón**

guía 1 *nmf (persona)* guide **2** *nf* (**a**) *(norma)* guideline (**b**) *(libro)* guide; *(lista)* directory; *Esp, RP* **g. telefónica** *o* **de teléfonos** telephone directory

guiar [29] **1** *vt* (**a**) *(indicar el camino)* to guide (**b**) *Aut* to drive; *Náut* to steer; *(caballo, bici)* to ride **2 guiarse** *vpr* **guiarse por** to be guided by, to go by

guijarro *nm* pebble

guillotina *nf* guillotine

guinda *nf (fruto)* morello (cherry)

guindilla *nf* chilli

guineo *nm Ándes, CAm* banana

guiñar *vt* to wink

guiñol *nm* puppet theatre

guión *nm* (**a**) *Cin, TV* script (**b**) *Ling* hyphen, dash (**c**) *(esquema)* sketch

guionista *nmf* scriptwriter

guiri *nmf Esp Fam* foreigner

guirnalda *nf* garland

guisado *nm Culin* stew

guisante *nm esp Esp* pea

guisar *vt* to cook

guiso *nm* dish; *(guisado)* stew

guitarra 1 *nf* guitar **2** *nmf* guitarist

guitarreada *nf CSur* singalong *(to guitars)*

guitarrista *nmf* guitarist

gurí, -isa *nm,f RP Fam (niño)* kid, child; *(chico)* lad, boy; *(chica)* lass, girl

gusano *nm* worm; *(oruga)* caterpillar; *Fam Pey (exiliado cubano)* = anti-Castro Cuban living in exile; **g. de seda** silkworm

gustar 1 *vt* (**a**) me gusta el vino I like wine; me gustaban los caramelos I used to like sweets; me gusta nadar I like swimming; me gustaría ir I would like to go (**b**) *Fml* ¿gustas? would you like some?; cuando gustes whenever you like **2** *vi* **g. de** to enjoy

gusto *nm* (**a**) *(sentido)* taste (**b**) *(en fórmulas de cortesía)* con (mucho) g. with (great) pleasure; tanto g. pleased to meet you (**c**) estar a g. to feel comfortable *o* at ease; por g. for the sake of it; ser de buen/mal g. to be in good/bad taste; tener buen/mal g. to have good/bad taste

Hh

haba *nf* broad bean

Takes the masculine articles **el** and **un**

habano *nm* Havana cigar

haber [14] **1** *v aux* (**a**) *(en tiempos compuestos)* to have; **lo he visto** I have seen it; **ya lo había hecho** he had already done it

(**b**) **h. de** + *infin (obligación)* to have to; **has de ser bueno** you must be good

2 *v impers* *(special form of present tense:* **hay**)

(**a**) *(existir, estar) (singular used also with plural nouns)* **hay** there is/are; **había** there was/were; **había un gato en el tejado** there was a cat on the roof; **había muchos libros** there were a lot of books; **hay 500 km entre Madrid y Granada** it's 500 km from Madrid to Granada

(**b**) **h. que** + *infin* it is necessary to; **hay que trabajar** you've got to o you must work; **habrá que comprobarlo** we will have to check it

(**c**) *(tener lugar)* **habrá una fiesta** there will be a party; **hoy hay partido** there's a match today; **los accidentes habidos en esta carretera** the accidents which have happened on this road

(**d**) **había una vez ...** once upon a time ...; **no hay de qué** you're welcome, don't mention it; **¿qué hay?** how are things?

3 *nm* (**a**) *Fin* credit; **haberes** assets (**b**) **en su h.** in his possession

habichuela *nf* *Esp, Carib, Col* bean

hábil *adj* (**a**) *(diestro)* skilful (**b**) *(astuto)* smart (**c**) **días hábiles** working days

habilidad *nf* (**a**) *(destreza)* skill (**b**) *(astucia)* cleverness

habiloso, -a *adj Chile* shrewd, astute

habitación *nf (cuarto)* room; *(dormitorio)* bedroom; **h. individual/doble** single/double room

habitante *nmf* inhabitant

habitar 1 *vt* to live in, to inhabit **2** *vi* to live

hábito *nm* (**a**) *(costumbre)* habit (**b**) *Rel* habit

habitual *adj* usual, habitual; *(cliente, lector)* regular

hablador, -a *adj (parlanchín)* talkative; *(chismoso)* gossipy

habladuría *nf (rumor)* rumour; *(chisme)* piece of gossip

hablar 1 *vi* (**a**) to speak, to talk; **h. con algn** to speak to sb (**b**) **¡ni h.!** certainly not!; *Fam* **¡quién fue a h.!** look who's talking!

2 *vt* (**a**) *(idioma)* to speak; **habla alemán** he speaks German (**b**) *(tratar un asunto)* to talk over, to discuss

3 hablarse *vpr* (**a**) to speak o talk to one another (**b**) **se habla español** *(en letrero)* Spanish spoken

hacendado, -a *nm,f* (**a**) *(terrateniente)* landowner (**b**) *CSur (ganadero)* rancher

hacer [15] **1** *vt* (**a**) *(crear, producir, fabricar)* to make; **h. una casa** to build a house

(**b**) *(obrar, ejecutar)* to do; **eso no se hace** it isn't done; **hazme un favor** do me a favour; **¿qué haces?** *(en este momento)* what are you doing?; **tengo mucho que h.** I have a lot to do; **h. deporte** to do sports; **h. una carrera/medicina** to do a degree/medicine

(**c**) *(conseguir) (amigos, dinero)* to make

(**d**) *(obligar)* to make; **hazle callar/trabajar** make him shut up/work (**e**) *(arreglar)* to make; **h. la cama** to make the bed

(**f**) *Mat (sumar)* to make; **y con éste hacen cien** and that makes a hundred

(**g**) *(dar aspecto)* to make look; **el negro le hace más delgado** black makes him look slimmer

(**h**) *(sustituyendo a otro verbo)* to do; **ya no puedo leer como solía hacerlo** I can't read as well as I used to

(**i**) *(representar)* to play

(**j**) **¡bien hecho!** well done!

2 *vi* (**a**) *(actuar)* **h. de** to play; **hizo de Desdémona** she played Desdemona (**b**) **h. por** o **para** + *infin* to try to; **hice por venir** I tried to come (**c**) *(fingir)* to pretend; **h. como si** to act as if (**d**) *(convenir)* to be suitable; **a las ocho si te hace** will eight o'clock be all right for you?

3 *v impers* (**a**) **hace calor/frío** it's hot/cold (**b**) *(tiempo transcurrido)* ago; **hace mucho (tiempo)** a long time ago; **hace dos días que no le veo** I haven't seen him for two days; **hace dos años que vivo en Glasgow** I've been living in Glasgow for two years

4 hacerse *vpr* (**a**) *(volverse)* to become, to grow; **hacerse viejo** to grow old

(**b**) *(simular)* to pretend; **hacerse el dormido** to pretend to be sleeping

(**c**) **hacerse con** *(apropiarse)* to get hold of

(**d**) **hacerse a** *(habituarse)* to get used to; **enseguida me hago a todo** I soon get used to anything

hacha *nf* (**a**) *(herramienta)* axe (**b**) *Fam* **ser un h. en algo** to be an ace o a wizard at sth

> Takes the masculine articles **el** and **un**

hachís *nm* hashish

hacia *prep* (**a**) *(dirección)* towards, to; **h. abajo** down, downwards; **h. adelante** forwards; **h. arriba** up, upwards; **h. atrás** back, backwards (**b**) *(tiempo)* at about, at around; **h. las tres** at about three o'clock

hacienda *nf* (**a**) *(finca)* country estate o property (**b**) *Fin* (**el Ministerio de**) **H.** *Br* ≃ the Treasury, *US* ≃ the

Department of the Treasury

hada *nf* fairy; **cuento de hadas** fairy tale; **h. madrina** fairy godmother

> Takes the masculine articles **el** and **un**

Haití *n* Haiti

hala *interj Esp (para dar ánimo, prisa)* come on!; *(para expresar incredulidad)* no!, you're joking!; *(para expresar admiración, sorpresa)* wow!

halago *nm* flattery

halcón *nm* falcon; **h. peregrino** peregrine (falcon)

hall [χol] *nm (pl* **halls***)* entrance hall, foyer

hallar 1 *vt (encontrar)* to find; *(averiguar)* to find out; *(descubrir)* to discover **2 hallarse** *vpr (estar)* to be, to find oneself; *(estar situado)* to be situated

halógeno, -a *adj Quím* halogenous

halterofilia *nf* weightlifting

hamaca *nf* hammock; *(mecedora)* rocking-chair

hambre *nf (apetito)* hunger; *(inanición)* starvation; *(catástrofe)* famine; **tener h.** to be hungry

> Takes the masculine articles **el** and **un**

hambriento, -a *adj* starving

hamburguesa *nf* hamburger, *Br* beefburger

hámster ['χamster] *nm (pl* **hámsters***)* hamster

hangar *nm* hangar

hardware ['χarwer] *nm Informát* hardware

harina *nf* flour

hartar 1 *vt* (**a**) *(cansar, fastidiar)* to annoy (**b**) *(atiborrar)* to satiate; **el dulce harta enseguida** sweet things soon fill you up **2 hartarse** *vpr* (**a**) *(saciar el apetito)* to eat one's fill (**b**) *(cansarse)* to get fed up (**de** with), to grow tired (**de** of)

harto, -a *adj* (**a**) *(de comida)* full (**b**) *(cansado)* fed up; **¡me tienes h.!** I'm fed up with you!; **estoy h. de trabajar** I'm fed up working (**c**) *Am salvo RP (mucho)* lots of; **tiene h. dinero** he's got lots of money **2** *adv* (**a**) *Esp Fml (muy)* very (**b**) *Am salvo RP (muy, mucho)* really

hasta 1 *prep* (**a**) *(lugar)* up to, as far as, down to (**b**) *(tiempo)* until, till, up to; **h. el domingo** until Sunday; **h. el final** right to the end; **h. la fecha** up to now; **h. luego** see you later (**c**) *(con cantidad)* up to, as many as (**d**) *(incluso)* even (**e**) *CAm, Col, Ecuad, Méx (no antes de)* **pintaremos la casa h. fin de mes** we won't paint the house till the end of the month **2** *conj* **h. que** until

haya¹ *nf* (**a**) *Bot (árbol)* beech (**b**) *(madera)* beech (wood)

Takes the masculine articles **el** and **un**

haya² *subj pres de* **haber**
haz¹ *nm* (**a**) *Agr* sheaf (**b**) *(de luz)* shaft
haz² *nf (de hoja)* top side
haz³ *imperat de* **hacer**
hazaña *nf* deed, exploit
he¹ *adv* **he ahí/aquí ...** there/here you have ...
he² *indic pres de* **haber**
hebilla *nf* buckle
hebra *nf* thread; *(de carne)* sinew; *(de madera)* grain; *Esp* **pegar la h.** to chat
hebreo, -a 1 *adj* Hebrew **2** *nm,f* Hebrew
hechizar [40] *vt* (**a**) *(embrujar)* to cast a spell on (**b**) *Fig (fascinar)* to bewitch, to charm
hechizo *nm* (**a**) *(embrujo)* spell (**b**) *Fig (fascinación)* fascination, charm
hecho, -a 1 *adj* (**a**) made, done; **¡bien h.!** well done! (**b**) *(carne)* done (**c**) *(persona)* mature (**d**) *(frase)* set; *(ropa)* ready-made **2** *nm* (**a**) *(realidad)* fact; **de h.** in fact; **el h. es que ...** the fact is that ... (**b**) *(acto)* act, deed (**c**) *(suceso)* event, incident
hectárea *nf* hectare
helada *nf* frost
heladera *nf CSur (nevera)* refrigerator, *Br* fridge, *US* icebox
heladería *nf* ice-cream parlour
helado, -a 1 *nm* ice cream **2** *adj* (**a**) *(muy frío)* frozen, freezing cold; **estoy**

h. (de frío) I'm frozen (**b**) *Fig* **quedarse h.** *(atónito)* to be flabbergasted
helar [1] **1** *vt (congelar)* to freeze
2 *v impers (congelarse)* to freeze; **anoche heló** there was a frost last night
3 **helarse** *vpr (congelarse)* to freeze
hélice *nf* (**a**) *Av, Náut* propeller (**b**) *Anat, Arquit, Mat* helix
helicóptero *nm Av* helicopter
hematoma *nm Med* haematoma
hembra *nf* (**a**) *Bot, Zool* female (**b**) *(mujer)* woman (**c**) *Téc* female; *(de tornillo)* nut; *(de enchufe)* socket
hemorragia *nf Med* haemorrhage
heno *nm* hay
hepatitis *nf inv* hepatitis
herboristería *nf* herbalist's (shop)
heredar *vt* (**a**) *Jur* to inherit (**b**) **ha heredado la sonrisa de su madre** she's got her mother's smile
heredero, -a *nm,f* heir, *f* heiress; **príncipe h.** crown prince
hereje *nmf Rel* heretic
herejía *nf Rel* heresy
herencia *nf* (**a**) *Jur* inheritance, legacy (**b**) *Biol* heredity
herida *nf (lesión)* injury; *(corte)* wound
herido, -a *nm,f* injured person; **no hubo heridos** there were no casualties
herir [5] **1** *vt* (**a**) *(físicamente) (lesionar)* to injure; *(cortar)* to wound (**b**) *(emocionalmente)* to hurt, to wound (**c**) *(vista)* to offend **2** **herirse** *vpr* to injure o hurt oneself
hermana *nf* (**a**) sister; (**b**) *(monja)* sister
hermanastro, -a *nm,f* stepbrother, *f* stepsister
hermano *nm* (**a**) brother; **h. político** brother-in-law; **primo h.** first cousin (**b**) *Rel (fraile)* brother (**c**) **hermanos** brothers and sisters
hermético, -a *adj* (**a**) *(cierre)* hermetic, airtight (**b**) *Fig (abstruso)* secretive
hermoso, -a *adj* beautiful, lovely; *(grande)* fine
hermosura *nf* beauty
héroe *nm* hero

heroico, -a *adj* heroic

heroína *nf* (**a**) *(mujer)* heroine (**b**) *(droga)* heroin

heroinómano, -a *nm,f* heroin addict

heroísmo *nm* heroism

herradura *nf* horseshoe

herramienta *nf Téc* tool; **caja de herramientas** toolbox

herrería *nf* forge, smithy

herrero *nm* blacksmith, smith

hervir [5] **1** *vt (hacer bullir)* to boil **2** *vi* (**a**) *Culin* to boil; **romper a h.** to come to the boil (**b**) *(abundar)* to swarm, to seethe (**de** with)

heterosexual *adj & nmf* heterosexual

hice *pt indef de* hacer

hidalgo *nm Hist* nobleman, gentleman

hidratante *adj* moisturizing; **crema/leche h.** moisturizing cream/lotion

hidratar *vt (piel)* to moisturize; *Quím* to hydrate

hiedra *nf* ivy

hielo *nm* ice; *Fig* **romper el h.** to break the ice

hiena *nf* hyena

hierba *nf* (**a**) grass; **mala h.** *Bot* weed; *Fig (persona)* bad lot; *Fam Hum* **y otras hierbas** among others (**b**) *Culin* herb; **h. luisa** lemon verbena (**c**) *Fam (marihuana)* grass

hierbabuena *nf* mint

hierro *nm* (**a**) *(metal)* iron; **h. forjado** wrought iron (**b**) *(punta de arma)* head, point (**c**) *(marca en el ganado)* brand

hígado *nm* (**a**) *Anat* liver (**b**) *Euf* guts

higiene *nf* hygiene

higiénico, -a *adj* hygienic; **papel h.** toilet paper

higo *nm* fig; *Fam* **hecho un h.** wizened, crumpled

higuera *nf Bot* fig tree

hija *nf* daughter

hijastro, -a *nm,f* stepson, *f* stepdaughter

hijo *nm* (**a**) son, child; *Pey* **h. de papá** rich kid; *Vulg* **h. de puta** *o Méx* **de la chingada** bastard, *US* asshole (**b**) **hijos** children

hilera *nf* line, row

hilo *nm* (**a**) *Cost* thread; *(grueso)* yarn (**b**) *Fig (de historia, discurso)* thread; *(de pensamiento)* train; **perder el h.** to lose the thread; **h. musical** background music (**c**) *Tex* linen

hilvanar *vt* (**a**) *Cost* *Br* to tack, *US* to baste (**b**) *Fig (ideas etc)* to outline

hincapié *nm* **hacer h. en** *(insistir)* to insist on; *(subrayar)* to emphasize, to stress

hincha *Fam* **1** *nmf Ftb* fan, supporter **2** *nf (antipatía)* grudge, dislike; *Esp* **me tiene h.** he's got it in for me

hinchado, -a *adj* (**a**) inflated, blown up (**b**) *Med (cara etc)* swollen, puffed up; *(estómago)* bloated (**c**) *Fig (estilo)* bombastic, pompous

hinchar **1** *vt* (**a**) *(inflar)* to inflate, to blow up (**b**) *Fig (exagerar)* to inflate, to exaggerate **2** **hincharse** *vpr* (**a**) *Med* to swell (up) (**b**) *Fam* **me hinché de comida** I stuffed myself; **me hinché de llorar** I cried for all I was worth

hinchazón *nf Med* swelling

hipermercado *nm* hypermarket

hipermetropía *nf* long-sightedness, *Espec* hypermetropia, *US* hypertropia

hipertensión *nf* high blood pressure

hípica *nf* (horse) riding

hipnotizar [40] *vt* to hypnotize

hipo *nm* hiccups; **me ha dado h.** it's given me the hiccups

hipocresía *nf* hypocrisy

hipócrita **1** *adj* hypocritical **2** *nmf* hypocrite

hipódromo *nm* racetrack, racecourse

hipopótamo *nm* hippopotamus

hipoteca *nf Fin* mortgage

hipótesis *nf inv* hypothesis

hipotético, -a *adj* hypothetical

hippy, hippie [ˈχipi] *adj & nmf* (*pl* **hippies**) hippy

hispánico, -a *adj* Hispanic, Spanish

hispano, -a **1** *adj (español)* Spanish; *(español y sudamericano)* Hispanic; *(sudamericano)* Spanish American **2** *nm,f (hispanoamericano)* Spanish

American; *(estadounidense)* Hispanic

Hispanoamérica *nf* Latin America

hispanoamericano, -a *adj & nm,f* Latin American

hispanohablante 1 *adj* Spanish-speaking **2** *nmf* Spanish speaker

histeria *nf* hysteria; **un ataque de h.** hysterics

histérico, -a *adj* hysterical; *Fam Fig* **me pones h.** you're driving me mad

historia *nf* (a) history; **esto pasará a la h.** this will go down in history (b) *(narración)* story, tale; *Fam* **¡déjate de historias!** don't give me that!

histórico, -a *adj* (a) historical (b) *(auténtico)* factual, true; **hechos históricos** true facts (c) *(de gran importancia)* historic, memorable

historieta *nf* (a) *(cuento)* short story, tale (b) *(tira cómica)* comic strip

hizo *pt indef de* **hacer**

hobby [ˈχoβi] *nm* hobby

hocico *nm* (a) *(de animal)* snout (b) *(de persona)* mug, snout; *Fam* **meter los hocicos en algo** to stick o poke one's nose into sth

hockey [ˈχokei] *nm* hockey; **h. sobre hielo** *Br* ice hockey, *US* hockey; **h. sobre hierba** *Br* hockey, *US* field hockey

hogar *nm* (a) *(casa)* home (b) *(de la chimenea)* hearth, fireplace (c) *Fig* **formar** o **crear un h.** *(familia)* to start a family

hogareño, -a *adj (vida)* home, family; *(persona)* home-loving, stay-at-home

hoguera *nf* bonfire

hoja *nf* (a) *Bot* leaf (b) *(pétalo)* petal (c) *(de papel)* sheet, leaf; **h. de cálculo** spreadsheet (d) *(de libro)* leaf, page (e) *(de metal)* sheet (f) *(de cuchillo, espada)* blade (g) *(impreso)* hand-out, printed sheet (h) *(de puerta o ventana)* leaf

hojalata *nf* tin, tin plate

hojaldre *nm Culin* puff pastry

hola *interj* hello!, hullo!, hi!

Holanda *n* Holland

holandés, -esa 1 *adj* Dutch **2** *nm,f* Dutchman, *f* Dutchwoman **3** *nm (idioma)* Dutch

holgado, -a *adj* (a) *(ropa)* loose, baggy (b) *(económicamente)* comfortable (c) *(espacio)* roomy; **andar h. de tiempo** to have plenty of time

holgazán, -ana 1 *adj* lazy, idle **2** *nm,f* lazybones, layabout

hombre 1 *nm* (a) man; **de h. a h.** man-to-man; **¡pobre h.!** poor *Br* chap o *US* guy!; **ser muy h.** to be every inch a man; **h. de estado** statesman; **h. de negocios** businessman (b) *(especie)* mankind, man **2** *interj* **¡h., Juan! ¡qué alegría verte!** hey Juan, how nice to see you!; **¡sí h.!** sure!

hombrera *nf* shoulder pad

hombrillo *nm Ven (arcén) (de carretera)* verge; *(de autopista) Br* hard shoulder, *US* shoulder

hombro *nm* shoulder; **a hombros** on one's shoulders; **encogerse de hombros** to shrug one's shoulders; **mirar a algn por encima del h.** to look down one's nose at sb

homenaje *nm* homage, tribute; **rendir h. a algn** to pay homage o tribute to sb

homeopatía *nf* homeopathy

homicida 1 *nmf* murderer, *f* murderess **2** *adj* homicidal; **el arma h.** the murder weapon

homicidio *nm* homicide

homosexual *adj & nmf* homosexual

hondo, -a *adj* (a) *(profundo)* deep; **plato h.** soup dish (b) *Fig (pesar)* profound, deep

Honduras *n* Honduras

hondureño, -a *adj & nm,f* Honduran

honestidad *nf* (a) *(honradez)* honesty, uprightness (b) *(decencia)* modesty

honesto, -a *adj* (a) *(honrado)* honest, upright (b) *(decente)* modest

hongo *nm* (a) *Bot* fungus; **h. venenoso** toadstool (b) *(sombrero) Br* bowler (hat), *US* derby

honor *nm* (a) *(virtud)* honour; **palabra de h.** word of honour (b) **en h. a**

la verdad ... to be fair ...; **es un h. para mí** it's an honour for me (**c**) **hacer h. a** to live up to

honorario, -a 1 *adj* honorary **2** *nmpl* **honorarios** fees, fee

honra *nf* (**a**) *(dignidad)* dignity, self-esteem (**b**) *(fama)* reputation, good name (**c**) *(honor)* honour; **me cabe la h. de ...** I have the honour of ...; **¡a mucha h.!** and proud of it!

honradez *nf* honesty, integrity

honrado, -a *adj* (**a**) *(de fiar)* honest (**b**) *(decente)* upright, respectable

honrar *vt* (**a**) *(respetar)* to honour (**b**) *(enaltecer)* to be a credit to

hora *nf* (**a**) hour; **media h.** half an hour; **a altas horas de la madrugada** in the small hours; **dar la h.** to strike the hour; **(trabajo) por horas** (work) paid by the hour; *Esp* **h. punta,** *Am* **h. pico** *(de mucho tráfico)* rush hour; *(de agua, electricidad)* peak times; **horas extra** overtime (hours)
(**b**) *Fig* time; **¿qué h. es?** what time is it?; **a última h.** at the last moment; *Esp, Andes, Carib, RP* **la h. de la verdad** the moment of truth
(**c**) *(cita)* appointment; **pedir h.** *(al médico etc)* to ask for an appointment

horario, -a 1 *nm Br* timetable, *US* schedule **2** *adj* time; *Rad* **señal horaria** pips

horca *nf* gallows *sing*

horchata *nf Culin* = cold drink made from ground tiger nuts, water and sugar

horizontal *adj* horizontal

horizonte *nm* horizon

horma *nf (de zapato)* last

hormiga *nf* ant

hormigón *nm Constr* concrete; **h. armado** reinforced concrete

hormigonera *nf* concrete mixer

hormiguero *nm* (**a**) anthill (**b**) *Fig* **ser un h.** *(lugar)* to be swarming (with people)

hormona *nf* hormone

hornear *vt* to bake

hornillo *nm (de cocinar)* stove; *(placa)* hotplate

horno *nm (cocina)* oven; *Téc* furnace; *(para cerámica, ladrillos)* kiln; *Culin* **pescado al h.** baked fish; *Fam Fig* **esta habitación es un h.** this room is boiling hot

horóscopo *nm* horoscope

horquilla *nf* (**a**) *(del pelo)* hairpin, *Br* hairgrip (**b**) *(estadística)* chart (**c**) **h. de precios** price range

hórreo *nm Agr* granary

horrible *adj* horrible, dreadful, awful

horror *nm* (**a**) horror, terror; **¡qué h.!** how awful!; *Fam* **tengo h. a las motos** I hate motorbikes (**b**) *Fam Fig* **me gusta horrores** *(muchísimo)* I like it an awful lot

horrorizar [40] *vt* to horrify, to terrify

horroroso, -a *adj* (**a**) *(que da miedo)* horrifying, terrifying (**b**) *Fam (muy feo)* hideous, ghastly (**c**) *Fam (malísimo)* awful, dreadful

hortaliza *nf* vegetable

hortelano, -a *nm,f Br* market gardener, *US* truck farmer

hortensia *nf Bot* hydrangea

hortera *adj Esp Fam (decoración, ropa, canción)* tacky, *Br* naff; **es muy h.** he has really tacky *o Br* naff taste

hospedar 1 *vt* to put up, to lodge **2** **hospedarse** *vpr* to stay (**en** at)

hospital *nm* hospital

hospitalario, -a *adj* (**a**) *(acogedor)* hospitable (**b**) *Med* hospital; **instalaciones hospitalarias** hospital facilities

hospitalidad *nf* hospitality

hospitalizar [40] *vt* to take *o* send into hospital, to hospitalize

hostal *nm* guesthouse

hostelería *nf (negocio)* catering business; *(estudios)* hotel management

hostería *nf CSur (hotel)* country hotel

hostia 1 *nf* (**a**) *Rel* host (**b**) *Esp Vulg (golpe)* bash (**c**) *Esp Vulg* **estar de mala h.** to be in a foul mood; **ser la h.** *(fantástico)* to be *Br* bloody *o US* goddamn amazing; *(penoso)* to be *Br* bloody *o US* goddamn awful **2** *interj Vulg* damn! *Br* bloody hell!

hostil *adj* hostile

hotel *nm* hotel

hotelero, -a 1 *adj* hotel; **el sector h.** the hotel sector **2** *nm,f* hotel-keeper, hotelier

hoy *adv* (a) *(día)* today (b) *Fig (presente)* now; **h. (en) día** nowadays; **h. por h.** at the present time

hoyo *nm* (a) *(agujero)* hole, pit (b) *(sepultura)* grave (c) *(de golf)* hole

hoz *nf Agr* sickle; **la h. y el martillo** the hammer and sickle

huacho = **guacho**

huasipungo *nm Andes* = small plot of land given by landowner to Indians in exchange for their labour

huaso, -a *nm,f Chile Fam* farmer, peasant

hubiera *subj imperf de* **haber**

hucha *nf Esp* piggy bank

hueco, -a 1 *adj* (a) *(vacío)* empty, hollow (b) *(sonido)* resonant **2** *nm* (a) *(cavidad)* hollow, hole (b) *(sitio no ocupado)* empty space (c) *(rato libre)* free time

huelga *nf* strike; **estar en** *o* **de h.** to be on strike; **h. de brazos caídos** go-slow; **h. de celo** *Br* work-to-rule, *US* job action

huella *nf* (a) *(del pie)* footprint; *(coche)* track; **h. dactilar** fingerprint (b) *Fig (vestigio)* trace, sign; **dejar h.** to leave one's mark

huérfano, -a *nm,f* orphan

huerta *nf Agr* (a) *(parcela)* *Br* market garden, *US* truck farm (b) *(región)* = irrigated area used for cultivation

huerto *nm (de verduras)* vegetable garden, kitchen garden; *(de frutales)* orchard

hueso *nm* (a) *Anat* bone; **estar en los huesos** to be all skin and bone (b) *(de fruto)* *Br* stone, *US* pit (c) *Fig (difícil)* hard work; *(profesor)* hard nut (d) *Méx (enchufe)* contact; *(trabajo fácil)* cushy job

huésped, -a *nm,f (invitado)* guest; *(en hotel etc)* lodger, boarder; **casa de huéspedes** guesthouse

huevada *nf Andes, RP muy Fam (dicho)* crap; **lo que dijiste es una h.** what you said is a load of crap

huevo *nm* (a) egg; **h. duro** hard-boiled egg; **h. escalfado** poached egg; **h. frito** fried egg; **h. pasado por agua**, *Méx* **h. tibio**, *Andes* **h. a la copa** soft-boiled egg; **huevos revueltos** scrambled eggs (b) *Vulg (usu pl)* balls *pl*; **hacer algo por huevos** to do sth even if it kills you; **tener huevos** to have guts

huevón, -ona *muy Fam nm,f* (a) *Cuba, Méx (vago)* **es un h.** *Br* he's a lazy sod *o* git, *US* he's so goddamn lazy (b) *Andes, Arg, Ven (tonto, torpe)* *Br* prat, *Br* pillock, *US* jerk

huida *nf* flight, escape

huipil *nm CAm, Méx* = colourful embroidered dress or blouse traditionally worn by Indian women

huir [37] *vi* to run away (**de** from), to flee; **h. de la cárcel** to escape from prison; **h. de algn** to avoid sb

hule *nm* (a) *(tela impermeable)* oilcloth, oilskin (b) *(de mesa)* table-cloth (c) *CAm, Méx (caucho)* rubber

humanidad *nf* (a) *(género humano)* humanity, mankind (b) *(cualidad)* humanity, humaneness (c) *(bondad)* compassion, kindness

humanitario, -a *adj* humanitarian

humano, -a 1 *adj* (a) *(relativo al hombre)* human (b) *(compasivo)* humane **2** *nm* human (being); **ser h.** human being

humareda *nf* cloud of smoke ¡**qué h.!** what a lot of smoke!, it's so smoky!

humedad *nf (atmosférica)* humidity; *(de lugar)* dampness; **a prueba de h.** damp-proof

humedecer [33] **1** *vt* to moisten, to dampen **2 humedecerse** *vpr* to become damp *o* wet *o* moist

húmedo, -a *adj (casa, ropa)* damp; *(clima)* humid, damp, moist

humilde *adj* humble, modest; *(pobre)* poor

humillación *nf* humiliation

humillante *adj* humiliating, humbling

humillar 1 *vt (rebajar)* to humiliate, to humble **2 humillarse** *vpr* **humillarse ante algn** to humble oneself before sb

humita *nf* (**a**) *Chile (pajarita)* bow tie (**b**) *Andes, Arg (pasta de maíz)* = paste made of mashed *Br* maize *o US* corn kernels mixed with cheese, chilli, onion and other ingredients, wrapped in a *Br* maize *o US* corn husk and steamed

humo *nm* (**a**) smoke; *(gas)* fumes; *(vapor)* vapour, steam (**b**) **¡qué humos tiene!** she thinks a lot of herself!

humor *nm* (**a**) *(genio)* mood; **estar de buen/mal h.** to be in a good/bad mood (**b**) *(carácter)* temper; **es persona de mal h.** he's bad-tempered (**c**) *(gracia)* humour; **sentido del h.** sense of humour

humorismo *nm* humour

humorista *nmf* humorist; **h. gráfico** cartoonist

humorístico, -a *adj* humorous, funny

hundir 1 *vt* (**a**) *(barco)* to sink (**b**) *(edificio)* to bring *o* knock down (**c**) *Fig (desmoralizar)* to demoralize **2 hundirse** *vpr* (**a**) *(barco)* to sink (**b**) *(edificio)* to collapse (**c**) *Fig (empresa)* to collapse, to crash

húngaro, -a 1 *adj & nm,f* Hungarian **2** *nm (idioma)* Hungarian

Hungría *n* Hungary

huracán *nm* hurricane

hurtadillas *adv* **a h.** stealthily, on the sly

hurto *nm* petty theft, pilfering

Ii

ibérico, -a *adj* Iberian

iceberg *nm* (*pl* **icebergs**) iceberg

Icona *nm Antes* (*abr* **Instituto Nacional para la Conservación de la Naturaleza**) = Spanish national institute for conservation, *Br* ≃ NCC

icono *nm* icon; *Informát* icon

ida *nf* (**billete de**) **i. y vuelta** *Br* return (ticket), *US* round-trip (ticket); **idas y venidas** comings and goings

idea *nf* (a) idea; **i. fija** fixed idea (b) (*noción*) idea; **hacerse a la i. de** to get used to the idea of; *Fam* **ni i.** no idea, not a clue (c) (*opinión*) opinion; **cambiar de i.** to change one's mind (d) (*intención*) intention; **a mala i.** on purpose

ideal *adj & nm* ideal

idealismo *nm* idealism

idealista 1 *adj* idealistic **2** *nmf* idealist

idéntico, -a *adj* identical

identidad *nf* (a) identity; **carnet de i.** identity card (b) (*semejanza*) identity, sameness

identificación *nf* identification

identificar [44] **1** *vt* to identify **2 identificarse** *vpr* to identify oneself; *Fig* **identificarse con** to identify with

ideología *nf* ideology

idilio *nm* (a) *Lit* idyll (b) *Fig* (*romance*) romance, love affair

idioma *nm* language

idiota 1 *adj* idiotic, stupid **2** *nmf* idiot, fool

ídolo *nm* idol

idóneo, -a *adj* suitable, fit

iglesia *nf* (a) (*edificio*) church (b) **la I.** (*institución*) the Church

ignorancia *nf* ignorance

ignorante 1 *adj* (a) (*sin instrucción*) ignorant (b) (*no informado*) ignorant, unaware (**de** of) **2** *nmf* ignoramus

ignorar 1 *vt* (a) (*algo*) not to know (b) (*a algn*) to ignore **2 ignorarse** *vpr* to be unknown

igual 1 *adj* (a) (*idéntico*) the same, alike; **son todos iguales** they're all the same; **es i.** it doesn't matter; **i. que** the same as (b) (*equivalente*) equal; **a partes iguales** fifty-fifty (c) *Dep* (*empatados*) even; **treinta iguales** thirty all (d) *Mat* equal; **tres más tres i. a seis** three plus three equals six (e) **al i. que** just like (f) **por i.** equally **2** *nm* equal; **sin i.** unique, unrivalled **3** *adv* (a) **lo haces i. que yo** you do it the same way I do (b) *Esp* (*posiblemente*) perhaps; **i. vengo** I'll probably come (c) *Andes, RP* (*aún así*) all the same; **estaba nublado pero i. fuimos** it was cloudy but we went all the same

igualdad *nf* (a) equality; **i. ante la ley** equality before the law (b) (*identidad*) sameness; **en i. de condiciones** on equal terms

igualmente *adv* equally; (*también*) also, likewise; *Fam* **encantado de conocerlo – ¡i.!** pleased to meet you – likewise!

ilegal *adj* illegal

ilegítimo, -a *adj* illegitimate

ileso, -a *adj* unhurt, unharmed

ilimitado, -a *adj* unlimited, limitless

ilógico, -a *adj* illogical

iluminación *nf* (*alumbrado*) illumination, lighting

iluminar *vt* (a) to illuminate, to light (up) (b) *Fig* (*a persona*) to enlighten; (*tema*) to throw light upon

ilusión *nf* (a) (*esperanza*) hope; (*esperanza vana*) illusion, delusion; **hacerse ilusiones** to build up one's hopes (**b**) *(sueño)* dream (**c**) *Esp (emoción)* excitement, thrill; **me hace i. verla** I'm looking forward to seeing her; **¡qué i.!** how exciting!

ilusionar 1 *vt* (**a**) *(esperanzar)* to build up sb's hopes (**b**) *(entusiasmar)* to excite, to thrill **2 ilusionarse** *vpr* (**a**) *(esperanzarse)* to build up one's hopes (**b**) *(entusiasmarse)* to be excited *o* thrilled (**con** about)

ilustración *nf* (**a**) *(grabado)* illustration, picture; *(ejemplo)* illustration (**b**) *(erudición)* learning, erudition; *Hist* **la I.** the Enlightenment

ilustrar 1 *vt* (**a**) to illustrate (**b**) *(aclarar)* to explain, to make clear **2 ilustrarse** *vpr* to acquire knowledge (**sobre** of), to learn (**sobre** about)

ilustre *adj* illustrious, distinguished

imagen *nf* (**a**) image; **ser la viva i. de algn** to be the spitting image of sb; **tener buena i.** to have a good image (**b**) *Rel* image, statue (**c**) *TV* picture

imaginación *nf* imagination; **eso son imaginaciones tuyas** you're imagining things

imaginar 1 *vt* to imagine **2 imaginarse** *vpr* to imagine; **me imagino que sí** I suppose so

imaginario, -a *adj* imaginary

imaginativo, -a *adj* imaginative

imán *nm* magnet

imbécil 1 *adj* stupid, silly **2** *nmf* idiot, imbecile

imitación *nf* imitation

imitar *vt* to imitate; *(gestos)* to mimic; **este collar imita al oro** this necklace is imitation gold

impaciencia *nf* impatience

impaciente *adj (deseoso)* impatient; *(intranquilo)* anxious

impar *adj Mat* odd; **número i.** odd number

imparable *adj Dep* unstoppable

imparcial *adj* impartial, unbiased

impasible *adj* impassive

impecable *adj* impeccable

impedimento *nm* impediment; *(obstáculo)* hindrance, obstacle

impedir [6] *vt (obstaculizar)* to impede, to hinder; *(imposibilitar)* to prevent, to stop; **i. el paso** to block the way

impensable *adj* unthinkable

imperativo, -a 1 *adj* imperative **2** *nm Ling* imperative

imperceptible *adj* imperceptible

imperdible *nm* safety pin

imperdonable *adj* unforgivable, inexcusable

imperfecto, -a *adj* (**a**) imperfect, fallible (**b**) *(defectuoso)* defective, faulty (**c**) *Ling* imperfect

imperial *adj* imperial

imperio *nm* empire; **el i. de la ley** the rule of law

impermeable 1 *adj* impermeable, impervious; *(ropa)* waterproof **2** *nm* raincoat, *Br* mac

impersonal *adj* impersonal

impertinencia *nf* impertinence

impertinente 1 *adj (insolente)* impertinent; *(inoportuno)* irrelevant **2** *nmpl* **impertinentes** lorgnette

ímpetu *nm* (**a**) *(impulso)* impetus, momentum (**b**) *(violencia)* violence (**c**) *(energía)* energy

implicancia *nf CSur* implication

implicar [44] *vt* (**a**) *(involucrar)* to involve, to implicate (**en** in) (**b**) *(conllevar)* to imply

implícito, -a *adj* implicit, implied

imponer [19] *(pp* impuesto*)* **1** *vt* (**a**) to impose (**b**) *(respeto)* to inspire (**c**) *Fin* to deposit
2 *vi (impresionar)* to be impressive;
3 imponerse *vpr* (**a**) *(infundir respeto)* to command respect (**b**) *(prevalecer)* to prevail (**c**) *(ser necesario)* to be necessary

importación *nf (mercancía)* import; *(acción)* importing; **artículos de i.** imported goods

importancia *nf* importance, significance; **dar i. a** to attach importance to; **sin i.** unimportant

importante *adj* important, significant; **una suma i.** a considerable sum

importar¹ 1 vi (**a**) (atañer) eso no te importa a tí that doesn't concern you, that's none of your business (**b**) (tener importancia) to be important; no importa it doesn't matter; Fam me importa un bledo o un pito I couldn't care less (**c**) (molestar) ¿te importaría repetirlo? would you mind repeating it?; ¿te importa si fumo? do you mind if I smoke?
2 vt (valer) to amount to; los libros importan 15 euros the books come to 15 euros

importar² vt to import

importe nm Com, Fin amount, total

imposibilidad nf impossibility

imposible adj impossible; me es i. hacerlo I can't (possibly) do it

impostor, -a nm,f (farsante) impostor

impotencia nf powerlessness, helplessness; Med impotence

impotente adj powerless, helpless; Med impotent

impreciso, -a adj imprecise, vague

impregnar 1 vt to impregnate (**de** with) **2 impregnarse** vpr to become impregnated

imprenta nf (**a**) (taller) printer's, print works (**b**) (aparato) printing press (**c**) libertad de i. freedom of the press

imprescindible adj essential, indispensable

impresión nf (**a**) Fig (efecto) impression; causar i. to make an impression (**b**) Fig (opinión) impression; cambiar impresiones to exchange impressions (**c**) Impr (acto) printing; (edición) edition (**d**) (huella) impression, imprint

impresionante adj impressive, striking; Fam un error i. (tremendo) a terrible mistake

impresionar vt (**a**) (causar admiración) to impress; (sorprender) to stun, to shock (**b**) Fot to expose

impreso, -a 1 adj printed **2** nm (**a**) (papel, folleto) printed matter (**b**) (formulario) form; i. de solicitud application form (**c**) impresos (de correos) printed matter

impresora nf Informát printer; i. láser laser printer; i. de chorro de tinta inkjet printer

imprevisto, -a 1 adj unforeseen, unexpected **2** nm (incidente) unforeseen event

imprimir (pp **impreso**) vt (**a**) Impr, Informát to print (**b**) (marcar) to stamp

improvisación nf improvisation; Mús extemporization

improvisado, -a adj (espontáneo) improvised, impromptu, ad lib; (provisional) makeshift; discurso i. impromptu speech

improvisar vt to improvise; Mús to extemporize

imprudente adj imprudent, unwise; (indiscreto) indiscreet

impuesto, -a 1 nm Fin tax; i. sobre la renta income tax; libre de impuestos tax-free; Esp i. sobre el valor añadido, Am i. al valor agregado value-added tax **2** adj imposed

impulsar vt to impel, to drive

impulsivo, -a adj impulsive

impulso nm impulse, thrust; Dep tomar i. to take a run-up

impuro, -a adj impure

inaceptable adj unacceptable

inadecuado, -a adj unsuitable, inappropriate

inadmisible adj inadmissible

inaguantable adj unbearable, intolerable

inauguración nf inauguration, opening

inaugurar vt to inaugurate, to open

incapacidad nf (**a**) incapacity, inability; i. física physical disability (**b**) (incompetencia) incompetence, inefficiency

incapaz adj (**a**) unable (**de** to), incapable (**de** of); soy i. de continuar I can't go on (**b**) Jur unfit

incendio nm fire; i. forestal forest fire

incentivo nm incentive

incidente nm incident

incinerador nm (de basura) incinerator

incinerar *vt (basura)* to incinerate; *(cadáveres)* to cremate

incitar *vt* to incite, to urge

inclinación *nf* (a) *(de terreno)* slope, incline; *(del cuerpo)* stoop (b) *(reverencia)* bow (c) *Fig (tendencia)* tendency, inclination, penchant

inclinar 1 *vt* (a) to incline, to bend; *(cabeza)* to nod (b) *Fig (persuadir)* to persuade, to induce **2 inclinarse** *vpr* (a) to lean, to slope, to incline (b) *(al saludar)* to bow; **inclinarse ante** to bow down to (c) *Fig (optar)* **inclinarse a** to be o feel inclined to; **me inclino por éste** I'd rather have this one, I prefer this one

incluido, -a *adj* (a) *(después del sustantivo)* included; *(antes del sustantivo)* including; **servicio no i.** service not included; **i. IVA** including VAT; **todos pagan, incluidos los niños** everyone has to pay, including children (b) *(adjunto)* enclosed

incluir [37] *vt* (a) to include (b) *(contener)* to contain, to comprise (c) *(adjuntar)* to enclose

inclusive *adv* (a) *(incluido)* inclusive; **de martes a viernes i.** from Tuesday to Friday inclusive; **hasta la lección ocho i.** up to and including lesson eight (b) *(incluso)* even

incluso *adv* even; **i. mi madre** even my mother

incógnita *nf* (a) *Mat* unknown quantity, unknown (b) *(misterio)* mystery

incoherente *adj* incoherent

incoloro, -a *adj* colourless

incómodo, -a *adj* uncomfortable; **sentirse i.** to feel uncomfortable o awkward

incomparable *adj* incomparable

incompatibilidad *nf* incompatibility; *Jur* **i. de caracteres** mutual incompatibility

incompetente *adj & nmf* incompetent

incomprensible *adj* incomprehensible

incomunicado, -a *adj* (a) *(aislado)* isolated; **el pueblo se quedó i.** the

town was cut off (b) *(en la cárcel)* in solitary confinement

incondicional 1 *adj* unconditional; *(apoyo)* wholehearted; *(amigo)* faithful; *(partidario)* staunch **2** *nm* die-hard

inconfundible *adj* unmistakable, obvious

inconsciencia *nf Med* unconsciousness; *Fig (irreflexión)* thoughtlessness; *(irresponsabilidad)* irresponsibility

inconsciente *adj* (a) *(con* **estar***)* *(desmayado)* unconscious (b) *(con* **ser***)* *(despreocupado)* unaware **(de** of); *Fig (irreflexivo)* thoughtless, irresponsible

incontable *adj* countless, innumerable

inconveniente 1 *adj* (a) inconvenient (b) *(inapropiado)* unsuitable **2** *nm* (a) *(objeción)* objection; **poner inconvenientes** to raise objections (b) *(desventaja)* disadvantage, drawback; *(problema)* difficulty; **¿tienes i. en acompañarme?** would you mind coming with me?

incorporación *nf* incorporation

incorporar 1 *vt* (a) to incorporate **(en** into) (b) *(levantar)* to help to sit up **2 incorporarse** *vpr* (a) **incorporarse a** *(sociedad)* to join; *(trabajo)* to start; *Mil* **incorporarse a filas** to join up (b) *(en la cama)* to sit up

incorrecto, -a *adj* (a) *(equivocado)* incorrect, inaccurate (b) *(grosero)* impolite, discourteous

incorregible *adj* incorrigible

incrédulo, -a 1 *adj* (a) incredulous, disbelieving (b) *Rel* unbelieving **2** *nm,f* (a) disbeliever (b) *Rel* unbeliever

increíble *adj* incredible, unbelievable

incremento *nm (aumento)* increase; *(crecimiento)* growth; **i. de la temperatura** rise in temperature

incubadora *nf* incubator

incubar *vt* to incubate

inculpado, -a *nm,f* **el i.** the accused

inculto, -a 1 *adj (ignorante)* uneducated, uncouth **2** *nm,f* ignoramus

incumbir *vi* to be incumbent **(a** upon); **esto no te incumbe** this is none of your business

incurable *adj también Fig* incurable

incurrir *vi (cometer)* to fall (**en** into); **i. en delito** to commit a crime; **i. en (un) error** to fall into error

incursionar *vi* (**a**) *(territorio)* to make an incursion (**en** into); *(en ciudad)* to make a raid (**en** into) (**b**) *(en tema, asunto)* to dabble

indecente *adj* (**a**) *(impúdico)* indecent (**b**) *(impresentable)* dreadful

indeciso, -a *adj* (**a**) *(vacilante)* hesitant, irresolute (**b**) *(resultados etc)* inconclusive

indefenso, -a *adj* defenceless, helpless

indefinido, -a *adj* (**a**) *(indeterminado)* indefinite; *(impreciso)* undefined, vague (**b**) *Ling* indefinite

indemnización *nf* (**a**) *(acto)* indemnification (**b**) *Fin (compensación)* indemnity, compensation; **i. por despido** redundancy payment

indemnizar [40] *vt* to indemnify, to compensate (**por** for)

independencia *nf* independence

independiente *adj (libre)* independent; *(individualista)* self-reliant

independizar [40] **1** *vt* to make independent, to grant independence to **2 independizarse** *vpr* to become independent

indeterminado, -a *adj* (**a**) indefinite; *(impreciso)* vague (**b**) *(persona)* irresolute (**c**) *Ling* indefinite

India *nf* (**la**) **I**. India

indicación *nf* (**a**) *(señal)* indication, sign (**b**) *(instrucción)* instruction, direction; **por i. de algn** at sb's suggestion

indicador *nm* (**a**) indicator (**b**) *Téc* gauge, meter; *Aut* **i. del nivel de aceite** (oil) dipstick; *Aut* **i. de velocidad** speedometer

indicar [44] *vt (señalar)* to indicate, to show, to point out; **¿me podría i. el camino?** could you show me the way?

indicativo, -a *adj* (**a**) indicative (**de** of) (**b**) *Ling* (**modo**) **i.** indicative (mood)

índice *nm* (**a**) *(de libro)* index, table of contents (**b**) *(relación)* rate; **í. de natalidad/mortalidad** birth/death rate; *Fin* **í. de precios** price index (**c**) *Anat* (**dedo**) **í.** index finger, forefinger

indicio *nm* (**a**) *(señal)* indication, sign, token (**de** of) (**b**) *Jur* **indicios** *(prueba)* evidence

indiferencia *nf* indifference, apathy

indiferente *adj* (**a**) *(no importante)* unimportant; **me es i.** it makes no difference to me (**b**) *(apático)* indifferent

indígena **1** *adj* indigenous, native (**de** to) **2** *nmf* native (**de** of)

indigestión *nf* indigestion

indigesto, -a *adj (comida)* indigestible, difficult to digest; **me siento i.** I've got indigestion

indignación *nf* indignation

indignado, -a *adj* indignant (**por** at *o* about)

indignante *adj* outrageous, infuriating

indio, -a *adj & nm,f* Indian; **en fila india** in single file; *Esp Fam* **hacer el i.** to play the fool

indirecta *nf Fam (insinuación)* hint, insinuation; **tirar** *o* **lanzar una i.** to drop a hint; **coger la i.** to get the message

indirecto, -a *adj* indirect; *Ling* **estilo i.** indirect *o* reported speech

indiscreto, -a *adj* indiscreet, tactless

indiscriminado, -a *adj* indiscriminate

indiscutible *adj* indisputable, unquestionable

indispensable *adj* indispensable, essential

indispuesto, -a *adj* indisposed, unwell

individual **1** *adj* individual; **habitación i.** single room **2** *nmpl Dep* **individuales** singles

individuo *nm* (**a**) individual (**b**) *(tío)* bloke, guy

índole *nf* (**a**) *(carácter)* character, nature (**b**) *(clase, tipo)* kind, sort

Indonesia *n* Indonesia

indumentaria *nf* clothing, clothes

industria *nf* industry

industrial 1 *adj* industrial **2** *nmf* industrialist

industrializado, -a *adj* industrialized; **países industrializados** industrialized countries

inédito, -a *adj* (a) *(libro, texto)* unpublished (b) *(nuevo)* completely new; *(desconocido)* unknown

inepto, -a 1 *adj* inept, incompetent **2** *nm,f* incompetent person

inequívoco, -a *adj* unmistakable, unequivocal

inesperado, -a *adj (fortuito)* unexpected, unforeseen; *(imprevisto)* sudden

inestable *adj* unstable, unsteady

inevitable *adj* inevitable, unavoidable

inexperto, -a *adj (inexperto)* inexpert; *(sin experiencia)* inexperienced

infalible *adj* infallible

infancia *nf* childhood, infancy

infanta *nf* infanta, princess

infantería *nf* Mil infantry; **la i. de marina** the marines

infantil *adj* (a) **literatura i.** *(para niños)* children's literature (b) *(aniñado)* Pey childish, infantile

infarto *nm* Med infarction, infarct; **i. (de miocardio)** heart attack, coronary thrombosis; *Fam* **de i.** thrilling, stunning

infección *nf* infection

infeccioso, -a *adj* infectious

infectar 1 *vt* to infect **2 infectarse** *vpr* to become infected **(de** with)

infeliz 1 *adj* unhappy; *(desdichado)* unfortunate **2** *nmf Fam* simpleton; **es un pobre i.** he is a poor devil

inferior 1 *adj* (a) *(más bajo)* lower (b) *(calidad)* inferior; **de calidad i.** of inferior quality (c) *(cantidad)* lower, less; **i. a la media** below average **2** *nmf (persona)* subordinate, inferior

inferioridad *nf* inferiority; **estar en i. de condiciones** to be at a disadvantage; **complejo de i.** inferiority complex

infición *nf Méx* pollution

infidelidad *nf* infidelity, unfaithfulness

infiel 1 *adj (desleal)* unfaithful **2** *nmf Rel* infidel

infierno *nm* (a) *Rel* hell (b) *Fig (tormento)* hell; **su vida es un i.** his life is sheer hell (c) *(horno)* inferno; **en verano esto es un i.** in summer it's like an inferno here; *Fam* **¡vete al i.!** go to hell!, get lost!

ínfimo, -a *adj Fml (mínimo)* extremely low; **detalle í.** smallest detail; **ínfima calidad** very poor quality

infinito, -a 1 *adj* infinite, endless **2** *nm* infinity **3** *adv Fam (muchísimo)* infinitely, immensely

inflación *nf* Econ inflation

inflar 1 *vt* (a) *(hinchar)* to inflate, to blow up; *Náut (vela)* to swell (b) *Fig (exagerar)* to exaggerate **2 inflarse** *vpr* (a) to inflate; *Náut (vela)* to swell (b) *Fam* **inflarse de** to overdo; **se inflaron de macarrones** they stuffed themselves with macaroni

inflexible *adj* inflexible

influencia *nf* influence; **ejercer** o **tener i. sobre algn** to have an influence on o upon sb; **tener influencias** to be influential

influenciar [43] *vt* to influence

influir [37] **1** *vt* to influence **2** *vi* (a) to have influence (b) **i. en** o **sobre** to influence, to have an influence on

influjo *nm* influence

influyente *adj* influential

información *nf* (a) information; **oficina de i.** information bureau (b) **una i.** *(noticia)* a piece of news, news *sing* (c) *Tel Br* directory enquiries, *US* information (d) *(referencias)* references

informal *adj* (a) *(reunión, cena)* informal (b) *(comportamiento)* casual (c) *(persona)* unreliable, untrustworthy

informalidad *nf (incumplimiento)* unreliability; *(desenfado)* informality

informar 1 *vt* to inform (**de** of); *(dar informes)* to report **2 informarse** *vpr (procurarse noticias)* to find out (**de** about); *(enterarse)* to inquire (**de** about)

informática *nf* computing, information technology

informático, -a 1 *adj* computer, computing **2** *nm,f* (computer) technician

informativo, -a 1 *adj* (**a**) *Rad, TV* news; **boletín i.** news (broadcast) (**b**) *(explicativo)* informative, explanatory **2** *nm Rad, TV* news bulletin

informe *nm* (**a**) report (**b**) **informes** references; **pedir informes sobre algn** to make inquiries about sb

infracción *nf (de ley)* infringement, breach (**de** of)

infundir *vt* to infuse; *Fig* to instil; **i. dudas** to give rise to doubt; **i. respeto** to command respect

infusión *nf* infusion

ingeniería *nf* engineering

ingeniero, -a *nm,f* engineer; **i. agrónomo** agricultural engineer; **i. de telecomunicaciones** telecommunications engineer; **i. técnico** technician

ingenio *nm* (**a**) *(talento)* talent; *(inventiva)* inventiveness, creativeness; *(agudeza)* wit (**b**) *(aparato)* device

ingenioso, -a *adj* ingenious, clever; *(vivaz)* witty

ingenuidad *nf* ingenuousness, naïveté

ingenuo, -a 1 *adj* ingenuous, naïve **2** *nm,f* naïve person

Inglaterra *n* England

ingle *nf Anat* groin

inglés, -esa 1 *adj* English **2** *nm,f* Englishman, *f* Englishwoman; **los ingleses** the English **3** *nm (idioma)* English

ingrato, -a 1 *adj* (**a**) *(persona)* ungrateful (**b**) *(noticia)* unpleasant (**c**) *(trabajo)* thankless, unrewarding (**d**) *(tierra)* unproductive **2** *nm,f* ungrateful person

ingrediente *nm* ingredient

ingresar 1 *vt* (**a**) *Esp (dinero)* to deposit, to pay in (**b**) *Med* to admit; **la ingresaron en el hospital** she was admitted to hospital **2** *vi* (**a**) to enter; **i. en el ejército** to enlist in the army, to join the army; **i. en un club** to join a club (**b**) *Esp* **i. cadáver** to be dead on arrival

ingreso *nm* (**a**) *(de dinero)* deposit; **hacer un i. en una cuenta** to pay money into an account (**b**) *(entrada)* entry (**en** to); *(admisión)* admission (**en** to) (**c**) **ingresos** *(sueldo, renta)* income; *(beneficios)* revenue

inhabitable *adj* uninhabitable

inhalar *vt* to inhale

inhibición *nf* inhibition

inhumano, -a *adj* inhumane; *(cruel)* inhuman

iniciación *nf* (**a**) *(ceremonia)* initiation (**b**) *(principio)* start, beginning

inicial *adj & nf* initial; **punto i.** starting point

iniciar [43] **1** *vt* (**a**) *(empezar)* to begin, to start; *(discusión)* to initiate; *(una cosa nueva)* to pioneer (**b**) *(introducir)* to initiate **2 iniciarse** *vpr* (**a**) **iniciarse en algo** *(aprender)* to start to study sth (**b**) *(empezar)* to begin, to start

iniciativa *nf* initiative; **i. privada** private enterprise; **por i. propia** on one's own initiative

inicio *nm* beginning, start; **a inicios de** at the beginning of

inimaginable *adj* unimaginable

injerto *nm* graft

injusticia *nf* injustice, unfairness

injusto, -a *adj* unjust, unfair

inmaduro, -a *adj* immature

inmediatamente *adv* immediately, at once

inmediato, -a *adj* (**a**) *(en el tiempo)* immediate; **de i.** at once (**b**) *(en el espacio)* next (**a** to), adjoining

inmejorable *adj (trabajo)* excellent; *(precio)* unbeatable

inmenso, -a *adj* immense, vast

inmigración *nf* immigration

inmigrante *adj & nmf* immigrant

inmigrar *vi* to immigrate

inmobiliaria *nf Br* estate agency *o* agent's, *US* real estate company

inmoral *adj* immoral

inmortal *adj & nmf* immortal

inmóvil *adj* motionless, immobile

inmovilizar [40] *vt* (**a**) *(persona, cosa)* to immobilize (**b**) *Fin (capital)* to immobilize, to tie up

inmueble 1 *adj* **bienes inmuebles** real estate **2** *nm* building

inmune *adj* immune (**a** to), exempt (**de** from)

inmunidad *nf* immunity (**contra** against); **i. diplomática/parlamentaria** diplomatic/parliamentary immunity

innato, -a *adj* innate, inborn

innecesario, -a *adj* unnecessary

innovación *nf* innovation

inocencia *nf* (**a**) innocence (**b**) *(ingenuidad)* naïveté

inocentada *nf Fam* ≃ April Fool's joke; **hacer una i. a algn** to play an April Fool's joke on sb

inocente 1 *adj* innocent **2** *nmf* innocent; **día de los Inocentes** Holy Innocents' Day, 28 December, ≃ April Fools' Day

inofensivo, -a *adj* harmless

inolvidable *adj* unforgettable

inoportuno, -a *adj* inappropriate; **llegó en un momento muy i.** he turned up at a very awkward moment

inoxidable *adj* **acero i.** stainless steel

inquietar 1 *vt* to worry **2 inquietarse** *vpr* to worry (**por** about)

inquieto, -a *adj* (**a**) *(preocupado)* worried (**por** about) (**b**) *(intranquilo)* restless (**c**) *(emprendedor)* eager

inquietud *nf* (**a**) *(preocupación)* worry (**b**) *(agitación)* restlessness (**c**) *(anhelo)* eagerness

inquilino, -a *nm,f* tenant

inquisición *nf* (**a**) *(indagación)* inquiry, investigation (**b**) **la I.** *(tribunal)* the (Spanish) Inquisition

insaciable *adj* insatiable

insalubre *adj* unhealthy

insatisfacción *nf* (**a**) *(disgusto, descontento)* dissatisfaction (**b**) *(falta, carencia)* lack of fulfilment

insatisfecho, -a *adj* dissatisfied

inscribir (*pp* **inscrito**) **1** *vt* (**a**) *(registrar)* to register; **i. a un niño en el registro civil** to register a child's birth (**b**) *(matricular)* to enrol (**c**) *(grabar)* to inscribe **2 inscribirse** *vpr* (**a**) *(registrarse)* to register; *(hacerse miembro)* to join (**b**) *(matricularse)* to enrol

inscripción *nf* (**a**) *(matriculación)* enrolment, registration (**b**) *(escrito etc)* inscription

insecticida *nm* insecticide

insecto *nm* insect

inseguridad *nf* (**a**) *(falta de confianza)* insecurity (**b**) *(duda)* uncertainty (**c**) *(peligro)* lack of safety; **la i. ciudadana** the breakdown of law and order

inseguro, -a *adj* (**a**) *(poco confiado)* insecure (**b**) *(dubitativo)* uncertain (**c**) *(peligroso)* unsafe

insensato, -a 1 *adj* foolish **2** *nm,f* fool

insensible *adj* (**a**) *(indiferente)* insensitive (**a** to), unfeeling (**b**) *(imperceptible)* imperceptible (**c**) *Med* numb

inseparable *adj* inseparable

insertar *vt* to insert

inservible *adj* useless

insignia *nf* (**a**) *(emblema)* badge (**b**) *(bandera)* flag

insignificante *adj* insignificant

insinuar [30] **1** *vt* to insinuate **2 insinuarse** *vpr* **insinuarse a algn** to make advances to sb

insípido, -a *adj* insipid; *Fig* dull, flat

insistencia *nf* insistence; **con i.** insistently

insistir *vi* to insist (**en** on); **insistió en ese punto** he stressed that point

insolación *nf Med* sunstroke; **coger una i.** to get sunstroke

insolencia *nf* insolence

insolente *adj* insolent

insólito, -a *adj* *(poco usual)* unusual;

(extraño) strange, odd

insolvente *adj Fin* insolvent

insomnio *nm* insomnia; **noche de i.** sleepless night

insoportable *adj* unbearable

inspeccionar *vt* to inspect

inspector, -a *nm,f* inspector; **i. de Hacienda** tax inspector

inspiración *nf* (a) inspiration (b) *(inhalación)* inhalation

inspirar 1 *vt* (a) to inspire (b) *(inhalar)* to inhale, to breathe in **2 inspirarse** *vpr* **inspirarse en** to be inspired by

instalación *nf* installation; **instalaciones deportivas** sports facilities

instalar 1 *vt* (a) to install (b) *(puesto, tienda)* to set up **2 instalarse** *vpr (persona)* to settle (down)

instancia *nf* (a) *(solicitud)* request; **a instancia(s) de** at the request of (b) *(escrito)* application form (c) *Jur* **tribunal de primera i.** court of first instance (d) **en primera i.** first of all; **en última i.** as a last resort

instantánea *nf* snapshot

instantáneo, -a *adj* instantaneous; **café i.** instant coffee

instante *nm* instant, moment; **a cada i.** constantly; **al i.** immediately, right away; **por instantes** with every second; **¡un i.!** just a moment!

instintivo, -a *adj* instinctive

instinto *nm* instinct; **por i.** instinctively; **i. de conservación** survival instinct

institución *nf* institution

institucional *adj* institutional

instituir [37] *vt* to institute

instituto *nm* (a) institute (b) *Esp (centro docente)* high school

institutriz *nf* governess

instrucción *nf* (a) *(educación)* education (b) *(usu pl) (indicación)* instruction; **instrucciones para el o de uso** directions for use (c) *Jur* preliminary investigation; **la i. del sumario** proceedings; **juez de i.** examining magistrate (d) *Mil* drill

instruir [37] *vt* (a) to instruct (b)

(enseñar) to educate (c) *Mil* to drill (d) *Jur* to investigate

instrumental *adj* instrumental

instrumento *nm* instrument

insuficiente 1 *adj* insufficient **2** *nm Educ (nota)* fail

insufrible *adj* insufferable

insultante *adj* insulting

insultar *vt* to insult

insulto *nm* insult

insuperable *adj* (a) *(inmejorable)* unsurpassable (b) *(problema)* insurmountable

intacto, -a *adj* intact

integración *nf también Mat* integration; **i. racial** racial integration

integrar 1 *vt (formar)* to compose, to make up; **el equipo lo integran once jugadores** there are eleven players in the team **2 integrarse** *vpr* to integrate (**en** with)

íntegro, -a *adj* (a) *(entero)* whole, entire; *Lit* **edición íntegra** unabridged edition (b) *(honrado)* upright

intelectual *adj & nmf* intellectual

inteligencia *nf (intelecto)* intelligence; **cociente de i.** intelligence quotient, IQ

inteligente *adj* intelligent

intemperie *nf* bad weather; **a la i.** in the open (air)

intención *nf* intention; **con i.** deliberately, on purpose; **con segunda o doble i.** with an ulterior motive; **tener la i. de hacer algo** to intend to do sth

intencionado, -a *adj* deliberate

intendencia *nf* (a) *RP (corporación municipal)* Br town council, US city council (b) *RP (edificio)* town hall, US city hall (c) *Chile (gobernación)* regional government

intendente *nm* (a) *RP (alcalde)* mayor (b) *Chile (gobernador)* provincial governor

intensivo, -a *adj* intensive; *Agr* **cultivo i.** intensive farming; *Educ* **curso i.** crash course

intenso, -a *adj* intense

intentar *vt* to try, to attempt; *Fam*

¡inténtalo! give it a go!

intento *nm* attempt; **i. de suicidio** attempted suicide

intercalar *vt* to insert

intercambio *nm* exchange; **i. comercial** trade

interceder *vi* to intercede

interceptar *vt* (**a**) *(detener)* to intercept (**b**) *(carretera)* to block; *(tráfico)* to hold up

interés *nm* (*pl* **intereses**) (**a**) interest; **poner i. en** to take an interest in; **tener i. en** o **por** to be interested in (**b**) *(provecho personal)* self-interest; **hacer algo (sólo) por i.** to do sth (purely) out of self-interest; **intereses creados** vested interests (**c**) *Fin* interest; **con un i. del 11 por ciento** at an interest of 11 percent; **tipos de i.** interest rates

interesado, -a 1 *adj* (**a**) interested (**en** in); **las partes interesadas** the interested parties (**b**) *(egoísta)* selfish **2** *nm,f* interested person; **los interesados** those interested o concerned

interesante *adj* interesting

interesar 1 *vt* (**a**) *(tener interés)* to interest; **la poesía no me interesa nada** poetry doesn't interest me at all (**b**) *(concernir)* to concern
   2 *vi* *(ser importante)* to be of interest, to be important; **interesaría llegar pronto** it is important to get there early
   3 interesarse *vpr* **interesarse por** o **en** to be interested in; **se interesó por ti** he asked about o after you

interferencia *nf* interference; *Rad, TV* jamming

interino, -a 1 *adj (persona)* acting **2** *nm,f* *(suplente)* stand-in, deputy; *(médico, juez)* locum; *(profesor)* *Br* supply teacher, *US* substitute teacher

interior 1 *adj* (**a**) inner, inside, interior; **habitación i.** inner room; **ropa i.** underwear (**b**) *Pol* domestic, internal (**c**) *Geog* inland **2** *nm* (**a**) inside, interior; **en su i. no estaba de acuerdo** deep down she disagreed (**b**) *Geog* interior; *Pol* **Ministerio del I.** *Br* ≃ Home Office, *US* ≃ Department of the Interior

interlocutor, -a *nm,f* speaker; *(negociador)* negotiator

intermediario *nm* *Com* middleman

intermedio, -a 1 *adj* intermediate **2** *nm* *TV (intervalo)* break

interminable *adj* endless

intermitente 1 *adj* intermittent **2** *nm* *Esp, Col (en vehículo)* *Br* indicator, *US* turn signal

internacional *adj* international

internado, -a 1 *nm,f* inmate **2** *nm* *(colegio)* boarding school

internauta *nmf* Net user

Internet *nf* *Informát* Internet; **está en I.** it's on the Internet

interno, -a 1 *adj* (**a**) internal; **por vía interna** internally (**b**) *Pol* domestic **2** *nm,f* *(alumno)* boarder; *Med (enfermo)* patient; *(preso)* inmate **3** *nm* *RP (extensión)* (telephone) extension; **i. 28, por favor** extension 28, please

interponer [19] *(pp* **interpuesto)** **1** *vt* to insert; *Jur* **i. un recurso** to give notice of appeal **2 interponerse** *vpr* to intervene

interpretación *nf* (**a**) interpretation (**b**) *Mús, Teatro* performance

interpretar *vt* (**a**) to interpret (**b**) *Teatro (papel)* to play; *(obra)* to perform; *Mús (concierto)* to play, to perform; *(canción)* to sing

intérprete *nmf* (**a**) *(traductor)* interpreter (**b**) *Teatro* performer; *Mús (cantante)* singer; *(músico)* performer

interrogación *nf* interrogation; *Ling* **(signo de) i.** question o interrogation mark

interrogante *nf* *Fig* question mark

interrogar [42] *vt* to question; *(testigo etc)* to interrogate

interrogatorio *nm* interrogation

interrumpir *vt* to interrupt; *(tráfico)* to block

interrupción *nf* interruption; **i. del embarazo** termination of pregnancy

interruptor *nm* *Elec* switch

interurbano, -a *adj* intercity; *Tel*

conferencia interurbana long-distance call

intervalo *nm* interval; **habrá intervalos de lluvia** there will be periods of rain

intervención *nf* (**a**) *(participación)* intervention, participation (**en** in); *(aportación)* contribution (**en** to) (**b**) *Med* intervention

intervenir [27] **1** *vi (mediar)* to intervene (**en** in); *(participar)* to take part (**en** in); *(contribuir)* to contribute (**en** to) **2** *vt* (**a**) *(confiscar)* to confiscate, to seize (**b**) *Tel (teléfono)* to tap (**c**) *Med* to operate on

interviú *nf* interview

intestino, -a 1 *adj (luchas)* internal **2** *nm Anat* intestine

intimidad *nf (amistad)* intimacy; *(vida privada)* private life; *(privacidad)* privacy; **en la i.** privately, in private

íntimo, -a 1 *adj* (**a**) intimate (**b**) *(vida)* private; **una boda íntima** a quiet wedding (**c**) *(amistad)* close **2** *nm,f* close friend, intimate

intocable *adj (persona, institución)* above criticism

intolerable *adj* intolerable

intolerante 1 *adj* intolerant **2** *nmf* intolerant person

intoxicación *nf* poisoning; **i. alimentaria** food poisoning

intoxicar [44] *vt* to poison

intranquilo, -a *adj (preocupado)* worried; *(agitado)* restless

intransigente *adj* intransigent

intransitable *adj* impassable

intrépido, -a *adj* intrepid

intriga *nf* intrigue; *Cin, Teatro* plot

intrigar [42] **1** *vt (interesar)* to intrigue, to interest **2** *vi (maquinar)* to plot

introducción *nf* introduction

introducir [10] *vt* (**a**) to introduce (**b**) *(meter)* to insert, to put in

introvertido, -a *adj* introverted **2** *nm,f* introvert

intruso, -a 1 *adj* intrusive **2** *nm,f* intruder; *Jur* trespasser

intuición *nf* intuition

inundación *nf* flood

inundar *vt* to flood; *Fig (de trabajo etc)* to swamp

inusual *adj* unusual

inútil 1 *adj* (**a**) useless; *(esfuerzo, intento)* vain, pointless (**b**) *Mil* unfit (for service) **2** *nmf Fam* good-for-nothing

invadir *vt* to invade; *Fig* **los estudiantes invadieron la calle** students poured out onto the street

inválido, -a 1 *adj* (**a**) *Jur (nulo)* invalid (**b**) *Med (minusválido)* disabled, handicapped **2** *nm,f Med* disabled *o* handicapped person

invasión *nf* invasion

invasor, -a 1 *adj* invading **2** *nm,f* invader

invención *nf (invento)* invention; *(mentira)* fabrication

inventar *vt* to invent; *(excusa, mentira)* to make up, to concoct

inventario *nm* inventory

invento *nm* invention

invernadero *nm* greenhouse; **efecto i.** greenhouse effect

inversión *nf* (**a**) inversion (**b**) *Fin* investment

inversionista *nmf* investor

inverso, -a *adj* opposite; **en sentido i.** in the opposite direction; **en orden i.** in reverse order

invertir [5] *vt* (**a**) *(orden)* to invert, to reverse (**b**) *(dinero)* to invest (**en** in); *(tiempo)* to spend (**en** on)

investigación *nf* (**a**) *(policial etc)* investigation (**b**) *(científica)* research

investigador, -a *nm,f* (**a**) *(detective)* investigator (**b**) *(científico)* researcher, research worker

investigar [42] *vt* to research; *(indagar)* to investigate

invidente 1 *adj* unsighted **2** *nmf* unsighted person

invierno *nm* winter

invisible *adj* invisible

invitación *nf* invitation

invitado, -a 1 *adj* invited; **artista i.**

guest artist **2** *nm,f* guest

invitar *vt* to invite; **hoy invito yo** it's on me today; **me invitó a una copa** he treated me to a drink

involucrar 1 *vt* to involve (**en** in) **2 involucrarse** *vpr* to get involved (**en** in)

invulnerable *adj* invulnerable

inyección *nf* injection; **poner una i.** to give an injection

ir [16] **1** *vi* (**a**) to go; **¡vamos!** let's go!; **voy a Lima** I'm going to Lima; **¡ya voy!** (I'm) coming!

(**b**) *(río, camino)* to lead; **esta carretera va a la frontera** this road leads to the border

(**c**) *(funcionar)* to work (properly); **el ascensor no va** the lift is out of order

(**d**) *(desenvolverse)* **¿cómo le va el nuevo trabajo?** how is he getting on in his new job?; **¿cómo te va?** how are things?, how are you doing?

(**e**) *(sentar bien)* to suit; **el verde te va mucho** green really suits you

(**f**) *(combinar)* to match; **el rojo no va con el verde** red doesn't go with green

(**g**) *(vestir)* to wear; **ir con falda** to wear a skirt; **ir de blanco/de uniforme** to be dressed in white/in uniform

(**h**) *Fam (importar, concernir)* to concern; **eso va por ti también** and the same goes for you; **ni me va ni me viene** I don't care one way or the other

(**i**) *Fam (comportarse)* to act; **ir de guapo por la vida** to be a flash Harry

(**j**) **va para abogado** he's studying to be a lawyer

(**k**) *(+ por)* **ir por la derecha** to keep (to the) right; *Esp (ir a buscar)* **ve (a) por agua** go and fetch some water; *(haber llegado)* **voy por la página 90** I've got as far as page 90

(**l**) *(locuciones)* **a eso iba** I was coming to that; **¡ahí va!** catch!; **en lo que va de año** so far this year; **ir a parar** to end up; **¡qué va!** of course not!, nothing of the sort!; **va a lo suyo** he looks after his own interests; **¡vamos a ver!** let's see!

2 *v aux* (**a**) *(+ gerundio)* **ir andando** to

go on foot; **va mejorando** she's improving

(**b**) *(+ pp)* **ya van rotos tres** three (of them) have already been broken

(**c**) *(a + inf)* **iba a decir que** I was going to say that; **va a llover** it's going to rain; **vas a caerte** you'll fall

3 irse *vpr* (**a**) *(marcharse)* to go away, to leave; **me voy** I'm off; **¡vámonos!** let's go!; **¡vete!** go away!; **vete a casa** go home (**b**) *(líquido, gas) (escaparse)* to leak (**c**) *(direcciones)* **¿por dónde se va a …?** which is the way to …? **por aquí se va al río** this is the way to the river

ira *nf* wrath, rage, anger

Irak *n* Iraq

Irán *n* Iran

Irlanda *n* Ireland; **I. del Norte** Northern Ireland

irlandés, -esa 1 *adj* Irish

2 *nm,f* Irishman, *f* Irishwoman; **los irlandeses** the Irish

3 *nm (idioma)* Irish

ironía *nf* irony

irónico, -a *adj* ironic

IRPF *nm Econ (abr* **impuesto sobre la renta de las personas físicas)** income tax

irracional *adj* irrational

irradiar [43] *vt* (**a**) *(luz, calor)* to radiate (**b**) *RP (emitir)* to broadcast

irrecuperable *adj* irretrievable

irregular *adj* irregular

irregularidad *nf* irregularity

irresistible *adj* (**a**) *(impulso, persona)* irresistible (**b**) *(insoportable)* unbearable

irresponsable *adj* irresponsible

irrestricto, -a *adj Am* unconditional, complete

irreversible *adj* irreversible

irrigar [42] *vt* to irrigate, to water

irritable *adj* irritable

irritación *nf* irritation

irritante *adj* irritating

irritar 1 *vt* (**a**) *(enfadar)* to irritate, to exasperate (**b**) *Med* to irritate **2 irritarse** *vpr* (**a**) *(enfadarse)* to lose one's temper, to get angry (**b**) *Med* to become irritated

isla *nf* island, isle

islam *nm Rel* Islam

islandés, -esa 1 *adj* Icelandic **2** *nm,f (persona)* Icelander **3** *nm (idioma)* Icelandic

Islandia *n* Iceland

islote *nm* small island

Israel *n* Israel

istmo *nm Geog* isthmus

itacate *nm Méx* packed lunch

Italia *n* Italy

italiano, -a 1 *adj & nm, f* Italian **2** *nm (idioma)* Italian

itinerario *nm* itinerary, route

IVA *nm Econ* (*abr Esp* **impuesto sobre el valor añadido,** *Am* **impuesto al valor agregado**) *Br* VAT, *US* ≃ sales tax

izqda., izqd^a (*abr* **izquierda**) left

izqdo., izqd^o (*abr* **izquierdo**) left

izquierda *nf* (**a**) left; **a la i.** on the left; **girar a la i.** to turn left (**b**) *(mano)* left hand (**c**) *Pol* **la i.** the left; *Esp* **de izquierdas** left-wing; *Am* **de i.** left-wing

izquierdo, -a *adj* (**a**) left; **brazo i.** left arm (**b**) *(zurdo)* left-handed

Jj

jabalí *nm* (*pl* **jabalíes**) wild boar

jabalina *nf Dep* javelin

jabato, -a *nm* (**a**) *(animal)* young wild boar (**b**) *Esp Fam (valiente)* daredevil

jabón *nm* soap; **j. de afeitar/tocador** shaving/toilet soap

jabonera *nf* soap dish

jacal *nm Méx* hut

jacuzzi® [ja'kusi] *nm* Jacuzzi®

jade *nm* jade

jadear *vi* to pant, to gasp

jaguar *nm* jaguar

jaiba *nf Am salvo RP (cangrejo)* crayfish

jalar *vt* (**a**) *Esp Fam (comer)* to eat, *Br* to scoff (**b**) *Am salvo RP (tirar de)* to pull

jalea *nf* jelly; **j. real** royal jelly

jaleo *nm (alboroto)* din, racket; *(riña)* row; *(confusión)* muddle; **armar j.** to make a racket

jalón *nm Am salvo RP* pull

Jamaica *n* Jamaica

jamás *adv* (**a**) never; **j. he estado allí** I have never been there; **nunca j.** never again (**b**) ever; **el mejor libro que j. se ha escrito** the best book ever written

jamón *nm* ham; **j. de York/serrano** boiled/cured ham

Japón *n* (**el**) **J.** Japan

japonés, -esa 1 *adj* Japanese **2** *nm,f (persona)* Japanese; **los japoneses** the Japanese **3** *nm (idioma)* Japanese

jarabe *nm* syrup; **j. para la tos** cough mixture

jardín *nm Br* garden, *US* yard; **j. botánico** botanical garden; **j. de infancia** nursery school, kindergarten

jardinera *nf* planter

jardinero *nm* gardener

jarra *nf* pitcher; **j. de cerveza** beer mug; *Fig* **de** *o* **en jarras** (with) arms akimbo, hands on hips

jarro *nm (recipiente)* jug; *(contenido)* jugful; *Fig* **echar un j. de agua fría a** to pour cold water on

jarrón *nm* vase; *(en arqueología)* urn

jaula *nf (para animales)* cage

jazmín *nm Bot* jasmine

jazz [jas] *nm inv* jazz

jefatura *nf* (**a**) *(cargo, dirección)* leadership (**b**) *(sede)* central office; **j. de policía** police headquarters

jefe *nm* (**a**) head, chief, boss; *Com* manager; **j. de estación** stationmaster; **j. de redacción** editor-in-chief; **j. de ventas** sales manager (**b**) *Pol* leader; **J. de Estado** Head of State (**c**) *Mil* officer in command; **comandante en j.** commander-in-chief

jején *nm Am* gnat

jerez *nm* sherry

jerga *nf (argot) (técnica)* jargon; *(vulgar)* slang; **la j. legal** legal jargon

jeringuilla *nf* (hypodermic) syringe

jeroglífico, -a 1 *adj* hieroglyphic **2** *nm* (**a**) *Ling* hieroglyph, hieroglyphic (**b**) *(juego)* rebus

jersey *nm* (*pl* **jerseys** *o* **jerséis**) *Esp* sweater, *Br* jumper

Jesucristo *nm* Jesus Christ

jesús *interj (sorpresa)* gosh!, good heavens!; *Esp (tras estornudo)* bless you!

jíbaro,-a *nm,f* (**a**) *(indio)* Jivaro (**b**) *Ven Fam (traficante)* pusher

jícama *nf* yam bean, jicama

jícara *nf CAm, Méx, Ven* (**a**) *(calabaza)* calabash, gourd (**b**) *(taza)* mug

jinete *nm* rider, horseman

jinetera *nf Cuba Fam* prostitute

jirafa *nf* (**a**) giraffe (**b**) *(de micrófono)* boom

jirón *nm* (**a**) *(trozo desgarrado)* shred, strip; *(pedazo suelto)* bit, scrap; **hecho jirones** in shreds o tatters (**b**) *Perú (calle)* street

jitomate *nm Méx* tomato

JJ.OO. *nmpl (abr* **Juegos Olímpicos**) Olympic Games

joda *nf RP, Ven muy Fam* (**a**) *(fastidio)* pain in the *Br* arse o *US* ass (**b**) *(broma)* piss-take; **¡no te enojes!, lo dije/hice en j.** don't be angry, I was just pissing around (**c**) *(fiesta)* **los espero el sábado en casa, va a haber j.** I'll see you at my place on Saturday, we're having a bash

joder *Vulg* **1** *interj* shit!, *Br* bloody hell! **2** *vt* (**a**) *(fastidiar)* to piss off; **¡no me jodas!** come on, don't give me that! (**b**) *Esp (copular)* to fuck (**c**) *(echar a perder)* to screw up; **¡la jodiste!** you screwed it up! (**d**) *(romper)* to bugger **3 joderse** *vpr* (**a**) *(aguantarse)* to put up with it; **¡hay que joderse!** you'll just have to grin and bear it! (**b**) *(echarse a perder)* to get screwed up; **¡que se joda!** to hell with him! (**c**) *(romperse)* to go bust

jogging *nm* (**a**) *(deporte)* jogging; **hacer j.** to go jogging (**b**) *RP (ropa)* tracksuit, jogging suit

Jordania *n* Jordan

jornada *nf* (**a**) **j. (laboral)** *(día de trabajo)* working day; **j. intensiva** continuous working day; **j. partida** working day with a lunch break; **trabajo de media j./j. completa** part-time/full-time work (**b**) **jornadas** conference

jornal *nm (paga)* day's wage; **trabajar a j.** to be paid by the day

jornalero, -a *nm,f* day labourer

jorongo *nm Méx* (**a**) *(manta)* blanket (**b**) *(poncho)* poncho

jota¹ *nf* (**a**) = name of the letter j in Spanish (**b**) *(cantidad mínima)* jot, scrap; **ni j.** not an iota; **no entiendo ni j.** I don't understand a thing

jota² *nf Mús* = Spanish dance and music

joven **1** *adj* young; **de aspecto j.** young-looking **2** *nmf* youth, young man, *f* girl, young woman; **de j.** as a young man/woman; **los jóvenes** young people, youth

joya *nf* (**a**) jewel, piece of jewellery; **joyas de imitación** imitation jewellery (**b**) *Fig* **ser una j.** *(persona)* to be a real treasure o gem

joyería *nf (tienda)* jewellery shop, jeweller's (shop)

joyero, -a **1** *nm,f* jeweller **2** *nm* jewel case o box

joystick ['joistik] *nm (pl* **joysticks**) joystick

jubilación *nf* (**a**) *(acción)* retirement; **j. anticipada** early retirement (**b**) *(pensión)* pension

jubilado, -a **1** *adj* retired **2** *nm,f Br* pensioner, *US* retiree; **los jubilados** retired people

jubilar **1** *vt (retirar)* to retire, to pension off; *Fam Fig* to get rid of, to ditch **2 jubilarse** *vpr (retirarse)* to retire, to go into retirement

judaísmo *nm* Judaism

judía *nf* bean; *Esp* **j. verde** green bean

judío, -a **1** *adj* Jewish **2** *nm,f* Jew

judo *nm Dep* judo

juego *nm* (**a**) game; **j. de azar** game of chance; **j. de cartas** card game; *Fig* **j. de manos** sleight of hand; *Fig* **j. de palabras** play on words, pun; **j. de rol** fantasy role-playing game; *Fig* **j. limpio/sucio** fair/foul play (**b**) *Dep* game; **Juegos Olímpicos** Olympic Games; **terreno de j.** *Ten* court; *Ftb* field; **fuera de j.** offside (**c**) *(apuestas)* gambling; *Fig.* **poner algo en j.** to put sth at stake (**d**) *(conjunto de piezas)* set; **j. de café/ té** coffee/tea service; *Fig* **ir a j. con** to match

juerga *nf Fam* binge, rave-up; **ir de j.** to go on a binge

jueves *nm inv* Thursday; **J. Santo** Maundy Thursday

juez *nmf* judge; **j. de instrucción** examining magistrate; **j. de paz** justice of the peace; *Dep* **j. de salida**

starter; **j. de línea** linesman

jugador, -a *nm,f* player; *(apostador)* gambler

jugar [32] **1** *vi* (**a**) to play; **j. a(l) fútbol/tenis** to play football/tennis; *Fig* **j. sucio** to play dirty (**b**) **j. con** *(no tomar en serio)* to toy with

2 *vt* (**a**) to play (**b**) *(apostar)* to bet, to stake

3 **jugarse** *vpr* (**a**) *(arriesgar)* to risk; *Fam* **jugarse el pellejo** to risk one's neck (**b**) *(apostar)* to bet, to stake

jugo *nm* juice; *Fig* **sacar el j. a** *(aprovechar)* to make the most of; *(explotar)* to squeeze dry

jugoso, -a *adj* (**a**) juicy; **un filete j.** a juicy steak (**b**) *Fig (sustancioso)* substantial, meaty; **un tema j.** a meaty topic

juguete *nm* toy; **pistola de j.** toy gun; *Fig* **ser el j. de algn** to be sb's plaything

juguetería *nf* toy shop

juguetón, -ona *adj* playful

juicio *nm* (**a**) *(facultad mental)* judgement, discernment; *(opinión)* opinion, judgement; **a j. de** in the opinion of; **a mi j.** in my opinion (**b**) *(sensatez)* reason, common sense; **en su sano j.** in one's right mind; **perder el j.** to go mad *o* insane (**c**) *Jur* trial, lawsuit; **llevar a algn a j.** to take legal action against sb, to sue sb

julepe *nm* (**a**) *(juego de naipes)* = type of card game (**b**) *PRico, RP Fam (susto)* scare, fright; **dar un j. a algn** to give sb a scare

julio *nm* July

junco *nm Bot* rush

jungla *nf* jungle

junio *nm* June

junta *nf* (**a**) *(reunión)* meeting, assembly; *Pol* **j. de gobierno** cabinet meeting (**b**) *(dirección)* board, committee; **j. directiva** board of directors (**c**) *Mil* junta; **j. militar** military junta (**d**) *(parlamento regional)* regional parliament (**e**) *Téc* joint

juntar **1** *vt* (**a**) *(unir)* to join, to put together; *(piezas)* to assemble (**b**) *(reunir) (sellos)* to collect; *(dinero)* to

raise **2** **juntarse** *vpr* (**a**) *(unirse)* to join; *(ríos, caminos)* to meet; *(personas)* to gather (**b**) *(amancebarse)* to live together

junto, -a **1** *adj* together; **dos mesas juntas** two tables side by side; **todos juntos** all together **2** *adv* **j. con** together with; **j. a** next to

jurado *nm* (**a**) *(tribunal)* jury; *(en un concurso)* panel of judges, jury (**b**) *(miembro del tribunal)* juror, member of the jury

jurar **1** *vi Jur, Rel* to swear, to take an oath **2** *vt* to swear; **j. el cargo** to take the oath of office; **j. por Dios** to swear to God **3** **jurarse** *vpr Fam* **jurársela(s) a algn** to have it in for sb

jurídico, -a *adj* legal

justicia *nf* justice; **tomarse la j. por su mano** to take the law into one's own hands

justificación *nf* justification

justificar [44] **1** *vt* to justify **2** **justificarse** *vpr* to clear oneself, to justify oneself

justo, -a **1** *adj* (**a**) just, fair, right; **un trato j.** a fair deal (**b**) *(apretado) (ropa)* tight; **estamos justos de tiempo** we're pressed for time (**c**) *(exacto)* right, accurate; **la palabra justa** the right word (**d**) *(preciso)* **llegamos en el momento j. en que salían** we arrived just as they were leaving (**e**) **lo j.** just enough

2 *nm,f* just *o* righteous person; **los justos** the just, the righteous

3 *adv (exactamente)* exactly, precisely; **j. al lado** right beside

juvenil **1** *adj (aspecto)* youthful, young; **ropa j.** young people's clothes; **delincuencia j.** juvenile delinquency **2** *nmf* **los juveniles** the juveniles

juventud *nf* (**a**) *(edad)* youth (**b**) *(jóvenes)* young people

juzgado *nm* court, tribunal; **j. de guardia** = court open during the night or at other times when ordinary courts are shut

juzgar [42] *vt* to judge; **a j. por ...** judging by ...

Kk

karaoke *nm* karaoke

kárate *nm Dep* karate

Kg, kg (*abr* **kilogramo(s)**) kg

kilo *nm* (**a**) *(medida)* kilo; *Fam* **pesa un k.** it weighs a ton (**b**) *Esp Antes Fam (millón)* a million (pesetas)

kilogramo *nm* kilogram, kilogramme

kilómetro *nm* kilometre

kimono *nm* kimono

kíndergarten, *Andes, Méx* **kínder** *nm* kindergarten, nursery school

kiwi *nm* (**a**) *Orn* kiwi (**b**) *(fruto)* kiwi (fruit), Chinese gooseberry

kleenex® ['klines, 'klineks] *nm inv* paper hanky, (paper) tissue

km (*abr* **kilómetro**) km

Ll

l (abr **litro(s)**) l

la¹ 1 art def f the; **la mesa** the table **2** pron dem the one; **la del vestido azul** the one in the blue dress; **la que vino ayer** the one who came yesterday; ver **el**

la² pron pers f (ella) her; (usted) you; (cosa) it; **la invitaré** I'll invite her along; **no la dejes abierta** don't leave it open; **ya la avisaremos, señora** we'll let you know, madam; ver **le**

la³ nm Mús la, A

laberinto nm labyrinth

labio nm lip

labor nf (a) job, task; **l. de equipo** teamwork; **profesión: sus labores** occupation: housewife (b) Agr farm-work (c) (de costura) needlework, sew-ing

laborable adj (a) día l. (no festivo) working day (b) Agr arable

laboral adj industrial; **accidente l.** industrial accident; **conflictividad l.** industrial unrest; **jornada l.** working day; **Universidad L.** technical training college

laboratorio nm laboratory

laborioso, -a adj (a) (persona) hardworking (b) (tarea) laborious

labrador, -a nm,f (granjero) farmer; (trabajador) farm worker

labrar 1 vt (a) Agr to till (b) (madera) to carve; (piedra) to cut; (metal) to work **2 labrarse** vpr Fig **labrarse un porvenir** to build a future for oneself

laburar vi RP Fam to work; **labura de vendedora** she works in a shop

laburo nm RP Fam job

laca nf (a) hair lacquer, hairspray; **l. de uñas** nail polish o varnish (b) Arte lacquer

lacio, -a adj (a) (pelo) lank, limp (b) **¡qué l.!** (soso) what a weed!

lácteo, -a adj **productos lácteos** milk o dairy products; Astron **Vía Láctea** Milky Way

ladera nf slope

ladino, -a 1 adj (astuto) crafty **2** nm,f CAm, Méx, Ven (no blanco) = non-white Spanish-speaking person

lado nm (a) side; **a un l.** aside; **al l.** close by, nearby; **al l. de** next to, beside; **ponte de l.** stand sideways (b) (en direcciones) direction; **por todos lados** on/from all sides (c) Fig **dar de l. a algn** to cold-shoulder sb; **por otro l.** (además) moreover; **por un l. …, por otro l. …** on the one hand …, on the other hand …

ladrar vi to bark

ladrido nm también Fig bark

ladrillo nm (a) Constr brick (b) Fam (pesado) bore, drag

ladrón, -ona 1 nm,f thief, robber; **¡al l.!** stop thief! **2** nm Elec multiple socket

lagartija nf small lizard

lagarto nm lizard

lago nm lake

lágrima nf (a) tear; **llorar a l. viva** to cry one's eyes out (b) (en lámpara) teardrop

laguna nf (a) small lake (b) Fig (hueco) gap

lamentable adj regrettable; (infame) lamentable

lamentar 1 vt to regret; **lo lamento** I'm sorry **2 lamentarse** vpr to com-plain

lamer vt to lick

lámina nf (a) sheet, plate; **l. de acero** steel sheet (b) Impr plate

lámpara nf (a) lamp; **l. de pie** Br

standard lamp, *US* floor lamp (**b**) *Elec (bombilla)* bulb (**c**) *Rad* valve

lana *nf* (**a**) *(de oveja)* wool; **pura l. virgen** pure new wool (**b**) *Andes, Méx Fam (dinero)* dough, cash

lanceta *nf Andes, Méx (aguijón)* sting

lancha *nf* motorboat, launch; **l. motora** speedboat; **l. neumática** rubber dinghy; **l. salvavidas** lifeboat

langosta *nf* (**a**) lobster (**b**) *(insecto)* locust

langostino *nm* king prawn

lanza *nf* spear, lance; **punta de l.** spearhead; *Fig* **romper una l. en favor de algn/de algo** to defend sb/ sth

lanzar [40] **1** *vt* (**a**) *(arrojar)* to throw, to fling (**b**) *Fig (grito)* to let out (**c**) *Náut, Com, Mil* to launch **2 lanzarse** *vpr* (**a**) *(arrojarse)* to throw *o* hurl oneself; **lanzarse al suelo** to throw oneself to the ground (**b**) *(emprender)* **lanzarse a** to embark on; **lanzarse a los negocios** to go into business (**c**) *Fam (irse, largarse)* to scram

lapa *nf* (**a**) *Zool* limpet (**b**) **es una verdadera l.** he sticks to you like glue

lapicera *nf CSur* ballpoint (pen), Biro®; **l. fuente** fountain pen

lapicero *nm* (**a**) *Esp (lápiz)* pencil (**b**) *CAm, Perú (bolígrafo)* ballpoint (pen), Biro®

lápida *nf* headstone

lápiz *nm* pencil; **l. labial** *o* **de labios** lipstick; **l. de ojos** eyeliner

largavistas *nm inv Bol, CSur* binoculars

largo, -a 1 *adj* (**a**) *(espacio)* long; *(tiempo)* long, lengthy; **pasamos un mes l. allí** we spent a good month there; **a lo l. de** *(espacio)* along; *(tiempo)* through; **a la larga** in the long run (**b**) *(excesivo)* too long; **se hizo l. el día** the day dragged on (**c**) **largos años** many years
 2 *nm* (**a**) *(longitud)* length; **¿cuánto tiene de l.?** how long is it? (**b**) *Mús* largo
 3 *adv* **l. y tendido** at length; *Fam* **¡l. (de aquí)!** clear off!; **esto va para l.**

this is going to last a long time

largometraje *nm* feature film, full-length film

laringe *nf* larynx

las¹ 1 *art def fpl* the; **l. sillas** the chairs; **lávate l. manos** wash your hands; *(no se traduce)* **me gustan l. flores** I like flowers **2** *pron dem* **l. que** *(personas)* the ones who, those who; *(objetos)* the ones that, those that; **toma l. que quieras** take whichever ones you want; *ver* **la¹** *y* **los**

las² *pron pers fpl (ellas)* them; *(ustedes)* you; **l. llamaré mañana (a ustedes)** I'll call you tomorrow; **no l. rompas** don't break them; **Pepa es de l. mías** Pepa thinks the way I do; *ver* **los**

lástima *nf* pity; **¡qué l.!** what a pity!, what a shame!; **es una l. que …** it's a pity (that) …; **estar hecho una l.** to be a sorry sight; **tener l. a algn** to feel sorry for sb

lata¹ *nf* (**a**) *(envase)* can, *esp Br* tin; **en l.** canned, *esp Br* tinned (**b**) *(hojalata)* tin(plate); **hecho de l.** made of tin

lata² *nf Esp Fam* nuisance, drag; **dar la l.** to be a nuisance *o* a pest

latido *nm (del corazón)* beat

látigo *nm* whip

latín *nm* Latin

Latinoamérica *nf* Latin America

latinoamericano, -a *adj & nm,f* Latin American

latir *vi* to beat

laucha *nf CSur* (**a**) *(ratón)* baby *o* small mouse (**b**) *Fam (persona)* **es una l.** he's a tiny little thing

laurel *nm Bot* laurel, (sweet) bay; *Culin* bay leaf; *Fig* **dormirse en los laureles** to rest on one's laurels

lava *nf* lava

lavabo *nm* (**a**) *(pila) Br* washbasin, *US* washbowl (**b**) *(retrete) Br* lavatory, *US* washroom

lavadero *nm (de coches)* car wash

lavado *nm* wash, washing; *Fig* **l. de cerebro** brainwashing; **l. en seco** dry-cleaning

lavadora *nf* washing machine

lavanda *nf* lavender

lavandería *nf* (**a**) *(automática)* launderette, *US* Laundromat® (**b**) *(atendida por personal)* laundry

lavaplatos *nm inv* dishwasher

lavar *vt* to wash; **l. en seco** to dry-clean

lavatorio *nm* (**a**) *(en misa)* lavabo (**b**) *Andes, RP (lavabo) Br* washbasin, *US* washbowl

lavavajillas *nm inv (aparato)* dishwasher

laxante *adj & nm* laxative

lazo *nm* (**a**) *(adorno)* bow (**b**) *(nudo)* knot; **l. corredizo** slipknot (**c**) *(para reses)* lasso (**d**) *Fig (usu pl) (vínculo)* tie, bond

le 1 *pron pers mf (objeto indirecto) (a él)* (to) him; *(a ella)* (to) her; *(a cosa)* (to) it; *(a usted)* (to) you; **lávale la cara** wash his face; **le compraré uno** I'll buy one for her; **¿qué le pasa (a usted)?** what's the matter with you? **2** *pron pers m Esp (objeto directo) (él)* him; *(usted)* you; **no le oigo** I can't hear him; **no quiero molestarle** I don't wish to disturb you

leal 1 *adj* loyal, faithful **2** *nmf* loyalist

lealtad *nf* loyalty, faithfulness

lección *nf* lesson; *Fig* **dar una l. a algn** to teach sb a lesson; *Fig* **te servirá de l.** let that be a lesson to you

lechal 1 *adj* sucking **2** *nm* sucking lamb

leche *nf* (**a**) milk; *Anat* **dientes de l.** milk teeth; **l. descremada** *o* **desnatada** skim *o* skimmed milk (**b**) *muy Fam* **estar de mala l.** to be in a *Br* bloody *o US* goddamn awful mood (**c**) **¡l.!** damn! (**d**) *Esp muy Fam (golpe)* knock; **dar** *o* **pegar una l. a algn** to clobber sb

lechera *nf* (**a**) *(vasija)* churn (**b**) *muy Fam* police car

lechería *nf* dairy, creamery

lechero, -a 1 *adj* milk, dairy; **central lechera** dairy co-operative; **vaca lechera** milk cow **2** *nm* milkman

lecho *nm Literario* bed; **l. del río** riverbed; **l. mortuorio** death-bed

lechosa *nf Carib* papaya

lechuga *nf* lettuce

lechuza *nf* owl

lector, -a 1 *nm,f* (**a**) *(persona)* reader (**b**) *Esp Univ* lector, (language) assistant **2** *nm* reader; **l. de CD-ROM** CD-ROM drive; **l. de DVD** DVD player

lectura *nf* reading

leer [36] *vt* to read; **léenos el menú** read out the menu for us; *Fig* **l. entre líneas** to read between the lines

legal *adj* (**a**) *Jur* legal, lawful; **requisitos legales** legal formalities (**b**) *Esp Fam (persona)* honest, decent

legalidad *nf* legality, lawfulness

legible *adj* legible

legislación *nf* legislation

legislatura *nf* legislature

legítimo, -a *adj* (**a**) *Jur* legitimate; **en legítima defensa** in self-defence (**b**) *(auténtico)* authentic, real; **oro l.** pure gold

legumbre *nf* pulse, pod vegetable; **legumbres secas** dried pulses; **legumbres verdes** green vegetables

lejano, -a *adj* distant, far-off; **parientes lejanos** distant relatives; **el L. Oriente** the Far East

lejía *nf* bleach

lejos *adv* far (away); **a lo l.** in the distance; **de l.** from a distance; *Fig* **ir demasiado l.** to go too far; *Fig* **llegar l.** to go a long way; *Fig* **sin ir más l.** to take an obvious example

lencería *nf* (**a**) *(prendas)* lingerie (**b**) *(ropa blanca)* linen (goods)

lengua *nf* (**a**) tongue; *Fig* **malas lenguas** gossips; *Fam Fig* **irse de la l.** to spill the beans; *Fam Fig* **tirarle a algn de la l.** to draw sb out (**b**) *Ling* language; **l. materna** native *o* mother tongue

lenguado *nm (pez)* sole

lenguaje *nm* language; *Informát* language; **l. corporal** body language

lengüeta *nf* (**a**) *(de zapato)* tongue (**b**) *Mús* reed

lente 1 *nf* lens; **lentes de contacto** contact lenses **2** *nmpl* **lentes** *Am* glasses; **lentes de contacto** contact lenses

lenteja *nf* lentil

lentilla *nf Esp* contact lens; **lentillas blandas/duras** soft/hard lenses

lentitud *nf* slowness; **con l.** slowly

lento, -a *adj* slow; **a fuego l.** on a low heat

leña *nf* (a) firewood; *Fig* **echar l. al fuego** to add fuel to the fire (b) *Fam (golpes)* knocks

leñador, -a *nm,f* woodcutter

leño *nm* (a) log (b) *Fam (persona)* blockhead, halfwit

Leo *nm* Leo

león *nm* lion

leopardo *nm* leopard

leotardos *nmpl Esp* thick tights

lépero, -a *Fam adj* (a) *CAm, Méx (vulgar)* coarse, vulgar (b) *Cuba (ladino)* smart, crafty

les 1 *pron pers mfpl (objeto indirecto) (a ellos, -as)* (to) them; *(a ustedes)* you; **dales el dinero** give them the money; **l. he comprado un regalo** I've bought you a present **2** *pron pers mpl Esp (objeto directo) (ellos)* them; *(ustedes)* you; **l. esperaré** I shall wait for you; **no quiero molestarles** I don't wish to disturb you

lesbiana *nf* lesbian

leseras *nfpl Chile Fam (tonterías)* nonsense, *Br* rubbish

lesión *nf* (a) *(corporal)* injury (b) *Jur (perjuicio)* damage

letal *adj* lethal, deadly

letra *nf* (a) letter; **l. de imprenta** block capitals; **l. mayúscula** capital letter; **l. minúscula** small letter; **l. pequeña** small print (b) *(escritura)* (hand) writing (c) *Mús (texto)* lyrics, words (d) *Fin* **l. (de cambio)** bill of exchange, draft (e) *Univ* **letras** arts

letrero *nm (aviso)* notice, sign; *(cartel)* poster; **l. luminoso** neon sign

levantamiento *nm* (a) raising, lifting; *Dep* **l. de pesos** weightlifting (b) *(insurrección)* uprising, insurrection

levantar 1 *vt* (a) to raise, to lift; *(mano, voz)* to raise; *(edificio)* to erect; *Fig (ánimos)* to raise; **l. los ojos** to look up (b) *(castigo)* to suspend **2 levantarse** *vpr* (a) *(ponerse de pie)* to stand up, to rise (b) *(salir de la cama)* to get up (c) *(concluir)* to finish; **se levanta la sesión** the meeting is closed (d) *Pol* to rise, to revolt; **levantarse en armas** to rise up in arms (e) *(viento)* to come up; *(tormenta)* to gather

levante *nm* (a) **(el) L.** Levante, = the regions of Valencia and Murcia (b) *(viento)* east wind, Levanter

léxico, -a *Ling* **1** *nm (diccionario)* lexicon; *(vocabulario)* vocabulary, word list **2** *adj* lexical

ley *nf (pl leyes)* (a) law; *Parl* bill, act; **aprobar una l.** to pass a bill (b) **oro de l.** pure gold; **plata de l.** sterling silver

leyenda *nf* (a) *(relato)* legend (b) *(en un mapa)* legend; *(en una moneda)* inscription; *(bajo ilustración)* caption

liar [29] **1** *vt* (a) *(envolver)* to wrap up; *(un cigarrillo)* to roll (b) *(enredar)* to muddle up; *(confundir)* to confuse **2 liarse** *vpr* (a) *(embarullarse)* to get muddled up (b) *Esp Fam (salir con)* to get involved; *(besarse)* to neck (c) *Esp* **liarse a bofetadas** to come to blows

Líbano *n* **el L.** the Lebanon

libélula *nf* dragonfly

liberal 1 *adj* (a) liberal; *(carácter)* open-minded; *Pol* **Partido L.** Liberal Party; **profesión l.** liberal profession (b) *(generoso)* generous, liberal **2** *nmf* liberal

liberar *vt (país)* to liberate; *(prisionero)* to free, to release

libertad *nf* freedom, liberty; **en l.** free; *Jur* **(en) l. bajo palabra/fianza** (on) parole/bail; *Jur* **(en) l. condicional** (on) parole; **l. de comercio** free trade; **l. de expresión** freedom of speech

libertador, -a *nm,f* liberator

Libia *n* Libya

Libra *nm* Libra

libra *nf (unidad de peso, moneda)* pound; **l. esterlina** pound sterling

librar 1 *vt* (a) to free; *Jur* to free, to

release (**b**) *Com (una letra)* to draw (**c**) **l. batalla** to do o join battle

2 *vi Esp* **libro los martes** *(no ir a trabajar)* I have Tuesdays off

3 librarse *vpr* to escape; **librarse de algn** to get rid of sb

libre *adj* free; **entrada l.** *(gratis)* admission free; *(sin restricción)* open to the public; **l. cambio** free trade; **l. de impuestos** tax-free

librería *nf* (**a**) *(tienda)* bookshop, *US* bookstore (**b**) *Esp (mueble)* bookcase

librero, -a 1 *nm,f* bookseller **2** *nm CAm, Col, Méx (mueble)* bookcase

libreta *nf* notebook; **l. (de ahorro)** savings book

libretista *nmf Am (guionista)* screen-writer, scriptwriter

libreto *nm Am (guión)* script

libro *nm* book; **l. de texto** textbook; *Com* **l. de caja** cashbook; *Fin* **l. mayor** ledger

liceal *nmf Urug,* **liceano, -a** *nm,f Chile,* **liceísta** *nmf Ven Br* secondary school o *US* high school pupil

licencia *nf* (**a**) *(permiso)* permission; *(documentos)* permit, licence; **l. de armas/caza** gun/hunting licence; *Carib, Chile, Ecuad* **l. de conducir,** *Méx* **l. para conducir** o **de conductor** *Br* driving licence, *US* driver's license; (**b**) *(libertad abusiva)* licence, licen-tiousness

licenciado, -a *nm,f* (**a**) *Univ* graduate; **l. en Ciencias** Bachelor of Science (**b**) *Am salvo RP (forma de tratamiento)* = form of address used to indicate respect; **el l. Pérez** Mr Pérez

licenciar [43] **1** *vt* (**a**) *Mil* to discharge (**b**) *Univ* to confer a degree on **2 licenciarse** *vpr Univ* to graduate

licenciatura *nf Univ (título)* (bach-elor's) degree (course); *(carrera)* degree (course)

liceo *nm* (**a**) *(sociedad literaria)* literary society (**b**) *(escuela) Br* secondary school, *US* high school

licor *nm* liquor, *US* spirits

licorería *nf* (**a**) *(fábrica)* distillery (**b**) *(tienda) Br* off-licence, *US* liquor store

licuadora *nf* (**a**) *Esp (para extraer zumo)* juice extractor, juicer (**b**) *Am (para batir)* blender, *Br* liquidizer

líder *nmf* leader

lidia *nf* bullfight, bullfighting

liebre *nf* hare

lienzo *nm* (**a**) *Tex* linen (**b**) *Arte* canvas

liga *nf* (**a**) *Dep, Pol* league; **hacer buena l.** to get on well together (**b**) *(para medias) (elástico)* garter; *(col-gante) Br* suspender, *US* garter

ligar [42] **1** *vt* (**a**) *(para join; Fig (dos personas)* to unite (**b**) *Fam (coger)* to get

2 *vi Fam* **l. con algn** *(entablar relaciones) Br* to get off with sb, *US* to make out with sb

3 ligarse *vpr Esp Fam* **ligarse a algn** *Br* to get off with sb, *US* to make out with sb

ligeramente *adv* (**a**) *(levemente)* lightly (**b**) *(un poco)* slightly

ligero, -a 1 *adj* (**a**) *(peso)* light, lightweight; **l. de ropa** lightly clad (**b**) *(ágil)* light on one's feet; *(veloz)* swift, quick (**c**) *(leve)* slight; **brisa/comida ligera** light breeze/meal (**d**) **a la ligera** lightly **2** *adv* *(rápido)* fast, swiftly

light [lait] *adj inv (tabaco)* mild; *Fig (persona)* lightweight

ligue *nm Esp Fam (novio) Br* bloke, *US* squeeze; *(novia) Br* bird, *US* squeeze

liguero, -a 1 *adj Dep* league; **partido l.** league match **2** *nm Br* suspender belt, *US* garter belt

lija *nf* sandpaper; **papel de l.** sandpaper

lijar *vt* to sand o sandpaper (down)

lila¹ 1 *nm (color)* lilac

2 *nf (flor)* lilac

3 *adj inv* lilac

lila² *Fam* **1** *adj (tonto)* dumb, stupid **2** *nmf (tonto)* twit

lima¹ *nf (fruto)* lime

lima² *nf (herramienta)* file; **l. de uñas** nail-file

límite *nm* limit; *Geog, Pol* boundary, border; **caso l.** borderline case; **fecha**

l. deadline; **velocidad l.** maximum speed

limón *nm* lemon

limonada *nf* lemonade, = iced, sweetened lemon juice drink

limonero *nm* lemon tree

limosna *nf* alms; **pedir l.** to beg

limpiabotas *nm inv* shoeshine, *Br* bootblack

limpiacristales *nm inv* window cleaner

limpiador, -a 1 *adj* cleansing **2** *nm,f (persona)* cleaner **3** *nm (producto)* cleaner

limpiaparabrisas *nm inv Br* windscreen *o US* windshield wiper

limpiar [43] *vt* (**a**) to clean; *(con un trapo)* to wipe; *(zapatos)* to polish; *Fig* to cleanse (**b**) *Fam (hurtar)* to pinch, to nick

limpieza *nf (calidad)* cleanliness; *(acción)* cleaning; *Fig (integridad)* integrity; **con l.** cleanly

limpio, -a 1 *adj* (**a**) *(aseado)* clean (**b**) *Dep* **juego l.** fair play (**c**) *Fin (neto)* net; **beneficios en l.** net profit (**d**) **pasar algo** *Esp* **a** *o Am* **en l.** to produce a fair copy of sth **2** *adv* fairly; **jugar l.** to play fair

linaje *nm* lineage

lince *nm* lynx; **tiene ojos de l.** he's eagle-eyed

lindo, -a 1 *adj esp Am (bonito)* pretty, lovely; **de lo l.** a great deal **2** *adv Am (bien)* very well, beautifully; **dibuja muy l.** he draws very well *o* beautifully

línea *nf* (**a**) line; **l. aérea** airline; **en líneas generales** roughly speaking; *Informát* **fuera de l.** off-line; *Informát* **en l.** on-line (**b**) **guardar la l.** to watch one's figure

lingote *nm* ingot; *(de oro, plata)* bar

lingüística *nf* linguistics *(sing)*

lingüístico, -a *adj* linguistic

lino *nm* (**a**) *Bot* flax (**b**) *Tex* linen

linterna *nf Br* torch, *US* flashlight

linyera *nmf RP (vagabundo)* tramp, *US* bum

lío *nm* (**a**) *(paquete)* bundle (**b**) *Fam*

(embrollo) mess, muddle; **hacerse un l.** to get mixed up; **meterse en líos** to get into trouble; **armar un l.** to kick up a fuss (**c**) *Fam (relación amorosa)* affair

liquidación *nf* (**a**) *Com (saldo)* clearance sale (**b**) *Fin* liquidation

liquidar 1 *vt Com (deuda, cuenta)* to settle; *(mercancías)* to sell off **2 liquidarse** *vpr Fam* (**a**) *(gastar)* to spend (**b**) **liquidarse a algn** *(matar)* to bump sb off

líquido, -a 1 *adj* (**a**) liquid (**b**) *Fin* net **2** *nm* (**a**) *(fluido)* liquid (**b**) *Fin* liquid assets; **l. imponible** taxable income

lira *nf Antes (moneda)* lira

lirio *nm* iris

liso, -a 1 *adj* (**a**) *(superficie)* smooth, even; *Esp* **los cien metros lisos** the one hundred metres sprint (**b**) *(pelo, falda)* straight (**c**) *(tela)* self-coloured **2** *nm,f Andes, CAm, Ven* cheeky; **es un l.** he's so cheeky

lista *nf* (**a**) *(relación)* list; **l. de espera** waiting list; *(en avión)* standby; **pasar l.** to call the register *o* the roll; *Informát* **l. de correo** mailing list (**b**) *(franja)* stripe; **a listas** striped

listar *vt* (**a**) *Informát* to list (**b**) *Am (hacer una lista de)* to list

listín *nm Esp* **l. telefónico** telephone directory

listo, -a *adj* (**a**) **ser l.** *(inteligente)* to be clever *o* smart (**b**) **estar l.** *(a punto)* to be ready

listón *nm Dep* bar; *Fig* **subir el l.** to raise the requirements level

lisura *nf* (**a**) *Andes, CAm, Ven (atrevimiento)* cheek (**b**) *Andes, CAm, Ven (dicho grosero)* rude remark (**c**) *Perú (donaire)* grace

litera *nf (cama)* bunk bed; *(en tren)* couchette

literal *adj* literal

literario, -a *adj* literary

literatura *nf* literature

litro *nm* litre

llaga *nf* sore; *(herida)* wound

llama *nf* flame; **en llamas** in flames, ablaze

llamada *nf* call; *Tel* **l. interurbana** long-distance call; **señal de l.** ringing tone

llamado, -a 1 *adj* so-called **2** *nm Am* (**a**) *(en general)* call; *(a la puerta)* knock; *(con timbre)* ring (**b**) *(telefónico)* call; **hacer un l.** to make a phone call (**c**) *(apelación)* appeal, call

llamar 1 *vt* (**a**) to call; **l. (por teléfono)** to ring up, to call (**b**) *(atraer)* to draw, to attract; **l. la atención** to attract attention **2** *vi (a la puerta)* to knock **3 llamarse** *vpr* to be called; **¿cómo te llamas?** what's your name?

llano, -a 1 *adj* (**a**) *(superficie)* flat, level (**b**) *(claro)* clear (**c**) *(sencillo)* simple; **el pueblo l.** the common people **2** *nm* plain

llanta *nf* (**a**) *(aro metálico)* rim (**b**) *Am (neumático)* tyre

llanura *nf* plain

llave *nf* (**a**) *(de cerradura)* key; **bajo l.** under lock and key; **echar la l., cerrar con l.** to lock up (**b**) *(grifo) Br* tap, *US* faucet; **l. de paso** stopcock; **cerrar la l. de paso** to turn the water/gas off at the mains (**c**) *(interruptor)* **l. de la luz** light switch (**d**) *(herramienta)* spanner; **l. allen** Allen key; **l. inglesa** monkey wrench, *Br* adjustable spanner (**e**) *(de judo)* hold, lock (**f**) *(signo ortográfico)* curly bracket

llegada *nf* arrival; *Dep* finish

llegar [42] **1** *vi* (**a**) to arrive; **l. a Madrid** to arrive in Madrid (**b**) *(ser bastante)* to be enough (**c**) *(alcanzar)* **l. a** to reach; **¿llegas al techo?** can you reach the ceiling? (**d**) *Fig* **l. a las manos** to come to blows; **l. a presidente** to become president (**e**) **l. a + *inf*** to go so far as to (**f**) **l. a ser** to become **2 llegarse** *vpr* to stop by

llenar 1 *vt* (**a**) to fill; *(cubrir)* to cover (**b**) *(satisfacer)* to satisfy **2** *vi (comida)* to be filling **3 llenarse** *vpr* to fill (up), to become full

lleno, -a 1 *adj* full (up); *Fig* **de l.** fully **2** *nm Teatro* full house

llevar 1 *vt* (**a**) to take; *(hacia el oyente)* to bring; **¿adónde llevas eso?** where are you taking that?; **te llevaré un regalo** I'll bring you a present (**b**) *(transportar)* to carry; **dejarse l.** to get carried away (**c**) *(prenda)* to wear; **llevaba falda** she was wearing a skirt (**d**) *(soportar)* to bear; **¿cómo lleva lo de su enfermedad?** how's he coping with his illness? (**e**) *(tiempo)* **llevo dos años aquí** I've been here for two years; **esto lleva mucho tiempo** this takes a long time (**f**) *(negocio)* to be in charge of **2** *v aux* (**a**) **l. + *gerundio*** to have been + *present participle*; **llevo dos años estudiando español** I've been studying Spanish for two years (**b**) **l. + *participio pasado*** to have + *past participle*; **llevaba escritas seis cartas** I had written six letters **3 llevarse** *vpr* (**a**) to take away; *(premio)* to win; *(recibir)* to get (**b**) *(arrastrar)* to carry away (**c**) *(estar de moda)* to be fashionable (**d**) **llevarse bien con algn** to get on well with sb

llorar *vi* to cry; *Lit* to weep

llorón, -ona *adj* **un bebé l.** a baby which cries a lot

llover [4] *v impers* to rain

llovizna *nf* drizzle

lloviznar *v impers* to drizzle

lluvia *nf* rain; **una l. de** lots of; **l. radiactiva** fallout; **l. ácida** acid rain

lluvioso, -a *adj* rainy

lo¹ *art neut* the; **lo mejor** the best (part); **lo mismo** the same thing; **lo mío** mine; **lo tuyo** yours

lo² *pron pers m & neut (pl* **los***)* (**a**) *(cosa)* it; **debes hacerlo** you must do it; **no lo creo** I don't think so; *(no se traduce)* **no se lo dije** I didn't tell her; *ver* **le** (**b**) **lo que ...** what ...; **no sé lo que pasa** I don't know what's going on (**c**) **lo cual ...** which ... (**d**) **lo de ...** the business of ...; **cuéntame lo del juicio** tell me about the trial

lobo *nm* wolf; **como boca de l.** pitch-dark; *Fam* **¡menos lobos!** pull the other one!

local 1 *adj* local **2** *nm (recinto)* premises, site

localidad *nf* (**a**) *(pueblo)* locality; *(en impreso)* place of residence (**b**) *Cin, Teatro (asiento)* seat; *(entrada)* ticket

localización *nf* localization

localizar [40] *vt* (**a**) *(encontrar)* to find (**b**) *(fuego, dolor)* to localize

loción *nf* lotion

loco, -a 1 *adj* mad, crazy; **a lo l.** crazily; **l. por** crazy about; **volverse l.** to go mad; *Fam* **¡ni l.!** I'd sooner die! **2** *nm,f* madman, *f* madwoman; **hacerse el l.** to act the fool **3** *nm Chile (molusco)* false abalone

locomotora *nf* locomotive

locura *nf (enfermedad)* madness, insanity; **con l.** madly; *Fam* **esto es una l.** this is crazy

locutor, -a *nm,f TV, Rad* presenter

locutorio *nm* telephone booth

lodo *nm* mud

lógica *nf* logic; **no tiene l.** there's no logic to it

lógico, -a *adj* logical; **era l. que ocurriera** it was bound to happen

logrado, -a *adj (bien hecho)* accomplished

lograr *vt* (**a**) to get, to obtain; *(premio)* to win; *(ambición)* to achieve (**b**) **l. hacer algo** to manage to do sth

logro *nm* achievement

lombriz *nf* worm, earthworm

lomo *nm* (**a**) back; **a lomo(s)** on the back (**b**) *Culin* loin (**c**) *(de libro)* spine

lona *nf* canvas

loncha *nf* slice; **l. de bacon** rasher of bacon

lonche *nm* (**a**) *Perú, Ven (merienda) (en escuela)* = snack eaten during break time; *(en casa)* (afternoon) tea (**b**) *Am (comida fría)* (packed) lunch (**c**) *Méx (torta)* filled roll

lonchería *nf Méx, Ven* = small fast food restaurant selling snacks, sandwiches etc

Londres *n* London

longaniza *nf* spicy (pork) sausage

longitud *nf* (**a**) length; **2 m de l.** 2 m

long; **l. de onda** wavelength; *Dep* **salto de l.** long jump (**b**) *Geog* longitude

lonja¹ *nf (loncha)* slice; **l. de bacon** rasher of bacon

lonja² *nf Esp* **l. de pescado** fish market

loro *nm* parrot

los¹ 1 *art def mpl* the; **l. libros** the books; **cierra l. ojos** close your eyes; **l. García** the Garcías; *ver* **el, las, lo¹** **2** *pron* **l. que** *(personas)* the ones who, those who; *(cosas)* the ones (that); **toma l. que quieras** take whichever ones you want; **esos son l. míos/ tuyos** these are mine/yours; *ver* **les**

los² *pron pers mpl* them; **¿l. has visto?** have you seen them?

lote *nm* (**a**) set (**b**) *Com* lot (**c**) *Informát* batch (**d**) *Esp Fam* **darse el l. (con)** to neck (with), *Br* to snog (**e**) *Am (solar)* plot (of land)

loteamiento *nm Bol, Urug* parcelling out, division into plots

loteo *nm Andes, Méx, RP* parcelling out, division into plots

lotería *nf* lottery; **me tocó la l.** I won a prize in the lottery

lotización *nf Ecuad, Perú* parcelling out, division into plots

loza *nf* (**a**) *(material)* earthenware (**b**) *(de cocina)* crockery

lubina *nf* sea bass

lubricante *nm* lubricant

lucha *nf* (**a**) fight, struggle; **l. de clases** class struggle (**b**) *Dep* wrestling; **l. libre** freestyle wrestling

luchador, -a *nm,f* (**a**) fighter (**b**) *Dep* wrestler

luchar *vi* (**a**) to fight, to struggle (**b**) *Dep* to wrestle

luciérnaga *nf* glow-worm

lucir [35] **1** *vi* (**a**) *(brillar)* to shine (**b**) *Am (parecer)* to look; **luces cansada** you seem o look tired (**c**) *Fam (compensar)* **no le luce lo que estudia** his studies don't get him anywhere **2** *vt (ropas)* to sport; *(talento)* to display **3 lucirse** *vpr* (**a**) *(hacer buen papel)* to do very well (**b**) *(pavonearse)* to show off

lucro *nm* profit, gain; **afán de l.** greed for money

lúdico, -a *adj* relating to games, recreational

luego 1 *adv* (**a**) *(después)* then, next, afterwards (**b**) *(más tarde)* later (on); **¡hasta l.!** so long!; **l. de** after (**c**) **desde l.** of course (**d**) *Chile, Ven (pronto)* soon; **acaba l., te estoy esperando** hurry up and finish, I'm waiting for you; *Méx Fam* **l. l., l. lueguito** immediately, straight away **2** *conj* therefore

lugar *nm* (**a**) place; **en primer l.** in the first place; **en l. de** instead of; **sin l. a dudas** without a doubt; **tener l.** to take place (**b**) **dar l. a** to cause, to give rise to

lujo *nm* luxury; **productos de l.** luxury products; **no puedo permitirme ese l.** I can't afford that

lujoso, -a *adj* luxurious

lujuria *nf* lust

lumbago *nm* lumbago

luminoso, -a *adj* luminous; *Fig* bright

luna *nf* (**a**) moon; *Fig* **estar en la l.** to have one's head in the clouds; **l. creciente/llena** crescent/full moon; *Fig* **l. de miel** honeymoon (**b**) *(de escaparate)* pane; *(espejo)* mirror

lunar 1 *adj* lunar **2** *nm (redondel)* dot; *(en la piel)* mole, beauty spot; **vestido de lunares** spotted dress

lunes *nm inv* Monday; **vendré el l.** I'll come on Monday

lupa *nf* magnifying glass

lustrabotas *nm inv,* **lustrador, -a** *nm,f Andes, RP* shoeshine, *Br* bootblack

luto *nm* mourning

luz *nf* (**a**) light; **apagar la l.** to put out the light; **a la l. de** in the light of; **a todas luces** obviously; *Fig* **dar a l.** to give birth to (**b**) *Aut* light; **luces de cruce** *Br* dipped headlights, *US* low beams; **luces de posición** sidelights (**c**) **luces** *(inteligencia)* intelligence; **corto de luces** dim-witted (**d**) **traje de luces** bullfighter's costume

lycra® *nf* Lycra®

Mm

m (**a**) (*abr* **metro(s)**) m (**b**) (*abr* **minuto(s)**) min

macana *nf* (**a**) *Andes, Carib, Méx (garrote)* wooden *Br* truncheon *o US* billy club (**b**) *CSur, Perú, Ven Fam (fastidio)* pain, drag (**c**) *CAm, Cuba (azada)* hoe

macanear *vt CSur, Ven (hacer mal)* to botch, to do badly

macanudo, -a *adj Fam* great, terrific

macarrones *nmpl* macaroni

macedonia *nf* fruit salad

maceta *nf (tiesto)* plant-pot, flower-pot

machacar [44] **1** *vt* (**a**) to crush; *Dep* to smash (**b**) *Esp Fam (estudiar) Br* to swot up on, *US* to bone up on (**c**) *Fam (insistir en)* to harp on about, to go on about **2** *vi* (**a**) *Fam (insistir mucho)* to harp on, to go on (**b**) *Fam (estudiar con ahínco) Br* to swot, *US* to grind (**c**) *(en baloncesto)* to smash

machete *nm* (**a**) *(arma)* machete (**b**) *Ven (amigo) Br* mate, *US* buddy (**c**) *Arg Fam (chuleta)* crib note

machismo *nm* machismo, male chauvinism

machista *adj & nm* male chauvinist

macho 1 *adj* (**a**) *(animal, planta)* male (**b**) *Fam (viril)* manly, virile, macho **2** *nm* (**a**) *(animal, planta)* male (**b**) *Téc (pieza)* male piece *o* part; *(de enchufe)* (male) plug (**c**) *Fam (hombre viril)* macho man, he-man

machote *nm CAm, Méx (borrador)* rough draft

macizo, -a 1 *adj* (**a**) *(sólido)* solid; **de oro m.** of solid gold (**b**) *(robusto)* solid, robust; *Fam (atractivo)* well-built **2** *nm (masa sólida)* mass

macramé *nm* macramé

macuto *nm (morral)* knapsack, haversack

madeja *nf (de lana etc)* hank, skein

madera *nf* (**a**) wood; *(de construcción)* timber, *US* lumber; **de m.** wood, wooden (**b**) *Fig* **tiene m. de líder** he has all the makings of a leader

madrastra *nf* stepmother

madre 1 *nf* (**a**) mother; **es m. de tres hijos** she is a mother of three (children); **m. de familia** mother, housewife; **m. política** mother-in-law; **m. soltera** unmarried mother; *Fig* **la m. patria** one's motherland (**b**) *(de río)* bed **2** *interj* **¡m. de Dios!, ¡m. mía!** good heavens!

madreselva *nf* honeysuckle

Madrid *n* Madrid

madriguera *nf* burrow, hole

madrileño, -a 1 *adj* of/from Madrid **2** *nm,f* person from Madrid

madrina *nf* (**a**) *(de bautizo)* godmother (**b**) *(de boda)* ≃ bridesmaid (**c**) *Fig (protectora)* protectress

madrugada *nf* (**a**) dawn; **de m.** in the wee small hours (**b**) early morning; **las tres de la m.** three o'clock in the morning

madrugador, -a 1 *adj* early-rising **2** *nm,f* early riser

madrugar [42] *vi* to get up early

madurar 1 *vt Fig (un plan)* to think out **2** *vi* (**a**) *(persona)* to mature (**b**) *(fruta)* to ripen

madurez *nf* (**a**) maturity (**b**) *(de la fruta)* ripeness

maduro, -a *adj* (**a**) mature; **de edad madura** middle-aged (**b**) *(fruta)* ripe

maestría *nf* mastery; **con m.** masterfully

maestro, -a 1 *nm,f* (**a**) *Educ* teacher;

m. de escuela schoolteacher (**b**) *Méx (en universidad) Br* lecturer, *US* professor (**c**) *(especialista)* master; **m. de obras** foreman (**d**) *Mús* maestro **2** *adj* **obra maestra** masterpiece; **llave maestra** master key

mafia *nf* mafia

magdalena *nf* bun, cake

magia *nf* magic; **por arte de m.** as if by magic

mágico, -a *adj* (**a**) magic (**b**) *Fig (maravilloso)* magical, wonderful

magistrado, -a *nm,f (juez)* judge

magistratura *nf (jueces)* magistrature; *(tribunal)* tribunal

magnate *nm* magnate, tycoon

magnesio *nm* magnesium

magnético, -a *adj* magnetic

magnetófono *nm* tape recorder

magnífico, -a *adj* magnificent, splendid

magnitud *nf* magnitude, dimension; **de primera m.** of the first order

magnolia *nf* magnolia

mago, -a *nm,f* wizard, magician; **los tres Reyes Magos** the Three Wise Men, the Three Kings

magro, -a 1 *nm (de cerdo)* lean meat **2** *adj (sin grasa)* lean

maillot [ma'jot] *nm (pl* **maillots**) *(malla)* leotard; *Dep* shirt

maíz *nm Br* maize, *US* (Indian) corn

majestuoso, -a *adj* majestic, stately

majo, -a *adj Esp (bonito)* pretty, nice; *Fam (simpático)* nice; **tiene un hijo muy m.** she's got a lovely little boy; *Fam* **ven aquí, m.** come here, dear

mal 1 *nm* (**a**) evil, wrong (**b**) *(daño)* harm; **no le deseo ningún m.** I don't wish him any harm (**c**) *(enfermedad)* illness, disease; *Fam* **el m. de las vacas locas** mad cow disease

2 *adj* bad; **un m. año** a bad year; *ver* **malo**

3 *adv* badly, wrong; **lo hizo muy m.** he did it very badly; **menos m. que ...** it's a good job (that) ...; **no está (nada) m.** it is not bad (at all); **te oigo/veo (muy) m.** I can hardly hear/see you;

tomar a m. *(enfadarse)* to take badly

malcriar [29] *vt* to spoil

maldad *nf* (**a**) badness, evil (**b**) *(acción perversa)* evil *o* wicked thing

maldición 1 *nf* curse **2** *interj* damnation!

maldito, -a *adj* (**a**) *Fam (molesto)* damned, *Br* bloody (**b**) *(endemoniado)* damned, cursed; **¡maldita sea!** damn it!

maleable *adj también Fig* malleable

malecón *nm (muelle)* jetty

maleducado, -a 1 *adj* bad-mannered **2** *nm,f* bad-mannered person

malentendido *nm* misunderstanding

malestar *nm* (**a**) *(molestia)* discomfort (**b**) *Fig (inquietud)* uneasiness; **tengo m.** I feel uneasy

maleta 1 *nf* suitcase, case; **hacer la m.** to pack one's things *o* case **2** *nm Fam (persona)* bungler

maletero *nm Esp, Cuba,* **maletera** *nf Am (de automóvil) Br* boot, *US* trunk

maletín *nm* briefcase

malformación *nf* malformation

malgastar *vt & vi* to waste, to squander

malhablado, -a 1 *adj* foul-mouthed **2** *nm,f* foul-mouthed person

malhechor, -a *nm,f* wrongdoer, criminal

malhumorado, -a *adj (de mal carácter)* bad-tempered; *(enfadado)* in a bad mood

malicia *nf* (**a**) *(mala intención)* malice, maliciousness (**b**) *(astucia)* cunning, slyness (**c**) *(maldad)* badness, evil

malintencionado, -a 1 *adj* ill-intentioned **2** *nm,f* ill-intentioned person

malla *nf* (**a**) *(prenda)* leotard (**b**) *(red)* mesh (**c**) *Ecuad, Perú, RP (traje de baño)* swimsuit

Mallorca *n* Majorca

malo, -a 1 *adj* (**a**) bad; **un año m.** a bad year; **estar a malas** to be on bad terms; **por las malas** by force (**b**) *(persona) (malvado)* wicked, bad;

(travieso) naughty (**c**) *(de poca calidad)* bad, poor; **una mala canción/comida** a poor song/meal (**d**) *(perjudicial)* harmful; **el tabaco es m.** tobacco is harmful (**e**) **lo m. es que …** the problem is that … (**f**) *(enfermo)* ill, sick

> **mal** is used instead of **malo** before masculine singular nouns (e.g. **un mal ejemplo** a bad example). The comparative form of **malo** (= worse) is **peor**, the superlative forms (= the worst) are **el peor** (masculine) and **la peor** (feminine)

2 *nm,f Fam* **el m.** the baddy *o* villain

malograr 1 *vt Andes (estropear)* to make a mess of, to ruin **2 malograrse** *vpr* (**a**) *(fracasar)* to fail, fall through (**b**) *Andes (estropearse) (máquina)* to break down; *(alimento)* to go off, to spoil; **se malogró el día** the day turned nasty

malpensado, -a 1 *adj* nasty-minded **2** *nm,f* nasty-minded person

maltratar *vt* to ill-treat, to mistreat

malviviente *nmf CSur* criminal

mamá *nf Fam Br* mum, *US* mom; *Col, Méx Fam* **m. grande** grandma

mamadera *nf RP (biberón)* feeding bottle

mamar *vt (leche)* to suck; **lo mamó desde pequeño** *(lo aprendió)* he was immersed in it as a child

mameluco *nm* (**a**) *Fam (torpe, necio)* idiot (**b**) *Méx (con mangas) Br* overalls, *US* coveralls; *CSur (de peto) Br* dungarees, *US* overalls

mamey *nm* (**a**) *(árbol)* mamey, mammee (**b**) *(fruto)* mamey, mammee (apple)

mamífero, -a *nm,f* mammal

mampara *nf* screen

mamut *nm (pl* **mamuts**) mammoth

manada *nf* (**a**) *Zool (de vacas, elefantes)* herd; *(de ovejas)* flock; *(de lobos, perros)* pack; *(de leones)* pride (**b**) *Fam (multitud)* crowd, mob; **en manada(s)** in crowds

manager *nmf (pl* **managers**) *Dep, Mús* manager

manantial *nm* spring

mancha *nf* stain, spot; **m. solar** sunspot; **m. de tinta/vino** ink/wine stain

manchar 1 *vt* to stain, to dirty; *Fig* to stain, to blemish **2 mancharse** *vpr* to get dirty

manco, -a 1 *adj* (**a**) *(de un brazo)* one-armed; *(sin brazos)* armless (**b**) *(de una mano)* one-handed; *(sin manos)* handless **2** *nm,f* (**a**) *(de brazos)* one-armed/armless person (**b**) *(de manos)* one-handed/handless person

mancorna *nf CAm, Chile, Col, Méx, Ven* cufflink

mancuerna *nf* (**a**) *(pesa)* dumbbell (**b**) *CAm, Chile, Col, Méx, Ven (gemelo)* cufflink

mandar *vt* (**a**) to order; *Fam* **¿mande?** pardon? (**b**) *(grupo)* to lead, to be in charge *o* command of; *Mil* to command (**c**) *(enviar)* to send; **m. (a) por** to send for; **m. algo por correo** to post sth, to send sth by post; **m. recuerdos** to send regards

mandarina *nf* mandarin (orange), tangerine

mandíbula *nf* jaw; *Fam* **reír a m. batiente** to laugh one's head off

Mandinga *nm Am* the devil

mando *nm* (**a**) *(autoridad)* command, control (**b**) **los altos mandos del ejército** high-ranking army officers (**c**) *Téc (control)* controls; *Aut* **cuadro** *o* **tablero de mandos** dashboard; **m. a distancia** remote control; **palanca de m.** *Téc* control lever; *(de avión, videojuego)* joystick

mandón, -ona 1 *adj Fam* bossy, domineering

2 *nm,f Fam* bossy *o* domineering person

3 *nm Chile (de mina)* foreman

manecilla *nf (de reloj)* hand

manejable *adj* manageable; *(herramienta)* easy-to-use; *(coche)* manoeuvrable

manejar 1 *vt* (**a**) *(máquina)* to handle, operate; *Fig (situación)* to handle (**b**) *(negocio)* to run, manage (**c**) *Fig (a otra* *persona)* to domineer, boss about (**d**) *Am (conducir)* to drive

2 *vi Am (conducir)* to drive

3 manejarse *vpr* to manage

manejo *nm* (**a**) *(uso)* handling, use; **de fácil m.** easy-to-use (**b**) *Am (de vehículo)* driving

manera *nf* (**a**) way, manner; **a mi/tu m.** (in) my/your way; **de cualquier m.** *(mal)* carelessly, any old how; *(en cualquier caso)* in any case; **de esta m.** in this way; **de ninguna m.** in no way, certainly not; **de todas maneras** anyway, at any rate, in any case; **es mi m. de ser** that's the way I am; **no hay m.** it's impossible (**b**) **de m. que** so; **de tal m. que** in such a way that (**c**) **maneras** manners; **de buenas maneras** politely

manga *nf* (**a**) sleeve; **de m. corta/ larga** short-/long-sleeved; **sin mangas** sleeveless; *Fig* **m. por hombro** messy and untidy; *Fig* **sacarse algo de la m.** to pull sth out of one's hat (**b**) *(de riego)* hose (**c**) *(del mar)* arm (**d**) *Dep* leg, round; *Ten* set

mango *nm* (**a**) *(asa)* handle (**b**) *RP Fam (dinero)* **no tengo un m.** I haven't got a bean, I'm broke

manguera *nf* hose

maní *nm* (*pl* **maníes**) peanut

manía *nf* (**a**) dislike, ill will; **me tiene m.** he has it in for me (**b**) *(costumbre)* habit; **tiene la m. de llegar tarde** he's always arriving late (**c**) *(afición exagerada)* craze; **la m. de las motos** the motorbike craze (**d**) *Med* mania

maniático, -a **1** *adj* fussy **2** *nm,f* fusspot

manicomio *nm* *Br* mental *o* psychiatric hospital, *US* insane asylum

manicura *nf* manicure

manifestación *nf* (**a**) demonstration (**b**) *(expresión)* manifestation, expression

manifestante *nmf* demonstrator

manifestar [1] *vt* (**a**) *(declarar)* to state, to declare (**b**) *(mostrar)* to show, to display **2 manifestarse** *vpr* (**a**) *(por la calle)* to demonstrate (**b**) *(declararse)*

to declare oneself; **se manifestó contrario a …** he spoke out against …

manifiesto, -a **1** *adj* clear, obvious; **poner de m.** *(revelar)* to reveal, to show; *(hacer patente)* to make clear **2** *nm* manifesto

manigua *nf*, **manigual** *nm* *Carib, Col (selva)* marshy tropical forest

manilla *nf* (**a**) *(de reloj)* hand (**b**) *esp Am (manivela)* crank

manillar *nm* handlebar

maniobra *nf* manoeuvre

manipular *vt* to manipulate; *(máquina)* to handle

maniquí *nm* (*pl* **maniquíes**) *(muñeco)* dummy

manito *nm* *Méx Fam* pal, *Br* mate, *US* buddy

manivela *nf* *Téc* crank

mano 1 *nf* (**a**) hand; **a m.** *(sin máquina)* by hand; *(asequible)* at hand; **escrito a m.** hand-written; **hecho a m.** handmade; **de segunda m.** second-hand; **echar una m. a algn** to give sb a hand; **meter m.** *(a un problema)* to tackle; *Vulg* to touch up; **traerse algo entre manos** to be up to sth; **equipaje de m.** hand luggage

(**b**) *(lado)* side; **a m. derecha/ izquierda** on the right/left(-hand side)

(**c**) **m. de pintura** coat of paint

(**d**) **m. de obra** labour (force)

(**e**) *RP (dirección)* direction *(of traffic)*; **calle de una/doble m.** one-/two-way street

2 *nm* *Am salvo RP Fam* pal, *Br* mate, *US* buddy

manopla *nf* mitten

manosear *vt* to touch repeatedly, to finger; *Fam* to paw

mansión *nf* mansion

manso, -a *adj* (**a**) *(persona)* gentle, meek (**b**) *(animal)* tame, docile (**c**) *Chile Fam (extraordinario)* tremendous; **tiene la mansa casa** he has a gigantic *o* massive house

manta 1 *nf* (**a**) blanket; **m. eléctrica** electric blanket (**b**) *(zurra)* beating, hiding (**c**) *Méx (algodón)* = coarse cotton cloth (**d**) *Ven (vestido)* =

traditional Indian woman's dress **2** *nmf Esp Fam* layabout

manteca *nf* (**a**) *Esp (de animal)* fat; **m. de cacao/cacahuete** cocoa/peanut butter; **m. de cerdo** lard (**b**) *RP, Ven (mantequilla)* butter

mantecado *nm Esp* = very crumbly shortbread biscuit

mantel *nm* tablecloth

mantelería *nf* set of table linen

mantener [24] **1** *vt* (**a**) *(conservar)* to keep; **mantén el fuego encendido** keep the fire burning; **m. la línea** to keep in trim (**b**) *(entrevista, reunión)* to have; **m. correspondencia con algn** to correspond with sb (**c**) *(ideas, opiniones)* to defend, to maintain (**d**) *(familia)* to support, to feed
2 mantenerse *vpr* (**a**) *(sostenerse)* to stand (**b**) **mantenerse firme** *(perseverar)* to hold one's ground (**c**) *(sustentarse)* to live (**de** on)

mantenimiento *nm* (**a**) *Téc* maintenance, upkeep; **servicio de m.** maintenance service (**b**) *(alimento)* sustenance, support (**c**) **gimnasia y m.** keep-fit

mantequilla *nf* butter

mantilla *nf* (**a**) *(de mujer)* mantilla (**b**) *(de bebé)* shawl

mantón *nm* shawl

manual 1 *adj* manual; **trabajo m.** manual labour; *Educ* **trabajos manuales** handicrafts **2** *nm* manual, hand-book

manubrio *nm Am (manillar)* handlebars

manuscrito *nm* manuscript

manzana *nf* (**a**) apple (**b**) *(de edificios)* block

manzanilla *nf* (**a**) *Bot* camomile (**b**) *(infusión)* camomile tea (**c**) *(vino)* manzanilla (sherry)

manzano *nm* apple tree

mañana 1 *nf* morning; **a las dos de la m.** at two in the morning; **de m.** early in the morning; **por la m.** in the morning
2 *nm* tomorrow, the future
3 *adv* tomorrow; **¡hasta m.!** see you

tomorrow! **m. por la m.** tomorrow morning; **pasado m.** the day after tomorrow

mañanitas *nfpl Méx* birthday song

mañoco *nm Ven* tapioca

mapa *nm* map; **m. mudo** blank map; *Fam* **borrar del m.** to wipe out

maqueta *nf* (**a**) *(miniatura)* scale model, maquette (**b**) *Mús* demo (tape)

maquila *nf CAm, Méx (de artículos electrónicos)* assembly; *(de ropa)* making-up

maquiladora *nf CAm, Méx* = bonded assembly plant set up by a foreign firm near the US border, *US* maquiladora

maquillaje *nm* make-up

maquillar 1 *vt* to make up **2 maquillarse** *vpr* (**a**) *(ponerse maquillaje)* to put one's make-up on, to make (oneself) up (**b**) *(usar maquillaje)* to wear make-up

máquina *nf* (**a**) machine; **escrito a m.** typewritten; **hecho a m.** machine-made; *Fam* **a toda m.** at full speed **m. de afeitar (eléctrica)** (electric) razor *o* shaver; **m. de coser** sewing machine; **m. de escribir** typewriter; **m. fotográfica** *o* **de fotos** camera; **m.** *Esp* **tragaperras** *o Am* **tragamonedas** slot machine, *Br* fruit machine (**b**) *Cuba (automóvil)* car

maquinaria *nf* (**a**) machinery, machines (**b**) *(de reloj etc)* *(mecanismo)* mechanism, works

maquinilla *nf* **m. de afeitar** safety razor

maquinista *nmf (de tren) Br* engine driver, *US* engineer

mar 1 *nm o nf* (**a**) sea; **en alta m.** on the high seas; **m. adentro** out to sea; **por m.** by sea; **m. gruesa** heavy sea; **m. picada** rough sea (**b**) *Fam* **está la m. de guapa** she's looking really beautiful; **llover a mares** to rain cats and dogs

---

Note that the feminine is used in literary language, by people such as fishermen with a close connection with the sea, and in some idiomatic expressions

2 *nm* sea; **M. del Norte** North Sea; **M. Muerto/Negro** Dead/Black Sea

maraca *nf* maraca

maratón *nm* marathon

maravilla *nf* marvel, wonder; **de m.** wonderfully; **¡qué m. de película!** what a wonderful film!; *Fam* **a las mil maravillas** marvellously

maravilloso, -a *adj* wonderful, marvellous

marca *nf* (a) mark, sign (b) *Com* brand, make; **ropa de m.** brand-name clothes; **m. de fábrica** trademark; **m. registrada** registered trademark (c) *Dep (récord)* record; **batir la m. mundial** to break the world record

marcador *nm* (a) marker (b) *Dep (tablero)* scoreboard (c) *Am (rotulador)* felt-tip pen; *Méx (fluorescente)* highlighter pen

marcapasos *nm inv Med* pacemaker

marcar [44] **1** *vt* (a) to mark (b) *Tel* to dial (c) *(indicar)* to indicate, to show; **el contador marca 1.327** the meter reads 1,327 (d) *Dep (gol, puntos)* to score; *(a jugador)* to mark (e) *(cabello)* to set **2 marcarse** *vpr Esp Fam* **marcarse un detalle** to do something nice o kind

marcha *nf* (a) march; **hacer algo sobre la m.** to do sth as one goes along (b) **estar en m.** *(vehículo)* to be in motion; *(máquina)* to be working; *(proyecto etc)* to be under way; **poner en m.** to start (c) *Aut (gear)* **m. atrás** reverse (gear) (d) *Mús* march (e) *Esp Fam (animación)* liveliness, life; **hay mucha m.** there's a great atmosphere

marchante, -a *nm,f* (a) *(de arte)* dealer (b) *CAm, Méx, Ven Fam (cliente)* customer, patron

marchar 1 *vi* (a) *(ir)* to go, to walk; *Fam* **¡marchando!** on your way!; **¡una cerveza! – ¡marchando!** a beer, please! – coming right up! (b) *(aparato)* to be on; **m. bien** *(negocio)* to be going well (c) *Mil* to march **2 marcharse** *vpr (irse)* to leave, to go away

marchitar *vt*, **marchitarse** *vpr* to shrivel, to wither

marchoso, -a *Esp Fam* **1** *adj (persona)* fun-loving, wild **2** *nm,f* raver, fun-lover

marciano, -a *adj & nm,f* Martian

marco *nm* (a) *(de cuadro etc)* frame (b) *Fig (ámbito)* framework; **acuerdo m.** framework agreement (c) *Fin (moneda)* mark

marea *nf* (a) tide; **m. alta/baja** high/low tide; **m. negra** oil slick (b) *Fig (multitud)* crowd, mob

mareado, -a *adj* (a) sick; *(en un avión)* airsick; *(en un coche)* car-sick, travel-sick; *(en el mar)* seasick (b) *Euf (bebido)* tipsy (c) *(aturdido)* dizzy

marear 1 *vt* (a) to make sick; *(en el mar)* to make seasick; *(en un avión)* to make airsick; *(en un coche)* to make car-sick o travel-sick (b) *(aturdir)* to make dizzy (c) *Fam (fastidiar)* to annoy, to pester **2 marearse** *vpr* (a) to get sick/seasick/airsick/car-sick o travel-sick (b) *(quedar aturdido)* to get dizzy (c) *Euf (emborracharse)* to get tipsy

marejada *nf* heavy sea

maremoto *nm* tidal wave

mareo *nm* (a) *(náusea)* sickness; *(en el mar)* seasickness; *(en un avión)* airsickness; *(en un coche)* car-sickness, travel-sickness (b) *(aturdimiento)* dizziness, light-headedness

marfil *nm* ivory

margarina *nf* margarine

margarita *nf* daisy

margen 1 *nm* (a) border, edge; *Fig* **dejar algn/algo al m.** to leave sb/sth out; *Fig* **mantenerse al m.** not to get involved; **al m. de** leaving aside (b) *(del papel)* margin (c) *Com* **m. de beneficio** profit margin **2** *nf (de río)* bank

marginación *nf* exclusion

marginado, -a 1 *adj* excluded **2** *nm,f* dropout

mariachi *nm* (a) *(música)* mariachi (music) (b) *(orquesta)* mariachi band; *(músico)* mariachi (musician)

maricón *nm muy Fam Br* poof, *US* fag

marido *nm* husband

marihuana *nf* marijuana

marina *nf* (**a**) *Náut* seamanship (**b**) *Mil* navy; **m. de guerra** navy; **m. mercante** merchant navy (**c**) *Geog (zona costera)* seacoast

marinero, -a 1 *nm* sailor, seaman **2** *adj* seafaring

marino, -a 1 *adj* marine; **brisa marina** sea breeze **2** *nm* sailor

marioneta *nf* marionette, puppet

mariposa *nf* (**a**) *(insecto)* butterfly (**b**) *(en natación)* butterfly

mariquita 1 *nf (insecto) Br* ladybird, *US* ladybug **2** *nm Fam (marica)* fairy

mariscada *nf* seafood meal

marisco *nm* shellfish; **mariscos** seafood

marisma *nf* marsh

marítimo, -a *adj* maritime, sea; **ciudad marítima** coastal town; **paseo m.** promenade

marketing ['marketin] *nm* (*pl* **marketings**) marketing

mármol *nm* marble

marqués *nm* marquis

marquesina *nf* canopy; **m. (del autobús)** bus shelter

marrano, -a 1 *adj (sucio)* filthy, dirty **2** *nm,f* (**a**) *Fam (persona)* dirty pig, slob (**b**) *(animal)* pig

marrón 1 *adj (color)* brown **2** *nm (color)* brown

marroquí *adj & nmf* (*pl* **marroquíes**) Moroccan

Marruecos *n* Morocco

martes *nm inv* Tuesday; **m. y trece** ≃ Friday the thirteenth

martillero *nm CSur* auctioneer

martillo *nm* hammer

mártir *nmf* martyr

marzo *nm* March

más 1 *adv* (**a**) *(adicional)* more; **no tengo m.** I haven't got any more (**b**) *(comparativo)* more; **es m. alta/inteligente que yo** she's taller/more intelligent than me; **tengo m. dinero que tú** I've more money than you; **m. gente de la que esperas** more

people than you're expecting; **m. de** *(con numerales, cantidad)* more than, over

(**c**) *(superlativo)* most; **es el m. bonito/caro** it's the prettiest/most expensive

(**d**) *interj* so ..., what a ...; **¡qué casa m. bonita!** what a lovely house! **¡está m. guapa!** she looks so beautiful!

(**e**) *(después de pron interr e indef)* else; **¿algo m.?** anything else?; **no, nada m.** no, nothing else; **¿quién m.?** who else?; **nadie/alguien m.** nobody/somebody else

(**f**) **cada día** *o* **vez m.** more and more; **estar de m.** to be unnecessary; **traje uno de m.** I brought a spare one; **es m.** what's more, furthermore; **lo m. posible** as much as possible; **m. bien** rather; **m. o menos** more or less; **m. aún** even more

(**g**) **por m.** (*+ adj/adv*) + **que** (*+ subjuntivo)* however (much), no matter how (much); **por m. fuerte que sea** however strong he may be; **por m. que grites no te oirá nadie** no matter how much you shout nobody will hear you

2 *nm inv* **los m.** the majority, most people; **sus m. y sus menos** its pros and cons

3 *prep Mat* plus; **dos m. dos** two plus *o* and two

masa *nf* (**a**) mass (**b**) *(de cosas)* bulk, volume; **m. salarial** total wage bill (**c**) *(gente)* mass; **en m.** en masse; **medios de comunicación de masas** mass media (**d**) *Culin* dough (**e**) *RP (pastelito)* cake

masaje *nm* massage; **dar masaje(s) (a)** to massage

masajista *nmf* masseur, *f* masseuse

mascar [44] *vt & vi* to chew, to masticate

máscara *nf* mask; **m. de gas** gas mask; **traje de m.** fancy dress

mascarilla *nf* (**a**) mask; **m. de oxígeno** oxygen mask (**b**) *Med* face mask (**c**) *(cosmética)* face pack

mascota *nf* mascot

masculino, -a *adj* (**a**) *Zool, Bot* male

(**b**) *(de hombre)* male; manly; **una voz masculina** a manly voice (**c**) *(para hombre)* men's; **ropa masculina** men's clothes, menswear (**d**) *Ling* masculine

masía *nf* = traditional Catalan or Aragonese farmhouse

master *nm* (*pl* **masters**) Master's (degree)

masticar [44] *vt* to chew

mástil *nm* (**a**) *(asta)* mast, pole (**b**) *Náut* mast (**c**) *(de guitarra)* neck

matadero *nm* slaughterhouse, abattoir

matador *nm* matador, bullfighter

matambre *nm Andes, RP* (**a**) *(carne)* flank *o Br* skirt steak (**b**) *(plato)* = flank steak rolled with boiled egg, olives, red pepper and cooked, then sliced and served cold

matamoscas *nm inv (pala)* fly swat

matanza *nf* slaughter

matar *vt* (**a**) to kill; *Fam* **m. el hambre/el tiempo** to kill one's hunger/the time (**b**) *(cigarro, bebida)* to finish off (**c**) *(sello)* to frank

matarratas *nm inv (veneno)* rat poison

matasellos *nm inv* postmark

mate¹ *adj (sin brillo)* matt

mate² *nm (en ajedrez)* mate; **jaque m.** checkmate

mate³ *nm (infusión)* maté

matemática *nf,* **matemáticas** *nfpl* mathematics *sing*

matemático, -a 1 *adj* mathematical **2** *nm,f* mathematician

materia *nf* (**a**) matter; **m. prima** raw material (**b**) *(tema)* matter, question; **índice de materias** table of contents (**c**) *Educ (asignatura)* subject

material 1 *adj* material, physical; **daños materiales** damage to property **2** *nm* (**a**) material; **m. escolar/de construcción** teaching/building material *o* materials (**b**) *(equipo)* equipment; **m. de oficina** office equipment

maternidad *nf* maternity, motherhood

materno, -a *adj* maternal; **abuelo m.** maternal grandfather; **lengua materna** native *o* mother tongue

matinal *adj* morning; **televisión m.** breakfast television

matiz *nm* (**a**) *(de color)* shade (**b**) *(de palabra)* shade of meaning, nuance; **un m. irónico** a touch of irony

matizar [40] *vt* (**a**) *Fig (precisar)* to be more precise *o* explicit about (**b**) *Arte* to blend, to harmonize (**c**) *Fig (palabras, discurso)* to tinge; *(voz)* to vary, to modulate

matón, -ona *nm,f Fam* thug, bully

matorral *nm* brushwood, thicket

matrero, -a *nm,f Andes, RP (fugitivo)* outlaw

matrícula *nf* (**a**) registration; **derechos de m.** registration fee; **m. de honor** distinction; **plazo de m.** registration period (**b**) *Aut Br* number plate, *US* license plate

matricular *vt,* **matricularse** *vpr* to register

matrimonio *nm* (**a**) marriage; **m. civil/religioso** registry office/church wedding; **contraer m.** to marry; **cama de m.** double bed (**b**) *(pareja casada)* married couple; **el m. y los niños** the couple and their children; **el m. Romero** Mr and Mrs Romero, the Romeros

matutino, -a *adj* morning; **prensa matutina** morning papers

maullar *vi* to miaow

maullido *nm* miaowing, miaow

máxima *nf* (**a**) *Met* maximum temperature (**b**) *(aforismo)* maxim

máximo, -a 1 *adj* maximum, highest; **la máxima puntuación** the highest score **2** *nm* maximum; **al m.** to the utmost; **como m.** *(como mucho)* at the most; *(lo más tarde)* at the latest

maya 1 *adj* Mayan **2** *nmf* Maya, Mayan **3** *nm (lengua)* Maya

mayo *nm* May

mayonesa *nf* mayonnaise

mayor 1 *adj* (**a**) *(comparativo)* *(tamaño)* larger, bigger (**que** than);

(edad) older, elder; **m. que yo** older than me

(**b**) *(superlativo) (tamaño)* largest, biggest; *(edad)* oldest, eldest; **la m. parte** the majority; **la m. parte de las veces** most often

(**c**) *(adulto)* grown-up; **ser m. de edad** to be of age

(**d**) *(maduro)* elderly, mature

(**e**) *(principal)* major, main

(**f**) *Mús* major

(**g**) *Com* **al por m.** wholesale

2 *nm* (**a**) *Mil* major

(**b**) **mayores** *(adultos)* grown-ups, adults

mayoreo *nm Am* wholesale

mayoría *nf* majority; **en su m.** in the main; **la m. de los niños** most children; **m. absoluta** absolute majority; **m. relativa** *Br* relative majority, *US* plurality; **m. de edad** majority

mayúscula *nf* capital letter

mazapán *nm* marzipan

mazo *nm* mallet

me *pron pers* (**a**) *(objeto directo)* me; **no me mires** don't look at me (**b**) *(objeto indirecto)* me, to me, for me; **¿me das un caramelo?** will you give me a sweet?; **me lo dio** he gave it to me; **me es difícil hacerlo** it is difficult for me to do it (**c**) *(pron reflexivo)* myself; **me he cortado** I've cut myself; **me voy/muero** *(no se traduce)* I'm off/dying

mear *Fam* **1** *vi* to (have a) piss **2 mearse** *vpr* to wet oneself; *Fig* **mearse de risa** to piss oneself (laughing)

mecánica *nf* (**a**) *(ciencia)* mechanics *sing* (**b**) *(mecanismo)* mechanism, works

mecánico, -a 1 *adj* mechanical **2** *nm,f* mechanic

mecanismo *nm* mechanism

mecanografía *nf* typewriting, typing

mecanógrafo, -a *nm,f* typist

mecapal *nm CAm, Méx* = porter's leather harness

mecedora *nf* rocking-chair

mecer [49] **1** *vt* to rock **2 mecerse** *vpr* to swing, to rock

mecha *nf* (**a**) *(de vela)* wick (**b**) *Mil, Min* fuse; *Fam* **aguantar m.** to grin and bear it (**c**) *(de pelo)* streak; **hacerse mechas** to have one's hair streaked

mechero *nm Esp* (cigarette) lighter

mechón *nm* (**a**) *(de pelo)* lock (**b**) *(de lana)* tuft

medalla 1 *nf* medal **2** *nmf Dep (campeón)* medallist

medallón *nm* medallion

media *nf* (**a**) *(prenda interior)* **medias** *(hasta la cintura) Br* tights, *US* pantyhose; *(hasta medio muslo)* stockings (**b**) *(calcetín) (hasta la rodilla)* (knee-length) sock; *Am (de cualquier longitud)* sock (**c**) *(promedio)* average; *Mat* mean; **m. aritmética/geométrica** arithmetic/geometric mean (**d**) **a medias** *(incompleto)* unfinished; *(entre dos)* half and half; **ir a medias** to go halves

mediado, -a *adj* half-full, half-empty; **a mediados de mes/semana** about the middle of the month/week

medialuna *nf* (**a**) *(símbolo musulmán)* crescent (**b**) *Am (bollo)* croissant

mediana *nf* (**a**) *Mat* median (**b**) *(de autopista) Br* central reservation, *US* median (strip)

mediano, -a *adj* (**a**) middling, average (**b**) *(tamaño)* medium-sized

medianoche *nf* midnight

mediante *prep* by means of, with the help of, using; **Dios m.** God willing

mediar [43] *vi* (**a**) *(intervenir)* to mediate, to intervene; **m. en favor de** *o* **por algn** to intercede on behalf of sb (**b**) *(tiempo)* to pass; **mediaron tres semanas** three weeks passed

medicamento *nm* medicine, medicament

medicina *nf* medicine; **estudiante de m.** medical student

medicinal *adj* medicinal

médico, -a 1 *nm,f* doctor; **m. de cabecera** family doctor, general practitioner **2** *adj* medical

medida *nf* (**a**) measure; **a (la) m. (ropa)** made-to-measure; **a m. que**

avanzaba as he advanced; **en gran m.** to a great extent (**b**) *(dimensión)* measurement (**c**) *(disposición)* measure; **adoptar** *o* **tomar medidas** to take steps; **m. represiva** deterrent

medidor *nm Am (contador)* meter

medieval *adj* medieval

medio, -a 1 *adj* (**a**) half; **m. kilo** half a kilo; **una hora y media** one and a half hours, an hour and a half (**b**) *(intermedio)* middle; **a media mañana/tarde** in the middle of the morning/afternoon; **clase media** middle class (**c**) *(normal)* average; **salario m.** average wage

2 *adv* half; **está m. muerta** she is half dead

3 *nm* (**a**) *(mitad)* half (**b**) *(centro)* middle; **en m. (de)** *(en el centro)* in the middle (of); *(entre dos)* in between (**c**) **medios de transporte** means of transport; **por m. de ...** by means of ...; **medios de comunicación** (mass) media (**d**) **m. ambiente** environment (**e**) *Dep (jugador)* half back

mediocre *adj* mediocre

mediocridad *nf* mediocrity

mediodía *nm* (**a**) *(hora exacta)* midday, noon (**b**) *(período aproximado)* early afternoon, lunch-time (**c**) *(sur)* south

medir [6] **1** *vt* (**a**) *(distancia, superficie, temperatura)* to measure (**b**) *(moderar)* to weigh; **mide tus palabras** weigh your words **2** *vi* to measure, to be; **¿cuánto mides?** how tall are you?; **mide 2 m** he is 2 m tall; **mide 2 m de alto/ancho/largo** it is 2 m high/wide/long

meditar *vt & vi* to meditate, to ponder; **m. sobre algo** to ponder over sth

mediterráneo, -a 1 *adj* Mediterranean **2** *nm* **el M.** the Mediterranean

médium *nmf inv* medium

medusa *nf* jellyfish

megáfono *nm* megaphone

mejilla *nf* cheek

mejillón *nm* mussel

mejor 1 *adj* (**a**) *(comparativo)* better (**que** than); **el m. de los dos** the better

of the two; **es m. no decírselo** it's better not to tell her; **es m. que vayas** you'd better go (**b**) *(superlativo)* best; **el m. de los tres** the best of the three; **tu m. amiga** your best friend; **lo m.** the best thing

2 *adv* (**a**) *(comparativo)* better (**que** than); **cada vez m.** better and better; **ella conduce m.** she drives better; **m. dicho** or rather; **¡mucho** *o* **tanto m.!** so much the better! (**b**) *(superlativo)* best; **es el que m. canta** he is the one who sings the best; **a lo m.** *(quizás)* perhaps; *(ojalá)* hopefully

mejora *nf* improvement

mejorar 1 *vt* to improve; **m. la red vial** to improve the road system; **m. una marca** *o* **un récord** to break a record

2 *vi* to improve, to get better

3 mejorarse *vpr* to get better; **¡que te mejores!** get well soon!

mejoría *nf* improvement

melancolía *nf* melancholy

melancólico, -a *adj* melancholic, melancholy

melena *nf* (head of) hair; *(de león)* mane

mella *nf* (**a**) *(hendedura)* nick, notch; *(en plato, taza etc)* chip (**b**) *(en dentadura)* gap (**c**) *Fig* impression; **hacer m. en algn** to make an impression on sb

mellizo, -a *adj & nm,f* twin

melocotón *nm esp Esp* peach

melocotonero *nm esp Esp* peach tree

melodía *nf* melody, tune

melodrama *nm* melodrama

melodramático, -a *adj* melodramatic

melón *nm* (**a**) *(fruto)* melon (**b**) *Fam (tonto)* ninny (**c**) *muy Fam* **melones** *(tetas)* boobs

membresía *nf Am* membership

membrillo *nm* (**a**) *Bot* quince; *(árbol)* quince tree; *(dulce)* quince preserve *o* jelly (**b**) *Fam (tonto)* dimwit

memela *nf Méx* = thick corn tortilla, oval in shape

memorable *adj* memorable

memoria *nf* (**a**) memory; **aprender/ saber algo de m.** to learn/know sth by heart; **irse de la m.** to slip one's mind (**b**) *(informe)* report, statement; **m. anual** annual report (**c**) *(recuerdo)* memory, recollection (**d**) **memorias** *(biografía)* memoirs

memorizar [40] *vt* to memorize

menaje *nm* furniture and furnishing; **m. de cocina** kitchen equipment *o* utensils

mención *nf* mention; **m. honorífica** honourable mention

mencionar *vt* to mention

mendigo, -a *nm,f* beggar

mendrugo *nm* (**a**) *(de pan)* crust (of bread) (**b**) *Esp Fam (idiota)* fathead, idiot

mene *nm Ven* = deposit of oil at surface level

menear 1 *vt (mover)* to move; *(cabeza)* to shake; *(cola)* to wag **2 menearse** *vpr (moverse)* to move (about); *(agitarse)* to shake

menestra *nf* vegetable stew

menor 1 *adj* (**a**) *(comparativo) (de tamaño)* smaller (**que** than); *(de edad)* younger (**que** than); **mal m.** the lesser of two evils; **ser m. de edad** to be a minor *o* under age (**b**) *(superlativo) (de tamaño)* smallest; *(de intensidad)* least, slightest; *(de edad)* youngest; **al m. ruido** at the slightest noise; **el m. de los tres** the youngest of the three; **es la m.** she's the youngest child (**c**) *Mús* minor (**d**) *Com* **al por m.** retail **2** *nmf* minor; *Jur* **tribunal de menores** juvenile court

Menorca *n* Minorca

menos 1 *adj* (**a**) *(comparativo) (con singular)* less; *(con plural)* fewer; **m. dinero/leche que** less money/milk than; **m. libros/pisos que** fewer books/flats than; *(con cláusula)* **tiene m. años de lo que parece** he's younger than he looks (**b**) *(superlativo)* **fui el que perdí m. dinero** I lost the least money **2** *adv* (**a**) **m. de** *(con singular)* less than; *(con plural)* fewer than, less than;

m. de media hora less than half an hour (**b**) *(superlativo) (con singular)* least; *(con plural)* the fewest; *(con cantidad)* the least; **el m. inteligente de la clase** the least intelligent boy in the class; **ayer fue cuando vinieron m. personas** yesterday was when the fewest people came

3 *(locuciones)* **a m. que** (+ *subjuntivo)* unless; **al** *o* **por lo m.** at least; **echar a algn de m.** to miss sb; **eso es lo de m.** that's the least of it; **¡m. mal!** just as well!; **nada m. que** no less *o* no fewer than

4 *prep* (**a**) but, except; **todo m. eso** anything but that (**b**) *Mat* minus; **tres m. uno** three minus one

menospreciar [43] *vt* to scorn, to disdain

menosprecio *nm* contempt, scorn, disdain

mensaje *nm* message

mensajero, -a *nm,f* messenger, courier

menso, -a *adj Méx Fam* foolish, stupid

menstruación *nf* menstruation

mensual *adj* monthly; **dos visitas mensuales** two visits a month

menta *nf* (**a**) *Bot* mint (**b**) *(licor)* crème de menthe

mental *adj* mental

mente *nf* mind; **se me quedó la m. en blanco** my mind went blank; **m. abierta/tolerante/cerrada** open/broad/closed mind

mentir [5] *vi* to lie, to tell lies

mentira *nf* lie; **aunque parezca m.** strange as it may seem; **parece m.** it is unbelievable

mentiroso, -a 1 *adj* lying **2** *nm,f* liar

mentón *nm Anat* chin

menú *nm* menu

menudeo *nm Andes, Méx* retailing

menudo, -a 1 *adj* minute, tiny; *(irónico)* tremendous; **la gente menuda** the little ones; **¡m. lío/ susto!** what a mess/fright! **2** *adv* **a m.** often

meñique *adj & nm* (**dedo**) **m.** little finger, *US, Scot* pinkie

mercadillo *nm* flea market

mercado *nm* market; **M. Común** Common Market; **m. negro** black market; **m. único** single market; **sacar algo al m.** to put sth on the market

mercancía *nf* merchandise, goods

mercantil *adj* mercantile, commercial

mercería *nf Br* haberdasher's (shop), *US* notions store

mercurio *nm* (**a**) *Quím* mercury, quicksilver (**b**) **M.** Mercury

merecer [33] **1** *vt* (**a**) to deserve (**b**) *(uso impers)* **no merece la pena hacerlo** it's not worthwhile doing it **2 merecerse** *vpr* to deserve

merendar [1] **1** *vt* to have as an afternoon snack, to have for tea **2** *vi* to have an afternoon snack, to have tea

merendero *nm (establecimiento)* tea room, snack bar; *(en el campo)* picnic spot

merengue *nm* (**a**) *Culin* meringue (**b**) *(música, baile)* merengue

meridiano *nm* meridian

meridional 1 *adj* southern **2** *nmf* southerner

merienda *nf* afternoon snack, tea

mérito *nm* merit, worth; **hacer méritos para algo** to strive to deserve sth

merluza *nf (pez)* hake

mermelada *nf* (**a**) jam; **m. de fresa** strawberry jam (**b**) *(de agrios)* marmalade; **m. de naranja** (orange) marmalade

mero, -a *adj* mere, pure; **por el m. hecho de** through the mere fact of

mes *nm* (**a**) month; **el m. pasado/que viene** last/next month (**b**) *(cobro)* monthly salary *o* wages; *(pago)* monthly payment (**c**) *Fam (menstruación)* period

mesa *nf* (**a**) table; **poner/recoger la m.** to set/clear the table; *(de despacho etc)* desk; **m. redonda** round table (**b**) *(junta directiva)* board, executive; **el presidente de la m.** the chairman; **m. electoral** electoral college

mesada *nf* (**a**) *Am (pago mensual)*

monthly payment, monthly instalment (**b**) *RP (para adolescentes)* pocket money, *US* allowance (**c**) *RP (encimera)* worktop

mesero, -a *nm,f Col, Guat, Méx, Salv* waiter, *f* waitress

meseta *nf* plateau, tableland, meseta; **la M.** the plateau of Castile

mesilla *nf* **m. de noche** bedside table

mesón *nm* = old-style tavern

mesonero, -a *nm,f* (**a**) *Esp (en mesón)* innkeeper (**b**) *Chile, Ven (camarero)* waiter, *f* waitress

mestizo, -a *adj & nm,f* half-breed, half-caste, mestizo

meta *nf* (**a**) *(objetivo)* goal, aim, objective (**b**) *(de carrera)* finish, finishing line (**c**) *Ftb (portería)* goal

metáfora *nf* metaphor

metal *nm* (**a**) metal; **metales preciosos** precious metals (**b**) *(timbre de la voz)* timbre (**c**) *Mús* brass

metálico, -a **1** *adj* metallic **2** *nm* cash; **pagar en m.** to pay (in) cash

metate *nm Guat, Méx* grinding stone

meteorito *nm* meteorite

meteorología *nf* meteorology

meter 1 *vt* (**a**) *(poner)* to put (**en** in); *Fig* **m. las narices en algo** to poke one's nose into sth (**b**) *(comprometer)* to involve (**en** in), to get mixed up (**en** in) (**c**) *Fam Fig (dar)* to give; **m. un rollo** to go on and on; **m. prisa a algn** to hurry sb up (**d**) *(hacer)* to make; **m. ruido** to make a noise

2 meterse *vpr* (**a**) *(entrar)* to go *o* come in, to get into (**b**) *(estar)* to be; **¿dónde te habías metido?** where have you been (all this time)? (**c**) *(entrometerse)* to meddle (**d**) **meterse con algn** *(en broma)* to get at sb

meterete *nmf RP Fam* busybody, *Br* nosy-parker

metete *nmf Andes, CAm Fam* busybody, *Br* nosy-parker

metiche *nmf Méx, Ven Fam* busybody, *Br* nosy-parker

método *nm* (**a**) method (**b**) *Educ* course

metralla *nf* shrapnel

metro *nm* (**a**) *(medida)* metre (**b**) *(tren) Br* underground, *US* subway

metrópoli *nf* metropolis

mexicano, -a *adj & nm,f* Mexican

México *n* Mexico

mezcla *nf* (**a**) *(acción)* mixing, blending; *Rad, Cin* mixing (**b**) *(producto)* mixture, blend

mezclar 1 *vt* (**a**) *(dos o más cosas)* to mix, to blend (**b**) *(desordenar)* to mix up (**c**) *(involucrar)* to involve, to mix up **2 mezclarse** *vpr* (**a**) *(cosas)* to get mixed up; *(gente)* to mingle (**b**) *(relacionarse)* to get involved (**con** with)

mezquino, -a *adj* (**a**) *(persona)* mean, stingy (**b**) *(sueldo)* miserable

mezquita *nf* mosque

mg *(abr* **miligramo)** mg

mi¹ *adj* my; **mi casa/trabajo** my house/ job; **mis cosas/libros** my things/ books

mi² *(pl* **mis)** *nm Mús* E; **mi menor** E minor

mí *pron pers* me; **a mí me dio tres** he gave me three; **compra otro para mí** buy one for me too; **por mí mismo** just by myself

miche *nm Ven (aguardiente)* = cane spirit flavoured with herbs and spices

mico *nm* (**a**) *Zool* (long-tailed) monkey (**b**) *Fam (pequeño)* **es un m.** he's a midget *o Br* titch

micro 1 *nm Fam* mike, microphone **2** *nm o nf Arg, Bol, Chile (autobús)* bus

microbio *nm* microbe

microbús *nm* (**a**) *(autobús)* minibus (**b**) *Méx (taxi)* (collective) taxi

micrófono *nm* microphone

microonda *nf* un (horno) **micro- ondas** a microwave (oven)

microscopio *nm* microscope

miedo *nm (pavor)* fear; *(temor)* apprehension; **una película de m.** a horror movie *o Br* film; **tener m. de algn/algo** to be afraid of sb/sth; *Esp Fam* **lo pasamos de m.** we had a fantastic time; **un calor de m.** sizzling heat

miedoso, -a *adj* fearful

miel *nf* honey; **luna de m.** honeymoon

miembro *nm* (**a**) *(socio)* member; **estado m.** member state (**b**) *Anat* limb; **m. viril** penis

mientras 1 *conj* (**a**) *(al mismo tiempo que)* while (**b**) *(durante el tiempo que)* when, while; **m. viví en Barcelona** when I lived in Barcelona (**c**) **m. que** *(por el contrario)* whereas (**d**) *Fam (cuanto más)* **m. más/menos …** the more/less … **2** *adv* **m. (tanto)** meanwhile, in the meantime

miércoles *nm inv* Wednesday; **M. de Ceniza** Ash Wednesday

mierda *nf Vulg* (**a**) shit; **ese libro es una m.** that book is crap; **¡vete a la m.!** piss off! (**b**) *Fig (porquería)* dirt, filth (**c**) *Esp (borrachera)* bender

miga *nf (de pan etc)* crumb; *Fig* **hacer buenas migas con algn** to get on well with sb

migaja *nf* (**a**) *(de pan)* crumb (**b**) *Fig* bit, scrap (**c**) **migajas** *(de pan)* crumbs; *Fig* leftovers

migra *nf Méx Fam Pey* **la m.** = US police border patrol

mil *adj & nm* thousand; **m. euros** a *o* one thousand euros

milagro *nm* miracle

milenario, -a 1 *adj* millenarian, millennial **2** *nm* millennium

milenio *nm* millennium

milésimo, -a *adj & nm,f* thousandth

mili *nf Esp Antes Fam* military *o* national service; **hacer la m.** to do one's military service

milico *nm Andes, RP* (**a**) *Fam Pey (militar)* soldier; **los milicos tomaron el poder** the military took power (**b**) *(policía)* pig

miligramo *nm* milligram

mililitro *nm* millilitre

milímetro *nm* millimetre

militante *adj & nmf* militant

militar 1 *adj* military
 2 *nm* military man, soldier
 3 *vi Pol (en un partido)* to be a member

milla *nf* mile

millar *nm* thousand

millón *nm* million

millonario, -a *adj & nm,f* millionaire

milpa *nf CAm, Méx* cornfield

mimado, -a *adj* spoilt

mimar *vt* to spoil, to pamper

mímica *nf* mimicry

mimosa *nf Bot* mimosa

mina *nf* (a) mine; **ingeniero de minas** mining engineer (b) *(explosivo)* mine; **campo de minas** minefield (c) *(de lápiz)* lead; **lápiz de m.** propelling pencil (d) *Fig (ganga)* gold mine

mineral 1 *adj* mineral **2** *nm* ore

minero, -a 1 *nm,f* miner **2** *adj* mining

miniatura *nf* miniature

minifalda *nf* miniskirt

mínimo, -a 1 *adj* (a) *(muy pequeño)* minute, tiny (b) *Mat, Téc* minimum, lowest; **m. común múltiplo** lowest common denominator **2** *nm* minimum; **como m.** at least; **ni lo más m.** not in the least

ministerio *nm* (a) *Pol Br* ministry, *US* department (b) *Rel* ministry

ministro, -a *nm,f* (a) *Pol Br* minister, *US* secretary; **primer m.** prime minister (b) *Rel* minister

minoría *nf* minority; *Jur* **m. de edad** minority

minoritario, -a *adj* minority

minucioso, -a *adj* (a) *(persona)* meticulous (b) *(informe, trabajo etc)* minute, detailed

minúscula *nf* small letter; *Impr* lower-case letter

minúsculo, -a *adj* minuscule, minute; **letra minúscula** lower-case *o* small letter

minusválido, -a 1 *adj* handicapped, disabled **2** *nm,f* handicapped person, disabled person

minuta *nf* (a) *(cuenta)* lawyer's bill (b) *(menú)* menu (c) *RP (comida rápida)* = single-course meal which usually consists of meat or fish accompanied by French fries and sometimes vegetables

minutero *nm* minute hand

minuto *nm* minute

mío, -a 1 *adj pos* of mine; **un amigo m.** a friend of mine; **no es asunto m.** it is none of my business **2** *pron pos* mine; **ese libro es m.** that book is mine; **lo m. es el tenis** tennis is my strong point; *Fam* **los míos** my people *o* folks

miope *nmf* short-sighted *o US* near-sighted person, *Espec* myopic person

miopía *nf* short-sightedness, *US* near-sightedness, *Espec* myopia

mirada *nf* look; **lanzar** *o* **echar una m. a** to glance at; **levantar la m.** to raise one's eyes; **m. fija** stare

mirador *nm* (a) *(lugar con vista)* viewpoint (b) *(balcón)* bay window, windowed balcony

mirar 1 *vt* (a) to look at (b) *(observar)* to watch (c) **m. por algn/algo** *(cuidar)* to look after sb/sth (d) *(procurar)* to see; **mira que no le pase nada** see that nothing happens to him **2** *vi (dar a)* to look, to face; **la casa mira al sur** the house faces south

mirilla *nf* spyhole, peephole

mirlo *nm* blackbird

mirón, -ona *Fam* **1** *adj (curioso)* nosey; *(con lascivia)* peeping **2** *nm,f (espectador)* onlooker; *(curioso)* busybody, *Br* nosy-parker; *(voyeur)* peeping Tom

misa *nf* mass

miscelánea *nf* (a) *(mezcla)* miscellany (b) *Méx (tienda)* = small general store

miserable 1 *adj* (a) *(mezquino) (persona)* despicable; *(sueldo etc)* miserable (b) *(pobre)* wretched, poor; **una vida m.** a wretched life **2** *nmf* (a) *(mezquino)* miser (b) *(canalla)* wretch

miseria *nf* (a) *(pobreza extrema)* extreme poverty (b) *(insignificancia)* pittance; **ganar una m.** to earn next to nothing (c) *(tacañería)* miserliness, meanness

misericordia *nf* mercy, compassion

misil *nm* missile; **m. tierra-aire** surface-to-air missile

misión *nf* mission; **m. cumplida**

mission accomplished

misionero, -a *nm,f* missionary

mismo, -a 1 *adj* (a) same (b) *(uso enfático)* **yo m.** I myself; **aquí m.** right here

2 *pron* same; **es el m. de ayer** it's the same one as yesterday; **lo m.** the same (thing); **dar** *o* **ser lo m.** to make no difference; **por eso m.** that is why; **por uno** *o* **sí m.** by oneself

3 *adv* (a) *(por ejemplo)* for instance; **que venga algn, Juan m.** ask one of them to come, Juan, for instance (b) **así m.** likewise

misterio *nm* mystery

misterioso, -a *adj* mysterious

mitad *nf* (a) half; **a m. de camino** halfway there; **a m. de precio** half-price (b) *(centro)* middle; **en la m. del primer acto** halfway through the first act; *Fam* **eso me parte por la m.** that really screws things up for me

mitin *nm Pol* meeting, rally

mito *nm* myth

mitología *nf* mythology

mitote *nm Méx* (a) *Fam (alboroto)* racket (b) *(fiesta)* house party

mixto, -a *adj* mixed

mobiliario *nm* furniture

mocasín *nm* moccasin

mochila *nf* rucksack, backpack

mochuelo *nm Zool* little owl

moco *nm* snot; **sonarse los mocos** to blow one's nose

moda *nf* (a) fashion; **a la m., de m.** in fashion; **pasado de m.** old-fashioned (b) *(furor pasajero)* craze

modalidad *nf* form, category; *Com* **m. de pago** method of payment; *Dep* **m. deportiva** sport

modelo 1 *adj inv & nm* model **2** *nmf* (fashion) model; **desfile de modelos** fashion show

módem *nm* (*pl* **modems**) *Informát* modem; **m. fax** fax modem

moderno, -a *adj* modern

modestia *nf* modesty; **m. aparte** without wishing to be immodest

modesto, -a *adj* modest

modificación *nf* alteration

modificar [44] *vt* to modify

modisto, -a *nm,f* (a) *(diseñador)* fashion designer (b) *(sastre)* couturier, *f* couturière

modo *nm* (a) *(manera)* way, manner; **m. de empleo** instructions for use (b) **modos** manners (c) *Ling* mood

moflete *nm* chubby cheek

mogollón *nm Esp Fam* (a) **m. de** loads of; **me gusta un m.** I like it loads (b) *(confusión)* commotion; *(ruido)* racket

moho *nm* (a) *Bot* mould (b) *(de metales)* rust

mojado, -a *adj (empapado)* wet; *(húmedo)* damp

mojar 1 *vt* (a) to wet; *(humedecer)* to damp; **m. pan en la leche** to dip *o* dunk bread in one's milk (b) *muy Fam* **mojarla** to have it off **2 mojarse** *vpr* to get wet

molcajete *nm Méx* mortar

molde *nm* mould; **letras de m.** printed letters; **pan de m.** ≃ sliced bread

moldear *vt* to mould

mole 1 *nf* mass, bulk **2** *nm Méx* (a) *(salsa)* = thick, cooked chilli sauce (b) *(guiso)* = dish served in "mole" sauce

molestar 1 *vt* (a) *(incomodar)* to disturb, to bother (b) *Fml* to bother; **¿le molestaría esperar fuera?** would you mind waiting outside? (c) *(causar malestar a)* to hurt **2 molestarse** *vpr* (a) *(tomarse la molestia)* to bother (b) *(ofenderse)* to take offence, to get upset

molestia *nf* (a) bother; **no es ninguna m.** it is no trouble at all; **perdone las molestias** forgive the inconvenience (b) *Med (dolor)* trouble, slight pain

molesto, -a *adj* (a) *(irritante)* annoying, upsetting (b) **estar m. con algn** *(enfadado)* to be annoyed *o* upset with sb

molino *nm* mill; **m. de agua** watermill; **m. de viento** windmill

molusco *nm* mollusc

momento *nm* (a) *(instante)* moment;

al m. at once; **por momentos** by the minute (**b**) *(periodo)* time; **de m.** for the time being; **en cualquier m.** at any time

momia *nf* mummy

monada *nf Fam* ¡qué m.! how cute!

monaguillo *nm Rel* altar boy

monarca *nmf* monarch

monarquía *nf* monarchy

monasterio *nm Rel* monastery

mondar 1 *vt* to peel **2 mondarse** *vpr Esp Fam* **mondarse (de risa)** to laugh one's head off

moneda *nf* (**a**) *(pieza)* coin; **m. suelta** small change; **acuñar m.** to mint money (**b**) *Fin* currency; **m. única** single currency

monedero *nm* purse

monitor, -a *nm,f* monitor; *(profesor)* instructor

monja *nf* nun

monje *nm* monk

mono, -a 1 *nm* (**a**) *(animal)* monkey (**b**) *(prenda) (con mangas) Br* overalls, *US* coveralls; *(con peto) Br* dungarees, *Br* boiler suit, *US* overalls; *Ven (de deporte)* tracksuit (**c**) *Esp Fam (síndrome de abstinencia)* cold turkey **2** *adj Fam (bonito)* pretty, cute

monobloque *nm Arg* tower block

monólogo *nm* monologue

monopatín *nm Esp* skateboard

monopolio *nm* monopoly

monótono, -a *adj* monotonous

monovolumen *nm* people carrier

monstruo *nm* (**a**) monster (**b**) *(genio)* genius

montacargas *nm inv Br* goods lift, *US* freight elevator

montaje *nm* (**a**) *Téc (instalación)* fitting; *(ensamblaje)* assembling; **cadena de m.** assembly line (**b**) *Cin* editing and mounting (**c**) *Teatro* staging (**d**) *Fot* montage (**e**) *Fam (farsa)* farce

montaña *nf* mountain; **m. rusa** big dipper

montañismo *nm* mountaineering

montañoso, -a *adj* mountainous

montar 1 *vi* (**a**) *(subirse)* to get in; *(en*

bici, a caballo) to ride (**b**) *Fin (ascender)* **m. a** to amount to, to come to
2 *vt* (**a**) *(colocar)* to put on (**b**) *(máquina etc)* to assemble, *(negocio)* to set up, to start (**c**) *Esp Culin (nata)* to whip (**d**) *Cin, Fot (película)* to edit, to mount; *(fotografía)* to mount (**e**) *Teatro (obra)* to stage, to mount (**f**) *Zool (cubrir)* to mount
3 montarse *vpr* (**a**) *(subirse)* to get on; *(en coche)* to get in (**en** to) (**b**) *Fam (armarse)* to break out; *Fam* **montárselo bien** to have things (nicely) worked out *o* set up

monte *nm* (**a**) *(montaña)* mountain; *(con nombre propio)* mount; **de m.** wild (**b**) **el m.** *(zona)* the hills

montera *nf* bullfighter's hat

montón *nm* heap, pile; **un m. de** a load of; *Fam* **me gusta un m.** I really love it; *Fam* **del m.** run-of-the-mill, nothing special

montura *nf* (**a**) *(cabalgadura)* mount (**b**) *(de gafas)* frame

monumental *adj* (**a**) *(ciudad, lugar)* famous for its monuments (**b**) *Fig (fracaso, éxito)* monumental

monumento *nm* monument

moño *nm* (**a**) *(de pelo)* bun (**b**) *Am (lazo)* bow (**c**) *Méx (pajarita)* bow tie

moqueta *nf Esp* fitted carpet

mora *nf (zarzamora)* blackberry

morado, -a 1 *adj* purple; *Esp Fam* **pasarlas moradas** to have a tough time; *Esp Fam* **ponerse m.** to stuff oneself **2** *nm* purple

moral 1 *adj* moral **2** *nf* (**a**) *(ética)* morals (**b**) *(ánimo)* morale, spirits; **levantar la m. a algn** to raise sb's spirits

moraleja *nf* moral

moralista 1 *adj* moralistic **2** *nmf* moralist

morcilla *nf Br* black pudding, *US* blood sausage; *Esp Fam* **que te/os den m.** you can stuff it, then!

mordaza *nf* gag

mordedura *nf* bite

morder [4] *vt* to bite; **me ha mordido**

it has bitten me; *Fig* **m. el anzuelo** to take the bait

mordida *nf CAm, Méx Fam (soborno)* bribe, *Br* backhander

mordisco *nm* bite

moreno, -a 1 *adj* (**a**) *(pelo)* dark-haired; *(piel)* dark-skinned (**b**) *(bronceado)* tanned; **ponerse m.** to get a suntan; **pan/azúcar m.** brown bread/ sugar **2** *nm,f (persona) (de pelo)* dark-haired person; *(de piel)* dark-skinned person

moribundo, -a *adj & nm,f* moribund

morir [7] **1** *vi* to die; **m. de frío/ hambre/cáncer** to die of cold/ hunger/cancer; **m. de amor** *o* **pena** to die from a broken heart
2 morirse *vpr* to die; **morirse de hambre** to starve to death; *Fig* to be starving; **morirse de aburrimiento** to be bored to death; **morirse de ganas (de hacer algo)** to be dying (to do sth); **morirse de risa** to die laughing

moro, -a *nm,f* (**a**) *Hist* Moor; *Fam* **no hay moros en la costa** the coast is clear (**b**) *Esp (árabe)* Arab, = pejorative term referring to a North African or Arab person

morocho, -a 1 *adj* (**a**) *Andes, RP (moreno)* dark-haired (**b**) *Andes, RP Euf (negro)* coloured (**c**) *Ven (gemelo)* twin **2** *nm,f* (**a**) *Andes, RP (moreno)* dark-haired person (**b**) *Andes, RP Euf (negro)* coloured person (**c**) *Ven (gemelo)* twin

moronga *nf CAm, Méx Br* black pudding, *US* blood sausage

moroso, -a *nm,f* bad debtor

morralla *nf* (**a**) *(cosas sin valor)* rubbish, junk (**b**) *(chusma)* scum

morro *nm* (**a**) *(de animal) (hocico)* snout (**b**) *Esp Fam (de persona)* mouth, (thick) lips; **caerse de m.** to fall flat on one's face; **por los morros** without so much as a by-your-leave; *Fam* **¡vaya m.!** what a cheek! (**c**) *Esp (de coche)* nose

morsa *nf* walrus

mortadela *nf* mortadella

mortal 1 *adj* (**a**) mortal (**b**) *(mortífero)*

fatal; **un accidente m.** a fatal accident **2** *nmf* mortal

mortero *nm Culin, Mil* mortar

mosaico *nm* mosaic

mosca *nf* fly; **peso m.** flyweight; *Esp Fam* **estar m.** *(suspicaz)* to be suspicious; *(borracho)* to be pissed; *Fam* **por si las moscas** just in case; *Fam* **¿qué m. te ha picado?** what's biting you?

moscatel *nm* Muscatel, = dessert wine made from muscat grapes; **uvas de m.** muscat grapes

mosquito *nm* mosquito

mostaza *nf Bot, Culin* mustard

mostrador *nm* (**a**) *(de tienda)* counter (**b**) *(de bar)* bar

mostrar 1 *vt* to show; **muéstramelo** show it to me **2 mostrarse** *vpr* to be; **se mostró muy comprensiva** she was very understanding

mote¹ *nm* nickname

mote² *nm Andes* stewed *Br* maize *o US* corn

motel *nm* motel

motivación *nf* motivation

motivar *vt* (**a**) *(causar)* to cause, to give rise to (**b**) *(inducir)* to motivate

motivo *nm* (**a**) *(causa)* reason; *(usu pl)* grounds; **con este** *o* **tal m.** for this reason; **con m. de** on the occasion of; **sin m.** for no reason at all; **bajo ningún m.** under no circumstances (**b**) *Arte, Mús* motif, leitmotiv

moto *nf Aut* motorbike, bike; **m. náutica** *o* **acuática** jet ski

motocicleta *nf* motorbike

motociclismo *nm* motorcycling

motociclista *nmf* motorcyclist

motocross *nm* motocross

motoneta *nf Am (motor)* scooter

motonetista *nmf Am* scooter rider

motor, -a 1 *nm (grande)* engine; *(pequeño)* motor; **m. de reacción** jet engine; **m. de explosión** internal combustion engine; **m. eléctrico** electric motor; *Informát* **m. de búsqueda** search engine **2** *adj Téc* motive

motora *nf* motorboat

motorista *nmf Esp* motorcyclist

mousse [mus] *nf, Esp nm* mousse

mover [4] **1** *vt* (**a**) to move; **m. algo de su sitio** to move sth out of its place (**b**) *(hacer funcionar)* to drive; **el motor mueve el coche** the engine drives the car **2 moverse** *vpr* (**a**) to move (**b**) *Fam (gestionar)* to do everything possible (**c**) *(darse prisa)* to hurry up; **¡muévete!** get a move on!

movida *nf Esp, RP Fam* **hay mucha m.** there's a lot going on

movido, -a *adj* (**a**) *Fot* blurred (**b**) *(ocupado)* busy

móvil 1 *adj* mobile; **teléfono m.** mobile phone; *TV, Rad* **unidad m.** outside broadcast unit **2** *nm* (**a**) *(de delito)* motive (**b**) *(teléfono)* mobile

movimiento *nm* (**a**) *(gen)* movement; *Fís, Téc* motion; **(poner algo) en m.** (to set sth) in motion; **m. sísmico** earth tremor (**b**) *(actividad)* activity (**c**) *Com, Fin (entradas y salidas)* operations (**d**) *Hist* **el M.** the Falangist Movement

mozárabe 1 *adj* Mozarabic, = Christian in the time of Moorish Spain **2** *nmf (habitante)* Mozarab, = Christian of Moorish Spain **3** *nm (lengua)* Mozarabic

mozo, -a *nm* (**a**) *(niño)* young boy, young lad; *(niña)* young girl (**b**) *(de estación)* porter; *(de hotel)* bellboy, *US* bellhop (**c**) *Mil* conscript (**d**) *Andes, RP (camarero)* waiter, *f* waitress (**e**) *Col (novio)* boyfriend; *(novia)* girlfriend

mucamo, -a *Andes, RP nm,f (en hotel)* chamberperson, *f* chambermaid

muchacha *nf* girl

muchachada *nf* bunch of kids

muchacho *nm* boy

muchedumbre *nf (de gente)* crowd

mucho, -a 1 *adj* (**a**) *sing (usu en frases afirmativas)* a lot of, lots of; *(usu en frases negativas)* much; **m. tiempo** a long time; **tengo m. sueño/mucha sed** I am very sleepy/thirsty; **¿bebes m. café? – no, no m.** do you drink a lot of coffee? – no, not much (**b**)

(demasiado) **es m. coche para mí** this car is a bit too much for me (**c**) **muchos** *(usu en frases afirmativas)* a lot of, lots of; *(usu en frases negativas)* many; **tiene muchos años** he is very old **2** *pron* (**a**) a lot, a great deal; **¿cuánta leche queda? – mucha** how much milk is there left? – a lot (**b**) **muchos** a lot, lots, many; **¿cuántos libros tienes? – muchos** how many books have you got? – lots *o* a lot; **muchos creemos que ...** many of us believe that ...

3 *adv* (**a**) a lot, very much; **lo siento m.** I'm very sorry; **como m.** at the most; **m. antes/después** long before/after; **¡ni m. menos!** no way!; **por m. (que)** (+ *subjuntivo*) however much (**b**) *(tiempo)* **hace m. que no viene por aquí** he has not been to see us for a long time (**c**) *(a menudo)* often; **vamos m. al cine** we go to the cinema quite often

mudanza *nf* move; **estar de m.** to be moving; **camión de m.** removal van

mudar 1 *vt* (**a**) *(ropa)* to change (**b**) *(plumas, pelo)* to moult; *(piel)* to shed, to slough **2 mudarse** *vpr* **mudarse de casa/ropa** to move house/to change one's clothes

mudéjar *adj & nmf* Mudejar

mudo, -a 1 *adj* (**a**) *(que no habla)* dumb; **cine m.** silent films (**b**) *Fig (callado)* speechless **2** *nm,f* mute

mueble 1 *nm* piece of furniture; **muebles** furniture; **con/sin muebles** furnished/unfurnished; **m. bar** cocktail cabinet **2** *adj* movable

mueca *nf* (**a**) *(de burla)* mocking face; **hacer muecas** to pull faces (**b**) *(de dolor, asco)* grimace

muela *nf* (**a**) *Anat* molar; **dolor de muelas** toothache; **m. del juicio** wisdom tooth (**b**) *Téc (de molino)* millstone

muelle¹ *nm* spring

muelle² *nm Náut* dock

muerte *nf* death; **m. natural** natural death; **dar m. a algn** to kill sb; **odiar a algn a m.** to loathe sb; *Esp* **de mala m.** badly; *Fam* **un susto de m.** the fright of one's life

muerto, -a 1 *adj* dead; **m. de hambre** starving; **m. de frío** frozen to death; **m. de miedo** scared stiff; **m. de risa** laughing one's head off; **horas muertas** spare time; *Aut* **(en) punto m.** (in) neutral **2** *nm,f (difunto)* dead person; **hacerse el m.** to pretend to be dead; *Fam* **cargar con el m.** to do the dirty work; **hubo dos muertos** two (people) died

muestra *nf* (a) *(espécimen)* sample, specimen (b) *(modelo a copiar)* model (c) *(prueba, señal)* sign; **dar muestras de** to show signs of; **m. de cariño/respeto** token of affection/respect; **una m. más de …** yet another example of …

mugido *nm (de vaca)* moo; *(de toro)* bellow

mugir [57] *vi (vaca)* to moo, to low; *(toro)* to bellow

mujer *nf* (a) woman; **dos mujeres** two women; **m. de la limpieza** cleaner; **m. de su casa** house-proud woman (b) *(esposa)* wife; **su futura m.** his bride-to-be

mulato, -a *adj & nm,f* mulatto

muleta *nf* (a) *(prótesis)* crutch (b) *Taurom* muleta

mulo *nm* mule

multa *nf* fine; *Aut* ticket

multar *vt* to fine

multinacional *adj & nf* multinational

múltiple *adj* (a) multiple; **accidente m.** pile-up (b) **múltiples** *(muchos)* many

multiplicación *nf Mat* multiplication

multiplicar [44] **1** *vt & vi* to multiply **(por** by) **2 multiplicarse** *vpr (reproducirse, aumentar)* to multiply

múltiplo, -a *adj & nm* multiple

multitud *nf* (a) *(de personas)* crowd (b) *(de cosas)* multitude

mundial 1 *adj* worldwide; **campeón m.** world champion; **de fama m.** world-famous **2** *nm* world championship

mundo *nm* world; **todo el m.** everyone; **correr** *o* **ver m.** to travel widely; **nada del otro m.** nothing

special; **el otro m.** the hereafter

munición *nf* ammunition

municipal 1 *adj* municipal **2** *nmf Esp (guardia)* policeman, *f* policewoman

municipio *nm* (a) *(corporación)* local council (b) *(territorio)* town, municipality

muñeca *nf* (a) *(del cuerpo)* wrist (b) *(juguete, muchacha)* doll (c) *Andes, RP Fam* **tener m.** *(enchufe)* to have friends in high places; *(habilidad)* to have the knack (d) *Méx (mazorca)* baby sweetcorn

muñeco *nm (juguete)* (little) boy doll; **m. de trapo** rag doll; **m. de nieve** snowman

muñeira *nf* = popular Galician dance and music

muñequera *nf* wristband

mural 1 *adj (pintura)* mural; *(mapa)* wall **2** *nm* mural

muralla *nf* wall

murciélago *nm Zool* bat

muro *nm* wall

musa *nf* muse

músculo *nm* muscle

museo *nm* museum; **m. de arte** *o* **pintura** art gallery

musgo *nm* moss

música *nf* music; **m. clásica** classical music; **m. de fondo** background music

musical 1 *adj* musical **2** *nm* musical

músico, -a 1 *adj* musical **2** *nm,f* musician

muslo *nm* thigh

musulmán, -ana *adj & nm,f* Muslim, Moslem

mutilado, -a *nm,f* disabled person; **m. de guerra** disabled serviceman

mutua *nf Br* friendly society, *US* mutual benefit society

mutual *nf CSur, Perú Br* friendly society, *US* mutual benefit society

muy *adv* very; **m. bueno/malo** very good/bad; **¡m. bien!** very good!; *Fam* **m. mucho** very much; **M. señor mío** Dear Sir; **m. de los andaluces** typically Andalusian; **m. de mañana/noche** very early/late

Nn

nº (*abr* **número**) no

nabo *nm* (**a**) *Bot* turnip (**b**) *muy Fam* *(pene)* tool, *Br* knob

nacer [60] *vi* (**a**) to be born; **al n.** at birth; **nací en Montoro** I was born in Montoro; *Fam Fig* **n. de pie** to be born under a lucky star (**b**) *(pájaro)* to hatch (out) (**c**) *(pelo)* to begin to grow (**d**) *(río)* to rise

nacimiento *nm* (**a**) birth; **sordo de n.** deaf from birth; **lugar de n.** birthplace, place of birth (**b**) *Fig (principio)* origin, beginning; *(de río)* source (**c**) *(belén)* Nativity scene, crib

nación *nf* nation; **las Naciones Unidas** the United Nations

nacional 1 *adj* (**a**) national (**b**) *(producto, mercado)* domestic; **vuelos nacionales** domestic flights **2** *nmf* national; *Hist* **los nacionales** the Francoist forces

nacionalidad *nf* nationality

nada 1 *pron* (**a**) *(como respuesta)* nothing; **¿qué quieres? – n.** what do you want? – nothing

(**b**) *(con verbo)* not … anything; *(enfático)* nothing; **no sé n.** I don't know anything

(**c**) *(con otro negativo)* anything; **no hace nunca n.** he never does anything; **nadie sabía n.** nobody knew anything

(**d**) *(en ciertas construcciones)* anything; **más que n.** more than anything; **sin decir n.** without saying anything; **casi n.** hardly anything

(**e**) **gracias – de n.** thanks – don't mention it; *Fam* **para n.** not at all; **casi n.** almost nothing; **un rasguño de n.** an insignificant little scratch; **n. de eso** nothing of the kind; **no es n.** nothing at all; **n. más verla** as soon as he saw her

2 *adv* not at all; **no me gusta n.** I don't like it at all; **no lo encuentro n. interesante** I don't find it remotely interesting

3 *nf* nothingness; **salir de la n.** to come out of nowhere

nadador, -a *nm,f* swimmer

nadar *vi* (**a**) *Dep* to swim; **n. a braza** to do the breaststroke (**b**) *(flotar)* to float

nadie 1 *pron* (**a**) *(como respuesta)* no one, nobody; **¿quién vino? – n.** who came? – no one

(**b**) *(con verbo)* not … anyone, not … anybody; *(enfático)* no one, nobody; **no conozco a n.** I don't know anyone *o* anybody; **no vi a n.** I saw no one

(**c**) *(con otro negativo)* anyone, anybody; **nunca habla con n.** he never speaks to anybody

(**d**) *(en ciertas construcciones)* anybody, anyone; **más que n.** more than anyone; **sin decírselo a n.** without telling anyone; **casi n.** hardly anyone

2 *nm* nobody; **ser un don n.** to be a nobody

nafta *nf RP (gasolina) Br* petrol, *US* gas, *US* gasoline

nailon *nm* nylon

naipe *nm* playing card

nalga *nf* buttock; **nalgas** bottom, buttocks

nana *nf* (**a**) *(canción)* lullaby (**b**) *Col, Méx (niñera)* nanny (**c**) *Col, Méx (nodriza)* wet nurse

naranja 1 *nf* orange; *Fig* **mi media n.** my better half **2** *adj & nm (color)* orange

naranjada *nf* orangeade

naranjo *nm* orange tree

narcotraficante *nmf* drug trafficker

narcotráfico *nm* drug trafficking

nariz *nf* (**a**) nose; *Fam* **me da en la n. que …** I've got this feeling that … (**b**) *Fam* **en mis (propias) narices** right under my very nose; *Fam* **estar hasta las narices de** to be totally fed up with; *Esp Fam* **tenemos que ir por narices** we have to go whether we like it or not

narración *nf* narration

narrador, -a *nm,f* narrator

narrar *vt* to narrate, to tell

narrativa *nf* narrative

nata *nf* (**a**) *Esp (crema de leche)* cream; **n. batida** *o* **montada** whipped cream (**b**) *(de leche hervida)* skin (**c**) *Fig* cream, best

natación *nf Dep* swimming

natillas *nfpl Esp* custard

nativo, -a *adj & nm,f* native

natural 1 *adj* natural; *(fruta, flor)* fresh; **de tamaño n.** life-size; **en estado n.** in its natural state; *Jur* **hijo n.** illegitimate child **2** *nmf* native

naturaleza *nf* (**a**) nature; **en plena n.** in the wild, in unspoilt countryside; *Arte* **n. muerta** still life (**b**) *(complexión)* physical constitution

naufragar [42] *vi (barco)* to sink, to be wrecked; *(persona)* to be shipwrecked

naufragio *nm Náut* shipwreck

náusea *nf (usu pl)* nausea, sickness; **me da n.** it makes me sick; **sentir náuseas** to feel sick

náutico, -a *adj* nautical

navaja *nf* (**a**) *(cuchillo)* penknife, pocketknife; **n. de afeitar** razor (**b**) *(molusco)* razor-shell

naval *adj* naval

nave *nf* (**a**) ship; **n. (espacial)** spaceship, spacecraft (**b**) *Ind* plant, building (**c**) *(de iglesia)* nave; **n. lateral** aisle

navegable *adj* navigable

navegador *nm Informát* browser

navegar [42] *vi* (**a**) to navigate, to sail (**b**) *Av* to navigate, to fly (**c**) **n. por Internet** to surf the Net

Navidad(es) *nf(pl)* Christmas; **árbol de Navidad** Christmas tree; **Feliz Navidad, Felices Navidades** Merry Christmas

nazareno, -a 1 *adj & nm,f* Nazarene **2** *nm* = penitent in Holy Week processions; **el N.** Jesus of Nazareth

neblina *nf* mist, thin fog

necedad *nf* (**a**) *(estupidez)* stupidity, foolishness (**b**) *(tontería)* stupid thing to say *o* to do

necesario, -a *adj* necessary; **es n. hacerlo** it has to be done; **es n. que vayas** you must go; **no es n. que vayas** there is no need for you to go; **si fuera n.** if need be

neceser *nm (de aseo)* toilet bag; *(de maquillaje)* make-up bag

necesidad *nf* (**a**) necessity, need; **artículos de primera n.** essentials; **por n.** of necessity; **tener n. de** to need (**b**) *(pobreza)* poverty, hardship (**c**) **hacer sus necesidades** to relieve oneself

necesitar *vt* to need; **se necesita chico** *(en anuncios)* boy wanted

necio, -a 1 *adj* (**a**) *(tonto)* silly, stupid (**b**) *Am (terco)* stubborn, pigheaded (**c**) *Méx (susceptible)* touchy **2** *nm,f* (**a**) *(tonto)* fool, idiot (**b**) *Am (terco)* stubborn *o* pigheaded person (**c**) *Méx (susceptible)* touchy person; **es un n.** he's really touchy

nécora *nf* = small edible crab

necrológica *nm,f* obituary; **necrológicas** *(sección de periódico)* obituaries, obituary column

necrológico, -a *adj* **nota necrológica** obituary

negación *nf* (**a**) negation (**b**) *(negativa)* denial; *(rechazo)* refusal (**c**) *Ling* negative

negado, -a 1 *adj* **ser n. para algo** to be hopeless *o* useless at sth **2** *nm,f* no-hoper

negar [1] **1** *vt* (**a**) to deny; **negó haberlo robado** he denied stealing it (**b**) *(rechazar)* to refuse, to deny; **le negaron la beca** they refused him the grant **2 negarse** *vpr* to refuse (**a** to)

negativa *nf* denial

negativo, -a *adj & nm* negative

negociable adj negotiable

negociación nf negotiation

negociado nm Andes, RP (chanchullo) shady deal

negociador, -a adj negotiating; **comité n.** negotiating committee

negociar [43] **1** vt Fin, Pol to negotiate **2** vi (comerciar) to do business, to deal

negocio nm Com, Fin business; (transacción) deal, transaction; (asunto) affair; **hombre de negocios** businessman; **mujer de negocios** businesswoman

negro, -a 1 adj (a) black; **estar n.** (bronceado) to be suntanned (b) Fig (suerte) awful; (desesperado) desperate; (furioso) furious; **verlo todo n.** to be very pessimistic; **vérselas negras para hacer algo** to have a tough time doing sth **2** nm,f (de raza negra) black man, f black woman **3** nm (color) black

nene, -a nm,f baby boy, f baby girl

nenúfar nm Bot waterlily

nervio nm (a) Anat, Bot nerve; (de la carne) sinew (b) Fig (fuerza, vigor) nerve, courage (c) **nervios** nerves; **ataque de nervios** fit of hysterics; **ser un manojo de nervios** to be a bundle of nerves; **tener los nervios de acero** to have nerves of steel

nerviosismo nm nerves

nervioso, -a adj nervous; **poner n. a algn** to get on sb's nerves

neto, -a adj (a) (peso, cantidad) net (b) (nítido) neat, clear

neumático, -a 1 adj pneumatic **2** nm tyre; **n. de recambio** spare tyre

neurosis nf inv neurosis

neutral adj neutral

neutro, -a adj (a) (imparcial) neutral (b) Ling neuter

nevada nf snowfall

nevar [1] v impers to snow

nevera nf (a) (frigorífico) refrigerator, Br fridge, US icebox (b) (portátil) cool box

ni conj (a) **no ... ni, ni ... ni** neither ... nor, not ... or; **no tengo tiempo ni dinero** I have got neither time nor money; **ni ha venido ni ha llamado** he hasn't come or phoned; **no vengas ni hoy ni mañana** don't come today or tomorrow (b) (ni siquiera) not even; **ni por dinero** not even for money; **ni se te ocurra** don't even think about it; **¡ni hablar!** no way!

Nicaragua n Nicaragua

nicaragüense adj & nmf Nicaraguan

nicho nm niche

nido nm nest

niebla nf fog; **hay mucha n.** it is very foggy

nieto, -a nm,f grandson, f granddaughter; **mis nietos** my grandchildren

nieve nf (a) Met snow; Culin **a punto de n.** (beaten) stiff (b) Fam (cocaína) snow (c) Carib, Méx (dulce) sorbet

ninguno, -a 1 adj (a) (con verbo) not ... any; **no leí ninguna revista** I didn't read any magazines; **no tiene ninguna gracia** it is not funny at all (b) **en ninguna parte** nowhere; **de ningún modo** no way

> **ningún** is used instead of **ninguno** before masculine singular nouns (e.g. **ningún hombre** no man)

2 pron (a) (persona) nobody, no one; **n. lo vio** no one saw it; **n. de los dos** neither of the two; **n. de ellos** none of them (b) (cosa) not ... any of them; (enfático) none of them; **me gusta n.** I don't like any of them; **no vi n.** I saw none of them

niña nf (a) girl; ver **niño, -a** (b) Anat pupil; Fig **es la n. de sus ojos** she's the apple of his eye

niñera nf nursemaid, nanny

niñez nf infancy; (a partir de los cuatro años) childhood

niño, -a nm,f (a) child; (muchacho) (small) boy; (muchacha) (little) girl; **de n.** as a child; **n. prodigio** child prodigy; Pey **n. bien** o **de papá** rich boy, rich kid; Pey **n. bonito** o **mimado** mummy's/daddy's boy (b) (bebé) baby (c) **niños** children; Fig **juego de ni-**

ños child's play (**d**) *Met* el N. el Niño

níquel *nm* nickel

níspero *nm (fruto)* medlar; *(árbol)* medlar tree

nítido, -a *adj (claro)* clear; *(imagen)* sharp

nitrógeno *nm* nitrogen

nivel *nm* (**a**) *(altura)* level; **a n. del mar** at sea level (**b**) *(categoría)* standard; **n. de vida** standard of living (**c**) *(instrumento)* level; **n. de aire** spirit level (**d**) *Ferroc* **paso a n.** *Br* level crossing, *US* grade crossing

no 1 *adv* (**a**) *(como respuesta)* no; **¿te gusta? – no** do you like it? – no (**b**) *(en otros contextos)* not; **no vi a nadie** I didn't see anyone; **aún no** not yet; **ya no** no longer, not any more; **¿por qué no?** why not?

(**c**) **no fumar/aparcar** *(en letrero)* no smoking/parking

(**d**) **no sea que** *(+ subjuntivo)* in case

(**e**) **es rubia, ¿no?** she's blonde, isn't she?; **llegaron anoche, ¿no?** they arrived yesterday, didn't they?

(**f**) *(como prefijo negativo)* non; **la no violencia** non-violence

2 *nm (pl* **noes***)* no; **un no rotundo** a definite no

noble 1 *adj* noble **2** *nmf (hombre)* nobleman; *(mujer)* noblewoman; **los nobles** the nobility

nobleza *nf* nobility

noche *nf* evening; *(después de las diez)* night, night-time; **de n.**, *Esp* **por la n.**, *Am* **en la n.** at night; **esta n.** tonight; **mañana por la n.** tomorrow night *o* evening; **buenas noches** *(saludo)* good evening; *(despedida)* good night; **son las nueve de la n.** it's nine p.m.

nochebuena *nf* Christmas Eve

nochero *nm* (**a**) *CSur (vigilante)* night watchman (**b**) *Col (mesilla de noche)* bedside table

nochevieja *nf* New Year's Eve

noción *nf* (**a**) notion, idea (**b**) **nociones** smattering, basic knowledge; **nociones de español** a smattering of Spanish

nocivo, -a *adj* noxious, harmful

noctámbulo, -a *nm,f* sleepwalker; *Fam* nightbird

nocturno, -a *adj* (**a**) night; **vida nocturna** night life; **clases nocturnas** evening classes (**b**) *Bot, Zool* nocturnal

nogal *nm Bot* walnut (tree)

nómada 1 *adj* nomadic **2** *nmf* nomad

nombrar *vt* (**a**) *(designar)* to name, to appoint; **n. a algn director** to appoint sb director (**b**) *(mencionar)* to name, to mention

nombre *nm* (**a**) name; **n. de pila** Christian name; **n. y apellidos** full name; *Informát* **n. de dominio** domain name; **a n. de** addressed to; **en n. de** on behalf of (**b**) *Ling* noun; **n. propio** proper noun

nomeolvides *nm inv* (**a**) *(flor)* forget-me-not (**b**) *(pulsera)* identity bracelet

nómina *nf* (**a**) *(de sueldo)* pay slip (**b**) *(plantilla)* payroll

nórdico, -a 1 *adj* (**a**) *(del norte)* northern (**b**) *(escandinavo)* Nordic **2** *nm,f* Nordic person

noreste *nm* northeast

noria *nf* (**a**) *Esp (de feria)* *Br* big wheel, *US* Ferris wheel (**b**) *(para agua)* water wheel

norma *nf* norm; **n. de seguridad** safety standard

normal *adj* normal, usual; **lo n.** the normal thing, what usually happens

noroeste *nm* northwest

norte *nm* (**a**) north; **al n. de** to the north of (**b**) *Fig* aim, goal

Norteamérica *n* North America

norteamericano, -a *adj & nm,f* (North) American

Noruega *n* Norway

noruego, -a 1 *adj & nm,f* Norwegian **2** *nm (idioma)* Norwegian

nos 1 *pron pers (directo)* us; *(indirecto)* (to) us; **n. ha visto** he has seen us; **n. trajo un regalo** he brought us a present; **n. lo dio** he gave it to us **2** *pron (reflexivo)* ourselves; *(recíproco)* each other; **n. hemos divertido mucho** we enjoyed ourselves a lot; **n.**

queremos mucho we love each other very much

nosotros, -as *pron pers pl* (a) *(sujeto)* we; **n. lo vimos** we saw it; **somos n.** it is us (b) *(complemento)* us; **con n.** with us

> Usually omitted in Spanish except for emphasis or contrast

nostalgia *nf* nostalgia; *(morriña)* homesickness

nostálgico, -a *adj* nostalgic; *(con morriña)* homesick

nota *nf* (a) *(anotación)* note (b) *(calificación)* mark, grade; **sacar** *o* **tener buenas notas** to get good marks (c) *Fig (detalle)* element, quality; **la n. dominante** the prevailing quality (d) *Mús* note; *Fam* **dar la n.** to make oneself noticed

notable 1 *adj (apreciable)* noticeable; *(destacado)* outstanding, remarkable **2** *nm (nota)* very good

notar *vt (percibir)* to notice, to note **2 notarse** *vpr* to be noticeable *o* evident, to show; **no se nota** it doesn't show; **se nota que ...** one can see that ...

notario, -a *nm,f* notary (public), solicitor

noticia *nf* news *sing*; **una n.** a piece of news; **una buena n.** good news; **no tengo n. de esto** I don't know anything about it

noticiario, *Am* **noticiero** *nm* (a) *Cin* newsreel (b) *Rad, TV* television news

novatada *nf* (a) *(broma)* rough joke, rag (b) **pagar la n.** to learn the hard way

novato, -a 1 *adj (persona)* inexperienced; *Fam* green **2** *nm,f* (a) *(principiante)* novice, beginner (b) *Univ* fresher

novecientos, -as *adj & nm* nine hundred

novedad *nf* (a) *(cosa nueva)* novelty; **últimas novedades** latest arrivals (b) *(cambio)* change, development (c) *(cualidad)* newness

novela *nf Lit* novel; **n. corta** short

story; **n. policíaca** detective story

novelesco, -a *adj* (a) *(de novela)* novelistic, fictional (b) *(extraordinario)* bizarre, fantastic

novelista *nmf* novelist

noveno, -a *adj & nm* ninth; **la** *o* **una novena parte** a ninth

noventa *adj & nm inv* ninety

novia *nf* (a) *(amiga)* girlfriend (b) *(prometida)* fiancée (c) *(en boda)* bride

noviar *vi CSur, Méx Fam* **n. con algn** to go out with sb, *US* to date sb; **novian hace tiempo** they've been going out together *o US* dating for a while

noviazgo *nm* engagement

noviembre *nm* November

novillada *nf Taurom* = bullfight with young bulls

novillero, -a *nm,f Taurom* apprentice matador

novillo, -a *nm,f* (a) *(toro)* young bull; *(vaca)* young cow (b) *Esp Fam* **hacer novillos** to play *Br* truant *o US* hookey

novio *nm* (a) *(amigo)* boyfriend (b) *(prometido)* fiancé (c) *(en boda)* bridegroom; **los novios** the bride and groom

nubarrón *nm Fam* storm cloud

nube *nf* cloud; *Fig* **vivir en las nubes** to have one's head in the clouds; *Fig* **poner a algn por las nubes** to praise sb to the skies

nublado, -a *adj* cloudy, overcast

nublarse *vpr* to become cloudy, to cloud over; *Fig* **se le nubló la vista** his eyes clouded over

nubosidad *nf* cloudiness, clouds

nuboso, -a *adj* cloudy

nuca *nf* nape, back of the neck

nuclear *adj* nuclear; **central n.** nuclear power station

núcleo *nm* nucleus; *(parte central)* core; **n. urbano** city centre

nudillo *nm (usu pl)* knuckle

nudismo *nm* nudism

nudista *adj & nmf* nudist

nudo *nm* (a) knot; **hacer un n.** to tie a knot; *Fig* **se me hizo un n. en la**

garganta I got a lump in my throat (**b**) *(punto principal)* crux, core (**c**) *(de comunicaciones)* centre

nuera *nf* daughter-in-law

nuestro, -a 1 *adj pos* (**a**) our; **nuestra familia** our family (**b**) *(después del sustantivo)* of ours; **un amigo n.** a friend of ours **2** *pron pos* ours; **este libro es n.** this book is ours

Nueva Zelanda *n* New Zealand

nueve *adj & nm inv* nine

nuevo, -a 1 *adj* (**a**) new; *Fam* **¿qué hay de n.?** what's new?; **de n.** again; **Nueva York** New York; **Nueva Zelanda** New Zealand (**b**) *(adicional)* further **2** *nm,f* newcomer; *(principiante)* beginner

nuez *nf* (**a**) walnut; **n. moscada** nutmeg (**b**) *Anat* **n. (de Adán)** Adam's apple

nulidad *nf* (**a**) *(ineptitud)* incompetence (**b**) *Jur* nullity

nulo, -a *adj* (**a**) *(inepto)* useless, totally incapable (**b**) *(sin valor)* null and void, invalid; **voto n.** invalid vote (**c**) **crecimiento n.** zero growth

núm. *(abr* **número)** no

número *nm* (**a**) number; **n. de**

matrícula *Br* registration number, *US* license number; **n. de serie** serial number; *Fig* **sin n.** countless (**b**) *Prensa* number, issue; **n. atrasado** back number (**c**) *(de zapatos)* size (**d**) *(en espectáculo)* sketch, act; *Fam* **montar un n.** to make a scene

numeroso, -a *adj* numerous

numismática *nf* *(estudio)* numismatics *(sing)*

nunca *adv* (**a**) *(como respuesta)* never; **¿cuándo volverás? – n.** when will you come back? – never (**b**) *(con verbo)* never; *(enfático)* not ... ever; **no he estado n. en España** I've never been to Spain; **yo no haría n. eso** I wouldn't ever do that (**c**) *(en ciertas construcciones)* ever; **casi n.** hardly ever; **más que n.** more than ever

nupcial *adj* wedding, nuptial; **marcha n.** wedding march

nupcias *nfpl Fml* wedding, nuptials; **casarse en segundas n.** to marry again

nutria *nf* otter

nutrición *nf* nutrition

nutritivo, -a *adj* nutritious, nourishing; **valor n.** nutritional value

Ññ

ñapa *Ven Fam nf* bonus, extra

ñato, -a *adj Andes, RP* snub-nosed

ñoñería, ñoñez *nf* inanity

ñoño, -a *adj* (**a**) *(remilgado)* squeamish; *(quejica)* whining (**b**) *(soso)* dull, insipid

ñoqui *nm Culin* gnocchi

Oo

o *conj* or; **jueves o viernes** Thursday or Friday; **o … o** either … or; **o sea** that is (to say), in other words

> **u** is used instead of **o** in front of words beginning with "o" or "ho" (e.g. **mujer u hombre** woman or man). Note that **ó** (with acute accent) is used between figures

oasis *nm inv* oasis

obedecer [33] **1** *vt* to obey **2** *vi* **o. a** *(provenir)* to be due to; **¿a qué obedece esa actitud?** what's the reason behind this attitude?

obediencia *nf* obedience

obediente *adj* obedient

obesidad *nf* obesity

obeso, -a *adj* obese

obispo *nm* bishop

objeción *nf* objection; **poner una o.** to raise an objection, to object

objetar *vt* to object to

objetividad *nf* objectivity

objetivo, -a 1 *nm* (**a**) *(fin, meta)* objective, aim (**b**) *Mil* target (**c**) *Cin, Fot* lens; **o. zoom** zoom lens **2** *adj* objective

objeto *nm* (**a**) object; **objetos perdidos** lost property, *US* lost and found; **mujer o.** sex object (**b**) *(fin)* aim, purpose; **con o. de …** in order to …; **tiene por o. …** it is designed to … (**c**) *Ling* object

obligación *nf* (**a**) *(deber)* obligation; **por o.** out of a sense of duty; **tengo o. de …** I have to … (**b**) *Fin* bond, security

obligar [42] *vt* to compel, to force

obligatorio, -a *adj* compulsory, obligatory

obra *nf* (**a**) *(trabajo)* (piece of) work; **por o. de** thanks to (**b**) *Arte* work; **o.**

maestra masterpiece (**c**) *(acto)* deed (**d**) *Constr* building site (**e**) **obras** *(arreglos)* repairs; **carretera en obras** *(en letrero)* roadworks; **cerrado por obras** *(en letrero)* closed for repairs

obrero, -a 1 *nm,f* worker, labourer **2** *adj* working; **clase obrera** working class; **movimiento o.** labour movement

obscuridad = oscuridad

obscuro, -a = oscuro

obsequiar [43] *vt Esp* **o. a algn con algo,** *Am* **o. algo a algn** to present sb with sth

obsequio *nm* gift, present

observación *nf* observation

observador, -a 1 *nm,f* observer **2** *adj* observant

observar *vt* (**a**) *(mirar)* to observe, to watch (**b**) *(notar)* to notice (**c**) *(cumplir)* to observe

observatorio *nm* observatory

obsesión *nf* obsession

obsesionar 1 *vt* to obsess; **estoy obsesionado con eso** I can't get it out of my mind **2 obsesionarse** *vpr* to get obsessed

obstáculo *nm* obstacle

obstante *adv* **no o.** nevertheless, however

obstinado, -a *adj* obstinate

obstruir [37] **1** *vt* (**a**) *(salida, paso)* to block, to obstruct (**b**) *(progreso)* to impede, to block **2 obstruirse** *vpr* to get blocked up

obtener [24] **1** *vt (alcanzar)* to obtain, to get **2 obtenerse** *vpr* **obtenerse de** *(provenir)* to come from

obvio, -a *adj* obvious

oca *nf* goose

ocasión *nf* (**a**) *(momento)* occasion;

con o. de ... on the occasion of ...; **en cierta o.** once (**b**) *(oportunidad)* opportunity, chance; **aprovechar una o.** to make the most of an opportunity (**c**) *Com* bargain; **de o.** cheap; **precios de o.** bargain prices

ocasional *adj* (**a**) *(eventual)* occasional; **trabajo o.** casual work; **de forma o.** occasionally (**b**) *(fortuito)* accidental, chance

ocaso *nm (anochecer)* sunset; *Fig (declive)* fall, decline

occidental *adj* western, occidental

occidente *nm* west; **el O.** the West

océano *nm* ocean

ochenta *adj & nm inv* eighty

ocho *adj & nm inv* eight

ochocientos, -as *adj & nm* eight hundred

ocio *nm* leisure; **en mis ratos de o.** in my spare *o* leisure time

ocioso, -a *adj* (**a**) *(inactivo)* idle (**b**) *(inútil)* pointless

ocre *nm* ochre

octavo, -a *adj & nm,f* eighth

octubre *nm* October

oculista *nmf* ophthalmologist

ocultar 1 *vt* to conceal, to hide; **o. algo a algn** to hide sth from sb **2 ocultarse** *vpr* to hide

oculto, -a *adj* concealed, hidden

ocupación *nf* occupation

ocupado, -a *adj (persona)* busy; *(asiento)* taken; *(teléfono) Br* engaged, *US* busy; *(lavabo)* engaged; *(puesto de trabajo)* filled

ocupar 1 *vt* (**a**) to occupy (**b**) *(espacio, tiempo)* to take up; *(cargo)* to hold, fill (**c**) *CAm, Méx (usar, emplear)* to use **2 ocuparse** *vpr* **ocuparse de** *(cuidar)* to look after; *(encargarse)* to see to

ocurrir 1 *v impers* to happen, to occur; **¿qué ocurre?** what's going on?; **¿qué te ocurre?** what's the matter with you? **2 ocurrirse** *vpr* **no se me ocurre nada** I can't think of anything; **se me ocurre que ...** it occurs to me that ...

odiar [43] *vt* to detest, to hate; **odio**

tener que ... I hate having to ...

odio *nm* hatred, loathing; **mirada de o.** hateful look

oeste *nm* west

ofensiva *nf* offensive

oferta *nf* offer; *Fin, Ind* bid, tender, proposal; *Com* **de** *o* **en o.** on (special) offer; **o. y demanda** supply and demand

oficial 1 *adj* official **2** *nmf* (**a**) *Mil, Náut* officer (**b**) *(empleado)* clerk (**c**) *(obrero)* skilled worker

oficialismo *nm Am* (**a**) **el o.** *(gobierno)* the Government (**b**) **el o.** *(partidarios del gobierno)* government supporters

oficialista *Am* **1** *adj* pro-government **2** *nm,f* government supporter

oficina *nf* office; **o. de empleo** *Br* job centre, *US* job office; **o. de turismo** tourist office; **o. de correos** post office; **horas/horario de o.** business hours

oficinista *nmf* office worker, clerk

oficio *nm* (**a**) *(ocupación)* job, occupation; *(profesión)* trade; **ser del o.** to be in the trade (**b**) *(comunicación oficial)* official letter *o* note; **de o.** ex-officio; **abogado de o.** state-appointed lawyer (**c**) *Rel* service

ofrecer [33] **1** *vt* (**a**) to offer (**b**) *(aspecto)* to present **2 ofrecerse** *vpr* (**a**) *(prestarse)* to offer, to volunteer (**b**) *(situación)* to present itself (**c**) *Fml* **¿qué se le ofrece?** what can I do for you?

oftalmología *nf* ophthalmology

ogro *nm también Fig* ogre

oído *nm* (**a**) *(sentido)* hearing (**b**) *(órgano)* ear; **aprender de o.** to learn by ear; *Fig* **hacer oídos sordos** to turn a deaf ear

oír [17] *vt* to hear; **¡oye!** hey!; **¡oiga!** excuse me!; *Fam* **como lo oyes** believe it or not

ojal *nm* buttonhole

ojalá 1 *interj* let's hope so!, I hope so! **2** *conj* (+ *subjuntivo*) **¡o. sea cierto!** I hope it's true!

ojeras *nfpl* rings *o* bags under the eyes

ojo 1 *nm* (**a**) eye; **o. morado** black eye; **ojos saltones** bulging eyes; *Fig* **a ojos vista** clearly, openly; *Fig* **calcular a o.** to guess; *Fam* **no pegué o.** I didn't sleep a wink (**b**) *(de aguja)* eye; *(de cerradura)* keyhole (**c**) *(de un puente)* span **2** *interj* careful!, look out!

ojota *nf* (**a**) *Andes (zapatilla)* sandal (**b**) *RP (chancleta) Br* flip-flop, *US, Austr* thong

okupa *nmf Esp Fam* squatter

ola *nf* wave; **o. de calor** heat wave

ole, olé *interj* bravo!

oleaje *nm* swell

óleo *nm Arte* oil; **pintura** *o* **cuadro al ó.** oil painting

oler [65] **1** *vt* (**a**) *(percibir olor)* to smell (**b**) *Fig (adivinar)* to smell, to feel
2 *vi* (**a**) *(exhalar)* to smell; **o. a** to smell of; **o. bien/mal** to smell good/bad (**b**) *Fig (parecer)* to smack (**a** of)
3 olerse *vpr Fig (adivinar)* to feel, to sense; **me lo olía** I thought as much

olfato *nm* sense of smell; *Fig* good nose, instinct

olimpiada *nf Dep* Olympiad, Olympic Games; **las olimpiadas** the Olympic Games

olímpico, -a *adj* Olympic; **Juegos Olímpicos** Olympic Games

oliva *nf* olive; **aceite de o.** olive oil

olivo *nm* olive (tree)

olla *nf* saucepan, pot; **o. exprés** *o* **a presión** pressure cooker

olmo *nm* smooth-leaved elm

olor *nm* smell; **o. corporal** body odour

olvidar 1 *vt* (**a**) to forget; *Fam* **¡olvídame!** leave me alone! (**b**) **olvidé el paraguas allí** I left my umbrella there **2 olvidarse** *vpr* to forget; **se me ha olvidado hacerlo** I forgot to do it

olvido *nm* (**a**) *(desmemoria)* oblivion (**b**) *(lapsus)* oversight

ombligo *nm* navel

omitir *vt* to omit, to leave out

ómnibus *nm* (*pl* **ómnibus** *o* **omnibuses**) *Cuba, Urug (urbano)* bus; *Andes, Cuba, Urug (interurbano, internacional) Br* coach, *US* bus

ONCE *nf (abr* **Organización Nacional de Ciegos Españoles**) ≃ RNIB

once *adj & nm inv* eleven

onda *nf* (**a**) *Fís* wave; *Fam Fig* **estar en la o.** to be with it; **o. expansiva** shock wave; *Rad* **o. larga/media/corta** long/medium/short wave (**b**) *(en el agua)* ripple (**c**) *(de pelo)* wave (**d**) *Méx, RP* **¿qué o.?** *(¿qué tal?)* how's it going?, how are things?; **captar** *o* **agarrar la onda** *(entender)* to catch the drift

ondulado, -a *adj (pelo)* wavy; *(paisaje)* rolling

ONU *nf (abr* **Organización de las Naciones Unidas**) UN(O)

opaco, -a *adj* opaque

opción *nf* (**a**) *(elección)* option, choice; *(alternativa)* alternative (**b**) *(posibilidad)* opportunity, chance

ópera *nf Mús* opera

operación *nf* (**a**) *Med* operation; **o. quirúrgica** surgical operation (**b**) *Fin* transaction, deal; **operaciones bursátiles** stock exchange transactions (**c**) *Mat* operation

operador, -a *nm,f* (**a**) *(técnico)* operator (**b**) *Cin (de cámara)* cameraman, *f* camerawoman; *(del proyector)* projectionist (**c**) *Tel* operator

operar 1 *vt* (**a**) *Med* **o. a algn (de algo)** to operate on sb (for sth) (**b**) *(cambio etc)* to bring about
2 *vi Fin* to deal, to do business (**con** with)
3 operarse *vpr* (**a**) *Med* to have an operation (**de** for) (**b**) *(producirse)* to occur, to come about

operario, -a *nm,f* operator; *(obrero)* worker

opinar *vi* (**a**) *(pensar)* to think (**b**) *(declarar)* to give one's opinion, to be of the opinion

opinión *nf (juicio)* opinion; **cambiar de o.** to change one's mind

oponer [19] (*pp* **opuesto**) **1** *vt* *(resistencia)* to offer **2 oponerse** *vpr* *(estar en contra)* to be opposed; **se opone a aceptarlo** he refuses to accept it

oportunidad *nf* opportunity, chance

oportuno, -a *adj* (**a**) *(adecuado)* timely; **¡qué o.!** what good timing! (**b**) *(conveniente)* appropriate; **si te parece o.** if you think it appropriate

oposición *nf* (**a**) opposition (**b**) *(examen)* competitive examination

oprimir *vt* (**a**) *(pulsar)* to press (**b**) *(subyugar)* to oppress

optar *vi* (**a**) *(elegir)* to choose (**entre** between); **opté por ir yo mismo** I decided to go myself (**b**) *(aspirar)* to apply (**a** for); **puede o. a medalla** he's in with a chance of winning a medal

optativo, -a *adj* optional, *US* elective

óptica *nf* (**a**) *(tienda)* optician's (shop) (**b**) *(punto de vista)* angle

optimismo *nm* optimism

optimista **1** *adj* optimistic **2** *nmf* optimist

óptimo, -a *adj* optimum, excellent

opuesto, -a *adj* (**a**) *(contrario)* contrary; **en direcciones opuestas** in opposite directions; **gustos opuestos** conflicting tastes (**b**) *(de enfrente)* opposite; **el extremo o.** the other end

oración *nf* (**a**) *Rel* prayer (**b**) *Ling* clause, sentence

orador, -a *nm,f* speaker, orator

oral *adj* oral; *Med* **por vía o.** to be taken orally

órale *interj Méx Fam* (**a**) *(venga)* come on! (**b**) *(de acuerdo)* right!, OK!

orangután *nm* orang-outang, orangutan

oratoria *nf* oratory

órbita *nf* (**a**) orbit (**b**) *Anat* eye socket

orca *nf* killer whale

orden **1** *nm* order; **o. público** law and order; **por o. alfabético** in alphabetical order; **de primer o.** first-rate; **o. del día** agenda; **del o. de** approximately **2** *nf* (**a**) *(mandato)* order; *Mil* **¡a la o.!** sir! (**b**) *Jur* warrant, order; **o. de registro** search warrant; **o. judicial** court order

ordenado, -a *adj* tidy

ordenador *nm Esp* computer; **o. personal** personal computer

ordenar **1** *vt* (**a**) *(organizar)* to put in order; *(habitación)* to tidy up (**b**) *(mandar)* to order (**c**) *Am (pedir)* to order **2** **ordenarse** *vpr Rel* to be ordained (**de** as), to take holy orders

ordeñar *vt* to milk

ordinario, -a *adj* (**a**) *(corriente)* ordinary, common (**b**) *(grosero)* vulgar, common

orégano *nm* oregano

oreja *nf* ear; *(de sillón)* wing

orgánico, -a *adj* organic

organillo *nm* barrel organ

organismo *nm* (**a**) *(ser vivo)* organism (**b**) *(institución)* organization, body

organización *nf* organization

organizador, -a **1** *adj* organizing **2** *nm,f* organizer

organizar [40] **1** *vt* to organize **2** **organizarse** *vpr (persona)* to organize oneself

órgano *nm* organ

orgullo *nm* (**a**) *(propia estima)* pride (**b**) *(arrogancia)* arrogance

orgulloso, -a *adj* (**a**) **estar o.** *(satisfecho)* to be proud (**b**) **ser o.** *(arrogante)* to be arrogant *o* haughty

oriental **1** *adj* (**a**) *(del este)* eastern, oriental; *(del Lejano Oriente)* oriental (**b**) *Am (uruguayo)* Uruguayan **2** *nmf* (**a**) *(del Lejano Oriente)* oriental (**b**) *Am (uruguayo)* Uruguayan

orientar **1** *vt* (**a**) *(enfocar)* to aim (**a** at), to intend (**a** for); **orientado al consumo** intended for consumption (**b**) *(indicar camino)* to give directions to; *Fig (aconsejar)* to advise (**c**) **una casa orientada al sur** a house facing south (**d**) *(esfuerzo)* to direct **2** **orientarse** *vpr (encontrar el camino)* to get one's bearings, to find one's way about

oriente *nm* East, Orient; **el Extremo** *o* **Lejano/Medio/Próximo O.** the Far/Middle/Near East

orificio *nm* hole, opening; *Anat, Téc* orifice; **o. de entrada** inlet; **o. de salida** outlet

origen *nm* origin; **país de o.** country

of origin; **dar o. a** to give rise to

original *adj & nm* original

originario, -a *adj* native

orilla *nf (borde)* edge; *(del río)* bank; *(del mar)* shore

orillero, -a *adj RP, Ven* common, low-class

orina *nf* urine

orinal *nm* chamberpot; *Fam* potty

orinar 1 *vi* to urinate **2 orinarse** *vpr* to wet oneself

oro *nm* (a) gold; **de o.** gold, golden; **o. de ley** fine gold (b) *Naipes* **oros** *(baraja española)* = suit in Spanish deck of cards, with the symbol of a gold coin

orquesta *nf* orchestra; *(de verbena)* dance band

orquestar *vt* to orchestrate

orquídea *nf* orchid

ortiga *nf* (stinging) nettle

ortodoxo, -a *adj* orthodox

oruga *nf* caterpillar

os *pron pers pl* (a) *(complemento directo)* you; **os veo mañana** I'll see you tomorrow (b) *(complemento indirecto)* you, to you; **os daré el dinero** I'll give you the money; **os escribiré** I'll write to you (c) *(con verbo reflexivo)* yourselves (d) *(con verbo recíproco)* each other; **os queréis mucho** you love each other very much

oscilar *vi* (a) *Fís* to oscillate (b) *(variar)* to vary, to fluctuate

oscuridad *nf* darkness; *Fig* obscurity

oscuro, -a *adj* (a) dark (b) *(origen, idea)* obscure; *(asunto)* shady; *(nublado)* overcast

oso *nm* bear; **o. polar** polar bear; **o. hormiguero** anteater; **o. marino** fur seal; *Fam Fig* **hacer el o.** to play the fool

ostión *nm* (a) *Méx (ostra)* Portuguese oyster, Pacific oyster (b) *Chile (vieira)* scallop

ostra *nf* oyster; *Fig* **aburrirse como una o.** to be bored stiff; *Esp Fam* **¡ostras!** *Br* crikey!, *US* gee!

OTAN *nf (abr* **Organización del Tratado del Atlántico Norte)** NATO

otoño *nm* autumn, *US* fall

otorrino, -a *nm,f Fam* ear, nose and throat specialist

otorrinolaringólogo, -a *nm,f* ear, nose and throat specialist

otro, -a 1 *adj indef* (a) *(sin artículo) (sing)* another; *(pl)* other; **o. coche** another car; **otras personas** other people *(pl)* *(con artículo definido)* other; **el o. coche** the other car (c) **otra cosa** something else; **otra vez** again

2 *pron indef* (a) *(sin artículo) (sing)* another (one); *(pl) (personas)* others; *(cosas)* other ones; **dame o.** give me another (one); **no es mío, es de o.** it's not mine, it's somebody else's (b) *(con artículo definido) (sing)* **el o./la otra** the other (one); *(pl) (personas)* **los otros/las otras** the others; *(cosas)* the other ones

ovalado, -a *adj* oval

ovario *nm* ovary

oveja *nf* sheep; *(hembra)* ewe; *Fig* **la o. negra** the black sheep

overol *nm Am (de peto) Br* dungarees, *US* overalls; *(completo)* overalls, *Br* boiler suit

OVNI *nm (abr* **objeto volador no identificado)** UFO

óxido *nm* (a) oxide; **ó. de carbono** carbon monoxide (b) *(orín)* rust

oxígeno *nm* oxygen; **bomba de o.** oxygen cylinder o tank

oyente *nmf* (a) *Rad* listener (b) *Univ Br* occasional student, *US* auditing student

ozono *nm* ozone; **capa de o.** ozone layer

Pp

pabellón *nm* (a) **p. de deportes** sports centre (b) *(en feria)* stand (c) *(bloque)* wing (d) *(bandera)* flag

pacer [60] *vt & vi* to graze, to pasture

pacharán *nm* = liqueur made from brandy and sloes

paciencia *nf* patience; **armarse de p.** to grin and bear it

paciente *adj & nmf* patient

pacificación *nf* pacification

pacífico, -a *adj* peaceful

pacifismo *nm* pacifism

pacifista *adj & nmf* pacifist

pack [pak] *nm* (*pl* **packs**) pack; **un p. de seis** a six-pack

paco, -a *nm,f Andes, Pan Fam (policía)* cop

pacto *nm* pact; **el P. de Varsovia** the Warsaw Pact; **p. de caballeros** gentlemen's agreement

padecer [33] *vt & vi* to suffer; **padece del corazón** he suffers from heart trouble

padrastro *nm* (a) stepfather (b) *(pellejo)* hangnail

padre 1 *nm* (a) father; **p. de familia** family man (b) **padres** parents **2** *adj Fam* (a) *Esp (tremendo)* huge; **fue el cachondeo p.** it was a great laugh (b) *Méx (genial)* great, fantastic

padrino *nm* (a) *(de bautizo)* godfather; *(de boda)* best man; **padrinos** godparents (b) *(espónsor)* sponsor

padrísimo, -a *adj Méx Fam* fantastic, great

padrote *nm* (a) *Méx Fam (proxeneta)* pimp (b) *CAm, Ven (caballo)* stallion

paella *nf* paella, = rice dish made with vegetables, meat and/or seafood

pág. *(abr* **página**) p

paga *nf (salario)* wage; *(de niños)* pocket money; **p. extra** bonus

pagadero, -a *adj* payable; *Fin* **cheque p. al portador** cheque payable to bearer

pagado, -a *adj* paid

pagano, -a *adj & nm,f* pagan, heathen

pagar [42] *vt* (a) to pay; **p. en metálico** *o* **al contado** to pay cash; **p. por** *(producto, mala acción)* to pay for; *Fig* **(ella) lo ha pagado caro** she's paid dearly for it (b) *(recompensar)* to repay

página *nf* page; **en la p. 3** on page 3; *Fig* **una p. importante de la historia** an important chapter in history; *Informát* **p. personal** home page; *Informát* **p. de inicio** home page; *Informát* **p. web** web page

pago *nm* payment; **p. adelantado** *o* **anticipado** advance payment; **p. contra reembolso** cash on delivery; **p. inicial** down payment; **p. por visión** pay-per-view

paila *nf Andes, CAm, Carib (sartén)* frying pan

país *nm* country, land; **vino del p.** local wine; **los Países Bajos** the Netherlands; **P. Vasco** Basque Country; **P. Valenciano** Valencia

paisaje *nm* landscape, scenery

paisano, -a 1 *adj* of the same country **2** *nm,f (compatriota)* fellow countryman/countrywoman, compatriot; **en traje de p.** in plain clothes

paja *nf* (a) straw (b) *Fam Fig (bazofia)* padding, waffle (c) *Vulg* **hacerse una** *o Am* **la p.** to jerk off, *Br* to have a wank

pajarita *nf* (a) *Esp (corbata)* bow tie (b) *(de papel)* paper bird

pájaro *nm* (a) bird; **Madrid a vista de p.** a bird's-eye view of Madrid; **p. carpintero** woodpecker (b) *Fam* **tener pájaros** to have daft ideas

paje nm page

pala nf (**a**) shovel; (de jardinero) spade; (de cocina) slice (**b**) Dep (de ping-pong, frontón) bat, US paddle; (de remo) blade

palabra nf (**a**) word; **de p.** by word of mouth; **dirigir la p. a algn** to address sb; **juego de palabras** pun (**b**) (promesa) word; **p. de honor** word of honour (**c**) (turno para hablar) right to speak; **tener la p.** to have the floor

palacio nm (grande) palace; (pequeño) mansion; **P. de Justicia** Law Courts

paladar nm (**a**) palate (**b**) (sabor) taste

paladear vt to savour, to relish

palanca nf (**a**) lever (**b**) (manecilla) handle, stick; Aut **p. de cambio** Br gear lever, gearstick, US gearshift, stick shift; **p. de mando** joystick (**c**) (trampolín) diving board

palangana nf Br washbasin, US washbowl

palco nm box

paleta nf (**a**) (espátula) slice (**b**) (de pintor) palette; (de albañil) trowel (**c**) Dep (de ping-pong) bat (**d**) Andes, CAm, Méx (piruli) lollipop; Bol, Col, Perú (polo) Br ice lolly, US Popsicle®

paletilla nf (**a**) shoulder blade (**b**) Culin shoulder

pálido, -a adj pale

palillo nm (**a**) (mondadientes) toothpick; **palillos chinos** chopsticks (**b**) Mús drumstick

paliza nf (**a**) (zurra) thrashing, beating; **darle a algn una p.** to beat sb up (**b**) (derrota) beating (**c**) Fam (pesadez) bore, pain (in the neck)

palma nf (**a**) Anat palm (**b**) Bot palm tree (**c**) **hacer palmas** to applaud

palmada nf (**a**) (golpe) slap (**b**) **palmadas** applause, clapping

palmera nf palm tree

palo nm (**a**) stick; (vara) rod; (de escoba) broomstick; Fig **a p. seco** on its own (**b**) (golpe) blow; Fig **dar un p. a algn** to let sb down (**c**) **de p.** wooden (**d**) Dep (de portería) woodwork (**e**) (de golf) club (**f**) Naipes suit

paloma nf pigeon; Literario dove; **p. mensajera** homing o carrier pigeon

palomar nm pigeon house, dovecot

palomitas (de maíz) nfpl popcorn

palpitar vi to palpitate, to throb

palta nf Andes, RP (fruto) avocado

pamela nf broad-brimmed hat

pampa nf pampa, pampas

pan nm bread; **p. de molde** loaf of bread; **p. integral** Br wholemeal o US wholewheat bread; **p. rallado** breadcrumbs pl; **p. dulce** Méx (bollo) bun; RP (panetone) panettone; Arg **p. lactal** sliced bread; Fam Fig **más bueno que el p.** as good as gold; Fam Fig **es p. comido** it's a piece of cake

panadería nf baker's (shop), bakery

panadero, -a nm,f baker

panal nm honeycomb

Panamá n Panama

panameño, -a adj & nm,f Panamanian

pancarta nf placard; (en manifestación) banner

pancho nm RP (perrito caliente) hot dog

panda 1 adj **oso p.** panda
  2 nm panda
  3 nf Esp (de amigos) crowd, gang; (de gamberros, delincuentes) gang

pandereta nf tambourine

pandilla nf Fam gang

panel nm panel

panera nf (para guardar) Br bread bin, US bread box; (para servir) bread basket

pánico nm panic; **sembrar el p.** to cause panic

panorama nm (vista) panorama, view; Fig panorama

panorámica nf panorama

panorámico, -a adj panoramic

panqueque nm Am pancake

pantaleta nf, **pantaletas** nfpl CAm, Carib, Méx (bragas) panties, Br knickers

pantalla nf (**a**) Cin, TV, Informát screen (**b**) (de lámpara) shade (**c**) Fig **servir de p.** to act as a decoy

pantalón nm (usu pl) trousers, US pants; **p. vaquero** jeans

pantano *nm Geog* (a) *(natural)* marsh, bog (b) *(artificial)* reservoir

pantera *nf* panther

pantimedias *nfpl Méx Br* tights, *US* pantyhose

pantorrilla *nf Anat* calf

pantry *nm Ven (comedor diario)* = family dining area off kitchen

pants *nmpl Méx (traje)* tracksuit, jogging suit; *(pantalón)* tracksuit bottoms *o US* pants

panty *nm (pl* **pantis** *o* **pantys**) *Br* tights, *US* pantyhose

pañal *nm Br* nappy, *US* diaper; *Fam Fig* **estar en pañales** to be in its infancy

paño *nm* (a) cloth, material; *(de lana)* woollen cloth; *(para polvo)* duster, rag; *(de cocina)* dishcloth; *Fig* **paños calientes** half-measures (b) **paños** *(ropa)* clothes; **en paños menores** in one's underclothes

pañuelo *nm* handkerchief; *(pañoleta)* shawl

Papa *nm* el P. the Pope

papa *nf esp Am* potato; *Fam* **no saber ni p. (de algo)** not to have the faintest idea (about sth)

papá *nm Fam* dad, daddy, *US* pop

papachar *vt Méx* to cuddle, to pamper

papagayo *nm* (a) *(animal)* parrot (b) *Carib, Méx (cometa)* kite

papalote *nm CAm, Méx* kite

papel *nm* (a) paper; *(hoja)* piece *o* sheet of paper; **papeles** *(documentos)* documents, identification papers; **p. higiénico** toilet paper; *Chile* **p. confort** toilet paper; **p. de aluminio/de estraza** aluminium foil/brown paper; **p. de fumar** cigarette paper; **p. de lija** sandpaper; *Fin* **p. moneda** paper money, banknotes *pl*; **p. pintado** wallpaper; *Guat, Ven* **p. toilette** *o* **tualé** toilet paper (b) *Cin, Teatro* role, part

papeleo *nm Fam* paperwork

papelera *nf* (a) *(en despacho)* wastepaper basket *o Br* bin; *(en calle)* litter bin (b) *Informát (en Windows)* recycle bin; *(en Macintosh) Br* wastebasket, *US* trash can

papelería *nf (tienda)* stationer's (shop)

papeleta *nf* (a) *(de rifa)* ticket; *(de votación)* ballot paper; *(de resultados)* report (b) *Fam (dificultad)* tricky problem, difficult job

paperas *nfpl Med* mumps *sing*

papilla *nf (de niños)* baby food, *US* formula

paquete *nm* (a) *(de cigarrillos etc)* packet; *(postal)* parcel, package (b) *(conjunto)* set, package; *Fin* **p. de acciones** share package (c) *Informát* software package (d) *Fam (castigo)* punishment (e) *Esp muy Fam (genitales)* packet, bulge

Paquistán *n* Pakistan

paquistaní *adj & nmf (pl* **paquistaníes**) Pakistani

par 1 *adj Mat* even **2** *nm* (a) *(pareja)* pair; *(dos)* couple (b) *Mat* even number; **pares y nones** odds and evens (c) *(noble)* peer (d) *(locuciones)* **a la p.** *(a la vez)* at the same time; **de p. en p.** wide open; *Fig* **sin p.** matchless

para *prep* (a) for; **bueno p. la salud** good for your health; **¿p. qué?** what for?; **p. ser inglés habla muy bien español** for an Englishman he speaks very good Spanish

(b) *(finalidad)* to, in order to; **p. terminar antes** to *o* in order to finish earlier; **p. que lo disfrutes** for you to enjoy

(c) *(tiempo)* by; **p. entonces** by then

(d) *(a punto de)* **está p. salir** it's about to leave

(e) *(locuciones)* **decir p. sí** to say to oneself; **ir p. viejo** to be getting old; **no es p. tanto** it's not as bad as all that; **p. mí** in my opinion

parabólica *nf* satellite dish

parabrisas *nm inv Br* windscreen, *US* windshield

paracaídas *nm inv* parachute

parachoques *nm inv* bumper, *US* fender

parada *nf* (a) stop; **p. de autobús** bus stop; **p. de taxis** taxi stand *o* rank (b) *Ftb* save, stop

paradero *nm* (**a**) *(lugar)* whereabouts sing (**b**) *Chile, Col, Méx, Perú (de autobús)* stop

parado, -a 1 *adj* (**a**) stopped, stationary; *(quieto)* still; *(fábrica)* at a standstill; *Fig* **salir bien/mal p.** to come off well/badly (**b**) *Esp (desempleado)* unemployed, out of work (**c**) *Fig (lento)* slow (**d**) *Am (en pie)* standing (**e**) *Chile, PRico (orgulloso)* vain, conceited **2** *nm,f Esp* unemployed person

paradoja *nf* paradox

paradójico, -a *adj* paradoxical

parador *nm* roadside inn; **p. (nacional)** = state-owned luxury hotel, usually a building of historic or artistic importance

paragolpes *nmpl inv RP* bumper, *US* fender

paraguas *nm inv* umbrella

Paraguay *n* Paraguay

paraguayo, -a 1 *adj & nm,f* Paraguayan **2** *nm (fruta)* = fruit similar to peach

paraíso *nm* (**a**) paradise; **p. terrenal** heaven on earth; *Fin* **p. fiscal** tax haven (**b**) *Teatro* gods, gallery

paraje *nm* spot, place

paralelo, -a *adj & nm* parallel

parálisis *nf inv* paralysis; **p. infantil** poliomyelitis

paralítico, -a *adj & nm,f* paralytic

paralizar [40] **1** *vt* to paralyse; *(circulación)* to stop **2 paralizarse** *vpr Fig* to come to a standstill

parapente *nm (desde montaña)* paragliding, parapenting

parar 1 *vt* (**a**) to stop (**b**) *Dep* to save (**c**) *Am (levantar)* to raise

2 *vi* (**a**) to stop; **p. de hacer algo** to stop doing sth; **sin p.** nonstop, without stopping; *Fam* **no p.** to be always on the go (**b**) *(alojarse)* to stay (**c**) *(acabar)* **fue a p. a la cárcel** he ended up in jail

3 pararse *vt* (**a**) to stop; **p. a pensar** to stop to think (**b**) *Am (ponerse en pie)* to stand up

pararrayos *nm inv* lightning rod *o* conductor

parasol *nm* sunshade, parasol

parchís *nm Br* ludo, *US* Parcheesi®

parcial 1 *adj* (**a**) *(partidario)* biased (**b**) *(no completo)* partial; **a tiempo p.** part-time **2** *nm* **(examen) p.** class examination

pardo, -a *adj (marrón)* brown; *(gris)* dark grey

parecer¹ *nm* (**a**) *(opinión)* opinion (**b**) *(aspecto)* appearance

parecer² [33] **1** *vi* to seem, to look (like); **parece difícil** it seems *o* looks difficult; **parecía (de) cera** it looked like wax; *(uso impers)* **parece que no arranca** it looks as if it won't start; **como te parezca** whatever you like; **parece que sí/no** I think/don't think so; **¿qué te parece?** what do you think of it?

2 parecerse (**a**) *vpr* to be alike; **no se parecen** they're not alike (**b**) **parecerse a** to look like, to resemble; **se parecen a su madre** they look like their mother

parecido, -a 1 *adj* (**a**) alike, similar (**b**) **bien p.** good-looking **2** *nm* likeness, resemblance; **tener p. con algn** to bear a resemblance to sb

pared *nf* wall

pareja *nf* (**a**) pair; **por parejas** in pairs (**b**) *(hombre y mujer)* couple; *(hijo e hija)* boy and girl; **hacen buena p.** they make a nice couple, they're well matched; **p. de hecho** = common-law heterosexual or homosexual relationship (**c**) *(en naipes)* pair; **doble p.** two pairs (**d**) *(de baile, juego)* partner

parentesco *nm* relationship, kinship

paréntesis *nm inv* (**a**) parenthesis, bracket; **entre p.** in parentheses *o* brackets (**b**) *(descanso)* break, interruption; *(digresión)* digression

pareo *nm* wraparound skirt

pariente *nmf* relative, relation

parir 1 *vi* to give birth; *Esp Fam* **poner algo/a algn a p.** *Br* to slag sth/sb off, *US* to badmouth sth/sb **2** *vt* to give birth to

parking *nm* (*pl* **parkings**) *Br* car park, *US* parking lot

parlamentario, -a 1 *adj* parliamentary **2** *nm,f Br* Member of Parliament, MP, *US* Congressman, *f* Congresswoman

parlamento *nm* parliament

parlanchín, -ina *adj Fam* talkative, chatty

paro *nm* (**a**) *(huelga)* strike, stoppage (**b**) *Esp (desempleo)* unemployment; **estar en p.** to be unemployed; **cobrar el p.** *Br* to be on the dole

parpadear *vi (ojos)* to blink; *Fig (luz)* to flicker

párpado *nm* eyelid

parque *nm* (**a**) park; **p. de atracciones** funfair; **p. zoológico** zoo; **p. nacional/natural** national park/nature reserve; **p. eólico** wind farm (**b**) *(de niños)* playpen (**c**) **p. móvil** total number of cars

parqué *nm* parquet (floor)

parqueadero *nm Col, Ecuad, Pan, Ven Br* car park, *US* parking lot

parquear *vt Bol, Carib, Col* to park

parquímetro *nm Aut* parking meter

parra *nf* grapevine

párrafo *nm* paragraph

parrilla *nf* (**a**) *Culin* grill; **pescado a la p.** grilled fish (**b**) *Téc* grate (**c**) *Aut, Dep* starting grid

parrillada *nf* mixed grill

parronal *nm Chile* vineyard

parroquia *nf* parish; *(iglesia)* parish church

parte 1 *nf* (**a**) *(sección)* part; *(en una repartición)* share
(**b**) *(lugar)* place, spot; **en** *o* **por todas partes** everywhere; **se fue por otra p.** he went another way
(**c**) *Jur* party
(**d**) *(bando)* side; **estoy de tu p.** I'm on your side
(**e**) *(locuciones)* **por mi p.** as far as I am concerned; **de p. de ...** on behalf of ...; *Tel* **¿de p. de quién?** who's calling?; **en gran p.** to a large extent; **en p.** partly; **la mayor p.** the majority; **por otra p.** on the other hand; **tomar p. en** to take part in
2 *nm (informe)* report

participación *nf* (**a**) participation (**b**) *Fin (acción)* share; **p. en los beneficios** profit-sharing (**c**) *(en lotería)* part of a lottery ticket (**d**) *(notificación)* notice, notification

participar 1 *vi* (**a**) to take part, to participate (**en** in) (**b**) *Fin* to have a share (**en** in) (**c**) *Fig* **p. de** to share **2** *vt (notificar)* to notify

partícula *nf* particle

particular 1 *adj* (**a**) *(concreto)* particular (**b**) *(privado)* private, personal (**c**) *(raro)* peculiar
2 *nmf (individuo)* private individual
3 *nm (asunto)* subject, matter

partida *nf* (**a**) *(salida)* departure (**b**) *Com (remesa)* batch, consignment (**c**) *(juego)* game (**d**) *Fin (entrada)* item (**e**) *Jur (certificado)* certificate; **p. de nacimiento** birth certificate

partidario, -a 1 *adj* **ser/no ser p. de algo** to be for/against sth **2** *nm,f* supporter, follower; **es p. del aborto** he is in favour of abortion

partidista *adj* biased, partisan

partido *nm* (**a**) *Pol* party (**b**) *Dep* game, *Br* match; **p. amistoso** friendly; **p. de vuelta** return match (**c**) *(provecho)* advantage; **sacar p. de** to profit from (**d**) *Jur (distrito)* district (**e**) **tomar p. por** to side with (**f**) **ser un buen p.** to be a good catch

partir 1 *vt* to break; *(dividir)* to split, to divide; *(cortar)* to cut; **p. a algn por la mitad** to mess things up for sb
2 *vi* (**a**) *(marcharse)* to leave, to set out *o* off (**b**) **a p. de** from
3 partirse *vpr* to split (up), to break (up); *Fam* **partirse de risa** to split one's sides laughing

partitura *nf Mús* score

parto *nm* childbirth, labour; **estar de p.** to be in labour

parvulario *nm* nursery school, kindergarten

pasa *nf* raisin; **p. de Corinto** currant

pasable *adj* passable, tolerable

pasaboca *nm Col* snack, appetizer

pasacalle *nm* (**a**) *(procesión)* street procession *(during town festival)* (**b**) *(banderola) Col, Urug* banner *(hung across street)*

pasada *nf* (a) **de p.** in passing (b) *(jugarreta)* dirty trick (c) *Esp Fam* **es una p.** *(una barbaridad)* it's way over the top

pasado, -a 1 *adj* (a) *(último)* last; **el año/lunes p.** last year/Monday (b) *(anticuado)* dated, old-fashioned; **p. (de moda)** out of date o fashion (c) *(alimento)* bad (d) *Culin* cooked; **lo quiero muy p.** I want it well done (e) **p. mañana** the day after tomorrow **2** *nm* past

pasaje *nm* (a) passage (b) *(calle)* alley (c) *(pasajeros)* passengers (d) *(billete)* ticket

pasajero, -a 1 *adj* passing, temporary; **aventura pasajera** fling **2** *nm,f* passenger

pasamanos *nm inv (barra)* handrail; *(de escalera)* banister, bannister

pasapalo *nm Ven* snack, appetizer

pasaporte *nm* passport

pasar 1 *vt* (a) to pass; *(mensaje)* to give; *(página)* to turn; **p. algo a limpio** to make a clean copy of sth (b) *(tiempo)* to spend, to pass; **p. el rato** to kill time (c) *(padecer)* to suffer, to endure; **p. hambre** to go hungry (d) *(río, calle)* to cross; *(barrera)* to pass through o over; *(límite)* to go beyond (e) *(perdonar)* to forgive, to tolerate; **p. algo (por alto)** to overlook sth (f) *(examen)* to pass

2 *vi* (a) to pass; **¿ha pasado el autobús?** has the bus gone by?; **ha pasado un hombre** a man has gone past; **p. de largo** to go by (without stopping); **el tren pasa por Burgos** the train goes via Burgos; **pasa por casa mañana** come round to my house tomorrow (b) **p. a** *(continuar)* to go on to; **p. a ser** to become (c) *(entrar)* to come in (d) *(tiempo)* to pass, to go by (e) **p. sin** to do without; *Fam* **paso de ti** I couldn't care less about you;

Fam **yo paso** count me out **3** *v impers (suceder)* to happen; **¿qué pasa aquí?** what's going on here?; *Fam* **¿qué pasa?** *(saludo)* how are you?; **¿qué te pasa?** what's the matter?; **pase lo que pase** whatever happens, come what may

4 pasarse *vpr* (a) **se me pasó la ocasión** I missed my chance; **se le pasó llamarme** he forgot to phone me (b) *(gastar tiempo)* to spend o pass time; **pasárselo bien/mal** to have a good/bad time (c) *(comida)* to go off (d) *Fam (excederse)* to go too far; **no te pases** don't overdo it (e) **pásate por mi casa** call round at my place

pasarela *nf (puente)* footbridge; *(de barco)* gangway; *(de moda) Br* catwalk, *US* runway

pasatiempo *nm* pastime, hobby

pascua *nf* (a) Easter (b) **pascuas** *(Navidad)* Christmas; **¡felices Pascuas!** Merry Christmas!

pascualina *nf RP, Ven* = tart with spinach and hard-boiled egg

pase *nm* (a) *(permiso)* pass, permit (b) *Esp (proyección)* showing

pasear 1 *vi* to go for a walk, to take a walk **2** *vt* (a) *(persona)* to take for a walk; *(perro)* to walk (b) *Fig (exhibir)* to show off **3 pasearse** *vpr* to go for a walk

paseíllo *nm Taurom* opening parade

paseo *nm* (a) walk; *(en bicicleta, caballo)* ride; *(en coche)* drive; **dar un p.** to go for a walk/a ride (b) *(avenida)* avenue

pasillo *nm* corridor; *Av* **p. aéreo** air corridor

pasión *nf* passion

pasividad *nf* passivity, passiveness

pasivo, -a 1 *adj* passive; *(inactivo)* inactive **2** *nm Com* liabilities

paso¹, -a *adj* **ciruela pasa** prune; **uva pasa** raisin

paso² *nm* (a) step; *(modo de andar)* gait, walk; *(ruido al andar)* footstep;

Fig **a dos pasos** a short distance away; *Fig* **seguir los pasos de algn** to follow in sb's footsteps

(**b**) *(camino)* passage, way; **abrirse p.** to force one's way through; **prohibido el p.** *(en letrero)* no entry; **p. de cebra** zebra crossing; **p. a nivel** *Br* level crossing, *US* grade crossing; **p. de peatones** *Br* pedestrian crossing, *US* crosswalk

(**c**) *(acción)* passage, passing; **a su p. por la ciudad** when he was in town; **el p. del tiempo** the passage of time; **estar de p.** to be just passing through

pasodoble *nm* paso doble

pasta *nf* (**a**) paste; **p. de dientes** *o* **dentífrica** toothpaste (**b**) *(de pasteles)* dough; *(italiana)* pasta (**c**) *(pastelito)* shortcake *Br* biscuit *o US* cookie (**d**) *Esp Fam (dinero)* dough

pastel *nm* (**a**) cake; *(de carne, fruta)* pie (**b**) *Arte* pastel (**c**) *Fam* **descubrir el p.** to spill the beans

pastelería *nf* (**a**) *(tienda)* confectioner's (shop) (**b**) *(dulces)* confectionery

pastelero, -a *nm,f* pastry cook, confectioner

pastilla *nf* (**a**) tablet, pill; **pastillas para la tos** cough drops (**b**) *(de jabón)* bar (**c**) *Esp Fam* **a toda p.** at top speed, *Br* like the clappers

pasto *nm* (**a**) *(hierba)* grass (**b**) *(alimento)* fodder; **ser p. de** to fall prey to (**c**) *Am (césped)* lawn, grass

pastor, -a 1 *nm,f* shepherd, *f* shepherdess; **perro p.** sheepdog **2** *nm* (**a**) *Rel* pastor, minister (**b**) *(perro)* **p. alemán** Alsatian

pastoreo *nm* shepherding

pata 1 *nf* leg; *Fig* **patas arriba** upside down; **estirar la p.** to kick the bucket; **mala p.** bad luck; **meter la p.** to put one's foot in it; **p. de gallo** crow's foot **2** *nm Perú Fam (amigo)* pal, *Br* mate, *US* buddy; *(tipo)* guy, *Br* bloke

patada *nf (puntapié)* kick, stamp

patata *nf Esp* potato; **patatas fritas** *(de sartén)* *Br* chips, *US* (French) fries; *(de bolsa)* *Br* crisps, *US* (potato) chips

paté *nm* pâté

patena *nf* paten; *Esp* **limpio** *o* **blanco como una p.** as clean as a new pin

patente 1 *nf* (**a**) *(autorización)* licence; *(de invención)* patent (**b**) *CSur (matrícula)* *Br* number plate, *US* license plate **2** *adj (evidente)* patent, obvious

paterno, -a *adj* paternal

patilla *nf* (**a**) *(de gafas)* leg (**b**) **patillas** *(pelo)* sideburns

patín *nm* (**a**) skate; *(patinete)* scooter; **p. de ruedas/de hielo** roller-/ice-skate; **p. en línea** rollerblade (**b**) *Esp (embarcación)* pedal boat

patinaje *nm* skating; **p. artístico** figure skating; **p. sobre hielo/ruedas** ice-/roller-skating

patinar *vi* (**a**) to skate; *(sobre ruedas)* to roller-skate; *(sobre hielo)* to ice-skate (**b**) *(deslizarse)* to slide; *(resbalar)* to slip; *(vehículo)* to skid (**c**) *Fam (equivocarse)* to put one's foot in it, to slip up

patinazo *nm* (**a**) skid (**b**) *Fam (equivocación)* blunder, boob

patinete *nm* scooter

patio *nm* (**a**) *(de una casa)* yard, patio; *(de recreo)* playground (**b**) *Esp Teatro, Cin* **p. de butacas** stalls

pato *nm* duck; *Fam* **pagar el p.** *Br* to carry the can, *US* to pick up the tab

patoso, -a *adj Esp* clumsy

patota *nf Perú, RP (de gamberros)* street gang

patria *nf* fatherland, native country; **madre p.** motherland; **p. chica** one's home town/region

patriota *nmf* patriot

patriótico, -a *adj* patriotic

patrocinador, -a 1 *adj* sponsoring **2** *nm,f* sponsor

patrón, -ona 1 *nm,f* (**a**) *(jefe)* boss (**b**) *Esp (de pensión)* landlord, *f* landlady (**c**) *Rel* patron saint **2** *nm* (**a**) pattern (**b**) *(medida)* standard

patronal 1 *adj* employers'; **cierre p.** lockout; **clase p.** managerial class **2** *nf (dirección)* management

patrono, -a *nm,f* (**a**) boss; *(empresario)* employer (**b**) *Rel* patron saint

patrulla *nf* (**a**) patrol; **estar de p.** to be on patrol; **coche p.** patrol car (**b**) *(grupo)* group, band; **p. de rescate** rescue party; **p. ciudadana** vigilante group

patrullero *nm* (**a**) *(barco)* patrol boat (**b**) *CSur (auto)* police (patrol) car, *US* cruiser

pausa *nf* pause, break; *Mús* rest

pauta *nf* guidelines

pava *nf* (**a**) *CAm (flequillo)* Br fringe, *US* bangs (**b**) *Chile, Perú (broma)* coarse o tasteless joke (**c**) *Arg (hervidor)* kettle

pavada *nf RP* (**a**) *Fam (estupidez)* **decir una pavada** to say something stupid; **decir pavadas** to talk nonsense (**b**) *(cosa sin importancia)* silly little thing

pavimento *nm (de carretera)* road (surface), *US* pavement; *(de acera)* paving; *(de habitación)* flooring

pavo *nm* (**a**) turkey; *Fam* **no ser moco de p.** to be nothing to scoff at (**b**) *Fam (tonto)* twit; *Fam* **estar en la edad del p.** to be growing up

pay *nm Chile, Méx, Ven* pie

payaso *nm* clown; **hacer el p.** to act the clown

paz *nf* peace; *(sosiego)* peacefulness; *Fam* **¡déjame en p.!** leave me alone!, **hacer las paces** to make (it) up

pazo *nm* = Galician mansion, belonging to noble family

PC *nm (abr* **personal computer)** PC

peaje *nm* toll; **autopista de p.** *Br* toll motorway, *US* turnpike

peatón *nm* pedestrian

peatonal *adj* pedestrian; **calle p.** pedestrian street

peca *nf* freckle

pecado *nm Rel* sin; **p. capital** o **mortal** deadly sin

pecador, -a *nm,f* sinner

pecar [44] *vi* to sin; *Fig* **p. por defecto** to fall short of the mark

pecera *nf* fish bowl, fish tank

pecho *nm* (**a**) chest; *(de mujer)* breast, bust; *(de animal)* breast; **dar el p. (a un bebé)** to breast-feed (a baby); *Fig* **tomar(se) (algo) a p.** to take (sth) to heart (**b**) *Am (en natación)* breaststroke; **nadar p.** to do the breaststroke

pechuga *nf* (**a**) *(de ave)* breast (**b**) *Fam (de mujer)* boob

pecoso, -a *adj* freckly

peculiar *adj (raro)* peculiar; *(característico)* characteristic

pedagogía *nf* pedagogy

pedagogo, -a *nm,f (especialista)* educationist; *(profesor)* teacher, educator

pedal *nm* pedal

pedalear *vi* to pedal

pedante **1** *adj* pedantic **2** *nmf* pedant

pedazo *nm* piece, bit; **a pedazos** in pieces; **caerse a pedazos** to fall apart o to pieces; **hacer pedazos** to break o tear to pieces, to smash (up); *Fam* **¡qué p. de coche!** what a terrific car!

pedestal *nm* pedestal

pediatra *nmf* paediatrician

pedido *nm* (**a**) *Com* order; **hacer un p. a** to place an order with (**b**) *(petición)* request

pedir [6] *vt* (**a**) to ask (for); **p. algo a algn** to ask sb for sth; **te pido que te quedes** I'm asking you to stay; **p. prestado** to borrow; *Fig* **p. cuentas** to ask for an explanation (**b**) *(mercancía, consumición)* to order (**c**) *(mendigar)* to beg

pedo *nm* (**a**) *(ventosidad)* fart; **tirarse un p.** to fart (**b**) *Fam (borrachera)* bender

pedregoso, -a *adj* stony, rocky

pedrisco *nm* hailstorm

pega *nf* (**a**) *Fam (obstáculo)* difficulty, hitch; **poner pegas (a)** to find problems (with) (**b**) **de p.** *(falso)* false, fake

pegajoso, -a *adj (pegadizo)* sticky; *Fig (persona)* tiresome, hard to get rid of

pegamento *nm* glue

pegar [42] **1** *vt* (**a**) *(adherir)* to stick;

(con pegamento) to glue; *Fam* **no pegó ojo** he didn't sleep a wink; **p. fuego** a to set fire to (**b**) *(golpear)* to hit (**c**) **p. un grito** to shout; **p. un salto** to jump (**d**) *Fam (contagiar)* to give; **me ha pegado sus manías** I've caught his bad habits (**e**) *(arrimar)* **p. algo a** o **contra algo** to put o place sth against sth

2 *vi* (**a**) *(adherirse)* to stick (**b**) *(armonizar)* to match, to go; **el azul no pega con el verde** blue and green don't go together o don't match; *Fig* **ella no pegaría aquí** she wouldn't fit in here (**c**) *(sol)* to beat down

3 pegarse *vpr* (**a**) *(adherirse)* to stick; *(pelearse)* to fight (**b**) *Fam (darse)* to have, to get; **pegarse un tiro** to shoot oneself (**c**) *(comida)* to get burnt; **se me ha pegado el sol** I've got a touch of the sun (**d**) *Esp Fam* **pegársela a algn** to trick o deceive sb (**e**) *(arrimarse)* to get close (**f**) *Med (enfermedad)* to be catching o contagious; *Fig (melodía)* to be catchy

pegatina *nf Esp* sticker

peinado *nm* hairstyle, *Fam* hairdo

peinar 1 *vt* (**a**) *(pelo)* to comb (**b**) *(registrar)* to comb **2 peinarse** *vpr* to comb one's hair

peine *nm* comb

peineta *nf* = ornamental comb worn in hair

p.ej. *(abr* **por ejemplo**) e.g.

peladilla *nf* sugared almond

pelado, -a 1 *adj* (**a**) *(cabeza)* shorn; *(piel, fruta)* peeled; *(terreno)* bare (**b**) *Fam* **saqué un cinco p.** *(en escuela)* I just scraped a pass; **a grito p.** shouting and bawling (**c**) *Fam (arruinado)* broke, *Br* skint

2 *nm Fam* haircut

3 *nm,f* (**a**) *Andes Fam (niño, adolescente)* kid (**b**) *CAm, Méx Fam (persona humilde)* common person, *Br* pleb, *Br* oik

pelar 1 *vt (cortar el pelo a)* to cut the hair of; *(fruta, patata)* to peel; *Fam* **hace un frío que pela** it's brass monkey weather

2 *vi (despellejar)* to peel

3 pelarse *vpr* (**a**) *(cortarse el pelo)* to get one's hair cut (**b**) *Fam* **corre que se las pela** she runs like the wind

peldaño *nm* step; *(de escalera de mano)* rung

pelea *nf* fight; *(riña)* row, quarrel; **buscar p.** to look for trouble

pelear 1 *vi* to fight; *(reñir)* to quarrel **2 pelearse** *vpr* (**a**) to fight; *(reñir)* to quarrel (**b**) *(enemistarse)* to fall out

peletería *nf* furrier's; *(tienda)* fur shop

pelícano *nm* pelican

película *nf* (**a**) *Cin* movie, *Br* film; **p. de miedo** o **terror** horror movie o *Br* film; **p. del Oeste** Western; *Fam* **de p.** fabulous (**b**) *Fot* film

peligro *nm* danger; *(riesgo)* risk; **con p. de …** at the risk of …; **correr (el) p. de …** to run the risk of …; **poner en p.** to endanger

peligroso, -a *adj* dangerous, risky

pelirrojo, -a 1 *adj* red-haired; *(anaranjado)* ginger-haired **2** *nm,f* redhead

pellejo *nm* (**a**) *(piel)* skin (**b**) *(odre)* wineskin (**c**) *Fam* **arriesgar** o **jugarse el p.** to risk one's neck

pellizcar [44] *vt* to pinch, to nip

pellizco *nm* pinch, nip

pelma *nmf,* **pelmazo, -a** *nm,f Esp (persona)* bore, drag

pelo *nm* (**a**) *(pelo)* hair; **cortarse el p.** *(en la peluquería)* to have one's hair cut; *Fig* **tomar el p. a algn** to pull sb's leg, to take the mickey out of sb; *Fam* **por los pelos** by the skin of one's teeth; *Fam* **me puso el p. de punta** it gave me the creeps (**b**) *(de animal)* fur, coat, hair (**c**) *Tex (de una tela)* nap, pile (**d**) *(cerda)* bristle

pelota 1 *nf* (**a**) ball; *Fam* **devolver la p.** to give tit for tat (**b**) *Dep* pelota (**c**) *Fam (cabeza)* nut (**d**) *Esp* **hacer la p. a algn** to toady to sb, to butter sb up (**e**) *muy Fam* **pelotas** *(testículos)* balls; **en pelotas** *Br* starkers, *US* butt-naked **2** *nmf Esp Fam (persona)* crawler

pelotari *nm* pelota player

pelotón *nm* (**a**) *Mil* squad (**b**) *Fam (grupo)* small crowd, bunch; *(en ciclismo)* pack (**c**) *(amasijo)* bundle

pelotudo, -a *adj RP Fam* (**a**) *(estúpido)* damn stupid (**b**) *(grande)* massive

peluca *nf* wig

peludo, -a *adj* hairy, furry

peluquería *nf* hairdresser's (shop)

peluquero, -a *nm,f* hairdresser

pelusa *nf (de tela)* fluff; *(de polvo)* ball of fluff

pelvis *nf inv* pelvis

pena *nf* (**a**) *(tristeza)* grief, sorrow; *Fig* **me da p. de ella** I feel sorry for her; **¡qué p.!** what a pity! (**b**) *(dificultad)* hardships *pl*, trouble; **no merece** o **vale la p. (ir)** it's not worthwhile (going); **a duras penas** with great difficulty (**c**) *(castigo)* punishment, penalty; **p. de muerte** death penalty (**d**) *CAm, Carib, Col, Méx (vergüenza)* embarrassment; **me da p.** I'm embarrassed about it

penalti *nm Dep* penalty; *Esp Fam* **casarse de p.** to have a shotgun wedding

pendejo, -a *nm,f* (**a**) *Am muy Fam (tonto)* jerk, *Br* tosser (**b**) *RP Fam Pey (adolescente)* spotty teenager

pendiente 1 *adj* (**a**) *(por resolver)* pending; *Educ* **asignatura p.** failed subject; *Com* **p. de pago** unpaid (**b**) **estar p. de** *(esperar)* to be waiting for; *(vigilar)* to be on the lookout for (**c**) *(colgante)* hanging (**de** from)
2 *nm Esp* earring
3 *nf* slope; *(de tejado)* pitch

péndulo *nm* pendulum

pene *nm* penis

penetrar 1 *vt* to penetrate; **p. un misterio** to get to the bottom of a mystery **2** *vi (entrar)* to go o get (**en** in)

penicilina *nf* penicillin

península *nf* peninsula

peninsular *adj* peninsular

penitencia *nf* penance

penitente *nmf* penitent

penoso, -a *adj* (**a**) *(lamentable)* sorry, distressing (**b**) *(laborioso)* laborious, difficult (**c**) *CAm, Carib, Col, Méx (embarazoso)* embarrassing (**d**) *CAm,* *Carib, Col, Méx (persona)* shy

pensador, -a *nm,f* thinker

pensamiento *nm* (**a**) thought (**b**) *(máxima)* saying, motto (**c**) *Bot* pansy

pensar [1] **1** *vi* to think (**en** o about; **sobre** about o over); *Fig* **sin p.** *(con precipitación)* without thinking; *(involuntariamente)* involuntarily
2 *vt* (**a**) to think (**de** of); *(considerar)* to think over o about; **piénsalo bien** think it over; *Fam* **¡ni pensarlo!** not on your life! (**b**) *(proponerse)* to intend; **pienso quedarme** I plan to stay (**c**) *(concebir)* to make; **p. un plan** to make a plan; **p. una solución** to find a solution

pensativo, -a *adj* pensive, thoughtful

pensión *nf* (**a**) *(residencia)* boarding house; *(hotel)* guesthouse; **media p.** half board; **p. completa** full board (**b**) *(paga)* pension, allowance; **p. vitalicia** life annuity

pensionista *nmf (jubilado)* pensioner

penthouse [pent'χaus] *nm CSur, Ven* penthouse

peña *nf* (**a**) rock, crag (**b**) *(de amigos)* club (**c**) *Esp Fam (gente)* people

peñasco *nm* rock, crag

peón *nm* (**a**) unskilled labourer; **p. agrícola** farmhand (**b**) *(en ajedrez)* pawn

peonza *nf* (spinning) top

peor 1 *adj* (**a**) *(comparativo)* worse (**b**) *(superlativo)* worst; **en el p. de los casos** if the worst comes to the worst; **lo p. es que** the worst of it is that **2** *adv* (**a**) *(comparativo)* worse; **¡p. para mí/ti/***etc***!** too bad! (**b**) *(superlativo)* worst

pepa *nf* (**a**) *Am salvo RP (pepita)* pip; *(hueso)* stone (**b**) *Méx, RP, Ven muy Fam (vulva)* pussy (**c**) *Ven (en la piel)* blackhead

pepenador, -a *nm,f CAm, Méx* scavenger *(on rubbish tip)*

pepián *nm Andes, CAm, Méx* (**a**) *(salsa)* = sauce thickened with ground nuts or seeds (**b**) *(guiso)* = type of stew in which the sauce is thickened with ground nuts or seeds

pepino *nm* cucumber; *Fam* **me importa un p.** I don't give a hoot

pepita *nf (de fruta)* pip, seed; *(de metal)* nugget

pepito *nm Esp (de carne)* grilled meat sandwich

pequeño, -a 1 *adj* small, little; *(bajo)* short **2** *nm,f* child; **de p.** as a child

pera *nf* (a) *Bot* pear; **p. de agua** juicy pear (b) *CSur Fam (mentón)* chin

peral *nm* pear tree

percebe *nm* (a) *(marisco)* goose barnacle (b) *Fam (persona)* twit

percha *nf (colgador)* (coat) hanger; *(de gallina)* perch

perchero *nm* clothes rack

percibir *vt* (a) *(notar)* to perceive, to notice (b) *(cobrar)* to receive

perdedor, -a 1 *adj* losing **2** *nm,f* loser

perder [3] **1** *vt* (a) to lose (b) *(tren, autobús)* to miss; *(tiempo)* to waste; *(oportunidad)* to miss (c) *(pervertir)* to be the ruin o downfall of
2 *vi* to lose; **echar (algo) a p.** to spoil (sth); **echarse a p.** to be spoilt; **salir perdiendo** to come off worst
3 perderse *vpr* (a) *(extraviarse) (persona)* to get lost; **se me ha perdido la llave** I've lost my key; **no te lo pierdas** don't miss it (b) *(pervertirse)* to go to rack and ruin

pérdida *nf* (a) loss; *Esp* **no tiene p.** you can't miss it (b) *(de tiempo, esfuerzos)* waste (c) *Mil* **pérdidas** losses

perdigón *nm* pellet

perdiz *nf* partridge

perdón *nm* pardon, forgiveness; **¡p.!** sorry!; **pedir p.** to apologize

perdonar *vt* (a) *(remitir)* to forgive (b) **¡perdone!** sorry!; **perdone que le moleste** sorry for bothering you (c) *(eximir)* to pardon; **perdonarle la vida a algn** to spare sb's life; **p. una deuda** to write off a debt

peregrinación *nf,* **peregrinaje** *nm* pilgrimage

peregrino, -a 1 *nm,f* pilgrim **2** *adj* **ideas peregrinas** crazy ideas

perejil *nm* parsley

pereza *nf* laziness, idleness

perezoso, -a *adj (vago)* lazy, idle

perfección *nf* perfection; **a la p.** to perfection

perfeccionista *adj & nmf* perfectionist

perfectamente *adv* perfectly; **¡p.!** *(de acuerdo)* agreed!, all right!

perfecto, -a *adj* perfect

perfil *nm* (a) profile; *(contorno)* outline, contour; **de p.** in profile (b) *Geom* cross-section

perforación *nf,* **perforado** *nm* perforation; *Min* drilling, boring; *Informát (de tarjetas)* punching

perforar *vt* to perforate; *Min* to drill, to bore; *Informát* to punch

perfumar 1 *vt* to perfume **2 perfumarse** *vpr* to put on perfume

perfume *nm* perfume, scent

perfumería *nf (tienda, arte)* perfumery

pergamino *nm* parchment

pérgola *nf* pergola

periferia *nf* periphery; *(alrededores)* outskirts

periférico, -a 1 *adj* peripheral **2** *nm* (a) *Informát* peripheral (b) *CAm, Méx (carretera) Br* ring road, *US* beltway

periódico, -a 1 *nm* newspaper **2** *adj* periodic(al); *Quím* **tabla periódica** periodic table

periodismo *nm* journalism

periodista *nmf* journalist, reporter

periodo, período *nm* period

periquito *nm* budgerigar, *Fam* budgie

peritaje *nm (estudios)* technical studies

perito, -a *nm,f* technician, expert; **p. industrial/agrónomo** ≃ industrial/agricultural expert

perjudicar [44] *vt* to harm, to injure; *(intereses)* to prejudice

perjuicio *nm* harm, damage; **en p. de** to the detriment of; **sin p. de** without prejudice to

perla *nf* pearl; *Fig (persona)* gem, jewel; *Fam* **me viene de perlas** it's just the ticket

permanecer [33] *vi* to remain, to stay

permanencia *nf* (**a**) *(inmutabilidad)* permanence (**b**) *(estancia)* stay

permanente 1 *adj* permanent **2** *nf (de pelo)* permanent wave, perm; **hacerse la p.** to have one's hair permed

permiso *nm* (**a**) *(autorización)* permission (**b**) *(licencia)* licence, permit; **p. de conducción** *o* **de conducir** *Br* driving licence, *US* driver's license; **p. de residencia/trabajo** residence/work permit (**c**) *Mil* leave; **estar de p.** to be on leave

permitir 1 *vt* to permit, to allow; **¿me permite?** may I? **2 permitirse** *vpr* (**a**) to permit *o* allow oneself; **me permito recordarle que** let me remind you that (**b**) **no se permite fumar** *(en letrero)* no smoking

pernoctar *vi* to stay overnight

pero 1 *conj* but; **p., ¿qué pasa aquí?** now, what's going on here? **2** *nm* objection

perpendicular *adj & nf* perpendicular

perpetuo, -a *adj* perpetual, everlasting; *Jur* **cadena perpetua** life imprisonment

perplejo, -a *adj* perplexed, bewildered

perra *nf* (**a**) bitch (**b**) *Esp Fam (dinero)* penny; **estar sin una p.** to be broke

perro, -a 1 *nm* dog; *Fam* **un día de perros** a lousy day; *Fam* **vida de perros** dog's life; *Culin* **p. caliente** hot dog **2** *adj Fam (vago)* lazy

persa 1 *adj & nmf* Persian **2** *nm (idioma)* Persian, Farsi

persecución *nf* (**a**) pursuit (**b**) *Pol (represión)* persecution

perseguir [6] *vt* (**a**) to pursue, to chase; *(correr tras)* to run after, to follow (**b**) *(reprimir)* to persecute

persiana *nf* blinds

persona *nf* person; **algunas personas** some people; *Fam* **p. mayor** grown-up

personaje *nm* (**a**) *Cin, Lit, Teatro* character (**b**) *(celebridad)* celebrity, important person

personal 1 *adj* personal, private **2** *nm* (**a**) *(plantilla)* staff, personnel (**b**) *Esp Fam (gente)* people

personalidad *nf* personality

personero, -a *nm,f Am* (**a**) *(representante)* representative (**b**) *(portavoz)* spokesperson

perspectiva *nf* (**a**) perspective (**b**) *(futuro)* prospect

persuadir *vt* to persuade; **estar persuadido de que** to be convinced that

persuasión *nf* persuasion

pertenecer [33] *vi* to belong (**a** to)

perteneciente *adj* belonging

pertenencia *nf* (**a**) possessions, property (**b**) *(a un partido etc)* affiliation, membership

pértiga *nf* pole; *Dep* **salto con p.** pole vault

Perú *n* Peru

peruano, -a *adj & nm,f* Peruvian

pesa *nf* weight; **levantamiento de pesas** weightlifting

pesadez *nf* (**a**) heaviness; *(de estómago)* fullness (**b**) *Fam (fastidio)* drag, nuisance

pesadilla *nf* nightmare; **de p.** nightmarish

pesado, -a 1 *adj* (**a**) heavy (**b**) *(aburrido)* tedious, dull; **¡qué p.!** what a drag! **2** *nm,f* bore

pesadumbre *nf* grief, affliction

pésame *nm* condolences, sympathy; **dar el p.** to offer one's condolences; **mi más sentido p.** my deepest sympathy

pesar 1 *vt* to weigh; *Fig (entristecer)* to grieve

2 *vi* (**a**) to weigh; **¿cuánto pesas?** how much do you weigh? (**b**) *(ser pesado)* to be heavy (**c**) *Fig (tener importancia)* **este factor pesa mucho** this is a very important factor

3 *nm* (**a**) *(pena)* sorrow, grief (**b**) *(arrepentimiento)* regret; **a su p.** to his regret (**c**) **a p. de** in spite of

pesca *nf* fishing; *Fam* **y toda la p.** and all that

pescadería *nf* fish shop, fishmonger's (shop)

pescadero, -a *nm,f* fishmonger

pescadilla *nf* whiting

pescado *nm* fish

pescador, -a 1 *adj* fishing **2** *nm,f* fisherman, *f* fisherwoman

pescar [44] **1** *vi* to fish **2** *vt* (**a**) to fish (**b**) *Fam (coger)* to catch

pesebre *nm* manger, stall

pesero *nm Méx* (**a**) *(vehículo)* collective taxi *(with a fixed rate and travelling a fixed route)* (**b**) *(persona)* collective taxi driver

peseta *nf Antes* peseta

pesimismo *nm* pessimism

pesimista 1 *adj* pessimistic **2** *nmf* pessimist

pésimo, -a *adj* very bad, awful, terrible

peso *nm* (**a**) weight; **al p.** by weight; **p. bruto/neto** gross/net weight; *Fig* **me quité un p. de encima** it took a load off my mind; **p. mosca/pesado** *(en boxeo)* flyweight/heavyweight (**b**) *(importancia)* importance; **de p.** *(persona)* influential; *(razón)* convincing

pesquero, -a 1 *adj* fishing **2** *nm* fishing boat

pestaña *nf* (**a**) eyelash, lash (**b**) *Téc (de neumático)* rim

peste *nf* (**a**) *(hedor)* stench, stink (**b**) *Med* plague; *Hist* **la p. negra** the Black Death (**c**) **decir** *o* **echar pestes de algn** *Br* to slag sb off, *US* to badmouth sb

pesticida *nm* pesticide

pestillo *nm* bolt, latch

petaca *nf* (**a**) *(para cigarrillos)* cigarette case; *(para bebidas)* flask (**b**) *Méx (maleta)* suitcase (**c**) *Méx Fam* **petacas** *(nalgas)* buttocks

pétalo *nm* petal

petanca *nf* petanque

petardo *nm* (**a**) firecracker, *Br* banger; *Mil* petard (**b**) *Fam (persona aburrida)* bore (**c**) *Esp Fam (porro)* joint

petenera *nf Esp Fam* **salir por peteneras** to go off at a tangent

petición *nf* request; *Jur* petition, plea

petiso, -a *adj Andes, RP Fam* short

peto *nm* **pantalón de p.** dungarees

petróleo *nm* petroleum, oil

petrolero *nm* oil tanker

petrolífero, -a *adj* oil; **pozo p.** oil well

petulancia *nf* arrogance

petulante *adj* arrogant, vain

petunia *nf* petunia

peúco *nm* bootee

pez¹ *nm* fish; **ella está como p. en el agua** she's in her element; **p. gordo** big shot

pez² *nf* pitch, tar

pezón *nm* nipple

pezuña *nf* hoof

pianista *nmf* pianist, piano player

piano *nm* piano

piar [29] *vi* to chirp, to tweet

pibe, -a *nm,f Fam* (**a**) *Esp (hombre)* guy; *(mujer)* girl (**b**) *Arg (niño)* kid, boy; *(niña)* kid, girl

pica *nf* (**a**) *(lanza)* pike (**b**) **picas** *(palo de baraja)* spades

picada *nf* (**a**) *RP (tapas)* appetizers, snacks (**b**) *RP Br* mince, *US* ground beef (**c**) *Am (de avión)* nose dive; **hacer una p.** to dive

picadillo *nm* (**a**) *(de carne)* minced meat; *(de verduras)* vegetable salad (**b**) *Chile (tapas)* appetizers, snacks

picador *nm Taurom* mounted bullfighter, picador

picadora *nf Esp, RP* mincer

picadura *nf* (**a**) *(mordedura)* bite; *(de avispa, abeja)* sting (**b**) *(en fruta)* spot; *Med (de viruela)* pockmark; *(en diente)* decay, caries *sing*; *(en metalurgia)* pitting

picante *adj* (**a**) *Culin* hot, spicy (**b**) *Fig (chiste etc)* risqué, spicy

picantería *nf Andes (restaurante)* cheap restaurant

picar [44] **1** *vt* (**a**) *(de insecto, serpiente)* to bite; *(de avispas, abejas)* to sting; *(barba)* to prick (**b**) *(comer) (aves)* to peck (at); *(persona)* to nibble, to pick at (**c**) *(de pez)* to bite (**d**) *(perforar)* to prick, to puncture (**e**) *Culin (carne) Br* to mince, *US* to grind (**f**) *(incitar)* to incite, to goad; **p. la curiosidad (de algn)** to arouse (sb's) curiosity

2 *vi* (**a**) *(escocer)* to itch; *(herida)* to smart; *(el sol)* to burn (**b**) *Culin* to be hot (**c**) *(pez)* to bite (**d**) *Fig (dejarse engañar)* to swallow it

3 picarse *vpr* (**a**) *(hacerse rivales)* to be at loggerheads (**b**) *(fruta)* to spot, to rot; *(ropa)* to become moth-eaten; *(dientes)* to decay (**c**) *(enfadarse)* to get cross (**d**) *(drogadicto)* to shoot up

pícaro, -a 1 *adj* (**a**) *(travieso)* naughty, mischievous; *(astuto)* sly, crafty (**b**) *(procaz)* risqué **2** *nm,f* rascal, rogue

pichincha *nf RP Fam* snip, bargain

pichón *nm* young pigeon; **tiro al** *o* **de p.** pigeon shooting

pickles *nmpl RP* pickles

picnic *nm* (*pl* **picnics**) picnic

pico *nm* (**a**) *(de ave)* beak, bill; *Fam (boca)* mouth, *esp Br* gob; **tener un p. de oro** to have the gift of the gab (**b**) *(punta)* corner (**c**) *Geog* peak (**d**) *(herramienta)* pick, pickaxe (**e**) *(cantidad)* odd amount; **cincuenta y p.** fifty-odd; **las dos y p.** just after two (**f**) *(drogas)* fix

picor *nm* itch, tingling

picoso, -a *adj Méx* spicy, hot

pie *nm* (**a**) foot; **pies** feet; **a p.** on foot; **de p.** standing up; **en p.** standing; **hacer p.** to touch the bottom; *Fig* **al p. de la letra** to the letter, word for word; *Fig* **dar p. a** to give cause for (**b**) *(de instrumento)* stand; *(de copa)* stem (**c**) *(de página)* foot; *(de ilustración)* caption (**d**) *(medida)* foot (**e**) *Teatro* cue

piedad *nf* (**a**) *(devoutness)* devoutness, piety (**b**) *(compasión)* compassion, pity

piedra *nf* stone; *(de mechero)* flint; **poner la primera p.** to lay the foundation stone; *Fam Fig* **me dejó** *o* **me quedé de p.** I was flabbergasted

piel *nf* (**a**) skin; **p. de gallina** goose pimples (**b**) *(de fruta, de patata)* skin, peel (**c**) *Esp, Méx (cuero)* leather (**d**) *(pelo)* fur

pierna *nf* leg

pieza *nf* (**a**) piece, part; **p. de**

recambio spare part, *US* extra; *Fig* **me dejó** *o* **me quedé de una p.** I was speechless *o* dumbfounded *o* flabbergasted (**b**) *(habitación)* room (**c**) *Teatro* play

pijama *nm* pyjamas

pila *nf* (**a**) *Elec* battery *(montón)* pile, heap; *Fig* **una p. de** *(muchos)* piles *o* heaps *o* loads of (**c**) *(lavadero)* basin (**d**) *Fig* **nombre de p.** Christian name

pilar *nm* (**a**) *Arquit* pillar (**b**) *(fuente)* waterhole

píldora *nf* pill; **p. abortiva** morning-after pill; *Fig* **dorar la p. a algn** to butter sb up

pileta *nf RP* (**a**) *(en baño)* washbasin; *(en cocina)* sink (**b**) *(piscina)* swimming pool

pillar 1 *vt* (**a**) *(robar)* to plunder, to loot (**b**) *(coger)* to catch; *(alcanzar)* to catch up with; **lo pilló un coche** he was run over by a car (**c**) *Fam* to be; **me pilla un poco lejos** it's a bit far for *o* from me **2 pillarse** *vpr* to catch; **pillarse un dedo/una mano** to catch one's finger/hand

pilotar *vt Av* to pilot, to fly; *Aut* to drive; *Náut* to pilot, to steer

piloto *nm* (**a**) *Av, Náut* pilot; *Aut* driver; **piso p.** show flat; **programa p.** pilot programme (**b**) *(luz)* pilot lamp *o* light

pimentón *nm* paprika, red pepper

pimienta *nf* pepper

pimiento *nm (fruto)* pepper; *(planta)* pimiento; **p. morrón** sweet pepper; *Fam* **me importa un p.** I don't give a damn, I couldn't care less

pin *nm* (*pl* **pins**) pin, (lapel) badge

pincel *nm* brush, paintbrush

pinchar 1 *vt* (**a**) *(punzar)* to prick; *(balón, globo)* to burst; *(rueda)* to puncture (**b**) *Fam (incitar)* to prod; *(molestar)* to get at, to nag (**c**) *Med* to inject, to give an injection to (**d**) *Tel* to bug **2** *vi Aut* to get a puncture

pinchazo *nm* (**a**) *(punzadura)* prick; *Aut* puncture, blowout (**b**) *(de dolor)* sudden *o* sharp pain

pinche *nm* (**a**) *(de cocina)* kitchen boy, f maid (**b**) *RP Fam (en oficina)* office junior

pincho *nm* (**a**) *(púa)* barb (**b**) *Esp (tapa)* **p. moruno** ≃ shish kebab; **p. de tortilla** = small portion of omelette

pinga *nf Andes, Méx, Ven Vulg* prick, cock

ping-pong [pim'pon] *nm* ping-pong, table-tennis

pingüino *nm* penguin

pino *nm* pine; *Esp Fig* **hacer el p.** to do a handstand; *Esp Fam* **en el quinto p.** in the back of beyond

pinol, pinole *nm CAm, Méx (harina)* Br maize flour, US corn flour

pintada *nf* graffiti

pintado, -a *adj* **recién p.** *(en letrero)* wet paint; *Fam Fig* **nos viene que ni p.** it is just the ticket; *Fam Fig* **te está que ni p.** it suits you to a tee

pintalabios *nm inv* lipstick

pintar 1 *vt* (**a**) *(dar color)* to paint (**b**) *(dibujar)* to draw, to sketch
2 *vi (importar)* to count; *Fig* **yo aquí no pinto nada** I am out of place here
3 pintarse *vpr* (**a**) *(maquillarse)* to put make-up on (**b**) *Fam* **pintárselas** to manage

pintor, -a *nm,f* painter

pintoresco, -a *adj* (**a**) *(lugar)* picturesque (**b**) *(raro)* eccentric, bizarre

pintura *nf* (**a**) painting; **p. rupestre** cave painting; *Fam Fig* **no la puedo ver ni en p.** I can't stand the sight of her (**b**) *(materia)* paint

pinza *nf (para tender)* Br clothes peg, US clothes pin; *(de animal)* pincer, claw; **pinzas** *(para depilar)* tweezers; *(para hielo)* tongs

piña *nf* (**a**) *(de pino)* pine cone; *(ananás)* pineapple (**b**) *Fig (grupo)* clan, clique (**c**) *Fam (golpe)* thump

piñón *nm* (**a**) pine seed o nut (**b**) *Téc* pinion

piojo *nm* louse

piola *adj RP Fam* (**a**) *(simpático)* fun (**b**) *Irón (listo)* smart, clever (**c**) *(lugar)* cosy

piolín *nm Andes, RP* cord

pipa *nf* (**a**) *(de fumar)* pipe; **fumar en p.** to smoke a pipe (**b**) *(de fruta)* pip; *(de girasol)* sunflower seed

pipí *nm Fam* pee, *Br* wee-wee; **hacer p.** to pee, *Br* to wee-wee

pipián = pepián

pique *nm* (**a**) resentment (**b**) *(rivalidad)* needle (**c**) **a p. de** on the point of (**d**) **irse a p.** *Náut* to sink; *(un plan)* to fall through; *(un negocio)* to go bust

piragua *nf* canoe

piragüismo *nm* canoeing

pirámide *nf* pyramid

piraña *nf* piranha

pirata *adj & nmf* pirate

piratear *vt Fig* to pirate

Pirineo(s) *nm(pl)* Pyrenees

pirómano, -a *nm,f Med* pyromaniac; *Jur* arsonist

piropo *nm* **echar un p.** to pay a compliment

pirueta *nf* pirouette; *Fig Pol* **hacer una p.** to do a U-turn

pisada *nf* step, footstep; *(huella)* footprint

pisar *vt* to tread on, to step on

piscina *nf* swimming pool

Piscis *nm* Pisces

pisco *nm* pisco, = Andean grape brandy

piso *nm* (**a**) *Esp (vivienda)* apartment, Br flat; *Pol* **p. franco** safe house (**b**) *(planta)* floor; *(de carretera)* surface

pisotón *nm* **me dio un p.** he stood on my foot

pista *nf* (**a**) track; **p. de baile** dance floor; *Dep* **p. de esquí** ski run o slope; *Dep* **p. de patinaje** ice rink; *Dep* **p. de tenis** tennis court; **p. de aterrizaje** landing strip; **p. de despegue** runway (**b**) *(rastro)* trail, track (**c**) **dame una p.** give me a clue

pistacho *nm* pistachio nut

pistola *nf* (**a**) gun, pistol (**b**) *(para pintar)* spray gun

pistolero *nm* gunman, gangster

pitada *nf* (**a**) *(silbidos de protesta)* booing, whistling (**b**) *Am Fam (calada)* drag, puff

pitar 1 *vt* (**a**) *(silbato)* to blow (**b**) *Dep* **el árbitro pitó un penalti** the referee awarded a penalty **2** *vi* (**a**) to whistle (**b**) *Aut* to toot one's horn (**c**) *Dep* to referee (**d**) *Esp Fam* **salir pitando** to fly off

pitillera *nf* cigarette case

pitillo *nm* (**a**) *(cigarrillo)* cigarette (**b**) *Col (paja)* drinking straw

pito *nm* (**a**) whistle; *Aut* horn; *Fam* **me importa un p.** I don't give a hoot (**b**) *Fam (cigarrillo) Br* fag (**c**) *Fam (pene) Br* willie, *US* peter

pitón *nm* (**a**) *(serpiente)* python (**b**) *(de toro)* horn

pizarra *nf* (**a**) *(encerado) Br* blackboard, *US* chalkboard (**b**) *(roca, material)* slate

pizarrón *nm Am Br* blackboard, *US* chalkboard

pizza ['pitsa] *nf* pizza

pizzería [pitse'ria] *nf* pizzeria, pizza parlour

placa *nf* (**a**) plate (**b**) *(conmemorativa)* plaque

placer [33] **1** *vt* to please **2** *nm* pleasure; **ha sido un p. (conocerle)** it's been a pleasure (meeting you); *Fml* **tengo el p. de** it gives me great pleasure to; **un viaje de p.** a holiday trip

plagiar [43] *vt* (**a**) *(copiar)* to plagiarize (**b**) *CAm, Col, Perú, Méx (secuestrar)* to kidnap

plagiario, -a *nm,f CAm, Col, Perú, Méx (secuestrador)* kidnapper

plan *nm* (**a**) *(proyecto)* plan (**b**) *(programa)* scheme, programme; *Educ* **p. de estudios** syllabus; **estar a p.** to be on a diet (**c**) *Fam* **en p. de broma** for a laugh; **si te pones en ese p.** if you're going to be like that (about it); **en p. barato** cheaply (**d**) *Fam (cita)* date

plancha *nf* (**a**) iron; *(de metal)* plate (**b**) *Culin* hotplate; **sardinas a la p.** grilled sardines (**c**) *Impr* plate

planchar *vt* to iron

planeta *nm* planet

planilla *nf* (**a**) *Am (formulario)* form

(**b**) *Am (nómina)* payroll

plano, -a 1 *nm* (**a**) *(de ciudad)* map; *Arquit* plan, draft (**b**) *Cin* shot; **un primer p.** a close-up; *Fig* **estar en primer/segundo p.** to be in the limelight/in the background (**c**) *Mat* plane **2** *adj* flat, even

planta *nf* (**a**) plant (**b**) *(del pie)* sole (**c**) *(piso)* floor, storey; **p. baja** *Br* ground floor, *US* first floor

plantar 1 *vt* (**a**) *(árboles, campo)* to plant (**b**) *(poner)* to put, to place; **p. cara a algn** to stand up to sb (**c**) *Fam* **p. a algn en la calle** to throw sb out; **le ha plantado su novia** his girlfriend has ditched him **2 plantarse** *vpr* (**a**) to stand (**b**) *(llegar)* to arrive; **en cinco minutos se plantó aquí** he got here in five minutes flat

planteamiento *nm (enfoque)* approach

plantear 1 *vt* (**a**) *(problema)* to pose, to raise (**b**) *(planear)* to plan (**c**) *(proponer)* to put forward (**d**) *(exponer)* to present **2 plantearse** *vpr* (**a**) *(considerar)* to consider (**b**) *(problema)* to arise

plantilla *nf* (**a**) *(personal)* staff, personnel (**b**) *(de zapato)* insole (**c**) *(patrón)* model, pattern

plástico, -a 1 *adj* plastic **2** *nm* (**a**) plastic (**b**) *(disco)* record

plastificar [44] *vt* to coat o cover with plastic

plastilina® *nf* Plasticine®

plata *nf* (**a**) silver; *(objetos de plata)* silverware; *Fam* **hablar en p.** to lay (it) on the line; **p. de ley** sterling silver (**b**) *Am Fam (dinero)* money

plataforma *nf* platform

plátano *nm* (**a**) *(fruta)* banana (**b**) *(árbol)* plane tree; **falso p.** sycamore

platea *nf Br* stalls, *US* orchestra

plateresco, -a *adj* plateresque

plática *nf CAm, Méx (charla)* talk, chat

platicar [44] *vi CAm, Méx* to chat, to talk

platillo *nm* (**a**) saucer; **p. volador,** *Esp* **p. volante** flying saucer (**b**) *Mús* cymbal

plato *nm* (**a**) plate, dish (**b**) *(parte de una comida)* course; **de primer p.** for starters; **p. fuerte** main course; **p. combinado** one-course meal (**c**) *(guiso)* dish (**d**) *(de balanza)* pan, tray (**e**) *(de tocadiscos)* turntable

platudo, -a *adj Am Fam* loaded, rolling in it

playa *nf* (**a**) beach; *(costa)* seaside (**b**) *Am* **p. de estacionamiento** *Br* car park, *US* parking lot

play-back ['pleiβak] *nm* (*pl* **play-backs**) **hacer p.** to mime (the lyrics)

playera *nf* (**a**) *(zapatilla) Br* sandshoe, *US* sneaker (**b**) *Méx (camiseta)* T-shirt

plaza *nf* (**a**) square (**b**) *(mercado)* market, marketplace (**c**) *Aut* seat (**d**) *(laboral)* post, position (**e**) **p. de toros** bullring

plazo *nm* (**a**) *(periodo)* time, period; *(término)* deadline; **a corto/largo p.** in the short term/in the long run; **el p. termina el viernes** Friday is the deadline (**b**) *Fin* **comprar a plazos** to buy on *Br* hire purchase *o US* an installment plan; **en seis plazos** in six instalments

plegable *adj* folding, collapsible

pleito *nm* (**a**) *Jur* lawsuit, litigation; **poner un p. (a algn)** to sue (sb) (**b**) *Am (discusión)* argument

plenitud *nf* plenitude, fullness; **en la p. de la vida** in the prime of life

pleno, -a 1 *adj* full; **en plena noche** in the middle of the night; **los empleados en p.** the entire staff **2** *nm* plenary meeting

pliegue *nm* (**a**) fold (**b**) *(de vestido)* pleat

plomería *nf Méx, RP, Ven* (**a**) *(negocio)* plumber's (**b**) *(instalación)* plumbing

plomero *nm Méx, RP, Ven* plumber

plomo *nm* (**a**) *(en metalurgia)* lead (**b**) *Elec (fusible)* fuse (**c**) *(bala)* slug, pellet

pluma *nf* (**a**) *(de ave)* feather (**b**) *(estilográfica)* fountain pen (**c**) *Carib, Méx (bolígrafo)* (ballpoint) pen (**d**) *Carib, Col, Méx (grifo) Br* tap, *US* faucet

plumaje *nm* plumage

plumero *nm* (**a**) *(para el polvo)* feather duster (**b**) *Fam* **se te ve el p.** I can see through you

plumier *nm* (*pl* **plumiers**) pencil box

plumón *nm (de ave)* down

plural *adj & nm* plural

pluralidad *nf* diversity

plusmarca *nf* record

plusmarquista *nmf* record breaker

PM *nf (abr* **policía militar**) MP

p.m. (*abr* **post meridiem**) p.m.

población *nf* (**a**) *(ciudad)* town; *(pueblo)* village (**b**) *(habitantes)* population (**c**) *Chile (barrio)* **p. (callampa)** shanty town

poblado, -a *adj* (**a**) populated; *Fig* **p. de** full of (**b**) *(barba)* bushy, thick

poblar [2] *vt* (**a**) *(con gente)* to settle, to people; *(con plantas)* to plant (**b**) *(vivir)* to inhabit

pobre 1 *adj* poor; **¡p.!** poor thing!; **un hombre p.** a poor man; **un p. hombre** a poor devil **2** *nmf* poor person; **los pobres** the poor

pobreza *nf* poverty; *Fig (de medios, recursos)* lack

pocho, -a *adj* (**a**) *(fruta)* bad, overripe (**b**) *Fig (persona) (débil)* off-colour; *(triste)* depressed, down (**c**) *Méx Fam (americanizado)* Americanized

pochoclo *nm Arg* popcorn

pocilga *nf* pigsty

pocillo *nm* (**a**) *RP (pequeño)* small cup (**b**) *Méx, Ven (grande)* enamel mug

poco, -a *nm* (**a**) **un p.** *(con adj o adv)* a little; **un p. tarde/frío** a little late/ cold (**b**) **un p.** *(con sustantivo)* a little; **un p. de azúcar** a little sugar

2 *adj* (**a**) not much, little; **p. sitio/ tiempo** not much *o* little space/time; **poca cosa** not much (**b**) **pocos** not many, few; **pocas personas** not many *o* few people (**c**) **unos pocos** a few

3 *pron* (**a**) *(escasa cantidad)* not much; **queda p.** there isn't much left (**b**) *(breve tiempo)* **p. antes/después** shortly *o* a little before/afterwards; **a p. de** shortly *o* a little after; **dentro de p.** soon (**c**) **pocos** *(cosas)* few, not many; **tengo muy pocos** I have very few, I don't have very many (**d**) **pocos**

(personas) few people, not many people; **vinieron pocos** few people came, not many people came

4 *adv* (**a**) *(con verbo)* not (very) much, little; **ella come p.** she doesn't eat much, she eats little (**b**) *(con adj)* not very; **es p. probable** it's not very likely (**c**) *(en frases)* **p. a p.** little by little, gradually; **por p.** almost

podadera, *Am* **podadora** *nf* garden shears

podar *vt* to prune

poder¹ *nm* power; *Econ* **p. adquisitivo** purchasing power

poder² [18] **1** *vi* (**a**) *(capacidad)* to be able to; **no puede hablar** she can't speak; **no podré llamarte** I won't be able to phone you; **no puedo más** I can't take any more

(**b**) *(permiso)* may, might; **¿puedo pasar?** can *o* may I come in?; **aquí no se puede fumar** you can't smoke here

(**c**) *(uso impers)* *(posibilidad)* may, might; **puede que no lo sepan** they may *o* might not know; **no puede ser** that's impossible; **puede (ser) (que sí)** maybe, perhaps

(**d**) *(deber)* **podrías haberme advertido** you might have warned me

(**e**) to cope (**con** with); **no puede con tanto trabajo** he can't cope with so much work

2 *vt* *(batir)* to be stronger than; **les puede a todos** he can take on anybody

poderoso, -a *adj* powerful

podio, pódium *nm Dep* podium

podrido, -a *adj* (**a**) *(putrefacto)* rotten, putrid (**b**) *(corrupto)* rotten; *Fam* **estar p. de dinero** *o Am* **en plata** to be filthy rich (**c**) *RP Fam (harto)* fed up, sick

poema *nm* poem

poesía *nf* (**a**) *(género)* poetry (**b**) *(poema)* poem

poeta *nmf* poet

poético, -a *adj* poetic

polar *adj* polar

polea *nf* pulley

polémica *nf* controversy

polémico, -a *adj* controversial

polen *nm* pollen

polera *nf* (**a**) *Arg, Chile (polo)* polo shirt (**b**) *Urug (de cuello alto)* turtleneck *o Br* polo neck sweater

polichinela *nm* (**a**) *(personaje)* Punchinello (**b**) *(títere)* puppet, marionette

policía 1 *nf* police (force) **2** *nmf* policeman, *f* policewoman

policíaco, -a, policiaco, -a, policial *adj* police; **novela/película policíaca** detective story/movie *o Br* film

polideportivo *nm* sports centre

poliéster *nm* polyester

políglota *adj & nmf* polyglot

polígono *nm* polygon; **p. industrial** *Br* industrial estate, *US* industrial area

politécnico, -a *adj & nm* polytechnic

política *nf* (**a**) politics *sing* (**b**) *(estrategia)* policy

político, -a 1 *adj* (**a**) political (**b**) *(pariente)* in-law; **hermano p.** brother-in-law; **su familia política** her in-laws **2** *nm,f* politician

póliza *nf* (**a**) *(sello)* stamp (**b**) **p. de seguros** insurance policy

pollera *nf* (**a**) *CSur (occidental)* skirt (**b**) *Andes (indígena)* = long skirt worn in layers by Indian women

pollo *nm* (**a**) chicken (**b**) *Fam (joven)* lad

polo *nm* (**a**) *Elec, Geog* pole; **P. Norte/ Sur** North/South Pole (**b**) *(helado) Br* ice lolly, *US* Popsicle® (**c**) *(prenda)* polo shirt (**d**) *Dep* polo

pololear *vi Chile Fam* to go out (together)

pololo, -a *nm,f Chile Fam* boyfriend, *f* girlfriend

Polonia *n* Poland

polución *nf* pollution

polvera *nf* powder compact

polvo *nm* (**a**) dust; **limpiar** *o* **quitar el p.** to dust; **en p.** powdered; **polvo(s) de talco** talcum powder (**b**) *Fam* **estar hecho p.** *(cansado)* to be *Br* knackered *o US* bushed; *(deprimido)* to be depressed (**c**) *muy Fam* **echar un p.** to have a screw *o Br* a shag

pólvora *nf* gunpowder

polvoriento, -a *adj* dusty

polvorón *nm* sweet pastry

pomada *nf* ointment

pomelo *nm (fruto)* grapefruit; *(árbol)* grapefruit tree

pomo *nm (de puerta)* knob

pompa *nf* (**a**) **p. (de jabón)** (soap) bubble (**b**) *(suntuosidad)* pomp (**c**) *Méx Fam* **pompas** behind, bottom

pómulo *nm* cheekbone

ponchar 1 *vt* (**a**) *CAm, Carib, Méx (rueda)* to puncture (**b**) *Am (en béisbol)* to strike out **2 poncharse** *vpr* (**a**) *CAm, Carib, Méx (rueda)* to blow (**b**) *Am (en béisbol)* to strike out

poner [19] *(pp* **puesto) 1** *vt* (**a**) to put; *(mesa, huevo)* to lay; *(gesto)* to make; *(multa)* to impose; *(telegrama)* to send; *(negocio)* to set up

(**b**) *(tele, radio etc)* to turn *o* switch on

(**c**) *(+ adj)* to make; **p. triste a algn** to make sb sad; **p. colorado a algn** to make sb blush

(**d**) **¿qué llevaba puesto?** what was he wearing?

(**e**) *Esp (decir)* **¿qué pone aquí?** what does it say here?

(**f**) *(suponer)* to suppose; **pongamos que Ana no viene** supposing Ana doesn't turn up

(**g**) *TV, Cin* to put on, to show; **¿qué ponen en la tele?** what's on the telly?

(**h**) *Esp Tel* **ponme con Manuel** put me through to Manuel

(**i**) *(nombrar)* **le pondremos (de nombre) Pilar** we are going to call her Pilar

2 *vi Am Fam (parecer)* **se me pone que ...** it seems to me that ...

3 ponerse *vpr* (**a**) to put oneself; **ponte en mi lugar** put yourself in my place; **ponte más cerca** come closer

(**b**) *(vestirse)* to put on; **se puso el jersey** she put her sweater on

(**c**) *(+ adj)* to become; **ponerse furioso/malo** to become furious/ill

(**d**) *(sol)* to set

(**e**) *Tel* **ponerse al teléfono** to answer the phone

(**f**) **ponerse a** to start to; **ponerse a trabajar** to get down to work

pongo *indic pres de* **poner**

poniente *nm* (**a**) *(occidente)* West (**b**) *(viento)* westerly (wind)

ponqué *nm Col, Ven* = fruit or custard-filled cake

popa *nf* stern; *Fig* **ir viento en p.** to go full speed ahead

popote *nm Méx* (drinking) straw

popular *adj* (**a**) folk; **arte/música p.** folk art/music (**b**) *(medida)* popular (**c**) *(actor)* well-known

popularidad *nf* popularity

póquer *nm* poker

por *prep* (**a**) *(agente)* by; **pintado p. Picasso** painted by Picasso

(**b**) **p. qué** why

(**c**) *(causa)* because of; **p. sus ideas** because of her ideas; **p. necesidad/amor** out of need/love; **suspendió p. no estudiar** he failed because he didn't study

(**d**) *(tiempo)* **p. la mañana/noche** in the morning/at night; **p. ahora** for the time being

(**e**) *(en favor de)* for; **lo hago p. mi hermano** I'm doing it for my brother('s sake)

(**f**) *(lugar)* **pasamos p. Córdoba** we went through Córdoba; **¿p. dónde vamos?** which way are we taking *o* going?; **p. la calle** in the street; **mirar p. la ventana** to look out the window; **entrar p. la ventana** to get in through the window

(**g**) *(medio)* by; **p. avión/correo** by plane/post

(**h**) *(a cambio de)* for; **cambiar algo p. otra cosa** to exchange sth for sth else

(**i**) *(distributivo)* **p. cabeza** a head, per person; **p. hora/mes** per hour/month

(**j**) *Mat* **dos p. tres, seis** two times three is six; **un 10 p. ciento** 10 percent

(**k**) *(+ infinitivo)* in order to, so as to; **hablar p. hablar** to talk for the sake of it

(**l**) *(locuciones)* **p. así decirlo** so to speak; **p. más *o* muy ... que sea** no matter how … he/she is; **p. mí** as far as I'm concerned

porcelana *nf* porcelain

porcentaje *nm* percentage

porche *nm* porch

porción *nf* portion, part

porno *adj inv Fam* porn

pornografía *nf* pornography

pornográfico, -a *adj* pornographic

poroto *nm Andes, RP* kidney bean

porque *conj* (**a**) *(causal)* because; **¡p. no!** just because! (**b**) *(final) (+ subjuntivo)* so that, in order that

porqué *nm* reason

porro *nm* (**a**) *Fam (de droga)* joint (**b**) *Am (puerro)* leek

porrón *nm* = glass wine vessel used for drinking wine from its long spout

portaaviones *nm inv* aircraft carrier

portada *nf* (**a**) *(de libro etc)* cover; *(de periódico)* front page; *(de disco)* sleeve (**b**) *(fachada)* front, facade

portador, -a *nm,f Com* bearer; *Med* carrier

portaequipajes *nm inv* (**a**) *Aut (maletero) Br* boot, *US* trunk; *(baca)* roof *o* luggage rack (**b**) *(carrito)* luggage trolley

portafolios *nm inv* briefcase

portal *nm* (**a**) *(zaguán)* porch, entrance hall (**b**) *(puerta de la calle)* main door (**c**) **p. de Belén** Nativity scene (**d**) *Informát* portal

portarse *vpr* to behave; **p. mal** to misbehave

portátil *adj* portable

portavoz *nmf* spokesperson, spokesman, *f* spokeswoman

portazo *nm* **oímos un p.** we heard a slam *o* bang; **dar un p.** to slam the door

portería *nf* (**a**) *(de casa, colegio) Br* caretaker's office, *US* super(intendent)'s office; *(de hotel, ministerio)* porter's office (**b**) *Dep* goal, goalmouth

portero, -a 1 *nm,f* (**a**) *(de casa, colegio) Br* caretaker, *US* super (intendent); *(de hotel, ministerio) (en recepción)* porter; *(a la puerta)* doorman; (**b**) *Dep* goalkeeper **2** *nm* **p.**

automático entryphone

Portugal *n* Portugal

portugués, -esa 1 *adj & nm,f* Portuguese **2** *nm (idioma)* Portuguese

porvenir *nm* future; **sin p.** with no prospects

posada *nf* inn

posar 1 *vi (para retrato etc)* to pose **2** *vt* to put *o* lay down **3** **posarse** *vpr* to settle, to alight

posavasos *nm inv* coaster

posdata *nf* postscript

pose *nf* (**a**) *(postura)* pose (**b**) *(afectación)* posing

poseedor, -a *nm,f* possessor

poseer [36] *vt* to possess, to own

posesión *nf* possession; **estar en p. de** to have; **tomar p. (de un cargo)** to take up (a post)

posesivo, -a *adj* possessive

posibilidad *nf* possibility; *(oportunidad)* chance

posible 1 *adj* possible; **de ser p.** if possible; **en (la medida de) lo p.** as far as possible; **haré todo lo p.** I'll do everything I can; **lo antes p.** as soon as possible; **es p. que venga** he might come **2** *nmpl* **posibles** means

posición *nf* position

positivo, -a *adj* positive

posmoderno, -a *adj* postmodern

poso *nm* dregs, sediment

postal 1 *adj* postal **2** *nf* postcard

poste *nm* pole; *Dep (de portería)* post

póster *nm* *(pl* **pósters** *o* **posters***)* poster

posterior *adj* (**a**) *(lugar)* posterior, rear (**b**) *(tiempo)* later (**a** than), subsequent (**a** to)

postre *nm* dessert, *Br* pudding

postular 1 *vt* (**a**) *(defender)* to call for (**b**) *Am (proponer de candidato)* to nominate **2** *vi (en colecta)* to collect **3** **postularse** *vpr Am* (**a**) *Pol (para cargo)* to stand, to run (**b**) *CSur (para trabajo)* to apply (**para** for)

póstumo, -a *adj* posthumous

postura *nf* (**a**) position, posture (**b**)

Fig (actitud) attitude

potable *adj* drinkable; **agua p./no p.** drinking water/not drinking water

potaje *nm* hotpot, stew

potencia *nf* power; **en p.** potential

potenciar [43] *vt* to promote, to strengthen

potrero *nm Am* field, pasture

potro *nm Zool* colt; *(de gimnasia)* horse

pozo *nm* well; *Min* shaft, pit

pozole *nm CAm, Carib, Méx (guiso)* = stew made with maize kernels, pork or chicken and vegetables

práctica *nf* (a) practice; **en la p.** in practice (b) *(formación)* placement; **período de prácticas** practical training period

practicante 1 *adj Rel* practising **2** *nmf Med* medical assistant

practicar [44] **1** *vt* to practise; *(operación)* to carry out **2** *vi* to practise

práctico, -a *adj* practical; *(útil)* handy, useful

pradera *nf* meadow

prado *nm* meadow, field

precario, -a *adj* precarious

precaución *nf* (a) *(cautela)* caution; **con p.** cautiously (b) *(medida)* precaution

precintar *vt* to seal

precinto *nm* seal

precio *nm* price; **p. de costo** cost price; **a cualquier p.** at any price

preciosidad *nf* (a) *(hermosura) (cosa)* lovely thing; *(persona)* darling (b) *Fml (cualidad)* preciousness

precioso, -a *adj* (a) *(hermoso)* lovely, beautiful (b) *(valioso)* precious, valuable

precipicio *nm* precipice

precipitación *nf* (a) *(prisa)* haste (b) *(lluvia)* rainfall

precipitado, -a *adj (apresurado)* hasty, hurried; *(irreflexivo)* rash

precipitar 1 *vt* (a) *(acelerar)* to hurry, to rush (b) *(arrojar)* to throw, to hurl down **2 precipitarse** *vpr* (a) *(persona)* to hurl oneself; *(acontecimientos)*

to gather speed (b) *(actuar irreflexivamente)* to hurry, to rush

precisamente *adv (con precisión)* precisely; *(exactamente)* exactly; **p. por eso** for that very reason

precisar *vt* (a) *(determinar)* to determine, to give full details of; *(especificar)* to specify (b) *(necesitar)* to require, to need

preciso, -a *adj* (a) *(necesario)* necessary, essential (b) *(exacto)* accurate, exact; **en este p. momento** at this very moment (c) *(claro)* concise, clear

precoz *adj* (a) *(persona)* precocious (b) *(fruta)* early

predicar [44] *vt* to preach

predilecto, -a *adj* favourite, preferred

predominar *vi* to predominate

preeminente *adj* preeminent

preescolar *adj* preschool; **en p.** in the nursery school

preferencia *nf* preference

preferible *adj* preferable; **es p. que no vengas** you'd better not come

preferir [5] *vt* to prefer

prefijo *nm* (a) *Tel Br* dialling code, *US* area code (b) *Ling* prefix

pregón *nm* (a) *(bando)* proclamation, announcement (b) *(discurso)* speech

pregonar *vt (anunciar)* to announce publicly; *Fig (divulgar)* to reveal, to disclose

pregonero, -a *nm,f (de pueblo)* town crier; *Fig (bocazas)* blabbermouth

pregunta *nf* question; **hacer una p.** to ask a question

preguntar 1 *vt* to ask; **p. algo a algn** to ask sb sth; **p. por algn** to ask after *o* about sb **2 preguntarse** *vpr* to wonder; **me pregunto si …** I wonder whether …

prehistórico, -a *adj* prehistoric

prejuicio *nm* prejudice; **tener prejuicios** to be prejudiced, to be biased

prematuro, -a *adj* premature

premeditación *nf* premeditation; **con p.** deliberately

premiar [43] *vt* (**a**) to award a prize to (**b**) *(recompensar)* to reward

premio *nm* prize, award; *(recompensa)* reward

premisa *nf* premise

prenatal *adj* antenatal, prenatal

prenda *nf* (**a**) *(prenda)* garment (**b**) *(garantía)* token, pledge

prensa *nf* press; *Fig* **tener buena/ mala p.** to have a good/bad press

preocupación *nf* worry, concern

preocupado, -a *adj* worried, concerned

preocupar 1 *vt* to worry; **me preocupa que llegue tan tarde** I'm worried about him arriving so late **2 preocuparse** *vpr* to worry, to get worried (**por** about); **no te preocupes** don't worry; **preocuparse de algn** to look after sb; **preocuparse de algo** to see to sth

preparación *nf* preparation; *(formación)* training

preparar 1 *vt* (**a**) to prepare, to get ready; **p. un examen** to prepare for an exam (**b**) *Dep (entrenar)* to train, to coach **2 prepararse** *vpr* (**a**) to prepare oneself, to get ready (**b**) *Dep (entrenarse)* to train

preparativo *nm* preparation

preparatorio, -a *adj* preparatory

preponderante *adj* preponderant

preposición *nf Ling* preposition

prepotente *adj* domineering; *(arrogante)* overbearing

presa *nf* (**a**) prey; *Fig* **ser p. de** to be a victim of; **p. del pánico** panic-stricken (**b**) *(embalse)* dam

prescindir *vi* **p. de** to do without

presencia *nf* presence; **hacer acto de p.** to put in an appearance; **p. de ánimo** presence of mind

presenciar [43] *vt (ver)* to witness

presentable *adj* presentable; **no estoy p.** I'm not dressed for the occasion

presentación *nf* presentation; *(aspecto)* appearance; *(de personas)* introduction

presentador, -a *nm,f Rad, TV* presenter, host, *f* hostess

presentar 1 *vt* (**a**) to present; *(mostrar)* to show, to display; *(ofrecer)* to offer (**b**) *(una persona a otra)* to introduce; **le presento al doctor Ruiz** may I introduce you to Dr Ruiz **2 presentarse** *vpr* (**a**) *(comparecer)* to present oneself; *(inesperadamente)* to turn *o* come up (**b**) *(ocasión, oportunidad)* to present itself, to arise (**c**) *(candidato)* to stand; **presentarse a unas elecciones** to stand for election, *US* to run for office; **presentarse a un examen** to sit an examination (**d**) *(darse a conocer)* to introduce oneself (**a** to)

presente 1 *adj* present; **la p. (carta)** this letter; **hacer p.** to declare, to state; **tener p.** *(tener en cuenta)* to bear in mind; *(recordar)* to remember **2** *nm* present

presentimiento *nm* presentiment, premonition; **tengo el p. de que …** I have the feeling that …

preservar *vt* to preserve, to protect (**de** from; **contra** against)

preservativo *nm* condom

presidencia *nf* (**a**) *Pol* presidency (**b**) *(de una reunión)* chairmanship

presidenciable *nmf esp Am* potential presidential candidate

presidencial *adj* presidential

presidente, -a *nm,f* (**a**) *Pol (de nación)* president; **p. (del gobierno)** prime minister (**b**) *(de una reunión)* chairperson

presidiario, -a *nm,f* prisoner, convict

presidir *vt* (**a**) *Pol* to rule, to head (**b**) *(reunión)* to chair, to preside over

presión *nf* pressure; **a** *o* **bajo p.** under pressure; **grupo de p.** pressure group, lobby; **p. arterial** *o* **sanguínea** blood pressure; **p. atmosférica** atmospheric pressure

preso, -a 1 *adj* imprisoned **2** *nm,f* prisoner

préstamo *nm* loan

prestar 1 *vt* (**a**) to lend, to loan; **¿me prestas tu pluma?** can I borrow your pen? (**b**) *(atención)* to pay; *(ayuda)* to give; *(servicio)* to do **2 prestarse** *vpr* (**a**) *(ofrecerse)* to offer oneself (**a** to) (**b**) **prestarse a** *(dar motivo)* to cause; **se presta a (crear) malentendidos** it makes for misunderstandings

prestigio *nm* prestige

presumido, -a 1 *adj* vain, conceited **2** *nm,f* vain person

presumir 1 *vt (suponer)* to presume, to suppose **2** *vi* (**a**) *(ser vanidoso)* to show off (**b**) **presume de guapo** he thinks he's good-looking

presunción *nf* (**a**) *(suposición)* presumption, supposition (**b**) *(vanidad)* vanity, conceit

presunto, -a *adj* supposed; *Jur* alleged

presuntuoso, -a *adj* (**a**) *(vanidoso)* vain, conceited (**b**) *(pretencioso)* pretentious, showy

presupuesto *nm* (**a**) *Fin* budget; *(cálculo)* estimate (**b**) *(supuesto)* supposition, assumption

pretencioso, -a *adj* pretentious

pretender *vt* (**a**) *(intentar)* to try; **¿qué pretendes insinuar?** what are you getting at? (**b**) *(afirmar)* to claim (**c**) *(aspirar a)* to try for (**d**) *(cortejar)* to court, to woo

pretendiente, -a *nm,f* (**a**) *(al trono)* pretender (**b**) *(a un cargo)* applicant, candidate (**c**) *(amante)* suitor

pretensión *nf* (**a**) *(aspiración)* aim, aspiration (**b**) *(presunción)* pretentiousness

pretexto *nm* pretext, excuse

prever [28] *(pp* **previsto**) *vt* (**a**) *(prevenir)* to foresee, to forecast (**b**) *(preparar de antemano)* to cater for

previo, -a *adj* previous, prior; **p. pago de su importe** only on payment; **sin p. aviso** without prior notice

previsión *nf* (**a**) *(predicción)* forecast; **p. del tiempo** weather forecast (**b**) *(precaución)* precaution; **en p. de** as a precaution against (**c**) *Andes, RP* **p. social** social security

previsor, -a *adj* careful, far-sighted

previsto, -a *adj* foreseen, forecast;

según lo p. as expected

prieto, -a *adj* (**a**) *(ceñido)* tight; **íbamos muy prietos en el coche** we were really squashed together in the car (**b**) *Méx (oscuro)* dark

primaria *nf (enseñanza)* primary education

primario, -a *adj* primary

primavera *nf* spring

primer *adj (delante de nm)* ver **primero, -a**

primera *nf* (**a**) *(en tren)* first class (**b**) *Aut (marcha)* first gear (**c**) **a la p.** at the first attempt; *Fam* **de p.** great, first-class

primero, -a 1 *adj* first; **a primera hora de la mañana** first thing in the morning; **primera página** *o* **plana** front page; **de primera necesidad** basic

---

primer is used instead of **primero** before masculine singular nouns (e.g. **el primer hombre** the first man)

---

2 *nm,f* first; **a primero(s) de mes** at the beginning of the month **3** *adv* (**a**) first (**b**) *(más bien)* rather, sooner; *ver* **primera**

primo, -a 1 *nm,f* (**a**) cousin; **p. hermano** first cousin (**b**) *Fam (tonto)* fool, drip, dunce **2** *adj* (**a**) **materia prima** raw material (**b**) *(número)* prime

primogénito, -a *adj & nm,f* first-born

princesa *nf* princess

principado *nm* principality

principal *adj* main, principal; **lo p. es que ...** the main thing is that ...; **puerta p.** front door

príncipe *nm* prince

principiante 1 *adj* novice **2** *nmf* beginner, novice

principio *nm* (**a**) beginning, start; **a principio(s) de** at the beginning of; **al p., en un p.** at first, in the beginning (**b**) *(fundamento)* principle; **en p.** in principle (**c**) **principios** rudiments, basics

pringoso, -a *adj (grasiento)* greasy; *(sucio)* dirty

prioridad *nf* priority

prisa *nf* (a) *(rapidez)* hurry; **date p.** hurry up; **tener p.** to be in a hurry; **de/a p.** in a hurry (b) **correr p.** to be urgent; **me corre mucha p.** I need it right away

prisión *nf* prison, jail

prisionero, -a *nm,f* prisoner

prisma *nm* prism

prismáticos *nmpl* binoculars, field glasses

privado, -a *adj* private

privar 1 *vt (despojar)* to deprive (**de** of)
2 *vi* (a) *Fam (gustar)* to like; *(estar de moda)* to be fashionable o popular (b) *Fam (beber)* to booze
3 privarse *vpr (abstenerse)* to deprive oneself (**de** of), to go without

privilegiado, -a 1 *adj* privileged **2** *nm,f* privileged person

privilegio *nm* privilege

proa *nf* prow, bows

probabilidad *nf* probability, likelihood; **tiene pocas probabilidades** he stands little chance

probable *adj* probable, likely; **es p. que llueva** it'll probably rain

probador *nm* fitting room

probar [2] **1** *vt* (a) *(comida, bebida)* to try (b) *(comprobar)* to test, to check (c) *(intentar)* to try (d) *(demostrar)* to prove, to show
2 *vi* to try; **p. a** to attempt o try to
3 probarse *vpr (ropa)* to try on

probeta *nf* test tube; **niño p.** test-tube baby

problema *nm* problem

problemático, -a *adj* problematic

procedencia *nf* origin, source

procedente *adj* (a) *(originario)* coming (**de** from) (b) *(adecuado)* appropriate; *Jur* proper

proceder 1 *vi* (a) **p. de** *(provenir)* to come from (b) *(actuar)* to act (c) *(ser oportuno)* to be advisable o appropriate; *Jur* **la protesta no procede** objection overruled (d) **p. a** *(conti-nuar)* to go on to **2** *nm (compor-tamiento)* behaviour

procedimiento *nm* (a) *(método)* procedure (b) *Jur (trámites)* proceedings

procesado, -a 1 *nm,f* accused **2** *nm Informát* processing

procesar *vt* (a) *Jur* to prosecute (b) *(elaborar, transformar)* to process; *Informát* to process

procesión *nf* procession

proceso *nm* (a) process; *Informát* **p. de datos** data processing (b) *Jur* trial

proclamación *nf* proclamation

proclamar *vt* to proclaim

procuraduría *nf Méx* **p. general de justicia** Ministry of Justice

procurar *vt* (a) *(intentar)* to try, to attempt; **procura que no te vean** make sure they don't see you (b) *(proporcionar)* (to manage) to get

prodigar [42] *Fml* **1** *vt (dar generosamente)* to lavish **2 prodigarse** *vpr* **prodigarse en** to be lavish in

producción *nf (acción)* production; *(producto)* product; *Cin* production; **p. en cadena/serie** assembly-line/mass production

producir [10] **1** *vt* (a) to produce; *(fruto, cosecha)* to yield, to bear; *(ganancias)* to yield (b) *Fig (originar)* to cause, to bring about **2 producirse** *vpr* to take place, to happen

productividad *nf* productivity

productivo, -a *adj* productive; *(beneficioso)* profitable

producto *nm* product; *Agr (produc-ción)* produce

productor, -a 1 *adj* producing **2** *nm,f* producer

profecía *nf* prophecy

profesión *nf* profession; **de p.** by profession

profesional *adj & nmf* professional

profesionista *adj & nmf Méx* professional

profesor, -a *nm,f* teacher; *Univ Br* lecturer, *US* professor

profeta *nm* prophet

profundidad *nf* depth; **un metro de p.** one metre deep o in depth; *Fig (de* *ideas etc)* profundity, depth

profundo, -a *adj* deep; *Fig (idea, sentimiento)* profound

programa *nm* programme; *Informát* program; *Educ* syllabus

programación *nf Rad, TV* programme planning

programador, -a *nm,f Informát* programmer

programar *vt* to programme; *Informát* to program

progresar *vi* to progress, to make progress

progresivo, -a *adj* progressive

progreso *nm* progress; **hace grandes progresos** he's making great progress

prohibición *nf* prohibition, ban

prohibido, -a *adj* forbidden, prohibited; **prohibida la entrada** *(en letrero)* no admittance; **p. aparcar/ fumar** *(en letrero)* no parking/smoking

prohibir *vt* to forbid, to prohibit; **se prohíbe pasar** *(en letrero)* no admittance *o* entry

prójimo, -a *nm,f* one's fellow man, one's neighbour

proliferación *nf* proliferation; **p. nuclear** proliferation (of nuclear arms)

prólogo *nm* prologue

prolongar [42] **1** *vt (alargar)* to prolong, to extend **2 prolongarse** *vpr (continuar)* to carry on

promedio *nm* average; **como p.** on average

promesa *nf* promise; *Fig* **la joven p. de la música** the promising young musician

prometer 1 *vt* to promise; **te lo prometo** I promise

  2 *vi* to be promising

  3 prometerse *vpr (pareja)* to get engaged

prometido, -a 1 *adj* promised **2** *nm,f* fiancé, *f* fiancée

promoción *nf* promotion; *Educ* **p. universitaria** class, year

promocionar *vt (cosas)* to promote; *(personas)* to give promotion to

promotor, -a *adj* promoting **2** *nm,f* promoter

pronóstico *nm (del tiempo)* forecast; *Med* prognosis

pronto, -a 1 *adj* quick, prompt; *Fml (dispuesto)* prepared

  2 *nm (impulso)* sudden impulse

  3 *adv* (**a**) *(deprisa)* quickly, rapidly; **al p.** at first; **de p.** suddenly; **por de** *o* **lo p.** *(para empezar)* to start with (**b**) *(dentro de poco)* soon; **¡hasta p.!** see you soon! (**c**) *Esp (temprano)* early; **salimos p.** we left early

pronunciación *nf* pronunciation

pronunciar [43] **1** *vt* to pronounce; *(discurso)* to deliver **2 pronunciarse** *vpr* (**a**) *(opinar)* to declare oneself (**b**) *(sublevarse)* to rise up

propaganda *nf (política)* propaganda; *(comercial)* advertising, publicity

propensión *nf* tendency, inclination

propenso, -a *adj* (**a**) *(inclinado)* prone, inclined (**b**) *Med* susceptible

propiciar [43] *vt (causar)* to cause

propicio, -a *adj* propitious, suitable; **ser p. a** to be inclined to

propiedad *nf* (**a**) *(posesión)* ownership; *(cosa poseída)* property (**b**) *(cualidad)* property, quality; *Fig* **con p.** properly, appropriately

propietario, -a *nm,f* owner

propina *nf* tip; **dar p. (a algn)** to tip (sb)

propio, -a *adj* (**a**) *(de uno)* own; **en su propia casa** in his own house (**b**) *(correcto)* suitable, appropriate; **juegos propios para su edad** games suitable for their age (**c**) *(característico)* typical, peculiar (**d**) *(mismo)* *(hombre)* himself; *(mujer)* herself; *(animal, cosa)* itself; **el p. autor** the author himself (**e**) **propios** themselves; **los propios inquilinos** the tenants themselves (**f**) *Ling* proper

proponer [19] *(pp* **propuesto)** **1** *vt* to propose, to suggest **2 proponerse** *vpr* to intend

proporcionado, -a *adj (mesurado)* proportionate, in proportion

proporcionar *vt (dar)* to give, to supply, to provide

proposición *nf* (**a**) *(propuesta)* proposal (**b**) *(oración)* clause

propósito *nm* (**a**) *(intención)* intention (**b**) **a p.** *(por cierto)* by the way; *(adrede)* on purpose, intentionally; **a p. de viajes …** speaking of travelling …

propuesta *nf* suggestion, proposal

propuesto, -a *pp de* **proponer**

prórroga *nf* (**a**) *(prolongación)* extension; *Dep Br* extra time, *US* overtime (**b**) *(aplazamiento)* postponement; *Mil* deferment

prorrogar [42] *vt* (**a**) *(prolongar)* to extend (**b**) *(aplazar)* to postpone; *Mil* to defer

prosa *nf* prose

proscrito, -a 1 *adj (persona)* exiled, banished; *(cosa)* banned **2** *nm,f* exile, outlaw

prospecto *nm* leaflet, prospectus

próspero, -a *adj* prosperous, thriving; **¡p. año nuevo!** Happy New Year!

prostíbulo *nm* brothel

prostitución *nf* prostitution

prostituta *nf* prostitute

protagonista *nmf* (**a**) main character, leading role; **¿quién es el p.?** who plays the lead? (**b**) *Fig (centro)* centre of attraction

protección *nf* protection

proteger [53] *vt* to protect, to defend

protegido, -a *nm,f (hombre)* protégé; *(mujer)* protégée

proteína *nf* protein

protesta *nf* protest; *Jur* objection

protestante *adj & nmf Rel* Protestant

protestar *vi* (**a**) to protest; *Jur* to object (**b**) *Fam (quejarse)* to complain

protocolo *nm* protocol

provecho *nm* profit, benefit; **¡buen p.!** enjoy your meal!; **sacar p. de algo** to benefit from sth

provechoso, -a *adj* beneficial

provenir [27] *vi* **p. de** to come from

proverbio *nm* proverb

provincia *nf* province

provisional, *Am* **provisorio, -a** *adj* provisional

provocación *nf* provocation

provocar [44] *vt* (**a**) *(causar)* to cause; **p. un incendio** to start a fire (**b**) *(instigar)* to provoke (**c**) *Carib, Col, Méx Fam (apetecer)* **¿te provoca ir al cine?** would you like to go to the movies?, *Br* do you fancy going to the cinema?

provocativo, -a *adj* provocative

próximo, -a *adj* (**a**) *(cercano)* near, close (**b**) *(siguiente)* next

proyección *nf* (**a**) projection (**b**) *Cin* showing

proyectar *vt* (**a**) *(luz)* to project (**b**) *(planear)* to plan (**c**) *Cin* to show

proyecto *nm (plan)* project, plan; **tener algo en p.** to be planning sth; **p. de ley** bill

proyector *nm Cin* projector

prudencia *nf* prudence, discretion; *(moderación)* care

prudente *adj* prudent, sensible; *(conductor)* careful; **a una hora p.** at a reasonable time

prueba *nf* (**a**) proof; **en p. de** as a sign of (**b**) *(examen etc)* test; **a p.** on trial; **a p. de agua/balas** waterproof/bulletproof; **haz la p.** try it (**c**) *Dep* event

psicoanálisis *nm inv* psychoanalysis

psicología *nf* psychology

psicológico, -a *adj* psychological

psicólogo, -a *nm,f* psychologist

psicópata *nmf* psychopath

psiquiatra *nmf* psychiatrist

psiquiátrico, -a 1 *adj* psychiatric; **hospital p.** psychiatric hospital **2** *nm* psychiatric hospital

psíquico, -a *adj* psychic

pta. (*pl* **ptas.**) *(abr* **peseta**) *Antes* peseta(s)

púa *nf* (**a**) *(de planta)* thorn; *(de animal)* quill, spine; *(de peine)* tooth; **alambre de púas** barbed wire (**b**) *Mús* plectrum

pub *nm* (*pl* **pubs**) pub

pubertad *nf* puberty

pubis *nm inv* pubes

publicación *nf* publication

publicar [44] *vt* (**a**) *(libro etc)* to publish (**b**) *(secreto)* to publicize

publicidad *nf* (**a**) *Com* advertising (**b**) *(conocimiento público)* publicity

publicitario, -a *adj* advertising

público, -a 1 *adj* public **2** *nm* public; *Teatro* audience; *Dep* spectators

pucha *interj* Andes, RP Fam Euf (**a**) *(lamento, enojo)* Br sugar!, US shoot! (**b**) *(sorpresa)* wow!

pucho *nm* Fam (**a**) Andes, RP *(cigarrillo)* cigarette, Br fag (**b**) Andes, RP *(colilla)* cigarette butt (**c**) Chile, Ecuad *(hijo menor)* youngest child

pudor *nm* modesty

pudrir *vt* defect, **pudrirse** *vpr* to rot, to decay

pueblo *nm* (**a**) *(población) (pequeña)* village; *(grande)* town (**b**) *(gente)* people; **el p. español** the Spanish people

puente *nm* (**a**) bridge; *Av* **p. aéreo** *(civil)* air shuttle service; *Mil* airlift; **p. colgante** suspension bridge; **p. levadizo** drawbridge (**b**) *(entre dos fiestas)* ≃ long weekend

puerco, -a 1 *adj* filthy **2** *nm,f* pig **3** *nm* **p. espín** porcupine

puerro *nm* leek

puerta *nf* door; *(verja, en aeropuerto)* gate; *Dep* goal; **p. corredera/ giratoria** sliding/revolving door; *Fig* **a las puertas, en puertas** imminent; *Fig* **a p. cerrada** behind closed doors

puerto *nm* (**a**) *(de mar)* port, harbour; **p. deportivo** marina (**b**) *(de montaña)* (mountain) pass

Puerto Rico *n* Puerto Rico

pues *conj* (**a**) *(puesto que)* as, since (**b**) *(por lo tanto)* therefore (**c**) *(entonces)* so (**d**) *(para reforzar)* **¡p. claro que sí!** but of course!; **p. como iba diciendo** well, as I was saying; **¡p. mejor!** so much the better!; **¡p. no!** certainly not!

puesta *nf* (**a**) **p. de sol** sunset (**b**) *Fig* **p. a punto** tuning, adjusting; *Fig* **p. al día** updating; *Teatro* **p. en escena** staging; **p. en marcha** starting-up, start-up; *ver* **puesto, -a**

puestero, -a *nm,f Am* stallholder

puesto, -a 1 *conj* **p. que** since, as **2** *nm* (**a**) *(lugar)* place; *(asiento)* seat (**b**) *(empleo)* position, post, job; **p. de trabajo** job, post (**c**) *(tienda)* stall (**d**) *Mil* post

3 *adj* (**a**) *(colocado)* set, put (**b**) **llevar p.** *(ropa)* to have on; *Fam* **ir muy p.** to be all dressed up (**c**) *Fam (borracho)* drunk (**d**) *Fam* **estar p. en una materia** to be well up in a subject

pulga *nf* flea; *Fam* **tener malas pulgas** to be bad-tempered, *Br* to be stroppy

pulgar *nm* thumb

pulidora *nf* polisher

pulir *vt* (**a**) *(metal, madera)* to polish (**b**) *(mejorar)* to polish up

pulmón *nm* lung

pulmonía *nf* pneumonia

pulpa *nf* pulp

pulpería *nf Am* general store

pulpo *nm* octopus

pulque *nm CAm, Méx* pulque, = fermented agave cactus juice

pulquería *nf CAm, Méx* "pulque" bar

pulsar *vt* *(timbre, botón)* to press; *(tecla)* to hit, to strike

pulsera *nf* *(aro)* bracelet; *(de reloj)* watchstrap; **reloj de p.** wristwatch

pulso *nm* (**a**) pulse; *Fig* **tomar el p. a la opinión pública** to sound out opinion (**b**) *(mano firme)* steady hand; **a p.** freehand; **ganarse algo a p.** to deserve sth (**c**) *Fig* trial of strength; **echarse un p.** to arm-wrestle

puma *nm* puma

puna *nf* Andes (**a**) *(llanura)* Andean plateau (**b**) *(mal de altura)* altitude sickness

punk [pank] *adj, nm & nmf* (*pl* **punks**) punk

punki ['panki] *adj & nmf* punk

punta *nf* (**a**) *(extremo)* tip; *(extremo afilado)* point; *(de cabello)* end; **sacar p. a un lápiz** to sharpen a pencil; **tecnología p.** state-of-the-art technology; **me pone los nervios de p.** he makes me very nervous (**b**) *(periodo)* peak; **hora p.** rush hour (**c**) *(pequeña cantidad)* bit; **una p. de sal** a pinch of salt (**d**) *(clavo)* nail

puntada *nf* (**a**) *(pespunte)* stitch (**b**) *RP (dolor)* stabbing pain (**c**) *Méx (broma)* witticism

puntaje *nf Am (calificación)* mark, *US* grade; *(en concursos, competiciones)* score

puntapié *nm* kick

puntera *nf (de zapato)* toecap; *(de calcetín)* toe

puntería *nf* aim; **tener buena/mala p.** to be a good/bad shot

puntero, -a 1 *adj* leading **2** *nm,f CSur Dep* winger

puntiagudo, -a *adj* pointed, sharp

puntilla *nf* (**a**) *(encaje)* lace (**b**) **dar la p.** *Taurom* to finish (the bull) off; *Fig (liquidar)* to finish off (**c**) **de puntillas** on tiptoe

punto *nm* (**a**) point; **a p.** ready; *Culin* **en su p.** just right; **a p. de** on the point of; **hasta cierto p.** to a certain *o* some extent; **p. muerto** *Aut* neutral; *Fig (impase)* deadlock; **p. de vista** point of view

(**b**) *(marca)* dot; **línea de puntos** dotted line

(**c**) *(lugar)* place, point

(**d**) **p. y aparte** *Br* full stop *o US* period, new paragraph; **p. y coma** semicolon; **p. y seguido** *Br* full stop, *US* period *(no new paragraph)*; **dos puntos** colon

(**e**) *(tiempo)* **en p.** sharp, on the dot

(**f**) *Dep (tanto)* point

(**g**) *Cost, Med* stitch; **hacer p.** to knit

puntuación *nf* (**a**) *Ling* punctuation (**b**) *Dep* score (**c**) *Educ* mark

puntual 1 *adj* (**a**) punctual (**b**) *(exacto)* accurate, precise (**c**) *(caso)* specific **2** *adv* punctually

puntualidad *nf* punctuality

puntualización *nf* clarification

puntualizar [40] *vt* to specify, to clarify

puntuar [30] **1** *vt (al escribir)* to punctuate **2** *vi* (**a**) *(marcar)* to score (**b**) *(ser puntuable)* to count

punzón *nm (herramienta)* punch

puñado *nm* handful; *Fam* **a puñados** by the score, galore

puñal *nm* dagger

puñalada *nf* stab; *Fig* **p. trapera** stab in the back

puñeta *nf Fam* **hacer la p. a algn** to pester sb, to annoy sb; **¡puñetas!** damn!; **¡vete a hacer puñetas!** go to hell!

puñetazo *nm* punch

puñetero, -a *Esp Fam* **1** *adj* (**a**) *(persona)* damn (**b**) *(cosa)* tricky, awkward **2** *nm,f* pain

puño *nm* (**a**) fist (**b**) *(de camisa etc)* cuff (**c**) *(de herramienta)* handle

pupa *nf* (**a**) *(herida)* cold sore (**b**) *Fam (daño)* pain

pupitre *nm* desk

puré *nm* purée; **p. de patata** mashed potatoes; **p. de verduras** thick vegetable soup

puritano, -a 1 *adj* puritanical **2** *nm,f* puritan, Puritan

puro, -a 1 *adj* (**a**) *(sin mezclas)* pure; **aire p.** fresh air; **la pura verdad** the plain truth; *Pol* **p. y duro** hardline (**b**) *(mero)* sheer, mere; **por pura curiosidad** out of sheer curiosity (**c**) *(casto)* chaste, pure **2** *nm (cigarro)* cigar

puta *nf Vulg* whore; **de p. madre** great, terrific; **de p. pena** *Br* bloody *o US* goddamn awful; **no tengo ni p. idea** I haven't (got) a *Br* bloody *o US* goddamn clue; **pasarlas putas** to go through hell, to have a rotten time

puteada *nf RP muy Fam (insulto)* swearword

putear *vt muy Fam* (**a**) *(fastidiar)* **p. a algn** to screw *o* bugger sb around (**b**) *Am (insultar)* **p. a algn** to call sb for everything, to call sb every name under the sun

puzzle *nm* jigsaw puzzle

PVP *nm (abr* **precio de venta al público***)* RRP

Pza. *(abr* **Plaza***)* Sq

Qq

que¹ *pron rel* (**a**) *(sujeto)* *(persona)* who; *(cosa)* that, which; **el hombre q. vino** the man who came; **la bomba q. estalló** the bomb that o which went off (**b**) *(complemento)* *(persona)* that, who, *Fml* whom; *(cosa)* that, which; **la chica q. conocí** the girl (that o who o whom) I met; **el coche q. compré** the car (that o which) I bought (**c**) **lo q.** what; **lo q. más me gusta** what I like best (**d**) *(+ infinitivo)* **hay mucho q. hacer** there's a lot to do

que² *conj* (**a**) that; **dijo q. llamaría** he said (that) he would call; **quiero q. vengas** I want you to come (**b**) *(consecutivo)* that; *(en comparativas)* than; **habla tan bajo q. no se le oye** he speaks so quietly (that) he can't be heard; **más alto q. yo** taller than me (**c**) *(causal)* **date deprisa q. no tenemos mucho tiempo** hurry up, we haven't got much time (**d**) *(enfático)* **¡q. no!** no!; **¡q. te calles!** I said be quiet! (**e**) *(deseo, mandato)* **¡q. te diviertas!** enjoy yourself! (**f**) *(final)* so that; **ven q. te dé un beso** come and let me give you a kiss (**g**) *(disyuntivo)* whether; **me da igual q. suba o no** it doesn't matter to me whether he comes up or not (**h**) *(locuciones)* **¿a q. no ...?** I bet you can't ...!; **q. yo sepa** as far as I know; **yo q. tú** if I were you

qué **1** *pron* (**a**) *(interrogativo)* what; **¿q. quieres?** what do you want?; *Fam* **¿y q.?** so what? (**b**) *(exclamativo)* *(+ adj)* how; **¡q. bonito!** how pretty! (**c**) *(+ nombre)* what a; **¡q. lástima!** what a pity! (**d**) *Fam* **¡q. de ...!** what a lot of ...! **2** *adj interr* which; **¿q. libro quieres?** which book do you want?

quebrada *nf Am (arroyo)* stream

quebrado *nm Mat* fraction

quebrar [1] **1** *vt (romper)* to break
2 *vi Fin* to go bankrupt
3 quebrarse *vpr* to break; *Med* to rupture oneself

quedar 1 *vi* (**a**) *(restar)* to be left, to remain; **quedan dos** there are two left (**b**) *(en un lugar)* to arrange to meet; **quedamos en el bar** I'll meet you in the bar (**c**) **me queda corta** *(ropa)* it is too short for me; **quedaría muy bien allí** *(objeto)* it would look very nice there (**d**) *(acordar)* to agree (**en** to); **¿en qué quedamos?** so what's it to be? (**e**) *(estar situado)* to be; **¿dónde queda la estación?** where's the station? (**f**) **q. bien/mal** to make a good/bad impression
2 quedarse *vpr* (**a**) *(permanecer)* to stay; **se quedó en casa** she stayed (at) home; **quedarse sin dinero/pan** to run out of money/bread; **quedarse con hambre** to still be hungry (**b**) **quedarse (con)** *(retener)* to keep; **quédese (con) el cambio** keep the change (**c**) *Esp Fam* **quedarse con algn** to make a fool of sb

quehacer *nm* task, chore

quejarse *vpr* to complain (**de** about)

quejido *nm* groan, cry

quemadura *nf* burn

quemar 1 *vt* to burn; *Fig (agotar)* to burn out
2 *vi* to be burning hot; **este café quema** this coffee's boiling hot
3 quemarse *vpr Fig* to burn out

quepa etc ver **caber**

quepo *indic pres de* **caber**

queque *nm Andes, CAm, Méx* sponge (cake)

querer [20] **1** *vt* (**a**) *(amar)* to love (**b**) *(desear)* to want; **¿cuánto quiere por la casa?** how much does he want for the house?; **sin q.** without meaning to; **queriendo** on purpose; **¡por lo que más quieras!** for heaven's sake!; **¿quiere pasarme el pan?** would you pass me the bread? (**c**) **q. decir** to mean (**d**) **no quiso darme permiso** he refused me permission

2 quererse *vpr* to love each other

3 *nm* love, affection

querido, -a 1 *adj* dear, beloved; **q. amigo** *(en carta)* dear friend **2** *nm,f (amante)* lover

quesadilla *nf* (**a**) *CAm, Méx (salada)* = filled fried tortilla (**b**) *Ecuad (dulce)* = sweet, cheese-filled pasty

queso *nm* cheese; **q. rallado** grated cheese; **q. de cerdo** *Br* brawn, *US* headcheese

quiebra *nf Fin (bancarrota)* bankruptcy; *(en Bolsa)* crash

quien *pron rel* (**a**) *(con prep)* **el hombre con q. vino** the man she came with; *Fml* the man with whom she came (**b**) *(indefinido)* whoever, anyone who; **q. quiera venir que venga** whoever wants to can come; **hay q. dice lo contrario** some people say the opposite; *Fig* **q. más q. menos** everybody

quién *pron interr* (**a**) *(sujeto)* who?; **¿q. es?** who is it? (**b**) *(complemento)* who, *Fml* whom; **¿para q. es?** who is it for?; **¿de q. es esa bici?** whose bike is that?

quienquiera (*pl* **quienesquiera**) *pron* whoever; **q. que venga** whoever comes

quieto, -a *adj* still; *(mar)* calm; **¡estáte q.!** keep still!, don't move!

quilla *nf* keel

quillango *nm Arg, Chile* fur blanket

quilo = **kilo**

quilombo *nm RP muy Fam* (**a**) *(burdel)* whorehouse (**b**) *(lío, desorden)* **se armó un gran q.** all hell broke loose

química *nf* chemistry

químico, -a 1 *adj* chemical **2** *nm,f* chemist

quince *adj & nm inv* fifteen

quincena *nf* fortnight, two weeks

quincho *nm Andes, RP* (**a**) *(techo)* thatched roof (**b**) *(refugio)* thatched shelter

quinielas *nfpl Esp Br* (football) pools, *US* sports lottery

quinientos, -as *adj & nm* five hundred

quinqué *nm* oil lamp

quinteto *nm* quintet

quinto, -a 1 *adj & nm,f* fifth **2** *nm Mil* conscript, recruit

quiosco *nm* kiosk; **q. de periódicos** newspaper stand

quipos, quipus *nmpl Andes* quipus, = knotted cords used for record keeping by the Incas

quirófano *nm* operating *Br* theatre *o US* room

quisquilloso, -a 1 *adj* fussy, finicky **2** *nm,f* fusspot

quitamanchas *nm inv* stain remover

quitar 1 *vt* (**a**) to remove; *(ropa)* to take off; *(la mesa)* to clear; *(mancha)* to remove; *(dolor)* to relieve; *(hipo)* to stop; *(sed)* to quench; *(hambre)* to take away (**b**) *(apartar)* to take away, to take off; *Fig* **q. importancia a algo** to play sth down; *Fig* **q. las ganas a algn** to put sb off (**c**) *(robar)* to steal, to take; *Fig (tiempo)* to take up; *(sitio)* to take (**d**) *(descontar)* to take off (**e**) *Fam (apagar)* to turn off (**f**) **eso no quita para que …** that's no reason not to be …

2 quitarse *vpr* (**a**) *(apartarse)* to move away (**b**) *(mancha)* to come out; *(dolor)* to go away; **se me han quitado las ganas** I don't feel like it any more (**c**) *(ropa, gafas)* to take off (**d**) **quitarse de beber/fumar** to give up drinking/smoking (**e**) **quitarse a algn de encima** to get rid of sb

quizá, quizás *adv* perhaps, maybe

Rr

rábano *nm* radish; *Fam* **me importa un r.** I couldn't care less

rabia *nf* (**a**) *Fig (ira)* fury, rage; **¡qué r.!** how annoying!; **me da r.** it gets up my nose; **me tiene r.** he's got it in for me (**b**) *Med* rabies *sing*

rabieta *nf Fam* tantrum; **coger una r.** to throw a tantrum

rabioso, -a *adj* (**a**) *Med* rabid; **perro r.** rabid dog (**b**) *Fig (enfadado)* furious (**c**) **de rabiosa actualidad** up-to-the-minute

rabo *nm* tail; *(de fruta etc)* stalk

racha *nf (de viento)* gust, squall; *Fam (período)* spell, patch; **a rachas** in fits and starts

racial *adj* **discriminación r.** racial discrimination; **disturbios raciales** race riots

racimo *nm* bunch, cluster

ración *nf* portion

racismo *nm* racism

racista *adj & nmf* racist

radar *nm Téc* radar

radiación *nf* radiation

radiador *nm* radiator

radial *adj* (**a**) *(en forma de estrella)* radial (**b**) *Am (de la radio)* radio

radiante *adj* radiant (**de** with)

radiar [43] *vt* to broadcast, to transmit

radical *adj* radical

radio 1 *nf (medio)* radio; *Esp, CSur (aparato)* radio (set) **2** *nm* (**a**) radius; **r. de acción** field of action, scope (**b**) *(de rueda)* spoke

radioaficionado, -a *nm,f* radio ham

radiocasete *nm* radio cassette

radiodespertador *nm* clock radio

radiodifusión *nf* broadcasting

radiograbador *nm*, **radiograba-**

dora *nf CSur* radio cassette

radiografía *nf (imagen)* X-ray

radiólogo, -a *nm,f* radiologist

radionovela *nf* radio soap opera

radiotaxi *nm (aparato de radio)* = taxi driver's two-way radio; *(taxi)* taxi *(fitted with two-way radio)*

radioyente *nmf* listener

ráfaga *nf (de viento)* gust, squall; *(de disparos)* burst

rafting *nm Dep* rafting

raíl *nm* rail

raíz *nf* root; **r. cuadrada** square root; *Fig* **a r. de** as a result of

raja *nf (corte)* cut, slit; *(hendidura)* crack, split

rajar 1 *vt (hender)* to crack, split; *Fam (acuchillar)* to cut up
2 *vi Esp Fam* to natter on, to witter on
3 rajarse *vpr* (**a**) *(partirse)* to crack (**b**) *Esp Fam (echarse atrás)* to back *o* pull out

rajatabla: a rajatabla *loc adv* to the letter, strictly

rallador *nm* grater

rallar *vt* to grate

rally ['rrali] *nm (pl* **rallys** *o* **rallies)** rally

rama *nf* branch; *Fam* **andarse** *o* **irse por las ramas** to beat about the bush

rambla *nf (avenida)* boulevard, avenue

ramo *nm* (**a**) *(de flores)* bunch, bouquet (**b**) *(sector)* branch

rampa *nf* ramp; **r. de lanzamiento** launch pad

rana *nf* frog; *Fam* **salir r.** to be a disappointment

ranchera *nf* (**a**) *Mús* = popular Mexican song (**b**) *(automóvil) Br* estate (car), *US* station wagon

rancho *nm* (**a**) *(granja)* ranch (**b**) *Mil (comida)* mess (**c**) *RP (en la playa)* =

thatched beachside building (**d**) *CSur,
Ven (en ciudad)* shack, shanty (**e**) *Méx
(pequeña finca)* = small farmhouse
and outbuildings

rancio, -a *adj* (**a**) *(comida)* stale (**b**)
(antiguo) ancient

rango *nm* rank; *(jerarquía elevada)*
high social standing

ranura *nf* slot

rape *nm* (**a**) *(pez)* angler fish (**b**) *Fam*
cortado al r. close-cropped

rápidamente *adv* quickly

rapidez *nf* speed, rapidity

rápido, -a 1 *adj* quick, fast, rapid
2 *adv* quickly
3 *nm* (**a**) *(tren)* fast train (**b**) **rápidos**
(de río) rapids

raptar *vt* to kidnap, to abduct

raqueta *nf* (**a**) *(de tenis)* racquet; *(de
ping-pong)* *Br* bat, *US* paddle (**b**) *(de
nieve)* snowshoe

raro, -a *adj* (**a**) rare; **rara vez** seldom
(**b**) *(extraño)* odd, strange

rascacielos *nm inv* skyscraper

rascador *nm (herramienta)* scraper

rascar [44] **1** *vt (con uñas)* to scratch;
(guitarra) to strum **2** *vi* to chafe

rasgar [42] *vt* to tear, to rip

rasgo *nm (característica)* characteristic, feature; *(de rostro)* feature; *Fig* **a
grandes rasgos** broadly speaking

raso, -a 1 *adj (llano)* flat, level; *(vuelo)*
low; *(cielo)* clear, cloudless; **soldado r.**
private **2** *nm* satin

rastrillo *nm* (**a**) rake (**b**) *(mercado)*
flea market

rastro *nm* (**a**) trace, sign; *(en el suelo)*
track, trail (**b**) **el R.** = the Madrid flea
market

rata 1 *nf* rat **2** *nm Fam (tacaño)* mean *o*
stingy person

ratero, -a *nm,f* pickpocket

rato *nm* (**a**) *(momento)* while, time; **a
ratos** at times; **al poco r.** shortly after;
hay para r. it'll take a while; **pasar un
buen/mal r.** to have a good/bad time;
ratos libres free time (**b**) *Esp Fam* **un r.**
(mucho) very, a lot

ratón *nm* mouse; *Esp Informát* mouse

raya *nf* (**a**) *(línea)* line; *(del pantalón)*
crease; *Esp, Andes, RP (del pelo)* *Br*
parting, *US* part; **camisa a rayas**
striped shirt (**b**) *Fig* **tener a r.** to keep
at bay; **pasarse de la r.** to go too far
(**c**) *(de droga)* fix, dose

rayo *nm* (**a**) ray, beam; **rayos X** X-rays
(**b**) *(relámpago)* (flash of) lightning;
¡mal r. la parta! to hell with her!

rayuela *nf* hopscotch

raza *nf* (**a**) *(humana)* race (**b**) *(de
animal)* breed (**c**) *Méx Pey (populacho)*
la r. the masses (**d**) *Perú (descaro)*
cheek, nerve

razón *nf* (**a**) *(facultad)* reason; **uso de
r.** power of reasoning (**b**) *(motivo)*
reason; **r. de más para** all the more
reason to (**c**) *(justicia)* rightness,
justice; **dar la r. a algn** to say that sb
is right; **tienes r.** you're right (**d**)
(proporción) ratio, rate; **a r. de** at the
rate of (**e**) **r. aquí** *(en letrero)* enquire
within, apply within

razonable *adj* reasonable

razonamiento *nm* reasoning

razonar 1 *vt (argumentar)* to reason
out **2** *vi (discurrir)* to reason

reacción *nf* reaction; **avión de r.** jet
(plane); **r. en cadena** chain reaction

reaccionar *vi* to react

reactor *nm* reactor; *(avión)* jet (plane)

real¹ *adj (efectivo, verdadero)* real; **en
la vida r.** in real life

real² *adj (regio)* royal

realeza *nf* royalty

realidad *nf* reality; **en r.** in fact,
actually; **la r. es que ...** the fact of the
matter is that ...

realismo *nm* realism

realización *nf (ejecución)* carrying
out; *Cin, TV* production

realizar [40] **1** *vt* (**a**) *(hacer)* to carry
out; *(ambición)* to achieve, to fulfil (**b**)
Cin, TV to produce (**c**) *Fin* to realize
2 realizarse *vpr (persona)* to fulfil
oneself; *(sueño)* to come true

realmente *adv* really; *(en realidad)*
actually, in fact

reanimación *nf* revival

rebaja *nf (descuento)* reduction, discount; **rebajas** sales; **precio de r.** sale price

rebajado, -a *adj* (**a**) *(precio)* reduced (**b**) *(diluido)* diluted (**con** with)

rebajar 1 *vt* (**a**) *(precio)* to cut, to reduce; *(cantidad)* to take off (**b**) *(color)* to tone down, to soften; *(intensidad)* to diminish (**c**) *(trabajador)* to excuse, to exempt (**de** from) (**d**) *(humillar)* to humiliate **2 rebajarse** *vpr (humillarse)* to humble oneself

rebanada *nf* slice

rebanar *vt* to slice, to cut into slices

rebaño *nm (de ovejas)* flock; *(de otros animales)* herd

rebelarse *vpr* to rebel, to revolt

rebelde 1 *nmf* rebel **2** *adj* rebellious; *Fig* **una tos r.** a persistent cough

rebeldía *nf* (**a**) rebelliousness (**b**) *Jur* default

rebelión *nf* rebellion, revolt

rebenque *nm RP (fusta)* (riding) crop, whip

rebotar *vi* to bounce (**en** off), to rebound (**en** off)

rebote *nm* (**a**) *(bote)* bounce, bouncing; *Fig* **de r.** by chance, indirectly (**b**) *Dep* rebound; **de r.** on the rebound

rebozado, -a *adj Culin* coated in batter *o* breadcrumbs; *Fig* **r. de** *o* **en** *(barro)* covered in

rebozo *nm Am* wrap, shawl; **sin r.** *(con franqueza)* frankly

recado *nm (mandado)* errand; *(mensaje)* message; **dejar un r.** to leave a message

recaer [39] *vi* (**a**) *Med* to relapse (**b**) *(culpa, responsabilidad)* to fall (**sobre** on)

recalcar [44] *vt* to stress, to emphasize

recalentar [1] *vt* *(comida)* to reheat, to warm up; *(calentar demasiado)* to overheat

recámara *nf* (**a**) *(de rueda)* tube (**b**) *(habitación)* dressing room (**c**) *CAm, Col, Méx (dormitorio)* bedroom

recamarera *nf CAm, Col, Méx* chambermaid

recambio *nm* (**a**) *(repuesto)* spare (part); **rueda de r.** spare wheel (**b**) *(de pluma etc)* refill

recargar [42] **1** *vt* (**a**) *Elec* to recharge (**b**) *(sobrecargar)* to overload; *(adornar mucho)* to overelaborate (**c**) *Fin* to increase **2 recargarse** *vpr Méx (apoyarse)* to lean (**contra** against)

recato *nm (cautela)* caution, prudence; *(pudor)* modesty

recepción *nf* reception; *(en hotel)* reception (desk)

recepcionista *nmf* receptionist

receptor, -a 1 *nm,f (persona)* recipient **2** *nm Rad, TV* receiver

recesión *nf* recession

receta *nf* recipe; *Med* prescription

recetar *vt Med* to prescribe

rechazar [40] *vt* to reject, to turn down; *Mil* to repel, to drive back

rechazo *nm* rejection

recibidor *nm* entrance hall

recibimiento *nm* reception, welcome

recibir 1 *vt* to receive; *(en casa)* to welcome; *(en la estación etc)* to meet **2 recibirse** *vpr Am (graduarse)* to graduate, to qualify (**de** as)

recibo *nm* (**a**) *(factura)* invoice, bill; *(resguardo)* receipt; **r. de la luz** electricity bill (**b**) **acusar r. de** to acknowledge receipt of

reciclado, -a 1 *adj* recycled **2** *nm (reciclaje)* recycling

reciclaje *nm (de residuos)* recycling; *Fig (renovación)* retraining; **curso de r.** refresher course

reciclar *vt (residuos)* to recycle; *Fig (profesores etc)* to retrain

recién *adv* (**a**) *(recientemente) (antes de pp)* recently, newly; **café r. hecho** freshly-made coffee; **r. casados** newly-weds; **r. nacido** newborn baby (**b**) *Am (apenas)* just now, recently; **regresó r. ayer** she only *o* just got back yesterday (**c**) *Am (ahora mismo)* (only) just; **r. me entero** I've (only) just heard (**d**) *Am (sólo)* only; **r. el martes sabremos el resultado** we'll only know the result on Tuesday, we won't know the result until Tuesday

reciente *adj* recent

recientemente *adv* recently, lately

recinto *nm (cercado)* enclosure; **r. comercial** shopping precinct

recipiente *nm* receptacle, container

recital *nm Mús* recital; *Lit* reading

recitar *vt* to recite

reclamación *nf* (**a**) *(demanda)* claim, demand (**b**) *(queja)* complaint

reclamar 1 *vt* to claim, to demand **2** *vi* (**a**) to protest (**contra** against) (**b**) *Jur* to appeal

reclamo *nm* (**a**) *(publicitario)* appeal (**b**) *(en caza)* decoy bird, lure; *Fig* inducement (**c**) *Am (queja)* complaint (**d**) *Am (reivindicación)* claim

recluir [37] *vt* to shut away, to lock away; *(encarcelar)* to imprison, to intern

reclusión *nf* seclusion; *(encarcelamiento)* imprisonment, internment

recobrar 1 *vt* to recover, to retrieve; *(conocimiento)* to regain; **r. el aliento** to get one's breath back **2 recobrarse** *vpr* to recover, to recuperate

recogedor *nm* dustpan

recoger [53] **1** *vt* (**a**) *(del suelo etc)* to pick up (**b**) *(datos etc)* to gather, to collect (**c**) *(ordenar, limpiar)* to clean; **r. la mesa** to clear the table (**d**) *(ir a buscar)* to pick up, to fetch (**e**) *(cosecha)* to gather, to pick **2 recogerse** *vpr* (**a**) *(irse a casa)* to go home (**b**) *(pelo)* to lift up

recogida *nf* collection; *Agr (cosecha)* harvest, harvesting

recolección *nf Agr* harvest, harvesting; *(recogida)* collection, gathering

recomendado, -a *adj Am (carta, paquete)* registered

recomendar [1] *vt* to recommend

recompensa *nf* reward

recompensar *vt* to reward

reconocer [34] *vt* (**a**) to recognize (**b**) *(admitir)* to recognize, to admit (**c**) *Med (paciente)* to examine

reconocimiento *nm* (**a**) recognition

(**b**) *Med* examination, checkup

reconquista *nf* reconquest

récord *nm (pl* **récords**) record

recordar [2] **1** *vt* (**a**) *(rememorar)* to remember (**b**) **r. algo a algn** to remind sb of sth **2** *vi* to remember

recorrer *vt (distancia)* to cover, to travel; *(país)* to tour, to travel through *o* round; *(ciudad)* to visit, to walk round

recorrido *nm*, *Am* **recorrida** *nf* *(distancia)* distance travelled; *(trayecto)* trip, journey; *(itinerario)* itinerary, route

recortar *vt* to cut out

recostar [2] **1** *vt* to lean **2 recostarse** *vpr (tumbarse)* to lie down

recreo *nm* (**a**) *(diversión)* recreation (**b**) *(en el colegio)* break, recreation

recta *nf Geom* straight line; *(de carretera)* straight stretch; *Dep* **la r. final** the home straight

rectangular *adj* rectangular

rectángulo *nm* rectangle

rectitud *nf* straightness; *Fig* uprightness, rectitude

recto, -a 1 *adj* (**a**) *(derecho)* straight (**b**) *(honesto)* upright, honest (**c**) *Geom* right

  2 *nm Anat* rectum

  3 *adv* straight (on)

rector, -a 1 *adj (principio)* guiding, ruling **2** *nm Rel* rector

recuerdo *nm* (**a**) *(memoria)* memory (**b**) *(regalo etc)* souvenir (**c**) **recuerdos** regards

recuperación *nf* recovery; *(examen)* resit

recuperar 1 *vt (salud)* to recover; *(conocimiento)* to regain; *(tiempo, clases)* to make up **2 recuperarse** *vpr* to recover

recurrir *vi* (**a**) *Jur* to appeal (**b**) **r. a** *(a algn)* to turn to; *(a algo)* to make use of, to resort to

recurso *nm* (**a**) resource; **recursos naturales** natural resources; **como último r.** as a last resort (**b**) *Jur* appeal

red *nf* net; *(sistema)* network; *Com (cadena)* chain of supermarkets; *Fig* *(trampa)* trap; **la R.** *(Internet)* the Net

redacción *nf (escrito)* composition, essay; *(acción)* writing; *Prensa* editing; *(redactores)* editorial staff

redactar *vt* to draft; *Prensa* to edit

redactor, -a *nm,f Prensa* editor

redil *nm* fold, sheepfold

redondeado, -a *adj* rounded

redondel *nm Fam (círculo)* circle, ring; *Taurom* ring, arena

redondo, -a *adj* (a) round; *Fig* caer r. to collapse (b) *(rotundo)* categorical; *(perfecto)* perfect

reducción *nf* reduction

reducir [10] 1 *vt (disminuir)* to reduce 2 **reducirse** *vpr* (a) *(disminuirse)* to be reduced, to diminish (b) *(limitarse)* to confine oneself

reembolsar *vt* to reimburse; *(deuda)* to repay; *(importe)* to refund

reembolso *nm* reimbursement; *(de deuda)* repayment; *(devolución)* refund; **contra r.** cash on delivery

reemplazar [40] *vt* to replace (**con** with)

reestreno *nm* (a) *Cin* rerun, rerelease; **cine de r.** second-run cinema (b) *Teatro* revival

reestructurar *vt* to restructure

refacción *nf* (a) *Andes, CAm, RP, Ven (reforma)* refurbishment (b) *Andes, CAm, RP, Ven (reparación)* restoration (c) *Méx (recambio)* spare part

refaccionar *vt Andes, CAm, Ven* (a) *(reformar)* to refurbish (b) *(reparar)* to restore

referencia *nf* reference; **con r. a** with reference to

referéndum *nm (pl* **referéndums)** referendum

referente *adj* r. a concerning, regarding

referir [5] 1 *vt* to tell, to relate 2 **referirse** *vpr (aludir)* to refer (a to); ¿a qué te refieres? what do you mean?

refinería *nf* refinery

reflector, -a 1 *adj* reflecting 2 *nm Elec* spotlight, searchlight

reflejar 1 *vt* to reflect 2 **reflejarse** *vpr*

to be reflected (**en** in)

reflejo, -a 1 *nm* (a) *(imagen)* reflection (b) *(destello)* gleam, glint (c) *Anat* reflex (d) **reflejos** *(en cabello)* streaks, highlights 2 *adj (movimiento)* reflex

reflexión *nf* reflection

reflexionar *vi* to reflect (**sobre** on), to think (**sobre** about)

reforma *nf* (a) reform; **r. fiscal** tax reform (b) *(reparación)* repair

reformar 1 *vt* to reform; *(edificio)* to renovate 2 **reformarse** *vpr* to reform

reforzar [2] *vt* to reinforce, to strengthen

refrán *nm* proverb, saying

refrescante *adj* refreshing

refresco *nm* soft drink

refrigerado, -a *adj* air-conditioned

refrigerador *nm* refrigerator, *Br* fridge, *US* icebox

refugiado, -a *adj & nm,f* refugee

refugiarse [43] *vpr* to shelter, to take refuge

refugio *nm* refuge

regadera *nf* (a) *(para regar)* watering can; *Esp Fam* **estar como una r.** to be as mad as a hatter (b) *Col, Méx, Ven (ducha)* shower

regadío *nm (tierra)* irrigated land

regalar *vt* (a) *(dar)* to give (as a present); *(en ofertas etc)* to give away (b) **r. el oído a algn** to flatter sb

regaliz *nm* liquorice

regalo *nm* (a) gift, present; **de r.** as a present (b) *(comodidad)* pleasure, comfort

regalón, -ona *adj CSur Fam (niño)* spoilt

regañar 1 *vt (reprender)* to tell off 2 *vi Esp (pelearse)* to nag

regar [1] *vt* to water

regata *nf* boat race

regatear 1 *vi* (a) to haggle, to bargain (b) *Dep* to dribble 2 *vt* **no r. esfuerzos** to spare no effort

regazo *nm* lap

regenerar *vt* to regenerate

regente 1 *nmf Pol* regent 2 *nmf* (a)

(director) manager (**b**) *Méx (alcalde)* mayor, *f* mayoress

régimen *nm* (*pl* **regímenes**) (**a**) *Pol* regime (**b**) *Med* diet; **estar a r.** to be on a diet

regio, -a *adj* (**a**) *(real)* royal, regal (**b**) *Andes, RP (genial)* great, fabulous

región *nf* region

regional *adj* regional

regir [58] **1** *vt* to govern
2 *vi* to be in force
3 regirse *vpr* to be guided, to go (**por** by)

registrado,-a *adj* (**a**) *(patentado, inscrito)* registered; **marca registrada** registered trademark (**b**) *Am (certificado)* registered

registradora *nf Am* cash register

registrar 1 *vt* (**a**) *(examinar)* to inspect; *(cachear)* to frisk (**b**) *(inscribir)* to register (**c**) *(grabar)* to record **2 registrarse** *vpr* (**a**) *(inscribirse)* to register, to enrol (**b**) *(detectarse)* to be recorded

registro *nm* (**a**) inspection (**b**) *(inscripción)* registration, recording; *(oficina)* registry office (**c**) *Mús* register

regla *nf* (**a**) *(norma)* rule; **en r.** in order; **por r. general** as a (general) rule; **r. de oro** golden rule (**b**) *(instrumento)* ruler (**c**) *Mat* rule (**d**) *Med (periodo)* period

reglamento *nm* regulations, rules

regresar 1 *vi* to return
2 *vt Am salvo RP (devolver)* to give back
3 regresarse *vpr Am salvo RP (yendo)* to go back, to return; *(viniendo)* to come back, to return

regreso *nm* return

regular 1 *vt* (**a**) to regulate, to control (**b**) *(ajustar)* to adjust
2 *adj* (**a**) regular; **por lo r.** as a rule; **vuelo r.** scheduled flight (**b**) *Fam (mediano)* average, so-so
3 *adv* so-so

regularidad *nf* regularity; **con r.** regularly

rehabilitar *vt* to rehabilitate; *(edificio)* to convert

rehén *nm* hostage

rehogar [42] *vt* to brown

reina *nf* queen

reinado *nm* reign

reinar *vi* to reign

reincorporarse *vpr* **r. al trabajo** to return to work

reino *nm* kingdom; **el R. Unido** the United Kingdom

reintegro *nm (en lotería)* winning of one's stake

reír [56] **1** *vi* to laugh **2 reírse** *vpr* (**a**) to laugh (**b**) *(mofarse)* to laugh (**de** at), to make fun (**de** of)

reivindicación *nf* claim, demand

reivindicar [44] *vt* to claim, to demand; **el atentado fue reivindicado por los terroristas** the terrorists claimed responsibility for the attack

reja *nf* (**a**) *(de ventana)* grill, grating; *Fam* **estar entre rejas** to be behind bars (**b**) *Agr* ploughshare

rejilla *nf (de ventana, ventilador, radiador)* grill; *(de horno)* gridiron; *(para equipaje)* luggage rack

rejuvenecer [33] *vt* to rejuvenate

relación *nf* (**a**) relationship; *(conexión)* connection, link; **con** o **en r. a** with regard to; **relaciones públicas** public relations (**b**) *(lista)* list (**c**) *(relato)* account (**d**) *Mat, Téc* ratio

relacionar 1 *vt* to relate (**con** to), to connect (**con** with) **2 relacionarse** *vpr* (**a**) to be related, to be connected (**b**) *(alternar)* to mix, to get acquainted

relajación *nf* relaxation

relajar 1 *vt* to relax **2 relajarse** *vpr* to relax; *(moral)* to deteriorate

relajo *nm* (**a**) *Am Fam (alboroto)* **se armó un r.** there was an almighty row; **esta mesa es un r.** this table is a complete mess (**b**) *Méx, RP (complicación)* nuisance, hassle (**c**) *CAm, Carib, Méx (broma)* joke

relámpago *nm* flash of lightning; *Fig* **pasó como un r.** he flashed past; *Fig* **visita r.** flying visit

relampaguear *v impers* to flash

relatar *vt* to narrate, to relate

relativo, -a *adj* relative (**a** to); **en lo r. a** with regard to, concerning

relato *nm (cuento)* tale, story

relevo *nm* relief; *Dep* relay

relieve *nm Arte* relief; *Fig* **poner de r.** to emphasize

religión *nf* religion

religioso, -a 1 *adj* religious **2** *nm,f (hombre)* monk; *(mujer)* nun

relinchar *vi* to neigh, to whinny

relincho *nm* neigh, whinny

rellano *nm* landing

rellenar *vt* (**a**) *(impreso etc)* to fill in (**b**) *(un ave)* to stuff; *(un pastel)* to fill

relleno, -a 1 *nm (de aves)* stuffing; *(de pasteles)* filling **2** *adj* stuffed

reloj *nm* clock; *(de pulsera)* watch; **r. de arena** hourglass; **r. de sol** sundial; **r. despertador** alarm clock

relojería *nf (tienda)* watchmaker's, clockmaker's; **bomba de r.** time bomb

relojero, -a *nm,f* watchmaker, clockmaker

remar *vi* to row

remediar [43] *vt* (**a**) to remedy; *(enmendar)* to repair, to make good (**b**) *(evitar)* to avoid, to prevent; **no pude remediarlo** I couldn't help it

remedio *nm (cura)* remedy, cure; *(solución)* solution; **¡qué r.!** what else can I do?; **no hay más r.** there's no choice; **sin r.** without fail; *Fam* **¡no tienes r.!** you're hopeless!

remendar [1] *vt (ropa)* to patch

remero, -a 1 *nm,f* rower **2** *nf RP (prenda)* T-shirt

remise *nm RP* taxi *(in private car without meter)*

remisero, -a *nm,f RP* taxi driver *(of private car without meter)*

remite *nm (en carta)* = sender's name and address

remitente *nmf* sender

remitir 1 *vt* (**a**) *(enviar)* to send (**b**) *(referir)* to refer

  2 *vi (fiebre, temporal)* to subside

  3 remitirse *vpr* **si nos remitimos a los hechos** if we look at the facts;

remítase a la página 10 see page 10

remo *nm* oar; *(deporte)* rowing

remoción *nf Andes, RP (de escombros)* removal; *(de heridos)* transport

remojar *vt* to soak (**en** in)

remojo *nm* **dejar** *o* **poner en r.** to soak, to leave to soak

remolacha *nf (planta) Br* beetroot, *US* beet

remolcador *nm* (**a**) *Náut* tug, tugboat (**b**) *Aut Br* breakdown van *o* truck; *US* tow truck

remolcar [44] *vt* to tow

remolque *nm (acción)* towing; *(vehículo)* trailer; *Fig* **ir a r. de algn** to trundle along behind sb

remontar 1 *vt* (**a**) *(subir)* to go up (**b**) *(superar)* to overcome **2 remontarse** *vpr* (**a**) *(pájaros, aviones)* to soar (**b**) *(datar)* to go back, to date back (**a** to)

remordimiento *nm* remorse

remoto, -a *adj* remote, faraway; **no tengo la más remota idea** I haven't got the faintest idea

remover [4] *vt* (**a**) *(trasladar)* to move over (**b**) *(tierra)* to turn over; *(líquido)* to shake up; *(comida etc)* to stir; *(asunto)* to stir up

remuneración *nf* remuneration

renacuajo *nm* tadpole; *Fam (niño pequeño)* shrimp

rencor *nm* rancour; *(resentimiento)* resentment; **guardar r. a algn** to have a grudge against sb

rendición *nf* surrender

rendimiento *nm (producción)* yield, output; *(de máquina, motor)* efficiency, performance

rendir [6] **1** *vt* (**a**) *(fruto, beneficios)* to yield, to produce (**b**) *(cansar)* to exhaust, to wear out (**c**) **r. culto a** to worship; **r. homenaje a** to pay homage to

  2 *vi (dar beneficios)* to pay, to be profitable

  3 rendirse *vpr* (**a**) to surrender, to give in; **¡me rindo!** I give up! (**b**) *(cansarse)* to wear oneself out

RENFE *nf (abr* **Red Nacional de los**

Ferrocarriles Españoles) = Spanish state railway company

rengo, -a *Andes, RP adj* lame

renguear *vi Andes, RP* to limp, to hobble

reno *nm* reindeer

renovación *nf (de contrato, pasaporte)* renewal; *(de una casa)* renovation

renovar [2] *vt* to renew; *(edificio)* to renovate

renta *nf* (a) *Fin (ingresos)* income; *(beneficio)* interest, return; **r. per cápita** per capita income; **r. fija** fixed-interest security (b) *(alquiler)* rent

rentable *adj* profitable

rentar 1 *vt* (a) *(rendir)* to produce, yield (b) *Méx (alquilar)* to rent; *(vehículo)* to hire **2** *vi* to be profitable

renunciar [43] *vi* (a) **r. a** to renounce, to give up; *(no aceptar)* to decline (b) *(dimitir)* to resign

reñir [6] **1** *vt (regañar)* to scold, to tell off **2** *vi (discutir)* to quarrel, to argue; *(pelear)* to fight; **r. con algn** to fall out with sb

reo *nmf (acusado)* defendant, accused; *(culpable)* culprit

reparación *nf* repair; *(compensación)* reparation, amends

reparar 1 *vt* to repair; *(ofensa, injuria)* to make amends for; *(daño)* to make good **2** *vi* **r. en** *(darse cuenta de)* to notice; *(reflexionar sobre)* to think about

repartidor, -a *nm,f* distributor

repartir *vt* (a) *(dividir)* to distribute, to share out (b) *(regalo, premio)* to give out, to hand out; *(correo)* to deliver; *Naipes* to deal

reparto *nm* (a) distribution, sharing out (b) *(distribución)* handing out; *(de mercancías)* delivery (c) *Cin, Teatro* cast

repasador *nm RP (trapo)* tea towel

repasar *vt* (a) to revise, to go over (b) *(ropa)* to mend

repaso *nm* revision

repelente *adj* repulsive, repellent; *Fam* **niño r.** little know-all

repente *nm Fam (arrebato)* fit, outburst; **de r.** suddenly, all of a sudden

repentino, -a *adj* sudden

repercusión *nf* repercussion

repertorio *nm* repertoire, repertory

repetición *nf* repetition; **r. de la jugada** action replay

repetidor, -a 1 *adj* repeating **2** *nm,f Fam Educ* = student who is repeating a year

repetir [6] **1** *vt* (a) to repeat (b) *(plato)* to have a second helping

2 *vi Educ* to repeat a year

3 repetirse *vpr* (a) *(persona)* to repeat oneself (b) *(hecho)* to recur (c) **el pepino se repite** cucumber repeats (on me/you/him *etc*)

réplica *nf* (a) answer, reply (b) *(copia)* replica

replicar [44] **1** *vt* to answer back **2** *vi* (a) to reply, to retort (b) *(objetar)* to argue (c) *Jur* to answer

repoblación *nf* repopulation; **r. forestal** reafforestation

repoblar [2] *vt* to repopulate; *(bosque)* to reafforest

reponer [19] **1** *vt* (a) to put back, to replace (b) *Teatro (obra)* to put on again; *Cin (película)* to rerun; *TV (programa)* to repeat **2 reponerse** *vpr* **reponerse de** to recover from, to get over

reportaje *nm Prensa & Rad* report; *(noticias)* article, news item

reportar 1 *vt* (a) *(beneficios etc)* to bring (b) *Andes, CAm, Méx, Ven (informar)* to report (c) *CAm, Méx (denunciar)* to report (to the police) **2 reportarse** *vpr CAm, Méx, Ven (presentarse)* to report (a to)

reporte *nm Andes, CAm, Méx, Ven (informe)* report; *(noticia)* news item o report; **recibí reportes de mi hermano** I was sent news by my brother; **el r. del tiempo** weather report o forecast

reportero, -a *nm,f* reporter

reposera *nf RP Br* sun-lounger, *US* beach recliner

reposo *nm* rest; **en r.** at rest

repostería *nf* confectionery; *(tienda)* confectioner's (shop)

representación *nf* (**a**) representation (**b**) *Teatro* performance

representante *nmf* representative

representar *vt* (**a**) to represent (**b**) *(significar)* to mean, to represent (**c**) *Teatro (obra)* to perform

representativo, -a *adj* representative

represión *nf* repression

reprimir *vt* to repress

reprobar [2] *vt (cosa)* to condemn; *(a persona)* to reproach, reprove; *Am (estudiante, examen)* to fail

reprochar *vt* to reproach; **r. algo a algn** to reproach sb for sth

reproche *nm* reproach

reproducción *nf* reproduction

reproducir [10] **1** *vt* to reproduce **2 reproducirse** *vpr* (**a**) to reproduce, to breed (**b**) *(repetirse)* to recur, to happen again

reptar *vi* to slither

reptil *nm* reptile

república *nf* republic; **la R. Dominicana** the Dominican Republic; **la R. Checa** the Czech Republic

republicano, -a *adj & nm,f* republican

repuesto *nm (recambio)* spare part, spare; *Aut* **rueda de r.** spare wheel

repugnar *vt* to disgust, to revolt

repuntar *vi Am (mejorar)* to improve

repunte *nm (aumento)* rise, increase; **un r. en las ventas** an improvement *o* increase in sales

reputación *nf* reputation

requerir [5] *vt* (**a**) to require (**b**) *(solicitar)* to request (**c**) *Jur (avisar)* to summon

requesón *nm* cottage cheese

res *nf* animal

resaca *nf* (**a**) hangover (**b**) *Náut* undertow, undercurrent

resbalada *nf Am Fam* slip; **dar** *o* **pegar una r.** to slip

resbaladizo, -a *adj* slippery

resbalar *vi,* **resbalarse** *vpr* to slip; *Aut* to skid

rescatar *vt (persona)* to rescue; *(objeto)* to recover

rescate *nm* (**a**) *(salvamento)* rescue; *(recuperación)* recovery (**b**) *(suma)* ransom

resentimiento *nm* resentment

reserva 1 *nf* (**a**) *(de entradas etc)* reservation, booking (**b**) *(provisión)* reserve, stock; **un vino de r.** a vintage wine (**c**) *Mil* reserve, reserves (**d**) *(duda)* reservation **2** *nmf Dep* reserve, substitute

reservación *nf Méx* reservation

reservado, -a 1 *adj (persona)* reserved, quiet **2** *nm* private room

reservar 1 *vt* (**a**) *(billetes etc)* to reserve, to book (**b**) *(dinero, tiempo etc)* to keep, to save **2 reservarse** *vpr* (**a**) to save oneself (**para** for) (**b**) *(sentimientos)* to keep to oneself (**c**) **reservarse el derecho de** to reserve the right to

resfriado, -a 1 *nm (catarro)* cold; **coger un r.** to catch (a) cold **2** *adj* **estar r.** to have a cold

resfriarse *vpr* to catch (a) cold

resfrío *nm Andes, RP* cold

resguardar *vt (proteger)* to protect, to shelter (**de** from)

resguardo *nm* (**a**) *(recibo)* receipt (**b**) *(protección)* protection, shelter

residencia *nf* residence; **r. de ancianos** old people's home

residuo *nm* (**a**) residue (**b**) **residuos** waste

resignarse *vpr* to resign oneself (**a** to)

resistencia *nf* (**a**) resistance (**b**) *(aguante)* endurance, stamina (**c**) *Elec* element

resistente *adj* (**a**) resistant (**a** to) (**b**) *(fuerte)* tough, hardy

resistir 1 *vi* (**a**) to resist (**b**) *(aguantar)* to hold (out)

2 *vt (situación, persona)* to put up with; *(tentación)* to resist

3 resistirse *vpr* to resist; *(oponerse)* to offer resistance; *(negarse)* to refuse

resolver [4] (*pp* **resuelto**) **1** *vt (problema)* to solve; *(asunto)* to settle **2** *vi (decidir)* to resolve, to decide **3 resolverse** *vpr* (**a**) *(solucionarse)* to be solved (**b**) *(decidirse)* to resolve, to make up one's mind (**a** to)

resonancia *nf* (**a**) *(sonora)* resonance (**b**) *(repercusión)* repercussions

resorte *nm* (**a**) *(muelle)* spring (**b**) *Fig* means

respaldo *nm* (*de silla etc*) back; *Fig (apoyo)* support, backing

respectivo, -a *adj* respective; **en lo r. a** with regard to, regarding

respecto *nm* **al r., a este r.** in this respect; **(con) r. a, r. de** with regard to; **r. a mí** as for me, as far as I am concerned

respetable 1 *adj* respectable **2** *nm Fam* **el r.** the audience

respetar *vt* to respect; **hacerse r. de todos** to command everyone's respect

respeto *nm* (**a**) respect; **por r.** out of consideration (**b**) *(recelo)* fear

respiración *nf (acción)* breathing, respiration; *(aliento)* breath; **r. artificial** artificial resuscitation

respirar *vi* to breathe; **¡por fin respiro!** well, that's a relief!

respiro *nm* (**a**) breathing (**b**) *(descanso)* breather, break

resplandor *nm (brillo)* brightness; *(muy intenso)* brilliance; *(de fuego)* glow, blaze

responder 1 *vt* to answer **2** *vi* (**a**) *(una carta)* to reply (**b**) *(reaccionar)* to respond (**c**) *(protestar)* to answer back (**d**) **r. de algn** to be responsible for sb; **r. por algn** to vouch for sb

responsabilidad *nf* responsibility

responsable 1 *adj* responsible **2** *nmf* **el/la r.** *(encargado)* the person in charge; *(de robo etc)* the perpetrator

respuesta *nf* answer, reply; *(reacción)* response

resta *nf* subtraction

restar 1 *vt* (**a**) *Mat* to subtract, to take away (**b**) **r. importancia a algo** to play sth down **2** *vi (quedar)* to be left, to remain

restauración *nf* restoration

restaurador, -a 1 *nm,f* restorer **2** *adj* restoring

restaurante *nm* restaurant

restaurar *vt* to restore

resto *nm* (**a**) rest, remainder; *Mat* remainder (**b**) **restos** remains; *(de comida)* leftovers

restricción *nf* restriction

resucitar *vt & vi* to resuscitate

resuelto, -a *adj (decidido)* resolute, determined

resultado *nm* result; *(consecuencia)* outcome; **dar buen r.** to work, to give results

resultar *vi* (**a**) *(ser)* to turn o work out; **así resulta más barato** it works out cheaper this way; **me resultó fácil** it turned out to be easy for me (**b**) *(ocurrir)* **resulta que ...** the thing is ...; **y ahora resulta que no puede venir** and now it turns out that she can't come (**c**) *(tener éxito)* to be successful; **la fiesta no resultó** the party wasn't a success

resumen *nm* summary; **en r.** in short, to sum up

resumir 1 *vt* to sum up; *(recapitular)* to summarize **2 resumirse** *vpr* (**a**) *(abreviarse)* **se resume en pocas palabras** it can be summed up in a few words (**b**) **resumirse en** *(saldarse con)* to result in

retablo *nm* altarpiece

retal *nm (pedazo)* scrap

retén *nm* (**a**) **r. (de bomberos)** squad (of firefighters) (**b**) *Am (de menores)* reformatory, reform school

retención *nf* retention; *Fin* withholding; **r. de tráfico** (traffic) hold-up, traffic jam

retirado, -a 1 *adj* (**a**) *(alejado)* remote (**b**) *(jubilado)* retired **2** *nm,f* retired person, *US* retiree

retirar 1 *vt* to take away, to remove; *(dinero)* to withdraw; *(ofensa)* to take back **2 retirarse** *vpr* (**a**) *(apartarse)* to withdraw, to draw back; *(irse)* to retire (**b**) *(jubilarse)* to retire (**c**) *Mil* to retreat, to withdraw

reto *nm* challenge

retocar [44] *vt* to touch up

retorcer [41] **1** *vt (cuerda, hilo)* to twist; *(ropa)* to wring (out) **2 retorcerse** *vpr* to twist, to become twisted; **retorcerse de dolor** to writhe in pain

retórica *nf* rhetoric

retornable *adj* returnable; **envase no r.** non-deposit bottle

retorno *nm* return

retransmisión *nf* broadcast, transmission

retransmitir *vt* to broadcast

retrasado, -a 1 *adj* (**a**) *(tren)* late; *(reloj)* slow; **voy r.** I'm behind schedule (**b**) *(país)* backward, underdeveloped (**c**) *(mental)* retarded, backward **2** *nm,f* **r. (mental)** mentally retarded person

retrasar 1 *vt* (**a**) *(retardar)* to slow down (**b**) *(atrasar)* to delay, to postpone (**c**) *(reloj)* to put back **2 retrasarse** *vpr* to be late, to be delayed; *(reloj)* to be slow

retraso *nm* delay; **con r.** late; **una hora de r.** an hour behind schedule; **r. mental** mental deficiency

retratar 1 *vt (pintar)* to paint a portrait of; *Fot* to take a photograph of; *Fig (describir)* to describe, to depict **2 retratarse** *vpr Fot* to have one's photograph taken

retrato *nm (pintura)* portrait; *Fot* photograph; **r. robot** Identikit® picture, *Br* Photofit® picture; **ser el vivo r. de** to be the spitting image of

retrete *nm Br* toilet, *US* bathroom

retroceder *vi* to move back, to back away

retrospectivo, -a *adj & nf* retrospective

retrovisor *nm Aut* rear-view mirror

reúma *nm* rheumatism

reunión *nf* meeting; *(reencuentro)* reunion

reunir 1 *vt* to gather together; *(dinero)* to raise; *(cualidades)* to have, to possess; *(requisitos)* to fulfil **2 reunirse** *vpr* to meet, to gather; **reunirse con algn** to meet sb

revancha *nf* revenge; *Dep* return match

revelado *nm Fot* developing

revelar *vt* (**a**) to reveal, to disclose (**b**) *Fot (película)* to develop

reventar [1] **1** *vt* (**a**) to burst (**b**) *(romper)* to break, to smash (**c**) *(fastidiar)* to annoy, to bother

2 *vi (estallar)* to burst; **r. de ganas de hacer algo** to be dying to do sth

3 reventarse *vpr (estallar)* to burst, to explode

reventón *nm (de neumático)* blowout, *Br* puncture, *US* flat

reverencia *nf* (**a**) *(respeto)* reverence (**b**) *(inclinación) (de hombre)* bow; *(de mujer)* curtsy

reversa *nf Méx* reverse

reversible *adj* reversible

reverso *nm* reverse, back

revés *nm* (**a**) *(reverso)* reverse; **al** *o* **del r.** *(al contrario)* the other way round; *(la parte interior en el exterior)* inside out; *(boca abajo)* upside down; *(la parte de detrás delante)* back to front; **al r. de lo que dicen** contrary to what they say

(**b**) *(bofetada)* slap; *Ten* backhand (stroke)

(**c**) *Fig (contrariedad)* setback, reverse; **los reveses de la vida** life's misfortunes; **reveses de fortuna** setbacks, blows of fate

revestimiento *nm Téc* covering, coating

revisar *vt* to check; *(coche)* to service

revisión *nf* checking; *(de coche)* service, overhaul; **r. médica** checkup

revisor, -a *nm,f* ticket inspector

revista *nf* (**a**) magazine (**b**) **pasar r. a** to inspect, to review (**c**) *Teatro* revue

revistero *nm (mueble)* magazine rack

revolcar [2] **1** *vt Fam (oponente)* to floor, to crush **2 revolcarse** *vpr* to roll about

revoltijo, revoltillo *nm* jumble

revoltoso, -a *adj (travieso)* mischievous, naughty

revolución *nf* revolution

revolucionario, -a *adj & nm,f* revolutionary

revolver [4] (*pp* **revuelto**) **1** *vt (mezclar)* to stir, to mix; *(desordenar)* to mess up; **me revuelve el estómago** it turns my stomach **2 revolverse** *vpr* (**a**) *(agitarse)* to roll (**b**) *Fig* **revolverse contra algn** to turn against sb (**c**) *(tiempo atmosférico)* to turn stormy; *(mar)* to become rough

revólver *nm* revolver

revuelta *nf* (**a**) *(insurrección)* revolt (**b**) *(curva)* bend, turn

revuelto, -a *adj* (**a**) *(desordenado)* jumbled, in a mess (**b**) *(tiempo)* stormy, unsettled; *(mar)* rough (**c**) *(agitado)* excited

rey *nm* (*pl* **reyes**) king; *Rel* (**el día de**) **Reyes** (the) Epiphany, 6 January

rezar [40] **1** *vi* (**a**) *(orar)* to pray (**b**) *(decir)* to say, to read **2** *vt (oración)* to say

rezo *nm* prayer

ría *nf* estuary

riachuelo *nm* brook, stream

riada *nf* flood

ribera *nf (de río)* bank; *(zona)* riverside, waterfront

ribete *nm* edging, border

rico, -a 1 *adj* (**a**) **ser r.** *(adinerado)* to be rich *o* wealthy; *(abundante)* to be rich; *(bonito)* to be lovely *o* adorable; *(fértil)* to be rich *o* fertile (**b**) **estar r.** *(delicioso)* to be delicious **2** *nm,f* rich person

ridículo, -a 1 *adj* ridiculous **2** *nm* ridicule; **hacer el r., quedar en r.** to make a fool of oneself; **poner a algn en r.** to make a fool of sb

riego *nm* watering, irrigation; **r. sanguíneo** blood circulation

rienda *nf* rein; *Fig* **dar r. suelta a** to give free rein to; *Fig* **llevar las riendas** to hold the reins, to be in control

riesgo *nm* risk; **correr el r. de** to run the risk of; **seguro a todo r.** fully comprehensive insurance

riesgoso, -a *adj Am* risky

rifar *vt* to raffle (off)

rigidez *nf* rigidity, stiffness; *Fig (severidad)* strictness, inflexibility

rígido, -a *adj* rigid, stiff; *Fig (severo)* strict, inflexible

rigor *nm* rigour; *(severidad)* severity; **con r.** rigorously; **de r.** indispensable

riguroso, -a *adj* rigorous; *(severo)* severe, strict

rima *nf* rhyme

rímel *nm* mascara

rincón *nm* corner; *Fam (lugar remoto)* nook

ring [rrin] *nm* (*pl* **rings**) (boxing) ring

rinoceronte *nm* rhinoceros

riña *nf (pelea)* fight; *(discusión)* row, quarrel

riñón *nm* kidney; *Fam* **costar un r.** to cost an arm and a leg; *Med* **r. artificial** kidney machine

riñonera *nf (pequeño bolso) Br* bum bag, *US* fanny pack

río *nm* river; **r. abajo** downstream; **r. arriba** upstream

rioja *nm* Rioja (wine)

RIP [rrip] (*abr* **requiescat in pace**) RIP

riqueza *nf* (**a**) wealth (**b**) *(cualidad)* wealthiness

risa *nf* laugh; *(carcajadas)* laughter; **es (cosa) de r.** it's laughable; **me da r.** it makes me laugh; **tomarse algo a r.** to laugh sth off; *Fig* **morirse** *o* **mondarse de r.** to die *o* fall about laughing; *Fam* **mi hermano es una r.** my brother is a laugh; *Fam Fig* **tener algo muerto de r.** to leave sth lying around

ristra *nf* string

ritmo *nm* (**a**) rhythm (**b**) *(paso)* rate; **llevar un buen r. de trabajo** to work at a good pace

rito *nm* (**a**) rite (**b**) *(ritual)* ritual

ritual *adj & nm* ritual

rival *adj & nmf* rival

rizado, -a *adj* (**a**) *(pelo)* curly (**b**) *(mar)* choppy

rizo *nm* (**a**) *(de pelo)* curl (**b**) *(en el agua)* ripple

RNE *nf* (*abr* **Radio Nacional de España**) = Spanish state radio station

robar *vt* (**a**) *(objeto)* to steal; *(banco,*

persona) to rob; *(casa)* to burgle; *Fig* **en aquel supermercado te roban** they really rip you off in that super-market (**b**) *Naipes* to draw

roble *nm* oak (tree)

robo *nm* robbery, theft; *(en casa)* burglary; *Fam (timo)* rip-off

robot *nm* (*pl* **robots**) robot; **r. de cocina** food processor

robusto, -a *adj* robust, sturdy

roca *nf* rock

roce *nm* (**a**) *(fricción)* rubbing; *(en la piel)* chafing (**b**) *(marca) (en la pared etc)* scuff mark; *(en la piel)* chafing mark, graze (**c**) *(contacto ligero)* brush, light touch (**d**) *Fam (trato entre personas)* contact (**e**) *Fam (discusión)* brush

rociar [29] *vt (salpicar)* to spray, to sprinkle

rocío *nm* dew

rock *nm inv* rock; **r. duro** hard rock; **r. and roll** rock and roll

rocoso, -a *adj* rocky, stony

rodaballo *nm (pez)* turbot

rodaje *nm* (**a**) *(filmación)* filming, shooting (**b**) *Aut* running-in

rodar [2] **1** *vt (película etc)* to film, to shoot **2** *vi* to roll, to turn

rodear 1 *vt* to surround, to encircle **2 rodearse** *vpr* to surround oneself (**de** with)

rodeo *nm* (**a**) *(desvío)* detour (**b**) *(al hablar)* evasiveness; **andarse con rodeos** to beat about the bush; **no andarse con rodeos** to get straight to the point (**c**) *(espectáculo)* rodeo

rodilla *nf* knee; **de rodillas** *(arro-dillado)* kneeling; **hincarse** *o* **ponerse de rodillas** to kneel down, to go down on one's knees

rodillo *nm* roller; **r. de cocina** rolling pin

roedor *nm* rodent

roer [38] *vt (hueso)* to gnaw; *(galleta)* to nibble at; *Fig (conciencia)* to gnaw at, to nag at; *Fig* **un hueso duro de r.** a hard nut to crack

rogar [2] *vt (pedir)* to request, to ask;

(implorar) to beg; **hacerse de r.** to play hard to get; **se ruega silencio** *(en letrero)* silence please; **rogamos disculpen la molestia** please forgive the inconvenience

rojo, -a 1 *adj* (**a**) red; *Fin* **estar en números rojos** to be in the red (**b**) *Pol (comunista)* red

2 *nm (color)* red; **al r. vivo** *(caliente)* red-hot; *Fig (tenso)* very tense

3 *nm,f Pol (comunista)* red

rollo *nm* (**a**) *(de papel etc)* roll (**b**) *Fam (pesadez)* drag, bore; **es el mismo r. de siempre** it's the same old story; **un r. de libro** a boring book (**c**) *Esp Fam (amorío)* affair

romana *nf* **calamares a la r.** = squid in batter

románico, -a *adj & nm* Romanesque

romano, -a 1 *adj* Roman; *Rel* Roman Catholic **2** *nm,f* Roman

romántico, -a *adj & nm,f* romantic

rombo *nm* rhombus

romería *nf Rel* pilgrimage

romero *nm Bot* rosemary

romo, -a *adj* (**a**) blunt (**b**) *(nariz)* snub

rompecabezas *nm inv (juego)* (jigsaw) puzzle; *Fig (problema)* riddle, puzzle

rompeolas *nm inv* breakwater, jetty

romper *(pp* **roto**) **1** *vt* (**a**) to break; *(papel, tela)* to tear; *(vajilla, cristal)* to smash, to shatter (**b**) *(relaciones)* to break off

2 *vi* (**a**) *(olas, día)* to break (**b**) *(acabar)* to break (**con** with); **rompió con su novio** she broke it off with her boyfriend (**c**) **r. a llorar** to burst out crying

3 romperse *vpr* to break; *(papel, tela)* to tear; **se rompió por la mitad** it broke *o* split in half; *Fig* **romperse la cabeza** to rack one's brains

rompevientos *nm RP (jersey)* Br polo neck, *US* turtleneck; *(anorak)* windcheater

rompimiento *nm Am* break

ron *nm* rum

roncar [44] *vi* to snore

ronco, -a *adj* hoarse; **quedarse r.** to lose one's voice

ronda *nf* (**a**) round; *(patrulla)* patrol (**b**) *(carretera)* ring road; *(paseo)* avenue (**c**) **pagar una r.** to pay for a round of drinks

rondín *nm* Andes (**a**) *(vigilante)* watchman, guard (**b**) *(armónica)* mouth organ

ronquido *nm* snore

ronronear *vi* to purr

ronroneo *nm* purring

ropa *nf* clothes, clothing; *Fig* **a quema r.** point-blank; **r. blanca** (household) linen; **r. interior** underwear

roquefort [rroke'for] *nm* Roquefort (cheese)

rosa 1 *adj inv (color)* pink; **novela r.** romantic novel
  2 *nf Bot* rose; *(en la piel)* birthmark; **r. de los vientos** compass (rose)
  3 *nm (color)* pink

rosado, -a 1 *adj (color)* pink, rosy; *(vino)* rosé **2** *nm (vino)* rosé

rosal *nm* rosebush

rosario *nm Rel* rosary; *(sarta)* string, series *sing*

rosco *nm* = ring-shaped bread roll; *Esp Fam* **nunca se come un r.** he never gets off with anyone

roscón *nm* = ring-shaped bread roll; **r. de Reyes** = ring-shaped pastry eaten on 6th January

rosetón *nm* rose window

rosquilla *nf* ring-shaped pastry; *Fam Fig* **venderse como rosquillas** to sell like hot cakes

rosticería *nf Chile, Méx* = shop selling roast chicken

rostro *nm* face; *Fam* **tener mucho r.** to have a lot of nerve; *Fam* **¡vaya r.!** what a cheek!

rotativo, -a 1 *adj* rotary, revolving **2** *nm* newspaper

roto, -a 1 *adj* broken; *(papel)* torn; *(ropa)* in tatters, tattered
  2 *nm (agujero)* hole, tear
  3 *nm,f Chile Fam* (**a**) *(tipo)* guy; *(mujer)* woman (**b**) *Pey (trabajador)* worker

rotonda *nf* (**a**) *(glorieta)* roundabout (**b**) *(plaza)* circus

rotoso, -a *Andes, RP adj* ragged, in tatters

rotulador *nm* felt-tip pen

rótulo *nm (letrero)* sign, notice; *(titular)* title, heading

rotundo, -a *adj* categorical; **éxito r.** resounding success; **un no r.** a flat refusal

rozar [40] **1** *vt* to touch, to rub against, to brush against
  2 *vi* to rub
  3 rozarse *vpr* to rub, to brush (**con** against)

Rte. (*abr* **remite, remitente**) sender

RTVE *nf* (*abr* **Radiotelevisión Española**) = Spanish state broadcasting company

ruana *nf* (**a**) *Andes (cerrado)* poncho (**b**) *RP (abierto)* wraparound poncho

rubí *nm* (*pl* **rubís** o **rubíes**) ruby

rubio, -a 1 *adj (pelo, persona)* fair, blond, *f* blonde; **r. de bote** peroxide blonde; **tabaco r.** Virginia tobacco **2** *nm,f* blond, *f* blonde

rubor *nm* blush, flush

ruborizarse [40] *vpr* to blush, to go red

rudimentario, -a *adj* rudimentary

rudo, -a *adj* rough, coarse

rueda *nf* (**a**) wheel; *Aut* **r. de recambio** spare wheel; *Aut* **r. delantera/trasera** front/rear wheel; **r. de prensa** press conference; *Fam* **ir sobre ruedas** to go very smoothly (**b**) *(rodaja)* round slice

ruedo *nm* (**a**) *Taurom* bullring, arena (**b**) *(de falda)* hem

ruego *nm* request

rugby *nm* rugby

rugido *nm (de animal)* roar; *(del viento)* howl; *(de tripas)* rumbling

rugir [57] *vi* to roar; *(viento)* to howl

rugoso, -a *adj* rough

ruido *nm* noise; *(sonido)* sound; *(jaleo)* din, row; *Fig* stir, commotion; **hacer r.** to make a noise

ruidoso, -a *adj* noisy, loud

ruin *adj* (**a**) *(vil)* vile, despicable (**b**) *(tacaño)* mean, stingy

ruina *nf* ruin; *(derrumbamiento)* collapse; *(de persona)* downfall

ruinoso, -a *adj* dilapidated, tumbledown

ruiseñor *nm* nightingale

ruleta *nf* roulette

ruletear *vi CAm, Méx Fam (en taxi)* to drive a taxi

ruletero *nm CAm, Méx Fam (de taxi)* taxi driver

rulo *nm* (**a**) *(para el pelo)* curler, roller (**b**) *Culin* rolling pin

ruma *nf Andes, Ven* heap, pile

rumba *nf* rhumba, rumba

rumbo *nm* direction, course; (**con**) **r. a** bound for, heading for

rumiante *nm* ruminant

rumiar [43] **1** *vt* (**a**) *(mascar)* to chew (**b**) *Fig (pensar)* to ruminate, to reflect on, to chew over **2** *vi* to ruminate, to chew the cud

rumor *nm* (**a**) rumour (**b**) *(murmullo)* murmur

rumorearse *v impers* to be rumoured

ruptura *nf* breaking; *(de relaciones)* breaking off

rural *adj* rural, country

Rusia *n* Russia

ruso, -a **1** *adj & nm,f* Russian **2** *nm (idioma)* Russian

ruta *nf* route, road

rutina *nf* routine; **por r.** as a matter of course

Ss

S (*abr* **Sur**) S

S.A. (*abr* **Sociedad Anónima**) *Br* $\simeq$ PLC, *US* $\simeq$ Inc

sábado *nm* Saturday

sábana *nf* sheet; *Fam* **se me pegaron las sábanas** I overslept

sabañón *nm* chilblain

saber¹ *nm* knowledge

saber² [21] **1** *vt* (**a**) to know; **hacer s.** to inform; **que yo sepa** as far as I know; **¡y yo qué sé!** how should I know!; *Fig* **a s.** namely (**b**) *(tener habilidad)* to be able to; **¿sabes cocinar?** can you cook?; **¿sabes hablar inglés?** can you speak English? (**c**) *(enterarse)* to learn, find out; **lo supe ayer** I found this out yesterday
2 *vi* (**a**) *(tener sabor a)* to taste (**a** of); **sabe a fresa** it tastes of strawberries; *Fig* **me sabe mal** I feel guilty *o* bad about that (**b**) *Am (soler)* **s. hacer algo** to be in the habit of doing sth

sabiduría *nf* wisdom

sabio, -a 1 *adj (prudente)* wise **2** *nm,f* scholar

sable *nm* sabre

sabor *nm (gusto)* taste, flavour; **con s. a limón** lemon-flavoured; **sin s.** tasteless; **me deja mal s. de boca** it leaves a bad taste in my mouth

saborear *vt (degustar)* to taste; *Fig (apreciar)* to savour

sabotaje *nm* sabotage

sabroso, -a *adj* (**a**) *(delicioso)* tasty; *(delicioso)* delicious (**b**) *(agradable)* delightful

sacacorchos *nm inv* corkscrew

sacapuntas *nm inv* pencil sharpener

sacar [44] *vt* (**a**) to take out; *(con más fuerza)* to pull out; **s. dinero del banco** to withdraw money from the bank; **s. la lengua** to stick one's tongue out; *Fig* **s. faltas a algo** to find fault with sth; **s. provecho de algo** to benefit from sth; **s. algo en claro** *o* **en limpio** to make sense of sth
(**b**) *(obtener)* to get; *(dinero)* to get, to make; *(conclusiones)* to draw, to reach; *(entrada)* to get, to buy
(**c**) *(producto, libro, disco)* to bring out; *(nueva moda)* to bring in
(**d**) *(fotografía)* to take; *(fotocopia)* to make
(**e**) *Ten* to serve; *Ftb* to kick off

sacarina *nf* saccharin

sacerdote *nm* priest; **sumo s.** high priest

saciar [43] *vt* to satiate; *(sed)* to quench; *(deseos, hambre)* to satisfy; *(ambiciones)* to fulfil

saco *nm* (**a**) sack; **s. de dormir** sleeping bag (**b**) *Mil* **entrar a s. en una ciudad** to pillage a town (**c**) *Am (abrigo) (de tela)* jacket; *(de punto)* cardigan

sacramento *nm* sacrament

sacrificar [44] **1** *vt* to sacrifice **2 sacrificarse** *vpr* to make a sacrifice *o* sacrifices

sacrificio *nm* sacrifice

sacristán *nm* verger, sexton

sacudida *nf* (**a**) shake; *(espasmo)* jolt, jerk; **s. eléctrica** electric shock (**b**) *(de terremoto)* tremor

sacudir *vt* (**a**) *(agitar)* to shake; *(alfombra, sábana)* to shake out; *(arena, polvo)* to shake off (**b**) *(golpear)* to beat (**c**) *(conmover)* to shock, to stun

safari *nm (cacería)* safari; *(parque)* safari park

Sagitario *nm* Sagittarius

sagrado, -a *adj* sacred

sal¹ *nf* (**a**) salt; **s. fina** table salt; **s.**

gema salt crystals; *Esp* **s. gorda** cooking salt (**b**) *Fig (gracia)* wit

sal² *imperat de* **salir**

sala *nf* room; *(en un hospital)* ward; *Jur* courtroom; **s. de estar** lounge, living room; **s. de espera** waiting room; **s. de exposiciones** exhibition hall; **s. de fiestas** nightclub, discotheque; **s. de lectura** reading room

saladito *nm RP* savoury snack *o* appetizer

salado, -a *adj* (**a**) *(con sal)* salted; *(con exceso de sal)* salty; **agua salada** salt water (**b**) *Esp (gracioso, simpático)* amusing; *(encantador)* charming (**c**) *CAm, Carib, Méx (desgraciado)* un-lucky

salamandra *nf* salamander

salar *vt* to salt, to add salt to

salario *nm* salary, wages; **s. mínimo** minimum wage

salchicha *nf* sausage

salchichón *nm* = salami-type saus-age

salchichonería *nf Méx* delicatessen

saldo *nm* (**a**) **saldos** sales; **a precio de s.** at bargain prices (**b**) *Fin* balance (**c**) *(de una deuda)* liquidation, settlement (**d**) *(resto de mercancía)* remainder, leftover

salero *nm* (**a**) *(recipiente)* saltcellar, *US* saltshaker (**b**) *Fig (gracia)* charm

salida *nf* (**a**) *(partida)* departure; *(puerta etc)* exit, way out; **callejón sin s.** dead end; **s. de emergencia** emerg-ency exit
(**b**) *Dep* start; **línea de s.** starting line
(**c**) **te vi a la s. del cine** I saw you leaving the cinema
(**d**) *(de astro)* rising; **s. del sol** sunrise
(**e**) *(profesional)* opening; *Com* outlet
(**f**) *(recurso)* solution, way out; **no tengo otra s.** I have no other option
(**g**) *Fam (ocurrencia)* witty remark, witticism
(**h**) *Informát* output

salina *nf* salt mine

salir [22] *vi* (**a**) *(de un sitio)* to go out, to leave; *(venir de dentro)* to come out; **salió de la habitación** she left the room; **s. de la carretera** to turn off the road
(**b**) *(tren etc)* to depart
(**c**) *(novios)* to go out (**con** with)
(**d**) *(aparecer)* to appear; *(revista, disco)* to come out; *(ley)* to come in; *(trabajo, vacante)* to come up
(**e**) *(resultar)* to turn out, to turn out to be; **el pequeño les ha salido muy listo** their son has turned out to be very clever; **¿cómo te salió el examen?** how did your exam go?; **s. ganando** to come out ahead *o* on top
(**f**) **s. a** *(precio)* to come to, to work out at; **s. barato/caro** to work out cheap/ expensive
(**g**) **ha salido al abuelo** she takes after her grandfather
(**h**) *(problema)* to work out; **esta cuenta no me sale** I can't work this sum out
(**i**) **¡con qué cosas sales!** the things you come out with!
2 salirse *vpr* (**a**) *(líquido, gas)* to leak (out); *Fig* **salirse de lo normal** to be out of the ordinary; **se salió de la carretera** he went off the road (**b**) *Fam* **salirse con la suya** to get one's own way

saliva *nf* saliva

salmón 1 *nm (pescado)* salmon **2** *adj inv (color)* salmon pink, salmon

salmonete *nm (pescado)* red mullet

salón *nm* (**a**) *(en una casa)* lounge, sitting room (**b**) **s. de actos** assembly hall; **s. de baile** dance hall (**c**) **s. del automóvil** motor show; **s. de belleza** beauty salon; **s. de té** tearoom, teashop

salpicadera *nf Méx Br* mudguard, *US* fender

salpicadero *nm Esp* dashboard

salpicar [44] *vt* (**a**) *(rociar)* to splash; **me salpicó el abrigo de barro** he splashed mud on my coat (**b**) *Fig (esparcir)* to sprinkle

salpicón *nm* (**a**) splash (**b**) *Culin* cocktail

salpimentar [1] *vt* to season

salsa *nf* sauce; *(de carne)* gravy; *Fig* **en su (propia) s.** in one's element

salsera *nf* gravy boat

saltamontes *nm inv* grasshopper

saltar 1 *vt* (*obstáculo, valla*) to jump (over)

2 *vi* (**a**) to jump; *Fig* **s. a la vista** to be obvious (**b**) (*cristal etc*) to break, to shatter; (*plomos*) to go, to blow (**c**) (*desprenderse*) to come off (**d**) (*encolerizarse*) to explode, to blow up

3 saltarse *vpr* (**a**) (*omitir*) to skip, to miss out; **saltarse el semáforo/turno** to jump the lights/the queue (**b**) (*botón*) to come off; **se me saltaron las lágrimas** tears came to my eyes

salteado, -a *adj* (**a**) (*espaciado*) spaced out (**b**) *Culin* sauté, sautéed

saltear *vt Culin* to sauté

salto *nm* (**a**) (*acción*) jump, leap; *Fig* (*paso adelante*) leap forward; **a saltos** in leaps and bounds; **dar** *o* **pegar un s.** to jump; to leap; **de un s.** in a flash; *Fig* **a s. de mata** every now and then; **s. de agua** waterfall; **s. de cama** negligée (**b**) *Dep* jump; **s. de altura** high jump; **s. de longitud** long jump; **s. mortal** somersault

salud *nf* health; **beber a la s. de algn** to drink to sb's health; *Fam* **¡s.!** cheers!

saludable *adj* (**a**) (*sano*) healthy, wholesome (**b**) *Fig* (*beneficioso*) good, beneficial

saludar *vt* (**a**) (*decir hola a*) to say hello to, to greet; **saluda de mi parte a** give my regards to; **le saluda atentamente** (*en una carta*) yours faithfully (**b**) *Mil* to salute

saludo *nm* (**a**) greeting; **un s. de** best wishes from (**b**) *Mil* salute

salvación *nf* salvation

Salvador *nm* (**a**) *Rel* **el S.** the Saviour (**b**) *Geog* **El S.** El Salvador

salvadoreño, -a *adj & nm,f* Salvadoran

salvaje *adj* (**a**) *Bot* wild, uncultivated; *Zool* wild; (*pueblo, tribu*) savage, uncivilized (**b**) *Fam* (*violento*) savage, wild

salvamanteles *nm inv* (*plano*) table mat; (*con pies*) trivet

salvar 1 *vt* (**a**) to save, to rescue

(**de** from) (**b**) (*obstáculo*) to clear; (*dificultad*) to get round, to overcome (**c**) (*exceptuar*) to exclude, to except; **salvando ciertos errores** except for a few mistakes

2 salvarse *vpr* (**a**) (*sobrevivir*) to survive, to come out alive; *Fam* (*escaparse*) to escape (**de** from); **¡sálvese quien pueda!** every man for himself! (**b**) *Rel* to be saved, to save one's soul

salvavidas *nm inv* life belt

salvo, -a 1 *adj* unharmed, safe; **a s.** safe **2** *adv* (*exceptuando*) except (for); **s. que** unless

san *adj* saint

sanatorio *nm* sanatorium

sanción *nf* (**a**) sanction (**b**) (*aprobación*) sanction, approval (**c**) *Jur* penalty

sancocho *nm Andes* (*comida*) = stew of beef, chicken or fish, vegetables and green bananas

sandalia *nf* sandal

sandía *nf* watermelon

sándwich ['sanwitʃ, 'sanwis] *nm* (*pl* **sándwiches**) sandwich

sangrar 1 *vt* (**a**) to bleed (**b**) *Fam* (*sacar dinero*) to bleed dry **2** *vi* to bleed

sangre *nf* blood; **donar s.** to give blood; **s. fría** sangfroid; **a s. fría** in cold blood

sangría *nf* (**a**) *Med* bleeding, bloodletting; *Fig* drain (**b**) (*timo*) rip-off (**c**) (*bebida*) sangria

sangriento, -a *adj* (*guerra etc*) bloody

sanidad *nf* health; **Ministerio de S.** Department of Health

sanitario, -a 1 *adj* health **2** *nm* toilet, *US* bathroom

sano, -a *adj* (**a**) (*bien de salud*) healthy; **s. y salvo** safe and sound (**b**) (*comida*) healthy, wholesome (**c**) **en su s. juicio** in one's right mind

Santa Claus, *Méx, Ven* **Santa Clos** *n* Santa Claus

santería *nf* (**a**) (*religión*) santería, = form of religion common in the Caribbean in which people allegedly have contact with the spirit world (**b**)

Am (tienda) = shop selling religious mementoes such as statues of saints

santiguarse [45] *vpr* to cross oneself

santo, -a 1 *adj* (**a**) holy, sacred (**b**) *(bueno)* saintly; **un s. varón** a saint **2** *nm,f* (**a**) saint; *Fam* **¡por todos los santos!** for heaven's sake!; *Fig* **se me fue el s. al cielo** I clean forgot (**b**) *(día onomástico)* saint's day; *Fig* **¿a s. de qué?** why on earth?

santuario *nm* sanctuary, shrine

sapo *nm* toad; *Fam* **echar sapos y culebras** to rant and rave

saque *nm* (**a**) *Ftb* **s. inicial** kick-off; **s. de banda** throw-in; **s. de esquina** corner kick (**b**) *Ten* service

saquear *vt (ciudad)* to sack, to plunder; *(casas, tiendas)* to loot

sarampión *nm* measles *sing*

sarcástico, -a *adj* sarcastic

sardana *nf* sardana, = Catalan dance and music

sardina *nf* sardine

sargento *nm* sergeant

sarna *nf Med* scabies *sing*; *Zool* mange

sarpullido *nm* rash

sarro *nm (sedimento)* deposit; *(en dientes)* tartar; *(en lengua)* fur

sartén *nf* frying pan, *US* fry-pan; *Fam Fig* **tener la s. por el mango** to call the shots

sastre *nm* tailor

sastrería *nf (oficio)* tailoring; *(taller)* tailor's (shop); *Cin, Teatro* wardrobe (department)

satélite *nm* satellite; *Fig* **país s.** satellite state; **televisión vía s.** satellite TV

sátira *nf* satire

satírico, -a *adj* satirical

satisfacción *nf* satisfaction; **s. de un deseo** fulfilment of a desire

satisfacer [15] *(pp* **satisfecho)** *vt* (**a**) *(deseos, necesidades)* to satisfy (**b**) *(requisitos)* to meet, to satisfy (**c**) *(deuda)* to pay

satisfecho, -a *adj* satisfied; **me doy por s.** that's good enough for me; **s. de sí mismo** self-satisfied, smug

sauce *nm* willow; **s. llorón** weeping willow

sauna *nf* sauna

saxofón *nm* saxophone

sazonar *vt* to season, to flavour

se¹ *pron* (**a**) *(reflexivo) (objeto directo) (a él mismo)* himself; *(animal)* itself; *(a ella misma)* herself; *(animal)* itself; *(a usted mismo)* yourself; *(a ellos mismos)* themselves; *(a ustedes mismos)* yourselves

(**b**) *(objeto indirecto) (a él mismo)* (to/for) himself; *(animal)* (to/for) itself; *(a ella misma)* (to/for) herself; *(animal)* (to/for) itself; *(a usted mismo)* (to/for) yourself; *(a ellos mismos)* (to/for) themselves; *(a ustedes mismos)* (to/for) yourselves; **se compró un nuevo coche** he bought himself a new car; **todos los días se lava el pelo** she washes her hair every day

(**c**) *(recíproco)* one another, each other (**d**) *(voz pasiva)* **el vino se guarda en cubas** wine is kept in casks

(**e**) *(impersonal)* **nunca se sabe** you never know; **se habla inglés** *(en letrero)* English spoken here; **se dice que …** it is said that …

se² *pron pers (a él)* (to/for) him; *(a ella)* (to/for) her; *(a usted o ustedes)* (to/for) you; *(a ellos)* (to/for) them; **se lo diré en cuanto les vea** I'll tell them as soon as I see them; **¿se lo explico?** shall I explain it to you?; **¿se lo has dado ya?** have you given it to him yet?

sé¹ *indic pres de* **saber**

sé² *imperat de* **ser**

sea *subj pres de* **ser**

secador *nm* dryer; **s. de pelo** hairdryer

secadora *nf* tumble dryer

secano *nm* dry land

secar [44] **1** *vt* to dry **2 secarse** *vpr* (**a**) to dry; **sécate** dry yourself; **secarse las manos** to dry one's hands (**b**) *(marchitarse)* to dry up, to wither

sección *nf* section

seco, -a *adj* (**a**) dry; **frutos secos** dried fruit; **limpieza en s.** drycleaning; *Fig* **a palo s.** on its own; *Fig*

a secas just, only (**b**) *(tono)* curt, sharp; *(golpe, ruido)* sharp; *Fig* **frenar en s.** to pull up sharply; *Fig* **parar en s.** to stop dead (**c**) *(delgado)* skinny

secretaría *nf (oficina)* secretary's office; **S. de Estado** *(en España)* = government department under the control of a *Br* junior minister o *US* under-secretary; *(en Latinoamérica)* ministry; *(en Estados Unidos)* State Department

secretariado *nm* (**a**) *(oficina)* secretariat (**b**) *Educ* secretarial course

secretario, -a *nm,f* secretary; **s. de dirección** secretary to the director; **s. de Estado** *(en España) Br* junior minister, *US* under-secretary; *(en Latinoamérica) Br* minister, *US* secretary; *(en Estados Unidos)* Secretary of State

secreto, -a 1 *adj* secret; **en s.** in secret, secretly **2** *nm* secret; **guardar un s.** to keep a secret; **con mucho s.** in great secrecy

secta *nf* sect

sector *nm* (**a**) sector (**b**) *(zona)* area; **un s. de la ciudad** an area of the city

secuestrador, -a *nm,f* (**a**) *(de persona)* kidnapper; *(de un avión)* hijacker (**b**) *Jur* sequestrator

secuestrar *vt* (**a**) *(persona)* to kidnap; *(aviones)* to hijack (**b**) *Jur* to confiscate

secuestro *nm* (**a**) *(de persona)* kidnapping; *(de un avión)* hijacking (**b**) *Jur* confiscation

secundario, -a *adj* secondary

sed *nf* thirst; **tener s.** to be thirsty

seda *nf* silk

sedante *adj & nm* sedative

sede *nf* (**a**) headquarters, head office; *(de gobierno)* seat (**b**) **la Santa S.** the Holy See

sedentario, -a *adj* sedentary

sediento, -a *adj* thirsty; *Fig* **s. de poder** hungry for power

seductor, -a 1 *adj* seductive; *(persuasivo)* tempting **2** *nm,f* seducer

segador, -a *nm,f (agricultor)* reaper

segadora *nf (máquina)* reaper, harvester

segar [1] *vt* to reap, to cut

segmento *nm* segment

seguido, -a 1 *adj* (**a**) *(continuo)* continuous (**b**) *(consecutivo)* consecutive, successive; **tres veces seguidas** on three consecutive occasions; **tres lunes seguidos** three Mondays in a row **2** *adv* (**a**) *(en línea recta)* straight on; **todo s.** straight on o ahead (**b**) *Am (a menudo)* often

seguir [6] **1** *vt* (**a**) to follow (**b**) *(camino)* to continue (**c**) *(perseguir)* to chase

2 *vi* (**a**) to follow (**b**) **s. + ger** *(continuar)* to continue, to go on, to keep on; **siguió hablando** he continued o went on o kept on speaking (**c**) **s. + adj/pp** to continue to be, to be still; **sigo resfriado** I've still got the cold; **sigue con vida** he's still alive

3 seguirse *vpr* to follow, to ensue

según 1 *prep* (**a**) according to; **s. la Biblia** according to the Bible (**b**) *(en función de)* depending on; **varía s. el tiempo (que haga)** it varies depending on the weather

2 *adv* (**a**) depending on; **s. estén las cosas** depending on how things stand; **¿vendrás mañana? – s.** will you come tomorrow? – it depends (**b**) *(tal como)* just as; **estaba s. lo dejé** it was just as I had left it (**c**) *(a medida que)* as; **s. iba leyendo ...** as I read on ...

segunda *nf* (**a**) *Aut* second (gear); **meter (la) s.** to go into second (gear) (**b**) *Av, Ferroc* second class; **viajar en s.** to travel second class

segundero *nm* second hand

segundo¹, -a 1 *adj* second; *Fig* **decir algo con segundas (intenciones)** to say sth with a double meaning **2** *nm,f (de una serie)* second (one)

segundo² *nm (tiempo)* second; **sesenta segundos** sixty seconds

seguramente *adv* (**a**) *(seguro)* surely (**b**) *(probablemente)* most probably; **s. no lloverá** it isn't likely to rain

seguridad *nf* (**a**) security; **cerradura**

de s. security lock (**b**) *(física)* safety; **s. en carretera** road safety; **para mayor s.** to be on the safe side (**c**) *(confianza)* confidence; **s. en sí mismo** self-confidence (**d**) *(certeza)* sureness; **con toda s.** most probably; **tener la s. de que ...** to be certain that ... (**e**) **S. Social** ≃ Social Security

seguro, -a 1 *adj* (**a**) *(cierto)* sure; **estoy s. de que ...** I am sure that ...; **dar algo por s.** to take sth for granted (**b**) *(libre de peligro)* safe; *Fig* **ir sobre s.** to play safe (**c**) *(protegido)* secure (**d**) *(fiable)* reliable (**e**) **está segura de ella misma** she has self-confidence (**f**) *(firme)* steady, firm
2 *nm* (**a**) *Seg* insurance; **s. a todo riesgo** fully comprehensive insurance; **s. de vida** life insurance (**b**) *(dispositivo)* safety catch o device (**c**) *CAm, Méx (imperdible)* safety pin
3 *adv* for sure, definitely

seis *adj & nm inv* six

seiscientos, -as *adj & nm* six hundred

selección *nf* (**a**) selection (**b**) *Dep* team

seleccionador, -a *nm,f* (**a**) selector (**b**) *Dep* manager

seleccionar *vt* to select

selectividad *nf* selectivity; *Esp (examen)* **(prueba de) s.** entrance examination

selecto, -a *adj* select; **ambiente s.** exclusive atmosphere

selector, -a 1 *adj* selecting **2** *nm* selector (button)

self-service *nm* self-service cafeteria

sello *nm* (**a**) *(de correos)* stamp; *(para documentos)* seal (**b**) *(precinto)* seal

selva *nf* jungle

semáforo *nm* traffic lights

semana *nf* week; **entre s.** during the week; **S. Santa** Holy Week

semanada *nf Am* (weekly) pocket money

semanal *adj & nm* weekly

semanario *nm* weekly magazine

sembrar [1] *vt* (**a**) *Agr* to sow (**b**) *Fig* **s. el pánico** to spread panic

semejante 1 *adj* (**a**) *(parecido)* similar; **nunca he visto nada s.** I've never seen anything like it (**b**) *Pey (comparativo)* such; **s. desvergüenza** such insolence **2** *nm (prójimo)* fellow being

semejanza *nf* similarity, likeness

semen *nm* semen

semestre *nm* six-month period, *US* semester

semidesnatado, -a *adj* semi-skimmed

semidirecto, -a 1 *adj* express **2** *nm (tren)* = through train, a section of which becomes a stopping train

semifinal *nf* semifinal

semilla *nf* seed

sémola *nf* semolina

senado *nm* senate

senador, -a *nm,f* senator

sencillo, -a 1 *adj* (**a**) *(fácil)* simple, easy (**b**) *(natural)* natural, unaffected (**c**) *(billete) Br* single, *US* one-way (**d**) *(sin adornos)* simple, plain **2** *nm Andes, CAm, Méx Fam (cambio)* loose change

senda *nf*, **sendero** *nm* path

seno *nm* (**a**) *(pecho)* breast (**b**) *Fig* bosom, heart; **en el s. de** within (**c**) *Mat* sine

sensación *nf* (**a**) sensation, feeling; **tengo la s. de que ...** I have a feeling that ... (**b**) *(impresión)* sensation; **causar s.** to cause a sensation

sensacional *adj* sensational

sensacionalismo *nm* sensationalism

sensacionalista *adj* sensationalist; **prensa s.** gutter press

sensato, -a *adj* sensible

sensibilidad *nf* (**a**) *(percepción)* feeling; **no tiene s. en los brazos** she has no feeling in her arms (**b**) *(emotividad)* sensitivity; **tener la s. a flor de piel** to be easily hurt, to be very sensitive

sensible *adj* (**a**) sensitive (**b**) *(perceptible)* perceptible

sensual *adj* sensual

sentado, -a *adj (establecido)* established, settled; **dar algo por s.** to take sth for granted; **dejar s. que ...** to make it clear that ...

sentar [1] **1** vt (**a**) to sit (**b**) *(establecer)* to establish; **s. las bases** to lay the foundations

2 vi (**a**) *(color, ropa etc)* to suit; **el pelo corto te sienta mal** short hair doesn't suit you (**b**) **s. bien/mal a** *(comida)* to agree/disagree with; **la sopa te sentará bien** the soup will do you good (**c**) **le sentó mal la broma** she didn't like the joke

3 sentarse vpr to sit, to sit down

sentencia nf (**a**) sentence; **visto para s.** ready for judgement (**b**) *(aforismo)* maxim, saying

sentenciar [43] vt Jur to sentence (**a to**)

sentido, -a 1 nm (**a**) sense; **los cinco sentidos** the five senses; **s. común** common sense; **s. del humor** sense of humour (**b**) *(significado)* meaning; **doble s.** double meaning; **no tiene s.** it doesn't make sense (**c**) *(dirección)* direction; (**de**) **s. único** one-way (**d**) *(conciencia)* consciousness; **perder el s.** to faint

2 adj deeply felt; Fml **mi más s. pésame** my deepest sympathy

sentimental 1 adj sentimental; **vida s.** love life **2** nmf sentimental person

sentimiento nm (**a**) feeling (**b**) *(pesar)* sorrow, grief; Fml **le acompaño en el s.** my deepest sympathy

sentir¹ nm (**a**) *(sentimiento)* feeling (**b**) *(opinión)* opinion, view

sentir² [5] **1** vt (**a**) to feel; **s. hambre/calor** to feel hungry/hot (**b**) *(lamentar)* to regret, to be sorry about; **lo siento (mucho)** I'm (very) sorry; **siento molestarle** I'm sorry to bother you **2 sentirse** vpr to feel; **me siento mal** I feel ill; **sentirse con ánimos de hacer algo** to feel like doing sth

seña nf (**a**) mark (**b**) *(gesto)* sign; **hacer señas a algn** to signal to sb (**c**) *(indicio)* sign (**d**) **señas** *(dirección)* address

señal nf (**a**) *(indicio)* sign, indication; **en s. de** as a sign of, as a token of (**b**) *(placa)* sign; **s. de tráfico** road sign (**c**) *(gesto etc)* signal, sign (**d**) *(marca)* mark; *(vestigio)* trace (**e**) Tel tone; **s. de llamada** Br dialling tone, US dial tone (**f**) Com deposit

señalado, -a adj *(importante)* important; **un día s.** a red-letter day

señalar vt (**a**) *(indicar)* to mark, to indicate; **s. con el dedo** to point at (**b**) *(resaltar)* to point out (**c**) *(precio, fecha)* to fix, to arrange

señalero nm Urug Br indicator, US turn signal

señor nm (**a**) *(hombre)* man; *(caballero)* gentleman (**b**) Rel **El S.** the Lord (**c**) *(con apellido)* Mr; *(tratamiento de respeto)* sir; **el Sr. Gutiérrez** Mr Gutiérrez; **muy s. mío** *(en carta)* Dear Sir (**d**) *(con título) (no se traduce)* **el s. ministro** the Minister

señora nf (**a**) *(mujer)* woman, Fml lady; **¡señoras y señores!** ladies and gentlemen! (**b**) Rel **Nuestra S.** Our Lady (**c**) *(con apellido)* Mrs; *(tratamiento de respeto)* madam; **la Sra. Salinas** Mrs Salinas; **muy s. mía** *(en carta)* Dear Madam (**d**) *(con título) (no se traduce)* **la s. ministra** the Minister (**e**) *(esposa)* wife

señorita nf (**a**) *(joven)* young woman, Fml young lady (**b**) *(tratamiento de respeto)* Miss; **S. Padilla** Miss Padilla (**c**) Educ **la s.** the teacher, Miss

señorito, -a 1 adj Fam Pey *(refinado)* lordly **2** nm (**a**) Anticuado *(hijo del amo)* master (**b**) Fam Pey *(niñato)* rich kid

sepa subj pres de **saber**

separación nf (**a**) separation; Jur **s. conyugal** legal separation (**b**) *(espacio)* space, gap

separado, -a adj (**a**) separate; **por s.** separately, individually (**b**) *(divorciado)* separated

separar 1 vt (**a**) to separate (**b**) *(desunir)* to detach, to remove (**c**) *(dividir)* to divide, to separate (**d**) *(apartar)* to move away **2 separarse** vpr (**a**) to separate, to part company (**b**) *(matrimonio)* to separate (**c**) *(apartarse)* to move away (**de** from)

separo nm Méx cell

sepia 1 *nf (pez)* cuttlefish **2** *adj & nm (color)* sepia

septentrional *adj* northern

septiembre *nm* September; **el 5 de s.** the 5th of September; **en s.** in September

séptimo, -a *adj & nm,f* seventh; **la o una séptima parte** a seventh

sepulcro *nm* tomb

sequía *nf* drought

ser¹ *nm* being; **s. humano** human being; **s. vivo** living being

ser² [23] *vi* (a) (+ *adj*) to be; **es alto y rubio** he is tall and fair; **el edificio es gris** the building is grey

(b) (+ *profesión*) to be a(n); **Rafael es músico** Rafael is a musician

(c) **s. de** *(procedencia)* to be o come from; **¿de dónde eres?** where are you from?, where do you come from?

(d) **s. de** (+ *material*) to be made of

(e) **s. de** (+ *poseedor*) to belong to; **el perro es de Miguel** the dog belongs to Miguel; **¿de quién es este abrigo?** whose coat is this?

(f) **s. para** *(finalidad)* to be for; **esta agua es para lavar** this water is for washing

(g) (+ *día, hora*) to be; **hoy es 2 de noviembre** today is the 2nd of November; **son las cinco de la tarde** it's five o'clock

(h) (+ *cantidad*) **¿cuántos estaremos en la fiesta?** how many of us will there be at the party?

(i) *(costar)* to be, to cost; **¿cuánto es?** how much is it?

(j) *(tener lugar)* to be; **el estreno será mañana** tomorrow is the opening night

(k) **¿qué es de Gonzalo?** what has become of Gonzalo?

(l) *(auxiliar en pasiva)* to be; **fue asesinado** he was murdered

(m) *(locuciones)* **es más** furthermore; **es que ...** it's just that ...; **como sea** anyhow; **lo que sea** whatever; **o sea** that is (to say); **sea como sea** in any case, be that as it may; **a no s. que** unless; **de no s. por ...** had it not been for ...

The auxiliary verb **ser** is used with the past participle of a verb to form the passive (e.g. **la película fue criticada** the film was criticized)

serenar 1 *vt (calmar)* to calm **2 serenarse** *vpr (calmarse)* to calm down

serenidad *nf* serenity

sereno¹ *nm (vigilante)* night watchman

sereno², -a *adj* (a) calm (b) *Fam* **estar s.** *(sobrio)* to be sober

serie *nf* (a) series *sing*; **fabricación en s.** mass production; **lleva ABS de s.** it has ABS fitted as standard; **fuera de s.** out of the ordinary (b) *Rad, TV* series *sing*

seriedad *nf* (a) seriousness (b) *(formalidad)* reliability, dependability; **falta de s.** irresponsibility

serio, -a *adj* (a) *(severo)* serious; **en s.** seriously (b) *(formal)* reliable, responsible

sermón *nm* sermon

serpentina *nf (de papel)* streamer

serpiente *nf* snake; **s. de cascabel** rattlesnake; **s. pitón** python

serrar [1] *vt* to saw

serrín *nm* sawdust

serrucho *nm* handsaw

servicio *nm* (a) service; **s. a domicilio** delivery service (b) *Mil* service; **s. militar** military service; **estar de s.** to be on duty (c) *Esp (WC)* toilet, *US* bathroom

servidumbre *nf* (a) *(criados)* servants (b) *(dependencia)* servitude

servilleta *nf* napkin, *Br* serviette

servir [6] **1** *vt* to serve; **¿en qué puedo servirle?** what can I do for you?, may I help you?; **¿te sirvo una copa?** will I pour you a drink?

2 *vi* (a) to serve (b) *(valer)* to be useful, to be suitable; **no sirve de nada llorar** it's no use crying; **ya no sirve** it's no use; **¿para qué sirve esto?** what is this (used) for? (c) **s. de** to serve as, to act as

3 servirse *vpr* (a) *(comida etc)* to help oneself (b) *Fml* **sírvase comunicarnos su decisión** please inform us of your decision

sesenta *adj & nm inv* sixty

sesión *nf* (**a**) *(reunión)* meeting, session; *Jur* session, sitting (**b**) *Cin* showing

seso *nm* brain

seta *nf Esp (comestible)* mushroom; **s. venenosa** toadstool

setecientos, -as *adj & nm* seven hundred

setenta *adj & nm inv* seventy

setiembre *nm* September

seto *nm* hedge

severidad *nf* severity

severo, -a *adj* severe

Sevilla *n* Seville

sevillana *nf* = Andalusian dance and song

sexismo *nm* sexism

sexista *adj* sexist

sexo *nm* (**a**) sex (**b**) *(órgano)* genitals

sexto, -a *adj & nm,f* sixth

sexual *adj* sexual; **vida s.** sex life

sexualidad *nf* sexuality

short *nm Am* shorts

shorts [ʃorts] *nmpl* shorts

show [ʃou, tʃou] *nm (pl* **shows***)* show

si¹ *conj* (**a**) *(condicional)* if; **como si** as if; **si no** if not; **si quieres** if you like, if you wish (**b**) *(pregunta indirecta)* whether, if; **me preguntó si me gustaba** he asked me if I liked it; **no sé si ir o no** *(disyuntivo)* I don't know whether to go or not (**c**) *(sorpresa)* **¡si está llorando!** but she's crying!

si² *nm (pl* **sis***) Mús* B; *(en solfeo)* ti

sí¹ *pron pers* (**a**) *(singular) (él)* himself; *(ella)* herself; *(cosa)* itself; *(plural)* themselves; **de por sí, en sí** in itself; **hablaban entre sí** they were talking among themselves *o* to each other; **por sí mismo** by himself (**b**) *(uno mismo)* oneself; **decir para sí** to say to oneself

sí² **1** *adv* (**a**) yes; **dije que sí** I said yes, I accepted, I agreed; **porque sí** just because; **¡que sí!** yes, I tell you!; **un día sí y otro no** every other day (**b**) *(uso enfático) (no se traduce)* **sí que me gusta** of course I like it; **¡eso sí que**

no! certainly not! **2** *nm (pl* **síes***)* yes; **los síes** *(en parlamento)* the ayes

sida *nm (abr* **síndrome de inmunodeficiencia adquirida***)* AIDS

sidecar *nm* sidecar

sidra *nf Br* cider, *US* hard cider

siega **1** *ver* **segar 2** *nf* (**a**) *(acción)* reaping, harvesting (**b**) *(época)* harvest (time)

siembra **1** *ver* **sembrar 2** *nf* (**a**) *(acción)* sowing (**b**) *(época)* sowing time

siempre *adv* (**a**) always; **s. pasa lo mismo** it's always the same; **como s.** as usual; **a la hora de s.** at the usual time; **para s.** forever; **s. que** *(cada vez que)* whenever; *(a condición de que)* provided, as long as; **s. y cuando** provided, as long as (**b**) *Am (todavía)* still; **s. viven allí** they still live there (**c**) *Méx Fam (enfático)* **s. sí quiero ir** I do still want to go; **s. no me marcho** I'm still not leaving

sien *nf* temple

sierra *nf* (**a**) saw; **s. mecánica** power saw (**b**) *Geog* mountain range, sierra

siesta *nf* siesta, nap; **dormir la s.** to have a siesta *o* an afternoon nap

siete **1** *adj & nm inv* seven **2** *nf RP Fam Euf* **¡la gran s.!** *Br* sugar!, *US* shoot!

sifón *nm* siphon; **whisky con s.** whisky and soda

sigla *nf* acronym

siglo *nm* century; **el s. veintiuno** the twenty-first century; *Fam* **hace siglos que no le veo** I haven't seen him for ages

significado *nm* meaning

significar [44] *vt* to mean

significativo, -a *adj* significant; *(expresivo)* meaningful

signo *nm* (**a**) sign; **s. del zodiaco** zodiac sign (**b**) *Ling* mark; **s. de interrogación** question mark

siguiente *adj* following, next; **¡el s.!** next, please!; **al día s.** the following day

sílaba *nf* syllable

silbar *vi* to whistle; *(abuchear)* to hiss, to boo

silbato *nm* whistle

silbido *nm* whistle, whistling; *(agudo)* hiss

silenciador *nm (de arma)* silencer; *(de coche, moto)* Br silencer, US muffler

silencio *nm* silence; **imponer s. a algn** to make sb be quiet

silencioso, -a *adj (persona)* quiet; *(motor etc)* silent

silicona *nf* silicone

silla *nf* (a) chair; **s. de ruedas** wheelchair; **s. giratoria** swivel chair (b) *(de montura)* saddle

sillín *nm* saddle

sillón *nm* armchair

silueta *nf* silhouette; *(de cuerpo)* figure

silvestre *adj* wild

símbolo *nm* symbol

simétrico, -a *adj* symmetrical

similar *adj* similar

similitud *nf* similarity

simpatía *nf* liking, affection; **le tengo mucha s.** I am very fond of him

simpático, -a *adj (amable)* nice, likeable; **me cae s.** I like him

simpatizante *nmf* sympathizer

simpatizar [40] *vi* (a) to sympathize (**con** with) (b) *(llevarse bien)* to hit it off (**con** with)

simple 1 *adj* (a) simple (b) *(fácil)* simple, easy (c) *(mero)* mere (d) *(persona)* simple, simple-minded **2** *nm (persona)* simpleton

simplicidad *nf* simplicity

simular *vt* to simulate

simultáneo, -a *adj* simultaneous

sin *prep* (a) without; **s. dinero/ti** without money/you; **estamos s. pan** we're out of bread; **s. hacer nada** without doing anything; **cerveza s.** alcohol-free beer; **s. más ni más** without further ado (b) *(+ infinitivo)* **está s. secar** it hasn't been dried

sinagoga *nf* synagogue

sinceridad *nf* sincerity; **con toda s.** in all sincerity

sincero, -a *adj* sincere

sincronizar [40] *vt* to synchronize

sindicar *vt Andes, RP, Ven* to accuse; **s. a algn de algo** to accuse sb of sth

sindicato *nm* (Br trade o US labor) union

sinfonía *nf* symphony

sinfónico, -a *adj* symphonic

singani *nm Bol* grape brandy

single *nm* (a) *(disco)* single, 7-inch (b) *CSur (habitación)* single room

singular 1 *adj* (a) singular (b) *(excepcional)* exceptional, unique (c) *(raro)* peculiar, odd **2** *nm Ling* singular; **en s.** in the singular

siniestro, -a 1 *adj* sinister, ominous **2** *nm* disaster, catastrophe

sinnúmero *nm* **un s. de** countless

sino¹ *nm Fml* fate, destiny

sino² *conj* (a) but; **no fui a Madrid, s. a Barcelona** I didn't go to Madrid but to Barcelona (b) *(excepto)* **nadie s. él** no one but him; **no quiero s. que me oigan** I only want them to listen (to me)

sinónimo, -a 1 *adj* synonymous **2** *nm* synonym

síntesis *nf inv* synthesis; **en s.** in short; *Informát, Ling* **s. del habla** speech synthesis

sintético, -a *adj* synthetic

sintetizador *nm* synthesizer

síntoma *nm* symptom

sintonía *nf* (a) *Elec, Rad* tuning (b) *Mús, Rad (de programa)* theme tune, Br signature tune (c) *Fig* harmony

sintonizar [40] *vt* (a) *Rad* to tune in to (b) *(simpatizar)* **sintonizaron muy bien** they clicked straight away

sinvergüenza 1 *adj (desvergonzado)* shameless; *(descarado)* cheeky **2** *nmf (desvergonzado)* rogue; *(caradura)* cheeky devil

siquiera 1 *adv (por lo menos)* at least; **ni s.** not even **2** *conj Fml (aunque)* although, even though

sirena *nf* (a) siren, mermaid (b) *(señal acústica)* siren

sirviente, -a *nm,f* servant

sisa *nf* (a) *(de manga)* armhole (b) *(de dinero)* pilfering

sistema *nm* system; **por s.** as a rule; **s.**

nervioso nervous system; **s. montañoso** mountain chain

sitiar [43] *vt* to besiege

sitio¹ *nm* (a) *(lugar)* place; **en cualquier s.** anywhere; **en todos los sitios** everywhere; *Fig* **quedarse en el s.** to die (b) *(espacio)* room; **hacer s.** to make room (c) *Méx (parada de taxis)* taxi *Br* rank o *US* stand (d) *Informát* site; **s. web** website

sitio² *nm* siege; **estado de s.** state of emergency

situación *nf* (a) situation; **su s. económica es buena** his financial position is good (b) *(ubicación)* situation, location

situar [30] **1** *vt* to locate **2 situarse** *vpr* to be situated o located

skinhead [es'kinχeð] *nmf* (*pl* **skinheads**) skinhead

S.L. (*abr* **Sociedad Limitada**) *Br* ≃ Ltd, *US* ≃ Inc

S.M. (*abr* **Su Majestad**) *(rey)* His Majesty; *(reina)* Her Majesty

s/n (*abr* **sin número**) = abbreviation used in addresses after the street name, where the building has no number

sobaco *nm* armpit

sobar *vt (tocar)* to finger, to paw; *Fam (persona)* to touch up, to fondle

soberbia *nf* pride

soberbio, -a *adj* (a) proud (b) *(magnífico)* splendid, magnificent

soborno *nm (acción)* bribery; *(dinero etc)* bribe

sobra *nf* (a) **de s.** *(no necesario)* superfluous; **tener de s.** to have plenty; **estar de s.** not to be needed; **saber algo de s.** to know sth only too well (b) **sobras** *(restos)* leftovers

sobrar *vi* (a) to be more than enough, *(sing)* to be too much, *(pl)* to be too many; **sobran tres sillas** there are three chairs too many; **sobran comentarios** I've nothing further to add; *Fam* **tú sobras aquí** you are not wanted here (b) *(quedar)* to be left over; **ha sobrado carne** there's still some meat left

sobrasada *nf* sausage spread

sobre¹ *nm* (a) *(para carta)* envelope (b) *(de sopa etc)* packet

sobre² *prep* (a) *(encima de)* on, upon, on top of (b) *(por encima)* over, above (c) *(acerca de)* about, on (d) *(aproximadamente)* about; **vendré s. las ocho** I'll come at about eight o'clock (e) **s. todo** especially, above all

sobrecarga *nf* overload

sobredosis *nf inv* overdose

sobrehumano, -a *adj* superhuman

sobremesa¹ *nf* afternoon

sobremesa² *nf* **ordenador de s.** desktop computer

sobrenombre *nm* nickname

sobrepasar 1 *vt* to exceed, to surpass; *(rival)* to beat **2 sobrepasarse** *vpr* to go too far

sobreponer [19] **1** *vt* (a) *(poner encima)* to put on top (b) *Fig (anteponer)* **s. algo a algo** to put sth before sth **2 sobreponerse** *vpr* **sobreponerse a algo** to overcome sth

sobresaliente 1 *nm (nota)* ≃ A **2** *adj (que destaca)* outstanding, excellent

sobresalir [22] *vi* to stick out, to protrude; *Fig (destacar)* to stand out, to excel

sobresalto *nm (movimiento)* start; *(susto)* fright

sobretiempo *nm Andes* (a) *(en trabajo)* overtime (b) *(en deporte) Br* extra time, *US* overtime

sobrevivir *vi* to survive

sobrevolar [2] *vt* to fly over

sobrino *nm* nephew

sobrio, -a *adj* sober

sociable *adj* sociable, friendly

social *adj* social

socialista *adj & nmf* socialist

sociedad *nf* (a) society; **s. de consumo** consumer society (b) *(asociación)* association, society (c) *Com* company; **s. anónima** *Br* public (limited) company, *US* incorporated company; **s. limitada** private limited company

socio, -a *nm,f* (a) *(miembro)* member;

hacerse s. de un club to become a member of a club, to join a club (**b**) *Com (asociado)* partner

sociología *nf* sociology

sociólogo, -a *nm,f* sociologist

socorrer *vt* to help, to assist

socorrismo *nm* first aid; *(en la playa)* lifesaving

socorrista *nmf* life-saver, lifeguard

socorro *nm* help, assistance; **¡s.!** help!; **puesto de s.** first-aid post

soda *nf* soda water

sofá *nm* sofa, settee; **s. cama** sofa bed, studio couch

sofisticado, -a *adj* sophisticated

sofocante *adj* suffocating, stifling; **hacía un calor s.** it was unbearably hot

sofoco *nm* (**a**) *Fig (vergüenza)* embarrassment; *(disgusto)* **le dio un s.** it gave her quite a turn (**b**) *Med* **sofocos** hot flushes

sofrito *nm* = fried tomato and onion sauce

software *nm* software

sol¹ *nm* (**a**) sun (**b**) *(luz)* sunlight; *(luz y calor)* sunshine; **hace s.** it's sunny, the sun is shining; **tomar el s.** to sunbathe; **al** *o* **bajo el s.** in the sun; **de s. a s.** from sunrise to sunset (**c**) *Fin* = standard monetary unit of Peru

sol² *nm Mús* G; *(solfeo)* so

solamente *adv* only; **no s.** not only; **s. con mirarte lo sé** I know just by looking at you; **s. que …** except that …

solapa *nf (de chaqueta)* lapel; *(de sobre, bolsillo, libro)* flap

solar¹ *adj* solar; **luz s.** sunlight

solar² *nm (terreno)* plot; *(en obras)* building site

solario, solárium *nm (pl* solariums) solarium

soldado *nm* soldier; **s. raso** private

soldador, -a 1 *nm,f* welder 2 *nm* soldering iron

soldar [2] *vt (cable)* to solder; *(chapa)* to weld

soleado, -a *adj* sunny

soledad *nf (estado)* solitude; *(sentimiento)* loneliness

solemne *adj* (**a**) *(majestuoso)* solemn (**b**) *Pey* downright

solemnidad *nf* solemnity

soler [4] *vi defect* (**a**) *(en presente)* to be in the habit of; **solemos ir en coche** we usually go by car; **sueles equivocarte** you are usually wrong (**b**) *(en pasado)* **solía pasear por aquí** he used to walk round here

solicitar *vt (información etc)* to request, to ask for; *(trabajo)* to apply for

solicitud *nf (petición)* request; *(de trabajo)* application

solidaridad *nf* solidarity

sólido, -a *adj* solid, strong

solista *nmf* soloist

solitario, -a 1 *adj (que está solo)* solitary, lone; *(que se siente solo)* lonely 2 *nm* (**a**) *(diamante)* solitaire (**b**) *Naipes Br* patience, *US* solitaire

sollozar [40] *vi* to sob

sollozo *nm* sob

solo, -a 1 *adj* (**a**) only, single; **ni un s. día** not a single day; **una sola vez** only once, just once (**b**) *(solitario)* lonely (**c**) **hablar s.** to talk to oneself; **se enciende s.** it switches itself on automatically; **a solas** alone, by oneself 2 *nm Mús* solo

sólo *adv* only; **tan s.** only; **no s. … sino (también)** not only … but (also); **con s., (tan) s. con** just by

Note that the adverb **sólo** can be written without an accent when there is no risk of confusion with the adjective

solomillo *nm* sirloin

soltar [2] 1 *vt* (**a**) *(desasir)* to let go of; **¡suéltame!** let me go! (**b**) *(prisionero)* to release (**c**) *(humo, olor)* to give off (**d**) *(bofetada)* to deal; *(carcajada)* to let out; **me soltó un rollo** he bored me to tears 2 **soltarse** *vpr* (**a**) *(desatarse)* to come loose (**b**) *(perro etc)* to get loose, to break loose (**c**) *(desprenderse)* to come off

soltero, -a 1 *adj* single, unmarried 2 *nm* bachelor, single man, *f* single woman, *f* spinster

solterón, -ona *nm,f* old bachelor, *f* old maid

soltura *nf (agilidad)* agility; *(seguridad)* confidence, assurance; **habla italiano con s.** he speaks Italian fluently

solución *nf* solution

solucionar *vt* to solve; *(arreglar)* to settle

solvente *adj* (a) *Fin* solvent (b) *(fiable)* reliable

sombra *nf* (a) shade (b) *(silueta proyectada)* shadow; **s. de ojos** eyeshadow; **sin s. de duda** beyond a shadow of doubt (c) **tener buena s.** *(tener suerte)* to be lucky

sombrero *nm* hat; **s. de copa** top hat; **s. hongo** *Br* bowler hat, *US* derby

sombrilla *nf* parasol, sunshade

someter 1 *vt* (a) to subject; **s. a prueba** to put to the test; **s. algo a votación** to put sth to the vote (b) *(rebeldes)* to subdue, to put down **2 someterse** *vpr* (a) *(subordinarse)* to submit (b) *(rendirse)* to surrender, to yield (c) **someterse a un tratamiento** to undergo treatment

somier *nm* spring mattress

somnífero *nm* sleeping pill

son *nm* sound; **al s. del tambor** to the sound of the drum; **venir en s. de paz** to come in peace

sonajero *nm* baby's rattle

sonar [2] **1** *vi* (a) to sound; **s. a** to sound like; **suena bien** it sounds good (b) *(timbre, teléfono)* to ring; **sonaron las cinco** the clock struck five (c) **tu nombre/cara me suena** your name/face rings a bell **2 sonarse** *vpr* **sonarse (la nariz)** to blow one's nose

sonido *nm* sound

sonoro, -a *adj* (a) *Cin* sound; **banda sonora** soundtrack (b) *(resonante)* loud, resounding (c) *Ling* voiced

sonreír [56] *vi*, **sonreírse** *vpr* to smile; **me sonrió** he smiled at me

sonriente *adj* smiling

sonrisa *nf* smile

sonrojarse *vpr* to blush

sonso, -a *adj Am* foolish, silly

soñar [2] *vt & vi* (a) to dream; **s. con** to dream of o about; *Fig* **¡ni soñarlo!** not on your life! (b) *(fantasear)* to daydream, to dream

sopa *nf* soup; **s. juliana** spring vegetable soup; *Fig* **quedar hecho una s.** to get soaked to the skin

sope *nm Méx* = fried corn tortilla, with beans and cheese or other toppings

sopera *nf* soup tureen

soplar 1 *vi (viento)* to blow **2** *vt* (a) *(polvo etc)* to blow away; *(para enfriar)* to blow on (b) *(para apagar)* to blow out (c) *(para inflar)* to blow up (d) *(en examen etc)* **me sopló las respuestas** he whispered the answers to me

soplete *nm* blowlamp, blowtorch

soplido *nm* blow, puff

soplo *nm* (a) *(acción)* blow, puff; *(de viento)* gust (b) *Med* murmur

soportal *nm* porch; **soportales** arcade

soportar *vt* (a) *(peso)* to support, to bear (b) *Fig (calor, ruido)* to bear, to endure; *(situación)* to put up with, to bear; **no te soporto** I can't stand you

soporte *nm* support; **s. publicitario** advertising medium

soprano *nmf* soprano

sorber *vt* (a) *(beber)* to sip (b) *(absorber)* to soak up, to absorb

sorbete *nm* sorbet, sherbet

sordo, -a 1 *adj* (a) *(persona)* deaf; **s. como una tapia** stone-deaf (b) *(golpe, ruido, dolor)* dull **2** *nm,f* deaf person; **los sordos** the deaf *pl*; *Fam Fig* **hacerse el s.** to turn a deaf ear

sordomudo, -a 1 *adj* deaf and dumb, deaf-mute **2** *nm,f* deaf and dumb person, deaf-mute

soroche *nm* (a) *Andes, Arg (mal de altura)* altitude sickness (b) *Chile (rubor)* blush, flush

sorprendente *adj* surprising

sorprender *vt* (a) *(extrañar)* to surprise (b) *(coger desprevenido)* to catch unawares, to take by surprise

sorpresa *nf* surprise; **coger de** o **por**

s. to take by surprise

sortear *vt* (**a**) to draw *o* cast lots for; *(rifar)* to raffle (off) (**b**) *(evitar)* to avoid, to get round

sorteo *nm* draw; *(rifa)* raffle

sortija *nf* ring

SOS *nm* SOS

sosiego *nm (calma)* calmness; *(paz)* peace, tranquillity

soso, -a *adj* lacking in salt; *Fig (persona)* insipid, dull

sospechar 1 *vi (desconfiar)* to suspect; **s. de algn** to suspect sb **2** *vt (pensar)* to suspect

sospechoso, -a 1 *adj* suspicious; **s. de** suspected of **2** *nm,f* suspect

sostén *nm* (**a**) *(apoyo)* support (**b**) *(sustento)* sustenance (**c**) *(prenda)* bra, brassière

sostener [24] **1** *vt* (**a**) *(sujetar)* to support, to hold up (**b**) *(con la mano)* to hold (**c**) *Fig (teoría etc)* to defend, to uphold; **s. que ...** to maintain that ... (**d**) *(conversación)* to hold, to sustain (**e**) *(familia)* to support **2 sostenerse** *vpr* (**a**) *(mantenerse)* to support oneself (**b**) *(permanecer)* to stay, to remain

sota *nf Naipes* jack, knave

sotana *nf* cassock, soutane

sótano *nm* basement, cellar

soy *indic pres de* **ser**

squash [es'kwas] *nm inv Dep* squash

Sr. *(abr* **Señor**) Mr

Sra. *(abr* **Señora**) Mrs

Sres. *(abr* **Señores**) Messrs

Srta. *(abr* **Señorita**) Miss

SS.MM. *(abr* **Sus Majestades**) their Royal Highnesses

Sta., sta. *(abr* **Santa**) St

Sto., sto. *(abr* **Santo**) St

stock [es'tok] *nm (pl* **stocks**) *Com* stock

stop [es'top] *nm (pl* **stops**) (**a**) *(señal de tráfico)* stop sign (**b**) *(en telegrama)* stop

su *(pl* **sus**) *adj pos (de él)* his; *(de ella)* her; *(de usted, ustedes)* your; *(de animales o cosas)* its; *(impersonal)* one's; *(de ellos)* their; **su coche** his/her/your/their car; **su pata** its leg; **sus**

libros his/her/your/their books; **sus patas** its legs

suave *adj* (**a**) smooth; *(luz, voz etc)* soft (**b**) *Met (templado)* mild

suavidad *nf* (**a**) smoothness; *(dulzura)* softness (**b**) *Met* mildness

suavizante *nm (para el pelo)* (hair) conditioner; *(para la ropa)* fabric softener

subasta *nf* auction

subcampeón *nm Dep* runner-up

subconsciente *adj & nm* subconscious

subdesarrollado, -a *adj* underdeveloped

subdesarrollo *nm* underdevelopment

subdirector, -a *nm,f* assistant director/manager

subdirectorio *nm Informát* subdirectory

súbdito, -a *nm,f* subject, citizen; **s. francés** French citizen

subida *nf* (**a**) *(de temperatura)* rise; *(de precios, salarios)* rise, increase (**b**) *(ascenso)* ascent, climb (**c**) *(pendiente)* slope, hill (**d**) *Fam (drogas)* high

subir 1 *vt* (**a**) to go up (**b**) *(llevar arriba)* to take up, to bring up (**c**) *(cabeza, mano)* to lift, to raise (**d**) *(precio, salario)* to raise, to put up (**e**) *(volumen)* to turn up; *(voz)* to raise **2** *vi* (**a**) *(ir arriba)* to go up, to come up (**b**) **s. a** *(un coche)* to get into; *(un autobús)* to get on; *(un barco, avión, tren)* to board, to get on (**c**) *(aumentar)* to rise, to go up **3 subirse** *vpr* (**a**) to climb up; *Fig* **el vino se le subió a la cabeza** the wine went to his head (**b**) **subirse a** *(un coche)* to get into; *(un autobús, avión, tren)* to get on, to board; *(caballo, bici)* to get on (**c**) *(cremallera)* to do up; *(mangas)* to roll up

súbito, -a *adj* sudden

subjetivo, -a *adj* subjective

subjuntivo, -a *adj & nm* subjunctive

sublevar 1 *vt Fig (indignar)* to infuriate, to enrage **2 sublevarse** *vpr* to rebel, to revolt

sublime *adj* sublime

submarinismo *nm* skin-diving

submarinista *nmf* scuba diver

submarino, -a 1 *adj* submarine, underwater **2** *nm* submarine

subrayar *vt* to underline; *Fig (recalcar)* to emphasize, to stress

subsidio *nm* allowance, benefit; **s. de desempleo** unemployment benefit

subsistencia *nf* subsistence

subsuelo *nm* subsoil

subte *nm RP* metro, *Br* underground, *US* subway

subterráneo, -a 1 *adj* underground **2** *nm (túnel)* tunnel, underground passage

subtítulo *nm* subtitle

suburbio *nm (barrio pobre)* slums; *(barrio periférico)* suburb

subvención *nf* subsidy

sucedáneo, -a *adj & nm* substitute

suceder 1 *vi* (a) *(ocurrir) (uso impers)* to happen, to occur; **¿qué sucede?** what's going on?, what's the matter? (b) *(seguir)* to follow, to succeed **2 sucederse** *vpr* to follow one another, to come one after the other

sucesión *nf* (a) *(serie)* series *sing,* succession (b) *(al trono)* succession (c) *(descendencia)* issue, heirs

sucesivo, -a *adj* following, successive; **en lo s.** from now on

suceso *nm (hecho)* event, occurrence; *(incidente)* incident; *Prensa* **sección de sucesos** accident and crime reports

sucesor, -a *nm,f* successor

suciedad *nf* (a) dirt (b) *(calidad)* dirtiness

sucio, -a 1 *adj* dirty; **en s.** in rough; *Fig* **juego s.** foul play; *Fig* **negocio s.** shady business **2** *adv* **jugar s.** to play dirty

suculento, -a *adj* succulent, juicy

sucumbir *vi* to succumb, to yield

sucursal *nf Com, Fin* branch, branch office

sudadera *nf* sweatshirt

Sudáfrica *n* South Africa

Sudamérica *n* South America

sudamericano, -a *adj & nm,f* South American

sudar *vt & vi* to sweat; *Fam Fig* **s. la gota gorda** to sweat blood

sudeste *nm* southeast

sudoeste *nm* southwest

sudor *nm* sweat; *Fig* **con el s. de mi frente** by the sweat of my brow

Suecia *n* Sweden

sueco, -a 1 *adj* Swedish **2** *nm,f (persona)* Swede **3** *nm (idioma)* Swedish

suegro *nm* father-in-law; **mis suegros** my in-laws

suela *nf (de zapato)* sole

sueldo *nm* salary, wages

suelo *nm* (a) *(superficie)* ground; *(de interior)* floor; *Fig* **estar por los suelos** *(precios)* to be rock-bottom (b) *(territorio)* soil, land (c) *(campo, terreno)* land; **s. cultivable** arable land (d) *(de carretera)* surface

suelto, -a 1 *adj* (a) loose; *(desatado)* undone (b) *Fig* **dinero s.** loose change; **hojas sueltas** loose sheets (of paper); **se venden sueltos** they are sold singly *o* separately *o* loose (c) *(en libertad)* free; *(huido)* at large (d) *(vestido, camisa)* loose, loose-fitting **2** *nm (dinero)* (loose) change

sueño *nm* (a) sleep; *(ganas de dormir)* sleepiness; **tener s.** to feel *o* be sleepy (b) *(cosa soñada)* dream

suero *nm Med* serum; *(de la leche)* whey

suerte *nf* (a) *(fortuna)* luck; **por s.** fortunately; **probar s.** to try one's luck; **tener s.** to be lucky; **¡que tengas s.!** good luck! (b) **echar algo** *Esp* **a suertes** *o Am* **a la s.** to draw lots for sth (c) *(destino)* fate, destiny (d) *Fml (género)* kind, sort, type

suéter *nm* sweater

suficiente 1 *adj (bastante)* sufficient, enough **2** *nm Educ* pass

sufragar [42] **1** *vt (gastos)* to pay, defray **2** *vi Am* to vote

sufragio *nm Pol* suffrage; *(voto)* vote

sufrido, -a *adj (persona)* long-suffering

sufrimiento *nm* suffering

sufrir 1 *vi* to suffer; **s. del corazón** to have a heart condition **2** *vt* (**a**) *(accidente)* to have; *(operación)* to undergo; *(dificultades, cambios)* to experience; **s. dolores de cabeza** to suffer from headaches (**b**) *(aguantar)* to bear, to put up with

sugerencia *nf* suggestion

sugerir [5] *vt* to suggest

suiche *nm Col, Ven* switch

suicidio *nm* suicide

suite *nf* suite

Suiza *n* Switzerland

suizo, -a 1 *adj & nm,f* Swiss **2** *nm Esp* *(bollo)* = type of sugared bun

sujetador *nm Esp* bra, brassière

sujetar 1 *vt* (**a**) *(agarrar)* to hold (**b**) *(fijar)* to hold down, to hold in place (**c**) *Fig (someter)* to restrain **2 sujetarse** *vpr (agarrarse)* to hold on

sujeto, -a 1 *nm* subject; *(individuo)* fellow, individual **2** *adj (atado)* fastened, secure; **s. a** *(sometido)* subject to, liable to

suma *nf* (**a**) *(cantidad)* sum, amount (**b**) *Mat* sum, addition; **s. total** sum total (**c**) **en s.** in short

sumar 1 *vt Mat* to add, to add up **2 sumarse** *vpr* **sumarse a** *(huelga)* to join; *(propuesta)* to support

sumario, -a 1 *adj* summary, brief; *Jur* **juicio s.** summary proceedings **2** *nm Jur* summary

sumergible *adj & nm* submersible

sumergir [57] **1** *vt* to submerge, to submerse; *(hundir)* to sink, to plunge **2 sumergirse** *vpr* to submerge, to go underwater; *(hundirse)* to sink

suministrar *vt* to supply, to provide; **s. algo a algn** to supply sb with sth

suministro *nm* supply

sumiso, -a *adj* submissive, obedient

súper *Fam* **1** *adj* super, great **2** *nm* (**a**) *(supermercado)* supermarket (**b**) *(gasolina) Br* four-star (petrol), *US* regular

superación *nf* overcoming; **afán de s.** drive to improve

superar 1 *vt* (**a**) *(obstáculo etc)* to

overcome, to surmount; *(prueba)* to pass (**b**) *(aventajar)* to surpass, to excel **2 superarse** *vpr* to improve o better oneself

superficial *adj* superficial

superficie *nf* surface; *(área)* area; *Com* **grandes superficies** hypermarkets

superfluo, -a *adj* superfluous

superior 1 *adj* (**a**) *(posición)* top, upper (**b**) *(cantidad)* greater, higher, larger (**a** than) (**c**) *(calidad)* superior; **calidad s.** top quality (**d**) *Educ* higher **2** *nm (jefe)* superior

supermercado *nm* supermarket

superponer [19] *vt* to superimpose

superpuesto, -a 1 *pp de ver* **superponer 2** *adj* superimposed

superstición *nf* superstition

supersticioso, -a *adj* superstitious

superviviente 1 *adj* surviving **2** *nmf* survivor

suplemento *nm* supplement; **sin s.** without extra charge

suplente *adj & nmf (sustituto)* substitute, stand-in; *Dep* substitute

supletorio, -a *adj* supplementary, additional; **cama supletoria** extra bed; **teléfono s.** extension

súplica *nf* entreaty, plea

suplir *vt* (**a**) *(reemplazar)* to replace, to substitute (**b**) *(compensar)* to make up for

suponer [19] *(pp* **supuesto**) *vt* (**a**) *(significar)* to mean (**b**) *(implicar)* to entail (**c**) *(representar)* to account for (**d**) *(pensar)* to suppose; **supongo que sí** I suppose so; **supongamos que ...** let's assume that ... (**e**) *(adivinar)* to guess; **(me) lo suponía** I guessed as much

suposición *nf* supposition

supositorio *nm* suppository

suprimir *vt* (**a**) *(ley, impuesto)* to abolish; *(restricción)* to lift; *(palabra)* to delete, to take/leave out; *(rebelión)* to suppress (**b**) *(omitir)* to omit

supuesto, -a 1 *adj* (**a**) *(asumido)* supposed, assumed; **¡por s.!** of course!; **dar algo por s.** to take sth for granted (**b**) *(presunto)* alleged **2** *nm* assumption; **en el s. de que** on the assumption that

sur *nm* south

surco *nm Agr* furrow; *(en un disco)* groove

sureño, -a 1 *adj* southern **2** *nm,f* southerner

surf, surfing *nm* surfing

surfista *nmf* surfer

surgir [57] *vi (aparecer)* to arise, to emerge, to appear; *(problema, dificultad)* to crop up

surtido, -a 1 *adj* (**a**) *(variado)* assorted (**b**) **bien s.** well-stocked **2** *nm* selection, assortment

surtidor *nm* spout; **s. de gasolina** *Br* petrol pump, *US* gas pump

susceptible *adj* susceptible; *(quisquilloso)* oversensitive, touchy

suscribir *(pp* **suscrito)** **1** *vt* (**a**) to subscribe to, to endorse (**b**) *Fml (firmar)* to sign **2 suscribirse** *vpr* to subscribe (**a** to)

suscripción *nf* subscription

suspender 1 *vt* (**a**) *(ley)* to suspend; *(reunión)* to adjourn (**b**) *Esp (examen)* to fail; **me han suspendido** I've failed (the exam) (**c**) *(colgar)* to hang, to suspend **2** *vi (alumno)* to fail

suspense *nm* suspense; **novela/**

película de s. thriller

suspenso *nm* (**a**) *(nota)* **sacar un s.** to fail (**b**) **en s.** *(asunto, trabajo)* pending; **estar en s.** to be pending

suspirar *vi* to sigh

suspiro *nm* sigh

sustancia *nf* substance

sustancial *adj* (**a**) substantial (**b**) *(fundamental)* essential, fundamental

sustantivo, -a 1 *adj* substantive **2** *nm Ling* noun

sustituir [37] *vt* to substitute, to replace

susto *nm* fright, scare; **llevarse** *o* **darse un s.** to get a fright

sustracción *nf* (**a**) *(robo)* theft (**b**) *Mat* subtraction

sustraer [25] *vt* (**a**) *Mat* to subtract (**b**) *(robar)* to steal, to remove

susurrar *vt* to whisper

suyo, -a *adj & pron pos (de él)* his; *(de ella)* hers; *(de usted, ustedes)* yours; *(de animal o cosa)* its; *(de ellos, ellas)* theirs; **los zapatos no son suyos** the shoes aren't hers; **varios amigos suyos** several friends of his/hers/yours/ theirs; *Fam* **es muy s.** he's very aloof; *Fam* **hacer de las suyas** to be up to one's tricks; *Fam* **ir (cada uno) a lo s.** to mind one's own business; *Fam* **salirse con la suya** to get one's (own) way

Tt

t (*abr* **tonelada(s)**) t

tabaco *nm* (**a**) *(planta, hoja)* tobacco; **t. rubio** Virginia tobacco (**b**) *(cigarrillos)* cigarettes

tábano *nm* horsefly

tabasco® *nm* Tabasco® *(sauce)*

taberna *nf* pub, bar; *(antiguamente)* tavern

tabique *nm* (**a**) *(pared)* partition (wall) (**b**) *Anat* **t. nasal** nasal wall

tabla *nf* (**a**) *(board;* *Dep* **t. de surf** surfboard; *Dep* **t. de windsurf** sailboard (**b**) *(de vestido)* pleat (**c**) *Mat* table (**d**) **tablas** *(en ajedrez)* stalemate, draw; **quedar en tablas** *(juego)* to end in a draw (**e**) *Taurom* **tablas** fence (**f**) *Teatro* **las tablas** the stage; *Fig* **tener (muchas) tablas** to be an old hand

tablao *nm* *Fam* = flamenco bar or show

tablero *nm* (**a**) *(tablón)* panel, board; **t. de mandos** *(de coche)* dash(board) (**b**) *(en juegos)* board; **t. de ajedrez** chessboard

tableta *nf* *(de chocolate)* bar

tablón *nm* plank; *(en construcción)* beam; **t. de anuncios** *Br* noticeboard, *US* bulletin board

tabú *adj & nm* (*pl* **tabúes**) taboo

taburete *nm* stool

tacaño, -a **1** *adj* mean, stingy **2** *nm,f* miser

tachar *vt* (**a**) to cross out (**b**) *Fig* **t. de** to accuse of

tachero *nm* *RP Fam (de taxi)* taxi driver

tacho *nm* *Andes, RP (metálico, de hojalata)* tin; *(de plástico)* container; *(papelera)* *Br* waste paper bin *o* basket, *US* waste basket

tácito, -a *adj* tacit

taco *nm* (**a**) plug; *(de billetes)* wad; *(de bota de fútbol)* stud; *(en billar)* cue (**b**) *(cubo) (de jamón, queso)* cube, piece (**c**) *Culin (tortilla de maíz)* taco, = rolled-up tortilla pancake (**d**) *Esp Fam (palabrota)* swearword (**e**) *Esp Fam (lío)* mess, muddle; **armarse** *o* **hacerse un t.** to get all mixed up (**f**) *Esp Fam* **tacos** *(años)* years

tacón *nm* heel; **zapatos de t.** high-heeled shoes

tacto *nm* (**a**) *(sentido)* touch (**b**) *Fig (delicadeza)* tact; **tener t.** to be tactful

taekwondo *nm* tae kwon do

Taiwán [tai'wan] *n* Taiwan

tajada *nf* (**a**) slice; *Fig* **sacar** *o* **llevarse t.** to take one's share (**b**) *Fam (borrachera)* drunkenness

tajo *nm* (**a**) *(corte)* deep cut (**b**) *Esp (trabajo)* workplace, work

tal 1 *adj* (**a**) *(semejante)* such; *(más sustantivo singular contable)* such a; **en tales condiciones** in such conditions; **nunca dije t. cosa** I never said such a thing (**b**) *(indeterminado)* such and such; **t. día y a t. hora** such and such a day and at such and such a time (**c**) *(persona)* **una t. Amelia** someone called Amelia (**d**) *(locuciones)* **t. vez** perhaps, maybe; **como si t. cosa** as if nothing had happened

2 *adv* (**a**) *(así)* just; **t. cual** just as it is; **t. (y) como** just as (**b**) **¿qué t.?** how are things?; **¿qué t. este vino?** how do you find this wine?

3 *conj* as; **con t. (de) que** (+ *subjuntivo*) so long as, provided

4 *pron (cosa)* something; *(persona)* someone, somebody; **t. para cual** two of a kind; **y t. y cual** and so on

taladradora *nf* drill

taladrar *vt* to drill; *(pared)* to bore

through; *(papeles)* to punch

taladro *nm* (**a**) *(herramienta)* drill (**b**) *(agujero)* hole

talco *nm* talc; **polvos de t.** talcum powder

talento *nm* talent

Talgo *nm* = fast passenger train

talla *nf* (**a**) *(de prenda)* size; **¿qué t. usas?** what size are you? (**b**) *(estatura)* height; *Fig* stature; *Fig* **dar la t.** to make the grade (**c**) *(escultura)* carving, sculpture (**d**) *(tallado)* cutting, carving

tallarines *nmpl* tagliatelle

taller *nm* (**a**) *(obrador)* workshop; *Aut* **t. de reparaciones** garage (**b**) *Ind* factory, mill

tallo *nm* stem, stalk

talón *nm* (**a**) *(de pie)* heel (**b**) *(cheque)* cheque

talonario *nm* *(de cheques)* cheque book; *(de billetes)* book of tickets

tamal *nm* *(comida)* tamale, = steamed maize dumpling with savoury or sweet filling, wrapped in maize husks or a banana leaf

tamaño, -a 1 *adj* such a big, so big a **2** *nm* size; **de gran t.** large; **del t. de** as large as, as big as

tambero *nm* (**a**) *RP (granjero)* dairy farmer (**b**) *(dueño)* *(de una tienda)* storekeeper; *(de un tenderete)* stall holder

también *adv* *(igualmente)* too, also, as well; **tú t. puedes venir** you can come too; **¿lo harás? yo t.** are you going to do it? so am I

tambo *nm* (**a**) *Andes (posada)* wayside inn (**b**) *Andes (tienda)* shop; *(tenderete)* stall (**c**) *RP (granja)* dairy farm (**d**) *Méx (recipiente)* drum

tambor *nm* (**a**) *(Mús, de lavadora, de freno)* drum (**b**) *Anat* eardrum

tampoco *adv* (**a**) *(en afirmativas)* nor, neither; **Juan no vendrá y María t.** Juan won't come and neither will Maria; **no lo sé – yo t.** I don't know – neither do I (**b**) *(en negativas)* either, not … either; **la Bolsa no sube, pero t. baja** the stock market isn't going up, but it's not going down either

tampón *nm* tampon

tan *adv* (**a**) such; *(más sustantivo singular contable)* such a; **es t. listo** he's such a clever fellow; **no me gusta t. dulce** I don't like it so sweet; **¡qué gente t. agradable!** such nice people!; **¡qué vestido t. bonito!** what a beautiful dress!

(**b**) *(comparativo)* **t. … como** as … as; **t. alto como tú** as tall as you (are)

(**c**) *(consecutivo)* so … (that); **iba t. deprisa que no lo vi** he was going so fast that I couldn't see him

(**d**) **t. siquiera** at least; **t. sólo** only

tanda *nf* *(conjunto)* batch, lot; *(serie)* series *sing*; **por tandas** in groups

tándem *nm* tandem

tanga *nm* tanga

tango *nm* tango

tanque *nm* tank

tanto, -a 1 *nm* (**a**) *(punto)* point (**b**) *(cantidad imprecisa)* so much, a certain amount; **t. por ciento** percentage (**c**) **un t.** a bit; **la casa es un t. pequeña** the house is rather *o* somewhat small (**d**) **estar al t.** *(informado)* to be informed; *(pendiente)* to be on the lookout

2 *adj* (**a**) *(+ singular)* so much; *(+ plural)* so many; **no le des t. dinero** don't give him so much money; **¡ha pasado t. tiempo!** it's been so long!; **no comas tantas manzanas** don't eat so many apples (**b**) **cincuenta y tantas personas** fifty-odd people; **en el año sesenta y tantos** in nineteen sixty-something (**c**) **t. como** as much as; **tantos como** as many as

3 *pron* (**a**) *(+ singular)* so much; **otro t.** as much again, the same again; **no es** *o* **hay para t.** it's not that bad (**b**) *(+ plural)* so many; **otros tantos** as many again; **uno de tantos** run-of-the-mill; *Fam* **a las tantas** very late, at an unearthly hour

4 *adv* (**a**) *(cantidad)* so much; **t. más cuanto que** all the more so because (**b**) *(tiempo)* so long (**c**) *(frecuencia)* so often (**d**) **t. … como** both … and; **t. tú como yo** both you and I; **t. si vienes como si no** whether you come or not

(e) *(locuciones)* **por lo t.** therefore; **¡y t.!** oh yes!, and how!

tapa *nf* **(a)** *(cubierta)* lid; *Andes, RP (de botella)* top; *(de libro)* cover; *(de zapato)* heelplate; *Aut (de cilindro)* head **(b)** *(aperitivo)* appetizer, snack

tapabarros *nm inv* **(a)** *(de hombre primitivo)* loincloth **(b)** *(tanga)* tanga briefs

tapadera *nf (tapa)* cover, lid; *Fig* cover, front

tapado *CSur (abrigo)* overcoat

tapar 1 *vt* **(a)** to cover; *(botella etc)* to put the lid/top on; *(con ropas o mantas)* to wrap up **(b)** *(ocultar)* to hide; *(vista)* to block **(c)** *(encubrir)* to cover up **2 taparse** *vpr (cubrirse)* to cover one-self; *(abrigarse)* to wrap up

tapete *nm* (table) cover; *Fig* **poner algo sobre el t.** to table sth

tapia *nf* garden wall

tapicería *nf* **(a)** tapestry; *(de muebles, coche)* upholstery **(b)** *(tienda)* uphol-sterer's shop/workshop

tapiz *nm* tapestry

tapizar [40] *vt* to upholster

tapón *nm* **(a)** *(de lavabo etc)* stopper, plug; *(de botella)* cap, cork; **t. de rosca** screw-on cap **(b)** *(de oídos)* earplug **(c)** *(en baloncesto)* block **(d)** *Aut* traffic jam **(e)** *Am (plomo)* fuse

taquería *nf Méx (quiosco)* taco stall; *(restaurante)* taco restaurant

taquigrafía *nf* shorthand

taquilla *nf* **(a)** ticket office, booking office; *Cin, Teatro* box office; **un éxito de t.** a box-office success **(b)** *(recau-dación)* takings **(c)** *(armario)* locker

taquillero, -a 1 *adj* popular; **película taquillera** box-office hit **2** *nm,f* book-ing o ticket clerk

tara *nf* **(a)** *(peso)* tare **(b)** *(defecto)* defect, fault

tardar 1 *vt (llevar tiempo)* to take; **¿cuánto va a t.?** how long will it take?; **tardé dos horas en venir** it took me two hours to get here **2** *vi (demorar)* to take long; **si tarda mucho, me voy** if it takes much longer, I'm going; **no tardes** don't be

long; **a más t.** at the latest

3 tardarse *vpr* **¿cuánto se tarda en llegar?** how long does it take to get there?

tarde 1 *nf* **(a)** *(hasta las cinco)* afternoon **(b)** *(después de las cinco)* evening **(c)** **la t. noche** late evening **2** *adv* **(a)** late; **siento llegar t.** sorry I'm late **(b)** *(locuciones)* **de t. en t.** very rarely, not very often; **(más) t. o (más) temprano** sooner or later

tarea *nf* job, task; **tareas** *(de ama de casa)* housework; *(de estudiante)* home-work

tarifa *nf* **(a)** *(precio)* tariff, rate; *(en transportes)* fare **(b)** *(lista de precios)* price list

tarima *nf* platform, dais

tarjeta *nf* card; **t. postal** postcard; **t. de crédito** credit card; **t. de visita** visiting card, *US* calling card; *Informát* **t. perforada** punch o punched card

tarro *nm* **(a)** *(vasija)* jar, pot **(b)** *Esp Fam (cabeza)* nut, *Br* bonce

tarta *nf* tart, pie

tartamudo, -a 1 *adj* stuttering, stammering **2** *nm,f* stutterer, stam-merer

tasa *nf* **(a)** *(precio)* fee; **tasas acadé-micas** course fees **(b)** *(impuesto)* tax; **tasas de aeropuerto** airport tax **(c)** *(índice)* rate; **t. de natalidad/ mortalidad** birth/death rate **(d)** *(va-loración)* valuation, appraisal

tasca *nf* cheap bar

tata 1 *nf Esp (niñera)* nanny **2** *nm Am Fam (papá)* dad, *US* pop

tatuaje *nm* tattoo

taurino, -a *adj* bullfighting

Tauro *nm* Taurus

tauromaquia *nf* tauromachy, (art of) bullfighting

taxi *nm* taxi

taxímetro *nm* taximeter, clock

taxista *nmf* taxi driver

taza *nf* **(a)** *(recipiente)* cup; **una t. de café** *(recipiente)* coffee cup; *(contenido)* a cup of coffee **(b)** *(de retrete)* bowl

tazón *nm* bowl

te *pron pers* (**a**) *(complemento directo)* you; *(complemento indirecto)* (to/for) you; **no quiero verte** I don't want to see you; **te compraré uno** I'll buy one for you, I'll buy you one; **te lo dije** I told you so (**b**) *(reflexivo)* yourself; **lávate** wash yourself; *(sin traducción)* **bébetelo todo** drink it up; **no te vayas** don't go

té *nm* tea; **té con limón** lemon tea

teatral *adj* (**a**) **grupo t.** theatre company; **obra t.** play (**b**) *Fig (teatrero)* theatrical

teatro *nm* (**a**) theatre; **obra de t.** play; **autor de t.** playwright (**b**) *Lit* drama

tebeo *nm Esp* (children's) comic

techo *nm (de habitación)* ceiling; *(tejado)* roof; *Aut* **t. corredizo** sun roof

tecla *nf* key; *Fig* **dar en la t.** to get it right

teclado *nm* keyboard; *Informát* **t. expandido** expanded keyboard

teclear 1 *vt* to key in **2** *vi* to drum with one's fingers

técnica *nf* (**a**) *(tecnología)* technology (**b**) *(método)* technique (**c**) *(habilidad)* skill

técnico, -a 1 *adj* technical **2** *nm,f* technician, technical expert

tecnología *nf* technology

tecnológico, -a *adj* technological

tecolote *nm CAm, Méx (búho)* owl

teja *nf Constr* tile; *Fam Fig* **a toca t.** on the nail

tejado *nm* roof

tejanos *nmpl* jeans

tejer *vt (en el telar)* to weave; *(hacer punto)* to knit; *(telaraña)* to spin; *Fig (plan)* to plot, to scheme

tejido *nm* (**a**) fabric; **t. de punto** knitted fabric (**b**) *Anat* tissue

tejo *nm Esp Fam* **tirar los tejos a algn** to make a play for sb

tel. *(abr* **teléfono***)* tel.

tela *nf* (**a**) *Tex* material, fabric, cloth; *(de la leche)* skin; **t. de araña** cobweb; **t. metálica** gauze (**b**) *Fam (dinero)* dough (**c**) *Arte* canvas (**d**) *Fig* **poner en t. de juicio** to question; *Fig* **tiene mucha t.** it's not an easy thing

telaraña *nf* cobweb, spider's web

tele *nf Fam* TV, *Br* telly

telearrastre *nm* ski lift

telebanca *nf* telephone banking, home banking

telecabina *nf* cable car

telecomunicaciones *nfpl* telecommunications

telediario *nm* television news

teledirigido, -a *adj* remote-controlled

telefax *nm* telefax, fax

teleférico *nm* cable car/railway

telefonazo *nm* **dar un t. (a algn)** to give (sb) a buzz *o Br* ring

telefonear *vt & vi* to phone, *Br* to ring

telefónico, -a *adj* telephone; **llamada telefónica** telephone call

telefonista *nmf* (telephone) operator

teléfono *nm* telephone, phone; **t. inalámbrico** cordless telephone; **t. portátil** portable telephone; **t. móvil** *or Am* **celular** *Br* mobile phone, *US* cellphone; **está hablando por t.** she's on the phone; **te llamó por t.** she phoned you

telégrafo *nm* (**a**) telegraph (**b**) **telégrafos** post office

telegrama *nm* telegram, cable

telenovela *nf* television serial

teleobjetivo *nm* telephoto lens *sing*

telepatía *nf* telepathy

telescopio *nm* telescope

telesilla *nm* chair lift

telespectador, -a *nm,f* TV viewer

telesquí *nm (pl* **telesquíes** *o* **telesquís)** ski lift

teletexto *nm* teletext

teletipo *nm* teleprinter

televidente *nmf* TV viewer

televisar *vt* to televise

televisión *nf* (**a**) *(sistema)* television (**b**) *Fam (aparato)* television set; **t. en color/en blanco y negro** colour/black-and-white television; **t. digital** digital television; **t. por cable** cable television; **ver la t.** to watch television

televisor *nm* television set

télex *nm inv* telex

telón *nm Teatro* curtain; *Hist* **t. de acero** Iron Curtain; **t. de fondo** *Teatro* backdrop; *Fig* background

tema *nm* (**a**) *(asunto)* topic, subject; *(de examen)* subject; **temas de actualidad** current affairs (**b**) *Mús* theme

temática *nf* subject matter

temático, -a *adj* thematic

temblar [1] *vi (de frío)* to shiver; *(de miedo)* to tremble (**de** with); *(voz)* to quiver; *(pulso)* to shake

temblor *nm* tremor, shudder; **t. de tierra** earth tremor

temer 1 *vt* to fear, to be afraid of; **temo que esté muerto** I fear he's dead; **temo que no podrá recibirte** I'm afraid (that) he won't be able to see you
2 *vi* to be afraid
3 temerse *vpr* to fear, to be afraid; **¡me lo temía!** I was afraid this would happen!

temor *nm* (**a**) fear (**b**) *(recelo)* worry, apprehension

temperamento *nm* temperament; **tener t.** to have a strong character

temperatura *nf* temperature

tempestad *nf* storm; *Fig* turmoil, uproar

templado, -a *adj* (**a**) *(agua)* lukewarm; *(clima)* mild, temperate (**b**) *Mús (afinado)* tuned

templo *nm* temple

temporada *nf* (**a**) season; **t. alta** high *o* peak season; **t. baja** low *o* off season (**b**) *(período)* period, time; **por temporadas** on and off

temporal 1 *adj* temporary, provisional **2** *nm* storm

temporario, -a *adj Am* temporary

temprano, -a *adj & adv* early

tenaza *nf,* **tenazas** *nfpl (herramienta)* pliers, pincers; *(para el fuego)* tongs

tendedero *nm* clothes line, drying place

tendencia *nf* tendency

tender [3] **1** *vt* (**a**) *(mantel etc)* to spread out; *(para secar)* to hang out (**b**) *Am (cama)* to make; *(mesa)* to set, to lay (**c**) *(red)* to cast; *(puente)* to build; *(vía, cable)* to lay; *(trampa)* to lay, set (**d**) *(mano)* to stretch *o* hold out (**e**) *(tumbar)* to lay
2 *vi* to tend (**a** to), have a tendency (**a** to)
3 tenderse *vpr* to lie down, stretch out

tenderete *nm (puesto)* market stall

tendero, -a *nm,f* shopkeeper

tendón *nm* tendon, sinew

tenedor *nm* fork

tener [24] **1** *vt* (**a**) to have, have got; **tenemos un examen** we've got *o* have an exam; **va a t. un niño** she's going to have a baby, she's expecting (**b**) *(poseer)* to own, possess (**c**) *(sostener)* to hold; **tenme el bolso un momento** hold my bag a minute; **ten, es para ti** take this *o* here you are, it's for you (**d**) **t. calor/frío** to be hot/cold; **t. cariño a algn** to be fond of sb; **t. miedo** to be frightened (**e**) *(edad)* to be; **tiene dieciocho (años)** he's eighteen (years old) (**f**) *Am (llevar)* **tengo tres años aquí** I've been here for three years (**g**) *(medida)* **la casa tiene cien metros cuadrados** the house is 100 square metres (**h**) *(mantener)* to keep; **me tuvo despierto toda la noche** he kept me up all night (**i**) **t. por** *(considerar)* to consider, think; **me tienen por estúpido** they think I'm a fool; **ten por seguro que lloverá** you can be sure it'll rain (**j**) **t. que** to have (got) to; **tengo que irme** I must leave; **tienes/tendrías que verlo** you must/should see it
2 tenerse *vpr* (**a**) **tenerse en pie** to stand (up) (**b**) **tenerse por** *(considerarse)* to think *o* consider oneself; **se tiene por muy inteligente** he thinks he's very intelligent

tenga *subj pres de* **tener**

tengo *indic pres de* **tener**

teniente *nm* (**a**) *Mil* lieutenant (**b**) **t.**

(de) alcalde deputy mayor

tenis *nm* tennis

tenista *nmf* tennis player

tenor¹ *nm Mús* tenor

tenor² *nm* **a t. de** according to

tensión *nf* (a) tension; **en t.** tense (b) *Elec* tension, voltage (c) *Med* **t. arterial** blood pressure; **t. nerviosa** nervous strain (d) *Téc* stress

tenso, -a *adj* (a) *(cuerda, cable)* tense, taut (b) *(persona)* tense; *(relaciones)* strained

tentación *nf* temptation

tentáculo *nm* tentacle

tentempié *nm Fam* (a) *(comida)* snack, bite (b) *(juguete)* tumbler

tenue *adj* (a) *(luz, sonido)* subdued, faint (b) *(delgado)* thin, light

teñir [6] **1** *vt* (a) *(pelo etc)* to dye (b) *Fig* to tinge with **2 teñirse** *vpr* **teñirse el pelo** to dye one's hair

teología *nf* theology

teoría *nf* theory; **en t.** theoretically

terapeuta *nmf* therapist

tercera *nf Aut* third (gear)

tercerización *nf Am Com* out-sourcing

tercermundista *adj* third-world

tercero, -a 1 *adj* third

> **tercer** is used instead of **tercero** before masculine singular nouns (e.g. **el tercer piso** the third floor)

2 *nm,f (de una serie)* third; *Esp* **a la tercera va la vencida** third time lucky **3** *nm (mediador)* mediator; *Jur* third party

tercio *nm* (a) *(parte)* (one) third (b) *(de cerveza)* = medium-sized bottle of beer (c) *Taurom* stage, part *(of a bullfight)*

terciopelo *nm* velvet

terco, -a *adj* stubborn, obstinate

tereré *nm Arg, Par (mate)* cold maté

tergal® *nm* = type of synthetic fibre containing polyester

termas *nfpl (baños)* spa, hot baths *o* springs

terminal 1 *adj* terminal **2** *nf* (a) *(de*

aeropuerto) terminal; *(de autobús)* terminus (b) *Elec, Informát* terminal

terminar 1 *vt (acabar)* to finish, to complete; *(completamente)* to finish off **2** *vi* (a) *(acabarse)* to finish, to end; **termina en seis** it ends with a six; **no termina de convencerse** he still isn't quite convinced (b) *(ir a parar)* to end up **(en** in); **terminó por comprarlo** he ended up buying it (c) **t. con** *(eliminar)* to put an end to **3 terminarse** *vpr* (a) to finish, to end, to be over (b) *(vino, dinero etc)* to run out

término *nm* (a) *(final)* end, finish (b) *(palabra)* term, word; **en otros términos** in other words; **en términos generales** generally speaking (c) **t. municipal** district (d) **por t. medio** on average (e) *Fig* **en último t.** as a last resort

terminología *nf* terminology

termita *nf* termite

termo *nm* Thermos® (flask), flask

termómetro *nm* thermometer

termostato *nm* thermostat

ternera *nf* calf; *(carne)* veal

ternero *nm* calf

terno *nm* (a) *(trío)* trio (b) *(traje)* three-piece suit

ternura *nf* tenderness

terraja *adj RP Fam (persona)* flashy, tacky; *(decoración, ropa, canción)* tacky, *Br* naff

terrajada *nf RP Fam* **esos zapatos son una t.** those shoes are tacky

terral *nm Am (polvareda)* dust cloud

terraplén *nm* embankment

terrateniente *nmf* landowner

terraza *nf* (a) *(balcón)* balcony (b) *(de café)* terrace, patio (c) *(azotea)* terrace roof

terremoto *nm* earthquake

terreno *nm* (a) *(tierra)* (piece of) land, ground; *Geol* terrain; *(campo)* field; **ganar/perder t.** to gain/lose ground (b) *Dep* field, *Br* pitch (c) *Fig* field, sphere

terrestre *adj* (a) *(de la tierra)*

terrestrial, earthly (**b**) *(por tierra)* by land; **por vía t.** by land

terrible *adj* terrible, awful

territorio *nm* territory

terrón *nm (de azúcar)* lump; *(de tierra)* clod

terror *nm* terror; *Cin* horror

terrorismo *nm* terrorism

terrorista *adj & nmf* terrorist

tertulia *nf* get-together; **t. literaria** literary gathering

tesis *nf inv* thesis; *(opinión)* view, theory

tesoro *nm* (**a**) treasure (**b**) *(erario)* exchequer; **T. Público** Treasury

test [test] *nm (pl* **tests**) test

testamento *nm* (**a**) *Jur* will; **hacer** o **otorgar t.** to make o draw up one's will (**b**) *Rel* Testament

testarudo, -a *adj* stubborn, obstinate

testear *vt CSur* to test

testículo *nm* testicle

testigo 1 *nmf* witness; *Jur* **t. de cargo/descargo** witness for the prosecution/defence; *Jur* **t. ocular/presencial** eyewitness; *Rel* **Testigos de Jehová** Jehovah's Witnesses **2** *nm Dep* baton

testimonio *nm Jur* testimony; *(prueba)* evidence, proof

teta *nf Fam* (**a**) tit, boob; **niño de t.** breast-feeding baby (**b**) *(de vaca)* udder

tetera *nf* teapot

tetero *nm Col, Ven (biberón)* baby's bottle

tetrabrik® *nm (pl* **tetrabriks**) tetrabrik®; **un t. de leche** a carton of milk

textil *adj & nm* textile

texto *nm* text; **libro de t.** textbook

textura *nf Tex* texture; *(en minerales)* structure

ti *pron pers* you; **es para ti** it's for you; **hazlo por ti** do it for your own sake; **piensas demasiado en ti mismo** you think too much about yourself

tianguis *nm inv CAm, Méx* open-air market

tibia *nf* shinbone, tibia

tibio, -a *adj* tepid, lukewarm; *Fam* **ponerse t. de cerveza** to get pissed

tiburón *nm* shark

ticket *nm (pl* **tickets**) *(billete)* ticket; *(recibo)* receipt

tiempo *nm* (**a**) time; **a t.** in time; **a su (debido) t.** in due course; **a un t., al mismo t.** at the same time; **al poco t.** soon afterwards; **antes de t.** (too) early o soon; **con el t.** in the course of time, with time; **¿cuánto t.?** how long?; **¿cuánto t. hace?** how long ago?; **demasiado t.** too long; **estar a t. de** to still have time to; **hacer t.** to kill time; **¿nos da t. de llegar?** have we got (enough) time to get there?; **t. libre** free time

(**b**) *(meteorológico)* weather; **¿qué t. hace?** what's the weather like?; **hace buen/mal t.** the weather is good/bad

(**c**) *(edad)* age; **¿cuánto** o **qué t. tiene tu niño?** how old is your baby/child?

(**d**) *Mús* movement

(**e**) *Dep* half

(**f**) *Ling* tense

tienda *nf* (**a**) shop, store; **ir de tiendas** to go shopping (**b**) **t. (de campaña)** tent

tierno, -a *adj* (**a**) *(blando)* tender, soft (**b**) *(reciente)* fresh

tierra *nf* (**a**) *(planeta)* earth (**b**) *Agr* land, soil (**c**) *(continente)* land; **tocar t.** to land (**d**) *(país)* country; **t. de nadie** no-man's-land (**e**) *(suelo)* ground; *Fig* **echar** o **tirar por t.** to spoil (**f**) *Elec* **(toma de) t.** *Br* earth, *US* ground

tierral *nm Am (polvareda)* dust cloud

tieso, -a *adj (rígido)* stiff, rigid; *(erguido)* upright, erect

tiesto *nm* flowerpot

tigre *nm* (**a**) tiger (**b**) *Am (jaguar)* jaguar

tijeras *nfpl* (pair of) scissors

tila *nf (flor)* lime o linden blossom; *(infusión)* lime o linden blossom tea

tilde *nf* written accent

tilma *nf Méx* woollen blanket

timbal *nm* kettledrum

timbre *nm* (**a**) *(de la puerta)* bell (**b**) *(sello)* stamp, seal; *Fin* fiscal o revenue stamp (**c**) *Mús (sonido)* timbre

tímido, -a *adj* shy, timid; *Fig (mejoría)* light; *(intento)* cautious

timo *nm* swindle, fiddle; **es un t.** it's a rip-off

timón *nm* (**a**) *(de barco) (palanca)* tiller, helm; *(rueda)* wheel, helm; *(pieza articulada)* rudder; **estar al t.** to be at the helm (**b**) *Andes, Cuba (de vehículo)* steering wheel

tímpano *nm Anat* eardrum

tina *nf* (**a**) *(tinaja)* pitcher (**b**) *(gran cuba)* vat (**c**) *CAm, Col, Méx (bañera)* bathtub

tino *nm* (**a**) *(puntería)* (good) aim; **tener buen t.** to be a good shot (**b**) *(tacto)* (common) sense, good judgement

tinta *nf* (**a**) ink; **t. china** Indian ink; **t. simpática** invisible ink (**b**) *Fig* **medias tintas** ambiguities, half-measures

tintero *nm* inkpot, inkwell; *Fig* **se quedó en el t.** it wasn't said

tinto 1 *adj (vino)* red **2** *nm* (**a**) *(vino)* red wine (**b**) *Col, Ven (café)* black coffee

tintorería *nf* dry-cleaner's

tío *nm* (**a**) *(pariente)* uncle; **mis tíos** my uncle and aunt (**b**) *Esp Fam* guy, *Br* bloke

tiovivo *nm* merry-go-round, *US* carousel

tipear *Am* **1** *vt* to type **2** *vi* to type

típico, -a *adj* (**a**) typical; **eso es t. de Antonio** that's just like Antonio (**b**) *(baile, traje)* traditional

tipo *nm* (**a**) *(clase)* type, kind (**b**) *Fam (persona)* guy, *Br* bloke; **t. raro** weirdo (**c**) *Anat (de hombre)* build, physique; *(de mujer)* figure (**d**) *Fin* rate; **t. de cambio/interés** rate of exchange/interest (**e**) **el político t. de la izquierda** the typical left-wing politician

tipografía *nf* typography

tira *nf* (**a**) *(banda, cinta)* strip (**b**) *(de dibujos)* comic strip (**c**) *Fam* **la t. de gente** a lot o loads of people (**d**) *Méx Fam* **la t.** *(la policía)* the law, *US* the heat (**e**) **t. y afloja** tug of war

tirabuzón *nm* ringlet

tirada *nf* (**a**) *(lanzamiento)* throw (**b**) *(impresión)* print run

tirador *nm* (**a**) *(persona)* marksman (**b**) *(pomo)* knob, handle; *(cordón)* bell pull (**c**) *(tirachinas) Br* catapult, *US* slingshot

tiraje *nm Am* print run

tiranía *nf* tyranny

tirano, -a *nm,f* tyrant

tirante 1 *adj (cable etc)* tight, taut; *(situación, relación)* tense **2** *nm* (**a**) *(de vestido etc)* strap; **tirantes** *Br* braces, *US* suspenders (**b**) *Téc* brace, stay

tirar 1 *vt* (**a**) *(echar)* to throw (**b**) *(dejar caer)* to drop (**c**) *(desechar)* to throw away; *Fig (dinero)* to squander (**d**) *(derribar)* to knock down; **t. la puerta (abajo)** to smash the door in (**e**) *(beso)* to blow

2 *vi* (**a**) **t. de** *(cuerda, puerta)* to pull (**b**) *(chimenea, estufa)* to draw (**c**) *(funcionar)* to work, to run (**d**) *ir tirando* to get by (**e**) **t. a** to tend towards; **tira a rojo** it's reddish (**f**) **tira a la izquierda** turn left; **¡venga, tira ya!** come on, get going! (**g**) *(disparar)* to shoot, to fire

3 tirarse *vpr* (**a**) *(lanzarse)* to throw o hurl oneself; **tirarse de cabeza al agua** to dive into the water (**b**) *(tumbarse)* to lie down (**c**) *Fam (tiempo)* to spend; **me tiré una hora esperando** I waited (for) a good hour (**d**) *Vulg* **tirarse a algn** to lay sb

tirita *nf Br* (sticking) plaster, *US* Band-aid®

tiritar *vi* to shiver, to shake

tiro *nm* (**a**) *(lanzamiento)* throw (**b**) *(disparo, ruido)* shot; *Ftb* **t. a gol** shot at goal; **t. al blanco** target shooting; **t. al plato** clay pigeon shooting; **t. con arco** archery (**c**) *(de vestido)* shoulder width (**d**) *(de chimenea)* draught; **animal de t.** draught animal

tirón *nm* pull, tug; *(del bolso)* snatch; *Fam* **de un t.** in one go

tisú *nm* tissue, paper hankie

títere *nm (marioneta)* puppet; **no dejar t. con cabeza** to spare no one

titular¹ 1 *nmf (persona)* holder

2 *nm Prensa* headline
3 *adj* appointed, official

titular² **1** *vt (poner título)* to call **2**
titularse *vpr* (**a**) *(película etc)* to be
called; **¿cómo se titula?** what is it
called? (**b**) *Educ* to graduate (**en** in)

título *nm* (**a**) title (**b**) *Educ* degree;
(diploma) diploma (**c**) *Prensa (titular)*
headline (**d**) **a t. de ejemplo** by way
of example

tiza *nf* chalk; **una t.** a piece of chalk

tlapalería *nf Méx* ironmonger's (shop)

toalla *nf* towel; **tirar la t.** to throw in
the towel

tobillo *nm* ankle

tobogán *nm* slide, chute

tocadiscos *nm inv* record player; **t.
digital** *o* **compacto** CD player

tocador *nm* (**a**) *(mueble)* dressing
table (**b**) *(habitación)* dressing room;
t. de señoras powder room

tocar [44] **1** *vt* (**a**) *(objeto, persona)* to
touch (**b**) *(instrumento, canción)* to
play; *(timbre, campana)* to ring;
(bocina) to blow (**c**) *(tema, asunto)* to
touch on (**d**) *(afectar)* to concern; **por
lo que a mí me toca** as far as I am
concerned

2 *vi* (**a**) **¿a quién le toca?** *(en juegos)*
whose turn is it? (**b**) **me tocó el gordo**
(en rifa) I won the jackpot (**c**) *Fig* **t. a su
fin** to be coming to an end (**d**) *(llamar)*
t. a la puerta to knock on the door

3 **tocarse** *vpr (una cosa con otra)* to
touch each other

tocino *nm* lard; **t. ahumado** smoked
bacon; **t. de cielo** = sweet made with
egg yolk

tocuyo *nm Andes, Arg* coarse cotton
cloth

todavía *adv* (**a**) *(aún)* still; *(en
negativas)* yet; **t. la quiere** he still
loves her; **t. no** not yet; **no mires t.**
don't look yet (**b**) *(para reforzar)* even,
still; **t. más/menos** even more/less

todo, -a **1** *adj* (**a**) all; **t. el pan** all the
bread; **t. el mundo** (absolutely) every-
body; **t. el día** all day, the whole *o* entire
day

(**b**) *(cada)* every; **t. ciudadano de**
más de dieciocho años every citizen
over eighteen years of age

(**c**) *(entero)* complete, thorough; **es
toda una mujer** she is every inch a
woman

(**d**) **todos** all; *(con expresiones de
tiempo)* every; **todos los niños** all the
children; **todos los martes** every
Tuesday

2 *nm (totalidad)* whole

3 *pron* (**a**) *(sin excluir nada)* all,
everything; **ante t.** first of all; **del t.**
completely; **después de t.** after all;
eso es t. that's all, that's it; **estar en t.**
to be really with it; **hay de t.** there are
all sorts; **lo sé t.** I know all about it; **t. lo
contrario** quite the contrary *o* opposite

(**b**) *(cualquiera)* anybody; **t. aquél** *o* **el
que quiera** anybody who wants (to)

(**c**) *(cada uno)* **todos aprobamos** we
all passed; **todos fueron** they all went

4 *adv* completely, totally; **volvió t.
sucio** he was all dirty when he got back

toga *nf* (**a**) gown, robe (**b**) *Hist* toga

toldo *nm (cubierta)* awning

tolerancia *nf* tolerance

tolerante *adj* tolerant

tolerar *vt* to tolerate; *(situación)* to
stand; *(gente)* to put up with

toma *nf* (**a**) *(acción)* taking; *Elec* **t. de
corriente** power point, socket (**b**) *Med*
dose (**c**) *Mil* capture (**d**) *Cin* take, shot
(**e**) **t. de posesión** swearing-in (**f**)
Fam Fig **t. y daca** give and take

tomado, -a *adj* (**a**) *(voz)* hoarse (**b**)
Am Fam (persona) tight, tanked up (**c**)
tenerla tomada con algn to have it in
for sb

tomar **1** *vt* (**a**) *(coger)* to take;
(autobús, tren) to catch; *(decisión)* to
make, take; **toma** here (you are); **t. el
sol** to sunbathe; *Av* **t. tierra** to land;
Fam **tomarla con algn** to have it in for
sb (**b**) *(comer, beber)* to have (**c**) **t. algo
a mal** to take sth badly; **t. en serio/
broma** to take seriously/as a joke (**d**)
(confundir) to take (**por** for) (**e**) *Mil* to
take

2 *vi Am (beber alcohol)* to drink

3 **tomarse** *vpr* (**a**) *(comer)* to eat;
(beber) to drink (**b**) *Fam* **no te lo**

tomes así don't take it like that

tomate nm tomato; **salsa de t.** (de lata) tomato sauce; (de botella) ketchup

tómbola nf tombola

tomillo nm thyme

tomo nm volume; Fam **de t. y lomo** utter, out-and-out

tonada nf (a) Mús tune, song (b) Am (acento) (regional) accent

tonel nm barrel, cask

tonelada nf ton; **t. métrica** tonne

tongo nm fix

tónico, -a 1 nm Med tonic; (cosmético) skin tonic

2 nf **tónica** (a) (tendencia) tendency, trend; **tónica general** overall trend (b) (bebida) tonic (water) (c) Mús tonic 3 adj (a) Ling tonic, stressed (b) Mús, Med tonic

tono nm tone; **a t. con** in tune o harmony with; **subir de t. o el t.** to speak louder; **un t. alto/bajo** a high/ low pitch; Fig **darse t.** to put on airs; Fig **fuera de t.** inappropriate, out of place; **dar el t.** to set the tone

tontería nf (a) stupidity, silliness (b) (dicho, hecho) silly o stupid thing (c) (insignificancia) trifle

tonto, -a 1 adj silly, dumb 2 nm,f fool, idiot; **t. de remate o de capirote** prize idiot

topadora nf RP bulldozer

tope 1 nm (a) (límite) limit, end; Fam **a t.** (al máximo) flat out; Fig **estar hasta los topes** to be full up; **fecha t.** deadline (b) Téc stop, check (c) Ferroc buffer 2 adv Fam incredibly; **t. difícil** really difficult

tópico, -a 1 nm cliché 2 adj Med, Farm for external use

topo nm mole

tórax nm thorax

torbellino nm (a) (de viento) whirl-wind (b) Fig (confusión) whirl, turmoil

torcer [41] 1 vt (a) (metal) to bend; (cuerda, hilo) to twist; Med to sprain; Fig (esquina) to turn (b) (inclinar) to slant

2 vi to turn (left o right)

3 **torcerse** vpr (a) (doblarse) to twist, to bend (b) Med **se me torció el tobillo** I sprained my ankle (c) (plan) to fall through (d) (desviarse) to go off to the side

torcido, -a adj twisted; (ladeado) slanted, lopsided; (corbata) crooked

tordo, -a 1 adj dapple-grey 2 nm Orn thrush

torear 1 vt to fight; Fam **t. a algn** to tease o confuse sb; Fam **t. un asunto** to tackle a matter skilfully 2 vi to fight

torera nf (prenda) bolero (jacket)

torero, -a nm,f bullfighter

tormenta nf storm

tormentoso, -a adj stormy

torneo nm (a) Dep tournament, US tourney (b) Hist tourney, joust

tornillo nm screw

torniquete nm (a) turnstile (b) Med tourniquet

toro nm bull; **¿te gustan los toros?** do you like bullfighting?

torpe adj (a) (sin habilidad) clumsy (b) (tonto) dim, thick (c) (movimiento) slow, awkward

torpedo nm torpedo

torpeza nf (a) (física) clumsiness; (mental) dimness, stupidity (b) (lentitud) slowness, heaviness (c) (error) blunder

torre nf (a) tower (b) Mil, Náut turret (c) (en ajedrez) rook, castle

torrente nm (a) (de agua) torrent (b) Fig **t. de voz** strong o powerful voice

torrija nf French toast

torta nf (a) Culin Esp (de harina) = flat, round plain cake; CSur, Ven (dulce) cake; Andes, CAm, Carib, RP (salada) pie; Méx (sandwich) filled roll (b) Fam (golpe) slap, punch

tortazo nm Fam (a) (bofetada) slap, punch (b) (golpe) whack, thump

tortilla nf (a) (de huevo) omelette; **t. española** Spanish o potato omelette **t. francesa** French o plain omelette (b) (de maíz) tortilla, = thin maize pancake

tórtola nf dove

tortuga nf (de tierra) tortoise, US

turtle; *(de mar)* turtle

torturar *vt* to torture

tos *nf* cough; **t. ferina** whooping cough

toser *vi* to cough

tostada *nf* (slice of) toast

tostador *nm* toaster

tostar [2] *vt (pan)* to toast; *(café)* to roast; *(carne, pescado)* to brown; *Fig (la piel)* to tan

total 1 *adj (completo)* total
2 *nm* (a) *(todo)* whole; **en t.** in all (b) *Mat* total
3 *adv* so, in short; **¿t. para qué?** what's the point anyhow?; *Fam* **t. que ...** so ...; **t., tampoco te hará caso** he won't listen to you anyway

totalidad *nf* whole, totality; **la t. de** all of; **en su t.** as a whole

tóxico, -a 1 *adj* toxic, poisonous **2** *nm* poison

toxicomanía *nf* drug addiction

toxicómano, -a *Med* **1** *adj* addicted to drugs **2** *nm,f* drug addict

trabajador, -a 1 *nm,f* worker, labourer **2** *adj* hard-working

trabajar 1 *vi* to work; **trabaja mucho** he works hard; **t. de camarera** to work as a waitress **2** *vt* (a) to work (on); *(la tierra)* to till (b) *(asignatura etc)* to work on (c) *Fam (convencer)* to (try to) persuade

trabajo *nm* (a) *(ocupación)* work; **t. a destajo** piecework; **t. eventual** casual labour; **trabajos manuales** arts and crafts (b) *(empleo)* employment, job (c) *(tarea)* task, job (d) *Educ (redacción)* report, paper (e) *(esfuerzo)* effort; **cuesta t. creerlo** it's hard to believe

trabalenguas *nm inv* tongue twister

traca *nf* string of firecrackers

tractor *nm* tractor

tradición *nf* tradition

tradicional *adj* traditional

traducción *nf* translation; **t. directa/inversa** translation from/into a foreign language

traducir [10] **1** *vt* to translate (**a** into) **2 traducirse** *vpr Fig* to result (**en** in)

traductor, -a *nm,f* translator

traer [25] **1** *vt* (a) to bring; **trae** give it to me (b) *(llevar puesto)* to wear (c) *(llevar consigo)* to carry (d) *(problemas)* to cause; **traerá como consecuencia ...** it will result in ... **2 traerse** *vpr (llevar consigo)* to bring along; *Fig* **¿qué se trae entre manos?** what is he up to?

traficante *nmf (de drogas etc)* trafficker, pusher

traficar [44] *vi (ilegalmente)* to traffic (**con** in)

tráfico *nm* (a) *Aut* traffic; **t. rodado** road traffic (b) *Com* traffic, trade; **t. de drogas** drug traffic

tragar [42] **1** *vt* (a) *(ingerir)* to swallow (b) *Fam (engullir)* to gobble up, to tuck away (c) *Fig (a una persona)* to stand, to stomach (d) *Fig (creer)* to believe, to swallow **2 tragarse** *vpr* (a) *(ingerir)* to swallow (b) *Fig (creer)* to believe, to swallow

tragedia *nf* tragedy

trágico, -a *adj* tragic

tragicomedia *nf* tragicomedy

trago *nm* (a) *(bebida)* swig; **de un t.** in one go (b) *Fig* **pasar un mal t.** to have a bad time of it

traición *nf* treason, betrayal; **a t.** treacherously; **alta t.** high treason

traje¹ *nm* (a) *(de hombre)* suit; **t. de baño** swimming costume, bathing suit *o Br* costume; **t. de paisano** civilian clothes; **t. de luces** bullfighter's costume (b) *(de mujer)* dress; **t. de chaqueta** two-piece suit; **t. de novia** wedding dress

traje² *pt indef de* **traer**

trama *nf* (a) *Tex* weft, woof (b) *Lit* plot

tramar *vt* to plot, to cook up; **¿qué tramas?** what are you up to?

tramitar *vt* (a) *(gestionar)* to take the necessary (legal) steps to obtain (b) *Fml (despachar)* to convey, to transmit (c) *Com, Jur, Fin* to carry out, to process

tramo *nm (de carretera)* section, stretch; *(de escalera)* flight

tramontana *nf* north wind

tramoya *nf (maquinaria)* stage

machinery; *(trama)* plot, scheme

trampa *nf* (a) *(de caza)* trap, snare (b) *(puerta)* trapdoor (c) *(engaño)* fiddle; **hacer trampa(s)** to cheat (d) *(truco)* trick

trampolín *nm* (a) *(de piscina)* diving board (b) *(de esquí)* ski jump

trancar 1 *vt* *(asegurar)* *(con cerrojo)* to bolt; *(con tranca)* to bar **2 trancarse** *vpr Am (atascarse)* to get stuck; **la llave se trancó en la cerradura** the key got stuck in the lock

trance *nm* (a) *(coyuntura)* (critical) moment; **estar en t. de ...** to be on the point of ... (b) *(éxtasis)* trance

tranquilidad *nf* calmness, tranquillity; **con t.** calmly; **pídemelo con toda t.** don't hesitate to ask me

tranquilo, -a *adj* (a) *(persona, lugar)* calm; *(agua)* still; *(conciencia)* clear; *Fam* **tú t.** don't you worry (b) *(despreocupado)* placid, easy-going

transar *Fam vi* (a) *Am (transigir)* to compromise, to give in (b) *Am (negociar)* to come to an arrangement, to reach a compromise (c) *RP (droga)* to deal

transbordador *nm* (car) ferry; **t. espacial** space shuttle

transbordar 1 *vt* to transfer; *Náut (mercancías)* to tranship **2** *vi Ferroc* to change trains, *US* to transfer

transbordo *nm* (a) *Ferroc* change, *US* transfer; **hacer t.** to change, *US* to transfer (b) *Náut* transhipment

transcurrir *vi* (a) *(tiempo)* to pass, to go by (b) *(acontecer)* to take place

transeúnte *nmf* (a) *(peatón)* passerby (b) *(residente temporal)* temporary resident

transferencia *nf* transference; *Fin* transfer; **t. bancaria** banker's order

transformación *nf* transformation

transformador *nm Elec* transformer

transformar 1 *vt* to transform, to change **2 transformarse** *vpr* to change, to turn (**en** into); *(algo plegable)* to convert

transfusión *nf* transfusion

transición *nf* transition

transigir [57] *vi* to compromise

transistor *nm* transistor

tránsito *nm* (a) *Aut* traffic (b) *(movimiento)* movement, passage; **pasajeros en t.** passengers in transit

translúcido, -a = traslúcido

transmitir *vt* (a) to transmit, to pass on (b) *Rad, TV* to transmit, to broadcast (c) *Jur* to transfer, to hand down

transparente 1 *adj* transparent; *Pol* open **2** *nm* (a) *(visillo)* net curtain (b) *(pantalla)* shade, blind

transplantar = trasplantar

transplante = trasplante

transportar *vt* to transport; *(pasajeros)* to carry; *(mercancías)* to ship

transporte *nm* (a) transport, *US* transportation (b) *Com* freight; **t. de mercancías** freight transport; **t. marítimo** shipment

transversal *adj* transverse, cross

tranvía *nm Br* tram, *US* streetcar

trapecio *nm* trapeze

trapecista *nmf* trapeze artist

trapo *nm* (a) *(viejo, roto)* rag (b) *(bayeta)* cloth; *Fam* **poner a algn como un t.** to tear sb to pieces; **t. de cocina** *Br* tea towel, *US* dish towel; **t. del polvo** dust cloth, *Br* duster

tráquea *nf* trachea, windpipe

tras *prep* (a) *(después de)* after; **uno t. otro** one after the other (b) *(detrás)* behind; **sentados uno t. otro** sitting one behind the other (c) **andar/ir t.** to be after; **la policía iba t. ella** the police were after her

trasero, -a 1 *adj* back, rear; **en la parte trasera** at the back **2** *nm Euf* backside

trasladar 1 *vt* *(cosa)* to move; *(persona)* to move, to transfer **2 trasladarse** *vpr* to go, to move

traslado *nm* *(de casa)* move, removal; *(de personal)* transfer; *Educ* **t. de expediente** transfer of student record

traslúcido, -a *adj* translucent

traspasar *vt* (a) *(atravesar)* to go through; *(río)* to cross (b) *(negocio, local)* to transfer; **se traspasa** *(en* *letrero)* for sale (**c**) *Fig (exceder)* to exceed, to go beyond

traspié *nm* stumble, trip; **dar un t.** to trip

trasplantar *vt* to transplant

trasplante *nm* transplant; **t. de corazón** heart transplant

traste¹ *nm Mús* fret

traste² *nm* (**a**) *Am salvo RP (utensilio de cocina)* cooking utensil; **fregar los trastes** to wash the dishes (**b**) *CSur Fam (trasero)* bottom, *US* tush (**c**) *Fig* **dar al t. (con un plan)** to spoil (a plan); **irse al t.** to fall through

trasto *nm (objeto cualquiera)* thing; *(cosa inservible)* piece of junk

tratado *nm* (**a**) *(pacto)* treaty (**b**) *(estudio)* treatise

tratamiento *nm* (**a**) treatment (**b**) *Téc* processing, treatment (**c**) *Informát* processing; **t. de textos** word processing

tratar 1 *vt* (**a**) *(atender)* to treat; **t. bien/mal** to treat well/badly (**b**) *Med* to treat (**c**) *(asunto)* to discuss (**d**) *Informát, Téc* to process (**e**) **me trata de tú** he addresses me as "tu"

2 *vi* (**a**) **t. de** *(intentar)* to try (**b**) **t. de** *o* **sobre** *o* **acerca** to be about; **¿de qué trata?** what is it about? (**c**) **t. con** *(tener tratos)* to deal with; *(negociar)* to negotiate with; *(relacionarse)* to move among

3 tratarse *vpr* (**a**) *(relacionarse)* to be on speaking terms (**b**) **se trata de** *(es cuestión de)* it's a question of; **se trata de un caso excepcional** it's an exceptional case

tratativas *nfpl CSur* negotiation

trato *nm* (**a**) *(de personas)* manner; *(contacto)* contact; **malos tratos** ill-treatment (**b**) *(acuerdo)* agreement; **¡t. hecho!** it's a deal! (**c**) *Com* deal

trauma *nm* trauma

través 1 *prep* (**a**) **a t. de** *(superficie)* across, over; *(agujero etc)* through; **a t. del río** across the river; **a t. del agujero** through the hole (**b**) *Fig* **a t. de** through; **a t. del periódico** through the newspaper **2** *adv* **de t.**

(transversalmente) crosswise; *(de lado)* sideways

travesaño *nm Ftb* crossbar

travesía *nf (viaje)* crossing

travestí *nmf* (*pl* **travestíes** *o* **travestís**), **travesti** transvestite

travieso, -a *adj* mischievous

trayecto *nm* (**a**) *(distancia)* distance; *(recorrido)* route; *(trecho)* stretch (**b**) *(viaje)* journey

trayectoria *nf* (**a**) *(de proyectil, geométrica)* trajectory (**b**) *Fig (orientación)* line, course

trazado *nm* (**a**) *(plano)* layout, plan (**b**) *(de carretera, ferrocarril)* route

trazar [40] *vt (línea)* to draw; *(plano)* to design; *Fig (plan)* to sketch out

trazo *nm* (**a**) *(línea)* line (**b**) *(de letra)* stroke

trébol *nm* (**a**) *(planta)* trefoil (**b**) *Naipes* club

trece 1 *adj inv* thirteen **2** *nm inv* thirteen; *Fig* **estar** *o* **mantenerse** *o* **seguir en sus t.** to stick to one's guns

tregua *nf Mil* truce; *Fig* respite

treinta *adj & nm inv* thirty

tremendo, -a *adj* (**a**) *(terrible)* terrible, dreadful (**b**) *(muy grande)* enormous; *Fig* tremendous

tren *nm* (**a**) train (**b**) *Av* **t. de aterrizaje** undercarriage; **t. de lavado** car wash (**c**) **t. de vida** lifestyle

trenza *nf (de pelo)* plait, *esp US* braid

trepar *vt & vi* to climb

tres 1 *adj inv (cardinal)* three; *(ordinal)* third; *Fam* **de t. al cuarto** cheap, of little value **2** *nm* three; **t. en raya** *Br* noughts and crosses, *US* tick-tack-toe

tresillo *nm* (**a**) *(mueble)* (three-piece) suite (**b**) *Mús* triplet

trial *nm Dep* trial

triangular *adj* triangular

triángulo *nm* triangle; *Fig* **t. amoroso** eternal triangle

tribu *nf* tribe

tribuna *nf* (**a**) *(plataforma)* rostrum, dais; **t. de (la) prensa** press box (**b**) *Dep* stand

tribunal *nm* (**a**) *Jur* court; **t. de apelación** court of appeal; **el T.**

Supremo *Br* ≃ the High Court, *US* ≃ the Supreme Court (**b**) *(de examen)* board of examiners

triciclo *nm* tricycle

trigo *nm* wheat

trigueño, -a *Am adj (pelo)* light brown, corn-coloured; *(persona)* light brown-skinned

trilladora *nf* threshing machine; **t. segadora** combine harvester

trillar *vt* to thresh

trillizo, -a *nm,f* triplet

trimestral *adj* quarterly, three-monthly

trimestre *nm* quarter; *Educ* term

trineo *nm* sledge, sleigh

trío *nm* trio

tripa *nf* (**a**) *(intestino)* gut, intestine; *Esp Fam* tummy; **dolor de t.** stomach ache (**b**) **tripas** innards

triple *adj & nm* triple

trípode *nm* tripod

tripulación *nf* crew

tripulante *nmf* crew member

triste *adj* (**a**) *(persona, situación)* sad (**b**) *(lugar)* gloomy

tristeza *nf* sadness

triturar *vt (machacar)* to grind (up)

triunfal *adj* triumphant

triunfar *vi* to triumph

triunfo *nm* (**a**) *(victoria)* triumph, victory; *Dep* win (**b**) *(éxito)* success

trivial *adj* trivial

triza *nf* bit, fragment; **hacer trizas** to tear to shreds

trocar [64] *vt* (**a**) *(transformar)* **t. algo (en algo)** to change sth (into sth) (**b**) *(intercambiar)* to swap, to exchange

trocha *nf Am* path

trofeo *nm* trophy

trombón *nm* trombone

trombosis *nf inv* thrombosis

trompa *nf* (**a**) *Mús* horn (**b**) *(de elefante)* trunk (**c**) *Anat* tube (**d**) *Fam* **estar t.** to be sloshed *o* plastered

trompazo *nm Fam* bump; **darse** *o* **pegarse un t.** to have a bump

trompeta *nf* trumpet

tronar [2] **1** *vi* to thunder **2** *vt Méx Fam* (**a**) *(destruir, acabar con)* to get rid of; **este remedio es para t. anginas** this remedy will clear up tonsillitis (**b**) *(suspender)* to fail

tronco *nm* (**a**) *Anat* trunk, torso (**b**) *Bot (de árbol)* trunk; *(leño)* log; *Fam Fig* **dormir como un t.** to sleep like a log

trono *nm* throne

tropa *nf* (**a**) squad (**b**) **tropas** troops

tropezar [1] *vi* (**a**) to trip, to stumble (**con** on) (**b**) **t. con algo** to come across sth; **t. con algn/dificultades** to run into sb/difficulties

tropezón *nm* (**a**) *(traspié)* trip, stumble; **dar un t.** to trip (**b**) *(error)* slip-up, faux pas (**c**) *(de comida)* chunk of meat

tropical *adj* tropical

trópico *nm* tropic

tropiezo **1** *nm* (**a**) *(obstáculo)* trip (**b**) *Fig (error)* blunder, faux pas **2** *indic pres de* **tropezar**

trotar *vi* to trot

trote *nm* (**a**) trot; **al t.** at a trot (**b**) *Fam* **ya no está para esos trotes** he cannot keep up the pace any more

trozar *vt Am (carne)* to cut up; *(res, tronco)* to butcher, to cut up

trozo *nm* piece

trucar [44] *vt* to doctor, to alter

trucha *nf* trout

truco *nm* (**a**) *(ardid)* trick; **aquí hay t.** there's something fishy going on here (**b**) **coger el t. (a algo)** to get the knack *o* hang (of sth)

trueno *nm* thunder; **un t.** a thunderclap

trufa *nf* truffle

trusa *nf* (**a**) *Carib (traje de baño)* swimsuit (**b**) *Perú (short)* briefs (**c**) *RP (faja)* girdle

tu *adj pos (pl* **tus)** your; **tu libro** your book; **tus libros** your books

tú *pron* you; **de tú a tú** on equal terms

> Usually omitted in Spanish except for emphasis or contrast

tuberculosis *nf inv* tuberculosis

tubería *nf* (**a**) *(de agua)* piping, pipes (**b**) *(de gas)* pipeline

tubo *nm* (**a**) tube; **t. de ensayo** test tube (**b**) *(tubería)* pipe; *Aut* **t. de escape** exhaust (pipe)

tuerca *nf* nut

tuerto, -a 1 *adj* one-eyed, blind in one eye **2** *nm,f* one-eyed person

tul *nm* tulle

tulipán *nm* tulip

tullido, -a *adj* crippled, disabled

tumba *nf* grave, tomb

tumbar 1 *vt* to knock down *o* over **2 tumbarse** *vpr (acostarse)* to lie down, to stretch out

tumbona *nf* *Br* sun-lounger, *US* (beach) recliner

tumor *nm* tumour

tumulto *nm* tumult, commotion

tuna *nf* (**a**) *(agrupación musical)* = group of student minstrels (**b**) *Am (higo chumbo)* prickly pear

túnel *nm* tunnel; **el t. del Canal de la Mancha** the Channel Tunnel

Túnez *n* (**a**) *(país)* Tunisia (**b**) *(ciudad)* Tunis

túnica *nf* tunic

tupido, -a *adj* thick, dense

turbina *nf* turbine

turbio, -a *adj (agua)* cloudy; *(negocio etc)* shady, dubious

turbulencia *nf* turbulence

turco, -a 1 *adj* Turkish

2 *nm,f (persona)* Turk; *Fig* **cabeza de t.** scapegoat

3 *nm (idioma)* Turkish

turismo *nm* (**a**) tourism; **ir de t.** to go touring; **t. rural** rural tourism (**b**) *Aut* car

turista *nmf* tourist

turístico, -a *adj* tourist; **de interés t.** of interest to tourists

túrmix® *nf inv* blender, liquidizer

turno *nm* (**a**) *(en juegos etc)* turn, go (**b**) *(de trabajo)* shift; **estar de t.** to be on duty; **t. de día/noche** day/night shift

Turquía *n* Turkey

turrón *nm* nougat

tute *nm* *Fam* **darse** *o* **pegarse un (buen) t.** to slog one's guts out

tutear 1 *vt* = to address as "tú" **2 tutearse** *vpr* = to address each other as "tú"

tutor *nm* (**a**) *Jur* guardian (**b**) *Educ* tutor

tuyo, -a 1 *adj pos (con personas)* of yours; *(con objetos)* one of your; **¿es amigo t.?** is he a friend of yours?; **unas amigas tuyas** some friends of yours; **un libro t.** one of your books **2** *pron pos* yours; **éste es t.** this one is yours; *Fam* **los tuyos** *(familiares)* your family

TV *nf* (*abr* **televisión**) TV

Uu

u *conj* or; *ver también* **o**

ubicar [44] **1** *vt* (**a**) *(situar) (edificio, fábrica)* to locate (**b**) *Am (colocar)* to put (**c**) *Am (encontrar)* to find, to locate; **no veo su ficha por acá, pero en cuanto la ubique le aviso** I can't see your card here, but as soon as I find it I'll let you know

2 ubicarse *vpr* (**a**) *(edificio)* to be situated *o* located (**b**) *Am (persona)* to get one's bearings; **¿ya te ubicas en la ciudad?** are you finding your way around the city all right?

UCI ['uθi] *nf (abr* **unidad de cuidados intensivos)** ICU, intensive care unit

Ud. *(abr* **usted)** you

Uds. *(abr* **ustedes)** you

UE *nf(abr* **Unión Europea)** EU

úlcera *nf* ulcer

ultimar *vt* (**a**) *(terminar)* to finalize (**b**) *Am (asesinar)* to kill

último, -a 1 *adj* (**a**) last; **el ú. día** the last day; **por ú.** finally (**b**) *(más reciente)* latest; **últimas noticias** latest news (**c**) *(más alto)* top; **el ú. piso** the top flat (**d**) *(más bajo)* lowest (**e**) *(más lejano)* back, last; **la última fila** the back row (**f**) *(definitivo)* final

2 *nm,f* **llegar el ú.** to arrive last; **a últimos de mes** at the end of the month; **en las últimas** on one's last legs; *Fam* **a la última** up to the minute; **el ú. de la lista** the lowest in the list

ultramarinos *nmpl* groceries; **tienda de u.** greengrocer's (shop)

ultravioleta *adj inv* ultraviolet

umbral *nm* threshold

un, -a 1 *art indef* (**a**) a; *(antes de vocal)* an; **un coche** a car; **un huevo** an egg; **una flor** a flower (**b**) **unos, -as** some; **unas flores** some flowers **2** *adj*
(delante de nm sing) one; **un chico y dos chicas** one boy and two girls; *ver también* **uno, -a**

unánime *adj* unanimous

UNED *nf (abr* **Universidad Nacional de Educación a Distancia)** = Spanish open university

únicamente *adv* only, solely

único, -a *adj* (**a**) *(solo)* only; **es el ú. que tengo** it's the only one I've got; **hijo ú.** only child; **lo ú. que quiero** the only thing I want; **el Mercado Ú.** the Single Market; **el Acta Única** the Single European Act (**b**) *(extraordinario)* unique

unidad *nf* (**a**) unit (**b**) *(cohesión)* unity

unido, -a *adj* united; **están muy unidos** they are very attached to one another; **una familia muy unida** a very close family

unifamiliar *adj* **vivienda u.** detached house

unificación *nf* unification

uniforme 1 *nm (prenda)* uniform **2** *adj* (**a**) *(igual)* uniform (**b**) *(superficie)* even

unión *nf* union

unir 1 *vt (juntar)* to unite, to join (together); **esta carretera une las dos comarcas** this road links both districts **2 unirse** *vpr (juntarse)* to unite, to join

unisex *adj inv* unisex

universal *adj* universal; **historia u.** world history

universidad *nf* university; **u. a distancia** = distance learning university, ≃ Open University; **u. laboral** technical college

universitario, -a 1 *adj* university **2** *nm,f* university student

universo *nm* universe

uno, -a 1 *nm inv* one; **el u.** (number) one; **el u. de mayo** the first of May
2 *nf* **es la una** *(hora)* it's one o'clock
3 *adj* **unos** some; **unas cajas** some boxes; **habrá unos veinte** there must be around twenty
4 *pron* (**a**) one; **u. (de ellos)** one of them; **unos cuantos** a few; **se miraron el u. al otro** they looked at each other; **de u. en u.** one by one (**b**) *(persona)* someone, somebody; **u. que pasaba por allí** some passer-by; **unos … otros** some people … others (**c**) *(impers)* you, one; **u. tiene que …** you have to …

untar *vt* to grease, to smear; *(mantequilla)* to spread

uña *nf* (**a**) nail; **morderse** *o* **comerse las uñas** to bite one's fingernails; *Fig* **ser u. y carne** to be hand in glove (**b**) *Zool (garra)* claw; *(pezuña)* hoof

uralita® *nf* = material made of asbestos and cement, usually corrugated and used mainly for roofing

uranio *nm* uranium

urbanización *nf* (**a**) *(barrio)* housing development *o* estate (**b**) *(proceso)* urbanization

urbano, -a *adj* urban, city; **guardia u.** (traffic) policeman

urgencia *nf* (**a**) urgency (**b**) *(emergencia)* emergency

urgente *adj* urgent; **correo u.** express mail

urinario *nm* urinal, *US* comfort station

urna *nf* (**a**) *Pol* ballot box (**b**) *(vasija)* urn

urraca *nf* magpie

urticaria *nf Med* hives

Uruguay *n* Uruguay

uruguayo, -a *adj & nm,f* Uruguayan

usado, -a *adj (ropa)* second-hand, used

usar 1 *vt* (**a**) to use (**b**) *(prenda)* to wear
2 usarse *vpr* to be used *o* in fashion

usina *nf Andes, RP* plant; **u. eléctrica** power station, power plant; **u. nuclear** nuclear power station, nuclear power plant

uso *nm* (**a**) use; *Farm* **u. externo/ tópico** external/local application (**b**) *(de poder, privilegio)* exercise (**c**) *(de prenda)* wearing; **haga u. del casco** wear a helmet (**d**) *(costumbre)* usage, custom; **al u.** conventional

usted *pron pers (pl* **ustedes**) *Fml* you; **¿quién es u.?, ¿quiénes son ustedes?** who are you?

> Usually omitted in Spanish except for emphasis or contrast. Although formal in peninsular Spanish, it is not necessarily so in Latin American Spanish

usual *adj* usual, common

usuario, -a *nm,f* user

utensilio *nm* utensil; *(herramienta)* tool

útero *nm* uterus, womb

útil 1 *adj* useful; *(día)* working **2** *nm (herramienta)* tool, instrument

utilidad *nf* usefulness, utility; *(beneficio)* profit

utilitario, -a 1 *nm (coche)* utility vehicle **2** *adj* utilitarian

utilizar [40] *vt* to use, to utilize

uva *nf* grape; **u. blanca** green grape

Vv

vaca *nf* (**a**) cow (**b**) *(carne)* beef

vacaciones *nfpl* holiday, *Br* holidays, *US* vacation; **durante las v.** during the holidays; **estar/irse de v.** to be/go on *Br* holiday *o US* vacation

vacacionista *nmf Am Br* holiday-maker, *US* vacationer

vacante 1 *adj* vacant **2** *nf* vacancy

vaciar [29] **1** *vt* (**a**) *(recipiente)* to empty; *(contenido)* to empty out (**b**) *(terreno)* to hollow out (**c**) *Arte* to cast, to mould **2 vaciarse** *vpr* to empty

vacilar *vi* (**a**) *(dudar)* to hesitate; **sin v.** without hesitation (**b**) *(voz)* to falter (**c**) *(luz)* to flicker (**d**) *Fam (jactarse)* to show off

vacilón, -ona *Fam* **1** *adj* (**a**) *(fanfarrón)* swanky (**b**) *Esp, Carib, Méx (bromista)* jokey, teasing
2 *nm,f* (**a**) *(fanfarrón)* show-off (**b**) *Esp, Carib, Méx (bromista)* tease
3 *nm CAm, Carib, Méx (fiesta)* party

vacío, -a 1 *adj* (**a**) empty; *(hueco)* hollow (**b**) *(sin ocupar)* vacant, unoccupied **2** *nm* (**a**) emptiness, void (**b**) *(hueco)* gap; *(espacio)* (empty) space (**c**) *Fís* vacuum; **envasado al v.** vacuum-packed

vacuna *nf* vaccine

vacunación *nf* vaccination

vacunar 1 *vt* to vaccinate (**contra** against); *Fig* to inure **2 vacunarse** *vpr* to get oneself vaccinated

vado *nm* (**a**) *(de un río)* ford (**b**) *Aut* **v. permanente** *(en letrero)* keep clear

vagabundo, -a 1 *adj (persona)* vagrant; **perro v.** stray dog **2** *nm,f (sin casa)* tramp, vagrant, *US* bum

vagina *nf* vagina

vago, -a 1 *adj* (**a**) *(perezoso)* lazy (**b**) *(indefinido)* vague **2** *nm,f* (**a**) *(holgazán)* layabout (**b**) *Jur* vagrant

vagón *nm (para pasajeros)* carriage, coach, *US* car; *(para mercancías)* truck, wagon, *US* freight car, *US* boxcar

vagoneta *nf* wagon

vaho *nm (de aliento)* breath; *(vapor)* vapour

vaina 1 *nf* (**a**) *(de espada)* sheath, scabbard (**b**) *Bot* pod (**c**) *Col, Perú, Ven muy Fam (persona o cosa molesta)* pain (in the neck); **ése es un v.** he's a pain **2** *nmf (persona)* dimwit

vainilla *nf* vanilla

vajilla *nf* crockery, dishes; **una v.** a set of dishes, a dinner service

vale¹ *interj Esp* all right!, OK!

vale² *nm* (**a**) *(comprobante)* voucher (**b**) *(pagaré)* promissory note, IOU (I owe you) (**c**) *Méx, Ven Fam (amigo)* pal, *Br* mate, *US* buddy

valenciano, -a 1 *adj & nm,f* Valencian **2** *nm (idioma)* Valencian

valentía *nf* courage, bravery

valer [26] **1** *vt* (**a**) *(ser válido)* to be worth; **no vale nada** it is worthless; **no vale la pena (ir)** it's not worthwhile (going) (**b**) *(costar)* to cost; **¿cuánto vale?** how much is it? (**c**) *(proporcionar)* to earn
2 *vi* (**a**) *(servir)* to be useful, to be of use (**b**) *(ser válido)* to be valid, to count; **no vale hacer trampa** cheating isn't on (**c**) **más vale** it is better; **más vale que te vayas ya** you had better leave now
3 valerse *vpr* **valerse de** to use, to make use of; **valerse por sí mismo** to be able to manage on one's own

valeriana *nf* valerian, allheal

validez *nf* validity

válido, -a *adj* valid

valiente *adj* (**a**) *(valeroso)* brave, courageous (**b**) *Irón* ¡**v. amigo eres tú!** a fine friend you are!

valioso, -a *adj* valuable

valla *nf* (**a**) *(cerca)* fence; *(muro)* wall; **v. publicitaria** billboard, *Br* hoarding (**b**) *Dep* hurdle; **los 100 metros vallas** the 100 metres hurdle race

valle *nm* valley

valor *nm* (**a**) *(valía)* value, worth; *(precio)* price; **objetos de v.** valuables; **sin v.** worthless; **v. alimenticio** food value (**b**) *(valentía)* courage (**c**) *Fin* **valores** securities, bonds

valoración *nf* valuation

valorar *vt* to value, to calculate the value of

vals *nm* waltz; **bailar el v.** to waltz

válvula *nf* valve; **v. de seguridad** safety valve

vanguardista **1** *adj* avant-garde **2** *nmf* avant-gardist

vanidad *nf* vanity

vanidoso, -a *adj* vain, conceited

vano, -a *adj* (**a**) *(vanidoso)* vain, conceited (**b**) *(esfuerzo, esperanza)* vain, futile; **en v.** in vain

vapor *nm* (**a**) *(de agua hirviendo)* steam; *Culin* **al v.** steamed (**b**) *(gas)* vapour; **v. de agua** water vapour

vaporizador *nm* vaporizer, spray

vaquero, -a **1** *nm* cowherd, cowboy **2** *adj* **pantalón v.** jeans, pair of jeans **3** *nmpl* **vaqueros** *(prenda)* jeans, pair of jeans

vara *nf* pole, rod

variable *adj & nf* variable

variado, -a *adj* varied; **galletas variadas** assorted *Br* biscuits *o US* cookies

variar [29] **1** *vt* to vary, to change **2** *vi* to vary, to change; *Irón* **para v.** as usual, just for a change

varicela *nf* chickenpox

variedad *nf* (**a**) variety (**b**) *Teatro* **variedades** variety, *Br* music hall

varios, -as *adj* several

variz *nf* varicose vein

varón *nm (hombre)* man; *(chico)* boy;

hijo v. male child; **sexo v.** male sex

varonil *adj* manly, virile

vasallo, -a *nm,f Hist* vassal

vasco, -a *adj* Basque; **el País V.** the Basque Country

vasija *nf* pot

vaso *nm* (**a**) *(para beber)* glass (**b**) *Anat* vessel

vasto, -a *adj* vast

Vaticano *nm* **el V.** the Vatican

vaya¹ *interj* ¡**v. lío!** what a mess!

vaya² *subj pres de* **ir**

Vd. *(abr* **usted)** you

Vds. *(abr* **ustedes)** you

ve **1** *imperat de* **ir** **2** *indic pres de* **ver**

vecindad *nf,* **vecindario** *nm* (**a**) *(área)* neighbourhood, vicinity (**b**) *(vecinos)* community, residents *pl* (**c**) *Méx (vivienda)* = communal dwelling where poor families each live in a single room and share a bathroom and kitchen with others

vecino, -a **1** *nm,f* (**a**) *(persona)* neighbour; **el v. de al lado** the next-door neighbour (**b**) *(residente)* resident **2** *adj* neighbouring, nearby

vegetación *nf* (**a**) *Bot* vegetation (**b**) *Med* **vegetaciones** adenoids

vegetal *nm* vegetable

vegetariano, -a *adj & nm,f* vegetarian

vehículo *nm* vehicle

veinte *adj & nm inv* twenty

vejez *nf* old age

vejiga *nf* bladder

vela¹ *nf* (**a**) candle (**b**) *Fam* **quedarse a dos velas** to be in the dark (**c**) **pasar la noche en v.** to have a sleepless night

vela² *nf Náut* sail

velador **1** *nm* (**a**) *(mesa)* table (**b**) *Andes, Méx (mesilla de noche)* bedside table (**c**) *Méx, RP (lámpara)* bedside lamp **2** *nm,f Méx (sereno)* night watchman

velcro® *nm* Velcro®

velero *nm* sailing boat *o* ship

veleta **1** *nf* weather vane, weathercock **2** *nmf Fam* fickle *o* changeable person

veliz *nf Méx* suitcase

vello *nm* hair

velo *nm* veil

velocidad *nf* (a) *(rapidez)* speed; *(de proyectil etc)* velocity; *Aut* **v. máxima** speed limit; *Informát* **v. de transmisión** bit rate; *Informát* **v. operativa** operating speed (b) *Aut (marcha)* gear

velódromo *nm* cycle track, velodrome

velomotor *nm* moped

velorio *nm* wake

veloz **1** *adj* swift, rapid **2** *adv* quickly, fast

vena *nf* vein

venado *nm* deer, stag; *Culin* venison

vencedor, -a **1** *nm,f* winner **2** *adj* winning

vencejo *nm Orn* swift

vencer [49] **1** *vt* (a) *(al enemigo)* to defeat; *(al contrincante)* to beat (b) *(dificultad)* to overcome, to surmount **2** *vi* (a) *(pago, deuda)* to fall due, to be payable (b) *(plazo)* to expire **3 vencerse** *vpr (torcerse)* to warp

vencido, -a *adj* (a) *Mil (derrotado)* defeated; *Dep* beaten; *Fig* **darse por v.** to give up, to accept defeat (b) *(pago, deuda)* due, payable (c) *(plazo)* expired (d) *Fam* **a la tercera va la vencida** third time lucky

vencimiento *nm* (a) *Com* maturity (b) *(de un plazo)* expiry

venda *nf* bandage

vendaje *nm* dressing

vendar *vt* to bandage; *Fig* **v. los ojos a algn** to blindfold sb

vendaval *nm* gale

vendedor, -a *nm,f* seller; *(de coches, seguros)* salesman, *f* saleswoman

vender **1** *vt* to sell; **v. a plazos/al contado** to sell on credit/for cash; **v. al por mayor/menor** to (sell) wholesale/retail **2 venderse** *vpr* (a) to sell; **este disco se vende bien** this record is selling well; **se vende** *(en letrero)* for sale (b) *(claudicar)* to sell out

vendimia *nf* grape harvest

vendimiador, -a *nm,f* grape picker

vendimiar [43] **1** *vt (uvas)* to harvest **2** *vi* to pick grapes

veneno *nm* poison; *(de serpiente)* venom

venenoso, -a *adj* poisonous

venezolano, -a *adj & nm,f* Venezuelan

Venezuela *n* Venezuela

venga *subj pres de* **venir**

venganza *nf* vengeance, revenge

vengar [42] **1** *vt* to avenge **2 vengarse** *vpr* to avenge oneself; **vengarse de algn** to take revenge on sb

vengo *indic pres de* **venir**

venida *nf* coming, arrival

venir [27] **1** *vi* (a) to come; *Fig* **v. a menos** to come down in the world; **el año que viene** next year; *Fig* **me viene a la memoria** I remember; *Fam* **¡venga ya!** *(vamos)* come on!; *(expresa incredulidad)* come off it!
  (b) **v. grande/pequeño** *(ropa)* to be too big/small; **v. mal/bien** to be inconvenient/convenient; **el metro me viene muy bien** I find the *Br* underground *o US* subway very handy
  (c) *(en pasivas)* **esto vino provocado por ...** this was brought about by ...
  (d) **esto viene ocurriendo desde hace mucho tiempo** this has been going on for a long time now
  2 venirse *vpr* **venirse abajo** to collapse

venta *nf* (a) sale; **en v.** for sale; **a la v.** on sale; **v. al contado** cash sale; **v. al por mayor/al por menor** wholesale/retail; **v. a plazos** sale by instalments, *Br* hire purchase (b) *(posada)* country inn

ventaja *nf* advantage; **llevar v. a** to have the advantage over; **le sacó 2 metros de v.** he beat him by 2 metres

ventana *nf* (a) window (b) *(de la nariz)* nostril

ventanilla *nf* (a) window (b) *(de la nariz)* nostril

ventilación *nf* ventilation; **sin v.** unventilated

ventilador *nm* ventilator; *(de coche)* fan

ventisca *nf* blizzard; *(de nieve)* snow-storm

ventosa *nf* sucker; *Med* cupping glass

ventoso, -a *adj* windy

ventrílocuo, -a *nm,f* ventriloquist

ver¹ *nm* de buen v. good-looking

ver² [28] **1** *vt* (**a**) to see; *(televisión)* to watch; **a v.** let me see, let's see; **a v. si escribes** I hope you'll write; **(ya) veremos** we'll see; *Fam* **había un jaleo que no veas** you should have seen the fuss that was made (**b**) **no tener nada que v. con** to have nothing to do with
2 verse *vpr* (**a**) *(imagen etc)* to be seen (**b**) *(encontrarse con algn)* to meet, see each other; **¡nos vemos!** see you later!

veraneante *nmf Br* holidaymaker, *US* (summer) vacationer

veranear *vi* **v. en** to spend one's summer *Br* holidays *o US* vacation in

veraneo *nm* summer *Br* holidays *o US* vacation

veraniego, -a *adj* summer

verano *nm* summer

veras *nfpl* de v. really, seriously

verbena *nf* street party

verbo *nm* verb

verdad *nf* (**a**) truth; **es v.** it is true; **a decir v.** to tell the truth; **¡de v!.** really!, truly!; **un amigo de v.** a real friend (**b**) *(en frase afirmativa)* **está muy bien, ¿(no es) v.?** it is very good, isn't it?; *(en frase negativa)* **no te gusta, ¿v.?** you don't like it, do you?

verdadero, -a *adj* true, real

verde 1 *adj* (**a**) green (**b**) *(fruta)* unripe (**c**) *Fam (chiste, película)* blue; **viejo v.** dirty old man (**d**) *Fam Fig* **poner v. a algn** to call sb every name under the sun **2** *nm* (**a**) *(color)* green (**b**) *Pol* **los verdes** the Greens

verdulería *nf* greengrocer's (shop)

verdulero, -a *nm,f* greengrocer

verdura *nf* vegetables, greens

vereda *nf* (**a**) *(camino)* path, lane (**b**) *CSur, Perú (acera) Br* pavement, *US* sidewalk (**c**) *Col (distrito)* area, district

veredicto *nm* verdict

vergonzoso, -a *adj* (**a**) *(penoso)* shameful, disgraceful (**b**) *(tímido)* shy, bashful

vergüenza *nf* (**a**) shame; **¿no te da v.?** aren't you ashamed?, have you no shame?; **¡es una v.!** it's a disgrace! (**b**) *(timidez)* shyness, bashfulness; **tener v.** to be shy; **me da v.** I'm too embarrassed

verificar [44] **1** *vt (comprobar)* to check **2 verificarse** *vpr* to take place, to occur

verja *nf (reja)* grating; *(cerca)* railing, railings; *(puerta)* iron gate

vermut *nm* (*pl* **vermuts**), **vermú** (*pl* **vermús**) (**a**) *(licor)* vermouth (**b**) *(aperitivo)* aperitif (**c**) *esp Andes, RP (en cine)* early-evening showing; *(en teatro)* early-evening performance

verosímil *adj* probable, likely; *(creíble)* credible

verruga *nf* wart

versión *nf* version; **película en v. original** movie *o Br* film in the original language

verso *nm* (**a**) *(poesía)* verse (**b**) *(línea)* line

vertedero *nm (de basura) Br* rubbish tip *o* dump, *US* garbage dump

verter [3] **1** *vt* (**a**) to pour (out) (**b**) *(basura)* to dump **2** *vi (río)* to flow, to run (**a** into)

vertical *adj* vertical

vértice *nm* vertex

vertido *nm (residuo)* waste; **vertidos radiactivos** radioactive waste

vertiente *nf* (**a**) *(de una montaña, un tejado)* slope; *Fig* aspect (**b**) *CSur (manantial)* spring

vértigo *nm* vertigo; **me da v.** it makes me dizzy

vestíbulo *nm (de casa)* hall; *(de edificio público)* foyer

vestido, -a 1 *nm (ropa)* clothes; *(de mujer)* dress **2** *adj* dressed; **policía v. de paisano** plain-clothes policeman

vestimenta *nf* clothes, garments

vestir [6] **1** *vt* (**a**) *(a algn)* to dress (**b**) *(llevar puesto)* to wear

2 *vi* (**a**) to dress; **ropa de (mucho) v.** formal dress (**b**) *Fam* **la seda viste mucho** silk always looks very elegant
3 vestirse *vpr* (**a**) to get dressed, to dress (**b**) **vestirse de** to wear, to dress in; *(disfrazarse)* to disguise oneself as, to dress up as

vestuario *nm* (**a**) *(conjunto de vestidos)* clothes, wardrobe; *Teatro* wardrobe, costumes (**b**) *(camerino)* dressing room (**c**) *Dep* changing room, *US* locker room

veterano, -a *adj & nm,f* veteran

veterinario, -a 1 *nm,f* vet, *Br* veterinary surgeon, *US* veterinarian **2** *nf* **veterinaria** veterinary medicine *o* science

vez *nf* (**a**) time; **una v.** once; **dos veces** twice; **cinco veces** five times; **a** *o* **algunas veces** sometimes; **cada v.** each *o* every time; **cada v. más** more and more; **de v. en cuando** now and again, every now and then; **¿le has visto alguna v.?** have you ever seen him?; **otra v.** again; **a la v.** at the same time; **tal v.** perhaps, maybe; **de una v.** in one go; **en v. de** instead of
(**b**) *(turno)* turn
(**c**) **hacer las veces de** to do duty as

vía 1 *nf* (**a**) *Ferroc* track, line (**b**) *(camino)* road; **v. pública** public thoroughfare; **V. Láctea** Milky Way (**c**) *Anat* passage, tract; *Farm* **(por) v. oral** to be taken orally (**d**) *Fig* **por v. oficial** through official channels; **por v. aérea/marítima** by air/sea (**e**) **en vías de** in the process of; **países en vías de desarrollo** developing countries
2 *prep (a través de)* via, through; **v. París** via Paris; **transmisión v. satélite** satellite transmission

viaducto *nm* viaduct

viajar *vi* to travel

viaje *nm* *(recorrido)* journey, trip; *(largo, en barco)* voyage; **¡buen v.!** bon voyage!, have a good trip!; **estar de v.** to be away (on a trip); **irse** *o* **marcharse de v.** to go on a journey *o* trip; **v. de negocios** business trip; **v. de novios** honeymoon

viajero, -a 1 *nm,f* (**a**) traveller (**b**) *(en transporte público)* passenger **2** *adj* **cheque v.** traveller's cheque

vianda *nf* (**a**) *Méx, RP (tentempié)* packed lunch (**b**) *Méx, RP (fiambrera)* lunchbox

víbora *nf* viper

vibrar *vt & vi* to vibrate

vicepresidente, -a *nm,f* (**a**) *Pol* vice-president (**b**) *(de compañía, comité)* vice-chairman, *f* vice-chairwoman, *US* vice-president

viciar [43] **1** *vt* (**a**) *(corromper)* to corrupt (**b**) *(estropear)* to waste **2** **viciarse** *vpr* (**a**) *(deformarse)* to go out of shape (**b**) *(corromperse)* to become corrupted

vicio *nm* (**a**) vice (**b**) *(mala costumbre)* bad habit (**c**) *Fam (destreza)* skill

vicioso, -a 1 *adj* (**a**) *(persona)* depraved, perverted (**b**) **círculo v.** vicious circle **2** *nm,f* depraved person; **v. del trabajo** workaholic

víctima *nf* victim

victimar *vt Am* to kill, to murder

victimario, -a *nm,f Am* killer, murderer

victoria *nf* victory

vid *nf* vine, grapevine

vida *nf* life; *(período)* lifetime; **de toda la v.** lifelong; **en mi v.** never in my life; **de por v.** for life; **ganarse la v.** to earn one's living; **¿qué es de tu v.?** how's life?; **estar con/sin v.** to be alive/dead

vidente *nmf* clairvoyant

vídeo, *Am* **video** *nm* video; **grabar en v.** to videotape

videocámara *nf* video camera

videocasete *nm* video, videocassette

videojuego *nm* video game

vidriera *nf* (**a**) stained-glass window (**b**) *Am (escaparate)* shop window

vidrio *nm* glass

vieira *nf* scallop

viejo, -a 1 *adj* old; **hacerse v.** to grow old; **un v. amigo** an old friend **2** *nm,f* (**a**) *(hombre, padre)* old man; *(mujer, madre)* old woman; **los viejos** old people; *Fam* **mis viejos** my parents (**b**) *Am Fam (amigo)* pal, *Br* mate, *US* buddy; *(amiga)* girl, *US* girlfriend (**c**) *Chile* **el V. Pascuero** Father Christmas

viento *nm* wind; **hace** o **sopla mucho v.** it is very windy; *Fam Fig* **¡vete a tomar v.!** get lost!

vientre *nm* (**a**) belly; **hacer de v.** to have a bowel movement (**b**) *(útero)* womb

viernes *nm inv* Friday; **V. Santo** Good Friday

Vietnam *n* Vietnam

viga *nf (de madera)* beam; *(de hierro)* girder

vigencia *nf* validity; **entrar en v.** to come into force o effect

vigente *adj* in force

vigilante *nm* watchman; *(de banco)* guard

vigilar 1 *vt* to watch; *(un lugar)* to guard; **vigila que no entren** make sure they don't get in **2** *vi (gen)* to keep watch

vigor *nm* (**a**) vigour; *(fuerza)* strength (**b**) **en v.** in force

vigoroso, -a *adj* vigorous

vil *adj Fml* vile, base

villa *nf* (**a**) *(población)* town (**b**) *(casa)* villa, country house (**c**) *Arg, Bol* **v. miseria** shanty town

villancico *nm* (Christmas) carol

vinagre *nm* vinegar

vinagreras *nfpl* cruet set

vinagreta *nf* vinaigrette sauce

vincha *nf Andes, RP* headband

vinculación *nf* link, connection

vincular *vt* to link, to bind; *(relacionar)* to relate, to connect

vino *nm* wine; **tomar un v.** to have a glass of wine; **v. blanco/tinto** white/red wine; **v. dulce/seco** sweet/dry wine; **v. rosado** rosé

viña *nf* vineyard

violación *nf* (**a**) *(de una persona)* rape (**b**) *(de ley, derecho)* violation, infringement

violador *nm* rapist

violar *vt* (**a**) *(persona)* to rape (**b**) *(ley, derecho)* to violate, to infringe

violencia *nf* (**a**) violence; **la no v.** non-violence (**b**) *(incomodidad)* embarrassment

violento, -a *adj* (**a**) violent (**b**) *(situación)* embarrassing, awkward (**c**) **sentirse v.** *(incómodo)* to feel embarrassed o awkward

violeta 1 *adj & nm (color)* violet **2** *nf (flor)* violet

violín *nm* violin; *Fam* fiddle

violinista *nmf* violinist

violoncelo, violonchelo *nm* violoncello, cello

VIP [bip] *nmf (abr* **very important person**) VIP

virgen 1 *adj* (**a**) *(persona, selva)* virgin (**b**) *(aceite, lana)* pure; *(cinta)* blank **2** *nmf* virgin; *Fam* **ser un viva la v.** to be a devil-may-care person

Virgo *nm* Virgo

virtud *nf* (**a**) virtue; *Fig* **en v. de** by virtue of (**b**) *(propiedad)* property, quality

viruela *nf* smallpox; **viruelas** pockmarks

virus *nm inv* virus

viruta *nf* shaving

visado *nm, Am* **visa** *nf* visa

víscera *nf* (**a**) internal organ (**b**) **vísceras** viscera, entrails

viscosa *nf (tejido)* viscose

visera *nf (de gorra)* peak; *(de casco)* visor

visible *adj* visible; *(evidente)* evident

visillo *nm* net curtain, lace curtain

visita *nf* (**a**) *(acción)* visit; **hacer una v.** to pay a visit; **estar de v.** to be visiting (**b**) *(invitado)* visitor, guest

visitante 1 *nmf* visitor **2** *adj (equipo)* away

visitar *vt* to visit

vislumbrar *vt* to glimpse

víspera *nf (día anterior)* day before; *(de festivo)* eve; **en vísperas de** in the period leading up to

vista *nf* (**a**) sight; **a la v.** visible; **a primera** o **simple v.** at first sight, on the face of it; **con vistas a** with a view to; **en v. de** in view of, considering;

corto de v. short-sighted; **conocer a algn de v.** to know sb by sight; *Fig* **tener mucha v. para** to have a good eye for; *Fam* **¡hasta la v.!** goodbye!, see you!

(**b**) *(panorama)* view; **con vista(s) al mar** overlooking the sea

(**c**) *Jur* trial, hearing

vistazo *nm* glance; **echar un v. a algo** *(ojear)* to have a (quick) look at sth; *(tener cuidado de)* to keep an eye on sth

visto, -a 1 *adj* (**a**) **está v. que ...** it is obvious that ...; **por lo v.** evidently, apparently; **v. que** in view of the fact that, seeing o given that (**b**) **estar bien v.** to be well looked upon, to be considered acceptable; **estar mal v.** to be frowned upon (**c**) **estar muy v.** to be old hat **2** *nm* **v. bueno** approval, OK

vistoso, -a *adj* eye-catching

vital *adj* (**a**) vital (**b**) *(persona)* full of vitality

vitalidad *nf* vitality

vitamina *nf* vitamin

vitrina *nf* *(aparador)* glass o display cabinet; *(de exposición)* glass case, showcase; *Am (escaparate)* shop window

viudo, -a *nm,f (hombre)* widower; *(mujer)* widow

viva *interj* hurrah!

víveres *nmpl* provisions, supplies

vivienda *nf* (**a**) housing (**b**) *(casa)* house; *(piso)* flat

vivir 1 *vi* to live; **vive de sus ahorros** she lives off her savings; **viven de la pesca** they make their living by fishing

2 *vt* to live through

3 *nm* life

vivo, -a 1 *adj* (**a**) alive; **de viva voz** verbally, by word of mouth; **en v.** *(programa)* live; *Fam* **es el v. retrato** o **la viva imagen de** she is the spitting image of (**b**) **al rojo v.** red-hot (**c**) *(vivaz)* lively, vivacious (**d**) *(listo)* sharp, clever (**e**) *(color)* vivid, bright (**f**) *(descripción)* lively, graphic **2** *nm,f* **los vivos** the living

vocabulario *nm* vocabulary

vocación *nf* vocation, calling; **con v.**

europea with leanings towards Europe

vocal 1 *nf Ling* vowel **2** *nmf* member

voceador, -a *nm,f Col, Ecuad, Méx* newspaper seller

vocero, -a *nm,f esp Am* spokesperson, spokesman, *f* spokeswoman

vodka *nm* vodka

vol. *(abr* **volumen***)* vol

volador, -a *adj* flying

volante 1 *nm* (**a**) *Aut* steering wheel; **ir al v.** to be driving (**b**) *Cost* frill, ruffle (**c**) *Esp (del médico)* (referral) note **2** *adj* flying; **platillo v.** flying saucer

volantín *nm Carib, Chile* kite

volar [2] **1** *vi* (**a**) to fly; *Fig* **lo hizo volando** he did it in a flash (**b**) *Fam (desaparecer)* to disappear, to vanish

2 *vt (edificios)* to blow up; *(caja fuerte)* to blow open; *Min* to blast

3 **volarse** *vpr (papel etc)* to be blown away

volcán *nm* volcano

volcánico, -a *adj* volcanic

volcar [2] **1** *vt* (**a**) *(cubo etc)* to knock over; *(barco, bote)* to capsize (**b**) *(vaciar)* to empty out (**c**) *(tiempo)* to invest

2 *vi (coche)* to turn over; *(barco)* to capsize

3 **volcarse** *vpr* (**a**) *(vaso, jarra)* to fall over, to tip over; *(coche)* to turn over; *(barco)* to capsize (**b**) *Fig* **volcarse con** to do one's utmost for

voleibol *nm* volleyball

volquete *nm* dumper truck, *US* dump truck

voltaje *nm* voltage

voltear 1 *vt* (**a**) *Am (derribar) (objeto)* to knock over; *(gobierno)* to overthrow, to bring down (**b**) *Am salvo RP (poner del revés) (boca abajo)* to turn upside down; *(lo de dentro fuera)* to turn inside out; *(lo de detrás delante)* to turn back to front (**c**) *Am salvo RP (cabeza, espalda)* to turn

2 *vi Méx (doblar la esquina)* to turn

3 **voltearse** *vpr* (**a**) *Am salvo RP (volverse)* to turn around (**b**) *Méx (vehículo)* to overturn

voltereta *nf* somersault

volumen *nm* volume

voluntad *nf* will; **fuerza de v.** willpower; **tiene mucha v.** he is very strong-willed; **a v.** at will

voluntario, -a 1 *adj* voluntary 2 *nm,f* volunteer; **ofrecerse v.** to volunteer

voluntarioso, -a *adj* willing

volver [4] (*pp* **vuelto**) 1 *vi* (**a**) to return; (*venir*) to come back; (*ir*) to go back; **v. en sí** to come round, to recover consciousness (**b**) **v. a hacer algo** to do sth again

2 *vt* (**a**) (*convertir*) to turn, to make; **me vas a v. loco** you are driving me mad (**b**) (*dar vuelta a*) to turn; (*boca abajo*) to turn upside down; (*de fuera adentro*) to turn inside out; (*de atrás adelante*) to turn back to front; (*dar la vuelta a*) to turn over; **volverle la espalda a algn** to turn one's back on sb; *Fig* **v. la vista atrás** to look back; **al v. la esquina** on turning the corner

3 volverse *vpr* (**a**) to turn (**b**) (*regresar*) (*venir*) to come back; (*ir*) to go back (**c**) (*convertirse*) to become; **volverse loco, -a** to go mad

vomitar 1 *vi* to vomit, to be sick; **tengo ganas de v.** I feel sick, I want to be sick 2 *vt* to vomit, to bring up

vos *pron pers Am* (*tú*) you

> The **vos** form is used alongside **tú** in many Latin American countries, and in some countries (Argentina, Paraguay and Uruguay) is the preferred form

V.O.S.E. *nf* (*abr* **versión original subtitulada en español**) = original language version subtitled in Spanish

vosotros, -as *pron pers pl Esp* (**a**) (*sujeto*) you (**b**) (*con prep*) you; **entre v.** among yourselves; **sin vosotras** without you

> Usually omitted in Spanish except for emphasis or contrast. In Latin America, **vosotros** is not used. Instead, **ustedes** is used as the second person plural in all contexts, without necessarily suggesting formality

votación *nf* (**a**) (*voto*) vote, ballot (**b**) (*acción*) voting

votante *nmf* voter

votar *vi* to vote; **v. a algn** to vote (for) sb

voto *nm* (**a**) vote; **tener v.** to have the right to vote; **v. secreto** secret ballot (**b**) *Rel* vow

voy *indic pres de* **ir**

voz *nf* (**a**) voice; **en v. alta** aloud; **en v. baja** in a low voice; **a media v.** in a low voice, softly; **de viva v.** verbally (**b**) (*grito*) shout; **a voces** shouting; **dar voces** to shout; *Fig* **estar pidiendo algo a voces** to be crying out for sth; *Fig* **secreto a voces** open secret; **a v. en grito** at the top of one's voice (**c**) **no tener ni v. ni voto** to have no say in the matter; *Fig* **llevar la v. cantante** to rule the roost (**d**) *Ling* **v. pasiva** passive voice

vuelo *nm* (**a**) flight; **v. chárter/regular** charter/scheduled flight; **v. sin motor** gliding; *Fig* **cazarlas** *o* **cogerlas al v.** to be quick on the uptake (**b**) *Cost* **una falda de v.** a full skirt

vuelta *nf* (**a**) (*regreso*) return; (*viaje*) return journey; **estar de v.** to be back; *Dep* **partido de v.** return match (**b**) (*giro*) turn; (*en carreras*) lap; *Dep* (*ciclista*) tour; **dar media v.** to turn round; *Fig* **la cabeza me da vueltas** my head is spinning; *Fig* **no le des más vueltas** stop worrying about it; **v. de campana** somersault (**c**) (*dinero*) change (**d**) **dar una v.** (*a pie*) to go for a walk *o* stroll; (*en coche*) to go for a drive *o* a spin (in the car)

vuelto, -a 1 *adj* **jersey de cuello v.** rollneck sweater 2 *nm Am* change

vuestro, -a *Esp* 1 *adj pos* (*antes del sustantivo*) your; (*después del sustantivo*) of yours; **v. libro** your book; **un amigo v.** a friend of yours 2 *pron pos* yours; **éstos son los vuestros** these are yours; **lo v.** what is yours, what belongs to you

vulgar *adj* (**a**) vulgar (**b**) **el término v.** the everyday term

Ww

walkman® ['walman] *nm* (*pl* **walkmans**) Walkman®

wáter *nm* (*pl* **wáteres**) *Fam* toilet

waterpolo *nm* water polo

WC [*Esp* uβe'θe, *Am* doβleβe'se] *nm* (*abr* water closet) WC

whisky ['wiski] *nm (escocés)* whisky; *(irlandés, US)* whiskey

windsurf, windsurfing *nm* windsurfing

Xx

xenofobia *nf* xenophobia
xenófobo, -a 1 *adj* xenophobic **2**
nm,f xenophobe

xerocopia *nf* photocopy

xilofón, xilófono *nm* xylophone

Yy

y *conj* (**a**) and; **una chica alta y
morena** a tall, dark-haired girl; **son
las tres y cuarto** it's a quarter past
three (**b**) **¿y qué?** so what?; **¿y si no
llega a tiempo?** what if he doesn't
arrive in time?; **¿y tú?** what about
you?; **¿y eso?** how come?; **y eso que**
although, even though; **¡y tanto!** you
bet!, and how!; *ver* **e**

ya 1 *adv* (**a**) already; **ya lo sabía** I
already knew; **ya en la Edad Media**
as far back as the Middle Ages
(**b**) *(ahora mismo)* now; **es preciso
actuar ya** it is vital that we act now;
¡hazlo ya! do it at once!; **ya mismo**
right away
(**c**) *(en el futuro)* **ya hablaremos
luego** we'll talk about it later; **ya nos
veremos** see you!
(**d**) **ya no** no longer; **ya no viene por
aquí** he doesn't come round here any
more
(**e**) *(refuerza el verbo)* **ya era hora**
about time too; **ya lo creo** of course, I
should think so; **¡ya voy!** coming!; **¡ya
está!** that's it!
2 *conj* **ya que** since

yacer [61] *vi* (**a**) *(estar tumbado,
enterrado)* to lie; **aquí yace ...** here
lies ... (**b**) *(tener relaciones sexuales)* to
lie together

yacimiento *nm* bed, deposit;
yacimientos petrolíferos oilfields

yanqui *Pey* **1** *adj* Yankee **2** *nmf*
Yankee, Yank

yaraví *nm Am* = type of melancholy
Indian song

yate *nm* yacht

yaya *nf* (**a**) *Perú (insecto)* mite (**b**) *Cuba,
PRico (árbol)* lancewood

yayo, -a *nm,f Fam* granddad, *f*
grandma

yegua *nf* mare

yema *nf* (**a**) *(de huevo)* yolk (**b**) *Bot* bud
(**c**) **y. del dedo** fingertip (**d**) *Culin* =
sweet made from sugar and egg yolk

yen *nm (moneda)* yen

yerba *nf* (**a**) = **hierba** (**b**) *RP* maté; **y.
mate** *(yerba)* maté leaves

yerbatero, -a 1 *nm,f Andes, Carib
(curandero)* witch doctor who uses
herbs; *(vendedor de hierbas)* herbalist
2 *adj RP* maté

yerno *nm* son-in-law

yeso *nm* (**a**) *Geol* gypsum (**b**) *Constr*
plaster

yo *pron pers* I; **entre tú y yo** between
you and me; **¿quién es? – soy yo**
who is it? – it's me; **yo no** not me; **yo
que tú** if I were you; **yo mismo** I myself

Usually omitted as a personal pronoun in Spanish except for emphasis or contrast

yodo *nm* iodine

yoga *nm* yoga

yogur *nm* (*pl* **yogures**), **yogurt** (*pl* **yogurts**) yogurt, yoghurt

Yugoslavia *n* Yugoslavia

yunque *nm* anvil

yunta *nf* yoke *o* team of oxen

yuyo *nm* (**a**) *CSur (mala hierba)* weed; *(hierba medicinal)* medicinal herb (**b**) *Andes (hierba silvestre)* wild herb

Zz

zacate *nm CAm, Méx* fodder

zafiro *nm* sapphire

zaguán *nm* hall, hallway

zambo, -a 1 *adj (piernas, persona)* knock-kneed **2** *nm,f Am (hijo de persona negra y otra india)* = person who has one Black and one Indian parent

zambullida *nf* plunge

zambullirse *vpr* to plunge

zanahoria *nf* carrot

zancadilla *nf* **ponerle la z. a algn** to trip sb up

zanco *nm* stilt

zancudo, -a 1 *adj* (**a**) long-legged (**b**) *Orn* wading; **ave zancuda** wading bird, wader **2** *nm Am* mosquito

zanja *nf* ditch, trench

zapallito *nm CSur Br* courgette, *US* zucchini

zapallo *nm* (**a**) *Andes, RP* **z. (italiano)** *Br* courgette, *US* zucchini (**b**) *Andes, RP (calabaza)* pumpkin (**c**) *RP Fam (bobo)* mug, *Br* wally

zapateado *nm* = type of flamenco dance where the dancers stamp their feet rhythmically

zapatería *nf* shoe shop

zapatero, -a *nm,f (vendedor)* shoe dealer; *(fabricante)* shoemaker, cobbler

zapatilla *nf* slipper; **zapatillas de deporte** *Br* trainers, *US* sneakers

zapato *nm* shoe; **zapatos de tacón** high-heeled shoes

zapping ['θapin] *nm inv Fam* channel-hopping, *US* channel-surfing; **hacer z.** to channel-hop

zarandear *vt* to shake

zarpar *vi* to weigh anchor, to set sail

zarpazo *nm* clawing; **dar** *o* **pegar un z. a** to claw

zarza *nf* bramble, blackberry bush

zarzamora *nf (zarza)* blackberry bush; *(fruto)* blackberry

zarzuela *nf* (**a**) = Spanish operetta (**b**) **la Z.** = royal residence in Madrid (**c**) *Culin* = fish stew

zenit *nm* zenith

zinc *nm* zinc

zíper *nm CAm, Méx Br* zip, *US* zipper

zipizape *nm Fam* squabble, set-to

zócalo *nm* (**a**) *(de pared)* skirting board (**b**) *(pedestal)* plinth

zodiaco, zodíaco *nm* zodiac

zona *nf* zone; *(región)* region; **z. euro** euro zone; **z. verde** park, green area

zoo *nm* zoo

zoología *nf* zoology

zoológico, -a 1 *adj* zoological; **parque z.** zoo **2** *nm* zoo

zopenco, -a *nm,f Fam* dope, halfwit

zopilote *nm CAm, Méx* black vulture

zoquete 1 *nmf Fam* blockhead **2** *nm CSur (calcetín)* ankle sock

zorra *nf* (**a**) vixen (**b**) *Esp Fam* slut

zorro, -a 1 *nm* fox **2** *adj* (**a**) *(astuto)*

cunning, sly (**b**) *Esp muy Fam* **no tengo ni zorra (idea)** I haven't got a *Br* bloody *o US* goddamn clue

zueco *nm* clog

zumbar 1 *vi* to buzz, to hum; **me zumban los oídos** my ears are buzzing; *Fam* **salir zumbando** to zoom off **2** *vt Fam* to thrash

zumbido *nm* buzzing, humming

zumo *nm Esp* juice

zurcir [52] *vt Cost* to darn; *Fam* **¡que te zurzan!** go to hell!

zurdo, -a 1 *nm,f (persona)* left-handed person **2** *adj* left-handed

zurrar *vt (pegar)* to beat, to flog